Managerial Accounting

Managerial Accounting

Sixteenth Edition

Ray H. Garrison, D.B.A., CPA

Professor Emeritus
Brigham Young University

Eric W. Noreen, Ph.D., CMA

Professor Emeritus
University of Washington

Peter C. Brewer, Ph.D.

Wake Forest University

Mc
Graw
Hill
Education

Dedication

To our families and to our many colleagues who use this book.

MANAGERIAL ACCOUNTING, SIXTEENTH EDITION

Published by McGraw-Hill Education, 2 Penn Plaza, New York, NY 10121. Copyright © 2018 by McGraw-Hill Education. All rights reserved. Printed in the United States of America. Previous editions © 2015, 2012, and 2010. No part of this publication may be reproduced or distributed in any form or by any means, or stored in a database or retrieval system, without the prior written consent of McGraw-Hill Education, including, but not limited to, in any network or other electronic storage or transmission, or broadcast for distance learning.

Some ancillaries, including electronic and print components, may not be available to customers outside the United States.

This book is printed on acid-free paper.

1 2 3 4 5 6 7 8 9 LWI 21 20 19 18 17

ISBN 978-1-259-30741-6
MHID 1-259-30741-7

Chief Product Officer, SVP Products & Markets: *G. Scott Virkler*
Vice President, General Manager, Products & Markets: *Marty Lange*
Managing Director: *Tim Vertovec*
Marketing Director: *Natalie King*
Brand Manager: *Pat Plumb*
Director, Product Development: *Rose Koos*
Director of Digital Content: *Peggy Hussey*
Associate Director of Digital Content: *Kevin Moran*
Lead Product Developer: *Kris Tibbetts*
Product Developer: *Erin Quinones*
Marketing Manager: *Cheryl Osgood*

Digital Product Analyst: *Xin Lin*
Director, Content Design & Delivery: *Linda Avenarius*
Program Manager: *Daryl Horrocks*
Lead Content Project Manager: *Pat Frederickson*
Senior Content Project Manager: *Angela Norris*
Buyer: *Sandy Ludovissy*
Design: *Matt Diamond*
Content Licensing Specialists: *Lori Slattery* and *Melissa Homer*
Cover Image: © *Eli Pascall-Willis/Getty Images*
Compositor: *SPi Global*
Printer: *LSC Communications*

All credits appearing on page or at the end of the book are considered to be an extension of the copyright page. About the Author images: *Courtesy of author.* Design element icons: banker's lamp and a stack of books, © *Janice Christine/Getty Images;* education icons, © *phipatbit/Shutterstock;* office icons, © *Ingram Publishing;* and justice icons, © *Turnervisual/Getty Images.*

Library of Congress Cataloging-in-Publication Data

Names: Garrison, Ray H., author. | Noreen, Eric W., author. | Brewer, Peter C, author.
Title: Managerial accounting / Ray H. Garrison, D.B.A., CPA, Professor Emeritus, Brigham Young University, Eric W. Noreen, Ph.D., CMA, Professor Emeritus, University of Washington, Peter C. Brewer, Ph.D., Wake Forest University.
Description: Sixteenth edition. | New York, NY : McGraw-Hill Education, [2018]
Identifiers: LCCN 2016040843 | ISBN 9781259307416 (alk. paper)
Subjects: LCSH: Managerial accounting.
Classification: LCC HF5657.4 .G37 2018 | DDC 658.15/11—dc23
LC record available at https://lccn.loc.gov/2016040843

The Internet addresses listed in the text were accurate at the time of publication. The inclusion of a website does not indicate an endorsement by the authors or McGraw-Hill Education, and McGraw-Hill Education does not guarantee the accuracy of the information presented at these sites.

About the
Authors

Ray H. Garrison is emeritus professor of accounting at Brigham Young University, Provo, Utah. He received his BS and MS degrees from Brigham Young University and his DBA degree from Indiana University.

As a certified public accountant, Professor Garrison has been involved in management consulting work with both national and regional accounting firms. He has published articles in *The Accounting Review, Management Accounting,* and other professional journals. Innovation in the classroom has earned Professor Garrison the Karl G. Maeser Distinguished Teaching Award from Brigham Young University.

Eric W. Noreen has taught at INSEAD in France and the Hong Kong Institute of Science and Technology and is emeritus professor of accounting at the University of Washington. Currently, he is the Accounting Circle Professor of Accounting, Fox School of Business, Temple University.

He received his BA degree from the University of Washington and MBA and PhD degrees from Stanford University. A Certified Management Accountant, he was awarded a Certificate of Distinguished Performance by the Institute of Certified Management Accountants.

Professor Noreen has served as associate editor of *The Accounting Review* and the *Journal of Accounting and Economics.* He has numerous articles in academic journals including: the *Journal of Accounting Research; The Accounting Review;* the *Journal of Accounting and Economics; Accounting Horizons; Accounting, Organizations and Society; Contemporary Accounting Research;* the *Journal of Management Accounting Research;* and the *Review of Accounting Studies.*

Professor Noreen has won a number of awards from students for his teaching.

Peter C. Brewer is a Lecturer in the Department of Accountancy at Wake Forest University. Prior to joining the faculty at Wake Forest, he was an accounting professor at Miami University for 19 years. He holds a BS degree in accounting from Penn State University, an MS degree in accounting from the University of Virginia, and a PhD from the University of Tennessee. He has published more than 40 articles in a variety of journals including: *Management Accounting Research;* the *Journal of Information Systems; Cost Management; Strategic Finance;* the *Journal of Accountancy; Issues in Accounting Education;* and the *Journal of Business Logistics.*

Professor Brewer has served on the editorial boards of the *Journal of Accounting Education* and *Issues in Accounting Education.* His article "Putting Strategy into the Balanced Scorecard" won the 2003 International Federation of Accountants' Articles of Merit competition, and his articles "Using Six Sigma to Improve the Finance Function" and "Lean Accounting: What's It All About?" were awarded the Institute of Management Accountants' Lybrand Gold and Silver Medals in 2005 and 2006. He has received Miami University's Richard T. Farmer School of Business Teaching Excellence Award.

Prior to joining the faculty at Miami University, Professor Brewer was employed as an auditor for Touche Ross in the firm's Philadelphia office. He also worked as an internal audit manager for the Board of Pensions of the Presbyterian Church (U.S.A.).

Let **Garrison** be Your Guide

For centuries, the lighthouse has provided guidance and safe passage for sailors. Similarly, Garrison/Noreen/Brewer has successfully guided millions of students through managerial accounting, lighting the way and helping them sail smoothly through the course.

Decades ago, lighthouses were still being operated manually. In these days of digital transformation, lighthouses are run using automatic lamp changers and other modern devices. In much the same way, Garrison/Noreen/Brewer has evolved over the years. Today, the Garrison book not only guides students—accounting majors and other business majors alike—safely through the course but is enhanced by a number of powerful tools to augment student learning and increase student motivation. Connect, which includes adaptive and interactive study features such as SmartBook, Concept Overview Videos, Auto-Graded Excel Simulations, and Guided Examples, as well as a repository of additional resources tied directly to the text, will improve students' engagement in and and out of class, help them maximize their study time, and make their learning experience more enjoyable. Animated, narrated Concept Overview Videos for each learning objective teach the core concepts of the text with auto-graded knowledge-check questions, and animated, narrated Guided Examples connected to practice exercises provide a step-by-step walk through of a similar exercise, assisting students when they need it most. Excel Simulations provide the student the opportunity to learn valuable Excel skills while solving problems specific to the text pedagogy.

Just as the lighthouse continues to provide reliable guidance to seafarers, the Garrison/Noreen/Brewer book continues its tradition of leading the way and helping students sail successfully through managerial accounting by always focusing on three important qualities: **relevance, accuracy,** and **clarity.**

I am a big fan of this book. I have taught this course with a few other books and this book does the best job tying all the concepts together. When asked I always refer to this book as being superior to the other books that I have used.

Garrison truly is the gold standard of managerial accounting texts.

Pamela Rouse,
Butler University

Christopher O'Byrne,
Cuyamaca College

Garrison is clearly the best managerial accounting text available.

Carleton Donchess,
Bridgewater State University

I have always liked this textbook in my over 20 years of teaching Accounting. It is quite readable and comprehensive and the end-of-chapter material is quite effective."

Rama Ramamurthy,
Georgetown University

RELEVANCE.

Every effort is made to help students relate the concepts in this book to the decisions made by working managers. In the sixteenth edition, the authors have added 13 new **Integration Exercises** that help students learn to think like managers. These exercises link learning objectives across chapters in ways that enable students to grasp how managerial accounting "all fits together" to provide enhanced managerial insights. New and revised In Business boxes throughout the book link chapter concepts to pertinent real-world examples. Service industry references appear throughout the chapter narrative and end-of-chapter material to provide students with relevant context for the material they are learning.

ACCURACY.

The Garrison book continues to set the standard for accurate and reliable material in its sixteenth edition. With each revision, the authors evaluate the book and its supplements in their entirety, working diligently to ensure that the end-of-chapter material, solutions manual, and test bank are consistent, current, and accurate.

CLARITY.

Generations of students have praised Garrison for the friendliness and readability of its writing, but that's just the beginning. In the sixteenth edition, the authors have rewritten various chapters with input and guidance from instructors around the country to ensure that teaching and learning from Garrison remains as easy as it can be.

The authors' steady focus on these three core elements has led to tremendous results. *Managerial Accounting* has consistently led the market, being used by over two million students and earning a reputation for reliability that other texts aspire to match.

Garrison's Powerful Pedagogy

Managerial Accounting includes pedagogical elements that engage and instruct students without cluttering the pages or interrupting student learning. Garrison's key pedagogical tools enhance and support students' understanding of the concepts rather than compete with the narrative for their attention.

NEW* Integration Exercises

We have added 13 new exercises (located in the back of the book) that integrate learning objectives across chapters. These exercises will increase the students' level of interest in the course because they forge the connections across chapters. Rather than seeing each chapter as an isolated set of learning objectives, students begin to see how "it all fits together" to provide greater managerial insight and more effective planning, controlling, and decision making. The integration exercises also are tailor-made for flipping the classroom because they offer challenging questions that require students to work in teams to derive solutions that synthesize what they have learning throughout the semester.

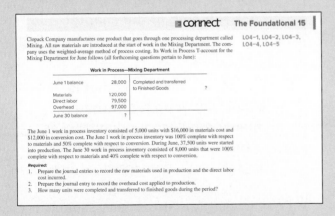

The Foundational 15

Each chapter contains one Foundational 15 exercise that includes 15 "building-block" questions related to one concise set of data. These exercises can be used for in-class discussion or as homework assignments. They are found before the Exercises and are available in **Connect.**

I like the "Foundational 15" and its integration of all the chapter objectives into one problem that can be reviewed in class.

Melanie Anderson, Slippery Rock University

Concept Overview Videos

New for the 16th edition of Garrison, the Concept Overview Videos cover each learning objective through narrated, animated presentations. Formerly Interactive Presentation, each Concept Overview Video has been enhanced for improved accessibility, and includes both the visual animations and transcript to accommodate all types of learners. The Concept Overview Videos also pause frequently to check for comprehension with assignable, auto-graded Knowledge Check questions..

CHAPTER 4

Process Costing

Costing the "Quicker-Picker-Upper"

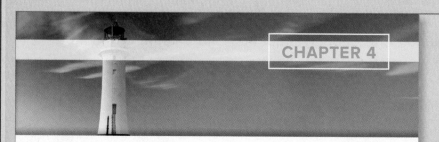

© Kristoffer Tripplaar/Alamy

If you have ever spilled milk, there is a good chance that you used Bounty paper towels to clean up the mess. **Procter & Gamble (P&G)** manufactures Bounty in two main processing departments—Paper Making and Paper Converting. In the Paper Making Department, wood pulp is converted into paper and then spooled into 2,000 pound rolls. In the Paper Converting Department, two of the 2,000 pound rolls of paper are simultaneously unwound into a machine that creates a two-ply paper towel that is decorated, perforated, and embossed to create texture. The large sheets of paper towels that emerge from this process are wrapped around a cylindrical cardboard core measuring eight feet in length. Once enough sheets wrap around the core, the eight foot roll is cut into individual rolls of Bounty that are sent down a conveyor to be wrapped, packed, and shipped.

In this type of manufacturing environment, costs cannot be readily traced to individual rolls of Bounty; however, given the homogeneous nature of the product, the total costs incurred in the Paper Making Department can be spread uniformly across its output of 2,000 pound rolls of paper. Similarly, the total costs incurred in the Paper Converting Department (including the cost of the 2,000 pound rolls that are transferred in from the Paper Making Department) can be spread uniformly across the number of cases of Bounty produced.

P&G uses a similar costing approach for many of its products such as Tide detergent, Crest toothpaste, and Dawn dishwashing liquid. ■

Source: Conversation with Brad Bays, formerly a Procter & Gamble financial executive.

LEARNING OBJECTIVES

After studying Chapter 4, you should be able to:

LO4–1	Record the flow of materials, labor, and overhead through a process costing system.
LO4–2	Compute the equivalent units of production using the weighted-average method.
LO4–3	Compute the cost per equivalent unit using the weighted-average method.
LO4–4	Assign costs to units using the weighted-average method.
LO4–5	Prepare a cost reconciliation report using the weighted-average method.
LO4–6	(Appendix 4A) Compute the equivalent units of production using the FIFO method.
LO4–7	(Appendix 4A) Compute the cost per equivalent unit using the FIFO method.
LO4–8	(Appendix 4A) Assign costs to units using the FIFO method.
LO4–9	(Appendix 4A) Prepare a cost reconciliation report using the FIFO method.
LO4–10	(Appendix 4B) Allocate service department costs to operating departments using the direct method.
LO4–11	(Appendix 4B) Allocate service department costs to operating departments using the step-down method.

Opening Vignette
Each chapter opens with a **Business Focus** feature that provides a real-world example for students, allowing them to see how the chapter's information and insights apply to the world outside the classroom. **Learning Objectives** alert students to what they should expect as they progress through the chapter.

I like how you engage the reader with the "Business Focus" at the beginning of the chapter.

Kathy Crusto-Way,
Tarrant County College

An excellent text that is especially good for introductory managerial accounting classes because it is organized in a logical topic development flow.

Elizabeth Widdison,
University of Washington, Seattle

Excellent coverage of the topics. Easy for students to read.

Sharon Bell,
The University of North Carolina at Pembroke

In Business Boxes

These helpful boxed features offer a glimpse into how real companies use the managerial accounting concepts discussed within the chapter. Each chapter contains multiple current examples.

MANAGERIAL ACCOUNTING IN ACTION
THE WRAP-UP

ACOUSTIC concepts inc

Prem Narayan and Bob Luchinni met to discuss the results of Bob's analysis.

Prem: Bob, everything you have shown me is pretty clear. I can see what impact the sales manager's suggestions would have on our profits. Some of those suggestions are quite good and others are not so good. I am concerned that our margin of safety is only 50 speakers. What can we do to increase this number?

Bob: Well, we have to increase total sales or decrease the break-even point or both.

Prem: And to decrease the break-even point, we have to either decrease our fixed expenses or increase our unit contribution margin?

Bob: Exactly.

Prem: And to increase our unit contribution margin, we must either increase our selling price or decrease the variable cost per unit?

Bob: Correct.

Prem: So what do you suggest?

Bob: Well, the analysis doesn't tell us which of these to do, but it does indicate we have a potential problem here.

Prem: If you don't have any immediate suggestions, I would like to call a general meeting next week to discuss ways we can work on increasing the margin of safety. I think everyone will be concerned about how vulnerable we are to even small downturns in sales.

Managerial Accounting in Action Vignettes

These vignettes depict cross-functional teams working together in real-life settings, working with the products and services that students recognize from their own lives. Students are shown step-by-step how accounting concepts are implemented in organizations and how these concepts are applied to solve everyday business problems. First, "The Issue" is introduced through a dialogue; the student then walks through the implementation process; finally, "The Wrap-up" summarizes the big picture.

In-depth, clear coverage; interesting updated examples in the "In Business" boxes.

Natalie Allen,
Texas A&M University

Extremely well written with great examples, including the "Managerial in Action" segments.

Loisanne Kattelman,
Weber State University

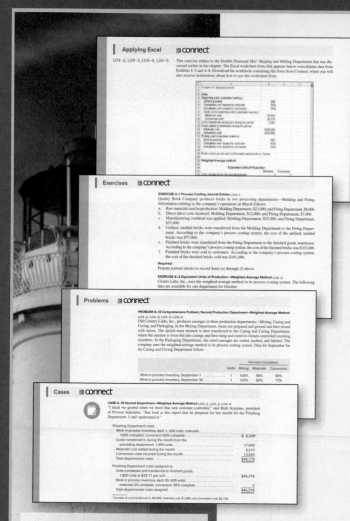

End-of-Chapter Material

Managerial Accounting has earned a reputation for the best end-of-chapter practice material of any text on the market. Our problem and case material continues to conform to AACSB recommendations and makes a great starting point for class discussions and group projects. When Ray Garrison first wrote *Managerial Accounting,* he started with the end-of-chapter material, then wrote the narrative in support of it. This unique approach to textbook authoring not only ensured consistency between the end-of-chapter material and text content but also underscored Garrison's fundamental belief in the importance of applying theory through practice. It is not enough for students to read, they must also understand. To this day, the guiding principle of that first edition remains, and Garrison's superior end-of-chapter material continues to provide accurate, current, and relevant practice for students.

Strong integration between chapter content and end-of-chapter exercises/problems. Clearly written and well-organized content.

Carleton Donchess, Bridgewater State University

Garrison has the best online material I have ever seen.

Minna Yu, Monmouth University

Utilizing the Icons

To reflect our service-based economy, the text is replete with examples from service-based businesses. A helpful icon distinguishes service-related examples in the text.

The IFRS icon highlights content that may be affected by the impending change to IFRS and possible convergence between U.S. GAAP and IFRS.

Ethics assignments and examples serve as a reminder that good conduct is vital in business. Icons call out content that relates to ethical behavior for students.

The writing icon denotes problems that require students to use critical thinking as well as writing skills to explain their decisions.

Author-Written Supplements

Unlike other managerial accounting texts, the book's authors write the major supplements such as the test bank and solution files, ensuring a perfect fit between text and supplements.

Guided Examples are one of my students' favorite features in Connect. They use them extensively to help with their homework.

Amy Bentley, Tallahassee Community College

I am a big proponent of including Excel® in the course. The students really need practice with Excel and this course really lends itself to providing good problems they can practice with.

Stacy Kline, Drexel University

Business Ethics are of growing importance and the coverage early in the book is commendable.

Heminigild Mpundu, University of Northern Iowa

Assurance of Learning Ready

Many educational institutions today are focused on the notion of assurance of learning, an important element of some accreditation standards. *Managerial Accounting,* 16e, is designed specifically to support your assurance of learning initiatives with a simple, yet powerful, solution.

Each question for *Managerial Accounting,* 16e, maps to a specific chapter learning outcome/objective listed in the text. The reporting features of **Connect** can aggregate student to make the collection and presentation of assurance of learning data simple and easy.

AACSB Statement

McGraw-Hill Education is a proud corporate member of AACSB International. Recognizing the importance and value of AACSB accreditation, we have sought to recognize the curricula guidelines detailed in AACSB standards for business accreditation by connecting selected questions in *Managerial Accounting,* 16e, to the general knowledge and skill guidelines found in the AACSB standards. The statements contained in *Managerial Accounting,* 16e, are provided only as a guide for the users of this text. The AACSB leaves content coverage and assessment clearly within the realm and control of individual schools, the mission of the school, and the faculty. The AACSB does also charge schools with the obligation of doing assessment against their own content and learning goals. While *Managerial Accounting,* 16e, and its teaching package make no claim of any specific AACSB qualification or evaluation, we have, within *Managerial Accounting,* 16e, tagged questions according to the six general knowledge and skills areas. The labels or tags within *Managerial Accounting,* 16e, are as indicated. There are, of course, many more within the test bank, the text, and the teaching package which might be used as a "standard" for your course. However, the labeled questions are suggested for your consideration.

New in the Sixteenth Edition

Faculty feedback helps us continue to improve *Managerial Accounting*. In response to reviewer suggestions, the authors have made the following changes to the text:

- We split the job-order costing chapter into two chapters to improve the students' ability to understand the material and to give professors greater flexibility in choosing how to cover the material.

- We reviewed all end-of-chapter exercises and problems and revised them as appropriate to better function within Connect.

- We added 13 Integration Exercises in the back of the book to help students connect the concepts. These exercises are suitable for both a flipped classroom model and in-class active learning environment as they engage students and encourage critical thinking.

- In-Business boxes are updated throughout to provide relevant and current real-world examples for use in classroom discussion and to support student understanding of key concepts as they read through a chapter.

Prologue
The Prologue has added coverage of the CGMA exam and an updated summary of the CMA exam content specifications.

Chapter 1
The high-low method has been removed from this chapter. We added an exhibit to visually depict product and period cost flows. We also made various changes to further emphasize the chapter's unifying theme of *different cost classifications for different purposes*. We have created 11 new end-of-chapter exercises/problems.

Chapter 2
This is a new chapter that explains how to use a job-order costing system to calculate unit product costs. It describes how to use plantwide and multiple overhead rates to apply overhead costs to individual jobs. The chapter has a strong managerial accounting orientation because it looks at how job-order costing systems serve the needs of internal managers.

Chapter 3
This is a new chapter that explains how job-order costing systems can be used to determine the value of ending inventories and cost of goods sold for external reporting purposes. The chapter has a strong financial accounting orientation because it uses journal entries and T-accounts to explain the flow of costs in a job-order costing system. The chapter also has a new appendix that uses Microsoft Excel® to explain the flow of costs in a job-order costing system.

Chapter 4

We revised the text in the main body of the chapter and Appendix 4A to better highlight the key concepts and steps needed to perform the weighted-average and FIFO process costing calculations. We also revised the first few paragraphs of Appendix 4B to better clarify its purpose and to better distinguish that purpose from the intent of the service department cost allocation coverage that appears later in the book.

Chapter 5

We added a new appendix that explains how to analyze mixed costs using the high-low method and the least-squares regression method.

Chapter 6

We added new text that better highlights this chapter's reliance on actual costing and contrasts it with the job-order costing chapters' reliance on normal costing.

Chapter 7

This chapter has a new appendix titled Time-Driven Activity-Based Costing: A Microsoft Excel-Based Approach.

Chapter 8

The end-of-chapter materials include three new exercises/problems (8-17, 8-18, and 8-27).

Chapter 9

We revised numerous end-of-chapter exercises and problems to better align them with Connect.

Chapter 10

We overhauled Appendix 10B to introduce students to a Microsoft Excel-based approach for creating an income statement using standard costing.

Chapter 11

This chapter includes four new In Business boxes.

Chapter 12

We revised the front-end of the chapter to better highlight the six key concepts that provide the foundation for effective decision making. We also revised the end-of-chapter exercises and problems to better dovetail with Connect and streamlined the coverage of sell or process further decisions to aid student comprehension. In addition, we relocated the Pricing appendix to this chapter and added new coverage of customer latitude and pricing and value-based pricing.

Chapter 13

We revised many end-of-chapter exercises and problems and extensively revised the formatting within Connect throughout all the chapters, (not just Chapter 13) to allow students greater flexibility for alternate methods of approaching a problem, such as performing net present value calculations.

Chapter 14

We added three new In Business boxes.

Chapter 15

We added four new In Business boxes.

Required=Results

©Getty Images/iStockphoto

McGraw-Hill Connect®
Learn Without Limits

Connect is a teaching and learning platform that is proven to deliver better results for students and instructors.

Connect empowers students by continually adapting to deliver precisely what they need, when they need it, and how they need it, so your class time is more engaging and effective.

73% of instructors who use **Connect** require it; instructor satisfaction **increases** by 28% when **Connect** is required.

Connect's Impact on Retention Rates, Pass Rates, and Average Exam Scores

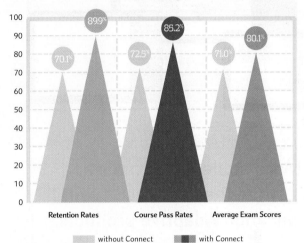

without Connect — with Connect

Using **Connect** improves retention rates by **19.8%**, passing rates by **12.7%**, and exam scores by **9.1%**.

Analytics

Connect Insight®

Connect Insight is Connect's new one-of-a-kind visual analytics dashboard—now available for both instructors and students—that provides at-a-glance information regarding student performance, which is immediately actionable. By presenting assignment, assessment, and topical performance results together with a time metric that is easily visible for aggregate or individual results, Connect Insight gives the user the ability to take a just-in-time approach to teaching and learning, which was never before available. Connect Insight presents data that empowers students and helps instructors improve class performance in a way that is efficient and effective.

Impact on Final Course Grade Distribution

without Connect		with Connect
22.9%	A	31.0%
27.4%	B	34.3%
22.9%	C	18.7%
11.5%	D	6.1%
15.4%	F	9.9%

Students can view their results for any **Connect** course.

Mobile

Connect's new, intuitive mobile interface gives students and instructors flexible and convenient, anytime–anywhere access to all components of the Connect platform.

Adaptive

THE **ADAPTIVE** READING EXPERIENCE DESIGNED TO TRANSFORM THE WAY STUDENTS READ

More students earn **A's** and **B's** when they use McGraw-Hill Education **Adaptive** products.

SmartBook®

Proven to help students improve grades and study more efficiently, SmartBook contains the same content within the print book, but actively tailors that content to the needs of the individual. SmartBook's adaptive technology provides precise, personalized instruction on what the student should do next, guiding the student to master and remember key concepts, targeting gaps in knowledge and offering customized feedback, and driving the student toward comprehension and retention of the subject matter. Available on tablets, SmartBook puts learning at the student's fingertips—anywhere, anytime.

Over **8 billion questions** have been answered, making McGraw-Hill Education products more intelligent, reliable, and precise.

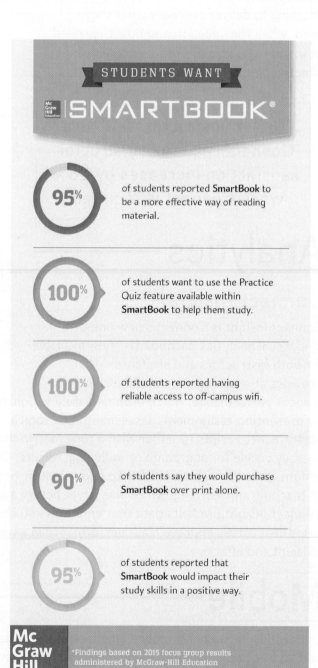

STUDENTS WANT

Mc Graw Hill Education **SMARTBOOK®**

95% of students reported SmartBook to be a more effective way of reading material.

100% of students want to use the Practice Quiz feature available within SmartBook to help them study.

100% of students reported having reliable access to off-campus wifi.

90% of students say they would purchase SmartBook over print alone.

95% of students reported that SmartBook would impact their study skills in a positive way.

Mc Graw Hill Education

*Findings based on 2015 focus group results administered by McGraw-Hill Education

Acknowledgments

Suggestions from professors, students, and the professional accounting community continue to drive the excellence and refinement of each edition of this book. Each of those who have offered comments and suggestions has our immense gratitude and thanks.

The efforts of many people are needed to continually refine a text and maintain its excellence. Among these people are the reviewers and consultants who point out areas of concern, cite areas of strength, and make recommendations for change. In this regard, the following academics have provided feedback that was enormously helpful in preparing the sixteenth edition of *Managerial Accounting:*

Dawn Addington, *Central New Mexico Community College*
Nasrollah Ahadiat, *California State PolytecnicUniversity*
Markus Ahrens, *St. Louis Community College–Meramec*
Akinloye Akindayomi, *University Of Massachusetts–Dartmouth*
David Albrecht, *Bowling Green State University*
Natalie Allen, *Texas A & M University*
Vern Allen, *Central Florida Community College*
Shamir Ally, *DeSales University*
Felix Amenkhienan, *Radford University*
Jane Austin, *Oklahoma City University*
John Babich, *Kankakee Community College*
Ibolya Balog, *Cedar Crest College*
Bonnie Banks, *Alabama A&M University*
Scottie Barty, *Northern Kentucky University*
Eric Bashaw, *University of Nevada–Las Vegas*
Lamrot Bekele, *Dallas County Community College*
Sharon Bell, *University of North Carolina–Pembroke*
Amy Bentley, *Tallahassee Community College Pamela Benner, Stark State College*
Stephen Benner, *Eastern Illinois University*
Scott Berube, *University of New Hampshire*
Kelly Blacker, *Mercy College*
Phillip Blanchard, *The University of Arizona*
Charles Blumer, *Saint Charles Community College*
Rachel Brassine, *East Carolina University*
Alison Jill Brock, *Imperial Valley College*
Ann Brooks, *University of New Mexico*
Rada Brooks, *University of California–Berkeley*
Myra Bruegger, *Southeastern Community College*
Georgia Buckles, *Manchester Community College*
Esther Bunn, *Stephen S. Austin State University*
Laurie Burney, *Mississippi State University*
Marci Butterfield, *University of Utah–Salt Lake City*
Charles Caliendo, *University of Minnesota*
Donald Campbell, *Brigham Young University–Idaho*
Don Campodonico, *Notre Dame de Namur University*
Dana Carpenter, *Madison Area Technical College*

Wanda Causseaux, *Valdosta State University*
David Centers, *Grand Valley State University*
Sandra Cereola, *James Madison University*
Gayle Chaky, *Dutchess Community College*
Pamela Champeau, *University of Wisconsin Whitewater*
Kathryn Chang, *Sonoma State University*
Valerie Chau, *Palomar College*
Clement Chen, *University of Michigan–Flint*
Carolyn Christesen, *Westchester Community College*
Star Ciccio, *Johnson & Wales University*
Richard S. Claire, *Canada College*
Robert Clarke, *Brigham Young University–Idaho*
Curtis Clements, *Abilene Christian University*
Darlene Coarts, *University of Northern Iowa*
Ron Collins, *Miami University–Ohio*
Carol Coman, *California Lutheran University*
Jackie Conrecode, *Florida Gulf Coast University*
Debora Constable, *Georgia Perimeter College*
Rita Cook, *University of Delaware*
Wendy Coons, *University of Maine*
Susan Corder, *Johnson County Community College*
Michael Cornick, *Winthrop University*
Deb Cosgrove, *University of Nebraska–Lincoln*
Kathy Crusto-Way, *Tarrant County College*
Robin D'Agati, *Palm Beach State College–Lake Worth*
Masako Darrough, *Baruch College*
Patricia Davis, *Keystone College*
Kathleen Davisson, *University of Denver*
Nina Doherty, *Arkansas Tech University*
Patricia Doherty, *Boston University*
Carleton Donchess, *Bridgewater State University*
Peter Dorff, *Kent State University*
David Doyon, *Southern New Hampshire University*
Emily Drogt, *Grand Valley State University*
Rita Dufour, *Northeast Wisconsin Technical College*
Barbara Durham, *University of Central Florida*
Dean Edmiston, *Emporia State University*
Barb Eide, *University of Wisconsin–Lacrosse*

Jerrilyn Eisenhauer, *Tulsa Community College*
Rafik Elias, *California State University–Los Angeles*
Dr. Gene Elrod, *University of Texas at Arlington*
Raymond Elson, *Valdosta State University*
Richard F. Emery, *Linfield College*
Ruth Epps, *Virginia Commonwealth University*
John Eubanks, *Independence Community College*
Christopher M. Fairchild, *Southeastern University*
Amanda Farmer, *University of Georgia*
Jack Fatica, *Terra Community College*
Christos Fatouros, *Curry College*
Susan Ferguson, *James Madison University*
Janice Fergusson, *University of South Carolina*
Jerry Ferry, *University of North Alabama*
Calvin Fink, *Bethune Cookman University*
Virginia Fullwood, *Texas A&M University–Commerce*
Robert Gannon, *Alvernia University*
Joseph Gerard, *University of Wisconsin Whitewater*
Frank Gersich, *Monmouth College*
Hubert Gill, *North Florida*
Jeff Gillespie, *University of Delaware*
Earl Godfrey, *Gardner–Webb University*
Nina Goza, *Arkansas Tech University*
Marina Grau, *Huston Community College–Northwest College*
Alfred C. Greenfield, Jr., *High Point University*
Olen Greer, *Missouri State University*
Connie Groer, *Frostburg State University*
Steve Groves, *Ivy Tech Community College of Indiana–Kokomo*
Thomas Guarino, *Plymouth State University*
Bob Gutschick, *College of Southern Nevada*
Ty Handy, *Vermont Technical College*
David Harr, *George Mason University*
Michael Haselkorn, *Bentley University*
Susan Hass, *Simmons College*
John Haverty, *St. Joseph's University*
Hassan Hefzi, *Cal Poly Pomona University*
Candice Heino, *Anoka Ramsey Community College*
Sueann Hely, *West Kentucky Community & Technical College*
David Henderson, *College of Charleston*
Donna Hetzel, *Western Michigan University–Kalamazoo*
Kristina Hoang, *Tulane University*
Cynthia Hollenbach, *University of Denver*
Peg Horan, *Wagner College*
Rong Huang, *Baruch College*
Steven Huddart, *Penn State*
George Hunt, *Stephen F Austin State University*
Marianne James, *California State University, Los Angeles*
Mary Jepperson, *College of Saint Benedict & Saint John's University*

Gene Johnson, *Clark College*
Becky Jones, *Baylor University*
Jeffrey Jones, *College of Southern Nevada*
Kevin Jones, *Drexel University*
Bill Joyce, *Minnesota State University–Mankato*
Celina Jozsi, *University of South Florida*
Robert L. Kachur, *Richard Stockton College of New Jersey*
Loisanne Kattelman, *Weber State University*
Sue Kattelus, *Michigan State University–East Lansing*
Gokham Karahan, *University of Anchorage Alaska*
Nancy Kelly, *Middlesex Community College*
Anna Kenner, *Brevard Community College*
Sara Kern, *Gonzaga University*
Lara Kessler, *Grand Valley State University*
Mozaffar Khan, *University of Minnesota*
Frank Klaus, *Cleveland State University*
Shirly Kleiner, *Johnson County Community College*
Stacy Kline, *Drexel University*
Christine Kloezeman, *Glendale Community College*
Bill Knowles, *University of New Hampshire*
Barbara Kren, *Marquette University*
Jerry Kreuze, *Western Michigan University*
David Krug, *Johnson County Community College*
Wikil Kwak, *Nebraska Omaha*
C. Andrew Lafond, *LaSalle University*
Dr. Ben Lansford, *Rice University*
Yvette Lazdowski, *Plymouth Statue University*
Ron Lazer, *University of Houston–Houston*
Raymond Levesque, *Bentley College*
Jing Lin, *Saint Joseph's University*
Dennis Lopez, *University of Texas–San Antonio*
Gina Lord, *Santa Rosa Junior College*
Don Lucy, *Indian River State College*
Cathy Lumbattis, *Southern Illinois University*
Joseph F. Lupino, *St. Mary's College of California*
Patrick M. Lynch, *Loyola University of New Orleans*
Suneel Maheshwari, *Marshall University*
Linda Malgeri, *Kennesaw State University*
Michael Manahan, *California State University–Dominquez Hills*
Carol Mannino, *Milwaukee School of Engineering*
Steven Markoff, *Montclair State University*
Linda Marquis, *Northern Kentucky University*
Melissa Martin, *Arizona State University*
Michele Martinez, *Hillsborough Community College*
Josephine Mathias, *Mercer Community College*
Florence McGovern, *Bergen Community College*
Annie McGowan, *Texas A&M University*
Michael McLain, *Hampton University*
Gloria McVay, *Winona State University*
Heidi Meier, *Cleveland State University*

Edna Mitchell, *Polk State College*
Kim Mollberg, *Minnesota State University–Moorhead*
Shirley Montagne, *Lyndon State College*
Andrew Morgret, *Christian Brothers University*
Jennifer Moriarty, *Hudson Valley Community College*
Kenneth Morlino, *Wilmington University*
Michael Morris, *University of Notre Dame*
Mark Motluck, *Anderson University*
Heminigild Mpundu, *University of Northern Iowa*
Matt Muller, *Adirondack Community College*
Michael Newman, *University of Houston–Houston*
Hossein Noorian, *Wentworth Institue of Technology*
Christopher O'Byrne, *Cuyamaca College*
Janet O'Tousa, *University of Notre Dame*
Mehmet Ozbilgin, *Bernard M. Baruch College*
Janet Papiernik, *Indiana University–Purdue University Fort Wayne*
Abbie Gail Parham, *Georgia Southern*
Mary Pearson, *Southern Utah University*
Judy Peterson, *Monmouth College*
Yvonne Phang, *Bernard M. Baruch College*
Debbie Pike, *Saint Louis University*
Jo Ann Pinto, *Montclair State University*
Janice Pitera, *Broome Community College*
Angela Pannell, *Mississippi State University*
Matthew Probst, *Ivy Tech Community College*
Laura Prosser, *Black Hills State University*
Herbert Purick, *Palm Beach State College–Lake Worth*
Rama Ramamurthy, *Georgetown University*
Paulette Ratliff-Miller, *Grand Valley State University*
Vasant Raval, *Creighton University*
Margaret Reed, *University of Cincinnati*
Vernon Richardson, *University of Arkansas–Fayetteville*
Marc B. Robinson, *Richard Stockton College of New Jersey*
Ramon Rodriguez, *Murray State University*
Alan Rogers, *Franklin University*
David Rogers, *Mesa State College*
Lawrence A. Roman, *Cuyahoga Community College*
Luther Ross, Sr., *Central Piedmont Community College*
Pamela Rouse, *Butler University*
Martin Rudnick, *William Paterson University*
Amal Said, *University of Toledo*
Yehia Salama, *University of Illinois–Chicago*
Mary Scarborough, *Tyler Junior College*
Rex Schildhouse, *Miramar College*
Nancy Schrumpf, *Parkland College*
Jeremy Schwartz, *Youngstown State University*
Pamela Schwer, *St. Xavier University*
Vineeta Sharma, *Florida International University–Miami*

Jeffrey Shields, *University of Southern Maine*
Kathe Shinham, *Northern Arizona University at Flagstaff*
Franklin Shuman, *Utah State University–Logan*
Danny Siciliano, *University of Nevada at Las Vegas*
Kenneth Sinclair, *LeHigh University*
Lakshmy Sivaratnam, *Kansas City Kansas Community College*
Talitha Smith, *Auburn University–Auburn*
Diane Stark, *Phoenix College*
Dennis Stovall, *Grand Valley State University*
Gracelyn Stuart-Tuggle, *Palm Beach State College–Boca Campus*
Suzy Summers, *Furman University*
Kenton Swift, *University of Montana*
Scott Szilagyi, *Fordham University–Rose Hill*
Karen Tabak, *Maryville University*
Rita Taylor, *University of Cincinnati*
Lisa Tekmetarovic, *Truman College*
Teresa Thamer, *Brenau University*
Amanda Thompson-Abbott, *Marshall University*
Jerry Thorne, *North Carolina A&T State University*
Don Trippeer, *State University of New York at Oneonta*
Robin Turner, *Rowan-Cabarrus Community College*
Tracy Campbell Tuttle, *San Diego Mesa Community College*
Eric Typpo, *University of the Pacific*
Suneel Udpa, *University of California–Berkeley*
Michael Van Breda, *Southern Methodist University*
Jayaraman Vijayakumar, *Virginia Commonwealth University*
Ron Vogel, *College of Eastern Utah*
David Vyncke, *Scott Community College*
Terri Walsh, *Seminole State College of Florida*
Lorry Wasserman, *University of Portland*
Richard Watson, *University of California–Santa Barbara*
Victoria Wattigny, *Midwestern State University*
Betsy Wenz, *Indiana University–Kokomo*
Robert Weprin, *Lourdes College*
Gwendolen White, *Ball State University*
Elizabeth Widdison, *University of Washington–Seattle*
Val Williams, *Duquesne University*
Janet Woods, *Macon State College*
John Woodward, *Polk State College*
Jia Wu, *University OF Massachusetts–Dartmouth*
Emily Xu, *University of New Hampshire*
Claire Yan, *University or Arkansas–Fayetteville*
James Yang, *Montclair State University*
Jeff Yu, *Southern Methodist University*
Bert Zarb, *Embry-Riddle Aeronautical University*
Thomas Zeller, *Loyola University–Chicago*

We are grateful for the outstanding support from McGraw-Hill. In particular, we would like to thank Tim Vertovec, Managing Director; Patricia Plumb, Brand Manager; Erin Quinones, Product Developer; Cheryl Osgood, Marketing Manager; Peggy Hussey, Director of Digital Development; Kevin Moran, Associate Director or Digital Content; Xin Lin, Senior Digital Product Analyst; Pat Frederickson, Lead Content Project Manager (core); Angela Norris, Senior Content Project Manager (assessments); Daryl Horrocks, Program Manager; Matt Diamond, Senior Designer; and Content Licensing Specialists Melissa Homer and Lori Slattery.

Special thanks also to the team of contributors who spend countless hours helping us build and test our digital assets and ancillary materials. This team includes the best and brightest in the business. Julie Hankins (as Lead Digital Contributor), deserves special mention for her tireless efforts in building, testing, and supporting others in producing the Connect assessment content. We also thank the following contributors: Patti Lopez (Valencia College), for her continued lead in building our adaptive products; Kay Poston (Francis Marion University), Beth Woods (subject matter and digital consultant), and Mark McCarthy (East Carolina University), for their detailed Connect accuracy reviews; Ilene Persoff (Long Island University); Ann Brooks (University of New Mexico), for her authoring contributions to the redesigned Concept Overview Videos and adaptive product testing; Jeannie Folk (member of the Illinois Board of Examiners), for her work on both the updates to the Lecture Notes and redesigned Concept Overview Videos; Jon A. Booker (Tennessee Technological University), Cynthia J. Rooney (University of New Mexico), and Susan C. Galbreath (Lipscomb University), for crafting PowerPoint presentations; Margaret Shackell-Dowell (Cornell University), for her continued authoring excellence of the Guided Examples; and Helen Roybark (Radford University), for her detailed text and instructor manual reviews.

We are grateful to the Institute of Certified Management Accountants for permission to use questions and/or unofficial answers from past Certificate in Management Accounting (CMA) examinations.

Ray H. Garrison • Eric Noreen • Peter Brewer

Brief Contents

Contents

Chapter **2**

Job-Order Costing: Calculating Unit Product Costs 67

Chapter **3**

Job-Order Costing: Cost Flows and External Reporting 110

Process Costing   154

Comparison of Job-Order and Process Costing   155

Similarities between Job-Order and
Process Costing   155

Differences between Job-Order and Process
Costing   155

Cost Flows in Process Costing   156

Processing Departments   156

The Flow of Materials, Labor, and Overhead Costs   157

Materials, Labor, and Overhead Cost Entries   158

   Materials Costs   158

   Labor Costs   158

   Overhead Costs   158

   Completing the Cost Flows   159

Process Costing Computations: Three Key Concepts   159

Key Concept #1   160

Key Concept #2   160

Key Concept #3   160

Cost-Volume-Profit Relationships   196

The Basics of Cost-Volume-Profit (CVP) Analysis   198

Contribution Margin   198

CVP Relationships in Equation Form   200

CVP Relationships in Graphic Form   201

   Preparing the CVP Graph   201

Contribution Margin Ratio (CM Ratio) and the Variable
Expense Ratio   203

   Applications of the Contribution Margin Ratio   205

Additional Applications of CVP Concepts   206

   *Example 1: Change in Fixed Cost and
Sales Volume   206*

   Alternative Solution 1   207

   Alternative Solution 2   207

   *Example 2: Change in Variable Costs and
Sales Volume   207*

   Solution   207

   *Example 3: Change in Fixed Cost, Selling Price, and
Sales Volume   207*

   Solution   208

Chapter 6

Variable Costing and Segment Reporting: Tools for Management 257

Chapter 7

Activity-Based Costing:
A Tool to Aid Decision Making   310

Activity-Based Costing: An Overview   311

Nonmanufacturing Costs and Activity-Based
Costing   311

Manufacturing Costs and Activity-Based Costing   312

Cost Pools, Allocation Bases, and Activity-Based
Costing   312

Designing an Activity-Based Costing (ABC) System   315

Steps for Implementing Activity-Based Costing: 317

Step 1: Define Activities, Activity Cost Pools, and
Activity Measures   318

The Mechanics of Activity-Based Costing   319

Step 2: Assign Overhead Costs to Activity Cost Pools   319

Step 3: Calculate Activity Rates   322

Step 4: Assign Overhead Costs to Cost Objects   323

Step 5: Prepare Management Reports   326

Comparison of Traditional and ABC Product
Costs   329

Product Margins Computed Using the Traditional Cost
System   329

The Differences between ABC and Traditional Product
Costs   330

Targeting Process Improvements   333

Activity-Based Costing and External Reports   334

The Limitations of Activity-Based Costing   334

Chapter 8

Master Budgeting   362

Why and How Do Organizations Create Budgets?   363

Advantages of Budgeting   363

Responsibility Accounting   363

Choosing a Budget Period   364

The Self-Imposed Budget   364

Human Factors in Budgeting   365

The Master Budget: An Overview   365

Seeing the Big Picture   367

Preparing the Master Budget   368

The Beginning Balance Sheet   369

The Budgeting Assumptions   369

The Sales Budget   372

The Production Budget   373

Inventory Purchases—Merchandising Company   374

The Direct Materials Budget   374

The Direct Labor Budget   376

The Manufacturing Overhead Budget   377

The Ending Finished Goods Inventory Budget   378

The Selling and Administrative Expense Budget   379

The Cash Budget   380

The Budgeted Income Statement   384

The Budgeted Balance Sheet   385

Flexible Budgets and Performance Analysis   413

Standard Costs and Variances   449

Performance Measurement in Decentralized Organizations   506

Chapter 12

Differential Analysis: The Key to Decision Making   560

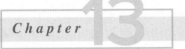

Chapter 13

Chapter 14

Financial Statement Analysis   725

Credits for Chapter Openers

(1) © Raymond Boyd/Getty Images; (2) Courtesy of University Tees, Inc.; (3) © Pixtal/AGE Fotostock; (4) © Kristoffer Tripplaar/Alamy; (5) © Everett Collection Inc/Alamy; (6) © Bloomberg/Getty Images; (7) © Scott Eells/Bloomberg/Getty Images; (8) © Sandee Noreen; (9) © Michael Sears/MCT/Newscom; (10) © Bloomberg/Getty Images; (11) © Luke Sharrett/Bloomberg/Getty Images; (12) © Ian Dagnall/Alamy; (13) © David Goldman/AP Images; (14) © Bloomberg/Getty Images; (15) © Lionel Bonaventure/AFP/Getty Images.

Managerial Accounting: An Overview

Managerial Accounting: It's More Than Just Crunching Numbers

© LuckyImages/Shutterstock.com

"Creating value through values" is the credo of today's management accountant. It means that management accountants should maintain an unwavering commitment to ethical values while using their knowledge and skills to influence decisions that create value for organizational stakeholders. These skills include managing risks and implementing strategy through planning, budgeting and forecasting, and decision support. Management accountants are strategic business partners who understand the financial and operational sides of the business. They report and analyze financial as well as nonfinancial measures of process performance and corporate social performance. Think of these responsibilities as relating to profits (financial statements), processes (customer focus and satisfaction), people (employee learning and satisfaction), and the planet (environmental stewardship). ∎

Source: Conversation with Jeff Thomson, president and CEO of the Institute of Management Accountants.

What Is Managerial Accounting?

The prologue explains why managerial accounting is important to the future careers of all business students. It begins by answering two questions: (1) What is managerial accounting? and (2) Why does managerial accounting matter to your career? It concludes by discussing six topics—ethics, strategic management, enterprise risk management, corporate social responsibility, process management, and leadership—that define the business context for applying the quantitative aspects of managerial accounting.

Many students enrolled in this course will have recently completed an introductory *financial accounting* course. **Financial accounting** is concerned with reporting financial information to external parties, such as stockholders, creditors, and regulators. **Managerial accounting** is concerned with providing information to managers for use within the organization. Exhibit P–1 summarizes seven key differences between financial and managerial accounting. It recognizes that the fundamental difference between financial and managerial accounting is that financial accounting serves the needs of those *outside* the organization, whereas managerial accounting serves the needs of managers employed *inside* the organization. Because of this fundamental difference in users, financial accounting emphasizes the financial consequences of past activities, objectivity and verifiability, precision, and

EXHIBIT P–1
Comparison of Financial and Managerial Accounting

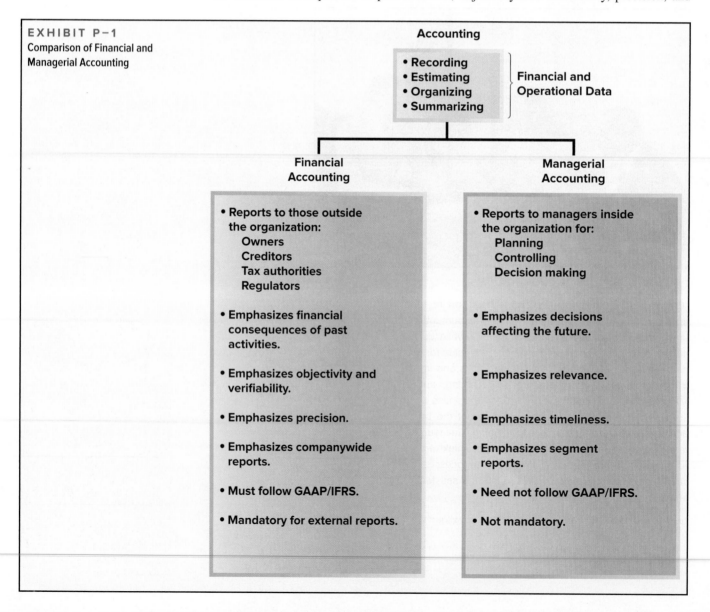

Accounting

- Recording
- Estimating
- Organizing
- Summarizing

Financial and Operational Data

Financial Accounting

- Reports to those outside the organization:
    Owners
    Creditors
    Tax authorities
    Regulators

- Emphasizes financial consequences of past activities.

- Emphasizes objectivity and verifiability.

- Emphasizes precision.

- Emphasizes companywide reports.

- Must follow GAAP/IFRS.

- Mandatory for external reports.

Managerial Accounting

- Reports to managers inside the organization for:
    Planning
    Controlling
    Decision making

- Emphasizes decisions affecting the future.

- Emphasizes relevance.

- Emphasizes timeliness.

- Emphasizes segment reports.

- Need not follow GAAP/IFRS.

- Not mandatory.

companywide performance, whereas managerial accounting emphasizes decisions affecting the future, relevance, timeliness, and *segment* performance. A **segment** is a part or activity of an organization about which managers would like cost, revenue, or profit data. Examples of business segments include product lines, customer groups (segmented by age, ethnicity, gender, volume of purchases, etc.), geographic territories, divisions, plants, and departments. Finally, financial accounting is mandatory for external reports and it needs to comply with rules, such as generally accepted accounting principles (GAAP) and international financial reporting standards (IFRS), whereas managerial accounting is not mandatory and it does not need to comply with externally imposed rules.

As mentioned in Exhibit P–1, managerial accounting helps managers perform three vital activities—*planning, controlling,* and *decision making.* **Planning** involves establishing goals and specifying how to achieve them. **Controlling** involves gathering feedback to ensure that the plan is being properly executed or modified as circumstances change. **Decision making** involves selecting a course of action from competing alternatives. Now let's take a closer look at these three pillars of managerial accounting.

Planning

Assume that you work for **Procter & Gamble (P&G)** and that you are in charge of the company's campus recruiting for all undergraduate business majors. In this example, your planning process would begin by establishing a goal such as: our goal is to recruit the "best and brightest" college graduates. The next stage of the planning process would require specifying how to achieve this goal by answering numerous questions such as:

- How many students do we need to hire in total and from each major?
- What schools do we plan to include in our recruiting efforts?
- Which of our employees will be involved in each school's recruiting activities?
- When will we conduct our interviews?
- How will we compare students to one another to decide who will be extended job offers?
- What salary will we offer our new hires? Will the salaries differ by major?
- How much money can we spend on our recruiting efforts?

As you can see, there are many questions that need to be answered as part of the planning process. Plans are often accompanied by a *budget.* A **budget** is a detailed plan for the future that is usually expressed in formal quantitative terms. As the head of recruiting at P&G, your budget would include two key components. First, you would have to work with other senior managers inside the company to establish a budgeted amount of total salaries that can be offered to all new hires. Second, you would have to create a budget that quantifies how much you intend to spend on your campus recruiting activities.

THE FINANCIAL SIDE OF RUNNING A COMMUNITY THEATRE

Formulating plans and creating budgets is an important part of running a community theater. For example, the **Manatee Players** is a theater group from Bradenton, Florida, that has seen its annual operating budget grow from $480,000 to $1.5 million over the last 10 years. The theater's ticket sales cover about 77% of its operating costs, with additional financial support coming from individual and corporate donors.

In additional to managing its revenues, the theater also seeks to control its costs in various ways—such as saving $3,000 per year by bringing the production of its programs in-house. Rather than promoting individual shows, the group has decided to focus its marketing dollars on touting the entire season of shows. It also shifted a portion of its marketing budget away from traditional methods to more cost-effective social-media outlets.

Source: Kevin Brass, "Let's Put on a Show," *The Wall Street Journal,* November 3, 2014, p. D7.

© McGraw-Hill Education/Christopher Kerrigan, photographer

Controlling

Once you established and started implementing P&G's recruiting plan, you would transition to the control process. This process would involve gathering, evaluating, and responding to feedback to ensure that this year's recruiting process meets expectations. It would also include evaluating the feedback in search of ways to run a more effective recruiting campaign next year. The control process would involve answering questions such as:

- Did we succeed in hiring the planned number of students within each major and at each school?
- Did we lose too many exceptional candidates to competitors?
- Did each of our employees involved in the recruiting process perform satisfactorily?
- Is our method of comparing students to one another working?
- Did the on-campus and office interviews run smoothly?
- Did we stay within our budget in terms of total salary commitments to new hires?
- Did we stay within our budget regarding spending on recruiting activities?

As you can see, there are many questions that need to be answered as part of the control process. When answering these questions your goal would be to go beyond simple yes or no answers in search of the underlying reasons why performance exceeded or failed to meet expectations. Part of the control process includes preparing *performance reports*. A **performance report** compares budgeted data to actual data in an effort to identify and learn from excellent performance and to identify and eliminate sources of unsatisfactory performance. Performance reports can also be used as one of many inputs to help evaluate and reward employees.

Although this example focused on P&G's campus recruiting efforts, we could have described how planning enables **FedEx** to deliver packages across the globe overnight, or how it helped **Apple** develop and market the iPad. We could have discussed how the control process helps **Pfizer**, **Eli Lilly**, and **Abbott Laboratories** ensure that their pharmaceutical drugs are produced in conformance with rigorous quality standards, or how **Kroger** relies on the control process to keep its grocery shelves stocked. We also could have looked at planning and control failures such as **Takata**'s recall of more than 30 million defective driver-side air bags installed by a variety of automakers such as **Honda**, **Ford**, **Toyota**, and **Subaru**. In short, all managers (and that probably includes you someday) perform planning and controlling activities.

Decision Making

Perhaps the most basic managerial skill is the ability to make intelligent, data-driven decisions. Broadly speaking, many of those decisions revolve around the following three questions. *What* should we be selling? *Who* should we be serving? *How* should we execute? Exhibit P–2 provides examples of decisions pertaining to each of these three categories.

The left-hand column of Exhibit P–2 suggests that every company must make decisions related to the products and services that it sells. For example, each year **Procter & Gamble** must decide how to allocate its marketing budget across numerous brands that each generates over $1 billion in sales as well as other brands that have promising growth potential. **Mattel** must decide what new toys to introduce to the market. **Southwest Airlines** must decide what ticket prices to establish for each of its thousands of flights per day. **General Motors** must decide whether to discontinue certain models of automobiles.

The middle column of Exhibit P–2 indicates that all companies must make decisions related to the customers that they serve. For example, **Sears** must decide how to allocate its marketing budget between products that tend to appeal to male versus female customers. **FedEx** must decide whether to expand its services into new markets across the globe. **Hewlett-Packard** must decide what price discounts to offer corporate clients that purchase large volumes of its products. A bank must decide whether to discontinue customers that may be unprofitable.

EXHIBIT P–2
Examples of Decisions

What should we be selling?	Who should we be serving?	How should we execute?
What products and services should be the focus of our marketing efforts?	Who should be the focus of our marketing efforts?	How should we supply our parts and services?
What new products and services should we offer?	Who should we start serving?	How should we expand our capacity?
What prices should we charge for our products and services?	Who should pay price premiums or receive price discounts?	How should we reduce our capacity?
What products and services should we discontinue?	Who should we stop serving?	How should we improve our efficiency and effectiveness?

The right-hand column of Exhibit P–2 shows that companies also make decisions related to how they execute. For example, Boeing must decide whether to rely on outside vendors such as Goodrich, Saab, and Rolls-Royce to manufacture many of the parts used to make its airplanes. Cintas must decide whether to expand its laundering and cleaning capacity in a given geographic region by adding square footage to an existing facility or by constructing an entirely new facility. In an economic downturn, a manufacturer might have to decide whether to eliminate one 8-hour shift at three plants or to close one plant. Finally, all companies have to decide among competing improvement opportunities. For example, a company may have to decide whether to implement a new software system, to upgrade a piece of equipment, or to provide extra training to its employees.

This portion of the chapter has explained that the three pillars of managerial accounting are planning, controlling, and decision making. This book helps prepare you to become an effective manager by explaining how to make intelligent data-driven decisions, how to create financial plans for the future, and how to continually make progress toward achieving goals by obtaining, evaluating, and responding to feedback.

Why Does Managerial Accounting Matter to Your Career?

Many students feel anxious about choosing a major because they are unsure if it will provide a fulfilling career. To reduce these anxieties, we recommend deemphasizing what you cannot control about the future; instead focusing on what you can control right now. More specifically, concentrate on answering the following question: What can you do now to prepare for success in an unknown future career? The best answer is to learn skills that will make it easier for you to adapt to an uncertain future. You need to become adaptable!

Whether you end up working in the United States or abroad, for a large corporation, a small entrepreneurial company, a nonprofit organization, or a governmental entity, you'll need to know how to plan for the future, how to make progress toward achieving goals, and how to make intelligent decisions. In other words, managerial accounting skills are useful in just about any career, organization, and industry. If you commit energy to this course, you'll be making a smart investment in your future—even though you cannot clearly envision it. Next, we will elaborate on this point by explaining how managerial accounting relates to the future careers of business majors and accounting majors.

Business Majors

Exhibit P–3 provides examples of how planning, controlling, and decision making affect three majors other than accounting—marketing, supply chain management, and human resource management.

EXHIBIT P–3
Relating Managerial Accounting to
Three Business Majors

	Marketing	Supply Chain Management	Human Resource Management
Planning	How much should we budget for TV, print, and Internet advertising?	How many units should we plan to produce next period?	How much should we plan to spend for occupational safety training?
	How many salespeople should we plan to hire to serve a new territory?	How much should we budget for next period's utility expense?	How much should we plan to spend on employee recruitment advertising?
Controlling	Is the budgeted price cut increasing unit sales as expected?	Did we spend more or less than expected for the units we actually produced?	Is our employee retention rate exceeding our goals?
	Are we accumulating too much inventory during the holiday shopping season?	Are we achieving our goal of reducing the number of defective units produced?	Are we meeting our goal of completing timely performance appraisals?
Decision Making	Should we sell our services as one bundle or sell them separately?	Should we transfer production of a component part to an overseas supplier?	Should we hire an on-site medical staff to lower our health care costs?
	Should we sell directly to customers or use a distributor?	Should we redesign our manufacturing process to lower inventory levels?	Should we hire temporary workers or full-time employees?

The left-hand column of Exhibit P–3 describes some planning, controlling, and decision-making applications in the marketing profession. For example, marketing managers make planning decisions related to allocating advertising dollars across various communication mediums and to staffing new sales territories. From a control standpoint, they may closely track sales data to see if a budgeted price cut is generating an anticipated increase in unit sales, or they may study inventory levels during the holiday shopping season so that they can adjust prices as needed to optimize sales. Marketing managers also make many important decisions such as whether to bundle services together and sell them for one price or to sell each service separately. They may also decide whether to sell products directly to the customer or to sell to a distributor, who then sells to the end consumer.

The middle column of Exhibit P–3 states that supply chain managers have to plan how many units to produce to satisfy anticipated customer demand. They also need to budget for operating expenses such as utilities, supplies, and labor costs. In terms of control, they monitor actual spending relative to the budget, and closely watch operational measures such as the number of defects produced relative to the plan. Supply chain managers make numerous decisions, such as deciding whether to transfer production of a component part to an overseas supplier. They also decide whether to invest in redesigning a manufacturing process to reduce inventory levels.

The right-hand column of Exhibit P–3 explains how human resource managers make a variety of planning decisions, such as budgeting how much to spend on occupational safety training and employee recruitment advertising. They monitor feedback related to numerous management concerns, such as employee retention rates and the timely completion of employee performance appraisals. They also help make many important decisions such as whether to hire on-site medical staff in an effort to lower health care costs, and whether to hire temporary workers or full-time employees in an uncertain economy.

For brevity, Exhibit P–3 does not include all business majors, such as finance, management information systems, and economics. Can you explain how planning, controlling, and decision-making activities would relate to these majors?

Accounting Majors

Many accounting graduates begin their careers working for public accounting firms that provide a variety of valuable services for their clients. Some of these graduates will build successful and fulfilling careers in the public accounting industry; however, most will leave public accounting at some point to work in other organizations. In fact, the **Institute of Management Accountants** (IMA) estimates that more than 80% of professional accountants in the United States work in nonpublic accounting environments (**www.imanet.org/about_ima/our_mission.aspx**).

The public accounting profession has a strong financial accounting orientation. Its most important function is to protect investors and other external parties by assuring them that companies are reporting historical financial results that comply with applicable accounting rules. Managerial accountants also have strong financial accounting skills. For example, they play an important role in helping their organizations design and maintain financial reporting systems that generate reliable financial disclosures. However, the primary role of managerial accountants is to partner with their co-workers within the organization to improve performance.

Given the 80% figure mentioned above, if you are an accounting major there is a very high likelihood that your future will involve working for a nonpublic accounting employer. Your employer will expect you to have strong financial accounting skills, but more importantly, it will expect you to help improve organizational performance by applying the planning, controlling, and decision-making skills that are the foundation of managerial accounting.

IN BUSINESS

A NETWORKING OPPORTUNITY

The **Institute of Management Accountants** (IMA) is a network of more than 70,000 accounting and finance professionals from over 120 countries. Every year the IMA hosts a student leadership conference that attracts 300 students from over 50 colleges and universities. Guest speakers at past conferences have discussed topics such as leadership, advice for a successful career, how to market yourself in a difficult economy, and excelling in today's multigenerational workforce. One student who attended the conference said, "I liked that I was able to interact with professionals who are in fields that could be potential career paths for me." For more information on this worthwhile networking opportunity, contact the IMA at the phone number and website shown below.

Source: Conversation with Jodi Ryan, the Institute of Management Accountants' Director, Education/Corporate Partnerships. (201) 474-1556 or visit its website at **www.imanet.org**.

Professional Certification—A Smart Investment If you plan to become an accounting major, the Certified Management Accountant (CMA) and Chartered Global Management Accountant (CGMA) designations are globally respected credentials that will increase your credibility, upward mobility, and compensation.

The CMA exam is sponsored by the Institute of Management Accountants (IMA) in Montvale, New Jersey. To become a CMA requires membership in the IMA, a bachelor's degree from an accredited college or university, two continuous years of relevant professional experience, and passage of the CMA exam. Exhibit P–4 summarizes the topics covered in the IMA's two-part CMA exam. For brevity, we are not going to define all the terms included in this exhibit. Its purpose is simply to emphasize that the CMA

EXHIBIT P–4
CMA Exam Content Specifications

Part 1　　*Financial Reporting, Planning, Performance and Control*
　　　　　　External financial reporting decisions
　　　　　　Planning, budgeting, and forecasting
　　　　　　Performance management
　　　　　　Cost management
　　　　　　Internal controls

Part 2　　*Financial Decision Making*
　　　　　　Financial statement analysis
　　　　　　Corporate finance
　　　　　　Decision analysis
　　　　　　Risk management
　　　　　　Investment decisions
　　　　　　Professional ethics

---

exam focuses on the planning, controlling, and decision-making skills that are critically important to all managers. Information about becoming a CMA is available on the IMA's website (**www.imanet.org**) or by calling 1-800-638-4427.

The CGMA designaton is co-sponsored by the **American Institute of Certified Public Accountants** (AICPA) and the **Chartered Institute of Management Accountants** (CIMA), each of whom provides a distinct pathway to becoming a CGMA. The AICPA pathway requires a bachelor's degree in accounting (accompanied by a total of 150 college credit-hours), passage of the Certified Public Accountant (CPA) exam, membership in the AICPA, three years of relevant management accounting work experience, and passage of the CGMA exam—which is a case-based exam that focuses on technical skills, business skills, leadership skills, people skills, and ethics, integrity, and professionalism. Notice that the AICPA's pathway to becoming a CGMA requires passage of the multi-part CPA exam, which emphasizes rule-based compliance—assurance standards, financial accounting standards, business law, and the tax code. Information on becoming a CGMA is available at **www.cgma.org**.

IN BUSINESS

HOW'S THE PAY?

The **Institute of Management Accountants** has created the following table that allows individuals to estimate what their salary would be as a management accountant.

			Your Calculation
Start with this base amount		$42,660	$42,660
If you are top-level management	ADD	$59,595	
OR, if you are senior-level management	ADD	$39,131	
OR, if you are middle-level management	ADD	$22,089	
Number of years in the field _____	TIMES	$979	
If you have an advanced degree	ADD	$20,102	
If you hold the CMA	ADD	$21,919	
If you hold the CPA	ADD	$5,907	
Your estimated salary level			

For example, if you make it to top-level management in 10 years, have an advanced degree and a CMA, your estimated salary would be $154,066 [$42,660 + $59,595 + (10 × 979) + $20,102 + $21,919].

Source: Kip Krumweide, "IMA's Global Salary Survey," *Strategic Finance* March 2016, pp. 27–35.

Managerial Accounting: Beyond the Numbers

Exhibit P–5 summarizes how each chapter of the book teaches measurement skills that managers use on the job every day. For example, Chapter 8 teaches you the measurement skills that managers use to answer the question—how should I create a financial plan for next year? Chapters 9 and 10 teach you the measurement skills that managers use to answer the question—how well am I performing relative to my plan? Chapter 7 teaches you measurement skills related to product, service, and customer profitability. However, it is vitally important that you also understand managerial accounting involves more than just "crunching numbers." To be successful, managers must complement their measurement skills with six business management perspectives that "go beyond the numbers" to enable intelligent planning, control, and decision making.

An Ethics Perspective

Ethical behavior is the lubricant that keeps the economy running. Without that lubricant, the economy would operate much less efficiently—less would be available to consumers, quality would be lower, and prices would be higher. In other words, without fundamental trust in the integrity of business, the economy would operate much less efficiently. Thus, for the good of everyone—including profit-making companies—it is vitally important that business be conducted within an ethical framework that builds and sustains trust.

Code of Conduct for Management Accountants The **Institute of Management Accountants** (IMA) of the United States has adopted an ethical code called the

Chapter Number	The Key Question from a Manager's Perspective
Chapter 1	What cost classifications do I use for different management purposes?
Chapter 2	How much does it cost us to manufacture customized jobs for each of our customers?
Chapters 3 & 4	What is the value of our ending inventory and cost of goods sold for external reporting purposes?
Chapter 5	How will my profits change if I change my selling price, sales volume, or costs?
Chapter 6	How should the income statement be presented?
Chapter 7	How profitable is each of our products, services, and customers?
Chapter 8	How should I create a financial plan for next year?
Chapters 9 & 10	How well am I performing relative to my plan?
Chapter 11	What performance measures should we monitor to ensure that we achieve our strategic goals?
Chapter 12	How do I quantify the financial impact of pursuing one course of action versus another?
Chapter 13	How do I make long-term capital investment decisions?
Chapter 14	What cash inflows and outflows explain the change in our cash balance?
Chapter 15	How can we analyze our financial statements to better understand our performance?

EXHIBIT P–5
Measurement Skills: A Manager's Perspective

Statement of Ethical Professional Practice that describes in some detail the ethical responsibilities of management accountants. Even though the standards were developed specifically for management accountants, they have much broader application. The standards consist of two parts that are presented in full in Exhibit P–6. The first part provides general guidelines for ethical behavior. In a nutshell, a management accountant has ethical responsibilities in four broad areas: first, to maintain a high level of professional competence; second, to treat sensitive matters with confidentiality; third, to maintain personal integrity; and fourth, to disclose information in a credible fashion. The second part of the standards specifies what should be done if an individual finds evidence of ethical misconduct.

The ethical standards provide sound, practical advice for management accountants and managers. Most of the rules in the ethical standards are motivated by a very practical consideration—if these rules were not generally followed in business, then the economy and all of us would suffer. Consider the following specific examples of the consequences of not abiding by the standards:

- Suppose employees could not be trusted with confidential information. Then top managers would be reluctant to distribute such information within the company and, as a result, decisions would be based on incomplete information and operations would deteriorate.
- Suppose employees accepted bribes from suppliers. Then contracts would tend to go to the suppliers who pay the highest bribes rather than to the most competent suppliers. Would you like to fly in aircraft whose wings were made by the subcontractor who paid the highest bribe? Would you fly as often? What would happen to the airline industry if its safety record deteriorated due to shoddy workmanship on contracted parts and subassemblies?
- Suppose the presidents of companies routinely lied in their annual reports and financial statements. If investors could not rely on the basic integrity of a company's financial statements, they would have little basis for making informed decisions. Suspecting the worst, rational investors would pay less for securities issued by companies and may not be willing to invest at all. As a consequence, companies would have less money for productive investments—leading to slower economic growth, fewer goods and services, and higher prices.

Not only is ethical behavior the lubricant for our economy, it is the foundation of managerial accounting. The numbers that managers rely on for planning, controlling, and decision making are meaningless unless they have been competently, objectively, and honestly gathered, analyzed, and reported. As your career unfolds, you will inevitably face decisions with ethical implications. Before making such decisions, consider performing the following steps. First, define your alternative courses of action. Second, identify all of the parties that will be affected by your decision. Third, define how each course of action will favorably or unfavorably impact each affected party. Once you have a complete understanding of the decision context, seek guidance from external sources such as the IMA Statement of Ethical Professional Practice (see Exhibit P–6), the IMA Ethics Helpline at (800) 245-1383, or a trusted confidant. Before executing your decision ask yourself one final question—would I be comfortable disclosing my chosen course of action on the front page of *The Wall Street Journal?*

A Strategic Management Perspective

Companies do not succeed by sheer luck; instead, they need to develop a *strategy* that defines how they intend to succeed in the marketplace. A **strategy** is a "game plan" that enables a company to attract customers by distinguishing itself from competitors. The focal point of a company's strategy should be its target customers. A company can only succeed if it creates a reason for its target customers to choose it over a competitor. These reasons, or what are more formally called *customer value propositions,* are the essence of strategy.

EXHIBIT P–6
Institute of Management Accountants (IMA) Statement of Ethical Professional Practice

Members of IMA shall behave ethically. A commitment to ethical professional practice includes: overarching principles that express our values, and standards that guide our conduct.

PRINCIPLES

IMA's overarching ethical principles include: Honesty, Fairness, Objectivity, and Responsibility. Members shall act in accordance with these principles and shall encourage others within their organizations to adhere to them.

STANDARDS

A member's failure to comply with the following standards may result in disciplinary action.

I. COMPETENCE

Each member has a responsibility to:
1. Maintain an appropriate level of professional expertise by continually developing knowledge and skills.
2. Perform professional duties in accordance with relevant laws, regulations, and technical standards.
3. Provide decision support information and recommendations that are accurate, clear, concise, and timely.
4. Recognize and communicate professional limitations or other constraints that would preclude responsible judgment or successful performance of an activity.

II. CONFIDENTIALITY

Each member has a responsibility to:
1. Keep information confidential except when disclosure is authorized or legally required.
2. Inform all relevant parties regarding appropriate use of confidential information. Monitor subordinates' activities to ensure compliance.
3. Refrain from using confidential information for unethical or illegal advantage.

III. INTEGRITY

Each member has a responsibility to:
1. Mitigate actual conflicts of interest. Regularly communicate with business associates to avoid apparent conflicts of interest. Advise all parties of any potential conflicts.
2. Refrain from engaging in any conduct that would prejudice carrying out duties ethically.
3. Abstain from engaging in or supporting any activity that might discredit the profession.

IV. CREDIBILITY

Each member has a responsibility to:
1. Communicate information fairly and objectively.
2. Disclose all relevant information that could reasonably be expected to influence an intended user's understanding of the reports, analyses, or recommendations.
3. Disclose delays or deficiencies in information, timeliness, processing, or internal controls in conformance with organization policy and/or applicable law.

RESOLUTION OF ETHICAL CONFLICT

In applying the Standards of Ethical Professional Practice, you may encounter problems identifying unethical behavior or resolving an ethical conflict. When faced with ethical issues, you should follow your organization's established policies on the resolution of such conflict. If these policies do not resolve the ethical conflict, you should consider the following courses of action:
1. Discuss the issue with your immediate supervisor except when it appears that the supervisor is involved. In that case, present the issue to the next level. If you cannot achieve a satisfactory resolution, submit the issue to the next management level. If your immediate superior is the chief executive officer or equivalent, the acceptable reviewing authority may be a group such as the audit committee, executive committee, board of directors, board of trustees, or owners. Contact with levels above the immediate superior should be initiated only with your superior's knowledge, assuming he or she is not involved. Communication of such problems to authorities or individuals not employed or engaged by the organization is not considered appropriate, unless you believe there is a clear violation of the law.
2. Clarify relevant ethical issues by initiating a confidential discussion with an IMA Ethics Counselor or other impartial advisor to obtain a better understanding of possible courses of action.
3. Consult your own attorney as to legal obligations and rights concerning the ethical conflict.

Customer value propositions tend to fall into three broad categories—*customer intimacy, operational excellence,* and *product leadership.* Companies that adopt a *customer intimacy* strategy are in essence saying to their customers, "You should choose us because we can customize our products and services to meet your individual needs better than our competitors." **Ritz-Carlton, Nordstrom,** and **Virtuoso** (a premium service travel agency) rely primarily on a customer intimacy value proposition for their success. Companies that pursue the second customer value proposition, called *operational excellence,* are saying to their target customers, "You should choose us because we deliver products and services faster, more conveniently, and at a lower price than our competitors." **Southwest Airlines, Walmart,** and **Google** are examples of companies that succeed first and foremost because of their operational excellence. Companies pursuing the third customer value proposition, called *product leadership,* are saying to their target customers, "You should choose us because we offer higher quality products than our competitors." **Apple, Cisco Systems,** and **W.L. Gore** (the creator of GORE-TEX® fabrics) are examples of companies that succeed because of their product leadership.[1]

The plans managers set forth, the variables they seek to control, and the decisions they make are all influenced by their company's strategy. For example, Walmart would not make plans to build ultraexpensive clothing boutiques because these plans would conflict with the company's strategy of operational excellence and "everyday low prices." Apple would not seek to control its operations by selecting performance measures that focus solely on cost-cutting because those measures would conflict with its product leadership customer value proposition. Finally, it is unlikely that **Rolex** would decide to implement drastic price reductions for its watches even if a financial analysis indicated that establishing a lower price might boost short-run profits. Rolex would oppose this course of action because it would diminish the luxury brand that forms the foundation of the company's product leadership customer value proposition.

An Enterprise Risk Management Perspective

Every strategy, plan, and decision involves risks. **Enterprise risk management** is a process used by a company to identify those risks and develop responses to them that enable it to be reasonably assured of meeting its goals. The left-hand column of Exhibit P–7 provides 10 examples of the types of business risks that companies face. They range from risks that relate to the weather to risks associated with computer hackers, complying with the law, supplier strikes, and products harming customers. The right-hand column of Exhibit P–7 provides an example of a control that could be implemented to help reduce each of the risks mentioned in the left-hand column of the exhibit.[2] Although these types of controls cannot completely eliminate risks, they enable companies to proactively manage their risks rather than passively reacting to unfortunate events that have already occurred.

In managerial accounting, companies use controls to reduce the risk that their plans will not be achieved. For example, if a company plans to build a new manufacturing facility within a predefined budget and time frame, it will establish and monitor control measures to ensure that the project is concluded on time and within the budget. Risk management is also a critically important aspect of decision making. For example, when a company quantifies the labor cost savings that it can realize by sending jobs overseas, it should complement its financial analysis with a prudent assessment of the accompanying risks. Will the overseas manufacturer use child labor? Will the product's quality decline, thereby leading to more warranty repairs, customer complaints, and lawsuits? Will the

---

[1] These three customer value propositions were defined by Michael Treacy and Fred Wiersema in "Customer Intimacy and Other Value Disciplines," *Harvard Business Review,* Volume 71 Issue 1, pp. 84–93.

[2] Besides using controls to reduce risks, companies can also choose other risk responses, such as accepting or avoiding a risk.

Examples of Business Risks	Examples of Controls to Reduce Business Risks
• Intellectual assets being stolen from computer files	• Create firewalls that prohibit computer hackers from corrupting or stealing intellectual property
• Products harming customers	• Develop a formal and rigorous new product testing program
• Losing market share due to the unforeseen actions of competitors	• Develop an approach for legally gathering information about competitors' plans and practices
• Poor weather conditions shutting down operations	• Develop contingency plans for overcoming weather-related disruptions
• A website malfunctioning	• Thoroughly test the website before going "live" on the Internet
• A supplier strike halting the flow of raw materials	• Establish a relationship with two companies capable of providing needed raw materials
• A poorly designed incentive compensation system causing employees to make bad decisions	• Create a balanced set of performance measures that motivates the desired behavior
• Poor environmental stewardship causing reputational and financial damage	• Create a reporting system that tracks key environmental performance indicators
• Inaccurate budget estimates causing excessive or insufficient production	• Implement a rigorous budget review process
• Failing to comply with equal employment opportunity laws	• Create a report that tracks key metrics related to compliance with the laws

EXHIBIT P–7
Identifying and Controlling Business Risks

elapsed time from customer order to delivery dramatically increase? Will terminating domestic employees diminish morale within the company and harm perceptions within the community? These are the types of risks that managers should incorporate into their decision-making processes.

Companies also use controls in financial accounting to safeguard assets and minimize the risk of financial reporting errors. Exhibit P–8 describes seven types of controls that companies use to safeguard their assets and to reduce their financial reporting risks. Each item in the exhibit is labeled as a *preventive control* and/or a *detective control*. A **preventive control** deters undesirable events from occurring. A **detective control** detects undesirable events that have already occurred.

As shown in Exhibit P–8, requiring *authorizations* for certain types of transactions is a preventive control. For example, companies frequently require that a specific senior manager sign all checks above a particular dollar amount to reduce the risk of an inappropriate cash disbursement. *Reconciliations* are a detective control. If you have ever compared a bank statement to your checkbook to resolve any discrepancies, then you have performed a type of reconciliation known as a bank reconciliation. This is a detective control because you are seeking to identify any mistakes already made by the bank or existing mistakes in your own records. Another type of reconciliation occurs when a company performs a physical count of its inventory. The value of the physical inventory on hand is compared to the accounting records so that any discrepancies can be identified and resolved.

Exhibit P–8 also mentions *segregation of duties,* which is a preventive control that separates responsibilities for authorizing transactions, recording transactions, and maintaining custody of the related assets. For example, the same employee should not have

EXHIBIT P–8
Types of Internal Controls for Financial Reporting

Type of Control	Classification	Description
Authorizations	Preventive	Requiring management to formally approve certain types of transactions.
Reconciliations	Detective	Relating data sets to one another to identify and resolve discrepancies.
Segregation of duties	Preventive	Separating responsibilities related to authorizing transactions, recording transactions, and maintaining custody of the related assets.
Physical safeguards	Preventive	Using cameras, locks, and physical barriers to protect assets.
Performance reviews	Detective	Comparing actual performance to various benchmarks to identify unexpected results.
Maintaining records	Detective	Maintaining written and/or electronic evidence to support transactions.
Information systems security	Preventive/ Detective	Using controls such as passwords and access logs to ensure appropriate data restrictions.

the ability to authorize inventory purchases, account for those purchases, and manage the inventory storeroom. *Physical safeguards* prevent unauthorized employees from having access to assets such as inventories and computer equipment. *Performance reviews* are a detective control performed by employees in supervisory positions to ensure that actual results are reasonable when compared to relevant benchmarks. If actual results unexpectedly deviate from expectations, then it triggers further analysis to determine the root cause of the deviation. Companies *maintain records* to provide evidence that supports each transaction. For example, companies use serially numbered checks (a detective control) so that they can readily track all of their cash disbursements. Finally, companies maintain *information systems security* by using passwords (a preventive control) and access logs (a detective control) to restrict electronic data access as appropriate.

It bears reemphasizing that these types of controls may help a company reduce its risks, but they cannot guarantee that a company will achieve its objectives. For example, two or more employees may collude to circumvent the control system, or a company's senior leaders may manipulate financial results by intentionally overriding prescribed policies and procedures. This reality highlights the importance of having senior leaders (including the chief executive officer and the chief financial officer) who are committed to creating an ethical "tone at the top" of the organization.

IN BUSINESS

MANAGING RISKS WHEN PATIENTS GO UNDER THE KNIFE

A study by researchers at **Johns Hopkins University** estimated that more than 4,000 claims are filed each year for what it referred to as never events—surgical errors that should never happen, such as operating on the wrong body part. The study found that over a 20-year period these never events led to death in 6.6% of patients and permanent injury in almost 33% of patients. The total payout from the ensuing lawsuits in these cases topped $1.3 billion.

Given these statistics, it is not surprising that many hospitals are paying greater attention to identifying risks and implementing controls to reduce those risks. For example, to reduce the risk that surgical objects are left inside a patient after the surgery concludes, hospitals are introducing controls such as counting instruments, needles, and sponges before and after each surgical procedure. Radio frequency identification tags are also being used to detect instruments inside a patient before wound closure.

Source: Laura Landro, "How to Make Surgery Safer," *The Wall Street Journal,* February 17, 2015, pp. R1–R2.

A Corporate Social Responsibility Perspective

Companies are responsible for creating strategies that produce financial results that satisfy stockholders. However, they also have a *corporate social responsibility* to serve other stakeholders—such as customers, employees, suppliers, communities, and environmental and human rights advocates—whose interests are tied to the company's performance. **Corporate social responsibility** (CSR) is a concept whereby organizations consider the needs of all stakeholders when making decisions. CSR extends beyond legal compliance to include voluntary actions that satisfy stakeholder expectations. Numerous companies, such as **Procter & Gamble, 3M, Eli Lilly and Company, Starbucks, Microsoft, Genentech, Johnson & Johnson, Baxter International, Abbott Laboratories, KPMG, PNC Bank, Deloitte, Southwest Airlines**, and **Caterpillar**, prominently describe their corporate social performance on their websites.

Exhibit P–9 presents examples of corporate social responsibilities that are of interest to six stakeholder groups.[3] If a company fails to meet the needs of these six stakeholder groups it can adversely affect its financial performance. For example, if a company pollutes the environment or fails to provide safe and humane working conditions for its employees, the negative publicity from environmental and human rights activists could cause the company's customers to defect and its "best and brightest" job candidates to apply elsewhere—both of which are likely to eventually harm financial performance. This explains why in managerial accounting a manager must establish plans, implement controls, and make decisions that consider impacts on all stakeholders.

EXHIBIT P–9
Examples of Corporate Social Responsibilities

Companies should provide *customers* with:
- Safe, high-quality products that are fairly priced.
- Competent, courteous, and rapid delivery of products and services.
- Full disclosure of product-related risks.
- Easy-to-use information systems for shopping and tracking orders.

Companies should provide *suppliers* with:
- Fair contract terms and prompt payments.
- Reasonable time to prepare orders.
- Hassle-free acceptance of timely and complete deliveries.
- Cooperative rather than unilateral actions.

Companies should provide *stockholders* with:
- Competent management.
- Easy access to complete and accurate financial information.
- Full disclosure of enterprise risks.
- Honest answers to knowledgeable questions.

Companies and their suppliers should provide *employees* with:
- Safe and humane working conditions.
- Nondiscriminatory treatment and the right to organize and file grievances.
- Fair compensation.
- Opportunities for training, promotion, and personal development.

Companies should provide *communities* with:
- Payment of fair taxes.
- Honest information about plans such as plant closings.
- Resources that support charities, schools, and civic activities.
- Reasonable access to media sources.

Companies should provide *environmental and human rights advocates* with:
- Greenhouse gas emissions data.
- Recycling and resource conservation data.
- Child labor transparency.
- Full disclosure of suppliers located in developing countries.

---

[3] Many of the examples in Exhibit P–9 were drawn from Terry Leap and Misty L. Loughry, "The Stakeholder-Friendly Firm," *Business Horizons*, March/April 2004, pp. 27–32.

© Phil Wills/Alamy

EVACUATION PLANNING: AN UNFORTUNATE BUT NECESSARY CORPORATE SOCIAL RESPONSIBILITY

Companies have responsibilities for their employees above and beyond paying them for services rendered. For example, when a company's globallydispersed employees are threatened by events such as a violent uprising due to political unrest, a terror attack, or an outbreak of Ebola, it has a responsibility to look out for their safety. To assist employers in this endeavor, companies such as Global Rescue and International SOS specialize in designing and executing contingency plans to remove (by air, land, or sea) employees from dangerous situations. In recognition of the seriousness of this corporate responsibility, the United Kingdom has passed a law that makes corporate manslaughter a criminal offense.

Source: Erika Fry, "The Great Escape Business," *Fortune,* December 1, 2014, p. 16.

A Process Management Perspective

Most companies organize themselves by functional departments, such as the Marketing Department, the Research and Development Department, and the Accounting Department. These departments tend to have a clearly defined "chain of command" that specifies superior and subordinate relationships. However, effective managers understand that *business processes,* more so than functional departments, serve the needs of a company's most important stakeholders—its customers. A **business process** is a series of steps that are followed in order to carry out some task in a business. These steps often span departmental boundaries, thereby requiring managers to cooperate across functional departments. The term *value chain* is often used to describe how an organization's functional departments interact with one another to form business processes. A **value chain,** as shown in Exhibit P–10, consists of the major business functions that add value to a company's products and services.

Managers need to understand the value chain to be effective in terms of planning, control, and decision making. For example, if a company's engineers plan to design a new product, they must communicate with the Manufacturing Department to ensure that the product can actually be produced, the Marketing Department to ensure that customers will buy the product, the Distribution Department to ensure that large volumes of the product can be cost-effectively transported to customers, and the Accounting Department to ensure that the product will increase profits. From a control and decision-making standpoint, managers also need to focus on process excellence instead of functional performance. For example, if the Purchasing Department focuses solely on minimizing the cost of purchased materials, this narrowly focused attempt at cost reduction may lead to greater scrap and rework in the Manufacturing Department, more complaints in the Customer Service Department, and greater challenges in the Marketing Department because dissatisfied customers are turning their attention to competitors.

Managers frequently use a process management method known as *lean thinking,* or what is called *Lean Production* in the manufacturing sector. **Lean Production** is a management approach that organizes resources such as people and machines around the

---

EXHIBIT P–10
Business Functions Making Up the Value Chain

Research and Development	Product Design	Manufacturing	Marketing	Distribution	Customer Service

flow of business processes and that only produces units in response to customer orders. It is often called *just-in-time* production (or *JIT*) because products are only manufactured in response to customer orders and they are completed just-in-time to be shipped to customers. Lean thinking differs from traditional manufacturing methods that organize work departmentally and that encourage departments to maximize their output even if it exceeds customer demand and bloats inventories. Because lean thinking only allows production in response to customer orders, the number of units produced tends to equal the number of units sold, thereby resulting in minimal inventory. The lean approach also results in fewer defects, less wasted effort, and quicker customer response times than traditional production methods.

A Leadership Perspective

An organization's employees bring diverse needs, beliefs, and goals to the workplace. Therefore, an important role for organizational leaders is to unite the behaviors of their fellow employees around two common themes—pursuing strategic goals and making optimal decisions. To fulfill this responsibility, leaders need to understand how *intrinsic motivation, extrinsic incentives,* and *cognitive bias* influence human behavior.

Intrinsic Motivation   Intrinsic motivation refers to motivation that comes from within us. Stop for a moment and identify the greatest accomplishment of your life. Then ask yourself what motivated you to achieve this goal? In all likelihood, you achieved it because you wanted to, not because someone forced you to do it. In other words, you were intrinsically motivated. Similarly, an organization is more likely to prosper when its employees are intrinsically motivated to pursue its interests. A leader, who employees perceive as *credible* and *respectful* of their value to the organization, can increase the extent to which those employees are intrinsically motivated to pursue strategic goals. As your career evolves, to be perceived as a credible leader you'll need to possess three attributes—technical competence (that spans the value chain), personal integrity (in terms of work ethic and honesty), and strong communication skills (including oral presentation skills and writing skills). To be perceived as a leader who is respectful of your co-workers' value to the organization, you'll need to possess three more attributes—strong mentoring skills (to help others realize their potential), strong listening skills (to learn from your co-workers and be responsive to their needs), and personal humility (in terms of deferring recognition to all employees who contribute to the organization's success). If you possess these six traits, then you'll have the potential to become a leader who inspires others to readily and energetically channel their efforts toward achieving organizational goals.

Extrinsic Incentives   Many organizations use *extrinsic incentives* to highlight important goals and to motivate employees to achieve them. For example, assume a company establishes the goal of reducing the time needed to perform a task by 20%. In addition, assume the company agrees to pay bonus compensation to its employees if they achieve the goal within three months. In this example, the company is using a type of extrinsic incentive known as a bonus to highlight a particular goal and to presumably motivate employees to achieve it.

While proponents of extrinsic incentives rightly assert that these types of rewards can have a powerful influence on employee behavior, many critics warn that they can also produce dysfunctional consequences. For example, suppose the employees mentioned above earned their bonuses by achieving the 20% time reduction goal within three months. However, let's also assume that during those three months the quality of the employees' output plummeted, thereby causing a spike in the company's repair costs, product returns, and customer defections. In this instance, did the extrinsic incentive work properly? The answer is yes and no. The bonus system did motivate employees to attain the time reduction goal; however, it also had the unintended consequences of causing employees to neglect product quality, thereby increasing repair costs, product returns, and customer defections. In other words, what may have seemed like a well-intended extrinsic incentive actually produced dysfunctional results for the company. This example highlights an important leadership challenge that you are likely to face someday—designing financial compensation systems that fairly reward employees for their efforts without inadvertently creating extrinsic incentives that motivate them to take actions that harm the company.

Cognitive Bias   Leaders need to be aware that all people (including themselves) possess *cognitive biases,* or distorted thought processes, that can adversely affect planning, controlling, and decision making. To illustrate how cognitive bias works, let's consider the scenario of a television "infomercial" where someone is selling a product with a proclaimed value of $200 for $19.99 if viewers call within the next 30 minutes. Why do you think the seller claims that the product has a $200 value? The seller is relying on a cognitive bias called *anchoring bias* in an effort to convince viewers that a $180 discount is simply too good to pass up. The "anchor" is the false assertion that the product is actually worth $200. If viewers erroneously attach credibility to this contrived piece of information, their distorted analysis of the situation may cause them to spend $19.99 on an item whose true economic value is much less than that amount.

While cognitive biases cannot be eliminated, effective leaders should take two steps to reduce their negative impacts. First, they should acknowledge their own susceptibility to cognitive bias. For example, a leader's judgment might be clouded by optimism bias (being overly optimistic in assessing the likelihood of future outcomes) or self-enhancement bias (overestimating ones strengths and underestimating ones weaknesses relative to others). Second, they should acknowledge the presence of cognitive bias in others and introduce techniques to minimize their adverse consequences. For example, to reduce the risks of confirmation bias (a bias where people pay greater attention to information that confirms their preconceived notions, while devaluing information that contradicts them) or groupthink bias (a bias where some group members support a course of action solely because other group members do), a leader may routinely appoint independent teams of employees to assess the credibility of recommendations set forth by other individuals and groups.

Summary

The prologue defined managerial accounting and explained why it is relevant to business and accounting majors. It also discussed six topics—ethics, strategic management, enterprise risk management, corporate social responsibility, process management, and leadership—that define the context for applying the quantitative aspects of managerial accounting. The most important goal of the prologue was to help you understand that managerial accounting matters to your future career regardless of your major. Accounting is the language of business and you'll need to speak it to communicate effectively with and influence fellow managers.

Glossary

Budget A detailed plan for the future that is usually expressed in formal quantitative terms. (p. 3)

Business process A series of steps that are followed in order to carry out some task in a business. (p. 16)

Controlling The process of gathering feedback to ensure that a plan is being properly executed or modified as circumstances change. (p. 3)

Corporate social responsibility A concept whereby organizations consider the needs of all stakeholders when making decisions. (p. 15)

Decision making Selecting a course of action from competing alternatives. (p. 3)

Detective control A control that detects undesirable events that have already occurred. (p. 13)

Enterprise risk management A process used by a company to identify its risks and develop responses to them that enable it to be reasonably assured of meeting its goals. (p. 12)

Financial accounting The phase of accounting that is concerned with reporting historical financial information to external parties, such as stockholders, creditors, and regulators. (p. 2)

Lean Production A management approach that organizes resources such as people and machines around the flow of business processes and that only produces units in response to customer orders. (p. 16)

Managerial accounting The phase of accounting that is concerned with providing information to managers for use within the organization. (p. 2)

Performance report A report that compares budgeted data to actual data to highlight instances of excellent and unsatisfactory performance. (p. 4)

Planning The process of establishing goals and specifying how to achieve them. (p. 3)

Preventive control A control that deters undesirable events from occurring. (p. 13)

Segment Any part or activity of an organization about which managers seek cost, revenue, or profit data. (p. 3)

Strategy A company's "game plan" for attracting customers by distinguishing itself from competitors. (p. 10)

Value chain The major business functions that add value to a company's products and services, such as research and development, product design, manufacturing, marketing, distribution, and customer service. (p. 16)

Questions

P–1 How does managerial accounting differ from financial accounting?

P–2 Pick any major television network and describe some planning and control activities that its managers would engage in.

P–3 If you had to decide whether to continue making a component part or to begin buying the part from an overseas supplier, what quantitative and qualitative factors would influence your decision?

P–4 Why do companies prepare budgets?

P–5 Why is managerial accounting relevant to business majors and their future careers?

P–6 Why is managerial accounting relevant to accounting majors and their future careers?

P–7 Pick any large company and describe its strategy using one of the three customer value propositions defined in the prologue.

P–8 Why do management accountants need to understand their company's strategy?

P–9 Pick any large company and describe three risks that it faces and how it responds to those risks.

P–10 Pick three industries and describe how the risks faced by companies within those industries can influence their planning, controlling, and decision-making activities.

P–11 Pick any large company and explain three ways that it could segment its companywide performance.

P–12 Locate the website of any company that publishes a corporate social responsibility report (also referred to as a sustainability report). Describe three nonfinancial performance measures included in the report. Why do you think the company publishes this report?

P–13 Why do companies that implement Lean Production tend to have minimal inventories?

P–14 Why are leadership skills important to managers?

P–15 Why is ethical behavior important to business?

P–16 If you were a restaurant owner, what internal controls would you implement to help maintain control of your cash?

P–17 As a form of internal control, what documents would you review prior to paying an invoice received from a supplier?

P–18 What internal controls would you implement to help maintain control of your credit sales and accounts receivable?

P–19 Why do companies take a physical count of their inventory on hand at least once per year?

P–20 Why do companies use sequential prenumbering for documents such as checks, sales invoices, and purchase orders?

Exercises

EXERCISE P–1 Planning and Control

Many companies use budgets for three purposes. First, they use them to plan how to deploy resources to best serve customers. Second, they use them to establish challenging goals, or stretch targets, to motivate employees to strive for exceptional results. Third, they use them to evaluate and reward employees.

Assume that you are a sales manager working with your boss to create a sales budget for next year. Once the sales budget is established, it will influence how other departments within the company plan to deploy their resources. For example, the manufacturing manager will plan to produce enough units to meet budgeted unit sales. The sales budget will also be instrumental in determining your pay raise, potential for promotion, and bonus. If actual sales exceed the sales budget, it bodes well for your career. If actual sales are less than budgeted sales, it will diminish your financial compensation and potential for promotion.

Required:

1. Do you think it would be appropriate for your boss to establish the sales budget without any input from you? Why?
2. Do you think the company would be comfortable with allowing you to establish the sales budget without any input from your boss? Why?
3. Assume the company uses its sales budget for only one purpose—planning to deploy resources in a manner that best serves customers. What thoughts would influence your estimate of future sales as well as your boss's estimate of future sales?
4. Assume the company uses its sales budget for only one purpose—motivating employees to strive for exceptional results. What thoughts would influence your estimate of future sales as well as your boss's estimate of future sales?
5. Assume the company uses its sales budget for only one purpose—to determine your pay raise, potential for promotion, and bonus. What thoughts would influence your estimate of future sales as well as your boss's estimate of future sales?
6. Assume the sales budget is used for all three purposes described in questions 3–5. Describe any conflicts or complications that might arise when using the sales budget for these three purposes.

EXERCISE P–2 Controlling

Assume that you work for an airline unloading luggage from airplanes. Your boss has said that, on average, each airplane contains 100 pieces of luggage. Furthermore, your boss has stated that you should be able to unload 100 pieces of luggage from an airplane in 10 minutes. Today an airplane arrived with 150 pieces of luggage and you unloaded all of it in 13 minutes. After finishing with the 150 pieces of luggage, your boss yelled at you for exceeding the 10 minute allowance for unloading luggage from an airplane.

Required:

How would you feel about being yelled at for taking 13 minutes to unload 150 pieces of luggage? How does this scenario relate to the larger issue of how companies design control systems?

EXERCISE P–3 Decision Making

Exhibit P–2 from within the Prologue includes 12 questions related to 12 types of decisions that companies often face. In the prologue, these 12 decisions were discussed within the context of for-profit companies; however, they are also readily applicable to nonprofit organizations. To illustrate this point, assume that you are a senior leader, such as a president, provost, or dean, in a university setting.

Required:

For each of the 12 decisions in Exhibit P–2, provide an example of how that type of decision might be applicable to a university setting.

EXERCISE P–4 Ethics and the Manager

Richmond, Inc., operates a chain of 44 department stores. Two years ago, the board of directors of Richmond approved a large-scale remodeling of its stores to attract a more upscale clientele.

Before finalizing these plans, two stores were remodeled as a test. Linda Perlman, assistant controller, was asked to oversee the financial reporting for these test stores, and she and other management personnel were offered bonuses based on the sales growth and profitability of these stores. While completing the financial reports, Perlman discovered a sizable inventory of outdated goods that should have been discounted for sale or returned to the manufacturer. She discussed the situation with her management colleagues; the consensus was to ignore reporting this inventory as obsolete because reporting it would diminish the financial results and their bonuses.

Required:
1. According to the IMA's Statement of Ethical Professional Practice, would it be ethical for Perlman *not* to report the inventory as obsolete?
2. Would it be easy for Perlman to take the ethical action in this situation?

(CMA, adapted)

EXERCISE P–5 Strategy
The table below contains the names of six companies.

Required:
For each company, categorize its strategy as being focused on customer intimacy, operational excellence, or product leadership. If you wish to improve your understanding of each company's customer value proposition before completing the exercise, review its most recent annual report. To obtain electronic access to this information, perform an Internet search on each company's name followed by the words "annual report."

	Company	Strategy
1.	Deere	?
2.	FedEx	?
3.	State Farm Insurance	?
4.	BMW	?
5.	Amazon.com	?
6.	Charles Schwab	?

EXERCISE P–6 Enterprise Risk Management
The table below refers to seven industries.

Required:
For each industry, provide an example of a business risk faced by companies that compete within that industry. Then, describe an example of a control that could be used to reduce the business risk that you have identified.

Industry	Example of Business Risk	Example of Control to Reduce the Business Risk
1. Airlines (e.g., Delta Airlines)		
2. Pharmaceutical drugs (e.g., Merck)		
3. Package delivery (e.g., United Parcel Service)		
4. Banking (e.g., Bank of America)		
5. Oil & gas (e.g., ExxonMobil)		
6. E-commerce (e.g., eBay)		
7. Automotive (e.g., Toyota)		

EXERCISE P–7 Ethics in Business
Consumers and attorney generals in more than 40 states accused a prominent nationwide chain of auto repair shops of misleading customers and selling them unnecessary parts and services, from brake jobs to front-end alignments. Lynn Sharpe Paine reported the situation as follows in "Managing for Organizational Integrity," *Harvard Business Review,* Volume 72 Issue 3:

> In the face of declining revenues, shrinking market share, and an increasingly competitive market . . . management attempted to spur performance of its auto centers. . . . The automotive service advisers were given product-specific sales quotas—sell so many springs, shock absorbers, alignments, or brake jobs per shift—and paid a commission based on sales. . . . [F]ailure to meet quotas could lead to a transfer or a reduction in work hours. Some employees spoke of the "pressure, pressure, pressure" to bring in sales.

This pressure-cooker atmosphere created conditions under which employees felt that the only way to satisfy top management was by selling products and services to customers that they didn't really need.

Suppose all automotive repair businesses routinely followed the practice of attempting to sell customers unnecessary parts and services.

Required:
1. How would this behavior affect customers? How might customers attempt to protect themselves against this behavior?
2. How would this behavior probably affect profits and employment in the automotive service industry?

EXERCISE P–8 Cognitive Bias

In the 1970s, one million college-bound students were surveyed and asked to compare themselves to their peers. Some of the key findings of the survey were as follows:
a. 70% of the students rated themselves as above average in leadership ability, while only 2% rated themselves as below average in this regard.
b. With respect to athletic skills, 60% of the students rated their skills as above the median and only 6% of students rated themselves as below the median.
c. 60% of the students rated themselves in the top 10% in terms of their ability to get along with others, while 25% of the students felt that they were in the top 1% in terms of this interpersonal skill.

Required:
1. What type of cognitive bias reveals itself in the data mentioned above?
2. How might this cognitive bias adversely influence a manager's planning, controlling, and decision-making activities?
3. What steps could managers take to reduce the possibility that this cognitive bias would adversely influence their actions?

Source: Dan Lovallo and Daniel Kahneman, "Delusions of Success: How Optimism Undermines Executives' Decisions," *Harvard Business Review,* July 2003, pp. 56–63.

EXERCISE P–9 Ethics and Decision Making

Assume that you are the chairman of the Department of Accountancy at Mountain State University. One of the accounting professors in your department, Dr. Candler, has been consistently and uniformly regarded by students as an awful teacher for more than 10 years. Other accounting professors within your department have observed Dr. Candler's classroom teaching and they concur that his teaching skills are very poor. However, Dr. Candler was granted tenure 12 years ago, thereby ensuring him life-long job security at Mountain State University.

Much to your surprise, today you received a phone call from an accounting professor at Oregon Coastal University. During this phone call you are informed that Oregon Coastal University is on the verge of making a job offer to Dr. Candler. However, before extending the job offer, the faculty at Oregon Coastal wants your input regarding Dr. Candler's teaching effectiveness while at Mountain State University.

Required:
How would you respond to the professor from Oregon Coastal University? What would you say about Dr. Candler's teaching ability? Would you describe your answer to this inquiry as being ethical? Why?

EXERCISE P–10 Corporate Social Responsibility

In his book *Capitalism and Freedom,* economist Milton Friedman wrote on page 133: "There is one and only one social responsibility of business—to use its resources and engage in activities designed to increase its profits so long as it . . . engages in open and free competition, without deception or fraud."

Required:
Explain why you agree or disagree with this quote.

EXERCISE P–11 Intrinsic Motivation and Extrinsic Incentives

In a *Harvard Business Review* article titled "Why Incentive Plans Cannot Work," (Volume 71, Issue 5) author Alfie Kohn wrote: "Research suggests that, by and large, rewards succeed at securing one thing only: temporary compliance. When it comes to producing lasting change in attitudes and behavior, however, rewards, like punishment, are strikingly ineffective. Once the rewards run out, people revert to their old behaviors. . . . Incentives, a version of what psychologists call extrinsic motivators, do not alter the attitudes that underlie our behaviors. They do not create an enduring *commitment* to any value or action. Rather, incentives merely—and temporarily—change what we do."

Required:
1. Do you agree with this quote? Why?
2. As a manager, how would you seek to motivate your employees?
3. As a manager, would you use financial incentives to compensate your employees? If so, what would be the keys to using them effectively? If not, then how would you compensate your employees?

EXERCISE P–12 Cognitive Bias and Decision Making

During World War II, the U.S. military was studying its combat-tested fighter planes to determine the parts of the plane that were most vulnerable to enemy fire. The purpose of the study was to identify the most vulnerable sections of each plane and then take steps to reinforce those sections to improve pilot safety and airplane durability. The data gathered by the U.S. military showed that certain sections of its combat-tested fighter planes were consistently hit more often with enemy fire than other sections of the plane.

Required:
1. Would you recommend reinforcing the sections of the plane that were hit most often by enemy fire, or would you reinforce the sections that were hit less frequently by enemy fire? Why?
2. Do you think cognitive bias had the potential to influence the U.S. military's decision-making process with respect to reinforcing its fighter planes?

Source: Jerker Denrell, "Selection Bias and the Perils of Benchmarking," *Harvard Business Review,* Volume 83, Issue 4, pp. 114–119.

EXERCISE P–13 Ethics and Decision Making

Assume that you just completed a December weekend vacation to a casino within the United States. During your trip you won $10,000 gambling. When the casino exchanged your chips for cash they did not record any personal information, such as your driver's license number or social security number. Four months later while preparing your tax returns for the prior year, you stop to contemplate the fact that the Internal Revenue Service requires taxpayers to report all gambling winnings on Form 1040.

Required:
Would you report your gambling winnings to the Internal Revenue Service so that you could pay federal income taxes on those winnings? Do you believe that your actions are ethical? Why?

Managerial Accounting and Cost Concepts

Curbing Administrative Expenses

© Raymond Boyd/Getty Images

When Eric Kaler was appointed as the University of Minnesota's President he promised to cut administrative expenses. Over an 11-year period, the university's administrative headcount had climbed by 1,000 employees, or 37%. This growth rate practically doubled the faculty and student growth rates during the same time period. Beyond the disparity in headcount growth rates, the executive administrators' pay raises exceeded the pay raises given to faculty members, while at the same time the university's in-state tuition and fees more than doubled.

Dr. Kaler's cost cutting efforts included closing dozens of extension school offices, freezing or reducing salaries, eliminating 14 car allowances, restructuring healthcare and retirement benefits, and eliminating the Office of Academic Administration—a move that cut 5.5 full-time positions including a senior vice-president who earned more than $300,000. ∎

Source: Douglas Belkin and Scott Thurm, "Dean's List: Hiring Spree Fattens College Bureaucracy—And Tuition," *The Wall Street Journal*, December 29–30, 2012, pp. A1 and A10.

LEARNING OBJECTIVES

After studying Chapter 1, you should be able to:

LO1–1 Understand cost classifications used for assigning costs to cost objects: direct costs and indirect costs.

LO1–2 Identify and give examples of each of the three basic manufacturing cost categories.

LO1–3 Understand cost classifications used to prepare financial statements: product costs and period costs.

LO1–4 Understand cost classifications used to predict cost behavior: variable costs, fixed costs, and mixed costs.

LO1–5 Understand cost classifications used in making decisions: differential costs, sunk costs, and opportunity costs.

LO1–6 Prepare income statements for a merchandising company using the traditional and contribution formats.

LO1–7 *(Appendix 1A) Identify the four types of quality costs and explain how they interact.*

LO1–8 *(Appendix 1A) Prepare and interpret a quality cost report.*

In accounting, costs can be classified differently depending on the needs of management. For example, the Prologue mentioned that **financial accounting** is concerned with reporting financial information to external parties, such as stockholders, creditors, and regulators. In this context, costs are classified in accordance with externally imposed rules to enable the preparation of financial statements. Conversely, **managerial accounting** is concerned with providing information to managers within an organization so that they can formulate plans, control operations, and make decisions. In these contexts, costs are classified in diverse ways that enable managers to predict future costs, to compare actual costs to budgeted costs, to assign costs to segments of the business (such as product lines, geographic regions, and distribution channels), and to properly contrast the costs associated with competing alternatives.

The notion of *different cost classifications for different purposes* is the most important unifying theme of this chapter and one of the key foundational concepts of the entire textbook. Exhibit 1–1 summarizes five types of cost classifications that will be used throughout the textbook, namely cost classifications (1) for assigning costs to cost objects, (2) for manufacturing companies, (3) for preparing financial statements, (4) for predicting cost behavior, and (5) for making decisions. As we begin defining the cost terminology related to each of these cost classifications, please refer back to this exhibit to help improve your understanding of the overall organization of the chapter.

Cost Classifications for Assigning Costs to Cost Objects

Costs are assigned to cost objects for a variety of purposes including pricing, preparing profitability studies, and controlling spending. A **cost object** is anything for which cost data are desired—including products, customers, and organizational subunits. For purposes of assigning costs to cost objects, costs are classified as either *direct* or *indirect*.

LO1–1
Understand cost classifications used for assigning costs to cost objects: direct costs and indirect costs.

EXHIBIT 1–1
Summary of Cost Classifications

Purpose of Cost Classification	Cost Classifications
Assigning costs to cost objects	• Direct cost (can be easily traced) • Indirect cost (cannot be easily traced)

Accounting for costs in manufacturing companies	• Manufacturing costs
	  • Direct materials
	  • Direct labor
	  • Manufacturing overhead
	• Nonmanufacturing costs
	  • Selling costs
	  • Administrative costs

Preparing financial statements	• Product costs (inventoriable) • Period costs (expensed)
Predicting cost behavior in response to changes in activity	• Variable cost (proportional to activity) • Fixed cost (constant in total) • Mixed cost (has variable and fixed elements)
Making decisions	• Differential cost (differs between alternatives) • Sunk cost (should be ignored) • Opportunity cost (foregone benefit)

Direct Cost

A **direct cost** is a cost that can be easily and conveniently traced to a specified cost object. For example, if Adidas is assigning costs to its various regional and national sales offices, then the salary of the sales manager in its Tokyo office would be a direct cost of that office. If a printing company made 10,000 brochures for a specific customer, then the cost of the paper used to make the brochures would be a direct cost of that customer.

Indirect Cost

An **indirect cost** is a cost that cannot be easily and conveniently traced to a specified cost object. For example, a Campbell Soup factory may produce dozens of varieties of canned soups. The factory manager's salary would be an indirect cost of a particular variety such as chicken noodle soup. The reason is that the factory manager's salary is incurred as a consequence of running the entire factory—it is not incurred to produce any one soup variety. *To be traced to a cost object such as a particular product, the cost must be caused by the cost object.* The factory manager's salary is called a *common cost* of producing the various products of the factory. A **common cost** is a cost that is incurred to support a number of cost objects but cannot be traced to them individually. A common cost is a type of indirect cost.

A particular cost may be direct or indirect, depending on the cost object. While the Campbell Soup factory manager's salary is an *indirect* cost of manufacturing chicken noodle soup, it is a *direct* cost of the manufacturing division. In the first case, the cost object is chicken noodle soup. In the second case, the cost object is the entire manufacturing division.

IN BUSINESS

THE HIGH PRICE OF SELLING ON MANHATTAN'S FIFTH AVENUE

The cost to buy retail real estate on Manhattan's Fifth Avenue exceeds $15,000 per square foot. Investors are willing to pay such a high price because they can turn around and rent their space to high-end retailers (such as **Dolce & Gabbana**, **Tommy Bahama**, and **Massimo Dutti**) for as much as $3,000 per square foot per year. **Abercrombie & Fitch**'s store at 720 Fifth Avenue is its single most profitable store—bringing in $100 million in annual sales while incurring annual rent of $12.5 million. When Abercrombie measures the profits earned at its Fifth Avenue location, the rental expense of $12.5 million is a direct cost of operating that particular store.

Source: Kris Hudson and Dana Mattioli, "Fifth Avenue's Eye-Popping Rents," *The Wall Street Journal*, November 21, 2012, pp. C1 and C10.

Cost Classifications for Manufacturing Companies

LO1–2
Identify and give examples of each of the three basic manufacturing cost categories.

Manufacturing companies such as Texas Instruments, Ford, and DuPont separate their costs into two broad categories—manufacturing and nonmanufacturing costs.

Manufacturing Costs

Most manufacturing companies further separate their manufacturing costs into two direct cost categories, direct materials and direct labor, and one indirect cost category, manufacturing overhead. A discussion of these three categories follows.

Direct Materials   The materials that go into the final product are called **raw materials**. This term is somewhat misleading because it seems to imply unprocessed natural resources like wood pulp or iron ore. Actually, raw materials refer to any materials that are used in the final product; and the finished product of one company can become the raw materials of another company. For example, the plastics produced by **DuPont** are a raw material used by **Hewlett-Packard** in its personal computers.

Direct materials refers to raw materials that become an integral part of the finished product and whose costs can be conveniently traced to the finished product. This would include, for example, the seats that **Airbus** purchases from subcontractors to install in its commercial aircraft, the electronic components that **Apple** uses in its iPhones, and the doors that **Whirlpool** installs on its refrigerators.

CHEAP PART COSTS GENERAL MOTORS A FORTUNE

A direct material component part, called a detent plunger, is used by General Motors (GM) in the manufacture of its automobile ignition switches. The part, which can be installed by direct laborers in a matter of minutes, costs GM between $2.00 and $5.00 per unit to manufacture. However, when this seemingly trivial component part caused ignition system failures that killed 12 people, its legal and financial impacts on GM became front-page news.

GM's troubles include a federal criminal probe that is investigating why the company did not act sooner to redesign, recall, and replace the flawed detent plunger. It appears as though GM learned of ignition switch failures in its Chevy Cobalt in 2004, but it did not redesign the detent plunger to eliminate the problem until 2007. Furthermore, the company did not issue a recall for cars that contained the faulty ignition switches until 2014. Beyond its legal matters, GM expects to spend $8 million replacing the ignition switches of 1.6 million recalled vehicles.

Source: Jeff Bennett, "For GM, Cheap Part Now a Pricey Fix," *The Wall Street Journal*, March 13, 2014, pp. B1–B2.

© Monty Rakusen/Getty Images RF

Direct Labor   **Direct labor** consists of labor costs that can be easily traced to individual units of product. Direct labor is sometimes called *touch labor* because direct labor workers typically touch the product while it is being made. Examples of direct labor include assembly-line workers at **Toyota**, carpenters at the home builder **KB Home**, and electricians who install equipment on aircraft at **Bombardier Learjet**.

Managers occasionally refer to their two direct manufacturing cost categories as *prime costs*. **Prime cost** is the sum of direct materials cost and direct labor cost.

Manufacturing Overhead   **Manufacturing overhead**, the third manufacturing cost category, includes all manufacturing costs except direct materials and direct labor. For example, manufacturing overhead includes a portion of raw materials know as *indirect materials* as well as *indirect labor*. **Indirect materials** are raw materials, such as the solder used to make electrical connections in a **Samsung** HDTV and the glue used to assemble an **Ethan Allen** chair, whose costs cannot be easily or conveniently traced to finished products. **Indirect labor** refers to employees, such as janitors, supervisors, materials handlers, maintenance workers, and night security guards, that play an essential role in running a manufacturing facility; however, the cost of compensating these people cannot be easily or conveniently traced to specific units of product. Since indirect materials and indirect labor are difficult to trace to specific products, their costs are included in manufacturing overhead.

Manufacturing overhead also includes other indirect costs that cannot be readily traced to finished products such as depreciation of manufacturing equipment and the utility costs, property taxes, and insurance premiums incurred to operate a manufacturing facility. Although companies also incur depreciation, utility costs, property taxes, and insurance premiums to sustain their nonmanufacturing operations, these costs are not included as part of manufacturing overhead. Only those indirect costs associated with *operating the factory* are included in manufacturing overhead.

In practice, managers use various names for manufacturing overhead, such as *indirect manufacturing cost*, *factory overhead*, and *factory burden*. All of these terms are synonyms for manufacturing overhead. Another term that managers frequently use in practice is *conversion cost*. **Conversion cost** refers to the sum of direct labor and manufacturing overhead. The term conversion cost is used to describe direct labor and manufacturing overhead because these costs are incurred to *convert* direct materials into finished products.

Nonmanufacturing Costs

Nonmanufacturing costs are often divided into two categories: (1) *selling costs* and (2) *administrative costs*. **Selling costs** include all costs that are incurred to secure customer orders and get the finished product to the customer. These costs are sometimes called *order-getting* and *order-filling* costs. Examples of selling costs include advertising, shipping, sales travel, sales commissions, sales salaries, and costs of finished goods warehouses. Selling costs can be either direct or indirect costs. For example, the cost of an advertising campaign dedicated to one specific product is a direct cost of that product, whereas the salary of a marketing manager who oversees numerous products is an indirect cost with respect to individual products.

Administrative costs include all costs associated with the *general management* of an organization rather than with manufacturing or selling. Examples of administrative costs include executive compensation, general accounting, secretarial, public relations, and similar costs involved in the overall, general administration of the organization *as a whole*. Administrative costs can be either direct or indirect costs. For example, the salary of an accounting manager in charge of accounts receivable collections in the East region is a direct cost of that region, whereas the salary of a chief financial officer who oversees all of a company's regions is an indirect cost with respect to individual regions.

Nonmanufacturing costs are also often called selling, general, and administrative (SG&A) costs or just selling and administrative costs.

Cost Classifications for Preparing Financial Statements

LO1–3
Understand cost classifications used to prepare financial statements: product costs and period costs.

When preparing a balance sheet and an income statement, companies need to classify their costs as *product costs* or *period costs*. To understand the difference between product costs and period costs, we must first discuss the matching principle from financial accounting.

Generally, costs are recognized as expenses on the income statement in the period that benefits from the cost. For example, if a company pays for liability insurance in advance for two years, the entire amount is not considered an expense of the year in which the payment is made. Instead, one-half of the cost would be recognized as an expense each year. The reason is that both years—not just the first year—benefit from the insurance payment. The unexpensed portion of the insurance payment is carried on the balance sheet as an asset called prepaid insurance.

The *matching principle* is based on the *accrual* concept that *costs incurred to generate a particular revenue should be recognized as expenses in the same period that the revenue is recognized*. This means that if a cost is incurred to acquire or make something that will eventually be sold, then the cost should be recognized as an expense only when the sale takes place—that is, when the benefit occurs. Such costs are called *product costs.*

Product Costs

For financial accounting purposes, **product costs** include all costs involved in acquiring or making a product. Product costs "attach" to a unit of product as it is purchased or manufactured and they stay attached to each unit of product as long as it remains in inventory awaiting sale. When units of product are sold, their costs are released from inventory as expenses (typically called cost of goods sold) and matched against sales on the income statement. Because product costs are initially assigned to inventories, they are also known as **inventoriable costs**.

For manufacturing companies, product costs include direct materials, direct labor, and manufacturing overhead.[1] A manufacturer's product costs flow through three inventory accounts on the balance sheet—*Raw Materials*, *Work in Process*, and *Finished Goods*—prior to being recorded in cost of goods sold on the income statement. Raw materials include any materials that go into the final product. **Work in process** consists of units of product that are only partially complete and will require further work before they are ready for sale to the customer. **Finished goods** consist of completed units of product that have not yet been sold to customers.

When direct materials are used in production, their costs are transferred from Raw Materials to Work in Process. Direct labor and manufacturing overhead costs are added to Work in Process to convert direct materials into finished goods. Once units of product are completed, their costs are transferred from Work in Process to Finished Goods. When a manufacturer sells its finished goods to customers, the costs are transferred from Finished Goods to Cost of Goods Sold.

We want to emphasize that product costs are not necessarily recorded as expenses on the income statement in the period in which they are incurred. Rather, as explained above, they are recorded as expenses in the period in which the related products *are sold.*

Period Costs

Period costs are all the costs that are not product costs. *All selling and administrative expenses are treated as period costs.* For example, sales commissions, advertising, executive salaries, public relations, and the rental costs of administrative offices are all period costs. Period costs are not included as part of the cost of either purchased or manufactured goods; instead, period costs are expensed on the income statement in the period in which they are incurred using the usual rules of accrual accounting. Keep in mind that the period in which a cost is incurred is not necessarily the period in which cash changes hands. For example, as discussed earlier, the cost of liability insurance is spread across the periods that benefit from the insurance—regardless of the period in which the insurance premium is paid.

Exhibit 1–2 summarizes the product and period cost flows for manufacturers that were just discussed. Notice that product costs flow through three inventory accounts on the balance sheet prior to being recognized as part of cost of goods sold in the income statement. Conversely, period costs do not flow through the inventory accounts on the balance sheet and they are not included in cost of goods sold in the income statement. Instead, they are recorded as selling and administrative expenses in the income statement during the period incurred.

---

[1] For internal management purposes, product costs may exclude some manufacturing costs. For example, see Appendix 2B and the discussion in Chapter 6.

EXHIBIT 1–2
Cost Flows and Classifications in a Manufacturing Company

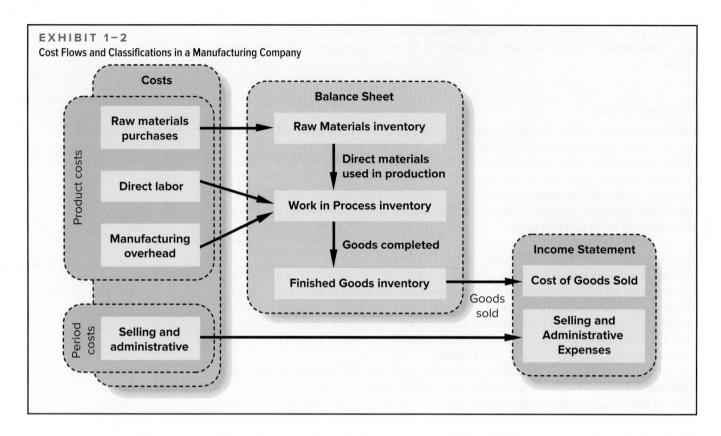

Cost Classifications for Predicting Cost Behavior

LO1–4
Understand cost classifications used to predict cost behavior: variable costs, fixed costs, and mixed costs.

It is often necessary to predict how a certain cost will behave in response to a change in activity. For example, a manager at **Under Armour** may want to estimate the impact a 5 percent increase in sales would have on the company's total direct materials cost. **Cost behavior** refers to how a cost reacts to changes in the level of activity. As the activity level rises and falls, a particular cost may rise and fall as well—or it may remain constant. For planning purposes, a manager must be able to anticipate which of these will happen; and if a cost can be expected to change, the manager must be able to estimate how much it will change. To help make such distinctions, costs are often categorized as *variable, fixed,* or *mixed.* The relative proportion of each type of cost in an organization is known as its **cost structure**. For example, an organization might have many fixed costs but few variable or mixed costs. Alternatively, it might have many variable costs but few fixed or mixed costs.

Variable Cost

A **variable cost** varies, in total, in direct proportion to changes in the level of activity. Common examples of variable costs include cost of goods sold for a merchandising company, direct materials, direct labor, variable elements of manufacturing overhead, such as indirect materials, supplies, and power, and variable elements of selling and administrative expenses, such as commissions and shipping costs.[2]

---

[2] Direct labor costs often can be fixed instead of variable for a variety of reasons. For example, in some countries, such as France, Germany, and Japan, labor regulations and cultural norms may limit management's ability to adjust the labor force in response to changes in activity. In this textbook, always assume that direct labor is a variable cost unless you are explicitly told otherwise.

For a cost to be variable, it must be variable *with respect to something.* That "something" is its *activity base.* An **activity base** is a measure of whatever causes the incurrence of a variable cost. An activity base is sometimes referred to as a *cost driver.* Some of the most common activity bases are direct labor-hours, machine-hours, units produced, and units sold. Other examples of activity bases (cost drivers) include the number of miles driven by salespersons, the number of pounds of laundry cleaned by a hotel, the number of calls handled by technical support staff at a software company, and the number of beds occupied in a hospital. *While there are many activity bases within organizations, throughout this textbook, unless stated otherwise, you should assume that the activity base under consideration is the total volume of goods and services provided by the organization. We will specify the activity base only when it is something other than total output.*

To provide an example of a variable cost, consider Nooksack Expeditions, a small company that provides daylong whitewater rafting excursions on rivers in the North Cascade Mountains. The company provides all of the necessary equipment and experienced guides, and it serves gourmet meals to its guests. The meals are purchased from a caterer for $30 a person for a daylong excursion. The behavior of this variable cost, on both a per unit and a total basis, is shown below:

Number of Guests	Cost of Meals per Guest	Total Cost of Meals
250	$30	$7,500
500	$30	$15,000
750	$30	$22,500
1,000	$30	$30,000

While total variable costs change as the activity level changes, it is important to note that a variable cost is constant if expressed on a *per unit* basis. For example, the per unit cost of the meals remains constant at $30 even though the total cost of the meals increases and decreases with activity. The graph on the left-hand side of Exhibit 1–3 illustrates that the total variable cost rises and falls as the activity level rises and falls. At an activity level of 250 guests, the total meal cost is $7,500. At an activity level of 1,000 guests, the total meal cost rises to $30,000.

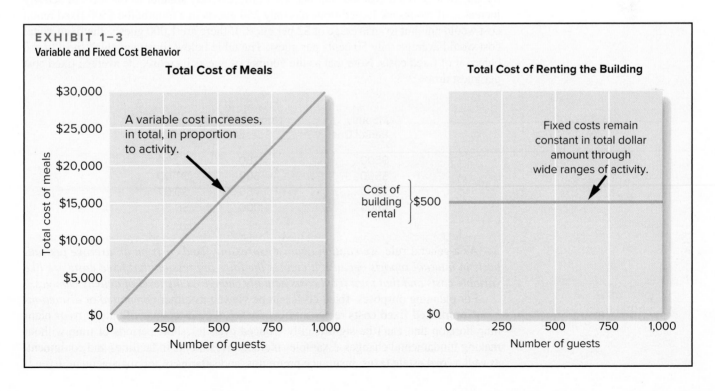

EXHIBIT 1–3
Variable and Fixed Cost Behavior

© Sandee Noreen

FOOD COSTS AT A LUXURY HOTEL

The **Sporthotel Theresa** (http://www.theresa.at/), owned and operated by the Egger family, is a four star hotel located in Zell im Zillertal, Austria. The hotel features access to hiking, skiing, biking, and other activities in the Ziller alps as well as its own fitness facility and spa.

Three full meals a day are included in the hotel room charge. Breakfast and lunch are served buffet-style while dinner is a more formal affair with as many as six courses. The chef, Stefan Egger, believes that food costs are roughly proportional to the number of guests staying at the hotel; that is, they are a variable cost. He must order food from suppliers two or three days in advance, but he adjusts his purchases to the number of guests who are currently staying at the hotel and their consumption patterns. In addition, guests make their selections from the dinner menu early in the day, which helps Stefan plan which foodstuffs will be required for dinner. Consequently, he is able to prepare just enough food so that all guests are satisfied and yet waste is held to a minimum.

Fixed Cost

A **fixed cost** is a cost that remains constant, in total, regardless of changes in the level of activity. Manufacturing overhead usually includes various fixed costs such as depreciation, insurance, property taxes, rent, and supervisory salaries. Similarly, selling and administrative costs often include fixed costs such as administrative salaries, advertising, and depreciation of nonmanufacturing assets. Unlike variable costs, fixed costs are not affected by changes in activity. Consequently, as the activity level rises and falls, total fixed costs remain constant unless influenced by some outside force, such as a landlord increasing your monthly rent. To continue the Nooksack Expeditions example, assume the company rents a building for $500 per month to store its equipment. The total amount of rent paid is the same regardless of the number of guests the company takes on its expeditions during any given month. The concept of a fixed cost is shown graphically on the right-hand side of Exhibit 1–3.

Because total fixed costs remain constant for large variations in the level of activity, the average fixed cost *per unit* becomes progressively smaller as the level of activity increases. If Nooksack Expeditions has only 250 guests in a month, the $500 fixed rental cost would amount to an average of $2 per guest. If there are 1,000 guests, the fixed rental cost would average only 50 cents per guest. The table below illustrates this aspect of the behavior of fixed costs. Note that as the number of guests increase, the average fixed cost per guest drops.

Monthly Rental Cost	Number of Guests	Average Cost per Guest
$500	250	$2.00
$500	500	$1.00
$500	750	$0.67
$500	1,000	$0.50

As a general rule, *we caution against expressing fixed costs on an average per unit basis in internal reports because it creates the false impression that fixed costs are like variable costs and that total fixed costs actually change as the level of activity changes.*

For planning purposes, fixed costs can be viewed as either *committed* or *discretionary*. **Committed fixed costs** represent organizational investments with a *multiyear* planning horizon that can't be significantly reduced even for short periods of time without making fundamental changes. Examples include investments in facilities and equipment, as well as real estate taxes, insurance premiums, and salaries of top management. Even if operations are interrupted or cut back, committed fixed costs remain largely unchanged in the short term because the costs of restoring them later are likely to be far greater than any short-run savings that might be realized. **Discretionary fixed costs** (often referred to as *managed fixed costs*) usually arise from *annual* decisions by management to spend on certain fixed cost items. Examples of discretionary fixed costs include advertising, research, public relations, management development programs, and internships for students. Discretionary fixed costs can be cut for short periods of time with minimal damage to the long-run goals of the organization.

The Linearity Assumption and the Relevant Range

Management accountants ordinarily assume that costs are strictly linear; that is, the relation between cost on the one hand and activity on the other can be represented by a straight line within a narrow band of activity known as the *relevant range*. The **relevant range** is the range of activity within which the assumption that cost behavior is strictly linear is reasonably valid.[3]

The concept of the relevant range is important in understanding fixed costs. For example, suppose the **Mayo Clinic** rents a machine for $20,000 per month that tests blood samples for the presence of leukemia cells. Furthermore, suppose that the capacity of the leukemia diagnostic machine is 3,000 tests per month. The assumption that the rent for the diagnostic machine is $20,000 per month is only valid within the relevant range of 0 to 3,000 tests per month. If the Mayo Clinic needed to test 5,000 blood samples per month, then it would need to rent another machine for an additional $20,000 per month. It would be difficult to rent half of a diagnostic machine; therefore, the step pattern depicted in Exhibit 1–4 is typical for such costs. This exhibit shows that the fixed rental cost is $20,000 for a relevant range of 0 to 3,000 tests. The fixed rental cost increases to $40,000 within the relevant range of 3,001 to 6,000 tests. The rental cost increases in discrete steps or increments of 3,000 tests, rather than increasing in a linear fashion per test.

This step-oriented cost behavior pattern can also be used to describe other costs, such as some labor costs. For example, the cost of compensating salaried employees can be characterized using a step pattern. Salaried employees are paid a fixed amount, such as $40,000 per year, for providing the capacity to work a prespecified amount of

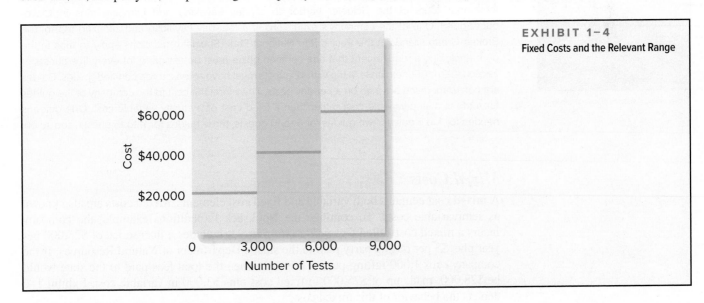

EXHIBIT 1–4
Fixed Costs and the Relevant Range

[3] Recent research has focused on how costs respond to changes in activity. That research is broadly consistent with the accountant's linear model, with anticipated activity outside of the relevant range often leading to adjustments in fixed costs. See Rajiv Banker and Dmitri Byzalov, "Asymmetric Cost Behavior", *Journal of Management Accounting Research,* 2014, Vol. 26, No. 2, pages 43–79, and Eric Noreen, "Capacity Constraints and Asymmetric Cost Behavior", working paper, 20145.

EXHIBIT 1–5
Summary of Variable and Fixed Cost Behavior

Cost	Behavior of the Cost (within the relevant range)	
	In Total	Per Unit
Variable cost	Total variable cost increases and decreases in proportion to changes in the activity level.	Variable cost per unit remains constant.
Fixed cost	Total fixed cost is not affected by changes in the activity level within the relevant range.	Fixed cost per unit decreases as the activity level rises and increases as the activity level falls.

time, such as 40 hours per week for 50 weeks a year (= 2,000 hours per year). In this example, the total salary cost is $40,000 within a relevant range of 0 to 2,000 hours of work. The total salary cost increases to $80,000 (or two employees) if the organization's work requirements expand to a relevant range of 2,001 to 4,000 hours of work. Cost behavior patterns such as salaried employees are often called *step-variable costs.* Step-variable costs can often be adjusted quickly as conditions change. Furthermore, the width of the steps for step-variable costs is generally so narrow that these costs can be treated essentially as variable costs for most purposes. The width of the steps for fixed costs, on the other hand, is so wide that these costs should be treated as entirely fixed within the relevant range.

Exhibit 1–5 summarizes four key concepts related to variable and fixed costs. Study it carefully before reading further.

IN BUSINESS

© Kuznetcov_Konstantin/Shutterstock.com

HOW MANY GUIDES?

Majestic Ocean Kayaking, of Ucluelet, British Columbia, is owned and operated by Tracy Morben-Eeftink. The company offers a number of guided kayaking excursions ranging from three-hour tours of the Ucluelet harbor to six-day kayaking and camping trips in Clayoquot Sound. One of the company's excursions is a four-day kayaking and camping trip to The Broken Group Islands in the Pacific Rim National Park. Special regulations apply to trips in the park—including a requirement that one certified guide must be assigned for every five guests or fraction thereof. For example, a trip with 12 guests must have at least three certified guides. Guides are not salaried and are paid on a per-day basis. Therefore, the cost to the company of the guides for a trip is a step-variable cost rather than a fixed cost or a strictly variable cost. One guide is needed for 1 to 5 guests, two guides for 6 to 10 guests, three guides for 11 to 15 guests, and so on.

Mixed Costs

A **mixed cost** contains both variable and fixed cost elements. Mixed costs are also known as semivariable costs. To continue the Nooksack Expeditions example, the company incurs a mixed cost called *fees paid to the state.* It includes a license fee of $25,000 per year plus $3 per rafting party paid to the state's Department of Natural Resources. If the company runs 1,000 rafting parties this year, then the total fees paid to the state would be $28,000, made up of $25,000 in fixed cost plus $3,000 in variable cost. Exhibit 1–6 depicts the behavior of this mixed cost.

Even if Nooksack fails to attract any customers, the company will still have to pay the license fee of $25,000. This is why the cost line in Exhibit 1–6 intersects the vertical cost axis at the $25,000 point. For each rafting party the company organizes, the total cost of the state fees will increase by $3. Therefore, the total cost line slopes upward as the variable cost of $3 per party is added to the fixed cost of $25,000 per year.

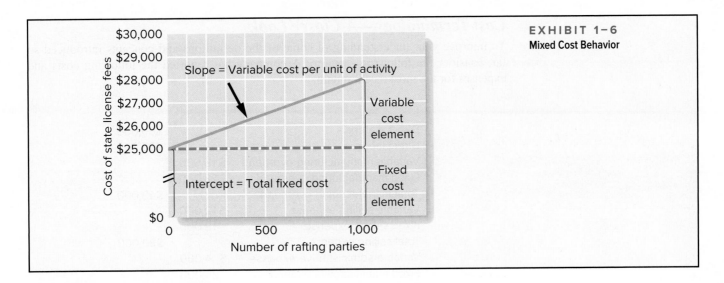

EXHIBIT 1–6
Mixed Cost Behavior

Because the mixed cost in Exhibit 1–6 is represented by a straight line, the following equation for a straight line can be used to express the relationship between a mixed cost and the level of activity:

$$Y = a + bX$$

In this equation,

Y = The total mixed cost

a = The total fixed cost (the vertical intercept of the line)

b = The variable cost per unit of activity (the slope of the line)

X = The level of activity

Because the variable cost per unit equals the slope of the straight line, the steeper the slope, the higher the variable cost per unit.

In the case of the state fees paid by Nooksack Expeditions, the equation is written as follows:

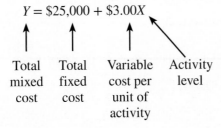

$$Y = \$25,000 + \$3.00X$$

| Total mixed cost | Total fixed cost | Variable cost per unit of activity | Activity level |

This equation makes it easy to calculate the total mixed cost for any activity level within the relevant range. For example, suppose that the company expects to organize 800 rafting parties in the next year. The total state fees would be calculated as follows:

$Y = \$25,000 + (\$3.00$ per rafting party $\times 800$ rafting parties)

$= \$27,400$

Cost Terminology—A Closer Look

To improve your understanding of some of the definitions and concepts introduced so far, consider the following scenario. A company has reported the following costs and expenses for the most recent month:

Direct materials		$69,000
Direct labor		$35,000
Variable manufacturing overhead	$15,000	
Fixed manufacturing overhead	28,000	
Total manufacturing overhead		$43,000
Variable selling expense	$12,000	
Fixed selling expense	18,000	
Total selling expense		$30,000
Variable administrative expense	$ 4,000	
Fixed administrative expense	25,000	
Total administrative expense		$29,000

These costs and expenses can be categorized in a number of ways, some of which are shown below:

Product cost	= Direct materials + Direct labor + Manufacturing overhead
	= $69,000 + $35,000 + $43,000
	= $147,000
Period cost	= Selling expense + Administrative expense
	= $30,000 + $29,000
	= $59,000
Conversion cost	= Direct labor + Manufacturing overhead
	= $35,000 + $43,000
	= $78,000
Prime cost	= Direct materials + Direct labor
	= $69,000 + $35,000
	= $104,000
Variable manufacturing cost	= Direct materials + Direct labor + Variable manufacturing overhead
	= $69,000 + $35,000 + $15,000
	= $119,000
Total fixed cost	= Fixed manufacturing overhead + Fixed selling expense + Fixed administrative expense
	= $28,000 + $18,000 + $25,000
	= $71,000

Cost Classifications for Decision Making

Decisions involve choosing between alternatives. To make intelligent choices, it is essential to consider *relevant costs* (and benefits) while ignoring *irrelevant costs* (and benefits). More specifically, it important to understand the terms *differential cost* and *revenue*, *sunk cost*, and *opportunity cost*.

LO1–5
Understand cost classifications used in making decisions: differential costs, sunk costs, and opportunity costs.

Differential Cost and Revenue

In business decisions, each alternative will have costs and benefits that must be compared to the costs and benefits of other available alternatives. A future cost that differs between any two alternatives is known as a **differential cost**. Differential costs are always relevant costs. Future revenue that differs between any two alternatives is known as **differential revenue**. Differential revenue is an example of a relevant benefit. Any future cost or benefit that does not differ between the alternatives is irrelevant and should be ignored.

A differential cost is also known as an **incremental cost**. Although technically an incremental cost should refer only to an increase in cost from one alternative to another, whereas decreases in cost should be referred to as *decremental costs*. Differential cost is a broader term, encompassing both cost increases (incremental costs) and cost decreases (decremental costs) between alternatives.

The accountant's differential cost concept can be compared to the economist's marginal cost concept. In speaking of changes in cost and revenue, the economist uses the terms *marginal cost* and *marginal revenue*. The revenue that can be obtained from selling one more unit of product is called marginal revenue, and the cost involved in producing one more unit of product is called marginal cost. The economist's marginal concept is basically the same as the accountant's differential concept applied to a single unit of output.

Differential costs can be either fixed or variable. To illustrate, assume that Natural Cosmetics, Inc., is thinking about changing its marketing method from distribution through retailers to distribution by a network of neighborhood sales representatives. Present costs and revenues are compared to projected costs and revenues in the following table:

	Retailer Distribution (present)	Sales Representatives (proposed)	Differential Costs and Revenues
Sales (*variable*)	$700,000	$800,000	$100,000
Cost of goods sold (*variable*)	350,000	400,000	50,000
Advertising (*fixed*)	80,000	45,000	(35,000)
Commissions (*variable*)	0	40,000	40,000
Warehouse depreciation (*fixed*)	50,000	80,000	30,000
Other expenses (*fixed*)	60,000	60,000	0
Total expenses	540,000	625,000	85,000
Net operating income	$160,000	$175,000	$ 15,000

According to the above analysis, the differential revenue is $100,000 and the differential costs total $85,000, leaving a positive differential net operating income of $15,000 in favor of using sales representatives.

In general, only the differences between alternatives are relevant in decisions. Those items that are the same under all alternatives and that are not affected by the decision can be ignored. For example, in the Natural Cosmetics, Inc., example above, the "Other expenses" category, which is $60,000 under both alternatives, can be ignored because it has no effect on the decision. If it were removed from the calculations, the sales representatives would still be preferred by $15,000. This is an extremely important principle in management accounting that we will revisit in later chapters.

Sunk Cost and Opportunity Cost

A **sunk cost** is a cost *that has already been incurred* and that cannot be changed by any decision made now or in the future. Because sunk costs cannot be changed by any decision, they are not differential costs. And because only differential costs are relevant in a decision, sunk costs should always be ignored.

To illustrate a sunk cost, assume that a company paid $50,000 several years ago for a special-purpose machine. The machine was used to make a product that is now obsolete and is no longer being sold. Even though in hindsight purchasing the machine may have been unwise, the $50,000 cost has already been incurred and cannot be undone. It would be folly to continue making the obsolete product in a misguided attempt to "recover" the original cost of the machine. In short, the $50,000 originally paid for the machine is a sunk cost that should be ignored in current decisions.

Opportunity cost is the potential benefit that is given up when one alternative is selected over another. For example, assume that you have a part-time job while attending college that pays $200 per week. If you spend one week at the beach during spring break without pay, then the $200 in lost wages would be an opportunity cost of taking the week off to be at the beach. Opportunity costs are not usually found in accounting records, but they are costs that must be explicitly considered in every decision a manager makes. Virtually every alternative involves an opportunity cost.

IN BUSINESS

NAVISTAR CLOSES ITS ENGINE PLANT IN ALABAMA

When **Navistar International**'s share of the medium-size truck market dropped from 30% to 17%, the company decided to eliminate excess capacity by closing its engine plant in Alabama. The plant closure resulted in a loss of 280 jobs and an annual cost savings of about $22 million per year. When making this decision Navistar was essentially choosing between two alternatives—keep the Alabama plant open or close the plant. When Navistar analyzed the differential costs and revenues associated with these two alternatives, it opted to close the plant.

Source: Bob Tita, "Truck Maker Navistar to Close Alabama Plant," *The Wall Street Journal*, February 21, 2014, p. B3.

Using Different Cost Classifications for Different Purposes

L01–6

Prepare income statements for a merchandising company using the traditional and contribution formats.

In this section of the chapter, we discuss how to prepare traditional and contribution format income statements for a merchandising company.[4] Merchandising companies do not manufacture the products that they sell to customers. For example, **Lowe's** and **Home Depot** are merchandising companies because they buy finished products from manufacturers and then resell them to end consumers.

Contrasting these two types of income statements enables us to illustrate the chapter's unifying theme of *different cost classifications for different purposes*. Traditional income statements are prepared primarily for *external reporting purposes*. They rely on cost classifications for preparing financial statements (product and period costs) to depict the financial consequences of *past* transactions. Contribution format income statements are prepared for *internal management purposes*. They use cost classifications for predicting costs behavior (variable and fixed costs) to better inform decisions affecting the *future*.

The two different purposes served by these income statements highlight what is arguably the most important difference between financial accounting and managerial accounting—an emphasis on recording past performance versus an emphasis on making predictions and decisions that affect future performance.

---

[4] Subsequent chapters compare the income statement formats for manufacturing companies.

The Traditional Format Income Statement

The left-hand side of Exhibit 1–7 shows a traditional income statement format for merchandising companies. This type of income statement organizes costs into two categories—cost of goods sold and selling and administrative expenses. Sales minus cost of goods sold equals the *gross margin.* The gross margin minus selling and administrative expenses equals net operating income.

The cost of goods sold reports the *product costs* attached to the merchandise sold during the period. The selling and administrative expenses report all *period costs* that have been expensed as incurred. The cost of goods sold for a merchandising company can be computed directly by multiplying the number of units sold by their unit cost or indirectly using the equation below:

$$\begin{matrix} \text{Cost of} \\ \text{goods sold} \end{matrix} = \begin{matrix} \text{Beginning} \\ \text{merchandise} \\ \text{inventory} \end{matrix} + \text{Purchases} - \begin{matrix} \text{Ending} \\ \text{merchandise} \\ \text{inventory} \end{matrix}$$

For example, let's assume that the company depicted in Exhibit 1–7 purchased $3,000 of merchandise inventory during the period and had beginning and ending merchandise inventory balances of $7,000 and $4,000, respectively. The equation above could be used to compute the cost of goods sold as follows:

$$\begin{matrix} \text{Cost of} \\ \text{goods sold} \end{matrix} = \begin{matrix} \text{Beginning} \\ \text{merchandise} \\ \text{inventory} \end{matrix} + \text{Purchases} - \begin{matrix} \text{Ending} \\ \text{merchandise} \\ \text{inventory} \end{matrix}$$

$$= \quad \$7{,}000 \quad + \quad \$3{,}000 \quad - \quad \$4{,}000$$

$$= \quad \$6{,}000$$

Although the traditional income statement is useful for external reporting purposes, it has serious limitations when used for internal purposes. It does not distinguish between fixed and variable costs. For example, under the heading "Selling and administrative expenses," both variable administrative costs ($400) and fixed administrative costs ($1,500) are lumped together ($1,900). Internally, managers need cost data organized by cost behavior to aid in planning, controlling, and decision making. The contribution format income statement has been developed in response to these needs.

EXHIBIT 1–7

Comparing Traditional and Contribution Format Income Statements for Merchandising Companies (all numbers are given)

Traditional Format			Contribution Format		
Sales		$12,000	Sales		$12,000
Cost of goods sold*		6,000	Variable expenses:		
Gross margin		6,000	Cost of goods sold	$6,000	
Selling and administrative expenses:			Variable selling	600	
Selling	$3,100		Variable administrative	400	7,000
Administrative	1,900	5,000	Contribution margin		5,000
Net operating income		$ 1,000	Fixed expenses:		
			Fixed selling	2,500	
			Fixed administrative	1,500	4,000
			Net operating income		$ 1,000

*For a manufacturing company, the cost of goods sold would include some variable costs, such as direct materials, direct labor, and variable overhead, and some fixed costs, such as fixed manufacturing overhead. Income statement formats for manufacturing companies will be explored in greater detail in a subsequent chapter.

The Contribution Format Income Statement

The crucial distinction between fixed and variable costs is at the heart of the **contribution approach** to constructing income statements. The unique thing about the contribution approach is that it provides managers with an income statement that clearly distinguishes between fixed and variable costs and therefore aids planning, controlling, and decision making. The right-hand side of Exhibit 1–7 shows a contribution format income statement for merchandising companies.

The contribution approach separates costs into fixed and variable categories, first deducting all variable expenses from sales to obtain the *contribution margin*. For a merchandising company, cost of goods sold is a variable cost that gets included in the "Variable expenses" portion of the contribution format income statement. The **contribution margin** is the amount remaining from sales revenues after all variable expenses have been deducted. This amount *contributes* toward covering fixed expenses and then toward profits for the period. The contribution margin can also be stated on a per unit basis. For example, if the company depicted in Exhibit 1–7 sold 500 units, then its contribution margin per unit would be $10 per unit (= $5,000 ÷ 500 units).

The contribution format income statement is used as an internal planning and decision-making tool. Its emphasis on cost behavior aids cost-volume-profit analysis, management performance appraisals, and budgeting. Moreover, the contribution approach helps managers organize data pertinent to numerous decisions such as product-line analysis, pricing, use of scarce resources, and make or buy analysis. All of these topics are covered in later chapters.

Summary

In this chapter, we have discussed ways in which managers classify costs. How the costs will be used—for assigning costs to cost objects, preparing external reports, predicting cost behavior, or decision making—will dictate how the costs are classified.

For purposes of assigning costs to cost objects such as products or departments, costs are classified as direct or indirect. Direct costs can be conveniently traced to cost objects. Indirect costs cannot be conveniently traced to cost objects.

For external reporting purposes, costs are classified as either product costs or period costs. Product costs are assigned to inventories and are considered assets until the products are sold. At the point of sale, product costs become cost of goods sold on the income statement. In contrast, period costs are taken directly to the income statement as expenses in the period in which they are incurred.

For purposes of predicting how costs will react to changes in activity, costs are classified into three categories—variable, fixed, and mixed. Variable costs, in total, are strictly proportional to activity. The variable cost per unit is constant. Fixed costs, in total, remain the same as the activity level changes within the relevant range. The average fixed cost per unit decreases as the activity level increases. Mixed costs consist of variable and fixed elements and can be expressed in equation form as $Y = a + bX$, where Y is the total mixed cost, a is the total fixed cost, b is the variable cost per unit of activity, and X is the activity level.

For purposes of making decisions, the concepts of differential cost and revenue, sunk cost, and opportunity cost are vitally important. Differential costs and revenues are the costs and revenues that differ between alternatives. Sunk cost is a cost that occurred in the past and cannot be altered. Opportunity cost is the benefit that is forgone when one alternative is selected over another. Differential costs and opportunity costs should be carefully considered in decisions. Sunk costs are always irrelevant in decisions and should be ignored.

Different cost classifications for different purposes is the unifying theme of this chapter and it can be highlighted by contrasting traditional and contribution format income statements. The traditional income statement format is used primarily for external reporting purposes. It organizes costs using product and period cost classifications. The contribution format income statement aids decision making because it organizes costs using variable and fixed cost classifications.

Review Problem 1: Cost Terms

Many new cost terms have been introduced in this chapter. It will take you some time to learn what each term means and how to properly classify costs in an organization. Consider the following example: Porter Company manufactures furniture, including tables. Selected costs are given below:

1. The tables are made of wood that costs $100 per table.
2. The tables are assembled by workers, at a wage cost of $40 per table.
3. Workers assembling the tables are supervised by a factory supervisor who is paid $38,000 per year.
4. Electrical costs are $2 per machine-hour. Four machine-hours are required to produce a table.
5. The depreciation on the machines used to make the tables totals $10,000 per year. The machines have no resale value and do not wear out through use.
6. The salary of the president of the company is $100,000 per year.
7. The company spends $250,000 per year to advertise its products.
8. Salespersons are paid a commission of $30 for each table sold.
9. Instead of producing the tables, the company could rent its factory space for $50,000 per year.

Required:

Classify these costs according to the various cost terms used in the chapter. *Carefully study the classification of each cost.* If you don't understand why a particular cost is classified the way it is, reread the section of the chapter discussing the particular cost term. The terms *variable cost* and *fixed cost* refer to how costs behave with respect to the number of tables produced in a year.

Solution to Review Problem 1

	Variable Cost	Fixed Cost	Period (Selling and Administrative) Cost	Direct Materials	Direct Labor	Manufacturing Overhead	Sunk Cost	Opportunity Cost
				Product Cost				
1. Wood used in a table ($100 per table)	X			X				
2. Labor cost to assemble a table ($40 per table)	X				X			
3. Salary of the factory supervisor ($38,000 per year)		X				X		
4. Cost of electricity to produce tables ($2 per machine-hour)	X					X		
5. Depreciation of machines used to produce tables ($10,000 per year)		X				X	X*	
6. Salary of the company president ($100,000 per year)		X	X					
7. Advertising expense ($250,000 per year)		X	X					
8. Commissions paid to salespersons ($30 per table sold)	X		X					
9. Rental income forgone on factory space ($50,000 per year)								X†

* This is a sunk cost because the outlay for the equipment was made in a previous period.

† This is an opportunity cost because it represents the potential benefit that is lost or sacrificed as a result of using the factory space to produce tables. Opportunity cost is a special category of cost that is not ordinarily recorded in an organization's accounting records. To avoid possible confusion with other costs, we will not attempt to classify this cost in any other way except as an opportunity cost.

Review Problem 2: Income Statement Formats

McFarland, Inc., is a merchandiser that provided the following information:

	Amount
Number of units sold	35,000
Selling price per unit	$40
Variable selling expense per unit	$3
Variable administrative expense per unit	$1
Total fixed selling expense	$45,000
Total fixed administrative expense	$28,000
Beginning merchandise inventory	$21,000
Ending merchandise inventory	$35,000
Merchandise purchases	$805,000

Required:
1. Prepare a traditional income statement.
2. Prepare a contribution format income statement.

Solution to Review Problem 2
1. Traditional income statement

McFarland, Inc.		
Traditional Income Statement		
Sales ($40 per unit × 35,000 units)		$1,400,000
Cost of goods sold ($21,000 + $805,000 − $35,000)		791,000
Gross margin		609,000
Selling and administrative expenses:		
Selling expense (($3 per unit × 35,000 units) + $45,000)	$150,000	
Administrative expense (($1 per unit × 35,000 units) + $28,000)	63,000	213,000
Net operating income		$ 396,000

2. Contribution format income statement

McFarland, Inc.		
Contribution Format Income Statement		
Sales		$1,400,000
Variable expenses:		
Cost of goods sold ($21,000 + $805,000 − $35,000)	$791,000	
Selling expense ($3 per unit × 35,000 units)	105,000	
Administrative expense ($1 per unit × 35,000 units)	35,000	931,000
Contribution margin		469,000
Fixed expenses:		
Selling expense	45,000	
Administrative expense	28,000	73,000
Net operating income		$ 396,000

Glossary

Activity base A measure of whatever causes the incurrence of a variable cost. For example, the total cost of surgical gloves in a hospital will increase as the number of surgeries increases. Therefore, the number of surgeries is the activity base that explains the total cost of surgical gloves. (p. 31)

Administrative costs All executive, organizational, and clerical costs associated with the general management of an organization rather than with manufacturing or selling. (p. 28)

Committed fixed costs Investments in facilities, equipment, and basic organizational structure that can't be significantly reduced even for short periods of time without making fundamental changes. (p. 32)

Common cost A cost that is incurred to support a number of cost objects but that cannot be traced to them individually. For example, the wage cost of the pilot of a 747 airliner is a common cost of all of the passengers on the aircraft. Without the pilot, there would be no flight and no passengers. But no part of the pilot's wage is caused by any one passenger taking the flight. (p. 26)

Contribution approach An income statement format that organizes costs by their behavior. Costs are separated into variable and fixed categories rather than being separated into product and period costs for external reporting purposes. (p. 40)

Contribution margin The amount remaining from sales revenues after all variable expenses have been deducted. (p. 40)

Conversion cost Direct labor cost plus manufacturing overhead cost. (p. 28)

Cost behavior The way in which a cost reacts to changes in the level of activity. (p. 30)

Cost object Anything for which cost data are desired. Examples of cost objects are products, customers, geographic regions, and parts of the organization such as departments or divisions. (p. 25)

Cost structure The relative proportion of fixed, variable, and mixed costs in an organization. (p. 30)

Differential cost A future cost that differs between any two alternatives. (p. 37)

Differential revenue Future revenue that differs between any two alternatives. (p. 37)

Direct cost A cost that can be easily and conveniently traced to a specified cost object. (p. 26)

Direct labor Factory labor costs that can be easily traced to individual units of product. Also called *touch labor*. (p. 27)

Direct materials Materials that become an integral part of a finished product and whose costs can be conveniently traced to it. (p. 27)

Discretionary fixed costs Those fixed costs that arise from annual decisions by management to spend on certain fixed cost items, such as advertising and research. (p. 33)

Financial accounting The phase of accounting that is concerned with reporting historical financial information to external parties, such as stockholders, creditors, and regulators. (p. 25)

Fixed cost A cost that remains constant, in total, regardless of changes in the level of activity within the relevant range. If a fixed cost is expressed on a per unit basis, it varies inversely with the level of activity. (p. 32)

Finished goods Units of product that have been completed but not yet sold to customers. (p. 29)

Incremental cost An increase in cost between two alternatives. Also see *Differential cost*. (p. 37)

Indirect cost A cost that cannot be easily and conveniently traced to a specified cost object. (p. 26)

Indirect labor The labor costs of janitors, supervisors, materials handlers, and other factory workers that cannot be conveniently traced to particular products. (p. 27)

Indirect materials Small items of material such as glue and nails that may be an integral part of a finished product, but whose costs cannot be easily or conveniently traced to it. (p. 27)

Inventoriable costs Synonym for product costs. (p. 29)

Managerial accounting The phase of accounting that is concerned with providing information to managers for use within the organization. (p. 25)

Manufacturing overhead All manufacturing costs except direct materials and direct labor. (p. 27)

Mixed cost A cost that contains both variable and fixed cost elements. (p. 34)

Opportunity cost The potential benefit that is given up when one alternative is selected over another. (p. 38)

Period costs Costs that are taken directly to the income statement as expenses in the period in which they are incurred or accrued. (p. 29)

Prime cost Direct materials cost plus direct labor cost. (p. 27)

Product costs All costs that are involved in acquiring or making a product. In the case of manufactured goods, these costs consist of direct materials, direct labor, and manufacturing overhead. Also see *Inventoriable costs*. (p. 29)

Raw materials Any materials that go into the final product. (p. 27)

Relevant range The range of activity within which assumptions about variable and fixed cost behavior are valid. (p. 33)

Selling costs All costs that are incurred to secure customer orders and get the finished product or service into the hands of the customer. (p. 28)

Sunk cost A cost that has already been incurred and that cannot be changed by any decision made now or in the future. (p. 38)

Variable cost A cost that varies, in total, in direct proportion to changes in the level of activity. A variable cost is constant per unit. (p. 30)

Work in process Units of product that are only partially complete and will require further work before they are ready for sale to the customer. (p. 29)

Questions

1–1 What are the three major types of product costs in a manufacturing company?

1–2 Define the following: (*a*) direct materials, (*b*) indirect materials, (*c*) direct labor, (*d*) indirect labor, and (*e*) manufacturing overhead.

1–3 Explain the difference between a product cost and a period cost.

1–4 Distinguish between (*a*) a variable cost, (*b*) a fixed cost, and (*c*) a mixed cost.

1–5 What effect does an increase in the activity level have on—
  a. Unit fixed costs?
  b. Unit variable costs?
  c. Total fixed costs?
  d. Total variable costs?

1–6 Define the following terms: (*a*) cost behavior and (*b*) relevant range.

1–7 What is meant by an *activity base* when dealing with variable costs? Give several examples of activity bases.

1–8 Managers often assume a strictly linear relationship between cost and the level of activity. How can this practice be defended in light of the fact that many costs are curvilinear?

1–9 Distinguish between discretionary fixed costs and committed fixed costs.

1–10 Does the concept of the relevant range apply to fixed costs? Explain.

1–11 What is the difference between a traditional format income statement and a contribution format income statement?

1–12 What is the contribution margin?

1–13 Define the following terms: differential cost, sunk cost, and opportunity cost.

1–14 Only variable costs can be differential costs. Do you agree? Explain.

Applying Excel

LO1–6 This Excel worksheet form is to be used to recreate Exhibit 1–7. Download the workbook containing this form from Connect, where you will also receive instructions.

	A	B	C	D
1	Chapter 1: Applying Excel			
2				
3	**Data**			
4	Sales	$12,000		
5	Variable costs:			
6	Cost of goods sold	$6,000		
7	Variable selling	$600		
8	Variable administrative	$400		
9	Fixed costs:			
10	Fixed selling	$2,500		
11	Fixed administrative	$1,500		
12				
13	Enter a formula into each of the cells marked with a ? below			
14	**Exhibit 1-7**			
15				
16	**Traditional Format Income Statement**			
17	Sales		?	
18	Cost of goods sold		?	
19	Gross margin		?	
20	Selling and administrative expenses:			
21	Selling	?		
22	Administrative	?	?	
23	Net operating income		?	
24				
25	**Contribution Format Income Statement**			
26	Sales		?	
27	Variable expenses:			
28	Cost of goods sold	?		
29	Variable selling	?		
30	Variable administration	?	?	
31	Contribution margin		?	
32	Fixed expenses:			
33	Fixed selling	?		
34	Fixed administrative	?	?	
35	Net operating income		?	
36				

Chapter 1 Form / Filled in Chapter 1 Form

Required:

1. Check your worksheet by changing the variable selling cost in the Data area to $900, keeping all of the other data the same as in Exhibit 1–7. If your worksheet is operating properly, the net operating income under the traditional format income statement and under the contribution format income statement should now be $700 and the contribution margin should now be $4,700. If you do not get these answers, find the errors in your worksheet and correct them.

    How much is the gross margin? Did it change? Why or why not?

2. Suppose that sales are 10% higher as shown below:

Sales	$13,200
Variable costs:	
Cost of goods sold	$6,600
Variable selling	$660
Variable administrative	$440
Fixed costs:	
Fixed selling	$2,500
Fixed administrative	$1,500

    Enter this new data into your worksheet. Make sure that you change all of the data that are different—not just the sales. Print or copy the income statements from your worksheet.

    What happened to the variable costs and to the fixed costs when sales increased by 10%? Why? Did the contribution margin increase by 10%? Why or why not? Did the net operating income increase by 10%? Why or why not?

---

connect° The Foundational 15

Martinez Company's relevant range of production is 7,500 units to 12,500 units. When it produces and sells 10,000 units, its average costs per unit are as follows:

LO1–1, LO1–2, LO1–3, LO1–4, LO1–5, LO1–6

	Average Cost per Unit
Direct materials	$6.00
Direct labor	$3.50
Variable manufacturing overhead	$1.50
Fixed manufacturing overhead	$4.00
Fixed selling expense	$3.00
Fixed administrative expense	$2.00
Sales commissions	$1.00
Variable administrative expense	$0.50

Required:

1. For financial accounting purposes, what is the total amount of product costs incurred to make 10,000 units?
2. For financial accounting purposes, what is the total amount of period costs incurred to sell 10,000 units?
3. If 8,000 units are produced and sold, what is the variable cost per unit produced and sold?
4. If 12,500 units are produced and sold, what is the variable cost per unit produced and sold?
5. If 8,000 units are produced and sold, what is the total amount of variable costs related to the units produced and sold?
6. If 12,500 units are produced and sold, what is the total amount of variable costs related to the units produced and sold?
7. If 8,000 units are produced, what is the average fixed manufacturing cost per unit produced?
8. If 12,500 units are produced, what is the average fixed manufacturing cost per unit produced?
9. If 8,000 units are produced, what is the total amount of fixed manufacturing cost incurred to support this level of production?
10. If 12,500 units are produced, what is the total amount of fixed manufacturing cost incurred to support this level of production?
11. If 8,000 units are produced, what is the total amount of manufacturing overhead cost incurred to support this level of production? What is this total amount expressed on a per unit basis?

12. If 12,500 units are produced, what is the total amount of manufacturing overhead cost incurred to support this level of production? What is this total amount expressed on a per unit basis?
13. If the selling price is $22 per unit, what is the contribution margin per unit?
14. If 11,000 units are produced, what are the total amounts of direct and indirect manufacturing costs incurred to support this level of production?
15. What incremental manufacturing cost will Martinez incur if it increases production from 10,000 to 10,001 units?

Exercises

EXERCISE 1–1 Identifying Direct and Indirect Costs LO1–1

Northwest Hospital is a full-service hospital that provides everything from major surgery and emergency room care to outpatient clinics.

Required:

For each cost incurred at Northwest Hospital, indicate whether it would most likely be a direct cost or an indirect cost of the specified cost object by placing an *X* in the appropriate column.

Cost	Cost Object	Direct Cost	Indirect Cost
Ex. Catered food served to patients	A particular patient	X	
1. The wages of pediatric nurses	The pediatric department		
2. Prescription drugs	A particular patient		
3. Heating the hospital	The pediatric department		
4. The salary of the head of pediatrics	The pediatric department		
5. The salary of the head of pediatrics	A particular pediatric patient		
6. Hospital chaplain's salary	A particular patient		
7. Lab tests by outside contractor	A particular patient		
8. Lab tests by outside contractor	A particular department		

EXERCISE 1–2 Classifying Manufacturing Costs LO1–2

The PC Works assembles custom computers from components supplied by various manufacturers. The company is very small and its assembly shop and retail sales store are housed in a single facility in a Redmond, Washington, industrial park. Listed below are some of the costs that are incurred at the company.

Required:

For each cost, indicate whether it would most likely be classified as direct materials, direct labor, manufacturing overhead, selling, or an administrative cost.
1. The cost of a hard drive installed in a computer.
2. The cost of advertising in the *Puget Sound Computer User* newspaper.
3. The wages of employees who assemble computers from components.
4. Sales commissions paid to the company's salespeople.
5. The salary of the assembly shop's supervisor.
6. The salary of the company's accountant.
7. Depreciation on equipment used to test assembled computers before release to customers.
8. Rent on the facility in the industrial park.

EXERCISE 1–3 Classifying Costs as Product or Period Costs LO1–3

Suppose that you have been given a summer job as an intern at Issac Aircams, a company that manufactures sophisticated spy cameras for remote-controlled military reconnaissance aircraft. The company, which is privately owned, has approached a bank for a loan to help finance its growth. The bank requires financial statements before approving the loan.

Required:

Classify each cost listed below as either a product cost or a period cost for the purpose of preparing financial statements for the bank.
1. Depreciation on salespersons' cars.
2. Rent on equipment used in the factory.

3. Lubricants used for machine maintenance.
4. Salaries of personnel who work in the finished goods warehouse.
5. Soap and paper towels used by factory workers at the end of a shift.
6. Factory supervisors' salaries.
7. Heat, water, and power consumed in the factory.
8. Materials used for boxing products for shipment overseas. (Units are not normally boxed.)
9. Advertising costs.
10. Workers' compensation insurance for factory employees.
11. Depreciation on chairs and tables in the factory lunchroom.
12. The wages of the receptionist in the administrative offices.
13. Cost of leasing the corporate jet used by the company's executives.
14. The cost of renting rooms at a Florida resort for the annual sales conference.
15. The cost of packaging the company's product.

EXERCISE 1–4 Fixed and Variable Cost Behavior LO1–4

Espresso Express operates a number of espresso coffee stands in busy suburban malls. The fixed weekly expense of a coffee stand is $1,200 and the variable cost per cup of coffee served is $0.22.

Required:

1. Fill in the following table with your estimates of the company's total cost and average cost per cup of coffee at the indicated levels of activity. Round off the average cost per cup of coffee to the nearest tenth of a cent.

	Cups of Coffee Served in a Week		
	2,000	2,100	2,200
Fixed cost	?	?	?
Variable cost	?	?	?
Total cost	?	?	?
Average cost per cup of coffee served	?	?	?

2. Does the average cost per cup of coffee served increase, decrease, or remain the same as the number of cups of coffee served in a week increases? Explain.

EXERCISE 1–5 Differential, Sunk, and Opportunity Costs LO1–5

Northeast Hospital's Radiology Department is considering replacing an old inefficient X-ray machine with a state-of-the-art digital X-ray machine. The new machine would provide higher quality X-rays in less time and at a lower cost per X-ray. It would also require less power and would use a color laser printer to produce easily readable X-ray images. Instead of investing the funds in the new X-ray machine, the Laboratory Department is lobbying the hospital's management to buy a new DNA analyzer.

Required:

For each of the items below, indicate by placing an X in the appropriate column whether it should be considered a differential cost, a sunk cost, or an opportunity cost in the decision to replace the old X-ray machine with a new machine. If none of the categories apply for a particular item, leave all columns blank.

Item	Differential Cost	Sunk Cost	Opportunity Cost
Ex. Cost of X-ray film used in the old machine	X		
1. Cost of the old X-ray machine			
2. The salary of the head of the Radiology Department			
3. The salary of the head of the Laboratory Department			
4. Cost of the new color laser printer			
5. Rent on the space occupied by Radiology			
6. The cost of maintaining the old machine			
7. Benefits from a new DNA analyzer			
8. Cost of electricity to run the X-ray machines			

EXERCISE 1–6 Traditional and Contribution Format Income Statements LO1–6

Cherokee Inc. is a merchandiser that provided the following information:

	Amount
Number of units sold	20,000
Selling price per unit........................	$30
Variable selling expense per unit.............	$4
Variable administrative expense per unit	$2
Total fixed selling expense	$40,000
Total fixed administrative expense	$30,000
Beginning merchandise inventory	$24,000
Ending merchandise inventory................	$44,000
Merchandise purchases......................	$180,000

Required:

1. Prepare a traditional income statement.
2. Prepare a contribution format income statement.

EXERCISE 1–7 Direct and Indirect Costs LO1–1

Kubin Company's relevant range of production is 18,000 to 22,000 units. When it produces and sells 20,000 units, its average costs per unit are as follows:

	Average Cost per Unit
Direct materials	$7.00
Direct labor............................	$4.00
Variable manufacturing overhead	$1.50
Fixed manufacturing overhead.............	$5.00
Fixed selling expense....................	$3.50
Fixed administrative expense	$2.50
Sales commissions	$1.00
Variable administrative expense...........	$0.50

Required:

1. Assume the cost object is units of production:
   a. What is the total direct manufacturing cost incurred to make 20,000 units?
   b. What is the total indirect manufacturing cost incurred to make 20,000 units?
2. Assume the cost object is the Manufacturing Department and that its total output is 20,000 units.
   a. How much total manufacturing cost is directly traceable to the Manufacturing Department?
   b. How much total manufacturing cost is an indirect cost that cannot be easily traced to the Manufacturing Department?
3. Assume the cost object is the company's various sales representatives. Furthermore, assume that the company spent $50,000 of its total fixed selling expense on advertising and the remainder of the total fixed selling expense comprised the fixed portion of the company's sales representatives' compensation.
   a. When the company sells 20,000 units, what is the total direct selling expense that can be readily traced to individual sales representatives?
   b. When the company sells 20,000 units, what is the total indirect selling expense that cannot be readily traced to individual sales representatives?
4. Are Kubin's administrative expenses always going to be treated as indirect costs in its internal management reports?

EXERCISE 1–8 Product Costs and Period Costs; Variable and Fixed Costs LO1–3, LO1–4

Refer to the data given in Exercise 1–7. Answer all questions independently.

Required:

1. For financial accounting purposes, what is the total amount of product costs incurred to make 20,000 units?
2. For financial accounting purposes, what is the total amount of period costs incurred to sell 20,000 units?

3. For financial accounting purposes, what is the total amount of product costs incurred to make 22,000 units?
4. For financial accounting purposes, what is the total amount of period costs incurred to sell 18,000 units?

EXERCISE 1–9 Fixed, Variable, and Mixed Costs LO1–4

Refer to the data given in Exercise 1–7. Answer all questions independently.

Required:
1. If 18,000 units are produced and sold, what is the variable cost per unit produced and sold?
2. If 22,000 units are produced and sold, what is the variable cost per unit produced and sold?
3. If 18,000 units are produced and sold, what is the total amount of variable cost related to the units produced and sold?
4. If 22,000 units are produced and sold, what is the total amount of variable cost related to the units produced and sold?
5. If 18,000 units are produced, what is the average fixed manufacturing cost per unit produced?
6. If 22,000 units are produced, what is the average fixed manufacturing cost per unit produced?
7. If 18,000 units are produced, what is the total amount of fixed manufacturing overhead incurred to support this level of production?
8. If 22,000 units are produced, what is the total amount of fixed manufacturing overhead incurred to support this level of production?

EXERCISE 1–10 Differential Costs and Sunk Costs LO1–5

Refer to the data given in Exercise 1–7. Answer all questions independently.

Required:
1. What is the incremental manufacturing cost incurred if the company increases production from 20,000 to 20,001 units?
2. What is the incremental cost incurred if the company increases production *and* sales from 20,000 to 20,001 units?
3. Assume that Kubin Company produced 20,000 units and expects to sell 19,800 of them. If a new customer unexpectedly emerges and expresses interest in buying the 200 extra units that have been produced by the company and that would otherwise remain unsold, what is the incremental manufacturing cost per unit incurred to sell these units to the customer?
4. Assume that Kubin Company produced 20,000 units and expects to sell 19,800 of them. If a new customer unexpectedly emerges and expresses interest in buying the 200 extra units that have been produced by the company and that would otherwise remain unsold, what incremental selling and administrative cost per unit is incurred to sell these units to the customer?

EXERCISE 1–11 Cost Behavior; Contribution Format Income Statement LO1–4, LO1–6

Harris Company manufactures and sells a single product. A partially completed schedule of the company's total costs and costs per unit over the relevant range of 30,000 to 50,000 units is given below:

	Units Produced and Sold		
	30,000	40,000	50,000
Total costs:			
Variable cost	$180,000	?	?
Fixed cost.............	300,000	?	?
Total cost	$480,000	?	?
Costs per unit:			
Variable cost	?	?	?
Fixed cost.............	?	?	?
Total cost per unit	?	?	?

Required:
1. Complete the above schedule of the company's total costs and costs per unit.
2. Assume that the company produces and sells 45,000 units during the year at a selling price of $16 per unit. Prepare a contribution format income statement for the year.

EXERCISE 1–12 Product and Period Cost Flows LO1–3

The Devon Motor Company produces automobiles. On April 1st the company had no beginning inventories and it purchased 8,000 batteries at a cost of $80 per battery. It withdrew 7,600 batteries from the storeroom during the month. Of these, 100 were used to replace batteries in cars being used by the company's traveling sales staff. The remaining 7,500 batteries withdrawn from the storeroom were placed in cars being produced by the company. Of the cars in production during April, 90 percent were completed and transferred from work in process to finished goods. Of the cars completed during the month, 30 percent were unsold at April 30th.

Required:

1. Determine the cost of batteries that would appear in each of the following accounts on April 30th.
    a.   Raw Materials
    b.   Work in Process
    c.   Finished Goods
    d.   Cost of Goods Sold
    e.   Selling Expense
2. Specify whether each of the above accounts would appear on the balance sheet or on the income statement at the end of the month.

EXERCISE 1–13 Variable and Fixed Cost Behavior LO1–4

Munchak Company's relevant range of production is 9,000–11,000 units. Last month the company produced 10,000 units. Its total manufacturing cost per unit produced was $70. At this level of activity the company's variable manufacturing costs are 40% of its total manufacturing costs.

Required:

Assume that next month Munchak produces 10,050 units and that its cost behavior patterns remain unchanged. Label each of the following statements as true or false with respect to next month. Do not use a calculator to answer items 1 through 6. You can use a calculator to answer items 7 through 12. Record your answers by placing an X under the appropriate heading.

	True	False
1. The variable manufacturing cost per unit will remain the same as last month.		
2. The total fixed manufacturing cost will be greater than last month.		
3. The total manufacturing cost will be greater than last month.		
4. The average fixed manufacturing cost per unit will be less than last month.		
5. The total variable manufacturing cost will be less than last month.		
6. The total manufacturing cost per unit will be greater than last month.		
7. The variable manufacturing cost per unit will equal $28.		
8. The total fixed manufacturing cost will equal $422,100.		
9. The total manufacturing cost will equal $701,400.		
10. The average fixed manufacturing cost per unit (rounded to the nearest cent) will equal $41.79.		
11. The total variable manufacturing cost will equal $280,000.		
12. The total manufacturing cost per unit (rounded to the nearest cent) will equal $69.79.		

EXERCISE 1–14 Cost Classification LO1–2, LO1–3, LO1–4, LO1–5

Wollogong Group Ltd. of New South Wales, Australia, acquired its factory building 10 years ago. For several years, the company has rented out a small annex attached to the rear of the building for $30,000 per year. The renter's lease will expire soon, and rather than renewing the lease, the company has decided to use the annex to manufacture a new product.

Direct materials cost for the new product will total $80 per unit. To have a place to store its finished goods, the company will rent a small warehouse for $500 per month. In addition, the company must rent equipment for $4,000 per month to produce the new product. Direct laborers will be hired and paid $60 per unit to manufacture the new product. As in prior years, the space in the annex will continue to be depreciated at $8,000 per year.

The annual advertising cost for the new product will be $50,000. A supervisor will be hired and paid $3,500 per month to oversee production. Electricity for operating machines will be $1.20 per unit. The cost of shipping the new product to customers will be $9 per unit.

To provide funds to purchase materials, meet payrolls, and so forth, the company will have to liquidate some temporary investments. These investments are presently yielding a return of $3,000 per year.

Required:

Using the table shown below, describe each of the costs associated with the new product decision in four ways. In terms of cost classifications for predicting cost behavior (column 1), indicate whether the cost is fixed or variable. With respect to cost classifications for manufacturers (column 2), if the item is a manufacturing cost, indicate whether it is direct materials, direct labor, or manufacturing overhead. If it is a nonmanufacturing cost, then select "none" as your answer. With respect to cost classifications for preparing financial statements (column 3), indicate whether the item is a product cost or period cost. Finally, in terms of cost classifications for decision making (column 4), identify any items that are sunk costs or opportunity costs. If you identify an item as an opportunity cost, then select "none" as your answer in columns 1–3.

		Cost Classifications for:		
	(1)	(2)	(3)	(4)
	Predicting		Preparing	
Cost Item	Cost Behavior	Manufacturers	Financial Statements	Decision Making

EXERCISE 1–15 Traditional and Contribution Format Income Statements LO1–6

The Alpine House, Inc., is a large retailer of snow skis. The company assembled the information shown below for the quarter ended March 31:

	Amount
Sales	$150,000
Selling price per pair of skis	$750
Variable selling expense per pair of skis.	$50
Variable administrative expense per pair of skis	$10
Total fixed selling expense	$20,000
Total fixed administrative expense.	$20,000
Beginning merchandise inventory	$30,000
Ending merchandise inventory	$40,000
Merchandise purchases.	$100,000

Required:

1. Prepare a traditional income statement for the quarter ended March 31.
2. Prepare a contribution format income statement for the quarter ended March 31.
3. What was the contribution margin per unit?

EXERCISE 1–16 Cost Classifications for Decision Making LO1–5

Warner Corporation purchased a machine 7 years ago for $319,000 when it launched product P50. Unfortunately, this machine has broken down and cannot be repaired. The machine could be replaced by a new model 300 machine costing $313,000 or by a new model 200 machine costing $275,000. Management has decided to buy the model 200 machine. It has less capacity than the model 300 machine, but its capacity is sufficient to continue making product P50. Management also considered, but rejected, the alternative of dropping product P50 and not replacing the old machine. If that were done, the $275,000 invested in the new machine could instead have been invested in a project that would have returned a total of $374,000.

Required:

1. What is the total differential cost regarding the decision to buy the model 200 machine rather than the model 300 machine?
2. What is the total sunk cost regarding the decision to buy the model 200 machine rather than the model 300 machine?
3. What is the total opportunity cost regarding the decision to invest in the model 200 machine?

EXERCISE 1–17 Classifying Variable and Fixed Costs and Product and Period Costs LO1–3, LO1–4

Below are listed various costs that are found in organizations.
1. Hamburger buns in a Wendy's restaurant.
2. Advertising by a dental office.
3. Apples processed and canned by Del Monte.
4. Shipping canned apples from a Del Monte plant to customers.
5. Insurance on a Bausch & Lomb factory producing contact lenses.
6. Insurance on IBM's corporate headquarters.

7. Salary of a supervisor overseeing production of printers at Hewlett-Packard.
8. Commissions paid to automobile salespersons.
9. Depreciation of factory lunchroom facilities at a General Electric plant.
10. Steering wheels installed in BMWs.

Required:

Using the table shown below, describe each of the costs mentioned above in two ways. In terms of cost classifications for predicting cost behavior (column 1), indicate whether the cost is fixed or variable with respect to the number of units produced and sold. With respect to cost classifications for preparing financial statements (column 2), indicate whether the item is a product cost or period cost (selling and administrative cost).

	Cost Classifications for:	
	(1)	(2)
Cost Item	Predicting Cost Behavior	Preparing Financial Statements

Problems   connect

PROBLEM 1–18 Direct and Indirect Costs; Variable Costs LO1–1, LO1–4

The following cost data pertain to the operations of Montgomery Department Stores, Inc., for the month of July.

Corporate legal office salaries	$56,000
Apparel Department cost of sales—Evendale Store	$90,000
Corporate headquarters building lease.	$48,000
Store manager's salary—Evendale Store	$12,000
Apparel Department sales commission—Evendale Store	$7,000
Store utilities—Evendale Store	$11,000
Apparel Department manager's salary—Evendale Store	$8,000
Central warehouse lease cost.	$15,000
Janitorial costs—Evendale Store.	$9,000

The Evendale Store is one of many stores owned and operated by the company. The Apparel Department is one of many departments at the Evendale Store. The central warehouse serves all of the company's stores.

Required:

1. What is the total amount of the costs listed above that are direct costs of the Apparel Department?
2. What is the total amount of the costs listed above that are direct costs of the Evendale Store?
3. What is the total amount of the Apparel Department's direct costs that are also variable costs with respect to total departmental sales?

PROBLEM 1–19 Traditional and Contribution Format Income Statements LO1–6

Todrick Company is a merchandiser that reported the following information based on 1,000 units sold:

Sales	$300,000
Beginning merchandise inventory	$20,000
Purchases.	$200,000
Ending merchandise inventory	$7,000
Fixed selling expense.	?
Fixed administrative expense	$12,000
Variable selling expense	$15,000
Variable administrative expense	?
Contribution margin	$60,000
Net operating income.	$18,000

Required:

1. Prepare a contribution format income statement.
2. Prepare a traditional format income statement.

3. Calculate the selling price per unit.
4. Calculate the variable cost per unit.
5. Calculate the contribution margin per unit.
6. Which income statement format (traditional format or contribution format) would be more useful to managers in estimating how net operating income will change in responses to changes in unit sales? Why?

PROBLEM 1–20 Variable and Fixed Costs; Subtleties of Direct and Indirect Costs LO1–1, LO1–4

Madison Seniors Care Center is a nonprofit organization that provides a variety of health services to the elderly. The center is organized into a number of departments, one of which is the Meals-On-Wheels program that delivers hot meals to seniors in their homes on a daily basis. Below are listed a number of costs of the center and the Meals-On-Wheels program.

example The cost of groceries used in meal preparation.
    a. The cost of leasing the Meals-On-Wheels van.
    b. The cost of incidental supplies such as salt, pepper, napkins, and so on.
    c. The cost of gasoline consumed by the Meals-On-Wheels van.
    d. The rent on the facility that houses Madison Seniors Care Center, including the Meals-On-Wheels program.
    e. The salary of the part-time manager of the Meals-On-Wheels program.
    f. Depreciation on the kitchen equipment used in the Meals-On-Wheels program.
    g. The hourly wages of the caregiver who drives the van and delivers the meals.
    h. The costs of complying with health safety regulations in the kitchen.
    i. The costs of mailing letters soliciting donations to the Meals-On-Wheels program.

Required:

For each cost listed above, indicate whether it is a direct or indirect cost of the Meals-On-Wheels program, whether it is a direct or indirect cost of particular seniors served by the program, and whether it is variable or fixed with respect to the number of seniors served. Use the form below for your answer.

Item	Description	Direct or Indirect Cost of the Meals-on-Wheels Program		Direct or Indirect Cost of Particular Seniors Served by the Meals-on-Wheels Program		Variable or Fixed with Respect to the Number of Seniors Served by the Meals-on-Wheels Program	
		Direct	Indirect	Direct	Indirect	Variable	Fixed
Example	The cost of groceries used in meal preparation...	X		X		X	

PROBLEM 1–21 Traditional and Contribution Format Income Statements LO1–6

Marwick's Pianos, Inc., purchases pianos from a large manufacturer for an average cost of $2,450 per unit and then sells them to retail customers for an average price of $3,125 each. The company's selling and administrative costs for a typical month are presented below:

Costs	Cost Formula
Selling:	
Advertising	$700 per month
Sales salaries and commissions	$950 per month, plus 8% of sales
Delivery of pianos to customers	$30 per piano sold
Utilities	$350 per month
Depreciation of sales facilities	$800 per month
Administrative:	
Executive salaries	$2,500 per month
Insurance	$400 per month
Clerical	$1,000 per month, plus $20 per piano sold
Depreciation of office equipment . . .	$300 per month

During August, Marwick's Pianos, Inc., sold and delivered 40 pianos.

Required:

1. Prepare a traditional format income statement for August.
2. Prepare a contribution format income statement for August. Show costs and revenues on both a total and a per unit basis down through contribution margin.
3. Refer to the income statement you prepared in (2) above. Why might it be misleading to show the fixed costs on a per unit basis?

PROBLEM 1–22 Cost Terminology; Contribution Format Income Statement LO1–2, LO1–4, LO1–6

Miller Company's total sales are $120,000. The company's direct labor cost is $15,000, which represents 30% of its total conversion cost and 40% of its total prime cost. Its total selling and administrative expense is $18,000 and its only variable selling and administrative expense is a sales commission of 5% of sales. The company maintains no beginning or ending inventories and its manufacturing overhead costs are entirely fixed costs.

Required:

1. What is the total manufacturing overhead cost?
2. What is the total direct materials cost?
3. What is the total manufacturing cost?
4. What is the total variable selling and administrative cost?
5. What is the total variable cost?
6. What is the total fixed cost?
7. What is the total contribution margin?

PROBLEM 1–23 Cost Classification LO1–1, LO1–3, LO1–4

Listed below are costs found in various organizations.

1. Property taxes, factory.
2. Boxes used for packaging detergent produced by the company.
3. Salespersons' commissions.
4. Supervisor's salary, factory.
5. Depreciation, executive autos.
6. Wages of workers assembling computers.
7. Insurance, finished goods warehouses.
8. Lubricants for production equipment.
9. Advertising costs.
10. Microchips used in producing calculators.
11. Shipping costs on merchandise sold.
12. Magazine subscriptions, factory lunchroom.
13. Thread in a garment factory.
14. Executive life insurance.
15. Ink used in textbook production.
16. Fringe benefits, materials handling workers.
17. Yarn used in sweater production.
18. Wages of receptionist, executive offices.

Required:

Prepare an answer sheet with column headings as shown below. For each cost item, indicate whether it would be variable or fixed with respect to the number of units produced and sold; and then whether it would be a selling cost, an administrative cost, or a manufacturing cost. If it is a manufacturing cost, indicate whether it is a direct cost or an indirect cost with respect to units of product. Three sample answers are provided for illustration.

Cost Item	Variable or Fixed	Selling Cost	Administrative Cost	Manufacturing (Product) Cost Direct	Manufacturing (Product) Cost Indirect
Direct labor	V			X	
Executive salaries	F		X		
Factory rent	F				X

PROBLEM 1–24 Different Cost Classifications for Different Purposes LO1–1, LO1–2, LO1–3, LO1–4, LO1–5

Dozier Company produced and sold 1,000 units during its first month of operations. It reported the following costs and expenses for the month:

Direct materials		$69,000
Direct labor.		$35,000
Variable manufacturing overhead	$15,000	
Fixed manufacturing overhead.	28,000	
Total manufacturing overhead		$43,000
Variable selling expense	$12,000	
Fixed selling expense.	18,000	
Total selling expense		$30,000
Variable administrative expense.	$ 4,000	
Fixed administrative expense	25,000	
Total administrative expense.		$29,000

Required:

1. With respect to cost classifications for preparing financial statements:
   a. What is the total product cost?
   b. What is the total period cost?
2. With respect to cost classifications for assigning costs to cost objects:
   a. What is total direct manufacturing cost?
   b. What is the total indirect manufacturing cost?
3. With respect to cost classifications for manufacturers:
   a. What is the total manufacturing cost?
   b. What is the total nonmanufacturing cost?
   c. What is the total conversion cost and prime cost?
4. With respect to cost classifications for predicting cost behavior:
   a. What is the total variable manufacturing cost?
   b. What is the total fixed cost for the company as a whole?
   c. What is the variable cost per unit produced and sold?
5. With respect to cost classifications for decision making:
   a. If Dozier had produced 1,001 units instead of 1,000 units, how much incremental manufacturing cost would it have incurred to make the additional unit?

PROBLEM 1–25 Traditional and Contribution Format Income Statements LO1–6

Milden Company is a merchandiser that plans to sell 12,000 units during the next quarter at a selling price of $100 per unit. The company also gathered the following cost estimates for the next quarter:

Cost	Cost Formula
Cost of good sold	$35 per unit sold
Advertising expense	$210,000 per quarter
Sales commissions	6% of sales
Shipping expense	$28,000 per quarter + $9.10 per unit sold
Administrative salaries	$145,000 per quarter
Insurance expense	$9,000 per quarter
Depreciation expense	$76,000 per quarter

Required:

1. Prepare a contribution format income statement for the next quarter.
2. Prepare a traditional format income statement for the next quarter.

connect Cases

CASE 1–26 Cost Classification and Cost Behavior LO1–1, LO1–2, LO1–3, LO1–4

The Dorilane Company produces a set of wood patio furniture consisting of a table and four chairs. The company has enough customer demand to justify producing its full capacity of 2,000 sets per year. Annual cost data at full capacity follow:

Direct labor.	$118,000
Advertising	$50,000
Factory supervision.	$40,000
Property taxes, factory building	$3,500
Sales commissions	$80,000
Insurance, factory	$2,500
Depreciation, administrative office equipment.	$4,000
Lease cost, factory equipment	$12,000
Indirect materials, factory.	$6,000
Depreciation, factory building.	$10,000
Administrative office supplies (billing)	$3,000
Administrative office salaries.	$60,000
Direct materials used (wood, bolts, etc.)	$94,000
Utilities, factory	$20,000

Required:

1. Prepare an answer sheet with the column headings shown below. Enter each cost item on your answer sheet, placing the dollar amount under the appropriate headings. As examples, this has been done already for the first two items in the list above. Note that each cost item is classified in two ways: first, as variable or fixed with respect to the number of units produced and sold; and second, as a selling and administrative cost or a product cost. (If the item is a product cost, it should also be classified as either direct or indirect as shown.)

	Cost Behavior		Period (Selling or Administrative)	Product Cost	
Cost Item	Variable	Fixed	Cost	Direct	Indirect*
Direct labor	$118,000			$118,000	
Advertising		$50,000	$50,000		

*To units of product.

2. Total the dollar amounts in each of the columns in (1) above. Compute the average product cost of one patio set.

3. Assume that production drops to only 1,000 sets annually. Would you expect the average product cost per set to increase, decrease, or remain unchanged? Explain. No computations are necessary.

4. Refer to the original data. The president's brother-in-law has considered making himself a patio set and has priced the necessary materials at a building supply store. The brother-in-law has asked the president if he could purchase a patio set from the Dorilane Company "at cost," and the president agreed to let him do so.

    a. Would you expect any disagreement between the two men over the price the brother-in-law should pay? Explain. What price does the president probably have in mind? The brother-in-law?

    b. Because the company is operating at full capacity, what cost term used in the chapter might be justification for the president to charge the full, regular price to the brother-in-law and still be selling "at cost"?

CASE 1–27 Ethics and the Manager LO1–3

M. K. Gallant is president of Kranbrack Corporation, a company whose stock is traded on a national exchange. In a meeting with investment analysts at the beginning of the year, Gallant had predicted that the company's earnings would grow by 20% this year. Unfortunately, sales have been less than expected for the year, and Gallant concluded within two weeks of the end of the fiscal year that it would be impossible to report an increase in earnings as large as predicted unless some drastic action was taken. Accordingly, Gallant has ordered that wherever possible, expenditures should be postponed to the new year—including canceling or postponing orders with suppliers, delaying planned maintenance and training, and cutting back on end-of-year advertising and travel. Additionally, Gallant ordered the company's controller to carefully scrutinize all costs that are currently classified as period costs and reclassify as many as possible as product costs. The company is expected to have substantial inventories at the end of the year.

Required:

1. Why would reclassifying period costs as product costs increase this period's reported earnings?

2. Do you believe Gallant's actions are ethical? Why or why not?

A company may have a product with a high-quality design that uses high-quality components, but if the product is poorly assembled or has other defects, the company will have high warranty repair costs and dissatisfied customers. People who are dissatisfied with a product are unlikely to buy the product again. They often tell others about their bad experiences. This is the worst possible sort of advertising. To prevent such problems, companies expend a great deal of effort to reduce defects. The objective is to have high *quality of conformance.*

Quality of Conformance

A product that meets or exceeds its design specifications and is free of defects that diminish its appearance or degrade its performance is said to have high **quality of conformance**. Note that if an economy car is free of defects, it can have a quality of conformance that is just as high as a defect-free luxury car. The purchasers of economy cars cannot expect their cars to be as opulently equipped as luxury cars, but they can and do expect them to be free of defects.

> Preventing, detecting, and dealing with defects causes costs that are called *quality costs* or the *cost of quality.* The use of the term *quality cost* is confusing to some people. It does not refer to costs such as using a higher-grade leather to make a wallet or using 14K gold instead of gold-plating in jewelry. Instead, the term **quality cost** refers to all of the costs that are incurred to prevent defects or that result from defects in products.

> Quality costs can be broken down into four broad groups. Two of these groups—known as *prevention costs* and *appraisal costs*—are incurred in an effort to keep defective products from falling into the hands of customers. The other two groups of costs—known as *internal failure costs* and *external failure costs*—are incurred because defects occur despite efforts to prevent them. Examples of specific costs involved in each of these four groups are given in Exhibit 1A–1.

LO1–7
Identify the four types of quality costs and explain how they interact.

EXHIBIT 1A–1
Typical Quality Costs

Prevention Costs	Internal Failure Costs
Systems development	Net cost of scrap
Quality engineering	Net cost of spoilage
Quality training	Rework labor and overhead
Quality circles	Reinspection of reworked products
Statistical process control activities	Retesting of reworked products
Supervision of prevention activities	Downtime caused by quality problems
Quality data gathering, analysis, and reporting	Disposal of defective products
Quality improvement projects	Analysis of the cause of defects in production
Technical support provided to suppliers	Re-entering data because of keying errors
Audits of the effectiveness of the quality system	Debugging software errors

Appraisal Costs	External Failure Costs
Test and inspection of incoming materials	Cost of field servicing and handling complaints
Test and inspection of in-process goods	Warranty repairs and replacements
Final product testing and inspection	Repairs and replacements beyond the warranty period
Supplies used in testing and inspection	Product recalls
Supervision of testing and inspection activities	Liability arising from defective products
Depreciation of test equipment	Returns and allowances arising from quality problems
Maintenance of test equipment	Lost sales arising from a reputation for poor quality
Plant utilities in the inspection area	
Field testing and appraisal at customer site	

Several things should be noted about the quality costs shown in the exhibit. First, quality costs don't relate to just manufacturing; rather, they relate to all the activities in a company from initial research and development (R&D) through customer service. Second, the number of costs associated with quality is very large; total quality cost can be very high unless management gives this area special attention. Finally, the costs in the four groupings are quite different. We will now look at each of these groupings more closely.

Prevention Costs

Generally, the most effective way to manage quality costs is to avoid having defects in the first place. It is much less costly to prevent a problem from ever happening than it is to find and correct the problem after it has occurred. **Prevention costs** support activities whose purpose is to reduce the number of defects.

Note from Exhibit 1A–1 that prevention costs include activities relating to quality circles and statistical process control. **Quality circles** consist of small groups of employees that meet on a regular basis to discuss ways to improve quality. Both management and workers are included in these circles. Quality circles are widely used and can be found in manufacturing companies, utilities, health care organizations, banks, and many other organizations.

Statistical process control is a technique that is used to detect whether a process is in or out of control. An out-of-control process results in defective units and may be caused by a miscalibrated machine or some other factor. In statistical process control, workers use charts to monitor the quality of units that pass through their workstations. With these charts, workers can quickly spot processes that are out of control and that are creating defects. Problems can be immediately corrected and further defects prevented rather than waiting for an inspector to catch the defects later.

Note also from the list of prevention costs in Exhibit 1A–1 that some companies provide technical support to their suppliers as a way of preventing defects. Particularly in *just-in-time (JIT) systems*, such support to suppliers is vital. In a JIT system, parts are delivered from suppliers just in time and in just the correct quantity to fill customer orders. There are no parts stockpiles. If a defective part is received from a supplier, the part cannot be used and the order for the ultimate customer cannot be filled on time. Hence, every part received from a supplier must be free of defects. Consequently, companies that use JIT often require that their suppliers use sophisticated quality control programs such as statistical process control and that their suppliers certify that they will deliver parts and materials that are free of defects.

Appraisal Costs

Any defective parts and products should be caught as early as possible in the production process. **Appraisal costs**, which are sometimes called *inspection costs,* are incurred to identify defective products *before* the products are shipped to customers. Unfortunately, performing appraisal activities doesn't keep defects from happening again, and most managers now realize that maintaining an army of inspectors is an expensive (and ineffective) approach to quality control. Therefore, production employees are increasingly being asked to oversee their own quality control. This approach, along with designing products that are easy to manufacture, prevents defects from occurring—which is less costly than relying on inspections to detect and correct defects.

Internal Failure Costs

Failure costs are incurred when a product fails to conform to its design specifications. Failure costs can be either internal or external. **Internal failure costs** result from identifying defects before they are shipped to customers. These costs include scrap, rejected products, reworking of defective units, and downtime caused by quality problems. In some companies, as little as 10% of the company's products make it through the production process without rework of some kind. Of course, the more effective a company's appraisal activities, the greater the chance of catching defects internally and the greater the level of internal failure costs. This is the price that is paid to avoid incurring external failure costs, which can be devastating.

External Failure Costs

External failure costs result when a defective product is delivered to a customer. Exhibit 1A–1includes examples of external failure costs such as warranty repairs and replacements, product recalls, liability arising from legal action against a company, and lost sales arising from a reputation for poor quality. Such costs can decimate profits.

In the past, some managers have taken the attitude, "Let's go ahead and ship everything to customers, and we'll take care of any problems under the warranty." This attitude generally results in high external failure costs, customer ill will, and declining market share and profits.

Distribution of Quality Costs

Quality costs for some companies range between 10% and 20% of total sales, whereas experts say that these costs should be more in the 2% to 4% range. How does a company reduce its total quality cost? The answer lies in how the quality costs are distributed. Refer to the graph in Exhibit 1A–2, which shows total quality costs as a function of the quality of conformance.

The graph shows that when the quality of conformance is low, total quality cost is high and that most of this cost consists of costs of internal and external failure. A low quality of conformance means that a high percentage of units are defective and hence the company has high failure costs. However, as a company spends more and more on prevention and appraisal, the percentage of defective units drops. This results in lower internal and external failure costs. Ordinarily, total quality cost drops rapidly as the quality of conformance increases. Thus, a company can reduce its total quality cost by focusing its efforts on prevention and appraisal. The cost savings from reduced defects usually swamp the costs of the additional prevention and appraisal efforts.

The graph in Exhibit 1A–2 has been drawn so that the total quality cost is minimized when the quality of conformance is less than 100%. However, some experts contend that the total quality cost is not minimized until the quality of conformance is 100% and there are no defects. Indeed, many companies have found that the total quality costs seem to keep dropping even when the quality of conformance approaches 100% and defect rates get as low as 1 in a million units. Others argue that total quality cost eventually increases as the quality of conformance increases. However, in most companies this does not seem to happen until the quality of conformance is very close to 100% and defect rates are very close to zero.

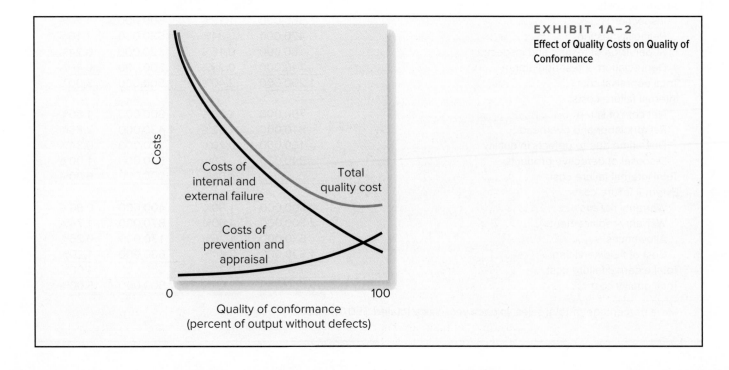

EXHIBIT 1A–2
Effect of Quality Costs on Quality of Conformance

Costs

Costs of internal and external failure

Total quality cost

Costs of prevention and appraisal

0   100

Quality of conformance
(percent of output without defects)

As a company's quality program becomes more refined and as its failure costs begin to fall, prevention activities usually become more effective than appraisal activities. Appraisal can only find defects, whereas prevention can eliminate them. The best way to prevent defects from happening is to design processes that reduce the likelihood of defects and to continually monitor processes using statistical process control methods.

Quality Cost Reports

LO1–8
Prepare and interpret a quality cost report.

As an initial step in quality improvement programs, companies often construct a *quality cost report* that provides an estimate of the financial consequences of the company's current level of defects. A **quality cost report** details the prevention costs, appraisal costs, and costs of internal and external failures that arise from the company's current quality control efforts. Managers are often shocked by the magnitude of these costs. An example of a quality cost report is shown in Exhibit 1A–3.

Several things should be noted from the data in the exhibit. First, Ventura Company's quality costs are poorly distributed in both years, with most of the costs due to either

EXHIBIT 1A–3
Quality Cost Report

	Ventura Company Quality Cost Report For Years 1 and 2			
	Year 1		Year 2	
	Amount	Percent*	Amount	Percent*
Prevention costs:				
Systems development	$ 270,000	0.54%	$ 400,000	0.80%
Quality training	130,000	0.26%	210,000	0.42%
Supervision of prevention activities	40,000	0.08%	70,000	0.14%
Quality improvement projects	210,000	0.42%	320,000	0.64%
Total prevention cost	650,000	1.30%	1,000,000	2.00%
Appraisal costs:				
Inspection	560,000	1.12%	600,000	1.20%
Reliability testing	420,000	0.84%	580,000	1.16%
Supervision of testing and inspection	80,000	0.16%	120,000	0.24%
Depreciation of test equipment	140,000	0.28%	200,000	0.40%
Total appraisal cost	1,200,000	2.40%	1,500,000	3.00%
Internal failure costs:				
Net cost of scrap	750,000	1.50%	900,000	1.80%
Rework labor and overhead	810,000	1.62%	1,430,000	2.86%
Downtime due to defects in quality	100,000	0.20%	170,000	0.34%
Disposal of defective products	340,000	0.68%	500,000	1.00%
Total internal failure cost	2,000,000	4.00%	3,000,000	6.00%
External failure costs:				
Warranty repairs	900,000	1.80%	400,000	0.80%
Warranty replacements	2,300,000	4.60%	870,000	1.74%
Allowances	630,000	1.26%	130,000	0.26%
Cost of field servicing	1,320,000	2.64%	600,000	1.20%
Total external failure cost	5,150,000	10.30%	2,000,000	4.00%
Total quality cost	$9,000,000	18.00%	$7,500,000	15.00%

*As a percentage of total sales. In each year, sales totaled $50,000,000.

internal failure or external failure. The external failure costs are particularly high in Year 1 in comparison to other costs.

Second, note that the company increased its spending on prevention and appraisal activities in Year 2. As a result, internal failure costs went up in that year (from $2 million in Year 1 to $3 million in Year 2), but external failure costs dropped sharply (from $5.15 million in Year 1 to only $2 million in Year 2). Because of the increase in appraisal activity in Year 2, more defects were caught inside the company before they were shipped to customers. This resulted in more cost for scrap, rework, and so forth, but saved huge amounts in warranty repairs, warranty replacements, and other external failure costs.

Third, note that as a result of greater emphasis on prevention and appraisal, *total* quality cost decreased in Year 2. As continued emphasis is placed on prevention and appraisal in future years, total quality cost should continue to decrease. That is, future increases in prevention and appraisal costs should be more than offset by decreases in failure costs. Moreover, appraisal costs should also decrease over time as more effort is placed into prevention.

Quality Cost Reports in Graphic Form

As a supplement to the quality cost report shown in Exhibit 1A–3, companies frequently prepare quality cost information in graphic form. Graphic presentations include pie charts, bar graphs, trend lines, and so forth. The data for Ventura Company from Exhibit 1A–3 are presented in bar graph form in Exhibit 1A–4.

The first set of bar graphs in Exhibit 1A–4 is scaled in terms of dollars of quality cost, and the second set is scaled in terms of quality cost as a percentage of sales. In both graphs, the data are "stacked" upward. That is, appraisal costs are stacked on top of prevention costs, internal failure costs are stacked on top of the sum of prevention costs plus appraisal costs, and so forth. The percentage figures in the second graph show that total quality cost equals 18% of sales in Year 1 and 15% of sales in Year 2, the same as reported earlier in Exhibit 1A–3.

Data in graphic form help managers to see trends more clearly and to see the magnitude of the various costs in relation to each other. Such graphs are easily prepared using computer graphics and spreadsheet applications.

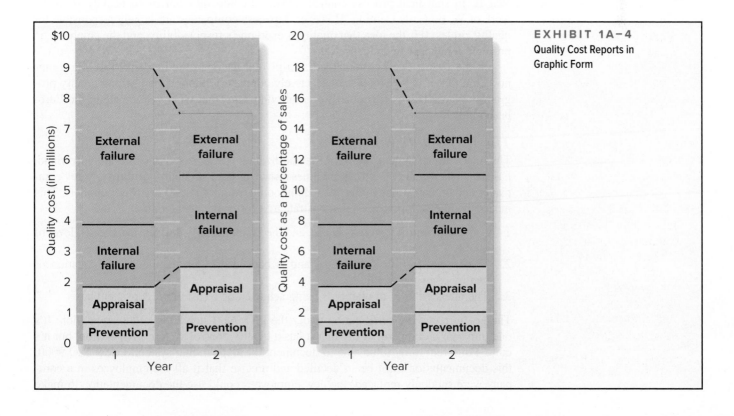

EXHIBIT 1A–4
Quality Cost Reports in Graphic Form

Uses of Quality Cost Information

A quality cost report has several uses. First, quality cost information helps managers see the financial significance of defects. Managers usually are not aware of the magnitude of their quality costs because these costs cut across departmental lines and are not normally tracked and accumulated by the cost system. Thus, when first presented with a quality cost report, managers often are surprised by the amount of cost attributable to poor quality.

Second, quality cost information helps managers identify the relative importance of the quality problems faced by their companies. For example, the quality cost report may show that scrap is a major quality problem or that the company is incurring huge warranty costs. With this information, managers have a better idea of where to focus their efforts.

Third, quality cost information helps managers see whether their quality costs are poorly distributed. In general, quality costs should be distributed more toward prevention and appraisal activities and less toward failures.

Counterbalancing these uses, three limitations of quality cost information should be recognized. First, simply measuring and reporting quality costs does not solve quality problems. Problems can be solved only by taking action. Second, results usually lag behind quality improvement programs. Initially, total quality cost may even increase as quality control systems are designed and installed. Decreases in quality costs may not begin to occur until the quality program has been in effect for some time. And third, the most important quality cost, lost sales arising from customer ill will, is usually omitted from the quality cost report because it is difficult to estimate.

Typically, during the initial years of a quality improvement program, the benefits of compiling a quality cost report outweigh the costs and limitations of the reports. As managers gain experience in balancing prevention and appraisal activities, the need for quality cost reports often diminishes.

International Aspects of Quality

Many of the tools used in quality management today were developed in Japan after World War II. In statistical process control, Japanese companies borrowed heavily from the work of W. Edwards Deming. However, Japanese companies are largely responsible for quality circles, JIT, the idea that quality is everyone's responsibility, and the emphasis on prevention rather than on inspection.

In the 1980s, quality reemerged as a pivotal factor in the market. Most companies now find that it is impossible to effectively compete without a very strong quality program in place. This is particularly true of companies that wish to compete in the European market.

The ISO 9000 Standards

The International Organization for Standardization (ISO), based in Geneva, Switzerland, has established quality control guidelines known as the **ISO 9000 standards**. Many companies and organizations in Europe will buy only from ISO 9000-certified suppliers. This means that the suppliers must demonstrate to a certifying agency that:

1. A quality control system is in use, and the system clearly defines an expected level of quality.
2. The system is fully operational and is backed up with detailed documentation of quality control procedures.
3. The intended level of quality is being achieved on a sustained, consistent basis.

The key to receiving certification under the ISO 9000 standards is documentation. It's one thing for a company to say that it has a quality control system in operation, but it's quite a different thing to be able to document the steps in that system. Under ISO 9000, this documentation must be so detailed and precise that if all the employees in a company were suddenly replaced, the new employees could use the documentation to make the product exactly as it was made by the old employees. Even companies with good quality control systems find that it takes up to two years of painstaking work to develop this detailed documentation. But companies often find that compiling this documentation results in improvements in their quality systems.

The ISO 9000 standards have become an international measure of quality. Although the standards were developed to control the quality of goods sold in European countries, they have become widely accepted elsewhere as well. Companies in the United States that export to Europe often expect their own suppliers to comply with ISO 9000 standards because these exporters must document the quality of the materials going into their products as part of their own ISO 9000 certification.

The ISO program for certification of quality management programs is not limited to manufacturing companies. The American Institute of Certified Public Accountants was the first professional membership organization in the United States to win recognition under an ISO certification program.

Summary (Appendix 1A)

Defects cause costs, which can be classified into prevention costs, appraisal costs, internal failure costs, and external failure costs. Prevention costs are incurred to keep defects from happening. Appraisal costs are incurred to ensure that defective products, once made, are not shipped to customers. Internal failure costs are incurred as a consequence of detecting defective products before they are shipped to customers. External failure costs are the consequences (in terms of repairs, servicing, and lost future business) of delivering defective products to customers. Most experts agree that management effort should be focused on preventing defects. Small investments in prevention can lead to dramatic reductions in appraisal costs and costs of internal and external failure.

Quality costs are summarized on a quality cost report. This report shows the types of quality costs being incurred and their significance and trends. The report helps managers understand the importance of quality costs, spot problem areas, and assess the way in which the quality costs are distributed.

Glossary (Appendix 1A)

Appraisal costs Costs that are incurred to identify defective products before the products are shipped to customers. (p. 58)

External failure costs Costs that are incurred when a product or service that is defective is delivered to a customer. (p. 59)

Internal failure costs Costs that are incurred as a result of identifying defective products before they are shipped to customers. (p. 58)

ISO 9000 standards Quality control requirements issued by the International Organization for Standardization that relate to products sold in European countries. (p. 62)

Prevention costs Costs that are incurred to keep defects from occurring. (p. 58)

Quality circles Small groups of employees that meet on a regular basis to discuss ways of improving quality. (p. 58)

Quality cost Costs that are incurred to prevent defective products from falling into the hands of customers or that are incurred as a result of defective units. (p. 57)

Quality cost report A report that details prevention costs, appraisal costs, and the costs of internal and external failures. (p. 60)

Quality of conformance The degree to which a product or service meets or exceeds its design specifications and is free of defects or other problems that mar its appearance or degrade its performance. (p. 57)

Statistical process control A charting technique used to monitor the quality of work being done in a workstation for the purpose of immediately correcting any problems. (p. 58)

Appendix 1A Exercises and Problems   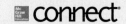 connect

EXERCISE 1A–1 Cost of Quality Terms LO1–7, LO1–8

A number of terms relating to the cost of quality and quality management are listed below:

Appraisal costs	Quality circles
Quality cost report	Prevention costs
Quality of conformance	External failure costs
Internal failure costs	Quality costs

Required:

Choose the term or terms that most appropriately complete the following statements. The terms can be used more than once and a blank can hold more than one word.

1. A product that has a high rate of defects is said to have a low _____.
2. All of the costs associated with preventing and dealing with defects once they occur are known as _____.
3. In many companies, small groups of employees, known as _____, meet on a regular basis to discuss ways to improve quality.
4. A company incurs _____ and _____ in an effort to keep defects from occurring.
5. A company incurs _____ and _____ because defects have occurred.
6. Of the four groups of costs associated with quality of conformance, _____ are generally the most damaging to a company.
7. Inspection, testing, and other costs incurred to keep defective products from being shipped to customers are known as _____.
8. _____ are incurred in an effort to eliminate poor product design, defective manufacturing practices, and the providing of substandard service.
9. The costs relating to defects, rejected products, and downtime caused by quality problems are known as _____.
10. When a product that is defective in some way is delivered to a customer, _____ are incurred.
11. Over time a company's total quality costs should decrease if it redistributes its quality costs by placing its greatest emphasis on _____ and _____.
12. One way to ensure that management is aware of the costs associated with quality is to summarize such costs on a _____.

EXERCISE 1A–2 Classification of Quality Costs LO1–7

A number of activities that are a part of a company's quality control system are listed below:

a. Product testing.	k. Net cost of scrap.
b. Product recalls.	l. Depreciation of test equipment.
c. Rework labor and overhead.	m. Returns and allowances arising from poor quality.
d. Quality circles.	
e. Downtime caused by defects.	n. Disposal of defective products.
f. Cost of field servicing.	o. Technical support to suppliers.
g. Inspection of goods.	p. Systems development.
h. Quality engineering.	q. Warranty replacements.
i. Warranty repairs.	r. Field testing at customer site.
j. Statistical process control.	s. Product design.

Required:

1. Classify the costs associated with each of these activities into one of the following categories: prevention cost, appraisal cost, internal failure cost, or external failure cost.
2. Which of the four types of costs in (1) above are incurred in an effort to keep poor quality of conformance from occurring? Which of the four types of costs in (1) above are incurred because poor quality of conformance has occurred?

PROBLEM 1A–3 Analyzing a Quality Cost Report LO1–8

Mercury, Inc., produces cell phones at its plant in Texas. In recent years, the company's market share has been eroded by stiff competition from overseas. Price and product quality are the two key areas in which companies compete in this market.

A year ago, the company's cell phones had been ranked low in product quality in a consumer survey. Shocked by this result, Jorge Gomez, Mercury's president, initiated an intense effort to improve product quality. Gomez set up a task force to implement a formal quality improvement program. Included on this task force were representatives from the Engineering, Marketing, Customer Service, Production, and Accounting departments. The broad representation was needed because Gomez believed that this was a companywide program and that all employees should share the responsibility for its success.

After the first meeting of the task force, Holly Elsoe, manager of the Marketing Department, asked John Tran, production manager, what he thought of the proposed program. Tran replied, "I have reservations. Quality is too abstract to be attaching costs to it and then to be holding you and me responsible for cost improvements. I like to work with goals that I can see and count! I'm nervous about having my annual bonus based on a decrease in quality costs; there are too many variables that we have no control over."

Mercury's quality improvement program has now been in operation for one year. The company's most recent quality cost report is shown below.

Mercury, Inc. Quality Cost Report (in thousands)	Last Year	This Year
Prevention costs:		
Machine maintenance	$ 70	$ 120
Training suppliers	0	10
Quality circles	0	20
Total prevention cost	70	150
Appraisal costs:		
Incoming inspection	20	40
Final testing	80	90
Total appraisal cost............	100	130
Internal failure costs:		
Rework	50	130
Scrap......................	40	70
Total internal failure cost	90	200
External failure costs:		
Warranty repairs	90	30
Customer returns	320	80
Total external failure cost........	410	110
Total quality cost	$ 670	$ 590
Total production cost	$4,200	$4,800

As they were reviewing the report, Elsoe asked Tran what he now thought of the quality improvement program. Tran replied. "I'm relieved that the new quality improvement program hasn't hurt our bonuses, but the program has increased the workload in the Production Department. It is true that customer returns are way down, but the cell phones that were returned by customers to retail outlets were rarely sent back to us for rework."

Required:
1. Expand the company's quality cost report by showing the costs in both years as percentages of both total production cost and total quality cost. Carry all computations to one decimal place. By analyzing the report, determine if Mercury, Inc.'s quality improvement program has been successful. List specific evidence to support your answer.
2. Do you expect the improvement program as it progresses to continue to increase the workload in the Production Department?
3. Jorge Gomez believed that the quality improvement program was essential and that Mercury, Inc., could no longer afford to ignore the importance of product quality. Discuss how Mercury, Inc., could measure the cost of *not* implementing the quality improvement program.

(CMA, adapted)

PROBLEM 1A–4 Quality Cost Report LO1–7, LO1–8

In response to intensive foreign competition, the management of Florex Company has attempted over the past year to improve the quality of its products. A statistical process control system has been installed and other steps have been taken to decrease the amount of warranty and other field costs, which have been trending upward over the past several years. Costs relating to quality and quality control over the last two years (in thousands) are given below:

	Costs (in thousands)	
	Last Year	This Year
Inspection.	$750	$900
Quality engineering	$420	$570
Depreciation of test equipment	$210	$240
Rework labor	$1,050	$1,500
Statistical process control	$0	$180
Cost of field servicing	$1,200	$900
Supplies used in testing	$30	$60
Systems development	$480	$750
Warranty repairs	$3,600	$1,050
Net cost of scrap	$630	$1,125
Product testing.	$810	$1,200
Product recalls	$2,100	$750
Disposal of defective products	$720	$975

Sales have been flat over the past few years, at $75,000,000 per year. A great deal of money has been spent in the effort to upgrade quality, and management is anxious to see whether or not the effort has been effective.

Required:
1. Prepare a quality cost report that contains data for both this year and last year. Carry percentage computations to two decimal places.
2. Prepare a bar graph showing the distribution of the various quality costs by category.
3. Prepare a written evaluation to accompany the reports you have prepared in (1) and (2) above. This evaluation should discuss the distribution of quality costs in the company, changes in this distribution that you see taking place, the reasons for changes in costs in the various categories, and any other information that would be of value to management.

Job-Order Costing: Calculating Unit Product Costs

University Tees: Serving Over 150 Campuses Nationwide

BUSINESS FOCUS

Courtesy of University Tees, Inc.

University Tees was founded in 2003 by two **Miami University** college students to provide screen-printing, embroidery, and promotional products for fraternities, sororities, and student organizations. Today, the company, which is headquartered in Cleveland, Ohio, employs as many as four Campus Managers on each of over 150 college campuses across America.

Accurately calculating the cost of each potential customer order is critically important to University Tees because the company needs to be sure that the sales price exceeds the cost associated with satisfying the order. The costs include the cost of the blank T-shirts themselves, printing costs (which vary depending on the quantity of shirts produced and the number of colors per shirt), screen costs (which also vary depending on the number of colors included in a design), shipping costs, and the artwork needed to create a design. The company also takes into account its competitors' pricing strategies when developing its own prices.

Given its success on college campuses, University Tees has introduced a sister company called **On Point Promos** to serve for-profit companies and nonprofit organizations. ■

Source: Conversation with Joe Haddad, cofounder of University Tees.

LEARNING OBJECTIVES

After studying Chapter 2, you should be able to:

LO2–1 Compute a predetermined overhead rate.

LO2–2 Apply overhead cost to jobs using a predetermined overhead rate.

LO2–3 Compute the total cost and the unit product cost of a job using a plantwide predetermined overhead rate.

LO2–4 Compute the total cost and the unit product cost of a job using multiple predetermined overhead rates

LO2–5 *(Appendix 2A) Use activity-based absorption costing to compute unit product costs.*

LO2–6 *(Appendix 2B) Understand the implications of basing the predetermined overhead rate on activity at capacity rather than on estimated activity for the period.*

Companies usually assign costs to their products and services for two main reasons. First, it helps them fulfill their planning, controlling, and decision-making responsibilities. For example, a company may use product cost information to better understand each product's profitability or to establish each product's selling price. Second, it helps them determine the value of ending inventories and cost of goods sold for external reporting purposes. The costs attached to products that have not been sold are included in ending inventories on the balance sheet, whereas the costs attached to units that have been sold are included in cost of goods sold on the income statement.

It is very common for external financial reporting requirements to heavily influence how companies assign costs to their products and services. Because most countries (including the United States) require some form of *absorption costing* for external financial reports, many companies use some form of absorption costing for product costing purposes. In **absorption costing**, all manufacturing costs, both fixed and variable, are assigned to units of product—units are said to *fully absorb manufacturing costs*. Conversely, all nonmanufacturing costs are treated as period costs and they are not assigned to units of product.

This chapter and the next explain a common type of absorption costing system known as *job-order costing*. In this chapter we'll discuss the role of job-order costing systems in planning, control, and decision making. Our focus will be on assigning manufacturing costs to individual jobs. In the next chapter, we will explain how job-order costing systems can be used to determine the value of ending inventories and cost of goods sold for external reporting purposes.

Job-Order Costing—An Overview

Job-order costing is used in situations where many *different* products, each with individual and unique features, are produced each period. For example, a **Levi Strauss** clothing factory would typically make many different types of jeans for both men and women during a month. A particular order might consist of 1,000 boot-cut men's blue denim jeans, style number A312. This order of 1,000 jeans is called a *job*. In a job-order costing system, costs are traced and allocated to jobs and then the costs of the job are divided by the number of units in the job to arrive at an average cost per unit. This average cost per unit is also referred to as the *unit product cost*.

Other examples of situations where job-order costing would be used include large-scale construction projects managed by **Bechtel International**, commercial aircraft produced by **Boeing**, greeting cards designed and printed by **Hallmark**, and airline meals prepared by **LSG SkyChefs**. All of these examples are characterized by diverse outputs. Each Bechtel project is unique and different from every other—the company may be simultaneously constructing a dam in Nigeria and a bridge in Indonesia. Likewise, each airline orders a different type of meal from LSG SkyChefs' catering service.

Job-order costing is also used extensively in service industries. For example, hospitals, law firms, movie studios, accounting firms, advertising agencies, and repair shops all use a variation of job-order costing to accumulate costs. Although the detailed example of job-order costing provided in the following section deals with a manufacturing company, the same basic concepts and procedures are used by many service organizations.

IS THIS REALLY A JOB?

VBT Bicycling Vacations of Bristol, Vermont, offers deluxe bicycling vacations in the United States, Canada, Europe, and other locations throughout the world. For example, the company offers a 10-day tour of the Puglia region of Italy—the "heel of the boot." The tour price includes international airfare, 10 nights of lodging, most meals, use of a bicycle, and ground transportation as needed. Each tour is led by at least two local tour leaders, one of whom rides with the guests along the tour route. The other tour leader drives a "sag wagon" that carries extra water, snacks, and bicycle repair equipment and is available for a shuttle back to the hotel or up a hill. The sag wagon also transports guests' luggage from one hotel to another.

Each specific tour can be considered a job. For example, Giuliano Astore and Debora Trippetti, two natives of Puglia, led a VBT tour with 17 guests over 10 days in late April. At the end of the tour, Giuliano submitted a report, a sort of job cost sheet, to VBT headquarters. This report detailed the on the ground costs incurred for this specific tour, including fuel and operating costs for the van, lodging costs for the guests, the costs of meals provided to guests, the costs of snacks, the cost of hiring additional ground transportation as needed, and the wages of the tour leaders. In addition to these costs, some costs are paid directly by VBT in Vermont to vendors. The total cost incurred for the tour is then compared to the total revenue collected from guests to determine the gross profit for the tour.

Sources: Giuliano Astore and Gregg Marston, President, VBT Bicycling Vacations. For more information about VBT, see www.vbt.com.

© Sandee Noreen

© Sandee Noreen

Job-Order Costing—An Example

To introduce job-order costing, we will follow a specific job as it progresses through the manufacturing process. This job consists of two experimental couplings that Yost Precision Machining has agreed to produce for Loops Unlimited, a manufacturer of roller coasters. Couplings connect the cars on the roller coaster and are a critical component in the performance and safety of the ride. Before we begin our discussion, it bears reemphasizing that companies generally classify manufacturing costs into three broad categories: (1) direct materials, (2) direct labor, and (3) manufacturing overhead. As we study the operation of a job-order costing system, we will see how each of these three types of product costs is assigned to jobs for purposes of computing unit product costs.

Yost Precision Machining is a small company in Michigan that specializes in fabricating precision metal parts that are used in a variety of applications ranging from deep-sea exploration vehicles to the inertial triggers in automobile air bags. The company's top managers gather every morning at 8:00 A.M. in the company's conference room for the daily planning meeting. Attending the meeting this morning are: Jean Yost, the company's president; David Cheung, the marketing manager; Debbie Turner, the production manager; and Marc White, the company controller. The president opened the meeting:

Jean: The production schedule indicates we'll be starting Job 2B47 today. Isn't that the special order for experimental couplings, David?

David: That's right. That's the order from Loops Unlimited for two couplings for their new roller coaster ride for Magic Mountain.

Debbie: Why only two couplings? Don't they need a coupling for every car?

David: Yes. But this is a completely new roller coaster. The cars will go faster and will be subjected to more twists, turns, drops, and loops than on any other existing roller coaster. To hold up under these stresses, Loops Unlimited's engineers completely redesigned the cars and couplings. They want us to make just two of these new couplings for testing purposes. If the design works, then we'll have the inside track on the order to supply couplings for the whole ride.

MANAGERIAL
ACCOUNTING IN ACTION
THE ISSUE

YOST
Precision Machining

Jean: We agreed to take on this initial order at our cost just to get our foot in the door. Marc, will there be any problem documenting our cost so we can get paid?

Marc: No problem. The contract with Loops stipulates that they will pay us an amount equal to each coupling's unit product cost as determined by our job-order costing system. I can finalize each coupling's direct materials, direct labor, and manufacturing overhead costs on the day the job is completed.

Jean: Good. Is there anything else we should discuss about this job at this time? No? Well then let's move on to the next item of business.

Measuring Direct Materials Cost

The blueprints submitted by Loops Unlimited indicate that each experimental coupling will require three parts that are classified as direct materials: two G7 Connectors and one M46 Housing. Since each coupling requires two connectors and one housing, the production of two couplings requires four connectors and two housings. This is a custom product that is being made for the first time, but if this were one of the company's standard products, it would have an established *bill of materials*. A **bill of materials** is a document that lists the quantity of each type of direct material needed to complete a unit of product.

When an agreement has been reached with the customer concerning the quantities, prices, and shipment date for the order, a *production order* is issued. The Production Department then prepares a *materials requisition form* similar to the form in Exhibit 2–1. The **materials requisition form** is a document that specifies the type and quantity of materials to be drawn from the storeroom and identifies the job that will be charged for the cost of the materials. The form is used to control the flow of materials into production and also for making journal entries in the accounting records (as will be demonstrated in the next chapter).

The Yost Precision Machining materials requisition form in Exhibit 2–1 shows that the company's Milling Department has requisitioned two M46 Housings and four G7 Connectors for the Loops Unlimited job, which has been designated as Job 2B47.

Job Cost Sheet

After a production order has been issued, the Accounting Department's job-order costing software system automatically generates a *job cost sheet* like the one presented in Exhibit 2–2. A **job cost sheet** records the materials, labor, and manufacturing overhead costs charged to that job.

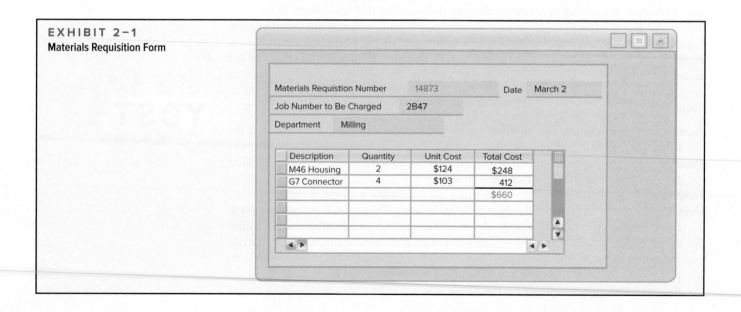

EXHIBIT 2–1
Materials Requisition Form

| Materials Requisition Number | 14873 | | Date | March 2 |

| Job Number to Be Charged | 2B47 |

| Department | Milling |

Description	Quantity	Unit Cost	Total Cost
M46 Housing	2	$124	$248
G7 Connector	4	$103	412
			$660

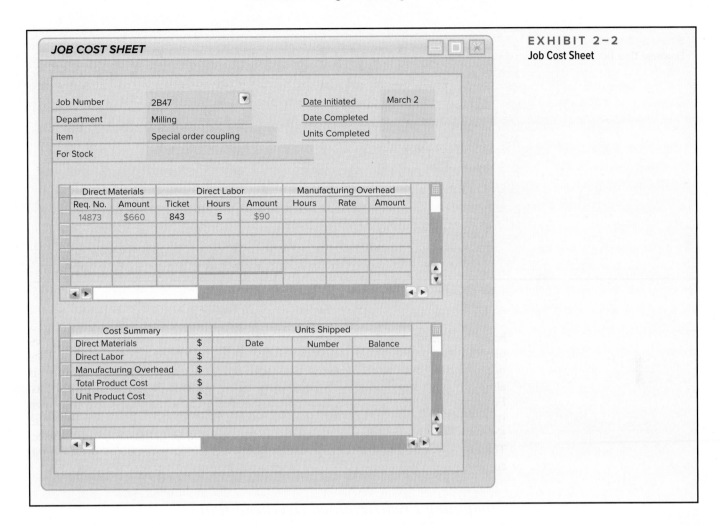

EXHIBIT 2–2
Job Cost Sheet

After direct materials are issued, the cost of these materials are automatically recorded on the job cost sheet. Note from Exhibit 2–2, for example, that the $660 cost for direct materials shown earlier on the materials requisition form has been charged to Job 2B47 on its job cost sheet. The requisition number 14873 from the materials requisition form appears on the job cost sheet to make it easier to identify the source document for the direct materials charge.

Measuring Direct Labor Cost

Direct labor consists of labor charges that are easily traced to a particular job. Labor charges that cannot be easily traced to specific jobs are treated as part of manufacturing overhead. As discussed in the previous chapter, this latter category of labor cost is called *indirect labor* and includes tasks such as maintenance, supervision, and cleanup.

Most companies rely on computerized systems to maintain employee *time tickets*. A completed **time ticket** is an hour-by-hour summary of the employee's activities throughout the day. One computerized approach to creating time tickets uses bar codes to capture data. Each employee and each job has a unique bar code. When beginning work on a job, the employee scans three bar codes using a handheld device much like the bar code readers at grocery store checkout stands. The first bar code indicates that a task is being started; the second is the unique bar code on the employee's identity badge; and the third is the unique bar code of the job itself. This information is fed automatically via an electronic network to a computer that notes the time and records all of the data. When the task is completed, the employee scans a bar code indicating the task is complete, the

EXHIBIT 2–3
Employee Time Ticket

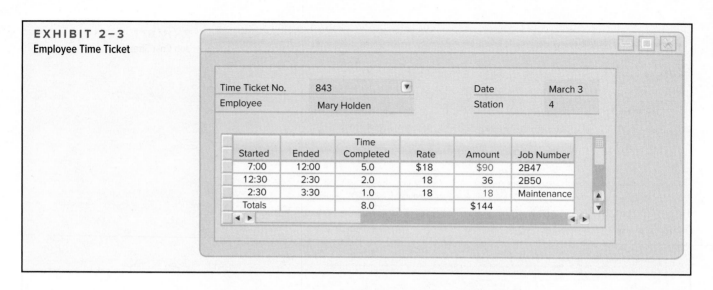

| | Time Ticket No. | 843 | ▾ | Date | March 3 |
| | Employee | Mary Holden | | Station | 4 |

	Started	Ended	Time Completed	Rate	Amount	Job Number
	7:00	12:00	5.0	$18	$90	2B47
	12:30	2:30	2.0	18	36	2B50
	2:30	3:30	1.0	18	18	Maintenance
	Totals		8.0		$144	

bar code on his or her identity badge, and the bar code attached to the job. This information is relayed to the computer that again notes the time, and a time ticket, such as the one shown in Exhibit 2–3, is automatically prepared. Because all of the source data is already in computer files, the labor costs can be automatically posted to job cost sheets. For example, Exhibit 2–3 shows $90 of direct labor cost related to Job 2B47. This amount is automatically posted to the job cost sheet shown in Exhibit 2–2. The time ticket in Exhibit 2–3 also shows $18 of indirect labor cost related to performing maintenance. This cost is treated as part of manufacturing overhead and does not get posted on a job cost sheet.

LO2–1

Compute a predetermined overhead rate.

Computing Predetermined Overhead Rates

Recall that in absorption costing, product costs include manufacturing overhead as well as direct materials and direct labor. Therefore, manufacturing overhead also needs to be recorded on the job cost sheet. However, assigning manufacturing overhead to a specific job is complicated by three circumstances:

1. Manufacturing overhead is an *indirect cost*. This means that it is either impossible or difficult to trace these costs to a particular product or job.
2. Manufacturing overhead consists of many different types of costs ranging from the grease used in machines to the annual salary of the production manager. Some of these costs are variable overhead costs because they vary in direct proportion to changes in the level of production (e.g., indirect materials, supplies, and power) and some are fixed overhead costs because they remain constant as the level of production fluctuates (e.g., heat and light, property taxes, and insurance).
3. Many companies have large amounts of fixed manufacturing overhead. Therefore, their total manufacturing overhead costs tend to remain relatively constant from one period to the next even though the number of units that they produce can fluctuate widely. Consequently, the average cost per unit will vary from one period to the next.

Given these circumstances, allocation is used to assign overhead costs to products. Allocation is accomplished by selecting an *allocation base* that is common to all of the company's products and services. An **allocation base** is a measure such as direct labor-hours (DLH) or machine-hours (MH) that is used to assign overhead costs to products and services. The most widely used allocation bases in manufacturing are direct labor-hours, direct labor cost, machine-hours, and (where a company has only a single product) units of product.

Manufacturing overhead is commonly assigned to products using a *predetermined overhead rate*. The **predetermined overhead rate** is computed by dividing the total estimated manufacturing overhead cost for the period by the estimated total amount of the allocation base as follows:

$$\text{Predetermined overhead rate} = \frac{\text{Estimated total manufacturing overhead cost}}{\text{Estimated total amount of the allocation base}}$$

The predetermined overhead rate is computed before the period begins using a four-step process. The first step is to estimate the total amount of the allocation base (the denominator) that will be required for next period's estimated level of production. The second step is to estimate the total fixed manufacturing overhead cost for the coming period and the variable manufacturing overhead cost per unit of the allocation base. The third step is to use the cost formula shown below to estimate the total manufacturing overhead cost (the numerator) for the coming period:

$$Y = a + bX$$

where,

Y = The estimated total manufacturing overhead cost
a = The estimated total fixed manufacturing overhead cost
b = The estimated variable manufacturing overhead cost per unit of the allocation base
X = The estimated total amount of the allocation base

The fourth step is to compute the predetermined overhead rate.[1] Notice, the estimated amount of the allocation base is determined before estimating the total manufacturing overhead cost. This needs to be done because total manufacturing overhead cost includes variable overhead costs that depend on the amount of the allocation base.

Applying Manufacturing Overhead

LO2–2
Apply overhead cost to jobs using a predetermined overhead rate.

To repeat, the predetermined overhead rate is computed *before* the period begins. The predetermined overhead rate is then used to apply overhead cost to jobs throughout the period. The process of assigning overhead cost to jobs is called **overhead application**. The formula for determining the amount of overhead cost to apply to a particular job is:

$$\text{Overhead applied to a particular job} = \text{Predetermined overhead rate} \times \text{Amount of the allocation base incurred by the job}$$

For example, if the predetermined overhead rate is $20 per direct labor-hour, then $20 of overhead cost is *applied* to a job for each direct labor-hour incurred on the job. When the allocation base is direct labor-hours, the formula becomes:

$$\text{Overhead applied to a particular job} = \text{Predetermined overhead rate} \times \text{Actual direct labor-hours worked on the job}$$

Note that the amount of overhead applied to a particular job is not the actual amount of overhead caused by the job. Actual overhead costs are not assigned to jobs—if that could be done, the costs would be direct costs, not overhead. The overhead assigned to the job is simply a share of the total overhead that was estimated at the beginning of the

---

[1] When there is more than one production department, each department may have a different variable manufacturing overhead cost per unit of the allocation base. In that case, the formula $Y = a + bX$ should be applied to each department separately. These departmental cost estimates (Y) can be combined in step 4 to calculate one overhead rate or they can be kept separate to calculate departmental overhead rates.

year. This approach to overhead application is known as *normal costing*. A **normal cost system** applies overhead costs to jobs by multiplying a predetermined overhead rate by the actual amount of the allocation base incurred by the jobs.

Manufacturing Overhead—A Closer Look

To illustrate the steps involved in computing and using a predetermined overhead rate, let's return to Yost Precision Machining and make the following assumptions. In step one, the company estimated that 40,000 direct labor-hours would be required to support the production planned for the year. In step two, it estimated $640,000 of total fixed manufacturing overhead cost for the coming year and $4.00 of variable manufacturing overhead cost per direct labor-hour. Given these assumptions, in step three the company used the cost formula shown below to estimate its total manufacturing overhead cost for the year:

$$Y = a + bX$$

$$Y = \$640,000 + (\$4.00 \text{ per direct labor-hour} \times 40,000 \text{ direct labor-hours})$$

$$Y = \$640,000 + \$160,000$$

$$Y = \$800,000$$

In step four, Yost Precision Machining computed its predetermined overhead rate for the year of $20 per direct labor-hour as shown below:

$$\text{Predetermined overhead rate} = \frac{\text{Estimated total manufacturing overhead cost}}{\text{Estimated total amount of the allocation base}}$$

$$= \frac{\$800,000}{40,000 \text{ direct labor-hours}}$$

$$= \$20 \text{ per direct labor-hour}$$

The job cost sheet in Exhibit 2–4 indicates that 27 direct labor-hours (i.e., DLHs) were charged to Job 2B47. Therefore, a total of $540 of manufacturing overhead cost would be applied to the job:

$$\begin{array}{c}\text{Overhead applied to} \\ \text{Job 2B47}\end{array} = \begin{array}{c}\text{Predetermined} \\ \text{overhead rate}\end{array} \times \begin{array}{c}\text{Actual direct labor-hours} \\ \text{charged to Job 2B47}\end{array}$$

$$= \$20 \text{ per DLH} \times 27 \text{ DLHs}$$

$$= \$540 \text{ of overhead applied to Job 2B47}$$

This amount of overhead has been entered on the job cost sheet in Exhibit 2–4.

The Need for a Predetermined Rate

Instead of using a predetermined rate based on estimates, why not base the overhead rate on the *actual* total manufacturing overhead cost and the *actual* total amount of the allocation base incurred on a monthly, quarterly, or annual basis? If an actual rate is computed monthly or quarterly, seasonal factors in overhead costs or in the allocation base can produce fluctuations in the overhead rate. For example, the costs of heating and cooling a factory in Illinois will be highest in the winter and summer months and lowest in the spring and fall. If the overhead rate is recomputed at the end of each month or each quarter based on actual costs and activity, the overhead rate would go up in the winter and summer and down in the spring and fall. As a result, two identical jobs, one completed in the winter and one completed in the spring, would be assigned different manufacturing overhead costs.

Many managers believe that such fluctuations in product costs serve no useful purpose. To avoid such fluctuations, actual overhead rates could be computed on an annual

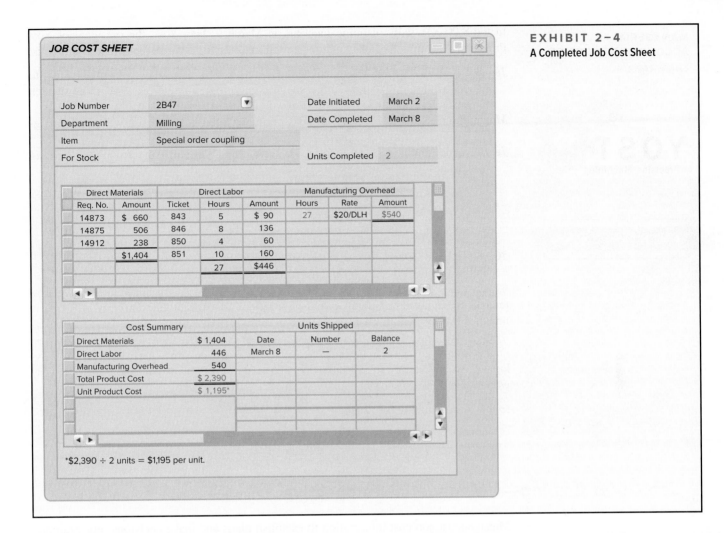

EXHIBIT 2–4
A Completed Job Cost Sheet

or less-frequent basis. However, if the overhead rate is computed annually based on the actual costs and activity for the year, the manufacturing overhead assigned to any particular job would not be known until the end of the year. For example, the cost of Job 2B47 at Yost Precision Machining would not be known until the end of the year, even though the job will be completed and shipped to the customer in March. For these reasons, most companies use predetermined overhead rates rather than actual overhead rates in their cost accounting systems.

Computation of Total Job Costs and Unit Product Costs

With the application of Yost Precision Machining's $540 of manufacturing overhead to the job cost sheet in Exhibit 2–4, the job cost sheet is complete except for two final steps. First, the totals for direct materials, direct labor, and manufacturing overhead are transferred to the Cost Summary section of the job cost sheet and added together to obtain the total cost for the job.[2] Then the total product cost ($2,390) is divided by the number of units (2) to obtain the unit product cost ($1,195). As indicated earlier, *this unit product cost is an average cost and should not be interpreted as the cost that would actually be incurred if another unit were produced.* The incremental cost of an additional unit is something less than the average unit cost of $1,195 because much of the actual overhead costs would not change if another unit were produced.

LO2–3
Compute the total cost and the unit product cost of a job using a plantwide predetermined overhead rate.

---

[2] Notice, we are assuming that Job 2B47 required direct materials and direct labor beyond the charges shown in Exhibits 2–1 and 2–3.

In the 8:00 A.M. daily planning meeting on March 9, Jean Yost, the president of Yost Precision Machining, once again drew attention to Job 2B47, the experimental couplings:

Jean: I see Job 2B47 is completed. Let's get those couplings shipped immediately to Loops Unlimited so they can get their testing program under way. Marc, how much are we going to bill Loops for those two units?

Marc: Because we agreed to sell the experimental couplings at cost, we will be charging Loops Unlimited just $1,195 a unit.

Jean: Fine. Let's hope the couplings work out and we make some money on the big order later.

IN BUSINESS

JOB-ORDER COSTING IN THE SERVICE INDUSTRY

Accenture is one of the world's largest consulting firms with annual revenues greater than $30 billion. Because the firm does not have any inventory on its balance sheet, it might be tempting to conclude that it does not need a job-order costing system. However, that is not true.

Accenture pays its consultants more than $20 billion per year to provide services for clients. Job-order costing enables the firm to compare each client's revenues to the costs of serving those clients. It also enables the firm to determine what portion of their consulting capacity was billable to clients and what portion was not billed to specific clients.

Source: Accenture 2014 Annual Report

Job-Order Costing—A Managerial Perspective

Managers use job cost information to establish plans and make decisions. For example, managers may use job profitability reports to develop sales and production plans for next year. If certain types of jobs, such as low-volume engineering-intensive jobs, appear to be highly profitable, managers may decide to dedicate future advertising expenditures to growing sales of these types of jobs. Conversely, if other types of jobs, such as high-volume labor-intensive jobs, appear to be unprofitable, managers may take actions to reduce the projected sales and production of these types of jobs.

Managers may also use job cost information to make pricing decisions. For example, if Job A has a total manufacturing cost of $100, managers often use a predefined markup percentage, say 50%, to establish a markup of $50 (= $100 × 50%) and a selling price of $150 (= $100 + $50). Under this approach, known as cost-plus pricing, the managers establish a markup percentage that they believe will generate enough revenue to cover all of a job's manufacturing costs and a portion of the company's nonmanufacturing costs, while generating some residual profit.

If a company's job-order costing system does not accurately assign manufacturing costs to jobs, it will adversely influence the types of planning and decision-making scenarios just described. In other words, distorted job cost data may cause managers to use additional advertising dollars to pursue certain types of jobs that they believe are profitable, but in actuality are not. Similarly, inaccurate job costs may cause managers to establish selling prices that are too high or too low relative to the prices established by more savvy competitors.

At this point, you may be wondering, how can this happen? How can a job-order costing system inaccurately assign costs to jobs? The key to answering this question is to focus on *indirect* manufacturing costs, also called manufacturing overhead costs. While job-order costing systems can accurately trace *direct* materials and *direct* labor costs to jobs, they often fail to accurately allocate the manufacturing overhead costs used during the production process to their respective jobs. The root cause of the problem often relates to the choice of an allocation base.

Choosing an Allocation Base—A Key to Job Cost Accuracy

Imagine going to a restaurant with three of your friends. The group orders an extra large pizza for $20 that is cut into ten slices. One of your friends eats five slices of pizza, your other two friends eat two slices each, and you eat one slice. When the bill arrives, the friend who ate five slices recommends paying the bill using "number of people seated at the table" as the allocation base, thereby requiring you to contribute $5 (= $20 ÷ 4) towards paying the bill. How would you feel about the accuracy of this cost allocation base? In all likelihood, you'd suggest distributing the bill among the four diners using another allocation base called "number of slices eaten." This approach would require each person seated at the table to pay $2 (= $20 ÷ 10) per slice consumed, thereby requiring you to contribute $2 towards paying the bill. While the distortion caused by using "number of people seated at the table" as the allocation base seems obvious, job-order costing systems often make the same error—they use allocation bases that do not reflect how jobs actually use overhead resources.

To improve job cost accuracy, the allocation base in the predetermined overhead rate should *drive* the overhead cost. A **cost driver** is a factor, such as machine-hours, beds occupied, computer time, or flight-hours, that causes overhead costs. If the base in the predetermined overhead rate does not "drive" overhead costs, it will not accurately measure the cost of overhead resources used by each job. Many companies use job-order costing systems that assume direct labor-hours (or direct labor cost) is the only manufacturing overhead cost driver. They use a single predetermined overhead rate, or what is called a **plantwide overhead rate**, to allocate all manufacturing overhead costs to jobs based on their usage of direct-labor hours. However, while direct labor-hours may indeed "drive" some of a company's manufacturing overhead costs, it is often overly simplistic and incorrect to assume that direct-labor hours is a company's *only* manufacturing overhead cost driver. When companies can identify more than one overhead cost driver they can improve job cost accuracy by using *multiple predetermined overhead rates.*

Job-Order Costing Using Multiple Predetermined Overhead Rates

A cost system with **multiple predetermined overhead rates** uses more than one overhead rate to apply overhead costs to jobs. For example, a company may choose to use a predetermined overhead rate for each of its production departments. Such a system, while more complex, is more accurate because it reflects differences across departments in terms of how jobs consume overhead costs. For example, in departments that are relatively labor-intensive, their overhead costs might be applied to jobs based on direct labor-hours and in departments that are relatively machine-intensive, their overhead costs might be applied to jobs based on machine-hours.

LO2–4
Compute the total cost and the unit product cost of a job using multiple predetermined overhead rates.

Multiple Predetermined Overhead Rates—A Departmental Approach

Dickson Company has two production departments, Milling and Assembly. The company uses a job-order costing system and computes a predetermined overhead rate in each production department. The predetermined overhead rate in the Milling Department is based on machine-hours and in the Assembly Department it is based on direct labor-hours. The company uses cost-plus pricing (and a markup percentage of 75% of total manufacturing cost) to establish selling prices for all of its jobs. At the beginning of the year, the company made the following estimates:

	Department	
	Milling	Assembly
Machine-hours	60,000	3,000
Direct labor-hours	8,000	80,000
Total fixed manufacturing overhead cost	$390,000	$500,000
Variable manufacturing overhead per machine-hour	$2.00	—
Variable manufacturing overhead per direct labor-hour	—	$3.75

During the current month the company started and completed Job 407. It wants to use its predetermined departmental overhead rates and the information pertaining to Job 407 that is shown below to establish a selling price for this job:

Job 407	Department	
	Milling	Assembly
Machine-hours	90	4
Direct labor-hours	5	20
Direct materials	$800	$370
Direct labor cost	$70	$280

Exhibit 2–5 explains how Dickson would compute a selling price for Job 407 using a five-step process, the first of which is to calculate the estimated total manufacturing overhead cost in each department using the equation

$$Y = a + bX$$

where:

Y = The estimated total manufacturing overhead cost
a = The estimated total fixed manufacturing overhead cost
b = The estimated variable manufacturing overhead cost per unit of the allocation base
X = The estimated total amount of the allocation base

As shown in step 1 in Exhibit 2–5, this equation provides the Milling Department's estimated total manufacturing overhead cost of $510,000 and the Assembly Department's estimated total overhead cost of $800,000.

The second step is to calculate the predetermined overhead rate for each department using the following formula:

$$\text{Predetermined overhead rate} = \frac{\text{Estimated total manufacturing overhead cost}}{\text{Estimated total amount of the allocation base}}$$

Per step 2 in Exhibit 2–5, this formula results in predetermined overhead rates in the Milling and Assembly Departments of $8.50 per machine-hour and $10.00 per direct labor-hour, respectively.

The third step is to use the general equation shown below to calculate the amount of overhead applied from each department to Job 407.

$$\text{Overhead applied to Job 407} = \text{Predetermined overhead rate} \times \text{Actual amount of the allocation base used by Job 407}$$

EXHIBIT 2–5
Dickson Company: An Example Using Multiple Predetermined Overhead Rates

Step 1: Calculate the estimated total manufacturing overhead cost for each department.

Milling Department Overhead Cost (Y):	*Assembly Department Overhead Cost (Y):*
= $390,000 + ($2.00 per MH × 60,000 MHs)	= $500,000 + ($3.75 per DLH × 80,000 DLHs)
= $390,000 + $120,000	= $500,000 + $300,000
= $510,000	= $800,000

Step 2: Calculate the predetermined overhead rate in each department.

Milling Department Overhead Rate:	*Assembly Department Overhead Rate:*
$= \dfrac{\$510{,}000}{60{,}000 \text{ machine-hours}}$	$= \dfrac{\$800{,}000}{80{,}000 \text{ direct labor-hours}}$
= $8.50 per machine-hour	= $10.00 per direct labor-hour

Step 3: Calculate the amount of overhead applied from both departments to Job 407.

Milling Department: Overhead Applied to Job 407	*Assembly Department: Overhead Applied to Job 407*
= $8.50 per MH × 90 MHs	= $10.00 per DLH × 20 DLHs
= $765	= $200

Step 4: Calculate the total job cost for Job 407.

	Milling	*Assembly*	*Total*
Direct materials	$800	$370	$1,170
Direct labor	$ 70	$280	350
Manufacturing overhead applied	$765	$200	965
Total cost of Job 407			$2,485

Step 5: Calculate the selling price for Job 407.

Total cost of Job 407	$2,485.00
Markup ($2,485 × 75%)	1,863.75
Selling price of Job 407	$4,348.75

As depicted in the middle of Exhibit 2–5, $765 of manufacturing overhead would be applied from the Milling Department to Job 407, whereas $200 would be applied from the Assembly Department to this same job.

Finally, Exhibit 2–5 also summarizes steps 4 and 5, which calculate the total job cost for Job 407 ($2,485) and the selling price of Job 407 ($4,348.75) using the markup percentage of 75%.

It is important to emphasize that using a departmental approach to overhead application results in a different selling price for Job 407 than would have been derived using a plantwide overhead rate based on either direct labor-hours or machine-hours. The appeal of using predetermined departmental overhead rates is that they presumably provide a more accurate accounting of the costs caused by jobs, which in turn, should enhance management planning and decision making.

Multiple Predetermined Overhead Rates—An Activity-Based Approach

Using departmental overhead rates is one approach to creating a job-order costing system that includes multiple predetermined overhead rates. Another approach is to create overhead rates related to the activities performed within departments. This approach usually results in more overhead rates than a departmental approach because each department may perform more than one activity. When a company creates overhead rates based on the activities that it performs, it is employing an approach called *activity-based costing*.

For now, our goal is to simply introduce you to the idea of activity-based costing—an alternative approach to developing multiple predetermined overhead rates. Managers use activity-based costing systems to more accurately measure the demands that jobs, products, customers, and other cost objects make on overhead resources. Appendix 2A provides an in-depth discussion of activity-based absorption costing and contrasts it with the plantwide approach described earlier in this chapter. Chapter 7 describes a more refined approach to activity-based costing that better serves the needs of management than the activity-based absorption costing approach discussed in Appendix 2A.

IN BUSINESS

COST SYSTEM DESIGN AT SALMON RIVER FOODS

© bogdanhoda/Shutterstock.com

Salmon River Foods' largest product line is called Dream Chocolates. The company's cost system uses a plantwide overhead rate that allocates overhead costs based on the number of chocolate bars produced. The manufacturing process consists of seven steps: (1) receiving, (2) pouring, (3) inspection, (4) foiling, (5) labeling and custom label designs, (6) finished product storage, and (7) shipping. The company is considering implementing a new cost system that would include multiple predetermined overhead rates. Based on Salmon River Foods' seven-step manufacturing process, can you think of any reasons why using more than one overhead rate may make sense?

Source: Kip R. Krumwiede and W. Darrell Walden, "Dream Chocolate Company: Choosing a Costing System," *Issues in Accounting Education*, March 2013, pp. 637–652.

Job-Order Costing—An External Reporting Perspective

This chapter focuses on using job-order costing systems to compute unit product costs for internal management purposes. However, job-order costing systems are also often used to create a balance sheet and income statement for external parties, such as shareholders and lenders. While the next chapter will provide a detailed explanation of how job-order costing systems facilitate external financial reporting, we'd like to take a moment to highlight two important points related to overhead application and subsidiary ledgers that, in some sense, connect this chapter to the next.

Overhead Application and the Income Statement

When a company uses predetermined overhead rates to apply overhead cost to jobs, it is almost a certainty that the amount of overhead applied to all jobs during a period will differ from the actual amount of overhead costs incurred during the period. When a company applies less overhead to production than it actually incurs, it creates what is known as *underapplied overhead*. When it applies more overhead to production than it actually incurs, it results in *overapplied overhead*.

The existence of underapplied or overapplied overhead has implications for how a company prepares its financial statements. For example, the cost of goods sold reported on a company's income statement must be adjusted to reflect underapplied or overapplied overhead. The adjustment for underapplied overhead increases cost of goods sold and decreases net operating income, whereas the adjustment for overapplied overhead decreases cost of goods sold and increases net operating income. The next chapter will provide a more in-depth numerical explanation of how to compute underapplied or overapplied overhead.

Job Cost Sheets: A Subsidiary Ledger

A job cost sheet accumulates the total direct materials, direct labor, and manufacturing overhead costs assigned to a job. When all of a company's job cost sheets are viewed collectively they form what is known as a subsidiary ledger. In other words, a company's job costs sheets provide an underlying set of financial records that explain what specific jobs comprise the amounts reported in *Work-in-Process* and *Finished Goods* on the balance sheet as well as *Cost of Goods Sold* on the income statement.

To illustrate, assume Dixon Company started six jobs during its first month of operations and incurred no underapplied or overapplied manufacturing overhead. Jobs A and B were incomplete at the end of the month, Job C was finished, but unsold, and Jobs D, E, and F, had been produced and sold during the month. In addition, assume the job cost sheets for these six jobs reported the following costs at the end of the month (in thousands):

| | Jobs | | | | | |
	A	B	C	D	E	F
Direct materials	$100	$ 90	$140	$110	$180	$160
Direct labor	80	60	90	70	120	100
Manufacturing overhead applied . . .	96	72	108	84	144	120
Total product cost	$276	$222	$338	$264	$444	$380

These six job costs would comprise Work in Process and Finished Goods on the balance sheet and Cost of Goods Sold on the income statement as follows:

Work In Process		Finished Goods		Cost of Goods Sold	
Job A	$276	Job C	$338	Job D	$ 264
Job B	222	Total	$338	Job E	444
Total	$498			Job F	380
				Total	$1,088

This brief example illustrates the interrelationship between a company's job cost sheets and its financial statements. For example, the combined costs of Jobs A and B equal Work in Process ($498) on the balance sheet, whereas the combined costs of Jobs D, E, and F equal Cost of Goods Sold ($1,088) on the income statement.

Job-Order Costing in Service Companies

This chapter has focused on manufacturing companies; however, job-order costing is also used in service organizations such as law firms, movie studios, hospitals, and repair shops. In a law firm, for example, each client is a "job," and the costs of that job are accumulated day by day on a job cost sheet as the client's case is handled by the firm. Legal forms and similar inputs represent the direct materials for the job; the time expended by attorneys is like direct labor; and the costs of secretaries and legal aids, rent, depreciation, and so forth, represent the overhead.

In a movie studio such as **Columbia Pictures**, each film produced by the studio is a "job," and costs of direct materials (costumes, props, film, etc.) and direct labor (actors, directors, and extras) are charged to each film's job cost sheet. A share of the studio's overhead costs, such as utilities, depreciation of equipment, wages of maintenance workers, and so forth, is also charged to each film.

In sum, job-order costing is a versatile and widely used costing method that may be encountered in virtually any organization that provides diverse products or services.

COMPUTING JOB COSTS AT FAST WRAP

Fast Wrap is a company that shrink-wraps everything from jet skis and recreation vehicles (RVs) to entire buildings. It generates more than $6 million in annual sales at its 64 locations across America.

The company's revenues far exceed its direct materials and direct labor costs. For example, Fast Wrap charges customers $400 to wrap a 20-foot boat that requires $25 worth of plastic and $30 worth of labor. Larger jobs are even more profitable. For example, Fast Wrap signed a $250,000 contract to shrink-wrap a 244,000-square-foot hospital under construction in Fontana, California. The materials and labor for this job cost Fast Wrap $44,000.

Source: Susan Adams, "It's a Wrap," *Forbes,* March 15, 2010, pp. 36–38.

Summary

Job-order costing is used in situations where the organization offers many different products or services, such as in furniture manufacturing, hospitals, and legal firms. When used in a manufacturing context, job-order costing systems accumulate a job's direct materials, direct labor, and manufacturing overhead costs on a job cost sheet. Selling and administrative costs are not assigned to jobs because they are treated as period costs.

Job-order costing systems use materials requisition forms and labor time tickets to trace direct materials and direct labor costs to jobs. Because manufacturing overhead costs are indirect costs, they must be allocated to jobs. Ideally, the allocation base used to allocate overhead costs to jobs should be a cost driver—it should cause the consumption of overhead costs. The most frequently used allocation bases in job-order costing systems are direct labor-hours and machine-hours.

Normal costing systems allocate overhead costs to jobs using predetermined overhead rates that are estimated before the period begins. A predetermined overhead rate is computed by dividing the estimated total manufacturing overhead cost for the period by the estimated total amount of the allocation base for the period. Job-order costing systems can use only one predetermined overhead rate (also called a plantwide rate) or multiple predetermined overhead rates.

Throughout the period, overhead is applied to jobs by multiplying the predetermined overhead rate by the actual amount of the allocation base recorded for each job. The total manufacturing costs assigned to a job (including direct materials, direct labor, and applied overhead) divided by the number of units within that job equals what is known as the unit product cost.

Review Problem: Calculating Unit Product Costs

Redhawk Company has two manufacturing departments—Assembly and Fabrication. The company considers all of its manufacturing overhead costs to be fixed costs. The first set of data shown below is based on estimates that were made at the beginning of the year for the expected total output. The second set of data relates to one particular job completed during the year—Job A200.

Estimated Data	Assembly	Fabrication	Total
Manufacturing overhead costs	$300,000	$400,000	$700,000
Direct labor-hours	25,000	15,000	40,000
Machine-hours	10,000	50,000	60,000

Job A200	Assembly	Fabrication	Total
Direct materials	$110	$50	$160
Direct labor	$70	$45	$115
Direct labor-hours	10 hours	2 hours	12 hours
Machine-hours	1 hour	7 hours	8 hours

Required:

1. If Redhawk uses a predetermined plantwide overhead rate with direct labor-hours as the allocation base, how much manufacturing overhead would be applied to Job A200?

2. If Redhawk uses predetermined departmental overhead rates with direct labor-hours as the allocation base in Assembly and machine-hours as the allocation base in Fabrication, how much total manufacturing overhead cost would be applied to Job A200?

3. Assume that Redhawk uses the departmental overhead rates mentioned in requirement 2 and that Job A200 includes 50 units. What is the unit product cost for Job A200?

Solution to Review Problem

1. The predetermined plantwide overhead rate is computed as follows:

$$\text{Predetermined overhead rate} = \frac{\text{Estimated total manufacturing overhead cost}}{\text{Estimated total amount of the allocation base}}$$

$$= \frac{\$700,000}{40,000 \text{ direct labor-hours}}$$

$$= \$17.50 \text{ per direct labor-hour}$$

The manufacturing overhead applied to Job A200 is computed as follows:

$$\frac{\text{Overhead applied to}}{\text{Job A200}} = \frac{\text{Predetermined}}{\text{overhead rate}} \times \frac{\text{Actual direct labor-hours}}{\text{charged to Job A200}}$$

$$= \$17.50 \text{ per DLH} \times 12 \text{ DLHs}$$

$$= \$210 \text{ of overhead applied to Job A200}$$

2. The predetermined departmental overhead rates are computed as follows:
Assembly Department:

$$\text{Predetermined overhead rate} = \frac{\text{Estimated total manufacturing overhead cost}}{\text{Estimated total amount of the allocation base}}$$

$$= \frac{\$300,000}{25,000 \text{ direct labor-hours}}$$

$$= \$12 \text{ per direct labor-hour}$$

Fabrication Department:

$$\text{Predetermined overhead rate} = \frac{\text{Estimated total manufacturing overhead cost}}{\text{Estimated total amount of the allocation base}}$$

$$= \frac{\$400,000}{50,000 \text{ machine-hours}}$$

$$= \$8.00 \text{ per machine-hour}$$

The manufacturing overhead applied to Job A200 is computed as follows:

Job A200	(1) Overhead Rate	(2) Actual Hours Used	Applied Overhead (1) × (2)
Assembly Department	$12 per DLH	10 hours	$120
Fabrication Department	$8 per MH	7 hours	56
Total applied overhead			$176

3. The unit product cost for Job A200 is computed as follows:

Job A200	Assembly	Fabrication	Total
Direct materials	$110	$50	$160
Direct labor	$70	$45	115
Applied overhead	$120	$56	176
Total job cost (a)			$451
Number of units in Job A200 (b)			50
Unit product cost (a) ÷ (b)			$9.02

Glossary

Absorption costing A costing method that includes all manufacturing costs—direct materials, direct labor, and both variable and fixed manufacturing overhead—in unit product costs. (p. 68)

Allocation base A measure of activity such as direct labor-hours or machine-hours that is used to assign costs to cost objects. (p. 72)

Bill of materials A document that shows the quantity of each type of direct material required to make a product. (p. 70)

Cost driver A factor, such as machine-hours, beds occupied, computer time, or flight-hours, that causes overhead costs. (p. 77)

Job cost sheet A form that records the direct materials, direct labor, and manufacturing overhead cost charged to a job. (p. 70)

Job-order costing A costing system used in situations where many different products, jobs, or services are produced each period. (p. 68)

Materials requisition form A document that specifies the type and quantity of materials to be drawn from the storeroom and that identifies the job that will be charged for the cost of those materials. (p. 70)

Multiple predetermined overhead rates A costing system with multiple overhead cost pools and a different predetermined overhead rate for each cost pool, rather than a single predetermined overhead rate for the entire company. Each production department may be treated as a separate overhead cost pool. (p. 77)

Normal cost system A costing system in which overhead costs are applied to a job by multiplying a predetermined overhead rate by the actual amount of the allocation base incurred by the job. (p. 74)

Overhead application The process of assigning overhead cost to specific jobs. (p. 73)

Plantwide overhead rate A single predetermined overhead rate that is used throughout a plant. (p. 77)

Predetermined overhead rate A rate used to charge manufacturing overhead cost to jobs that is established in advance for each period. It is computed by dividing the estimated total manufacturing overhead cost for the period by the estimated total amount of the allocation base for the period. (p. 73)

Time ticket A document that is used to record the amount of time an employee spends on various activities. (p. 71)

Questions

2–1   What is job-order costing?

2–2   What is absorption costing?

2–3   What is normal costing?

2–4   How is the unit product cost of a job calculated?

2–5   Explain the four-step process used to compute a predetermined overhead rate.

2–6   What is the purpose of the job cost sheet in a job-order costing system?

2–7   Explain why some production costs must be assigned to products through an allocation process.

2–8   Why do companies use predetermined overhead rates rather than actual manufacturing overhead costs to apply overhead to jobs?

2–9   What factors should be considered in selecting an allocation base to be used in computing a predetermined overhead rate?

2–10 If a company fully allocates all of its overhead costs to jobs, does this guarantee that a profit will be earned for the period?

2–11 Would you expect the amount of applied overhead for a period to equal the actual overhead costs of the period? Why or why not?

2–12 What is underapplied overhead? Overapplied overhead?

2–13 What is a plantwide overhead rate? Why are multiple overhead rates, rather than a plantwide overhead rate, used in some companies?

Applying Excel   connect

LO2–1, LO2–2, LO2–3, LO2–4

This Excel worksheet relates to the Dickson Company example that is summarized in Exhibit 2–5. Download the workbook containing this form from Connect, where you will also find instructions about how to use this worksheet form.

	A	B	C	D	E
1	Chapter 2: Applying Excel				
2					
3	Data				
4	Markup on job cost	75%			
5					
6		Department			
7		Milling	Assembly		
8	Machine-hours	60,000	3,000		
9	Direct labor-hours	8,000	80,000		
10	Total fixed manufacturing overhead cost	$390,000	$500,000		
11	Variable manufacturing overhead per machine-hour	$2.00			
12	Variable manufacturing overhead per direct labor-hour		$3.75		
13					
14	Cost summary for Job 407	Department			
15		Milling	Assembly		
16	Machine-hours	90	4		
17	Direct labor-hours	5	20		
18	Direct materials	$800	$370		
19	Direct labor cost	$70	$280		
20					
21	Enter a formula into each of the cells marked with a ? below				
22					
23	Step 1: Calculate the estimated total manufacturing overhead cost for each department				
24		Milling	Assembly		
25	Total fixed manufacturing overhead cost	?	?		
26	Variable manufacturing overhead per machine-hour or direct labor-hour	?	?		
27	Total machine-hours or direct labor-hours	?	?		
28	Total variable manufacturing overhead	?	?		
29	Total manufacturing overhead	?	?		
30					
31	Step 2: Calculate the predetermined overhead rate in each department				
32		Milling	Assembly		
33	Total manufacturing overhead	?	?		
34	Total machine-hours or direct labor-hours	?	?		
35	Predetermined overhead rate per machine-hour or direct labor-hour	?	?		
36					
37	Step 3: Calculate the amount of overhead applied from both departments to Job 407				
38		Milling	Assembly		
39	Predetermined overhead rate per machine-hour or direct labor-hour	?	?		
40	Machine-hours or direct labor-hours for the job	?	?		
41	Manufacturing overhead applied	?	?		
42					
43	Step 4: Calculate the total job cost for Job 407				
44		Milling	Assembly	Total	
45	Direct materials	?	?	?	
46	Direct labor cost	?	?	?	
47	Manufacturing overhead applied	?	?	?	
48	Total cost of Job 407			?	
49					
50	Step 5: Calculate the selling price for Job 407				
51	Total cost of Job 407			?	
52	Markup			?	
53	Selling price of Job 407			?	
54					

H ◀ ▶ H Chapter 2 Form / Filled in Chapter 2 Form

You should proceed to the requirements below only after completing your worksheet.

Required:

1. Check your worksheet by changing the total fixed manufacturing overhead cost for the Milling Department in the Data area to $300,000, keeping all of the other data the same as in the original example. If your worksheet is operating properly, the total cost of Job 407 should now be $2,350. If you do not get this answer, find the errors in your worksheet and correct them.

   How much is the selling price of Job 407? Did it change? Why or why not?

2. Change the total fixed manufacturing overhead cost for the Milling Department in the Data area back to $390,000, keeping all of the other data the same as in the original example. Determine the selling price for a new job, Job 408, with the following characteristics. You need not bother changing the job number from 407 to 408 in the worksheet.

	Department	
Cost summary for Job 408	Milling	Assembly
Machine-hours	40	10
Direct labor-hours	2	6
Direct materials	$700	$360
Direct labor cost	$50	$150

3. What happens to the selling price for Job 408 if the total number of machine-hours in the Assembly Department increases from 3,000 machine-hours to 6,000 machine-hours? Does it increase, decrease, or stay the same as in part 2 above? Why?
4. Restore the total number of machine-hours in the Assembly Department to 3,000 machine-hours. What happens to the selling price for Job 408 if the total number of direct labor-hours in the Assembly Department decreases from 80,000 direct labor-hours to 50,000 direct labor-hours? Does it increase, decrease, or stay the same as in part 2 above? Why?

Foundational 15   ■connect

LO2–1, LO2–2, LO2–3, LO2–4

Sweeten Company had no jobs in progress at the beginning of March and no beginning inventories. The company has two manufacturing departments—Molding and Fabrication. It started, completed, and sold only two jobs during March—Job P and Job Q. The following additional information is available for the company as a whole and for Jobs P and Q (all data and questions relate to the month of March):

	Molding	Fabrication	Total
Estimated total machine-hours used	2,500	1,500	4,000
Estimated total fixed manufacturing overhead	$10,000	$15,000	$25,000
Estimated variable manufacturing overhead per machine-hour	$1.40	$2.20	

	Job P	Job Q
Direct materials	$13,000	$8,000
Direct labor cost	$21,000	$7,500
Actual machine-hours used:		
Molding	1,700	800
Fabrication	600	900
Total	2,300	1,700

Sweeten Company had no underapplied or overapplied manufacturing overhead costs during the month.

Required:

For questions 1–8, assume that Sweeten Company uses a plantwide predetermined overhead rate with machine-hours as the allocation base. For questions 9–15, assume that the company uses departmental predetermined overhead rates with machine-hours as the allocation base in both departments.

1. What was the company's plantwide predetermined overhead rate?
2. How much manufacturing overhead was applied to Job P and how much was applied to Job Q?
3. What was the total manufacturing cost assigned to Job P?
4. If Job P included 20 units, what was its unit product cost?
5. What was the total manufacturing cost assigned to Job Q?
6. If Job Q included 30 units, what was its unit product cost?
7. Assume that Sweeten Company used cost-plus pricing (and a markup percentage of 80% of total manufacturing cost) to establish selling prices for all of its jobs. What selling price would the company have established for Jobs P and Q? What are the selling prices for both jobs when stated on a per unit basis?
8. What was Sweeten Company's cost of goods sold for March?
9. What were the company's predetermined overhead rates in the Molding Department and the Fabrication Department?
10. How much manufacturing overhead was applied from the Molding Department to Job P and how much was applied to Job Q?
11. How much manufacturing overhead was applied from the Fabrication Department to Job P and how much was applied to Job Q?
12. If Job P included 20 units, what was its unit product cost?

13. If Job Q included 30 units, what was its unit product cost?
14. Assume that Sweeten Company used cost-plus pricing (and a markup percentage of 80% of total manufacturing cost) to establish selling prices for all of its jobs. What selling price would the company have established for Jobs P and Q? What are the selling prices for both jobs when stated on a per unit basis?
15. What was Sweeten Company's cost of goods sold for March?

connect   **Exercises**

EXERCISE 2–1 Compute a Predetermined Overhead Rate LO2–1

Harris Fabrics computes its plantwide predetermined overhead rate annually on the basis of direct labor-hours. At the beginning of the year, it estimated that 20,000 direct labor-hours would be required for the period's estimated level of production. The company also estimated $94,000 of fixed manufacturing overhead cost for the coming period and variable manufacturing overhead of $2.00 per direct labor-hour. Harris's actual manufacturing overhead cost for the year was $123,900 and its actual total direct labor was 21,000 hours.

Required:
Compute the company's plantwide predetermined overhead rate for the year.

EXERCISE 2–2 Apply Overhead Cost to Jobs LO2–2

Luthan Company uses a plantwide predetermined overhead rate of $23.40 per direct labor-hour. This predetermined rate was based on a cost formula that estimated $257,400 of total manufacturing overhead cost for an estimated activity level of 11,000 direct labor-hours.

The company incurred actual total manufacturing overhead cost of $249,000 and 10,800 total direct labor-hours during the period.

Required:
Determine the amount of manufacturing overhead cost that would have been applied to all jobs during the period.

EXERCISE 2–3 Computing Total Job Costs and Unit Product Costs Using a Plantwide Predetermined Overhead Rate LO2–3

Mickley Company's plantwide predetermined overhead rate is $14.00 per direct labor-hour and its direct labor wage rate is $17.00 per hour. The following information pertains to Job A-500:

Direct materials	$231
Direct labor	$153

Required:
1. What is the total manufacturing cost assigned to Job A-500?
2. If Job A-500 consists of 40 units, what is the unit product cost for this job?

EXERCISE 2–4 Computing Total Job Costs and Unit Product Costs Using Multiple Predetermined Overhead Rates LO2–4

Fickel Company has two manufacturing departments—Assembly and Testing & Packaging. The predetermined overhead rates in Assembly and Testing & Packaging are $16.00 per direct labor-hour and $12.00 per direct labor-hour, respectively. The company's direct labor wage rate is $20.00 per hour. The following information pertains to Job N-60:

	Assembly	Testing & Packaging
Direct materials	$340	$25
Direct labor	$180	$40

Required:
1. What is the total manufacturing cost assigned to Job N-60?
2. If Job N-60 consists of 10 units, what is the unit product cost for this job?

EXERCISE 2–5 Computing Total Job Costs and Unit Product Costs Using Multiple Predetermined Overhead Rates LO2–4

Braverman Company has two manufacturing departments—Finishing and Fabrication. The predetermined overhead rates in Finishing and Fabrication are $18.00 per direct labor-hour and 110% of direct materials cost, respectively. The company's direct labor wage rate is $16.00 per hour. The following information pertains to Job 700:

	Finishing	Fabrication
Direct materials	$410	$60
Direct labor	$128	$48

Required:

1. What is the total manufacturing cost assigned to Job 700?
2. If Job 700 consists of 15 units, what is the unit product cost for this job?

EXERCISE 2–6 Job-Order Costing for a Service Company LO2–1, LO2–2, LO2–3

Tech Solutions is a consulting firm that uses a job-order costing system. Its direct materials consist of hardware and software that it purchases and installs on behalf of its clients. The firm's direct labor includes salaries of consultants that work at the client's job site, and its overhead consists of costs such as depreciation, utilities, and insurance related to the office headquarters as well as the office supplies that are consumed serving clients.

Tech Solutions computes its predetermined overhead rate annually on the basis of direct labor-hours. At the beginning of the year, it estimated that 80,000 direct labor-hours would be required for the period's estimated level of client service. The company also estimated $680,000 of fixed overhead cost for the coming period and variable overhead of $0.50 per direct labor-hour. The firm's actual overhead cost for the year was $692,000 and its actual total direct labor was 83,000 hours.

Required:

1. Compute the predetermined overhead rate.
2. During the year, Tech Solutions started and completed the Xavier Company engagement. The following information was available with respect to this job:

Direct materials	$38,000
Direct labor cost	$21,000
Direct labor-hours worked	280

Compute the total job cost for the Xavier Company engagement.

EXERCISE 2–7 Job-Order Costing; Working Backwards LO2–1, LO2–2, LO2–3

Hahn Company uses a job-order costing system. Its plantwide predetermined overhead rate uses direct labor-hours as the allocation base. The company pays its direct laborers $15 per hour. During the year, the company started and completed only two jobs—Job Alpha, which used 54,500 direct labor-hours, and Job Omega. The job cost sheets for these two jobs are shown below:

Job Alpha	
Direct materials	?
Direct labor	?
Manufacturing overhead applied	?
Total job cost	$1,533,500

Job Omega	
Direct materials	$235,000
Direct labor	345,000
Manufacturing overhead applied	184,000
Total job cost	$764,000

Required:

1. Calculate the plantwide predetermined overhead rate.
2. Complete the job cost sheet for Job Alpha.

EXERCISE 2–8 Applying Overhead Cost; Computing Unit Product Cost LO2–2, LO2–3

Newhard Company assigns overhead cost to jobs on the basis of 125% of direct labor cost. The job cost sheet for Job 313 includes $10,000 in direct materials cost and $12,000 in direct labor cost. A total of 1,000 units were produced in Job 313.

Required:

What is the total manufacturing cost assigned to Job 313? What is the unit product cost for Job 313?

EXERCISE 2–9 Job-Order Costing and Decision Making LO2–1, LO2–2, LO2–3

Taveras Corporation is currently operating at 50% of its available manufacturing capacity. It uses a job-order costing system with a plantwide predetermined overhead rate based on machine-hours. At the beginning of the year, the company made the following estimates:

Machine-hours required to support estimated production	165,000
Fixed manufacturing overhead cost	$1,980,000
Variable manufacturing overhead cost per machine-hour	$2.00

Required:
1. Compute the plantwide predetermined overhead rate.
2. During the year, Job P90 was started, completed, and sold to the customer for $2,500. The following information was available with respect to this job:

Direct materials	$1,150
Direct labor cost	$830
Machine-hours used	72

   Compute the total manufacturing cost assigned to Job P90.
3. Upon comparing Job P90's sales revenue to its total manufacturing cost, the company's chief financial officer said "If this exact same opportunity walked through our front door tomorrow, I'd turn it down rather than making it and selling it for $2,500."
   a. Construct an argument (supported by numerical analysis) that refutes the chief financial officer's assertion.
   b. Construct an argument (accompanied by numerical analysis) that supports the chief financial officer's assertion.

EXERCISE 2–10 Applying Overhead Cost to a Job LO2–2

Sigma Corporation applies overhead cost to jobs on the basis of direct labor cost. Job V, which was started and completed during the current period, shows charges of $5,000 for direct materials, $8,000 for direct labor, and $6,000 for overhead on its job cost sheet. Job W, which is still in process at year-end, shows charges of $2,500 for direct materials and $4,000 for direct labor.

Required:
1. Should any overhead cost be applied to Job W at year-end? If so, how much? Explain.
2. How will the costs included in Job W's job cost sheet be reported within Sigma Corporation's financial statements at the end of the year?

EXERCISE 2–11 Varying Plantwide Predetermined Overhead Rates LO2–1, LO2–2, LO2–3

Kingsport Containers Company makes a single product that is subject to wide seasonal variations in demand. The company uses a job-order costing system and computes plantwide predetermined overhead rates on a quarterly basis using the number of units to be produced as the allocation base. Its estimated costs, by quarter, for the coming year are given below:

	Quarter			
	First	Second	Third	Fourth
Direct materials	$240,000	$120,000	$ 60,000	$180,000
Direct labor	128,000	64,000	32,000	96,000
Manufacturing overhead	300,000	220,000	180,000	?
Total manufacturing costs (a)	$668,000	$404,000	$272,000	$?
Number of units to be produced (b)	80,000	40,000	20,000	60,000
Estimated unit product cost (a) ÷ (b)	$8.35	$10.10	$13.60	?

Management finds the variation in quarterly unit product costs to be confusing and difficult to work with. It has been suggested that the problem lies with manufacturing overhead because it is the largest element of total manufacturing cost. Accordingly, you have been asked to find a more appropriate way of assigning manufacturing overhead cost to units of product.

Required:

1. Assuming the estimated variable manufacturing overhead cost per unit is $2.00, what must be the estimated total fixed manufacturing overhead cost per quarter?
2. Assuming the assumptions about cost behavior from the first three quarters hold constant, what is the estimated unit product cost for the fourth quarter?
3. What is causing the estimated unit product cost to fluctuate from one quarter to the next?
4. How would you recommend stabilizing the company's unit product cost? Support your answer with computations.

EXERCISE 2–12 Computing Predetermined Overhead Rates and Job Costs LO2–1, LO2–2, LO2–3

Moody Corporation uses a job-order costing system with a plantwide predetermined overhead rate based on machine-hours. At the beginning of the year, the company made the following estimates:

Machine-hours required to support estimated production	100,000
Fixed manufacturing overhead cost	$650,000
Variable manufacturing overhead cost per machine-hour	$3.00

Required:

1. Compute the plantwide predetermined overhead rate.
2. During the year, Job 400 was started and completed. The following information was available with respect to this job:

Direct materials	$450
Direct labor cost	$210
Machine-hours used	40

Compute the total manufacturing cost assigned to Job 400.

3. If Job 400 includes 52 units, what is the unit product cost for this job?
4. If Moody uses a markup percentage of 120% of its total manufacturing cost, then what selling price per unit would it have established for Job 400?
5. If Moody hired you as a consultant to critique its pricing methodology, what would you say?

EXERCISE 2–13 Departmental Predetermined Overhead Rates LO2–1, LO2–2, LO2–4

White Company has two departments, Cutting and Finishing. The company uses a job-order costing system and computes a predetermined overhead rate in each department. The Cutting Department bases its rate on machine-hours, and the Finishing Department bases its rate on direct labor-hours. At the beginning of the year, the company made the following estimates:

	Department	
	Cutting	Finishing
Direct labor-hours	6,000	30,000
Machine-hours	48,000	5,000
Total fixed manufacturing overhead cost	$264,000	$366,000
Variable manufacturing overhead per machine-hour	$2.00	—
Variable manufacturing overhead per direct labor-hour ...	—	$4.00

Required:

1. Compute the predetermined overhead rate for each department.
2. The job cost sheet for Job 203, which was started and completed during the year, showed the following:

	Department	
	Cutting	Finishing
Direct labor-hours	6	20
Machine-hours	80	4
Direct materials	$500	$310
Direct labor cost	$108	$360

Using the predetermined overhead rates that you computed in (1) above, compute the total manufacturing cost assigned to Job 203.

3. Would you expect substantially different amounts of overhead cost to be assigned to some jobs if the company used a plantwide predetermined overhead rate based on direct labor-hours, rather than using departmental rates? Explain. No computations are necessary.

EXERCISE 2–14 Job-Order Costing for a Service Company LO2–1, LO2–2, LO2–3

Yancey Productions is a film studio that uses a job-order costing system. The company's direct materials consist of items such as costumes and props. Its direct labor includes each film's actors, directors, and extras. The company's overhead costs include items such as utilities, depreciation of equipment, senior management salaries, and wages of maintenance workers. Yancey applies its overhead cost to films based on direct labor-dollars.

At the beginning of the year, Yancey made the following estimates:

Direct labor-dollars to support all productions	$8,000,000
Fixed overhead cost	$4,800,000
Variable overhead cost per direct labor-dollar	$0.05

Required:

1. Compute the predetermined overhead rate.
2. During the year, Yancey produced a film titled *You Can Say That Again* that incurred the following costs:

Direct materials	$1,259,000
Direct labor cost	$2,400,000

Compute the total job cost for this particular film.

EXERCISE 2–15 Plantwide and Departmental Predetermined Overhead Rates; Job Costs LO2–1, LO2–2, LO2–3, LO2–4

Delph Company uses a job-order costing system and has two manufacturing departments—Molding and Fabrication. The company provided the following estimates at the beginning of the year:

	Molding	Fabrication	Total
Machine-hours	20,000	30,000	50,000
Fixed manufacturing overhead cost	$700,000	$210,000	$910,000
Variable manufacturing overhead cost per machine-hour	$3.00	$1.00	

During the year, the company had no beginning or ending inventories and it started, completed, and sold only two jobs—Job D-70 and Job C-200. It provided the following information related to those two jobs:

Job D-70	Molding	Fabrication	Total
Direct materials cost	$375,000	$325,000	$700,000
Direct labor cost	$200,000	$160,000	$360,000
Machine-hours	14,000	6,000	20,000

Job C-200	Molding	Fabrication	Total
Direct materials cost	$300,000	$250,000	$550,000
Direct labor cost	$175,000	$225,000	$400,000
Machine-hours	6,000	24,000	30,000

Delph had no underapplied or overapplied manufacturing overhead during the year.

Required:

1. Assume Delph uses a plantwide predetermined overhead rate based on machine-hours.
    a. Compute the plantwide predetermined overhead rate.
    b. Compute the total manufacturing cost assigned to Job D-70 and Job C-200.

   c.   If Delph establishes bid prices that are 150% of total manufacturing cost, what bid prices
        would it have established for Job D-70 and Job C-200?
   d.   What is Delph's cost of goods sold for the year?
2. Assume Delph uses departmental predetermined overhead rates based on machine-hours.
   a.   Compute the departmental predetermined overhead rates.
   b.   Compute the total manufacturing cost assigned to Job D-70 and Job C-200.
   c.   If Delph establishes bid prices that are 150% of total manufacturing costs, what bid prices
        would it have established for Job D-70 and Job C-200?
   d.   What is Delph's cost of goods sold for the year?
3. What managerial insights are revealed by the computations that you performed in this problem? (*Hint:* Do the cost of goods sold amounts that you computed in requirements 1 and 2
   differ from one another? Do the bid prices that you computed in requirements 1 and 2 differ
   from one another? Why?)

Problems

 connect

PROBLEM 2–16 Plantwide Predetermined Overhead Rates; Pricing LO2–1, LO2–2, LO2–3

Landen Corporation uses a job-order costing system. At the beginning of the year, the company
made the following estimates:

Direct labor-hours required to support estimated production	140,000
Machine-hours required to support estimated production	70,000
Fixed manufacturing overhead cost	$784,000
Variable manufacturing overhead cost per direct labor-hour	$2.00
Variable manufacturing overhead cost per machine-hour	$4.00

During the year, Job 550 was started and completed. The following information is available
with respect to this job:

Direct materials	$175
Direct labor cost	$225
Direct labor-hours	15
Machine-hours	5

Required:
1. Assume that Landen has historically used a plantwide predetermined overhead rate with direct
   labor-hours as the allocation base. Under this approach:
   a.   Compute the plantwide predetermined overhead rate.
   b.   Compute the total manufacturing cost of Job 550.
   c.   If Landen uses a markup percentage of 200% of its total manufacturing cost, what selling
        price would it establish for Job 550?
2. Assume that Landen's controller believes that machine-hours is a better allocation base than
   direct labor-hours. Under this approach:
   a.   Compute the plantwide predetermined overhead rate.
   b.   Compute the total manufacturing cost of Job 550.
   c.   If Landen uses a markup percentage of 200% of its total manufacturing cost, what selling
        price would it establish for Job 550?
3. Assume that Landen's controller is right about machine-hours being a more accurate overhead
   cost allocation base than direct labor-hours. If the company continues to use direct labor-hours
   as its only overhead cost allocation base what implications does this have for pricing jobs such
   as Job 550?

PROBLEM 2–17 Plantwide and Departmental Predetermined Overhead Rates; Overhead
Application LO2–1, LO2–2

Wilmington Company has two manufacturing departments—Assembly and Fabrication. It considers all of its manufacturing overhead costs to be fixed costs. The first set of data that is shown

below is based on estimates from the beginning of the year. The second set of data relates to one particular job completed during the year—Job Bravo.

Estimated Data	Assembly	Fabrication	Total
Manufacturing overhead costs	$600,000	$800,000	$1,400,000
Direct labor-hours	50,000	30,000	80,000
Machine-hours	20,000	100,000	120,000

Job Bravo	Assembly	Fabrication	Total
Direct labor-hours	11	3	14
Machine-hours	3	6	9

Required:

1. If Wilmington used a plantwide predetermined overhead rate based on direct labor-hours, how much manufacturing overhead would be applied to Job Bravo?
2. If Wilmington uses departmental predetermined overhead rates with direct labor-hours as the allocation base in Assembly and machine-hours as the allocation base in Fabrication, how much manufacturing overhead would be applied to Job Bravo?

PROBLEM 2–18 Job-Order Costing for a Service Company LO2–1, LO2–2, LO2–3
Speedy Auto Repairs uses a job-order costing system. The company's direct materials consist of replacement parts installed in customer vehicles, and its direct labor consists of the mechanics' hourly wages. Speedy's overhead costs include various items, such as the shop manager's salary, depreciation of equipment, utilities, insurance, and magazine subscriptions and refreshments for the waiting room.

The company applies all of its overhead costs to jobs based on direct labor-hours. At the beginning of the year, it made the following estimates:

Direct labor-hours required to support estimated output	20,000
Fixed overhead cost	$350,000
Variable overhead cost per direct labor-hour	$1.00

Required:

1. Compute the predetermined overhead rate.
2. During the year, Mr. Wilkes brought in his vehicle to replace his brakes, spark plugs, and tires. The following information was available with respect to his job:

Direct materials	$590
Direct labor cost	$109
Direct labor-hours used	6

Compute Mr. Wilkes' total job cost.

3. If Speedy establishes its selling prices using a markup percentage of 40% of its total job cost, then how much would it have charged Mr. Wilkes?

PROBLEM 2–19 Multiple Predetermined Overhead Rates; Applying Overhead LO2–1, LO2–2, LO2–4
High Desert Potteryworks makes a variety of pottery products that it sells to retailers. The company uses a job-order costing system in which departmental predetermined overhead rates are used to apply manufacturing overhead cost to jobs. The predetermined overhead rate in the Molding Department is based on machine-hours, and the rate in the Painting Department is based on direct labor-hours. At the beginning of the year, the company provided the following estimates:

	Department	
	Molding	Painting
Direct labor-hours	12,000	60,000
Machine-hours	70,000	8,000
Fixed manufacturing overhead cost	$497,000	$615,000
Variable manufacturing overhead per machine-hour	$1.50	–
Variable manufacturing overhead per direct labor-hour	–	$2.00

Job 205 was started on August 1 and completed on August 10. The company's cost records show the following information concerning the job:

	Department	
	Molding	Painting
Direct labor-hours	30	84
Machine-hours	110	20
Direct materials	$770	$1,332
Direct labor cost	$525	$1,470

Required:
1. Compute the predetermined overhead rates used in the Molding Department and the Painting Department.
2. Compute the total overhead cost applied to Job 205.
3. What would be the total manufacturing cost recorded for Job 205? If the job contained 50 units, what would be the unit product cost?

PROBLEM 2–20 Plantwide versus Multiple Predetermined Overhead Rates: Service Industry LO2–1, LO2–2, LO2–3, LO2–4

McCullough Hospital uses a job-order costing system to assign costs to its patients. Its direct materials include a variety of items such as pharmaceutical drugs, heart valves, artificial hips, and pacemakers. Its direct labor costs (e.g., surgeons, anesthesiologists, radiologists, and nurses) associated with specific surgical procedures and tests are traced to individual patients. All other costs, such as depreciation of medical equipment, insurance, utilities, incidental medical supplies, and the labor costs associated with around-the-clock monitoring of patients are treated as overhead costs.

Historically, McCullough has used one predetermined overhead rate based on the number of patient-days (each night that a patient spends in the hospital counts as one patient-day) to allocate overhead costs to patients. Recently a member of the hospital's accounting staff has suggested using two predetermined overhead rates (allocated based on the number of patient-days) to improve the accuracy of the costs allocated to patients. The first overhead rate would include all overhead costs within the Intensive Care Unit (ICU) and the second overhead rate would include all Other overhead costs. Information pertaining to the hospital's estimated number of patient-days, its estimated overhead costs, and two of its patients—Patient A and Patient B—is provided below:

	ICU	Other	Total
Estimated number of patient-days	2,000	18,000	20,000
Estimated fixed overhead cost	$3,200,000	$14,000,000	$17,200,000
Estimated variable overhead cost per patient-day	$236	$96	

	Patient A	Patient B
Direct materials	$4,500	$6,200
Direct labor	$25,000	$36,000
Total number of patient-days (including ICU)	14	21
Number of patient-days spent in ICU	0	7

Required:
1. Assuming McCullough uses only one predetermined overhead rate, calculate:
   a. The predetermined overhead rate.
   b. The total cost, including direct materials, direct labor and applied overhead, assigned to Patient A and Patient B.
2. Assuming McCullough calculates two overhead rates as recommended by the staff accountant, calculate:
   a. The ICU and Other overhead rates.
   b. The total cost, including direct materials, direct labor and applied overhead, assigned to Patient A and Patient B.
3. What insights are revealed by the staff accountant's approach?

PROBLEM 2–21 Plantwide Versus Multiple Predetermined Overhead Rates LO2–1, LO2–2

Mason Company has two manufacturing departments—Machining and Assembly. The company considers all of its manufacturing overhead costs to be fixed costs. It provided the following estimates at the beginning of the year as well as the following information with respect to Jobs A and B:

Estimated Data	Machining	Assembly	Total
Manufacturing overhead	$500,000	$100,000	$600,000
Direct labor-hours	10,000	50,000	60,000
Machine-hours	50,000	5,000	55,000

Job A	Machining	Assembly	Total
Direct labor-hours	5	10	15
Machine-hours	11	2	13

Job B	Machining	Assembly	Total
Direct labor-hours	4	5	9
Machine-hours	12	3	15

Required:
1. If Mason Company uses a plantwide predetermined overhead rate with direct labor-hours as the allocation base, how much manufacturing overhead cost would be applied to Job A? Job B?
2. Assume that Mason Company uses departmental predetermined overhead rates. The Machining Department is allocated based on machine-hours and the Assembly Department is allocated based on direct labor-hours. How much manufacturing overhead cost would be applied to Job A? Job B?
3. If Mason multiplies its job costs by a markup percentage to establish selling prices, how might plantwide overhead allocation adversely affect the company's pricing decisions?

connect   **Case**

CASE 2–22 Plantwide versus Departmental Overhead Rates; Pricing LO2–1, LO2–2, LO2–3, LO2–4

"Blast it!" said David Wilson, president of Teledex Company. "We've just lost the bid on the Koopers job by $2,000. It seems we're either too high to get the job or too low to make any money on half the jobs we bid."

Teledex Company manufactures products to customers' specifications and uses a job-order costing system. The company uses a plantwide predetermined overhead rate based on direct labor cost to apply its manufacturing overhead (assumed to be all fixed) to jobs. The following estimates were made at the beginning of the year:

	Department			
	Fabricating	Machining	Assembly	Total Plant
Manufacturing overhead	$350,000	$400,000	$90,000	$840,000
Direct labor	$200,000	$100,000	$300,000	$600,000

Jobs require varying amounts of work in the three departments. The Koopers job, for example, would have required manufacturing costs in the three departments as follows:

	Department			
	Fabricating	Machining	Assembly	Total Plant
Direct materials	$3,000	$200	$1,400	$4,600
Direct labor	$2,800	$500	$6,200	$9,500
Manufacturing overhead	?	?	?	?

Required:

1. Using the company's plantwide approach:
    a. Compute the plantwide predetermined rate for the current year.
    b. Determine the amount of manufacturing overhead cost that would have been applied to the Koopers job.
2. Suppose that instead of using a plantwide predetermined overhead rate, the company had used departmental predetermined overhead rates based on direct labor cost. Under these conditions:
    a. Compute the predetermined overhead rate for each department for the current year.
    b. Determine the amount of manufacturing overhead cost that would have been applied to the Koopers job.
3. Explain the difference between the manufacturing overhead that would have been applied to the Koopers job using the plantwide approach in question 1 (b) and using the departmental approach in question 2 (b).
4. Assume that it is customary in the industry to bid jobs at 150% of total manufacturing cost (direct materials, direct labor, and applied overhead). What was the company's bid price on the Koopers job using a plantwide predetermined overhead rate? What would the bid price have been if departmental predetermined overhead rates had been used to apply overhead cost?

Appendix 2A: Activity-Based Absorption Costing

LO2–5

Use activity-based absorption costing to compute unit product costs.

Chapter 2 described how manufacturing companies use traditional absorption costing systems to calculate unit product costs. In this appendix, we contrast traditional absorption costing with an alternative approach called *activity-based absorption costing*. **Activity-based absorption costing** assigns all manufacturing overhead costs to products based on the *activities* performed to make those products. An **activity** is an event that causes the consumption of manufacturing overhead resources. Rather than relying on plantwide or departmental cost pools, the activity-based approach accumulates each activity's overhead costs in *activity cost pools*. An **activity cost pool** is a "bucket" in which costs are accumulated that relate to a single activity. Each activity cost pool has one *activity measure*. An **activity measure** is an allocation base that is used as the denominator for an activity cost pool. The costs accumulated in the numerator of an activity cost pool divided by the quantity of the activity measure in its denominator equals what is called an *activity rate*. An activity rate is used to assign costs from an activity cost pool to products.

Activity-based absorption costing differs from traditional absorption costing in two ways. First, the activity-based approach uses more cost pools than a traditional approach. Second, the activity-based approach includes some activities and activity measures that *do not* relate to the volume of units produced, whereas the traditional approach relies exclusively on allocation bases that are driven by the volume of production. For example, the activity-based approach may include *batch-level activities*. A **batch-level activity** is performed each time a batch is handled or processed, regardless of how many units are in the batch. Batch-level activities include tasks such as placing purchase orders, setting up equipment, and transporting batches of component parts. Costs at the batch level depend on the number of batches processed rather than the number of units produced. The activity-based approach may also include *product-level activities*. A **product-level activity** relates to specific products and typically must be carried out regardless of how many batches are run or units of product are produced and sold. Product-level activities include tasks such as designing a product and making engineering design changes to a product. Costs at the product-level depend on the number of products supported rather than the number of batches run or the number of units of product produced and sold.

To illustrate the differences between traditional and activity-based absorption costing, we'll use an example focused on Maxtar Industries, a manufacturer of high-quality smoker/

EXHIBIT 2A–1
Maxtar Industries' Traditional Costing System

Basic Data		
Total estimated manufacturing overhead cost	$1,520,000	
Total estimated direct labor-hours	400,000 DLHs	

	Premium	Standard
Direct materials per unit	$40.00	$30.00
Direct labor per unit	$24.00	$18.00
Direct labor-hours per unit	2.0 DLHs	1.5 DLHs
Units produced	50,000	200,000 units

Computation of the Plantwide Predetermined Overhead Rate

$$\text{Predetermined overhead rate} = \frac{\text{Total estimated manufacturing overhead}}{\text{Total estimated amount of the allocation base}}$$

$$= \frac{\$1,520,000}{400,000 \text{ DLHs}} = \$3.80 \text{ per DLH}$$

Traditional Unit Product Costs		
	Premium	Standard
Direct materials	$40.00	$30.00
Direct labor	24.00	18.00
Manufacturing overhead (2.0 DLHs × $3.80 per DLH; 1.5 DLHs × $3.80 per DLH)	7.60	5.70
Unit product cost	$71.60	$53.70

barbecue units. The company has two product lines—Premium and Standard. The company has traditionally applied manufacturing overhead costs to these products using a plantwide predetermined overhead rate based on direct labor-hours. Exhibit 2A–1 details how the unit product costs of the two product lines are computed using the company's traditional costing system. The unit product cost of the Premium product line is $71.60 and the unit product cost of the Standard product line is $53.70 according to this traditional costing system.

Maxtar Industries has recently experimented with an activity-based absorption costing system that has three activity cost pools: (1) supporting direct labor; (2) setting up machines; and (3) parts administration. The top of Exhibit 2A–2 displays basic data concerning these activity cost pools. Note that the total estimated overhead cost in these three costs pools, $1,520,000, agrees with the total estimated overhead cost in the company's traditional costing system. The company's activity-based approach simply provides an alternative way to allocate the company's manufacturing overhead across the two products.

The activity rates for the three activity cost pools are computed in the second table in Exhibit 2A–2. For example, the total cost in the "setting up machines" activity cost pool, $480,000, is divided by the total activity associated with that cost pool, 800 setups, to determine the activity rate of $600 per setup.

The activity rates are used to allocate overhead costs to the two products in the third table in Exhibit 2A–2. For example, the activity rate for the "setting up machines" activity cost pool, $600 per setup, is multiplied by the Premium product line's 600 setups to determine the $360,000 machine setup cost allocated to the Premium product line.

The table at the bottom of Exhibit 2A–2 displays the overhead costs per unit and the activity-based unit product costs. The overhead cost per unit is determined by dividing the total overhead cost by the number of units produced. For example, the Premium product line's total overhead cost of $728,000 is divided by 50,000 units to determine the $14.56 overhead cost per unit. Note that the unit product costs differ from those

EXHIBIT 2A–2
Maxtar Industries' Activity-Based
Absorption Costing System

Basic Data

Activity Cost Pools and Activity Measures	Estimated Overhead Cost	Expected Activity		
		Premium	Standard	Total
Supporting direct labor (DLHs).......	$ 800,000	100,000	300,000	400,000
Setting up machines (setups)........	480,000	600	200	800
Parts administration (part types)......	240,000	140	60	200
Total manufacturing overhead cost ...	$1,520,000			

Computation of Activity Rates

Activity Cost Pools	(a) Estimated Overhead Cost	(b) Total Expected Activity	(a) ÷ (b) Activity Rate
Supporting direct labor ...	$800,000	400,000 DLHs	$2 per DLH
Setting up machines	$480,000	800 setups	$600 per setup
Parts administration	$240,000	200 part types	$1,200 per part type

Assigning Overhead Costs to Products

The Premium Product

Activity Cost Pools	(a) Activity Rate	(b) Activity	(a) × (b) ABC Cost
Supporting direct labor ...	$2 per DLH	100,000 DLHs	$200,000
Setting up machines	$600 per setup	600 setups	360,000
Parts administration	$1,200 per part type	140 part types	168,000
Total			$728,000

The Standard Product

Activity Cost Pools	(a) Activity Rate	(b) Activity	(a) × (b) ABC Cost
Supporting direct labor...	$2 per DLH	300,000 DLHs	$600,000
Setting up machines	$600 per setup	200 setups	120,000
Parts administration	$1,200 per part type	60 part types	72,000
Total...................			$792,000

Activity-Based Absorption Costing Product Costs

	Premium	Standard
Direct materials	$40.00	$30.00
Direct labor	24.00	18.00
Manufacturing overhead ($728,000 ÷ 50,000 units; $792,000 ÷ 200,000 units)	14.56	3.96
Unit product cost	$78.56	$51.96

computed using the company's traditional costing system in Exhibit 2A–1. Because the activity-based approach contains both a batch-level (setting up machines) and a product-level (parts administration) activity cost pool, the unit product costs under the activity-based approach follow the usual pattern in which overhead costs are shifted from the high-volume to the low-volume product. The unit product cost of the Standard product line, the high-volume product, has gone down from $53.70 under the traditional costing system to $51.96 under activity-based costing. In contrast, the unit product cost of the Premium product line, the low-volume product, has increased from $71.60 under the traditional costing system to $78.56 under activity-based costing. Instead of using direct labor-hours (which moves in tandem with the volume of the production) to assign all manufacturing overhead costs to products, the activity-based approach uses a batch-level activity measure and a product-level activity measure to assign the batch-level and product-level activity cost pools to the two products.

Glossary (Appendix 2A)

Activity An event that causes the consumption of overhead resources in an organization. (p. 96)

Activity-based absorption costing A costing method that assigns all manufacturing overhead costs to products based on the *activities* performed to make those products. (p. 96)

Activity cost pool A "bucket" in which costs are accumulated that relate to a single activity measure in an activity-based costing system. (p. 96)

Activity measure An allocation base in an activity-based costing system; ideally, a measure of the amount of activity that drives the costs in an activity cost pool. (p. 96)

Batch-level activity An activity that is performed each time a batch is handled or processed, regardless of how many units are in the batch. The amount of resources consumed depends on the number of batches run rather than on the number of units in the batch. (p. 96)

Product-level activity An activity that relates to specific products and typically must be carried out regardless of how many batches are run or units of product are produced and sold. (p. 96)

connect   Appendix 2A: Exercises, Problems, and Case

EXERCISE 2A–1 Activity-Based Absorption Costing LO2–5

Fogerty Company makes two products—titanium Hubs and Sprockets. Data regarding the two products follow:

	Direct Labor-Hours per Unit	Annual Production
Hubs	0.80	10,000 units
Sprockets	0.40	40,000 units

Additional information about the company follows:
a. Hubs require $32 in direct materials per unit, and Sprockets require $18.
b. The direct labor wage rate is $15 per hour.
c. Hubs are more complex to manufacture than Sprockets and they require special processing.
d. The company's activity-based absorption costing system has the following activity cost pools:

		Expected Activity		
Activity Cost Pool (and Activity Measure)	Estimated Overhead Cost	Hubs	Sprockets	Total
Machine setups (number of setups)	$72,000	100	300	400
Special processing (machine-hours)	$200,000	5,000	0	5,000
General factory (Direct labor-hours)	$816,000	8,000	16,000	24,000

Required:
1. Compute the activity rate for each activity cost pool.
2. Compute the unit product cost for Hubs and Sprockets using activity-based absorption costing.

EXERCISE 2A–2 Activity-Based Absorption Costing as an Alternative to Traditional Product Costing LO2–5

Harrison Company makes two products and uses a traditional costing system in which a single plantwide predetermined overhead rate is computed based on direct labor-hours. Data for the two products for the upcoming year follow:

	Rascon	Parcel
Direct materials cost per unit	$13.00	$22.00
Direct labor cost per unit	$6.00	$3.00
Direct labor-hours per unit	0.40	0.20
Number of units produced	20,000	80,000

These products are customized to some degree for specific customers.

Required:
1. The company's manufacturing overhead costs for the year are expected to be $576,000. Using the company's traditional costing system, compute the unit product costs for the two products.
2. Management is considering an activity-based absorption costing system in which half of the overhead would continue to be allocated based on direct labor-hours and half would be allocated based on engineering design time. This time is expected to be distributed as follows during the upcoming year:

	Rascon	Parcel	Total
Engineering design time (in hours)	3,000	3,000	6,000

Compute the unit product costs for the two products using the proposed activity-based absorption costing system.
3. Explain why the product costs differ between the two systems.

EXERCISE 2A–3 Activity-Based Absorption Costing as an Alternative to Traditional Product Costing LO2–5

Stillicum Corporation makes ultralightweight backpacking tents. Data concerning the company's two product lines appear below:

	Deluxe	Standard
Direct materials per unit	$72.00	$53.00
Direct labor per unit	$19.00	$15.20
Direct labor-hours per unit	1.0 DLHs	0.8 DLHs
Estimated annual production	10,000 units	50,000 units

The company has a traditional costing system in which manufacturing overhead is applied to units based on direct labor-hours. Data concerning manufacturing overhead and direct labor-hours for the upcoming year appear below:

Estimated total manufacturing overhead	$325,000
Estimated total direct labor-hours	50,000 DLHs

Required:
1. Determine the unit product costs of the Deluxe and Standard products under the company's traditional costing system.
2. The company is considering replacing its traditional costing system with an activity-based absorption costing system that would have the following three activity cost pools:

Activity Cost Pools (and Activity Measures)	Estimated Overhead Cost	Expected Activity		
		Deluxe	Standard	Total
Supporting direct labor (direct labor-hours)	$200,000	10,000	40,000	50,000
Batch setups (setups)	75,000	200	100	300
Safety testing (tests)	50,000	30	70	100
Total manufacturing overhead cost	$325,000			

Determine the unit product costs of the Deluxe and Standard products under the activity-based absorption costing system.

PROBLEM 2A–4 Activity-Based Absorption Costing as an Alternative to Traditional Product Costing LO2–5

Ellix Company manufactures two models of ultra-high fidelity speakers—the X200 model and the X99 model. Data regarding the two products follow:

Product	Direct Labor-Hours	Annual Production	Total Direct Labor-Hours
X200	1.8 DLHs per unit	5,000 units	9,000 DLHs
X99	0.9 DLHs per unit	30,000 units	27,000 DLHs
			36,000 DLHs

Additional information about the company follows:
a. Model X200 requires $72 in direct materials per unit, and model X99 requires $50.
b. The direct labor workers are paid $20 per hour.
c. The company has always used direct labor-hours as the base for applying manufacturing overhead cost to products.
d. Model X200 is more complex to manufacture than model X99 and requires the use of special equipment.
e. Because of the special work required in (d) above, the company is considering the use of activity-based absorption costing to apply manufacturing overhead cost to products. Three activity cost pools have been identified as follows:

Activity Cost Pool	Activity Measure	Estimated Total Cost	Estimated Total Activity		
			X200	X99	Total
Machine setups	Number of setups	$ 360,000	50	100	150
Special processing	Machine-hours	180,000	12,000	0	12,000
General factory	Direct labor-hours	1,260,000	9,000	27,000	36,000
		$1,800,000			

Required:
1. Assume that the company continues to use direct labor-hours as the base for applying overhead cost to products.
    a. Compute the plantwide predetermined overhead rate.
    b. Compute the unit product cost of each model.
2. Assume that the company decides to use activity-based absorption costing to apply overhead cost to products.
    a. Compute the activity rate for each activity cost pool and determine the amount of overhead cost that would be applied to each model using the activity-based approach.
    b. Compute the unit product cost of each model.
3. Explain why overhead cost shifted from the high-volume model to the low-volume model under the activity-based approach.

PROBLEM 2A–5 Activity-Based Absorption Costing as an Alternative to Traditional Product Costing LO2–5

Siegel Company manufactures a product that is available in both a deluxe model and a regular model. The company has manufactured the regular model for years. The deluxe model was introduced several years ago to tap a new segment of the market. Since introduction of the deluxe model, the company's profits have steadily declined and management has become increasingly concerned about the accuracy of its costing system. Sales of the deluxe model have been increasing rapidly.

Manufacturing overhead is assigned to products on the basis of direct labor-hours. For the current year, the company has estimated that it will incur $900,000 in manufacturing overhead cost and produce 5,000 units of the deluxe model and 40,000 units of the regular model. The deluxe model requires two hours of direct labor time per unit, and the regular model requires one hour. Material and labor costs per unit are as follows:

| | Model | |
	Deluxe	Regular
Direct materials	$40	$25
Direct labor	$38	$19

Required:

1. Compute the predetermined overhead rate using direct labor-hours as the allocation base. Using this rate and other data from the problem, calculate the unit product cost of each model.
2. Management is considering using activity-based absorption costing to apply manufacturing overhead cost to products. The activity-based system would have the following four activity cost pools:

Activity Cost Pool	Activity Measure	Estimated Overhead Cost
Purchasing	Purchase orders issued	$204,000
Processing	Machine-hours	182,000
Scrap/rework	Scrap/rework orders issued	379,000
Shipping	Number of shipments	135,000
		$900,000

| | Expected Activity | | |
Activity Measure	Deluxe	Regular	Total
Purchase orders issued	200	400	600
Machine-hours	20,000	15,000	35,000
Scrap/rework orders issued	1,000	1,000	2,000
Number of shipments	250	650	900

Determine the predetermined overhead rate for each of the four activity cost pools.
3. Using the predetermined overhead rates you computed in part (2), do the following:
   a. Compute the total amount of manufacturing overhead cost that would be applied to each model using the activity-based absorption costing system. After these totals have been computed, determine the amount of manufacturing overhead cost per unit of each model.
   b. Compute the unit product cost of each model (direct materials, direct labor, and manufacturing overhead).
4. From the data you have developed in parts (1) through (3), identify factors that may account for the company's declining profits.

CASE 2A–6 Activity-Based Absorption Costing and Pricing LO2–5

Java Source, Inc., (JSI) buys coffee beans from around the world and roasts, blends, and packages them for resale. Some of JSI's coffees are very popular and sell in large volumes, while a few of the newer blends sell in very low volumes. JSI prices its coffees at manufacturing cost plus a markup of 25%.

For the coming year, JSI's budget includes estimated manufacturing overhead cost of $2,200,000. JSI assigns manufacturing overhead to products on the basis of direct labor-hours. The expected direct labor cost totals $600,000, which represents 50,000 hours of direct labor time.

The expected costs for direct materials and direct labor for one-pound bags of two of the company's coffee products appear below.

	Kenya Dark	Viet Select
Direct materials	$4.50	$2.90
Direct labor (0.02 hours per bag)	$0.34	$0.34

JSI's controller believes that the company's traditional costing system may be providing misleading cost information. To determine whether or not this is correct, the controller has prepared an analysis of the year's expected manufacturing overhead costs, as shown in the following table:

Activity Cost Pool	Activity Measure	Expected Activity for the Year	Expected Cost for the Year
Purchasing	Purchase orders	2,000 orders	$ 560,000
Material handling	Number of setups	1,000 setups	193,000
Quality control	Number of batches	500 batches	90,000
Roasting	Roasting hours	95,000 roasting hours	1,045,000
Blending	Blending hours	32,000 blending hours	192,000
Packaging	Packaging hours	24,000 packaging hours	120,000
Total manufacturing overhead cost			$2,200,000

Data regarding the expected production of Kenya Dark and Viet Select coffee are presented below.

	Kenya Dark	Viet Select
Expected sales	80,000 pounds	4,000 pounds
Batch size	5,000 pounds	500 pounds
Setups	2 per batch	2 per batch
Purchase order size	20,000 pounds	500 pounds
Roasting time per 100 pounds	1.5 roasting hours	1.5 roasting hours
Blending time per 100 pounds	0.5 blending hours	0.5 blending hours
Packaging time per 100 pounds	0.3 packaging hours	0.3 packaging hours

Required:
1. Using direct labor-hours as the manufacturing overhead cost allocation base, do the following:
   a. Determine the plantwide predetermined overhead rate that will be used during the year.
   b. Determine the unit product cost of one pound of Kenya Dark coffee and one pound of Viet Select coffee.
2. Using the activity-based absorption costing approach, do the following:
   a. Determine the total amount of manufacturing overhead cost assigned to Kenya Dark coffee and to Viet Select coffee for the year.
   b. Using the data developed in (2a) above, compute the amount of manufacturing overhead cost per pound of Kenya Dark coffee and Viet Select coffee.
   c. Determine the unit product cost of one pound of Kenya Dark coffee and one pound of Viet Select coffee.
3. Write a brief memo to the president of JSI that explains what you found in (1) and (2) above and that discusses the implications of using direct labor-hours as the only manufacturing overhead cost allocation base.

(CMA, adapted)

Appendix 2B: The Predetermined Overhead Rate and Capacity

This appendix contrasts two methods of computing predetermined overhead rates. The first method (which was used throughout the chapter) demonstrates the absorption costing approach that company's use for external reporting purposes.[3] It bases the denominator

LO2–6
Understand the implications of basing the predetermined overhead rate on activity at capacity rather than on estimated activity for the period.

---

[3] Statement of Financial Accounting Standards No. 151: *Inventory Costs* and International Accounting Standard 2: *Inventories* require allocating fixed manufacturing overhead costs to products based on normal capacity. Normal capacity reflects the level of output expected to be produced over numerous periods under normal circumstances. This definition mirrors the language used in this book that refers to basing the predetermined overhead rate on the estimated, or budgeted, amount of the allocation base for the upcoming period.

volume for overhead rates on the estimated, or budgeted, amount of the allocation base for the upcoming period. The second method, often used for internal management purposes, bases the denominator volume for overhead rates on the estimated total amount of the allocation base at capacity. To simplify our forthcoming comparison of these two methods, we make two important assumptions that will hold true throughout the entire appendix: (1) all manufacturing overhead costs are fixed; and (2) the estimated, or budgeted, fixed manufacturing overhead at the beginning of the period equals the actual fixed manufacturing overhead at the end of the period.

Let's assume that Prahad Corporation manufactures DVDs for local production studios. The company's DVD duplicating machine is capable of producing a new DVD every 10 seconds from a master DVD. The company leases the DVD duplicating machine for a fixed cost of $180,000 per year, and this is the company's only estimated (and actual) manufacturing overhead cost. With allowances for setups and maintenance, the machine is theoretically capable of producing up to 900,000 DVDs per year. However, due to a business downturn, Prahad's customers are unlikely to order more than 600,000 DVDs next year. The company uses machine time as the allocation base for applying manufacturing overhead to DVDs. These data are summarized below:

Prahad Corporation Data	
Total estimated and actual manufacturing overhead cost . . .	$180,000 per year
Allocation base—machine time per DVD	10 seconds per DVD
Capacity	900,000 DVDs per year
Budgeted output for next year	600,000 DVDs

If Prahad uses the first method mentioned above, which computes predetermined overhead rates using the estimated or budgeted activity for the period, then its predetermined overhead rate for next year would be $0.03 per second of machine time computed as follows:

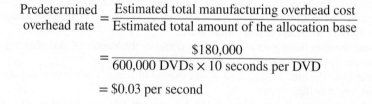

$$\text{Predetermined overhead rate} = \frac{\text{Estimated total manufacturing overhead cost}}{\text{Estimated total amount of the allocation base}}$$

$$= \frac{\$180,000}{600,000 \text{ DVDs} \times 10 \text{ seconds per DVD}}$$

$$= \$0.03 \text{ per second}$$

Because each DVD requires 10 seconds of machine time, each DVD will be charged for $0.30 of overhead cost.

While this absorption approach is commonly used for external reporting purposes, it has two important limitations from a managerial accounting standpoint. First, if predetermined overhead rates are based on budgeted activity and overhead includes significant fixed costs, then the unit product costs will fluctuate depending on the budgeted level of activity for the period. For example, if Prahad's budgeted output for the year was only 300,000 DVDs (instead of 600,000 DVDs), its predetermined overhead rate would be $0.06 per second of machine time or $0.60 per DVD rather than $0.30 per DVD. Notice that as the company's budgeted output falls, its overhead cost per unit increases. This in turn makes it appear as though the cost of producing DVDs has increased, which may tempt managers to raise prices at the worst possible time—just as demand is falling.

The second limitation of the absorption approach is that it charges products for resources that they don't use. When the fixed costs of capacity are spread over estimated activity, the units that are produced must shoulder the costs of any unused capacity. If the level of activity falls, a company's shrinking output of products must absorb a growing share of idle capacity cost that is above and beyond their actual production cost.

Basing the predetermined overhead rate on the estimated total amount of the allocation base at capacity overcomes the two limitations just discussed. It is computed as follows[4]:

$$\text{Predetermined overhead rate based on capacity} = \frac{\text{Estimated total manufacturing overhead cost at capacity}}{\text{Estimated total amount of the allocation base at capacity}}$$

$$= \frac{\$180,000}{900,000 \text{ DVDs} \times 10 \text{ seconds per DVD}}$$

$$= \$0.02 \text{ per second}$$

When Prahad bases its predetermined overhead rate on activity at capacity, its overhead rate is $0.02 per second instead of $0.03 per second as computed under the absorption approach. Consequently, the overhead cost that Prahad will apply to each DVD using the capacity-based approach would be $0.20 (= $0.02 × 10 seconds) per unit instead of $0.30 per unit under the absorption method. Notice that the capacity-based amounts per second and per unit are lower than the absorption-based amounts. This occurs because the capacity-based approach uses a higher denominator volume that reflects Prahad's capacity to produce DVDs—9,000,000 seconds.

Prahad's capacity-based rate of $0.02 per second will remain constant even if its budgeted level of activity fluctuates from one period to another. So, if the company's estimated level of activity drops from 600,000 DVDs to 300,000 DVDs, its capacity-based rate would stay at $0.02 per second. The company's unused capacity cost would increase in this situation, but its unit cost to make DVD's would stay constant at $0.20 per unit.

Whenever a company operates at less than full capacity and allocates fixed overhead costs using a capacity-based denominator volume it will report some amount of unused capacity cost that is computed as follows:

$$\text{Cost of unused capacity} = \left(\begin{array}{c} \text{Amount of the allocation} \\ \text{base at capacity} \end{array} - \begin{array}{c} \text{Actual amount of the} \\ \text{allocation base} \end{array} \right) \times \begin{array}{c} \text{Predetermined} \\ \text{overhead rate} \end{array}$$

For example, let's assume that Prahad Company actually used 6,000,000 seconds on the DVD duplicating machine to produce 600,000 DVDs. At this level of output, the company would compute its cost of unused capacity as follows:

$$\text{Cost of unused capacity} = \left(\begin{array}{c} \text{Amount of the allocation} \\ \text{base at capacity} \end{array} - \begin{array}{c} \text{Actual amount of the} \\ \text{allocation base} \end{array} \right) \times \begin{array}{c} \text{Predetermined} \\ \text{overhead rate} \end{array}$$

$$\text{Cost of unused capacity} = (9,000,000 \text{ seconds} - 6,000,000 \text{ seconds}) \times \$0.02 \text{ per second}$$

$$\text{Cost of unused capacity} = 3,000,000 \text{ seconds} \times \$0.02 \text{ per second}$$

$$\text{Cost of unused capacity} = \$60,000$$

Exhibit 2B–1 illustrates how Prahad would disclose this cost of unused capacity ($60,000) within an income statement prepared for internal management purposes. Rather than treating it as a product cost (as is done in the absorption approach), Prahad's

---

[4] Ordinarily, because of variable overhead costs, the estimated total manufacturing overhead cost at capacity will be larger than the estimated total manufacturing overhead cost at the estimated level of activity. However, for simplicity we assume in this appendix that all overhead costs are fixed. Then the total manufacturing overhead cost will be the same regardless of the level of activity.

EXHIBIT 2B–1

Prahad Corporation: An Income Statement That Recognizes the Cost of Unused Capacity

Prahad Corporation
Income Statement
For the Year Ended December 31

Sales[1]		$1,200,000
Cost of goods sold[2]		1,080,000
Gross margin		120,000
Other expenses:		
Cost of unused capacity	$60,000	
Selling and administrative expenses[3]	90,000	150,000
Net operating loss		$ (30,000)

[1] Assume sales of 600,000 CDs at $2 per CD.
[2] Assume the unit product cost of the CDs is $1.80, including $0.20 for manufacturing overhead.
[3] Assume selling and administrative expenses total $90,000.

capacity-based approach would treat this cost as a period expense that is reported below the gross margin. By separately disclosing the *Cost of unused capacity* as a lump sum of $60,000 on the income statement, instead of burying it in Cost of Goods Sold, the need to effectively manage capacity is highlighted for the company's managers. Generally speaking, a company's managers should respond to large unused capacity costs by either seeking new business opportunities that consume the capacity, or by cutting costs and shrinking the amount of available capacity.

Appendix 2B: Exercises, Problem, and Case

EXERCISE 2B–1 Overhead Rate Based on Capacity LO2–6

Wixis Cabinets makes custom wooden cabinets for high-end stereo systems from specialty woods. The company uses a job-order costing system. The capacity of the plant is determined by the capacity of its constraint, which is time on the automated bandsaw that makes finely beveled cuts in wood according to the preprogrammed specifications of each cabinet. The bandsaw can operate up to 180 hours per month. The estimated total manufacturing overhead cost at capacity is $14,760 per month. The company bases its predetermined overhead rate on capacity, so its predetermined overhead rate is $82 per hour of bandsaw use.

The results of a recent month's operations appear below:

Sales	$43,740
Beginning inventories	$0
Ending inventories	$0
Direct materials	$5,350
Direct labor	$8,860
Manufacturing overhead incurred	$14,760
Selling and administrative expense	$8,180
Actual hours of bandsaw use	150

Required:

1. Prepare an income statement following the example in Exhibit 2B–1 that records the cost of unused capacity on the income statement as a period expense.
2. Why do unused capacity costs arise when the predetermined overhead rate is based on capacity?

EXERCISE 2B–2 Overhead Rates and Capacity Issues LO2–1, LO2–2, LO2–6

Security Pension Services helps clients to set up and administer pension plans that are in compliance with tax laws and regulatory requirements. The firm uses a job-order costing system in which overhead is applied to clients' accounts on the basis of professional staff hours charged to the accounts. Data concerning two recent years appear below:

	Last Year	This Year
Estimated professional staff hours to be charged to clients' accounts	4,600	4,500
Estimated overhead cost	$310,500	$310,500
Professional staff hours available	6,000	6,000

"Professional staff hours available" is a measure of the capacity of the firm. Any hours available that are not charged to clients' accounts represent unused capacity. All of the firm's overhead is fixed.

Required:

1. Marta Brinksi is an established client whose pension plan was set up many years ago. In both this year and last year, only 2.5 hours of professional staff time were charged to Ms. Brinksi's account. If the company bases its predetermined overhead rate on the estimated overhead cost and the estimated professional staff hours to be charged to clients, how much overhead cost would have been applied to Ms. Brinksi's account last year? This year?

2. Suppose that the company bases its predetermined overhead rate on the estimated overhead cost and the estimated professional staff hours to be charged to clients as in (1) above. Also suppose that the actual professional staff hours charged to clients' accounts and the actual overhead costs turn out to be exactly as estimated in both years. How much unused capacity cost would the company report last year? How about for this year?

3. Refer back to the data concerning Ms. Brinksi in (1) above. If the company bases its predetermined overhead rate on the *professional staff hours available,* how much overhead cost would have been applied to Ms. Brinksi's account last year? This year?

4. Suppose that the company bases its predetermined overhead rate on the professional staff hours available as in (3) above. Also suppose that the actual professional staff hours charged to clients' accounts and the actual overhead costs turn out to be exactly as estimated in both years. How much unused capacity cost would the company report last year? How about for this year?

PROBLEM 2B–3 Predetermined Overhead Rate and Capacity LO2–1, LO2–2, LO2–6

Platinum Tracks, Inc., is a small audio recording studio located in Los Angeles. The company handles work for advertising agencies—primarily for radio ads—and has a few singers and bands as clients. Platinum Tracks handles all aspects of recording from editing to making a digital master from which CDs can be copied. The competition in the audio recording industry in Los Angeles has always been tough, but it has been getting even tougher over the last several years. The studio has been losing customers to newer studios that are equipped with more up-to-date equipment and that are able to offer very attractive prices and excellent service. Summary data concerning the last two years of operations follow:

	Last Year	This Year
Estimated hours of studio service	1,000	800
Estimated studio overhead cost	$160,000	$160,000
Actual hours of studio service provided	750	500
Actual studio overhead cost incurred	$160,000	$160,000
Hours of studio service at capacity	1,600	1,600

The company applies studio overhead to recording jobs on the basis of the hours of studio service provided. For example, 40 hours of studio time were required to record, edit, and master the *Verde Baja* music CD for a local Latino band. All of the studio overhead cost is fixed, and the actual overhead cost incurred was exactly as estimated at the beginning of the year in last year and this year.

Required:

1. Platinum Tracks computes its predetermined overhead rate at the beginning of each year based on the estimated studio overhead cost and the estimated hours of studio service for the year. Using this approach, how much overhead would have been applied to the Verde Baja job last year? How about this year?

2. The president of Platinum Tracks has heard that some companies in the industry have changed to a system of computing the predetermined overhead rate based on the hours of studio service that could be provided at capacity. He would like to know what effect this method would have on job costs. How much overhead would have been applied using this method to the Verde Baja job if it had been done last year? This year?

3. If Platinum Tracks computes its predetermined overhead rate based on the hours of studio service that could be provided at capacity as in (2) above, how much unused capacity cost would the company have incurred last year? This year?

4. What fundamental business problem is Platinum Tracks facing? Which method of computing the predetermined overhead rate is likely to be more helpful in facing this problem? Explain.

CASE 2B–4 Ethics; Predetermined Overhead Rate and Capacity LO2–2, LO2–6

Pat Miranda, the new controller of Vault Hard Drives, Inc., has just returned from a seminar on the choice of the activity level in the predetermined overhead rate. Even though the subject did not sound exciting at first, she found that there were some important ideas presented that should get a hearing at her company. After returning from the seminar, she arranged a meeting with the production manager, J. Stevens, and the assistant production manager, Marvin Washington.

Pat: I ran across an idea that I wanted to check out with both of you. It's about the way we compute predetermined overhead rates.

J.: We're all ears.

Pat: We compute the predetermined overhead rate by dividing the estimated total factory overhead for the coming year, which is all a fixed cost, by the estimated total units produced for the coming year.

Marvin: We've been doing that as long as I've been with the company.

J.: And it has been done that way at every other company I've worked at, except at most places they divide by direct labor-hours.

Pat: We use units because it is simpler and we basically make one product with minor variations. But, there's another way to do it. Instead of basing the overhead rate on the estimated total units produced for the coming year, we could base it on the total units produced at capacity.

Marvin: Oh, the Marketing Department will love that. It will drop the costs on all of our products. They'll go wild over there cutting prices.

Pat: That is a worry, but I wanted to talk to both of you first before going over to Marketing.

J.: Aren't you always going to have a lot of unused capacity costs?

Pat: That's correct, but let me show you how we would handle it. Here's an example based on our budget for next year.

Budgeted (estimated) production	160,000 units
Budgeted sales	160,000 units
Capacity	200,000 units
Selling price	$60 per unit
Variable manufacturing cost	$15 per unit
Total manufacturing overhead cost (all fixed)	$4,000,000
Selling and administrative expenses (all fixed)	$2,700,000
Beginning inventories	$0

Traditional Approach to Computation of the Predetermined Overhead Rate

$$\frac{\text{Estimated total manufacturing overhead cost, \$4,000,000}}{\text{Estimated total units produced, 160,000}} = \$25 \text{ per unit}$$

Budgeted Income Statement		
Revenue (160,000 units × $60 per unit)		$9,600,000
Cost of goods sold:		
Variable manufacturing (160,000 units × $15 per unit)	$2,400,000	
Manufacturing overhead applied		
(160,000 units × $25 per unit)	4,000,000	6,400,000
Gross margin		3,200,000
Selling and administrative expenses		2,700,000
Net operating income		$ 500,000

New Approach to Computation of the Predetermined Overhead Rate
Using Capacity in the Denominator

$$\frac{\text{Estimated total manufacturing overhead cost at capacity, \$4,000,000}}{\text{Total units at capacity, 200,000}} = \$20 \text{ per unit}$$

Budgeted Income Statement		
Revenue (160,000 units × $60 per unit)		$9,600,000
Cost of goods sold:		
Variable manufacturing (160,000 units × $15 per unit)	$2,400,000	
Manufacturing overhead applied		
(160,000 units × $20 per unit)	3,200,000	5,600,000
Gross margin		4,000,000
Cost of unused capacity [(200,000 units − 160,000 units)		
× $20 per unit]		800,000
Selling and administrative expenses		2,700,000
Net operating income		$ 500,000

J.: Whoa!! I don't think I like the looks of that "Cost of unused capacity." If that thing shows up on the income statement, someone from headquarters is likely to come down here looking for some people to lay off.

Marvin: I'm worried about something else too. What happens when sales are not up to expectations? Can we pull the "hat trick"?

Pat: I'm sorry, I don't understand.

J.: Marvin's talking about something that happens fairly regularly. When sales are down and profits look like they are going to be lower than the president told the owners they were going to be, the president comes down here and asks us to deliver some more profits.

Marvin: And we pull them out of our hat.

J.: Yeah, we just increase production until we get the profits we want.

Pat: I still don't understand. You mean you increase sales?

J.: Nope, we increase production. We're the production managers, not the sales managers.

Pat: I get it. Because you have produced more, the sales force has more units it can sell.

J.: Nope, the marketing people don't do a thing. We just build inventories and that does the trick.

Required:
In all of the questions below, assume that the predetermined overhead rate under the traditional method is $25 per unit, and under the new capacity-based method it is $20 per unit.

1. Assume actual sales is 150,000 units and the actual production in units, actual selling price, actual variable manufacturing cost per unit, and actual fixed costs all equal their respective budgeted amounts. Given these assumptions:
   a. Compute net operating income using the traditional income statement format.
   b. Compute net operating income using the new income statement format.
2. Assume that actual sales is 150,000 units and the actual selling price, actual variable manufacturing cost per unit, and actual fixed costs all equal their respective budgeted amounts. Under the traditional approach, how many units would have to be produced to realize net operating income of $500,000?
3. Assume that actual sales is 150,000 units and the actual selling price, actual variable manufacturing cost per unit, and actual fixed costs all equal their respective budgeted amounts. Under the new capacity-based approach, how many units would have to be produced to realize net operating income of $500,000?
4. What effect does the new capacity-based approach have on the volatility of net operating income?
5. Will the "hat trick" be easier or harder to perform if the new capacity-based method is used?
6. Do you think the "hat trick" is ethical?

Job-Order Costing: Cost Flows and External Reporting

Inventory Accounting at Toll Brothers

© Pixtal/AGE Fotostock

LEARNING OBJECTIVES

After studying Chapter 3, you should be able to:

LO3–1 Understand the flow of costs in a job-order costing system and prepare appropriate journal entries to record costs.

LO3–2 Use T-accounts to show the flow of costs in a job-order costing system.

LO3–3 Prepare schedules of cost of goods manufactured and cost of goods sold and an income statement.

LO3–4 Compute underapplied or overapplied overhead cost and prepare the journal entry to close the balance in Manufacturing Overhead to the appropriate accounts.

LO3–5 (Appendix 3A) Use Microsoft Excel to summarize the flow of costs in a job-order costing system.

Toll Brothers is one of America's largest home builders with annual revenues in excess of $3.9 billion. The company's inventory consists of land acquisition costs, land development costs, home construction costs, and overhead costs related to development and construction. In accordance with generally accepted accounting principles (GAAP), Toll Brothers treats its inventory as a long-lived asset rather than a current asset because its master planned communities can take up to 10 years to fully develop.

While Toll Brothers' industry has some unique attributes relative to most manufacturers, it is an industry well-suited for job-order costing. For example, each new home that the company builds can be accounted for as a job that gets assigned direct material costs (such as lumber, shingles, and bricks), direct labor (such as subcontracted electricians, plumbers, and roofers), and overhead costs (such as the costs of construction supervisors and the equipment that they use to perform their jobs). ∎

Chapter 2 discussed how companies use job-order costing to assign manufacturing costs to individual jobs. This chapter describes how companies use job-order costing to prepare a balance sheet and an income statement for external reporting purposes.

Exhibit 3–1 summarizes seven important vocabulary terms that were introduced in the previous chapter. Please take a moment to review these terms, each of which is included in the Glossary at the end of this chapter, because it will help you understand the forthcoming learning objectives.

EXHIBIT 3–1
Summary of Important Vocabulary Terms

Vocabulary Term	Definition
Job-order costing	A costing system used in situations where many different products, jobs, or services are produced each period.
Absorption costing	A costing method that includes all manufacturing costs—direct materials, direct labor, and both variable and fixed manufacturing overhead—in the cost of a product.
Allocation base	A measure of activity such as direct labor-hours or machine-hours that is used to assign costs to cost objects.
Predetermined overhead rate	A rate used to charge manufacturing overhead cost to jobs that is established in advance for each period. It is computed using the following equation: $$\text{Predetermined overhead rate} = \frac{\text{Estimated total manufacturing overhead cost}}{\text{Estimated total amount of the allocation base}}$$
Overhead application	The process of assigning overhead costs to specific jobs using the following formula: $$\begin{array}{l}\text{Overhead applied} \\ \text{to a particular job}\end{array} = \begin{array}{l}\text{Predetermined} \\ \text{overhead rate}\end{array} \times \begin{array}{l}\text{Amount of the allocation} \\ \text{base incurred by the job}\end{array}$$
Normal costing	A costing system in which overhead costs are applied to a job by multiplying a predetermined overhead rate by the actual amount of the allocation base incurred by the job.
Job cost sheet	A form that records the direct materials, direct labor, and manufacturing overhead cost charged to a job.

Job-Order Costing—The Flow of Costs

In Chapter 1, we used Exhibit 1–2 to illustrate the cost flows and classifications in a manufacturing company. Now we are going to use a similar version of that exhibit, as shown in Exhibit 3–2, to introduce the cost flows and classifications in a manufacturing company that uses job-order costing.

Exhibit 3–2 shows that in job-order costing a company's *product costs* flow through three inventory accounts on the balance sheet and then on to cost of goods sold in the income statement. More specifically, raw materials purchases are recorded in the *Raw Materials* inventory account. **Raw materials** include any materials that go into the final product. When raw materials are used in production as direct materials, their costs are transferred to *Work in Process* inventory.[1] **Work in process** consists of units of product that are only partially complete and will require further work before they are ready for sale to the customer. To transform direct materials into completed jobs, direct labor cost is added to Work in Process and manufacturing overhead cost is applied to Work in Process by multiplying the predetermined overhead rate by the actual quantity of the allocation base consumed by each job.[2] When jobs are completed, their costs are transferred

> **LO3–1**
> Understand the flow of costs in a job-order costing system and prepare appropriate journal entries to record costs.

---

[1] Indirect materials are accounted for as part of manufacturing overhead.

[2] For simplicity, Exhibit 3–2 assumes that Cost of Goods Sold does not need to be adjusted as discussed later in the chapter.

EXHIBIT 3–2
Cost Flows and Classifications in a Manufacturing Company That Uses Job-Order Costing

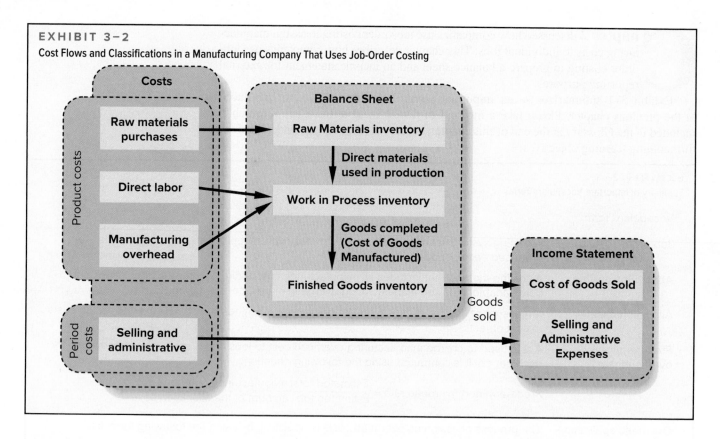

from Work in Process to *Finished Goods* inventory. **Finished goods** consist of completed units of product that have not yet been sold to customers.

The amount transferred from Work in Process to Finished Goods is referred to as the *cost of goods manufactured*. The **cost of goods manufactured** includes the manufacturing costs associated with units of product that were finished during the period. As jobs are sold, their costs are transferred from Finished Goods to Cost of Goods Sold. At this point, the various costs attached to each job are finally recorded as an expense on the income statement. Until that point, these costs are in inventory accounts on the balance sheet. Period costs (or selling and administrative expenses) do not flow through inventories on the balance sheet. They are recorded as expenses on the income statement in the period incurred.

To illustrate the cost flows within a job-order costing system, we will record Ruger Corporation's transactions for the month of April. Ruger is a producer of gold and silver commemorative medallions and it worked on only two jobs in April. Job A, a special minting of 1,000 gold medallions commemorating the invention of motion pictures, was started during March and completed in April. As of March 31, Job A had been assigned $30,000 in manufacturing costs, which corresponds with Ruger's Work in Process balance on April 1 of $30,000. Job B, an order for 10,000 silver medallions commemorating the fall of the Berlin Wall, was started in April and was incomplete at the end of the month.

The Purchase and Issue of Materials

On April 1, Ruger Corporation had $7,000 in raw materials on hand. During the month, the company purchased on account an additional $60,000 in raw materials. The purchase is recorded in journal entry (1) below:

(1)

Raw Materials	60,000	
Accounts Payable		60,000

Remember that Raw Materials is an asset account. Thus, when raw materials are purchased, they are initially recorded as an asset—not as an expense.

Issue of Direct and Indirect Materials   During April, *materials requisition forms* were prepared to authorize withdrawing $52,000 in raw materials from the storeroom for use in production. These raw materials included $50,000 of direct and $2,000 of indirect materials. Entry (2) records issuing the materials to the production departments.

(2)

Work in Process..	50,000	
Manufacturing Overhead............................	2,000	
Raw Materials.....................................		52,000

The materials charged to Work in Process represent direct materials for specific jobs. These costs are also recorded on the appropriate job cost sheets. This point is illustrated in Exhibit 3–3, where $28,000 of the $50,000 in direct materials is charged to Job A's cost sheet and the remaining $22,000 is charged to Job B's cost sheet. (In this example, all data are presented in summary form and the job cost sheet is abbreviated.)

The $2,000 charged to Manufacturing Overhead in entry (2) represents indirect materials. The debit side of the Manufacturing Overhead account is always used to record the actual manufacturing overhead costs, such as indirect materials, that are incurred during the period. The credit side of this account, as you will see in transaction (7), is always used to record the manufacturing overhead applied to work in process.

Before leaving Exhibit 3–3, we need to provide one additional comment. Notice from the exhibit that the job cost sheet for Job A contains a beginning balance of $30,000. We stated earlier that this balance represents the cost of work done during March that has been carried forward to April. Also note that the Work in Process account contains the same $30,000 balance. Thus, the Work in Process account summarizes all of the costs appearing on the job cost sheets of the jobs that are in process. Job A was the only job in process at the beginning of April, so the beginning balance in the Work in Process account equals Job A's beginning balance of $30,000.

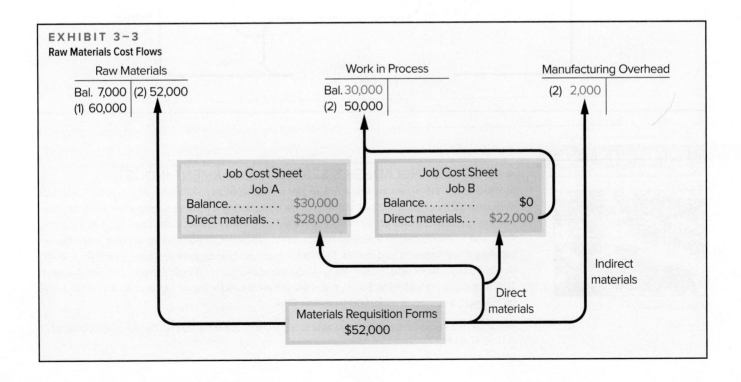

EXHIBIT 3–3
Raw Materials Cost Flows

Labor Cost

In April, the employee *time tickets* (which provide hourly summaries of each employee's activities throughout the day) included $60,000 recorded for direct labor and $15,000 for indirect labor. The following entry summarizes these costs:

(3)

Work in Process......................................	60,000	
Manufacturing Overhead..............................	15,000	
Salaries and Wages Payable........................		75,000

Only the direct labor cost of $60,000 is added to the Work in Process account. At the same time that direct labor costs are added to Work in Process, they are also added to the individual job cost sheets, as shown in Exhibit 3–4. During April, $40,000 of direct labor cost was charged to Job A and the remaining $20,000 was charged to Job B.

The $15,000 charged to Manufacturing Overhead represents the indirect labor costs of the period, such as supervision, janitorial work, and maintenance.

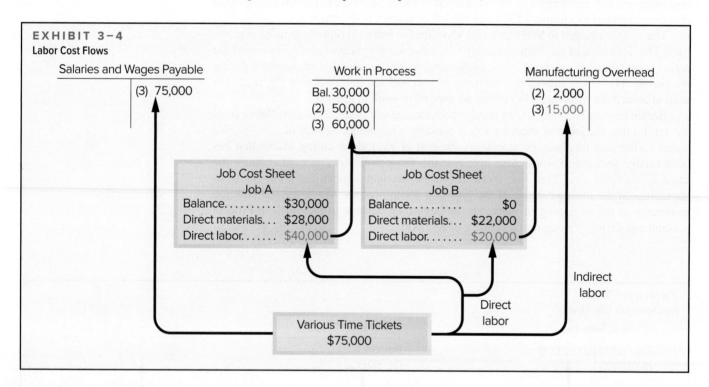

EXHIBIT 3–4
Labor Cost Flows

IN BUSINESS

© Joerg Boethling/Alamy

A LOOK AT BANGLADESH'S $20 BILLION GARMENT INDUSTRY

In Bangladesh the minimum wage is $38 per month. A highly-skilled sewing machine operator may earn as much as $100 per month before considering overtime. Companies such as **Fakir Apparels**, a T-shirt manufacturer in Bangladesh, can readily attract customers such as **Walmart**, **Gap**, and **Primark**, due to these low labor costs. However, in addition to serving mass market retailers, Fakir Apparels also makes T-shirts for premium brands such as **Tommy Hilfiger**, **Giorgio Armani**, **Hugo Boss**, and **G-Star Raw**. While the manufacturing cost for one of Fakir Apparels T-shirts ranges from $1.60 to $6.00, the retail selling prices for these T-shirts can vary from $6.00 (at Walmart) to as much as $91.00 (at G-Star Raw).

Source: Christina Passariello, Tripti Lahiri, Sean McLain, "Bangladesh's Tale of the T-Shirts," *The Wall Street Journal*, July 1, 2013, pp. B1 and B8.

Manufacturing Overhead Costs

Recall that all manufacturing costs other than direct materials and direct labor are classified as manufacturing overhead costs. These costs are entered directly into the Manufacturing Overhead account as they are incurred. To illustrate, assume that Ruger Corporation incurred the following general factory costs during April:

Utilities (heat, water, and power).	$21,000
Rent on factory equipment	16,000
Miscellaneous factory overhead costs	3,000
Total.	$40,000

The following entry records these costs:

(4)

Manufacturing Overhead.	40,000	
Accounts Payable*		40,000

---

*Accounts such as Cash may also be credited

In addition, assume that during April, Ruger Corporation recognized $13,000 in accrued property taxes and that $7,000 in prepaid insurance expired on factory buildings and equipment. The following entry records these items:

(5)

Manufacturing Overhead.	20,000	
Property Taxes Payable		13,000
Prepaid Insurance.		7,000

Finally, assume that the company recognized $18,000 in depreciation on factory equipment during April. The following entry records the accrual of this depreciation:

(6)

Manufacturing Overhead.	18,000	
Accumulated Depreciation		18,000

In short, all actual manufacturing overhead costs are debited to the Manufacturing Overhead account as they are incurred.

Applying Manufacturing Overhead

Because actual manufacturing overhead costs are charged to the Manufacturing Overhead account rather than to Work in Process, it begs the question how are manufacturing overhead costs assigned to Work in Process? The answer is, they are assigned by using the predetermined overhead rate—which is calculated by dividing the estimated total manufacturing overhead cost for the period by the estimated total amount of the allocation base. For example, if we assume that machine-hours is the allocation base, then overhead cost would be applied to jobs by multiplying the predetermined overhead rate by the number of machine-hours charged to each job.

To illustrate, assume that Ruger Corporation's predetermined overhead rate is $6 per machine-hour. Also assume that during April, 10,000 machine-hours were worked on Job A and 5,000 machine-hours were worked on Job B (a total of 15,000 machine-hours). Thus, $90,000 in overhead cost ($6 per machine-hour × 15,000 machine-hours = $90,000) would be applied to Work in Process. The following entry records the application of Manufacturing Overhead to Work in Process:

(7)

Work in Process.	90,000	
Manufacturing Overhead.		90,000

The flow of costs through the Manufacturing Overhead account is shown in Exhibit 3–5. The actual overhead costs on the debit side in the Manufacturing Overhead account in Exhibit 3–5 are the costs that were added to the account in entries (2)–(6). Observe that recording these actual overhead costs [entries (2)–(6)] and the application of overhead to Work in Process [entry (7)] represent two separate and entirely distinct processes.

The Concept of a Clearing Account   The Manufacturing Overhead account operates as a clearing account. As we have noted, actual manufacturing overhead costs are debited to the account as they are incurred throughout the year. When jobs are completed (or at the end of an accounting period), overhead cost is applied to the jobs using the predetermined overhead rate—Work in Process is debited and Manufacturing Overhead is credited. This sequence of events is illustrated below:

Manufacturing Overhead
(a clearing account)

Actual overhead costs are charged to this account as they are incurred throughout the period.	Overhead is applied to Work in Process using the predetermined overhead rate.

As we emphasized earlier, the predetermined overhead rate is based entirely on estimates of what the level of activity and overhead costs are *expected* to be, and it is established before the year begins. As a result, the overhead cost applied during a year will almost certainly turn out to be more or less than the actual overhead cost incurred. For example, notice from Exhibit 3–5 that Ruger Corporation's actual overhead costs for the period are $5,000 greater than the overhead cost that has been applied to Work in Process, resulting in a $5,000 debit balance in the Manufacturing Overhead account. We will reserve discussion of what to do with this $5,000 balance until later in the chapter.

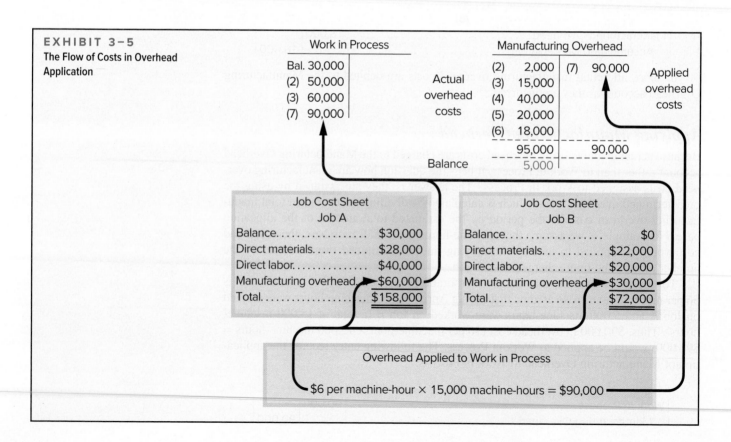

EXHIBIT 3–5
The Flow of Costs in Overhead Application

For the moment, we can conclude from Exhibit 3–5 that the cost of a completed job consists of the actual direct materials cost of the job, the actual direct labor cost of the job, and the manufacturing overhead cost *applied* to the job. Pay particular attention to the following subtle but important point: *Actual overhead costs are not charged to jobs; actual overhead costs do not appear on the job cost sheet nor do they appear in the Work in Process account. Only the applied overhead cost, based on the predetermined overhead rate, appears on the job cost sheet and in the Work in Process account.*

USING TECHNOLOGY TO IMPROVE MANUFACTURING EFFICIENCY

Roland DG, a Japanese manufacturer that employs 966 people, has developed an advanced production system that it refers to as D-shop. This technology-intensive system enables a single worker to assemble products from start to finish. Each worker refers to a computer screen that provides step-by-step instructions accompanied by 3-D drawings to properly assemble products. A computerized rotating parts rack automatically rotates to the appropriate component part for each step in the assembly process. Digital screwdrivers monitor how many times and how tightly screws are turned. The computer screen does not advance to the next step until the correct screws are turned the pre-specified number of times.

Thus far, the D-shop has increased the company's productivity by 60% with a long-term goal of doubling productivity. In essence, Roland has developed an innovative production method that invests in automated manufacturing overhead costs to reduce the direct labor cost per unit produced.

© igor terekhov/Alamy

Source: Mayumi Negishi, "No More Assembly Line," *The Wall Street Journal*, June 2, 2014, p. R3.

Nonmanufacturing Costs

In addition to manufacturing costs, companies also incur selling and administrative costs. These costs should be treated as period expenses and charged directly to the income statement. *Nonmanufacturing costs should not go into the Manufacturing Overhead account.* To illustrate the correct treatment of nonmanufacturing costs, assume that Ruger Corporation incurred $30,000 in selling and administrative salary costs during April. The following entry summarizes the accrual of those salaries:

(8)

Salaries Expense.....................................	30,000	
Salaries and Wages Payable........................		30,000

Assume that depreciation on office equipment during April was $7,000. The entry is as follows:

(9)

Depreciation Expense	7,000	
Accumulated Depreciation		7,000

Pay particular attention to the difference between this entry and entry (6) where we recorded depreciation on factory equipment. In journal entry (6), depreciation on factory equipment was debited to Manufacturing Overhead and is therefore a product cost. In journal entry (9) above, depreciation on office equipment is debited to Depreciation Expense. Depreciation on office equipment is a period expense rather than a product cost.

Finally, assume that advertising was $42,000 and that other selling and administrative expenses in April totaled $8,000. The following entry records these items:

(10)

Advertising Expense..................................	42,000	
Other Selling and Administrative Expense	8,000	
Accounts Payable*		50,000

*Other accounts such as Cash may also be credited

The amounts in entries (8) through (10) are recorded directly into expense accounts—they have no effect on product costs. The same will be true of any other selling and administrative expenses incurred during April, including sales commissions, depreciation on sales equipment, rent on office facilities, insurance on office facilities, and related costs.

Cost of Goods Manufactured

When a job has been completed, the finished output is transferred from the production departments to the finished goods warehouse. By this time, the accounting department will have charged the job with direct materials and direct labor cost, and manufacturing overhead will have been applied using the predetermined overhead rate. A transfer of costs is made within the costing system that *parallels* the physical transfer of goods to the finished goods warehouse. The costs of the completed job are transferred out of the Work in Process account and into the Finished Goods account. The sum of all amounts transferred between these two accounts represents the *cost of goods manufactured* for the period.

In the case of Ruger Corporation, remember that Job A was completed during April and Job B was incomplete at the end of the month. Thus, the following entry transfers the cost of Job A from Work in Process to Finished Goods:

(11)

Finished Goods	158,000	
Work in Process.		158,000

The $158,000 represents the completed cost of Job A, as shown on the job cost sheet in Exhibit 3–5. Because Job A was the only job completed during April, the $158,000 also represents the cost of goods manufactured for the month.

Because Job B was not completed by the end of the month, its assigned costs will remain in Work in Process and carry over to the next month. If a balance sheet were prepared at the end of April, the cost accumulated thus far on Job B ($72,000) would appear in the asset account Work in Process.

Cost of Goods Sold

As completed jobs are shipped to customers, their accumulated costs are transferred from Finished Goods to Cost of Goods Sold. If an entire job is shipped at one time, then the entire cost appearing on the job cost sheet is transferred to Cost of Goods Sold. However, sometimes only a portion of the units involved in a particular job will be immediately sold. In these situations, the unit product cost must be used to determine how much product cost should be removed from Finished Goods and charged to Cost of Goods Sold.

For Ruger Corporation, we will assume 750 of the 1,000 gold medallions in Job A were shipped to customers by the end of the month for total sales revenue of $225,000. Because 1,000 units were produced and the total cost of the job from the job cost sheet was $158,000, the unit product cost was $158. The following journal entries would record the sale (all sales were on account):

(12)

Accounts Receivable	225,000	
Sales		225,000

(13)

Cost of Goods Sold.	118,500	
Finished Goods		118,500
(750 units × $158 per unit = $118,500)		

Entry (13) completes the flow of costs through the job-order costing system. To pull the entire Ruger Corporation example together, journal entries (1) through (13) are summarized in Exhibit 3–6. In addition, Exhibit 3–7 presents the flow of costs through the accounts in T-account form.

LO3–2
Use T-accounts to show the flow of costs in a job-order costing system.

EXHIBIT 3–6
Summary of Journal Entries—Ruger Corporation

(1)

Raw Materials	60,000	
Accounts Payable		60,000

(2)

Work in Process	50,000	
Manufacturing Overhead	2,000	
Raw Materials		52,000

(3)

Work in Process	60,000	
Manufacturing Overhead	15,000	
Salaries and Wages Payable		75,000

(4)

Manufacturing Overhead	40,000	
Accounts Payable		40,000

(5)

Manufacturing Overhead	20,000	
Property Taxes Payable		13,000
Prepaid Insurance		7,000

(6)

Manufacturing Overhead	18,000	
Accumulated Depreciation		18,000

(7)

Work in Process	90,000	
Manufacturing Overhead		90,000

(8)

Salaries Expense	30,000	
Salaries and Wages Payable		30,000

(9)

Depreciation Expense	7,000	
Accumulated Depreciation		7,000

(10)

Advertising Expense	42,000	
Other Selling and Administrative Expense	8,000	
Accounts Payable		50,000

(11)

Finished Goods	158,000	
Work in Process		158,000

(12)

Accounts Receivable	225,000	
Sales		225,000

(13)

Cost of Goods Sold	118,500	
Finished Goods		118,500

EXHIBIT 3-7
Summary of Cost Flows—Ruger Corporation

Accounts Receivable

| Bal. | XX | |
| (12) | 225,000 | |

Prepaid Insurance

| Bal. | XX | | |
| | | (5) | 7,000 |

Raw Materials

Bal.	7,000	(2)	52,000
(1)	60,000		
Bal.	15,000		

Work in Process

Bal.	30,000	(11)	158,000
(2)	50,000		
(3)	60,000		
(7)	90,000		
Bal.	72,000		

Finished Goods

Bal.	0	(13)	118,500
(11)	158,000		
Bal.	39,500		

Accumulated Depreciation

		Bal.	XX
		(6)	18,000
		(9)	7,000

Manufacturing Overhead

(2)	2,000	(7)	90,000
(3)	15,000		
(4)	40,000		
(5)	20,000		
(6)	18,000		
	95,000		90,000
Bal.	5,000		

Accounts Payable

		Bal.	XX
		(1)	60,000
		(4)	40,000
		(10)	50,000

Salaries and Wages Payable

		Bal.	XX
		(3)	75,000
		(8)	30,000

Property Taxes Payable

| | | Bal. | XX |
| | | (5) | 13,000 |

Sales

| | | (12) | 225,000 |

Cost of Goods Sold

| (13) | 118,500 | |

Salaries Expense

| (8) | 30,000 | |

Depreciation Expense

| (9) | 7,000 | |

Advertising Expense

| (10) | 42,000 | |

Other Selling and Administrative Expense

| (10) | 8,000 | |

Explanation of entries:
(1) Raw materials purchased.
(2) Direct and indirect materials issued into production.
(3) Direct and indirect factory labor cost incurred.
(4) Utilities and other factory costs incurred.
(5) Property taxes and insurance incurred on the factory.
(6) Depreciation recorded on factory assets.
(7) Overhead cost applied to Work in Process.
(8) Administrative salaries expense incurred.
(9) Depreciation recorded on office equipment.
(10) Advertising and other selling and administrative expense incurred.
(11) Cost of goods manufactured transferred to finished goods.
(12) Sale of Job A recorded.
(13) Cost of goods sold recorded for Job A.

Schedules of Cost of Goods Manufactured and Cost of Goods Sold

This section uses the Ruger Corporation example to explain how to prepare schedules of cost of goods manufactured and cost of goods sold as well as an income statement. The **schedule of cost of goods manufactured** contains three elements of product costs—direct materials, direct labor, and manufacturing overhead—and it summarizes the portions of those costs that remain in ending Work in Process inventory and that are transferred out of Work in Process into Finished Goods. The **schedule of cost of goods sold** also contains three elements of product costs—direct materials, direct labor, and manufacturing overhead—and it summarizes the portions of those costs that remain in ending Finished Goods inventory and that are transferred out of Finished Goods into Cost of Goods Sold.

Exhibit 3–8 presents Ruger Corporation's schedules of cost of goods manufactured and cost of goods sold. We want to draw your attention to three equations that are embedded within the schedule of cost of goods manufactured. First, the *raw materials used in production* are computed using the following equation:

LO3–3
Prepare schedules of cost of goods manufactured and cost of goods sold and an income statement.

$$\text{Raw materials used in production} = \text{Beginning raw materials inventory} + \text{Purchases of raw materials} - \text{Ending raw materials inventory}$$

For Ruger Corporation, the beginning raw materials inventory of $7,000 plus the purchases of raw materials of $60,000 minus the ending raw materials inventory of $15,000

EXHIBIT 3–8
Schedules of Cost of Goods Manufactured and Cost of Goods Sold

Cost of Goods Manufactured

Direct materials:

Beginning raw materials inventory	$ 7,000	
Add: Purchases of raw materials	60,000	
Total raw materials available	67,000	
Deduct: Ending raw materials inventory	15,000	
Raw materials used in production	52,000	
Deduct: Indirect materials included in manufacturing overhead	2,000	$ 50,000
Direct labor		60,000
Manufacturing overhead applied to work in process		90,000
Total manufacturing costs		200,000
Add: Beginning work in process inventory		30,000
		230,000
Deduct: Ending work in process inventory		72,000
Cost of goods manufactured		$158,000

Cost of Goods Sold

Beginning finished goods inventory		$ 0
Add: Cost of goods manufactured		158,000
Cost of goods available for sale		158,000
Deduct: Ending finished goods inventory		39,500
Unadjusted cost of goods sold		118,500
Add: Underapplied overhead		5,000
Adjusted cost of goods sold		$123,500

*Note that the underapplied overhead is added to cost of goods sold. If overhead were overapplied, it would be deducted from cost of goods sold.

equals the raw materials used in production of $52,000. Second, the *total manufacturing costs* are computed using the following equation:

$$\text{Total manufacturing costs} = \text{Direct materials} + \text{Direct labor} + \text{Manufacturing overhead applied to work in process}$$

For Ruger Corporation, the direct materials of $50,000 plus the direct labor of $60,000 plus the manufacturing overhead applied to work in process of $90,000 equals the total manufacturing costs of $200,000. Notice, the direct materials used in production ($50,000) is included in total manufacturing costs instead of raw materials purchases ($60,000). The direct materials used in production will usually differ from the amount of raw material purchases when the raw materials inventory balance changes or indirect materials are withdrawn from raw materials inventory. You should also make a note that *this equation includes manufacturing overhead applied to work in process rather than actual manufacturing overhead costs.* For Ruger Corporation, its manufacturing overhead applied to work in process of $90,000 is computed by multiplying the predetermined overhead rate of $6 per machine-hour by the actual amount of the allocation base recorded on all jobs, or 15,000 machine-hours. *The actual manufacturing overhead costs incurred during the period are not added to the Work in Process account.*

The third equation included in the schedule of cost of goods manufactured relates to computing the cost of goods manufactured:

$$\text{Cost of goods manufactured} = \text{Total manufacturing costs} + \text{Beginning work in process inventory} - \text{Ending work in process inventory}$$

For Ruger, the total manufacturing costs of $200,000 plus the beginning work in process inventory of $30,000 minus the ending work in process inventory of $72,000 equals the cost of goods manufactured of $158,000. The cost of goods manufactured represents the cost of the goods completed during the period and transferred from Work in Process to Finished Goods.

The schedule of cost of goods sold shown in Exhibit 3–8 relies on the following equation to compute the unadjusted cost of goods sold:

$$\text{Unadjusted cost of goods sold} = \text{Beginning finished goods inventory} + \text{Cost of goods manufactured} - \text{Ending finished goods inventory}$$

The beginning finished goods inventory ($0) plus the cost of goods manufactured ($158,000) equals the cost of goods available for sale ($158,000). The cost of goods available for sale ($158,000) minus the ending finished goods inventory ($39,500) equals the unadjusted cost of goods sold ($118,500). Finally, the unadjusted cost of goods sold ($118,500) plus the underapplied overhead ($5,000) equals adjusted cost of goods sold ($123,500). The next section of the chapter takes a closer look at why cost of goods sold needs to be adjusted for the amount of underapplied or overapplied overhead.

Exhibit 3–9 presents Ruger Corporation's income statement for April. Notice that the cost of goods sold on this statement is carried over from Exhibit 3–8. The selling and administrative expenses (which total $87,000) did not flow through the schedules of cost of goods manufactured and cost of goods sold. Journal entries 8–10 show that these items were immediately debited to expense accounts rather than being debited to inventory accounts.

EXHIBIT 3–9
Income Statement

Ruger Corporation Income Statement For the Month Ending April 30		
Sales		$225,000
Cost of goods sold ($118,500 + $5,000).		123,500
Gross margin		101,500
Selling and administrative expenses:		
Salaries expense.	$30,000	
Depreciation expense	7,000	
Advertising expense.	42,000	
Other expense.	8,000	87,000
Net operating income.		$ 14,500

Underapplied and Overapplied Overhead—A Closer Look

This section explains how to compute underapplied and overapplied overhead and how to dispose of any balance remaining in the Manufacturing Overhead account at the end of a period.

Computing Underapplied and Overapplied Overhead

Because the predetermined overhead rate is established before the period begins and is based entirely on estimated data, the overhead cost applied to Work in Process will generally differ from the amount of overhead cost actually incurred. In the case of Ruger Corporation, for example, the predetermined overhead rate of $6 per machine-hour was used to apply $90,000 of overhead cost to Work in Process, whereas actual overhead costs for April proved to be $95,000 (see Exhibit 3–5). The difference between the overhead cost applied to Work in Process and the actual overhead costs of a period is called either **underapplied overhead** or **overapplied overhead**. For Ruger Corporation, overhead was underapplied by $5,000 because the applied cost ($90,000) was $5,000 less than the actual cost ($95,000). If the situation had been reversed and the company had applied $95,000 in overhead cost to Work in Process while incurring actual overhead cost of only $90,000, then the overhead would have been overapplied.

What is the cause of underapplied or overapplied overhead? Basically, the method of applying overhead to jobs using a predetermined overhead rate assumes that actual overhead costs will be proportional to the actual amount of the allocation base incurred during the period. If, for example, the predetermined overhead rate is $6 per machine-hour, then it is assumed that actual overhead costs incurred will be $6 for every machine-hour that is actually worked. There are at least two reasons why this may not be true. First, much of the overhead often consists of fixed costs that do not change as the number of machine-hours incurred goes up or down. Second, spending on overhead items may or may not be under control. If individuals who are responsible for overhead costs do a good job, those costs should be less than were expected at the beginning of the period. If they do a poor job, those costs will be more than expected.

To illustrate these concepts, suppose that two companies—Turbo Crafters and Black & Howell—have prepared the following estimated data for the coming year:

	Turbo Crafters	Black & Howell
Allocation base	Machine-hours	Direct materials cost
Estimated manufacturing overhead cost (a).	$300,000	$120,000
Estimated total amount of the allocation base (b)	75,000 machine-hours	$80,000 direct materials cost
Predetermined overhead rate (a) ÷ (b).	$4 per machine-hour	150% of direct materials cost

Note that when the allocation base is dollars (such as direct materials cost in the case of Black & Howell) the predetermined overhead rate is expressed as a percentage of the allocation base. When dollars are divided by dollars, the result is a percentage.

Now assume that because of unexpected changes in overhead spending and unit sales, the *actual* overhead cost incurred and the actual amount of the allocation base used during the year in each company are as follows:

	Turbo Crafters	Black & Howell
Actual manufacturing overhead cost...................	$290,000	$130,000
Actual total amount of the allocation base..............	68,000 machine-hours	$90,000 direct materials cost

Given this actual data and each company's predetermined overhead rate, the manufacturing overhead applied to Work in Process during the year would be computed as follows:

	Turbo Crafters	Black & Howell
Predetermined overhead rate (a)....................	$4 per machine-hour	150% of direct materials cost
Actual total amount of the allocation base (b)........	68,000 machine-hours	$90,000 direct materials cost
Manufacturing overhead applied (a) × (b)............	$272,000	$135,000

This results in underapplied and overapplied overhead as shown below:

	Turbo Crafters	Black & Howell
Actual manufacturing overhead cost.............	$290,000	$130,000
Manufacturing overhead applied................	272,000	135,000
Underapplied (overapplied) manufacturing overhead..................................	$ 18,000	$ (5,000)

For Turbo Crafters, the overhead cost applied to Work in Process of $272,000 is less than the actual overhead cost for the year of $290,000; therefore, overhead is underapplied by $18,000.

For Black & Howell, the overhead cost applied to Work in Process of $135,000 is greater than the actual overhead cost for the year of $130,000, so overhead is overapplied by $(5,000).

A summary of these concepts is presented in Exhibit 3–10.

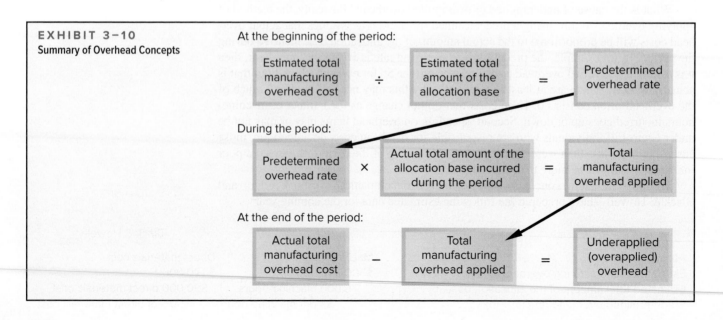

EXHIBIT 3–10
Summary of Overhead Concepts

At the beginning of the period:

Estimated total manufacturing overhead cost ÷ Estimated total amount of the allocation base = Predetermined overhead rate

During the period:

Predetermined overhead rate × Actual total amount of the allocation base incurred during the period = Total manufacturing overhead applied

At the end of the period:

Actual total manufacturing overhead cost − Total manufacturing overhead applied = Underapplied (overapplied) overhead

Disposition of Underapplied or Overapplied Overhead Balances

The Turbo Crafters and Black & Howell examples demonstrate one way to calculate underapplied or overapplied overhead. However, another equivalent method of determining the amount of underapplied or overapplied overhead is to properly analyze the Manufacturing Overhead T-account. Explaining this second method also enables us to discuss the topic of preparing a journal entry to dispose of underapplied or overapplied overhead for financial reporting purposes.

If we return to the Ruger Corporation example and look at the Manufacturing Overhead T-account in Exhibit 3–7, you will see that there is a debit balance of $5,000. Remember that debit entries to this account represent actual overhead costs, whereas credit entries represent applied overhead costs. In this case, the applied overhead costs (the credits) are less than the actual overhead costs (the debits) by $5,000—hence, the debit balance indicates that manufacturing overhead is underapplied. In other words, if there is a *debit* balance in the Manufacturing Overhead account of X dollars, then the overhead is *underapplied* by X dollars. On the other hand, if there is a *credit* balance in the Manufacturing Overhead account of Y dollars, then the overhead is *overapplied* by Y dollars.

Once we have quantified the amount of underapplied or overapplied overhead, the corresponding amount remaining in the Manufacturing Overhead account at the end of a period must be disposed of in one of two ways:

1. It can be closed to Cost of Goods Sold.
2. It can be closed proportionally to Work in Process, Finished Goods, and Cost of Goods Sold.

Closed to Cost of Goods Sold   Closing the balance in Manufacturing Overhead to Cost of Goods Sold is the simpler of the two methods. In the Ruger Corporation example, the entry to close the $5,000 of underapplied overhead to Cost of Goods Sold is:

(14)

Cost of Goods Sold......................................	5,000	
Manufacturing Overhead...............................		5,000

Note that because the Manufacturing Overhead account has a debit balance, Manufacturing Overhead must be credited to close out the account. This has the effect of increasing April's Cost of Goods Sold by $5,000 as shown below:

Unadjusted cost of goods sold [from entry (13)]	$118,500
Add underapplied overhead [from entry (14)]	5,000
Adjusted cost of goods sold	$123,500

Ruger Corporation's adjusted cost of goods sold of $123,500 as shown here agrees with the company's income statement that was presented earlier in Exhibit 3–9.

Keep in mind that unadjusted cost of goods sold is based on the amount of manufacturing overhead cost applied to jobs, not the amount of actual manufacturing overhead cost incurred. So, when overhead is underapplied it means two things—not enough overhead cost was applied to jobs and the cost of goods sold is understated. Adding the underapplied overhead to the cost of goods sold corrects this understatement.

Closed Proportionally to Work in Process, Finished Goods, and Cost of Goods Sold   Closing underapplied or overapplied overhead proportionally to Work in Process, Finished Goods, and Cost of Goods Sold is more accurate than closing the entire balance into Cost of Goods Sold; however, it is also more complex. We'll explain the proportional allocation of underapplied or overapplied overhead using a three-step process.

The first step is to take the total overhead cost applied to production during the period and break it into three pieces—the portion included in Work in Process at the end of the period, the portion included in Finished Goods at the end of the period, and the portion applied to Cost of Goods Sold during the period. The second step is to state each of these three amounts as a percent of the total overhead cost applied to production during the period. The third step is to derive the amounts needed for the journal entry by multiplying the percentages from step two by the amount of underapplied or overapplied overhead.

Exhibit 3–11 illustrates this three-step process for Ruger Corporation. As you may remember, Ruger worked on only two jobs in April—Job A and Job B. Job A consisted of

EXHIBIT 3–11
Ruger Corporation: Closing Underapplied Overhead Proportionally to Work in Process, Finished Goods, and Cost of Goods Sold

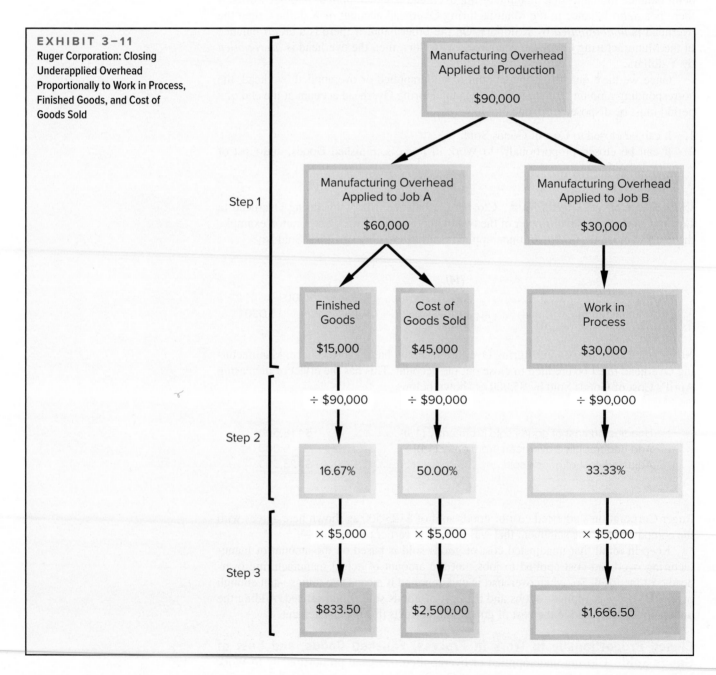

1,000 gold medallions, 750 of which were sold to customers and 250 of which remained in Finished Goods at the end of the month. Job B consisted of 10,000 silver medallions and it was incomplete at the end of April.

In step one of Exhibit 3–11, Ruger takes its total manufacturing overhead applied to production from Exhibit 3–5 ($90,000) and splits it between Job A ($60,000) and Job B ($30,000). Because Job B was incomplete at the end of April, all of its applied overhead cost ($30,000) resides in Work in Process at the end of the month, whereas the $60,000 of overhead cost applied to Job A needs to be split into two accounts. A total of 25% of Job A's gold medallions (= 250 ÷ 1,000) were in Finished Goods at the end of April; therefore, 25% of Job A's applied overhead cost, or $15,000 (= $60,000 × 25%), also remains in Finished Goods. Similarly, 75% of Job A's gold medallions (= 750 ÷ 1,000) were sold during April; thus, 75% of Job A's applied overhead cost, or $45,000 (= $60,000 × 75%), is included in Cost of Goods Sold.

In step 2 of Exhibit 3–11, the amounts of applied overhead cost in Work in Process ($30,000), Finished Goods ($15,000), and Cost of Goods Sold ($45,000) are each stated as a percent of the total manufacturing overhead cost applied to production during the period ($90,000). In other words, 33.33% of the period's total applied overhead cost resides in Work in Process at the end of April. Similarly, 16.67% of the total remains in Finished Goods and 50% is included in Cost of Goods Sold.

Step 3 from Exhibit 3–11 uses the percentages from step 2 to proportionally allocate the $5,000 of underapplied overhead to Work in Process, Finished Goods, and Cost of Goods Sold. Work in Process is allocated $1,666.50 of underapplied overhead, whereas Finished Goods and Cost of Goods Sold are allocated $833.50 and $2,500, respectively. Using these dollar amounts, the journal entry would be recorded as follows:

Work in Process...............................	1,666.50	
Finished Goods	833.50	
Cost of Goods Sold...........................	2,500.00	
Manufacturing Overhead.....................		5,000.00

Note that the $5,000 credit to Manufacturing Overhead ensures that this account concludes the month with a zero balance. Furthermore, it bears emphasizing that if Ruger's overhead had been overapplied rather than underapplied, the entry above would have been just the reverse. The Manufacturing Overhead account would have had a credit balance, thus necessitating a reversal of the debits and credits shown above.

Comparing the Two Methods for Disposing of Underapplied or Overapplied Overhead

Closing the underapplied or overapplied overhead to Work in Process, Finished Goods, and Cost of Goods Sold is more accurate than the simpler approach of closing it out to Cost of Goods Sold. For example, the simpler approach overstates Ruger Corporation's Cost of Goods Sold by $2,500 (= $5,000 – $2,500) and understates its net operating income by the same amount.

A General Model of Product Cost Flows

Exhibit 3–12 presents a T-account model of the flow of manufacturing costs in a job-order costing system. This model can be very helpful in understanding how manufacturing costs flow through a normal costing system and finally end up as Cost of Goods Sold on the income statement.

EXHIBIT 3–12
A General Model of Cost Flows (Using Normal Costing)

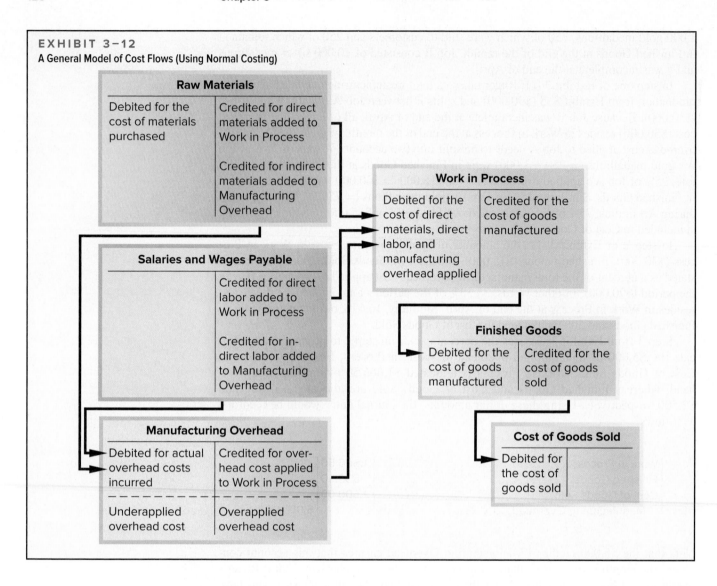

Summary

Perhaps the most important concept to understand in this chapter is the flow of costs for manufacturers. Raw materials purchased from suppliers are stored in raw materials inventory until requisitioned for use in production. Direct materials are added to work in process along with direct labor and applied overhead. Once units of production are complete, their manufacturing costs are transferred from Work in Process to Finished Goods. When units of production are sold their associated costs are transferred from Finished Goods to Cost of Goods Sold on the income statement. Selling and administrative expenses are not attached to units of production. Instead, they are recorded as expenses on the income statement as incurred.

Manufacturing overhead costs are applied to jobs using a predetermined overhead rate. Because the predetermined overhead rate is based on estimates, the actual overhead cost incurred during a period may be more or less than the amount of overhead cost applied to production. Such a difference is referred to as underapplied or overapplied overhead. The underapplied or overapplied overhead for a period can be either closed out to Cost of Goods Sold or closed proportionally to Work in Process, Finished Goods, and Cost of Goods Sold. When overhead is underapplied, manufacturing overhead costs have been understated and therefore inventories and/or cost of goods sold must be adjusted upwards. When overhead is overapplied, manufacturing overhead costs have been overstated and therefore inventories and/or cost of goods sold must be adjusted downwards.

Review Problem: The Flow of Costs in a Job-Order Costing System

Hogle Corporation is a manufacturer that uses job-order costing. On January 1, the company's inventory balances were as follows:

Raw materials......................	$20,000
Work in process....................	$15,000
Finished goods	$30,000

The company applies overhead cost to jobs on the basis of machine-hours worked. For the current year, the company's predetermined overhead rate was based on a cost formula that estimated $450,000 of total manufacturing overhead for an estimated activity level of 75,000 machine-hours. The following transactions were recorded for the year:

a. Raw materials were purchased on account, $410,000.
b. Raw materials were used in production, $380,000 ($360,000 direct materials and $20,000 indirect materials).
c. The following costs were accrued for employee services: direct labor, $75,000; indirect labor, $110,000; sales commissions, $90,000; and administrative salaries, $200,000.
d. Sales travel costs (on account) were $17,000.
e. Utility costs (on account) in the factory were $43,000.
f. Advertising costs (on account) were $180,000.
g. Depreciation was recorded for the year, $350,000 (80% relates to factory assets, and 20% relates to selling and administrative assets).
h. Insurance expired during the year, $10,000 (70% relates to factory operations, and the remaining 30% relates to selling and administrative activities).
i. Manufacturing overhead was applied to production. Due to greater than expected demand for its products, the company worked 80,000 machine-hours on all jobs during the year.
j. Jobs costing $900,000 to manufacture according to their job cost sheets were completed during the year.
k. Jobs were sold on account to customers during the year for a total of $1,500,000. The jobs cost $870,000 to manufacture according to their job cost sheets.

Required:
1. Prepare journal entries to record the preceding transactions.
2. Post the entries in (1) above to T-accounts (don't forget to enter the beginning balances in the inventory accounts).
3. Is Manufacturing Overhead underapplied or overapplied for the year? Prepare a journal entry to close any balance in the Manufacturing Overhead account to Cost of Goods Sold. Do not allocate the balance between Work in Process, Finished Goods, and Cost of Goods Sold.
4. Prepare an income statement for the year.

Solution to Review Problem

1.	a.	Raw Materials	410,000	
		Accounts Payable...............................		410,000
	b.	Work in Process	360,000	
		Manufacturing Overhead	20,000	
		Raw Materials		380,000
	c.	Work in Process	75,000	
		Manufacturing Overhead	110,000	
		Sales Commissions Expense	90,000	
		Administrative Salaries Expense	200,000	
		Salaries and Wages Payable........................		475,000
	d.	Sales Travel Expense	17,000	
		Accounts Payable................................		17,000
	e.	Manufacturing Overhead	43,000	
		Accounts Payable................................		43,000
	f.	Advertising Expense	180,000	
		Accounts Payable................................		180,000

g. Manufacturing Overhead   280,000
        Depreciation Expense   70,000
            Accumulated Depreciation.   350,000
h. Manufacturing Overhead   7,000
        Insurance Expense   3,000
        Prepaid Insurance.   10,000

i. The predetermined overhead rate for the year is computed as follows:

$$\frac{\text{Predetermined}}{\text{overhead rate}} = \frac{\text{Estimated total manufacturing overhead cost}}{\text{Estimated total amount of the allocation base}}$$

$$= \frac{\$450,000}{75,000 \text{ machine-hours}}$$

$$= \$6 \text{ per machine-hour}$$

Based on the 80,000 machine-hours actually worked during the year, the company applied $480,000 in overhead cost to production: $6 per machine-hour × 80,000 machine-hours = $480,000. The following entry records this application of overhead cost:

Work in Process   480,000
    Manufacturing Overhead   480,000
j. Finished Goods   900,000
        Work in Process   900,000
k. Accounts Receivable   1,500,000
        Sales.   1,500,000
    Cost of Goods Sold   870,000
        Finished Goods   870,000

2.

Accounts Receivable

(k)	1,500,000		

Prepaid Insurance

		(h)	10,000

Raw Materials

Bal.	20,000	(b)	380,000
(a)	410,000		
Bal.	50,000		

Work in Process

Bal.	15,000	(j)	900,000
(b)	360,000		
(c)	75,000		
(i)	480,000		
Bal.	30,000		

Finished Goods

Bal.	30,000	(k)	870,000
(j)	900,000		
Bal.	60,000		

Manufacturing Overhead

(b)	20,000	(i)	480,000
(c)	110,000		
(e)	43,000		
(g)	280,000		
(h)	7,000		
	460,000		480,000
		Bal.	20,000

Accumulated Depreciation

		(g)	350,000

Accounts Payable

		(a)	410,000
		(d)	17,000
		(e)	43,000
		(f)	180,000

Salaries and Wages Payable

		(c)	475,000

Sales

		(k)	1,500,000

Cost of Goods Sold

(k)	870,000		

Sales Commissions Expense

(c)	90,000		

Administrative Salaries Expense

(c)	200,000		

Sales Travel Expense

(d)	17,000		

Advertising Expense

(f)	180,000		

Depreciation Expense

(g)	70,000		

Insurance Expense

(h)	3,000		

3. Manufacturing overhead is overapplied for the year. The entry to close it out to Cost of Goods Sold is as follows:

Manufacturing Overhead   20,000
   Cost of Goods Sold   20,000

4.

Hogle Corporation Income Statement For the Year Ended December 31		
Sales		$1,500,000
Cost of goods sold ($870,000 − $20,000)		850,000
Gross margin		650,000
Selling and administrative expenses:		
Sales commissions expense	$ 90,000	
Administrative salaries expense	200,000	
Sales travel expense	17,000	
Advertising expense	180,000	
Depreciation expense	70,000	
Insurance expense	3,000	560,000
Net operating income		$ 90,000

Glossary

Absorption costing A costing method that includes all manufacturing costs—direct materials, direct labor, and both variable and fixed manufacturing overhead—in unit product costs. (p. 111)

Allocation base A measure of activity such as direct labor-hours or machine-hours that is used to assign costs to cost objects. (p. 111)

Cost of goods manufactured The manufacturing costs associated with units of product that were finished during the period. (p. 112)

Finished goods Units of product that have been completed but not yet sold to customers. (p. 112)

Job cost sheet A form that records the direct materials, direct labor, and manufacturing overhead cost charged to a job. (p. 111)

Job-order costing A costing system used in situations where many different products, jobs, or services are produced each period. (p. 111)

Normal costing A costing system in which overhead costs are applied to a job by multiplying a predetermined overhead rate by the actual amount of the allocation base incurred by the job (p. 111).

Overapplied overhead A credit balance in the Manufacturing Overhead account that occurs when the amount of overhead cost applied to Work in Process exceeds the amount of overhead cost actually incurred during a period. (p. 123)

Overhead application The process of assigning overhead cost to specific jobs. (p. 111)

Predetermined overhead rate A rate used to charge manufacturing overhead cost to jobs that is established in advance for each period. It is computed by dividing the estimated total manufacturing overhead cost for the period by the estimated total amount of the allocation base for the period. (p. 111)

Raw materials Any materials that go into the final product. (p. 111)

Schedule of cost of goods manufactured A schedule that contains three elements of product costs—direct materials, direct labor, and manufacturing overhead—and that summarizes the portions of those costs that remain in ending Work in Process inventory and that are transferred out of Work in Process into Finished Goods. (p. 121)

Schedule of cost of goods sold A schedule that contains three elements of product costs—direct materials, direct labor, and manufacturing overhead—and that summarizes the portions of those costs that remain in ending Finished Goods inventory and that are transferred out of Finished Goods into Cost of Goods Sold. (p. 121)

Underapplied overhead A debit balance in the Manufacturing Overhead account that occurs when the amount of overhead cost actually incurred exceeds the amount of overhead cost applied to Work in Process during a period. (p. 123)

Work in process Units of product that are only partially complete and will require further work before they are ready for sale to the customer. (p. 111)

Questions

3–1   What is the link that connects the schedule of cost of goods manufactured to the schedule of cost of goods sold?

3–2   What account is credited when overhead cost is applied to Work in Process? Would you expect the amount of overhead applied for a period to equal the actual overhead costs of the period? Why or why not?

3–3   What is underapplied overhead? Overapplied overhead? What disposition is made of these amounts at the end of the period?

3–4   Provide two reasons why overhead might be underapplied in a given year.

3–5   What adjustment is made for underapplied overhead on the schedule of cost of goods sold? What adjustment is made for overapplied overhead?

3–6   How do you compute the raw materials used in production?

3–7   How do you compute the total manufacturing costs within a schedule of cost of goods manufactured?

3–8   How do you compute the cost of goods manufactured?

3–9   How do you compute the unadjusted cost of goods sold?

3–10 How do direct labor costs flow through a job-order costing system?

Applying Excel   connect

LO3–1, LO3–4   The Excel worksheet form that appears below is to be used to recreate part of the example relating to Turbo Crafters that appears earlier in the chapter. Download the workbook containing this form from Connect, where you will also receive instructions about how to use this worksheet form.

	A	B	C	D
1	Chapter 3: Applying Excel			
2				
3	**Data**			
4	Allocation base	Machine-hours		
5	Estimated manufacturing overhead cost	$300,000		
6	Estimated total amount of the allocation base	75,000 machine-hours		
7	Actual manufacturing overhead cost	$290,000		
8	Actual total amount of the allocation base	68,000 machine-hours		
9				
10	*Enter a formula into each of the cells marked with a ? below*			
11				
12	**Computation of the predetermined overhead rate**			
13	Estimated manufacturing overhead cost	?		
14	Estimated total amount of the allocation base	? machine-hours		
15	Predetermined overhead rate	? per machine-hour		
16				
17	**Computation of underapplied or overapplied manufacturing overhead**			
18	Actual manufacturing overhead cost	?		
19	Manufacturing overhead cost applied to Work in Process during the year:			
20	Predetermined overhead rate	? per machine-hour		
21	Actual total amount of the allocation base	? machine-hours		
22	Manufacturing overhead applied	?		
23	Underapplied (overapplied) manufacturing overhead	?		
24				

Chapter 3 Form / Filled in Chapter 3 Form / Chapter 3 Formulas

You should proceed to the requirements below only after completing your worksheet.

Required:

1. Check your worksheet by changing the estimated total amount of the allocation base in the Data area to 60,000 machine-hours, keeping all of the other data the same as in the original example. If your worksheet is operating properly, the predetermined overhead rate should now be $5.00 per machine-hour. If you do not get this answer, find the errors in your worksheet and correct them.

    How much is the underapplied (overapplied) manufacturing overhead? Did it change? Why or why not?

2. Determine the underapplied (overapplied) manufacturing overhead for a different company with the following data:

Allocation base	Machine-hours
Estimated manufacturing overhead cost..............	$100,000
Estimated total amount of the allocation base........	50,000 machine-hours
Actual manufacturing overhead cost.................	$90,000
Actual total amount of the allocation base	40,000 machine-hours

3. What happens to the underapplied (overapplied) manufacturing overhead from part (2) if the estimated total amount of the allocation base is changed to 40,000 machine-hours and everything else remains the same? Why is the amount of underapplied (overapplied) manufacturing overhead different from part (2)?

4. Change the estimated total amount of the allocation base back to 50,000 machine-hours so that the data look exactly like they did in part (2). Now change the actual manufacturing overhead cost to $100,000. What is the underapplied (overapplied) manufacturing overhead now? Why is the amount of underapplied (overapplied) manufacturing overhead different from part (2)?

---

connect   **The Foundational 15**

Bunnell Corporation is a manufacturer that uses job-order costing. On January 1, the company's inventory balances were as follows:

LO3–1, LO3–2,
LO3–3, LO3–4

Raw materials......................	$40,000
Work in process....................	$18,000
Finished goods	$35,000

The company applies overhead cost to jobs on the basis of direct labor-hours. For the current year, the company's predetermined overhead rate of $16.25 per direct labor-hour was based on a cost formula that estimated $650,000 of total manufacturing overhead for an estimated activity level of 40,000 direct labor-hours. The following transactions were recorded for the year:

a. Raw materials were purchased on account, $510,000.
b. Raw materials used in production, $480,000. All of of the raw materials were used as direct materials.
c. The following costs were accrued for employee services: direct labor, $600,000; indirect labor, $150,000; selling and administrative salaries, $240,000.
d. Incurred various selling and administrative expenses (e.g., advertising, sales travel costs, and finished goods warehousing), $367,000.
e. Incurred various manufacturing overhead costs (e.g., depreciation, insurance, and utilities), $500,000.
f. Manufacturing overhead cost was applied to production. The company actually worked 41,000 direct labor-hours on all jobs during the year.
g. Jobs costing $1,680,000 to manufacture according to their job cost sheets were completed during the year.
h. Jobs were sold on account to customers during the year for a total of $2,800,000. The jobs cost $1,690,000 to manufacture according to their job cost sheets.

Required:

1. What is the journal entry to record raw materials used in production?
2. What is the ending balance in Raw Materials?
3. What is the journal entry to record the labor costs incurred during the year?
4. What is the total amount of manufacturing overhead applied to production during the year?

5. What is the total manufacturing cost added to Work in Process during the year?
6. What is the journal entry to record the transfer of completed jobs that is referred to in item g above?
7. What is the ending balance in Work in Process?
8. What is the total amount of actual manufacturing overhead cost incurred during the year?
9. Is manufacturing overhead underapplied or overapplied for the year? By how much?
10. What is the cost of goods available for sale during the year?
11. What is the journal entry to record the cost of goods sold referred to in item h above?
12. What is the ending balance in Finished Goods?
13. Assuming that the company closes its underapplied or overapplied overhead to Cost of Goods Sold, what is the adjusted cost of goods sold for the year?
14. What is the gross margin for the year?
15. What is the net operating income for the year?

Exercises    connect

EXERCISE 3–1 Prepare Journal Entries LO3–1
Larned Corporation recorded the following transactions for the just completed month.
a. $80,000 in raw materials were purchased on account.
b. $71,000 in raw materials were used in production. Of this amount, $62,000 was for direct materials and the remainder was for indirect materials.
c. Total labor wages of $112,000 were paid in cash. Of this amount, $101,000 was for direct labor and the remainder was for indirect labor.
d. Depreciation of $175,000 was incurred on factory equipment.

Required:
Record the above transactions in journal entries.

EXERCISE 3–2 Prepare T-Accounts LO3–2, LO3–4
Jurvin Enterprises recorded the following transactions for the just completed month. The company had no beginning inventories.
a. $94,000 in raw materials were purchased for cash.
b. $89,000 in raw materials were used in production. Of this amount, $78,000 was for direct materials and the remainder was for indirect materials.
c. Total labor wages of $132,000 were incurred and paid. Of this amount, $112,000 was for direct labor and the remainder was for indirect labor.
d. Additional manufacturing overhead costs of $143,000 were incurred and paid.
e. Manufacturing overhead of $152,000 was applied to production using the company's predetermined overhead rate.
f. All of the jobs in process at the end of the month were completed.
g. All of the completed jobs were shipped to customers.
h. Any underapplied or overapplied overhead for the period was closed to Cost of Goods Sold.

Required:
1. Post the above transactions to T-accounts.
2. Determine the adjusted cost of goods sold for the period.

EXERCISE 3–3 Schedules of Cost of Goods Manufactured and Cost of Goods Sold LO3–3
Primare Corporation has provided the following data concerning last month's manufacturing operations.

Purchases of raw materials	$30,000
Indirect materials included in manufacturing overhead	$5,000
Direct labor.	$58,000
Manufacturing overhead applied to work in process	$87,000
Underapplied overhead.	$4,000

Inventories	Beginning	Ending
Raw materials.	$12,000	$18,000
Work in process.	$56,000	$65,000
Finished goods	$35,000	$42,000

Required:
1. Prepare a schedule of cost of goods manufactured for the month.
2. Prepare a schedule of cost of goods sold for the month. Assume the underapplied or overapplied overhead is closed to Cost of Goods Sold.

EXERCISE 3–4 Underapplied and Overapplied Overhead LO3–4

Osborn Manufacturing uses a predetermined overhead rate of $18.20 per direct labor-hour. This predetermined rate was based on a cost formula that estimates $218,400 of total manufacturing overhead for an estimated activity level of 12,000 direct labor-hours.

The company actually incurred $215,000 of manufacturing overhead and 11,500 direct labor-hours during the period.

Required:
1. Determine the amount of underapplied or overapplied manufacturing overhead for the period.
2. Assume that the company's underapplied or overapplied overhead is closed to Cost of Goods Sold. Would the journal entry to dispose of the underapplied or overapplied overhead increase or decrease the company's gross margin? By how much?

EXERCISE 3–5 Journal Entries and T-accounts LO3–1, LO3–2

The Polaris Company uses a job-order costing system. The following transactions occurred in October:
a. Raw materials purchased on account, $210,000.
b. Raw materials used in production, $190,000 ($178,000 direct materials and $12,000 indirect materials).
c. Accrued direct labor cost of $90,000 and indirect labor cost of $110,000.
d. Depreciation recorded on factory equipment, $40,000.
e. Other manufacturing overhead costs accrued during October, $70,000.
f. The company applies manufacturing overhead cost to production using a predetermined rate of $8 per machine-hour. A total of 30,000 machine-hours were used in October.
g. Jobs costing $520,000 according to their job cost sheets were completed during October and transferred to Finished Goods.
h. Jobs that had cost $480,000 to complete according to their job cost sheets were shipped to customers during the month. These jobs were sold on account at 25% above cost.

Required:
1. Prepare journal entries to record the transactions given above.
2. Prepare T-accounts for Manufacturing Overhead and Work in Process. Post the relevant transactions from above to each account. Compute the ending balance in each account, assuming that Work in Process has a beginning balance of $42,000.

EXERCISE 3–6 Schedules of Cost of Goods Manufactured and Cost of Goods Sold; Income Statement LO3–3

The following data from the just completed year are taken from the accounting records of Mason Company:

Sales	$524,000
Direct labor cost	$70,000
Raw material purchases	$118,000
Selling expenses	$140,000
Administrative expenses	$63,000
Manufacturing overhead applied to work in process	$90,000
Actual manufacturing overhead costs	$80,000

Inventories	Beginning	Ending
Raw materials	$7,000	$15,000
Work in process	$10,000	$5,000
Finished goods	$20,000	$35,000

Required:

1. Prepare a schedule of cost of goods manufactured. Assume all raw materials used in production were direct materials.
2. Prepare a schedule of cost of goods sold. Assume that the company's underapplied or overapplied overhead is closed to Cost of Goods Sold.
3. Prepare an income statement.

EXERCISE 3–7 Applying Overhead; Cost of Goods Manufactured LO3–3, LO3–4

The following cost data relate to the manufacturing activities of Chang Company during the just completed year:

Manufacturing overhead costs incurred:	
Indirect materials...	$ 15,000
Indirect labor	130,000
Property taxes, factory...	8,000
Utilities, factory	70,000
Depreciation, factory	240,000
Insurance, factory	10,000
Total actual manufacturing overhead costs incurred	$473,000
Other costs incurred:	
Purchases of raw materials (both direct and indirect).................	$400,000
Direct labor cost	$60,000
Inventories:	
Raw materials, beginning...	$20,000
Raw materials, ending	$30,000
Work in process, beginning..	$40,000
Work in process, ending	$70,000

The company uses a predetermined overhead rate of $25 per machine-hour to apply overhead cost to jobs. A total of 19,400 machine-hours were used during the year.

Required:

1. Compute the amount of underapplied or overapplied overhead cost for the year.
2. Prepare a schedule of cost of goods manufactured for the year.

EXERCISE 3–8 Applying Overhead; Journal Entries; Disposing of Underapplied or Overapplied Overhead LO3–1, LO3–2, LO3–4

The following information is taken from the accounts of Latta Company. The entries in the T-accounts are summaries of the transactions that affected those accounts during the year.

Manufacturing Overhead				
(a)	460,000	(b)	390,000
Bal.	70,000		

Work in Process				
Bal.	15,000	(c)	710,000
	260,000		
	85,000		
(b)	390,000		
Bal.	40,000		

Finished Goods				
Bal.	50,000	(d)	640,000
(c)	710,000		
Bal.	120,000		

Cost of Goods Sold		
(d)	640,000

The overhead that had been applied to production during the year is distributed among Work in Process, Finished Goods, and Cost of Goods Sold as of the end of the year as follows:

Work in Process, ending	$ 19,500
Finished Goods, ending.........................	58,500
Cost of Goods Sold............................	312,000
Overhead applied..............................	$390,000

For example, of the $40,000 ending balance in Work in Process, $19,500 was overhead that had been applied during the year.

Required:
1. Identify reasons for entries (a) through (d).
2. Assume that the underapplied or overapplied overhead is closed to Cost of Goods Sold. Prepare the necessary journal entry.
3. Assume that the underapplied or overapplied overhead is closed proportionally to Work in Process, Finished Goods, and Cost of Goods Sold. Prepare the necessary journal entry. Provide supporting computations.

EXERCISE 3–9 Applying Overhead; T-accounts; Journal Entries LO3–1, LO3–2, LO3–4

Harwood Company uses a job-order costing system that applies overhead cost to jobs on the basis of machine-hours. The company's predetermined overhead rate of $2.40 per machine-hour was based on a cost formula that estimates $192,000 of total manufacturing overhead for an estimated activity level of 80,000 machine-hours.

Required:
1. Assume that during the year the company works only 75,000 machine-hours and incurs the following costs in the Manufacturing Overhead and Work in Process accounts:

Manufacturing Overhead				Work in Process		
(Maintenance)	21,000	?		(Direct materials)	710,000	
(Indirect materials)	8,000			(Direct labor)	90,000	
(Indirect labor)	60,000			(Overhead)	?	
(Utilities)	32,000					
(Insurance)	7,000					
(Depreciation)	56,000					

   Copy the data in the T-accounts above onto your answer sheet. Compute the amount of overhead cost that would be applied to Work in Process for the year and make the entry in your T-accounts.
2. Compute the amount of underapplied or overapplied overhead for the year and show the balance in your Manufacturing Overhead T-account. Prepare a journal entry to close the company's underapplied or overapplied overhead to Cost of Goods Sold.
3. Explain why the manufacturing overhead was underapplied or overapplied for the year.

EXERCISE 3–10 Applying Overhead; Journal Entries; T-accounts LO3–1, LO3–2

Dillon Products manufactures various machined parts to customer specifications. The company uses a job-order costing system and applies overhead cost to jobs on the basis of machine-hours. At the beginning of the year, the company used a cost formula to estimate that it would incur $4,800,000 in manufacturing overhead cost at an activity level of 240,000 machine-hours.

The company spent the entire month of January working on a large order for 16,000 custom-made machined parts. The company had no work in process at the beginning of January. Cost data relating to January follow:

a. Raw materials purchased on account, $325,000.
b. Raw materials used in production, $290,000 (80% direct materials and 20% indirect materials).
c. Labor cost accrued in the factory, $180,000 (one-third direct labor and two-thirds indirect labor).
d. Depreciation recorded on factory equipment, $75,000.
e. Other manufacturing overhead costs incurred on account, $62,000.
f. Manufacturing overhead cost was applied to production on the basis of 15,000 machine-hours actually worked during the month.
g. The completed job for 16,000 custom-made machined parts was moved into the finished goods warehouse on January 31 to await delivery to the customer. (In computing the dollar amount for this entry, remember that the cost of a completed job consists of direct materials, direct labor, and *applied* overhead.)

Required:

1. Prepare journal entries to record items (a) through (f) above [ignore item (g) for the moment].
2. Prepare T-accounts for Manufacturing Overhead and Work in Process. Post the relevant items from your journal entries to these T-accounts.
3. Prepare a journal entry for item (g) above.
4. If 10,000 of the custom-made machined parts are shipped to the customer in February, how much of this job's cost will be included in cost of goods sold for February?

Problems   connect

PROBLEM 3–11 T-Account Analysis of Cost Flows LO3–2, LO3–3, LO3–4

Selected T-accounts of Moore Company are given below for the just completed year:

Raw Materials

Bal. 1/1	15,000	Credits	?
Debits	120,000		
Bal. 12/31	25,000		

Manufacturing Overhead

Debits	230,000	Credits	?

Work in Process

Bal. 1/1	20,000	Credits	470,000
Direct materials	90,000		
Direct labor	150,000		
Overhead	240,000		
Bal. 12/31	?		

Factory Wages Payable

Debits	185,000	Bal. 1/1	9,000
		Credits	180,000
		Bal. 12/31	4,000

Finished Goods

Bal. 1/1	40,000	Credits	?
Debits	?		
Bal. 12/31	60,000		

Cost of Goods Sold

Debits	?

Required:

1. What was the cost of raw materials used in production during the year?
2. How much of the materials in (1) above consisted of indirect materials?
3. How much of the factory labor cost for the year consisted of indirect labor?
4. What was the cost of goods manufactured for the year?
5. What was the unadjusted cost of goods sold for the year? Do not include any underapplied or overapplied overhead in your answer.
6. If overhead is applied to production on the basis of direct labor cost, what predetermined overhead rate was in effect during the year?
7. Was manufacturing overhead underapplied or overapplied? By how much?
8. Compute the ending balance in Work in Process. Assume that this balance consists entirely of goods started during the year. If $8,000 of this balance is direct labor cost, how much of it is direct materials cost? Applied overhead cost?

PROBLEM 3–12 Predetermined Overhead Rate; Disposing of Underapplied or Overapplied Overhead LO3–4

Luzadis Company makes furniture using the latest automated technology. The company uses a job-order costing system and applies manufacturing overhead cost to products on the basis of machine-hours. The predetermined overhead rate was based on a cost formula that estimates $900,000 of total manufacturing overhead for an estimated activity level of 75,000 machine-hours.

During the year, a large quantity of furniture on the market resulted in cutting back production and a buildup of furniture in the company's warehouse. The company's cost records revealed the following actual cost and operating data for the year:

Machine-hours..	60,000
Manufacturing overhead cost......................................	$850,000
Inventories at year-end:	
Raw materials..	$30,000
Work in process (includes overhead applied of $36,000)...............	$100,000
Finished goods (includes overhead applied of $180,000)	$500,000
Cost of goods sold (includes overhead applied of $504,000)	$1,400,000

Required:

1. Compute the underapplied or overapplied overhead.
2. Assume that the company closes any underapplied or overapplied overhead to Cost of Goods Sold. Prepare the appropriate journal entry.
3. Assume that the company allocates any underapplied or overapplied overhead proportionally to Work in Process, Finished Goods, and Cost of Goods Sold. Prepare the appropriate journal entry.
4. How much higher or lower will net operating income be if the underapplied or overapplied overhead is allocated to Work in Process, Finished Goods, and Cost of Goods Sold rather than being closed to Cost of Goods Sold?

PROBLEM 3–13 Schedules of Cost of Goods Manufactured and Cost of Goods Sold; Income Statement LO3–3

Superior Company provided the following data for the year ended December 31 (all raw materials are used in production as direct materials):

Selling expenses..	$140,000
Purchases of raw materials	$290,000
Direct labor..	?
Administrative expenses	$100,000
Manufacturing overhead applied to work in process	$285,000
Actual manufacturing overhead cost.................................	$270,000

Inventory balances at the beginning and end of the year were as follows:

	Beginning	Ending
Raw materials................	$40,000	$10,000
Work in process..............	?	$35,000
Finished goods	$50,000	?

The total manufacturing costs for the year were $683,000; the cost of goods available for sale totaled $740,000; the unadjusted cost of goods sold totaled $660,000; and the net operating income was $30,000. The company's underapplied or overapplied overhead is closed to Cost of Goods Sold.

Required:

Prepare schedules of cost of goods manufactured and cost of goods sold and an income statement. (*Hint:* Prepare the income statement and schedule of cost of goods sold first followed by the schedule of cost of goods manufactured.)

PROBLEM 3–14 Schedule of Cost of Goods Manufactured; Overhead Analysis LO3–3, LO3–4

Gitano Products operates a job-order costing system and applies overhead cost to jobs on the basis of direct materials *used in production* (*not* on the basis of raw materials purchased). Its predetermined overhead rate was based on a cost formula that estimated $800,000 of manufacturing overhead for an estimated allocation base of $500,000 direct material dollars to be used in production. The company has provided the following data for the just completed year:

Purchase of raw materials	$510,000
Direct labor cost	$90,000
Manufacturing overhead costs:	
Indirect labor	$170,000
Property taxes	$48,000
Depreciation of equipment	$260,000
Maintenance	$95,000
Insurance	$7,000
Rent, building.	$180,000

	Beginning	Ending
Raw Materials.	$20,000	$80,000
Work in Process.	$150,000	$70,000
Finished Goods	$260,000	$400,000

Required:
1. Compute the predetermined overhead rate for the year.
2. Compute the amount of underapplied or overapplied overhead for the year.
3. Prepare a schedule of cost of goods manufactured for the year. Assume all raw materials are used in production as direct materials.
4. Compute the unadjusted cost of goods sold for the year. Do not include any underapplied or overapplied overhead in your answer. What options are available for disposing of underapplied or overapplied overhead?
5. Assume that the $70,000 ending balance in Work in Process includes $24,000 of direct materials. Given this assumption, supply the information missing below:

Direct materials	$24,000
Direct labor.	?
Manufacturing overhead	?
Work in process inventory	$70,000

PROBLEM 3–15 Journal Entries; T-Accounts; Financial Statements LO3–1, LO3–2, LO3–3, LO3–4
Froya Fabrikker A/S of Bergen, Norway, is a small company that manufactures specialty heavy equipment for use in North Sea oil fields. The company uses a job-order costing system that applies manufacturing overhead cost to jobs on the basis of direct labor-hours. Its predetermined overhead rate was based on a cost formula that estimated $360,000 of manufacturing overhead for an estimated allocation base of 900 direct labor-hours. The following transactions took place during the year:
a. Raw materials purchased on account, $200,000.
b. Raw materials used in production (all direct materials), $185,000.
c. Utility bills incurred on account, $70,000 (90% related to factory operations, and the remainder related to selling and administrative activities).
d. Accrued salary and wage costs:

Direct labor (975 hours)	$230,000
Indirect labor	$90,000
Selling and administrative salaries	$110,000

e. Maintenance costs incurred on account in the factory, $54,000.
f. Advertising costs incurred on account, $136,000.
g. Depreciation was recorded for the year, $95,000 (80% related to factory equipment, and the remainder related to selling and administrative equipment).
h. Rental cost incurred on account, $120,000 (85% related to factory facilities, and the remainder related to selling and administrative facilities).
i. Manufacturing overhead cost was applied to jobs, $? .

j.   Cost of goods manufactured for the year, $770,000.

k.   Sales for the year (all on account) totaled $1,200,000. These goods cost $800,000 according to their job cost sheets.

The balances in the inventory accounts at the beginning of the year were:

Raw Materials..............................	$30,000
Work in Process...........................	$21,000
Finished Goods	$60,000

Required:

1.   Prepare journal entries to record the preceding transactions.

2.   Post your entries to T-accounts. (Don't forget to enter the beginning inventory balances above.) Determine the ending balances in the inventory accounts and in the Manufacturing Overhead account.

3.   Prepare a schedule of cost of goods manufactured.

4.   Prepare a journal entry to close any balance in the Manufacturing Overhead account to Cost of Goods Sold. Prepare a schedule of cost of goods sold.

5.   Prepare an income statement for the year.

PROBLEM 3–16 Comprehensive Problem LO3–1, LO3–2, LO3–4

Gold Nest Company of Guandong, China, is a family-owned enterprise that makes birdcages for the South China market. The company sells its birdcages through an extensive network of street vendors who receive commissions on their sales.

The company uses a job-order costing system in which overhead is applied to jobs on the basis of direct labor cost. Its predetermined overhead rate is based on a cost formula that estimated $330,000 of manufacturing overhead for an estimated activity level of $200,000 direct labor dollars. At the beginning of the year, the inventory balances were as follows:

Raw materials.............................	$25,000
Work in process...........................	$10,000
Finished goods	$40,000

During the year, the following transactions were completed:

a.   Raw materials purchased for cash, $275,000.

b.   Raw materials used in production, $280,000 (materials costing $220,000 were charged directly to jobs; the remaining materials were indirect).

c.   Cash paid to employees as follows:

Direct labor...............................	$180,000
Indirect labor	$72,000
Sales commissions	$63,000
Administrative salaries	$90,000

d.   Cash paid for rent during the year was $18,000 ($13,000 of this amount related to factory operations, and the remainder related to selling and administrative activities).

e.   Cash paid for utility costs in the factory, $57,000.

f.   Cash paid for advertising, $140,000.

g.   Depreciation recorded on equipment, $100,000. ($88,000 of this amount related to equipment used in factory operations; the remaining $12,000 related to equipment used in selling and administrative activities.)

h.   Manufacturing overhead cost was applied to jobs, $__?__.

i.   Goods that had cost $675,000 to manufacture according to their job cost sheets were completed.

j.   Sales for the year (all paid in cash) totaled $1,250,000. The total cost to manufacture these goods according to their job cost sheets was $700,000.

Required:

1.   Prepare journal entries to record the transactions for the year.

2.   Prepare T-accounts for each inventory account, Manufacturing Overhead, and Cost of Goods Sold. Post relevant data from your journal entries to these T-accounts (don't forget to enter the beginning balances in your inventory accounts). Compute an ending balance in each account.

3. Is Manufacturing Overhead underapplied or overapplied for the year? Prepare a journal entry to close any balance in the Manufacturing Overhead account to Cost of Goods Sold.

4. Prepare an income statement for the year. (Do not prepare a schedule of cost of goods manufactured; all of the information needed for the income statement is available in the journal entries and T-accounts you have prepared.)

PROBLEM 3–17 Cost Flows; T-Accounts; Income Statement LO3–2, LO3–3, LO3–4

Supreme Videos, Inc., produces short musical videos for sale to retail outlets. The company's balance sheet accounts as of January 1, are given below.

Supreme Videos, Inc.		
Balance Sheet		
January 1		
Assets		
Current assets:		
Cash		$ 63,000
Accounts receivable		102,000
Inventories:		
Raw materials (film, costumes)	$ 30,000	
Videos in process	45,000	
Finished videos awaiting sale	81,000	156,000
Prepaid insurance		9,000
Total current assets		330,000
Studio and equipment	730,000	
Less accumulated depreciation	210,000	520,000
Total assets		$850,000
Liabilities and Stockholders' Equity		
Accounts payable		$160,000
Capital stock	$420,000	
Retained earnings	270,000	690,000
Total liabilities and stockholders' equity		$850,000

Because the videos differ in length and in complexity of production, the company uses a job-order costing system to determine the cost of each video produced. Studio (manufacturing) overhead is charged to videos on the basis of camera-hours of activity. The company's predetermined overhead rate for the year is based on a cost formula that estimated $280,000 in manufacturing overhead for an estimated allocation base of 7,000 camera-hours. The following transactions occurred during the year:

a. Film, costumes, and similar raw materials purchased on account, $185,000.

b. Film, costumes, and other raw materials used in production, $200,000 (85% of this material was considered direct to the videos in production, and the other 15% was considered indirect).

c. Utility costs incurred in the production studio, $72,000.

d. Depreciation recorded on the studio, cameras, and other equipment, $84,000. Three-fourths of this depreciation related to production of the videos, and the remainder related to equipment used in marketing and administration.

e. Advertising expense incurred, $130,000.

f. Costs for salaries and wages were incurred as follows:

Direct labor (actors and directors)	$82,000
Indirect labor (carpenters to build sets, costume designers, and so forth)	$110,000
Administrative salaries	$95,000

g. Prepaid insurance expired during the year, $7,000 (80% related to production of videos, and 20% related to marketing and administrative activities).

h. Miscellaneous marketing and administrative expenses incurred, $8,600.

i. Studio (manufacturing) overhead was applied to videos in production. The company used 7,250 camera-hours during the year.

j. Videos that cost $550,000 to produce according to their job cost sheets were transferred to the finished videos warehouse to await sale and shipment.

k. Sales for the year totaled $925,000 and were all on account. The total cost to produce these videos according to their job cost sheets was $600,000.

l. Collections from customers during the year totaled $850,000.

m. Payments to suppliers on account during the year, $500,000; payments to employees for salaries and wages, $285,000.

Required:

1. Prepare a T-account for each account on the company's balance sheet and enter the beginning balances.

2. Record the transactions directly into the T-accounts. Prepare new T-accounts as needed. Key your entries to the letters (a) through (m) above. Compute the ending balance in each account.

3. Is the Studio (manufacturing) Overhead account underapplied or overapplied for the year? Make an entry in the T-accounts to close any balance in the Studio Overhead account to Cost of Goods Sold.

4. Prepare a schedule of cost of goods manufactured. If done correctly, the cost of goods manufactured from your schedule should agree with which of the above transactions?

5. Prepare a schedule of cost of goods sold. If done correctly, the unadjusted cost of goods sold from your schedule should agree with which of the above transactions?

6. Prepare an income statement for the year.

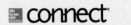 **Cases**

CASE 3–18 Ethics and the Manager LO3–4

Terri Ronsin had recently been transferred to the Home Security Systems Division of National Home Products. Shortly after taking over her new position as divisional controller, she was asked to develop the division's predetermined overhead rate for the upcoming year. The accuracy of the rate is important because it is used throughout the year and any underapplied or overapplied overhead is closed out to Cost of Goods Sold at the end of the year. National Home Products uses direct labor-hours in all of its divisions as the allocation base for manufacturing overhead.

To compute the predetermined overhead rate, Terri divided her estimate of the total manufacturing overhead for the coming year by the production manager's estimate of the total direct labor-hours for the coming year. She took her computations to the division's general manager for approval but was quite surprised when he suggested a modification in the allocation base. Her conversation with the general manager of the Home Security Systems Division, Harry Irving, went like this:

Ronsin: Here are my calculations for next year's predetermined overhead rate. If you approve, we can enter the rate into the computer on January 1 and be up and running in the job-order costing system right away this year.

Irving: Thanks for coming up with the calculations so quickly, and they look just fine. There is, however, one slight modification I would like to see. Your estimate of the total direct labor-hours for the year is 440,000 hours. How about cutting that to about 420,000 hours?

Ronsin: I don't know if I can do that. The production manager says she will need about 440,000 direct labor-hours to meet the sales projections for the year. Besides, there are going to be over 430,000 direct labor-hours during the current year and sales are projected to be higher next year.

Irving: Teri, I know all of that. I would still like to reduce the direct labor-hours in the allocation base to something like 420,000 hours. You probably don't know that I had an agreement with your predecessor as divisional controller to shave 5% or so off the estimated direct labor-hours every year. That way, we kept a reserve that usually resulted in a big boost to net operating income at the end of the year in December. We called it our Christmas bonus. Corporate headquarters always seemed to be pleased that we could pull off such a miracle at the end of the year. This system has worked well for many years, and I don't want to change it now.

Required:

1. Explain how shaving 5% off the estimated direct labor-hours in the allocation base for the predetermined overhead rate usually results in a big boost in net operating income at the end of the year.

2. Should Terri Ronsin go along with the general manager's request to reduce the direct labor-hours in the predetermined overhead rate computation to 420,000 direct labor-hours?

Appendix 3A: Job-Order Costing: A Microsoft Excel-Based Approach

LO3–5

Use Microsoft Excel to summarize the flow of costs in a job-order costing system.

In this appendix, we use Microsoft Excel to depict how the transactions in a job-order costing system impact a company's balance sheet. While the main body of the chapter focused on using journal entries to record transactions, the approach demonstrated in this appendix will help you develop a new and valuable managerial skill—analyzing how transactions affect the balance sheet without having to prepare formal journal entries.

To set the stage for the forthcoming example, we need to review your understanding of two fundamental accounting equations and we need to specify three important assumptions.

Fundamental Accounting Equations

A company's balance sheet is based on the following accounting equation that is the bedrock of double-entry bookkeeping:

$$\text{Assets} = \text{Liabilities} + \text{Stockholders' Equity}$$

In the Excel spreadsheets that we'll be using in this appendix, one column will always be populated with an "=" sign. The accounts on the left-hand side of the "=" sign will be asset accounts and the accounts on the right-hand side will be liability and stockholders' equity accounts. After we record every transaction, the amounts on the left-hand side of the "=" sign must equal the amounts on the right-hand side.

The second foundational equation relates to the Retained Earnings account on a company's balance sheet. The ending balance in retained earnings is computed using the following equation:

$$\text{Ending balance in retained earnings} = \text{Beginning balance in retained earnings} + \text{Net operating income} - \text{Dividends}$$

This equation highlights the connection between the balance sheet and the income statement. It recognizes the fact that net operating income from the income statement is embedded within retained earnings on the balance sheet. Thus, in our Microsoft Excel-based approach, any transactions involving sales or expenses will be recorded in the Retained Earnings column of the balance sheet.

Three Key Assumptions

The first assumption in the appendix is that we will always use only one predetermined overhead rate. In other words, we are going to use the same approach that was demonstrated in the main body of this chapter. This requires using an account titled Manufacturing Overhead within our Microsoft Excel spreadsheets that will serve the same purpose as the Manufacturing Overhead clearing account discussed earlier in the chapter.

The second assumption is that any underapplied or overapplied manufacturing overhead will always be closed to Cost of Goods Sold as reported in the income statement. Because the income statement is embedded in the Retained Earnings account on the balance sheet, we will always close underapplied or overapplied overhead to Retained Earnings.

Our third assumption is that we'll record transactions within Microsoft Excel by using positive numbers to increase balance sheet accounts and negative numbers (shown in parentheses) to decrease balance sheet accounts. This is a slightly different approach than we used in the main body of the chapter where all transactions were depicted using the language of debits and credits—in journal entry form and in T-account form. This appendix replaces the language of debits and credits with an equivalent alternative. Instead, it identifies the balance sheet accounts affected by each transaction and it determines if those account balances should increase or decrease.

Sapphire Company—Setting the Stage

Sapphire Company uses a job-order costing system to assign manufacturing costs to jobs. Its balance sheet on January 1 is as follows:

Sapphire Company Balance Sheet January 1		
Assets		
Cash.		$ 15,000
Raw materials.	$8,000	
Work in process.	5,000	
Finished goods	13,000	26,000
Prepaid expenses		3,000
Property, plant, and equipment (net)		240,000
Total assets.		$284,000
Liabilities and Stockholders' Equity		
Accounts payable		$ 4,000
Retained earnings		280,000
Total liabilities and stockholders' equity		$284,000

Exhibit 3A–1 contains a Microsoft Excel spreadsheet that includes the beginning balances shown in the balance sheet above. Notice that column "J" of the spreadsheet contains "=" signs (see cells J1 and J2). This means that after we record each of the forthcoming transactions, the amounts on the left-hand side of column "J" will always need to equal the amounts on the right-hand side of column "J."

Also, notice that the spreadsheet contains all of the accounts shown in the January 1 balance sheet plus an account called Manufacturing Overhead. As discussed earlier in the chapter, Manufacturing Overhead is a clearing account that always has a beginning and ending balance of zero. This account is used to record two things—all actual overhead costs and the amount of manufacturing overhead applied to production using the predetermined overhead rate. The difference between the actual overhead cost and the amount of overhead applied to production is the underapplied or overapplied overhead.

Finally, to conserve space, the Excel spreadsheet abbreviates Property, Plant, and Equipment (net) as PP&E (net). The term *net* implies that the acquisition cost of property, plant, and equipment is being reported *net* of accumulated depreciation.

Sapphire Company—Transaction Analysis

The remainder of the appendix proceeds in three steps. First, it lists Sapphire Company's transactions for the month of January. Second, it explains how each of these transactions is recorded in the Microsoft Excel spreadsheet. Finally, it explains how to use the

---

EXHIBIT 3A–1
Sapphire Company: Transaction Analysis

	A	B	C	D	E	F	G	H	I	J	K	L
1						Sapphire Company						
2						Transaction Analysis						
3						For the Month Ended January 31						
5	Transactions		Cash	Raw Materials	Work in Process	Finished Goods	Manufacturing Overhead	Prepaid Expenses	PP&E (net)	=	Accounts Payable	Retained Earnings
6	Beginning balances @ 1/1		$ 15,000	$ 8,000	$ 5,000	$ 13,000	$ -	$ 3,000	$240,000	=	$ 4,000	$280,000
7												

Exhibit 3A-1 Exhibit 3A-2 Exhibit 3A-3 Exhibit 3A-4 Exhibit 3A-5

information depicted in the spreadsheet to prepare a schedule of cost of goods manufactured, a schedule of cost of goods sold, and an income statement for the month of January.

To begin our illustration, let's assume that Sapphire Company has a predetermined overhead rate of $25 per direct labor-hour that was based on a cost formula that estimated $100,000 in manufacturing overhead cost for an estimated allocation base of 4,000 direct labor-hours. During January, the company completed the following transactions:

a. Purchased raw materials on account, $80,000.
b. Raw materials used in production, $78,000 ($70,000 was direct materials and $8,000 was indirect materials).
c. Paid $135,000 of salaries and wages in cash ($68,000 was direct labor, $45,000 was indirect labor, and $22,000 was related to employees responsible for selling and administration).
d. Utility costs incurred (on account) to support production, $15,000.
e. Depreciation recorded on property, plant, and equipment, $40,000 (70% related to manufacturing equipment and 30% related to assets that support selling and administration).
f. Advertising expenses paid in cash, $18,000.
g. Prepaid insurance expired during the month, $1,000 (80% related to production, and 20% related to selling and administration).
h. Manufacturing overhead applied to production, $102,500. This amount was computed by multiplying 4,100 direct labor-hours worked in January by the predetermined overhead rate of $25 per direct labor-hour.
i. Cost of goods manufactured, $235,000.
j. Cash sales, $320,000.
k. Cost of goods sold, $245,000.
l. Cash payments to creditors, $92,000.
m. Close overapplied overhead of $5,700 to cost of goods sold.

Exhibit 3A–2 summarizes how each of the transactions just described would be recorded in the Microsoft Excel spreadsheet. The underlying explanations for each transaction are as follows (each transaction includes a parenthetical reference to its row within the Microsoft Excel spreadsheet):

a. (*row 7*) Purchasing raw materials on account for $80,000 will increase Raw Materials and Accounts Payable by $80,000.
b. (*row 8*) When raw materials are used in production, it decreases Raw Materials by $78,000. The direct materials of $70,000 are added to Work in Process, whereas the

EXHIBIT 3A–2
Sapphire Company: Completed Transaction Analysis

	Transactions	Cash	Raw Materials	Work in Process	Finished Goods	Manufacturing Overhead	Prepaid Expenses	PP&E (net)	=	Accounts Payable	Retained Earnings
6	Beginning balances @ 1/1	$ 15,000	$ 8,000	$ 5,000	$ 13,000	$ -	$ 3,000	$240,000	=	$ 4,000	$280,000
7	(a) Raw material purchases		80,000						=	80,000	
8	(b) Raw materials used in production		(78,000)	70,000		8,000			=		
9	(c) Salaries and wages	(135,000)		68,000		45,000			=		(22,000)
10	(d) Utility costs					15,000			=	15,000	
11	(e) Depreciation					28,000		(40,000)	=		(12,000)
12	(f) Advertising	(18,000)							=		(18,000)
13	(g) Expiration of prepaid insurance					800	(1,000)		=		(200)
14	(h) Manufacturing overhead applied			102,500		(102,500)			=		
15	(i) Cost of goods manufactured			(235,000)	235,000				=		
16	(j) Sales	320,000							=		320,000
17	(k) Cost of goods sold				(245,000)				=		(245,000)
18	(l) Payments to creditors	(92,000)							=	(92,000)	
19	(m) Overapplied overhead					5,700			=		5,700
20	Ending balances @ 1/31	$ 90,000	$ 10,000	$ 10,500	$ 3,000	$ -	$ 2,000	$200,000	=	$ 7,000	$308,500

Exhibit 3A-1 **Exhibit 3A-2** Exhibit 3A-3 Exhibit 3A-4 Exhibit 3A-5

indirect materials of $8,000 are added to Manufacturing Overhead. Notice that actual manufacturing overhead costs, such as the $8,000 of indirect materials, *are not* added to Work in Process. As you will see in a later transaction, manufacturing overhead is applied to Work in Process using the predetermined overhead rate.

c. (*row 9*) The salaries and wages decrease Cash by $135,000. The direct labor cost of $68,000 increases Work in Process, whereas the indirect labor cost of $45,000 increases Manufacturing Overhead. The $22,000 paid to employees working in selling and administrative roles is a period cost that should be recorded on January's income statement. Because the income statement is embedded in Retained Earnings, we decrease Retained Earnings by $22,000.

d. (*row 10*) The utility costs support production, so they are treated as a product cost rather than a period cost. Thus, Manufacturing Overhead increases by $15,000 and Accounts Payable increases by the same amount.

e. (*row 11*) The depreciation reduces Property, Plant, and Equipment (net) by $40,000. This is equivalent to recording accumulated depreciation of $40,000. The depreciation on manufacturing equipment of $28,000 (a product cost) increases Manufacturing Overhead, whereas the depreciation on selling and administrative assets of $12,000 (a period cost) decreases Retained Earnings.

f. (*row 12*) Advertising is a period cost so Cash and Retained Earnings decrease by $18,000.

g. (*row 13*) The expired insurance coverage decreases Prepaid Expenses by $1,000. The insurance related to production (a product cost) increases Manufacturing Overhead by $800. The insurance related to selling and administration of $200 (a period cost) decreases Retained Earnings by $200.

h. (*row 14*) The manufacturing overhead applied increases Work in Process and decreases Manufacturing Overhead by $102,500. Notice that manufacturing overhead is applied to Work in Process using the predetermined overhead rate. Actual manufacturing overhead costs are not recorded in Work in Process. In a later transaction, the actual overhead costs will be compared to the applied overhead to determine the amount of underapplied or overapplied overhead for the month.

i. (*row 15*) The cost of goods manufactured refers to the cost of the goods that were transferred from work in process to finished goods during the period. This transaction decreases Work in Process by $235,000 and increases Finished Goods by the same amount.

j. (*row 16*) The sales will increase Cash by $320,000, and given that sales appear on the income statement, Retained Earnings will increase by the same amount.

k. (*row 17*) The cost of goods sold must be removed from finished goods; therefore, Finished Goods decreases by $245,000. Because cost of goods sold appears on the income statement, Retained Earnings decreases by the same amount.

l. (*row 18*) The cash payments to creditors decrease Cash and Accounts Payable by $92,000.

m. (*row 19*) The manufacturing overhead applied of $102,500 is $5,700 greater than the actual overhead costs incurred during the month of $96,800 (= $8,000 + $45,000 + $15,000 + $28,000 + $800). Therefore, manufacturing overhead is overapplied by $5,700. We record this transaction by increasing Manufacturing Overhead by $5,700 and increasing Retained Earnings by the same amount. The increase in Retained Earnings reflects the fact that we are decreasing Cost of Goods Sold (which increases net operating income).

Once we have recorded all transactions, the company's balance sheet at January 31 can be derived by summing each column in the spreadsheet (see row 20 for the ending balances that would be reported on Sapphire Company's balance sheet at January 31).

Sapphire Company—Schedules of Cost of Goods Manufactured and Cost of Goods Sold

The transactions recorded in Exhibit 3A–2 can be used to create schedules of cost of goods manufactured and cost of goods sold. Exhibit 3A–3 shows Sapphire Company's schedule of cost of goods manufactured. Each row heading in this exhibit contains a cell reference that indicates where the number appears in Exhibit 3A–2.

EXHIBIT 3A–3
Sapphire Company: Schedule of Cost of Goods Manufactured

	A	B	C
1	**Sapphire Company**		
2	**Schedule of Cost of Goods Manufactured**		
3	**For the Month Ended January 31**		
5	Direct materials:		
6	Beginning raw materials inventory (D6)	$ 8,000	
7	Add: Purchases of raw materials (D7)	80,000	
8	Total raw materials available	88,000	
9	Deduct: Ending raw materials inventory (D20)	10,000	
10	Raw materials used production	78,000	
11	Deduct: Indirect materials included in manufacturing overhead (G8)	8,000	$ 70,000
12	Direct labor (E9)		68,000
13	Manufacturing overhead applied to work in process (E14)		102,500
14	Total manufacturing costs		240,500
15	Add: Beginning work in process inventory (E6)		5,000
16			245,500
17	Deduct: Ending work in process inventory (E20)		10,500
18	Cost of goods manufactured		$ 235,000
19			

Exhibit 3A-1 | Exhibit 3A-2 | **Exhibit 3A-3** | Exhibit 3A-4 | Exhibit 3A-5

Notice that the cost of goods manufactured of $235,000 as shown in Exhibit 3A–3 equals the cost of goods manufactured mentioned in transaction "i" and recorded in row 15 of Exhibit 3A–2.

Exhibit 3A–4 shows Sapphire Company's schedule of cost of goods sold. Each row heading in this exhibit contains a cell reference that indicates where the number appears in Exhibit 3A–2.

EXHIBIT 3A–4
Sapphire Company: Schedule of
Cost of Goods Sold

	A	B
1	**Sapphire Company**	
2	**Schedule of Cost of Goods Sold**	
3	**For the Month Ended January 31**	
5	Beginning finished goods inventory (F6)	$ 13,000
6	Add: Cost of goods manufactured (F15)	235,000
7	Cost of goods available for sale	248,000
8	Deduct: Ending finished goods inventory (F20)	3,000
9	Unadjusted cost of goods sold	245,000
10	Deduct: Overapplied overhead (G19)	5,700
11	Adjusted cost of goods sold	$ 239,300
12		

Exhibit 3A-1 | Exhibit 3A-2 | Exhibit 3A-3 | **Exhibit 3A-4** | Exhibit 3A-5

	A	B	C	
1	Sapphire Company			
2	Income Statement			
3	For the Month Ended January 31			
5	Sales (L16)		$ 320,000	
6	Cost of goods sold		239,300	
7	Gross margin		80,700	
8	Selling and administrative expenses:			
9	Salaries expense (L9)	$ 22,000		
10	Depreciation expense (L11)	12,000		
11	Advertising expense (L12)	18,000		
12	Insurance expense (L13)	200	52,200	
13	Net operating income		$ 28,500	
14				

H ◄ ► H   Exhibit 3A-1   Exhibit 3A-2   Exhibit 3A-3   Exhibit 3A-4   **Exhibit 3A-5**

EXHIBIT 3A–5
Sapphire Company: Income Statement

In the schedule of cost of goods sold, we subtract overapplied overhead of $5,700 from unadjusted cost of good sold because overapplied overhead means that too much overhead was added to production during the period, and hence, the cost of goods sold was overstated. In Exhibit 3A–2, we add overapplied overhead to retained earnings (see row 19) because lowering cost of goods sold increases net operating income, which in turn increases retained earnings.

Sapphire Company—Income Statement

Exhibit 3A–5 shows Sapphire Company's income statement for the month of January. The sales and selling and administrative expenses come from the transaction analysis in Exhibit 3A–2 and they each contain a corresponding parenthetical cell reference. The cost of goods sold ($239,300) is carried over from the schedule of cost of goods sold in Exhibit 3A–4.

connect   **Appendix 3A: Exercises and Problems**

EXERCISE 3A–1 Transaction Analysis LO3–5

Carmen Company is a manufacturer that completed numerous transactions during the month, some of which are shown below:

a. Raw materials used in production as direct materials, $56,000.
b. Paid direct laborers $40,000 in cash for their work on various jobs during the month.
c. Applied $35,000 of manufacturing overhead to production during the month.
d. Various jobs costing a total of $110,000 were completed during the month and transferred to Finished Goods.
e. Various completed jobs costing a total of $90,000 were sold to customers.
f. Cash sales for the month totaled $160,000.
g. Selling and administrative expenses paid in cash, $18,000.

Required:

The table shown below includes a subset of Carmen Company's balance sheet accounts. Record each of the above transactions using the accounts that are given. If a transaction increases an account balance, then record the amount as a positive number. If it decreases an account balance, then record the amount in parentheses.

Transaction	Cash	Raw Materials	Work in Process	Finished Goods	Manufacturing Overhead		Retained Earnings
a.						=	
b.						=	
c.						=	
d.						=	
e.						=	
f.						=	
g.						=	

EXERCISE 3A–2 Transaction Analysis LO3–5

Adams Company is a manufacturer that completed numerous transactions during the month, some of which are shown below:
a. Manufacturing overhead costs incurred on account, $80,000.
b. Depreciation was recorded for the month, $35,000 (80% related to factory equipment, and the remainder related to selling and administrative equipment).
c. Prepaid insurance expired during the month, $2,500 (75% related to production, and 25% related to selling and administration).
d. Applied $115,000 of manufacturing overhead to production during the month.
e. Closed $5,125 of overapplied overhead to cost of goods sold.

Required:
The table shown below includes a subset of Adams Company's balance sheet accounts. Record each of the above transactions using the accounts that are given. If a transaction increases an account balance, then record the amount as a positive number. If it decreases an account balance, then record the amount in parentheses.

Transaction	Work in Process	Manufacturing Overhead	Prepaid Expenses	PP&E (net)		Accounts Payable	Retained Earnings
a.					=		
b.					=		
c.					=		
d.					=		
e.					=		

EXERCISE 3A–3 Transaction Analysis LO3–5

Dixon Company is a manufacturer that completed numerous transactions during the month, some of which are shown below:
a. Raw materials purchased on account, $100,000.
b. Raw materials used in production, $78,000 direct materials, and $16,000 indirect materials.
c. Sales commissions paid in cash, $45,000.
d. Depreciation was recorded for the month, $60,000 (65% related to factory equipment, and the remainder related to selling and administrative equipment).
e. Sales for the month, $450,000 (70% cash sales and the remainder were sales on account).
f. Factory utilities paid in cash, $12,000.
g. Applied $138,000 of manufacturing overhead to production during the month.
h. Various jobs costing a total of $190,000 were completed during the month and transferred to Finished Goods.
i. Cash receipts from customers who had previously purchased on credit, $115,000.
j. Various completed jobs costing a total of $220,000 were sold to customers.
k. Cash paid to raw material suppliers, $90,000.

Required:
The table shown below includes only one account from Dixon Company's balance sheet—Retained Earnings. For each of the above transactions, select "No" if it would not affect Retained Earnings. Conversely if the transaction would affect Retained Earnings, then record the amount of the increase or (decrease) to this account under the "Yes" column.

	Retained Earnings	
Transaction	Yes	No
a.		
b.		
c.		
d.		
e.		
f.		
g.		
h.		
i.		
j.		
k.		

PROBLEM 3A–4 Transaction Analysis LO3–5

Morrison Company uses a job-order costing system to assign manufacturing costs to jobs. Its balance sheet on January 1 is as follows:

Morrison Company
Balance Sheet
January 1

Assets		
Cash.		$ 32,000
Raw materials.	$ 9,000	
Work in process.	4,000	
Finished goods	17,000	30,000
Prepaid expenses		2,000
Property, plant, and equipment (net)		190,000
Total assets.		$254,000
Liabilities and Stockholders' Equity		
Accounts payable		$ 7,000
Retained earnings		247,000
Total liabilities and stockholders' equity		$254,000

During January the company completed the following transactions:

a. Purchased raw materials on account, $74,000.

b. Raw materials used in production, $77,000 ($67,000 was direct materials and $10,000 was indirect materials).

c. Paid $167,000 of salaries and wages in cash ($95,000 was direct labor, $35,000 was indirect labor, and $37,000 was related to employees responsible for selling and administration).

d. Various manufacturing overhead costs incurred (on account) to support production, $33,000.

e. Depreciation recorded on property, plant, and equipment, $90,000 (70% related to manufacturing equipment and 30% related to assets that support selling and administration).

f. Various selling expenses paid in cash, $27,000.

g. Prepaid insurance expired during the month, $1,200 (80% related to production, and 20% related to selling and administration).

h. Manufacturing overhead applied to production, $132,000.

i. Cost of goods manufactured, $288,000.

j. Cash sales to customers, $395,000.

k. Cost of goods sold (unadjusted), $285,000.

l. Cash payments to creditors, $62,000.

m. Underapplied or overapplied overhead $? .

Required:

1. Calculate the ending balances that would be reported on the company's balance sheet on January 31. You can derive your answers using Microsoft Excel and Exhibit 3A–2 as your guide, or you can use paper, pencil, and a calculator. (Hint: Be sure to calculate the underapplied or overapplied overhead and then account for its affect on the balance sheet.)

2. What is Morrison Company's net operating income for the month of January?

PROBLEM 3A–5 Transaction Analysis LO3–5

Star Videos, Inc., produces short musical videos for sale to retail outlets. The company's balance sheet accounts as of January 1 are given below.

Star Videos, Inc.		
Balance Sheet		
January 1		
Assets		
Cash.		$ 73,000
Accounts receivable		96,000
Inventories:		
Raw materials (film, costumes)	$33,000	
Videos in process	47,000	
Finished videos awaiting sale	78,000	158,000
Prepaid insurance		8,000
Studio and equipment (net)		530,000
Total assets.		$865,000
Liabilities and Stockholders' Equity		
Accounts payable		$150,000
Retained earnings		715,000
Total liabilities and stockholders' equity		$865,000

Because the videos differ in length and in complexity of production, the company uses a job-order costing system to determine the cost of each video produced. Studio (manufacturing) overhead is charged to videos on the basis of camera-hours of activity. The company's predetermined overhead rate for the year ($40 per camera-hour) is based on a cost formula that estimated $280,000 in manufacturing overhead for an estimated allocation base of 7,000 camera-hours. Any underapplied or overapplied overhead is closed to cost of goods sold. The following transactions were recorded for the year:

a. Film, costumes, and similar raw materials purchased on account, $183,000.
b. Film, costumes, and other raw materials issued to production, $210,000 (85% of this material was considered direct to the videos in production, and the other 15% was considered indirect).
c. Utility costs incurred (on account) in the production studio, $78,000.
d. Depreciation recorded on the studio, cameras, and other equipment, $82,000. Three-fourths of this depreciation related to actual production of the videos, and the remainder related to equipment used in marketing and administration.
e. Advertising expense incurred (on account), $131,000.
f. Salaries and wages paid in cash as follows:

Direct labor (actors and directors)	$84,000
Indirect labor (carpenters to build sets,	
costume designers, and so forth)	$105,000
Administrative salaries	$95,000

g. Prepaid insurance expired during the year, $7,000 (70% related to production of videos, and 30% related to marketing and administrative activities).
h. Miscellaneous marketing and administrative expenses incurred (on account), $9,600.
i. Studio (manufacturing) overhead was applied to videos in production. The company recorded 7,250 camera-hours of activity during the year.
j. Videos that cost $565,000 to produce according to their job cost sheets were transferred to the finished videos warehouse to await sale and shipment.
k. Sales for the year totaled $930,000 and were all on account.
l. The total cost to produce the videos that were sold according to their job cost sheets was $610,000.
m. Collections from customers during the year totaled $880,000.
n. Payments to suppliers on account during the year, $515,000.
o. Underapplied or overapplied overhead $? .

Required:
1. Using Exhibit 3A–2 as your guide, prepare a transaction analysis that records all of the above transactions. Calculate the ending balances at December 31 for all balance sheet accounts.
2. Using Exhibit 3A–3 as your guide, prepare a schedule of cost of goods manufactured for the year. If done correctly, your cost of goods manufactured should equal what amount mentioned in the transactions above?

3.   Using Exhibit 3A–4 as your guide, prepare a schedule of cost of goods sold for the year. If done correctly, your unadjusted cost of goods sold should equal what amount mentioned in the transactions above?
4.   Using Exhibit 3A–5 as your guide, prepare an income statement for the year.

PROBLEM 3A–6 Transaction Analysis LO3–5

Brooks Corporation uses a job-order costing system to apply manufacturing costs to jobs. The company closes its underapplied or overapplied overhead to cost of goods sold. Its balance sheet on March 1 is as follows:

Brooks Corporation		
Balance Sheet		
March 1		
Assets		
Cash.		$ 83,000
Raw materials.	$18,000	
Work in process.	14,000	
Finished goods	22,000	54,000
Prepaid expenses		1,800
Property, plant, and equipment (net)		175,000
Total assets.		$313,800
Liabilities and Stockholders' Equity		
Accounts payable		$ 12,000
Retained earnings.		301,800
Total liabilities and stockholders' equity		$313,800

During March the company completed the following transactions:
a.   Purchased raw materials for cash, $69,000.
b.   Raw materials used in production, $77,000 ($67,000 was direct materials and $10,000 was indirect materials).
c.   Paid $178,000 of salaries and wages in cash ($102,000 was direct labor, $23,000 was indirect labor, and $53,000 was related to employees responsible for selling and administration).
d.   Various manufacturing overhead costs paid in cash to support production, $41,000.
e.   Depreciation recorded on property, plant, and equipment, $35,000 (85% related to manufacturing equipment and 15% related to assets that support selling and administration).
f.   Various selling expenses incurred on account, $27,000.
g.   Prepaid insurance expired during the month, $450 (60% related to production, and 40% related to selling and administration).
h.   Manufacturing overhead applied to production, $101,000.
i.   Cost of goods manufactured, $___?___. (Hint: The Work in Process balance on March 31 is $5,000.)
j.   Cash sales to customers, $429,000.
k.   Cost of goods sold (unadjusted), $___?___. (Hint: The Finished Goods balance at March 31 is $6,000.)
l.   Cash payments to creditors, $35,000.
m.   Underapplied or overapplied overhead $___?___.

Required:
1.   Calculate the ending balances that would be reported on the company's balance sheet at March 31. You can derive your answers using Microsoft Excel and Exhibit 3A–2 as your guide, or you can use paper, pencil, and a calculator. (Hint: Be sure to calculate the underapplied or overapplied overhead and then account for its affect on the balance sheet.)
2.   Prepare Brooks Corporation's schedule of cost of goods manufactured for the month ended March 31. You can derive your answers using Microsoft Excel and Exhibit 3A–3 as your guide, or you can use paper, pencil, and a calculator.
3.   Prepare Brooks Corporation's schedule of cost of goods sold for the month ended March 31. You can derive your answers using Microsoft Excel and Exhibit 3A–4 as your guide, or you can use paper, pencil, and a calculator.
4.   Prepare Brooks Corporation's income statement for the month ended March 31. You can derive your answers using Microsoft Excel and Exhibit 3A–5 as your guide, or you can use paper, pencil, and a calculator.

Process Costing

Costing the "Quicker-Picker-Upper"

© Kristoffer Tripplaar/Alamy

If you have ever spilled milk, there is a good chance that you used Bounty paper towels to clean up the mess. **Procter & Gamble (P&G)** manufactures Bounty in two main processing departments—Paper Making and Paper Converting. In the Paper Making Department, wood pulp is converted into paper and then spooled into 2,000 pound rolls. In the Paper Converting Department, two of the 2,000 pound rolls of paper are simultaneously unwound into a machine that creates a two-ply paper towel that is decorated, perforated, and embossed to create texture. The large sheets of paper towels that emerge from this process are wrapped around a cylindrical cardboard core measuring eight feet in length. Once enough sheets wrap around the core, the eight foot roll is cut into individual rolls of Bounty that are sent down a conveyor to be wrapped, packed, and shipped.

In this type of manufacturing environment, costs cannot be readily traced to individual rolls of Bounty; however, given the homogeneous nature of the product, the total costs incurred in the Paper Making Department can be spread uniformly across its output of 2,000 pound rolls of paper. Similarly, the total costs incurred in the Paper Converting Department (including the cost of the 2,000 pound rolls that are transferred in from the Paper Making Department) can be spread uniformly across the number of cases of Bounty produced.

P&G uses a similar costing approach for many of its products such as Tide detergent, Crest toothpaste, and Dawn dishwashing liquid. ∎

Source: Conversation with Brad Bays, formerly a Procter & Gamble financial executive.

LEARNING OBJECTIVES

After studying Chapter 4, you should be able to:

LO4–1	Record the flow of materials, labor, and overhead through a process costing system.
LO4–2	Compute the equivalent units of production using the weighted-average method.
LO4–3	Compute the cost per equivalent unit using the weighted-average method.
LO4–4	Assign costs to units using the weighted-average method.
LO4–5	Prepare a cost reconciliation report using the weighted-average method.
LO4–6	*(Appendix 4A) Compute the equivalent units of production using the FIFO method.*
LO4–7	*(Appendix 4A) Compute the cost per equivalent unit using the FIFO method.*
LO4–8	*(Appendix 4A) Assign costs to units using the FIFO method.*
LO4–9	*(Appendix 4A) Prepare a cost reconciliation report using the FIFO method.*
LO4–10	*(Appendix 4B) Allocate service department costs to operating departments using the direct method.*
LO4–11	*(Appendix 4B) Allocate service department costs to operating departments using the step-down method.*

Job-order costing and process costing are two common methods for determining unit product costs. As explained in previous chapters, job-order costing is used when many different jobs or products are worked on each period. Examples of industries that use job-order costing include furniture manufacturing, special-order printing, shipbuilding, and many types of service organizations.

By contrast, **process costing** is used most commonly in industries that convert raw materials into homogeneous (i.e., uniform) products, such as bricks, soda, or paper, on a continuous basis. Examples of companies that would use process costing include **Reynolds Consumer Products** (aluminum ingots), **Scott Paper** (paper towels), **General Mills** (flours), **ExxonMobil** (gasoline and lubricating oils), **Coppertone** (sunscreens), and **Kellogg's** (breakfast cereals). In addition, process costing is sometimes used in companies with assembly operations. A form of process costing may also be used in utilities that produce gas, water, and electricity.

Our purpose in this chapter is to explain how product costing works in a process costing system.

Comparison of Job-Order and Process Costing

In some ways process costing is very similar to job-order costing, and in some ways it is very different. In this section, we focus on these similarities and differences to provide a foundation for the detailed discussion of process costing that follows.

Similarities between Job-Order and Process Costing

Much of what you learned in previous chapters about costing and cost flows applies equally well to process costing in this chapter. We are not throwing out all that we have learned about costing and starting from "scratch" with a whole new system. The similarities between job-order and process costing are as follows:

1. Both systems have the same basic purposes—to assign material, labor, and manufacturing overhead costs to products and to provide a mechanism for computing unit product costs.
2. Both systems use the same basic manufacturing accounts, including Manufacturing Overhead, Raw Materials, Work in Process, and Finished Goods.
3. The flow of costs through the manufacturing accounts is basically the same in both systems.

As can be seen from this comparison, much of what you have already learned about costing is applicable to a process costing system. Our task now is to refine and extend your knowledge to process costing.

Differences between Job-Order and Process Costing

Exhibit 4–1 summarizes three differences between job-order and process costing. First, job-order costing is used when a company produces many different jobs that have unique production requirements. Process costing is used when a company produces a continuous flow of units that are indistinguishable from one another. Second, job-order costing uses job cost sheets to accumulate costs for individual jobs. Process costing accumulates costs by department (rather than by job) and assigns these costs uniformly to all identical units that pass through the department during a period. Third, job-order costing uses job cost sheets to compute units costs for each job. Process costing systems compute unit costs by department.

EXHIBIT 4–1
Differences between Job-Order and Process Costing

Job-Order Costing	Process Costing
1. Many different jobs are worked on during each period, with each job having unique production requirements.	1. A single product is produced either on a continuous basis or for long periods of time. All units of product are identical.
2. Costs are accumulated by individual job.	2. Costs are accumulated by department.
3. Unit costs are computed *by job* on the job cost sheet.	3. Unit costs are computed *by department*.

Cost Flows in Process Costing

Before going through a detailed example of process costing, it will be helpful to see how, in a general way, manufacturing costs flow through a process costing system.

Processing Departments

A **processing department** is an organizational unit where work is performed on a product and where materials, labor, or overhead costs are added to the product. For example, a **Nalley's** potato chip factory might have three processing departments—one for preparing potatoes, one for cooking, and one for inspecting and packaging. A brick factory might have two processing departments—one for mixing and molding clay into bricks and one for firing the molded bricks. Some products and services may go through a number of processing departments, while others may go through only one or two. Regardless of the number of processing departments, they all have two essential features. First, the activity in the processing department is performed uniformly on all of the units passing through it. Second, the output of the processing department is homogeneous; in other words, all of the units produced are identical.

Products in a process costing environment, such as bricks or potato chips, typically flow in sequence from one department to another as in Exhibit 4–2.

EXHIBIT 4–2
Sequential Processing Departments

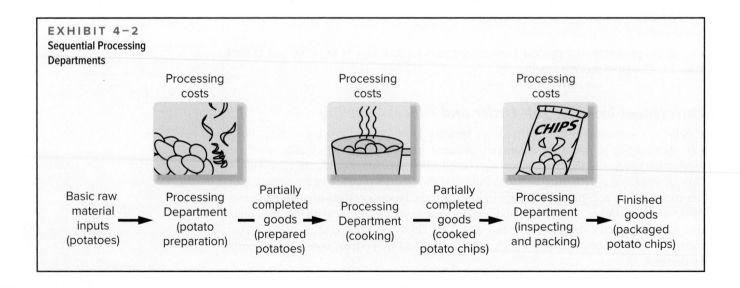

GET THE DOOR! IT'S PAPA JOHNS

On Super Bowl Sunday 12.5 million pizzas are delivered to American households. Each pizza comes in a box, many of which are manufactured in one of 17 plants owned by **Rock-Tenn Company** in Norcross, Georgia. The company's Atlanta plant uses a production line that spans more than one and a half football fields to convert "58-inch diameter rolls of heavy paper into a ribbon of corrugated cardboard that runs through a printing press and then through high-speed die cutters that crease, cut and trim it into individual boxes." A total of 50 employees keep this production line churning out 400 unfolded boxes per minute for 24 hours a day and seven days a week.

© A.Penkov/Shutterstock.com

This type of manufacturing process is conducive to process costing because the pizza boxes being produced at 400 units per minute are indistinguishable from one another. It stands in stark contrast to job-order manufacturing where customized outputs are produced in response to unique customer demands.

Source: Bob Tita, "It's Crunch Time for Pizza Boxes," *The Wall Street Journal,* January 30, 2015, pp. B1 and B6.

The Flow of Materials, Labor, and Overhead Costs

Cost accumulation is simpler in a process costing system than in a job-order costing system. In a process costing system, instead of having to assign costs to hundreds of different jobs, costs are assigned to only a few processing departments.

Exhibit 4–3 shows a T-account model of materials, labor, and overhead cost flows in a process costing system. Several key points should be noted from this exhibit. First, note that a separate Work in Process account is maintained for *each processing department.*

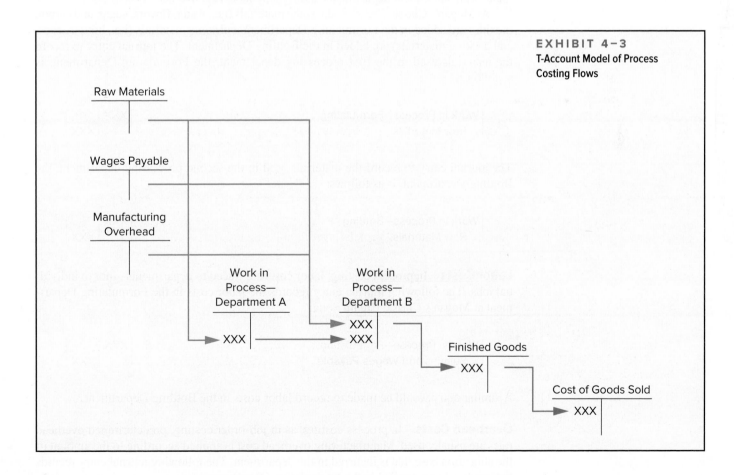

EXHIBIT 4–3
T-Account Model of Process Costing Flows

In contrast, in a job-order costing system the entire company may have only one Work in Process account. Second, note that the completed production of the first processing department (Department A in the exhibit) is transferred to the Work in Process account of the second processing department (Department B). After further work in Department B, the completed units are then transferred to Finished Goods. (In Exhibit 4–3, we show only two processing departments, but a company can have many processing departments.)

Finally, note that materials, labor, and overhead costs can be added in *any* processing department—not just the first. Costs in Department B's Work in Process account consist of the materials, labor, and overhead costs incurred in Department B plus the costs assigned to the units transferred in from Department A (called transferred-in costs).

Materials, Labor, and Overhead Cost Entries

LO4–1
Record the flow of materials, labor, and overhead through a process costing system.

To complete our discussion of cost flows in a process costing system, in this section we show journal entries relating to materials, labor, and overhead costs at Megan's Classic Cream Soda, a company that has two processing departments—Formulating and Bottling. In the Formulating Department, ingredients are checked for quality and then mixed and injected with carbon dioxide to create bulk cream soda. In the Bottling Department, bottles are checked for defects, filled with cream soda, capped, visually inspected again for defects, and then packed for shipping.

Materials Costs   As in job-order costing, materials are drawn from the storeroom using a materials requisition form. Materials can be added in any processing department, although it is not unusual for materials to be added only in the first processing department, with subsequent departments adding only labor and overhead costs.

At Megan's Classic Cream Soda, some materials (i.e., water, flavors, sugar, and carbon dioxide) are added in the Formulating Department and some materials (i.e., bottles, caps, and packing materials) are added in the Bottling Department. The journal entry to record the materials used in the first processing department, the Formulating Department, is as follows:

Work in Process—Formulating	XXX	
Raw Materials...		XXX

The journal entry to record the materials used in the second processing department, the Bottling Department, is as follows:

Work in Process—Bottling	XXX	
Raw Materials...		XXX

Labor Costs   In process costing, labor costs are traced to departments—not to individual jobs. The following journal entry records the labor costs in the Formulating Department at Megan's Classic Cream Soda:

Work in Process—Formulating	XXX	
Salaries and Wages Payable.............................		XXX

A similar entry would be made to record labor costs in the Bottling Department.

Overhead Costs   In process costing, as in job-order costing, predetermined overhead rates are usually used. Manufacturing overhead cost is applied according to the amount of the allocation base that is incurred in the department. The following journal entry records the overhead cost applied in the Formulating Department:

Work in Process—Formulating	XXX	
Manufacturing Overhead..................................		XXX

A similar entry would be made to apply manufacturing overhead cost in the Bottling Department.

Completing the Cost Flows   Once processing has been completed in a department, the units are transferred to the next department for further processing, as illustrated in the T-accounts in Exhibit 4–3. The following journal entry transfers the cost of the units that have been completed within the Formulating Department to the Bottling Department:

Work in Process—Bottling	XXX	
Work in Process—Formulating		XXX

After processing has been finished in the Bottling Department, the costs of the completed units are transferred to the Finished Goods inventory account:

Finished Goods	XXX	
Work in Process—Bottling		XXX

Finally, when a customer's order is filled and units are sold, the cost of the units is transferred to Cost of Goods Sold:

Cost of Goods Sold.......................................	XXX	
Finished Goods		XXX

To summarize, the cost flows between accounts are basically the same in a process costing system as they are in a job-order costing system. The only difference at this point is that in a process costing system each department has a separate Work in Process account.

JUNK FOOD GOES ON A HEALTH KICK

Candy manufacturers are feeling pressure from customers to remove unhealthy ingredients from their snack food. For example, **Nestlé** has been working on removing artificial colors (such as Red 40 and Yellow 5) and artificial flavors (such as Vanillin) from its more than 250 chocolate products. The company plans to use Annatto (which comes from achiote trees) instead of artificial food colors and it intends to replace vanillin with natural vanilla flavor. While these natural ingredients cost more, Nestlé says that it will not offset these higher material costs with higher prices. In addition to Nestlé, **Mondelez International**, the makers of Oreo cookies and Cadbury chocolate, plans to reduce the saturated fat and sodium in its products by 10% by 2020.

Source: Annie Gasparro, "Nestle Bars Artificial Color, Flavors," *The Wall Street JournaL,* February 18, 2015, p. B6.

© Ryan Remiorz/The Canadian Press/AP Images

Process Costing Computations: Three Key Concepts

In process costing, each department needs to calculate two numbers for financial reporting purposes—the cost of its ending work in process inventory and the cost of its completed units that were transferred to the next stage of the production process. The key to deriving these two numbers is calculating *unit costs* within each department. On the surface, these departmental unit cost calculations may seem very straightforward—simply divide the department's costs (the numerator) by its outputs, or units produced (the denominator). However, to set the stage for correctly performing this seemingly simple computation, you will need to understand three key foundational concepts.

Key Concept #1

There is more than one way to calculate departmental unit costs. This chapter explains two methods for performing these calculations, the *weighted-average method* and the *FIFO method*. The **weighted-average method** of process costing, which will be explained in the main body of the chapter, calculates unit costs by combining costs and outputs from the current and prior periods. The **FIFO method** of process costing, which will be covered in Appendix 4A, calculates unit costs based solely on the costs and outputs from the current period.

Key Concept #2

Each department needs to calculate a separate unit cost for each type of manufacturing cost that it incurs. For example, if a given department adds materials cost, labor cost, and overhead cost to the production process it would need to compute a unit cost for each of these three cost categories. To simplify things, companies often consolidate these three cost categories into two groups by combining labor and overhead costs into a category called *conversion costs* (or conversion for short). **Conversion cost**, as defined in an earlier chapter, is direct labor cost plus manufacturing overhead cost.

Key Concept #3

Quantifying each department's number of units produced during a period is complicated by the fact that most departments usually have some partially completed units on hand at the end of the period. Because it would be an overstatement to count these partially completed units as equivalent to fully completed units when counting the department's output, these partially completed units are translated into an *equivalent* number of fully completed units. In process costing, this translation is done using the following formula:

$$\text{Equivalent units} = \text{Number of partially completed units} \times \text{Percentage completion}$$

As the formula states, **equivalent units** is the product of the number of partially completed units and the percentage completion of those units with respect to the processing in the department. Roughly speaking, the equivalent units is the number of complete units that could have been obtained from the materials and effort that went into the partially complete units.

For example, suppose Department A has 500 units in its ending work in process inventory that are 60% complete with respect to processing in the department. These 500 partially complete units are equivalent to 300 fully complete units (500 × 60% = 300). Therefore, Department A's ending work in process inventory would contain 300 equivalent units that are included within its output for the period.

The Weighted-Average Method: An Example

We now turn our attention to Double Diamond Skis, a company that manufactures a high-performance deep-powder ski, and that uses process costing to determine its unit product costs. The company's production process is illustrated in Exhibit 4–4. Skis go through a sequence of five processing departments, starting with the Shaping and Milling Department and ending with the Finishing and Pairing Department.

We will use the Double Diamond Skis example to explain the weighted-average method of process costing in four steps:

    Step 1: Compute the equivalent units of production.
    Step 2: Compute the cost per equivalent unit.
    Step 3: Assign costs to units.
    Step 4: Prepare a cost reconciliation report.

EXHIBIT 4–4
The Production Process at Double Diamond Skis*

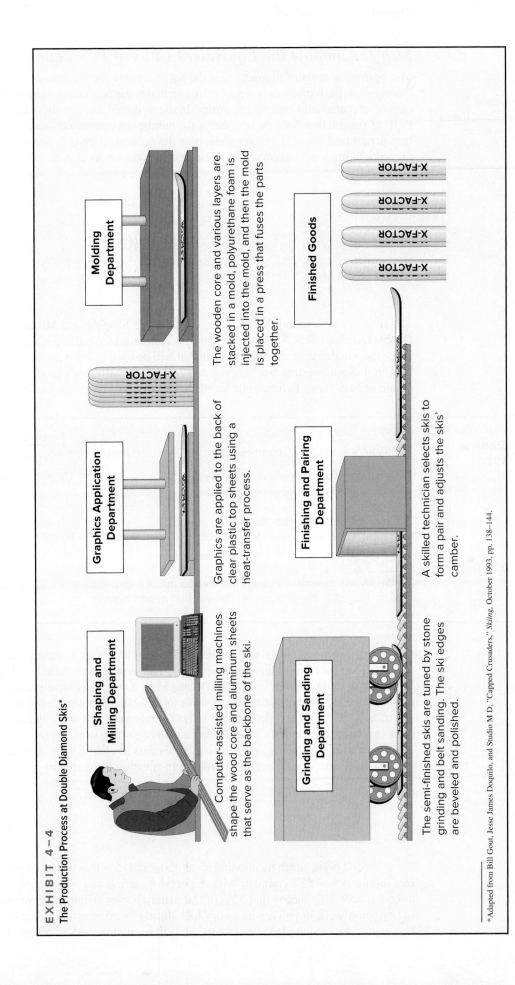

Shaping and Milling Department

Computer-assisted milling machines shape the wood core and aluminum sheets that serve as the backbone of the ski.

Graphics Application Department

Graphics are applied to the back of clear plastic top sheets using a heat-transfer process.

Molding Department

The wooden core and various layers are stacked in a mold, polyurethane foam is injected into the mold, and then the mold is placed in a press that fuses the parts together.

Grinding and Sanding Department

The semi-finished skis are tuned by stone grinding and belt sanding. The ski edges are beveled and polished.

Finishing and Pairing Department

A skilled technician selects skis to form a pair and adjusts the skis' camber.

Finished Goods

*Adapted from Bill Gout, Jesse James Doquilo, and Studio M D, "Capped Crusaders," *Skiing*, October 1993, pp. 138–144.

Step 1: Compute the Equivalent Units of Production

LO4–2

Compute the equivalent units of production using the weighted-average method.

The *equivalent units of production* is the name we use for the denominator in unit cost calculations. Each processing department calculates the equivalent units of production for each of its manufacturing cost categories. In the weighted-average method, the **equivalent units of production** for a department is the number of completed units transferred to the next department (or to finished goods) plus the equivalent units in the department's ending work in process inventory. This definition in equation form is as follows:

Weighted–Average Method
(a separate calculation is made for each cost category in
each processing department)

$$\text{Equivalent units of production} = \text{Units transferred to the next department or to finished goods} + \text{Equivalent units in ending work in process inventory}$$

To better understand this formula, consider the Shaping and Milling Department at Double Diamond Skis. This department uses computerized milling machines to precisely shape the wooden core and metal sheets that will be used to form the backbone of the ski. Exhibit 4–5 summarizes the Shaping and Milling Department's production data for the month of May for its two manufacturing cost categories, materials and conversion.

EXHIBIT 4–5
Shaping and Milling Department Production Data for May

Shaping and Milling Department	Units	Percent Complete	
		Materials	Conversion
Beginning work in process inventory	200	55%	30%
Units started into production during May	5,000		
Units completed during May and transferred to the next department.	4,800	100%*	100%*
Ending work in process inventory	400	40%	25%

*We always assume that units transferred out of a department are 100% complete with respect to the processing done in that department.

The first thing to note about Exhibit 4–5 is the flow of units through the department (focus on the data under the Units heading). The department started with 200 units in beginning work in process inventory. During May, 5,000 units were started into production. This made a total of 5,200 units. Of this total, 4,800 units were completed during May and transferred to the next department and 400 units were still in the department's ending work in process inventory. In general, the units in beginning work in process inventory plus the units started into production must equal the units in ending work in process inventory plus the units completed and transferred out. In equation form, this is:

Units in beginning work in process inventory + Units started into production
or transferred in = Units in ending work in process inventory + Units completed
and transferred out

A second point worth mentioning about Exhibit 4–5 is that its beginning work in process inventory was 55% complete with respect to materials and 30% complete with respect to conversion. This means that 55% of the materials cost required to complete the units in beginning work in process inventory had already been incurred. Likewise, 30% of the conversion costs required to complete the units in beginning work in process inventory had

Shaping and Milling Department	Materials	Conversion
Units transferred to the next department	4,800	4,800
Equivalent units in ending work in process inventory:		
Materials: 400 units × 40% complete	160	
Conversion: 400 units × 25% complete		100
Equivalent units of production	4,960	4,900

EXHIBIT 4–6
Equivalent Units of Production: Weighted-Average Method

already been incurred. However, when using the weighted-average method to compute the equivalent units of production, these two completion percentages pertaining to the beginning work in process inventory (55% for materials and 30% for conversion) will be ignored.

The third point to highlight from Exhibit 4–5 is that the Shaping and Milling Department's ending work in process inventory is 40% complete with respect to materials and 25% complete with respect to conversion. This means that 40% of the materials cost and 25% of the conversion costs required to complete the units in ending work in process inventory have already been incurred. Under the weighted-average method, these two completion percentages pertaining to the ending work in process inventory (40% for materials and 25% for conversion) will be included in the computation of equivalent units of production.

Exhibit 4–6 summarizes the equivalent units of production calculations within the Shaping and Milling Department for materials and conversion. Notice that these calculations ignore the fact that the units in the beginning work in process inventory were partially complete with respect to materials and conversion. For example, the 200 units in beginning inventory were already 30% complete with respect to conversion costs. However, the weighted-average method is concerned only with the 100 equivalent units that are in ending inventories and the 4,800 units that were transferred to the next department (for a total of 4,900 equivalent units of production); it is not concerned with the fact that the beginning work in process inventory was already partially complete. In other words, the 4,900 equivalent units of production computed using the weighted-average method include work that was accomplished in the prior period. This is a key point concerning the weighted-average method and it is easy to overlook.

Exhibit 4–7 provides another way of looking at the computation of equivalent units of production. It depicts the computations for conversion costs. Study it carefully before going on.

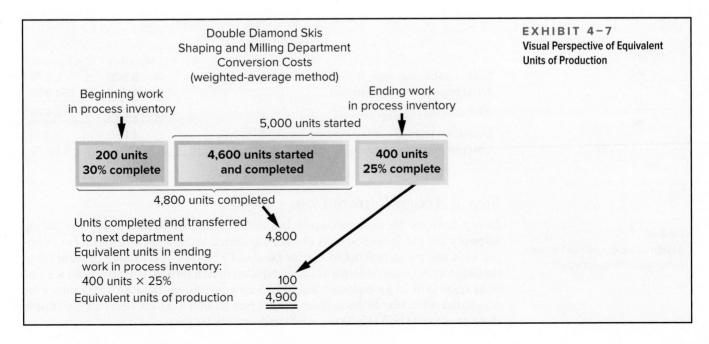

EXHIBIT 4–7
Visual Perspective of Equivalent Units of Production

LO4–3

Compute the cost per equivalent unit using the weighted-average method.

Step 2: Compute the Cost per Equivalent Unit

In step 2 we need to determine the total cost to include in the numerator and then divide it by the equivalent units of production that we already calculated in step 1 to derive the cost per equivalent unit for materials and conversion. To help us with this step, Exhibit 4–8 displays the Shaping and Milling Department's cost data for the Month of May.

EXHIBIT 4–8
Shaping and Milling Department Cost Data for May

	Materials	Conversion	Total
Cost of beginning work in process inventory	$ 9,600	$ 5,575	$ 15,175
Costs added during the period	368,600	350,900	719,500
Total cost	$378,200	$ 356,475	$734,675

Given this cost data, we can now compute the Shaping and Milling Department's cost per equivalent unit for materials and conversion using the following equation:

Weighted-Average Method
(a separate calculation is made for each cost category in each processing department)

$$\text{Cost per equivalent unit} = \frac{\text{Cost of beginning work in process inventory} + \text{Cost added during the period}}{\text{Equivalent units of production}}$$

Note that the numerator is the sum of the cost of beginning work in process inventory and of the cost added during the period. Thus, the weighted-average method blends together costs from the prior and current periods. That is why it is called the weighted-average method; it averages together costs and outputs from the current and prior periods.

Using this equation, the Shaping and Milling Department's costs per equivalent unit for materials and conversion for May are computed as follows:

Shaping and Milling Department Costs per Equivalent Unit		
	Materials	Conversion
Cost of beginning work in process inventory	$ 9,600	$ 5,575
Costs added during the period	368,600	350,900
Total cost (a)	$378,200	$ 356,475
Equivalent units of production (see Exhibit 4–6) (b)	4,960	4,900
Cost per equivalent unit (a) ÷ (b)	$76.25	$72.75

Step 3: Assign Costs to Units

LO4–4

Assign costs to units using the weighted-average method.

In step 3 we use the costs per equivalent unit to value the equivalent units in ending inventory and the completed units that are transferred to the next department. For example, each unit transferred out of Double Diamond's Shaping and Milling Department to the Graphics Application Department, as depicted in Exhibit 4–4, will carry with it a cost of $149.00 ($76.25 for materials and $72.75 for conversion). Because 4,800 units were transferred out in May to the next department (see Exhibit 4–5), the total cost assigned to those units would be $715,200 (= 4,800 units × $149.00 per unit).

A complete accounting of the costs of both ending work in process inventory and the units transferred out appears below:

Shaping and Milling Department Costs of Ending Work in Process Inventory and the Units Transferred Out			
	Materials	Conversion	Total
Ending work in process inventory:			
Equivalent units (see Exhibit 4–6) (a)	160	100	
Cost per equivalent unit (b)	$76.25	$72.75	
Cost of ending work in process inventory (a) × (b)	$12,200	$7,275	$19,475
Units completed and transferred out:			
Units transferred to the next department (see Exhibit 4–6) (a)	4,800	4,800	
Cost per equivalent unit (b)	$76.25	$72.75	
Cost of units transferred out (a) × (b)	$366,000	$349,200	$715,200

For materials and conversion, the equivalent units in ending work in process inventory and the completed units transferred to the next department are multiplied by the cost per equivalent unit to determine the cost assigned to the units. For example, the 100 equivalent units of conversion in ending work in process inventory are multiplied by the cost per equivalent unit of $72.75 to determine the conversion costs included in ending work in process inventory of $7,275. Similarly, the 4,800 units completed and transferred out are multiplied by the conversion cost per equivalent unit of $72.75 to determine the conversion costs attached to the completed units transferred out of $349,200.

Step 4: Prepare a Cost Reconciliation Report

The costs assigned to the equivalent units in ending work in process inventory and to the completed units transferred out reconcile with the costs we started with in Exhibit 4–8 as shown below:

LO4–5
Prepare a cost reconciliation report using the weighted-average method.

Shaping and Milling Department Cost Reconciliation	
Costs to be accounted for:	
Cost of beginning work in process inventory (Exhibit 4–8)	$ 15,175
Costs added to production during the period (Exhibit 4–8)	719,500
Total cost to be accounted for	$734,675
Costs accounted for as follows:	
Cost of ending work in process inventory (see above)	$ 19,475
Cost of units transferred out (see above)	715,200
Total cost accounted for	$734,675

The $715,200 cost of the units transferred to the next department, Graphics Application, will be accounted for in that department as "costs transferred in." It will be treated in the process costing system as just another category of costs like materials or conversion costs. The only difference is that the costs transferred in will always be 100% complete with respect to the work done in the Shaping and Milling Department. Costs are passed on from one department to the next in this fashion, until they reach the last processing department, Finishing and Pairing. When the products are completed in this last department, their costs are transferred to finished goods.

GETTING LESS FOR THE SAME PRICE

When the prices of raw materials such as sugar and cotton increase during an economic downturn, companies realize that they cannot pass these cost increases on to customers in the form of higher prices. Instead, companies often respond to these circumstances by holding their prices constant while giving customers less for their money. For example, when the price of cotton increased **Georgia-Pacific** responded by decreasing the width of its Angel Soft Double Roll toilet paper from 4.27 inches to 4.00 inches. The company also reduced the number of sheets per roll from 352 to 300. Similarly, **Procter & Gamble** decreased the number of sheets in a roll of Charmin Ultra Soft Big Roll from 200 to 176.

These product size reductions not only lower raw material costs, but they also reduce shipping costs. Georgia-Pacific estimates that its smaller rolls of toilet paper enable it to transport 12–17% more units per truck, thereby saving 345,000 gallons of gasoline per year.

Source: Beth Kowitt, "When Less is . . . Less?" *Fortune,* November 15, 2010, p. 21.

Operation Costing

Job-order costing and process costing represent the two ends of a continuum. On one end is job-order costing, which is used by companies that produce many different products in one facility. On the other end is process costing, which is used by companies that produce homogeneous products in large quantities. Between these two extremes there are many hybrid systems that include characteristics of both job-order and process costing. One of these hybrids is called *operation costing.*

Operation costing is used in situations where products have some common characteristics and some individual characteristics. Shoes, for example, have common characteristics in that all styles involve cutting and sewing that can be done on a repetitive basis, using the same equipment and following the same basic procedures. Shoes also have individual characteristics—some are made of expensive leathers and others may be made using inexpensive synthetic materials. In a situation such as this, where products have some common characteristics but also must be processed individually, operation costing may be used to determine product costs.

As mentioned above, operation costing is a hybrid system that employs aspects of both job-order and process costing. Products are typically processed in batches when operation costing is used, with each batch charged for its own specific materials. In this sense, operation costing is similar to job-order costing. However, labor and overhead costs are accumulated by operation or by department, and these costs are assigned to units as in process costing. If shoes are being produced, each shoe is charged the same per unit conversion cost, regardless of the style involved, but it is charged with its specific materials cost. Thus, the company is able to distinguish between styles in terms of materials, but it is able to employ the simplicity of a process costing system for labor and overhead costs.

Examples of other products for which operation costing may be used include electronic equipment (such as semiconductors), textiles, clothing, and jewelry (such as rings, bracelets, and medallions). Products of this type are typically produced in batches, but they can vary considerably from model to model or from style to style in terms of the cost of materials.

Summary

Process costing is used in situations where homogeneous products or services are produced on a continuous basis. Costs flow through the manufacturing accounts in basically the same way in a process costing system as in a job-order costing system. However, costs are accumulated by department rather than by job in process costing.

In process costing, the equivalent units of production must be determined for each cost category in each department. Under the weighted-average method, the equivalent units of production equals the number of completed units transferred out to the next department or to finished goods plus the equivalent units in ending work in process inventory. The equivalent units in ending work in process inventory equals the product of the number of partially completed units and the percentage completion of those units with respect to the specific cost category.

Under the weighted-average method, the cost per equivalent unit for a specific cost category is computed by combining the cost of beginning work in process inventory and the cost added during the period and then dividing this sum by the equivalent units of production. The cost per equivalent unit then is used to value the ending work in process inventory and the units transferred out to the next department or to finished goods.

The cost reconciliation report reconciles the cost of beginning inventory and the costs added to production during the period to the cost of ending inventory and the cost of units transferred out.

Costs are transferred from one department to the next until the last processing department. At that point, the cost of completed units is transferred to finished goods.

Review Problem: Process Cost Flows and Costing Units

Luxguard Home Paint Company produces exterior latex paint, which it sells in one-gallon containers. The company has two processing departments—Base Fab and Finishing. White paint, which is used as a base for all the company's paints, is mixed from raw ingredients in the Base Fab Department. Pigments are then added to the basic white paint, the pigmented paint is squirted under pressure into one-gallon containers, and the containers are labeled and packed for shipping in the Finishing Department. Information relating to the company's operations for April follows:

a. Raw materials used in production: Base Fab Department, $851,000; and Finishing Department, $629,000.
b. Incurred direct labor costs: Base Fab Department, $330,000; and Finishing Department, $270,000.
c. Applied manufacturing overhead cost: Base Fab Department, $665,000; and Finishing Department, $405,000.
d. Transferred basic white paint from the Base Fab Department to the Finishing Department, $1,850,000.
e. Transferred paint that had been prepared for shipping from the Finishing Department to Finished Goods, $3,200,000.

Required:

1. Prepare journal entries to record items (a) through (e) above.
2. Post the journal entries from (1) above to T-accounts. The balance in the Base Fab Department's Work in Process account on April 1 was $150,000; the beginning balance in the Finishing Department's Work in Process account was $70,000. After posting entries to the T-accounts, find the ending balance in each department's Work in Process account.
3. Compute the Base Fab Department's cost of ending work in process inventory for materials, labor, overhead, and in total for April. Also, compute the Base Fab Department's cost of the completed units transferred to the next department for materials, labor, overhead, and in total for April. The following additional information is available regarding production in the Base Fab Department during April:

Production data:	
Units (gallons) in process, April 1: materials 100% complete;	
labor and overhead 60% complete.	30,000
Units (gallons) started into production during April	420,000
Units (gallons) completed and transferred to the Finishing Department	370,000
Units (gallons) in process, April 30: materials 50% complete;	
labor and overhead 25% complete.	80,000
Cost data:	
Work in process inventory, April 1:	
Materials	$ 92,000
Labor	21,000
Overhead	37,000
Total cost of work in process inventory	$ 150,000
Cost added during April:	
Materials	$ 851,000
Labor	330,000
Overhead.	665,000
Total cost added during April	$1,846,000

4.   Prepare a cost reconciliation report for April.

Solution to Review Problem

1.   a.   Work in Process—Base Fab Department   851,000
          Work in Process—Finishing Department   629,000
              Raw Materials   1,480,000
     b.   Work in Process—Base Fab Department   330,000
          Work in Process—Finishing Department   270,000
              Salaries and Wages Payable   600,000
     c.   Work in Process—Base Fab Department   665,000
          Work in Process—Finishing Department   405,000
              Manufacturing Overhead   1,070,000
     d.   Work in Process—Finishing Department   1,850,000
              Work in Process—Base Fab Department   1,850,000
     e.   Finished Goods   3,200,000
              Work in Process—Finishing Department   3,200,000

2.

Raw Materials			
Bal.	XXX	(a)	1,480,000

Salaries and Wages Payable		
	(b)	600,000

Work in Process— Base Fab Department			
Bal.	150,000	(d)	1,850,000
(a)	851,000		
(b)	330,000		
(c)	665,000		
Bal.	146,000		

Manufacturing Overhead			
(Various actual			
costs)		(c)	1,070,000

Work in Process—Finishing Department			
Bal.	70,000	(e)	3,200,000
(a)	629,000		
(b)	270,000		
(c)	405,000		
(d)	1,850,000		
Bal.	24,000		

Finished Goods		
Bal.	XXX	
(e)	3,200,000	

3.   First, we must compute the equivalent units of production for each cost category:

Base Fab Department Equivalent Units of Production			
	Materials	Labor	Overhead
Units transferred to the next department	370,000	370,000	370,000
Equivalent units in ending work in process inventory (materials: 80,000 units × 50% complete; labor: 80,000 units × 25% complete; overhead: 80,000 units × 25% complete).	40,000	20,000	20,000
Equivalent units of production	410,000	390,000	390,000

Then we must compute the cost per equivalent unit for each cost category:

Base Fab Department Costs per Equivalent Unit			
	Materials	Labor	Overhead
Costs:			
Cost of beginning work in process inventory	$ 92,000	$ 21,000	$ 37,000
Costs added during the period	851,000	330,000	665,000
Total cost (a)	$943,000	$351,000	$ 702,000
Equivalent units of production (b)	410,000	390,000	390,000
Cost per equivalent unit (a) ÷ (b)	$2.30	$0.90	$1.80

The costs per equivalent unit can then be assigned to the units in ending work in process inventory and the units transferred out as follows:

Base Fab Department Costs of Ending Work in Process Inventory and the Units Transferred Out	Materials	Labor	Overhead	Total
Ending work in process inventory:				
Equivalent units	40,000	20,000	20,000	
Cost per equivalent unit	$2.30	$0.90	$1.80	
Cost of ending work in process inventory	$92,000	$18,000	$36,000	$146,000
Units completed and transferred out:				
Units transferred to the next department	370,000	370,000	370,000	
Cost per equivalent unit	$2.30	$0.90	$1.80	
Cost of units completed and transferred out ...	$851,000	$333,000	$666,000	$1,850,000

4.

Base Fab Department Cost Reconciliation	
Costs to be accounted for:	
Cost of beginning work in process inventory	$ 150,000
Costs added to production during the period	1,846,000
Total cost to be accounted for	$1,996,000
Costs accounted for as follows:	
Cost of ending work in process inventory	$ 146,000
Cost of units transferred out	1,850,000
Total cost accounted for	$1,996,000

Glossary

Conversion cost Direct labor cost plus manufacturing overhead cost. (p. 160)

Equivalent units The product of the number of partially completed units and their percentage of completion with respect to a particular cost. Equivalent units are the number of complete whole units that could be obtained from the materials and effort contained in partially completed units. (p. 160)

Equivalent units of production (weighted-average method) The units transferred to the next department (or to finished goods) during the period plus the equivalent units in the department's ending work in process inventory. (p. 162)

FIFO method A process costing method that calculates unit costs based solely on the costs and outputs from the current period. (p. 160)

Operation costing A hybrid costing system used when products have some common characteristics and some individual characteristics. (p. 166)

Process costing A costing method used when essentially homogeneous products are produced on a continuous basis. (p. 155)

Processing department An organizational unit where work is performed on a product and where materials, labor, or overhead costs are added to the product. (p. 156)

Weighted-average method A process costing method that calculates unit costs by combining costs and outputs from the current and prior periods. (p. 160)

Questions

4–1   Under what conditions would it be appropriate to use a process costing system?

4–2   In what ways are job-order and process costing similar?

4–3   Why is cost accumulation simpler in a process costing system than it is in a job-order costing system?

4–4   How many Work in Process accounts are maintained in a company that uses process costing?

4–5   Assume that a company has two processing departments—Mixing followed by Firing. Prepare a journal entry to show a transfer of work in process from the Mixing Department to the Firing Department.

4-6   Assume that a company has two processing departments—Mixing followed by Firing. Explain what costs might be added to the Firing Department's Work in Process account during a period.

4-7   What is meant by the term *equivalent units of production* when the weighted-average method is used?

4-8   Watkins Trophies, Inc., produces thousands of medallions made of bronze, silver, and gold. The medallions are identical except for the materials used in their manufacture. What costing system would you advise the company to use?

Applying Excel   ■ connect

LO4-2, LO4-3, LO4-4, LO4-5

This exercise relates to the Double Diamond Skis' Shaping and Milling Department that was discussed earlier in the chapter. The Excel worksheet form that appears below consolidates data from Exhibits 4–5 and 4–8. Download the workbook containing this form from Connect, where you will also receive instructions about how to use this worksheet form.

	A	B	C	D
1	Chapter 4: Applying Excel			
2				
3	**Data**			
4	Beginning work in process inventory:			
5	Units in process	200		
6	Completion with respect to materials	55%		
7	Completion with respect to conversion	30%		
8	Costs in the beginning work in process inventory:			
9	Materials cost	$9,600		
10	Conversion cost	$5,575		
11	Units started into production during the period	5,000		
12	Costs added to production during the period:			
13	Materials cost	$368,600		
14	Conversion cost	$350,900		
15	Ending work in process inventory:			
16	Units in process	400		
17	Completion with respect to materials	40%		
18	Completion with respect to conversion	25%		
19				
20	*Enter a formula into each of the cells marked with a ? below*			
21				
22	**Weighted-Average method:**			
23				
24	*Equivalent Units of Production*			
25		Materials	Conversion	
26	Units transferred to the next department	?	?	
27	Ending work in process inventory:			
28	Materials	?		
29	Conversion		?	
30	Equivalent units of production	?	?	
31				
32	*Costs per Equivalent Unit*			
33		Materials	Conversion	
34	Cost of beginning work in process inventory	?	?	
35	Costs added during the period	?	?	
36	Total cost	?	?	
37	Equivalent units of production	?	?	
38	Cost per equivalent unit	?	?	
39				
40	*Costs of Ending Work in Process Inventory and the Units Transferred Out*			
41		Materials	Conversion	Total
42	Ending work in process inventory:			
43	Equivalent units of production	?	?	
44	Cost per equivalent unit	?	?	
45	Cost of ending work in process inventory	?	?	?
46				
47	Units completed and transferred out:			
48	Units transferred to the next department	?	?	
49	Cost per equivalent unit	?	?	
50	Cost of units transferred out	?	?	?
51				
52	*Cost Reconciliation*			
53	Costs to be accounted for:			
54	Cost of beginning work in process inventory	?		
55	Costs added to production during the period	?		
56	Total cost to be accounted for	?		
57	Costs accounted for as follows:			
58	Cost of ending work in process inventory	?		
59	Cost of units transferred out	?		
60	Total cost accounted for	?		

Chapter 4 Form Chapter 4 Formulas Chapter

You should proceed to the requirements below only after completing your worksheet.

Required:

1. Check your worksheet by changing the beginning work in process inventory to 100 units, the units started into production during the period to 2,500 units, and the units in ending work in process inventory to 200 units, keeping all of the other data the same as in the original example. If your worksheet is operating properly, the cost per equivalent unit for materials should now be $152.50 and the cost per equivalent unit for conversion should be $145.50. If you do not get these answers, find the errors in your worksheet and correct them.

    How much is the total cost of the units transferred out? Did it change? Why or why not?

2. Enter the following data from a different company into your worksheet:

Beginning work in process inventory:	
Units in process	200
Completion with respect to materials	100%
Completion with respect to conversion	20%
Costs in the beginning work in process inventory:	
Materials cost	$2,000
Conversion cost	$800
Units started into production during the period	1,800
Costs added during the period:	
Materials cost	$18,400
Conversion cost	$38,765
Ending work in process inventory:	
Units in process	100
Completion with respect to materials	100%
Completion with respect to conversion	30%

    What is the cost of the units transferred out?

3. What happens to the cost of the units transferred out in part (2) above if the percentage completion with respect to conversion for the beginning inventory is changed from 20% to 40% and everything else remains the same? What happens to the cost per equivalent unit for conversion? Explain.

---

connect   **The Foundational 15**

Clopack Company manufactures one product that goes through one processing department called Mixing. All raw materials are introduced at the start of work in the Mixing Department. The company uses the weighted-average method of process costing. Its Work in Process T-account for the Mixing Department for June follows (all forthcoming questions pertain to June):

LO4–1, LO4–2, LO4–3, LO4–4, LO4–5

Work in Process—Mixing Department

June 1 balance	28,000	Completed and transferred to Finished Goods	?
Materials	120,000		
Direct labor	79,500		
Overhead	97,000		
June 30 balance	?		

The June 1 work in process inventory consisted of 5,000 units with $16,000 in materials cost and $12,000 in conversion cost. The June 1 work in process inventory was 100% complete with respect to materials and 50% complete with respect to conversion. During June, 37,500 units were started into production. The June 30 work in process inventory consisted of 8,000 units that were 100% complete with respect to materials and 40% complete with respect to conversion.

Required:

1. Prepare the journal entries to record the raw materials used in production and the direct labor cost incurred.
2. Prepare the journal entry to record the overhead cost applied to production.
3. How many units were completed and transferred to finished goods during the period?

4. Compute the equivalent units of production for materials.
5. Compute the equivalent units of production for conversion.
6. What is the cost of beginning work in process inventory plus the cost added during the period for materials?
7. What is the cost of beginning work in process inventory plus the cost added during the period for conversion?
8. What is the cost per equivalent unit for materials?
9. What is the cost per equivalent unit for conversion?
10. What is the cost of ending work in process inventory for materials?
11. What is the cost of ending work in process inventory for conversion?
12. What is the cost of materials transferred to finished goods?
13. What is the amount of conversion cost transferred to finished goods?
14. Prepare the journal entry to record the transfer of costs from Work in Process to Finished Goods.
15. What is the total cost to be accounted for? What is the total cost accounted for?

Exercises   connect

EXERCISE 4–1 Process Costing Journal Entries LO4–1

Quality Brick Company produces bricks in two processing departments—Molding and Firing. Information relating to the company's operations in March follows:

a. Raw materials used in production: Molding Department, $23,000; and Firing Department, $8,000.
b. Direct labor costs incurred: Molding Department, $12,000; and Firing Department, $7,000.
c. Manufacturing overhead was applied: Molding Department, $25,000; and Firing Department, $37,000.
d. Unfired, molded bricks were transferred from the Molding Department to the Firing Department. According to the company's process costing system, the cost of the unfired, molded bricks was $57,000.
e. Finished bricks were transferred from the Firing Department to the finished goods warehouse. According to the company's process costing system, the cost of the finished bricks was $103,000.
f. Finished bricks were sold to customers. According to the company's process costing system, the cost of the finished bricks sold was $101,000.

Required:
Prepare journal entries to record items (a) through (f) above.

EXERCISE 4–2 Equivalent Units of Production—Weighted-Average Method LO4–2

Clonex Labs, Inc., uses the weighted-average method in its process costing system. The following data are available for one department for October:

	Units	Percent Completed	
		Materials	Conversion
Work in process, October 1	30,000	65%	30%
Work in process, October 31	15,000	80%	40%

The department started 175,000 units into production during the month and transferred 190,000 completed units to the next department.

Required:
Compute the equivalent units of production for October.

EXERCISE 4–3 Cost per Equivalent Unit—Weighted-Average Method LO4–3

Superior Micro Products uses the weighted-average method in its process costing system. Data for the Assembly Department for May appear below:

	Materials	Labor	Overhead
Work in process, May 1	$18,000	$5,500	$27,500
Cost added during May	$238,900	$80,300	$401,500
Equivalent units of production	35,000	33,000	33,000

Required:
Compute the cost per equivalent unit for materials, labor, overhead, and in total.

EXERCISE 4–4 Assigning Costs to Units—Weighted-Average Method LO4–4

Data concerning a recent period's activity in the Prep Department, the first processing department in a company that uses process costing, appear below:

	Materials	Conversion
Equivalent units in ending work in process inventory	2,000	800
Cost per equivalent unit	$13.86	$4.43

A total of 20,100 units were completed and transferred to the next processing department during the period.

Required:

1. Compute the cost of ending work in process inventory for materials, conversion, and in total.
2. Compute the cost of the units completed and transferred out for materials, conversion, and in total.

EXERCISE 4–5 Cost Reconciliation Report—Weighted-Average Method LO4–5

Maria Am Corporation uses the weighted-average method in its process costing system. The Baking Department is one of the processing departments in its strudel manufacturing facility. In June in the Baking Department, the cost of beginning work in process inventory was $3,570, the cost of ending work in process inventory was $2,860, and the cost added to production was $43,120.

Required:

Prepare a cost reconciliation report for the Baking Department for June.

EXERCISE 4–6 Equivalent Units of Production—Weighted-Average Method LO4–2

Highlands Company uses the weighted-average method in its process costing system. It processes wood pulp for various manufacturers of paper products. Data relating to tons of pulp processed during June are provided below:

		Percent Completed	
	Tons of Pulp	Materials	Labor and Overhead
Work in process, June 1	20,000	90%	80%
Work in process, June 30	30,000	60%	40%
Started into production during June	190,000		

Required:

1. Compute the number of tons of pulp completed and transferred out during June.
2. Compute the equivalent units of production for materials and for labor and overhead for June.

EXERCISE 4–7 Process Costing Journal Entries LO4–1

Chocolaterie de Geneve, SA, is located in a French-speaking canton in Switzerland. The company makes chocolate truffles that are sold in popular embossed tins. The company has two processing departments—Cooking and Molding. In the Cooking Department, the raw ingredients for the truffles are mixed and then cooked in special candy-making vats. In the Molding Department, the melted chocolate and other ingredients from the Cooking Department are carefully poured into molds and decorative flourishes are applied by hand. After cooling, the truffles are packed for sale. The company uses a process costing system. The T-accounts below show the flow of costs through the two departments in April:

Work in Process—Cooking

Balance 4/1	8,000	Transferred out	160,000
Direct materials	42,000		
Direct labor	50,000		
Overhead	75,000		

Work in Process—Molding

Balance 4/1	4,000	Transferred out	240,000
Transferred in	160,000		
Direct labor	36,000		
Overhead	45,000		

Required:
Prepare journal entries showing the flow of costs through the two processing departments during April.

EXERCISE 4–8 Equivalent Units; Cost per Equivalent Unit; Assigning Costs to Units—Weighted-Average Method LO4–2, LO4–3, LO4–4
Helix Corporation uses the weighted-average method in its process costing system. It produces prefabricated flooring in a series of steps carried out in production departments. All of the material that is used in the first production department is added at the beginning of processing in that department. Data for May for the first production department follow:

		Percent Complete	
	Units	Materials	Conversion
Work in process inventory, May 1	5,000	100%	40%
Work in process inventory, May 31	10,000	100%	30%
Materials cost in work in process inventory, May 1		$1,500	
Conversion cost in work in process inventory, May 1		$4,000	
Units started into production		180,000	
Units transferred to the next production department		175,000	
Materials cost added during May		$54,000	
Conversion cost added during May		$352,000	

Required:
1. Calculate the first production department's equivalent units of production for materials and conversion for May.
2. Compute the first production department's cost per equivalent unit for materials and conversion for May.
3. Compute the first production department's cost of ending work in process inventory for materials, conversion, and in total for May.
4. Compute the first production department's cost of the units transferred to the next production department for materials, conversion, and in total for May.

EXERCISE 4–9 Equivalent Units and Cost per Equivalent Unit—Weighted-Average Method LO4–2, LO4–3
Pureform, Inc., uses the weighted-average method in its process costing system. It manufactures a product that passes through two departments. Data for a recent month for the first department follow:

	Units	Materials	Labor	Overhead
Work in process inventory, beginning	5,000	$4,320	$1,040	$1,790
Units started in process	45,000			
Units transferred out	42,000			
Work in process inventory, ending	8,000			
Cost added during the month		$52,800	$21,500	$32,250

The beginning work in process inventory was 80% complete with respect to materials and 60% complete with respect to labor and overhead. The ending work in process inventory was 75% complete with respect to materials and 50% complete with respect to labor and overhead.

Required:
1. Compute the first department's equivalent units of production for materials, labor, and overhead for the month.
2. Determine the first department's cost per equivalent unit for materials, labor, and overhead for the month.

EXERCISE 4–10 Equivalent Units of Production—Weighted-Average Method LO4–2
Alaskan Fisheries, Inc., processes salmon for various distributors and it uses the weighted-average method in its process costing system. The company has two processing departments—Cleaning

and Packing. Data relating to pounds of salmon processed in the Cleaning Department during July are presented below:

| | Pounds of Salmon | Percent Completed | |
		Materials	Labor and Overhead
Work in process inventory, July 1	20,000	100%	30%
Work in process inventory, July 31	25,000	100%	60%

A total of 380,000 pounds of salmon were started into processing during July. All materials are added at the beginning of processing in the Cleaning Department.

Required:
Compute the Cleaning Department's equivalent units of production for materials and for labor and overhead in the month of July.

EXERCISE 4–11 Comprehensive Exercise; Second Production Department—Weighted-Average Method LO4–2, LO4–3, LO4–4, LO4–5
Scribners Corporation produces fine papers in three production departments—Pulping, Drying, and Finishing. In the Pulping Department, raw materials such as wood fiber and rag cotton are mechanically and chemically treated to separate their fibers. The result is a thick slurry of fibers. In the Drying Department, the wet fibers transferred from the Pulping Department are laid down on porous webs, pressed to remove excess liquid, and dried in ovens. In the Finishing Department, the dried paper is coated, cut, and spooled onto reels. The company uses the weighted-average method in its process costing system. Data for March for the Drying Department follow:

| | Units | Percent Completed | |
		Pulping	Conversion
Work in process inventory, March 1	5,000	100%	20%
Work in process inventory, March 31	8,000	100%	25%
Pulping cost in work in process inventory, March 1			$4,800
Conversion cost in work in process inventory, March 1			$500
Units transferred to the next production department			157,000
Pulping cost added during March			$102,450
Conversion cost added during March			$31,300

No materials are added in the Drying Department. Pulping cost represents the costs of the wet fibers transferred in from the Pulping Department. Wet fiber is processed in the Drying Department in batches; each unit in the above table is a batch and one batch of wet fibers produces a set amount of dried paper that is passed on to the Finishing Department.

Required:
1. Compute the Drying Department's equivalent units of production for pulping and conversion in March.
2. Compute the Drying Department's cost per equivalent unit for pulping and conversion in March.
3. Compute the Drying Department's cost of ending work in process inventory for pulping, conversion, and in total for March.
4. Compute the Drying Department's cost of units transferred out to the Finishing Department for pulping, conversion, and in total in March.
5. Prepare a cost reconciliation report for the Drying Department for March.

EXERCISE 4–12 Equivalent Units; Assigning Costs; Cost Reconciliation—Weighted-Average Method LO4–2, LO4–4, LO4–5
Superior Micro Products uses the weighted-average method in its process costing system. During January, the Delta Assembly Department completed its processing of 25,000 units and transferred them to the next department. The cost of beginning work in process inventory and the costs added during January amounted to $599,780 in total. The ending work in process inventory in January

consisted of 3,000 units, which were 80% complete with respect to materials and 60% complete with respect to labor and overhead. The costs per equivalent unit for the month were as follows:

	Materials	Labor	Overhead
Cost per equivalent unit	$12.50	$3.20	$6.40

Required:

1. Compute the equivalent units of materials, labor, and overhead in the ending work in process inventory for the month.
2. Compute the cost of ending work in process inventory for materials, labor, overhead, and in total for January.
3. Compute the cost of the units transferred to the next department for materials, labor, overhead, and in total for January.
4. Prepare a cost reconciliation for January. (Note: You will not be able to break the cost to be accounted for into the cost of beginning work in process inventory and costs added during the month.)

Problems

PROBLEM 4–13 Comprehensive Problem; Second Production Department—Weighted-Average Method
LO4–2, LO4–3, LO4–4, LO4–5

Old Country Links, Inc., produces sausages in three production departments—Mixing, Casing and Curing, and Packaging. In the Mixing Department, meats are prepared and ground and then mixed with spices. The spiced meat mixture is then transferred to the Casing and Curing Department, where the mixture is force-fed into casings and then hung and cured in climate-controlled smoking chambers. In the Packaging Department, the cured sausages are sorted, packed, and labeled. The company uses the weighted-average method in its process costing system. Data for September for the Casing and Curing Department follow:

| | | Percent Completed | | |
	Units	Mixing	Materials	Conversion
Work in process inventory, September 1	1	100%	90%	80%
Work in process inventory, September 30	1	100%	80%	70%

	Mixing	Materials	Conversion
Work in process inventory, September 1	$1,670	$90	$605
Cost added during September	$81,460	$6,006	$42,490

Mixing cost represents the costs of the spiced meat mixture transferred in from the Mixing Department. The spiced meat mixture is processed in the Casing and Curing Department in batches; each unit in the above table is a batch and one batch of spiced meat mixture produces a set amount of sausages that are passed on to the Packaging Department. During September, 50 batches (i.e., units) were completed and transferred to the Packaging Department.

Required:

1. Determine the Casing and Curing Department's equivalent units of production for mixing, materials, and conversion for the month of September. Do not round off your computations.
2. Compute the Casing and Curing Department's cost per equivalent unit for mixing, materials, and conversion for the month of September.
3. Compute the Casing and Curing Department's cost of ending work in process inventory for mixing, materials, conversion, and in total for September.
4. Compute the Casing and Curing Department's cost of units transferred out to the Packaging Department for mixing, materials, conversion, and in total for September.
5. Prepare a cost reconciliation report for the Casing and Curing Department for September.

PROBLEM 4–14 Analysis of Work in Process T-account—Weighted-Average Method LO4–1, LO4–2, LO4–3, LO4–4

Weston Products manufactures an industrial cleaning compound that goes through three processing departments—Grinding, Mixing, and Cooking. All raw materials are introduced at the start of work in the Grinding Department. The Work in Process T-account for the Grinding Department for May is given below:

Work in Process—Grinding Department

Inventory, May 1	21,800	Completed and transferred to the Mixing Department	?
Materials	133,400		
Conversion	225,500		
Inventory, May 31	?		

The May 1 work in process inventory consisted of 18,000 pounds with $14,600 in materials cost and $7,200 in conversion cost. The May 1 work in process inventory was 100% complete with respect to materials and 30% complete with respect to conversion. During May, 167,000 pounds were started into production. The May 31 inventory consisted of 15,000 pounds that were 100% complete with respect to materials and 60% complete with respect to conversion. The company uses the weighted-average method in its process costing system.

Required:
1. Compute the Grinding Department's equivalent units of production for materials and conversion in May.
2. Compute the Grinding Department's costs per equivalent unit for materials and conversion for May.
3. Compute the Grinding Department's cost of ending work in process inventory for materials, conversion, and in total for May.
4. Compute the Grinding Department's cost of units transferred out to the Mixing Department for materials, conversion, and in total for May.

PROBLEM 4–15 Comprehensive Problem—Weighted-Average Method LO4–2, LO4–3, LO4–4, LO4–5

Sunspot Beverages, Ltd., of Fiji uses the weighted-average method in its process costing system. It makes blended tropical fruit drinks in two stages. Fruit juices are extracted from fresh fruits and then blended in the Blending Department. The blended juices are then bottled and packed for shipping in the Bottling Department. The following information pertains to the operations of the Blending Department for June.

		Percent Completed	
	Units	Materials	Conversion
Work in process, beginning	20,000	100%	75%
Started into production	180,000		
Completed and transferred out	160,000		
Work in process, ending	40,000	100%	25%

	Materials	Conversion
Work in process, beginning	$25,200	$24,800
Cost added during June	$334,800	$238,700

Required:
1. Calculate the Blending Department's equivalent units of production for materials and conversion in June.
2. Calculate the Blending Department's cost per equivalent unit for materials and conversion in June.
3. Calculate the Blending Department's cost of ending work in process inventory for materials, conversion, and in total for June.
4. Calculate the Blending Department's cost of units transferred out to the Bottling Department for materials, conversion, and in total for June.
5. Prepare a cost reconciliation report for the Blending Department for June.

PROBLEM 4–16 Comprehensive Problem—Weighted-Average Method LO4–2, LO4–3, LO4–4, LO4–5

Builder Products, Inc., uses the weighted-average method in its process costing system. It manufactures a caulking compound that goes through three processing stages prior to completion. Information on work in the first department, Cooking, is given below for May:

Production data:

Pounds in process, May 1; materials 100% complete; conversion 80% complete	10,000
Pounds started into production during May	100,000
Pounds completed and transferred out	?
Pounds in process, May 31; materials 60% complete; conversion 20% complete	15,000

Cost data:

Work in process inventory, May 1:

Materials cost	$1,500
Conversion cost	$7,200

Cost added during May:

Materials cost	$154,500
Conversion cost	$90,800

Required:
1. Compute the equivalent units of production for materials and conversion for May.
2. Compute the cost per equivalent unit for materials and conversion for May.
3. Compute the cost of ending work in process inventory for materials, conversion, and in total for May.
4. Compute the cost of units transferred out to the next department for materials, conversion, and in total for May.
5. Prepare a cost reconciliation report for May.

PROBLEM 4–17 Cost Flows LO4–1

Lubricants, Inc., produces a special kind of grease that is widely used by race car drivers. The grease is produced in two processing departments—Refining and Blending. Raw materials are introduced at various points in the Refining Department.

The following incomplete Work in Process account is available for the Refining Department for March:

Work in Process—Refining Department

March 1 balance	38,000	Completed and transferred to Blending	?
Materials	495,000		
Direct labor	72,000		
Overhead	181,000		
March 31 balance	?		

The March 1 work in process inventory in the Refining Department consists of the following elements: materials, $25,000; direct labor, $4,000; and overhead, $9,000.

Costs incurred during March in the Blending Department were: materials used, $115,000; direct labor, $18,000; and overhead cost applied to production, $42,000.

Required:
1. Prepare journal entries to record the costs incurred in both the Refining Department and Blending Department during March. Key your entries to the items (a) through (g) below.
   a. Raw materials used in production.
   b. Direct labor costs incurred.
   c. Manufacturing overhead costs incurred for the entire factory, $225,000. (Credit Accounts Payable.)
   d. Manufacturing overhead was applied to production using a predetermined overhead rate.
   e. Units that were complete with respect to processing in the Refining Department were transferred to the Blending Department, $740,000.

f. Units that were complete with respect to processing in the Blending Department were transferred to Finished Goods, $950,000.

g. Completed units were sold on account, $1,500,000. The Cost of Goods Sold was $900,000.

2. Post the journal entries from (1) above to T-accounts. The following account balances existed at the beginning of March. (The beginning balance in the Refining Department's Work in Process is given in the T-account shown above.)

Raw Materials	$618,000
Work in Process—Blending Department	$65,000
Finished Goods.	$20,000

After posting the entries to the T-accounts, find the ending balance in the inventory accounts and the Manufacturing Overhead account.

PROBLEM 4–18 Interpreting a Report—Weighted-Average Method LO4–2, LO4–3, LO4–4

Cooperative San José of southern Sonora state in Mexico makes a unique syrup using cane sugar and local herbs. The syrup is sold in small bottles and is prized as a flavoring for drinks and for use in desserts. The bottles are sold for $12 each. The first stage in the production process is carried out in the Mixing Department, which removes foreign matter from the raw materials and mixes them in the proper proportions in large vats. The company uses the weighted-average method in its process costing system.

A hastily prepared report for the Mixing Department for April appears below:

Units to be accounted for:	
Work in process, April 1 (materials 90% complete;	
conversion 80% complete)	30,000
Started into production	200,000
Total units to be accounted for	230,000
Units accounted for as follows:	
Transferred to next department	190,000
Work in process, April 30 (materials 75% complete;	
conversion 60% complete).	40,000
Total units accounted for	230,000

Cost Reconciliation

Cost to be accounted for:	
Work in process, April 1	$ 98,000
Cost added during the month	827,000
Total cost to be accounted for	$925,000
Cost accounted for as follows:	
Work in process, April 30	$119,400
Transferred to next department.	805,600
Total cost accounted for	$925,000

Management would like some additional information about Cooperative San José's operations.

Required:

1. What were the Mixing Department's equivalent units of production for materials and conversion for April?

2. What were the Mixing Department's cost per equivalent unit for materials and conversion for April? The beginning inventory consisted of the following costs: materials, $67,800; and conversion cost, $30,200. The costs added during the month consisted of: materials, $579,000; and conversion cost, $248,000.

3. How many of the units transferred out of the Mixing Department in April were started and completed during that month?

4. The manager of the Mixing Department stated, "Materials prices jumped from about $2.50 per unit in March to $3 per unit in April, but due to good cost control I was able to hold our materials cost to less than $3 per unit for the month." Should this manager be rewarded for good cost control? Explain.

Cases   connect

CASE 4–19 Second Department—Weighted-Average Method LO4–2, LO4–3, LO4–4

"I think we goofed when we hired that new assistant controller," said Ruth Scarpino, president of Provost Industries. "Just look at this report that he prepared for last month for the Finishing Department. I can't understand it."

Finishing Department costs:	
Work in process inventory, April 1, 450 units; materials	
100% complete; conversion 60% complete	$ 8,208*
Costs transferred in during the month from the	
preceding department, 1,950 units	17,940
Materials cost added during the month	6,210
Conversion costs incurred during the month	13,920
Total departmental costs	$46,278
Finishing Department costs assigned to:	
Units completed and transferred to finished goods,	
1,800 units at $25.71 per unit......................................	$46,278
Work in process inventory, April 30, 600 units;	
materials 0% complete; conversion 35% complete	0
Total departmental costs assigned	$46,278

*Consists of cost transferred in, $4,068; materials cost, $1,980; and conversion cost, $2,160.

"He's struggling to learn our system," replied Frank Harrop, the operations manager. "The problem is that he's been away from process costing for a long time, and it's coming back slowly."

"It's not just the format of his report that I'm concerned about. Look at that $25.71 unit cost that he's come up with for April. Doesn't that seem high to you?" said Ms. Scarpino.

"Yes, it does seem high; but on the other hand, I know we had an increase in materials prices during April, and that may be the explanation," replied Mr. Harrop. "I'll get someone else to redo this report and then we can see what's going on."

Provost Industries manufactures a ceramic product that goes through two processing departments—Molding and Finishing. The company uses the weighted-average method in its process costing.

Required:
1. Prepare a report for the Finishing Department showing how much cost should have been assigned to the units completed and transferred to finished goods, and how much cost should have been assigned to ending work in process inventory in the Finishing Department.
2. Explain to the president why the unit cost on the new assistant controller's report is so high.

CASE 4–20 Ethics and the Manager, Understanding the Impact of Percentage Completion on Profit—Weighted-Average Method LO4–2, LO4–3, LO4–4

Gary Stevens and Mary James are production managers in the Consumer Electronics Division of General Electronics Company, which has several dozen plants scattered in locations throughout the world. Mary manages the plant located in Des Moines, Iowa, while Gary manages the plant in El Segundo, California. Production managers are paid a salary and get an additional bonus equal to 5% of their base salary if the entire division meets or exceeds its target profits for the year. The bonus is determined in March after the company's annual report has been prepared and issued to stockholders.

Shortly after the beginning of the new year, Mary received a phone call from Gary that went like this:

Gary: How's it going, Mary?

Mary: Fine, Gary. How's it going with you?

Gary: Great! I just got the preliminary profit figures for the division for last year and we are within $200,000 of making the year's target profits. All we have to do is pull a few strings, and we'll be over the top!

Mary: What do you mean?

Gary: Well, one thing that would be easy to change is your estimate of the percentage completion of your ending work in process inventories.

Mary: I don't know if I can do that, Gary. Those percentage completion figures are supplied by Tom Winthrop, my lead supervisor, who I have always trusted to provide us with good estimates. Besides, I have already sent the percentage completion figures to corporate headquarters.

Gary: You can always tell them there was a mistake. Think about it, Mary. All of us managers are doing as much as we can to pull this bonus out of the hat. You may not want the bonus check, but the rest of us sure could use it.

The final processing department in Mary's production facility began the year with no work in process inventory. During the year, 210,000 units were transferred in from the prior processing department and 200,000 units were completed and sold. Costs transferred in from the prior department totaled $39,375,000. No materials are added in the final processing department. A total of $20,807,500 of conversion cost was incurred in the final processing department during the year.

Required:

1. Tom Winthrop estimated that the units in ending work in process inventory in the final processing department were 30% complete with respect to the conversion costs of the final processing department. If this estimate of the percentage completion is used, what would be the cost of goods sold for the year?
2. Does Gary Stevens want the estimated percentage completion to be increased or decreased? Explain why.
3. What percentage completion would result in increasing reported net operating income by $200,000 over the net operating income that would be reported if the 30% figure were used?
4. Do you think Mary James should go along with the request to alter estimates of the percentage completion? Why or why not?

Appendix 4A: FIFO Method

The FIFO method of process costing is generally considered more accurate than the weighted-average method, but it is more complex. It calculates unit costs using only the costs and outputs from the current period, whereas the weighted-average method calculates unit costs using costs and outputs from the current and prior periods.

     We will illustrate the FIFO method using the data from Exhibits 4–5 and 4–8 pertaining to Double Diamond Skis' Shaping and Milling Department. We will also organize our explanation using the same four-step process that we used for the weighted-average method.

Step 1: Compute the Equivalent Units of Production

The computation of equivalent units of production under the FIFO method differs from the computation under the weighted-average method in two ways.

> **LO4–6**
> Compute the equivalent units of production using the FIFO method.

     First, the "units transferred out" is divided into two parts. One part consists of the units from the beginning inventory that were completed and transferred out, and the other part consists of the units that were both *started* and *completed* during the current period.

     Second, full consideration is given to the amount of work expended during the current period on units in the *beginning* work in process inventory as well as on units in the ending work in process inventory. Thus, under the FIFO method, both beginning and ending work in process inventories are converted to equivalent units. For the beginning inventory, the equivalent units represent the work done to *complete* the units; for the ending inventory, the equivalent units represent the work done to bring the units to a stage of partial completion at the end of the period (the same as with the weighted-average method).

The formula for computing the equivalent units of production under the FIFO method is more complex than under the weighted-average method:

> **FIFO Method**
> **(a separate calculation is made for each cost category**
> **in each processing department)**
>
> Equivalent units of production = Equivalent units to complete beginning work in process inventory*
>
> + Units started and completed during the period
>
> + Equivalent units in ending work in process inventory
>
> *Equivalent units to complete beginning work in process inventory = Units in beginning work in process inventory × $\left(100\% - \text{Percentage completion of beginning work in process inventory}\right)$

Or, the equivalent units of production can also be determined as follows:

> Equivalent units of production = Units transferred out
>
> + Equivalent units in ending work in process inventory
>
> − Equivalent units in beginning work in process inventory

To illustrate the FIFO method, refer again to the data in Exhibit 4–5 for the Shaping and Milling Department at Double Diamond Skis. The department completed and transferred 4,800 units to the Graphics Application Department during May. Because 200 of these units came from the beginning inventory, the Shaping and Milling Department must have started and completed 4,600 units during May. The 200 units in the beginning inventory were 55% complete with respect to materials and only 30% complete with respect to conversion costs when the month started. Thus, to complete these units the department must have added another 45% of materials costs (100% − 55% = 45%) and another 70% of conversion costs (100% − 30% = 70%). Following this line of reasoning, the equivalent units of production for the Shaping and Milling Department for May would be computed as shown in Exhibit 4A–1.

EXHIBIT 4A–1
Equivalent Units of Production:
FIFO Method

	Materials	Conversion
Equivalent units needed to complete beginning work in process inventory:		
Materials: 200 units × (100% − 55%)*	90	
Conversion: 200 units × (100% − 30%)*		140
Units started and completed during the period	4,600[†]	4,600[†]
Equivalent units in ending work in process inventory:		
Materials: 400 units × 40% complete...................	160	
Conversion: 400 units × 25% complete................		100
Equivalent units of production	4,850	4,840

----

*This is the work needed to complete the units in beginning inventory.
[†]5,000 units started − 400 units in ending work in process = 4,600 units started and completed. This can also be computed as 4,800 units completed and transferred to the next department − 200 units in beginning work in process inventory. The FIFO method assumes that the units in beginning inventory are finished first.

Stop at this point and compare the data in Exhibit 4A–1 with the data in Exhibit 4–6 in the chapter, which shows the computation of equivalent units of production under the weighted-average method. Also refer to Exhibit 4A–2, which compares the two methods.

The essential difference between the two methods is that the weighted-average method blends costs and outputs from the current period with costs and outputs from the prior period, whereas the FIFO method separates the two periods. To see this more clearly, consider the following reconciliation of the two calculations of equivalent units of production:

Shaping and Milling Department	Materials	Conversion
Equivalent units of production—weighted-average method.....	4,960	4,900
Less equivalent units in beginning work in process inventory:		
200 units × 55%..	110	
200 units × 30%..		60
Equivalent units of production—FIFO method................	4,850	4,840

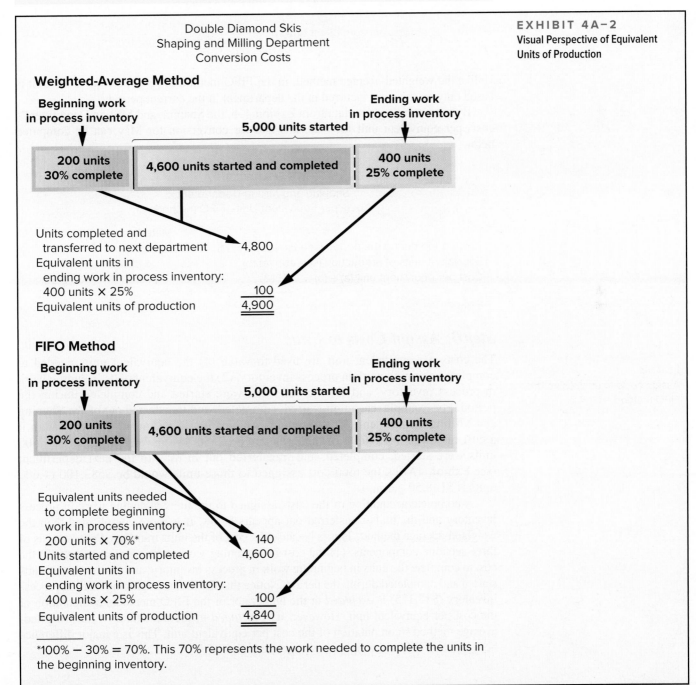

EXHIBIT 4A–2
Visual Perspective of Equivalent
Units of Production

Double Diamond Skis
Shaping and Milling Department
Conversion Costs

Weighted-Average Method

Beginning work in process inventory

Ending work in process inventory

5,000 units started

| 200 units 30% complete | 4,600 units started and completed | 400 units 25% complete |

Units completed and transferred to next department — 4,800
Equivalent units in ending work in process inventory:
400 units × 25% — 100
Equivalent units of production — 4,900

FIFO Method

Beginning work in process inventory

Ending work in process inventory

5,000 units started

| 200 units 30% complete | 4,600 units started and completed | 400 units 25% complete |

Equivalent units needed to complete beginning work in process inventory:
200 units × 70%* — 140
Units started and completed — 4,600
Equivalent units in ending work in process inventory:
400 units × 25% — 100
Equivalent units of production — 4,840

*100% − 30% = 70%. This 70% represents the work needed to complete the units in the beginning inventory.

As shown in the reconciliation of the two costing methods, it is evident that the FIFO method removes the equivalent units that were already in beginning inventory from the equivalent units of production as defined using the weighted-average method. Thus, the FIFO method isolates the equivalent units of production that are due to work performed during the current period. The weighted-average method blends together the equivalent units already in beginning inventory with the work performed in the current period.

Step 2: Compute the Cost per Equivalent Unit

LO4–7
Compute the cost per equivalent unit using the FIFO method.

In the FIFO method, the cost per equivalent unit is computed as follows:

FIFO Method
(a separate calculation is made for each cost category in each processing department)

$$\text{Cost per equivalent unit} = \frac{\text{Cost added during the period}}{\text{Equivalent units of production}}$$

Unlike the weighted-average method, in the FIFO method the cost per equivalent unit is based only on the costs incurred in the department in the current period.

By incorporating cost data from Exhibit 4–8, the Shaping and Milling Department's costs per equivalent unit for materials and for conversion for May can be computed below:

Shaping and Milling Department Costs per Equivalent Unit—FIFO method		
	Materials	Conversion
Cost added during the period (see Exhibit 4–8) (a)	$368,600	$350,900
Equivalent units of production (see above) (b)	4,850	4,840
Cost per equivalent unit (a) ÷ (b)	$76.00	$72.50

Step 3: Assign Costs to Units

LO4–8
Assign costs to units using the FIFO method.

The costs per equivalent unit are used to value (1) the equivalent units needed to complete beginning work in process inventory, (2) the equivalent units in ending work in process inventory, and (3) the units that were started and completed during the period. For example, each unit started, completed, and transferred out of the Shaping and Milling Department to the Graphics Application Department will carry with it a cost of $148.50—$76.00 for materials and $72.50 for conversion. Because 4,600 units were started, completed, and transferred out in May to the next department (see Exhibit 4A–1), the total cost assigned to those units would be $683,100 (4,600 units × $148.50 per unit).

A complete accounting of the costs assigned to the units in ending work in process inventory and the units transferred out appears below. It is more complicated than the weighted-average method. This is because the cost of the units transferred out consists of three separate components: (1) the cost in beginning work in process inventory; (2) the cost to complete the units in beginning work in process inventory; and (3) the cost of units started and completed during the period. Notice that the cost in beginning work in process inventory ($15,175) is *excluded* in the numerator of the FIFO method's computation of the cost per equivalent unit. However, it is *included* in the numerator of the weighted-average method's computation of the cost per equivalent unit. This is a major difference between the FIFO and weighted-average methods.

Shaping and Milling Department Costs of Ending Work in Process Inventory and Units Transferred Out—FIFO Method			
	Materials	Conversion	Total
Ending work in process inventory:			
Equivalent units in ending work in process inventory (see Exhibit 4A–1) (a)	160	100	
Cost per equivalent unit (b)	$76.00	$72.50	
Cost of ending work in process inventory (a) × (b)	$12,160	$7,250	$19,410
Units transferred out:			
Cost in beginning work in process inventory	$9,600	$5,575	$15,175
Cost to complete the units in beginning work in process inventory:			
Equivalent units needed to complete beginning work in process inventory (see Exhibit 4A–1) (a)	90	140	
Cost per equivalent unit (b)	$76.00	$72.50	
Cost to complete the units in beginning work in process inventory (a)	$6,840	$10,150	$16,990
Cost of units started and completed this period:			
Units started and completed this period (see Exhibit 4A–1) (a)	4,600	4,600	
Cost per equivalent unit (b)	$76.00	$72.50	
Cost of units started and completed this period (a) × (b)	$349,600	$333,500	$683,100
Total cost of units transferred out			$715,265

Step 4: Prepare a Cost Reconciliation Report

The costs assigned to ending work in process inventory and to the units transferred out reconcile with the costs we started with in Exhibit 4–8 as shown below:

LO4–9
Prepare a cost reconciliation report using the FIFO method.

Shaping and Milling Department Cost Reconciliation	
Costs to be accounted for:	
Cost of beginning work in process inventory (Exhibit 4–8)	$ 15,175
Costs added to production during the period (Exhibit 4–8)	719,500
Total cost to be accounted for	$734,675
Costs accounted for as follows:	
Cost of ending work in process inventory (see above)	$ 19,410
Cost of units transferred out (see above)	715,265
Total cost accounted for	$734,675

The $715,265 cost of the units transferred to the next department, Graphics Application, will be accounted for in that department as "costs transferred in." As in the weighted-average method, this cost will be treated in the process costing system as just another category of costs, like materials or conversion costs. The only difference is that the costs transferred in will always be 100% complete with respect to the work done in the Shaping and Milling Department. Costs are passed on from one department to the next in this fashion, until they reach the last processing department, Finishing and Pairing. When the products are completed in this last department, their costs are transferred to finished goods.

A Comparison of Costing Methods

In most situations, the weighted-average and FIFO methods will produce very similar unit costs. If there never are any ending inventories, the two methods will produce identical results. The reason for this is that without any ending inventories, no costs can be carried forward into the next period and the weighted-average method will base unit costs on just the current period's costs—just as in the FIFO method. If there *are* ending inventories, either erratic input prices or erratic production levels would also be required to generate much of a difference in unit costs under the two methods. This is because the weighted-average method will blend the unit costs from the prior period with the unit costs of the current period. Unless these unit costs differ greatly, the blending will not make much difference.

Nevertheless, from the standpoint of cost control, the FIFO method is better than the weighted-average method. Current performance should be evaluated based on costs of the current period only but the weighted-average method mixes costs of the current period with costs of the prior period. Thus, under the weighted-average method, the manager's apparent performance in the current period is influenced by what happened in the prior period. This problem does not arise under the FIFO method because the FIFO method makes a clear distinction between costs of prior periods and costs incurred during the current period. For the same reason, the FIFO method also provides more up-to-date cost data for decision-making purposes.

On the other hand, the weighted-average method is simpler to apply than the FIFO method, but computers can handle the additional calculations with ease once they have been appropriately programmed.

Appendix 4A: Exercises, Problems, and Case

EXERCISE 4A–1 Computation of Equivalent Units of Production—FIFO Method LO4–6
Refer to the data for Clonex Labs, Inc., in Exercise 4–2.

Required:
Assuming the company uses the FIFO method, compute the equivalent units of production for materials and conversion for October.

EXERCISE 4A–2 Cost per Equivalent Unit—FIFO Method LO4–7
Superior Micro Products uses the FIFO method in its process costing system. Data for the Assembly Department for May appear below:

	Materials	Labor	Overhead
Cost added during May...............	$193,320	$62,000	$310,000
Equivalent units of production	27,000	25,000	25,000

Required:
Compute the cost per equivalent unit for materials, labor, overhead, and in total.

EXERCISE 4A–3 Assigning Costs to Units—FIFO Method LO4–8
Data concerning a recent period's activity in the Assembly Department, the first processing department in a company that uses the FIFO method in its process costing, appear below:

	Materials	Conversion
Cost of work in process inventory at the beginning of the period ...	$3,200	$650
Equivalent units in the ending work in process inventory...........	400	200
Equivalent units required to complete the beginning work in process inventory.....................................	600	1,200
Cost per equivalent unit for the period	$2.32	$0.75

A total of 26,000 units were completed and transferred to the next processing department during the period. Beginning work in process inventory consisted of 2,000 units and ending work in process inventory consisted of 1,000 units.

Required:
1. Compute the Assembly Department's cost of ending work in process inventory for materials, conversion, and in total for the period.
2. Compute the Assembly Department's cost of units transferred out to the next department for materials, conversion, and in total for the period.

EXERCISE 4A–4 Cost Reconciliation Report—FIFO Method LO4–9
Schroeder Baking Corporation uses a process costing system in its large-scale baking operations. The Mixing Department is one of the company's processing departments. In the Mixing Department in July, the cost of beginning work in process inventory was $1,460, the cost of ending work in process inventory was $3,120, and the cost added to production was $36,540.

Required:
Prepare a cost reconciliation report for the Mixing Department for July.

EXERCISE 4A–5 Computation of Equivalent Units of Production—FIFO Method LO4–6
MediSecure, Inc., uses the FIFO method in its process costing system. It produces clear plastic containers for pharmacies in a process that starts in the Molding Department. Data concerning that department's operations in the most recent period appear below:

Beginning work in process:	
Units in process	500
Completion with respect to materials	80%
Completion with respect to conversion	40%
Units started into production during the month	153,600
Units completed and transferred out	153,700
Ending work in process:	
Units in process	400
Completion with respect to materials	75%
Completion with respect to conversion	20%

Required:
Compute the Molding Department's equivalent units of production for materials and conversion for the period.

EXERCISE 4A–6 Equivalent Units of Production—FIFO Method LO4–6
Refer to the data for Alaskan Fisheries, Inc., in Exercise 4–10.

Required:
Compute the Cleaning Department's equivalent units of production for materials and for labor and overhead for July.

EXERCISE 4A–7 Equivalent Units of Production and Cost per Equivalent Unit—FIFO Method
LO4–6, LO4–7
Refer to the data for Pureform, Inc., in Exercise 4–9.

Required:
Assume that the company uses the FIFO method in its process costing system.
1. Compute the first department's equivalent units of production for materials, labor, and overhead for the month.
2. Compute the first department's cost per equivalent unit for materials, labor, overhead, and in total for the month.

EXERCISE 4A–8 Equivalent Units of Production—FIFO Method LO4–6
Refer to the data for Highlands Company in Exercise 4–6. Assume that the company uses the FIFO method in its process costing system.

Required:
1. Compute the number of tons of pulp completed and transferred out during June.
2. Compute the equivalent units of production for materials and for labor and overhead for June.

EXERCISE 4A–9 Equivalent Units; Equivalent Units of Production; Assigning Costs—FIFO Method
LO4–6, LO4–7, LO4–8

Jarvene Corporation uses the FIFO method in its process costing system. The following data are for the most recent month of operations in one of the company's processing departments:

Units in beginning inventory	400
Units started into production	3,000
Units in ending inventory	300
Units transferred to the next department	3,100

	Materials	Conversion
Percentage completion of beginning inventory	80%	40%
Percentage completion of ending inventory	70%	60%

The cost of beginning inventory according to the company's costing system was $11,040 of which $8,120 was for materials and the remainder was for conversion cost. The costs added during the month amounted to $132,730. The costs per equivalent unit for the month were:

	Materials	Conversion
Cost per equivalent unit	$25.40	$18.20

Required:

1. Compute the total cost per equivalent unit for the month.
2. Compute the equivalent units of material and conversion in the ending inventory.
3. Compute the equivalent units of material and conversion that were required to complete the beginning inventory.
4. Compute the number of units started and completed during the month.
5. Compute the cost of ending work in process inventory for materials, conversion, and in total for the month.
6. Compute the cost of the units transferred to the next department for materials, conversion, and in total for the month.

PROBLEM 4A–10 Equivalent Units of Production; Assigning Costs; Cost Reconciliation Report—FIFO Method LO4–6, LO4–7, LO4–8, LO4–9

Selzik Company makes super-premium cake mixes that go through two processing departments—Blending and Packaging. The following activity was recorded in the Blending Department during July:

Production data:	
Units in process, July 1 (materials 100% complete; conversion 30% complete)	10,000
Units started into production	170,000
Units in process, July 31 (materials 100% complete; conversion 40% complete) ...	20,000
Cost data:	
Work in process inventory, July 1:	
Materials cost...	$8,500
Conversion cost	$4,900
Cost added during the month:	
Materials cost...	$139,400
Conversion cost..	$244,200

All materials are added at the beginning of work in the Blending Department. The company uses the FIFO method in its process costing system.

Required:

1. Calculate the Blending Department's equivalent units of production for materials and conversion for July.
2. Calculate the Blending Department's cost per equivalent unit for materials and conversion for July.
3. Calculate the Blending Department's cost of ending work in process inventory for materials, conversion, and in total for July.
4. Calculate the Blending Department's cost of units transferred out to the next department for materials, conversion, and in total for July.
5. Prepare a cost reconciliation report for the Blending Department for July.

PROBLEM 4A–11 Equivalent Units of Production; Cost per Equivalent Unit; Assigning Costs—FIFO Method LO4–6, LO4–7, LO4–8, LO4–9

Refer to the data for the Blending Department of Sunspots Beverages, Ltd., in Problem 4–15. Assume that the company uses the FIFO method in its process costing system.

Required:

1. Compute the Blending Department's equivalent units of production for materials and conversion for June.
2. Compute the Blending Department's cost per equivalent unit for materials and conversion for June.
3. Calculate the Blending Department's cost of ending work in process inventory for materials, conversion, and in total for June.
4. Calculate the Blending Department's cost of units transferred out to the next department for materials, conversion, and in total for June
5. Prepare a cost reconciliation report for the Blending Department for June.

CASE 4A–12 Second Department—FIFO Method LO4–6, LO4–7, LO4–8

Refer to the data for Provost Industries in Case 4–19. Assume that the company uses the FIFO method in its process costing system.

Required:

1. Prepare a report for the Finishing Department for April showing how much cost should have been assigned to the units completed and transferred to finished goods and how much cost should have been assigned to the ending work in process inventory.
2. As stated in the case, the company experienced an increase in materials prices during April. Would the effects of this price increase tend to show up more under the weighted-average method or under the FIFO method? Why?

Appendix 4B: Service Department Cost Allocations

Most large organizations have both *operating departments* and *service departments*. The central purposes of the organization are carried out in the operating departments. In contrast, service departments do not directly engage in operating activities. Instead, they provide services or assistance to the operating departments. Examples of operating departments include the Surgery Department at **Mt. Sinai Hospital**, the Geography Department at the **University of Washington**, the Marketing Department at **Allstate Insurance Company**, and production departments at manufacturers such as **Mitsubishi**, **Hewlett-Packard**, and **Michelin**. In process costing, the processing departments are all operating departments. Examples of service departments include Cafeteria, Internal Auditing, Human Resources, Cost Accounting, and Purchasing.

Companies allocate service department costs to operating departments for various reasons such as motivating and evaluating managerial performance, encouraging efficient use of service department resources, and calculating unit costs. Appendix 11B focuses on service department cost allocations for the first two reasons mentioned above—motivating and evaluating managerial performance and encouraging efficient use of service department resources. This appendix focuses on allocating service department costs to operating departments to enable calculating various types of unit costs.

For example, a manufacturer may incur service department costs that need to be included in the unit product cost calculations that it uses to value inventories and cost of goods sold for external reporting purposes. Service companies also incur service department costs that they may wish to incorporate into unit cost calculations within their operating departments. For example, hospitals often calculate unit costs such as the cost per patient-day or the cost per laboratory test. Allocating service department costs to the operating departments that directly serve patients or perform laboratory tests provides a more comprehensive understanding of the hospital's various unit costs.

This appendix illustrates two methods that are often used to allocate service department costs to other departments: the direct method and the step-down method.[1] However, before getting into the details of these two methods, we need to explain the concept of *interdepartmental services*.

Interdepartmental Services   Many service departments provide services to each other, as well as to operating departments. For example, the Cafeteria Department provides meals for all employees, including those working in other service departments, as well as those working in operating departments. In turn, the Cafeteria Department may receive services from other service departments, such as from Custodial Services or from Personnel. Services provided between service departments are known as *interdepartmental* or *reciprocal services.*

Direct Method

LO4–10
Allocate service department costs to operating departments using the direct method.

The *direct method* is simpler than the step-down method because it ignores any services provided by one service department to another service department (e.g., interdepartmental services). Even if a service department (such as Personnel) provides a large amount of service to another service department (such as the Cafeteria), the direct method does not allow for any cost allocations between these two departments. Rather, the direct method allocates all service department costs *directly* to the operating departments, bypassing the other service departments; hence, the term *direct method.*

For an example of the direct method, consider Mountain View Hospital, which has two service departments and two operating departments as shown below. The hospital allocates its Hospital Administration costs on the basis of employee-hours and its Custodial Services costs on the basis of square feet occupied.

	Service Departments		Operating Departments		
	Hospital Administration	Custodial Services	Laboratory	Patient Care	Total
Departmental costs before allocation	$360,000	$90,000	$261,000	$689,000	$1,400,000
Employee-hours	12,000	6,000	18,000	30,000	66,000
Space occupied— square feet	10,000	200	5,000	45,000	60,200

The direct method of allocating the hospital's service department costs to the operating departments is shown in Exhibit 4B–1. Several things should be noted in this exhibit. First, the employee-hours of the Hospital Administration Department and the Custodial Services Department are ignored when allocating the costs of Hospital Administration using the direct method. *Under the direct method, any of the allocation base attributable to the service departments themselves is ignored; only the amount of the allocation base attributable to the operating departments is used in the allocation.* Note that the same rule is used when allocating the costs of the Custodial Services Department. Even though the Hospital Administration and Custodial Services departments occupy some space, this is ignored when the Custodial Services costs are allocated. Finally, note that after all allocations have been completed, all of the service department costs are contained in the two operating departments.

---

[1] The reciprocal method can also be used to allocate service department costs to operating departments. However, this method requires the use of simultaneous linear equations that are beyond the scope of this book.

EXHIBIT 4B–1
Direct Method of Allocation

	Service Departments		Operating Departments		
	Hospital Administration	Custodial Services	Laboratory	Patient Care	Total
Departmental costs before allocation	$360,000	$90,000	$ 261,000	$689,000	$1,400,000
Allocation:					
Hospital Administration costs ($^{18}/_{48}$, $^{30}/_{48}$)*	(360,000)		135,000	225,000	
Custodial Services costs ($^{5}/_{50}$, $^{45}/_{50}$)†		(90,000)	9,000	81,000	
Total cost after allocation	$ 0	$ 0	$ 405,000	$995,000	$1,400,000

*Based on the employee-hours in the two operating departments, which are 18,000 hours + 30,000 hours = 48,000 hours.
†Based on the square feet occupied by the two operating departments, which is 5,000 square feet + 45,000 square feet = 50,000 square feet.

Step-Down Method

Unlike the direct method, the *step-down method* provides for allocation of a service department's costs to other service departments, as well as to operating departments. The step-down method is sequential. The sequence typically begins with the department that provides the greatest amount of service to other service departments. After its costs have been allocated, the process continues, step-by-step, ending with the department that provides the least amount of services to other service departments. This step procedure is illustrated in Exhibit 4B–2.

Exhibit 4B–3 shows the details of the step-down method. Note the following three key points about these allocations. First, under the Allocation heading in Exhibit 4B–3, you see two allocations, or steps. In the first step, the costs of Hospital Administration are allocated to another service department (Custodial Services) as well as to the operating departments. In contrast to the direct method, the allocation base for Hospital Administration costs now includes the employee-hours for Custodial Services as well as for the

LO4–11
Allocate service department costs to operating departments using the step-down method.

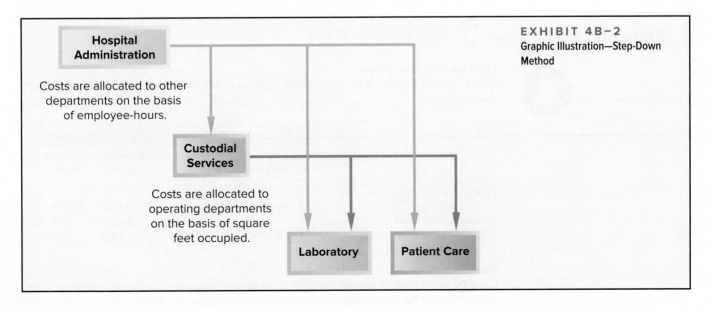

EXHIBIT 4B–2
Graphic Illustration—Step-Down Method

EXHIBIT 4B–3
Step-Down Method of Allocation

	Service Departments		Operating Departments		
	Hospital Administration	Custodial Services	Laboratory	Patient Care	Total
Departmental costs before allocation	$360,000	$ 90,000	$261,000	$ 689,000	$1,400,000
Allocation:					
Hospital Administration costs ($\frac{6}{54}$, $\frac{18}{54}$, $\frac{30}{54}$)*	(360,000)	40,000	120,000	200,000	
Custodial Services costs ($\frac{5}{50}$, $\frac{45}{50}$)†		(130,000)	13,000	117,000	
Total cost after allocation	$ 0	$ 0	$394,000	$1,006,000	$1,400,000

*Based on the employee-hours in Custodial Services and the two operating departments, which are 6,000 hours + 18,000 hours + 30,000 hours = 54,000 hours.
†As in Exhibit 4B–1, this allocation is based on the square feet occupied by the two operating departments.

operating departments. However, the allocation base still excludes the employee-hours for Hospital Administration itself. *In both the direct and step-down methods, any amount of the allocation base attributable to the service department whose cost is being allocated is always ignored.*

Second, looking again at Exhibit 4B–3, note that in the second step under the Allocation heading, the cost of Custodial Services is allocated to the two operating departments, and none of the cost is allocated to Hospital Administration even though Hospital Administration occupies space in the building. *In the step-down method, any amount of the allocation base that is attributable to a service department whose cost has already been allocated is ignored.* After a service department's costs have been allocated, costs of other service departments are not reallocated back to it. Third, note that the cost of Custodial Services allocated to other departments in the second step ($130,000) in Exhibit 4B–3 includes the costs of Hospital Administration that were allocated to Custodial Services in the first step in Exhibit 4B–3.

Appendix 4B: Exercises, Problems, and Case

EXERCISE 4B–1 Direct Method LO4–10

Seattle Western University has provided the following data to be used in its service department cost allocations:

	Service Departments		Operating Departments	
	Administration	Facility Services	Undergraduate Programs	Graduate Programs
Departmental costs before allocations	$2,400,000	$1,600,000	$26,800,000	$5,700,000
Student credit-hours			20,000	5,000
Space occupied—square feet	25,000	10,000	70,000	30,000

Required:

Using the direct method, allocate the costs of the service departments to the two operating departments. Allocate the Administration cost on the basis of student credit-hours and the Facility Services cost on the basis of space occupied.

EXERCISE 4B–2 Step-Down Method LO4–11

Madison Park Co-op, a whole foods grocery and gift shop, has provided the following data to be used in its service department cost allocations:

	Service Departments		Operating Departments	
	Administration	Janitorial	Groceries	Gifts
Departmental costs before allocations ...	$150,000	$40,000	$2,320,000	$950,000
Employee-hours........................	320	160	3,100	740
Space occupied—square feet	250	100	4,000	1,000

Required:

Using the step-down method, allocate the costs of the service departments to the two operating departments. Allocate Administration first on the basis of employee-hours and then Janitorial on the basis of space occupied.

EXERCISE 4B–3 Step-Down Method LO4–11

The Ferre Publishing Company has three service departments and two operating departments. Selected data from a recent period on the five departments follow:

	Service Departments			Operating Departments		
	Administration	Janitorial	Maintenance	Binding	Printing	Total
Costs	$140,000	$105,000	$48,000	$275,000	$430,000	$998,000
Number of employees....................	60	35	140	315	210	760
Square feet of space occupied	15,000	10,000	20,000	40,000	100,000	185,000
Hours of press time				30,000	60,000	90,000

The company allocates service department costs by the step-down method in the following order: Administration (number of employees), Janitorial (space occupied), and Maintenance (hours of press time).

Required:

Using the step-down method, allocate the service department costs to the operating departments.

EXERCISE 4B–4 Direct Method LO4–10

Refer to the data for the Ferre Publishing Company in Exercise 4B–3.

Required:

Assuming that the company uses the direct method rather than the step-down method to allocate service department costs, how much cost would be assigned to each operating department?

PROBLEM 4B–5 Step-Down Method LO4–11

Woodbury Hospital has three service departments and three operating departments. Estimated cost and operating data for all departments in the hospital for the forthcoming quarter are presented in the table below:

	Service Departments			Operating Departments			
	Housekeeping Services	Food Services	Admin. Services	Laboratory	Radiology	General Hospital	Total
Total cost.....................	$87,000	$301,060	$249,020	$405,900	$520,500	$475,800	$2,039,280
Meals served			800	2,000	1,000	68,000	71,800
Square feet of space	5,000	13,000	6,500	10,000	7,500	108,000	150,000
Files processed				14,000	7,000	25,000	46,000

The costs of the service departments are allocated by the step-down method using the allocation bases and in the order shown in the following table:

Service Department	Allocation Bases
Housekeeping Services	Square feet of space
Food Services	Meals served
Administrative Services	Files processed

All billing in the hospital is done through Laboratory, Radiology, or General Hospital. The hospital's administrator wants the costs of the three service departments allocated to these three billing centers.

Required:

Using the step-down method, prepare the cost allocation desired by the hospital administrator. Include under each billing center the direct costs of the center, as well as the costs allocated from the service departments.

PROBLEM 4B–6 Step-Down Method versus Direct Method; Predetermined Overhead Rates LO4–10, LO4–11

The Sendai Co., Ltd., of Japan has budgeted costs in its various departments as follows for the coming year:

Factory Administration	$270,000
Custodial Services	68,760
Personnel.	28,840
Maintenance	45,200
Machining—overhead	376,300
Assembly—overhead.	175,900
Total cost	$965,000

The company allocates service department costs to other departments in the order listed below.

Department	Number of Employees	Total Labor-Hours	Square Feet of Space Occupied	Direct Labor-Hours	Machine-Hours
Factory Administration	12	—	5,000	—	—
Custodial Services	4	3,000	2,000	—	—
Personnel.	5	5,000	3,000	—	—
Maintenance	25	22,000	10,000	—	—
Machining	40	30,000	70,000	20,000	70,000
Assembly.	60	90,000	20,000	80,000	10,000
	146	150,000	110,000	100,000	80,000

Machining and Assembly are operating departments; the other departments are service departments. Factory Administration is allocated based on labor-hours; Custodial Services based on square feet occupied; Personnel based on number of employees; and Maintenance based on machine-hours.

Required:

1. Allocate service department costs to consuming departments by the step-down method. Then compute predetermined overhead rates in the operating departments using machine-hours as the allocation base in Machining and direct labor-hours as the allocation base in Assembly.
2. Repeat (1) above, this time using the direct method. Again compute predetermined overhead rates in Machining and Assembly.
3. Assume that the company doesn't bother with allocating service department costs but simply computes a single plantwide overhead rate that divides the total overhead costs (both service department and operating department costs) by the total direct labor-hours. Compute the plantwide overhead rate.
4. Suppose a job requires machine and labor time as follows:

	Machine-Hours	Direct Labor-Hours
Machining Department	190	25
Assembly Department.	10	75
Total hours.	200	100

Using the overhead rates computed in (1), (2), and (3) above, compute the amount of overhead cost that would be assigned to the job if the overhead rates were developed using the step-down method, the direct method, and the plantwide method.

CASE 4B–7 Step-Down Method versus Direct Method LO4–10, LO4–11

"This is really an odd situation," said Jim Carter, general manager of Highland Publishing Company. "We get most of the jobs we bid on that require a lot of press time in the Printing Department, yet profits on those jobs are never as high as they ought to be. On the other hand, we lose most of the jobs we bid on that require a lot of time in the Binding Department. I would be inclined to think that the problem is with our overhead rates, but we're already computing separate overhead rates for each department. So what else could be wrong?"

Highland Publishing Company is a large organization that offers a variety of printing and binding work. The Printing and Binding departments are supported by three service departments. The costs of these service departments are allocated to other departments in the order listed below. The Personnel cost is allocated based on number of employees. The Custodial Services cost is allocated based on square feet of space occupied and the Maintenance cost is allocated based on machine-hours.

Department	Total Labor-Hours	Square Feet of Space Occupied	Number of Employees	Machine- Hours	Direct Labor- Hours
Personnel	20,000	4,000	10		
Custodial Services	30,000	6,000	15		
Maintenance	50,000	20,000	25		
Printing	90,000	80,000	40	150,000	60,000
Binding	260,000	40,000	120	30,000	175,000
	450,000	150,000	210	180,000	235,000

Budgeted overhead costs in each department for the current year are shown below:

Personnel	$ 360,000
Custodial Services.	141,000
Maintenance	201,000
Printing	525,000
Binding	373,500
Total budgeted cost	$1,600,500

Because of its simplicity, the company has always used the direct method to allocate service department costs to the two operating departments.

Required:

1. Using the step-down method, allocate the service department costs to the consuming departments. Then compute predetermined overhead rates in the two operating departments. Use machine-hours as the allocation base in the Printing Department and direct labor-hours as the allocation base in the Binding Department.

2. Repeat (1) above, this time using the direct method. Again compute predetermined overhead rates in the Printing and Binding departments.

3. Assume that during the current year the company bids on a job that requires machine and labor time as follows:

	Machine- Hours	Direct Labor-Hours
Printing Department	15,400	900
Binding Department	800	2,000
Total hours	16,200	2,900

   a. Determine the amount of overhead cost that would be assigned to the job if the company used the overhead rates developed in (1) above. Then determine the amount of overhead cost that would be assigned to the job if the company used the overhead rates developed in (2) above.

   b. Explain to Mr. Carter, the general manager, why the step-down method provides a better basis for computing predetermined overhead rates than the direct method.

CHAPTER 5

Cost-Volume-Profit Relationships

Kid Rock and Live Nation Entertainment Pull the CVP Levers

© Everett Collection Inc/Alamy

Live Nation Entertainment (LNE) owns and operates outdoor amphitheaters. When hosting music concerts the company usually pays a large amount of guaranteed upfront compensation to musical artists to safeguard them from poor attendance. However, rapper-turned-country rocker Kid Rock suggested a different financial arrangement. In exchange for bypassing his up-front fee (which usually ranged between $250,000 and $350,000) and agreeing to share a portion of his ticket revenues with LNE, Kid Rock asked for a share of the revenues from food, drinks, and parking. He then lowered his ticket prices to $20 in an effort to increase attendance and the amount of discretionary spending per customer for food, drinks, and his $20 concert T-shirts. Kid Rock's ultimate goal was to design a financial model that gave fans a more affordable evening of entertainment while still providing his band and LNE adequate profits. ∎

Source: John Jurgensen, "Kid Rock's Plan to Change the Economics of Touring," *The Wall Street Journal*, June 7, 2013, pp. D1–D8.

LEARNING OBJECTIVES

After studying Chapter 5, you should be able to:

LO5–1 Explain how changes in activity affect contribution margin and net operating income.

LO5–2 Prepare and interpret a cost-volume-profit (CVP) graph and a profit graph.

LO5–3 Use the contribution margin ratio (CM ratio) to compute changes in contribution margin and net operating income resulting from changes in sales volume.

LO5–4 Show the effects on net operating income of changes in variable costs, fixed costs, selling price, and volume.

LO5–5 Determine the break-even point.

LO5–6 Determine the level of sales needed to achieve a desired target profit.

LO5–7 Compute the margin of safety and explain its significance.

LO5–8 Compute the degree of operating leverage at a particular level of sales and explain how it can be used to predict changes in net operating income.

LO5–9 Compute the break-even point for a multiproduct company and explain the effects of shifts in the sales mix on contribution margin and the break-even point.

LO5–10 *(Appendix 5A) Analyze a mixed cost using a scattergraph plot and the high-low method.*

LO5–11 *(Appendix 5A) Analyze a mixed cost using a scattergraph plot and the least-squares regression method.*

Cost-volume-profit (CVP) analysis helps managers make many important decisions such as what products and services to offer, what prices to charge, what marketing strategy to use, and what cost structure to maintain. Its primary purpose is to estimate how profits are affected by the following five factors:

1. Selling prices.
2. Sales volume.
3. Unit variable costs.
4. Total fixed costs.
5. Mix of products sold.

To simplify CVP calculations, managers typically adopt the following assumptions with respect to these factors[1]:

1. Selling price is constant. The price of a product or service will not change as volume changes.
2. Costs are linear and can be accurately divided into variable and fixed components. The variable costs are constant per unit and the fixed costs are constant in total over the entire relevant range.
3. In multiproduct companies, the mix of products sold remains constant.

While these assumptions may be violated in practice, the results of CVP analysis are often "good enough" to be quite useful. Perhaps the greatest danger lies in relying on simple CVP analysis when a manager is contemplating a large change in sales volume that lies outside the relevant range. However, even in these situations the CVP model can be adjusted to take into account anticipated changes in selling prices, variable costs per unit, total fixed costs, and the sales mix that arise when the estimated sales volume falls outside the relevant range.

To help explain the role of CVP analysis in business decisions, we'll now turn our attention to the case of Acoustic Concepts, Inc., a company founded by Prem Narayan.

MANAGERIAL ACCOUNTING IN ACTION
THE ISSUE

ACOUSTIC concepts inc

Prem, who was a graduate student in engineering at the time, started Acoustic Concepts, Inc., to market a radical new speaker he had designed for automobile sound systems. The speaker, called the Sonic Blaster, uses an advanced microprocessor and proprietary software to boost amplification to awesome levels. Prem contracted with a Taiwanese electronics manufacturer to produce the speaker. With seed money provided by his family, Prem placed an order with the manufacturer and ran advertisements in auto magazines.

The Sonic Blaster was an immediate success, and sales grew to the point that Prem moved the company's headquarters out of his apartment and into rented quarters in a nearby industrial park. He also hired a receptionist, an accountant, a sales manager, and a small sales staff to sell the speakers to retail stores. The accountant, Bob Luchinni, had worked for several small companies where he had acted as a business advisor as well as accountant and bookkeeper. The following discussion occurred soon after Bob was hired:

Prem: Bob, I've got a lot of questions about the company's finances that I hope you can help answer.

Bob: We're in great shape. The loan from your family will be paid off within a few months.

Prem: I know, but I am worried about the risks I've taken on by expanding operations. What would happen if a competitor entered the market and our sales slipped? How far could sales drop without putting us into the red? Another question I've been trying to resolve is how much our sales would have to increase to justify the big marketing campaign the sales staff is pushing for.

Bob: Marketing always wants more money for advertising.

---

[1] One additional assumption often used in manufacturing companies is that inventories do not change. The number of units produced equals the number of units sold.

Prem: And they are always pushing me to drop the selling price on the speaker. I agree with them that a lower price will boost our sales volume, but I'm not sure the increased volume will offset the loss in revenue from the lower price.

Bob: It sounds like these questions are all related in some way to the relationships among our selling prices, our costs, and our volume. I shouldn't have a problem coming up with some answers.

Prem: Can we meet again in a couple of days to see what you have come up with?

Bob: Sounds good. By then I'll have some preliminary answers for you as well as a model you can use for answering similar questions in the future.

The Basics of Cost-Volume-Profit (CVP) Analysis

Bob Luchinni's preparation for his forthcoming meeting with Prem Narayan begins with the contribution format income statement that was introduced in an earlier chapter. The contribution income statement emphasizes the behavior of costs and therefore is extremely helpful to managers in judging the impact on profits of changes in selling price, cost, or volume. Bob will base his analysis on the following contribution income statement he prepared last month:

Acoustic Concepts, Inc. Contribution Income Statement For the Month of June		
	Total	Per Unit
Sales (400 speakers)	$100,000	$250
Variable expenses.	60,000	150
Contribution margin	40,000	$100
Fixed expenses	35,000	
Net operating income.	$ 5,000	

Notice that sales, variable expenses, and contribution margin are expressed on a per unit basis as well as in total on this contribution income statement. The per unit figures will be very helpful to Bob in some of his calculations. Note that this contribution income statement has been prepared for management's use inside the company and would not ordinarily be made available to those outside the company.

Contribution Margin

LO5–1
Explain how changes in activity affect contribution margin and net operating income.

Contribution margin is the amount remaining from sales revenue after variable expenses have been deducted. Thus, it is the amount available to cover fixed expenses and then to provide profits for the period. Notice the sequence here—contribution margin is used *first* to cover the fixed expenses, and then whatever remains goes toward profits. If the contribution margin is not sufficient to cover the fixed expenses, then a loss occurs for the period. To illustrate with an extreme example, assume that Acoustic Concepts sells only one speaker during a particular month. The company's income statement would appear as follows:

Contribution Income Statement Sales of 1 Speaker		
	Total	Per Unit
Sales (1 speaker).	$ 250	$250
Variable expenses.	150	150
Contribution margin	100	$100
Fixed expenses	35,000	
Net operating loss.	$(34,900)	

For each additional speaker the company sells during the month, $100 more in contribution margin becomes available to help cover the fixed expenses. If a second speaker is sold, for example, then the total contribution margin will increase by $100 (to a total of $200) and the company's loss will decrease by $100, to $34,800:

Contribution Income Statement Sales of 2 Speakers		
	Total	Per Unit
Sales (2 speakers).........................	$ 500	$250
Variable expenses..........................	300	150
Contribution margin	200	$100
Fixed expenses	35,000	
Net operating loss.........................	$(34,800)	

If enough speakers can be sold to generate $35,000 in contribution margin, then all of the fixed expenses will be covered and the company will *break even* for the month—that is, it will show neither profit nor loss but just cover all of its costs. To reach the break-even point, the company will have to sell 350 speakers in a month because each speaker sold yields $100 in contribution margin:

Contribution Income Statement Sales of 350 Speakers		
	Total	Per Unit
Sales (350 speakers)	$87,500	$250
Variable expenses..........................	52,500	150
Contribution margin	35,000	$100
Fixed expenses	35,000	
Net operating income......................	$ 0	

Computation of the break-even point is discussed in detail later in the chapter; for the moment, note that the **break-even point** is the level of sales at which profit is zero.

Once the break-even point has been reached, net operating income will increase by the amount of the unit contribution margin for each additional unit sold. For example, if 351 speakers are sold in a month, then the net operating income for the month will be $100 because the company will have sold 1 speaker more than the number needed to break even:

Contribution Income Statement Sales of 351 Speakers		
	Total	Per Unit
Sales (351 speakers)	$87,750	$250
Variable expenses..........................	52,650	150
Contribution margin	35,100	$100
Fixed expenses	35,000	
Net operating income......................	$ 100	

If 352 speakers are sold (2 speakers above the break-even point), the net operating income for the month will be $200. If 353 speakers are sold (3 speakers above the break-even point), the net operating income for the month will be $300, and so forth. To estimate the profit at any sales volume above the break-even point, multiply the number of units sold in excess of the break-even point by the unit contribution margin. The result represents the anticipated profits for the period. Or, to estimate the effect of a planned increase in sales on profits, simply multiply the increase in units sold by the unit contribution margin. The result will be the expected increase in profits. To illustrate, if Acoustic Concepts is currently selling 400 speakers per month and plans to increase sales to 425 speakers per month, the anticipated impact on profits can be computed as follows:

Additional speakers to be sold	25
Contribution margin per speaker	× $100
Increase in net operating income	$2,500

These calculations can be verified as follows:

	Sales Volume			
	400 Speakers	425 Speakers	Difference (25 Speakers)	Per Unit
Sales (@ $250 per speaker)	$100,000	$106,250	$6,250	$250
Variable expenses (@ $150 per speaker)	60,000	63,750	3,750	150
Contribution margin	40,000	42,500	2,500	$100
Fixed expenses	35,000	35,000	0	
Net operating income	$ 5,000	$ 7,500	$2,500	

To summarize, if sales are zero, the company's loss would equal its fixed expenses. Each unit that is sold reduces the loss by the amount of the unit contribution margin. Once the break-even point has been reached, each additional unit sold increases the company's profit by the amount of the unit contribution margin.

CVP Relationships in Equation Form

The contribution format income statement can be expressed in equation form as follows:

$$\text{Profit} = (\text{Sales} - \text{Variable expenses}) - \text{Fixed expenses}$$

For brevity, we use the term *profit* to stand for net operating income in equations.

When a company has only a *single* product, as at Acoustic Concepts, we can further refine the equation as follows:

$$\text{Sales} = \text{Selling price per unit} \times \text{Quantity sold} = P \times Q$$

$$\text{Variable expenses} = \text{Variable expenses per unit} \times \text{Quantity sold} = V \times Q$$

$$\text{Profit} = (P \times Q - V \times Q) - \text{Fixed expenses}$$

We can do all of the calculations of the previous section using this simple equation. For example, earlier we computed that the net operating income (profit) at sales of 351 speakers would be $100. We can arrive at the same conclusion using the above equation as follows:

$$\text{Profit} = (P \times Q - V \times Q) - \text{Fixed expenses}$$

$$\text{Profit} = (\$250 \times 351 - \$150 \times 351) - \$35{,}000$$

$$= (\$250 - \$150) \times 351 - \$35{,}000$$

$$= (\$100) \times 351 - \$35{,}000$$

$$= \$35{,}100 - \$35{,}000$$

$$= \$100$$

It is often useful to express the simple profit equation in terms of the unit contribution margin (Unit CM) as follows:

$$\text{Unit CM} = \text{Selling price per unit} - \text{Variable expenses per unit} = P - V$$

$$\text{Profit} = (P \times Q - V \times Q) - \text{Fixed expenses}$$

$$\text{Profit} = (P - V) \times Q - \text{Fixed expenses}$$

$$\text{Profit} = \text{Unit CM} \times Q - \text{Fixed expenses}$$

We could also have used this equation to determine the profit at sales of 351 speakers as follows:

$$\text{Profit} = \text{Unit CM} \times Q - \text{Fixed expenses}$$

$$= \$100 \times 351 - \$35,000$$

$$= \$35,100 - \$35,000$$

$$= \$100$$

For those who are comfortable with algebra, the quickest and easiest approach to solving the problems in this chapter may be to use the simple profit equation in one of its forms.

CVP Relationships in Graphic Form

The relationships among revenue, cost, profit, and volume are illustrated on a **cost-volume-profit (CVP) graph**. A CVP graph highlights CVP relationships over wide ranges of activity. To help explain his analysis to Prem Narayan, Bob Luchinni prepared a CVP graph for Acoustic Concepts.

LO5–2
Prepare and interpret a cost-volume-profit (CVP) graph and a profit graph.

Preparing the CVP Graph In a CVP graph (sometimes called a *break-even chart*), unit volume is represented on the horizontal (X) axis and dollars on the vertical (Y) axis. Preparing a CVP graph involves the three steps depicted in Exhibit 5–1:

1. Draw a line parallel to the volume axis to represent total fixed expense. For Acoustic Concepts, total fixed expenses are $35,000.
2. Choose some volume of unit sales and plot the point representing total expense (fixed and variable) at the sales volume you have selected. In Exhibit 5–1, Bob Luchinni chose a volume of 600 speakers. Total expense at that sales volume is:

Fixed expense	$ 35,000
Variable expense (600 speakers × $150 per speaker)	90,000
Total expense.	$125,000

After the point has been plotted, draw a line through it back to the point where the fixed expense line intersects the dollars axis.
3. Again choose some sales volume and plot the point representing total sales dollars at the activity level you have selected. In Exhibit 5–1, Bob Luchinni again chose a volume of 600 speakers. Sales at that volume total $150,000 (600 speakers × $250 per speaker). Draw a line through this point back to the origin.

The interpretation of the completed CVP graph is given in Exhibit 5–2. The anticipated profit or loss at any given level of sales is measured by the vertical distance between the total revenue line (sales) and the total expense line (variable expense plus fixed expense).

EXHIBIT 5–1
Preparing the CVP Graph

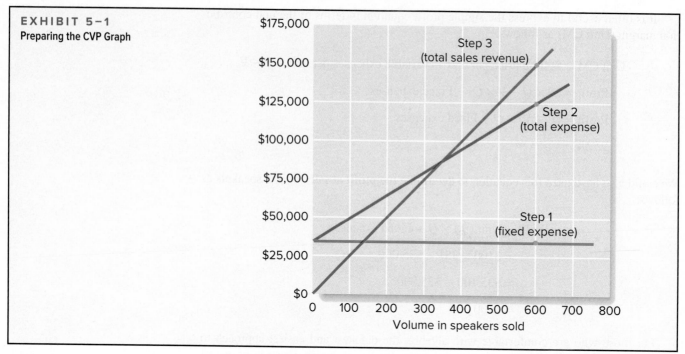

EXHIBIT 5–2
The Completed CVP Graph

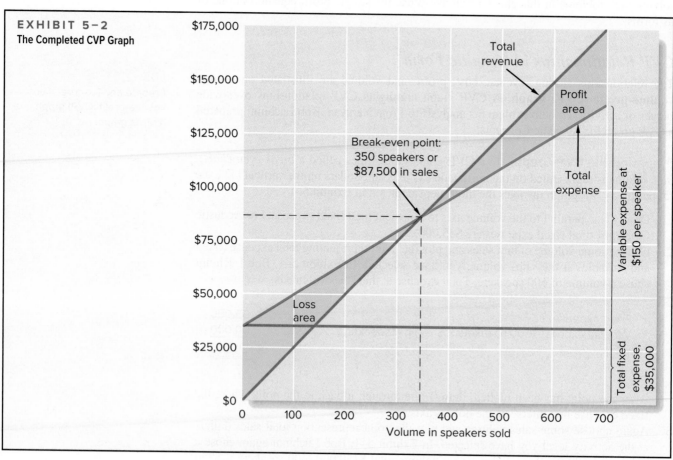

The break-even point is where the total revenue and total expense lines cross. The break-even point of 350 speakers in Exhibit 5–2 agrees with the break-even point computed earlier.

When sales are below the break-even point—in this case, 350 units—the company suffers a loss. Note that the loss (represented by the vertical distance between the total

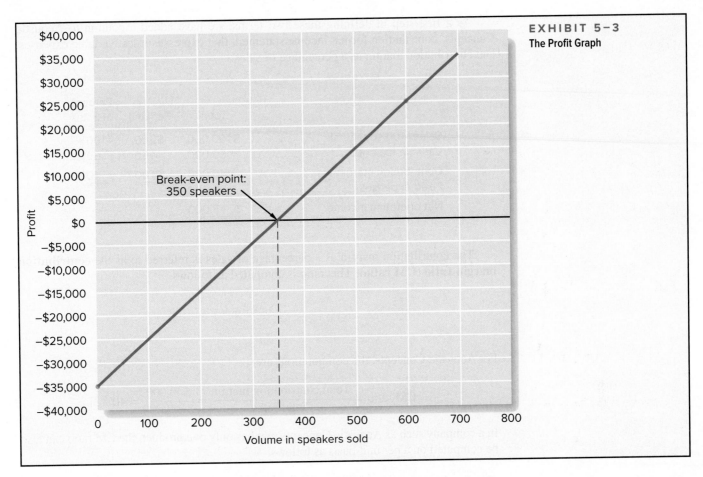

EXHIBIT 5–3
The Profit Graph

expense and total revenue lines) gets bigger as sales decline. When sales are above the break-even point, the company earns a profit and the size of the profit (represented by the vertical distance between the total revenue and total expense lines) increases as sales increase.

An even simpler form of the CVP graph, which we call a profit graph, is presented in Exhibit 5–3. That graph is based on the following equation:

$$\text{Profit} = \text{Unit CM} \times Q - \text{Fixed expenses}$$

In the case of Acoustic Concepts, the equation can be expressed as:

$$\text{Profit} = \$100 \times Q - \$35,000$$

Because this is a linear equation, it plots as a single straight line. To plot the line, compute the profit at two different sales volumes, plot the points, and then connect them with a straight line. For example, when the sales volume is zero (i.e., $Q = 0$), the profit is $-\$35,000$ ($= \$100 \times 0 - \$35,000$). When Q is 600, the profit is $\$25,000$ ($= \$100 \times 600 - \$35,000$). These two points are plotted in Exhibit 5–3 and a straight line has been drawn through them.

The break-even point on the profit graph is the volume of sales at which profit is zero and is indicated by the dashed line on the graph. Note that the profit steadily increases to the right of the break-even point as the sales volume increases and that the loss becomes steadily worse to the left of the break-even point as the sales volume decreases.

Contribution Margin Ratio (CM Ratio) and the Variable Expense Ratio

In the previous section, we explored how CVP relationships can be visualized. This section begins by defining the *contribution margin ratio* and the *variable expense ratio*. Then it demonstrates how to use the contribution margin ratio in CVP calculations.

As a first step in defining these two terms, we have added a column to Acoustic Concepts' contribution format income statement that expresses sales, variable expenses, and contribution margin as a percentage of sales:

	Total	Per Unit	Percent of Sales
Sales (400 speakers)	$100,000	$250	100%
Variable expenses.	60,000	150	60%
Contribution margin	40,000	$100	40%
Fixed expenses	35,000		
Net operating income.	$ 5,000		

The contribution margin as a percentage of sales is referred to as the **contribution margin ratio (CM ratio)**. This ratio is computed as follows:

$$\text{CM ratio} = \frac{\text{Contribution margin}}{\text{Sales}}$$

For Acoustic Concepts, the computations are:

$$\text{CM ratio} = \frac{\text{Total contribution margin}}{\text{Total sales}} = \frac{\$40,000}{\$100,000} = 40\%$$

In a company such as Acoustic Concepts that has only one product, the CM ratio can also be computed on a per unit basis as follows:

$$\text{CM ratio} = \frac{\text{Unit contribution margin}}{\text{Unit selling price}} = \frac{\$100}{\$250} = 40\%$$

Similarly, the variable expenses as a percentage of sales is referred to as the **variable expense ratio**. This ratio is computed as follows:

$$\text{Variable expense ratio} = \frac{\text{Variable expenses}}{\text{Sales}}$$

For Acoustic Concepts, the computations are:

$$\text{Variable expense ratio} = \frac{\text{Total variable expenses}}{\text{Total sales}} = \frac{\$60,000}{\$100,000} = 60\%$$

Because Acoustic Concepts has only one product, the variable expense ratio can also be computed on a per unit basis as follows:

$$\text{Variable expense ratio} = \frac{\text{Variable expense per unit}}{\text{Unit selling price}} = \frac{\$150}{\$250} = 60\%$$

Having defined the two terms, it bears emphasizing that the contribution margin ratio and the variable expense ratio can be mathematically related to one another:

$$\text{CM ratio} = \frac{\text{Contribution margin}}{\text{Sales}}$$

$$\text{CM ratio} = \frac{\text{Sales} - \text{Variable expenses}}{\text{Sales}}$$

$$\text{CM ratio} = 1 - \text{Variable expense ratio}$$

So, in the case of Acoustic Concepts, this relationship would be as follows:

$$\text{CM ratio} = 1 - \text{Variable expense ratio}$$
$$= 1 - 60\,\%$$
$$= 40\,\%$$

Applications of the Contribution Margin Ratio   The CM ratio shows how the contribution margin will be affected by a change in total sales. Acoustic Concepts' CM ratio of 40% means that for each dollar increase in sales, total contribution margin will increase by 40 cents ($1 sales × CM ratio of 40%). Net operating income will also increase by 40 cents, assuming that fixed costs are not affected by the increase in sales. Generally, the effect of a change in sales on the contribution margin is expressed in equation form as:

LO5–3

Use the contribution margin ratio (CM ratio) to compute changes in contribution margin and net operating income resulting from changes in sales volume.

$$\text{Change in contribution margin} = \text{CM ratio} \times \text{Change in sales}$$

As this illustration suggests, *the impact on net operating income of any given dollar change in total sales can be computed by applying the CM ratio to the dollar change.* For example, if Acoustic Concepts plans a $30,000 increase in sales during the coming month, the contribution margin should increase by $12,000 ($30,000 increase in sales × CM ratio of 40%). As we noted above, net operating income also will increase by $12,000 if fixed costs do not change. This is verified by the following table:

	Present	Expected	Increase	Percent of Sales
Sales	$100,000	$130,000	$30,000	100%
Variable expenses	60,000	78,000*	18,000	60%
Contribution margin	40,000	52,000	12,000	40%
Fixed expenses	35,000	35,000	0	
Net operating income	$ 5,000	$ 17,000	$12,000	

Sales Volume (column grouping over Present, Expected, Increase)

*$130,000 expected sales ÷ $250 per unit = 520 units. 520 units × $150 per unit = $78,000.

The relation between profit and the CM ratio can also be expressed using the following equation:

$$\text{Profit} = \text{CM ratio} \times \text{Sales} - \text{Fixed expenses}^{2}$$

or, in terms of changes,

$$\text{Change in profit} = \text{CM ratio} \times \text{Change in sales} - \text{Change in fixed expenses}$$

---

[2] This equation can be derived using the basic profit equation and the definition of the CM ratio as follows:

$$\text{Profit} = (\text{Sales} - \text{Variable expenses}) - \text{Fixed expenses}$$

$$\text{Profit} = \text{Contribution margin} - \text{Fixed expenses}$$

$$\text{Profit} = \frac{\text{Contribution margin}}{\text{Sales}} \times \text{Sales} - \text{Fixed expenses}$$

$$\text{Profit} = \text{CM ratio} \times \text{Sales} - \text{Fixed expenses}$$

For example, at sales of $130,000, the profit is expected to be $17,000 as shown below:

$$\begin{aligned}
\text{Profit} &= \text{CM ratio} \times \text{Sales} - \text{Fixed expenses} \\
&= 0.40 \times \$130,000 - \$35,000 \\
&= \$52,000 - \$35,000 \\
&= \$17,000
\end{aligned}$$

Again, if you are comfortable with algebra, this approach will often be quicker and easier than constructing contribution format income statements.

The CM ratio is particularly valuable in situations where the dollar sales of one product must be traded off against the dollar sales of another product. In this situation, products that yield the greatest amount of contribution margin per dollar of sales should be emphasized.

LO5–4

Show the effects on net operating income of changes in variable costs, fixed costs, selling price, and volume.

Additional Applications of CVP Concepts

Having demonstrated how to use the contribution margin ratio in CVP calculations, Bob Luchinni, the accountant at Acoustic Concepts, wanted to offer the company's president, Prem Narayan, five additional examples of how CVP analysis can be used to answer the types of questions that their company is facing. So, he began by reminding Prem that the company's fixed expenses are $35,000 per month and he restated the following key pieces of data:

	Per Unit	Percent of Sales
Selling price	$250	100%
Variable expenses...........................	150	60%
Contribution margin	$100	40%

Example 1: Change in Fixed Cost and Sales Volume Acoustic Concepts is currently selling 400 speakers per month at $250 per speaker for total monthly sales of $100,000. The sales manager feels that a $10,000 increase in the monthly advertising budget would increase monthly sales by $30,000 to a total of 520 units. Should the advertising budget be increased? The table below shows the financial impact of the proposed change in the monthly advertising budget.

	Current Sales	Sales with Additional Advertising Budget	Difference	Percent of Sales
Sales	$100,000	$130,000	$30,000	100%
Variable expenses...............	60,000	78,000*	18,000	60%
Contribution margin	40,000	52,000	12,000	40%
Fixed expenses	35,000	45,000†	10,000	
Net operating income............	$ 5,000	$ 7,000	$ 2,000	

*520 units × $150 per unit = $78,000.
†$35,000 + additional $10,000 monthly advertising budget = $45,000.

Assuming no other factors need to be considered, the increase in the advertising budget should be approved because it would increase net operating income by $2,000. There are two shorter ways to arrive at this solution. The first alternative solution follows:

Alternative Solution 1

Expected total contribution margin:	
$130,000 × 40% CM ratio	$52,000
Present total contribution margin:	
$100,000 × 40% CM ratio..........................	40,000
Increase in total contribution margin....................	12,000
Change in fixed expenses:	
Less incremental advertising expense	10,000
Increased net operating income........................	$ 2,000

Because in this case only the fixed costs and the sales volume change, the solution can also be quickly derived as follows:

Alternative Solution 2

Incremental contribution margin:	
$30,000 × 40% CM ratio.........................	$12,000
Less incremental advertising expense	10,000
Increased net operating income.......................	$ 2,000

Notice that this approach does not depend on knowledge of previous sales. Also note that it is unnecessary under either shorter approach to prepare an income statement. Both of the alternative solutions involve **incremental analysis**—that is, they consider only the costs and revenues that will change if the new program is implemented. Although in each case a new income statement could have been prepared, the incremental approach is simpler and more direct and focuses attention on the specific changes that would occur as a result of the decision.

Example 2: Change in Variable Costs and Sales Volume   Refer to the original data. Recall that Acoustic Concepts is currently selling 400 speakers per month. Prem is considering the use of higher-quality components, which would increase variable costs (and thereby reduce the contribution margin) by $10 per speaker. However, the sales manager predicts that using higher-quality components would increase sales to 480 speakers per month. Should the higher-quality components be used?

The $10 increase in variable costs would decrease the unit contribution margin by $10—from $100 down to $90.

Solution

Expected total contribution margin	
with higher-quality components:	
480 speakers × $90 per speaker	$43,200
Present total contribution margin:	
400 speakers × $100 per speaker	40,000
Increase in total contribution margin....................	$ 3,200

According to this analysis, the higher-quality components should be used. Because fixed costs would not change, the $3,200 increase in contribution margin shown above should result in a $3,200 increase in net operating income.

Example 3: Change in Fixed Cost, Selling Price, and Sales Volume   Refer to the original data and recall again that Acoustic Concepts is currently selling 400 speakers per month. To increase sales, the sales manager would like to cut the selling price by $20 per speaker and increase the advertising budget by $15,000 per month. The sales manager believes that if these two steps are taken, unit sales will increase by 50% to 600 speakers per month. Should the changes be made?

A decrease in the selling price of $20 per speaker would decrease the unit contribution margin by $20 down to $80.

Solution

Expected total contribution margin with lower selling price:	
600 speakers × $80 per speaker	$48,000
Present total contribution margin:	
400 speakers × $100 per speaker	40,000
Incremental contribution margin.	8,000
Change in fixed expenses:	
Less incremental advertising expense	15,000
Reduction in net operating income	$ (7,000)

According to this analysis, the changes should not be made. The $7,000 reduction in net operating income that is shown above can be verified by preparing comparative contribution format income statements as shown here:

	Present 400 Speakers per Month		Expected 600 Speakers per Month		
	Total	Per Unit	Total	Per Unit	Difference
Sales	$100,000	$250	$138,000	$230	$38,000
Variable expenses.	60,000	150	90,000	150	30,000
Contribution margin	40,000	$100	48,000	$ 80	8,000
Fixed expenses	35,000		50,000*		15,000
Net operating income (loss)	$ 5,000		$ (2,000)		$ (7,000)

*35,000 + Additional monthly advertising budget of $15,000 = $50,000.

Example 4: Change in Variable Cost, Fixed Cost, and Sales Volume Refer to Acoustic Concepts' original data. As before, the company is currently selling 400 speakers per month. The sales manager would like to pay salespersons a sales commission of $15 per speaker sold, rather than the flat salaries that now total $6,000 per month. The sales manager is confident that the change would increase monthly sales by 15% to 460 speakers per month. Should the change be made?

Solution Changing the sales staff's compensation from salaries to commissions would affect both variable and fixed expenses. Variable expenses per unit would increase by $15, from $150 to $165, and the unit contribution margin would decrease from $100 to $85. Fixed expenses would decrease by $6,000, from $35,000 to $29,000.

Expected total contribution margin	
with sales staff on commissions:	
460 speakers × $85 per speaker	$39,100
Present total contribution margin:	
400 speakers × $100 per speaker	40,000
Decrease in total contribution margin	(900)
Change in fixed expenses:	
Add salaries avoided if a commission is paid.	6,000
Increase in net operating income.	$ 5,100

According to this analysis, the changes should be made. Again, the same answer can be obtained by preparing comparative contribution income statements:

	Present 400 Speakers per Month		Expected 460 Speakers per Month		
	Total	Per Unit	Total	Per Unit	Difference
Sales	$100,000	$250	$115,000	$250	$15,000
Variable expenses.	60,000	150	75,900	165	15,900
Contribution margin	40,000	$100	39,100	$ 85	900
Fixed expenses	35,000		29,000		(6,000)*
Net operating income.	$ 5,000		$ 10,100		$ 5,100

*Note: A reduction in fixed expenses has the effect of increasing net operating income.

Example 5: Change in Selling Price   Refer to the original data where Acoustic Concepts is currently selling 400 speakers per month. The company has an opportunity to make a bulk sale of 150 speakers to a wholesaler if an acceptable price can be negotiated. This sale would not alter the company's regular sales and would not affect the company's total fixed expenses. What price per speaker should be quoted to the wholesaler if Acoustic Concepts is seeking a profit of $3,000 on the bulk sale?

Solution

Variable cost per speaker	$150
Desired profit per speaker:	
$3,000 ÷ 150 speakers	20
Quoted price per speaker	$170

Notice that fixed expenses are not included in the computation. This is because fixed expenses are not affected by the bulk sale, so all of the additional contribution margin increases the company's profits.

IN BUSINESS

NEWSPAPER CIRCULARS: STILL WORTH THE INVESTMENT

In the digital era, it might be easy to assume that retailers should abandon the advertising inserts (called newspaper circulars) that accompany print newspapers. However, Wanderful Media estimates that 80% of people who read print newspapers look at the circulars inside, whereas only 1% of online readers click through to digital circulars. Walmart acquainted itself with these statistics when it discontinued print circulars in Fargo, North Dakota, Madison, Wisconsin, and Tucson, Arizona and redirected its advertising dollars in those markets to digital media. The ensuing drop in sales motivated Walmart to immediately reinstate its circular ads in print newspapers.

© Robert Barnes/Getty Images

    Kohl's hopes to decrease the cost of producing and distributing its circulars by 40% while largely retaining its existing sales volumes. Its plan is to use data from past purchases to identify the zip codes with the highest concentrations of loyal Kohl's shoppers and then to limit its distribution of circulars to the most profitable zip codes (rather than relying on more expensive mass distribution in all zip codes). The company will probably use cost-volume-profit analysis to determine if its plan increases profits.

Source: Suzanne Kapner, "Retailers Can't Shake Their Circular Habit," *The Wall Street Journal*, March 12, 2015, p. B8.

Break-Even and Target Profit Analysis

Managers use break-even and target profit analysis to answer questions such as how much would we have to sell to avoid incurring a loss or how much would we have to sell to make a profit of $10,000 per month? We'll discuss break-even analysis first followed by target profit analysis.

Break-Even Analysis

LO5–5

Determine the break-even point.

Earlier in the chapter we defined the break-even point as *the level of sales at which the company's profit is zero*. To calculate the break-even point (in unit sales and dollar sales), managers can use either of two approaches, the equation method or the formula method. We'll demonstrate both approaches using the data from Acoustic Concepts.

The Equation Method

The equation method relies on the basic profit equation introduced earlier in the chapter. Because Acoustic Concepts has only one product, we'll use the contribution margin form of this equation to perform the break-even calculations. Remembering that Acoustic Concepts' unit contribution margin is $100, and its fixed expenses are $35,000, the company's break-even point is computed as follows:

$$\text{Profit} = \text{Unit CM} \times Q - \text{Fixed expense}$$
$$\$0 = \$100 \times Q - \$35,000$$
$$\$100 \times Q = \$0 + \$35,000$$
$$Q = \$35,000 \div \$100$$
$$Q = 350$$

Thus, as we determined earlier in the chapter, Acoustic Concepts will break even (or earn zero profit) at a sales volume of 350 speakers per month.

The Formula Method

The formula method is a shortcut version of the equation method. It centers on the idea discussed earlier in the chapter that each unit sold provides a certain amount of contribution margin that goes toward covering fixed expenses. In a single product situation, the formula for computing the unit sales to break even is:

$$\text{Unit sales to break even} = \frac{\text{Fixed expenses}[3]}{\text{Unit CM}}$$

In the case of Acoustic Concepts, the unit sales needed to break even is computed as follows:

$$\text{Unit sales to break even} = \frac{\text{Fixed expenses}}{\text{Unit CM}}$$
$$= \frac{\$35,000}{\$100}$$
$$= 350$$

---

[3] This formula can be derived as follows:
$$\text{Profit} = \text{Unit CM} \times Q - \text{Fixed expenses}$$
$$\$0 = \text{Unit CM} \times Q - \text{Fixed expenses}$$
$$\text{Unit CM} \times Q = \$0 + \text{Fixed expenses}$$
$$Q = \text{Fixed expenses} \div \text{Unit CM}$$

Notice that 350 units is the same answer that we got when using the equation method. This will always be the case because the formula method and equation method are mathematically equivalent. The formula method simply skips a few steps in the equation method.

Break-Even in Dollar Sales   In addition to finding the break-even point in unit sales, we can also find the break-even point in dollar sales using three methods. First, we could solve for the break-even point in *unit* sales using the equation method or formula method and then simply multiply the result by the selling price. In the case of Acoustic Concepts, the break-even point in dollar sales using this approach would be computed as 350 speakers × $250 per speaker, or $87,500 in total sales.

Second, we can use the equation method to compute the break-even point in dollar sales. Remembering that Acoustic Concepts' contribution margin ratio is 40% and its fixed expenses are $35,000, the equation method calculates the break-even point in dollar sales as follows:

$$\text{Profit} = \text{CM ratio} \times \text{Sales} - \text{Fixed expenses}$$
$$\$0 = 0.40 \times \text{Sales} - \$35,000$$
$$0.40 \times \text{Sales} = \$0 + \$35,000$$
$$\text{Sales} = \$35,000 \div 0.40$$
$$\text{Sales} = \$87,500$$

Third, we can use the formula method to compute the dollar sales needed to break even as shown below:

$$\text{Dollar sales to break even} = \frac{\text{Fixed expenses}^4}{\text{CM ratio}}$$

In the case of Acoustic Concepts, the computations are performed as follows:

$$\text{Dollar sales to break even} = \frac{\text{Fixed expenses}}{\text{CM ratio}}$$
$$= \frac{\$35,000}{0.40}$$
$$= \$87,500$$

Again, you'll notice that the break-even point in dollar sales ($87,500) is the same under all three methods. This will always be the case because these methods are mathematically equivalent.

Target Profit Analysis

Target profit analysis is one of the key uses of CVP analysis. In **target profit analysis**, we estimate what sales volume is needed to achieve a specific target profit. For example, suppose Prem Narayan of Acoustic Concepts, Inc., would like to estimate the sales needed to attain a target profit of $40,000 per month. To determine the unit sales and

LO5–6
Determine the level of sales needed to achieve a desired target profit.

---

[4] This formula can be derived as follows:
$$\text{Profit} = \text{CM ratio} \times \text{Sales} - \text{Fixed expenses}$$
$$\$0 = \text{CM ratio} \times \text{Sales} - \text{Fixed expenses}$$
$$\text{CM ratio} \times \text{Sales} = \$0 + \text{Fixed expenses}$$
$$\text{Sales} = \text{Fixed expenses} \div \text{CM ratio}$$

dollar sales needed to achieve a target profit, we can rely on the same two approaches that we have been discussing thus far, the equation method or the formula method.

The Equation Method   To compute the unit sales required to achieve a target profit of $40,000 per month, Acoustic Concepts can use the same profit equation that was used for its break-even analysis. Remembering that the company's contribution margin per unit is $100 and its total fixed expenses are $35,000, the equation method could be applied as follows:

$$\text{Profit} = \text{Unit CM} \times Q - \text{Fixed expense}$$
$$\$40,000 = \$140 \times Q - \$35,000$$
$$\$100 \times Q = \$40,000 + \$35,000$$
$$Q = \$75,000 \div \$100$$
$$Q = 750$$

Thus, the target profit can be achieved by selling 750 speakers per month. Notice that the only difference between this equation and the equation used for Acoustic Concepts' break-even calculation is the profit figure. In the break-even scenario, the profit is $0, whereas in the target profit scenario the profit is $40,000.

The Formula Method   In general, in a single product situation, we can compute the sales volume required to attain a specific target profit using the following formula:

$$\text{Unit sales to attain the target profit} = \frac{\text{Target profit} + \text{Fixed expenses}}{\text{Unit CM}}$$

In the case of Acoustic Concepts, the unit sales needed to attain a target profit of 40,000 is computed as follows:

$$\text{Unit sales to attain the target profit} = \frac{\text{Target profit} + \text{Fixed expenses}}{\text{Unit CM}}$$
$$= \frac{\$40,000 + \$35,000}{\$100}$$
$$= 750$$

Target Profit Analysis in Terms of Dollar Sales   When quantifying the dollar sales needed to attain a target profit we can apply the same three methods that we used for calculating the dollar sales needed to break even. First, we can solve for the *unit* sales needed to attain the target profit using the equation method or formula method and then simply multiply the result by the selling price. In the case of Acoustic Concepts, the dollar sales to attain its target profit would be computed as 750 speakers × $250 per speaker, or $187,500 in total sales.

Second, we can use the equation method to compute the dollar sales needed to attain the target profit. Remembering that Acoustic Concepts' target profit is $40,000, its contribution margin ratio is 40%, and its fixed expenses are $35,000, the equation method calculates the answer as follows:

$$\text{Profit} = \text{CM ratio} \times \text{Sales} - \text{Fixed expenses}$$
$$\$40,000 = 0.40 \times \text{Sales} - \$35,000$$
$$0.40 \times \text{Sales} = \$40,000 + \$35,000$$
$$\text{Sales} = \$75,000 \div 0.40$$
$$\text{Sales} = \$187,500$$

Third, we can use the formula method to compute the dollar sales needed to attain the target profit as shown below:

$$\text{Dollar sales to attain the target profit} = \frac{\text{Target profit} + \text{Fixed expenses}}{\text{CM ratio}}$$

In the case of Acoustic Concepts, the computations would be:

$$\begin{aligned}\text{Dollar sales to attain the target profit} &= \frac{\text{Target profit} + \text{Fixed expenses}}{\text{CM ratio}} \\ &= \frac{\$40{,}000 + \$35{,}000}{0.40} \\ &= \$187{,}500\end{aligned}$$

Again, you'll notice that the answers are the same regardless of which method we use. This is because all of the methods discussed are simply different roads to the same destination.

The Margin of Safety

The **margin of safety** is the excess of budgeted or actual sales dollars over the break-even volume of sales dollars. It is the amount by which sales can drop before losses are incurred. The higher the margin of safety, the lower the risk of not breaking even and incurring a loss. The formula for the margin of safety is:

$$\text{Margin of safety in dollars} = \text{Total budgeted (or actual) sales} - \text{Break-even sales}$$

The margin of safety also can be expressed in percentage form by dividing the margin of safety in dollars by total dollar sales:

$$\text{Margin of safety percentage} = \frac{\text{Margin of safety in dollars}}{\text{Total budgeted (or actual) sales in dollars}}$$

The calculation of the margin of safety for Acoustic Concepts is:

Sales (at the current volume of 400 speakers) (a)	$100,000
Break-even sales (at 350 speakers)	87,500
Margin of safety in dollars (b)	$ 12,500
Margin of safety percentage, (b) ÷ (a)	12.5%

LO5–7
Compute the margin of safety and explain its significance.

This margin of safety means that at the current level of sales and with the company's current prices and cost structure, a reduction in sales of $12,500, or 12.5%, would result in just breaking even.

In a single-product company like Acoustic Concepts, the margin of safety also can be expressed in terms of the number of units sold by dividing the margin of safety in dollars by the selling price per unit. In this case, the margin of safety is 50 speakers ($12,500 ÷ $250 per speaker = 50 speakers).

MANAGERIAL ACCOUNTING IN ACTION
THE WRAP-UP

ACOUSTIC
concepts

inc

Prem Narayan and Bob Luchinni met to discuss the results of Bob's analysis.

Prem: Bob, everything you have shown me is pretty clear. I can see what impact the sales manager's suggestions would have on our profits. Some of those suggestions are quite good and others are not so good. I am concerned that our margin of safety is only 50 speakers. What can we do to increase this number?

Bob: Well, we have to increase total sales or decrease the break-even point or both.

Prem: And to decrease the break-even point, we have to either decrease our fixed expenses or increase our unit contribution margin?

Bob: Exactly.

Prem: And to increase our unit contribution margin, we must either increase our selling price or decrease the variable cost per unit?

Bob: Correct.

Prem: So what do you suggest?

Bob: Well, the analysis doesn't tell us which of these to do, but it does indicate we have a potential problem here.

Prem: If you don't have any immediate suggestions, I would like to call a general meeting next week to discuss ways we can work on increasing the margin of safety. I think everyone will be concerned about how vulnerable we are to even small downturns in sales.

CVP Considerations in Choosing a Cost Structure

Cost structure refers to the relative proportion of fixed and variable costs in an organization. Managers often have some latitude in trading off between these two types of costs. For example, fixed investments in automated equipment can reduce variable labor costs. In this section, we discuss the choice of a cost structure. We also introduce the concept of *operating leverage*.

Cost Structure and Profit Stability

Which cost structure is better—high variable costs and low fixed costs, or the opposite? No single answer to this question is possible; each approach has its advantages. To show what we mean, refer to the following contribution format income statements for two blueberry farms. Bogside Farm depends on migrant workers to pick its berries by hand, whereas Sterling Farm has invested in expensive berry-picking machines. Consequently, Bogside Farm has higher variable costs, but Sterling Farm has higher fixed costs:

	Bogside Farm		Sterling Farm	
	Amount	Percent	Amount	Percent
Sales	$100,000	100%	$100,000	100%
Variable expenses..............	60,000	60%	30,000	30%
Contribution margin	40,000	40%	70,000	70%
Fixed expenses	30,000		60,000	
Net operating income...........	$ 10,000		$ 10,000	

Which farm has the better cost structure? The answer depends on many factors, including the long-run trend in sales, year-to-year fluctuations in the level of sales, and the attitude of the owners toward risk. If sales are expected to exceed $100,000 in the future, then Sterling Farm probably has the better cost structure. The reason is that its CM ratio is higher, and its profits will therefore increase more rapidly as sales increase. To illustrate, assume that each farm experiences a 10% increase in sales without any increase in fixed costs. The new contribution income statements would be as follows:

	Bogside Farm		Sterling Farm	
	Amount	Percent	Amount	Percent
Sales	$110,000	100%	$110,000	100%
Variable expenses.	66,000	60%	33,000	30%
Contribution margin	44,000	40%	77,000	70%
Fixed expenses	30,000		60,000	
Net operating income.	$ 14,000		$ 17,000	

Sterling Farm has experienced a greater increase in net operating income due to its higher CM ratio even though the increase in sales was the same for both farms.

What if sales drop below $100,000? What are the farms' break-even points? What are their margins of safety? The computations needed to answer these questions are shown below using the formula method:

	Bogside Farm	Sterling Farm
Fixed expenses	$ 30,000	$ 60,000
Contribution margin ratio.	÷ 0.40	÷ 0.70
Dollar sales to break even.	$ 75,000	$ 85,714
Total current sales (a)	$100,000	$100,000
Break-even sales.	75,000	85,714
Margin of safety in sales dollars (b)	$ 25,000	$ 14,286
Margin of safety percentage (b) ÷ (a).	25.0%	14.3%

Bogside Farm's margin of safety is greater and its contribution margin ratio is lower than Sterling Farm. Therefore, Bogside Farm is less vulnerable to downturns than Sterling Farm. Due to its lower contribution margin ratio, Bogside Farm will not lose contribution margin as rapidly as Sterling Farm when sales decline. Thus, Bogside Farm's profit will be less volatile. We saw earlier that this is a drawback when sales increase, but it provides more protection when sales drop. And because its break-even point is lower, Bogside Farm can suffer a larger sales decline before losses emerge.

To summarize, without knowing the future, it is not obvious which cost structure is better. Both have advantages and disadvantages. Sterling Farm, with its higher fixed costs and lower variable costs, will experience wider swings in net operating income as sales fluctuate, with greater profits in good years and greater losses in bad years. Bogside Farm, with its lower fixed costs and higher variable costs, will enjoy greater profit stability and will be more protected from losses during bad years, but at the cost of lower net operating income in good years. Moreover, if the higher fixed costs in Sterling Farm reflect greater capacity, Sterling Farm will be better able than Bogside Farm to profit from unexpected surges in demand.

Operating Leverage

A lever is a tool for multiplying force. Using a lever, a massive object can be moved with only a modest amount of force. In business, *operating leverage* serves a similar purpose. **Operating leverage** is a measure of how sensitive net operating income is to a given

LO5–8

Compute the degree of operating leverage at a particular level of sales and explain how it can be used to predict changes in net operating income.

percentage change in dollar sales. Operating leverage acts as a multiplier. If operating leverage is high, a small percentage increase in sales can produce a much larger percentage increase in net operating income.

Operating leverage can be illustrated by returning to the data for the two blueberry farms. We previously showed that a 10% increase in sales (from $100,000 to $110,000 in each farm) results in a 70% increase in the net operating income of Sterling Farm (from $10,000 to $17,000) and only a 40% increase in the net operating income of Bogside Farm (from $10,000 to $14,000). Thus, for a 10% increase in sales, Sterling Farm experiences a much greater percentage increase in profits than does Bogside Farm. Therefore, Sterling Farm has greater operating leverage than Bogside Farm.

The **degree of operating leverage** at a given level of sales is computed by the following formula:

$$\text{Degree of operating leverage} = \frac{\text{Contribution margin}}{\text{Net operating income}}$$

The degree of operating leverage is a measure, at a given level of sales, of how a percentage change in sales volume will affect profits. To illustrate, the degree of operating leverage for the two farms at $100,000 sales would be computed as follows:

$$\text{Bogside Farm}: \frac{\$40,000}{\$10,000} = 4$$

$$\text{Sterling Farm}: \frac{\$70,000}{\$10,000} = 7$$

Because the degree of operating leverage for Bogside Farm is 4, the farm's net operating income grows four times as fast as its sales. In contrast, Sterling Farm's net operating income grows seven times as fast as its sales. Thus, if sales increase by 10%, then we can expect the net operating income of Bogside Farm to increase by four times this amount, or by 40%, and the net operating income of Sterling Farm to increase by seven times this amount, or by 70%. In general, this relation between the percentage change in sales and the percentage change in net operating income is given by the following formula:

$$\begin{array}{c}\text{Percentage change in} \\ \text{net operating income}\end{array} = \begin{array}{c}\text{Degree of} \\ \text{operating leverage}\end{array} \times \begin{array}{c}\text{Percentage} \\ \text{change in sales}\end{array}$$

Bogside Farm : Percentage change in net operating income = 4 × 10% = 40%

Sterling Farm : Percentage change in net operating income = 7 × 10% = 70%

What is responsible for the higher operating leverage at Sterling Farm? The only difference between the two farms is their cost structure. If two companies have the same total revenue and same total expense but different cost structures, then the company with the higher proportion of fixed costs in its cost structure will have higher operating leverage. Referring back to the original data, when both farms have sales of $100,000 and total expenses of $90,000, one-third of Bogside Farm's costs are fixed but two-thirds of Sterling Farm's costs are fixed. As a consequence, Sterling's degree of operating leverage is higher than Bogside's.

The degree of operating leverage is not a constant; it is greatest at sales levels near the break-even point and decreases as sales and profits rise. The following table shows the degree of operating leverage for Bogside Farm at various sales levels. (Data used earlier for Bogside Farm are shown in color.)

Sales	$75,000	$80,000	$100,000	$150,000	$225,000
Variable expenses	45,000	48,000	60,000	90,000	135,000
Contribution margin (a)	30,000	32,000	40,000	60,000	90,000
Fixed expenses	30,000	30,000	30,000	30,000	30,000
Net operating income (b)	$ 0	$ 2,000	$ 10,000	$ 30,000	$ 60,000
Degree of operating leverage, (a) ÷ (b)	∞	16	4	2	1.5

Thus, a 10% increase in sales would increase profits by only 15% (10% × 1.5) if sales were previously $225,000, as compared to the 40% increase we computed earlier at the $100,000 sales level. The degree of operating leverage will continue to decrease the farther the company moves from its break-even point. At the break-even point, the degree of operating leverage is infinitely large ($30,000 contribution margin ÷ $0 net operating income = ∞).

The degree of operating leverage can be used to quickly estimate what impact various percentage changes in sales will have on profits, without the necessity of preparing detailed contribution format income statements. As shown by our examples, the effects of operating leverage can be dramatic. If a company is near its break-even point, then even small percentage increases in sales can yield large percentage increases in profits. *This explains why management will often work very hard for only a small increase in sales volume.* If the degree of operating leverage is 5, then a 6% increase in sales would translate into a 30% increase in profits.

COMPARING THE COST STRUCTURES OF TWO ONLINE GROCERS

Perhaps the biggest flop of the dot.com era was an online grocer called Webvan. The company burned through $800 million in cash before filing for bankruptcy in 2001 and halting operations. Part of Webvan's downfall was a cost structure heavily skewed towards fixed costs. For example, Webvan stored huge amounts of inventory in refrigerated warehouses that cost $40 million each to build. The company had 4,500 salaried employees with benefits (including warehouse workers and delivery personnel) and a fleet of its own delivery trucks.

Fast forward more than 15 years, and now Instacart Inc. is trying to become a profitable online grocer. Only this time Instacart is avoiding the kinds of huge fixed cost investments that plagued Webvan. Instead of hiring salaried employees with benefits, Instacart uses drivers who are independent contractors to deliver groceries to customers. The company pays its drivers $10 per order delivered plus additional compensation based on order size and delivery speed. Since the drivers use their own vehicles to pick up groceries directly from the supermarket, it eliminates the need for a fleet of delivery trucks, as well as the need for expensive refrigerated warehouses and the associated working capital tied up in perishable inventories.

© MachineHeadz/Getty Images RF

Source: Greg Benninger, "Rebuilding History's Biggest Dot-Com Bust," *The Wall Street Journal,* January 13, 2015, pp. B1–B2.

Structuring Sales Commissions

Companies usually compensate salespeople by paying them a commission based on sales, a salary, or a combination of the two. Commissions based on sales dollars can lead to lower profits. To illustrate, consider Pipeline Unlimited, a producer of surfing equipment. Salespersons sell the company's products to retail sporting goods stores throughout North America and the Pacific Basin. Data for two of the company's surfboards, the XR7 and Turbo models, appear below:

	Model	
	XR7	Turbo
Selling price	$695	$749
Variable expenses...................	344	410
Contribution margin	$351	$339

Which model will salespeople push hardest if they are paid a commission of 10% of sales revenue? The answer is the Turbo because it has the higher selling price and hence the larger commission. On the other hand, from the standpoint of the company, profits will be greater if salespeople steer customers toward the XR7 model because it has the higher contribution margin.

To eliminate such conflicts, commissions can be based on contribution margin rather than on selling price. If this is done, the salespersons will want to sell the mix of products that maximizes contribution margin. Providing that fixed costs remain constant, maximizing the contribution margin will also maximize the company's profit.[5] In effect, by maximizing their own compensation, salespersons will also maximize the company's profit.

Sales Mix

LO5–9

Compute the break-even point for a multiproduct company and explain the effects of shifts in the sales mix on contribution margin and the break-even point.

Before concluding our discussion of CVP concepts, we need to consider the impact of changes in *sales mix* on a company's profit.

The Definition of Sales Mix

The term **sales mix** refers to the relative proportions in which a company's products are sold. The idea is to achieve the combination, or mix, that will yield the greatest profits. Most companies have many products, and often these products are not equally profitable. Hence, profits will depend to some extent on the company's sales mix. Profits will be greater if high-margin rather than low-margin items make up a relatively large proportion of total sales.

Changes in the sales mix can cause perplexing variations in a company's profits. A shift in the sales mix from high-margin items to low-margin items can cause total profits to decrease even though total sales may increase. Conversely, a shift in the sales mix from low-margin items to high-margin items can cause the reverse effect—total profits may increase even though total sales decrease. It is one thing to achieve a particular sales volume; it is quite another to sell the most profitable mix of products.

---

[5] This also assumes the company has no production constraint. If it does, the sales commissions should be modified.

NETBOOK SALES CANNIBALIZE PC SALES

When computer manufacturers introduced the "netbook," they expected it to serve as a consumer's third computer—complementing home and office personal computers (PCs) rather than replacing them. However, when the economy soured many customers decided to buy lower-priced netbooks instead of PCs, which in turn adversely affected the financial performance of many companies. For example, when **Microsoft** failed to achieve its sales goals, the company partially blamed growing netbook sales and declining PC sales for its troubles. Microsoft's Windows operating system for netbooks sells for $15–$25 per device, which is less than half the cost of the company's least expensive Windows operating system for PCs.

Source: Olga Kharif, "Small, Cheap—and Frighteningly Popular," *BusinessWeek,* December 8, 2008, p. 64.

Sales Mix and Break-Even Analysis

If a company sells more than one product, break-even analysis is more complex than discussed to this point. The reason is that different products will have different selling prices, different costs, and different contribution margins. Consequently, the break-even point depends on the mix in which the various products are sold. To illustrate, consider Virtual Journeys Unlimited, a small company that sells two DVDs: the Monuments DVD, a tour of the United States' most popular National Monuments; and the Parks DVD, which tours the United States' National Parks. The company's September sales, expenses, and break-even point are shown in Exhibit 5–4.

As shown in the exhibit, the break-even point is $60,000 in sales, which was computed by dividing the company's fixed expenses of $27,000 by its overall CM ratio of 45%. However, this is the break-even only if the company's sales mix does not change. Currently, the Monuments DVD is responsible for 20% and the Parks DVD for 80% of the company's dollar sales. Assuming this sales mix does not change, if total sales are $60,000, the sales of the Monuments DVD would be $12,000 (20% of $60,000) and the sales of the Parks DVD would be $48,000 (80% of $60,000). As shown in Exhibit 5–4, at these levels of sales, the company would indeed break even. But $60,000 in sales represents the break-even point for the company only if the sales mix does not change. *If the sales mix changes, then the break-even point will also usually change.* This is illustrated by the results for October in which the sales mix shifted away from the more profitable Parks DVD (which has a 50% CM ratio) toward the less profitable Monuments DVD (which has a 25% CM ratio). These results appear in Exhibit 5–5.

Although sales have remained unchanged at $100,000, the sales mix is exactly the reverse of what it was in Exhibit 5–4, with the bulk of the sales now coming from the less profitable Monuments DVD. Notice that this shift in the sales mix has caused both the overall CM ratio and total profits to drop sharply from the prior month even though total sales are the same. The overall CM ratio has dropped from 45% in September to only 30% in October, and net operating income has dropped from $18,000 to only $3,000. In addition, with the drop in the overall CM ratio, the company's break-even point is no longer $60,000 in sales. Because the company is now realizing less average contribution margin per dollar of sales, it takes more sales to cover the same amount of fixed costs. Thus, the break-even point has increased from $60,000 to $90,000 in sales per year.

In preparing a break-even analysis, an assumption must be made concerning the sales mix. Usually the assumption is that it will not change. However, if the sales mix is expected to change, then this must be explicitly considered in any CVP computations.

EXHIBIT 5–4
Multiproduct Break-Even Analysis

Virtual Journeys Unlimited
Contribution Income Statement
For the Month of September

	Monuments DVD		Parks DVD		Total	
	Amount	Percent	Amount	Percent	Amount	Percent
Sales............................	$20,000	100%	$80,000	100%	$100,000	100%
Variable expenses.................	15,000	75%	40,000	50%	55,000	55%
Contribution margin	$ 5,000	25%	$40,000	50%	45,000	45%
Fixed expenses...................					27,000	
Net operating income					$ 18,000	

Computation of the break-even point:

$$\frac{\text{Fixed expenses}}{\text{Overall CM ratio}} = \frac{\$27,000}{0.45} = \$60,000$$

Verification of the break-even point:

	Monuments DVD	Parks DVD	Total
Current dollar sales	$20,000	$80,000	$100,000
Percentage of total dollar sales	20%	80%	100%
Sales at the break-even point......	$12,000	$48,000	$60,000

	Monuments DVD		Parks DVD		Total	
	Amount	Percent	Amount	Percent	Amount	Percent
Sales............................	$12,000	100%	$48,000	100%	$ 60,000	100%
Variable expenses.................	9,000	75%	24,000	50%	33,000	55%
Contribution margin	$ 3,000	25%	$24,000	50%	27,000	45%
Fixed expenses...................					27,000	
Net operating income					$ 0	

EXHIBIT 5–5
Multiproduct Break-Even Analysis: A Shift in Sales Mix (see Exhibit 5–4)

Virtual Journeys Unlimited
Contribution Income Statement
For the Month of October

	Monuments DVD		Parks DVD		Total	
	Amount	Percent	Amount	Percent	Amount	Percent
Sales............................	$80,000	100%	$20,000	100%	$100,000	100%
Variable expenses.................	60,000	75%	10,000	50%	70,000	70%
Contribution margin	$20,000	25%	$10,000	50%	30,000	30%
Fixed expenses...................					27,000	
Net operating income					$ 3,000	

Computation of the break-even point:

$$\frac{\text{Fixed expenses}}{\text{Overall CM ratio}} = \frac{\$27,000}{0.30} = \$90,000$$

Summary

CVP analysis is based on a simple model of how profits respond to prices, costs, and volume. This model can be used to answer a variety of critical questions such as what is the company's break-even volume, what is its margin of safety, and what is likely to happen if specific changes are made in prices, costs, and volume.

A CVP graph depicts the relationships between unit sales on the one hand and fixed expenses, variable expenses, total expenses, total sales, and profits on the other hand. The profit graph is simpler than the CVP graph and shows how profits depend on sales. The CVP and profit graphs are useful for developing intuition about how costs and profits respond to changes in sales.

The contribution margin ratio is the ratio of contribution margin to sales. This ratio can be used to quickly estimate what impact a change in total sales would have on net operating income. The ratio is also useful in break-even analysis.

Break-even analysis is used to estimate the sales needed to break even. The unit sales required to break even can be estimated by dividing the fixed expense by the unit contribution margin. Target profit analysis is used to estimate the sales needed to attain a specified target profit. The unit sales required to attain the target profit can be estimated by dividing the sum of the target profit and fixed expense by the unit contribution margin.

The margin of safety is the amount by which the company's budgeted (or actual) sales exceeds break-even sales.

The degree of operating leverage allows quick estimation of what impact a given percentage change in sales would have on the company's net operating income. The higher the degree of operating leverage, the greater is the impact on the company's profits. The degree of operating leverage is not constant—it depends on the company's current level of sales.

The profits of a multiproduct company are affected by its sales mix. Changes in the sales mix can affect the break-even point, margin of safety, and other critical factors.

Review Problem: CVP Relationships

Voltar Company manufactures and sells a specialized cordless telephone for high electromagnetic radiation environments. The company's contribution format income statement for the most recent year is given below:

	Total	Per Unit	Percent of Sales
Sales (20,000 units)	$1,200,000	$60	100%
Variable expenses.	900,000	45	? %
Contribution margin	300,000	$15	? %
Fixed expenses	240,000		
Net operating income.	$ 60,000		

Management is anxious to increase the company's profit and has asked for an analysis of a number of items.

Required:

1. Compute the company's CM ratio and variable expense ratio.
2. Compute the company's break-even point in both unit sales and dollar sales. Use the equation method.
3. Assume that sales increase by $400,000 next year. If cost behavior patterns remain unchanged, by how much will the company's net operating income increase? Use the CM ratio to compute your answer.
4. Refer to the original data. Assume that next year management wants the company to earn a profit of at least $90,000. How many units will have to be sold to earn this target profit?
5. Refer to the original data. Compute the company's margin of safety in both dollar and percentage form.

6. a. Compute the company's degree of operating leverage at the present level of sales.
    b. Assume that through a more intense effort by the sales staff, the company's sales increase by 8% next year. By what percentage would you expect net operating income to increase? Use the degree of operating leverage to obtain your answer.
    c. Verify your answer to (b) by preparing a new contribution format income statement showing an 8% increase in sales.

7. Refer to the original data. In an effort to increase sales and profits, management is considering the use of a higher-quality speaker. The higher-quality speaker would increase variable costs by $3 per unit, but management could eliminate one quality inspector who is paid a salary of $30,000 per year. The sales manager estimates that the higher-quality speaker would increase annual sales by at least 20%.
    a. Assuming that changes are made as described above, prepare a projected contribution format income statement for next year. Show data on a total, per unit, and percentage basis.
    b. Compute the company's new break-even point in both unit sales and dollar sales. Use the formula method.
    c. Would you recommend that the changes be made?

Solution to Review Problem

1.
$$\text{CM ratio} = \frac{\text{Unit contribution margin}}{\text{Unit selling price}} = \frac{\$15}{\$60} = 25\%$$

$$\text{Variable expense ratio} = \frac{\text{Variable expense}}{\text{Selling price}} = \frac{\$45}{\$60} = 75\%$$

2.
$$\text{Profit} = \text{Unit CM} \times Q - \text{Fixed expenses}$$

$$\$0 = \$15 \times Q - \$240{,}000$$

$$\$15Q = \$240{,}000$$

$$Q = \$240{,}000 \div \$15$$

$$Q = 16{,}000 \text{ units; or, at } \$60 \text{ per unit, } \$960{,}000$$

3.

Increase in sales	$400,000
Contribution margin ratio	× 25%
Expected increase in contribution margin	$100,000

Because the fixed expenses are not expected to change, net operating income will increase by the entire $100,000 increase in contribution margin computed above.

4. Equation method:

$$\text{Profit} = \text{Unit CM} \times Q - \text{Fixed expense}$$

$$\$90{,}000 = \$15 \times Q - \$240{,}000$$

$$\$15Q = \$90{,}000 + \$240{,}000$$

$$Q = \$330{,}000 \div \$15$$

$$Q = 22{,}000 \text{ units}$$

Formula method:

$$\frac{\text{Unit sales to attain}}{\text{the target profit}} = \frac{\text{Target profit} + \text{Fixed expenses}}{\text{Contribution margin per unit}} = \frac{\$90{,}000 + \$240{,}000}{\$15 \text{ per unit}} = 22{,}000 \text{ units}$$

5.
$$\text{Margin of safety in dollars} = \text{Total sales} - \text{Break-even sales}$$

$$= \$1{,}200{,}000 - \$960{,}000 = \$240{,}000$$

$$\text{Margin of safety percentage} = \frac{\text{Margin of safety in dollars}}{\text{Total sales}} = \frac{\$240{,}000}{\$1{,}200{,}000} = 20\%$$

6. a. Degree of operating leverage $= \dfrac{\text{Contribution margin}}{\text{Net operating income}} = \dfrac{\$300,000}{\$60,000} = 5$

   b.

Expected increase in sales	8%
Degree of operating leverage.	× 5
Expected increase in net operating income.	40%

   c. If sales increase by 8%, then 21,600 units (20,000 × 1.08 = 21,600) will be sold next year. The new contribution format income statement would be as follows:

	Total	Per Unit	Percent of Sales
Sales (21,600 units)	$1,296,000	$60	100%
Variable expenses	972,000	45	75%
Contribution margin	324,000	$15	25%
Fixed expenses	240,000		
Net operating income	$ 84,000		

Thus, the $84,000 expected net operating income for next year represents a 40% increase over the $60,000 net operating income earned during the current year:

$$\dfrac{\$84,000 - \$60,000}{\$60,000} = \dfrac{\$24,000}{\$60,000} = 40\% \text{ increase}$$

Note that the increase in sales from 20,000 to 21,600 units has increased *both* total sales and total variable expenses.

7. a. A 20% increase in sales would result in 24,000 units being sold next year: 20,000 units × 1.20 = 24,000 units.

	Total	Per Unit	Percent of Sales
Sales (24,000 units)	$1,440,000	$60	100%
Variable expenses.	1,152,000	48*	80%
Contribution margin	288,000	$12	20%
Fixed expenses	210,000†		
Net operating income.	$ 78,000		

*$45 + $3 = $48; $48 ÷ $60 = 80%.
†$240,000 − $30,000 = $210,000.

Note that the change in per unit variable expenses results in a change in both the per unit contribution margin and the CM ratio.

   b. Unit sales to break even $= \dfrac{\text{Fixed expenses}}{\text{Unit contribution margin}}$

$$= \dfrac{\$210,000}{\$12 \text{ per unit}} = 17,500 \text{ units}$$

Dollar sales to break even $= \dfrac{\text{Fixed expenses}}{\text{CM ratio}}$

$$= \dfrac{\$210,000}{0.20} = \$1,050,000$$

   c. Yes, based on these data, the changes should be made. The changes increase the company's net operating income from the present $60,000 to $78,000 per year. Although the changes also result in a higher break-even point (17,500 units as compared to the present 16,000 units), the company's margin of safety actually becomes greater than before:

Margin of safety in dollars = Total sales − Break-even sales
= $1,440,000 − $1,050,000 = $390,000

As shown in (5), the company's present margin of safety is only $240,000. Thus, several benefits will result from the proposed changes.

Glossary

Break-even point The level of sales at which profit is zero. (p. 199)

Contribution margin ratio (CM ratio) A ratio computed by dividing contribution margin by sales. (p. 204)

Cost-volume-profit (CVP) graph A graphical representation of the relationships between an organization's revenues, costs, and profits on the one hand and its sales volume on the other hand. (201)

Degree of operating leverage A measure, at a given level of sales, of how a percentage change in sales will affect profits. The degree of operating leverage is computed by dividing contribution margin by net operating income. (p. 216)

Incremental analysis An analytical approach that focuses only on those costs and revenues that change as a result of a decision. (p. 207)

Margin of safety The excess of budgeted or actual dollar sales over the break-even dollar sales. (p. 213)

Operating leverage A measure of how sensitive net operating income is to a given percentage change in dollar sales. (p. 215)

Sales mix The relative proportions in which a company's products are sold. Sales mix is computed by expressing the sales of each product as a percentage of total sales. (p. 218)

Target profit analysis Estimating what sales volume is needed to achieve a specific target profit. (p. 212)

Variable expense ratio A ratio computed by dividing variable expenses by sales. (p. 204)

Questions

5–1 What is the meaning of *contribution margin ratio*? How is this ratio useful in planning business operations?

5–2 Often the most direct route to a business decision is an incremental analysis. What is meant by an *incremental analysis?*

5–3 In all respects, Company A and Company B are identical except that Company A's costs are mostly variable, whereas Company B's costs are mostly fixed. When sales increase, which company will tend to realize the greatest increase in profits? Explain.

5–4 What is the meaning of *operating leverage?*

5–5 What is the meaning of *break-even point?*

5–6 In response to a request from your immediate supervisor, you have prepared a CVP graph portraying the cost and revenue characteristics of your company's product and operations. Explain how the lines on the graph and the break-even point would change if (*a*) the selling price per unit decreased, (*b*) fixed cost increased throughout the entire range of activity portrayed on the graph, and (*c*) variable cost per unit increased.

5–7 What is the meaning of *margin of safety*?

5–8 What is meant by the term *sales mix?* What assumption is usually made concerning sales mix in CVP analysis?

5–9 Explain how a shift in the sales mix could result in both a higher break-even point and a lower net operating income.

Applying Excel

connect

LO5–5, LO5–7, LO5–8

The Excel worksheet form that appears below is to be used to recreate portions of the Review Problem relating to Voltar Company. Download the workbook containing this form from Connect, where you will also receive instructions about how to use this worksheet form.

	A	B	C	D
1	Chapter 5: Applying Excel			
2				
3	Data			
4	Unit sales	20,000	units	
5	Selling price per unit	$60	per unit	
6	Variable expenses per unit	$45	per unit	
7	Fixed expenses	$240,000		
8				
9	Enter a formula into each of the cells marked with a ? below			
10	Review Problem: CVP Relationships			
11				
12	Compute the CM ratio and variable expense ratio			
13	Selling price per unit		? per unit	
14	Variable expenses per unit		? per unit	
15	Contribution margin per unit		? per unit	
16				
17	CM ratio		?	
18	Variable expense ratio		?	
19				
20	Compute the break-even			
21	Break-even in unit sales		? units	
22	Break-even in dollar sales		?	
23				
24	Compute the margin of safety			
25	Margin of safety in dollars		?	
26	Margin of safety percentage		?	
27				
28	Compute the degree of operating leverage			
29	Sales		?	
30	Variable expenses		?	
31	Contribution margin		?	
32	Fixed expenses		?	
33	Net operating income		?	
34				
35	Degree of operating leverage		?	
36				

Chapter 5 Form / Filled in Chapter 5 Form

You should proceed to the requirements below only after completing your worksheet.

Required:

1. Check your worksheet by changing the fixed expenses to $270,000. If your worksheet is operating properly, the degree of operating leverage should be 10. If you do not get this answer, find the errors in your worksheet and correct them. How much is the margin of safety percentage? Did it change? Why or why not?

2. Enter the following data from a different company into your worksheet:

Unit sales	10,000
Selling price per unit.	$120
Variable expenses per unit	$72
Fixed expenses	$420,000

What is the margin of safety percentage? What is the degree of operating leverage?

3. Using the degree of operating leverage and without changing anything in your worksheet, calculate the percentage change in net operating income if unit sales increase by 15%.

4. Confirm the calculations you made in part (3) above by increasing the unit sales in your worksheet by 15%. What is the new net operating income and by what percentage did it increase?

5. Thad Morgan, a motorcycle enthusiast, has been exploring the possibility of relaunching the Western Hombre brand of cycle that was popular in the 1930s. The retro-look cycle would be sold for $10,000 and at that price, Thad estimates that he could sell 600 units each year. The variable cost to produce and sell the cycles would be $7,500 per unit. The annual fixed cost would be $1,200,000.

    a. Using your worksheet, what would be the unit sales to break even, the margin of safety in dollars, and the degree of operating leverage?

    b. Thad is worried about the selling price. Rumors are circulating that other retro brands of cycles may be revived. If so, the selling price for the Western Hombre would have to be reduced to $9,000 to compete effectively. In that event, Thad also would reduce fixed expenses by $300,000 by reducing advertising expenses, but he still hopes to sell 600 units per year. Do you think this is a good plan? Explain. Also, explain the degree of operating leverage that appears on your worksheet.

The Foundational 15 connect

LO5–1, LO5–3, LO5–4, LO5–5, LO5–6, LO5–7, LO5–8

Oslo Company prepared the following contribution format income statement based on a sales volume of 1,000 units (the relevant range of production is 500 units to 1,500 units):

Sales	$20,000
Variable expenses	12,000
Contribution margin	8,000
Fixed expenses	6,000
Net operating income	$ 2,000

Required:

(Answer each question independently and always refer to the original data unless instructed otherwise.)

1. What is the contribution margin per unit?
2. What is the contribution margin ratio?
3. What is the variable expense ratio?
4. If sales increase to 1,001 units, what would be the increase in net operating income?
5. If sales decline to 900 units, what would be the net operating income?
6. If the selling price increases by $2 per unit and the sales volume decreases by 100 units, what would be the net operating income?
7. If the variable cost per unit increases by $1, spending on advertising increases by $1,500, and unit sales increase by 250 units, what would be the net operating income?
8. What is the break-even point in unit sales?
9. What is the break-even point in dollar sales?
10. How many units must be sold to achieve a target profit of $5,000?
11. What is the margin of safety in dollars? What is the margin of safety percentage?
12. What is the degree of operating leverage?
13. Using the degree of operating leverage, what is the estimated percent increase in net operating income of a 5% increase in sales?
14. Assume that the amounts of the company's total variable expenses and total fixed expenses were reversed. In other words, assume that the total variable expenses are $6,000 and the total fixed expenses are $12,000. Under this scenario and assuming that total sales remain the same, what is the degree of operating leverage?
15. Using the degree of operating leverage that you computed in the previous question, what is the estimated percent increase in net operating income of a 5% increase in sales?

EXERCISE 5–1 The Effect of Changes in Activity on Net Operating Income LO5–1

Whirly Corporation's contribution format income statement for the most recent month is shown below:

	Total	Per Unit
Sales (10,000 units)	$350,000	$ 35.00
Variable expenses	200,000	20.00
Contribution margin	150,000	$ 15.00
Fixed expenses..................................	135,000	
Net operating income	$ 15,000	

Required:

(Consider each case independently):

1. What would be the revised net operating income per month if the sales volume increases by 100 units?
2. What would be the revised net operating income per month if the sales volume decreases by 100 units?
3. What would be the revised net operating income per month if the sales volume is 9,000 units?

EXERCISE 5–2 Prepare a Cost-Volume-Profit (CVP) Graph LO5–2

Karlik Enterprises distributes a single product whose selling price is $24 per unit and whose variable expense is $18 per unit. The company's monthly fixed expense is $24,000.

Required:

1. Prepare a cost-volume-profit graph for the company up to a sales level of 8,000 units.
2. Estimate the company's break-even point in unit sales using your cost-volume-profit graph.

EXERCISE 5–3 Prepare a Profit Graph LO5–2

Jaffre Enterprises distributes a single product whose selling price is $16 per unit and whose variable expense is $11 per unit. The company's fixed expense is $16,000 per month.

Required:

1. Prepare a profit graph for the company up to a sales level of 4,000 units.
2. Estimate the company's break-even point in unit sales using your profit graph.

EXERCISE 5–4 Computing and Using the CM Ratio LO5–3

Last month when Holiday Creations, Inc., sold 50,000 units, total sales were $200,000, total variable expenses were $120,000, and fixed expenses were $65,000.

Required:

1. What is the company's contribution margin (CM) ratio?
2. What is the estimated change in the company's net operating income if it can increase total sales by $1,000?

EXERCISE 5–5 Changes in Variable Costs, Fixed Costs, Selling Price, and Volume LO5–4

Data for Hermann Corporation are shown below:

	Per Unit	Percent of Sales
Selling price	$90	100%
Variable expenses	63	70
Contribution margin	$27	30%

Fixed expenses are $30,000 per month and the company is selling 2,000 units per month.

Required:

1. How much will net operating income increase (decrease) per month if the monthly advertising budget increases by $5,000 and monthly sales increase by $9,000?
2. Refer to the original data. How much will net operating income increase (decrease) per month if the company uses higher-quality components that increase the variable expense by $2 per unit and increase unit sales by 10%.

EXERCISE 5–6 Break-Even Analysis LO5–5

Mauro Products distributes a single product, a woven basket whose selling price is $15 per unit and whose variable expense is $12 per unit. The company's monthly fixed expense is $4,200.

Required:

1. Calculate the company's break-even point in unit sales.
2. Calculate the company's break-even point in dollar sales.
3. If the company's fixed expenses increase by $600, what would become the new break-even point in unit sales? In dollar sales?.

EXERCISE 5–7 Target Profit Analysis LO5–6

Lin Corporation has a single product whose selling price is $120 per unit and whose variable expense is $80 per unit. The company's monthly fixed expense is $50,000.

Required:

1. Calculate the unit sales needed to attain a target profit of $10,000.
2. Calculate the dollar sales needed to attain a target profit of $15,000.

EXERCISE 5–8 Compute the Margin of Safety LO5–7

Molander Corporation is a distributor of a sun umbrella used at resort hotels. Data concerning the next month's budget appear below:

Selling price per unit...	$30
Variable expense per unit	$20
Fixed expense per month	$7,500
Unit sales per month...	1,000

Required:

1. What is the company's margin of safety?
2. What is the company's margin of safety as a percentage of its sales?

EXERCISE 5–9 Compute and Use the Degree of Operating Leverage LO5–8

Engberg Company installs lawn sod in home yards. The company's most recent monthly contribution format income statement follows:

	Amount	Percent of Sales
Sales	$80,000	100%
Variable expenses	32,000	40%
Contribution margin	48,000	60%
Fixed expenses.............................	38,000	
Net operating income	$10,000	

Required:

1. What is the company's degree of operating leverage?
2. Using the degree of operating leverage, estimate the impact on net operating income of a 5% increase in sales.
3. Verify your estimate from part (2) above by constructing a new contribution format income statement for the company assuming a 5% increase in sales.

EXERCISE 5–10 Multiproduct Break-Even Analysis LO5–9

Lucido Products markets two computer games: Claimjumper and Makeover. A contribution format income statement for a recent month for the two games appears below:

	Claimjumper	Makeover	Total
Sales	$30,000	$70,000	$100,000
Variable expenses...............	20,000	50,000	70,000
Contribution margin	$10,000	$20,000	30,000
Fixed expenses			24,000
Net operating income.............			$ 6,000

Required:
1. What is the overall contribution margin (CM) ratio for the company?
2. What is the company's overall break-even point in dollar sales?
3. Verify the overall break-even point for the company by constructing a contribution format income statement showing the appropriate levels of sales for the two products.

EXERCISE 5–11 Missing Data; Basic CVP Concepts LO5–1, LO5–9

Fill in the missing amounts in each of the eight case situations below. Each case is independent of the others. (*Hint:* One way to find the missing amounts would be to prepare a contribution format income statement for each case, enter the known data, and then compute the missing items.)

a. Assume that only one product is being sold in each of the four following case situations:

Case	Units Sold	Sales	Variable Expenses	Contribution Margin per Unit	Fixed Expenses	Net Operating Income (Loss)
1..........	15,000	$180,000	$120,000	?	$50,000	?
2..........	?	$100,000	?	$10	$32,000	$8,000
3..........	10,000	?	$70,000	$13	?	$12,000
4..........	6,000	$300,000	?	?	$100,000	$(10,000)

b. Assume that more than one product is being sold in each of the four following case situations:

Case	Sales	Variable Expenses	Average Contribution Margin Ratio	Fixed Expenses	Net Operating Income (Loss)
1....................	$500,000	?	20%	?	$7,000
2....................	$400,000	$260,000	?	$100,000	?
3....................	?	?	60%	$130,000	$20,000
4....................	$600,000	$420,000	?	?	$(5,000)

EXERCISE 5–12 Multiproduct Break-Even Analysis LO5–9

Olongapo Sports Corporation distributes two premium golf balls—Flight Dynamic and Sure Shot. Monthly sales and the contribution margin ratios for the two products follow:

	Product		
	Flight Dynamic	Sure Shot	Total
Sales	$150,000	$250,000	$400,000
CM ratio	80%	36%	?

Fixed expenses total $183,750 per month.

Required:

1. Prepare a contribution format income statement for the company as a whole. Carry computations to one decimal place.
2. What is the company's break-even point in dollar sales based on the current sales mix?
3. If sales increase by $100,000 a month, by how much would you expect the monthly net operating income to increase? What are your assumptions?

EXERCISE 5–13 Changes in Selling Price, Sales Volume, Variable Cost per Unit, and Total Fixed Costs LO5–1, LO5–4

Miller Company's contribution format income statement for the most recent month is shown below:

	Total	Per Unit
Sales (20,000 units)	$300,000	$15.00
Variable expenses	180,000	9.00
Contribution margin	120,000	$ 6.00
Fixed expenses	70,000	
Net operating income	$ 50,000	

Required:

(Consider each case independently):

1. What is the revised net operating income if unit sales increase by 15%?
2. What is the revised net operating income if the selling price decreases by $1.50 per unit and the number of units sold increases by 25%?
3. What is the revised net operating income if the selling price increases by $1.50 per unit, fixed expenses increase by $20,000, and the number of units sold decreases by 5%?
4. What is the revised net operating income if the selling price per unit increases by 12%, variable expenses increase by 60 cents per unit, and the number of units sold decreases by 10%?

EXERCISE 5–14 Break-Even and Target Profit Analysis LO5–3, LO5–4, LO5–5, LO5–6

Lindon Company is the exclusive distributor for an automotive product that sells for $40 per unit and has a CM ratio of 30%. The company's fixed expenses are $180,000 per year. The company plans to sell 16,000 units this year.

Required:

1. What are the variable expenses per unit?
2. What is the break-even point in unit sales and in dollar sales?
3. What amount of unit sales and dollar sales is required to attain a target profit of $60,000 per year?
4. Assume that by using a more efficient shipper, the company is able to reduce its variable expenses by $4 per unit. What is the company's new break-even point in unit sales and in dollar sales? What dollar sales is required to attain a target profit of $60,000?

EXERCISE 5–15 Operating Leverage LO5–1, LO5–8

Magic Realm, Inc., has developed a new fantasy board game. The company sold 15,000 games last year at a selling price of $20 per game. Fixed expenses associated with the game total $182,000 per year, and variable expenses are $6 per game. Production of the game is entrusted to a printing contractor. Variable expenses consist mostly of payments to this contractor.

Required:

1. Prepare a contribution format income statement for the game last year and compute the degree of operating leverage.
2. Management is confident that the company can sell 18,000 games next year (an increase of 3,000 games, or 20%, over last year). Given this assumption:
    a. What is the expected percentage increase in net operating income for next year?
    b. What is the expected amount of net operating income for next year? (Do not prepare an income statement; use the degree of operating leverage to compute your answer.)

EXERCISE 5–16 Break-Even Analysis and CVP Graphing LO5–2, LO5–4, LO5–5

The Hartford Symphony Guild is planning its annual dinner-dance. The dinner-dance committee has assembled the following expected costs for the event:

Dinner (per person).	$18
Favors and program (per person).	$2
Band	$2,800
Rental of ballroom.	$900
Professional entertainment during intermission.	$1,000
Tickets and advertising	$1,300

The committee members would like to charge $35 per person for the evening's activities.

Required:
1. What is the break-even point for the dinner-dance (in terms of the number of persons who must attend)?
2. Assume that last year only 300 persons attended the dinner-dance. If the same number attend this year, what price per ticket must be charged in order to break even?
3. Refer to the original data ($35 ticket price per person). Prepare a CVP graph for the dinner-dance from zero tickets up to 600 tickets sold.

EXERCISE 5–17 Break-Even and Target Profit Analysis LO5–4, LO5–5, LO5–6

Outback Outfitters sells recreational equipment. One of the company's products, a small camp stove, sells for $50 per unit. Variable expenses are $32 per stove, and fixed expenses associated with the stove total $108,000 per month.

Required:
1. What is the break-even point in unit sales and in dollar sales?
2. If the variable expenses per stove increase as a percentage of the selling price, will it result in a higher or a lower break-even point? Why? (Assume that the fixed expenses remain unchanged.)
3. At present, the company is selling 8,000 stoves per month. The sales manager is convinced that a 10% reduction in the selling price would result in a 25% increase in monthly sales of stoves. Prepare two contribution format income statements, one under present operating conditions, and one as operations would appear after the proposed changes. Show both total and per unit data on your statements.
4. Refer to the data in (3) above. How many stoves would have to be sold at the new selling price to attain a target profit of $35,000 per month?

EXERCISE 5–18 Break-Even and Target Profit Analysis; Margin of Safety; CM Ratio LO5–1, LO5–3, LO5–5, LO5–6, LO5–7

Menlo Company distributes a single product. The company's sales and expenses for last month follow:

	Total	Per Unit
Sales	$450,000	$30
Variable expenses.	180,000	12
Contribution margin	270,000	$18
Fixed expenses	216,000	
Net operating income.	$ 54,000	

Required:
1. What is the monthly break-even point in unit sales and in dollar sales?
2. Without resorting to computations, what is the total contribution margin at the break-even point?
3. How many units would have to be sold each month to attain a target profit of $90,000? Verify your answer by preparing a contribution format income statement at the target sales level.
4. Refer to the original data. Compute the company's margin of safety in both dollar and percentage terms.
5. What is the company's CM ratio? If sales increase by $50,000 per month and there is no change in fixed expenses, by how much would you expect monthly net operating income to increase?

Problems

PROBLEM 5–19 Break-Even Analysis; Pricing LO5–1, LO5–4, LO5–5

Minden Company introduced a new product last year for which it is trying to find an optimal selling price. Marketing studies suggest that the company can increase sales by 5,000 units for each $2 reduction in the selling price. The company's present selling price is $70 per unit, and variable expenses are $40 per unit. Fixed expenses are $540,000 per year. The present annual sales volume (at the $70 selling price) is 15,000 units.

Required:

1. What is the present yearly net operating income or loss?
2. What is the present break-even point in unit sales and in dollar sales?
3. Assuming that the marketing studies are correct, what is the maximum annual profit that the company can earn? At how many units and at what selling price per unit would the company generate this profit?
4. What would be the break-even point in unit sales and in dollar sales using the selling price you determined in (3) above (e.g., the selling price at the level of maximum profits)? Why is this break-even point different from the break-even point you computed in (2) above?

PROBLEM 5–20 CVP Applications: Break-Even Analysis; Cost Structure; Target Sales LO5–1, LO5–3, LO5–4, LO5–5, LO5–6, LO5–8

Northwood Company manufactures basketballs. The company has a ball that sells for $25. At present, the ball is manufactured in a small plant that relies heavily on direct labor workers. Thus, variable expenses are high, totaling $15 per ball, of which 60% is direct labor cost.

Last year, the company sold 30,000 of these balls, with the following results:

Sales (30,000 balls)	$750,000
Variable expenses	450,000
Contribution margin	300,000
Fixed expenses	210,000
Net operating income	$ 90,000

Required:

1. Compute (a) the CM ratio and the break-even point in balls, and (b) the degree of operating leverage at last year's sales level.
2. Due to an increase in labor rates, the company estimates that variable expenses will increase by $3 per ball next year. If this change takes place and the selling price per ball remains constant at $25, what will be the new CM ratio and break-even point in balls?
3. Refer to the data in (2) above. If the expected change in variable expenses takes place, how many balls will have to be sold next year to earn the same net operating income, $90,000, as last year?
4. Refer again to the data in (2) above. The president feels that the company must raise the selling price of its basketballs. If Northwood Company wants to maintain the same CM ratio as last year, what selling price per ball must it charge next year to cover the increased labor costs?
5. Refer to the original data. The company is discussing the construction of a new, automated manufacturing plant. The new plant would slash variable expenses per ball by 40%, but it would cause fixed expenses per year to double. If the new plant is built, what would be the company's new CM ratio and new break-even point in balls?
6. Refer to the data in (5) above.
   a. If the new plant is built, how many balls will have to be sold next year to earn the same net operating income, $90,000, as last year?
   b. Assume the new plant is built and that next year the company manufactures and sells 30,000 balls (the same number as sold last year). Prepare a contribution format income statement and compute the degree of operating leverage.
   c. If you were a member of top management, would you have been in favor of constructing the new plant? Explain.

PROBLEM 5–21 Sales Mix; Multiproduct Break-Even Analysis LO5–9

Gold Star Rice, Ltd., of Thailand exports Thai rice throughout Asia. The company grows three varieties of rice—White, Fragrant, and Loonzain. Budgeted sales by product and in total for the coming month are shown below:

	Product								
	White		Fragrant		Loonzain		Total	
Percentage of total sales....................	20%		52%		28%		100%	
Sales.......................................	$150,000	100%	$390,000	100%	$210,000	100%	$750,000	100%
Variable expenses...........................	108,000	72%	78,000	20%	84,000	40%	270,000	36%
Contribution margin	$ 42,000	28%	$312,000	80%	$126,000	60%	480,000	64%
Fixed expenses.............................							449,280	
Net operating income.......................							$ 30,720	

$$\text{Dollar sales to break-even} = \frac{\text{Fixed expenses}}{\text{CM ratio}} = \frac{\$449,280}{0.64} = \$702,000$$

As shown by these data, net operating income is budgeted at $30,720 for the month and the estimated break-even sales is $702,000.

Assume that actual sales for the month total $750,000 as planned. Actual sales by product are: White, $300,000; Fragrant, $180,000; and Loonzain, $270,000.

Required:

1. Prepare a contribution format income statement for the month based on the actual sales data. Present the income statement in the format shown above.
2. Compute the break-even point in dollar sales for the month based on your actual data.
3. Considering the fact that the company met its $750,000 sales budget for the month, the president is shocked at the results shown on your income statement in (1) above. Prepare a brief memo for the president explaining why the net operating income (loss) and the break-even point in dollar sales are different from what was budgeted.

PROBLEM 5–22 CVP Applications; Contribution Margin Ratio; Break-Even Analysis; Cost Structure LO5–1, LO5–3, LO5–4, LO5–5, LO5–6

Due to erratic sales of its sole product—a high-capacity battery for laptop computers—PEM, Inc., has been experiencing financial difficulty for some time. The company's contribution format income statement for the most recent month is given below:

Sales (19,500 units × $30 per unit)........................	$585,000
Variable expenses..	409,500
Contribution margin	175,500
Fixed expenses..	180,000
Net operating loss...	$ (4,500)

Required:

1. Compute the company's CM ratio and its break-even point in unit sales and dollar sales.
2. The president believes that a $16,000 increase in the monthly advertising budget, combined with an intensified effort by the sales staff, will result in an $80,000 increase in monthly sales. If the president is right, what will be the increase (decrease) in the company's monthly net operating income?
3. Refer to the original data. The sales manager is convinced that a 10% reduction in the selling price, combined with an increase of $60,000 in the monthly advertising budget, will double unit sales. If the sales manager is right, what will be the revised net operating income (loss)?
4. Refer to the original data. The Marketing Department thinks that a fancy new package for the laptop computer battery would grow sales. The new package would increase packaging costs by 75 cents per unit. Assuming no other changes, how many units would have to be sold each month to attain a target profit of $9,750?

5. Refer to the original data. By automating, the company could reduce variable expenses by $3 per unit. However, fixed expenses would increase by $72,000 each month.
    a. Compute the new CM ratio and the new break-even point in unit sales and dollar sales.
    b. Assume that the company expects to sell 26,000 units next month. Prepare two contribution format income statements, one assuming that operations are not automated and one assuming that they are. (Show data on a per unit and percentage basis, as well as in total, for each alternative.)
    c. Would you recommend that the company automate its operations? Explain.

PROBLEM 5–23 CVP Applications; Contribution Margin Ratio: Degree of Operating Leverage LO5–1, LO5–3, LO5–4, LO5–5, LO5–8

Feather Friends, Inc., distributes a high-quality wooden birdhouse that sells for $20 per unit. Variable expenses are $8 per unit, and fixed expenses total $180,000 per year. Its operating results for last year were as follows:

Sales	$400,000
Variable expenses	160,000
Contribution margin	240,000
Fixed expenses	180,000
Net operating income	$ 60,000

Required:

Answer each question independently based on the original data:

1. What is the product's CM ratio?
2. Use the CM ratio to determine the break-even point in dollar sales.
3. If this year's sales increase by $75,000 and fixed expenses do not change, how much will net operating income increase?
4. a. What is the degree of operating leverage based on last year's sales?
    b. Assume the president expects this year's sales to increase by 20%. Using the degree of operating leverage from last year, what percentage increase in net operating income will the company realize this year?
5. The sales manager is convinced that a 10% reduction in the selling price, combined with a $30,000 increase in advertising, would increase this year's unit sales by 25%. If the sales manager is right, what would be this year's net operating income if his ideas are implemented? Do you recommend implementing the sales manager's suggestions? Why?
6. The president does not want to change the selling price. Instead, he wants to increase the sales commission by $1 per unit. He thinks that this move, combined with some increase in advertising, would increase this year's sales by 25%. How much could the president increase this year's advertising expense and still earn the same $60,000 net operating income as last year?

PROBLEM 5–24 Break-Even and Target Profit Analysis LO5–5, LO5–6

The Shirt Works sells a large variety of tee shirts and sweatshirts. Steve Hooper, the owner, is thinking of expanding his sales by hiring high school students, on a commission basis, to sell sweatshirts bearing the name and mascot of the local high school.

These sweatshirts would have to be ordered from the manufacturer six weeks in advance, and they could not be returned because of the unique printing required. The sweatshirts would cost Hooper $8 each with a minimum order of 75 sweatshirts. Any additional sweatshirts would have to be ordered in increments of 75.

Since Hooper's plan would not require any additional facilities, the only costs associated with the project would be the costs of the sweatshirts and the costs of the sales commissions. The selling price of the sweatshirts would be $13.50 each. Hooper would pay the students a commission of $1.50 for each shirt sold.

Required:

1. What level of unit sales and dollar sales is needed to attain a target profit of $1,200?
2. Assume that Hooper places an initial order for 75 sweatshirts. What is his break-even point in unit sales and dollar sales?

PROBLEM 5–25 Changes in Fixed and Variable Costs; Break-Even and Target Profit Analysis LO5–4, LO5–5, LO5–6

Neptune Company produces toys and other items for use in beach and resort areas. A small, inflatable toy has come onto the market that the company is anxious to produce and sell. The new toy will sell for $3 per unit. Enough capacity exists in the company's plant to produce 16,000 units of the toy each month. Variable expenses to manufacture and sell one unit would be $1.25, and fixed expenses associated with the toy would total $35,000 per month.

The company's Marketing Department predicts that demand for the new toy will exceed the 16,000 units that the company is able to produce. Additional manufacturing space can be rented from another company at a fixed expense of $1,000 per month. Variable expenses in the rented facility would total $1.40 per unit, due to somewhat less efficient operations than in the main plant.

Required:
1. What is the monthly break-even point for the new toy in unit sales and dollar sales.
2. How many units must be sold each month to attain a target profit of $12,000 per month?
3. If the sales manager receives a bonus of 10 cents for each unit sold in excess of the break-even point, how many units must be sold each month to attain a target profit that equals a 25% return on the monthly investment in fixed expenses?

PROBLEM 5–26 CVP Applications; Break-Even Analysis; Graphing LO5–1, LO5–2, LO5–4, LO5–5

The Fashion Shoe Company operates a chain of women's shoe shops that carry many styles of shoes that are all sold at the same price. Sales personnel in the shops are paid a sales commission on each pair of shoes sold plus a small base salary.

The following data pertains to Shop 48 and is typical of the company's many outlets:

	Per Pair of Shoes
Selling price	$30.00
Variable expenses:	
Invoice cost	$13.50
Sales commission	4.50
Total variable expenses	$18.00

	Annual
Fixed expenses:	
Advertising	$ 30,000
Rent	20,000
Salaries	100,000
Total fixed expenses	$150,000

Required:
1. What is Shop 48's annual break-even point in unit sales and dollar sales?
2. Prepare a CVP graph showing cost and revenue data for Shop 48 from zero shoes up to 17,000 pairs of shoes sold each year. Clearly indicate the break-even point on the graph.
3. If 12,000 pairs of shoes are sold in a year, what would be Shop 48's net operating income (loss)?
4. The company is considering paying the Shop 48 store manager an incentive commission of 75 cents per pair of shoes (in addition to the salesperson's commission). If this change is made, what will be the new break-even point in unit sales and dollar sales?
5. Refer to the original data. As an alternative to (4) above, the company is considering paying the Shop 48 store manager 50 cents commission on each pair of shoes sold in excess of the break-even point. If this change is made, what will be Shop 48's net operating income (loss) if 15,000 pairs of shoes are sold?
6. Refer to the original data. The company is considering eliminating sales commissions entirely in its shops and increasing fixed salaries by $31,500 annually. If this change is made, what will be Shop 48's new break-even point in unit sales and dollar sales? Would you recommend that the change be made? Explain.

PROBLEM 5–27 Sales Mix; Break-Even Analysis; Margin of Safety LO5–7, LO5–9

Island Novelties, Inc., of Palau makes two products—Hawaiian Fantasy and Tahitian Joy. Each product's selling price, variable expense per unit and annual sales volume are as follows:

	Hawaiian Fantasy	Tahitian Joy
Selling price per unit............................	$15	$100
Variable expense per unit	$9	$20
Number of units sold annually......................	20,000	5,000

Fixed expenses total $475,800 per year.

Required:

1. Assuming the sales mix given above, do the following:
   a. Prepare a contribution format income statement showing both dollar and percent columns for each product and for the company as a whole.
   b. Compute the company's break-even point in dollar sales. Also, compute its margin of safety in dollars and its margin of safety percentage.
2. The company has developed a new product called Samoan Delight that sells for $45 each and that has variable expenses of $36 per unit. If the company can sell 10,000 units of Samoan Delight without incurring any additional fixed expenses:
   a. Prepare a revised contribution format income statement that includes Samoan Delight. Assume that sales of the other two products does not change.
   b. Compute the company's revised break-even point in dollar sales. Also, compute its revised margin of safety in dollars and margin of safety percentage.
3. The president of the company examines your figures and says, "There's something strange here. Our fixed expenses haven't changed and you show greater total contribution margin if we add the new product, but you also show our break-even point going up. With greater contribution margin, the break-even point should go down, not up. You've made a mistake somewhere." Explain to the president what has happened.

PROBLEM 5–28 Sales Mix; Commission Structure; Multiproduct Break-Even Analysis LO5–9

Carbex, Inc., produces cutlery sets out of high-quality wood and steel. The company makes a Standard set and a Deluxe set and sells them to retail department stores throughout the country. The Standard set sells for $60, and the Deluxe set sells for $75. The variable expenses associated with each set are given below.

	Standard	Deluxe
Variable production costs	$15.00	$30.00
Sales commissions (15% of sales price)	$9.00	$11.25

The company's fixed expenses each month are:

Advertising...............................	$105,000
Depreciation	$21,700
Administrative	$63,000

Mary Parsons, the financial vice president, watches sales commissions carefully and has noted that they have risen steadily over the last year. For this reason, she was shocked to find that even though sales have increased, profits for the current month—May—are down substantially from April. Sales, in sets, for the last two months are given below:

	Standard	Deluxe	Total
April.......................	4,000	2,000	6,000
May	1,000	5,000	6,000

Required:

1. Prepare contribution format income statements for April and May. Use the following headings:

	Standard		Deluxe		Total	
	Amount	Percent	Amount	Percent	Amount	Percent
Sales						
Etc.						

Place the fixed expenses only in the Total column. Do not show percentages for the fixed expenses.

2. Explain the difference in net operating incomes between the two months, even though the same total number of sets was sold in each month.

3. What can be done to the sales commissions to improve the sales mix?
    a. Using April's sales mix, what is the break-even point in dollar sales?
    b. Without doing any calculations, explain whether the break-even point in May would be higher or lower than the break-even point in April. Why?

PROBLEM 5–29 Changes in Cost Structure; Break-Even Analysis; Operating Leverage; Margin of Safety LO5–4, LO5–5, LO5–7, LO5–8

Morton Company's contribution format income statement for last month is given below:

Sales (15,000 units × $30 per unit)	$450,000
Variable expenses.	315,000
Contribution margin	135,000
Fixed expenses	90,000
Net operating income.	$ 45,000

The industry in which Morton Company operates is quite sensitive to cyclical movements in the economy. Thus, profits vary considerably from year to year according to general economic conditions. The company has a large amount of unused capacity and is studying ways of improving profits.

Required:

1. New equipment has come onto the market that would allow Morton Company to automate a portion of its operations. Variable expenses would be reduced by $9 per unit. However, fixed expenses would increase to a total of $225,000 each month. Prepare two contribution format income statements, one showing present operations and one showing how operations would appear if the new equipment is purchased. Show an Amount column, a Per Unit column, and a Percent column on each statement. Do not show percentages for the fixed expenses.

2. Refer to the income statements in (1). For the present operations and the proposed new operations, compute (a) the degree of operating leverage, (b) the break-even point in dollar sales, and (c) the margin of safety in dollars and the margin of safety percentage.

3. Refer again to the data in (1). As a manager, what factor would be paramount in your mind in deciding whether to purchase the new equipment? (Assume that enough funds are available to make the purchase.)

4. Refer to the original data. Rather than purchase new equipment, the marketing manager argues that the company's marketing strategy should be changed. Rather than pay sales commissions, which are currently included in variable expenses, the company would pay salespersons fixed salaries and would invest heavily in advertising. The marketing manager claims this new approach would increase unit sales by 30% without any change in selling price; the company's new monthly fixed expenses would be $180,000; and its net operating income would increase by 20%. Compute the company's break-even point in dollar sales under the new marketing strategy. Do you agree with the marketing manager's proposal?

PROBLEM 5–30 Graphing; Incremental Analysis; Operating Leverage LO5–2, LO5–4, LO5–5, LO5–6, LO5–8

Angie Silva has recently opened The Sandal Shop in Brisbane, Australia, a store that specializes in fashionable sandals. In time, she hopes to open a chain of sandal shops. As a first step, she has gathered the following data for her new store:

Sales price per pair of sandals	$40
Variable expenses per pair of sandals	16
Contribution margin per pair of sandals	$24
Fixed expenses per year:	
Building rental	$15,000
Equipment depreciation	7,000
Selling	20,000
Administrative	18,000
Total fixed expenses	$60,000

Required:

1. What is the break-even point in unit sales and dollar sales?
2. Prepare a CVP graph or a profit graph for the store from zero pairs up to 4,000 pairs of sandals sold each year. Indicate the break-even point on your graph.
3. Angie has decided that she must earn a profit of $18,000 the first year to justify her time and effort. How many pairs of sandals must be sold to attain this target profit?
4. Angie now has two salespersons working in the store—one full time and one part time. It will cost her an additional $8,000 per year to convert the part-time position to a full-time position. Angie believes that the change would increase annual sales by $25,000. Should she convert the position? Use the incremental approach. (Do not prepare an income statement.)
5. Refer to the original data. During the first year, the store sold only 3,000 pairs of sandals and reported the following operating results:

Sales (3,000 pairs)	$120,000
Variable expenses	48,000
Contribution margin	72,000
Fixed expenses	60,000
Net operating income	$ 12,000

  a. What is the store's degree of operating leverage?
  b. Angie is confident that with a more intense sales effort and with a more creative advertising program she can increase sales by 50% next year. Using the degree of operating leverage, what would be the expected percentage increase in net operating income if Angie is able to increase sales by 50%?

PROBLEM 5–31 Interpretive Questions on the CVP Graph LO5–2, LO5–5

A CVP graph such as the one shown below is a useful technique for showing relationships among an organization's costs, volume, and profits.

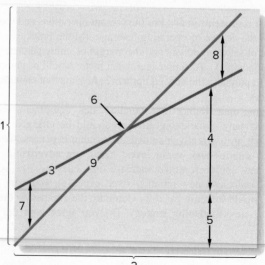

Required:

1. Identify the numbered components in the CVP graph.
2. State the effect of each of the following actions on line 3, line 9, and the break-even point. For line 3 and line 9, state whether the action will cause the line to:

> Remain unchanged.
> Shift upward.
> Shift downward.
> Have a steeper slope (i.e., rotate upward).
> Have a flatter slope (i.e., rotate downward).
> Shift upward *and* have a steeper slope.
> Shift upward *and* have a flatter slope.
> Shift downward *and* have a steeper slope.
> Shift downward *and* have a flatter slope.

In the case of the break-even point, state whether the action will cause the break-even point to:

> Remain unchanged.
> Increase.
> Decrease.
> Probably change, but the direction is uncertain.

Treat each case independently.

- x.   *Example.* Fixed expenses are reduced by $5,000 per period.
  Answer (see choices above):   Line 3:   Shift downward.
  Line 9:   Remain unchanged.
  Break-even point: Decrease.

- a.   The unit selling price is increased from $18 to $20.
- b.   Unit variable expenses are decreased from $12 to $10.
- c.   Fixed expenses are increased by $3,000 per period.
- d.   Two thousand more units are sold during the period than were budgeted.
- e.   Due to paying salespersons a commission rather than a flat salary, fixed expenses are reduced by $8,000 per period and unit variable expenses are increased by $3.
- f.   Due to an increase in the cost of materials, both unit variable expenses and the selling price are increased by $2.
- g.   Advertising costs are increased by $10,000 per period, resulting in a 10% increase in the number of units sold.
- h.   Due to automating an operation previously done by workers, fixed expenses are increased by $12,000 per period and unit variable expenses are reduced by $4.

Mc Graw Hill Education ▐ connect Cases

CASE 5–32 Break-Even Analysis for Individual Products in a Multiproduct Company LO5–5, LO5–9

Cheryl Montoya picked up the phone and called her boss, Wes Chan, the vice president of marketing at Piedmont Fasteners Corporation: "Wes, I'm not sure how to go about answering the questions that came up at the meeting with the president yesterday."

"What's the problem?"

"The president wanted to know the break-even point for each of the company's products, but I am having trouble figuring them out."

"I'm sure you can handle it, Cheryl. And, by the way, I need your analysis on my desk tomorrow morning at 8:00 sharp in time for the follow-up meeting at 9:00."

Piedmont Fasteners Corporation makes three different clothing fasteners in its manufacturing facility in North Carolina. Data concerning these products appear below:

	Velcro	Metal	Nylon
Annual sales volume....................	100,000	200,000	400,000
Unit selling price	$1.65	$1.50	$0.85
Variable expense per unit	$1.25	$0.70	$0.25

Total fixed expenses are $400,000 per year.

All three products are sold in highly competitive markets, so the company is unable to raise prices without losing an unacceptable numbers of customers.

The company has an extremely effective lean production system, so there are no beginning or ending work in process or finished goods inventories.

Required:

1. What is the company's over-all break-even point in dollar sales?
2. Of the total fixed expenses of $400,000, $20,000 could be avoided if the Velcro product is dropped, $80,000 if the Metal product is dropped, and $60,000 if the Nylon product is dropped. The remaining fixed expenses of $240,000 consist of common fixed expenses such as administrative salaries and rent on the factory building that could be avoided only by going out of business entirely.
    a. What is the break-even point in unit sales for each product?
    b. If the company sells exactly the break-even quantity of each product, what will be the overall profit of the company? Explain this result.

CASE 5–33 Cost Structure; Break-Even and Target Profit Analysis LO5–4, LO5–5, LO5–6

Pittman Company is a small but growing manufacturer of telecommunications equipment. The company has no sales force of its own; rather, it relies completely on independent sales agents to market its products. These agents are paid a sales commission of 15% for all items sold.

Barbara Cheney, Pittman's controller, has just prepared the company's budgeted income statement for next year as follows:

Pittman Company		
Budgeted Income Statement		
For the Year Ended December 31		
Sales		$16,000,000
Manufacturing expenses:		
Variable.............................	$7,200,000	
Fixed overhead	2,340,000	9,540,000
Gross margin		6,460,000
Selling and administrative expenses:		
Commissions to agents	2,400,000	
Fixed marketing expenses................	120,000*	
Fixed administrative expenses	1,800,000	4,320,000
Net operating income......................		2,140,000
Fixed interest expenses....................		540,000
Income before income taxes................		1,600,000
Income taxes (30%)........................		480,000
Net income...............................		$ 1,120,000

*Primarily depreciation on storage facilities.

As Barbara handed the statement to Karl Vecci, Pittman's president, she commented, "I went ahead and used the agents' 15% commission rate in completing these statements, but we've just learned that they refuse to handle our products next year unless we increase the commission rate to 20%."

"That's the last straw," Karl replied angrily. "Those agents have been demanding more and more, and this time they've gone too far. How can they possibly defend a 20% commission rate?"

"They claim that after paying for advertising, travel, and the other costs of promotion, there's nothing left over for profit," replied Barbara.

"I say it's just plain robbery," retorted Karl. "And I also say it's time we dumped those guys and got our own sales force. Can you get your people to work up some cost figures for us to look at?"

"We've already worked them up," said Barbara. "Several companies we know about pay a 7.5% commission to their own salespeople, along with a small salary. Of course, we would have to handle all promotion costs, too. We figure our fixed expenses would increase by $2,400,000 per year, but that would be more than offset by the $3,200,000 (20% × $16,000,000) that we would avoid on agents' commissions."

The breakdown of the $2,400,000 cost follows:

Salaries:	
Sales manager...	$ 100,000
Salespersons..	600,000
Travel and entertainment................................	400,000
Advertising..	1,300,000
Total..	$2,400,000

"Super," replied Karl. "And I noticed that the $2,400,000 equals what we're paying the agents under the old 15% commission rate."

"It's even better than that," explained Barbara. "We can actually save $75,000 a year because that's what we're paying our auditors to check out the agents' reports. So our overall administrative expenses would be less."

"Pull all of these numbers together and we'll show them to the executive committee tomorrow," said Karl. "With the approval of the committee, we can move on the matter immediately."

Required:

1. Compute Pittman Company's break-even point in dollar sales for next year assuming:
   a. The agents' commission rate remains unchanged at 15%.
   b. The agents' commission rate is increased to 20%.
   c. The company employs its own sales force.
2. Assume that Pittman Company decides to continue selling through agents and pays the 20% commission rate. Determine the dollar sales that would be required to generate the same net income as contained in the budgeted income statement for next year.
3. Determine the dollar sales at which net income would be equal regardless of whether Pittman Company sells through agents (at a 20% commission rate) or employs its own sales force.
4. Compute the degree of operating leverage that the company would expect to have at the end of next year assuming:
   a. The agents' commission rate remains unchanged at 15%.
   b. The agents' commission rate is increased to 20%.
   c. The company employs its own sales force.
   Use income *before* income taxes in your operating leverage computation.
5. Based on the data in (1) through (4) above, make a recommendation as to whether the company should continue to use sales agents (at a 20% commission rate) or employ its own sales force. Give reasons for your answer.

(CMA, adapted)

Appendix 5A: Analyzing Mixed Costs

The main body of Chapter 5 assumed that all costs could be readily classified as variable or fixed. In reality, many costs contain both variable *and* fixed components—they are *mixed costs*. The purpose of this appendix is to describe various methods that companies can use to separate mixed costs into their variable and fixed components, thereby enabling cost-volume-profit (CVP) analysis.

Mixed costs are very common in most organizations. For example, the overall cost of performing surgeries for patients at the Harvard Medical School Hospital is a mixed cost. The costs of equipment depreciation and surgeons' and nurses' salaries are fixed, but the costs of surgical gloves, power, and other supplies are variable. At Southwest Airlines, maintenance costs are a mixed cost. The company incurs fixed costs for renting maintenance facilities and for keeping skilled mechanics on the payroll, but the costs of replacement parts, lubricating oils, tires, and so forth, are variable with respect to how often and how far the company's aircraft are flown.

The fixed portion of a mixed cost represents the minimum cost of having a service *ready and available* for use. The variable portion represents the cost incurred for *actual consumption* of the service, thus it varies in proportion to the amount of service actually consumed.

Managers can use a variety of methods to estimate the fixed and variable components of a mixed cost such as *account analysis,* the *engineering approach,* the *high-low method,* and *least-squares regression analysis.* In **account analysis**, an account is classified as either variable or fixed based on the analyst's prior knowledge of how the cost in the account behaves. For example, direct materials would be classified as variable and a building lease cost would be classified as fixed because of the nature of those costs. The **engineering approach** to cost analysis involves a detailed analysis of what cost behavior should be, based on an industrial engineer's evaluation of the production methods to be used, the materials specifications, labor requirements, equipment usage, production efficiency, power consumption, and so on.

The high-low method and least-squares regression method estimate the fixed and variable elements of a mixed cost by analyzing past records of cost and activity data. Throughout the remainder of this appendix, we will define these two cost estimation methods and use an example from Brentline Hospital to illustrate how they each derive their respective fixed and variable cost estimates. The least-squares regression computations will be explained using Microsoft Excel because it can perform the underlying mathematics much faster than using a pencil and a calculator.

LO5–10

Analyze a mixed cost using a scattergraph plot and the high-low method.

Diagnosing Cost Behavior with a Scattergraph Plot

Assume that Brentline Hospital is interested in predicting future monthly maintenance costs for budgeting purposes. The senior management team believes that maintenance cost is a mixed cost and that the variable portion of this cost is driven by the number of patient-days. Each day a patient is in the hospital counts as one patient-day. The hospital's chief financial officer gathered the following data for the most recent seven-month period:

The first step in applying the high-low method or the least-squares regression method is to diagnose cost behavior with a scattergraph plot. The scattergraph plot of maintenance costs versus patient-days at Brentline Hospital is shown in Exhibit 5A–1. Two things should be noted about this scattergraph:

Month	Activity Level: Patient-Days	Maintenance Cost Incurred
January	5,600	$7,900
February	7,100	$8,500
March	5,000	$7,400
April	6,500	$8,200
May	7,300	$9,100
June	8,000	$9,800
July	6,200	$7,800

1. The total maintenance cost, *Y,* is plotted on the vertical axis. Cost is known as the **dependent variable** because the amount of cost incurred during a period depends on the level of activity for the period. (That is, as the level of activity increases, total cost also will ordinarily increase.)
2. The activity, *X* (patient-days in this case), is plotted on the horizontal axis. Activity is known as the **independent variable** because it causes variations in the cost.

From the scattergraph plot, it is evident that maintenance costs do increase with the number of patient-days in an approximately *linear* fashion. In other words, the points lie more or less along a straight line that slopes upward and to the right. **Linear cost behavior** exists whenever a straight line is a reasonable approximation for the relation between cost and activity.

Plotting the data on a scattergraph is an essential diagnostic step that should be performed before performing the high-low or least-squares regression calculations. If the scattergraph plot reveals linear cost behavior, then it makes sense to perform the high-low or least-squares regression calculations to separate the mixed cost into its variable and fixed components. If the scattergraph plot does not depict linear cost behavior, then it makes no sense to proceed any further in analyzing the data.

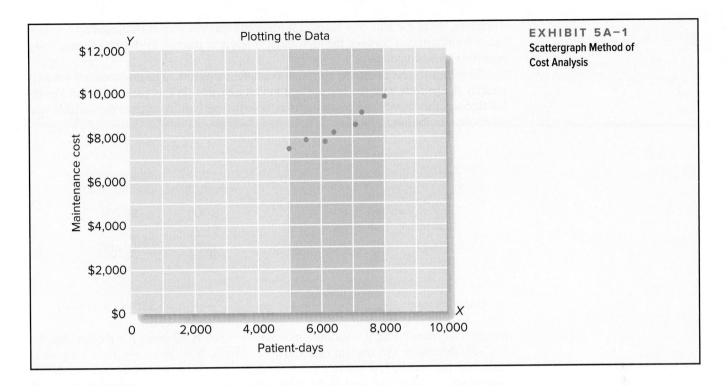

Once we determine that the dependent and independent variables have a linear relationship, the high-low and least-squares regression methods both rely on the following equation for a straight line (as introduced in Chapter 1) to express the relationship between a mixed cost and the level of activity:

$$Y = a + bX$$

In this equation ,
Y = The total mixed cost
a = The total fixed cost (the vertical intercept of the line)
b = The variable cost per unit of activity (the slope of the line)
X = The level of activity

The High-Low Method

The high-low method is based on the rise-over-run formula for the slope of a straight line. Assuming that the relation between cost and activity can be represented by a straight line, then the slope of the straight line is equal to the variable cost per unit of activity. Consequently, the following formula can be used to estimate the variable cost:

$$\text{Variable cost} = \text{Slope of the line} = \frac{\text{Rise}}{\text{Run}} = \frac{Y_2 - Y_1}{X_2 - X_1}$$

To analyze mixed costs with the **high-low method**, begin by identifying the period with the lowest level of activity and the period with the highest level of activity. The period with the lowest activity is selected as the first point in the above formula and the period with the highest activity is selected as the second point. Consequently, the formula becomes:

$$\text{Variable cost} = \frac{Y_2 - Y_1}{X_2 - X_1} = \frac{\text{Cost at the high activity level} - \text{Cost at the low activity level}}{\text{High activity level} - \text{Low activity level}}$$

or

$$\text{Variable cost} = \frac{\text{Change in cost}}{\text{Change in activity}}$$

Therefore, when the high-low method is used, the variable cost is estimated by dividing the difference in cost between the high and low levels of activity by the change in activity between those two points.

To return to the Brentline Hospital example, using the high-low method, we first identify the periods with the highest and lowest *activity*—in this case, June and March. We then use the activity and cost data from these two periods to estimate the variable cost component as follows:

	Patient-Days	Maintenance Cost Incurred
High activity level (June)	8,000	$9,800
Low activity level (March).	5,000	7,400
Change	3,000	$2,400

$$\text{Variable cost} = \frac{\text{Change in cost}}{\text{Change in activity}} = \frac{\$2,400}{3,000 \text{ patient-days}} = \$0.80 \text{ per patient-day}$$

Having determined that the variable maintenance cost is 80 cents per patient-day, we can now determine the amount of fixed cost. This is done by taking the total cost at *either* the high or the low activity level and deducting the variable cost element. In the computation below, total cost at the high activity level is used in computing the fixed cost element:

Fixed cost element = Total cost − Variable cost element
= $9,800 − ($0.80 per patient-day × 8,000 patient-days)
= $3,400

Given that we have estimated the variable and fixed cost elements, the maintenance cost can now be expressed as $3,400 per month plus 80 cents per patient-day, or as:

$$Y = \$3,400 + \$0.80X$$

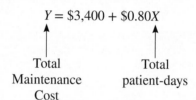

Total Maintenance Cost   Total patient-days

The data used in this illustration are shown graphically in Exhibit 5A–2. Notice that a straight line has been drawn through the points corresponding to the low and high levels of activity. In essence, that is what the high-low method does—it draws a straight line through those two points.

Sometimes the high and low levels of activity don't coincide with the high and low amounts of cost. For example, the period that has the highest level of activity may not have the highest amount of cost. Nevertheless, the costs at the highest and lowest levels of *activity* are always used to analyze a mixed cost under the high-low method. The reason is that the analyst would like to use data that reflect the greatest possible variation in activity.

The high-low method is very simple to apply, but it suffers from a major (and sometimes critical) defect—it utilizes only two data points. Generally, two data points are not enough to produce accurate estimates. Additionally, the periods with the highest and lowest activity tend to be unusual. A cost formula that is estimated solely using data from these unusual periods may misrepresent the true cost behavior during normal periods. Such a distortion is evident in Exhibit 5A–2. The straight line should probably be shifted down somewhat so that it is closer to more of the data points. For these reasons, least-squares regression will generally be more accurate than the high-low method.

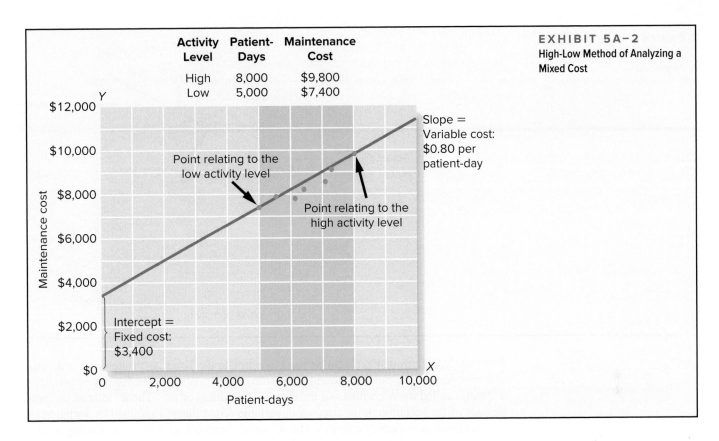

Activity Level	Patient- Days	Maintenance Cost
High	8,000	$9,800
Low	5,000	$7,400

Slope =
Variable cost:
$0.80 per
patient-day

Point relating to the low activity level

Point relating to the high activity level

Intercept =
Fixed cost:
$3,400

Maintenance cost

Patient-days

The Least-Squares Regression Method

The **least-squares regression method**, unlike the high-low method, uses all of the data to separate a mixed cost into its fixed and variable components. A *regression line* of the form $Y = a + bX$ is fitted to the data, where a (the intercept) represents the total fixed cost and b (the slope) represents the variable cost per unit of activity. The basic idea underlying the least-squares regression method is illustrated in Exhibit 5A–3 using hypothetical data points. Notice from the exhibit that the deviations from the plotted points to the regression line are measured vertically on the graph. These vertical deviations are called the regression errors. There is nothing mysterious about the least-squares regression method. It simply computes the regression line that minimizes the sum of these squared errors.

While the basic idea underlying least-squares regression analysis is pretty simple, the formulas that calculate a (the intercept) and b (the slope) are quite complex as shown below:

LO5–11
Analyze a mixed cost using
a scattergraph plot and the
least-squares regression
method.

$$b = \frac{n\left(\Sigma XY\right) - \left(\Sigma X\right)\left(\Sigma Y\right)}{n\left(\Sigma X^2\right) - \left(\Sigma X\right)^2}$$

$$a = \frac{\left(\Sigma Y\right) - b(\Sigma X)}{n}$$

where:

X = The level of activity (independent variable)
Y = The total mixed cost (dependent variable)
a = The total fixed cost (the vertical intercept of the line)
b = The variable cost per unit of activity (the slope of the line)
n = Number of observations
Σ = Sum across all n observations

EXHIBIT 5A–3
The Concept of Least-Squares Regression

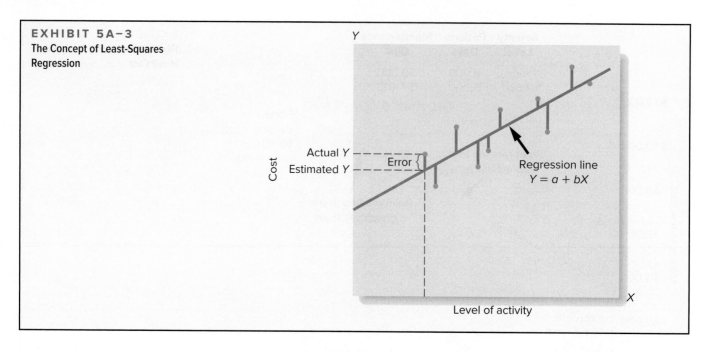

Fortunately, Microsoft Excel can be used to estimate the fixed cost (intercept) and variable cost per unit (slope) that minimize the sum of the squared errors. Excel also provides a statistic called the R^2, which is a measure of "goodness of fit." The R^2 tells us the percentage of the variation in the dependent variable (cost) that is explained by variation in the independent variable (activity). The R^2 varies from 0% to 100%, and the higher the percentage, the better.

As mentioned earlier, you should always plot the data in a scattergraph, but it is particularly important to check the data visually when the R^2 is low. A quick look at the scattergraph can reveal that there is little relation between the cost and the activity or that the relation is something other than a simple straight line. In such cases, additional analysis would be required.

Exhibit 5A–4 uses Excel to depict the Brentline Hospital data that we used earlier to illustrate the high-low method. We'll be using this same data set to illustrate how Excel can be used to create a scattergraph plot and to calculate the intercept a, the slope b, and the R^2 using least-squares regression.[6]

EXHIBIT 5A–4
The Least-Squares Regression Worksheet for Brentline Hospital

	A	B	C
1		Patient	Maintenance
2		Days	Cost
3	*Month*	*X*	*Y*
4	January	5,600	$ 7,900
5	February	7,100	$ 8,500
6	March	5,000	$ 7,400
7	April	6,500	$ 8,200
8	May	7,300	$ 9,100
9	June	8,000	$ 9,800
10	July	6,200	$ 7,800
11			

⏮ ◀ ▶ ⏭   Least-squares regression

[6] The authors wish to thank Don Schwartz, Professor of Accounting at National University, for providing suggestions that were instrumental in creating this appendix.

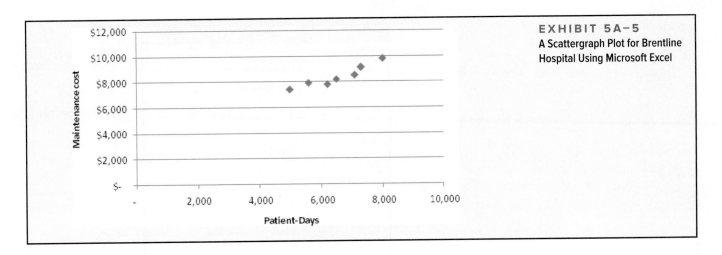

To prepare a scattergraph plot in Excel, begin by highlighting the data in cells B4 through C10 (as shown in Exhibit 5A–4). From the Charts group within the Insert tab, select the "Scatter" subgroup and then click on the choice that has no lines connecting the data points. This should produce a scattergraph plot similar to the one shown in Exhibit 5A–5. Notice that the number of patient-days is plotted on the X-axis and the maintenance cost is plotted on the Y-axis.[7] As we saw verified earlier in Exhibit 5A–1, the data is approximately linear, so it makes sense to proceed with estimating a regression equation that minimizes the sum of the squared errors.

To determine the intercept a, the slope b, and the R^2, begin by right clicking on any data point in the scattergraph plot and selecting "Add Trendline." This should produce the screen that is shown in Exhibit 5A–6. Notice that under "Trend/Regression Type" you should select "Linear." Similarly, under "Trendline Name" you should select "Automatic." Next to the word "Backward" you should input the lowest value for the independent variable, which in this example is 5000 patient-days. Taking this particular step instructs Excel to extend your fitted line until it intersects the Y-axis. Finally, you should check the two boxes at the bottom of Exhibit 5A–6 that say "Display Equation on chart" and "Display R-squared value on chart."

Once you have established these settings, then click "Close." As shown in Exhibit 5A–7, this will automatically insert a line within the scattergraph plot that minimizes the sum of the squared errors. It will also cause the estimated least-squares regression equation and R^2 to be inserted into your scattergraph plot. Instead of depicting the results using the form $Y = a + bX$, Excel uses an equivalent form of the equation depicted as $Y = bX + a$. In other words, Excel reverses the two terms shown to the right of the equals sign. So, in Exhibit 5A–7, Excel shows a least-squares regression equation of $y = 0.7589x + 3,430.9$. The slope b in this equation of \$0.7589 represents the estimated variable maintenance cost per patient-day. The intercept a in this equation of \$3,430.90 (or approximately \$3,431) represents the estimated fixed monthly maintenance cost. Note that the R^2 is approximately 0.90, which is quite good and indicates that 90% of the variation in maintenance cost is explained by the variation in patient-days.

---

[7] To insert labels for the X-axis and Y-axis, go to the Layout tab in Excel. Then, within the Labels group, select Axis Titles.

EXHIBIT 5A-6
Trendline Options in Microsoft Excel

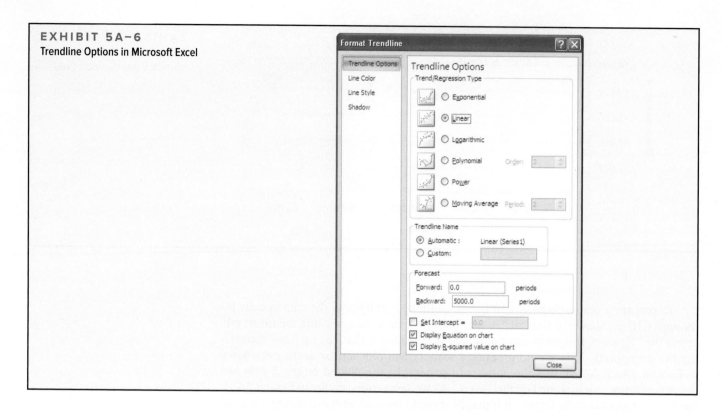

EXHIBIT 5A-7
Brentline Hospital: Least-Squares Regression Results Using Microsoft Excel

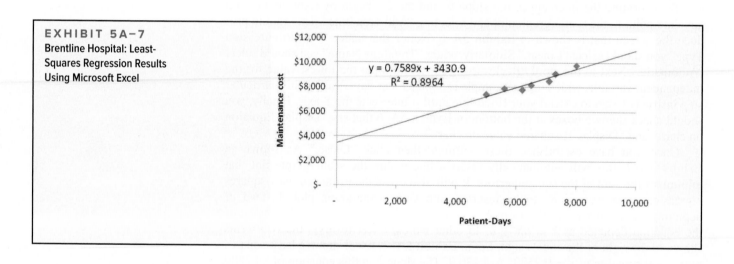

Comparing the High-Low and Least-Squares Regression Methods

The table below compares Brentline Hospital's cost estimates using the high-low method and the least-squares regression method:

	High-Low Method	Least-Squares Regression Method
Variable cost estimate per patient-day	$0.800	$0.759
Fixed cost estimate per month	$3,400	$3,431

When Brentline uses the least-squares regression method to create a straight line that minimizes the sum of the squared errors, it results in estimated fixed costs that are $31 higher than the amount derived using the high-low method. It also decreases the slope of the straight line resulting in a lower variable cost estimate of $0.759 per patient-day rather than $0.80 per patient-day as derived using the high-low method.

Glossary (Appendix 5A)

Account analysis A method for analyzing cost behavior in which an account is classified as either variable or fixed based on the analyst's prior knowledge of how the cost in the account behaves. (p. 242)

Dependent variable A variable that responds to some causal factor; total cost is the dependent variable, as represented by the letter Y, in the equation $Y = a + bX$. (p. 242)

Engineering approach A detailed analysis of cost behavior based on an industrial engineer's evaluation of the inputs that are required to carry out a particular activity and of the prices of those inputs. (p. 242)

High-low method A method of separating a mixed cost into its fixed and variable elements by analyzing the change in cost between the high and low activity levels. (p. 243)

Independent variable A variable that acts as a causal factor; activity is the independent variable, as represented by the letter X, in the equation $Y = a + bX$. (p. 242)

Least-squares regression method A method of separating a mixed cost into its fixed and variable elements by fitting a regression line that minimizes the sum of the squared errors. (p. 245)

Linear cost behavior Cost behavior is said to be linear whenever a straight line is a reasonable approximation for the relation between cost and activity. (p. 242)

R^2 A measure of goodness of fit in least-squares regression analysis. It is the percentage of the variation in the dependent variable that is explained by variation in the independent variable. (p. 246)

connect Appendix 5A: Exercises and Problems

EXERCISE 5A–1 High-Low Method LO5–10

The Cheyenne Hotel in Big Sky, Montana, has accumulated records of the total electrical costs of the hotel and the number of occupancy-days over the last year. An occupancy-day represents a room rented for one day. The hotel's business is highly seasonal, with peaks occurring during the ski season and in the summer.

Month	Occupancy-Days	Electrical Costs
January.............................	1,736	$4,127
February............................	1,904	$4,207
March...............................	2,356	$5,083
April................................	960	$2,857
May	360	$1,871
June.................................	744	$2,696
July	2,108	$4,670
August..............................	2,406	$5,148
September	840	$2,691
October.............................	124	$1,588
November...........................	720	$2,454
December...........................	1,364	$3,529

Required:

1. Using the high-low method, estimate the fixed cost of electricity per month and the variable cost of electricity per occupancy-day. Round off the fixed cost to the nearest whole dollar and the variable cost to the nearest whole cent.

2. What other factors in addition to occupancy-days are likely to affect the variation in electrical costs from month to month?

EXERCISE 5A–2 Least-Squares Regression LO5–11

Bargain Rental Car offers rental cars in an off-airport location near a major tourist destination in California. Management would like to better understand the variable and fixed portions of it car washing costs. The company operates its own car wash facility in which each rental car that is returned is thoroughly cleaned before being released for rental to another customer. Management believes that the variable portion of its car washing costs relates to the number of rental returns. Accordingly, the following data have been compiled:

Month	Rental Returns	Car Wash Costs
January	2,380	$10,825
February	2,421	$11,865
March.	2,586	$11,332
April.	2,725	$12,422
May	2,968	$13,850
June.	3,281	$14,419
July	3,353	$14,935
August.	3,489	$15,738
September	3,057	$13,563
October.	2,876	$11,889
November.	2,735	$12,683
December.	2,983	$13,796

Required:
1. Prepare a scattergraph plot. (Place car wash costs on the vertical axis and rental returns on the horizontal axis.)
2. Using least-squares regression, estimate the variable cost per rental return and the monthly fixed cost incurred to wash cars. The total fixed cost should be estimated to the nearest dollar and the variable cost per rental return to the nearest cent.

EXERCISE 5A–3 Cost Behavior; High-Low Method LO5–10

Hoi Chong Transport, Ltd., operates a fleet of delivery trucks in Singapore. The company has determined that if a truck is driven 105,000 kilometers during a year, the average operating cost is 11.4 cents per kilometer. If a truck is driven only 70,000 kilometers during a year, the average operating cost increases to 13.4 cents per kilometer.

Required:
1. Using the high-low method, estimate the variable operating cost per kilometer and the annual fixed operating cost associated with the fleet of trucks.
2. Express the variable and fixed costs in the form $Y = a + bX$.
3. If a truck were driven 80,000 kilometers during a year, what total operating cost would you expect to be incurred?

EXERCISE 5A–4 High-Low Method; Scattergraph Analysis LO5–10

Archer Company is a wholesaler of custom-built air-conditioning units for commercial buildings. It gathered the following monthly data relating to units shipped and total shipping expense:

Month	Units Shipped	Total Shipping Expense
January	3	$1,800
February	6	$2,300
March.	4	$1,700
April.	5	$2,000
May	7	$2,300
June.	8	$2,700
July	2	$1,200

Required:

1. Prepare a scattergraph using the data given above. Plot cost on the vertical axis and activity on the horizontal axis. Is there an approximately linear relationship between shipping expense and the number of units shipped?
2. Using the high-low method, estimate the cost formula for shipping expense. Draw a straight line through the high and low data points shown in the scattergraph that you prepared in requirement (1). Make sure your line intersects the *Y*-axis.
3. Comment on the accuracy of your high-low estimates assuming a least-squares regression analysis estimated the total fixed costs to be $910.71 per month and the variable cost to be $217.86 per unit. How would the straight line that you drew in requirement 2 differ from a straight line that minimizes the sum of the squared errors?
4. What factors, other than the number of units shipped, are likely to affect the company's shipping expense? Explain.

EXERCISE 5A–5 Least-Squares Regression LO5–11

George Caloz & Frères, located in Grenchen, Switzerland, makes luxury custom watches in small lots. One of the company's products, a platinum diving watch, goes through an etching process. The company has recorded etching costs as follows over the last six weeks:

Week	Units	Total Etching Cost
1............................	4	$ 18
2............................	3	17
3............................	8	25
4............................	6	20
5............................	7	24
6............................	2	16
	30	$120

For planning purposes, management would like to know the variable etching cost per unit and the total fixed etching cost per week.

Required:

1. Prepare a scattergraph plot. (Plot etching costs on the vertical axis and units on the horizontal axis.)
2. Using the least-squares regression method, estimate the variable etching cost per unit and the total fixed etching cost per week. Express these estimates in the form $Y = a + bX$.
3. If the company processes five units next week, what would be the expected total etching cost? (Round your answer to the nearest cent.)

PROBLEM 5A–6 Least-Squares Regression; Scattergraph; Comparison of Activity Bases LO5–11

The Hard Rock Mining Company is developing cost formulas for management planning and decision-making purposes. The company's cost analyst has concluded that utilities cost is a mixed cost, and he is attempting to find a base that correlates with the cost. The controller has suggested that tons mined might be a good base to use in developing a cost formula. The production superintendent disagrees; she thinks that direct labor-hours would be a better base. The cost analyst has decided to try both bases and has assembled the following information:

Quarter	Tons Mined	Direct Labor-Hours	Utilities Cost
Year 1:			
First	15,000	5,000	$50,000
Second	11,000	3,000	$45,000
Third	21,000	4,000	$60,000
Fourth	12,000	6,000	$75,000
Year 2:			
First	18,000	10,000	$100,000
Second	25,000	9,000	$105,000
Third	30,000	8,000	$85,000
Fourth	28,000	11,000	$120,000

Required:

1. Using tons mined as the independent variable, prepare a scattergraph that plots tons mined on the horizontal axis and utilities cost on the vertical axis. Using the least-squares regression method, estimate the variable utilities cost per ton mined and the total fixed utilities cost per quarter. Express these estimates in the form $Y = a + bX$.
2. Using direct labor-hours as the independent variable, prepare a scattergraph that plots direct labor-hours on the horizontal axis and utilities cost on the vertical axis. Using the least-squares regression method, estimate the variable utilities cost per ton mined and the total fixed utilities cost per quarter. Express these estimates in the form $Y = a + bX$.
3. Would you recommend that the company use tons mined or direct labor-hours as a base for planning utilities cost?

PROBLEM 5A–7 Cost Behavior; High-Low Method; Contribution Format Income Statement LO5–10

Morrisey & Brown, Ltd., of Sydney is a merchandising company that is the sole distributor of a product that is increasing in popularity among Australian consumers. The company's income statements for the three most recent months follow:

Morrisey & Brown, Ltd. Income Statements For the Three Months Ended September 30			
	July	August	September
Sales in units	4,000	4,500	5,000
Sales	$400,000	$450,000	$500,000
Cost of goods sold	240,000	270,000	300,000
Gross margin	160,000	180,000	200,000
Selling and administrative expenses:			
Advertising expense.............................	21,000	21,000	21,000
Shipping expense................................	34,000	36,000	38,000
Salaries and commissions	78,000	84,000	90,000
Insurance expense	6,000	6,000	6,000
Depreciation expense	15,000	15,000	15,000
Total selling and administrative expenses	154,000	162,000	170,000
Net operating income................................	$ 6,000	$ 18,000	$ 30,000

Required:

1. By analyzing the data from the company's income statements, classify each of its expenses (including cost of goods sold) as either variable, fixed, or mixed.
2. Using the high-low method, separate each mixed expense into variable and fixed elements. Express the variable and fixed portions of each mixed expense in the form $Y = a + bX$.
3. Redo the company's income statement at the 5,000-unit level of activity using the contribution format.

PROBLEM 5A–8 High-Low Method; Predicting Cost LO5–10

Nova Company's total overhead cost at various levels of activity are presented below:

Month	Machine-Hours	Total Overhead Cost
April	70,000	$198,000
May	60,000	$174,000
June............................	80,000	$222,000
July	90,000	$246,000

Assume that the total overhead cost above consists of utilities, supervisory salaries, and maintenance. The breakdown of these costs at the 60,000 machine-hour level of activity is:

Utilities (variable)............................	$ 48,000
Supervisory salaries (fixed)	21,000
Maintenance (mixed).........................	105,000
Total overhead cost..........................	$174,000

Nova Company's management wants to break down the maintenance cost into its variable and fixed cost elements.

Required:
1. Estimate how much of the $246,000 of overhead cost in July was maintenance cost. (*Hint:* to do this, it may be helpful to first determine how much of the $246,000 consisted of utilities and supervisory salaries. Think about the behavior of variable and fixed costs.)
2. Using the high-low method, estimate a cost formula for maintenance in the form $Y = a + bX$.
3. Express the company's *total* overhead cost in the form $Y = a + bX$.
4. What *total* overhead cost would you expect to be incurred at an activity level of 75,000 machine-hours?

PROBLEM 5A–9 High-Low Method; Contribution Format Income Statement LO5–10
Milden Company is a distributor who wants to start using a contribution format income statement for planning purposes. The company has analyzed its expenses and developed the following cost formulas:

Cost	Cost Formula
Cost of good sold	$35 per unit sold
Advertising expense...........................	$210,000 per quarter
Sales commissions	6% of sales
Shipping expense..............................	?
Administrative salaries	$145,000 per quarter
Insurance expense	$9,000 per quarter
Depreciation expense	$76,000 per quarter

Because shipping expense is a mixed cost, the company needs to estimate the variable shipping expense per unit sold and the fixed shipping expense per quarter using the following data:

Quarter	Units Sold	Shipping Expense
Year 1:		
First	10,000	$119,000
Second	16,000	$175,000
Third	18,000	$190,000
Fourth	15,000	$164,000
Year 2:		
First	11,000	$130,000
Second	17,000	$185,000
Third	20,000	$210,000
Fourth	13,000	$147,000

Required:
1. Using the high-low method, estimate a cost formula for shipping expense in the form $Y = a + bX$.
2. In the first quarter of Year 3, the company plans to sell 12,000 units at a selling price of $100 per unit. Prepare a contribution format income statement for the quarter.

PROBLEM 5A–10 Least-Squares Regression Method; Scattergraph; Cost Behavior LO5–11

Professor John Morton has just been appointed chairperson of the Finance Department at Westland University. In reviewing the department's cost records, Professor Morton has found the following total cost associated with Finance 101 over the last five terms:

Term	Number of Sections Offered	Total Cost
Fall, last year	4	$10,000
Winter, last year	6	$14,000
Summer, last year	2	$7,000
Fall, this year	5	$13,000
Winter, this year	3	$9,500

Professor Morton knows that there are some variable costs, such as amounts paid to graduate assistants, associated with the course. He would like to have the variable and fixed costs separated for planning purposes.

Required:

1. Prepare a scattergraph plot. (Plot total cost on the vertical axis and number of sections offered on the horizontal axis.)
2. Using the least-squares regression method, estimate the variable cost per section and the total fixed cost per term for Finance 101. Express these estimates in the form $Y = a + bX$.
3. Assume that because of the small number of sections offered during the Winter Term this year, Professor Morton will have to offer eight sections of Finance 101 during the Fall Term. Compute the expected total cost for Finance 101. Can you see any problem with using the cost formula from (2) above to derive this total cost figure? Explain.

CASE 5A–11 Mixed Cost Analysis and the Relevant Range LO5–10

The Ramon Company is a manufacturer that is interested in developing a cost formula to estimate the variable and fixed components of its monthly manufacturing overhead costs. The company wishes to use machine-hours as its measure of activity and has gathered the data below for this year and last year:

Month	Last Year Machine-Hours	Last Year Overhead Costs	This Year Machine-Hours	This Year Overhead Costs
January	21,000	$84,000	21,000	$86,000
February	25,000	$99,000	24,000	$93,000
March	22,000	$89,500	23,000	$93,000
April	23,000	$90,000	22,000	$87,000
May	20,500	$81,500	20,000	$80,000
June	19,000	$75,500	18,000	$76,500
July	14,000	$70,500	12,000	$67,500
August	10,000	$64,500	13,000	$71,000
September	12,000	$69,000	15,000	$73,500
October	17,000	$75,000	17,000	$72,500
November	16,000	$71,500	15,000	$71,000
December	19,000	$78,000	18,000	$75,000

The company leases all of its manufacturing equipment. The lease arrangement calls for a flat monthly fee up to 19,500 machine-hours. If the machine-hours used exceeds 19,500, then the fee becomes strictly variable with respect to the total number of machine-hours consumed during the month. Lease expense is a major element of overhead cost.

Required:

1. Using the high-low method, estimate a manufacturing overhead cost formula in the form $Y = a + bX$.
2. Prepare a scattergraph using all of the data for the two-year period. Fit a straight line or lines to the plotted points using a ruler. Describe the cost behavior pattern revealed by your scattergraph plot.

3. Assume a least-squares regression analysis using all of the given data points estimated the total fixed cost to be $40,102 and the variable cost to be $2.13 per machine-hour. Do you have any concerns about the accuracy of the high-low estimates that you have computed or the least-squares regression estimates that have been provided?

4. Assume that the company consumes 22,500 machine-hours during a month. Using the high-low method, estimate the total overhead cost that would be incurred at this level of activity. Be sure to consider only the data points contained in the relevant range of activity when performing your computations.

5. Comment on the accuracy of your high-low estimates assuming a least-squares regression analysis using only the data points in the relevant range of activity estimated the total fixed cost to be $10,090 and the variable cost to be $3.53 per machine-hour.

CASE 5A–12 Analysis of Mixed Costs in a Pricing Decision LO5–11

Maria Chavez owns a catering company that serves food and beverages at parties and business functions. Chavez's business is seasonal, with a heavy schedule during the summer months and holidays and a lighter schedule at other times.

One of the major events Chavez's customers request is a cocktail party. She offers a standard cocktail party and has estimated the cost per guest as follows:

Food and beverages	$15.00
Labor (0.5 hrs. @ $10.00/hr.)..................	5.00
Overhead (0.5 hrs. @ $13.98/hr.)...............	6.99
Total cost per guest..........................	$26.99

The standard cocktail party lasts three hours and Chavez hires one worker for every six guests, so that works out to one-half hour of labor per guest. These workers are hired only as needed and are paid only for the hours they actually work.

When bidding on cocktail parties, Chavez adds a 15% markup to yield a price of about $31 per guest. She is confident about her estimates of the costs of food and beverages and labor but is not as comfortable with the estimate of overhead cost. The $13.98 overhead cost per labor-hour was determined by dividing total overhead expenses for the last 12 months by total labor-hours for the same period. Monthly data concerning overhead costs and labor-hours follow:

Month	Labor-Hours	Overhead Expenses
January	2,500	$ 55,000
February	2,800	59,000
March.........................	3,000	60,000
April.........................	4,200	64,000
May	4,500	67,000
June.........................	5,500	71,000
July	6,500	74,000
August.........................	7,500	77,000
September	7,000	75,000
October.........................	4,500	68,000
November.........................	3,100	62,000
December.........................	6,500	73,000
Total.........................	57,600	$805,000

Chavez has received a request to bid on a 180-guest fundraising cocktail party to be given next month by an important local charity. (The party would last the usual three hours.) She would like to win this contract because the guest list for this charity event includes many prominent individuals that she would like to secure as future clients. Maria is confident that these potential customers would be favorably impressed by her company's services at the charity event.

Required:

1. Prepare a scattergraph plot that puts labor-hours on the X-axis and overhead expenses on the Y-axis. What insights are revealed by your scattergraph?

2. Use the least-squares regression method to estimate the fixed and variable components of overhead expenses. Express these estimates in the form $Y = a + bX$.

3. If Chavez charges her usual price of $31 per guest for the 180-guest cocktail party, how much contribution margin will she earn by serving this event?

4. How low could Chavez bid for the charity event in terms of a price per guest and still break even on the event itself?

5. The individual who is organizing the charity's fundraising event has indicated that he has already received a bid under $30 from another catering company. Do you think Chavez should bid below her normal $31 per guest price for the charity event? Why or why not?

(CMA, adapted)

Variable Costing and Segment Reporting: Tools for Management

Misguided Incentives in the Auto Industry

© Bloomberg/Getty Images

When the economy tanks, automakers, such as **General Motors** and **Chrysler**, often "flood the market" with a supply of vehicles that far exceeds customer demand. They pursue this course of action even though it tarnishes their brand image and increases their auto storage costs, tire replacement costs, customer rebate costs, and advertising costs. This begs the question why would managers knowingly produce more vehicles than are demanded by customers?

In the auto industry, a manager's bonus is often influenced by her company's reported profits; thus, there is a strong incentive to boost profits by producing more units. How can this be done you ask? It would seem logical that producing more units would have no impact on profits unless the units were sold, right? Wrong! As we will discover in this chapter, absorption costing—the most widely used method of determining unit product costs—can artificially increase profits when managers choose to increase the quantity of units produced. ■

Source: Marielle Segarra, "Lots of Trouble," *CFO*, March 2012, pp. 29–30.

LEARNING OBJECTIVES

After studying Chapter 6, you should be able to:

LO6–1 Explain how variable costing differs from absorption costing and compute unit product costs under each method.

LO6–2 Prepare income statements using both variable and absorption costing.

LO6–3 Reconcile variable costing and absorption costing net operating incomes and explain why the two amounts differ.

LO6–4 Prepare a segmented income statement that differentiates traceable fixed costs from common fixed costs and use it to make decisions.

LO6–5 Compute companywide and segment break-even points for a company with traceable fixed costs.

LO6–6 *(Appendix 6A) Prepare an income statement using super-variable costing and reconcile this approach with variable costing.*

This chapter describes two applications of the contribution format income statement that was introduced in earlier chapters. First, it explains how manufacturing companies can prepare *variable costing* income statements, which rely on the contribution format, for internal decision making purposes. The variable costing approach will be contrasted with *absorption costing* income statements, which are generally used for external reports. Ordinarily, variable costing and absorption costing produce different net operating income figures, and the difference can be quite large. In addition to showing how these two methods differ, we will describe the advantages of variable costing for internal reporting purposes and we will show how management decisions can be affected by the costing method chosen.

Second, the chapter explains how the contribution format can be used to prepare segmented income statements. In addition to companywide income statements, managers need to measure the profitability of individual *segments* of their organizations. A **segment** is a part or activity of an organization about which managers would like cost, revenue, or profit data. This chapter explains how to create contribution format income statements that report profit data for business segments, such as divisions, individual stores, geographic regions, customers, and product lines.

Overview of Variable and Absorption Costing

LO6–1

Explain how variable costing differs from absorption costing and compute unit product costs under each method.

As you begin to read about variable and absorption costing income statements in the coming pages, focus your attention on three key concepts. First, both income statement formats include product costs and period costs, although they define these cost classifications differently. Second, variable costing income statements are grounded in the contribution format. They categorize expenses based on cost behavior—variable expenses are reported separately from fixed expenses. Absorption costing income statements ignore variable and fixed cost distinctions. Third, as mentioned in the paragraph above, variable and absorption costing net operating incomes often differ from one another. The reason for the difference always relates to the fact that variable costing and absorption costing income statements account for fixed manufacturing overhead differently. *Pay very close attention to the two different ways that variable costing and absorption costing account for fixed manufacturing overhead.*

Variable Costing

Under **variable costing**, only those manufacturing costs that vary with output are treated as product costs. This would usually include direct materials, direct labor, and the variable portion of manufacturing overhead. Fixed manufacturing overhead is not treated as a product cost under this method. Rather, fixed manufacturing overhead is treated as a period cost and, like selling and administrative expenses, it is reported as an expense on the income statement in its entirety each period. Consequently, the cost of a unit of product in inventory or in cost of goods sold under the variable costing method does not contain any fixed manufacturing overhead cost. Variable costing is sometimes referred to as *direct costing* or *marginal costing*.

Absorption Costing

Absorption costing treats *all* manufacturing costs as product costs, regardless of whether they are variable or fixed. The cost of a unit of product under the absorption costing method consists of direct materials, direct labor, and *both* variable and fixed manufacturing overhead. Thus, absorption costing allocates a portion of fixed manufacturing overhead cost to each unit of product, along with the variable manufacturing costs. Because absorption costing includes all manufacturing costs in product costs, it is frequently referred to as the *full cost* method.

Selling and Administrative Expenses

Selling and administrative expenses are never treated as product costs, regardless of the costing method. Thus, under absorption and variable costing, variable and fixed selling and administrative expenses are always treated as period costs and are reported as expenses on the income statement as incurred.

Summary of Differences   The reason variable costing and absorption costing often report different net operating incomes, as illustrated in Exhibit 6–1, is because the two methods account for fixed manufacturing overhead costs differently—all other costs have the same affect on net operating income under the two methods. In absorption costing, fixed manufacturing overhead costs are included in work in process inventory. When units are completed, these costs are transferred to finished goods and only when the units are sold do these costs flow through to the income statement as part of cost of goods sold. In variable costing, fixed manufacturing overhead costs are considered to be period costs—just like selling and administrative costs—and are taken immediately to the income statement as period expenses.

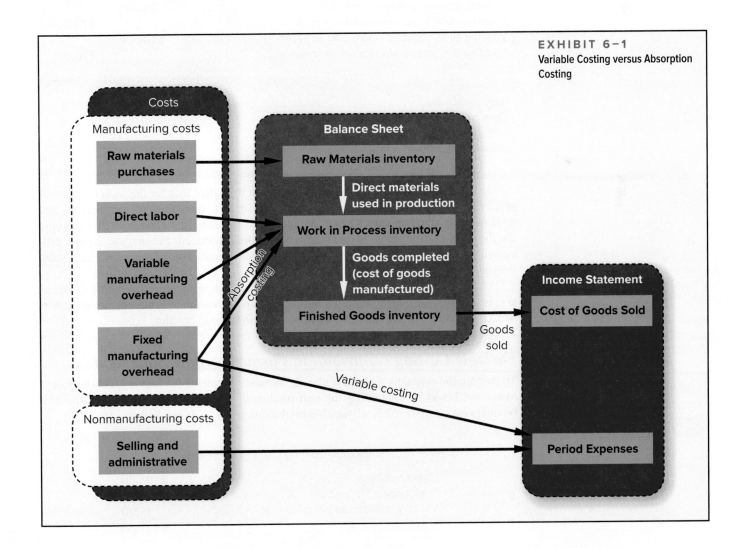

EXHIBIT 6–1
Variable Costing versus Absorption Costing

Variable and Absorption Costing—An Example

We will be making three simplifying assumptions throughout the forthcoming example and the entire chapter. First, this chapter uses *actual costing* rather than the *normal costing* approach that was used in the job-order costing chapters. In other words, rather than relying on predetermined overhead rates to apply overhead costs to products, this chapter assigns *actual* variable and fixed manufacturing overhead costs to products. Second, this chapter always uses the actual *number of units produced* as the allocation base for assigning actual fixed manufacturing overhead costs to products. Third, this chapter always assumes that the variable manufacturing costs per unit and the total fixed manufacturing overhead cost per period remain constant.

Having stated those assumptions, now let's illustrate the difference between variable costing and absorption costing by considering Weber Light Aircraft, a company that produces light recreational aircraft. Data concerning the company's operations appear below:

	Per Aircraft	Per Month
Selling price	$100,000	
Direct materials	$19,000	
Direct labor	$5,000	
Variable manufacturing overhead	$1,000	
Fixed manufacturing overhead		$70,000
Variable selling and administrative expense	$10,000	
Fixed selling and administrative expense		$20,000

	January	February	March
Beginning inventory	0	0	1
Units produced	1	2	4
Units sold	1	1	5
Ending inventory	0	1	0

As you review the data above, it is important to realize that for the months of January, February, and March, the selling price per aircraft, variable costs per aircraft, and total monthly fixed expenses never change. The only data that change in this example are the number of units produced (January = 1 unit produced; February = 2 units produced; March = 4 units produced) and the number of units sold (January = 1 unit sold; February = 1 unit sold; March = 5 units sold).

We will first construct the company's variable costing income statements for January, February, and March. Then we will show how the company's net operating income would be determined for the same months using absorption costing.

Variable Costing Contribution Format Income Statement

To prepare the company's variable costing income statements for January, February, and March we begin by computing the unit product cost. Under variable costing, the unit product cost consists solely of variable production costs as shown below:

Variable Costing Unit Product Cost	
Direct materials	$19,000
Direct labor	5,000
Variable manufacturing overhead	1,000
Unit product cost	$25,000

Because each month's unit product cost is $25,000 per aircraft, the variable costing cost of goods sold for all three months can be computed as follows:

Variable Costing Cost of Goods Sold	January	February	March
Unit product cost (a)	$25,000	$25,000	$25,000
Units sold (b)	1	1	5
Variable cost of goods sold (a) × (b).	$25,000	$25,000	$125,000

And the company's total selling and administrative expense would be derived as follows:

Selling and Administravtive Expenses	January	February	March
Variable selling and administrative expense (@ $10,000 per unit sold)	$10,000	$10,000	$50,000
Fixed selling and administrative expense	20,000	20,000	20,000
Total selling and administrative expense	$30,000	$30,000	$70,000

Putting it all together, the variable costing income statements would appear as shown in Exhibit 6–2. Notice, the contribution format has been used in these income statements. Also, the monthly fixed manufacturing overhead cost ($70,000) has been recorded as a period expense in the month incurred.

Variable Costing Contribution Format Income Statements	January	February	March
Sales	$100,000	$100,000	$500,000
Variable expenses:			
Variable cost of goods sold	25,000	25,000	125,000
Variable selling and administrative expense	10,000	10,000	50,000
Total variable expenses	35,000	35,000	175,000
Contribution margin	65,000	65,000	325,000
Fixed expenses:			
Fixed manufacturing overhead	70,000	70,000	70,000
Fixed selling and administrative expense . . .	20,000	20,000	20,000
Total fixed expenses	90,000	90,000	90,000
Net operating income (loss)	$ (25,000)	$ (25,000)	$235,000

EXHIBIT 6–2
Variable Costing Income Statements

A simple method for understanding how Weber Light Aircraft computed its variable costing net operating income for each month is to focus on the contribution margin per aircraft sold, which is computed as follows:

Contribution Margin per Aircraft Sold		
Selling price per aircraft.		$100,000
Variable cost of goods sold per aircraft.	$25,000	
Variable selling and administrative expense per aircraft	10,000	35,000
Contribution margin per aircraft		$ 65,000

The variable costing net operating income for each period can always be computed by multiplying the number of units sold by the contribution margin per unit and then subtracting total fixed expenses. For Weber Light Aircraft these computations would appear as follows:

	January	February	March
Number of aircraft sold.	1	1	5
Contribution margin per aircraft	× $ 65,000	× $ 65,000	× $ 65,000
Total contribution margin	$ 65,000	$ 65,000	$325,000
Total fixed expenses	90,000	90,000	90,000
Net operating income (loss).	$(25,000)	$(25,000)	$235,000

Notice, January and February have the same net operating loss. This occurs because one aircraft was sold in each month and, as previously mentioned, the selling price per aircraft, variable costs per aircraft, and total monthly fixed expenses remain constant.

Absorption Costing Income Statement

As we begin the absorption costing portion of the example, remember that the only reason absorption costing income differs from variable costing is that the two methods account for fixed manufacturing overhead differently. Under absorption costing, fixed manufacturing overhead is included in product costs. In variable costing, fixed manufacturing overhead is not included in product costs and instead is treated as a period expense just like selling and administrative expenses.

The first step in preparing Weber's absorption costing income statements for January, February, and March is to determine the company's unit product costs for each month as follows:

Absorption Costing Unit Product Cost			
	January	February	March
Direct materials	$19,000	$19,000	$19,000
Direct labor.	5,000	5,000	5,000
Variable manufacturing overhead	1,000	1,000	1,000
Fixed manufacturing overhead ($70,000 ÷ 1 unit produced in January; $70,000 ÷ 2 units produced in February; $70,000 ÷ 4 units produced in March) . . .	70,000	35,000	17,500
Unit product cost.	$95,000	$60,000	$42,500

Notice that in each month, Weber's fixed manufacturing overhead cost of $70,000 is divided by the number of units produced to determine the fixed manufacturing overhead cost per unit.

Given these unit product costs, the company's absorption costing net operating income in each month would be determined as shown in Exhibit 6–3.

The sales for all three months in Exhibit 6–3 are the same as the sales shown in the variable costing income statements. The January cost of goods sold consists of one unit produced during January at a cost of $95,000 according to the absorption costing system. The February cost of goods sold consists of one unit produced during February at a cost of $60,000 according to the absorption costing system. The March cost of goods sold ($230,000) consists of one unit produced during February at an absorption cost of $60,000 plus four units produced in March with a total absorption cost of $170,000

Absorption Costing Income Statements				EXHIBIT 6–3
	January	February	March	**Absorption Costing Income Statements**
Sales	$100,000	$100,000	$500,000	
Cost of goods sold ($95,000 × 1 unit; $60,000 × 1 unit; $60,000 × 1 unit + $42,500 × 4 units)....	95,000	60,000	230,000	
Gross margin	5,000	40,000	270,000	
Selling and administrative expenses	30,000	30,000	70,000	
Net operating income (loss)...............	$ (25,000)	$ 10,000	$200,000	

(= 4 units produced × $42,500 per unit). The selling and administrative expenses equal the amounts reported in the variable costing income statements; however they are reported as one amount rather than being separated into variable and fixed components.

Note that even though sales were exactly the same in January and February and the cost structure did not change, net operating income was $35,000 higher in February than in January under absorption costing. This occurs because one aircraft produced in February is not sold until March. This aircraft has $35,000 of fixed manufacturing overhead attached to it that was incurred in February, but will not be recorded as part of cost of goods sold until March.

Contrasting the variable costing and absorption costing income statements in Exhibits 6–2 and 6–3, note that net operating income is the same in January under variable costing and absorption costing, but differs in the other two months. We will discuss this in more depth shortly. Also note that the format of the variable costing income statement differs from the absorption costing income statement. An absorption costing income statement categorizes costs by function—manufacturing versus selling and administrative. All of the manufacturing costs flow through the absorption costing cost of goods sold and all of the selling and administrative expenses are listed separately as period expenses. In contrast, in the contribution approach, costs are categorized according to how they behave. All of the variable expenses are listed together and all of the fixed expenses are listed together. The variable expenses category includes manufacturing costs (i.e., variable cost of goods sold) as well as selling and administrative expenses. The fixed expenses category also includes both manufacturing costs and selling and administrative expenses.

IN BUSINESS

SUPER GLUE: THE VARIABLE OVERHEAD COST THAT HOLDS OUR PRODUCTS TOGETHER

Adhesives are gradually replacing welds, rivets, screws, and bolts in automobiles and airplanes. For companies that manufacture structural adhesives, such as Henkel AG, Dow Chemical, and 3M, the 4%–5% annual growth rate in this $2 billion market is good news. Automakers are replacing heavy metal fasteners with lighter adhesives in an effort to meet tougher fuel-economy standards. For example, the Ford Motor Company's F-150 pickup truck is using three times as much adhesive as prior models. In the aerospace industry, the Boeing 787 Dreamliner uses between 200,000 and 250,000 fewer metal fasteners than conventional airplanes thanks to its reliance on structural adhesives, which in turn lightens the plane and lowers fuel costs.

Source: James R. Hagerty and Mike Ramsey, "Super Glues, Not Bolts, Hold Cars Together," *The Wall Street Journal*, September 9, 2014, pp. B1 and B4.

Reconciliation of Variable Costing with Absorption Costing Income

As noted earlier, variable costing and absorption costing net operating incomes may not be the same. In the case of Weber Light Aircraft, the net operating incomes are the same in January, but differ in the other two months. These differences occur because under absorption costing some fixed manufacturing overhead is capitalized in inventories (i.e., included in product costs) rather than being immediately expensed on the income statement. If inventories increase during a period, under absorption costing some of the fixed manufacturing overhead of the current period will be *deferred* in ending inventories. For example, in February two aircraft were produced and each carried with it $35,000 (= $70,000 ÷ 2 aircraft produced) in fixed manufacturing overhead. Since only one aircraft was sold, $35,000 of this fixed manufacturing overhead was on February's absorption costing income statement as part of cost of goods sold, whereas the other $35,000 attached to the unsold aircraft would be included in February's ending finished goods inventory on the balance sheet. In contrast, under variable costing *all* of the $70,000 of fixed manufacturing overhead appeared on the February income statement as a period expense. Consequently, net operating income was higher under absorption costing than under variable costing by $35,000 in February. This was reversed in March when four units were produced, but five were sold. In March, under absorption costing $105,000 of fixed manufacturing overhead was included in cost of goods sold ($35,000 for the unit produced in February and sold in March plus $17,500 for each of the four units produced and sold in March), but only $70,000 was recognized as a period expense under variable costing. Hence, the net operating income in March was $35,000 lower under absorption costing than under variable costing.

In general, when the units produced exceed the units sold and hence inventories increase, net operating income is higher under absorption costing than under variable costing. This occurs because some of the fixed manufacturing overhead of the period is *deferred* in inventories under absorption costing. In contrast, when the units sold exceed the units produced and hence inventories decrease, net operating income is lower under absorption costing than under variable costing. This occurs because some of the fixed manufacturing overhead of previous periods is *released* from inventories under absorption costing. When the units produced and the units sold are equal, no change in inventories occurs and absorption costing and variable costing net operating incomes are the same.[1]

Variable costing and absorption costing net operating incomes can be reconciled by determining how much fixed manufacturing overhead was deferred in, or released from, inventories during the period:

Fixed Manufacturing Overhead Deferred in, or Released from, Inventories under Absorption Costing			
	January	February	March
Fixed manufacturing overhead in ending inventories	$0	$35,000	$ 0
Deduct: Fixed manufacturing overhead in beginning inventories.	0	0	35,000
Fixed manufacturing overhead deferred in (released from) inventories	$0	$35,000	$(35,000)

---

[1] These general statements about the relation between variable costing and absorption costing net operating income assume LIFO is used to value inventories. Even when LIFO is not used, the general statements tend to be correct. Although U.S. GAAP allows LIFO and FIFO inventory flow assumptions, International Financial Reporting Standards do not allow a LIFO inventory flow assumption.

Reconciliation of Variable Costing and Absorption Costing Net Operating Incomes			
	January	February	March
Variable costing net operating income (loss)	$(25,000)	$(25,000)	$235,000
Add (deduct) fixed manufacturing overhead deferred in (released from) inventory under absorption costing	0	35,000	(35,000)
Absorption costing net operating income (loss). . .	$(25,000)	$ 10,000	$200,000

EXHIBIT 6–4
Reconciliation of Variable Costing and Absorption Costing Net Operating Incomes

In equation form, the fixed manufacturing overhead that is deferred in or released from inventories can be determined as follows:

$$\begin{array}{c} \text{Manufacturing overhead} \\ \text{deferred in} \\ \text{(released from) inventory} \end{array} = \begin{array}{c} \text{Fixed manufacturing} \\ \text{overhead in} \\ \text{ending inventories} \end{array} - \begin{array}{c} \text{Fixed manufacturing} \\ \text{overhead in} \\ \text{beginning inventories} \end{array}$$

The reconciliation would then be reported as shown in Exhibit 6–4.

Again note that the difference between variable costing net operating income and absorption costing net operating income is entirely due to the amount of fixed manufacturing overhead that is deferred in, or released from, inventories during the period under absorption costing. Changes in inventories affect absorption costing net operating income—they do not affect variable costing net operating income, providing that variable manufacturing costs per unit are stable.

The reasons for differences between variable and absorption costing net operating incomes are summarized in Exhibit 6–5. When the units produced equal the units sold, as in January for Weber Light Aircraft, absorption costing net operating income will equal

Relation between Production and Sales for the Period	Effect on Inventories	Relation between Absorption and Variable Costing Net Operating Incomes
Units produced = Units sold	No change in inventories	Absorption costing net operating income = Variable costing net operating income
Units produced > Units sold	Inventories increase	Absorption costing net operating income > Variable costing net operating income*
Units produced < Units sold	Inventories decrease	Absorption costing net operating income < Variable costing net operating income'

*Net operating income is higher under absorption costing because fixed manufacturing overhead cost is *deferred* in inventory under absorption costing as inventories increase.
' Net operating income is lower under absorption costing because fixed manufacturing overhead cost is *released* from inventory under absorption costing as inventories decrease.

EXHIBIT 6–5
Comparative Income Effects—Absorption and Variable Costing

variable costing net operating income. This occurs because when production equals sales, all of the fixed manufacturing overhead incurred in the current period flows through to the income statement under both methods. For companies that use Lean Production, the number of units produced tends to equal the number of units sold. This occurs because goods are produced in response to customer orders, thereby eliminating finished goods inventories and reducing work in process inventory to almost nothing. So, when a company uses Lean Production differences in variable costing and absorption costing net operating income will largely disappear.

When the units produced exceed the units sold, absorption costing net operating income will exceed variable costing net operating income. This occurs because inventories have increased; therefore, under absorption costing some of the fixed manufacturing overhead incurred in the current period is deferred in ending inventories on the balance sheet, whereas under variable costing all of the fixed manufacturing overhead incurred in the current period flows through to the income statement. In contrast, when the units produced are less than the units sold, absorption costing net operating income will be less than variable costing net operating income. This occurs because inventories have decreased; therefore, under absorption costing fixed manufacturing overhead that had been deferred in inventories during a prior period flows through to the current period's income statement together with all of the fixed manufacturing overhead incurred during the current period. Under variable costing, just the fixed manufacturing overhead of the current period flows through to the income statement.

INVENTORY MANAGEMENT IS A DELICATE BALANCING ACT

Manufacturers are constantly striving to maintain optimal inventories. If they make too many units, it ties up working capital, whereas if they make too few units it can lead to lengthy customer delivery times and lost sales. The same challenges hold true for merchandisers such as Seattle-based web retailer **Zulily**. The company had been ordering items from vendors only after its customers ordered them. While this approach helped Zulily avoid the need to store inventories, it also led to order delivery times ranging from 14–18 days—which pales in comparison to **Amazon.com**, **QVC**, and **overstock.com** whose order delivery times range from 2–5 days.

To shorten its delivery times. Zulily decided to order and store items from vendors prior to their sale to end consumers. Although the items will reside in Zulily's warehouses, the goods will not be recorded on the company's balance sheet. The vendors will continue to own the merchandise stored in Zulily's warehouses until it is sold to end consumers.

Source: Serena Ng, "Zulily Nips Business Model in the Bud," *The Wall Street Journal*, March 24, 2015, p. B4.

Advantages of Variable Costing and the Contribution Approach

Variable costing, together with the contribution approach, offers appealing advantages for internal reports. This section discusses three of those advantages.

Enabling CVP Analysis

Cost-volume-profit (CVP) analysis requires that we break costs down into their variable and fixed components. Because variable costing income statements categorize costs as variable and fixed, it is much easier to use this income statement format to perform CVP analysis than attempting to use the absorption costing format, which mixes together variable and fixed costs.

Moreover, absorption costing net operating income may or may not agree with the results of CVP analysis. For example, let's suppose that you are interested in computing the sales that would be necessary to attain a target profit of $235,000 at Weber Light Aircraft. A CVP analysis based on the January variable costing income statement from Exhibit 6–2 would proceed as follows:

Sales (a).............................	$100,000
Contribution margin (b)...............	$65,000
Contribution margin ratio (b) ÷ (a).......	65%
Total fixed expenses.................	$90,000

$$\text{Dollar sales to attain target profit} = \frac{\text{Target profit} + \text{Fixed expenses}}{\text{CM ratio}}$$

$$= \frac{\$235,000 + \$90,000}{0.65} = \$500,000$$

Thus, a CVP analysis based on the January variable costing income statement predicts that the net operating income would be $235,000 when sales are $500,000. And indeed, the net operating income under variable costing *is* $235,000 when the sales are $500,000 in March. However, the net operating income under absorption costing is *not* $235,000 in March, even though the sales are $500,000. Why is this? The reason is that under absorption costing, net operating income can be distorted by changes in inventories. In March, inventories decreased, so some of the fixed manufacturing overhead that had been deferred in February's ending inventories was released to the March income statement, resulting in a net operating income that is $35,000 lower than the $235,000 predicted by CVP analysis. If inventories had increased in March, the opposite would have occurred—the absorption costing net operating income would have been higher than the $235,000 predicted by CVP analysis.

Explaining Changes in Net Operating Income

The variable costing income statements in Exhibit 6–2 are clear and easy to understand. All other things the same, when sales go up, net operating income goes up. When sales go down, net operating income goes down. When sales are constant, net operating income is constant. The number of units produced does not affect net operating income.

Absorption costing income statements can be confusing and are easily misinterpreted. Look again at the absorption costing income statements in Exhibit 6–3. A manager might wonder why net operating income went up from January to February even though sales were exactly the same. Was it a result of lower selling costs, more efficient operations, or was it some other factor? In fact, it was simply because the number of units produced exceeded the number of units sold in February and so some of the fixed manufacturing overhead costs were deferred in inventories in that month. These costs have not gone away—they will eventually flow through to the income statement in a later period when inventories go down. There is no way to tell this from the absorption costing income statements.

To avoid mistakes when absorption costing is used, readers of financial statements should be alert to changes in inventory levels. Under absorption costing, if inventories increase, fixed manufacturing overhead costs are deferred in inventories, which in turn increases net operating income. If inventories decrease, fixed manufacturing overhead costs are released from inventories, which in turn decreases net operating income. Thus, when absorption costing is used, fluctuations in net operating income can be caused by changes in inventories as well as changes in unit sales.

Supporting Decision Making

The variable costing method correctly identifies the additional variable costs that will be incurred to make one more unit. It also emphasizes the impact of fixed costs on profits. The total amount of fixed manufacturing costs appears explicitly on the income statement, highlighting that the whole amount of fixed manufacturing costs must be covered for the company to be truly profitable. In the Weber Light Aircraft example, the variable costing income statements correctly report that the cost of producing another unit is $25,000 and they explicitly recognize that $70,000 of fixed manufactured overhead must be covered to earn a profit.

Under absorption costing, fixed manufacturing overhead costs appear to be variable with respect to the number of units sold, but they are not. For example, in January, the absorption unit product cost at Weber Light Aircraft is $95,000, but the variable portion of this cost is only $25,000. The fixed overhead costs of $70,000 are commingled with variable production costs, thereby obscuring the impact of fixed overhead costs on profits. Because absorption unit product costs are stated on a per unit basis, managers may mistakenly believe that if another unit is produced, it will cost the company $95,000. But of course it would not. The cost of producing another unit would be only $25,000. Misinterpreting absorption unit product costs as variable can lead to many problems, including inappropriate pricing decisions and decisions to drop products that are in fact profitable.

Segmented Income Statements and the Contribution Approach

LO6–4
Prepare a segmented income statement that differentiates traceable fixed costs from common fixed costs and use it to make decisions.

In the remainder of the chapter, we'll learn how to use the contribution approach to construct income statements for business segments. These segmented income statements are useful for analyzing the profitability of segments, making decisions, and measuring the performance of segment managers.

Traceable and Common Fixed Costs and the Segment Margin

You need to understand three new terms to prepare segmented income statements using the contribution approach—*traceable fixed cost, common fixed cost,* and *segment margin.*

A **traceable fixed cost** of a segment is a fixed cost that is incurred because of the existence of the segment—if the segment had never existed, the fixed cost would not have been incurred; and if the segment were eliminated, the fixed cost would disappear. Examples of traceable fixed costs include the following:

- The salary of the Fritos product manager at **PepsiCo** is a *traceable* fixed cost of the Fritos business segment of PepsiCo.
- The maintenance cost for the building in which Boeing 747s are assembled is a *traceable* fixed cost of the 747 business segment of **Boeing**.
- The liability insurance at Disney World is a *traceable* fixed cost of the Disney World business segment of **The Walt Disney Corporation**.

A **common fixed cost** is a fixed cost that supports the operations of more than one segment, but is not traceable in whole or in part to any one segment. Even if a segment were entirely eliminated, there would be no change in a true common fixed cost. For example:

- The salary of the CEO of **General Motors** is a *common* fixed cost of the various divisions of General Motors.
- The cost of heating a **Safeway** or **Kroger** grocery store is a *common* fixed cost of the store's various departments—groceries, produce, bakery, meat, and so forth.
- The cost of the receptionist's salary at an office shared by a number of doctors is a *common* fixed cost of the doctors. The cost is traceable to the office, but not to individual doctors.

To prepare a segmented income statement, variable expenses are deducted from sales to yield the contribution margin for the segment. The contribution margin tells us what happens to profits as sales volume changes—holding a segment's capacity and fixed costs constant. The contribution margin is especially useful in decisions involving temporary uses of capacity such as special orders. These types of decisions often involve only sales and variable costs—the two components of contribution margin.

The **segment margin** is obtained by deducting the traceable fixed costs of a segment from the segment's contribution margin. It represents the margin available after a segment has covered all of its own costs. *The segment margin is the best gauge of the long-run profitability of a segment* because it includes only those costs that are caused by the segment. If a segment can't cover its own costs, then that segment probably should be dropped (unless it has important side effects on other segments). Notice, common fixed costs are not allocated to segments.

From a decision-making point of view, the segment margin is most useful in major decisions that affect capacity such as dropping a segment. By contrast, as we noted earlier, the contribution margin is most useful in decisions involving short-run changes in sales volume, such as pricing special orders that involve temporary use of existing capacity.

J. C. PENNEY IS BRINGING BACK ITS CATALOG

In 2010, **J.C. Penney** discontinued its catalog that was first published and distributed in 1963. However, once the company realized that many of its online sales came from customers responding to what they saw in print, it reintroduced the catalog in 2015. In other words, J.C. Penney realized that catalog shoppers and internet shoppers are not independent customer segments. If retailers such as J.C. Penney separately analyze catalog sales and internet sales, they may discontinue the catalogs segment while overlooking the adverse impact of this decision on internet segment margins.

Source: Suzanne Kapner, "Catalog Makes a Comeback at Penney," *The Wall Street Journal,* January 20, 2015, pp. B1 and B7.

© TRBfoto/Getty Images RF

Identifying Traceable Fixed Costs

The distinction between traceable and common fixed costs is crucial in segment reporting because traceable fixed costs are charged to segments and common fixed costs are not. In an actual situation, it is sometimes hard to determine whether a cost should be classified as traceable or common.

The general guideline is to treat as traceable costs *only those costs that would disappear over time if the segment itself disappeared.* For example, if one division within a company were sold or discontinued, it would no longer be necessary to pay that division manager's salary. Therefore the division manager's salary would be classified as a traceable fixed cost of the division. On the other hand, the president of the company undoubtedly would continue to be paid even if one of many divisions was dropped. In fact, he or she might even be paid more if dropping the division was a good idea. Therefore, the president's salary is common to the company's divisions and should not be charged to them.

When assigning costs to segments, the key point is to resist the temptation to allocate costs (such as depreciation of corporate facilities) that are clearly common and that will continue regardless of whether the segment exists or not. *Any allocation of common costs to segments reduces the value of the segment margin as a measure of long-run segment profitability and segment performance.*

Traceable Fixed Costs Can Become Common Fixed Costs

Fixed costs that are traceable to one segment may be a common cost of another segment. For example, **United Airlines** might want a segmented income statement that shows the segment margin for a particular flight from Chicago to Paris further broken down into first-class, business-class, and economy-class segment margins. The airline must pay a substantial landing fee at Charles DeGaulle airport in Paris. This fixed landing fee is a traceable cost of the flight, but it is a common cost of the first-class, business-class, and economy-class segments. Even if the first-class cabin is empty, the entire landing fee must be paid. So the landing fee is not a traceable cost of the first-class cabin. But on the other hand, paying the fee is necessary in order to have any first-class, business-class, or economy-class passengers. So the landing fee is a common cost of these three classes.

SEGMENT REPORTING AT THE VILAR PERFORMING ARTS CENTER

The **Vilar Performing Arts Center** is a 535-seat theater located in Beaver Creek, Colorado, that presents an unusually wide variety of performances categorized into six business segments—Family Series, Broadway Series, Theatre/Comedy Series, Dance Series, Classical Series, and Concert Series. The executive director of the Vilar, Kris Sabel, must decide which shows to book, what financial terms to offer to the artists, what contributions are likely from underwriters (i.e., donors), and what prices to charge for tickets. He evaluates the profitability of the segments using segmented income statements that include traceable costs (such as the costs of transporting, lodging, and feeding the artists) and exclude common costs (such as his salary, the salaries of his staff, depreciation on the theater, and general marketing expenses).

Data concerning the Classical Series segment for one season appears below:

Number of shows		4
Number of seats budgeted		863
Number of seats sold		655
Average seats sold per show		164
Ticket sales.	$46,800	
Underwriting (donors).	65,000	
Total revenue		$111,800
Artists fees	$78,870	
Other traceable expenses	11,231	
Total expenses.		90,101
Classical Series segment margin		$ 21,699

Although the Classical Series sold an average of only 164 seats per show, its overall segment margin ($21,699) is positive thanks to $65,000 of underwriting revenues from donors. Had common costs been allocated to the Classical Series, it may have appeared unprofitable and been discontinued—resulting in fewer shows during the season; less diverse programming; disappointment among a small, but dedicated, number of fans; and lower overall income for the Vilar due to the loss of its Classical Series segment margin.

Segmented Income Statements—An Example

ProphetMax, Inc., is a rapidly growing computer software company. Exhibit 6–6 shows its variable costing income statement for the most recent month. As the company has grown, its senior managers have asked for segmented income statements that could be used to make decisions and evaluate managerial performance. ProphetMax's controller responded by creating examples of contribution format income statements segmented by the company's divisions, product lines, and sales channels. She created Exhibit 6–7 to explain that ProphetMax's profits can be segmented into its two divisions—the Business Products Division and the Consumer Products Division. The Consumer Products Division's profits can be further segmented into the Clip Art and Computer Games product lines. Finally, the Computer Games product line's profits (within the Consumer Products Division) can be segmented into the Online Sales and Retail Stores sales channels.

EXHIBIT 6–6
ProphetMax, Inc. Variable Costing Income Statement

ProphetMax, Inc.
Variable Costing Income Statement

Sales	$500,000
Variable expenses:	
Variable cost of goods sold	180,000
Other variable expenses	50,000
Total variable expenses	230,000
Contribution margin	270,000
Fixed expenses	256,500
Net operating income	$ 13,500

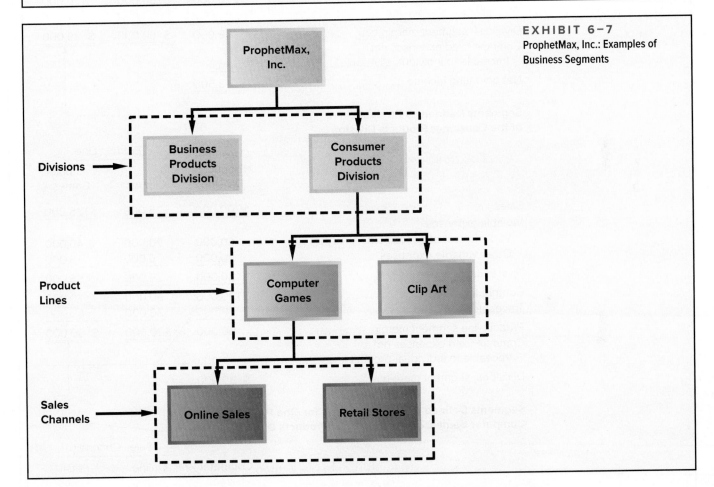

EXHIBIT 6–7
ProphetMax, Inc.: Examples of Business Segments

Levels of Segmented Income Statements

Exhibit 6–8 contains the controller's segmented income statements for the segments depicted in Exhibit 6–7. The contribution format income statement for the entire company appears at the very top of the exhibit under the column labeled Total Company. Notice, the net operating income shown in this column ($13,500) is the same as the net operating income shown in Exhibit 6–6. Immediately to the right of the Total Company column are two columns—one for each of the two divisions. We can see that the Business Products Division's traceable fixed expenses are $90,000 and the Consumer Products Division's are $81,000. These $171,000 of traceable fixed expenses (as shown in the Total Company column) plus the $85,500 of common fixed expenses not traceable to individual divisions equals ProphetMax's total fixed expenses ($256,500) as shown in Exhibit 6–6. We can also

EXHIBIT 6–8
ProphetMax, Inc.—Segmented
Income Statements in the
Contribution Format

Segments Defined as Divisions

	Total Company	Divisions	
		Business Products Division	Consumer Products Division
Sales	$500,000	$300,000	$200,000
Variable expenses:			
Variable cost of goods sold	180,000	120,000	60,000
Other variable expenses	50,000	30,000	20,000
Total variable expenses	230,000	150,000	80,000
Contribution margin	270,000	150,000	120,000
Traceable fixed expenses	171,000	90,000	81,000
Divisional segment margin	99,000	$ 60,000	$ 39,000
Common fixed expenses not traceable to individual divisions	85,500		
Net operating income	$ 13,500		

**Segments Defined as Product Lines
of the Consumer Products Division**

	Consumer Products Division	Product Line	
		Clip Art	Computer Games
Sales	$200,000	$75,000	$125,000
Variable expenses:			
Variable cost of goods sold	60,000	20,000	40,000
Other variable expenses	20,000	5,000	15,000
Total variable expenses	80,000	25,000	55,000
Contribution margin	120,000	50,000	70,000
Traceable fixed expenses	70,000	30,000	40,000
Product-line segment margin	50,000	$20,000	$ 30,000
Common fixed expenses not traceable to individual product lines ...	11,000		
Divisional segment margin	$ 39,000		

**Segments Defined as Sales Channels for One Product Line,
Computer Games, of the Consumer Products Division**

	Computer Games	Sales Channels	
		Online Sales	Retail Stores
Sales	$125,000	$100,000	$25,000
Variable expenses:			
Variable cost of goods sold	40,000	32,000	8,000
Other variable expenses	15,000	5,000	10,000
Total variable expenses	55,000	37,000	18,000
Contribution margin	70,000	63,000	7,000
Traceable fixed expenses	25,000	15,000	10,000
Sales-channel segment margin	45,000	$ 48,000	$ (3,000)
Common fixed expenses not traceable to individual sales channels ...	15,000		
Product-line segment margin	$ 30,000		

see that the Business Products Division's segment margin is $60,000 and the Consumer Products Division's is $39,000. These segment margins show the company's divisional managers how much each of their divisions is contributing to the company's profits.

The middle portion of Exhibit 6–8 further segments the Consumer Products Division into its two product lines—Clip Art and Computer Games. The dual nature of some fixed costs can be seen in this portion of the exhibit. Notice, in the top portion of Exhibit 6–8 when segments are defined as divisions, the Consumer Products Division has $81,000 in traceable fixed expenses. However, when we drill down to the product lines (in the middle portion of the exhibit), only $70,000 of the $81,000 expense that was traceable to the Consumer Products Division is traceable to the product lines. The other $11,000 becomes a common fixed expense of the two product lines of the Consumer Products Division.

Why would $11,000 of traceable fixed expense become a common fixed expense when the division is divided into product lines? The $11,000 is the monthly depreciation expense on a machine that is used to encase products in tamper-proof packages for the consumer market. The depreciation expense is a traceable cost of the Consumer Products Division as a whole, but it is a common cost of the division's two product lines. Even if one of the product lines were discontinued entirely, the machine would still be used to wrap the remaining products. Therefore, none of the depreciation expense can really be traced to individual products. Conversely, the $70,000 traceable fixed expense can be traced to the individual product lines because it consists of the costs of product-specific advertising. A total of $30,000 was spent on advertising clip art and $40,000 was spent on advertising computer programs.

The bottom portion of Exhibit 6–8 further segments the Computer Games product line into two sales channels—Online Sales and Retail Stores. The dual nature of some fixed costs can also be seen in this portion of the exhibit. In the middle portion of Exhibit 6–8 when segments are defined as product lines, the Computer Games product line has $40,000 in traceable fixed expenses. However, when we look at the sales channels in the bottom portion of the exhibit, only $25,000 of the $40,000 that was traceable to Computer Games is traceable to the sales channels. The other $15,000 becomes a common fixed expense of the two sales channels for the Computer Games product line.

Segmented Income Statements—Decision Making and Break-Even Analysis

Once a company prepares contribution format segmented income statements, it can use those statements to make decisions and perform break-even analysis.

Decision Making

Let's refer again to the bottom portion of Exhibit 6–8 to illustrate how segmented income statements support decision making. Notice that the Online Sales segment has a segment margin of $48,000 and the Retail Stores segment has a segment margin of $(3,000). Let's assume that ProphetMax wants to know the profit impact of discontinuing the sale of computer games through its Retail Stores sales channel. The company believes that Online Sales of its computer games will increase 10% if it discontinues the Retail Stores sales channel. It also believes that the Business Products Division and Clip Art product line will be unaffected by this decision. How would you compute the profit impact of this decision?

The first step is to calculate the profit impact of discontinuing the Retail Stores sales channel. If this sales channel is eliminated, we assume its sales, variable expenses, and traceable fixed expenses would all go away. The quickest way to summarize these financial impacts is to focus on the Retail Stores' segment margin. In other words, if the Retail Stores sales channel discontinued, then its negative segment margin of $3,000 would also be avoided. This would increase ProphetMax's net operating income by $3,000. The second step is to calculate the profit impact of increasing Online Sales of computer games by 10%. To perform this calculation, we assume that the Online Sales total traceable fixed expenses ($15,000) remain constant and its contribution margin ratio remains constant at 63% (= $63,000 ÷ $100,000). If Online Sales increase $10,000 (= $100,000 × 10%), then the Online Sales segment's contribution margin will increase by \$6,300 (= \$10,000 × 63%). The overall profit impact of discontinuing the Retail Stores sales channel can be summarized as follows:

Avoidance of the Retail Stores' segment loss	\$3,000
Increase in Online Sales contribution margin.	6,300
Increase in ProphetMax's net operating income	\$9,300

Break-Even Analysis

LO6–5

Compute companywide and segment break-even points for a company with traceable fixed costs.

In Chapter 5, we learned how to compute a companywide break-even point for a multiproduct company with no traceable fixed expenses. Now we are going to use the ProphetMax, Inc., data in Exhibit 6–8 to explain how to compute companywide and segment break-even points for a company with traceable fixed expenses. Beginning with the companywide perspective, the formula for computing the break-even point for a multiproduct company with traceable fixed expenses is as follows:

$$\text{Dollar sales for company to break even} = \frac{\text{Traceable fixed expenses} + \text{Common fixed expenses}}{\text{Overall CM ratio}}$$

In the case of ProphetMax, we should begin by reviewing the information in the Total Company column in the top portion of Exhibit 6–8. This column of data indicates that ProphetMax's total traceable fixed expenses are \$171,000 and its total common fixed expenses are \$85,500. Furthermore, the company's overall contribution margin of \$270,000 divided by its total sales of \$500,000 equals its overall CM ratio of 0.54. Given this information, ProphetMax's companywide break-even point is computed as follows:

$$\text{Dollar sales for company to break even} = \frac{\text{Traceable fixed expenses} + \text{Common fixed expenses}}{\text{Overall CM ratio}}$$

$$= \frac{\$171,000 + \$85,500}{0.54}$$

$$= \frac{\$256,500}{0.54}$$

$$= \$475,000$$

It is important to emphasize that this computation assumes a constant sales mix. In other words, in the ProphetMax example, it assumes that 60% of the total sales (\$300,000 ÷ \$500,000) will always come from the Business Products Division and 40% of the total sales (\$200,000 ÷ \$500,000) will always come from the Consumer Products Division.

To compute the break-even point for a business segment, the formula is as follows:

$$\text{Dollar sales for a segment to break even} = \frac{\text{Segment traceable fixed expenses}}{\text{Segment CM ratio}}$$

In the case of ProphetMax's Business Products Division, we should begin by reviewing the information in the Business Products Division column in the top portion of Exhibit 6–8. This column of data indicates that the Business Products Division's traceable fixed expenses are \$90,000 and its CM ratio is 0.50 (\$150,000 ÷ \$300,000). Given this information, the Business Products Division's break-even point is computed as follows:

$$\text{Dollar sales for a segment to break even} = \frac{\text{Segment traceable fixed expenses}}{\text{Segment CM ratio}}$$

$$= \frac{\$90,000}{0.50}$$

$$= \$180,000$$

The same calculation can be performed for the Consumer Products Division using data from the Consumer Products Division column in the top portion of Exhibit 6–8. Given that the Consumer Products Division's traceable fixed expenses are $81,000 and its CM ratio is 0.60 ($120,000 ÷ $200,000), its break-even point is computed as follows:

$$\text{Dollar sales for a segment to break even} = \frac{\text{Segment traceable fixed expenses}}{\text{Segment CM ratio}}$$

$$= \frac{\$81,000}{0.60}$$

$$= \$135,000$$

Notice that the sum of the segment break-even sales figures of $315,000 ($180,000 + $135,000) is less than the companywide break-even point of $475,000. This occurs because the segment break-even calculations *do not include the company's common fixed expenses.* The exclusion of the company's common fixed expenses can be verified by preparing income statements based on each segment's break-even dollar sales as follows:

	Total Company	Business Products Division	Consumer Products Division
Sales	$315,000	$180,000	$135,000
Variable expenses	144,000	90,000	54,000
Contribution margin	171,000	90,000	81,000
Traceable fixed expenses	171,000	90,000	81,000
Segment margin	0	$ 0	$ 0
Common fixed expenses	85,500		
Net operating loss	$ (85,500)		

When each segment achieves its break-even point, the company's overall net operating loss of $85,500 equals its common fixed expenses of $85,500. This reality can often lead managers astray when making decisions. In an attempt to "cover the company's common fixed expenses," managers will often allocate common fixed expenses to business segments when performing break-even calculations and making decisions. *This is a mistake!* Allocating common fixed expenses to business segments artificially inflates each segment's break-even point. This may cause managers to erroneously discontinue business segments where the inflated break-even point appears unobtainable. The decision to retain or discontinue a business segment should be based on the sales and expenses that would disappear if the segment were dropped. Because common fixed expenses *will persist even if a business segment is dropped,* they should not be allocated to business segments when making decisions.

Segmented Income Statements—Common Mistakes

All of the costs attributable to a segment—and only those costs—should be assigned to the segment. Unfortunately, companies often make mistakes when assigning costs to segments. They omit some costs, inappropriately assign traceable fixed costs, and arbitrarily allocate common fixed costs.

Omission of Costs

The costs assigned to a segment should include all costs attributable to that segment from the company's entire value chain. All of these functions, from research and development, through product design, manufacturing, marketing, distribution, and customer service, are required to bring a product or service to the customer and generate sales.

However, only manufacturing costs are included in product costs under absorption costing, which is widely regarded as required for external financial reporting. To avoid having to maintain two costing systems and to provide consistency between internal and external reports, many companies also use absorption costing for their internal reports such as segmented income statements. As a result, such companies omit from their profitability analysis part or all of the "upstream" costs in the value chain, which consist of research and development and product design, and the "downstream" costs, which consist of marketing, distribution, and customer service. Yet these nonmanufacturing costs are just as essential in determining product profitability as are the manufacturing costs. These upstream and downstream costs, which are usually included in selling and administrative expenses on absorption costing income statements, can represent half or more of the total costs of an organization. If either the upstream or downstream costs are omitted in profitability analysis, then the product is undercosted and management may unwittingly develop and maintain products that in the long run result in losses.

Inappropriate Methods for Assigning Traceable Costs among Segments

In addition to omitting costs, many companies do not correctly handle traceable fixed expenses on segmented income statements. First, they do not trace fixed expenses to segments even when it is feasible to do so. Second, they use inappropriate allocation bases to allocate traceable fixed expenses to segments.

Failure to Trace Costs Directly   Costs that can be traced directly to a specific segment should be charged directly to that segment and should not be allocated to other segments. For example, the rent for a branch office of an insurance company should be charged directly to the branch office rather than included in a companywide overhead pool and then spread throughout the company.

Inappropriate Allocation Base   Some companies use arbitrary allocation bases to allocate costs to segments. For example, some companies allocate selling and administrative expenses on the basis of sales revenues. Thus, if a segment generates 20% of total company sales, it would be allocated 20% of the company's selling and administrative expenses as its "fair share." This same basic procedure is followed if cost of goods sold or some other measure is used as the allocation base.

Costs should be allocated to segments for internal decision-making purposes only when the allocation base actually drives the cost being allocated (or is very highly correlated with the real cost driver). For example, sales should be used to allocate selling and administrative expenses only if a 10% increase in sales will result in a 10% increase in selling and administrative expenses. To the extent that selling and administrative expenses are not driven by sales volume, these expenses will be improperly allocated—with a disproportionately high percentage of the selling and administrative expenses assigned to the segments with the largest sales.

Arbitrarily Dividing Common Costs among Segments

The third business practice that leads to distorted segment costs is the practice of assigning nontraceable costs to segments. For example, some companies allocate the common costs of the corporate headquarters building to products on segment reports. However, in a multiproduct company, no single product is likely to be responsible for any significant amount of this cost. Even if a product were eliminated entirely, there would usually be no significant effect on any of the costs of the corporate headquarters building. In short, there is no cause-and-effect relation between the cost of the corporate headquarters building and the existence of any one product. As a consequence, any allocation of the cost of the corporate headquarters building to the products must be arbitrary.

Common costs like the costs of the corporate headquarters building are necessary, of course, to have a functioning organization. The practice of arbitrarily allocating common costs to segments is often justified on the grounds that "someone" has to "cover the common costs." While it is undeniably true that a company must cover its common costs to earn a profit, arbitrarily allocating common costs to segments does not ensure that this will happen. In fact, adding a share of common costs to the real costs of a segment may make an otherwise profitable segment appear to be unprofitable. If a manager eliminates the apparently unprofitable segment, the real traceable costs of the segment will be saved, but its sales will be lost. And what happens to the common fixed costs that were allocated to the segment? They don't disappear; they are reallocated to the remaining segments of the company. That makes all of the remaining segments appear to be less profitable— possibly resulting in dropping other segments. The net effect will be to reduce the overall profits of the company and make it even more difficult to "cover the common costs."

Additionally, common fixed costs are not manageable by the manager to whom they are arbitrarily allocated; they are the responsibility of higher-level managers. When common fixed costs are allocated to managers, they are held responsible for those costs even though they cannot control them.

Income Statements—An External Reporting Perspective

Companywide Income Statements

Practically speaking, absorption costing is required for external reports according to U.S. generally accepted accounting principles (GAAP).[2] Furthermore, International Financial Reporting Standards (IFRS) explicitly require companies to use absorption costing. Probably because of the cost and possible confusion of maintaining two separate costing systems—one for external reporting and one for internal reporting—most companies use absorption costing for their external and internal reports.

With all of the advantages of the contribution approach, you may wonder why the absorption approach is used at all. While the answer is partly due to adhering to tradition, absorption costing is also attractive to many accountants and managers because they believe it better matches costs with sales. Advocates of absorption costing argue that *all* manufacturing costs must be assigned to products in order to properly match the costs of producing units of product with their sales. The fixed costs of depreciation, taxes, insurance, supervisory salaries, and so on, are just as essential to manufacturing products as are the variable costs.

Advocates of variable costing argue that fixed manufacturing costs are not really the costs of any particular unit of product. These costs are incurred to have the *capacity* to make products during a particular period and will be incurred even if nothing is made during the period. Moreover, whether a unit is made or not, the fixed manufacturing costs will be exactly the same. Therefore, variable costing advocates argue that fixed manufacturing costs are not part of the costs of producing a particular unit of product, and thus, the matching principle dictates that fixed manufacturing costs should be recognized as an expense in the current period.

---

[2] The Financial Accounting Standards Board (FASB) has created a single source of authoritative nongovernmental U.S. generally accepted accounting principles (GAAP) called the FASB Accounting Standards Codification (FASB codification). Although the FASB codification does not explicitly disallow variable costing, it does explicitly prohibit companies from excluding all manufacturing overhead costs from product costs. It also provides an in-depth discussion of fixed overhead allocation to products, thereby implying that absorption costing is required for external reports. Although some companies expense significant elements of fixed manufacturing costs on their external reports, practically speaking, U.S. GAAP requires absorption costing for external reports.

Segmented Financial Information

U.S. GAAP and IFRS require that publicly traded companies include segmented financial and other data in their annual reports and that the segmented reports prepared for external users *must use the same methods and definitions that the companies use in internal segmented reports that are prepared to aid in making operating decisions.* This is a very unusual stipulation because companies are not ordinarily required to report the same data to external users that are used for internal decision-making purposes. This requirement creates incentives for publicly traded companies to avoid using the contribution format for internal segmented reports. Segmented contribution format income statements contain vital information that companies are often very reluctant to release to the public (and hence competitors). In addition, this requirement creates problems in reconciling internal and external reports.

IN BUSINESS

© Duncan Smith/Getty Images

AMAZON.COM TO REPORT ITS CLOUD-COMPUTING SERVICES AS A SEPARATE SEGMENT

For years, **Amazon.com** lumped revenues from one of its most important divisions—Amazon Web Services—in the "other" line of its financial statements. Now the company has decided to separately report this division's sales in external financial reports. Although companies spend more than $300 billion on servers, software, and IT services per year, growth in those markets has flattened out. Conversely, the infrastructure services market (that Amazon.com currently dominates) is expected to grow from $9 billion to $16 billion within one year. To put Amazon.com's growth in this market into perspective, the company has said that each day it is adding computing capacity that is equivalent to its entire capacity in 2004. Although Amazon.com plans to disclose Amazon Web Services' sales, it does not plan to report the segment's profits.

Source: Robert McMillan, "Amazon's AWS Aims to Be the Dominant Data Center for American Businesses," *The Wall Street Journal,* April 23, 2015, p. B5.

Summary

Variable and absorption costing are alternative methods of determining unit product costs. Under variable costing, only those manufacturing costs that vary with output are treated as product costs. This includes direct materials, variable overhead, and ordinarily direct labor. Fixed manufacturing overhead is treated as a period cost and is expensed on the income statement as incurred. By contrast, absorption costing treats fixed manufacturing overhead as a product cost, along with direct materials, direct labor, and variable overhead. Under both costing methods, selling and administrative expenses are treated as period costs and are expensed on the income statement as incurred.

Because absorption costing treats fixed manufacturing overhead as a product cost, a portion of fixed manufacturing overhead is assigned to each unit as it is produced. If units of product are unsold at the end of a period, then the fixed manufacturing overhead cost attached to those units is carried in ending inventory on the balance sheet rather than being recognized as an expense within cost of goods sold on the income statement. When these units are sold in a subsequent period, the fixed manufacturing overhead cost attached to them is released from the inventory account and recorded as part of cost of goods sold. Thus, under absorption costing, it is possible to defer a portion of the fixed manufacturing overhead cost from one period to a future period through the inventory account.

Unfortunately, this shifting of fixed manufacturing overhead cost between periods can cause erratic fluctuations in net operating income and can result in confusion and unwise decisions. To guard against mistakes when they interpret income statement data, managers should be alert to changes in inventory levels or unit product costs during the period.

Segmented income statements provide information for evaluating the profitability and performance of divisions, product lines, sales territories, and other segments of a company. Under the contribution approach, variable costs and fixed costs are clearly distinguished from each other and only those costs that are traceable to a segment are assigned to the segment. A cost is considered traceable to a segment only if the cost is caused by the segment and could be avoided by eliminating the segment. Fixed common costs are not allocated to segments. The segment margin consists of sales, less variable expenses, and less traceable fixed expenses of the segment.

The dollar sales required for a segment to break even is computed by dividing the segment's traceable fixed expenses by its contribution margin ratio. A company's common fixed expenses should not be allocated to segments when performing break-even calculations because they will not change in response to segment-level decisions.

Review Problem 1: Contrasting Variable and Absorption Costing

Dexter Corporation produces and sells a single product, a wooden hand loom for weaving small items such as scarves. Selected cost and operating data relating to the product for two years are given below:

Selling price per unit.	$50
Manufacturing costs:	
Variable manufacturing cost per unit produced:	
Direct materials	$11
Direct labor.	$6
Variable manufacturing overhead	$3
Fixed manufacturing overhead per year	$120,000
Selling and administrative expenses:	
Variable selling and administrative per unit sold	$4
Fixed selling and administrative per year	$70,000

	Year 1	Year 2
Units in beginning inventory	0	2,000
Units produced during the year	10,000	6,000
Units sold during the year	8,000	8,000
Units in ending inventory	2,000	0

Required:
1. Assume the company uses absorption costing.
   a. Compute the unit product cost in each year.
   b. Prepare an income statement for each year.
2. Assume the company uses variable costing.
   a. Compute the unit product cost in each year.
   b. Prepare an income statement for each year.
3. Reconcile the variable costing and absorption costing net operating incomes.

Solution to Review Problem 1

1. a. Under absorption costing, all manufacturing costs, variable and fixed, are included in unit product costs:

	Year 1	Year 2
Direct materials	$11	$11
Direct labor.	6	6
Variable manufacturing overhead	3	3
Fixed manufacturing overhead		
($120,000 ÷ 10,000 units)	12	
($120,000 ÷ 6,000 units).		20
Unit product cost.	$32	$40

b. The absorption costing income statements follow:

	Year 1	Year 2
Sales (8,000 units × $50 per unit)	$400,000	$400,000
Cost of goods sold (8,000 units × $32 per unit);		
(2,000 units × $32 per unit) +		
(6,000 units × $40 per unit)	256,000	304,000
Gross margin	144,000	96,000
Selling and administrative expenses		
(8,000 units × $4 per unit + $70,000)	102,000	102,000
Net operating income (loss).	$ 42,000	$ (6,000)

2. a.   Under variable costing, only the variable manufacturing costs are included in unit product costs:

	Year 1	Year 2
Direct materials	$11	$11
Direct labor.	6	6
Variable manufacturing overhead	3	3
Unit product cost.	$20	$20

b.   The variable costing income statements follow:

	Year 1		Year 2	
Sales (8,000 units × $50 per unit)		$400,000		$400,000
Variable expenses:				
Variable cost of goods sold				
(8,000 units × $20 per unit)	$160,000		$160,000	
Variable selling and administrative				
expenses (8,000 units × $4 per unit).	32,000	192,000	32,000	192,000
Contribution margin		208,000		208,000
Fixed expenses:				
Fixed manufacturing overhead.	120,000		120,000	
Fixed selling and administrative				
expenses	70,000	190,000	70,000	190,000
Net operating income.		$ 18,000		$ 18,000

3.   The reconciliation of the variable and absorption costing net operating incomes follows:

	Year 1	Year 2
Fixed manufacturing overhead in ending inventories		
(2,000 units × $12 per unit; 0 units × $20 per unit)	$24,000	$ 0
Deduct: Fixed manufacturing overhead in beginning		
inventories (0; 2,000 units × $12 per unit).	0	24,000
Fixed manufacturing overhead deferred in		
(released from) inventories	$24,000	$ (24,000)

	Year 1	Year 2
Variable costing net operating income	$18,000	$ 18,000
Add: Fixed manufacturing overhead costs deferred		
in inventory under absorption costing		
(2,000 units × $12 per unit)	24,000	
Deduct: Fixed manufacturing overhead costs released		
from inventory under absorption costing		
(2,000 units × $12 per unit)		(24,000)
Absorption costing net operating income (loss).	$42,000	$ (6,000)

Review Problem 2: Segmented Income Statements

The business staff of the law firm Frampton, Davis & Smythe has constructed the following report that breaks down the firm's overall results for last month into two business segments—family law and commercial law:

	Company Total	Family Law	Commercial Law
Revenues from clients	$1,000,000	$400,000	$600,000
Variable expenses..................	220,000	100,000	120,000
Contribution margin	780,000	300,000	480,000
Traceable fixed expenses	670,000	280,000	390,000
Segment margin	110,000	20,000	90,000
Common fixed expenses	60,000	24,000	36,000
Net operating income (loss).........	$ 50,000	$ (4,000)	$ 54,000

However, this report is not quite correct. The common fixed expenses such as the managing partner's salary, general administrative expenses, and general firm advertising have been allocated to the two segments based on revenues from clients.

Required:
1. Redo the segment report, eliminating the allocation of common fixed expenses. Would the firm be better off financially if the family law segment were dropped? (Note: Many of the firm's commercial law clients also use the firm for their family law requirements such as drawing up wills.)
2. The firm's advertising agency has proposed an ad campaign targeted at boosting the revenues of the family law segment. The ad campaign would cost $20,000, and the advertising agency claims it would increase family law revenues by $100,000. The managing partner of Frampton, Davis & Smythe believes this increase in business could be accommodated without any increase in fixed expenses. Estimate the effect this ad campaign would have on the family law segment margin and on the firm's overall net operating income.
3. Compute the companywide break-even point in dollar sales and the dollar sales required for each business segment to break even.

Solution to Review Problem 2
1. The corrected segmented income statement appears below:

	Company Total	Family Law	Commercial Law
Revenues from clients	$1,000,000	$400,000	$600,000
Variable expenses....................	220,000	100,000	120,000
Contribution margin	780,000	300,000	480,000
Traceable fixed expenses	670,000	280,000	390,000
Segment margin	110,000	$ 20,000	$ 90,000
Common fixed expenses...............	60,000		
Net operating income.................	$ 50,000		

No, the firm would not be better off financially if the family law practice were dropped. The family law segment is covering all of its own costs and is contributing $20,000 per month to covering the common fixed expenses of the firm. While the segment margin for family law is much lower than for commercial law, it is still profitable. Moreover, family law may be a service that the firm must provide to its commercial clients in order to remain competitive.

2. The ad campaign would increase the family law segment margin by $55,000 as follows:

Increased revenues from clients.	$100,000
Family law contribution margin ratio ($300,000 ÷ $400,000). . . .	× 75%
Increased contribution margin	$ 75,000
Less cost of the ad campaign	20,000
Increased segment margin	$ 55,000

Because there would be no increase in fixed expenses (including common fixed expenses), the increase in overall net operating income is also $55,000.

3. The companywide break-even point is computed as follows:

$$\frac{\text{Dollar sales for company}}{\text{to break even}} = \frac{\text{Traceable fixed expenses} + \text{Common fixed expenses}}{\text{Overall CM ratio}}$$

$$= \frac{\$670,000 + \$60,000}{0.78}$$

$$= \frac{\$730,000}{0.78}$$

$$= \$935,897 \text{ (rounded)}$$

The break-even point for the family law segment is computed as follows:

$$\frac{\text{Dollar sales for a segment}}{\text{to break even}} = \frac{\text{Segment traceable fixed expenses}}{\text{Segment CM ratio}}$$

$$= \frac{\$280,000}{0.75}$$

$$= \$373,333 \text{ (rounded)}$$

The break-even point for the commercial law segment is computed as follows:

$$\frac{\text{Dollar sales for a segment}}{\text{to break even}} = \frac{\text{Segment traceable fixed expenses}}{\text{Segment CM ratio}}$$

$$= \frac{\$390,000}{0.80}$$

$$= \$487,500$$

Glossary

Absorption costing A costing method that includes all manufacturing costs—direct materials, direct labor, and both variable and fixed manufacturing overhead—in unit product costs. (p. 258)

Common fixed cost A fixed cost that supports more than one business segment, but is not traceable in whole or in part to any one of the business segments. (p. 268)

Segment Any part or activity of an organization about which managers seek cost, revenue, or profit data. (p. 258)

Segment margin A segment's contribution margin less its traceable fixed costs. It represents the margin available after a segment has covered all of its own traceable costs. (p. 269)

Traceable fixed cost A fixed cost that is incurred because of the existence of a particular business segment and that would be eliminated if the segment were eliminated. (p. 268)

Variable costing A costing method that includes only variable manufacturing costs—direct materials, direct labor, and variable manufacturing overhead—in unit product costs. (p. 258)

Questions

6–1 What is the difference between absorption costing and variable costing?

6–2 Are selling and administrative expenses treated as product costs or as period costs under variable costing?

6–3 Explain how fixed manufacturing overhead costs are shifted from one period to another under absorption costing.

6–4 What are the arguments in favor of treating fixed manufacturing overhead costs as product costs?

6–5 What are the arguments in favor of treating fixed manufacturing overhead costs as period costs?

6–6 If the units produced equals the units sold, which method would you expect to show the higher net operating income, variable costing or absorption costing? Why?

6–7 If the units produced exceed the units sold, which method would you expect to show the higher net operating income, variable costing or absorption costing? Why?

6–8 If fixed manufacturing overhead costs are released from inventory under absorption costing, what does this tell you about the level of production in relation to the level of unit sales?

6–9 Under absorption costing, how is it possible to increase net operating income without increasing sales?

6–10 How does Lean Production reduce or eliminate the difference in reported net operating income between absorption and variable costing?

6–11 What is a segment of an organization? Give several examples of segments.

6–12 What costs are assigned to a segment under the contribution approach?

6–13 Distinguish between a traceable fixed cost and a common fixed cost. Give several examples of each.

6–14 Explain how the contribution margin differs from the segment margin.

6–15 Why aren't common fixed costs allocated to segments under the contribution approach?

6–16 How is it possible for a fixed cost that is traceable to a segment to become a common fixed cost if the segment is divided into further segments?

6–17 Should a company allocate its common fixed costs to business segments when computing the break-even point for those segments? Why?

CONNECT Applying Excel

LO6–2

The Excel worksheet form that appears below is to be used to recreate portions of Review Problem 1 relating to Dexter Corporation. Download the workbook containing this form from Connect, where you will also receive instructions about how to use this worksheet form.

	A	B	C	D	E	F
1	Chapter 6: Applying Excel					
2						
3	**Data**					
4	Selling price per unit	$50				
5	Manufacturing costs:					
6	Variable per unit produced:					
7	Direct materials	$11				
8	Direct labor	$6				
9	Variable manufacturing overhead	$3				
10	Fixed manufacturing overhead per year	$120,000				
11	Selling and administrative expenses:					
12	Variable per unit sold	$4				
13	Fixed per year	$70,000				
14						
15		Year 1	Year 2			
16	Units in beginning inventory	0				
17	Units produced during the year	10,000	6,000			
18	Units sold during the year	8,000	8,000			
19						
20	*Enter a formula into each of the cells marked with a ? below*					
21	**Review Problem 1: Contrasting Variable and Absorption Costing**					
22						
23	*Compute the Ending Inventory*					
24		Year 1	Year 2			
25	Units in beginning inventory	0	?			
26	Units produced during the year	?	?			
27	Units sold during the year	?	?			
28	Units in ending inventory	?	?			
29						
30	*Compute the Absorption Costing Unit Product Cost*					
31		Year 1	Year 2			
32	Direct materials	?	?			
33	Direct labor	?	?			
34	Variable manufacturing overhead	?	?			
35	Fixed manufacturing overhead	?	?			
36	Absorption costing unit product cost	?	?			
37						
38	*Construct the Absorption Costing Income Statement*					
39		Year 1	Year 2			
40	Sales	?	?			
41	Cost of goods sold	?	?			
42	Gross margin	?	?			
43	Selling and administrative expenses	?	?			
44	Net operating income	?	?			
45						
46	*Compute the Variable Costing Unit Product Cost*					
47		Year 1	Year 2			
48	Direct materials	?	?			
49	Direct labor	?	?			
50	Variable manufacturing overhead	?	?			
51	Variable costing unit product cost	?	?			
52						
53	*Construct the Variable Costing Income Statement*					
54		Year 1		Year 2		
55	Sales		?		?	
56	Variable expenses:					
57	Variable cost of goods sold	?		?		
58	Variable selling and administrative expenses	?	?	?	?	
59	Contribution margin		?		?	
60	Fixed expenses:					
61	Fixed manufacturing overhead	?		?		
62	Fixed selling and administrative expenses	?	?	?	?	
63	Net operating income		?		?	
64						

H ◀ ▶ H **Chapter 6 Form** / Filled in Chapter 6 Form / Chapter 6

You should proceed to the requirements below only after completing your worksheet. The LIFO inventory flow assumption is used throughout this problem.

Required:

1. Check your worksheet by changing the units sold in the Data to 6,000 for Year 2. The cost of goods sold under absorption costing for Year 2 should now be $240,000. If it isn't, check cell C41. The formula in this cell should be =IF(C26<C27,C26*C36+(C27−C26)*B36,C27*C36). If your worksheet is operating properly, the net operating income under both absorption costing and variable costing should be $(34,000) for Year 2. That is, the loss in Year 2 is $34,000 under both methods. If you do not get these answers, find the errors in your worksheet and correct them.

   Why is the absorption costing net operating income now equal to the variable costing net operating income in Year 2?

2. Enter the following data from a different company into your worksheet:

Data		
Selling price per unit.............................	$75	
Manufacturing costs:		
Variable per unit produced:......................		
Direct materials	$12	
Direct labor..................................	$5	
Variable manufacturing overhead	$7	
Fixed manufacturing overhead per year...........	$150,000	
Selling and administrative expenses:		
Variable per unit sold	$1	
Fixed per year	$60,000	
	Year 1	Year 2
Units in beginning inventory	0	
Units produced during the year	15,000	10,000
Units sold during the year	12,000	12,000

   Is the net operating income under variable costing different in Year 1 and Year 2? Why or why not? Explain the relation between the net operating income under absorption costing and variable costing in Year 1. Explain the relation between the net operating income under absorption costing and variable costing in Year 2.

3. At the end of Year 1, the company's board of directors set a target for Year 2 of net operating income of $500,000 under absorption costing. If this target is met, a hefty bonus would be paid to the CEO of the company. Keeping everything else the same from part (2) above, change the units produced in Year 2 to 50,000 units. Would this change result in a bonus being paid to the CEO? Do you think this change would be in the best interests of the company? What is likely to happen in Year 3 to the absorption costing net operating income if sales remain constant at 12,000 units per year?

connect **The Foundational 15**

Diego Company manufactures one product that is sold for $80 per unit in two geographic regions— the East and West regions. The following information pertains to the company's first year of operations in which it produced 40,000 units and sold 35,000 units.

LO6–1, LO6–2, LO6–3, LO6–4, LO6–5

Variable costs per unit:		
Manufacturing:		
Direct materials	$24	
Direct labor	$14	
Variable manufacturing overhead	$2	
Variable selling and administrative	$4	
Fixed costs per year:		
Fixed manufacturing overhead	$800,000	
Fixed selling and administrative expense.......	$496,000	

The company sold 25,000 units in the East region and 10,000 units in the West region. It determined that $250,000 of its fixed selling and administrative expense is traceable to the West region, $150,000 is traceable to the East region, and the remaining $96,000 is a common fixed expense. The company will continue to incur the total amount of its fixed manufacturing overhead costs as long as it continues to produce any amount of its only product.

Required:

Answer each question independently based on the original data unless instructed otherwise. You do not need to prepare a segmented income statement until question 13.

1. What is the unit product cost under variable costing?
2. What is the unit product cost under absorption costing?
3. What is the company's total contribution margin under variable costing?
4. What is the company's net operating income under variable costing?
5. What is the company's total gross margin under absorption costing?
6. What is the company's net operating income under absorption costing?
7. What is the amount of the difference between the variable costing and absorption costing net operating incomes? What is the cause of this difference?
8. What is the company's break-even point in unit sales? Is it above or below the actual unit sales? Compare the break-even point in unit sales to your answer for question 6 and comment.
9. If the sales volumes in the East and West regions had been reversed, what would be the company's overall break-even point in unit sales?
10. What would have been the company's variable costing net operating income if it had produced and sold 35,000 units? You do not need to perform any calculations to answer this question.
11. What would have been the company's absorption costing net operating income if it had produced and sold 35,000 units? You do not need to perform any calculations to answer this question.
12. If the company produces 5,000 fewer units than it sells in its second year of operations, will absorption costing net operating income be higher or lower than variable costing net operating income in Year 2? Why? No calculations are necessary.
13. Prepare a contribution format segmented income statement that includes a Total column and columns for the East and West regions.
14. Diego is considering eliminating the West region because an internally generated report suggests the region's total *gross margin* in the first year of operations was $50,000 less than its traceable fixed selling and administrative expenses. Diego believes that if it drops the West region, the East region's sales will grow by 5% in Year 2. Using the contribution approach for analyzing segment profitability and assuming all else remains constant in Year 2, what would be the profit impact of dropping the West region in Year 2?
15. Assume the West region invests $30,000 in a new advertising campaign in Year 2 that increases its unit sales by 20%. If all else remains constant, what would be the profit impact of pursuing the advertising campaign?

Exercises   connect

EXERCISE 6–1 Variable and Absorption Costing Unit Product Costs LO6–1

Ida Sidha Karya Company is a family-owned company located in the village of Gianyar on the island of Bali in Indonesia. The company produces a handcrafted Balinese musical instrument called a gamelan that is similar to a xylophone. The gamelans are sold for $850. Selected data for the company's operations last year follow:

Units in beginning inventory	0
Units produced	250
Units sold	225
Units in ending inventory	25
Variable costs per unit:	
Direct materials	$100
Direct labor	$320
Variable manufacturing overhead	$40
Variable selling and administrative	$20
Fixed costs:	
Fixed manufacturing overhead	$60,000
Fixed selling and administrative	$20,000

Required:

1. Assume that the company uses absorption costing. Compute the unit product cost for one gamelan.
2. Assume that the company uses variable costing. Compute the unit product cost for one gamelan.

EXERCISE 6–2 Variable Costing Income Statement; Explanation of Difference in Net Operating Income LO6–2

Refer to the data in Exercise 6–1 for Ida Sidha Karya Company. The absorption costing income statement prepared by the company's accountant for last year appears as shown:

Sales	$191,250
Cost of goods sold	157,500
Gross margin	33,750
Selling and administrative expense	24,500
Net operating income........................	$ 9,250

Required:

1. Under absorption costing, how much fixed manufacturing overhead cost is included in the company's inventory at the end of last year?
2. Prepare an income statement for last year using variable costing. Explain the difference in net operating income between the two costing methods.

EXERCISE 6–3 Reconciliation of Absorption and Variable Costing Net Operating Incomes LO6–3

Jorgansen Lighting, Inc., manufactures heavy-duty street lighting systems for municipalities. The company uses variable costing for internal management reports and absorption costing for external reports to shareholders, creditors, and the government. The company has provided the following data:

	Year 1	Year 2	Year 3
Inventories:			
Beginning (units)	200	170	180
Ending (units)	170	180	220
Variable costing net operating income	$1,080,400	$1,032,400	$996,400

The company's fixed manufacturing overhead per unit was constant at $560 for all three years.

Required:

1. Calculate each year's absorption costing net operating income. Present your answer in the form of a reconciliation report.
2. Assume in Year 4 that the company's variable costing net operating income was $984,400 and its absorption costing net operating income was $1,012,400.
   a. Did inventories increase or decrease during Year 4?
   b. How much fixed manufacturing overhead cost was deferred or released from inventory during Year 4?

EXERCISE 6–4 Basic Segmented Income Statement LO6–4

Royal Lawncare Company produces and sells two packaged products—Weedban and Greengrow. Revenue and cost information relating to the products follow:

	Product	
	Weedban	Greengrow
Selling price per unit	$6.00	$7.50
Variable expenses per unit	$2.40	$5.25
Traceable fixed expenses per year	$45,000	$21,000

288

Chapter 6

Common fixed expenses in the company total $33,000 annually. Last year the company produced and sold 15,000 units of Weedban and 28,000 units of Greengrow.

Required:

Prepare a contribution format income statement segmented by product lines.

EXERCISE 6–5 Companywide and Segment Break-Even Analysis LO6–5

Piedmont Company segments its business into two regions—North and South. The company prepared the contribution format segmented income statement as shown below:

	Total Company	North	South
Sales	$600,000	$400,000	$200,000
Variable expenses	360,000	280,000	80,000
Contribution margin	240,000	120,000	120,000
Traceable fixed expenses	120,000	60,000	60,000
Segment margin	120,000	$ 60,000	$ 60,000
Common fixed expenses	50,000		
Net operating income	$ 70,000		

Required:

1. Compute the companywide break-even point in dollar sales.
2. Compute the break-even point in dollar sales for the North region.
3. Compute the break-even point in dollar sales for the South region.

EXERCISE 6–6 Variable and Absorption Costing Unit Product Costs and Income Statements LO6–1, LO6–2

Lynch Company manufactures and sells a single product. The following costs were incurred during the company's first year of operations:

Variable costs per unit:	
Manufacturing:	
Direct materials	$6
Direct labor	$9
Variable manufacturing overhead	$3
Variable selling and administrative	$4
Fixed costs per year:	
Fixed manufacturing overhead	$300,000
Fixed selling and administrative	$190,000

During the year, the company produced 25,000 units and sold 20,000 units. The selling price of the company's product is $50 per unit.

Required:

1. Assume that the company uses absorption costing:
   a. Compute the unit product cost.
   b. Prepare an income statement for the year.
2. Assume that the company uses variable costing:
   a. Compute the unit product cost.
   b. Prepare an income statement for the year.

EXERCISE 6–7 Segmented Income Statement LO6–4

Shannon Company segments its income statement into its North and South Divisions. The company's overall sales, contribution margin ratio, and net operating income are $500,000, 46%, and $10,000, respectively. The North Division's contribution margin and contribution margin ratio are $150,000 and 50%, respectively. The South Division's segment margin is $30,000. The company has $90,000 of common fixed expenses that cannot be traced to either division.

Required:

Prepare an income statement for Shannon Company that uses the contribution format and is segmented by divisions. In addition, for the company as a whole and for each segment, show each item on the segmented income statements as a percent of sales.

EXERCISE 6–8 Deducing Changes in Inventories LO6–3

Parker Products, Inc. is a manufacturer whose absorption costing income statement reported sales of $123 million and a net operating loss of $18 million. According to a CVP analysis prepared for management, the company's break-even point is $115 million in sales.

Required:

Assuming that the CVP analysis is correct, is it likely that the company's inventory level increased, decreased, or remained unchanged during the year? Explain.

EXERCISE 6–9 Variable and Absorption Costing Unit Product Costs and Income Statements LO6–1, LO6–2, LO6–3

Walsh Company manufactures and sells one product. The following information pertains to each of the company's first two years of operations:

Variable costs per unit:	
Manufacturing:	
Direct materials	$25
Direct labor.	$15
Variable manufacturing overhead	$5
Variable selling and administrative.	$2
Fixed costs per year:	
Fixed manufacturing overhead.	$250,000
Fixed selling and administrative expenses.	$80,000

During its first year of operations, Walsh produced 50,000 units and sold 40,000 units. During its second year of operations, it produced 40,000 units and sold 50,000 units. The selling price of the company's product is $60 per unit.

Required:

1. Assume the company uses variable costing:
   a. Compute the unit product cost for Year 1 and Year 2.
   b. Prepare an income statement for Year 1 and Year 2.
2. Assume the company uses absorption costing:
   a. Compute the unit product cost for Year 1 and Year 2.
   b. Prepare an income statement for Year 1 and Year 2.
3. Explain the difference between variable costing and absorption costing net operating income in Year 1. Also, explain why the two net operating incomes differ in Year 2.

EXERCISE 6–10 Companywide and Segment Break-Even Analysis LO6–5

Crossfire Company segments its business into two regions—East and West. The company prepared a contribution format segmented income statement as shown below:

	Total Company	East	West
Sales	$900,000	$600,000	$300,000
Variable expenses.	675,000	480,000	195,000
Contribution margin	225,000	120,000	105,000
Traceable fixed expenses	141,000	50,000	91,000
Segment margin	84,000	$ 70,000	$ 14,000
Common fixed expenses.	59,000		
Net operating income.	$ 25,000		

Required:

1. Compute the companywide break-even point in dollar sales.
2. Compute the break-even point in dollar sales for the East region.
3. Compute the break-even point in dollar sales for the West region.
4. Prepare a new segmented income statement based on the break-even dollar sales that you computed in requirements 2 and 3. Use the same format as shown above. What is Crossfire's net operating income (loss) in your new segmented income statement?
5. Do you think that Crossfire should allocate its common fixed expenses to the East and West regions when computing the break-even points for each region? Why?

EXERCISE 6–11 Segmented Income Statement LO6–4

Wingate Company, a wholesale distributor of electronic equipment, has been experiencing losses for some time, as shown by its most recent monthly contribution format income statement:

Sales	$1,000,000
Variable expenses.	390,000
Contribution margin	610,000
Fixed expenses	625,000
Net operating income (loss).	$ (15,000)

In an effort to resolve the problem, the company would like to prepare an income statement segmented by division. Accordingly, the Accounting Department has developed the following information:

	Division		
	East	Central	West
Sales	$250,000	$400,000	$350,000
Variable expenses as a percentage of sales	52%	30%	40%
Traceable fixed expenses	$160,000	$200,000	$175,000

Required:

1. Prepare a contribution format income statement segmented by divisions.
2. The Marketing Department has proposed increasing the West Division's monthly advertising by $15,000 based on the belief that it would increase that division's sales by 20%. Assuming these estimates are accurate, how much would the company's net operating income increase (decrease) if the proposal is implemented?

EXERCISE 6–12 Variable Costing Income Statement; Reconciliation LO6–2, LO6–3

Whitman Company has just completed its first year of operations. The company's absorption costing income statement for the year follows:

Whitman Company	
Income Statement	
Sales (35,000 units × $25 per unit).	$875,000
Cost of goods sold (35,000 units × $16 per unit).	560,000
Gross margin	315,000
Selling and administrative expenses.	280,000
Net operating income.	$ 35,000

The company's selling and administrative expenses consist of $210,000 per year in fixed expenses and $2 per unit sold in variable expenses. The $16 unit product cost given above is computed as follows:

Direct materials	$ 5
Direct labor.	6
Variable manufacturing overhead	1
Fixed manufacturing overhead ($160,000 ÷ 40,000 units).	4
Absorption costing unit product cost.	$16

Required:
1. Redo the company's income statement in the contribution format using variable costing.
2. Reconcile any difference between the net operating income on your variable costing income statement and the net operating income on the absorption costing income statement above.

EXERCISE 6–13 Inferring Costing Method; Unit Product Cost LO6–1

Sierra Company incurs the following costs to produce and sell its only product.

Variable costs per unit:	
Direct materials	$9
Direct labor	$10
Variable manufacturing overhead	$5
Variable selling and administrative expenses	$3
Fixed costs per year:	
Fixed manufacturing overhead	$150,000
Fixed selling and administrative expenses	$400,000

During this year, 25,000 units were produced and 22,000 units were sold. The Finished Goods inventory account at the end of this year shows a balance of $72,000 for the 3,000 unsold units.

Required:
1. Calculate this year's ending balance in Finished Goods inventory two ways—using variable costing and using absorption costing. Does it appear that the company is using variable costing or absorption costing to assign costs to the 3,000 units in its Finished Goods inventory?
2. Assume that the company wishes to prepare this year's financial statements for its stockholders.
   a. Is Finished Goods inventory of $72,000 the correct amount to include on the balance sheet for external reporting purposes? Explain.
   b. What balance should be reported in the Finished Goods inventory account for external reporting purposes?

EXERCISE 6–14 Variable Costing Unit Product Cost and Income Statement; Break-Even Analysis LO6–1, LO6–2

Chuck Wagon Grills, Inc., makes a single product—a handmade specialty barbecue grill that it sells for $210. Data for last year's operations follow:

Units in beginning inventory	0
Units produced	20,000
Units sold	19,000
Units in ending inventory	1,000
Variable costs per unit:	
Direct materials	$ 50
Direct labor	80
Variable manufacturing overhead	20
Variable selling and administrative	10
Total variable cost per unit	$160
Fixed costs:	
Fixed manufacturing overhead	$700,000
Fixed selling and administrative	285,000
Total fixed costs	$985,000

Required:
1. Assume that the company uses variable costing. Compute the unit product cost for one barbecue grill.
2. Assume that the company uses variable costing. Prepare a contribution format income statement for last year.
3. What is the company's break-even point in terms of the number of barbecue grills sold?

EXERCISE 6–15 Absorption Costing Unit Product Cost and Income Statement LO6–1, LO6–2

Refer to the data in Exercise 6–14 for Chuck Wagon Grills. Assume in this exercise that the company uses absorption costing.

Required:

1. Compute the unit product cost for one barbecue grill.
2. Prepare an income statement for last year.

EXERCISE 6–16 Working with a Segmented Income Statement; Break-Even Analysis LO6–4, LO6–5

Raner, Harris & Chan is a consulting firm that specializes in information systems for medical and dental clinics. The firm has two offices—one in Chicago and one in Minneapolis. The firm classifies the direct costs of consulting jobs as variable costs. A contribution format segmented income statement for the company's most recent year is given:

	Total Company		Office			
			Chicago		Minneapolis	
Sales	$450,000	100%	$150,000	100%	$300,000	100%
Variable expenses..	225,000	50%	45,000	30%	180,000	60%
Contribution margin	225,000	50%	105,000	70%	120,000	40%
Traceable fixed expenses	126,000	28%	78,000	52%	48,000	16%
Office segment margin.....................................	99,000	22%	$ 27,000	18%	$ 72,000	24%
Common fixed expenses not traceable to offices..............	63,000	14%				
Net operating income.....................................	$ 36,000	8%				

Required:

1. Compute the companywide break-even point in dollar sales. Also, compute the break-even point for the Chicago office and for the Minneapolis office. Is the companywide break-even point greater than, less than, or equal to the sum of the Chicago and Minneapolis break-even points? Why?
2. By how much would the company's net operating income increase if Minneapolis increased its sales by $75,000 per year? Assume no change in cost behavior patterns.
3. Refer to the original data. Assume that sales in Chicago increase by $50,000 next year and that sales in Minneapolis remain unchanged. Assume no change in fixed costs.
    a. Prepare a new segmented income statement for the company using the above format. Show both amounts and percentages.
    b. Observe from the income statement you have prepared that the contribution margin ratio for Chicago has remained unchanged at 70% (the same as in the above data) but that the segment margin ratio has changed. How do you explain the change in the segment margin ratio?

EXERCISE 6–17 Working with a Segmented Income Statement LO6–4

Refer to the data in Exercise 6–16. Assume that Minneapolis' sales by major market are:

	Minneapolis		Market			
			Medical		Dental	
Sales	$300,000	100%	$200,000	100%	$100,000	100%
Variable expenses...	180,000	60%	128,000	64%	52,000	52%
Contribution margin	120,000	40%	72,000	36%	48,000	48%
Traceable fixed expenses	33,000	11%	12,000	6%	21,000	21%
Market segment margin....................................	87,000	29%	$ 60,000	30%	$ 27,000	27%
Common fixed expenses not traceable to markets..............	15,000	5%				
Office segment margin....................................	$ 72,000	24%				

The company would like to initiate an intensive advertising campaign in one of the two market segments during the next month. The campaign would cost $5,000. Marketing studies indicate that such a campaign would increase sales in the Medical market by $40,000 or increase sales in the Dental market by $35,000.

Required:

1. How much would the company's profits increase (decrease) if it implemented the advertising campaign in the Medical Market?
2. How much would the company's profits increase (decrease) if it implemented the advertising campaign in the Dental Market?
3. In which of the markets would you recommend that the company focus its advertising campaign?
4. In Exercise 6–16, Minneapolis shows $48,000 in traceable fixed expenses. What happened to the $48,000 in this exercise?

connect   **Problems**

PROBLEM 6–18 Variable and Absorption Costing Unit Product Costs and Income Statements LO6–1, LO6–2

Haas Company manufactures and sells one product. The following information pertains to each of the company's first three years of operations:

Variable costs per unit:	
Manufacturing:	
Direct materials	$20
Direct labor	$12
Variable manufacturing overhead	$4
Variable selling and administrative	$2
Fixed costs per year:	
Fixed manufacturing overhead	$960,000
Fixed selling and administrative expenses	$240,000

During its first year of operations, Haas produced 60,000 units and sold 60,000 units. During its second year of operations, it produced 75,000 units and sold 50,000 units. In its third year, Haas produced 40,000 units and sold 65,000 units. The selling price of the company's product is $58 per unit.

Required:

1. Compute the company's break-even point in unit sales.
2. Assume the company uses variable costing:
   a. Compute the unit product cost for Year 1, Year 2, and Year 3.
   b. Prepare an income statement for Year 1, Year 2, and Year 3.
3. Assume the company uses absorption costing:
   a. Compute the unit product cost for Year 1, Year 2, and Year 3.
   b. Prepare an income statement for Year 1, Year 2, and Year 3.
4. Compare the net operating incomes that you computed in requirements 2 and 3 to the break-even point in unit sales that you computed in requirement 1. Which net operating income figures (variable costing or absorption costing) seem counterintuitive? Why?

PROBLEM 6–19 Variable Costing Income Statement; Reconciliation LO6–2, LO6–3

During Heaton Company's first two years of operations, it reported absorption costing net operating income as follows:

	Year 1	Year 2
Sales (@ $25 per unit)	$1,000,000	$1,250,000
Cost of goods sold (@ $18 per unit)	720,000	900,000
Gross margin	280,000	350,000
Selling and administrative expenses*	210,000	230,000
Net operating income	$ 70,000	$ 120,000

*$2 per unit variable; $130,000 fixed each year.

The company's $18 unit product cost is computed as follows:

Direct materials	$ 4
Direct labor...	7
Variable manufacturing overhead	1
Fixed manufacturing overhead ($270,000 ÷ 45,000 units).........	6
Absorption costing unit product cost...........................	$18

Forty percent of fixed manufacturing overhead consists of wages and salaries; the remainder consists of depreciation charges on production equipment and buildings.

Production and cost data for the first two years of operations are:

	Year 1	Year 2
Units produced	45,000	45,000
Units sold	40,000	50,000

Required:
1. Using variable costing, what is the unit product cost for both years?
2. What is the variable costing net operating income in Year 1 and in Year 2?
3. Reconcile the absorption costing and the variable costing net operating income figures for each year.

PROBLEM 6–20 Variable and Absorption Costing Unit Product Costs and Income Statements; Explanation of Difference in Net Operating Income LO6–1, LO6–2, LO6–3

High Country, Inc., produces and sells many recreational products. The company has just opened a new plant to produce a folding camp cot that will be marketed throughout the United States. The following cost and revenue data relate to May, the first month of the plant's operation:

Beginning inventory	0
Units produced	10,000
Units sold	8,000
Selling price per unit..	$75
Selling and administrative expenses:	
Variable per unit	$6
Fixed (per month)	$200,000
Manufacturing costs:	
Direct materials cost per unit	$20
Direct labor cost per unit	$8
Variable manufacturing overhead cost per unit	$2
Fixed manufacturing overhead cost (per month).............	$100,000

Management is anxious to assess the profitability of the new camp cot during the month of May.

Required:
1. Assume that the company uses absorption costing.
   a. Determine the unit product cost.
   b. Prepare an income statement for May.
2. Assume that the company uses variable costing.
   a. Determine the unit product cost.
   b. Prepare a contribution format income statement for May.
3. Explain the reason for any difference in the ending inventory balances under the two costing methods and the impact of this difference on reported net operating income.

PROBLEM 6–21 Segment Reporting and Decision-Making LO6–4

Vulcan Company's contribution format income statement for June is as follows:

Vulcan Company	
Income Statement	
For the Month Ended June 30	
Sales	$750,000
Variable expenses......................	336,000
Contribution margin	414,000
Fixed expenses	378,000
Net operating income..................	$ 36,000

Management is disappointed with the company's performance and is wondering what can be done to improve profits. By examining sales and cost records, you have determined the following:

a.   The company is divided into two sales territories—Northern and Southern. The Northern territory recorded $300,000 in sales and $156,000 in variable expenses during June; the remaining sales and variable expenses were recorded in the Southern territory. Fixed expenses of $120,000 and $108,000 are traceable to the Northern and Southern territories, respectively. The rest of the fixed expenses are common to the two territories.

b.   The company is the exclusive distributor for two products—Paks and Tibs. Sales of Paks and Tibs totaled $50,000 and $250,000, respectively, in the Northern territory during June. Variable expenses are 22% of the selling price for Paks and 58% for Tibs. Cost records show that $30,000 of the Northern territory's fixed expenses are traceable to Paks and $40,000 to Tibs, with the remainder common to the two products.

Required:

1.   Prepare contribution format segmented income statements first showing the total company broken down between sales territories and then showing the Northern territory broken down by product line. In addition, for the company as a whole and for each segment, show each item on the segmented income statements as a percent of sales.

2.   Look at the statement you have prepared showing the total company segmented by sales territory. What insights revealed by this statement should be mentioned to management?

3.   Look at the statement you have prepared showing the Northern territory segmented by product lines. What insights revealed by this statement should be mentioned to management?

PROBLEM 6–22 Variable Costing Income Statements; Income Reconciliation LO6–1, LO6–2, LO6–3
Denton Company manufactures and sells a single product. Cost data for the product are given:

Variable costs per unit:	
Direct materials	$ 7
Direct labor......................................	10
Variable manufacturing overhead	5
Variable selling and administrative...............	3
Total variable cost per unit......................	$25
Fixed costs per month:	
Fixed manufacturing overhead....................	$315,000
Fixed selling and administrative	245,000
Total fixed cost per month	$560,000

The product sells for $60 per unit. Production and sales data for July and August, the first two months of operations, follow:

	Units Produced	Units Sold
July	17,500	15,000
August..................	17,500	20,000

The company's Accounting Department has prepared the following absorption costing income statements for July and August:

	July	August
Sales	$900,000	$1,200,000
Cost of goods sold	600,000	800,000
Gross margin	300,000	400,000
Selling and administrative expenses	290,000	305,000
Net operating income.	$ 10,000	$ 95,000

Required:
1. Determine the unit product cost under:
   a. Absorption costing.
   b. Variable costing.
2. Prepare contribution format variable costing income statements for July and August.
3. Reconcile the variable costing and absorption costing net operating incomes.
4. The company's Accounting Department has determined the company's break-even point to be 16,000 units per month, computed as follows:

$$\frac{\text{Fixed cost per month}}{\text{Unit contribution margin}} = \frac{\$560,000}{\$35 \text{ per unit}} = 16,000 \text{ units}$$

"I'm confused," said the president. "The accounting people say that our break-even point is 16,000 units per month, but we sold only 15,000 units in July, and the income statement they prepared shows a $10,000 profit for that month. Either the income statement is wrong or the break-even point is wrong." Prepare a brief memo for the president, explaining what happened on the July absorption costing income statement.

PROBLEM 6–23 Absorption and Variable Costing; Production Constant, Sales Fluctuate LO6–1, LO6–2, LO6–3

Tami Tyler opened Tami's Creations, Inc., a small manufacturing company, at the beginning of the year. Getting the company through its first quarter of operations placed a considerable strain on Ms. Tyler's personal finances. The following income statement for the first quarter was prepared by a friend who has just completed a course in managerial accounting at State University.

Tami's Creations, Inc. Income Statement For the Quarter Ended March 31		
Sales (28,000 units)		$1,120,000
Variable expenses:		
Variable cost of goods sold.	$462,000	
Variable selling and administrative.	168,000	630,000
Contribution margin		490,000
Fixed expenses:		
Fixed manufacturing overhead.	300,000	
Fixed selling and administrative	200,000	500,000
Net operating loss.		$ (10,000)

Ms. Tyler is discouraged over the loss shown for the quarter, particularly because she had planned to use the statement as support for a bank loan. Another friend, a CPA, insists that the company should be using absorption costing rather than variable costing and argues that if absorption costing had been used the company probably would have reported at least some profit for the quarter.

At this point, Ms. Tyler is manufacturing only one product—a swimsuit. Production and cost data relating to the swimsuit for the first quarter follow:

Units produced	30,000
Units sold	28,000
Variable costs per unit:	
Direct materials	$3.50
Direct labor...................................	$12.00
Variable manufacturing overhead	$1.00
Variable selling and administrative..............	$6.00

Required:
1. Complete the following:
    a. Compute the unit product cost under absorption costing.
    b. What is the company's absorption costing net operating income (loss) for the quarter?
    c. Reconcile the variable and absorption costing net operating income (loss) figures.
2. Was the CPA correct in suggesting that the company really earned a "profit" for the quarter? Explain.
3. During the second quarter of operations, the company again produced 30,000 units but sold 32,000 units. (Assume no change in total fixed costs.)
    a. What is the company's variable costing net operating income (loss) for the second quarter?
    b. What is the company's absorption costing net operating income (loss) for the second quarter?
    c. Reconcile the variable costing and absorption costing net operating incomes for the second quarter.

PROBLEM 6–24 Companywide and Segment Break-Even Analysis; Decision Making LO6–4, LO6–5
Toxaway Company is a merchandiser that segments its business into two divisions—Commercial and Residential. The company's accounting intern was asked to prepare segmented income statements that the company's divisional managers could use to calculate their break-even points and make decisions. She took the prior month's companywide income statement and prepared the absorption format segmented income statement shown below:

	Total Company	Commercial	Residential
Sales	$750,000	$250,000	$500,000
Cost of goods sold	500,000	140,000	360,000
Gross margin	250,000	110,000	140,000
Selling and administrative expenses............	240,000	104,000	136,000
Net operating income........................	$ 10,000	$ 6,000	$ 4,000

In preparing these statements, the intern determined that Toxaway's only variable selling and administrative expense is a 10% sales commission on all sales. The company's total fixed expenses include $72,000 of common fixed expenses that would continue to be incurred even if the Commercial or Residential segments are discontinued, $55,000 of fixed expenses that would be avoided if the Commericial segment is dropped, and $38,000 of fixed expenses that would be avoided if the Residential segment is dropped.

Required:
1. Do you agree with the intern's decision to use an absorption format for her segmented income statement? Why?
2. Based on a review of the intern's segmented income statement:
    a. How much of the company's common fixed expenses did she allocate to the Commercial and Residential segments?
    b. Which of the following three allocation bases did she most likely use to allocate common fixed expenses to the Commercial and Residential segments: (a) sales, (b) cost of goods sold, or (c) gross margin?

3. Do you agree with the intern's decision to allocate the common fixed expenses to the Commercial and Residential segments? Why?
4. Redo the intern's segmented income statement using the contribution format.
5. Compute the companywide break-even point in dollar sales.
6. Compute the break-even point in dollar sales for the Commercial Division and for the Residential Division.
7. Assume the company decided to pay its sales representatives in the Commercial and Residential Divisions a total monthly salary of $15,000 and $30,000, respectively, and to lower its companywide sales commission percentage from 10% to 5%. Calculate the new break-even point in dollar sales for the Commercial Division and the Residential Division.

PROBLEM 6–25 Prepare and Interpret Income Statements; Changes in Both Sales and Production; Lean Production LO6–1, LO6–2, LO6–3

Starfax, Inc., manufactures a small part that is widely used in various electronic products such as home computers. Results for the first three years of operations were as follows (absorption costing basis):

	Year 1	Year 2	Year 3
Sales	$800,000	$640,000	$800,000
Cost of goods sold	580,000	400,000	620,000
Gross margin	220,000	240,000	180,000
Selling and administrative expenses	190,000	180,000	190,000
Net operating income (loss)	$ 30,000	$ 60,000	$ (10,000)

In the latter part of Year 2, a competitor went out of business and in the process dumped a large number of units on the market. As a result, Starfax's sales dropped by 20% during Year 2 even though production increased during the year. Management had expected sales to remain constant at 50,000 units; the increased production was designed to provide the company with a buffer of protection against unexpected spurts in demand. By the start of Year 3, management could see that it had excess inventory and that spurts in demand were unlikely. To reduce the excessive inventories, Starfax cut back production during Year 3, as shown below:

	Year 1	Year 2	Year 3
Production in units	50,000	60,000	40,000
Sales in units	50,000	40,000	50,000

Additional information about the company follows:
a. The company's plant is highly automated. Variable manufacturing expenses (direct materials, direct labor, and variable manufacturing overhead) total only $2 per unit, and fixed manufacturing overhead expenses total $480,000 per year.
b. A new fixed manufacturing overhead rate is computed each year based that year's actual fixed manufacturing overhead costs divided by the actual number of units produced.
c. Variable selling and administrative expenses were $1 per unit sold in each year. Fixed selling and administrative expenses totaled $140,000 per year.
d. The company uses a FIFO inventory flow assumption. (FIFO means first-in first-out. In other words, it assumes that the oldest units in inventory are sold first.)

Starfax's management can't understand why profits doubled during Year 2 when sales dropped by 20% and why a loss was incurred during Year 3 when sales recovered to previous levels.

Required:
1. Prepare a contribution format variable costing income statement for each year.
2. Refer to the absorption costing income statements above.
   a. Compute the unit product cost in each year under absorption costing. Show how much of this cost is variable and how much is fixed.
   b. Reconcile the variable costing and absorption costing net operating income figures for each year.
3. Refer again to the absorption costing income statements. Explain why net operating income was higher in Year 2 than it was in Year 1 under the absorption approach, in light of the fact that fewer units were sold in Year 2 than in Year 1.

4. Refer again to the absorption costing income statements. Explain why the company suffered a loss in Year 3 but reported a profit in Year 1 although the same number of units was sold in each year.

5. a. Explain how operations would have differed in Year 2 and Year 3 if the company had been using Lean Production, with the result that ending inventory was zero.

   b. If Lean Production had been used during Year 2 and Year 3, what would the company's net operating income (or loss) have been in each year under absorption costing? No computations are necessary.

PROBLEM 6–26 Restructuring a Segmented Income Statement LO6–4

Millard Corporation is a wholesale distributor of office products. It purchases office products from manufacturers and distributes them in the West, Central, and East regions. Each of these regions is about the same size and each has its own manager and sales staff.

The company has been experiencing losses for many months. In an effort to improve performance, management has requested that the monthly income statement be segmented by sales region. The company's first effort at preparing a segmented income statement for May is given below.

	Sales Region		
	West	Central	East
Sales	$450,000	$800,000	$ 750,000
Regional expenses (traceable):			
Cost of goods sold	162,900	280,000	376,500
Advertising.......................................	108,000	200,000	210,000
Salaries...	90,000	88,000	135,000
Utilities	13,500	12,000	15,000
Depreciation......................................	27,000	28,000	30,000
Shipping expense...............................	17,100	32,000	28,500
Total regional expenses........................	418,500	640,000	795,000
Regional income (loss) before corporate expenses	31,500	160,000	(45,000)
Corporate expenses:			
Advertising (general)............................	18,000	32,000	30,000
General administrative expense..................	50,000	50,000	50,000
Total corporate expenses	68,000	82,000	80,000
Net operating income (loss)......................	$ (36,500)	$ 78,000	$(125,000)

The cost of goods sold and shipping expense are both variable. All other costs are fixed.

Required:

1. List any weaknesses that you see in the company's segmented income statement given above.

2. Explain the basis that is apparently being used to allocate the corporate expenses to the regions. Do you agree with these allocations? Explain.

3. Prepare a new contribution format segmented income statement for May. Show a Total column as well as data for each region. In addition, for the company as a whole and for each sales region, show each item on the segmented income statement as a percent of sales.

4. Analyze the statement that you prepared in part (3) above. What insights do those statements reveal that you would bring to management's attention?

PROBLEM 6–27 Incentives Created by Absorption Costing; Ethics and the Manager LO6–2

Carlos Cavalas, the manager of Echo Products' Brazilian Division, is trying to set the production schedule for the last quarter of the year. The Brazilian Division had planned to sell 3,600 units during the year, but by September 30 only the following activity had been reported:

	Units
Inventory, January 1	0
Production	2,400
Sales	2,000
Inventory, September 30	400

The division can rent warehouse space to store up to 1,000 units. The minimum inventory level that the division should carry is 50 units. Mr. Cavalas is aware that production must be at least 200 units per quarter in order to retain a nucleus of key employees. Maximum production capacity is 1,500 units per quarter.

Demand has been soft, and the sales forecast for the last quarter is only 600 units. Due to the nature of the division's operations, fixed manufacturing overhead is a major element of product cost.

Required:

1. Assume that the division is using variable costing. How many units should be scheduled for production during the last quarter of the year? (The basic formula for computing the required production for the quarter is: Required production = Expected sales + Desired ending inventory − Beginning inventory.) Show computations and explain your answer. Will the number of units scheduled for production affect the division's reported income or loss for the year? Explain.
2. Assume that the division is using absorption costing and that the divisional manager is given an annual bonus based on divisional operating income. If Mr. Cavalas wants to maximize his division's operating income for the year, how many units should be scheduled for production during the last quarter? [See the formula in (1) above.] Explain.
3. Identify the ethical issues involved in the decision Mr. Cavalas must make about the level of production for the last quarter of the year.

PROBLEM 6–28 Segment Reporting; Activity-Based Cost Assignment LO6–4

Diversified Products, Inc., has recently acquired a small publishing company that offers three books for sale—a cookbook, a travel guide, and a handy speller. Each book sells for $10. The publishing company's most recent monthly income statement is shown below.

		Product Line		
	Total Company	Cookbook	Travel Guide	Handy Speller
Sales	$300,000	$90,000	$150,000	$60,000
Expenses:				
Printing costs	102,000	27,000	63,000	12,000
Advertising	36,000	13,500	19,500	3,000
General sales	18,000	5,400	9,000	3,600
Salaries	33,000	18,000	9,000	6,000
Equipment depreciation	9,000	3,000	3,000	3,000
Sales commissions	30,000	9,000	15,000	6,000
General administration	42,000	14,000	14,000	14,000
Warehouse rent	12,000	3,600	6,000	2,400
Depreciation—office facilities	3,000	1,000	1,000	1,000
Total expenses	285,000	94,500	139,500	51,000
Net operating income (loss)	$ 15,000	$ (4,500)	$ 10,500	$ 9,000

The following additional information is available:

a. Only printing costs and sales commissions are variable; all other costs are fixed. The printing costs (which include materials, labor, and variable overhead) are traceable to the three product lines as shown in the income statement above. Sales commissions are 10% of sales.
b. The same equipment is used to produce all three books, so the equipment depreciation expense has been allocated equally among the three product lines. An analysis of the company's activities indicates that the equipment is used 30% of the time to produce cookbooks, 50% of the time to produce travel guides, and 20% of the time to produce handy spellers.
c. The warehouse is used to store finished units of product, so the rental cost has been allocated to the product lines on the basis of sales dollars. The warehouse rental cost is $3 per square foot per year. The warehouse contains 48,000 square feet of space, of which 7,200 square feet is used by the cookbook line, 24,000 square feet by the travel guide line, and 16,800 square feet by the handy speller line.

d. The general sales cost above includes the salary of the sales manager and other sales costs not traceable to any specific product line. This cost has been allocated to the product lines on the basis of sales dollars.

e. The general administration cost and depreciation of office facilities both relate to administration of the company as a whole. These costs have been allocated equally to the three product lines.

f. All other costs are traceable to the three product lines in the amounts shown on the income statement above.

The management of Diversified Products, Inc., is anxious to improve the publishing company's 5% return on sales.

Required:

1. Prepare a new contribution format segmented income statement for the month. Adjust allocations of equipment depreciation and of warehouse rent as indicated by the additional information provided.

2. Based on the segmented income statements given in the problem, management plans to eliminate the cookbook because it is not returning a profit, and to focus all available resources on promoting the travel guide. However, based on the new contribution format segmented income statement that you prepared:

   a. Do you agree with management's plan to eliminate the cookbook? Explain.

   b. Do you agree with the decision to focus all available resources on promoting the travel guide? Assume that an ample market is available for all three product lines. (*Hint:* Compute the contribution margin ratio for each product.)

connect **Cases**

CASE 6–29 Variable and Absorption Costing Unit Product Costs and Income Statements LO6–1, LO6–2

O'Brien Company manufactures and sells one product. The following information pertains to each of the company's first three years of operations:

Variable costs per unit:	
Manufacturing:	
Direct materials	$32
Direct labor	$20
Variable manufacturing overhead	$4
Variable selling and administrative	$3
Fixed costs per year:	
Fixed manufacturing overhead	$660,000
Fixed selling and administrative expenses	$120,000

During its first year of operations, O'Brien produced 100,000 units and sold 80,000 units. During its second year of operations, it produced 75,000 units and sold 90,000 units. In its third year, O'Brien produced 80,000 units and sold 75,000 units. The selling price of the company's product is $75 per unit.

Required:

1. Assume the company uses variable costing and a FIFO inventory flow assumption (FIFO means first-in first-out. In other words, it assumes that the oldest units in inventory are sold first):

   a. Compute the unit product cost for Year 1, Year 2, and Year 3.

   b. Prepare an income statement for Year 1, Year 2, and Year 3.

2. Assume the company uses variable costing and a LIFO inventory flow assumption (LIFO means last-in first-out. In other words, it assumes that the newest units in inventory are sold first):

   a. Compute the unit product cost for Year 1, Year 2, and Year 3.

   b. Prepare an income statement for Year 1, Year 2, and Year 3.

3. Assume the company uses absorption costing and a FIFO inventory flow assumption (FIFO means first-in first-out. In other words, it assumes that the oldest units in inventory are sold first):

   a. Compute the unit product cost for Year 1, Year 2, and Year 3.
   b. Prepare an income statement for Year 1, Year 2, and Year 3.

4. Assume the company uses absorption costing and a LIFO inventory flow assumption (LIFO means last-in first-out. In other words, it assumes that the newest units in inventory are sold first):

   a. Compute the unit product cost for Year 1, Year 2, and Year 3.
   b. Prepare an income statement for Year 1, Year 2, and Year 3.

CASE 6–30 Service Organization; Segment Reporting LO6–4

Music Teachers, Inc., is an educational association for music teachers that has 20,000 members. The association operates from a central headquarters but has local membership chapters throughout the United States. Monthly meetings are held by the local chapters to discuss recent developments on topics of interest to music teachers. The association's magazine, *Teachers' Forum,* is issued monthly with features about recent developments in the field. The association publishes books and reports and also sponsors professional courses that qualify for continuing professional education credit. The association's statement of revenues and expenses for the current year is presented below.

Music Teachers, Inc. Statement of Revenues and Expenses For the Year Ended November 30	
Revenues	$3,275,000
Expenses:	
Salaries	920,000
Personnel costs....................................	230,000
Occupancy costs....................................	280,000
Reimbursement of member costs to local chapters	600,000
Other membership services	500,000
Printing and paper..................................	320,000
Postage and shipping................................	176,000
Instructors' fees....................................	80,000
General and administrative	38,000
Total expenses......................................	3,144,000
Excess of revenues over expenses	$ 131,000

The board of directors of Music Teachers, Inc., has requested that a segmented income statement be prepared showing the contribution of each segment to the association. The association has four segments: Membership Division, Magazine Subscriptions Division, Books and Reports Division, and Continuing Education Division. Mike Doyle has been assigned responsibility for preparing the segmented income statement, and he has gathered the following data:

a. The 20,000 members of the association pay dues of $100 per year, of which $20 covers a one-year subscription to the *Teachers' Forum.* Other benefits include membership in the association and chapter affiliation. The portion of the dues covering the magazine subscription ($20) should be assigned to the Magazine Subscriptions Division.

b. A total of 2,500 one-year subscriptions to *Teachers' Forum* were also sold last year to non-members and libraries at $30 per subscription. In addition to subscriptions, the journal generated $100,000 in advertising revenues.

c. The costs to produce the *Teachers' Forum* magazine included $7 per subscription for printing and paper and $4 per subscription for postage and shipping.

d. A total of 28,000 technical reports and professional texts were sold by the Books and Reports Division at an average selling price per unit of $25. Average costs per publication were $4 for printing and paper and $2 for postage and shipping.

e. The association offers a variety of continuing education courses to both members and non-members. The one-day courses had a tuition cost of $75 each and were attended by 2,400 students. A total of 1,760 students took two-day courses at a tuition cost of $125 for each student. Outside instructors were paid to teach some courses.

f.　Salary costs and space occupied by division follow:

	Salaries	Space Occupied (square feet)
Membership.....................	$210,000	2,000
Magazine Subscriptions............	150,000	2,000
Books and Reports	300,000	3,000
Continuing Education..............	180,000	2,000
Corporate staff...................	80,000	1,000
Total........................	$920,000	10,000

Personnel costs are 25% of salaries in the separate divisions as well as for the corporate staff. The $280,000 in occupancy costs includes $50,000 in rental cost for a warehouse used by the Books and Reports Division for storage purposes.

g.　Printing and paper costs other than for magazine subscriptions and for books and reports relate to the Continuing Education Division.

h.　General and administrative expenses include costs relating to overall administration of the association as a whole. The company's corporate staff does some mailing of materials for general administrative purposes.

The expenses that can be traced or assigned to the corporate staff, as well as any other expenses that are not traceable to the segments, will be treated as common costs. It is not necessary to distinguish between variable and fixed costs.

Required:

1.　Prepare a segmented income statement for Music Teachers, Inc. This statement should show the segment margin for each division as well as results for the association as a whole.

2.　Give arguments for and against allocating all costs of the association to the four divisions.

(CMA, adapted)

Appendix 6A: Super-Variable Costing

In the discussion of variable costing in this chapter we have assumed that direct labor and a portion of manufacturing overhead are variable costs that should be attached to products. However, these assumptions about cost behavior may not be true. For example, it may be easier and more accurate to assume that *all* manufacturing overhead costs are fixed costs because the variable portion of these costs is insignificant or too difficult to estimate. Furthermore, many companies' labor costs (including direct and indirect labor) are more fixed than variable due to labor regulations, labor contracts, or management policy. In countries such as France, Germany, Spain, and Japan, management often has little flexibility in adjusting the labor force to changes in business activity. Even in countries such as the United States and the United Kingdom, where management usually has greater latitude to adjust the size of its labor force, many managers choose to view labor as a fixed cost. They make this choice because the cost savings from terminating or laying off employees during a short-term business downturn may be swamped by the negative effects on employee morale and by the costs of later finding and training suitable replacements. Moreover, treating employees as variable costs subtly fosters the attitude that employees are expendable and replaceable like materials rather than unique, difficult-to-replace assets.

Super-variable costing is a variation on variable costing in which direct labor and manufacturing overhead costs are considered to be fixed. **Super-variable costing** classifies all direct labor and manufacturing overhead costs as fixed period costs and *only direct materials as a variable product cost*. To simplify, in this appendix we also assume that selling and administrative expenses are entirely fixed.

LO6–6

Prepare an income statement using super-variable costing and reconcile this approach with variable costing.

Super-Variable Costing and Variable Costing—An Example

To illustrate the difference between treating direct labor as a fixed cost (as in super-variable costing) and treating direct labor as a variable cost (as in variable costing), we will use a modified version of the Weber Light Aircraft example from the main body of the chapter. Data concerning the company's operations appear below:

	Per Aircraft	Per Month
Selling price	$100,000	
Direct materials	$19,000	
Direct labor		$20,000
Fixed manufacturing overhead		$74,000
Fixed selling and administrative expense		$40,000

	January	February	March
Beginning inventory	0	0	1
Units produced	2	2	2
Units sold	2	1	3
Ending inventory	0	1	0

The key thing to notice here is that direct labor is a fixed cost—$20,000 per month. Also, notice that Weber Light Aircraft has no variable manufacturing overhead costs and no variable selling and administrative expenses. For the months of January, February, and March, the company's selling price per aircraft, variable cost per aircraft, monthly production in units, and total monthly fixed expenses never change. The only thing that changes in this example is the number of units sold (January = 2 units sold; February = 1 unit sold; March = 3 units sold).

We first will construct the company's super-variable costing income statements for January, February, and March. Then we will show how the company's net operating income would be determined for the same months using variable costing if it were incorrectly assumed that direct labor is a variable cost. As you'll see, both income statements rely on the contribution format.

Super-Variable Costing Income Statements

To prepare the company's super-variable costing income statements for each month we follow four steps. First, we compute sales by multiplying the number of units sold by the selling price per unit, which in this example is $100,000 per unit. Second, we compute the variable cost of goods sold by multiplying the number of units sold by the unit product cost, which in this example is the direct materials cost of $19,000 per unit. Third, we compute the contribution margin by subtracting variable cost of goods sold from sales. Fourth, we compute net operating income by subtracting total fixed expenses, which in this example is $134,000 per month (= $20,000 + $74,000 + $40,000), from the contribution margin.

Using these four steps, Weber's super-variable costing income statements for each month would appear as shown in Exhibit 6A–1. Notice that the only variable expense is variable cost of goods sold, which is the $19,000 of direct materials per unit sold. For example, in March, the unit product cost of $19,000 is multiplied by three units sold to obtain the variable cost of goods sold of $57,000. The total monthly fixed manufacturing expenses of $94,000 include $20,000 of direct labor and $74,000 of fixed manufacturing overhead.

Variable Costing Income Statements

The variable costing income statements in this example differ from the super-variable costing income statements in one important respect—we will assume that direct labor is incorrectly classified as a variable cost and is included in unit product costs. Because the monthly direct labor cost is $20,000 and two aircraft are produced each month, if direct labor costs are included in unit product costs, then Weber Light Aircraft will assign

	January	February	March
Sales (@ $100,000 per unit)	$200,000	$100,000	$300,000
Variable cost of goods sold			
(@ $19,000 per unit).....................	38,000	19,000	57,000
Contribution margin	162,000	81,000	243,000
Fixed expenses:			
Fixed manufacturing expenses.............	94,000	94,000	94,000
Fixed selling and administrative expenses...	40,000	40,000	40,000
Total fixed expenses.......................	134,000	134,000	134,000
Net operating income (loss)................	$ 28,000	$ (53,000)	$109,000

EXHIBIT 6A-1
Super-Variable Costing Income Statements

$10,000 of direct labor cost to each aircraft that it produces. Thus, the company's unit product costs under variable costing would be computed as follows:

	January	February	March
Direct materials	$19,000	$19,000	$19,000
Direct labor...............	10,000	10,000	10,000
Unit product cost..........	$29,000	$29,000	$29,000

Given these unit product cost figures, the company's variable costing income statements would be computed as shown in Exhibit 6A–2. For example, in March, the unit product cost of $29,000 is multiplied by three units sold to obtain the variable cost of goods sold of $87,000. The total fixed manufacturing overhead of $74,000 and total fixed selling and administrative expenses of $40,000 are both recorded as period expenses.

Reconciliation of Super-Variable Costing and Variable Costing Income

The super-variable costing and variable costing net operating incomes are both $28,000 in January. However, in February, the super-variable costing income is $10,000 lower than the variable costing income and the opposite holds true in March. In other words, the super-variable costing income in March is $10,000 higher than the variable costing income.

	January	February	March
Sales (@ $100,000 per unit)	$200,000	$100,000	$300,000
Variable cost of goods sold			
(@ $29,000 per unit).....................	58,000	29,000	87,000
Contribution margin	142,000	71,000	213,000
Fixed expenses:			
Fixed manufacturing overhead.............	74,000	74,000	74,000
Fixed selling and administrative expenses...	40,000	40,000	40,000
Total fixed expenses.......................	114,000	114,000	114,000
Net operating income (loss)................	$ 28,000	$ (43,000)	$ 99,000

EXHIBIT 6A-2
Variable Costing Income Statements

Why do these two costing methods produce different net operating incomes? The answer can be found in the accounting for direct labor costs. Super-variable costing treats direct labor as a fixed period expense whereas variable costing treats direct labor as a variable product cost. In other words, super-variable costing records the entire direct labor cost of $20,000 as an expense on each month's income statement. Conversely, variable costing assigns $10,000 of direct labor cost to each unit produced. The $10,000 assigned to each unit produced remains in inventory on the balance sheet until the unit is sold—at which point the $10,000 assigned to it is transferred to variable cost of goods sold on the income statement. Given this background, the super-variable costing and variable costing incomes for each month can be reconciled as follows:

	January	February	March
Direct labor cost in ending inventory (@ $10,000 per unit)......................	$ 0	$10,000	$ 0
Deduct: Direct labor cost in beginning inventory (@ $10,000 per unit)......................	0	0	10,000
Direct labor cost deferred in (released from) inventory..................	$ 0	$10,000	$(10,000)

	January	February	March
Super-variable costing net operating income (loss)	$28,000	$(53,000)	$109,000
Direct labor deferred in (released from) inventory.....................................	0	10,000	(10,000)
Variable costing net operating income (loss)	$28,000	$(43,000)	$ 99,000

In January, both costing methods report the same net operating income ($28,000). This occurs because the unit produced in January was also sold in January and, as a result, both methods expense $20,000 of direct labor in the income statement. In February, two units are produced, but only one unit is sold; therefore, super-variable costing income is $10,000 less than variable costing income. This difference arises because super-variable costing expenses $20,000 of direct labor in the income statement, whereas variable costing expenses only $10,000 of direct labor in the income statement ($10,000 per unit × 1 unit sold) while deferring the other $10,000 of direct labor in inventory ($10,000 per unit × 1 unit produced but not sold). In March, two units are produced and three units are sold; hence, super-variable costing income is $10,000 greater than variable costing income. This difference arises because super-variable costing expenses $20,000 of direct labor on the income statement, whereas variable costing expenses $30,000 of direct labor on the income statement ($10,000 per unit × 3 unit sold). Notice that one of the units sold in March was actually produced in February. Under variable costing, the $10,000 of direct labor attached to the unit produced in February is released from inventory and included in variable cost of goods sold for March.

In summary, the key issue considered in this appendix is how a company treats direct labor costs. If a company treats direct labor as a variable cost, the cost system may encourage managers to treat labor costs as an expense to be minimized when sales decline and this may result in reduced morale and eventual problems when business picks up. Second, in practice management may have little ability to adjust the direct labor force even if they wanted to, resulting in a situation in which direct labor costs are in fact fixed. In either case, treating direct labor costs as variable can lead to bad decisions. The super-variable costing approach overcomes this problem by treating labor costs as fixed costs.

Glossary (Appendix 6A)

Super-variable costing A costing method that classifies all direct labor and manufacturing overhead costs as fixed period costs and *only direct materials as a variable product cost.* (p. 303)

Appendix 6A: Exercises and Problems

EXERCISE 6A–1 Super-Variable Costing Income Statement LO6–6

Zola Company manufactures and sells one product. The following information pertains to the company's first year of operations:

Variable cost per unit:	
Direct materials	$18
Fixed costs per year:	
Direct labor.	$200,000
Fixed manufacturing overhead	$250,000
Fixed selling and administrative expenses	$80,000

The company does not incur any variable manufacturing overhead costs or variable selling and administrative expenses. During its first year of operations, Zola produced 25,000 units and sold 20,000 units. The selling price of the company's product is $50 per unit.

Required:

1. Assume the company uses super-variable costing:
   a. Compute the unit product cost for the year.
   b. Prepare an income statement for the year.

EXERCISE 6A–2 Super-Variable Costing and Variable Costing Unit Product Costs and Income Statements LO6–2, LO6–6

Lyons Company manufactures and sells one product. The following information pertains to the company's first year of operations:

Variable cost per unit:	
Direct materials	$13
Fixed costs per year:	
Direct labor.	$750,000
Fixed manufacturing overhead	$420,000
Fixed selling and administrative expenses	$110,000

The company does not incur any variable manufacturing overhead costs or variable selling and administrative expenses. During its first year of operations, Lyons produced 60,000 units and sold 52,000 units. The selling price of the company's product is $40 per unit.

Required:

1. Assume the company uses super-variable costing:
   a. Compute the unit product cost for the year.
   b. Prepare an income statement for the year.
2. Assume the company uses a variable costing system that assigns $12.50 of direct labor cost to each unit produced:
   a. Compute the unit product cost for the year.
   b. Prepare an income statement for the year.
3. Prepare a reconciliation that explains the difference between the super-variable costing and variable costing net operating incomes.

EXERCISE 6A–3 Super-Variable Costing and Variable Costing Unit Product Costs and Income Statements LO6–2, LO6–6

Kelly Company manufactures and sells one product. The following information pertains to each of the company's first two years of operations:

Variable cost per unit:	
Direct materials	$12
Fixed costs per year:	
Direct labor................................	$500,000
Fixed manufacturing overhead................	$450,000
Fixed selling and administrative expenses......	$180,000

The company does not incur any variable manufacturing overhead costs or variable selling and administrative expenses. During its first year of operations, Kelly produced 50,000 units and sold 40,000 units. During its second year of operations, it produced 50,000 units and sold 60,000 units. The selling price of the company's product is $50 per unit.

Required:

1. Assume the company uses super-variable costing:
    a. Compute the unit product cost for Year 1 and Year 2.
    b. Prepare an income statement for Year 1 and Year 2.
2. Assume the company uses a variable costing system that assigns $10 of direct labor cost to each unit produced:
    a. Compute the unit product cost for Year 1 and Year 2.
    b. Prepare an income statement for Year 1 and Year 2.
3. Prepare a reconciliation that explains the difference between the super-variable costing and variable costing net operating incomes in Years 1 and 2.

PROBLEM 6A–4 Super-Variable Costing and Variable Costing Unit Product Costs and Income Statements LO6–2, LO6–6

Ogilvy Company manufactures and sells one product. The following information pertains to each of the company's first three years of operations:

Variable cost per unit:	
Direct materials	$16
Fixed costs per year:	
Direct labor................................	$540,000
Fixed manufacturing overhead................	$822,000
Fixed selling and administrative expenses.......	$370,000

The company does not incur any variable manufacturing overhead costs or variable selling and administrative expenses. During its first year of operations, Ogilvy produced 60,000 units and sold 60,000 units. During its second year of operations, it produced 60,000 units and sold 55,000 units. In its third year, Ogilvy produced 60,000 units and sold 65,000 units. The selling price of the company's product is $45 per unit.

Required:

1. Assume the company uses super-variable costing:
    a. Compute the unit product cost for Year 1, Year 2, and Year 3.
    b. Prepare an income statement for Year 1, Year 2, and Year 3.
2. Assume the company uses a variable costing system that assigns $9 of direct labor cost to each unit produced:
    a. Compute the unit product cost for Year 1, Year 2, and Year 3.
    b. Prepare an income statement for Year 1, Year 2, and Year 3.
3. Prepare a reconciliation that explains the difference between the super-variable costing and variable costing net operating incomes in Years 1, 2, and 3.

PROBLEM 6A–5 Super-Variable Costing, Variable Costing, and Absorption Costing Income Statements LO6–2, LO6–6

Bracey Company manufactures and sells one product. The following information pertains to the company's first year of operations:

Variable cost per unit:	
Direct materials	$19
Fixed costs per year:	
Direct labor.	$250,000
Fixed manufacturing overhead.	$300,000
Fixed selling and administrative expenses	$90,000

The company does not incur any variable manufacturing overhead costs or variable selling and administrative expenses. During its first year of operations, Bracey produced 20,000 units and sold 18,000 units. The selling price of the company's product is $55 per unit.

Required:

1. Assume the company uses super-variable costing:
    a. Compute the unit product cost for the year.
    b. Prepare an income statement for the year.
2. Assume the company uses a variable costing system that assigns $12.50 of direct labor cost to each unit produced:
    a. Compute the unit product cost for the year.
    b. Prepare an income statement for the year.
3. Assume the company uses an absorption costing system that assigns $12.50 of direct labor cost and $15.00 of fixed manufacturing overhead cost to each unit produced:
    a. Compute the unit product cost for the year.
    b. Prepare an income statement for the year.
4. Prepare a reconciliation that explains the difference between the super-variable costing and variable costing net operating incomes. Prepare another reconciliation that explains the difference between the super-variable costing and absorption costing net operating incomes.

Activity-Based Costing:
A Tool to Aid Decision Making

Airline Fuel Cost Drivers

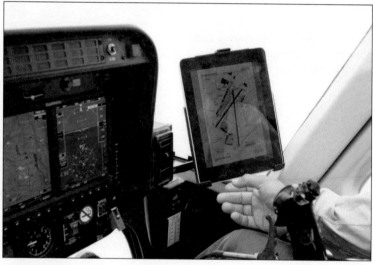

© Scott Eells/Bloomberg/Getty Images

Stop for a moment to identify as many airline fuel cost drivers as you can. Perhaps you readily thought of two important cost drivers—the number of flights and the number of miles flown. However, did you consider the weight of the plane in flight given the fact that heavier planes consume more fuel? While you may have overlooked weight as a cost driver, rest assured that the airline industry has not. Regulators have given airlines clearance for its pilots to replace the bulky navigation charts and manuals that they have hauled around for years with an iPad. American Airlines estimates that the switch to iPads will eliminate 3,000 pages of paper per pilot, which translates to annual savings of 400,000 gallons of fuel and $1.2 million dollars.

In this chapter, you'll learn how companies implement activity-based costing systems to better understand and manage the cost drivers that influence the profitability of various cost objects such as products and customers. ■

Source: Susan Carey, "Airlines Jettison a Costly Load of Paper," *The Wall Street Journal*, June 27, 2013, p. B6.

LEARNING OBJECTIVES

After studying Chapter 7, you should be able to:

LO7–1 Understand activity-based costing and how it differs from a traditional costing system.

LO7–2 Assign costs to cost pools using a first-stage allocation.

LO7–3 Compute activity rates for cost pools.

LO7–4 Assign costs to a cost object using a second-stage allocation.

LO7–5 Use activity-based costing to compute product and customer margins.

LO7–6 (Appendix 7A) Use time-driven activity-based costing to assign costs to cost objects.

LO7–7 (Appendix 7A) Use time-driven activity-based costing to analyze capacity.

This chapter introduces the concept of *activity-based costing* which has been embraced by a wide variety of organizations including **Charles Schwab**, **Citigroup**, **Lowe's**, **Coca-Cola**, **J&B Wholesale**, **Fairchild Semi-conductor**, **Assan Aluminum**, **Sysco Foods**, **Fisher Scientific International**, and **Peregrine Outfitters**. **Activity-based costing (ABC)** is a costing method that is designed to provide managers with cost information for strategic and other decisions that potentially affect capacity and therefore "fixed" as well as variable costs. Activity-based costing is ordinarily used as a supplement to, rather than as a replacement for, a company's usual costing system. Most organizations that use activity-based costing have two costing systems—the official costing system that is used for preparing external financial reports and the activity-based costing system that is used for internal decision making and for managing activities.

This chapter focuses primarily on ABC applications in manufacturing to provide a contrast with the material presented in earlier chapters. More specifically, Chapters 3 and 4 focused on traditional absorption costing systems used by manufacturing companies to calculate unit product costs for the purpose of valuing inventories and determining cost of goods sold for external financial reports. In contrast, this chapter explains how manufacturing companies can use activity-based costing rather than traditional methods to calculate unit product costs for the purposes of managing overhead and making decisions. Chapter 6 had a similar purpose. That chapter focused on how to use variable costing to aid decisions that do not affect fixed costs. This chapter extends that idea to show how activity-based costing can be used to aid decisions that potentially affect fixed costs as well as variable costs.

Activity-Based Costing: An Overview

As stated above, traditional absorption costing is designed to provide data for external financial reports. In contrast, activity-based costing is designed to be used for internal decision making. As a consequence, activity-based costing differs from traditional absorption costing in three ways. In activity-based costing:

> **LO7–1**
> Understand activity-based costing and how it differs from a traditional costing system.

1. Nonmanufacturing as well as manufacturing costs may be assigned to products, but only on a cause-and-effect basis.
2. Some manufacturing costs may be excluded from product costs.
3. Numerous overhead cost pools are used, each of which is allocated to products and other cost objects using its own unique measure of activity.

Each of these departures from traditional absorption costing will be discussed in turn.

Nonmanufacturing Costs and Activity-Based Costing

In traditional absorption costing, manufacturing costs are assigned to products and nonmanufacturing costs are not assigned to products. Conversely, in activity-based costing, we recognize that many nonmanufacturing costs relate to selling, distributing, and servicing specific products. Thus, ABC includes manufacturing *and* nonmanufacturing costs when calculating the entire cost of a product rather than just its manufacturing cost.

There are two types of nonmanufacturing costs that ABC systems assign to products. First, ABC systems trace all direct nonmanufacturing costs to products. Commissions paid to salespersons, shipping costs, and warranty repair costs are examples of nonmanufacturing costs that can be directly traced to individual products. Second, ABC systems allocate indirect nonmanufacturing costs to products whenever the products have presumably caused the costs to be incurred. In fact, in this chapter, we emphasize this point by expanding the definition of *overhead* to include all indirect costs—manufacturing and nonmanufacturing.

In summary, ABC product cost calculations include all direct costs that can be traced to products and all indirect costs that are caused by products. The need to distinguish between manufacturing and nonmanufacturing costs disappears—which is very different from earlier chapters that focused solely on determining the manufacturing cost of a product.

Manufacturing Costs and Activity-Based Costing

In traditional absorption costing systems, *all* manufacturing costs are assigned to products—even manufacturing costs that are not caused by the products. For example, in Chapters 2 and 3 we learned that a predetermined plantwide overhead rate is computed by dividing *all* budgeted manufacturing overhead costs by the budgeted amount of the allocation base. So, in the case of a company that uses budgeted direct labor-hours as its allocation base, this approach will assign *all* of the company's manufacturing overhead costs to its products based on each product's direct labor-hour usage. In contrast, activity-based costing systems purposely do not assign two types of manufacturing overhead costs to products—*organization-sustaining costs* and *unused capacity costs* (also called idle capacity costs).

Organization-sustaining costs include costs such as the factory security guard's wages, the plant controller's salary, and the cost of supplies used by the plant manager's secretary. These types of manufacturing overhead costs are assigned to products in a traditional absorption costing system even though they are totally unaffected by which products are made during a period. In contrast, activity-based costing systems treat these types of organization-sustaining costs as period expenses rather than arbitrarily assigning them to products.

Additionally, in a traditional absorption costing system, the cost of unused capacity is assigned to products. If the budgeted level of activity declines, the overhead rate and unit product costs rise thereby ensuring that the shrinking volume of output absorbs the increasing cost of idle capacity. In contrast, in activity-based costing, products are charged only for the cost of the capacity they use—not for the cost of the capacity they don't use. This provides more stable unit product costs and is consistent with the goal of assigning to products only the costs of the resources that they use.[1]

Exhibit 7–1 summarizes the two departures from traditional absorption costing that we have discussed thus far. The top portion of the exhibit shows that traditional absorption costing treats all manufacturing costs as product costs and all nonmanufacturing costs as period costs. The bottom portion of the exhibit shows that activity-based costing expands the definition of *overhead* to include all indirect costs—manufacturing and nonmanufacturing. The overhead costs that are caused by products are allocated to them, whereas any overhead costs that are not caused by products are treated as period costs. It also shows that ABC treats direct nonmanufacturing costs as product costs rather than period costs.

Now we turn our attention to the third and final difference between traditional absorption costing and activity-based costing.

Cost Pools, Allocation Bases, and Activity-Based Costing

Throughout the 19th century and most of the 20th century, cost system designs were simple and satisfactory. Typically, either one plantwide overhead cost pool or a number of departmental overhead cost pools were used to assign overhead costs to products. The plantwide and departmental approaches always had one thing in common—they relied on allocation bases such as direct labor-hours and machine-hours for allocating overhead

---

[1] Appendix 2B discusses how the cost of unused capacity can be accounted for as a period cost in an income statement. This treatment highlights the cost of unused capacity rather than burying it in inventory and cost of goods sold. The procedures laid out in this chapter for activity-based costing have the same end effect.

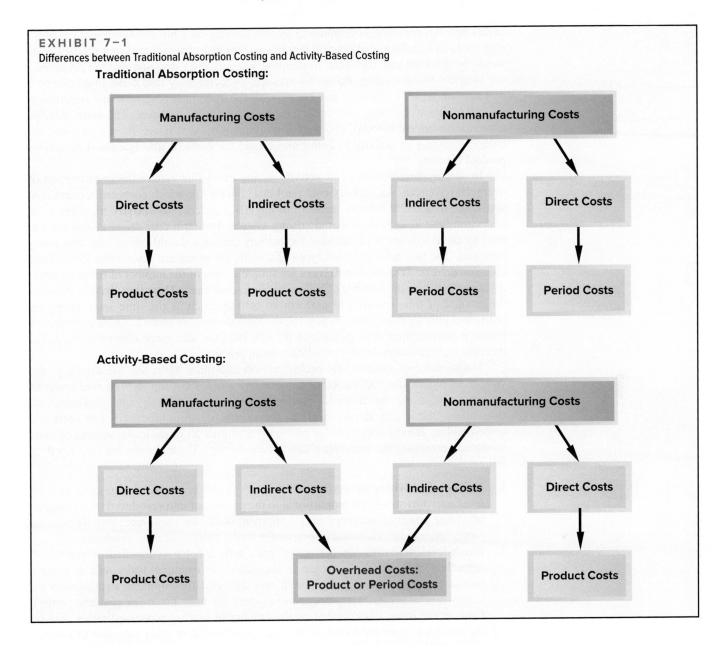

EXHIBIT 7–1
Differences between Traditional Absorption Costing and Activity-Based Costing

costs to products. In the labor-intensive production processes of many years ago, direct labor was the most common choice for an overhead allocation base because it represented a large component of product costs, direct labor-hours were closely tracked, and many managers believed that direct labor-hours, the total volume of units produced, and overhead costs were highly correlated. (Three variables, such as direct labor-hours, the total volume of units produced, and overhead costs, are highly correlated if they tend to move together.) Given that most companies at the time were producing a very limited variety of products that required similar resources to produce, allocation bases such as direct labor-hours, or even machine-hours, worked fine because, in fact, there was probably little difference in the overhead costs attributable to different products.

Then conditions began to change. As a percentage of total cost, direct labor began declining and overhead began increasing. Many tasks previously done by direct laborers were being performed by automated equipment—a component of overhead. Companies began creating new products and services at an ever-accelerating rate that differed in volume, batch size, and complexity. Managing and sustaining this product diversity required investing in many more overhead resources, such as production schedulers and product design engineers, that had no obvious connection to direct labor-hours or machine-hours.

In this new environment, continuing to rely exclusively on a limited number of overhead cost pools and traditional allocation bases posed the risk that reported unit product costs would be distorted and, therefore, misleading when used for decision-making purposes.

Activity-based costing, thanks to advances in technology that make more complex cost systems feasible, provides an alternative to the traditional plantwide and departmental approaches to defining cost pools and selecting allocation bases. The activity-based approach has appeal in today's business environment because it uses more cost pools and unique measures of activity to better understand the costs of managing and sustaining product diversity.

In activity-based costing, an **activity** is any event that causes the consumption of overhead resources. An **activity cost pool** is a "bucket" in which costs are accumulated that relate to a single activity measure in the ABC system. An **activity measure** is an allocation base in an activity-based costing system. The term *cost driver* is also used to refer to an activity measure because the activity measure should "drive" the cost being allocated. The two most common types of activity measures are *transaction drivers* and *duration drivers*. **Transaction drivers** are simple counts of the number of times an activity occurs, such as the number of bills sent out to customers. **Duration drivers** measure the amount of time required to perform an activity, such as the time spent preparing individual bills for customers. In general, duration drivers are more accurate measures of resource consumption than transaction drivers, but they take more effort to record. For that reason, transaction drivers are often used in practice.

Traditional cost systems rely exclusively on allocation bases that are driven by the volume of production. On the other hand, activity-based costing defines five levels of activity—unit-level, batch-level, product-level, customer-level, and organization-sustaining—that largely do *not* relate to the volume of units produced. The costs and corresponding activity measures for unit-level activities do relate to the volume of units produced; however, the remaining categories do not. These levels are described as follows:[2]

1. **Unit-level activities** are performed each time a unit is produced. The costs of unit-level activities should be proportional to the number of units produced. For example, providing power to run processing equipment would be a unit-level activity because power tends to be consumed in proportion to the number of units produced.

2. **Batch-level activities** are performed each time a batch is handled or processed, regardless of how many units are in the batch. For example, tasks such as placing purchase orders, setting up equipment, and arranging for shipments to customers are batch-level activities. They are incurred once for each batch (or customer order). Costs at the batch level depend on the number of batches processed rather than on the number of units produced, the number of units sold, or other measures of volume. For example, the cost of setting up a machine for batch processing is the same regardless of whether the batch contains one or thousands of items.

3. **Product-level activities** relate to specific products and typically must be carried out regardless of how many batches are run or units of product are produced or sold. For example, activities such as designing a product, advertising a product, and maintaining a product manager and staff are all product-level activities.

4. **Customer-level activities** relate to specific customers and include activities such as sales calls, catalog mailings, and general technical support that are not tied to any specific product.

5. **Organization-sustaining activities** are carried out regardless of which customers are served, which products are produced, how many batches are run, or how many units are made. This category includes activities such as heating the factory, cleaning executive offices, providing a computer network, arranging for loans, preparing annual reports to shareholders, and so on.

---

[2] Robin Cooper, "Cost Classification in Unit-Based and Activity-Based Manufacturing Cost Systems," *Journal of Cost Management*, Fall 1990, pp. 4–14.

Many companies throughout the world continue to base overhead allocations on direct labor-hours or machine-hours. In situations where overhead costs and direct labor-hours are highly correlated or in situations where the goal of the overhead allocation process is to prepare external financial reports, this practice makes sense. However, if plantwide overhead costs do not move in tandem with plantwide direct labor-hours or machine-hours, product costs will be distorted—with the potential of distorting decisions made within the company.

DINING IN THE CANYON

Western River Expeditions (www.westernriver.com) runs river rafting trips on the Colorado, Green, and Salmon rivers. One of its most popular trips is a six-day trip down the Grand Canyon, which features famous rapids such as Crystal and Lava Falls as well as the awesome scenery accessible only from the bottom of the Grand Canyon. The company runs trips of one or two rafts, each of which carries two guides and up to 18 guests. The company provides all meals on the trip, which are prepared by the guides.

In terms of the hierarchy of activities, a guest can be considered as a unit and a raft as a batch. In that context, the wages paid to the guides are a batch-level cost because each raft requires two guides regardless of the number of guests in the raft. Each guest is given a mug to use during the trip and to take home at the end of the trip as a souvenir. The cost of the mug is a unit-level cost because the number of mugs given away is strictly proportional to the number of guests on a trip.

What about the costs of food served to guests and guides—is this a unit-level cost, a batch-level cost, a product-level cost, or an organization-sustaining cost? At first glance, it might be thought that food costs are a unit-level cost—the greater the number of guests, the higher the food costs. However, that is not quite correct. Standard menus have been created for each day of the trip. For example, the first night's menu might consist of shrimp cocktail, steak, cornbread, salad, and cheesecake. The day before a trip begins, all of the food needed for the trip is taken from the central warehouse and packed in modular containers. It isn't practical to finely adjust the amount of food for the actual number of guests planned to be on a trip—most of the food comes prepackaged in large lots. For example, the shrimp cocktail menu may call for two large bags of frozen shrimp per raft and that many bags will be packed regardless of how many guests are expected on the raft. Consequently, the costs of food are not a unit-level cost that varies with the number of guests actually on a trip. Instead, the costs of food are a batch-level cost.

© Sandee Noreen

Designing an Activity-Based Costing (ABC) System

There are three essential characteristics of a successful activity-based costing implementation. First, top managers must strongly support the ABC implementation because their leadership is instrumental in properly motivating all employees to embrace the need to change. Second, top managers should ensure that ABC data is linked to how people are evaluated and rewarded. If employees continue to be evaluated and rewarded using traditional (non-ABC) cost data, they will quickly get the message that ABC is not important and they will abandon it. Third, a cross-functional team should be created to design and implement the ABC system. The team should include representatives from each area that will use ABC data, such as the marketing, production, engineering, and accounting departments. These cross-functional employees possess intimate knowledge of many parts of an organization's operations that is necessary for designing an effective ABC system. Furthermore, tapping the knowledge of cross-functional managers lessens their resistance to ABC because they feel included in the implementation process. Time after time, when accountants have attempted to implement an ABC system on their own without top-management support and cross-functional involvement, the results have been ignored.

Classic Brass, Inc., makes two main product lines for luxury yachts—standard stanchions and custom compass housings. The president of the company, John Towers, recently attended a management conference at which activity-based costing was discussed. Following the conference, he called a meeting of the company's top managers to discuss what he had learned. Attending the meeting were production manager Susan Richter, the marketing manager Tom Olafson, and the accounting manager Mary Goodman. He began the conference by distributing the company's income statement that Mary Goodman had prepared a few hours earlier (see Exhibit 7–2):

John: Well, it's official. Our company has sunk into the red for the first time in its history—a loss of $1,250.

Tom: I don't know what else we can do! Given our successful efforts to grow sales of the custom compass housings, I was expecting to see a boost to our bottom line, not a net loss. Granted, we have been losing even more bids than usual for standard stanchions because of our recent price increase, but . . .

John: Do you think our prices for standard stanchions are too high?

Tom: No, I don't think our prices are too high. I think our competitors' prices are too low. In fact, I'll bet they are pricing below their cost.

Susan: Why would our competitors price below their cost?

Tom: They are out to grab market share.

Susan: What good is more market share if they are losing money on every unit sold?

John: I think Susan has a point. Mary, what is your take on this?

Mary: If our competitors are pricing standard stanchions below cost, shouldn't they be losing money rather than us? If our company is the one using accurate information to make informed decisions while our competitors are supposedly clueless, then why is our "bottom line" taking a beating? Unfortunately, I think we may be the ones relying on distorted cost data, not our competitors.

John: Based on what I heard at the conference that I just attended, I am inclined to agree. One of the presentations at the conference dealt with activity-based costing. As the speaker began describing the usual insights revealed by activity-based costing systems, I was sitting in the audience getting an ill feeling in my stomach.

EXHIBIT 7–2
Classic Brass Income Statement

Classic Brass
Income Statement
Year Ended December 31, 2017

Sales		$3,200,000
Cost of goods sold:		
Direct materials	$ 975,000	
Direct labor.	351,250	
Manufacturing overhead*	1,000,000	2,326,250
Gross margin		873,750
Selling and administrative expenses:		
Shipping expense	65,000	
General administrative expense.	510,000	
Marketing expense.	300,000	875,000
Net operating loss.		$ (1,250)

*The company's traditional cost system allocates manufacturing overhead to products using a plantwide overhead rate and machine-hours as the allocation base. Inventory levels did not change during the year.

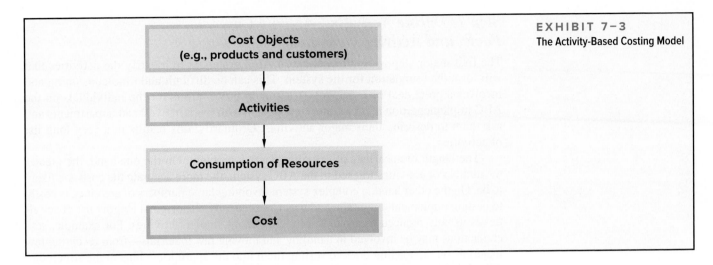

EXHIBIT 7–3
The Activity-Based Costing Model

Mary: Honestly John, I have been claiming for years that our existing cost system is okay for external reporting, but it is dangerous to use it for internal decision making. It sounds like you are on board now, right?

John: Yes.

Mary: Well then, how about if all of you commit the time and energy to help me build a fairly simple activity-based costing system that may shed some light on the problems we are facing?

John: Let's do it. I want each of you to appoint one of your top people to a special "ABC team" to investigate how we cost products.

Like most other ABC implementations, the ABC team decided that its new ABC system would supplement, rather than replace, the existing cost accounting system, which would continue to be used to prepare financial statements for external parties. The new ABC system would be used to prepare special reports for management decisions such as bidding on new business.

The accounting manager drew the chart appearing in Exhibit 7–3 to explain the general structure of the ABC model to her team members. Cost objects such as products generate activities. For example, a customer order for a custom compass housing requires the activity of preparing a production order. Such an activity consumes resources. A production order uses a sheet of paper and takes time to fill out. And consumption of resources causes costs. The greater the number of sheets used to fill out production orders and the greater the amount of time devoted to filling out such orders, the greater the cost. Activity-based costing attempts to trace through these relationships to identify how products and customers affect costs.

As in most other companies, the ABC team at Classic Brass felt that the company's traditional cost accounting system adequately measured the direct materials and direct labor costs of products because these costs are directly traced to products. Therefore, the ABC study would be concerned solely with the other costs of the company—manufacturing overhead and selling and administrative costs.

The team felt it was important to carefully plan how it would go about implementing the new ABC system at Classic Brass. Accordingly, it broke down the implementation process into five steps:

Steps for Implementing Activity-Based Costing:

1. Define activities, activity cost pools, and activity measures.
2. Assign overhead costs to activity cost pools.
3. Calculate activity rates.
4. Assign overhead costs to cost objects.
5. Prepare management reports.

Step 1: Define Activities, Activity Cost Pools, and Activity Measures

The first major step in implementing an ABC system is to identify the activities that will form the foundation for the system. This can be difficult and time-consuming and involves a great deal of judgment. A common procedure is for the individuals on the ABC implementation team to interview people who work in overhead departments and ask them to describe their major activities. Ordinarily, this results in a very long list of activities.

The length of such lists of activities poses a problem. On the one hand, the greater the number of activities tracked in the ABC system, the more accurate the costs are likely to be. On the other hand, a complex system involving large numbers of activities is costly to design, implement, maintain, and use. Consequently, the original lengthy list of activities is usually reduced to a handful by combining similar activities. For example, several actions may be involved in handling and moving raw materials—from receiving raw materials on the loading dock to sorting them into the appropriate bins in the storeroom. All of these activities might be combined into a single activity called material handling.

When combining activities in an ABC system, activities should be grouped together at the appropriate level. Batch-level activities should not be combined with unit-level activities or product-level activities with batch-level activities and so on. In general, it is best to combine only those activities that are highly correlated with each other within a level. For example, the number of customer orders received is likely to be highly correlated with the number of completed customer orders shipped, so these two batch-level activities (receiving and shipping orders) can usually be combined with little loss of accuracy.

At Classic Brass, the ABC team, in consultation with top managers, selected the following *activity cost pools* and *activity measures:*

Activity Cost Pools at Classic Brass	
Activity Cost Pool	Activity Measure
Customer orders	Number of customer orders
Product design	Number of product designs
Order size	Machine-hours
Customer relations	Number of active customers
Other	Not applicable

The *Customer Orders* cost pool will be assigned all costs of resources that are consumed by taking and processing customer orders, including costs of processing paperwork and any costs involved in setting up machines for specific orders. The activity measure for this cost pool is the number of customer orders received. This is a batch-level activity because each order generates work that occurs regardless of whether the order is for one unit or 1,000 units.

The *Product Design* cost pool will be assigned all costs of resources consumed by designing products. The activity measure for this cost pool is the number of product designs. This is a product-level activity because the amount of design work on a new product does not depend on the number of units ultimately ordered or batches ultimately run.

The *Order Size* cost pool will be assigned all costs of resources consumed as a consequence of the number of units produced, including the costs of miscellaneous factory supplies, power to run machines, and some equipment depreciation. This is a unit-level activity because each unit requires some of these resources. The activity measure for this cost pool is machine-hours.

The *Customer Relations* cost pool will be assigned all costs associated with maintaining relations with customers, including the costs of sales calls and the costs of entertaining customers. The activity measure for this cost pool is the number of customers the company has on its active customer list. The Customer Relations cost pool represents a customer-level activity.

The *Other* cost pool will be assigned all overhead costs that are not associated with customer orders, product design, the size of the orders, or customer relations. These costs mainly consist of organization-sustaining costs and the costs of unused, idle capacity. These costs *will not* be assigned to products because they represent resources that are *not* consumed by products.

It is unlikely that any other company would use exactly the same activity cost pools and activity measures that were selected by Classic Brass. Because of the amount of judgment involved, the number and definitions of the activity cost pools and activity measures used by companies vary considerably.

The Mechanics of Activity-Based Costing

Step 2: Assign Overhead Costs to Activity Cost Pools

Exhibit 7–4 shows the annual overhead costs (both manufacturing and nonmanufacturing) that Classic Brass intends to assign to its activity cost pools. Notice the data in the exhibit are organized by department (e.g., Production, General Administrative, and Marketing). This is because the data have been extracted from the company's general ledger. General ledgers usually classify costs within the departments where the costs are incurred. For example, salaries, supplies, rent, and so forth incurred in the marketing department are charged to that department. The functional orientation of the general ledger mirrors the presentation of costs in the absorption income statement in Exhibit 7–2. In fact, you'll notice the total costs for the Production Department in Exhibit 7–4 ($1,000,000) equal the total manufacturing overhead costs from the income statement in Exhibit 7–2. Similarly, the total costs for the General Administrative and Marketing Departments in Exhibit 7–4 ($510,000 and $300,000) equal the marketing and general and administrative expenses shown in Exhibit 7–2.

Three costs included in the income statement in Exhibit 7–2 —direct materials, direct labor, and shipping expenses—are excluded from the costs shown in Exhibit 7–4. The ABC team purposely excluded these costs from Exhibit 7–4 because the existing cost system can accurately trace direct materials, direct labor, and shipping costs to products. There is no need to incorporate these direct costs in the activity-based allocations of indirect costs.

LO7–2
Assign costs to cost pools using a first-stage allocation.

Production Department:			
Indirect factory wages	$500,000		
Factory equipment depreciation	300,000		
Factory utilities...............................	120,000		
Factory building lease	80,000	$1,000,000	
General Administrative Department:			
Administrative wages and salaries..............	400,000		
Office equipment depreciation.................	50,000		
Administrative building lease	60,000	510,000	
Marketing Department:			
Marketing wages and salaries	250,000		
Selling expenses.............................	50,000	300,000	
Total overhead cost...........................		$1,810,000	

EXHIBIT 7–4
Annual Overhead Costs (Both Manufacturing and Nonmanufacturing) at Classic Brass

Classic Brass's activity-based costing system will divide the nine types of overhead costs in Exhibit 7–4 among its five aforementioned activity cost pools via an allocation process called *first-stage allocation*. The **first-stage allocation** in an ABC system is the process of assigning functionally organized overhead costs derived from a company's general ledger to the activity cost pools.

First-stage allocations are usually based on the results of interviews with employees who have first-hand knowledge of the activities. For example, Classic Brass needs to allocate $500,000 of indirect factory wages to its five activity cost pools. These allocations will be more accurate if the employees who are classified as indirect factory workers (e.g., supervisors, engineers, and quality inspectors) are asked to estimate what percentage of their time is spent dealing with customer orders, with product design, with processing units of product (i.e., order size), and with customer relations. These interviews are conducted with considerable care. Those who are interviewed must thoroughly understand what the activities encompass and what is expected of them in the interview. In addition, departmental managers are typically interviewed to determine how the non-personnel costs should be distributed across the activity cost pools. For example, the Classic Brass production manager would be interviewed to determine how the $300,000 of factory equipment depreciation (shown in Exhibit 7–4) should be allocated to the activity cost pools. The key question that the production manager would need to answer is "What percentage of the available machine capacity is consumed by each activity such as the number of customer orders or the number of units processed (i.e., size of orders)?"

The results of the interviews at Classic Brass are displayed in Exhibit 7–5. For example, factory equipment depreciation is distributed 20% to Customer Orders, 60% to Order Size, and 20% to the Other cost pool. The resource in this instance is machine time. According to the estimates made by the production manager, 60% of the total available machine time was used to actually process units to fill orders. This percentage is entered in the Order Size column. Each customer order requires setting up, which also requires machine time. This activity consumes 20% of the total available machine time and is entered under the Customer Orders column. The remaining 20% of available machine time represents idle time and is entered under the Other column.

Exhibit 7–5 and many of the other exhibits in this chapter are presented in the form of Excel spreadsheets. All of the calculations required in activity-based costing can be done by hand. Nevertheless, setting up an activity-based costing system on a spreadsheet or using special ABC software can save a lot of work—particularly in situations involving many activity cost pools and in organizations that periodically update their ABC systems.

We will not go into the details of how all of the percentages in Exhibit 7–5 were determined. However, note that 100% of the factory building lease has been assigned to the Other cost pool. Classic Brass has a single production facility. It has no plans to expand or to sublease any excess space. The cost of this production facility is treated as an organization-sustaining cost because there is no way to avoid even a portion of this cost if a particular product or customer were to be dropped. (Remember that organization-sustaining costs are assigned to the Other cost pool and are not allocated to products.) In contrast, some companies have separate facilities for manufacturing specific products. The costs of these separate facilities could be directly traced to the specific products.

Once the percentage distributions in Exhibit 7–5 have been established, it is easy to allocate costs to the activity cost pools. The results of this first-stage allocation are displayed in Exhibit 7–6. Each cost is allocated across the activity cost pools by multiplying it by the percentages in Exhibit 7–5. For example, the indirect factory wages of $500,000 are multiplied by the 25% entry under Customer Orders in Exhibit 7–5 to arrive at the $125,000 entry under Customer Orders in Exhibit 7–6. Similarly, the indirect factory wages of $500,000 are multiplied by the 40% entry under Product Design in Exhibit 7–5 to arrive at the $200,000 entry under Product Design in Exhibit 7–6. All of the entries in Exhibit 7–6 are computed in this way.

Now that the first-stage allocations to the activity cost pools have been completed, the next step is to compute the activity rates.

EXHIBIT 7–5
Results of Interviews: Distribution
of Resource Consumption across
Activity Cost Pools

	A	B	C	D	E	F	G	H
1				Activity Cost Pools				
2		Customer Orders	Product Design	Order Size	Customer Relations	Other	Totals	
3								
4	Production Department:							
5	Indirect factory wages	25%	40%	20%	10%	5%	100%	
6	Factory equipment depreciation	20%	0%	60%	0%	20%	100%	
7	Factory utilities	0%	10%	50%	0%	40%	100%	
8	Factory building lease	0%	0%	0%	0%	100%	100%	
9								
10	General Administrative Department:							
11	Administrative wages and salaries	15%	5%	10%	30%	40%	100%	
12	Office equipment depreciation	30%	0%	0%	25%	45%	100%	
13	Administrative building lease	0%	0%	0%	0%	100%	100%	
14								
15	Marketing Department:							
16	Marketing wages and salaries	22%	8%	0%	60%	10%	100%	
17	Selling expenses	10%	0%	0%	70%	20%	100%	
18								

Exhibit 7-5 / Exhibit 7-6 / Exhibit 7-7 / Exhibit 7-9 / Exhibit 7-10 / Exhibit 7-11 / Exhibit 7-11 (2)

EXHIBIT 7–6
First-Stage Allocations to Activity
Cost Pools

	A	B	C	D	E	F	G	H
1				Activity Cost Pools				
2		Customer Orders	Product Design	Order Size	Customer Relations	Other	Totals	
3								
4	Production Department:							
5	Indirect factory wages	$ 125,000	$ 200,000	$ 100,000	$ 50,000	$ 25,000	$ 500,000	
6	Factory equipment depreciation	60,000	0	180,000	0	60,000	300,000	
7	Factory utilities	0	12,000	60,000	0	48,000	120,000	
8	Factory building lease	0	0	0	0	80,000	80,000	
9								
10	General Administrative Department:							
11	Administrative wages and salaries	60,000	20,000	40,000	120,000	160,000	400,000	
12	Office equipment depreciation	15,000	0	0	12,500	22,500	50,000	
13	Administrative building lease	0	0	0	0	60,000	60,000	
14								
15	Marketing Department:							
16	Marketing wages and salaries	55,000	20,000	0	150,000	25,000	250,000	
17	Selling expenses	5,000	0	0	35,000	10,000	50,000	
18								
19	Total	$ 320,000	$ 252,000	$ 380,000	$ 367,500	$ 490,500	$ 1,810,000	
20								
21								

Exhibit 7-5 / **Exhibit 7-6** / Exhibit 7-7 / Exhibit 7-9 / Exhibit 7-10 / Exhibit 7-11 / Exhibit 7-11 (2)

Exhibit 7–5 shows that Customer Orders consume 25% of the
resources represented by the $500,000 of indirected factory wages.

25% × $500,000 = $125,000

Other entries in the table are computed in a similar fashion.

AN ABC APPLICATION IN THE CONSTRUCTION INDUSTRY

Researchers from the United States and the Republic of Korea studied how a Korean manufacturer assigned the indirect costs of supplying reinforced steel bars (also called *rebar*) to various construction projects. The company's traditional cost system assigned all indirect costs to projects using rebar tonnage as the allocation base. Its ABC system had 10 activities that assigned indirect costs to projects using activity measures such as number of orders, number of sheets, number of distributing runs, number of production runs, and number of inspections.

The traditional and ABC systems assigned the following overhead costs to three construction projects called Commercial, High-Rise Condo, and Heavy Civil:

	Commercial	High-Rise Condo	Heavy Civil
Traditional cost system allocations	$ 64,587	$ 50,310	$91,102
ABC allocations	90,466	61,986	53,548
Difference	$(25,879)	$(11,676)	$37,554

Notice that the traditional cost system was undercosting the Commercial and High-Rise Condo projects relative to the ABC system. It was also overcosting the Heavy Civil project by $37,554 when compared to the ABC system.

Source: Yong-Woo Kim, Seungheon Han, "Sungwon Shin, and Kunhee Choi, "A Case Study of Activity-Based Costing in Allocation Rebar Fabrication Costs to Projects," *Construction Management and Economics,* May 2010, pp. 449–461.

Step 3: Calculate Activity Rates

The activity rates that will be used for assigning overhead costs to products and customers are computed in Exhibit 7–7. The ABC team determined the total activity for each cost pool that would be required to produce the company's present product mix and to serve its present customers. These numbers are listed in column C of Exhibit 7–7. For example, the ABC team found that 400 new product designs are required each year to serve the company's present customers. The activity rates are computed by dividing the *total* cost for each activity by its *total* activity. For example, the $320,000 total annual cost for the Customer Orders cost pool (which was computed in Exhibit 7–6) is divided by the total of 1,000 customer orders per year to arrive at the activity rate of $320 per customer order. Similarly, the $252,000 *total* cost for the Product Design cost pool is divided by the *total* number of designs (i.e., 400 product designs) to determine the activity rate of $630 per design. Note that an activity rate is not computed for the Other category of costs. This is because the *Other* cost pool consists of organization-sustaining costs and unused capacity costs that are not allocated to products and customers.

The rates in Exhibit 7–7 indicate that *on average* a customer order consumes resources that cost $320; a product design consumes resources that cost $630; a unit of product consumes resources that cost $19 per machine-hour; and maintaining relations with a customer consumes resources that cost $1,470. Note that these are *average* figures. Some members of the ABC design team at Classic Brass argued that it would be unfair to charge all new products the same $630 product design cost regardless of how much design time they actually require. After discussing the pros and cons, the team concluded that it would not be worth the effort at the present time to keep track of actual design time spent on each new product. They felt that the benefits of increased accuracy would not be great enough to justify the higher cost of implementing and maintaining the more detailed costing system. Similarly, some team members were uncomfortable assigning the same $1,470 cost to each customer. Some customers are undemanding—ordering standard products well in advance of their needs. Others are very demanding and consume large amounts of marketing and administrative staff time. These are generally customers who order customized products, who tend to order at the last minute, and who

EXHIBIT 7–7
Computation of Activity Rates

	A	B	C	D	E	F	G
		(a)	*(b)*		*(a) ÷ (b)*		
1	*Activity Cost Pools*	*Total Cost**	*Total Activity*		*Activity Rate*		
2	Customer orders	$320,000	1,000	orders	$320	per order	
3	Product design	$252,000	400	designs	$630	per design	
4	Order size	$380,000	20,000	MHs	$19	per MH	
5	Customer relations	$367,500	250	customers	$1,470	per customer	
6	Other	$490,500	Not applicable		Not applicable		
7							
8	*From Exhibit 7-6.						
9							

Exhibit 7-5 | Exhibit 7-6 | **Exhibit 7-7** | Exhibit 7-9 | Exhibit 7-10 | Exhibit 7-11 | Exhibit

EXHIBIT 7–7
Computation of Activity Rates

change their minds. While everyone agreed with this observation, the data that would be required to measure individual customers' demands on resources were not currently available. Rather than delay implementation of the ABC system, the team decided to defer such refinements to a later date.

Before proceeding further, it would be helpful to get a better idea of the overall process of assigning costs to products and other cost objects in an ABC system. Exhibit 7–8 provides a visual perspective of the ABC system at Classic Brass. We recommend that you carefully go over this exhibit. In particular, note that the Other category, which contains organization-sustaining costs and unused capacity costs, is not allocated to products or customers.

Step 4: Assign Overhead Costs to Cost Objects

The fourth step in the implementation of activity-based costing is called *second-stage allocation*. In the **second-stage allocation**, activity rates are used to apply overhead costs to products and customers. First, we will illustrate how to assign costs to products followed by an example of how to assign costs to customers.

LO7–4
Assign costs to a cost object using a second-stage allocation.

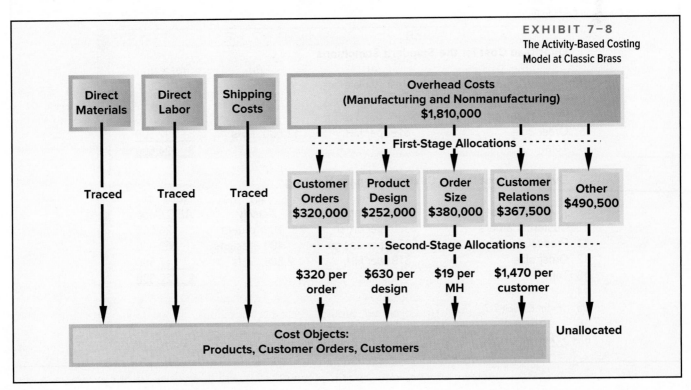

EXHIBIT 7–8
The Activity-Based Costing Model at Classic Brass

The data needed by the ABC team to assign overhead costs to Classic Brass's two products—standard stanchions and custom compass housings—are as follows:

Standard Stanchions

1. This product line does not require any new product design resources.
2. 30,000 units were ordered during the year, comprising 600 separate orders.
3. Each stanchion requires 35 minutes of machine time for a total of 17,500 machine-hours.

Custom Compass Housings

1. This is a custom product that requires new product design resources.
2. There were 400 orders for custom compass housings. Orders for this product are placed separately from orders for standard stanchions.
3. There were 400 custom designs prepared. One custom design was prepared for each order.
4. Because some orders were for more than one unit, a total of 1,250 custom compass housings were produced during the year. A custom compass housing requires an average of 2 machine-hours for a total of 2,500 machine-hours.

Notice, 600 customer orders were placed for standard stanchions and 400 customer orders were placed for custom compass housings, for a total of 1,000 customer orders. All 400 product designs related to custom compass housings; none related to standard stanchions. Producing 30,000 standard stanchions required 17,500 machine-hours and producing 1,250 custom compass housings required 2,500 machine-hours, for a total of 20,000 machine-hours.

Exhibit 7–9 illustrates how overhead costs are assigned to the standard stanchions and custom compass housings. For example, the exhibit shows that $192,000 of overhead costs are assigned from the Customer Orders activity cost pool to the standard stanchions

EXHIBIT 7–9
Assigning Overhead Costs to Products

	A	B	C	D	E	F	G
1	**Overhead Cost for the Standard Stanchions**						
2	*Activity Cost Pools*	*(a)* *Activity Rate**		*(b)* *Activity*		*(a) × (b)* *ABC Cost*	
3	Customer orders	$320	per order	600	orders	$ 192,000	
4	Product design	$630	per design	0	designs	0	
5	Order size	$19	per MH	17,500	MHs	332,500	
6	Total					$ 524,500	
7							
8	**Overhead Cost for the Custom Compass Housing**						
9	*Activity Cost Pools*	*(a)* *Activity Rate**		*(b)* *Activity*		*(a) × (b)* *ABC Cost*	
10	Customer orders	$320	per order	400	orders	$ 128,000	
11	Product design	$630	per design	400	designs	252,000	
12	Order size	$19	per MH	2,500	MHs	47,500	
13	Total					$ 427,500	
14							
15	*From Exhibit 7-7.						
16							

Exhibit 7-5 | Exhibit 7-6 | Exhibit 7-7 | **Exhibit 7-9** | Exhibit 7-10 | Exhibit

($320 per order × 600 orders). Similarly, $128,000 of overhead costs are assigned from the Customer Orders activity cost pool to the custom compass housings ($320 per order × 400 orders). The Customer Orders cost pool contained a total of $320,000 (see Exhibit 7–6 or 7–7) and this total amount has been assigned to the two products ($192,000 + $128,000 = $320,000).

Exhibit 7–9 shows that a total of $952,000 of overhead costs is assigned to Classic Brass's two product lines—$524,500 to standard stanchions and $427,500 to custom compass housings. This amount is less than the $1,810,000 of overhead costs included in the ABC system. Why? The total amount of overhead assigned to products does not match the total amount of overhead cost in the ABC system because the ABC team purposely did not assign the $367,500 of Customer Relations and $490,500 of Other costs to products. The Customer Relations activity is a customer-level activity and the Other activity is an organization-sustaining activity—neither activity is caused by products. As shown below, when the Customer Relations and Other activity costs are added to the $952,000 of overhead costs assigned to products, the total is $1,810,000.

	Standard Stanchions	Custom Compass Housings	Total
Overhead Costs Assigned to Products			
Customer orders	$ 192,000	$128,000	$ 320,000
Product design	0	252,000	252,000
Order size	332,500	47,500	380,000
Subtotal (a).............................	$ 524,500	$427,500	952,000
Overhead Costs not Assigned to Products			
Customer relations			367,500
Other..................................			490,500
Subtotal (b)			858,000
Total overhead cost (a) + (b)			$1,810,000

Next, we describe another example of second-stage allocation—assigning activity costs to customers. The data needed by Classic Brass to assign overhead costs to one of its customers—Windward Yachts—are as follows:

Windward Yachts

1. The company placed a total of three orders.
   a. Two orders were for 150 standard stanchions per order.
   b. One order was for a single custom compass housing unit.
2. A total of 177 machine-hours were used to fulfill the three customer orders.
   a. The 300 standard stanchions required 175 machine-hours.
   b. The custom compass housing required 2 machine-hours.
3. Windward Yachts is one of 250 customers served by Classic Brass.

Exhibit 7–10 illustrates how the ABC system assigns overhead costs to this customer. As shown in Exhibit 7–10, the ABC team calculated that $6,423 of overhead costs should be assigned to Windward Yachts. The exhibit shows that Windward Yachts is assigned $960 ($320 per order × 3 orders) of overhead costs from the Customer Orders activity cost pool; $630 ($630 per design × 1 design) from the Product Design cost pool; $3,363 ($19 per machine-hour × 177 machine-hours) from the Order Size cost pool; and $1,470 ($1,470 per customer × 1 customer) from the Customer Relations cost pool.

EXHIBIT 7–10
Assigning Overhead Costs to Customers

	A	B	C	D	E	F
1	**Overhead Cost for Windward Yachts**					
2						
3	*Activity Cost Pools*	*(a)* *Activity Rate**		*(b)* *Activity*		*(a) × (b)* *ABC Cost*
4	Customer orders	$320	per order	3	orders	$ 960
5	Product design	$630	per design	1	designs	630
6	Order size	$19	per MH	177	MHs	3,363
7	Customer relations	$1,470	per customer	1	customer	1,470
8	Total overhead cost assigned to customer					$ 6,423
9						
10	*From Exhibit 7-7.					
11						

Exhibit 7-5   Exhibit 7-6   Exhibit 7-7   Exhibit 7-9   **Exhibit 7-10**   Exhibit 7-11   Exhibit 7-

With second-stage allocations complete, the ABC design team was ready to turn its attention to creating reports that would help explain the company's first ever net operating loss.

IN BUSINESS

© Charles Knowles/Alamy

CARE FOR A TWINKIE?

When **Hostess Brands** was facing its second bankruptcy proceeding and eventual liquidation, the company ran 11 factories each operating at 50% of its capacity. Now that the company has re-emerged with new private equity ownership, it plans to operate only four factories at 85%–90% of their capacity. The owners expect the savings realized from their leaner production operations to offset some value-added increases in ingredient costs. For example, the company reformulated its Cup Cakes recipe to use dark chocolate instead of milk to enhance flavor and texture. This change, coupled with other product line upgrades, has increased Hostess' ingredients costs by 9%. The company expects its products to eventually reach 110,000 convenience stores as well as dollar stores, drug stores, club stores, and vending machines.

Activity-based costing helps companies improve their understanding of used and unused capacity costs so that they can more efficiently deliver products and services to customers.

Source: Julie Jargon, "The Return of Hostess," *The Wall Street Journal*, July 9, 2013, pp. B1–B2.

Step 5: Prepare Management Reports

LO7–5

Use activity-based costing to compute product and customer margins.

The most common management reports prepared with ABC data are product and customer profitability reports. These reports help companies channel their resources to their most profitable growth opportunities while at the same time highlighting products and customers that drain profits. We begin by illustrating a product profitability report followed by a customer profitability report.

The Classic Brass ABC team realized that the profit from a product, also called the *product margin,* is a function of the product's sales and the direct and indirect costs that the product causes. The ABC cost allocations shown in Exhibit 7–9 only summarize each product's indirect (i.e., overhead) costs. Therefore, to compute a product's profit (i.e., product margin), the design team needed to gather each product's sales and direct costs in addition to the overhead costs previously computed. The pertinent sales and direct cost data for each product are shown below. Notice the numbers in the total column agree with the income statement in Exhibit 7–2.

	Standard Stanchions	Custom Compass Housings	Total
Sales	$2,660,000	$540,000	$3,200,000
Direct costs:			
Direct materials	$905,500	$69,500	$975,000
Direct labor................	$263,750	$87,500	$351,250
Shipping	$60,000	$5,000	$65,000

Having gathered the above data, the design team created the product profitability report shown in Exhibit 7–11. The report revealed that standard stanchions are profitable, with a positive product margin of $906,250, whereas the custom compass housings are unprofitable, with a negative product margin of $49,500. Keep in mind that the product profitability report purposely does not include the costs in the Customer Relations and Other activity cost pools. These costs, which total $858,000, were excluded from the report because they are not caused by the products. Customer Relations costs are caused by customers, not products. The Other costs are organization-sustaining costs and unused capacity costs that are not caused by any particular product.

The product margins can be reconciled with the company's net operating loss as follows:

	Standard Stanchions	Custom Compass Housings	Total
Sales (See Exhibit 7–11)	$2,660,000	$540,000	$3,200,000
Total costs (See Exhibit 7–11)	1,753,750	589,500	2,343,250
Product margins (See Exhibit 7–11)	$ 906,250	$ (49,500)	856,750
Overhead costs not assigned to products:			
Customer relations			367,500
Other			490,500
Total			858,000
Net operating loss			$ (1,250)

EXHIBIT 7–11
Product Margins—Activity-Based Costing

	A	B	C	D	E	F
1	Product Margins—Activity-Based Costing					
2		Standard Stanchions			Custom Compass Housings	
3	Sales		$ 2,660,000			$ 540,000
4	Costs:					
5	Direct materials	$ 905,500			$ 69,500	
6	Direct labor	263,750			87,500	
7	Shipping	60,000			5,000	
8	Customer orders (from Exhibit 7-9)	192,000			128,000	
9	Product design (from Exhibit 7-9)	-			252,000	
10	Order size (from Exhibit 7-9)	332,500			47,500	
11	Total cost		1,753,750			589,500
12	Product margin		$ 906,250			$ (49,500)
13						

Exhibit 7-5 | Exhibit 7-6 | Exhibit 7-7 | Exhibit 7-9 | Exhibit 7-10 | **Exhibit 7-11** | Exhib

Next, the design team created a customer profitability report for Windward Yachts. Similar to the product profitability report, the design team needed to gather data concerning sales to Windward Yachts and the direct material, direct labor, and shipping costs associated with those sales. Those data are presented below:

	Windward Yachts
Sales	$11,350
Direct costs:	
Direct materials	$2,123
Direct labor	$1,900
Shipping	$205

Using these data and the data from Exhibit 7–10, the design team created the customer profitability report shown in Exhibit 7–12. The report revealed that the customer margin for Windward Yachts is $699. A similar report could be prepared for each of Classic Brass's 250 customers, thereby enabling the company to cultivate relationships with its most profitable customers, while taking steps to reduce the negative impact of unprofitable customers.

EXHIBIT 7–12
Customer Margin—Activity-Based Costing

	A	B	C
1	**Customer Margin—Activity-Based Costing**		
2			*Windward Yachts*
3	Sales		$11,350
4	Costs:		
5	Direct materials	$ 2,123	
6	Direct labor	1,900	
7	Shipping	205	
8	Customer orders (from Exhibit 7-10)	960	
9	Product design (from Exhibit 7-10)	630	
10	Order size (from Exhibit 7-10)	3,363	
11	Customer relations (from Exhibit 7-10)	1,470	10,651
12	Customer margin		$ 699
13			

Exhibit 7-12 / Exhibit 7-13 / Exhibit 7-14 / Exhibit 7A-1 / Ex

IN BUSINESS

ACTIVITY-BASED COSTING IN A GOVERNMENTAL ORGANIZATION

Activity-based costing is often studied in the context of for-profit companies; however, it can also be applied by governmental organizations. For example, the city of Somerville, MA, used activity-based costing to help manage its Traffic Unit Department. It assigned the Traffic Unit Department's operating costs to six activities: (1) investigate accidents, (2) manage tow companies, (3) traffic enforcement, (4) staff and supervise crossing guard posts, (5) process data, and (6) organize special events. The city also applied an activity-based costing perspective to the Electric, Water, and Building and Grounds programs within its Public Works Department. For example, the five activities within the Water Program included (1) maintain water quality and pressure, (2) maintain gate valves, (3) maintain and read meters, (4) track and issue water permits, and (5) maintain hydrants.

Source: Linda J. Bilmes, "City of Somerville: Using Activity-Based Budgeting to Improve Performance in the Somerville Traffic Unit," *Harvard Business School Publishing*, August 2013, pp. 1–29.

Comparison of Traditional and ABC Product Costs

The ABC team used a two-step process to compare its traditional and ABC product costs. First, the team reviewed the product margins reported by the traditional cost system. Then, it contrasted the differences between the traditional and ABC product margins.

Product Margins Computed Using the Traditional Cost System

Classic Brass's traditional cost system assigns only manufacturing costs to products—this includes direct materials, direct labor, and manufacturing overhead. Selling and administrative costs are not assigned to products. Exhibit 7–13 shows the product margins reported by Classic Brass's traditional cost system. We will explain how these margins were calculated in three steps. First, the sales, direct materials, and direct labor cost data are the same numbers used by the ABC team to prepare Exhibit 7–11. In other words, the traditional cost system and the ABC system treat these three pieces of revenue and cost data identically.

Second, the traditional cost system uses a plantwide overhead rate to assign manufacturing overhead costs to products. The numerator for the plantwide overhead rate is $1,000,000, which is the total amount of manufacturing overhead shown on the income statement in Exhibit 7–2. The footnote in Exhibit 7–2 mentions that the traditional cost system uses machine-hours to assign manufacturing overhead costs to products. The Order Size activity in Exhibit 7–7 used 20,000 machine-hours as its level of activity. These same 20,000 machine-hours would be used in the denominator of the plantwide overhead rate, which is computed as follows:

$$\text{Plantwide overhead rate} = \frac{\text{Total estimated manufacturing overhead}}{\text{Total estimated machine-hours}}$$

$$= \frac{\$1,000,000}{20,000 \text{ machine-hours}}$$

$$= \$50 \text{ per machine-hour}$$

Because 17,500 machine-hours were worked on standard stanchions, this product line is assigned $875,000 (17,500 machine-hours × $50 per machine-hour) of manufacturing

---

EXHIBIT 7–13
Product Margins—Traditional Cost System

A	B	C	D	E	F	G	H	I
1 Product Margins—Traditional Cost System								
2	Standard Stanchions			Custom Compass Housings			Total	
3 Sales		$2,660,000			$ 540,000			$3,200,000
4 Cost of goods sold:								
5 Direct materials	$ 905,500			$ 69,500			$ 975,000	
6 Direct labor	263,750			87,500			351,250	
7 Manufacturing overhead	875,000	2,044,250		125,000	282,000		1,000,000	2,326,250
8 Product margin		$ 615,750			$ 258,000			873,750
9 Selling and administrative								875,000
10 Net operating income								$ (1,250)
11								

◄ ◄ ► ►| / Exhibit 7-12 / **Exhibit 7-13** / Exhibit 7-14 / Exhibit 7A-1 / Exhibit 7A-2 / Exhibit 7A-3A / Exhibit 7A-3B

overhead cost. Similarly, the custom compass housings required 2,500 machine-hours, so this product line is assigned $125,000 (2,500 machine-hours × $50 per machine-hour) of manufacturing overhead cost. The sales of each product minus its cost of goods sold equals the product margin of $615,750 for standard stanchions and $258,000 for custom compass housings.

Notice, the net operating loss of $1,250 shown in Exhibit 7–13 agrees with the loss reported in the income statement in Exhibit 7–2 and with the loss shown in the table beneath Exhibit 7–11. The company's *total* sales, *total* costs, and its resulting net operating loss are the same regardless of whether you are looking at the absorption income statement in Exhibit 7–2, the ABC product profitability analysis, or the traditional product profitability analysis in Exhibit 7–13. Although the "total pie" remains constant across the traditional and ABC systems, what differs is how the pie is divided between the two product lines. The traditional product margin calculations suggest that standard stanchions are generating a product margin of $615,750 and the custom compass housings a product margin of $258,000. However, these product margins differ from the ABC product margins reported in Exhibit 7–11. Indeed, the traditional cost system is sending misleading signals to Classic Brass's managers about each product's profitability. Let's explain why.

The Differences between ABC and Traditional Product Costs

The changes in product margins caused by switching from the traditional cost system to the activity-based costing system are shown below:

	Standard Stanchions	Custom Compass Housings
Product margins—traditional	$615,750	$ 258,000
Product margins—ABC	906,250	(49,500)
Change in reported product margins	$290,500	$(307,500)

The traditional cost system overcosts the standard stanchions and consequently reports an artificially low product margin for this product. The switch to an activity-based view of product profitability increases the product margin on standard stanchions by $290,500. In contrast, the traditional cost system undercosts the custom compass housings and reports an artificially high product margin for this product. The switch to activity-based costing decreases the product margin on custom compass housings by $307,500.

The reasons for the change in reported product margins between the two costing methods are revealed in Exhibit 7–14. The top portion of the exhibit shows each product's direct and indirect cost assignments as reported by the traditional cost system in Exhibit 7–13. For example, Exhibit 7–14 includes the following costs for standard stanchions: direct materials, $905,500; direct labor, $263,750; and manufacturing overhead, $875,000. Each of these costs corresponds with those reported in Exhibit 7–13. Notice, the selling and administrative costs of $875,000 are purposely not allocated to products because these costs are considered to be period costs when using traditional costing. Similarly, the bottom portion of Exhibit 7–14 summarizes the direct and indirect cost assignments as reported by the activity-based costing system in Exhibit 7–11. The only new information in Exhibit 7–14 is shown in the two columns of percentages. The first column of percentages shows the percentage of each cost assigned to standard stanchions. For example, the $905,500 of direct materials cost traced to standard stanchions is 92.9% of the company's total direct materials cost of $975,000. The second column of percentages does the same thing for custom compass housings.

EXHIBIT 7-14
A Comparison of Traditional and
Activity-Based Cost Assignments

	A	B	C	D	E	F	G	H	I	
1			Standard Stanchions			Custom Compass Housings				
2	**Traditional Cost System**		(a) Amount	(a) ÷ (c) %		(b) Amount	(b) ÷ (c) %		(c) Total	
3	Direct materials		$ 905,500	92.9%		$ 69,500	7.1%		$ 975,000	
4	Direct labor		263,750	75.1%		87,500	24.9%		351,250	
5	Manufacturing overhead		875,000	87.5%		125,000	12.5%		1,000,000	
6	Total cost assigned to products		$ 2,044,250			$ 282,000			2,326,250	
7	Selling and administrative								875,000	
8	Total cost								$ 3,201,250	
9										
10	**Activity-Based Costing System**									
11	Direct costs:									
12	Direct materials		$ 905,500	92.9%		$ 69,500	7.1%		$ 975,000	
13	Direct labor		263,750	75.1%		87,500	24.9%		351,250	
14	Shipping		60,000	92.3%		5,000	7.7%		65,000	
15	Indirect costs:									
16	Customer orders		192,000	60.0%		128,000	40.0%		320,000	
17	Product design		-	0.0%		252,000	100.0%		252,000	
18	Order size		332,500	87.5%		47,500	12.5%		380,000	
19	Total cost assigned to products		$ 1,753,750			$ 589,500			2,343,250	
20	Costs not assigned to products:									
21	Customer relations								367,500	
22	Other								490,500	
23	Total cost								$ 3,201,250	
24										

Tabs: Exhibit 7-12 / Exhibit 7-13 / **Exhibit 7-14** / Exhibit 7A-1 / Exhibit 7A-2

There are three reasons why the traditional and activity-based costing systems report different product margins. First, Classic Brass's traditional cost system allocates all manufacturing overhead costs to products. This forces both products to absorb all manufacturing overhead costs regardless of whether they actually consumed the costs that were allocated to them. The ABC system does not assign the manufacturing overhead costs consumed by the Customer Relations activity to products because these costs are caused by customers, not specific products. It also does not assign the manufacturing overhead costs included in the Other activity to products because these organization-sustaining and unused capacity costs are not caused by any particular product. From an ABC point of view, assigning these costs to products is inherently arbitrary and counterproductive.

Second, Classic Brass's traditional cost system allocates all of the manufacturing overhead costs using a volume-related allocation base—machine-hours—that may or may not reflect what actually causes the costs. In other words, in the traditional system, 87.5% of each manufacturing overhead cost is implicitly assigned to standard stanchions and 12.5% is assigned to custom compass housings. For example, the traditional cost system inappropriately assigns 87.5% of the costs of the Customer Orders activity (a batch-level activity) to standard stanchions even though the ABC system revealed that standard stanchions caused only 60% of these costs. Conversely, the traditional cost system assigns only 12.5% of these costs to custom compass housings even though this product caused

40% of these costs. Similarly, the traditional cost system assigns 87.5% of the costs of the Product Design activity (a product-level activity) to standard stanchions even though the standard stanchions caused none (0%) of these costs. All (100%) of the costs of the Product Design activity, rather than just 12.5%, should be assigned to custom compass housings. The result is that traditional cost systems overcost high-volume products (such as the standard stanchions) and undercost low-volume products (such as the custom compass housings) because they assign batch-level and product-level costs using volume-related allocation bases.

The third reason the product margins differ between the two cost systems is that the ABC system assigns the nonmanufacturing overhead costs caused by products to those products on a cause-and-effect basis. The traditional cost system disregards these costs because they are classified as period costs. The ABC system directly traces shipping costs to products and includes the nonmanufacturing overhead costs caused by products in the activity cost pools that are assigned to products.

**MANAGERIAL
ACCOUNTING IN ACTION
THE WRAP-UP**

The ABC design team presented the results of its work in a meeting attended by all of the top managers of Classic Brass, including the president John Towers, the production manager Susan Richter, the marketing manager Tom Olafson, and the accounting manager Mary Goodman. The ABC team brought with them copies of the chart showing the ABC design (Exhibit 7–8), and the table comparing the traditional and ABC cost assignments (Exhibit 7–14). After the formal presentation by the ABC team, the following discussion took place:

John: I would like to personally thank the ABC team for all of the work they have done and for an extremely interesting presentation. I am now beginning to wonder about a lot of the decisions we have made in the past using our old cost accounting system. According to the ABC analysis, we had it all backwards. We are losing money on the custom products and making a fistful on the standard products.

Mary: I have to admit that I had no idea that the Product Design work for custom compass housings was so expensive! I knew burying these costs in our plantwide overhead rate was penalizing standard stanchions, but I didn't understand the magnitude of the problem.

Susan: I never did believe we were making a lot of money on the custom jobs. You ought to see all of the problems they create for us in production.

Tom: I hate to admit it, but the custom jobs always seem to give us headaches in marketing, too.

John: If we are losing money on custom compass housings, why not suggest to our customers that they go elsewhere for that kind of work?

Tom: Wait a minute, we would lose a lot of sales.

Susan: So what, we would save a lot more costs.

Mary: Maybe yes, maybe no. Some of the costs would not disappear if we were to drop the custom business.

Tom: Like what?

Mary: Well Tom, I believe you said that about 10% of your time is spent dealing with new products. As a consequence, 10% of your salary was allocated to the Product Design cost pool. If we were to drop all of the products requiring design work, would you be willing to take a 10% pay cut?

Tom: I trust you're joking.

Mary: Do you see the problem? Just because 10% of your time is spent on custom products doesn't mean that the company would save 10% of your salary if the custom products were dropped. Before we take a drastic action like dropping the custom products, we should identify which costs are really relevant.

John: I think I see what you are driving at. We wouldn't want to drop a lot of products only to find that our costs really haven't changed much. It is true that dropping the products would free up resources like Tom's time, but we had better be sure we have some good use for those resources *before* we take such an action.

As this discussion among the managers of Classic Brass illustrates, caution should be exercised before taking action based on an ABC analysis such as the one shown in Exhibit 7–11 and Exhibit 7–12. The product and customer margins computed in these exhibits are a useful starting point for further analysis, but managers need to know what costs are really affected before taking any action such as dropping a product or customer or changing the prices of products or services. For example, if an ABC system assigns some unavoidable fixed costs to products or customers, those costs should be ignored when making decisions with respect to those cost objects.

AN ABC IMPLEMENTATION IN THAILAND

APS, a parawood furniture factory located in the Songkhla Province of Southern Thailand, employs over 250 workers to make more than 100 types of furniture. The company's traditional cost system assigns indirect manufacturing costs to products based on each product's total sales. Its ABC system relies on various volume-related and non-volume-related activity measures, such as direct labor-hours, number of setups, and number of trips, to assign overhead costs to products.

The company's traditional and ABC systems assigned per-unit overhead costs to its five best-selling products as follows:

	Tile Top Table	Side Chair	Telephone Table	Plant Tree with Grooves	Computer Desk
Traditional cost system allocations	$7.08	$2.21	$3.53	$3.65	$ 4.53
ABC allocations	2.18	1.13	1.32	1.80	6.07
Difference	$4.90	$1.08	$2.21	$1.85	$(1.54)

Given that all five of these products have high sales volumes, it is not surprising to see that the traditional cost system has overcosted four of them.

Source: Sakesun Suthummanon, Wanida Ratanamanee, Nirachara Boonyanuwat, and Pieanpon Saritprit, "Applying Activity-Based Costing (ABC) to a Parawood Furniture Factory," *The Engineering Economist,* Volume 56 (2011), pp. 80–93.

Targeting Process Improvements

Activity-based costing can also be used to identify activities that would benefit from process improvements. When used in this way, activity-based costing is often called *activity-based management*. Basically, **activity-based management** involves focusing on activities to eliminate waste, decrease processing time, and reduce defects. Activity-based management is used in organizations as diverse as manufacturing companies, hospitals, and the **U.S. Marine Corps**.

The first step in any improvement program is to decide what to improve. The activity rates computed in activity-based costing can provide valuable clues concerning where there is waste and opportunity for improvement. For example, looking at the activity rates in Exhibit 7–7, managers at Classic Brass may conclude that $320 to process a customer order is far too expensive for an activity that adds no value to the product. As a consequence, they may target their process improvement efforts toward the Customer Orders activity.[3]

---

[3] Chapter 12 discusses another approach to improving processes and growing sales that focuses on effectively managing organizational constraints.

Benchmarking is another way to leverage the information in activity rates. **Benchmarking** is a systematic approach to identifying the activities with the greatest room for improvement. It is based on comparing the performance in an organization with the performance of other, similar organizations known for their outstanding performance. If a particular part of the organization performs far below the world-class standard, managers will be likely to target that area for improvement.

Activity-Based Costing and External Reports

Although activity-based costing generally provides more accurate product costs than traditional costing methods, it is infrequently used for external reports for a number of reasons. First, external reports are less detailed than internal reports prepared for decision making. On the external reports, individual product costs are not reported. Cost of goods sold and inventory valuations are disclosed, but they are not broken down by product. If some products are undercosted and some are overcosted, the errors tend to offset each other when the product costs are added together.

Second, it is often very difficult to make changes in a company's accounting system. The official cost accounting systems in most large companies are usually embedded in complex computer programs that have been modified in-house over the course of many years. It is extremely difficult to make changes in such computer programs without causing numerous bugs.

Third, an ABC system such as the one described in this chapter does not conform to generally accepted accounting principles (GAAP). As discussed in prior chapters, product costs computed for external reports must include all of the manufacturing costs and only manufacturing costs; but in an ABC system as described in this chapter, product costs exclude some manufacturing costs and include some nonmanufacturing costs. It is possible to adjust the ABC data at the end of the period to conform to GAAP, but that requires more work.

Fourth, auditors are likely to be uncomfortable with allocations that are based on interviews with the company's personnel. Such subjective data can be easily manipulated by management to make earnings and other key variables look more favorable.

For all of these reasons, most companies confine their ABC efforts to special studies for management, and they do not attempt to integrate activity-based costing into their formal cost accounting systems.

The Limitations of Activity-Based Costing

Implementing an activity-based costing system is a major project that requires substantial resources. And once implemented, an activity-based costing system is more costly to maintain than a traditional costing system—data concerning numerous activity measures must be periodically collected, checked, and entered into the system. The benefits of increased accuracy may not outweigh these costs.

Activity-based costing produces numbers, such as product margins, that are at odds with the numbers produced by traditional costing systems. But managers are accustomed to using traditional costing systems to run their operations and traditional costing systems are often used in performance evaluations. Essentially, activity-based costing changes the rules of the game. It is a fact of human nature that changes in organizations, particularly those that alter the rules of the game, inevitably face resistance. This underscores the importance of top management support and the full participation of line managers, as well as the accounting staff, in any activity-based costing initiative. If activity-based costing is viewed as an accounting initiative that does not have the full support of top management, it is doomed to failure.

In practice, most managers insist on fully allocating all costs to products, customers, and other costing objects in an activity-based costing system—including the organization-sustaining costs and unused capacity costs. This results in overstated costs and understated margins and mistakes in pricing and other critical decisions.

Activity-based costing data can easily be misinterpreted and must be used with care when used in making decisions. Costs assigned to products, customers, and other cost objects are only *potentially* relevant. Before making any significant decisions using activity-based costing data, managers must identify which costs are really relevant for the decision at hand. For example, if an ABC system assigns some unavoidable fixed costs to cost objects, those costs should be ignored when making decisions.

As discussed in the previous section, reports generated by the best activity-based costing systems do not conform to external reporting requirements. Consequently, an organization involved in activity-based costing should have two cost systems—one for internal use and one for preparing external reports. This is costlier than maintaining just one system and may cause confusion about which system is to be believed and relied on.

Summary

Traditional cost accounting methods suffer from several limitations that can result in distorted costs for decision-making purposes. All manufacturing costs—even those that are not caused by any specific product—are allocated to products. Nonmanufacturing costs that are caused by products are not assigned to products. And finally, traditional methods tend to place too much reliance on unit-level allocation bases such as direct labor and machine-hours. This results in overcosting high-volume products and undercosting low-volume products and can lead to mistakes when making decisions.

Activity-based costing estimates the costs of the resources consumed by cost objects such as products and customers. The activity-based costing approach assumes that cost objects generate activities that in turn consume costly resources. Activities form the link between costs and cost objects. Activity-based costing is concerned with overhead—both manufacturing overhead and selling and administrative overhead. The accounting for direct labor and direct materials is usually the same under traditional and ABC costing methods.

To build an ABC system, companies typically choose a small set of activities that summarize much of the work performed in overhead departments. Associated with each activity is an activity cost pool. To the extent possible, overhead costs are directly traced to these activity cost pools. The remaining overhead costs are allocated to the activity cost pools in the first-stage allocation. Interviews with managers often form the basis for these allocations.

An activity rate is computed for each cost pool by dividing the costs assigned to the cost pool by the measure of activity for the cost pool. Activity rates provide useful information to managers concerning the costs of performing overhead activities. A particularly high cost for an activity may trigger efforts to improve the way the activity is carried out in the organization.

In the second-stage allocation, activity rates are used to apply costs to cost objects such as products and customers. The costs computed under activity-based costing are often quite different from the costs generated by a company's traditional cost accounting system. While the ABC system is almost certainly more accurate, managers should nevertheless exercise caution before making decisions based on the ABC data. Some of the costs may not be avoidable and hence would not be relevant.

Review Problem: Activity-Based Costing

Ferris Corporation makes a single product—a fire-resistant commercial filing cabinet—that it sells to office furniture distributors. The company has a simple ABC system that it uses for internal decision making. The company has two overhead departments whose costs are as follows:

Manufacturing overhead	$500,000
Selling and administrative overhead	300,000
Total overhead costs.	$800,000

The company's ABC system has the following activity cost pools and activity measures:

Activity Cost Pool	Activity Measure
Assembling units	Number of units
Processing orders	Number of orders
Supporting customers	Number of customers
Other	Not applicable

Costs assigned to the "Other" activity cost pool have no activity measure; they consist of organization-sustaining costs and unused capacity costs—neither of which are assigned to orders, customers, or the product.

Ferris Corporation distributes the costs of manufacturing overhead and selling and administrative overhead to the activity cost pools based on employee interviews, the results of which are reported below:

Distribution of Resource Consumption Across Activity Cost Pools					
	Assembling Units	Processing Orders	Supporting Customers	Other	Total
Manufacturing overhead	50%	35%	5%	10%	100%
Selling and administrative overhead ...	10%	45%	25%	20%	100%
Total activity	1,000 units	250 orders	100 customers		

Required:

1. Perform the first-stage allocation of overhead costs to the activity cost pools as in Exhibit 7–6.
2. Compute activity rates for the activity cost pools as in Exhibit 7–7.
3. OfficeMart is one of Ferris Corporation's customers. Last year, OfficeMart ordered filing cabinets four different times. OfficeMart ordered a total of 80 filing cabinets during the year. Construct a table as in Exhibit 7–10 showing the overhead costs attributable to OfficeMart.
4. The selling price of a filing cabinet is $595. The cost of direct materials is $180 per filing cabinet, and direct labor is $50 per filing cabinet. What is the customer margin of OfficeMart? See Exhibit 7–12 for an example of how to complete this report.

Solution to Review Problem

1. The first-stage allocation of costs to the activity cost pools appears below:

	Activity Cost Pools				
	Assembling Units	Processing Orders	Supporting Customers	Other	Total
Manufacturing overhead	$ 250,000	$ 175,000	$ 25,000	$ 50,000	$500,000
Selling and administrative overhead	30,000	135,000	75,000	60,000	300,000
Total cost	$ 280,000	$ 310,000	$ 100,000	$110,000	$800,000

2. The activity rates for the activity cost pools are:

Activity Cost Pools	(a) Total Cost	(b) Total Activity	(a) ÷ (b) Activity Rate
Assembling units......................	$280,000	1,000 units	$280 per unit
Processing orders....................	$310,000	250 orders	$1,240 per order
Supporting customers	$100,000	100 customers	$1,000 per customer

3. The overhead cost attributable to OfficeMart would be computed as follows:

Activity Cost Pools	(a) Activity Rate	(b) Activity	(a) × (b) ABC Cost
Assembling units........................	$280 per unit	80 units	$22,400
Processing orders......................	$1,240 per order	4 orders	$4,960
Supporting customers	$1,000 per customer	1 customer	$1,000

4. The customer margin can be computed as follows:

Sales ($595 per unit x 80 units)		$47,600
Costs:		
Direct materials ($180 per unit x 80 units)	$14,400	
Direct labor ($50 per unit x 80 units)..................	4,000	
Assembling units (above)...........................	22,400	
Processing orders (above)..........................	4,960	
Supporting customers (above)	1,000	46,760
Customer margin..................................		$ 840

Glossary

Activity An event that causes the consumption of overhead resources in an organization. (p. 314)

Activity-based costing (ABC) A costing method based on activities that is designed to provide managers with cost information for strategic and other decisions that potentially affect capacity and therefore fixed as well as variable costs. (p. 311)

Activity-based management (ABM) A management approach that focuses on managing activities as a way of eliminating waste and reducing delays and defects. (p. 333)

Activity cost pool A "bucket" in which costs are accumulated that relate to a single activity measure in an activity-based costing system. (p. 314)

Activity measure An allocation base in an activity-based costing system; ideally, a measure of the amount of activity that drives the costs in an activity cost pool. (p. 314)

Batch-level activities Activities that are performed each time a batch of goods is handled or processed, regardless of how many units are in the batch. The amount of resource consumed depends on the number of batches run rather than on the number of units in the batch. (p. 314)

Benchmarking A systematic approach to identifying the activities with the greatest potential for improvement. (p. 334)

Customer-level activities Activities that are carried out to support customers, but that are not related to any specific product. (p. 314)

Duration driver A measure of the amount of time required to perform an activity. (p. 314)

First-stage allocation The process by which overhead costs are assigned to activity cost pools in an activity-based costing system. (p. 320)

Organization-sustaining activities Activities that are carried out regardless of which customers are served, which products are produced, how many batches are run, or how many units are made. (p. 314)

Product-level activities Activities that relate to specific products that must be carried out regardless of how many units are produced and sold or batches run. (p. 314)

Second-stage allocation The process by which activity rates are used to apply costs to products and customers in activity-based costing. (p. 323)

Transaction driver A simple count of the number of times an activity occurs. (p. 314)

Unit-level activities Activities that are performed each time a unit is produced. (p. 314)

Questions

7–1   In what fundamental ways does activity-based costing differ from traditional costing methods such as job-order costing as described in Chapters 2 and 3?

7–2   Why is direct labor a poor base for allocating overhead in many companies?

7–3   Why are top management support and cross-functional involvement crucial when attempting to implement an activity-based costing system?

7–4   What are unit-level, batch-level, product-level, customer-level, and organization-sustaining activities?

7–5   What types of costs should not be assigned to products in an activity-based costing system?

7–6   What are the two stages of allocation in activity-based costing?

7–7   Why is the first stage of the allocation process in activity-based costing often based on interviews?

7–8   When activity-based costing is used, why do manufacturing overhead costs often shift from high-volume products to low-volume products?

7–9   How can the activity rates (i.e., cost per activity) for the various activities be used to target process improvements?

7–10   Why is the form of activity-based costing described in this chapter unacceptable for external financial reports?

Applying Excel   Mc Graw Hill Education **connect**

LO7–1, LO7–2, LO7–3, LO7–4, LO7–5

The Excel worksheet form that appears below is to be used to recreate the Review Problem pertaining to Ferris Corporation. Download the workbook containing this form from Connect, where you will also receive instructions about how to use this worksheet form.

You should proceed to the requirements below only after completing your worksheet.

Required:

1. Check your worksheet by doubling the units ordered in cell B16 to 160. The customer margin under activity-based costing should now be $7,640 and the traditional costing product margin should be $(21,600). If you do not get these results, find the errors in your worksheet and correct them.

    a. Why has the customer margin under activity-based costing more than doubled when the number of units ordered is doubled?

    b. Why has the traditional costing product margin exactly doubled from a loss of $10,800 to a loss of $21,600?

    c. Which costing system, activity-based costing or traditional costing, provides a more accurate picture of what happens to profits as the number of units ordered increases? Explain.

	A	B	C	D	E	F	G
1	Chapter 7: Applying Excel						
2							
3	Data						
4	Manufacturing overhead	$500,000					
5	Selling and administrative overhead	$300,000					
6							
7		Assembling Units	Processing Orders	Supporting Customers	Other		
8	Manufacturing overhead	50%	35%	5%	10%		
9	Selling and administrative overhead	10%	45%	25%	20%		
10	Total activity	1,000	250	100			
11		units	orders	customers			
12							
13	OfficeMart orders:						
14	Customers	1	customer				
15	Orders	4	orders				
16	Number of filing cabinets ordered in total	80	units				
17	Selling price	$595					
18	Direct materials	$180					
19	Direct labor	$50					
20							
21	Enter a formula into each of the cells marked with a ? below						
22	Review Problem: Activity-Based Costing						
23							
24	Perform the first stage allocations						
25		Assembling Units	Processing Orders	Supporting Customers	Other	Total	
26	Manufacturing overhead	?	?	?	?	?	
27	Selling and administrative overhead	?	?	?	?	?	
28	Total cost	?	?	?	?	?	
29							
30	Compute the activity rates						
31	Activity Cost Pools	Total Cost	Total Activity		Activity Rate		
32	Assembling units	?	? units		? per unit		
33	Processing orders	?	? orders		? per order		
34	Supporting customers	?	? customers		? per customer		
35							
36	Compute the overhead cost attributable to the OfficeMart orders						
37	Activity Cost Pools	Activity Rate		Activity		ABC Cost	
38	Assembling units	? per unit		? units		?	
39	Processing orders	? per order		? orders		?	
40	Supporting customers	? per customer		? customer		?	
41							
42	Determine the customer margin for the OfficeMart orders under Activity-Based Costing						
43	Sales		?				
44	Costs:						
45	Direct materials	?					
46	Direct labor	?					
47	Unit-related overhead	?					
48	Order-related overhead	?					
49	Customer-related overhead	?	?				
50	Customer margin		?				
51							
52	Determine the product margin for the OfficeMart orders under a traditional cost system						
53	Manufacturing overhead	?					
54	Total activity	? units					
55	Manufacturing overhead per unit	? per unit					
56							
57	Sales		?				
58	Costs:						
59	Direct materials	?					
60	Direct labor	?					
61	Manufacturing overhead	?	?				
62	Traditional costing product margin		?				
63							

2. Let's assume that OfficeMart places different orders next year, purchasing higher-end filing cabinets more frequently, but in smaller quantities per order. Enter the following data into your worksheet:

Data				
Manufacturing overhead	$500,000			
Selling and administrative overhead	$300,000			

	Assembling Units	Processing Orders	Supporting Customers	Other
Manufacturing overhead	50%	35%	5%	10%
Selling and administrative overhead	10%	45%	25%	20%
Total activity	1,000 units	250 orders	100 customers	

OfficeMart orders:	
Customers	1 customer
Orders	20 orders
Total number of filing cabinets ordered ...	80 units
Selling price	$795
Direct materials	$185
Direct labor	$90

   a. What is the customer margin under activity-based costing?
   b. What is the product margin under the traditional cost system?
   c. Explain why the profitability picture looks much different now than it did when OfficeMart was ordering less expensive filing cabinets less frequently, but in larger quantities per order.

3. Using the data you entered in part (2), change the percentage of selling and administrative overhead attributable to processing orders from 45% to 30% and the percentage attributable to supporting customers from 25% to 40%. That portion of the worksheet should look like this:

	Assembling Units	Processing Orders	Supporting Customers	Other
Manufacturing overhead	50%	35%	5%	10%
Selling and administrative overhead	10%	30%	40%	20%
Total activity	1,000 units	250 orders	100 customers	

   a. Relative to the results from part (2), what has happened to the customer margin under activity-based costing? Why?
   b. Relative to the results from part (2), what has happened to the product margin under the traditional cost system? Why?

The Foundational 15 ![Mc Graw Hill Education] **connect**

L07–1, L07–3, L07–4

Hickory Company manufactures two products—14,000 units of Product Y and 6,000 units of Product Z. The company uses a plantwide overhead rate based on direct labor-hours. It is considering implementing an activity-based costing (ABC) system that allocates all $684,000 of its manufacturing overhead to four cost pools. The following additional information is available for the company as a whole and for Products Y and Z:

Activity Cost Pool	Activity Measure	Estimated Overhead Cost	Expected Activity
Machining	Machine-hours	$200,000	10,000 MHs
Machine setups	Number of setups	$100,000	200 setups
Product design	Number of products	$84,000	2 products
General factory	Direct labor-hours	$300,000	12,000 DLHs

Activity Measure	Product Y	Product Z
Machine-hours	7,000	3,000
Number of setups	50	150
Number of products	1	1
Direct labor-hours	8,000	4,000

Required:

1. What is the company's plantwide overhead rate?
2. Using the plantwide overhead rate, how much manufacturing overhead cost is allocated to Product Y? How much is allocated to Product Z?
3. What is the activity rate for the Machining activity cost pool?
4. What is the activity rate for the Machine Setups activity cost pool?
5. What is the activity rate for the Product Design activity cost pool?
6. What is the activity rate for the General Factory activity cost pool?
7. Which of the four activities is a batch-level activity? Why?
8. Which of the four activities is a product-level activity? Why?
9. Using the ABC system, how much total manufacturing overhead cost would be assigned to Product Y?
10. Using the ABC system, how much total manufacturing overhead cost would be assigned to Product Z?
11. Using the plantwide overhead rate, what percentage of the total overhead cost is allocated to Product Y? What percentage is allocated to Product Z?
12. Using the ABC system, what percentage of the Machining costs is assigned to Product Y? What percentage is assigned to Product Z? Are these percentages similar to those obtained in requirement 11? Why?
13. Using the ABC system, what percentage of Machine Setups cost is assigned to Product Y? What percentage is assigned to Product Z? Are these percentages similar to those obtained in requirement 11? Why?
14. Using the ABC system, what percentage of the Product Design cost is assigned to Product Y? What percentage is assigned to Product Z? Are these percentages similar to those obtained in requirement 11? Why?
15. Using the ABC system, what percentage of the General Factory cost is assigned to Product Y? What percentage is assigned to Product Z? Are these percentages similar to those obtained in requirement 11? Why?

 **Exercises**

EXERCISE 7–1 ABC Cost Hierarchy LO7–1

The following activities occur at Greenwich Corporation, a company that manufactures a variety of products.

a. Receive raw materials from suppliers.
b. Manage parts inventories.
c. Do rough milling work on products.
d. Interview and process new employees in the personnel department.
e. Design new products.
f. Perform periodic preventive maintenance on general-use equipment.
g. Use the general factory building.
h. Issue purchase orders for a job.

Required:

Classify each of the activities above as either a unit-level, batch-level, product-level, or organization-sustaining activity.

EXERCISE 7–2 First Stage Allocation LO7–2

SecuriCorp operates a fleet of armored cars that make scheduled pickups and deliveries in the Los Angeles area. The company is implementing an activity-based costing system that has four activity cost pools: Travel, Pickup and Delivery, Customer Service, and Other. The activity measures are miles for the Travel cost pool, number of pickups and deliveries for the Pickup and Delivery cost pool, and number of customers for the Customer Service cost pool. The Other cost pool has no activity measure because it is an organization-sustaining activity. The following costs will be assigned using the activity-based costing system:

Driver and guard wages	$ 720,000
Vehicle operating expense	280,000
Vehicle depreciation	120,000
Customer representative salaries and expenses	160,000
Office expenses	30,000
Administrative expenses	320,000
Total cost	$1,630,000

The distribution of resource consumption across the activity cost pools is as follows:

	Travel	Pickup and Delivery	Customer Service	Other	Totals
Driver and guard wages	50%	35%	10%	5%	100%
Vehicle operating expense	70%	5%	0%	25%	100%
Vehicle depreciation	60%	15%	0%	25%	100%
Customer representative salaries and expenses	0%	0%	90%	10%	100%
Office expenses	0%	20%	30%	50%	100%
Administrative expenses	0%	5%	60%	35%	100%

Required:

Complete the first stage allocations of costs to activity cost pools as illustrated in Exhibit 7–6.

EXERCISE 7–3 Compute Activity Rates LO7–3

Green Thumb Gardening is a small gardening service that uses activity-based costing to estimate costs for pricing and other purposes. The proprietor of the company believes that costs are driven primarily by the size of customer lawns, the size of customer garden beds, the distance to travel to customers, and the number of customers. In addition, the costs of maintaining garden beds depends on whether the beds are low maintenance beds (mainly ordinary trees and shrubs) or high maintenance beds (mainly flowers and exotic plants). Accordingly, the company uses the five activity cost pools listed below:

Activity Cost Pool	Activity Measure
Caring for lawn	Square feet of lawn
Caring for garden beds–low maintenance	Square feet of low maintenance beds
Caring for garden beds–high maintenance	Square feet of high maintenance beds
Travel to jobs	Miles
Customer billing and service	Number of customers

The company already has completed its first stage allocations of costs and has summarized its annual costs and activity as follows:

Activity Cost Pool	Estimated Overhead Cost	Expected Activity
Caring for lawn	$72,000	150,000 square feet of lawn
Caring for garden beds–low maintenance	$26,400	20,000 square feet of low maintenance beds
Caring for garden beds–high maintenance	$41,400	15,000 square feet of high maintenance beds
Travel to jobs	$3,250	12,500 miles
Customer billing and service	$8,750	25 customers

Required:
Compute the activity rate for each of the activity cost pools.

EXERCISE 7–4 Second-Stage Allocation LO7–4
Klumper Corporation is a diversified manufacturer of industrial goods. The company's activity-based costing system contains the following six activity cost pools and activity rates:

Activity Cost Pool	Activity Rates
Supporting direct labor	$6 per direct labor-hour
Machine processing	$4 per machine-hour
Machine setups	$50 per setup
Production orders	$90 per order
Shipments	$14 per shipment
Product sustaining	$840 per product

Activity data have been supplied for the following two products:

	Total Expected Activity	
	K425	M67
Number of units produced per year	200	2,000
Direct labor-hours	80	500
Machine-hours	100	1,500
Machine setups	1	4
Production orders	1	4
Shipments	1	10
Product sustaining	1	1

Required:
How much total overhead cost would be assigned to K425 and M67 using the activity-based costing system?

EXERCISE 7–5 Product and Customer Profitability Analysis LO7–4, LO7–5
Thermal Rising, Inc., makes paragliders for sale through specialty sporting goods stores. The company has a standard paraglider model, but also makes custom-designed paragliders. Management has designed an activity-based costing system with the following activity cost pools and activity rates:

Activity Cost Pool	Activity Rate
Supporting direct labor	$26 per direct labor-hour
Order processing	$284 per order
Custom design processing	$186 per custom design
Customer service	$379 per customer

Management would like an analysis of the profitability of a particular customer, Big Sky Outfitters, which has ordered the following products over the last 12 months:

	Standard Model	Custom Design
Number of gliders	20	3
Number of orders	1	3
Number of custom designs	0	3
Direct labor-hours per glider	26.35	28.00
Selling price per glider	$1,850	$2,400
Direct materials cost per glider	$564	$634

The company's direct labor rate is $19.50 per hour.

Required:

Using the company's activity-based costing system, compute the customer margin of Big Sky Outfitters.

EXERCISE 7–6 Cost Hierarchy LO7–1

CD Express, Inc., provides CD duplicating services for its customers. An order from a customer can be for a single copy or for thousands of copies. Most jobs are broken down into batches to allow smaller jobs, with higher priorities, to have access to the machines.

A number of activities carried out at CD Express are listed below.

a. Sales representatives' periodic visits to customers to keep them informed about the services provided by CD Express.
b. Ordering labels from the printer for a particular CD.
c. Setting up the CD duplicating machine to make copies from a particular master CD.
d. Loading the automatic labeling machine with labels for a particular CD.
e. Visually inspecting CDs and placing them by hand into protective plastic cases prior to shipping.
f. Preparation of the shipping documents for the order.
g. Periodic maintenance of equipment.
h. Lighting and heating the company's production facility.
i. Preparation of quarterly financial reports.

Required:

Classify each of the activities above as either a unit-level, batch-level, product-level, customer-level, or organization-sustaining activity. An order to duplicate a particular CD is a product-level activity. Assume the order is large enough that it must be broken down into batches.

EXERCISE 7–7 First-Stage Allocations LO7–2

The operations vice president of Security Home Bank has been interested in investigating the efficiency of the bank's operations. She has been particularly concerned about the costs of handling routine transactions at the bank and would like to compare these costs at the bank's various branches. If the branches with the most efficient operations can be identified, their methods can be studied and then replicated elsewhere. While the bank maintains meticulous records of wages and other costs, there has been no attempt thus far to show how those costs are related to the various services provided by the bank. The operations vice president has asked your help in conducting an activity-based costing study of bank operations. In particular, she would like to know the cost of opening an account, the cost of processing deposits and withdrawals, and the cost of processing other customer transactions.

The Westfield branch of Security Home Bank has submitted the following cost data for last year:

Teller wages	$160,000
Assistant branch manager salary	75,000
Branch manager salary	80,000
Total	$315,000

Virtually all other costs of the branch—rent, depreciation, utilities, and so on—are organization-sustaining costs that cannot be meaningfully assigned to individual customer transactions such as depositing checks.

In addition to the cost data above, the employees of the Westfield branch have been interviewed concerning how their time was distributed last year across the activities included in the activity-based costing study. The results of those interviews appear below:

Distribution of Resource Consumption Across Activities					
	Opening Accounts	Processing Deposits and Withdrawals	Processing Other Customer Transactions	Other Activities	Total
Teller wages	5%	65%	20%	10%	100%
Assistant branch manager salary	15%	5%	30%	50%	100%
Branch manager salary	5%	0%	10%	85%	100%

Required:
Prepare the first-stage allocation for the activity-based costing study. (See Exhibit 7–6 for an example of a first-stage allocation.)

EXERCISE 7–8 Computing and Interpreting Activity Rates LO7–3

(This exercise is a continuation of Exercise 7–7; it should be assigned *only* if Exercise 7–7 also is assigned.) The manager of the Westfield branch of Security Home Bank has provided the following data concerning the transactions of the branch during the past year:

Activity	Total Activity at the Westfield Branch
Opening accounts	500 new accounts opened
Processing deposits and withdrawals	100,000 deposits and withdrawals processed
Processing other customer transactions ...	5,000 other customer transactions processed

The lowest costs reported by other branches for these activities are displayed below:

Activity	Lowest Cost among All Security Home Bank Branches
Opening accounts	$26.75 per new account
Processing deposits and withdrawals	$1.24 per deposit or withdrawal
Processing other customer transactions	$11.86 per other customer transaction

Required:
1. Using the first-stage allocation from Exercise 7–7 and the above data, compute the activity rates for the activity-based costing system. (Use Exhibit 7–7 as a guide.) Round all computations to the nearest whole cent.
2. What do these results suggest to you concerning operations at the Westfield branch?

EXERCISE 7–9 Second-Stage Allocation to an Order LO7–4

Durban Metal Products, Ltd., of the Republic of South Africa makes specialty metal parts used in applications ranging from the cutting edges of bulldozer blades to replacement parts for Land Rovers. The company uses an activity-based costing system for internal decision-making purposes. The company has four activity cost pools as listed below:

Activity Cost Pool	Activity Measure	Activity Rate
Order size	Number of direct labor-hours	$16.85 per direct labor-hour
Customer orders	Number of customer orders	$320.00 per customer order
Product testing	Number of testing hours	$89.00 per testing hour
Selling	Number of sales calls	$1,090.00 per sales call

The managing director of the company would like information concerning the cost of a recently completed order for heavy-duty trailer axles. The order required 200 direct labor-hours, 4 hours of product testing, and 2 sales calls.

Required:
What is the total overhead cost assigned to the order for heavy-duty trailer axles?

EXERCISE 7–10 Customer Profitability Analysis LO7–3, LO7–4, LO7–5

Worley Company buys surgical supplies from a variety of manufacturers and then resells and delivers these supplies to hundreds of hospitals. Worley sets its prices for all hospitals by marking up its cost of goods sold to those hospitals by 5%. For example, if a hospital buys supplies from Worley that cost Worley $100 to buy from manufacturers, Worley would charge the hospital $105 to purchase these supplies.

For years, Worley believed that the 5% markup covered its selling and administrative expenses and provided a reasonable profit. However, in the face of declining profits Worley decided to implement an activity-based costing system to help improve its understanding of customer profitability. The company broke its selling and administrative expenses into five activities as shown:

Activity Cost Pool (Activity Measure)	Total Cost	Total Activity
Customer deliveries (Number of deliveries)	$ 500,000	5,000 deliveries
Manual order processing (Number of manual orders)	248,000	4,000 orders
Electronic order processing (Number of electronic orders)	200,000	12,500 orders
Line item picking (Number of line items picked)	450,000	450,000 line items
Other organization-sustaining costs (None)	602,000	
Total selling and administrative expenses	$2,000,000	

Worley gathered the data below for two of the many hospitals that it serves—University and Memorial (each hospital purchased medical supplies that had cost Worley $30,000 to buy from manufacturers):

	Activity	
Activity Measure	University	Memorial
Number of deliveries	10	25
Number of manual orders	0	30
Number of electronic orders	15	0
Number of line items picked	120	250

Required:
1. Compute the total revenue that Worley would receive from University and Memorial.
2. Compute the activity rate for each activity cost pool.
3. Compute the total activity costs that would be assigned to University and Memorial.
4. Compute Worley's customer margin for University and Memorial. (*Hint:* Do not overlook the $30,000 cost of goods sold that Worley incurred serving each hospital.)
5. Describe the purchasing behaviors that are likely to characterize Worley's least profitable customers.

EXERCISE 7–11 Second-Stage Allocation and Margin Calculations LO7–4, LO7–5
Foam Products, Inc., makes foam seat cushions for the automotive and aerospace industries. The company's activity-based costing system has four activity cost pools, which are listed below along with their activity measures and activity rates:

Activity Cost Pool	Activity Measure	Activity Rate
Supporting direct labor	Number of direct labor-hours	$5.55 per direct labor-hour
Batch processing	Number of batches	$107.00 per batch
Order processing	Number of orders	$275.00 per order
Customer service	Number of customers	$2,463.00 per customer

The company just completed a single order from Interstate Trucking for 1,000 custom seat cushions. The order was produced in two batches. Each seat cushion required 0.25 direct labor-hours. The selling price was $20 per unit, the direct materials cost was $8.50 per unit, and the direct labor cost was $6.00 per unit. This was Interstate Trucking's only order during the year.

Required:
Using Exhibit 7–12 as a guide, calculate the customer margin on sales to Interstate Trucking for the year.

EXERCISE 7–12 Activity Measures LO7–1

Various activities at Ming Corporation, a manufacturing company, are listed below. Each activity has been classified as a unit-level, batch-level, product-level, or customer-level activity.

Activity	Level of Activity	Examples of Activity Measures
a. Direct labor workers assemble a product	Unit	
b. Products are designed by engineers	Product	
c. Equipment is set up	Batch	
d. Machines are used to shape and cut materials	Unit	
e. Monthly bills are sent out to regular customers	Customer	
f. Materials are moved from the receiving dock to production lines	Batch	
g. All completed units are inspected for defects	Unit	

Required:

Complete the table by providing an example of an activity measure for each activity.

EXERCISE 7–13 Computing ABC Product Costs LO7–3, LO7–4

Fogerty Company makes two products—titanium Hubs and Sprockets. Data regarding the two products follow:

	Direct Labor-Hours per Unit	Annual Production
Hubs	0.80	10,000 units
Sprockets	0.40	40,000 units

Additional information about the company follows:
a. Hubs require $32 in direct materials per unit, and Sprockets require $18.
b. The direct labor wage rate is $15 per hour.
c. Hubs require special equipment and are more complex to manufacture than Sprockets.
d. The ABC system has the following activity cost pools:

	Estimated Overhead Cost	Activity		
Activity Cost Pool (Activity Measure)		Hubs	Sprockets	Total
Machine setups (number of setups)	$72,000	100	300	400
Special processing (machine-hours)	$200,000	5,000	0	5,000
General factory (organization-sustaining)	$816,000	NA	NA	NA

Required:

1. Compute the activity rate for each activity cost pool. Did you compute an activity rate for all of the activity cost pools? Why?
2. Determine the unit product cost of each product according to the ABC system.

EXERCISE 7–14 Calculating and Interpreting Activity-Based Costing Data LO7–3, LO7–4

Hiram's Lakeside is a popular restaurant located on Lake Washington in Seattle. The owner of the restaurant has been trying to better understand costs at the restaurant and has hired a student intern to conduct an activity-based costing study. The intern, in consultation with the owner, identified three major activities and then completed the first-stage allocations of costs to the activity cost pools. The results appear below.

Activity Cost Pool	Activity Measure	Total Cost	Total Activity
Serving a party of diners	Number of parties served	$33,000	6,000 parties
Serving a diner	Number of diners served	$138,000	15,000 diners
Serving drinks	Number of drinks ordered	$24,000	10,000 drinks

The above costs include all of the costs of the restaurant except for organization-sustaining costs such as rent, property taxes, and top-management salaries.

Some costs, such as the cost of cleaning the linens that cover the restaurant's tables, vary with the number of parties served. Other costs, such as washing plates and glasses, depend on the number of diners served or the number of drinks served.

Prior to the activity-based costing study, the owner knew very little about the costs of the restaurant. She knew that the total cost for the month (including organization-sustaining costs) was $240,000 and that 15,000 diners had been served. Therefore, the average cost per diner was $16.

Required:

1. According to the activity-based costing system, what is the total cost of serving each of the following parties of diners?
   a. A party of four diners who order three drinks in total.
   b. A party of two diners who do not order any drinks.
   c. A party of one diner who orders two drinks.
2. Convert the total costs you computed in (1) above to costs per diner. In other words, what is the average cost per diner for serving each of the following parties?
   a. A party of four diners who order three drinks in total.
   b. A party of two diners who do not order any drinks.
   c. A party of one diner who orders two drinks.
3. Why do the costs per diner for the three different parties differ from each other and from the overall average cost of $16 per diner?

EXERCISE 7–15 Comprehensive Activity-Based Costing Exercise LO7–2, LO7–3, LO7–4, LO7–5

Advanced Products Corporation has supplied the following data from its activity-based costing system:

Overhead Costs	
Wages and salaries	$300,000
Other overhead costs	100,000
Total overhead costs	$400,000

Activity Cost Pool	Activity Measure	Total Activity for the Year
Supporting direct labor	Number of direct labor-hours	20,000 DLHs
Order processing	Number of customer orders	400 orders
Customer support	Number of customers	200 customers
Other	This is an organization-sustaining activity	Not applicable

Distribution of Resource Consumption Across Activities

	Supporting Direct Labor	Order Processing	Customer Support	Other	Total
Wages and salaries	40%	30%	20%	10%	100%
Other overhead costs	30%	10%	20%	40%	100%

During the year, Advanced Products completed one order for a new customer, Shenzhen Enterprises. This customer did not order any other products during the year. Data concerning that order follow:

Data concerning the Shenzhen Enterprises Order	
Units ordered	10 units
Direct labor-hours	2 DLHs per unit
Selling price	$300 per unit
Direct materials	$180 per unit
Direct labor	$50 per unit

Required:

1. Using Exhibit 7–6 as a guide, prepare a report showing the first-stage allocations of overhead costs to the activity cost pools.
2. Using Exhibit 7–7 as a guide, compute the activity rates for the activity cost pools.
3. Calculate the total overhead costs for the order from Shenzhen Enterprises including customer support costs.
4. Using Exhibit 7–12 as a guide, calculate the customer margin for Shenzhen Enterprises.

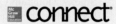 **connect**

Problems

PROBLEM 7–16 Comparing Traditional and Activity-Based Product Margins LO7–1, LO7–3, LO7–4, LO7–5

Hi-Tek Manufacturing, Inc., makes two types of industrial component parts—the B300 and the T500. An absorption costing income statement for the most recent period is shown:

Hi-Tek Manufacturing Inc. Income Statement	
Sales	$2,100,000
Cost of goods sold	1,600,000
Gross margin	500,000
Selling and administrative expenses	550,000
Net operating loss	$ (50,000)

Hi-Tek produced and sold 70,000 units of B300 at a price of $20 per unit and 17,500 units of T500 at a price of $40 per unit. The company's traditional cost system allocates manufacturing overhead to products using a plantwide overhead rate and direct labor dollars as the allocation base. Additional information relating to the company's two product lines is shown below:

	B300	T500	Total
Direct materials	$436,300	$251,700	$ 688,000
Direct labor	$200,000	$104,000	304,000
Manufacturing overhead			608,000
Cost of goods sold			$1,600,000

The company has created an activity-based costing system to evaluate the profitability of its products. Hi-Tek's ABC implementation team concluded that $50,000 and $100,000 of the company's advertising expenses could be directly traced to B300 and T500, respectively. The remainder of the selling and administrative expenses was organization-sustaining in nature. The ABC team also distributed the company's manufacturing overhead to four activities as shown:

Activity Cost Pool (and Activity Measure)	Manufacturing Overhead	Activity		
		B300	T500	Total
Machining (machine-hours)	$213,500	90,000	62,500	152,500
Setups (setup hours)	157,500	75	300	375
Product-sustaining (number of products)	120,000	1	1	2
Other (organization-sustaining costs)	117,000	NA	NA	NA
Total manufacturing overhead cost	$608,000			

Required:

1. Using Exhibit 7–13 as a guide, compute the product margins for the B300 and T500 under the company's traditional costing system.
2. Using Exhibit 7–11 as a guide, compute the product margins for B300 and T500 under the activity-based costing system.
3. Using Exhibit 7–14 as a guide, prepare a quantitative comparison of the traditional and activity-based cost assignments. Explain why the traditional and activity-based cost assignments differ.

PROBLEM 7–17 Comparing Traditional and Activity-Based Product Margins LO7–1, LO7–3, LO7–4, LO7–5

Smoky Mountain Corporation makes two types of hiking boots—the Xtreme and the Pathfinder. Data concerning these two product lines appear below:

	Xtreme	Pathfinder
Selling price per unit	$140.00	$99.00
Direct materials per unit	$72.00	$53.00
Direct labor per unit	$24.00	$12.00
Direct labor-hours per unit	2.0 DLHs	1.0 DLHs
Estimated annual production and sales	20,000 units	80,000 units

The company has a traditional costing system in which manufacturing overhead is applied to units based on direct labor-hours. Data concerning manufacturing overhead and direct labor-hours for the upcoming year appear below:

Estimated total manufacturing overhead	$1,980,000
Estimated total direct labor-hours	120,000 DLHs

Required:

1. Using Exhibit 7–13 as a guide, compute the product margins for the Xtreme and the Pathfinder products under the company's traditional costing system.
2. The company is considering replacing its traditional costing system with an activity-based costing system that would assign its manufacturing overhead to the following four activity cost pools (the Other cost pool includes organization-sustaining costs and idle capacity costs):

	Estimated	Expected Activity		
Activities and Activity Measures	Overhead Cost	Xtreme	Pathfinder	Total
Supporting direct labor (direct labor-hours)	$ 783,600	40,000	80,000	120,000
Batch setups (setups)	495,000	200	100	300
Product sustaining (number of products)	602,400	1	1	2
Other	99,000	NA	NA	NA
Total manufacturing overhead cost	$1,980,000			

Using Exhibit 7–11 as a guide, compute the product margins for the Xtreme and the Pathfinder products under the activity-based costing system.
3. Using Exhibit 7–14 as a guide, prepare a quantitative comparison of the traditional and activity-based cost assignments. Explain why the traditional and activity-based cost assignments differ.

PROBLEM 7–18 Activity-Based Costing and Bidding on Jobs LO7–2, LO7–3, LO7–4

Mercer Asbestos Removal Company removes potentially toxic asbestos insulation and related products from buildings. There has been a long-simmering dispute between the company's estimator and the work supervisors. The on-site supervisors claim that the estimators do not adequately distinguish between routine work, such as removal of asbestos insulation around heating pipes in older homes, and nonroutine work, such as removing asbestos-contaminated ceiling plaster in industrial buildings. The on-site supervisors believe that nonroutine work is far more expensive than routine work and should bear higher customer charges. The estimator sums up his position in this way: "My job is to measure the area to be cleared of asbestos. As directed by top management, I simply multiply the square footage by $2.50 to determine the bid price. Since our average cost is only $2.175 per square foot, that leaves enough cushion to take care of the additional costs of nonroutine work that shows up. Besides, it is difficult to know what is routine or not routine until you actually start tearing things apart."

To shed light on this controversy, the company initiated an activity-based costing study of all of its costs. Data from the activity-based costing system follow:

Activity Cost Pool	Activity Measure	Total Activity
Removing asbestos	Thousands of square feet	800 thousand square feet
Estimating and job setup	Number of jobs	500 jobs
Working on nonroutine jobs	Number of nonroutine jobs	100 nonroutine jobs
Other (organization-sustaining costs and idle capacity costs)	None	

Note: The 100 nonroutine jobs are included in the total of 500 jobs. Both nonroutine jobs and routine jobs require estimating and setup.

Costs for the Year	
Wages and salaries	$ 300,000
Disposal fees	700,000
Equipment depreciation	90,000
On-site supplies	50,000
Office expenses	200,000
Licensing and insurance	400,000
Total cost	$1,740,000

Distribution of Resource Consumption Across Activities

	Removing Asbestos	Estimating and Job Setup	Working on Nonroutine Jobs	Other	Total
Wages and salaries	50%	10%	30%	10%	100%
Disposal fees	60%	0%	40%	0%	100%
Equipment depreciation	40%	5%	20%	35%	100%
On-site supplies	60%	30%	10%	0%	100%
Office expenses	10%	35%	25%	30%	100%
Licensing and insurance	30%	0%	50%	20%	100%

Required:
1. Using Exhibit 7–6 as a guide, perform the first-stage allocation of costs to the activity cost pools.
2. Using Exhibit 7–7 as a guide, compute the activity rates for the activity cost pools.
3. Using the activity rates you have computed, determine the total cost and the average cost per thousand square feet of each of the following jobs according to the activity-based costing system.
   a. A routine 1,000-square-foot asbestos removal job.
   b. A routine 2,000-square-foot asbestos removal job.
   c. A nonroutine 2,000-square-foot asbestos removal job.
4. Given the results you obtained in (3) above, do you agree with the estimator that the company's present policy for bidding on jobs is adequate?

PROBLEM 7–19 Second-Stage Allocations and Product Margins LO7–4, LO7–5

Pixel Studio, Inc., is a small company that creates computer-generated animations for films and television. Much of the company's work consists of short commercials for television, but the company also does realistic computer animations for special effects in movies.

The young founders of the company have become increasingly concerned with the economics of the business—particularly since many competitors have sprung up recently in the local area. To help understand the company's cost structure, an activity-based costing system has been designed. Three major activities are carried out in the company: animation concept, animation production, and contract administration. The animation concept activity is carried out at the contract proposal stage when the company bids on projects. This is an intensive activity that involves individuals from all parts of the company in creating story boards and prototype stills to be shown to the prospective client. Once a project is accepted by the client, the animation goes into production and contract administration begins. Almost all of the work involved in animation production is done by the technical staff, whereas the administrative staff is largely responsible for contract administration. The activity cost pools and their activity measures are listed below:

Activity Cost Pool	Activity Measure	Activity Rate
Animation concept	Number of proposals	$6,040 per proposal
Animation production	Minutes of completed animation	$7,725 per minute
Contract administration	Number of contracts	$6,800 per contract

These activity rates include all of the company's costs, except for its organization-sustaining costs and idle capacity costs. There are no direct labor or direct materials costs.

Preliminary analysis using these activity rates has indicated that the local commercial segment of the market may be unprofitable. This segment is highly competitive. Producers of local commercials may ask three or four companies like Pixel Studio to bid, which results in an unusually low ratio of accepted contracts to bids. Furthermore, the animation sequences tend to be much shorter for local commercials than for other work. Since animation work is billed at fairly standard rates according to the running time of the completed animation, this means that the revenues from these short projects tend to be below average. Data concerning activity in the local commercial market appear below:

Activity Measure	Local Commercials
Number of proposals	25
Minutes of completed animation	5
Number of contracts	10

The total sales from the 10 contracts for local commercials was $180,000.

Required:
1. Calculate the cost of serving the local commercial market.
2. Calculate the margin earned serving the local commercial market. (Remember, this company has no direct materials or direct labor costs.)
3. What would you recommend to management concerning the local commercial market?

PROBLEM 7–20 Evaluating the Profitability of Services LO7–2, LO7–3, LO7–4, LO7–5

Gallatin Carpet Cleaning is a small, family-owned business operating out of Bozeman, Montana. For its services, the company has always charged a flat fee per hundred square feet of carpet cleaned. The current fee is $28 per hundred square feet. However, there is some question about whether the company is actually making any money on jobs for some customers—particularly those located on remote ranches that require considerable travel time. The owner's daughter, home for the summer from college, has suggested investigating this question using activity-based costing. After some discussion, she designed a simple system consisting of four activity cost pools. The activity cost pools and their activity measures appear below:

Activity Cost Pool	Activity Measure	Activity for the Year
Cleaning carpets	Square feet cleaned (00s)	20,000 hundred square feet
Travel to jobs	Miles driven	60,000 miles
Job support	Number of jobs	2,000 jobs
Other (organization-sustaining costs and idle capacity costs) ...	None	Not applicable

The total cost of operating the company for the year is $430,000, which includes the following costs:

Wages	$150,000
Cleaning supplies	40,000
Cleaning equipment depreciation	20,000
Vehicle expenses	80,000
Office expenses	60,000
Presidents compensation	80,000
Total cost	$430,000

Resource consumption is distributed across the activities as follows:

Distribution of Resource Consumption Across Activities					
	Cleaning Carpets	Travel to Jobs	Job Support	Other	Total
Wages	70%	20%	0%	10%	100%
Cleaning supplies	100%	0%	0%	0%	100%
Cleaning equipment depreciation	80%	0%	0%	20%	100%
Vehicle expenses	0%	60%	0%	40%	100%
Office expenses	0%	0%	45%	55%	100%
President's compensation	0%	0%	40%	60%	100%

Job support consists of receiving calls from potential customers at the home office, scheduling jobs, billing, resolving issues, and so on.

Required:
1. Using Exhibit 7–6 as a guide, prepare the first-stage allocation of costs to the activity cost pools.
2. Using Exhibit 7–7 as a guide, compute the activity rates for the activity cost pools.
3. The company recently completed a 500 square foot carpet-cleaning job at the Flying N Ranch—a 75-mile round-trip journey from the company's offices in Bozeman. Compute the cost of this job using the activity-based costing system.
4. The revenue from the Flying N Ranch was $140 (500 square feet @ $28 per hundred square feet). Using Exhibit 7–12 as a guide, calculate the customer margin earned on this job.
5. What do you conclude concerning the profitability of the Flying N Ranch job? Explain.
6. What advice would you give the president concerning pricing jobs in the future?

Appendix 7A: Time-Driven Activity-Based Costing: A Microsoft Excel-Based Approach

The purpose of this appendix is to introduce you to *time-driven activity-based costing* (TDABC). The approach demonstrated in this appendix overcomes two important limitations that accompany the activity-based costing (ABC) model described in the main body of the chapter. First, TDABC does not require extensive interviews with employees (as depicted in Exhibit 7–5) to perform stage one allocations. For a company that employs thousands of people, these interviews can be very time-consuming—which limits a company's ability to frequently update its cost model. Second, the ABC model depicted in Exhibits 7–5 and 7–6 assumes that employees will self-report their own idle time within the "Other" cost pool. In reality, most employees are very averse to reporting their own idle time because it may signal to management that the size of the labor force can be reduced.

This appendix will demonstrate how TDABC can be used to assign indirect costs to cost objects such as products and customers. We'll also explain how TDABC can be used for capacity analysis purposes. For simplicity, we limit the scope of this appendix to focus solely on labor costs. While TDABC systems can include other types of indirect costs such as equipment costs and utility costs, we purposely omit these kinds of costs to simplify our capacity analysis discussion.

Ridley Company: An Example

Ridley Company would like to improve its understanding of customer profitability and capacity utilization. As an initial pilot project, the company has decided to use TDABC to analyze its Customer Service Department labor costs. The goals of the project are to obtain a better understanding of how customer service labor costs are used by individual customers and to obtain a more informed basis for making employee staffing decisions within the department. In the past, the company has relied on "educated guesses" to make staffing decisions, which often resulted in an imbalance between the number of employees on the payroll and the number of employees needed to serve customers. Ridley hopes that TDABC will enable it to estimate the financial implications of better aligning its labor capacity with its customer demand.

The Data Inputs

Exhibit 7A–1 summarizes three types of data inputs for Ridley's TDABC model—resource data, activity data, and cost object data. The resource data includes the number of employees in the Customer Service Department (30), the average salary per employee ($29,952), the number of weeks in a year (52), the minutes available per week (2,400), and the practical capacity percentage (80%). The practical capacity percentage acknowledges that employees are not serving customers 100% of their available minutes. They spend some of their available time on vacation, on breaks, in training, attending to personal needs, etc. Thus, Ridley estimates that 80% of an employee's available minutes are spent actually serving customers.

The activity data contained in Exhibit 7A–1 specifies three activities within the Customer Service Department, namely order processing (cell B13), query resolution (cell C13), and credit reviews (cell D13). It also states the average number of minutes required to perform each activity one time. For example, on average it takes 10 minutes to process one order, 30 minutes to resolve one query from a customer, and 40 minutes to review one customer's credit worthiness.[4] The cost object data that is shown in Exhibit 7A–1 provides activity data for customers A, B, and C as well as all customers served by the Customer Service Department during the year. For example, customers A, B, and C placed 30, 18, and 7 orders, respectively. A total of 200,000 orders were placed by all of Ridley's customers during the year.

---

[4] For simplicity, we assume that all orders, queries, and credit reviews consume the same amount of minutes per unit of the activity.

EXHIBIT 7A-1
Ridley Company: The Data
Inputs

	A	B	C	D	E
1	Ridley Company				
2	Customer Service Department				
3	Data Inputs				
4					
5	*Resource Data:*				
6	Number of employees	30			
7	Average salary per employee	$ 29,952			
8					
9	Weeks per year	52			
10	Minutes available per week (40 hours × 60 minutes)	2,400			
11	Practical capacity percentage	80%			
12					
13	*Activity Data:*	Order processing	Query resolution	Credit reviews	
14	Minutes per unit of the activity	10	30	40	
15					
16	*Cost Object Data:*	Customer A	Customer B	Customer C	All Customers
17	Number of orders processed	30	18	7	200,000
18	Number of customer queries	17	10	8	4,500
19	Number of credit reviews	1	1	1	8,900
20					

Exhibit 7A-1 Exhibit 7A-2 Exhibit 7/

Customer Cost Analysis

Exhibit 7A–2 summarizes the three-step TDABC process that Ridley Company uses to assign Customer Service Department labor costs to customers A, B, and C. The first step is to divide the total cost of the resources supplied in cell B10 ($898,560) by the practical capacity of the resources supplied in cell B14 (2,995,200 minutes) to obtain the cost per minute of the resource supplied in cell B16 ($0.30). Notice that cell B12 shows a practical capacity per employee of 99,840 minutes. This amount is obtained by multiplying together three cells from the data inputs tab shown in Exhibit 7A–1—cell B9 (52 weeks), cell B10 (2,400 minutes per week), and cell B11 (80%).

The second step in Exhibit 7A–2 is to calculate the time-driven activity rate for each of the three activities. For example, the time-driven activity rate for the order processing activity of $3.00 per order (cell B21) is derived by multiplying 10 minutes per unit of the activity (cell B19) by the cost per minute of the resource supplied of $0.30 (cell B20). Similarly, the time-driven activity rate for the query resolution activity of $9.00 per query (cell C21) is derived by multiplying 30 minutes per unit of the activity (cell C19) by the cost per minute of the resource supplied of $0.30 (cell C20).

The third step in Exhibit 7A–2 is to assign customer service labor costs to customers A, B, and C. For example, the total customer service costs assigned to Customer A of $255 (cell B36) is the sum of the order processing costs of $90 (cell B26), the query resolution costs of $153 (cell B30), and the credit review costs of $12 (cell B34). Notice that the number of orders processed in cell B24 (30), the number of customer queries in cell B28 (17), and the number of credit reviews in cell B32 (1) are linked to cells B17 through B19 in the data inputs tab shown in Exhibit 7A–1.

The type of cost assignments summarized in Exhibit 7A–2 could be useful to Ridley Company in larger initiatives, such as measuring customer profitability and managing its customer mix based on those insights. Furthermore, the cost assignments shown in Exhibit 7A–2 were performed without having to interview the 30 employees within the Customer Services Department. Instead, Ridley Company only needed to make a reasonable estimate regarding its practical capacity percentage (80%) and to estimate the amount of time required to perform each activity one time in order to compute its time-driven activity rates.

However, the data in Exhibit 7A–2 does not help Ridley quantify and manage its used and unused capacity costs, nor does it enable the company to estimate the number of customer service department employees that it would need to meet future customer

LO7-6
Use time-driven activity-based costing to assign costs to cost objects.

EXHIBIT 7A–2
Ridley Company: Customer Cost
Analysis

	A	B	C	D
1	Ridley Company			
2	Customer Service Department			
3	Customer Cost Analysis			
4				
5	Step 1: Calculate the cost per minute of the resource supplied			
6				
7	*Customer Service Department:*			
8	Number of employees (a)	30		
9	Average salary per employee (b)	$ 29,952		
10	Total cost of resources supplied (a) × (b)	$ 898,560		
11				
12	Practical capacity per employee (in minutes) (a)	99,840		
13	Number of employees (b)	30		
14	Practical capacity of resources supplied (in minutes) (a) × (b)	2,995,200		
15				
16	Cost per minute of the resource supplied	$ 0.30		
17				
18	Step 2: Calculate the time-driven activity rate	Order processing	Query resolution	Credit reviews
19	Minutes per unit of the activity (a)	10	30	40
20	Cost per minute of the resource supplied (b)	$ 0.30	$ 0.30	$ 0.30
21	Time-driven activity rate (a) × (b)	$ 3.00	$ 9.00	$ 12.00
22				
23	Step 3: Assign costs to cost objects	Customer A	Customer B	Customer C
24	Number of orders processed (a)	30	18	7
25	Time-driven activity rate (b)	$ 3.00	$ 3.00	$ 3.00
26	Order processing costs assigned (a) × (b)	$ 90.00	$ 54.00	$ 21.00
27				
28	Number of customer queries (a)	17	10	8
29	Time-driven activity rate (b)	$ 9.00	$ 9.00	$ 9.00
30	Query resolution costs assigned (a) × (b)	$ 153.00	$ 90.00	$ 72.00
31				
32	Number of credit checks (a)	1	1	1
33	Time-driven activity rate (b)	$ 12.00	$ 12.00	$ 12.00
34	Credit review costs assigned (a) × (b)	$ 12.00	$ 12.00	$ 12.00
35				
36	Total customer service costs assigned	$ 255.00	$ 156.00	$ 105.00
37				

⏮ ◀ ▶ ▶| Exhibit 7A-1   **Exhibit 7A-2**   Exhibit ◀

demand. To glean these types of insights from Ridley's TDABC system, we turn our attention to the topic of capacity analysis.

Capacity Analysis

LO7–7
Use time-driven activity-based costing to analyze capacity.

Exhibit 7A–3 shows the four-step process that Ridley Company uses for capacity management purposes. It focuses on *all* of Ridley's customers rather than just customers A, B, and C. The first step is to calculate the total used capacity in minutes of 2,491,000 (= 2,000,000 + 135,000 + 356,000). The second step is to take the total minutes available of 2,995,200 from cell B11 (and as previously computed in cell B14 in Exhibit 7A–2) minus the minutes used of 2,491,000 (from cell B12) to derive the 504,200 minutes of unused capacity shown in cell B13.

The third step translates the unused capacity in minutes to unused capacity in terms of employees. We perform this calculation because customer service employees are a step-fixed cost rather than a variable cost. In other words, Ridley does not purchase customer service capacity by the minute. Instead, it hires individual employees who each provide 99,840 minutes of practical capacity per year. Because the unused capacity in minutes is 504,200 and the practical capacity of one employee is 99,840 minutes, the total unused capacity equates with 5.05 employees (= 504,200 ÷ 99,840).

		A	B	C	D	E	
1		Ridley Company					
2		Customer Service Department					
3		Capacity Analysis					
4							
5	Step 1: Calculate the used capacity in minutes		Order processing	Query resolution	Credit reviews	Total	
6	Customer demand for each activity (a)		200,000	4,500	8,900		
7	Customer service minutes required per unit of each activity (b)		10	30	40		
8	Customer service minutes used to meet demand (a) × (b)		2,000,000	135,000	356,000	2,491,000	
9							
10	Step 2: Calculate the unused capacity in minutes						
11	Total customer service minutes available to meet demand (a)		2,995,200				
12	Total customer service minutes used to meet demand (b)		2,491,000				
13	Unused capacity in minutes (a) − (b)		504,200				
14							
15	Step 3: Calculate the unused capacity in number of employees						
16	Unused capacity in minutes (a)		504,200				
17	Practical capacity per employee (in minutes) (b)		99,840				
18	Unused capacity in number of employees (a) ÷ (b)		5.05				
19							
20	Step 4: Calculate the financial impact of matching capacity with demand						
21	Potential adjustment in number of employees (rounded) (a)		(5.00)				
22	Average salary per employee (b)		$ 29,952				
23	Impact on expenses of matching capacity with demand (a) × (b)		$(149,760)				
24							
25	Note: Cell B21 uses the formula =If(B18>0,rounddown(-B18,0),roundup(-B18,0))						
26							

Exhibit 7A-2 | **Exhibit 7A-3** | Exhibit 7A-4 | Exhi

EXHIBIT 7A-3
Ridley Company: Capacity Analysis

The fourth step calculates the financial impact of matching capacity with demand. The key to this step is the formula in cell B21 of Exhibit 7A–3, which rounds the value reported in cell B18 to a whole number. We perform this rounding function because Ridley alters its step-fixed employee headcount in terms of whole employees, not portions of an employee. So, for example, cell B18 shows an unused capacity of 5.05 employees; however, Ridley cannot eliminate .05 employees. It could possibly eliminate five or six employees, but nothing in between. Since eliminating six employees would leave the Customer Service Department a little short-handed, we round down to five employees. Given the average salary per employee of $29,952, the impact on expenses of matching labor capacity with demand is a savings of $149,760 (= 5.00 × $29,952).

"What-If" Analysis

The data inputs in Exhibit 7A–1 also enable Ridley to answer some interesting "what if" questions. For example, what if the company was able to lower its credit review time from 40 minutes to 30 minutes? How would this effect the costs assigned to customers A, B, and C? To answer this question, we would change cell D14 in Exhibit 7A–1 from 40 minutes to 30 minutes. The revised customer cost analysis that would be instantly generated is shown in Exhibit 7A–4.

Notice that cell D19 shows 30 minutes per credit review instead of the 40 minutes shown in the same cell in Exhibit 7A–2. This in turn lowers the cost per credit review to $9.00 (as shown in cell D21) rather than the $12.00 shown in the same cell in Exhibit 7A–2. The lower time-driven activity rate of $9.00 carries forward to cells B33 through D33 and in turn lowers each customer's total customer service costs by $3. For example, customer A's total customer service cost is $252 in cell B36 of Exhibit 7A–4, whereas the corresponding total in cell B36 of Exhibit 7A–2 is $255.

Let's further assume that Ridley Company wants to answer the question: What if we also increase the number of orders processed from 200,000 (as shown in cell E17 in Exhibit 7A–1) to 265,000? How would the projected increase in the number of orders processed affect our staffing needs in the Customer Service Department? After making the appropriate change in cell E17 of Exhibit 7A–1, Exhibit 7A–5 provides the answer to this question—Ridley Company would need to hire one more employee at an estimated cost of $29,952.

EXHIBIT 7A–4
Ridley Company's Customer Cost
Analysis: A "What If" Analysis

	A	B	C	D
1	Ridley Company			
2	Customer Service Department			
3	Customer Cost Analysis			
4				
5	**Step 1: Calculate the cost per minute of the resource supplied**			
6				
7	*Customer Service Department:*			
8	Number of employees (a)	30		
9	Average salary per employee (b)	$ 29,952		
10	Total cost of resources supplied (a) × (b)	$ 898,560		
11				
12	Practical capacity per employee (in minutes) (a)	99,840		
13	Number of employees (b)	30		
14	Practical capacity of resources supplied (in minutes) (a) × (b)	2,995,200		
15				
16	Cost per minute of the resource supplied	$ 0.30		
17				
18	**Step 2: Calculate the time-driven activity rate**	Order processing	Query resolution	Credit reviews
19	Minutes per unit of the activity (a)	10	30	30
20	Cost per minute of the resource supplied (b)	$ 0.30	$ 0.30	$ 0.30
21	Time-driven activity rate (a) × (b)	$ 3.00	$ 9.00	$ 9.00
22				
23	**Step 3: Assign costs to cost objects**	Customer A	Customer B	Customer C
24	Number of orders processed (a)	30	18	7
25	Time-driven activity rate (b)	$ 3.00	$ 3.00	$ 3.00
26	Order processing costs assigned (a) × (b)	$ 90.00	$ 54.00	$ 21.00
27				
28	Number of customer queries (a)	17	10	8
29	Time-driven activity rate (b)	$ 9.00	$ 9.00	$ 9.00
30	Query resolution costs assigned (a) × (b)	$ 153.00	$ 90.00	$ 72.00
31				
32	Number of credit checks (a)	1	1	1
33	Time-driven activity rate (b)	$ 9.00	$ 9.00	$ 9.00
34	Credit review costs assigned (a) × (b)	$ 9.00	$ 9.00	$ 9.00
35				
36	Total customer service costs assigned	$ 252.00	$ 153.00	$ 102.00
37				

Exhibit 7A-4　Exhibit 7A-5　Exerci

To understand how this answer is derived, let's start with Step 1 within Exhibit 7A–5, which shows 265,000 orders processed in cell B6. This increase in the number of orders processed increases the number of customer service minutes needed to meet customer demand to 3,052,000 (cell E8). Step 2 shows that the total customer service minutes available of 2,995,200 (cell B11) is now less than the number of minutes used to meet demand of 3,052,000 (cell B12), which results in unused capacity of (56,800) minutes as shown in cell B13. Because the unused capacity is a negative number, it implies that Ridley does not have enough capacity available to satisfy the estimated customer demand. Step 3 in Exhibit 7A–5 translates the shortage in minutes to a shortfall stated in terms of number of employees—or (0.57) employees as shown in cell B18. Given that Ridley cannot hire slightly more than one-half of an employee, cell B21 rounds this number to 1.00 and then cell B23 translates the estimated cost of hiring one additional employee to $29,952.

This concludes our introduction to TDABC. The strengths of this methodology include (1) it is easy to update because it does not require employee interviews, (2) it quantifies unused capacity costs in an objective fashion that does not require employees to self-report their own idle time, and (3) it helps companies estimate the financial impact of aligning capacity with demand, particularly with respect to step-fixed resources such as the customer service employees in the Ridley Company example.

EXHIBIT 7A–5
Ridley Company's Capacity Analysis: A "What If" Analysis

	A	B	C	D	E
1	Ridley Company				
2	Customer Service Department				
3	Capacity Analysis				
4					
5	Step 1: Calculate the used capacity in minutes	Order processing	Query resolution	Credit reviews	Total
6	Customer demand for each activity (a)	265,000	4,500	8,900	
7	Customer service minutes required per unit of each activity (b)	10	30	30	
8	Customer service minutes used to meet demand (a) × (b)	2,650,000	135,000	267,000	3,052,000
9					
10	Step 2: Calculate the unused capacity in minutes				
11	Total customer service minutes available to meet demand (a)	2,995,200			
12	Total customer service minutes used to meet demand (b)	3,052,000			
13	Unused capacity in minutes (a) – (b)	(56,800)			
14					
15	Step 3: Calculate the unused capacity in number of employees				
16	Unused capacity in minutes (a)	(56,800)			
17	Practical capacity per employee (in minutes) (b)	99,840			
18	Unused capacity in number of employees (a) ÷ (b)	(0.57)			
19					
20	Step 4: Calculate the financial impact of matching capacity with demand				
21	Potential adjustment in number of employees (rounded) (a)	1.00			
22	Average salary per employee (b)	$ 29,952			
23	Impact on expenses of matching capacity with demand (a) × (b)	$ 29,952			
24					
25	Note: Cell B21 uses the formula =If(B18>0,rounddown(-B18,0),roundup(-B18,0))				
26					

Exhibit 7A-4   **Exhibit 7A-5**   Exercise 7A-1 Inputs

---

connect   **Appendix 7A: Exercises and Problems**

EXERCISE 7A–1 Time-Driven Activity-Based Costing LO 7–6

Saratoga Company manufactures jobs to customer specifications. The company is conducting a time-driven activity-based costing study in its Purchasing Department to better understand how Purchasing Department labor costs are consumed by individual jobs. To aid the study, the company provided the following data regarding its Purchasing Department and three of its many jobs:

Number of employees	12
Average salary per employee	$28,000
Weeks of employment per year	52
Hours worked per week	40
Practical capacity percentage	85%

	Requisition Processing	Bid Evaluation	Inspection
Minutes per unit of the activity	15	45	30

	Job X	Job Y	Job Z
Number of requisitions processed	8	5	4
Number of bid evaluations	3	2	4
Number of inspections	6	2	6

Required:
1.   Calculate the cost per minute of the resource supplied in the Purchasing Department.
2.   Calculate the time-driven activity rate for each of Saratoga's three activities.
3.   Calculate the total purchasing labor costs assigned to Job X, Job Y, and Job Z.

EXERCISE 7A–2 Time-Driven Activity-Based Costing LO 7–7
Refer to the data in Exercise 7A–1. In addition, assume that Saratoga Company provided the following activity data for *all* jobs produced during the year:

	Requisition Processing	Bid Evaluation	Inspection
Activity demands for all jobs	7,000	9,400	10,000

Required:
1.   Calculate Saratoga's used capacity in minutes.
2.   Calculate Saratoga's unused capacity in minutes.
3.   Calculate Saratoga's unused capacity in number of employees. (Do not round your answer to a whole number.)
4.   Calculate the impact on expenses of matching capacity with demand. (Be sure to round your potential adjustment in the number of employees to a whole number.)

EXERCISE 7A–3 Time-Driven Activity-Based Costing LO 7–6, LO 7–7
Refer to the data in Exercises 7A–1 and 7A–2. Now assume that Saratoga Company would like to answer the following "what if" question using its time-driven activity-based costing system: Assuming our estimated activity demands for all jobs in the next period will be as shown below, how will this affect our job costs and our staffing levels within the Purchasing Department?

	Requisition Processing	Bid Evaluation	Inspection
Activity demands for all jobs	7,600	9,900	11,000

Required:
1.   How will these revised activity demands affect the total Purchasing Department labor costs assigned to Job X, Job Y, and Job Z? No calculations are necessary
2.   Using the revised activity demands, calculate Saratoga's used capacity in minutes.
3.   Using the revised activity demands, calculate Saratoga's unused capacity in minutes.
4.   Using the revised activity demands, calculate Saratoga's unused capacity in number of employees. (Do not round your answer to a whole number.)
5.   Based on the revised activity demands, calculate the impact on expenses of matching capacity with demand. (Be sure to round your potential adjustment in the number of employees to a whole number.)

PROBLEM 7A–4 Time-Driven Activity-Based Costing LO 7–6, LO 7–7
Stahl Company is conducting a time-driven activity-based costing study in its Shipping Department. To aid the study, the company provided the following data regarding its Shipping Department and the customers served by the department:

Number of employees	34
Average salary per employee	$34,000
Weeks of employment per year	52
Hours worked per week	40
Practical capacity percentage	80%

	Line-Item Picking	Packaging	Loading Deliveries
Minutes per unit of the activity	5	15	30

	Customer L	Customer M	Customer N	All Customers
Number of line items picked	280	160	90	335,000
Number of boxes packaged	50	20	15	46,800
Number of deliveries loaded	6	2	10	12,100

Required:

1. Using the customer cost analysis shown in Exhibit 7A–2 as your guide, compute the following:
    a. The cost per minute of the resource supplied in the Shipping Department.
    b. The time-driven activity rate for each of Stahl's three activities.
    c. The total labor costs consumed by Customer L, Customer M, and Customer N.
2. Using the capacity analysis shown in Exhibit 7A–3 as your guide, compute the following:
    a. The used capacity in minutes.
    b. The unused capacity in minutes.
    c. The unused capacity in number of employees. (Do not round your answer to a whole number.)
    d. The impact on expenses of matching capacity with demand. (Be sure to round your potential adjustment in the number of employees to a whole number.)

PROBLEM 7A–5 Time-Driven Activity-Based Costing LO 7–6, LO 7–7

Athens Company is conducting a time-driven activity-based costing study in its Engineering Department. To aid the study, the company provided the following data regarding its Engineering Department and the customers served by the department:

Number of employees.	10
Average salary per employee	$90,000
Weeks of employment per year	52
Hours worked per week	40
Practical capacity percentage	85%

	New Product Design	Engineering Change Orders	Product Testing
Hours per unit of the activity	40	20	8

	Customer A	Customer B	Customer C	All Customers
Number of new products designed	3	2	4	180
Number of engineering change orders	5	2	2	250
Number of products tested	8	4	6	160

Required:

1. Using the customer cost analysis shown in Exhibit 7A–2 as your guide, compute the following:
    a. The cost per hour of the resource supplied in the Engineering Department.
    b. The time-driven activity rate per hour for each of Athens' three activities.
    c. The total engineering costs consumed by Customer A, Customer B, and Customer C.
2. Using the capacity analysis shown in Exhibit 7A–3 as your guide, compute the following:
    a. The used capacity in hours.
    b. The unused capacity in hours.
    c. The unused capacity in number of employees. (Do not round your answer to a whole number.)
    d. The impact on expenses of matching capacity with demand. (Be sure to round your potential adjustment in the number of employees to a whole number.)
3. Assume that Athens is considering expanding its business such that the estimated number of new products designed would increase to 250, the number of engineering change orders would jump to 320, and the number of products tested would rise to 240. Using these revised figures, calculate the following:
    a. The used capacity in hours.
    b. The unused capacity in hours.
    c. The unused capacity in number of employees. (Do not round your answer to a whole number.)
    d. The impact on expenses of matching capacity with demand. (Be sure to round your potential adjustment in the number of employees to a whole number.)

CHAPTER 8

Master Budgeting

Planning for a Crisis—Civil War Trust

© Sandee Noreen

The **Civil War Trust** (CWT) is a private, nonprofit organization with 70,000 members that works to preserve the nation's remaining Civil War battlefields—many of which are threatened by commercial development such as shopping centers, houses, industrial parks, and casinos. To forestall development, the CWT typically purchases the land or development rights to the land. The CWT has saved over 25,000 acres from development, including, for example, 698 acres of battlefield at Gettysburg.

The CWT is wholly supported by contributions from its members. When the economy stagnates it complicates the CWT's ability to predict the amount of future donations. The CWT responds to this uncertainty by creating an annual budget that contains three variations based on progressively pessimistic economic assumptions. The more pessimistic budgets were called contingent budgets. If member contributions decline somewhat due to economic woes, the CWT can switch to its first contingent budget. In the past, rolling to the contingent budget has required a number of actions to reduce costs including a hiring freeze and a salary freeze while maintaining an aggressive program of protecting battlefield acreage through purchases of land and development rights. In more dire circumstances, the CWT can switch to its most pessimistic budget—which would involve layoffs and other extraordinary cost-saving measures.

Instead of reacting in a panic mode to unfavorable developments, CWT uses the budgeting process to carefully plan in advance for a number of possible contingencies. ■

Sources: Communications with James Lighthizer, president, and David Duncan, director of membership and development, Civil War Trust; and the CWT website, www.civilwar.org.

LEARNING OBJECTIVES

After studying Chapter 8, you should be able to:

LO8–1 Understand why organizations budget and the processes they use to create budgets.

LO8–2 Prepare a sales budget, including a schedule of expected cash collections.

LO8–3 Prepare a production budget.

LO8–4 Prepare a direct materials budget, including a schedule of expected cash disbursements for purchases of materials.

LO8–5 Prepare a direct labor budget.

LO8–6 Prepare a manufacturing overhead budget.

LO8–7 Prepare a selling and administrative expense budget.

LO8–8 Prepare a cash budget.

LO8–9 Prepare a budgeted income statement.

LO8–10 Prepare a budgeted balance sheet.

In this chapter, we describe how organizations strive to achieve their financial goals by preparing *budgets*. A **budget** is a detailed plan for the future that is usually expressed in formal quantitative terms. Individuals sometimes create household budgets that balance their income and expenditures for food, clothing, housing, and so on while providing for some savings. Once the budget is established, actual spending is compared to the budget to make sure the plan is being followed. Companies use budgets in a similar way, although the amount of work and underlying details far exceed a personal budget.

Why and How Do Organizations Create Budgets?

Budgets are used for two distinct purposes—*planning* and *control*. **Planning** involves developing goals and preparing various budgets to achieve those goals. **Control** involves gathering feedback to ensure that the plan is being properly executed or modified as circumstances change. To be effective, a good budgeting system must provide for both planning and control. Good planning without effective control is a waste of time and effort.

Advantages of Budgeting

Organizations realize many benefits from budgeting, including:

1. Budgets *communicate* management's plans throughout the organization.
2. Budgets force managers to *think about* and *plan* for the future. In the absence of the necessity to prepare a budget, many managers would spend all of their time dealing with day-to-day emergencies.
3. The budgeting process provides a means of *allocating resources* to those parts of the organization where they can be used most effectively.
4. The budgeting process can uncover potential *bottlenecks* before they occur.
5. Budgets *coordinate* the activities of the entire organization by *integrating* the plans of its various parts. Budgeting helps to ensure that everyone in the organization is pulling in the same direction.
6. Budgets define goals and objectives that can serve as *benchmarks* for evaluating subsequent performance.

IN BUSINESS

A CRITICAL PERSPECTIVE OF HOW COMPANIES USE BUDGETS

Most, if not all, companies operate in dynamic environments where the only constant is change. The large majority of these companies also rely on annual budgets to manage themselves. The question becomes: at what point do changes in the business environment render an annual budget obsolete? When 152 business professionals were asked this question 13% of them said their company's annual budget becomes obsolete before the new budget year begins. Another 46% of respondents said the budget becomes obsolete before the second quarter of the budget year concludes, whereas 25% of those surveyed said the budget never becomes obsolete.

© Morsa Images/Getty Images RF

Given that approximately 60% of respondents expressed concerns over obsolescence, it begged a related question for the 152 respondents: how many "what if" forecasts does your company prepare in response to changing market conditions? About 20% of the respondents said their company did not evaluate any "what if" scenarios. Another 60% of respondents said their employers evaluated no more than six "what if" scenarios.

Source: Kenneth A. Merchant, "Companies Get Budgets All Wrong," *The Wall Street Journal,* July 22, 2013, p. R5.

Responsibility Accounting

Most of what we say in this chapter and in the next three chapters is concerned with *responsibility accounting*. The basic idea underlying **responsibility accounting** is that a manager should be held responsible for those items—and *only* those items—that the manager can actually control to a significant extent. Each line item (i.e., revenue or cost) in the budget is the responsibility of a manager who is held responsible for subsequent deviations between budgeted goals and actual results. In effect, responsibility accounting *personalizes* accounting information by holding individuals responsible for revenues and costs. This concept is central to any effective planning and control system. Someone must be held responsible for each cost or else no one will be responsible and the cost will inevitably grow out of control.

What happens if actual results do not measure up to the budgeted goals? The manager is not necessarily penalized. However, the manager should take the initiative to understand the sources of significant favorable or unfavorable discrepancies, should take steps to correct unfavorable discrepancies and to exploit and replicate favorable discrepancies, and should be prepared to explain discrepancies and the steps taken to correct or exploit them to higher management. The point of an effective responsibility accounting system is to make sure that nothing "falls through the cracks," that the organization reacts quickly and appropriately to deviations from its plans, and that the organization learns from the feedback it gets by comparing budgeted goals to actual results. The point is *not* to penalize individuals for missing targets.

Choosing a Budget Period

Operating budgets ordinarily cover a one-year period corresponding to the company's fiscal year. Many companies divide their budget year into four quarters. The first quarter is then subdivided into months, and monthly budgets are developed. The last three quarters may be carried in the budget as quarterly totals only. As the year progresses, the figures for the second quarter are broken down into monthly amounts, then the third-quarter figures are broken down, and so forth. This approach has the advantage of requiring periodic review and reappraisal of budget data throughout the year.

Continuous or *perpetual budgets* are sometimes used. A **continuous** or **perpetual budget** is a 12-month budget that rolls forward one month (or quarter) as the current month (or quarter) is completed. In other words, one month (or quarter) is added to the end of the budget as each month (or quarter) comes to a close. This approach keeps managers focused at least one year ahead so that they do not become too narrowly focused on short-term results.

In this chapter, we will look at one-year operating budgets. However, using basically the same techniques, operating budgets can be prepared for periods that extend over many years. It may be difficult to accurately forecast sales and other data much beyond a year, but even rough estimates can be invaluable in uncovering potential problems and opportunities that would otherwise be overlooked.

The Self-Imposed Budget

The success of a budget program is largely determined by the way a budget is developed. Oftentimes, the budget is imposed from above, with little participation by lower-level managers. However, in the most successful budget programs, managers actively participate in preparing their own budgets. Imposing expectations from above and then penalizing employees who do not meet those expectations will generate resentment rather than cooperation and commitment. In fact, many managers believe that being empowered to create their own *self-imposed budgets* is the most effective method of budget preparation. A **self-imposed budget** or **participative budget** is a budget that is prepared with the full cooperation and participation of managers at all levels.

Self-imposed budgets have a number of advantages:

1. Individuals at all levels of the organization are recognized as members of the team whose views and judgments are valued by top management.
2. Budget estimates prepared by front-line managers are often more accurate and reliable than estimates prepared by top managers who have less intimate knowledge of markets and day-to-day operations.
3. Motivation is generally higher when individuals participate in setting their own goals than when the goals are imposed from above. Self-imposed budgets create commitment.

4. A manager who is not able to meet a budget that has been imposed from above can always say that the budget was unrealistic and impossible to meet. With a self-imposed budget, this claim cannot be made.

Self-imposed budgeting has two important limitations. First, lower-level managers may make suboptimal budgeting recommendations if they lack the broad strategic perspective possessed by top managers. Second, self-imposed budgeting may allow lower-level managers to create too much *budgetary slack*. Because the manager who creates the budget will be held accountable for actual results that deviate from the budget, the manager will have a natural tendency to submit a budget that is easy to attain (i.e., the manager will build slack into the budget). For this reason, budgets prepared by lower-level managers should be scrutinized by higher levels of management. Questionable items should be discussed and modified as appropriate. Without such a review, self-imposed budgets may fail to support the organization's strategy or may be too slack, resulting in suboptimal performance.

Unfortunately, many companies do not use self-imposed budgeting. Instead, top managers often initiate the budgeting process by issuing profit targets. Lower-level managers are directed to prepare budgets that meet those targets. The difficulty is that the targets set by top managers may be unrealistically high or may allow too much slack. If the targets are too high and employees know they are unrealistic, motivation will suffer. If the targets allow too much slack, waste will occur. Unfortunately, top managers often are not in a position to know whether the targets are appropriate. Admittedly, a self-imposed budgeting system may lack sufficient strategic direction and lower-level managers may be tempted to build slack into their budgets. Nevertheless, because of the motivational advantages of self-imposed budgets, top managers should be cautious about imposing inflexible targets from above.

Human Factors in Budgeting

The success of a budget program also depends on whether top management uses the budget to pressure or blame employees. Using budgets to blame employees breeds hostility, tension, and mistrust rather than cooperation and productivity. Unfortunately, the budget is too often used as a pressure device and excessive emphasis is placed on "meeting the budget" under all circumstances. Rather than being used as a weapon, the budget should be used as a positive instrument to assist in establishing goals, measuring operating results, and isolating areas that need attention.

The budgeting process also is influenced by the fact that bonuses are often based on meeting and exceeding budgets. Typically, no bonus is paid unless the budget is met. The bonus often increases when the budget target is exceeded, but the bonus is usually capped out at some level. For obvious reasons, managers who have such a bonus plan or whose performance is evaluated based on meeting budget targets usually prefer to be evaluated based on highly achievable budgets. Moreover, highly achievable budgets may help build a manager's confidence and generate greater commitment to the budget while also reducing the likelihood that a manager will engage in undesirable behavior at the end of budgetary periods to secure bonus compensation. So, while some experts argue that budget targets should be very challenging and should require managers to stretch to meet their goals, in practice, most companies set their budget targets at "highly achievable" levels.

The Master Budget: An Overview

For the remainder of the chapter, we are going to illustrate a type of integrated business plan known as a *master budget*. The **master budget** consists of a number of separate but interdependent budgets that formally lay out the company's sales, production, and financial goals. The master budget culminates in a cash budget, a budgeted income statement, and a budgeted balance sheet. Exhibit 8–1 provides an overview of the various parts of the master budget and how they are related.

EXHIBIT 8–1
The Master Budget Interrelationships

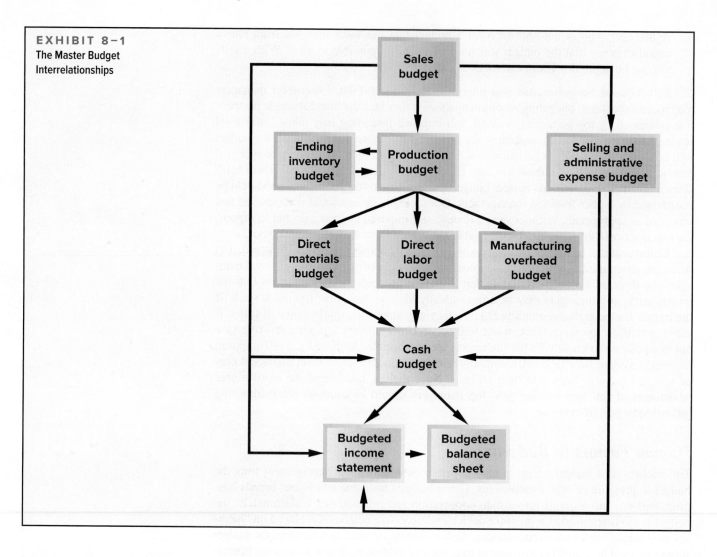

The first step in the budgeting process is preparing a **sales budget**, which is a detailed schedule showing the expected sales for the budget period. An accurate sales budget is the key to the entire budgeting process. As illustrated in Exhibit 8–1, all other parts of the master budget depend on the sales budget. If the sales budget is inaccurate, the rest of the budget will be inaccurate. The sales budget is based on the company's sales forecast, which may require the use of sophisticated mathematical models and statistical tools that are beyond the scope of this course.

The sales budget influences the variable portion of the selling and administrative expense budget and it feeds into the production budget, which defines how many units need to be produced during the budget period. The production budget in turn is used to determine the direct materials, direct labor, and manufacturing overhead budgets. Once a company has prepared these three manufacturing cost budgets, it can prepare the ending finished goods inventory budget.

The master budget concludes with the preparation of a cash budget, income statement, and balance sheet. Information from the sales budget, selling and administrative expense budget, and the manufacturing cost budgets all influence the preparation of the *cash budget*. A **cash budget** is a detailed plan showing how cash resources will be acquired and used. The budgeted income statement provides an estimate of net income for the budget period and it relies on information from the sales budget, ending finished goods inventory budget, selling and administrative expense budget, and the cash budget. The final schedule of the master budget is the balance sheet, which estimates a company's assets, liabilities, and stockholders' equity at the end of a budget period.

Seeing the Big Picture

The 10 schedules contained in a master budget can be overwhelming; therefore, it is important to see the big picture in two respects. First, a master budget for a manufacturing company is designed to answer 10 key questions as follows:

1. How much sales will we earn?
2. How much cash will we collect from customers?
3. How much raw material will we need to purchase?
4. How much manufacturing cost (including direct materials, direct labor, and manufacturing overhead) will we incur?
5. How much cash will we pay to our suppliers and our direct laborers, and how much will we pay for manufacturing overhead resources?
6. What is the total cost that will be transferred from finished goods inventory to cost of goods sold?
7. How much selling and administrative expense will we incur and how much cash will we pay related to those expenses?
8. How much money will we borrow from or repay to lenders—including interest?
9. How much net operating income will we earn?
10. What will our balance sheet look like at the end of the budget period?

Second, it is important to understand that many of the schedules in a master budget hinge on a variety of estimates and assumptions that managers must make when preparing those schedules. Exhibit 8–2 summarizes the questions that underlie these estimates and assumptions for seven of the schedules included in a master budget. As you study the forthcoming

---

EXHIBIT 8–2
Estimates and Assumptions for a Master Budget

Sales budget:
1. What are the budgeted unit sales?
2. What is the budgeted selling price per unit?
3. What percentage of accounts receivable will be collected in the current and subsequent periods?

Production budget:
1. What percentage of next period's unit sales needs to be maintained in ending finished goods inventory?

Direct materials budget:
1. How many units of raw material are needed to make one unit of finished goods?
2. What is the budgeted cost for one unit of raw material?
3. What percentage of next period's production needs should be maintained in ending raw materials inventory?
4. What percentage of raw material purchases will be paid in the current and subsequent periods?

Direct labor budget:
1. How many direct labor-hours are required per unit of finished goods?
2. What is the budgeted direct labor wage rate per hour?

Manufacturing overhead budget:
1. What is the budgeted variable overhead cost per unit of the allocation base?
2. What is the total budgeted fixed overhead cost per period?
3. What is the budgeted depreciation expense on factory assets per period?

Selling and administrative expense budget:
1. What is the budgeted variable selling and administrative expense per unit sold?
2. What is the total budgeted fixed selling and administrative expense per period?
3. What is the budgeted depreciation expense on non-factory assets per period?

Cash budget:
1. What is the budgeted minimum cash balance?
2. What are our estimated expenditures for noncurrent asset purchases and dividends?
3. What is the estimated interest rate on borrowed funds?

budget schedules, keep these two "big picture" insights in mind—that the budget is designed to answer 10 key questions and that it is based on various estimates and assumptions—because they will help you understand *why* and *how* a master budget is created.

Preparing the Master Budget

Tom Wills is the majority stockholder and chief executive officer of Hampton Freeze, Inc., a company he started in 2015. The company makes premium popsicles using only natural ingredients and featuring exotic flavors such as tangy tangerine and minty mango. The company's business is highly seasonal, with most of the sales occurring in spring and summer.

In 2016, the company's second year of operations, a major cash crunch in the first and second quarters almost forced the company into bankruptcy. In spite of this cash crunch, 2016 turned out to be a very successful year in terms of both cash flow and net income. Partly as a result of that harrowing experience, Tom decided toward the end of 2016 to hire a professional financial manager. Tom interviewed several promising candidates for the job and settled on Larry Giano, who had considerable experience in the packaged foods industry. In the job interview, Tom questioned Larry about the steps he would take to prevent a recurrence of the 2016 cash crunch:

Tom: As I mentioned earlier, we are going to end 2016 with a very nice profit. What you may not know is that we had some very big financial problems this year.

Larry: Let me guess. You ran out of cash sometime in the first or second quarter.

Tom: How did you know?

Larry: Most of your sales are in the second and third quarter, right?

Tom: Sure, everyone wants to buy popsicles in the spring and summer, but nobody wants them when the weather turns cold.

Larry: So you don't have many sales in the first quarter?

Tom: Right.

Larry: And in the second quarter, which is the spring, you are producing like crazy to fill orders?

Tom: Sure.

Larry: Do your customers, the grocery stores, pay you the day you make your deliveries?

Tom: Are you kidding? Of course not.

Larry: So in the first quarter, you don't have many sales. In the second quarter, you are producing like crazy, which eats up cash, but you aren't paid by your customers until long after you have paid your employees and suppliers. No wonder you had a cash problem. I see this pattern all the time in food processing because of the seasonality of the business.

Tom: So what can we do about it?

Larry: The first step is to predict the magnitude of the problem before it occurs. If we can predict early in the year what the cash shortfall is going to be, we can go to the bank and arrange for credit before we really need it. Bankers tend to be leery of panicky people who show up begging for emergency loans. They are much more likely to make the loan if you look like you are in control of the situation.

Tom: How can we predict the cash shortfall?

Larry: You can put together a cash budget. In fact, while you're at it, you might as well do a master budget. You'll find it well worth the effort because we can use a master budget to estimate the financial statement implications of numerous "what if" questions. For example, with the click of a mouse we can answer questions such as: What if unit sales are 10% less than our original forecast, what will be the impact on profits? Or, what if we increase our selling price by 15% and unit sales drop by 5%, what will be the impact on profits?

Tom: That sounds great Larry! Not only do we need a cash budget, but I would love to have a master budget that could quickly answer the types of "what if" questions that you just described. As far as I'm concerned, the sooner you get started, the better.

With the full backing of Tom Wills, Larry Giano set out to create a master budget for the company for the year 2017. In his planning for the budgeting process, Larry drew up the following list of documents that would be a part of the master budget:

1. A sales budget, including a schedule of expected cash collections.
2. A production budget (a merchandise purchases budget would be used in a merchandising company).
3. A direct materials budget, including a schedule of expected cash disbursements for purchases of materials.
4. A direct labor budget.
5. A manufacturing overhead budget.
6. An ending finished goods inventory budget.
7. A selling and administrative expense budget.
8. A cash budget.
9. A budgeted income statement.
10. A budgeted balance sheet.

Larry felt it was important to have everyone's cooperation in the budgeting process, so he asked Tom to call a companywide meeting to explain the budgeting process. At the meeting there was initially some grumbling, but Tom was able to convince nearly everyone of the necessity for planning and getting better control over spending. It helped that the cash crisis earlier in the year was still fresh in everyone's minds. As much as some people disliked the idea of budgets, they liked their jobs more.

In the months that followed, Larry worked closely with all of the managers involved in the master budget, gathering data from them and making sure that they understood and fully supported the parts of the master budget that would affect them.

The interdependent documents that Larry Giano prepared for Hampton Freeze are Schedules 1 through 10 of the company's master budget. In this section, we will study these schedules as well as the beginning balance sheet and the budgeting assumptions that Larry included in his master budget to help answer the types of "what if" questions that he discussed with Tom Wills.

The Beginning Balance Sheet

Exhibit 8–3 shows the first tab included in Larry's Microsoft Excel master budget file. It contains Hampton Freeze's beginning balance sheet as of December 31, 2016. Larry included this balance sheet in his master budget file so he could link some of this data to subsequent schedules. For example, as you'll eventually see, he used cell references within Excel to link the beginning accounts receivable balance of $90,000 to the schedule of expected cash collections. He also used cell references to link the beginning cash balance of $42,500 to the cash budget.

The Budgeting Assumptions

Exhibit 8–4 shows the second tab included in Larry's master budget file. It is labeled Budgeting Assumptions and it contains all of Hampton Freeze's answers to the questions summarized in Exhibit 8–2. The data included in Exhibit 8–4 summarize the estimates and assumptions that provide the foundation for Hampton Freeze's entire master budget, so it is important to familiarize yourself with this information now. Beginning with the estimates underlying the sales budget, Exhibit 8–4 shows that Hampton Freeze's budgeted quarterly unit sales are 10,000, 30,000, 40,000, and 20,000 cases. Its budgeted selling price is $20 per case. The company expects to collect 70% of its credit sales in the quarter of sale, and the remaining 30% of credit sales will be collected in the quarter after sale. The company's bad debts are negligible.

Exhibit 8–4 also shows that the production budget is based on the assumption that Hampton Freeze will maintain ending finished goods inventory equal to 20% of the next quarter's unit sales. In terms of the company's only direct material, high fructose sugar, it

EXHIBIT 8–3

Hampton Freeze: The Beginning Balance Sheet

	A	B	C
1	Hampton Freeze, Inc.		
2	Balance Sheet		
3	December 31, 2016		
4			
5	Assets		
6	Current assets:		
7	Cash	$ 42,500	
8	Accounts receivable	90,000	
9	Raw materials inventory (21,000 pounds)	4,200	
10	Finished goods inventory (2,000 cases)	26,000	
11	Total current assets		$ 162,700
12	Plant and equipment:		
13	Land	80,000	
14	Buildings and equipment	700,000	
15	Accumulated depreciation	(292,000)	
16	Plant and equipment, net		488,000
17	Total assets		$ 650,700
18			
19	Liabilities and Stockholders' Equity		
20	Current liabilities:		
21	Accounts payable		$ 25,800
22	Stockholders' equity:		
23	Common stock	$ 175,000	
24	Retained earnings	449,900	
25	Total stockholders' equity		624,900
26	Total liabilities and stockholders' equity		$ 650,700
27			

Beginning Balance Sheet / Budgeting Assump|

budgets 15 pounds of sugar per case of popsicles at a cost of $0.20 per pound.[1] It expects to maintain ending raw materials inventory equal to 10% of the raw materials needed to satisfy the following quarter's production. In addition, the company plans to pay for 50% of its material purchases within the quarter of purchase and the remaining 50% in the following quarter.

Continuing with a summary of Exhibit 8–4, the two key assumptions underlying the direct labor budget are that 0.40 direct labor-hours are required per case of popsicles and the direct labor cost per hour is $15. The manufacturing overhead budget is based on three underlying assumptions—the variable overhead cost per direct labor-hour is $4.00, the total fixed overhead per quarter is $60,600, and the quarterly depreciation on factory assets is $15,000. Exhibit 8–4 also shows that the budgeted variable selling and administrative expense per case of popsicles is $1.80 and the fixed selling and administrative expenses per quarter include advertising ($20,000), executive salaries ($55,000), insurance ($10,000), property tax ($4,000), and depreciation expense ($10,000). The remaining budget assumptions depicted in Exhibit 8–4 pertain to the cash budget. The company expects to maintain a minimum cash balance each quarter of $30,000; it plans to make quarterly equipment purchases of $50,000, $40,000, $20,000, and $20,000;[2] it plans to pay quarterly dividends of $8,000; and it expects to pay simple interest on borrowed money of 3% per quarter.

---

[1] While popsicle manufacturing is likely to involve other raw materials, such as popsicle sticks and packaging materials, for simplicity, we have limited our scope to high fructose sugar.

[2] For simplicity, we assume that depreciation on these newly acquired assets is included in the quarterly depreciation estimates included in the Budgeting Assumptions tab.

EXHIBIT 8–4
Hampton Freeze: Budgeting Assumptions

	A	B	C	D	E	F
1		Hampton Freeze, Inc.				
2		Budgeting Assumptions				
3		For the Year Ended December 31, 2017				
4						
5		*All 4 Quarters*		*Quarter*		
			1	*2*	*3*	*4*
6	*Sales Budget*					
7	Budgeted sales in cases		10,000	30,000	40,000	20,000
8	Selling price per case	$ 20.00				
9	Percentage of sales collected in the quarter of sale	70%				
10	Percentage of sales collected in the quarter after sale	30%				
11						
12	*Production Budget*					
13	Percentage of next quarter's sales in ending finished goods inventory	20%				
14						
15	*Direct Materials Budget*					
16	Pounds of sugar per case	15				
17	Cost per pound of sugar	$ 0.20				
18	Percentage of next quarter's production needs in ending inventory	10%				
19	Percentage of purchases paid in the quarter purchased	50%				
20	Percentage of purchases paid in the quarter after purchase	50%				
21						
22	*Direct Labor Budget*					
23	Direct labor-hours required per case	0.40				
24	Direct labor cost per hour	$ 15.00				
25						
26	*Manufacturing Overhead Budget*					
27	Variable manufacturing overhead per direct labor-hour	$ 4.00				
28	Fixed manufacturing overhead per quarter	$ 60,600				
29	Depreciation per quarter	$ 15,000				
30						
31						
32	*Selling and Administrative Expense Budget*					
33	Variable selling and administrative expense per case	$ 1.80				
34	Fixed selling and administrative expense per quarter:					
35	Advertising	$ 20,000				
36	Executive salaries	$ 55,000				
37	Insurance	$ 10,000				
38	Property tax	$ 4,000				
39	Depreciation	$ 10,000				
40						
41	*Cash Budget*					
42	Minimum cash balance	$ 30,000				
43	Equipment purchases		$ 50,000	$ 40,000	$ 20,000	$ 20,000
44	Dividends	$ 8,000				
45	Simple interest rate per quarter	3%				
46						

Beginning Balance Sheet | **Budgeting Assumptions** | Schedule 1 | Schedule 2 | Sche...

*For simplicity, we assume that all quarterly estimates, except quarterly unit sales and equipment purchases, will be the same for all four quarters.

Before reading further, it is important to understand why Larry created the Budgeting Assumptions tab shown in Exhibit 8–4. He did it because it simplifies the process of using a master budget to answer "what if" questions. For example, assume that Larry wanted to answer the question: What if we increase the selling price per unit by $2 and expect sales to drop by 1,000 units per quarter, what would be the impact on profits? With a properly constructed Budgeting Assumptions tab, Larry would only need to make a few adjustments to the data within this tab and the formulas embedded in each of the budget schedules would automatically update the projected financial results. This is much simpler than attempting to adjust data inputs within each of the master budget schedules.

The Sales Budget

LO8–2

Prepare a sales budget, including a schedule of expected cash collections.

Schedule 1 contains Hampton Freeze's sales budget for 2017. As you study this schedule, keep in mind that all of its numbers are derived from cell references to the Budgeting Assumptions tab and formulas—none of the numbers appearing in the schedule were actually keyed into their respective cells. Furthermore, it bears emphasizing that all remaining schedules in the master budget are prepared in the same fashion—they rely almost exclusively on cell references and formulas.

For the year, Hampton Freeze expects to sell 100,000 cases of popsicles at a price of $20 per case for total budgeted sales of $2,000,000. The budgeted unit sales for each quarter (10,000, 30,000, 40,000, and 20,000) come from cells C7 through F7 in the Budgeting Assumptions tab shown in Exhibit 8–4, and the selling price per case ($20.00) comes from cell B8 in the Budgeting Assumptions tab. Schedule 1 also shows that the company's expected cash collections for 2017 are $1,970,000. The accounts receivable balance of $90,000 that is collected in the first quarter comes from cell B8 of the beginning balance sheet shown in Exhibit 8–3. All other cash collections rely on the estimated cash collection percentages from cells B9 and B10 of the Budgeting Assumptions tab. For example, Schedule 1 shows that the budgeted sales for the first quarter equal $200,000. In the first quarter, Hampton Freeze expects to collect 70% of this amount, or $140,000. In the second quarter, the company expects to collect the remaining 30% of this amount, or $60,000.

SCHEDULE 1

	A	B	C	D	E	F
1			Hampton Freeze, Inc.			
2			Sales Budget			
3			For the Year Ended December 31, 2017			
4						
5				*Quarter*		
6			*1*	*2*	*3*	*4*	*Year*
7	Budgeted unit sales (in cases)		10,000	30,000	40,000	20,000	100,000
8	Selling price per unit		$ 20.00	$ 20.00	$ 20.00	$ 20.00	$ 20.00
9	Total sales		$200,000	$600,000	$800,000	$400,000	$2,000,000
10						
11			70%	30%		
12			Schedule of Expected Cash Collections			
13	Beginning accounts receivable[1]		$ 90,000				$ 90,000
14	First-quarter sales[2]		140,000	$ 60,000			200,000
15	Second-quarter sales[3]			420,000	$180,000		600,000
16	Third-quarter sales[4]				560,000	$240,000	800,000
17	Fourth-quarter sales[5]		-	-	-	280,000	280,000
18	Total cash collections[6]		$230,000	$480,000	$740,000	$520,000	$1,970,000

◄ ◄ ► ►| / Budgeting Assumptions / **Schedule 1** / Schedule 2 / Schedule 3 / Sc ◄ | ►

[1]Cash collections from last year's fourth-quarter sales. See the beginning balance sheet in Exhibit 8–3.
[2]$200,000 × 70%; $200,000 × 30%.
[3]$600,000 × 70%; $600,000 × 30%.
[4]$800,000 × 70%; $800,000 × 30%.
[5]$400,000 × 70%.
[6]Uncollected fourth-quarter sales ($120,000) appear as accounts receivable on the company's end-of-year budgeted balance sheet (see Schedule 10).

BUDGETING FOR SALES RETURNS

In addition to preparing sales budgets, companies need to budget for the expense of managing sales returns. Optoro, a logistics provider, estimates that companies process $60 billion in customer returns during the holiday season. The U.S. Postal Service and United Parcel Service transport 3.2 million and 4 million returns, respectively, in the two weeks after Christmas. Best Buy estimates that returns, damaged goods, and replaced merchandise cost the company $400 million per year, or 10% of its revenue.

When it comes to internet commerce, 82% of shoppers say they are more likely to complete online purchases if the company offers free returns via pre-paid shipping labels or free in-store returns. For some high-end apparel retailers, the return rate for online purchases can reach 50% of the transactions processed.

Source: Laura Stevens, "For Retailers, It's Many Unhappy Returns," *The Wall Street Journal,* December 27–28, 2014, p. B3.

The Production Budget

The production budget is prepared after the sales budget. The **production budget** lists the number of units that must be produced to satisfy sales needs and to provide for the desired ending finished goods inventory. Production needs can be determined as follows:

Budgeted unit sales	XXX
Add desired units of ending finished goods inventory	XXX
Total needs	XXX
Less units of beginning finished goods inventory	XXX
Required production in units	XXX

Note the production requirements are influenced by the desired level of the ending finished goods inventory. Inventories should be carefully planned. Excessive inventories tie up funds and create storage problems. Insufficient inventories can lead to lost sales or last-minute, high-cost production efforts.

Schedule 2 contains the production budget for Hampton Freeze. The budgeted sales data come from cells B7 through E7 of the sales budget. The desired ending finished goods inventory for the first quarter of 6,000 cases is computed by multiplying budgeted sales from the second quarter (30,000 cases) by the desired ending finished goods inventory percentage (20%) shown in cell B13 of the Budgeting Assumptions tab. The total needs for the first quarter (16,000 cases) are determined by adding together the budgeted sales of 10,000 cases for the quarter and the desired ending inventory of 6,000 cases. As discussed above, the ending inventory is intended to provide some cushion in the event that problems develop in production, or sales increase unexpectedly. Because the company already has 2,000 cases in beginning finished goods inventory (as shown in the beginning balance sheet in Exhibit 8–3), only 14,000 cases need to be produced in the first quarter.

Pay particular attention to the Year column to the right of the production budget in Schedule 2. In some cases (e.g., budgeted unit sales and required production in units), the amount listed for the year is the sum of the quarterly amounts for the item. In other cases, (e.g., desired units of ending finished goods inventory and units of beginning finished goods inventory), the amount listed for the year is not simply the sum of the quarterly amounts. From the standpoint of the entire year, the ending finished goods inventory, which Larry Giano assumed to be 3,000 units, is the same as the ending finished goods inventory for the fourth quarter—it is *not* the sum of the ending finished goods inventories for all four quarters. Similarly, from the standpoint of the entire year, the beginning finished goods inventory (2,000 units) is the same as the beginning finished goods inventory for the first quarter—it is *not* the sum of the beginning finished goods inventories for all four quarters. It is important to pay attention to such distinctions in all schedules that follow.

SCHEDULE 2

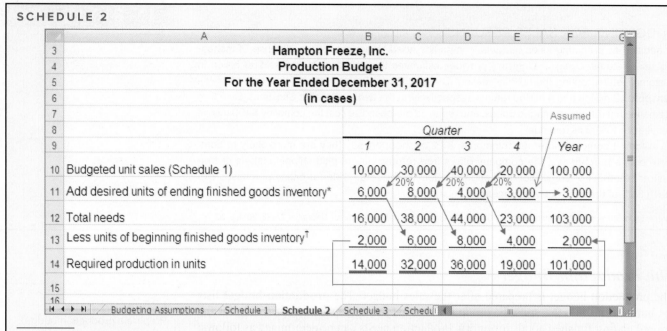

	A	B	C	D	E	F	G
3	Hampton Freeze, Inc.						
4	Production Budget						
5	For the Year Ended December 31, 2017						
6	(in cases)						
7						Assumed	
8			Quarter				
9		1	2	3	4	Year	
10	Budgeted unit sales (Schedule 1)	10,000	30,000	40,000	20,000	100,000	
11	Add desired units of ending finished goods inventory*	6,000	8,000	4,000	3,000	3,000	
12	Total needs	16,000	38,000	44,000	23,000	103,000	
13	Less units of beginning finished goods inventory†	2,000	6,000	8,000	4,000	2,000	
14	Required production in units	14,000	32,000	36,000	19,000	101,000	
15							
16							

20%   20%   20%

Budgeting Assumptions   Schedule 1   **Schedule 2**   Schedule 3   Schedu

*Twenty percent of next quarter's sales. For example, the second-quarter sales are 30,000 cases. Therefore, the desired ending inventory of finished goods for the first quarter would be 20% × 30,000 cases = 6,000 cases.
†The beginning inventory in each quarter is the same as the prior quarter's ending inventory.

Inventory Purchases—Merchandising Company

Hampton Freeze prepares a production budget because it is a *manufacturing* company. If it were a *merchandising* company, instead it would prepare a **merchandise purchases budget** showing the amount of goods to be purchased from suppliers during the period.

The format of the merchandise purchases budget is shown below:

Budgeted cost of goods sold	XXX
Add desired ending merchandise inventory	XXX
Total needs.	XXX
Less beginning merchandise inventory.	XXX
Required purchases	XXX

A merchandising company would prepare a merchandise purchases budget, such as the one above, for each item carried in stock. The merchandise purchases budget can be expressed in dollars (using the headings shown above) or in units. The top line of a merchandise purchases budget based on units would say Budgeted unit sales instead of Budgeted cost of goods sold.

A merchandise purchases budget is usually accompanied by a schedule of expected cash disbursements for merchandise purchases. The format of this schedule mirrors the approach used for the schedule of expected cash disbursements for purchases of materials that is illustrated at the bottom of Schedule 3.

LO8–4
Prepare a direct materials budget, including a schedule of expected cash disbursements for purchases of materials.

The Direct Materials Budget

A *direct materials budget* is prepared after the production requirements have been computed. The **direct materials budget** details the raw materials that must be purchased to fulfill the production budget and to provide for adequate inventories. The required purchases of raw materials are computed as follows:

Required production in units of finished goods	XXX
Units of raw materials needed per unit of finished goods	XXX
Units of raw materials needed to meet production	XXX
Add desired units of ending raw materials inventory	XXX
Total units of raw materials needed	XXX
Less units of beginning raw materials inventory	XXX
Units of raw materials to be purchased	XXX
Unit cost of raw materials	XXX
Cost of raw materials to be purchased	XXX

Schedule 3 contains the direct materials budget for Hampton Freeze. The first line of this budget contains the required production for each quarter, which is taken directly from cells B14 through E14 of the production budget (Schedule 2). The second line of the direct materials budget recognizes that 15 pounds of sugar (see cell B16 from the Budgeting Assumptions tab) are required to make one case of popsicles. The third line

SCHEDULE 3

Hampton Freeze, Inc.
Direct Materials Budget
For the Year Ended December 31, 2017

	Quarter 1	2	3	4	Year
Required production in cases (Schedule 2)	14,000	32,000	36,000	19,000	101,000
Units of raw materials needed per case	15	15	15	15	15
Units of raw materials needed to meet production	210,000	480,000	540,000	285,000	1,515,000
Add desired units of ending raw materials inventory¹	48,000	54,000	28,500	22,500	22,500
Total units of raw materials needed	258,000	534,000	568,500	307,500	1,537,500
Less units of beginning raw materials inventory	21,000	48,000	54,000	28,500	21,000
Units of raw materials to be purchased	237,000	486,000	514,500	279,000	1,516,500
Cost of raw materials per pound	$ 0.20	$ 0.20	$ 0.20	$ 0.20	$ 0.20
Cost of raw materials to be purchased	$47,400	$97,200	$102,900	$55,800	$ 303,300

Schedule of Expected Cash Disbursements for Purchases of Materials

	1	2	3	4	Year
Beginning accounts payable²	$25,800				$ 25,800
First-quarter purchases³	23,700	$23,700			47,400
Second-quarter purchases⁴		48,600	$ 48,600		97,200
Third-quarter purchases⁵			51,450	$51,450	102,900
Fourth-quarter purchases⁶	-	-	-	27,900	27,900
Total cash disbursements for materials	$49,500	$72,300	$100,050	$79,350	$ 301,200

Schedule 3 / Schedule 4 / Schedule 5 / Schedule 6 / Schedule 7

¹Ten percent of the next quarter's production needs. For example, the second-quarter production needs are 480,000 pounds. Therefore, the desired ending inventory for the first quarter would be 10% × 480,000 pounds = 48,000 pounds. The desired ending inventory for quarter 4 (22,500 pounds) assumes the first quarter production needs in 2018 are 225,000 pounds (= 225,000 pounds × 10% = 22,500 pounds).
²Cash payments for last year's fourth-quarter purchases. See the beginning-of-year balance sheet in Exhibit 8–3.
³$47,400 × 50%; $47,400 × 50%.
⁴$97,200 × 50%; $97,200 × 50%.
⁵$102,900 × 50%; $102,900 × 50%.
⁶$55,800 × 50%. Unpaid fourth-quarter purchases ($27,900) appear as accounts payable on the company's end-of-year budgeted balance sheet (see Schedule 10).

of the budget presents the raw materials needed to meet production. For example, in the first quarter, the required production of 14,000 cases is multiplied by 15 pounds to equal 210,000 pounds of sugar needed to meet production. The fourth line shows the desired units of ending raw materials inventory. For the first quarter this amount is computed by multiplying the raw materials needed to meet production in the second quarter of 480,000 pounds by the desired ending inventory percentage of 10% as shown in cell B18 of the Budgeting Assumptions tab. The desired units of ending raw materials inventory of 48,000 pounds is added to 210,000 pounds to provide the total units of raw materials needed of 258,000 pounds. However, because the company already has 21,000 pounds of sugar in beginning inventory (as shown in cell A9 in the beginning balance sheet in Exhibit 8–3), only 237,000 pounds of sugar need to be purchased in the first quarter. Because the budgeted cost of raw materials per pound is $0.20 (see cell B17 from the Budgeting Assumptions tab), the cost of raw material to be purchased in the first quarter is $47,400. For the entire year, the company plans to purchase $303,300 of raw materials.

Schedule 3 also shows that the company's expected cash disbursements for material purchases for 2017 are $301,200. The accounts payable balance of $25,800 that is paid in the first quarter comes from cell C21 of the beginning balance sheet shown in Exhibit 8–3. All other cash disbursement computations rely on the estimated cash payment percentages (both of which are 50%) from cells B19 and B20 of the Budgeting Assumptions tab. For example, Schedule 3 shows that the budgeted raw material purchases for the first quarter equal $47,400. In the first quarter, Hampton Freeze expects to pay 50% of this amount, or $23,700. In the second quarter, the company expects to pay the remaining 50% of this amount, or $23,700.

The Direct Labor Budget

LO8–5

Prepare a direct labor budget.

The **direct labor budget** shows the direct labor-hours required to satisfy the production budget. By knowing in advance how much labor time will be needed throughout the budget year, the company can develop plans to adjust the labor force as the situation requires. Companies that neglect the budgeting process run the risk of facing labor shortages or having to hire and lay off workers at awkward times. Erratic labor policies lead to insecurity, low morale, and inefficiency.

The direct labor budget for Hampton Freeze is shown in Schedule 4. The first line in the direct labor budget consists of the required production for each quarter, which is taken directly from cells B14 through E14 of the production budget (Schedule 2). The direct labor requirement for each quarter is computed by multiplying the number of units to be produced in each quarter by the 0.40 direct labor-hours required to make one unit (see cell B23 from the Budgeting Assumptions tab). For example, 14,000 cases are to be produced in the first quarter and each case requires 0.40 direct labor-hours, so a total of 5,600 direct labor-hours (14,000 cases × 0.40 direct labor-hours per case) will be required in the first quarter. The direct labor requirements are then translated into budgeted direct labor costs, which we

SCHEDULE 4

	A	B	C	D	E	F	G
1		Hampton Freeze, Inc.					
2		Direct Labor Budget					
3		For the Year Ended December 31, 2017					
4							
5				Quarter			
6		1	2	3	4	Year	
7	Required production in cases (Schedule 2)	14,000	32,000	36,000	19,000	101,000	
8	Direct labor-hours per case	0.40	0.40	0.40	0.40	0.40	
9	Total direct labor-hours needed	5,600	12,800	14,400	7,600	40,400	
10	Direct labor cost per hour	$ 15.00	$ 15.00	$ 15.00	$ 15.00	$ 15.00	
11	Total direct labor cost	$ 84,000	$ 192,000	$ 216,000	$ 114,000	$ 606,000	
12							

Schedule 1 / Schedule 2 / Schedule 3 / **Schedule 4** / Schedule 5 / Schedule

*This schedule assumes that the direct labor workforce will be fully adjusted to the total direct labor-hours needed each quarter.

will assume are paid in the quarter incurred. How this is done will depend on the company's labor policy. In Schedule 4, Hampton Freeze has assumed that the direct labor force will be adjusted as the work requirements change from quarter to quarter. In that case, the direct labor cost is computed by simply multiplying the direct labor-hour requirements by the direct labor rate of $15 per hour (see cell B24 from the Budgeting Assumptions tab). For example, the direct labor cost in the first quarter is $84,000 (5,600 direct labor-hours × $15 per direct labor-hour).

However, many companies have employment policies or contracts that prevent them from laying off and rehiring workers as needed. Suppose, for example, that Hampton Freeze has 25 workers who are classified as direct labor, but each of them is guaranteed at least 480 hours of pay each quarter at a rate of $15 per hour. In that case, the minimum direct labor cost for a quarter would be computed as follows:

25 workers × 480 hours per worker × $15 per hour = $180,000

Note that in this case the direct costs shown in the first and fourth quarters of Schedule 4 would have to be increased to $180,000.

The Manufacturing Overhead Budget

The **manufacturing overhead budget** lists all costs of production other than direct materials and direct labor. Schedule 5 shows the manufacturing overhead budget for Hampton Freeze. At Hampton Freeze, manufacturing overhead is separated into variable and fixed components. As shown in the Budgeting Assumptions tab (Exhibit 8–4), the variable component is $4 per direct labor-hour and the fixed component is $60,600 per quarter. Because the variable component of manufacturing overhead depends on direct labor, the first line in the manufacturing overhead budget consists of the budgeted direct labor-hours from cells B9 through E9 of the direct labor budget (Schedule 4). The budgeted direct labor-hours in each quarter are multiplied by the variable overhead rate to determine the variable component of manufacturing overhead. For example, the variable manufacturing overhead for the first quarter is $22,400 (5,600 direct labor-hours × $4.00 per direct labor-hour). This is added to the fixed manufacturing overhead for the quarter to determine the total manufacturing overhead for the quarter of $83,000 ($22,400 + $60,600).

The last line of Schedule 5 for Hampton Freeze shows the budgeted cash disbursements for manufacturing overhead. Because some of the overhead costs are not cash outflows, the total budgeted manufacturing overhead costs must be adjusted to determine the

LO8–6
Prepare a manufacturing overhead budget.

SCHEDULE 5

	A	B	C	D	E	F
1		Hampton Freeze, Inc.				
2		Manufacturing Overhead Budget				
3		For the Year Ended December 31, 2017				
4						
5				Quarter		
6		1	2	3	4	Year
7	Budgeted direct labor-hours (Schedule 4)	5,600	12,800	14,400	7,600	40,400
8	Variable manufacturing overhead rate	$ 4.00	$ 4.00	$ 4.00	$ 4.00	$ 4.00
9	Variable manufacturing overhead	$ 22,400	$ 51,200	$ 57,600	$ 30,400	$ 161,600
10	Fixed manufacturing overhead	60,600	60,600	60,600	60,600	242,400
11	Total manufacturing overhead	83,000	111,800	118,200	91,000	404,000
12	Less depreciation	15,000	15,000	15,000	15,000	60,000
13	Cash disbursements for manufacturing overhead	$ 68,000	$ 96,800	$ 103,200	$ 76,000	$ 344,000
14						
15	Total manufacturing overhead (a)					$ 404,000
16	Budgeted direct labor-hours (b)					40,400
17	Predetermined overhead rate for the year (a)÷(b)					$10.00
18						
19						

Schedule 3 / Schedule 4 / **Schedule 5** / Schedule 6 / Schedule 7 / Schedule 8

cash disbursements for manufacturing overhead. At Hampton Freeze, the only significant noncash manufacturing overhead cost is depreciation, which is $15,000 per quarter (see cell B29 in the Budgeting Assumptions tab). These noncash depreciation charges are deducted from the total budgeted manufacturing overhead to determine each quarter's expected cash disbursements. Hampton Freeze pays all overhead costs involving cash disbursements in the quarter incurred. Note that the company's predetermined overhead rate for the year is $10 per direct labor-hour, which is determined by dividing the total budgeted manufacturing overhead for the year ($404,000) by the total budgeted direct labor-hours for the year (40,400).

The Ending Finished Goods Inventory Budget

After completing Schedules 1–5, Larry Giano had all of the data he needed to compute the absorption unit product cost for the units produced during the budget year. This computation was needed for two reasons: first, to help determine cost of goods sold on the budgeted income statement; and second, to value ending inventories on the budgeted balance sheet. The cost of unsold units is computed on the **ending finished goods inventory budget**.[3]

Schedule 6 shows that Hampton Freeze's absorption unit product cost is $13 per case of popsicles—consisting of $3 of direct materials, $6 of direct labor, and $4 of manufacturing overhead. Notice that manufacturing overhead has been applied to units of product using the rate of $10 per direct labor-hour from cell F17 of the Manufacturing Overhead budget. The budgeted carrying cost of the ending inventory is $39,000.

---

[3] For simplicity, the beginning balance sheet and the ending finished goods inventory budget both report a unit product cost of $13. For purposes of answering "what-if" questions, this schedule would assume a FIFO inventory flow. In other words, the ending inventory would consist solely of units that are produced during the budget year.

SCHEDULE 6

	A	B	C	D	E	F	G	H	I
1				Hampton Freeze, Inc.					
2				Ending Finished Goods Inventory Budget					
3				(absorption costing basis)					
4				For the Year Ended December 31, 2017					
5									
6	*Item*	*Quantity*			*Cost*			*Total*	
7	Production cost per case:								
8	Direct materials	15.00	pounds		$ 0.20	per pound		$ 3.00	
9	Direct labor	0.40	hours		$15.00	per hour		6.00	
10	Manufacturing overhead	0.40	hours		$10.00	per hour		4.00	
11	Unit product cost							$ 13.00	
12									
13	Budgeted finished goods inventory:								
14	Ending finished goods inventory in cases (Schedule 2)							3,000	
15	Unit product cost (see above)							$ 13.00	
16	Ending finished goods inventory in dollars							$ 39,000	
17									

Schedule 3   Schedule 4   Schedule 5   **Schedule 6**   Sch

The Selling and Administrative Expense Budget

The **selling and administrative expense budget** lists the budgeted expenses for areas other than manufacturing. In large organizations, this budget would be a compilation of many smaller, individual budgets submitted by department heads and other persons responsible for selling and administrative expenses. For example, the marketing manager would submit a budget detailing the advertising expenses for each budget period.

LO8–7
Prepare a selling and administrative expense budget.

Schedule 7 contains the selling and administrative expense budget for Hampton Freeze. Like the manufacturing overhead budget, the selling and administrative expense budget is divided into variable and fixed cost components. Consequently, budgeted sales in cases for each quarter are entered at the top of the schedule. These data are taken from cells B7 through E7 of the sales budget (Schedule 1). The budgeted variable selling and administrative expenses are determined by multiplying the budgeted cases sold by the variable selling and administrative expense of $1.80 per case (see cell B33 from the Budgeting Assumptions tab). For example, the budgeted variable selling and administrative expense for the first quarter is $18,000 (10,000 cases × $1.80 per case). The fixed selling and administrative expenses of $99,000 per quarter (see cells B35 through B39 from the Budgeting Assumptions tab) are then added to the variable selling and administrative expenses to arrive at the total budgeted selling and administrative expenses. Finally, to determine the cash disbursements for selling and administrative items, the total budgeted selling and administrative expense is adjusted by subtracting any noncash selling and administrative expenses (in this case, just depreciation).[4]

---

[4] Other adjustments might need to be made for differences between cash flows on the one hand and revenues and expenses on the other hand. For example, if property taxes are paid twice a year in installments of $8,000 each, the expense for property tax would have to be "backed out" of the total budgeted selling and administrative expenses and the cash installment payments added to the appropriate quarters to determine the cash disbursements. Similar adjustments might also need to be made in the manufacturing overhead budget. We generally ignore these complications in this chapter.

SCHEDULE 7

	A	B	C	D	E	F
				Hampton Freeze, Inc.		
1				Hampton Freeze, Inc.		
2			Selling and Administrative Expense Budget			
3			For the Year Ended December 31, 2017			
4						
5				Quarter		
6		1	2	3	4	Year
7	Budgeted units sales (Schedule 1)	10,000	30,000	40,000	20,000	100,000
8	Variable selling and administrative expense per case	$ 1.80	$ 1.80	$ 1.80	$ 1.80	$ 1.80
9	Variable selling and administrative expense	$ 18,000	$ 54,000	$ 72,000	$ 36,000	$180,000
10	Fixed selling and administrative expenses:					
11	Advertising	20,000	20,000	20,000	20,000	80,000
12	Executive salaries	55,000	55,000	55,000	55,000	220,000
13	Insurance	10,000	10,000	10,000	10,000	40,000
14	Property taxes	4,000	4,000	4,000	4,000	16,000
15	Depreciation	10,000	10,000	10,000	10,000	40,000
16	Total fixed selling and administrative expenses	99,000	99,000	99,000	99,000	396,000
17	Total selling and administrative expenses	117,000	153,000	171,000	135,000	576,000
18	Less depreciation	10,000	10,000	10,000	10,000	40,000
19	Cash disbursements for selling and administrative expenses	$107,000	$143,000	$161,000	$125,000	$536,000
20						

Schedule 5   Schedule 6   **Schedule 7**   Schedule 8   Schedule 9   Schedule 10

The Cash Budget

LO8–8
Prepare a cash budget.

The cash budget is composed of four main sections:

1. The cash receipts section.
2. The cash disbursements section.
3. The cash excess or deficiency section.
4. The financing section.

The receipts section lists all of the cash inflows, except from financing, expected during the budget period. Generally, the major source of receipts is from sales. The disbursements section summarizes all cash payments that are planned for the budget period. These payments include raw materials purchases, direct labor payments, manufacturing overhead costs, and so on, as contained in their respective budgets. In addition, other cash disbursements such as equipment purchases and dividends are listed.

The cash excess or deficiency section is computed as follows:

Beginning cash balance....................................	XXX
Add cash receipts..	XXX
Total cash available.....................................	XXX
Less cash disbursements..................................	XXX
Excess (deficiency) of cash available over disbursements....	XXX

If a cash deficiency exists during any budget period or if there is a cash excess during any budget period that is less than the minimum required cash balance, the company will need to borrow money. Conversely, if there is a cash excess during any budget period that is greater than the minimum required cash balance, the company can invest the excess funds or repay principal and interest to lenders.

MISMATCHED CASH FLOWS—CLIMBING THE HILLS AND VALLEYS

The **Washington Trails Association (WTA)** is a private, nonprofit organization primarily concerned with protecting and maintaining hiking trails in the state of Washington. Some 2,000 WTA volunteer workers donate more than 80,000 hours per year maintaining trails in rugged landscapes on federal, state, and private lands. The organization is supported by membership dues, voluntary contributions, grants, and some contract work for government.

The organization's income and expenses are erratic—although somewhat predictable—over the course of the year as shown in the following chart. Expenses tend to be highest in the spring and summer when most of the trail maintenance work is done. However, income spikes in December well after the expenses have been incurred. With cash outflows running ahead of cash inflows for much of the year, it is very important for the WTA to carefully plan its cash budget and to maintain adequate cash reserves to be able to pay its bills.

© Eric Noreen

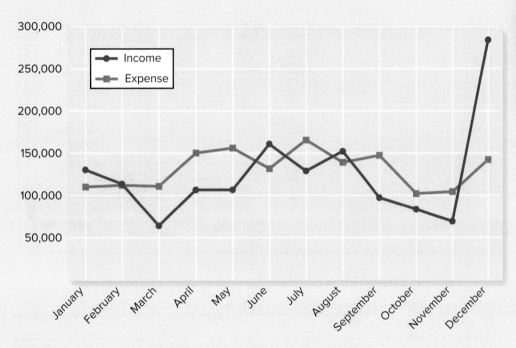

Note: Total income and total expense are approximately equal over the course of the year.

Sources: Conversation with Elizabeth Lunney, President of the Washington Trails Association; WTA documents; and the WTA website www.wta.org.

The financing section of the cash budget details the borrowings and principal and interest repayments projected to take place during the budget period. *In this chapter unless explicitly stated otherwise, we'll always assume that all borrowings take place on the first day of the borrowing period and all repayments take place on the last day of the final period included in the cash budget.* To calculate borrowings and interest payments, you'll need to pay attention to the company's desired minimum cash balance and to the terms of the company's loan agreement with the bank. For example, Hampton Freeze's desired minimum cash balance is $30,000 (see cell B42 in the Budgeting Assumptions tab). Furthermore, *we are going to assume that Hampton Freeze's loan agreement stipulates that it must borrow money in increments of $10,000* and that it must pay simple interest of 3% per quarter (as shown in cell B45 in Exhibit 8–4).[5]

The cash balances at both the beginning and end of the year may be adequate even though a serious cash deficit occurs at some point during the year. Consequently, the cash budget should be broken down into time periods that are short enough to capture major

---

[5] We use simple interest rather than compound interest throughout the chapter for simplicity.

SCHEDULE 8

	A	B	C	D	E	F	G
1		Hampton Freeze, Inc.					
2		Cash Budget					
3		For the Year Ended December 31, 2017					
4							
5					Quarter		
6		Schedule	1	2	3	4	Year
7	Beginning cash balance		$ 42,500	$ 36,000	$ 33,900	$ 165,650	$ 42,500
8	Add cash receipts:						
9	Collections from customers	1	230,000	480,000	740,000	520,000	1,970,000
10	Total cash available		272,500	516,000	773,900	685,650	2,012,500
11	Less cash disbursements:						
12	Direct materials	3	49,500	72,300	100,050	79,350	301,200
13	Direct labor	4	84,000	192,000	216,000	114,000	606,000
14	Manufacturing overhead	5	68,000	96,800	103,200	76,000	344,000
15	Selling and administrative	7	107,000	143,000	161,000	125,000	536,000
16	Equipment purchases		50,000	40,000	20,000	20,000	130,000
17	Dividends		8,000	8,000	8,000	8,000	32,000
18	Total cash disbursements		366,500	552,100	608,250	422,350	1,949,200
19	Excess (deficiency) of cash available over disbursements		(94,000)	(36,100)	165,650	263,300	63,300
20	Financing:						
21	Borrowings (at the beginnings of quarters)		130,000	70,000	-	-	200,000
22	Repayments (at end of the year)		-	-	-	(200,000)	(200,000)
23	Interest		-	-	-	(21,900)	(21,900)
24	Total financing		130,000	70,000	-	(221,900)	(21,900)
25	Ending cash balance		$ 36,000	$ 33,900	$ 165,650	$ 41,400	$ 41,400
26							
27							

Schedule 5 / Schedule 6 / Schedule 7 / **Schedule 8** / Schedule 9 / Schedule 10

fluctuations in cash balances. While a monthly cash budget is most common, some organizations budget cash on a weekly or even daily basis. At Hampton Freeze, Larry Giano has prepared a quarterly cash budget that can be further refined as necessary. This budget appears in Schedule 8.[6]

The beginning cash balance in the first quarter of $42,500 agrees with cell B7 of the beginning balance sheet in Exhibit 8–3. Each quarter's collections from customers come from cells B18 through E18 of the schedule of expected cash collections in Schedule 1. Each quarter's beginning cash balance plus the collections from customers equals the total cash available. For example, in the first quarter, the beginning cash balance of $42,500 plus the collections from customers of $230,000 equals the total cash available of $272,500.

The disbursements section of the cash budget includes six types of cash disbursements. Each quarter's cash disbursements for direct materials come from cells B27 through E27 of the schedule of expected cash disbursements for materials (see Schedule 3). The quarterly cash payments for direct labor were calculated in cells B11 through E11 of the direct labor budget (see Schedule 4), whereas the quarterly cash payments related to manufacturing overhead were calculated in cells B13 through E13 of the manufacturing overhead budget (see Schedule 5). The quarterly cash payments for selling and administrative expenses come from cells B19 through E19 of the selling and administrative expense budget (see Schedule 7). So putting it all together, in the first quarter, the cash disbursements for direct materials ($49,500), direct labor ($84,000), manufacturing overhead ($68,000), selling and administrative expenses ($107,000), equipment purchases ($50,000), and the dividend ($8,000) (see cells C43 and B44 in Exhibit 8–4) equals the total cash disbursements of $366,500.

---

[6] The format for the statement of cash flows, which is discussed in a later chapter, may also be used for the cash budget.

Each quarter's total cash available minus its total disbursements equals the excess (deficiency) of cash available over disbursements. For example, in the first quarter the total cash available of $272,500 minus the total disbursements of $366,500 results in a cash deficiency of $94,000. The excess or deficiency of cash directly influences whether Hampton Freeze will need to borrow money as shown in the Financing section of the cash budget.

The first row in the financing section of the cash budget relates to projected borrowings. In any period where a company's excess of cash available over disbursements is greater than its desired minimum cash balance, the company will not need to borrow money during that period. In the case of Hampton Freeze, the company wants to maintain a minimum cash balance of $30,000; therefore, it will not need to borrow money in any quarter where its excess of cash available over disbursements is greater than $30,000. However, in the first quarter of 2017 Hampton Freeze estimates that it will have a cash deficiency of $94,000; consequently, the company's minimum required borrowings at the beginning of the first quarter would be computed as follows:

Required Borrowings at the Beginning of the First Quarter:	
Desired ending cash balance	$ 30,000
Plus deficiency of cash available over disbursements	94,000
Minimum required borrowings	$124,000

Recall that the bank requires that loans be made in increments of $10,000. Because Hampton Freeze needs to borrow at least $124,000, it will have to borrow $130,000.

In the second quarter of 2017 Hampton Freeze estimates that it will have another cash deficiency of $36,100; therefore, the company's minimum required borrowings at the beginning of the second quarter would be computed as follows:

Required Borrowings at the Beginning of the Second Quarter:	
Desired ending cash balance	$30,000
Plus deficiency of cash available over disbursements	36,100
Minimum required borrowings	$66,100

Again, recall that the bank requires loans be made in increments of $10,000. Because Hampton Freeze needs to borrow at least $66,100 at the beginning of the second quarter, the company will have to borrow $70,000 from the bank.

In the third and fourth quarters, Hampton Freeze has an excess of cash available over disbursements that is greater than $30,000, so it will not need to borrow money in these two quarters. Notice that in the third quarter Hampton Freeze has excess cash of $165,650, yet the cash budget does not include any principal or interest repayments during this quarter. This occurs because, unless stated otherwise, we always assume that the company will, as far as it is able, repay the loan plus accumulated interest on the *last day of the final period* included in the cash budget. Because Hampton Freeze has excess cash of $263,300 in the fourth quarter, on the last day of the fourth quarter, it would be able to repay the $200,000 that it borrowed from the lender plus $21,900 of interest computed as follows:

Interest on the $130,000 borrowed at the beginning of the first quarter:	
$130,000 × 0.03 per quarter × 4 quarters*	$15,600
Interest on the $70,000 borrowed at the beginning of the second quarter:	
$70,000 × 0.03 per quarter × 3 quarters*	6,300
Total interest accrued to the end of the fourth quarter	$21,900

*Simple, rather than compounded, interest is assumed for simplicity

The ending cash balance for each period is computed by taking the excess (deficiency) of cash available over disbursements plus the total financing. For example, in the first quarter, Hampton Freeze's cash deficiency of $(94,000) plus its total financing of $130,000 equals its ending cash balance of $36,000. The ending cash balance for each quarter then becomes the beginning cash balance for the next quarter. Also notice that the amounts under the Year column in the cash budget are not always the sum of the amounts for the four quarters. In particular, the beginning cash balance for the year is the same as the beginning cash balance for the first quarter and the ending cash balance for the year is the same as the ending cash balance for the fourth quarter.

IN BUSINESS

© GDA/AP Images

CINNABON MANAGES SEASONAL DEMAND

Cinnabon Inc. has over 1,000 franchise locations worldwide including one of its most recent new store openings in Tripoli, Libya. The company's annual sales exceed $900 million with 60% of those revenues being earned in November and December. Seasonal demand impacts a variety of supporting schedules within a company's master budget. For example, materials and labor budgets are likely to differ in months with slack versus peak sales. In Cinnabon's case, the cash budget will show a spike in cash receipts during the last two months of the year with more modest cash inflows throughout the remainder of the year.

Source: Leslie Kwoh, "Cinnabon Finds Sweet Success in Russia, Mideast," *The Wall Street Journal*, December 26, 2012, p. B5.

The Budgeted Income Statement

LO8–9

Prepare a budgeted income statement.

Schedule 9 contains the budgeted income statement for Hampton Freeze. All of the sales and expenses shown on the budgeted income statement come from the data in the beginning balance sheet and the data developed in Schedules 1–8. The sales of $2,000,000 come from cell F9 of the sales budget (Schedule 1). Given that the unit product cost of the year's beginning inventory and the year's production both equal $13 per unit, the cost of goods sold of $1,300,000 can be computed by multiplying 100,000 units sold (see cell F7 from Schedule 1) by the unit product cost of $13 per unit (see cell H11 in Schedule 6).[7] The selling and administrative expenses of $576,000 come from cell F17 of the selling and administrative expenses budget (Schedule 7). Finally, the interest expense of $21,900 comes from cell G23 of the cash budget (Schedule 8).

The budgeted income statement is one of the key schedules in the budget process. It shows the company's planned profit and serves as a benchmark against which subsequent company performance can be measured. Because Larry Giano created a Budgeting Assumptions tab in his Excel file (see Exhibit 8–4) and linked all of his budget schedules together using properly constructed Excel formulas, he can make changes to his underlying budgeting assumptions and instantly see the impact of the change on all of the schedules and on net income. For example, if Larry wanted to estimate the profit impact if fourth quarter sales are 18,000 cases instead of 20,000 cases, he would simply change the 20,000 cases shown in cell F7 of his Budgeting Assumptions worksheet to 18,000 cases. The revised net income of $87,045 would instantly appear in cell C12 of the budgeted income statement.

---

[7] Cost of goods sold can also be computed using equations introduced in earlier chapters. Manufacturing companies can use the equation: Cost of goods sold = Beginning finished goods inventory + Cost of goods manufactured − Ending finished goods inventory. Merchandising companies can use the equation: Cost of goods sold = Beginning merchandise inventory + Purchases − Ending merchandise inventory.

	A	B	C
1	Hampton Freeze, Inc.		
2	Budgeted Income Statement		
3	For the Year Ended December 31, 2017		
4			
5		*Schedules*	
6	Sales	1	$ 2,000,000
7	Cost of goods sold	1, 6	1,300,000
8	Gross margin		700,000
9	Selling and administrative expenses	7	576,000
10	Net operating Income		124,000
11	Interest expense	8	21,900
12	Net Income		$ 102,100
13			

Schedule 7   Schedule 8   **Schedule 9**   S

The Budgeted Balance Sheet

The budgeted balance sheet is developed using data from the balance sheet from the beginning of the budget period (see Exhibit 8–3) and data contained in the various schedules. Hampton Freeze's budgeted balance sheet accompanied by explanations of how the numbers were derived is presented in Schedule 10.

After completing the master budget, Larry Giano took the documents to Tom Wills, chief executive officer of Hampton Freeze, for his review.

LO8–10
Prepare a budgeted balance sheet.

MANAGERIAL
ACCOUNTING IN ACTION
THE WRAP-UP

Larry: Here's the budget. Overall, the income is excellent, and the net cash flow for the entire year is positive.

Tom: Yes, but I see on this cash budget that we have the same problem with negative cash flows in the first and second quarters that we had last year.

Larry: That's true. I don't see any way around that problem. However, there is no doubt in my mind that if you take this budget to the bank today, they'll approve an open line of credit that will allow you to borrow enough money to make it through the first two quarters without any problem.

Tom: Are you sure? They didn't seem very happy to see me last year when I came in for an emergency loan.

Larry: Did you repay the loan on time?

Tom: Sure.

Larry: I don't see any problem. You won't be asking for an emergency loan this time. The bank will have plenty of warning. And with this budget, you have a solid plan that shows when and how you are going to pay off the loan. Trust me, they'll go for it. Also, keep in mind that the master budget contains all the embedded formulas you'll need to answer the types of "what if" questions that we discussed earlier. If you want to calculate the financial impact of changing any of your master budget's underlying estimates or assumptions, you can do it with the click of a mouse!

Tom: This sounds fabulous Larry. Thanks for all of your work on this project.

SCHEDULE 10

	A	B	C	D	E
1	Hampton Freeze, Inc.				
2	Budgeted Balance Sheet				
3	December 31, 2017				
4					
5	*Assets*				
6	Current assets:				
7	Cash	$ 41,400	(a)		
8	Accounts receivable	120,000	(b)		
9	Raw materials inventory	4,500	(c)		
10	Finished goods inventory	39,000	(d)		
11	Total current assets			$ 204,900	
12	Plant and equipment:				
13	Land	80,000	(e)		
14	Buildings and equipment	830,000	(f)		
15	Accumulated depreciation	(392,000)	(g)		
16	Plant and equipment, net			518,000	
17	Total assets			$ 722,900	
18					
19	*Liabilities and Stockholders' Equity*				
20	Current liabilities:				
21	Accounts payable (raw materials)			$ 27,900	(h)
22	Stockholders' equity:				
23	Common stock, no par	$ 175,000	(i)		
24	Retained earnings	520,000	(j)		
25	Total stockholders' equity			695,000	
26	Total liabilities and stockholders' equity			$ 722,900	
27					

Schedule 8   Schedule 9   **Schedule 10**

Explanations of December 31, 2017, balance sheet figures:
(a) From cell G25 of the cash budget (Schedule 8).
(b) Thirty percent of fourth-quarter sales, from Schedule 1 ($400,000 × 30% = $120,000).
(c) From the direct materials budget (Schedule 3). Cell E12 multiplied by cell E16. In other words, 22,500 pounds × $0.20 per pound = $4,500.
(d) From cell H16 of the ending finished goods inventory budget (Schedule 6).
(e) From cell B13 of the beginning balance sheet (Exhibit 8–3).
(f) Cell B14 of the beginning balance sheet (Exhibit 8–3) plus cell G16 from the cash budget (Schedule 8). In other words, $700,000 + $130,000 = $830,000.
(g) The beginning balance of $292,000 (from cell B15 of the beginning balance sheet in Exhibit 8–3) plus the depreciation of $60,000 included in cell F12 of the manufacturing overhead budget (Schedule 5) plus depreciation expense of $40,000 included in cell F18 in the selling and administrative expense budget (Schedule 7). In other words, $292,000 + $60,000 + $40,000 = $392,000.
(h) One-half of fourth-quarter raw materials purchases, from Schedule 3 ($55,800 × 50% = $27,900).
(i) From cell B23 of the beginning balance sheet (Exhibit 8–3).
(j)

December 31, 2016, balance, from cell B24 of Exhibit 8–3......	$449,900
Add net income, from cell C12 of Schedule 9.................	102,100
	552,000
Deduct dividends paid, from cell G17 of Schedule 8............	32,000
December 31, 2017, balance...............................	$520,000

This chapter describes the budgeting process and shows how the various operating budgets relate to each other. The sales budget is the foundation for a master budget. Once the sales budget has been set, the production budget and the selling and administrative expense budget can be prepared because they depend on how many units are to be sold. The production budget determines how many units are to be produced, so after it is prepared, the various manufacturing cost budgets can be prepared. All of these budgets feed into the cash budget and the budgeted income statement and balance sheet. The parts of the master budget are connected in many ways. For example, the schedule of expected cash collections, which is completed in connection with the sales budget, provides data for both the cash budget and the budgeted balance sheet.

The material in this chapter is just an introduction to master budgeting. In later chapters, we will see how budgets are used to control day-to-day operations and how they are used in performance evaluation.

Review Problem: Budget Schedules |

Mynor Corporation manufactures and sells a seasonal product that has peak sales in the third quarter. The following information concerns operations for Year 2—the coming year—and for the first two quarters of Year 3:

a. The company's single product sells for $8 per unit. Budgeted unit sales for the next six quarters are as follows (all sales are on credit):

	Year 2 Quarter				Year 3 Quarter	
	1	2	3	4	1	2
Budgeted unit sales	40,000	60,000	100,000	50,000	70,000	80,000

b. Sales are collected in the following pattern: 75% in the quarter the sales are made, and the remaining 25% in the following quarter. On January 1, Year 2, the company's balance sheet showed $65,000 in accounts receivable, all of which will be collected in the first quarter of the year. Bad debts are negligible and can be ignored.

c. The company desires an ending finished goods inventory at the end of each quarter equal to 30% of the budgeted unit sales for the next quarter. On December 31, Year 1, the company had 12,000 units on hand.

d. Five pounds of raw materials are required to complete one unit of product. The company requires ending raw materials inventory at the end of each quarter equal to 10% of the following quarter's production needs. On December 31, Year 1, the company had 23,000 pounds of raw materials on hand.

e. The raw material costs $0.80 per pound. Raw material purchases are paid for in the following pattern: 60% paid in the quarter the purchases are made, and the remaining 40% paid in the following quarter. On January 1, Year 2, the company's balance sheet showed $81,500 in accounts payable for raw material purchases, all of which will be paid for in the first quarter of the year.

Required:

Prepare the following budgets and schedules for the year, showing both quarterly and total figures:

1. A sales budget and a schedule of expected cash collections.
2. A production budget.
3. A direct materials budget and a schedule of expected cash payments for purchases of materials.

Solution to Review Problem

1. The sales budget is prepared as follows:

	Year 2 Quarter				
	1	2	3	4	Year 2
Budgeted unit sales	40,000	60,000	100,000	50,000	250,000
Selling price per unit.......	× $8	× $8	× $8	× $8	× $8
Total sales...............	$320,000	$480,000	$800,000	$400,000	$2,000,000

Based on the budgeted sales above, the schedule of expected cash collections is prepared as follows:

	Year 2 Quarter				Year 2
	1	2	3	4	
Beginning accounts receivable........................	$ 65,000				$ 65,000
First-quarter sales ($320,000 × 75%, 25%)...............	240,000	$ 80,000			320,000
Second-quarter sales ($480,000 × 75%, 25%)............		360,000	$120,000		480,000
Third-quarter sales ($800,000 × 75%, 25%).............			600,000	$200,000	800,000
Fourth-quarter sales ($400,000 × 75%).................				300,000	300,000
Total cash collections..................................	$305,000	$440,000	$720,000	$500,000	$1,965,000

2. Based on the sales budget in units, the production budget is prepared as follows:

	Year 2 Quarter					Year 3 Quarter	
	1	2	3	4	Year 2	1	2
Budgeted unit sales	40,000	60,000	100,000	50,000	250,000	70,000	80,000
Add desired ending finished goods inventory*..........	18,000	30,000	15,000	21,000†	21,000	24,000	
Total needs..	58,000	90,000	115,000	71,000	271,000	94,000	
Less beginning finished goods inventory	12,000	18,000	30,000	15,000	12,000	21,000	
Required production...................................	46,000	72,000	85,000	56,000	259,000	73,000	

*30% of the following quarter's budgeted unit sales.
†30% of the budgeted Year 3 first-quarter sales.

3. Based on the production budget, raw materials will need to be purchased during the year as follows:

	Year 2 Quarter				Year 2	Year 3 Quarter 1
	1	2	3	4		
Required production in units of finished goods.........	46,000	72,000	85,000	56,000	259,000	73,000
Units of raw materials needed per unit of finished goods	× 5	× 5	× 5	× 5	× 5	× 5
Units of raw materials needed to meet production......	230,000	360,000	425,000	280,000	1,295,000	365,000
Add desired units of ending raw materials inventory* ...	36,000	42,500	28,000	36,500†	36,500	
Total units of raw materials needed...................	266,000	402,500	453,000	316,500	1,331,500	
Less units of beginning raw materials inventory	23,000	36,000	42,500	28,000	23,000	
Units of raw materials to be purchased...............	243,000	366,500	410,500	288,500	1,308,500	
Unit cost of raw materials............................	× $0.80	× $0.80	× $0.80	× $0.80	× $0.80	
Cost of raw materials to be purchased	$194,400	$293,200	$328,400	$230,800	$1,046,800	

*10% of the following quarter's production needs in pounds.
†10% of the Year 3 first-quarter production needs in pounds.

Based on the raw material purchases above, expected cash payments are computed as follows:

	Year 2 Quarter				Year 2
	1	2	3	4	
Beginning accounts payable..............................	$ 81,500				$ 81,500
First-quarter purchases ($194,400 × 60%, 40%)..............	116,640	$ 77,760			194,400
Second-quarter purchases ($293,200 × 60%, 40%)..........		175,920	$117,280		293,200
Third-quarter purchases ($328,400 × 60%, 40%)............			197,040	$131,360	328,400
Fourth-quarter purchases ($230,800 × 60%)................				138,480	138,480
Total cash disbursements	$198,140	$253,680	$314,320	$269,840	$1,035,980

Budget A detailed plan for the future that is usually expressed in formal quantitative terms. (p. 363)

Cash budget A detailed plan showing how cash resources will be acquired and used over a specific time period. (p. 366)

Continuous budget A 12-month budget that rolls forward one month as the current month is completed. (p. 364)

Control The process of gathering feedback to ensure that a plan is being properly executed or modified as circumstances change. (p. 363)

Direct labor budget A detailed plan that shows the direct labor-hours required to fulfill the production budget. (p. 376)

Direct materials budget A detailed plan showing the amount of raw materials that must be purchased to fulfill the production budget and to provide for adequate inventories. (p. 374)

Ending finished goods inventory budget A budget showing the dollar amount of unsold finished goods inventory that will appear on the ending balance sheet. (p. 378)

Manufacturing overhead budget A detailed plan showing the production costs, other than direct materials and direct labor, that will be incurred over a specified time period. (p. 377)

Master budget A number of separate but interdependent budgets that formally lay out the company's sales, production, and financial goals and that culminates in a cash budget, budgeted income statement, and budgeted balance sheet. (p. 365)

Merchandise purchases budget A detailed plan used by a merchandising company that shows the amount of goods that must be purchased from suppliers during the period. (p. 374)

Participative budget See *Self-imposed budget*. (p. 364)

Perpetual budget See *Continuous budget*. (p. 364)

Planning The process of establishing goals and specifying how to achieve them. (p. 363)

Production budget A detailed plan showing the number of units that must be produced during a period in order to satisfy both sales and inventory needs. (p. 373)

Responsibility accounting A system of accountability in which managers are held responsible for those items of revenue and cost—and only those items—over which they can exert significant control. The managers are held responsible for differences between budgeted and actual results. (p. 363)

Sales budget A detailed schedule showing expected sales expressed in both dollars and units. (p. 366)

Self-imposed budget A method of preparing budgets in which managers prepare their own budgets. These budgets are then reviewed by higher-level managers, and any issues are resolved by mutual agreement. (p. 364)

Selling and administrative expense budget A detailed schedule of planned expenses that will be incurred in areas other than manufacturing during a budget period. (p. 379)

8–1 What is a budget? What is budgetary control?

8–2 Discuss some of the major benefits to be gained from budgeting.

8–3 What is meant by the term *responsibility accounting?*

8–4 What is a master budget? Briefly describe its contents.

8–5 Why is the sales forecast the starting point in budgeting?

8–6 "As a practical matter, planning and control mean exactly the same thing." Do you agree? Explain.

8–7 Why is it a good idea to create a "Budgeting Assumptions" tab when creating a master budget in Microsoft Excel?

8–8 What is a self-imposed budget? What are the major advantages of self-imposed budgets? What caution must be exercised in their use?

8–9 How can budgeting assist a company in planning its workforce staffing levels?

8–10 "The principal purpose of the cash budget is to see how much cash the company will have in the bank at the end of the year." Do you agree? Explain.

Applying Excel   Connect

LO8-2, LO8-3, LO8-4   The Excel worksheet form that appears below is to be used to recreate the Review Problem related to Mynor Corporation. Download the workbook containing this form from Connect, where you will also receive instructions about how to use this worksheet form.

	A	B	C	D	E	F	G	H	I
1	Chapter 8: Applying Excel								
2									
3	Data			Year 2 Quarter		Year 3 Quarter			
4		1	2	3	4	1	2		
5	Budgeted unit sales	40,000	60,000	100,000	50,000	70,000	80,000		
6									
7	• Selling price per unit	$8							
8	• Accounts receivable, beginning balance	$65,000							
9	• Sales collected in the quarter sales are made	75%							
10	• Sales collected in the quarter after sales are made	25%							
11	• Desired ending finished goods inventory is		30% of the budgeted unit sales of the next quarter						
12	• Finished goods inventory, beginning	12,000	units						
13	• Raw materials required to produce one unit	5	pounds						
14	• Desired ending inventory of raw materials is		10% of the next quarter's production needs						
15	• Raw materials inventory, beginning	23,000	pounds						
16	• Raw material costs	$0.80	per pound						
17	• Raw materials purchases are paid		60% in the quarter the purchases are made						
18	and		40% in the quarter following purchase						
19	• Accounts payable for raw materials, beginning balance	$81,500							
20									
21	*Enter a formula into each of the cells marked with a ? below*								
22	**Review Problem: Budget Schedules**								
23									
24	*Construct the sales budget*			Year 2 Quarter		Year 3 Quarter			
25		1	2	3	4	1	2		
26	Budgeted unit sales	?	?	?	?	?	?		
27	Selling price per unit	?	?	?	?	?	?		
28	Total sales	?	?	?	?	?	?		
29									
30	*Construct the schedule of expected cash collections*			Year 2 Quarter					
31		1	2	3	4	Year			
32	Beginning balance accounts receivable	?				?			
33	First-quarter sales	?	?			?			
34	Second-quarter sales		?	?		?			
35	Third-quarter sales			?	?	?			
36	Fourth-quarter sales				?	?			
37	Total cash collections	?	?	?	?	?			
38									
39	*Construct the production budget*			Year 2 Quarter			Year 3 Quarter		
40		1	2	3	4	Year	1	2	
41	Budgeted unit sales	?	?	?	?	?	?	?	
42	Add desired ending finished goods inventory	?	?	?	?	?	?		
43	Total needs	?	?	?	?	?	?		
44	Less beginning finished goods inventory	?	?	?	?	?	?		
45	Required production in units	?	?	?	?	?	?		
46									
47	*Construct the raw materials purchases budget*			Year 2 Quarter			Year 3 Quarter		
48		1	2	3	4	Year	1		
49	Required production (units)	?	?	?	?	?	?		
50	Raw materials required to produce one unit (pounds)	?	?	?	?	?	?		
51	Production needs (pounds)	?	?	?	?	?	?		
52	Add desired ending inventory of raw materials (pounds)	?	?	?	?	?			
53	Total needs (pounds)	?	?	?	?	?			
54	Less beginning inventory of raw materials (pounds)	?	?	?	?	?			
55	Raw materials to be purchased (pounds)	?	?	?	?	?			
56	Cost of raw materials per pound	?	?	?	?	?			
57	Cost of raw materials to be purchased	?	?	?	?	?			
58									
59	*Construct the schedule of expected cash payments*			Year 2 Quarter					
60		1	2	3	4	Year			
61	Beginning balance accounts payable	?				?			
62	First-quarter purchases	?	?			?			
63	Second-quarter purchases		?	?		?			
64	Third-quarter purchases			?	?	?			
65	Fourth-quarter purchases				?	?			
66	Total cash disbursements	?	?	?	?	?			
67									

Chapter 8 Form | Filled in Chapter 8 Form | Chapter 8 Formulas | Chapter 8 Requirement

You should proceed to the requirements below only after completing your worksheet.

Required:

1. Check your worksheet by changing the budgeted unit sales in Quarter 2 of Year 2 in cell C5 to 75,000 units. The total expected cash collections for the year should now be $2,085,000. If you do not get this answer, find the errors in your worksheet and correct them. Have the total cash disbursements for the year changed? Why or why not?

2. The company has just hired a new marketing manager who insists that unit sales can be dramatically increased by dropping the selling price from $8 to $7. The marketing manager would like to use the following projections in the budget:

Data	Year 2 Quarter				Year 3 Quarter	
	1	2	3	4	1	2
Budgeted unit sales	50,000	70,000	120,000	80,000	90,000	100,000
Selling price per unit.........	$7					

   a. What are the total expected cash collections for the year under this revised budget?
   b. What is the total required production for the year under this revised budget?
   c. What is the total cost of raw materials to be purchased for the year under this revised budget?
   d. What are the total expected cash disbursements for raw materials for the year under this revised budget?
   e. After seeing this revised budget, the production manager cautioned that due to the limited availability of a complex milling machine, the plant can produce no more than 90,000 units in any one quarter. Is this a potential problem? If so, what can be done about it?

---

connect **The Foundational 15**

Morganton Company makes one product and it provided the following information to help prepare the master budget:

LO8–2, LO8–3, LO8–4, LO8–5, LO8–7, LO8–9, LO8–10

   a. The budgeted selling price per unit is $70. Budgeted unit sales for June, July, August, and September are 8,400, 10,000, 12,000, and 13,000 units, respectively. All sales are on credit.
   b. Forty percent of credit sales are collected in the month of the sale and 60% in the following month.
   c. The ending finished goods inventory equals 20% of the following month's unit sales.
   d. The ending raw materials inventory equals 10% of the following month's raw materials production needs. Each unit of finished goods requires 5 pounds of raw materials. The raw materials cost $2.00 per pound.
   e. Thirty percent of raw materials purchases are paid for in the month of purchase and 70% in the following month.
   f. The direct labor wage rate is $15 per hour. Each unit of finished goods requires two direct labor-hours.
   g. The variable selling and administrative expense per unit sold is $1.80. The fixed selling and administrative expense per month is $60,000.

Required:

1. What are the budgeted sales for July?
2. What are the expected cash collections for July?
3. What is the accounts receivable balance at the end of July?
4. According to the production budget, how many units should be produced in July?
5. If 61,000 pounds of raw materials are needed to meet production in August, how many pounds of raw materials should be purchased in July?
6. What is the estimated cost of raw materials purchases for July?
7. In July what are the total estimated cash disbursements for raw materials purchases? Assume the cost of raw material purchases in June is $88,880.
8. What is the estimated accounts payable balance at the end of July?
9. What is the estimated raw materials inventory balance at the end of July?
10. What is the total estimated direct labor cost for July assuming the direct labor workforce is adjusted to match the hours required to produce the forecasted number of units produced?

11. If we assume that there is no fixed manufacturing overhead and the variable manufacturing overhead is $10 per direct labor-hour, what is the estimated unit product cost?
12. What is the estimated finished goods inventory balance at the end of July?
13. What is the estimated cost of goods sold and gross margin for July?
14. What is the estimated total selling and administrative expense for July?
15. What is the estimated net operating income for July?

Exercises   ▪ connect

EXERCISE 8–1 Schedule of Expected Cash Collections LO8–2

Silver Company makes a product that is very popular as a Mother's Day gift. Thus, peak sales occur in May of each year, as shown in the company's sales budget for the second quarter given below:

	April	May	June	Total
Budgeted sales (all on account)	$300,000	$500,000	$200,000	$1,000,000

From past experience, the company has learned that 20% of a month's sales are collected in the month of sale, another 70% are collected in the month following sale, and the remaining 10% are collected in the second month following sale. Bad debts are negligible and can be ignored. February sales totaled $230,000, and March sales totaled $260,000.

Required:
1. Using Schedule 1 as your guide, prepare a schedule of expected cash collections from sales, by month and in total, for the second quarter.
2. What is the accounts receivable balance on June 30th?

EXERCISE 8–2 Production Budget LO8–3

Down Under Products, Ltd., of Australia has budgeted sales of its popular boomerang for the next four months as follows:

	Unit Sales
April	50,000
May	75,000
June	90,000
July	80,000

The company is now in the process of preparing a production budget for the second quarter. Past experience has shown that end-of-month inventory levels must equal 10% of the following month's unit sales. The inventory at the end of March was 5,000 units.

Required:
Using Schedule 2 as your guide, prepare a production budget by month and in total, for the second quarter.

EXERCISE 8–3 Direct Materials Budget LO8–4

Three grams of musk oil are required for each bottle of Mink Caress, a very popular perfume made by a small company in western Siberia. The cost of the musk oil is $1.50 per gram. Budgeted production of Mink Caress is given below by quarters for Year 2 and for the first quarter of Year 3:

	Year 2				Year 3
	First	Second	Third	Fourth	First
Budgeted production, in bottles	60,000	90,000	150,000	100,000	70,000

Musk oil has become so popular as a perfume ingredient that it has become necessary to carry large inventories as a precaution against stock-outs. For this reason, the inventory of musk oil at the end of a quarter must be equal to 20% of the following quarter's production needs. Some 36,000 grams of musk oil will be on hand to start the first quarter of Year 2.

Required:
Using Schedule 3 as your guide, prepare a direct materials budget for musk oil, by quarter and in total, for Year 2.

EXERCISE 8–4 Direct Labor Budget LO8–5
The production manager of Rordan Corporation has submitted the following quarterly production forecast for the upcoming fiscal year:

	1st Quarter	2nd Quarter	3rd Quarter	4th Quarter
Units to be produced	8,000	6,500	7,000	7,500

Each unit requires 0.35 direct labor-hours, and direct laborers are paid $12.00 per hour.

Required:
1. Using Schedule 4 as your guide, prepare the company's direct labor budget for the upcoming fiscal year. Assume that the direct labor workforce is adjusted each quarter to match the number of hours required to produce the forecasted number of units produced.
2. Prepare the company's direct labor budget for the upcoming fiscal year, assuming that the direct labor workforce is not adjusted each quarter. Instead, assume that the company's direct labor workforce consists of permanent employees who are guaranteed to be paid for at least 2,600 hours of work each quarter. If the number of required direct labor-hours is less than this number, the workers are paid for 2,600 hours anyway. Any hours worked in excess of 2,600 hours in a quarter are paid at the rate of 1.5 times the normal hourly rate for direct labor.

EXERCISE 8–5 Manufacturing Overhead Budget LO8–6
The direct labor budget of Yuvwell Corporation for the upcoming fiscal year contains the following details concerning budgeted direct labor-hours:

	1st Quarter	2nd Quarter	3rd Quarter	4th Quarter
Budgeted direct labor-hours	8,000	8,200	8,500	7,800

The company uses direct labor-hours as its overhead allocation base. The variable portion of its predetermined manufacturing overhead rate is $3.25 per direct labor-hour and its total fixed manufacturing overhead is $48,000 per quarter. The only noncash item included in fixed manufacturing overhead is depreciation, which is $16,000 per quarter.

Required:
1. Using Schedule 5 as your guide, prepare the company's manufacturing overhead budget for the upcoming fiscal year.
2. Compute the company's predetermined overhead rate (including both variable and fixed manufacturing overhead) for the upcoming fiscal year. Round off to the nearest whole cent.

EXERCISE 8–6 Selling and Administrative Expense Budget LO8–7
Weller Company's budgeted unit sales for the upcoming fiscal year are provided below:

	1st Quarter	2nd Quarter	3rd Quarter	4th Quarter
Budgeted unit sales	15,000	16,000	14,000	13,000

The company's variable selling and administrative expense per unit is $2.50. Fixed selling and administrative expenses include advertising expenses of $8,000 per quarter, executive salaries of $35,000 per quarter, and depreciation of $20,000 per quarter. In addition, the company will make insurance payments of $5,000 in the first quarter and $5,000 in the third quarter. Finally, property taxes of $8,000 will be paid in the second quarter.

Required:
Using Schedule 7 as your guide, prepare the company's selling and administrative expense budget for the upcoming fiscal year.

EXERCISE 8–7 Cash Budget LO8–8

Garden Depot is a retailer that is preparing its budget for the upcoming fiscal year. Management has prepared the following summary of its budgeted cash flows:

	1st Quarter	2nd Quarter	3rd Quarter	4th Quarter
Total cash receipts	$180,000	$330,000	$210,000	$230,000
Total cash disbursements	$260,000	$230,000	$220,000	$240,000

The company's beginning cash balance for the upcoming fiscal year will be $20,000. The company requires a minimum cash balance of $10,000 and may borrow any amount needed from a local bank at a quarterly interest rate of 3%. The company may borrow any amount at the beginning of any quarter and may repay its loans, or any part of its loans, at the end of any quarter. Interest payments are due on any principal at the time it is repaid. For simplicity, assume that interest is not compounded.

Required:

Using Schedule 8 as your guide, prepare the company's cash budget for the upcoming fiscal year.

EXERCISE 8–8 Budgeted Income Statement LO8–9

Gig Harbor Boating is the wholesale distributor of a small recreational catamaran sailboat. Management has prepared the following summary data to use in its annual budgeting process:

Budgeted unit sales	460
Selling price per unit......................................	$1,950
Cost per unit..	$1,575
Variable selling and administrative expense (per unit)..........	$75
Fixed selling and administrative expense (per year)............	$105,000
Interest expense for the year	$14,000

Required:

Using Schedule 9 as your guide, prepare the company's budgeted income statement for the year.

EXERCISE 8–9 Budgeted Balance Sheet LO8–10

The management of Mecca Copy, a photocopying center located on University Avenue, has compiled the following data to use in preparing its budgeted balance sheet for next year:

	Ending Balances
Cash................................	?
Accounts receivable..................	$8,100
Supplies inventory....................	$3,200
Equipment	$34,000
Accumulated depreciation.............	$16,000
Accounts payable	$1,800
Common stock.......................	$5,000
Retained earnings...................	?

The beginning balance of retained earnings was $28,000, net income is budgeted to be $11,500, and dividends are budgeted to be $4,800.

Required:

Prepare the company's budgeted balance sheet.

EXERCISE 8–10 Production and Direct Materials Budgets LO8–3, LO8–4

Pearl Products Limited of Shenzhen, China, manufactures and distributes toys throughout South East Asia. Three cubic centimeters (cc) of solvent H300 are required to manufacture each unit of Supermix, one of the company's products. The company now is planning raw materials needs for the third quarter, the quarter in which peak sales of Supermix occur. To keep production and sales moving smoothly, the company has the following inventory requirements:

a. The finished goods inventory on hand at the end of each month must equal 3,000 units of Supermix plus 20% of the next month's sales. The finished goods inventory on June 30 is budgeted to be 10,000 units.

b. The raw materials inventory on hand at the end of each month must equal one-half of the following month's production needs for raw materials. The raw materials inventory on June 30 is budgeted to be 54,000 cc of solvent H300.

c. The company maintains no work in process inventories.

A monthly sales budget for Supermix for the third and fourth quarters of the year follows.

	Budgeted Unit Sales
July	35,000
August......................	40,000
September	50,000
October.....................	30,000
November..................	20,000
December..................	10,000

Required:

1. Prepare a production budget for Supermix for the months July, August, September, and October.

2. Examine the production budget that you prepared in (1) above. Why will the company produce more units than it sells in July and August, and fewer units than it sells in September and October?

3. Prepare a direct materials budget showing the quantity of solvent H300 to be purchased for July, August, and September, and for the quarter in total.

EXERCISE 8–11 Cash Budget Analysis LO8–8

A cash budget, by quarters, is given below for a retail company (000 omitted). The company requires a minimum cash balance of at least $5,000 to start each quarter.

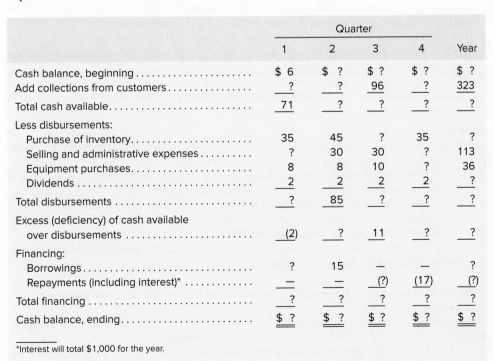

	Quarter				
	1	2	3	4	Year
Cash balance, beginning	$ 6	$?	$?	$?	$?
Add collections from customers...............	?	?	96	?	323
Total cash available............................	71	?	?	?	?
Less disbursements:					
Purchase of inventory......................	35	45	?	35	?
Selling and administrative expenses..........	?	30	30	?	113
Equipment purchases......................	8	8	10	?	36
Dividends	2	2	2	2	?
Total disbursements	?	85	?	?	?
Excess (deficiency) of cash available over disbursements	(2)	?	11	?	?
Financing:					
Borrowings..................................	?	15	—	—	?
Repayments (including interest)*	—	—	(?)	(17)	(?)
Total financing	?	?	?	?	?
Cash balance, ending..........................	$?	$?	$?	$?	$?

*Interest will total $1,000 for the year.

Required:

Fill in the missing amounts in the above table.

EXERCISE 8–12 Schedules of Expected Cash Collections and Disbursements; Income Statement; Balance Sheet LO8–2, LO8–4, LO8–9, LO8–10

Beech Corporation is a merchandising company that is preparing a master budget for the third quarter of the calendar year. The company's balance sheet as of June 30th is shown below:

	Beech Corporation Balance Sheet June 30

Assets

Cash.	$ 90,000
Accounts receivable	136,000
Inventory.	62,000
Plant and equipment, net of depreciation.	210,000
Total assets.	$498,000

Liabilities and Stockholders' Equity

Accounts payable	$ 71,100
Common stock.	327,000
Retained earnings.	99,900
Total liabilities and stockholders' equity	$498,000

Beech's managers have made the following additional assumptions and estimates:

1. Estimated sales for July, August, September, and October will be $210,000, $230,000, $220,000, and $240,000, respectively.
2. All sales are on credit and all credit sales are collected. Each month's credit sales are collected 35% in the month of sale and 65% in the month following the sale. All of the accounts receivable at June 30 will be collected in July.
3. Each month's ending inventory must equal 30% of the cost of next month's sales. The cost of goods sold is 60% of sales. The company pays for 40% of its merchandise purchases in the month of the purchase and the remaining 60% in the month following the purchase. All of the accounts payable at June 30 will be paid in July.
4. Monthly selling and administrative expenses are always $60,000. Each month $5,000 of this total amount is depreciation expense and the remaining $55,000 relates to expenses that are paid in the month they are incurred.
5. The company does not plan to borrow money or pay or declare dividends during the quarter ended September 30. The company does not plan to issue any common stock or repurchase its own stock during the quarter ended September 30.

Required:

1. Prepare a schedule of expected cash collections for July, August, and September. Also compute total cash collections for the quarter ended September 30.
2. a. Prepare a merchandise purchases budget for July, August, and September. Also compute total merchandise purchases for the quarter ended September 30.
   b. Prepare a schedule of expected cash disbursements for merchandise purchases for July, August, and September. Also compute total cash disbursements for merchandise purchases for the quarter ended September 30.
3. Using Schedule 9 as your guide, prepare an income statement for the quarter ended September 30.
4. Prepare a balance sheet as of September 30.

EXERCISE 8–13 Schedules of Expected Cash Collections and Disbursements; Income Statement; Balance Sheet LO8–2, LO8–4, LO8–9, LO8–10

Refer to the data for Beech Corporation in Exercise 8–12. The company is considering making the following changes to the assumptions underlying its master budget:

1. Each month's credit sales are collected 45% in the month of sale and 55% in the month following the sale.
2. Each month's ending inventory must equal 20% of the cost of next month's sales.
3. The company pays for 30% of its merchandise purchases in the month of the purchase and the remaining 70% in the month following the purchase.

All other information from Exercise 8–12 that is not mentioned above remains the same.

Required:

Using the new assumptions described above, complete the following requirements:
1. Prepare a schedule of expected cash collections for July, August, and September. Also compute total cash collections for the quarter ended September 30.
2. a. Prepare a merchandise purchases budget for July, August, and September. Also compute total merchandise purchases for the quarter ended September 30.
   b. Prepare a schedule of expected cash disbursements for merchandise purchases for July, August, and September. Also compute total cash disbursements for merchandise purchases for the quarter ended September 30.
3. Using Schedule 9 as your guide, prepare an income statement for the quarter ended September 30.
4. Prepare a balance sheet as of September 30.

EXERCISE 8–14 Sales and Production Budgets LO8–2, LO8–3

The marketing department of Jessi Corporation has submitted the following sales forecast for the upcoming fiscal year (all sales are on account):

	1st Quarter	2nd Quarter	3rd Quarter	4th Quarter
Budgeted unit sales	11,000	12,000	14,000	13,000

The selling price of the company's product is $18.00 per unit. Management expects to collect 65% of sales in the quarter in which the sales are made, 30% in the following quarter, and 5% of sales are expected to be uncollectible. The beginning balance of accounts receivable, all of which is expected to be collected in the first quarter, is $70,200.

The company expects to start the first quarter with 1,650 units in finished goods inventory. Management desires an ending finished goods inventory in each quarter equal to 15% of the next quarter's budgeted sales. The desired ending finished goods inventory for the fourth quarter is 1,850 units.

Required:
1. Calculate the estimated sales for each quarter of the fiscal year and for the year as a whole. (Hint: Refer to Schedule 1 for guidance.)
2. Calculate the expected cash collections for each quarter of the fiscal year and for the year as a whole. (Hint: Refer to Schedule 1 for guidance.)
3. Calculate the required production in units of finished goods for each quarter of the fiscal year and for the year as a whole. (Hint: Refer to Schedule 2 for guidance.)

EXERCISE 8–15 Direct Labor and Manufacturing Overhead Budgets LO8–5, LO8–6

The Production Department of Hruska Corporation has submitted the following forecast of units to be produced by quarter for the upcoming fiscal year:

	1st Quarter	2nd Quarter	3rd Quarter	4th Quarter
Units to be produced	12,000	10,000	13,000	14,000

Each unit requires 0.2 direct labor-hours and direct laborers are paid $12.00 per hour.

In addition, the variable manufacturing overhead rate is $1.75 per direct labor-hour. The fixed manufacturing overhead is $86,000 per quarter. The only noncash element of manufacturing overhead is depreciation, which is $23,000 per quarter.

Required:
1. Calculate the company's total estimated direct labor cost for each quarter of the the upcoming fiscal year and for the year as a whole. Assume that the direct labor workforce is adjusted each quarter to match the number of hours required to produce the estimated number of units produced (Hint: Refer to Schedule 4 for guidance).
2. Calculate the company's total estimated manufacturing overhead cost for each quarter of the upcoming fiscal year and for the year as a whole (Hint: Refer to Schedule 5 for guidance).
3. Calculate the company's cash disbursements for manufacturing overhead for each quarter of the the upcoming fiscal year and for the year as a whole (Hint: Refer to Schedule 5 for guidance).

EXERCISE 8–16 Direct Materials and Direct Labor Budgets LO8–4, LO8–5

The production department of Zan Corporation has submitted the following forecast of units to be produced by quarter for the upcoming fiscal year:

	1st Quarter	2nd Quarter	3rd Quarter	4th Quarter
Units to be produced	5,000	8,000	7,000	6,000

In addition, 6,000 grams of raw materials inventory is on hand at the start of the 1st Quarter and the beginning accounts payable for the 1st Quarter is $2,880.

Each unit requires 8 grams of raw material that costs $1.20 per gram. Management desires to end each quarter with an inventory of raw materials equal to 25% of the following quarter's production needs. The desired ending inventory for the 4th Quarter is 8,000 grams. Management plans to pay for 60% of raw material purchases in the quarter acquired and 40% in the following quarter. Each unit requires 0.20 direct labor-hours and direct laborers are paid $11.50 per hour.

Required:
1. Calculate the estimated grams of raw material that need to be purchased each quarter and for the year as a whole (Hint: Refer to Schedule 3 for guidance).
2. Calculate the cost of raw material purchases for each quarter and for the year as a whole (Hint: Refer to Schedule 3 for guidance).
3. Calculate the expected cash disbursements for purchases of materials for each quarter and for the year as a whole (Hint: Refer to Schedule 3 for guidance).
4. Calculate the estimated direct labor cost for each quarter and for the year as a whole. Assume that the direct labor workforce is adjusted each quarter to match the number of hours required to produce the estimated number of units produced (Hint: Refer to Schedule 4 for guidance).

EXERCISE 8–17 Cash Flows; Budgeted Income Statement and Balance Sheet LO 8–2, LO 8–3, LO 8–4, LO8–9, LO8–10

Wheeling Company is a merchandiser that provided a balance sheet as of September 30 as shown below:

Wheeling Company Balance Sheet September 30	
Assets	
Cash.	$ 59,000
Accounts receivable	90,000
Inventory.	32,400
Buildings and equipment, net of depreciation	214,000
Total assets.	$395,400
Liabilities and Stockholders' Equity	
Accounts payable	$ 73,000
Common stock.	216,000
Retained earnings.	106,400
Total liabilities and stockholders' equity	$395,400

The company is in the process of preparing a budget for October and has assembled the following data:
1. Sales are budgeted at $240,000 for October and $250,000 for November. Of these sales, 35% will be for cash; the remainder will be credit sales. Forty percent of a month's credit sales are collected in the month the sales are made, and the remaining 60% is collected in the following month. All of the September 30 accounts receivable will be collected in October.
2. The budgeted cost of goods sold is always 45% of sales and the ending merchandise inventory is always 30% of the following month's cost of goods sold.
3. All merchandise purchases are on account. Thirty percent of all purchases are paid for in the month of purchase and 70% are paid for in the following month. All of the September 30 accounts payable to suppliers will be paid during October.
4. Selling and administrative expenses for October are budgeted at $78,000, exclusive of depreciation. These expenses will be paid in cash. Depreciation is budgeted at $2,000 for the month.

Required:
1. Using the information provided, calculate or prepare the following:
   a. The budgeted cash collections for October.
   b. The budgeted merchandise purchases for October.
   c. The budgeted cash disbursements for merchandise purchases for October.
   d. The budgeted net operating income for October.
   e. A budgeted balance sheet at October 31.
2. Assume the following changes to the underlying budgeting assumptions: (1) 50% of a month's credit sales are collected in the month the sales are made and the remaining 50% is collected in the following month, (2) the ending merchandise inventory is always 10% of the following month's cost of goods sold, and (3) 20% of all purchases are paid for in the month of purchase and 80% are paid for in the following month. Using these new assumptions, calculate or prepare the following:
   a. The budgeted cash collections for October.
   b. The budgeted merchandise purchases for October.
   c. The budgeted cash disbursements for merchandise purchases for October.
   d. Net operating income for the month of October.
   e. A budgeted balance sheet at October 31.
3. Compare your answers in requirement 1 to those that you obtained in requirement 2. If Wheeling Company is able to achieve the budgeted projections described in requirement 2, will it improve the company's financial performance relative to the projections that you derived in requirement 1?

EXERCISE 8–18 Cash Flows; Budgeted Income Statement and Balance Sheet LO 8–2, LO 8–3, LO8–9, LO8–10
Wolfpack Company is a merchandising company that is preparing a budget for the month of July. It has provided the following information:

Wolfpack Company Balance Sheet June 30	
Assets	
Cash.	$ 75,000
Accounts receivable	50,000
Inventory.	30,000
Buildings and equipment, net of depreciation	150,000
Total assets.	$305,000
Liabilities and Stockholders' Equity	
Accounts payable	$ 35,300
Retained earnings.	269,700
Total liabilities and stockholders' equity	$305,000

Budgeting Assumptions:
1. All sales are on account. Thirty percent of the credit sales are collected in the month of sale and the remaining 70% are collected in the month subsequent to the sale. The accounts receivable at June 30 will be collected in July.
2. All merchandise purchases are on account. Twenty percent of merchandise inventory purchases are paid in the month of the purchase and the remaining 80% is paid in the month after the purchase.
3. The budgeted inventory balance at July 31 is $22,000.
4. Depreciation expense is $3,000 per month. All other selling and administrative expenses are paid in full in the month the expense is incurred.
5. The company's cash budget for July shows expected cash collections of $77,000, expected cash disbursements for merchandise purchases of $44,500, and cash paid for selling and administrative expenses of $15,000.

Required:
1. For the month of July, calculate the following:
   a. Budgeted sales
   b. Budgeted merchandise purchases
   c. Budgeted cost of goods sold
   d. Budgeted net operating income
2. Prepare a budgeted balance sheet as of July 31.

Problems   **connect**

PROBLEM 8–19 Cash Budget; Income Statement; Balance Sheet LO8–2, LO8–4, LO8–8, LO8–9, LO8–10

Minden Company is a wholesale distributor of premium European chocolates. The company's balance sheet as of April 30 is given below:

Minden Company Balance Sheet April 30	
Assets	
Cash...	$ 9,000
Accounts receivable...........................	54,000
Inventory.....................................	30,000
Buildings and equipment, net of depreciation.......	207,000
Total assets..................................	$300,000
Liabilities and Stockholders' Equity	
Accounts payable	$ 63,000
Note payable	14,500
Common stock.................................	180,000
Retained earnings.............................	42,500
Total liabilities and stockholders' equity	$300,000

The company is in the process of preparing a budget for May and has assembled the following data:
a. Sales are budgeted at $200,000 for May. Of these sales, $60,000 will be for cash; the remainder will be credit sales. One-half of a month's credit sales are collected in the month the sales are made, and the remainder is collected in the following month. All of the April 30 accounts receivable will be collected in May.
b. Purchases of inventory are expected to total $120,000 during May. These purchases will all be on account. Forty percent of all purchases are paid for in the month of purchase; the remainder are paid in the following month. All of the April 30 accounts payable to suppliers will be paid during May.
c. The May 31 inventory balance is budgeted at $40,000.
d. Selling and administrative expenses for May are budgeted at $72,000, exclusive of depreciation. These expenses will be paid in cash. Depreciation is budgeted at $2,000 for the month.
e. The note payable on the April 30 balance sheet will be paid during May, with $100 in interest. (All of the interest relates to May.)
f. New refrigerating equipment costing $6,500 will be purchased for cash during May.
g. During May, the company will borrow $20,000 from its bank by giving a new note payable to the bank for that amount. The new note will be due in one year.

Required:
1. Calculate the expected cash collections for May.
2. Calculate the expected cash disbursements for merchandise purchases for May.
3. Prepare a cash budget for May.
4. Using Schedule 9 as your guide, prepare a budgeted income statement for May.
5. Prepare a budgeted balance sheet as of May 31.

PROBLEM 8–20 Cash Budget; Income Statement; Balance Sheet; Changing Assumptions LO8–2, LO8–4, LO8–8, LO8–9, LO8–10

Refer to the data for Minden Company in Problem 8–19. The company is considering making the following changes to the assumptions underlying its master budget:
1. Sales are budgeted for $220,000 for May.
2. Each month's credit sales are collected 60% in the month of sale and 40% in the month following the sale.
3. The company pays for 50% of its merchandise purchases in the month of the purchase and the remaining 50% in the month following the purchase.
All other information from Problem 8–19 that is not mentioned above remains the same.

Required:

Using the new assumptions described above, complete the following requirements:
1. Calculate the expected cash collections for May.
2. Calculate the expected cash disbursements for merchandise purchases for May.
3. Prepare a cash budget for May.
4. Using Schedule 9 as your guide, prepare a budgeted income statement for May.
5. Prepare a budgeted balance sheet as of May 31.

PROBLEM 8–21 Schedules of Expected Cash Collections and Disbursements LO8–2, LO8–4, LO8–8

You have been asked to prepare a December cash budget for Ashton Company, a distributor of exercise equipment. The following information is available about the company's operations:
a. The cash balance on December 1 is $40,000.
b. Actual sales for October and November and expected sales for December are as follows:

	October	November	December
Cash sales	$65,000	$70,000	$83,000
Sales on account......	$400,000	$525,000	$600,000

Sales on account are collected over a three-month period as follows: 20% collected in the month of sale, 60% collected in the month following sale, and 18% collected in the second month following sale. The remaining 2% is uncollectible.
c. Purchases of inventory will total $280,000 for December. Thirty percent of a month's inventory purchases are paid during the month of purchase. The accounts payable remaining from November's inventory purchases total $161,000, all of which will be paid in December.
d. Selling and administrative expenses are budgeted at $430,000 for December. Of this amount, $50,000 is for depreciation.
e. A new web server for the Marketing Department costing $76,000 will be purchased for cash during December, and dividends totaling $9,000 will be paid during the month.
f. The company maintains a minimum cash balance of $20,000. An open line of credit is available from the company's bank to increase its cash balance as needed.

Required:

1. Calculate the expected cash collections for December.
2. Calculate the expected cash disbursements for merchandise purchases for December.
3. Prepare a cash budget for December. Indicate in the financing section any borrowing that will be needed during the month. Assume that any interest will not be paid until the following month.

PROBLEM 8–22 Evaluating a Company's Budget Procedures LO8–1

Springfield Corporation operates on a calendar-year basis. It begins the annual budgeting process in late August, when the president establishes targets for total sales dollars and net operating income before taxes for the next year.

The sales target is given to the Marketing Department, where the marketing manager formulates a sales budget by product line in both units and dollars. From this budget, sales quotas by product line in units and dollars are established for each of the corporation's sales districts.

The marketing manager also estimates the cost of the marketing activities required to support the target sales volume and prepares a tentative marketing expense budget.

The executive vice president uses the sales and profit targets, the sales budget by product line, and the tentative marketing expense budget to determine the dollar amounts that can be devoted to manufacturing and corporate office expense. The executive vice president prepares the budget for corporate expenses, and then forwards to the Production Department the product-line sales budget in units and the total dollar amount that can be devoted to manufacturing.

The production manager meets with the factory managers to develop a manufacturing plan that will produce the required units when needed within the cost constraints set by the executive vice president. The budgeting process usually comes to a halt at this point because the Production Department does not consider its allocated financial resources to be adequate.

When this standstill occurs, the vice president of finance, the executive vice president, the marketing manager, and the production manager meet to determine the final budgets for each of the areas. This normally results in a modest increase in the total amount available for manufacturing costs, while the marketing expense and corporate office expense budgets are cut. The total sales and net operating income figures proposed by the president are seldom changed. Although the participants are seldom pleased with the compromise, these budgets are final. Each executive then develops a new detailed budget for the operations in his or her area.

None of the areas has achieved its budget in recent years. Sales often run below the target. When budgeted sales are not achieved, each area is expected to cut costs so that the president's profit target can still be met. However, the profit target is seldom met because costs are not cut enough. In fact, costs often run above the original budget in all functional areas. The president is disturbed that Springfield has not been able to meet the sales and profit targets. He hired a consultant with considerable relevant industry experience. The consultant reviewed the budgets for the past four years. He concluded that the product-line sales budgets were reasonable and that the cost and expense budgets were adequate for the budgeted sales and production levels.

Required:

1. Discuss how Springfield Corporation's budgeting process contributes to its failure to achieve the president's sales and profit targets.
2. Suggest how Springfield Corporation's budgeting process could be revised to correct the problem.
3. Should the functional areas be expected to cut their costs when sales volume falls below budget? Explain your answer.

(CMA, adapted)

PROBLEM 8–23 Schedule of Expected Cash Collections; Cash Budget LO8–2, LO8–8

The president of the retailer Prime Products has just approached the company's bank with a request for a $30,000, 90-day loan. The purpose of the loan is to assist the company in acquiring inventories. Because the company has had some difficulty in paying off its loans in the past, the loan officer has asked for a cash budget to help determine whether the loan should be made. The following data are available for the months April through June, during which the loan will be used:

a. On April 1, the start of the loan period, the cash balance will be $24,000. Accounts receivable on April 1 will total $140,000, of which $120,000 will be collected during April and $16,000 will be collected during May. The remainder will be uncollectible.

b. Past experience shows that 30% of a month's sales are collected in the month of sale, 60% in the month following sale, and 8% in the second month following sale. The other 2% is bad debts that are never collected. Budgeted sales and expenses for the three-month period follow:

	April	May	June
Sales (all on account)	$300,000	$400,000	$250,000
Merchandise purchases.	$210,000	$160,000	$130,000
Payroll	$20,000	$20,000	$18,000
Lease payments.	$22,000	$22,000	$22,000
Advertising	$60,000	$60,000	$50,000
Equipment purchases.	—	—	$65,000
Depreciation.	$15,000	$15,000	$15,000

c. Merchandise purchases are paid in full during the month following purchase. Accounts payable for merchandise purchases during March, which will be paid in April, total $140,000.

d. In preparing the cash budget, assume that the $30,000 loan will be made in April and repaid in June. Interest on the loan will total $1,200.

Required:

1. Calculate the expected cash collections for April, May, and June, and for the three months in total.
2. Prepare a cash budget, by month and in total, for the three-month period.
3. If the company needs a minimum cash balance of $20,000 to start each month, can the loan be repaid as planned? Explain.

PROBLEM 8–24 Cash Budget with Supporting Schedules LO8–2, LO8–4, LO8–8

Garden Sales, Inc., sells garden supplies. Management is planning its cash needs for the second quarter. The company usually has to borrow money during this quarter to support peak sales of lawn care equipment, which occur during May. The following information has been assembled to assist in preparing a cash budget for the quarter:

a. Budgeted monthly absorption costing income statements for April–July are:

	April	May	June	July
Sales	$600,000	$900,000	$500,000	$400,000
Cost of goods sold	420,000	630,000	350,000	280,000
Gross margin	180,000	270,000	150,000	120,000
Selling and administrative expenses:				
Selling expense........................	79,000	120,000	62,000	51,000
Administrative expense*	45,000	52,000	41,000	38,000
Total selling and administrative expenses ...	124,000	172,000	103,000	89,000
Net operating income....................	$ 56,000	$ 98,000	$ 47,000	$ 31,000

*Includes $20,000 of depreciation each month.

b. Sales are 20% for cash and 80% on account.

c. Sales on account are collected over a three-month period with 10% collected in the month of sale; 70% collected in the first month following the month of sale; and the remaining 20% collected in the second month following the month of sale. February's sales totaled $200,000, and March's sales totaled $300,000.

d. Inventory purchases are paid for within 15 days. Therefore, 50% of a month's inventory purchases are paid for in the month of purchase. The remaining 50% is paid in the following month. Accounts payable at March 31 for inventory purchases during March total $126,000.

e. Each month's ending inventory must equal 20% of the cost of the merchandise to be sold in the following month. The merchandise inventory at March 31 is $84,000.

f. Dividends of $49,000 will be declared and paid in April.

g. Land costing $16,000 will be purchased for cash in May.

h. The cash balance at March 31 is $52,000; the company must maintain a cash balance of at least $40,000 at the end of each month.

i. The company has an agreement with a local bank that allows the company to borrow in increments of $1,000 at the beginning of each month, up to a total loan balance of $200,000. The interest rate on these loans is 1% per month and for simplicity we will assume that interest is not compounded. The company would, as far as it is able, repay the loan plus accumulated interest at the end of the quarter.

Required:

1. Prepare a schedule of expected cash collections for April, May, and June, and for the quarter in total.

2. Prepare the following for merchandise inventory:
    a. A merchandise purchases budget for April, May, and June.
    b. A schedule of expected cash disbursements for merchandise purchases for April, May, and June, and for the quarter in total.

3. Prepare a cash budget for April, May, and June as well as in total for the quarter.

PROBLEM 8–25 Cash Budget with Supporting Schedules; Changing Assumptions LO8–2, LO8–4, LO8–8

Refer to the data for Garden Sales, Inc., in Problem 8–24. The company's president is interested in knowing how reducing inventory levels and collecting accounts receivable sooner will impact the cash budget. He revises the cash collection and ending inventory assumptions as follows:

1. Sales continue to be 20% for cash and 80% on credit. However, credit sales from April, May, and June are collected over a three-month period with 25% collected in the month of sale, 65% collected in the month following sale, and 10% in the second month following sale. Credit sales from February and March are collected during the second quarter using the collection percentages specified in Problem 8–24.

2.   The company maintains its ending inventory levels for April, May, and June at 15% of the cost of merchandise to be sold in the following month. The merchandise inventory at March 31 remains $84,000 and accounts payable for inventory purchases at March 31 remains $126,000.

All other information from Problem 8–24 that is not referred to above remains the same.

Required:

1.   Using the president's new assumptions in (1) above, prepare a schedule of expected cash collections for April, May, and June and for the quarter in total.
2.   Using the president's new assumptions in (2) above, prepare the following for merchandise inventory:
     a.   A merchandise purchases budget for April, May, and June.
     b.   A schedule of expected cash disbursements for merchandise purchases for April, May, and June and for the quarter in total.
3.   Using the president's new assumptions, prepare a cash budget for April, May, and June, and for the quarter in total.
4.   Prepare a brief memorandum for the president explaining how his revised assumptions affect the cash budget.

PROBLEM 8–26 Behavioral Aspects of Budgeting; Ethics and the Manager LO8–1

Norton Company, a manufacturer of infant furniture and carriages, is in the initial stages of preparing the annual budget for next year. Scott Ford has recently joined Norton's accounting staff and wants to learn as much as possible about the company's budgeting process. During a recent lunch with Marge Atkins, sales manager, and Pete Granger, production manager, Ford initiated the following conversation.

Ford: Since I'm new around here and am going to be involved with the preparation of the annual budget, I'd be interested to learn how the two of you estimate sales and production numbers.
Atkins: We start out very methodically by looking at recent history, discussing what we know about current accounts, potential customers, and the general state of consumer spending. Then, we add that usual dose of intuition to come up with the best forecast we can.
Granger: I usually take the sales projections as the basis for my projections. Of course, we have to make an estimate of what this year's ending inventories will be, which is sometimes difficult.
Ford: Why does that present a problem? There must have been an estimate of ending inventories in the budget for the current year.
Granger: Those numbers aren't always reliable because Marge makes some adjustments to the sales numbers before passing them on to me.
Ford: What kind of adjustments?
Atkins: Well, we don't want to fall short of the sales projections so we generally give ourselves a little breathing room by lowering the initial sales projection anywhere from 5% to 10%.
Granger: So, you can see why this year's budget is not a very reliable starting point. We always have to adjust the projected production rates as the year progresses and, of course, this changes the ending inventory estimates. By the way, we make similar adjustments to expenses by adding at least 10% to the estimates; I think everyone around here does the same thing.

Required:

1.   Marge Atkins and Pete Granger have described the use of what is sometimes called *budgetary slack.*
     a.   Explain why Atkins and Granger behave in this manner and describe the benefits they expect to realize from the use of budgetary slack.
     b.   Explain how the use of budgetary slack can adversely affect Atkins and Granger.
2.   As a management accountant, Scott Ford believes that the behavior described by Marge Atkins and Pete Granger may be unethical. By referring to the IMA's Statement of Ethical Professional Practice in the Prologue, explain why the use of budgetary slack may be unethical.

(CMA, adapted)

PROBLEM 8–27 Cash Collections; Cash Disbursements; Budgeted Balance Sheet LO8–2, LO8–3, LO8–4, 8–10

Deacon Company is a merchandising company that is preparing a budget for the three-month period ended June 30. The following information is available:

Deacon Company
Balance Sheet
March 31

Assets

Cash.	$ 55,000
Accounts receivable.	36,000
Inventory.	40,000
Buildings and equipment, net of depreciation.	100,000
Total assets.	$231,000

Liabilities and Stockholders' Equity

Accounts payable	$ 51,300
Retained earnings.	179,700
Total liabilities and stockholders' equity	$231,000

Budgeted Income Statements

	April	May	June
Sales	$100,000	$110,000	$130,000
Cost of goods sold	60,000	66,000	78,000
Gross margin	40,000	44,000	52,000
Selling and administrative expenses	15,000	16,500	19,500
Net operating income.	$ 25,000	$ 27,500	$ 32,500

Budgeting Assumptions:
1. 60% of sales are cash sales and 40% of sales are credit sales. Twenty percent of all credit sales are collected in the month of sale and the remaining 80% are collected in the month subsequent to the sale.
2. Budgeted sales for July are $140,000.
3. 10% of merchandise inventory purchases are paid in cash at the time of the purchase. The remaining 90% of purchases are credit purchases. All purchases on credit are paid in the month subsequent to the purchase.
4. Each month's ending merchandise inventory should equal $10,000 plus 50% of the next month's cost of goods sold.
5. Depreciation expense is $1,000 per month. All other selling and administrative expenses are paid in full in the month the expense is incurred.

Required:
1. Calculate the expected cash collections for April, May, and June.
2. Calculate the budgeted merchandise purchases for April, May, and June.
3. Calculate the expected cash disbursements for merchandise purchases for April, May, and June.
4. Prepare a budgeted balance sheet at June 30. (Hint: You need to calculate the cash paid for selling and administrative expenses during April, May, and June to determine the cash balance in your June 30 balance sheet.)

PROBLEM 8–28 Cash Budget with Supporting Schedules LO8–2, LO8–4, LO8–7, LO8–8

Westex Products is a wholesale distributor of industrial cleaning products. When the treasurer of Westex Products approached the company's bank late in the current year seeking short-term financing, he was told that money was very tight and that any borrowing over the next year would have to be supported by a detailed statement of cash collections and disbursements. The treasurer also was told that it would be very helpful to the bank if borrowers would indicate the quarters in which they would be needing funds, as well as the amounts that would be needed, and the quarters in which repayments could be made.

Because the treasurer is unsure as to the particular quarters in which bank financing will be needed, he has assembled the following information to assist in preparing a detailed cash budget:

a. Budgeted sales and merchandise purchases for next year, as well as actual sales and purchases for the last quarter of the current year, are:

	Sales	Merchandise Purchases
Current Year:		
Fourth quarter actual	$200,000	$126,000
Next Year:		
First quarter estimated...........	$300,000	$186,000
Second quarter estimated........	$400,000	$246,000
Third quarter estimated	$500,000	$305,000
Fourth quarter estimated........	$200,000	$126,000

b. All sales are on account. The company normally collects 65% of a quarter's sales before the quarter ends and another 33% in the following quarter. The remainder is uncollectible. This pattern of collections is now being experienced in the current year's fourth-quarter actual data.

c. Eighty percent of a quarter's merchandise purchases are paid for within the quarter. The remainder is paid for in the following quarter.

d. Selling and administrative expenses for next year are budgeted at $50,000 per quarter plus 15% of sales. Of the fixed amount, $20,000 each quarter is depreciation.

e. The company will pay $10,000 in dividends each quarter.

f. Land purchases of $75,000 will be made in the second quarter, and purchases of $48,000 will be made in the third quarter. These purchases will be for cash.

g. The Cash account contained $10,000 at the end of the current year. The treasurer feels that this represents a minimum balance that must be maintained.

h. The company's bank allows borrowing in increments of $1,000 at the beginning of each quarter, up to a total loan balance of $100,000. The interest rate on these loans is 2.5% per quarter and for simplicity we will assume that interest is not compounded. The company would, as far as it is able, repay the loan plus accumulated interest at the end of the year.

i. At present, the company has no loans outstanding.

Required:

1. Calculate the expected cash collections by quarter and in total for next year.
2. Calculate the expected cash disbursements for merchandise purchases by quarter and in total for next year.
3. Calculate the expected cash disbursements for selling and administrative expenses, by quarter and in total for next year.
4. Prepare a cash budget by quarter and in total for next year.

PROBLEM 8–29 Completing a Master Budget LO8–2, LO8–4, LO8–7, LO8–8, LO8–9, LO8–10

The following data relate to the operations of Shilow Company, a wholesale distributor of consumer goods:

Current assets as of March 31:	
Cash	$8,000
Accounts receivable...............	$20,000
Inventory.......................	$36,000
Building and equipment, net...........	$120,000
Accounts payable	$21,750
Common stock.....................	$150,000
Retained earnings..................	$12,250

a. The gross margin is 25% of sales.

b. Actual and budgeted sales data:

March (actual)..............	$50,000
April......................	$60,000
May	$72,000
June.......................	$90,000
July	$48,000

c. Sales are 60% for cash and 40% on credit. Credit sales are collected in the month following sale. The accounts receivable at March 31 are a result of March credit sales.
d. Each month's ending inventory should equal 80% of the following month's budgeted cost of goods sold.
e. One-half of a month's inventory purchases is paid for in the month of purchase; the other half is paid for in the following month. The accounts payable at March 31 are the result of March purchases of inventory.
f. Monthly expenses are as follows: commissions, 12% of sales; rent, $2,500 per month; other expenses (excluding depreciation), 6% of sales. Assume that these expenses are paid monthly. Depreciation is $900 per month (includes depreciation on new assets).
g. Equipment costing $1,500 will be purchased for cash in April.
h. Management would like to maintain a minimum cash balance of at least $4,000 at the end of each month. The company has an agreement with a local bank that allows the company to borrow in increments of $1,000 at the beginning of each month, up to a total loan balance of $20,000. The interest rate on these loans is 1% per month and for simplicity we will assume that interest is not compounded. The company would, as far as it is able, repay the loan plus accumulated interest at the end of the quarter.

Required:
Using the preceding data:
1. Complete the following schedule:

Schedule of Expected Cash Collections	April	May	June	Quarter
Cash sales	$36,000			
Credit sales........................	20,000	____	____	____
Total collections....................	$56,000	====	====	====

2. Complete the following:

Merchandise Purchases Budget	April	May	June	Quarter
Budgeted cost of goods sold	$45,000*	$54,000		
Add desired ending inventory.........	43,200†	____	____	____
Total needs........................	88,200			
Less beginning inventory.............	36,000	____	____	____
Required purchases	$52,200	====	====	====

*For April sales: $60,000 sales × 75% cost ratio = $45,000.
†$54,000 × 80% = $43,200

Schedule of Expected Cash Disbursements—Merchandise Purchases	April	May	June	Quarter
March purchases.....................	$21,750			$21,750
April purchases	26,100	$26,100		52,200
May purchases.......................				
June purchases......................		____	____	____
Total disbursements	$47,850	====	====	====

3. Complete the following cash budget:

Cash Budget				
	April	May	June	Quarter
Beginning cash balance....................	$8,000			
Add cash collections......................	56,000	_____	_____	_____
Total cash available......................	64,000	_____	_____	_____
Less cash disbursements:				
For inventory	47,850			
For expenses............................	13,300			
For equipment..........................	1,500	_____	_____	_____
Total cash disbursements	62,650	_____	_____	_____
Excess (deficiency) of cash	1,350			
Financing:				
Etc.				

4. Using Schedule 9 as your guide, prepare an absorption costing income statement for the quarter ended June 30.
5. Prepare a balance sheet as of June 30.

PROBLEM 8–30 Integration of the Sales, Production, and Direct Materials Budgets LO8–2, LO8–3, LO8–4

Milo Company manufactures beach umbrellas. The company is preparing detailed budgets for the third quarter and has assembled the following information to assist in the budget preparation:

a. The Marketing Department has estimated sales as follows for the remainder of the year (in units):

July	30,000	October..................	20,000
August..................	70,000	November...............	10,000
September	50,000	December...............	10,000

The selling price of the beach umbrellas is $12 per unit.

b. All sales are on account. Based on past experience, sales are collected in the following pattern:

30% in the month of sale
65% in the month following sale
5% uncollectible

Sales for June totaled $300,000.

c. The company maintains finished goods inventories equal to 15% of the following month's sales. This requirement will be met at the end of June.

d. Each beach umbrella requires 4 feet of Gilden, a material that is sometimes hard to acquire. Therefore, the company requires that the ending inventory of Gilden be equal to 50% of the following month's production needs. The inventory of Gilden on hand at the beginning and end of the quarter will be:

June 30.................. 72,000 feet
September 30 .... ? feet

e. Gilden costs $0.80 per foot. One-half of a month's purchases of Gilden is paid for in the month of purchase; the remainder is paid for in the following month. The accounts payable on July 1 for purchases of Gilden during June will be $76,000.

Required:
1. Calculate the estimated sales, by month and in total, for the third quarter (Hint: Refer to Schedule 1 for guidance).
2. Calculate the expected cash collections, by month and in total, for the third quarter (Hint: Refer to Schedule 1 for guidance).
3. Calculate the estimated quantity of beach umbrellas that need to be produced in July, August, September, and October (Hint: Refer to Schedule 2 for guidance).

4. Calculate the quantity of Gilden (in feet) that needs to be purchased by month and in total, for the third quarter (Hint: Refer to Schedule 3 for guidance).
5. Calculate the cost of the raw material (Gilden) purchases by month and in total, for the third quarter (Hint: Refer to Schedule 3 for guidance).
6. Calculate the expected cash disbursements for raw material (Gilden) purchases, by month and in total, for the third quarter (Hint: Refer to Schedule 3 for guidance).

PROBLEM 8–31 Completing a Master Budget LO8–2, LO8–4, LO8–7, LO8–8, LO8–9, LO8–10

Hillyard Company, an office supplies specialty store, prepares its master budget on a quarterly basis. The following data have been assembled to assist in preparing the master budget for the first quarter:

a. As of December 31 (the end of the prior quarter), the company's general ledger showed the following account balances:

	Debits	Credits
Cash.	$ 48,000	
Accounts receivable	224,000	
Inventory	60,000	
Buildings and equipment (net)	370,000	
Accounts payable		$ 93,000
Common stock.		500,000
Retained earnings		109,000
	$702,000	$702,000

b. Actual sales for December and budgeted sales for the next four months are as follows:

December (actual)	$280,000
January	$400,000
February	$600,000
March.	$300,000
April	$200,000

c. Sales are 20% for cash and 80% on credit. All payments on credit sales are collected in the month following sale. The accounts receivable at December 31 are a result of December credit sales.
d. The company's gross margin is 40% of sales. (In other words, cost of goods sold is 60% of sales.)
e. Monthly expenses are budgeted as follows: salaries and wages, $27,000 per month: advertising, $70,000 per month; shipping, 5% of sales; other expenses, 3% of sales. Depreciation, including depreciation on new assets acquired during the quarter, will be $42,000 for the quarter.
f. Each month's ending inventory should equal 25% of the following month's cost of goods sold.
g. One-half of a month's inventory purchases is paid for in the month of purchase; the other half is paid in the following month.
h. During February, the company will purchase a new copy machine for $1,700 cash. During March, other equipment will be purchased for cash at a cost of $84,500.
i. During January, the company will declare and pay $45,000 in cash dividends.
j. Management wants to maintain a minimum cash balance of $30,000. The company has an agreement with a local bank that allows the company to borrow in increments of $1,000 at the beginning of each month. The interest rate on these loans is 1% per month and for simplicity we will assume that interest is not compounded. The company would, as far as it is able, repay the loan plus accumulated interest at the end of the quarter.

Required:

Using the data above, complete the following statements and schedules for the first quarter:

1. Schedule of expected cash collections:

	January	February	March	Quarter
Cash sales	$ 80,000			
Credit sales.	224,000			
Total cash collections	$304,000			

2. a. Merchandise purchases budget:

	January	February	March	Quarter
Budgeted cost of goods sold	$240,000*	$360,000		
Add desired ending inventory.	90,000†			
Total needs.	330,000			
Less beginning inventory.	60,000			
Required purchases	$270,000			

*$400,000 sales × 60% cost ratio = $240,000.
†$360,000 × 25% = $90,000.

b. Schedule of expected cash disbursements for merchandise purchases:

	January	February	March	Quarter
December purchases	$ 93,000			$ 93,000
January purchases	135,000	135,000		270,000
February purchases	—			
March purchases.	—			
Total cash disbursements				
for purchases.	$228,000			

3. Cash budget:

	January	February	March	Quarter
Beginning cash balance.	$ 48,000			
Add cash collections.	304,000			
Total cash available.	352,000			
Less cash disbursements:				
Inventory purchases	228,000			
Selling and administrative expenses	129,000			
Equipment purchases.	—			
Cash dividends	45,000			
Total cash disbursements	402,000			
Excess (deficiency) of cash	(50,000)			
Financing:				
Etc.				

4. Using Schedule 9 as your guide, prepare an absorption costing income statement for the quarter ending March 31.

5. Prepare a balance sheet as of March 31.

Cases   connect

CASE 8–32 Evaluating a Company's Budget Procedures LO8–1

Tom Emory and Jim Morris strolled back to their plant from the administrative offices of Ferguson & Son Manufacturing Company. Tom is manager of the machine shop in the company's factory; Jim is manager of the equipment maintenance department.

The men had just attended the monthly performance evaluation meeting for plant department heads. These meetings had been held on the third Tuesday of each month since Robert Ferguson, Jr., the president's son, had become plant manager a year earlier.

As they were walking, Tom Emory spoke: "Boy, I hate those meetings! I never know whether my department's accounting reports will show good or bad performance. I'm beginning to expect the worst. If the accountants say I saved the company a dollar, I'm called 'Sir,' but if I spend even a little too much—boy, do I get in trouble. I don't know if I can hold on until I retire."

Tom had just been given the worst evaluation he had ever received in his long career with Ferguson & Son. He was the most respected of the experienced machinists in the company. He had been with Ferguson & Son for many years and was promoted to supervisor of the machine shop when the company expanded and moved to its present location. The president (Robert Ferguson, Sr.) had often stated that the company's success was due to the high-quality work of machinists like Tom. As supervisor, Tom stressed the importance of craftsmanship and told his workers that he wanted no sloppy work coming from his department.

When Robert Ferguson, Jr., became the plant manager, he directed that monthly performance comparisons be made between actual and budgeted costs for each department. The departmental budgets were intended to encourage the supervisors to reduce inefficiencies and to seek cost reduction opportunities. The company controller was instructed to have his staff "tighten" the budget slightly whenever a department attained its budget in a given month; this was done to reinforce the plant manager's desire to reduce costs. The young plant manager often stressed the importance of continued progress toward attaining the budget; he also made it known that he kept a file of these performance reports for future reference when he succeeded his father.

Tom Emory's conversation with Jim Morris continued as follows:

Emory: I really don't understand. We've worked so hard to meet the budget, and the minute we do so they tighten it on us. We can't work any faster and still maintain quality. I think my men are ready to quit trying. Besides, those reports don't tell the whole story. We always seem to be interrupting the big jobs for all those small rush orders. All that setup and machine adjustment time is killing us. And quite frankly, Jim, you were no help. When our hydraulic press broke down last month, your people were nowhere to be found. We had to take it apart ourselves and got stuck with all that idle time.

Morris: I'm sorry about that, Tom, but you know my department has had trouble making budget, too. We were running well behind at the time of that problem, and if we'd spent a day on that old machine, we would never have made it up. Instead we made the scheduled inspections of the forklift trucks because we knew we could do those in less than the budgeted time.

Emory: Well, Jim, at least you have some options. I'm locked into what the scheduling department assigns to me and you know they're being harassed by sales for those special orders. Incidentally, why didn't your report show all the supplies you guys wasted last month when you were working in Bill's department?

Morris: We're not out of the woods on that deal yet. We charged the maximum we could to other work and haven't even reported some of it yet.

Emory: Well, I'm glad you have a way of getting out of the pressure. The accountants seem to know everything that's happening in my department, sometimes even before I do. I thought all that budget and accounting stuff was supposed to help, but it just gets me into trouble. It's all a big pain. I'm trying to put out quality work; they're trying to save pennies.

Required:
1. Identify the problems that appear to exist in Ferguson & Son Manufacturing Company's budgetary control system and explain how the problems are likely to reduce the effectiveness of the system.
2. Explain how Ferguson & Son Manufacturing Company's budgetary control system could be revised to improve its effectiveness.

(CMA, adapted)

CASE 8–33 Master Budget with Supporting Schedules LO8–2, LO8–4, LO8–8, LO8–9, LO8–10

You have just been hired as a new management trainee by Earrings Unlimited, a distributor of earrings to various retail outlets located in shopping malls across the country. In the past, the company has done very little in the way of budgeting and at certain times of the year has experienced a shortage of cash. Since you are well trained in budgeting, you have decided to prepare a master budget for the upcoming second quarter. To this end, you have worked with accounting and other areas to gather the information assembled below.

The company sells many styles of earrings, but all are sold for the same price—$10 per pair. Actual sales of earrings for the last three months and budgeted sales for the next six months follow (in pairs of earrings):

January (actual)	20,000	June (budget)	50,000
February (actual)	26,000	July (budget)	30,000
March (actual)	40,000	August (budget)	28,000
April (budget)	65,000	September (budget)	25,000
May (budget)	100,000		

The concentration of sales before and during May is due to Mother's Day. Sufficient inventory should be on hand at the end of each month to supply 40% of the earrings sold in the following month.

Suppliers are paid $4 for a pair of earrings. One-half of a month's purchases is paid for in the month of purchase; the other half is paid for in the following month. All sales are on credit. Only 20% of a month's sales are collected in the month of sale. An additional 70% is collected in the following month, and the remaining 10% is collected in the second month following sale. Bad debts have been negligible.

Monthly operating expenses for the company are given below:

Variable:	
Sales commissions	4% of sales
Fixed:	
Advertising	$200,000
Rent	$18,000
Salaries	$106,000
Utilities	$7,000
Insurance	$3,000
Depreciation.	$14,000

Insurance is paid on an annual basis, in November of each year.

The company plans to purchase $16,000 in new equipment during May and $40,000 in new equipment during June; both purchases will be for cash. The company declares dividends of $15,000 each quarter, payable in the first month of the following quarter.

The company's balance sheet as of March 31 is given below:

Assets

Cash.	$ 74,000
Accounts receivable ($26,000 February sales;	
$320,000 March sales)	346,000
Inventory.	104,000
Prepaid insurance	21,000
Property and equipment (net)	950,000
Total assets.	$1,495,000

Liabilities and Stockholders' Equity

Accounts payable	$ 100,000
Dividends payable.	15,000
Common stock.	800,000
Retained earnings	580,000
Total liabilities and stockholders' equity	$1,495,000

The company maintains a minimum cash balance of $50,000. All borrowing is done at the beginning of a month; any repayments are made at the end of a month.

The company has an agreement with a bank that allows the company to borrow in increments of $1,000 at the beginning of each month. The interest rate on these loans is 1% per month and for simplicity we will assume that interest is not compounded. At the end of the quarter, the company would pay the bank all of the accumulated interest on the loan and as much of the loan as possible (in increments of $1,000), while still retaining at least $50,000 in cash.

Required:
Prepare a master budget for the three-month period ending June 30. Include the following detailed schedules:
1.   a.   A sales budget, by month and in total.
    b.   A schedule of expected cash collections, by month and in total.
    c.   A merchandise purchases budget in units and in dollars. Show the budget by month and in total.
    d.   A schedule of expected cash disbursements for merchandise purchases, by month and in total.
2.   A cash budget. Show the budget by month and in total. Determine any borrowing that would be needed to maintain the minimum cash balance of $50,000.
3.   A budgeted income statement for the three-month period ending June 30. Use the contribution approach.
4.   A budgeted balance sheet as of June 30.

Flexible Budgets and Performance Analysis

Why Do Companies Need Flexible Budgets?

© Michael Sears/MCT/Newscom

The difficulty of accurately predicting future financial performance can be readily understood by reading the annual report of any publicly traded company. For example, **Nucor Corporation**, a steel manufacturer headquartered in Charlotte, North Carolina, cites numerous reasons why its actual results may differ from expectations, including the following: (1) changes in the supply and cost of raw materials; (2) changes in the availability and cost of electricity and natural gas; (3) changes in the market demand for steel products; (4) fluctuations in currency conversion rates; (5) significant changes in laws or government regulations; and (6) the cyclical nature of the steel industry. ■

Source: Nucor Corporation 2014 Annual Report.

LEARNING OBJECTIVES

After studying Chapter 9, you should be able to:

LO9–1 Prepare a planning budget and a flexible budget and understand how they differ from one another.

LO9–2 Calculate and interpret activity variances.

LO9–3 Calculate and interpret revenue and spending variances.

LO9–4 Prepare a performance report that combines activity variances and revenue and spending variances.

LO9–5 Prepare a flexible budget with more than one cost driver.

LO9–6 Understand common errors made in preparing performance reports based on budgets and actual results.

In the last chapter we explored how budgets are developed before a period begins. In this chapter, we explain how budgets can be adjusted to help guide actual operations and influence the performance evaluation process. For example, an organization's actual expenses will rarely equal its budgeted expenses as estimated at the beginning of the period. The reason is that the actual level of activity (such as unit sales) will rarely be the same as the budgeted activity; therefore, many actual expenses and revenues will naturally differ from what was budgeted. Should a manager be penalized for spending 10% more than budgeted for a variable expense like direct materials if unit sales are 10% higher than budgeted? Of course not. After studying this chapter, you'll know how to adjust a budget to enable meaningful comparisons to actual results.

The Variance Analysis Cycle

Companies use the *variance analysis cycle,* as illustrated in Exhibit 9–1, to evaluate and improve performance. The cycle begins with the preparation of performance reports in the accounting department. These reports highlight variances, which are the differences between the actual results and what should have occurred according to the budget. The variances raise questions. Why did this variance occur? Why is this variance larger than it was last period? The significant variances are investigated so that their root causes can be either replicated or eliminated. Then, next period's operations are carried out and the cycle begins again with the preparation of a new performance report for the latest period. The emphasis should be on highlighting superior and unsatisfactory results, finding the root causes of these outcomes, and then replicating the sources of superior achievement and eliminating the sources of unsatisfactory performance. The variance analysis cycle should not be used to assign blame for poor performance.

Managers frequently use the concept of *management by exception* in conjunction with the variance analysis cycle. **Management by exception** is a management system that compares actual results to a budget so that significant deviations can be flagged as exceptions and investigated further. This approach enables managers to focus on the most important variances while bypassing trivial discrepancies between the budget and actual results. For example, a variance of $5 is probably not big enough to warrant attention, whereas a variance of $5,000 might be worth tracking down. Another clue is the size of the variance relative to the amount of spending. A variance that is only 0.1% of spending on an item is probably caused by random factors. On the other hand, a variance of 10% of spending is much more likely to be a signal that something is wrong. In addition to

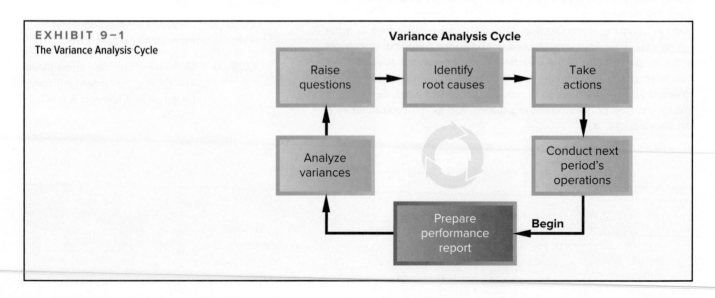

EXHIBIT 9–1
The Variance Analysis Cycle

Variance Analysis Cycle

watching for unusually large variances, the pattern of the variances should be monitored. For example, a run of steadily mounting variances should trigger an investigation even though none of the variances is large enough by itself to warrant investigation.

Next, we explain how organizations use flexible budgets to compare actual results to what should have occurred according to the budget.

Flexible Budgets

Characteristics of a Flexible Budget

The budgets that we explored in the last chapter were *planning budgets*. A **planning budget** is prepared before the period begins and is valid for only the planned level of activity. A static planning budget is suitable for planning but is inappropriate for evaluating how well costs are controlled. If the actual level of activity differs from what was planned, it would be misleading to compare actual costs to the static, unchanged planning budget. If activity is higher than expected, variable costs should be higher than expected; and if activity is lower than expected, variable costs should be lower than expected.

Flexible budgets take into account how changes in activity affect costs. A **flexible budget** is an estimate of what revenues and costs should have been, given the actual level of activity for the period. When a flexible budget is used in performance evaluation, actual costs are compared to what the costs *should have been for the actual level of activity during the period* rather than to the static planning budget. This is a very important distinction. If adjustments for the level of activity are not made, it is very difficult to interpret discrepancies between budgeted and actual costs.

> **LO9–1**
> Prepare a planning budget and a flexible budget and understand how they differ from one another.

IN BUSINESS

WINNERS AND LOSERS FROM THE NBA LOCKOUT

A company's actual net operating income can deviate from the budget for numerous and often uncontrollable reasons. For example, when the **National Basketball Association** (NBA) decided to suspend play because of a dispute between its team owners and players, many small businesses suffered—caterers, sports bars, apparel retailers, and parking lot owners all experienced a drop in revenues. **BestSportsApparel.com** experienced a substantial drop in NBA apparel sales due to the work stoppage. Rather than hiring 12 extra employees for the NBA season, the company reduced the size of its workforce.

While some companies lost revenues when the NBA shut down, others benefited from the situation. Andrew Zimbalist, professor of economics at Smith College, notes that "local economies are not impacted by sports work stoppages" because people choose to spend their entertainment dollars at other venues such as the theater, the zoo, or the museum.

Source: Emily Maltby and Sarah E. Needleman, "NBA Lockout: Local Firms Lose Big," *The Wall Street Journal*, October 13, 2011, p. B5.

© Jason O. Watson/Getty Images

Deficiencies of the Static Planning Budget

To illustrate the difference between a static planning budget and a flexible budget, consider Rick's Hairstyling, an upscale hairstyling salon located in Beverly Hills that is owned and managed by Rick Manzi. Recently Rick has been attempting to get better control of his revenues and costs, and at the urging of his accounting and business adviser, Victoria Kho, he has begun to prepare monthly budgets.

At the end of February, Rick prepared the March budget that appears in Exhibit 9–2. Rick believes that the number of customers served in a month (also known as the number of client-visits) is the best way to measure the overall level of activity in his salon. A customer who comes into the salon and has his or her hair styled is counted as one client-visit.

EXHIBIT 9–2
Planning Budget

Rick's Hairstyling Planning Budget For the Month Ended March 31	
Budgeted client-visits *(q)*	1,000
Revenue ($180.00*q*)	$180,000
Expenses:	
Wages and salaries ($65,000 + $37.00*q*)	102,000
Hairstyling supplies ($1.50*q*)	1,500
Client gratuities ($4.10*q*)	4,100
Electricity ($1,500 + $0.10*q*)	1,600
Rent ($28,500)	28,500
Liability insurance ($2,800)	2,800
Employee health insurance ($21,300)	21,300
Miscellaneous ($1,200 + $0.20*q*)	1,400
Total expense	163,200
Net operating income	$ 16,800

Note that the term *revenue* is used in the planning budget rather than *sales.* We use the term revenue throughout the chapter because some organizations have sources of revenue other than sales. For example, donations, as well as sales, are counted as revenue in nonprofit organizations.

Rick has identified eight major categories of costs—wages and salaries, hairstyling supplies, client gratuities, electricity, rent, liability insurance, employee health insurance, and miscellaneous. Client gratuities consist of flowers, candies, and glasses of champagne that Rick gives to his customers while they are in the salon.

Working with Victoria, Rick estimated a cost formula for each cost. For example, the cost formula for electricity is $1,500 + $0.10q$, where q equals the number of client-visits. In other words, electricity is a mixed cost with a $1,500 fixed element and a $0.10 per client-visit variable element. Once the budgeted level of activity was set at 1,000 client-visits, Rick computed the budgeted amount for each line item in the budget. For example, using the cost formula, he set the budgeted cost for electricity at $1,600 (= $1,500 + $0.10 × 1,000). To finalize his budget, Rick computed his expected net operating income for March of $16,800.

At the end of March, Rick prepared the income statement in Exhibit 9–3, which shows that 1,100 clients actually visited his salon in March and that his actual net operating income for the month was $21,230. It is important to realize that the actual results are *not* determined by plugging the actual number of client-visits into the revenue and cost formulas. The formulas are simply estimates of what the revenues and costs should be for a given level of activity. What actually happens usually differs from what is supposed to happen.

The first thing Rick noticed when comparing Exhibits 9–2 and 9–3 is that the actual profit of $21,230 (from Exhibit 9–3) was substantially higher than the budgeted profit of $16,800 (from Exhibit 9–2). This was, of course, good news, but Rick wanted to know more. Business was up by 10%—the salon had 1,100 client-visits instead of the budgeted 1,000 client-visits. Could this alone explain the higher net operating income? The answer is no. An increase in net operating income of 10% would have resulted in net operating income of only $18,480 (= 1.1 × $16,800), not the $21,230 actually earned during the month. What is responsible for this better outcome? Higher prices? Lower costs? Something else? Whatever the cause, Rick would like to know the answer and then hopefully repeat the same performance next month.

In an attempt to analyze what happened in March, Rick prepared the report comparing actual to budgeted costs that appears in Exhibit 9–4. Note that most of the variances in this report are labeled unfavorable (U) rather than favorable (F) even though net

EXHIBIT 9–3
Actual Results—Income Statement

Rick's Hairstyling
Income Statement
For the Month Ended March 31

Actual client-visits	1,100
Revenue	$194,200
Expenses:	
Wages and salaries	106,900
Hairstyling supplies	1,620
Client gratuities	6,870
Electricity	1,550
Rent	28,500
Liability insurance	2,800
Employee health insurance	22,600
Miscellaneous	2,130
Total expense	172,970
Net operating income	$ 21,230

EXHIBIT 9–4
Comparison of Actual Results to the
Static Planning Budget

Rick's Hairstyling
Comparison of Actual Results to the Planning Budget
For the Month Ended March 31

	Actual Results	Planning Budget	Variances*
Client-visits	1,100	1,000	
Revenue	$194,200	$180,000	$14,200 F
Expenses:			
Wages and salaries	106,900	102,000	4,900 U
Hairstyling supplies	1,620	1,500	120 U
Client gratuities	6,870	4,100	2,770 U
Electricity	1,550	1,600	50 F
Rent	28,500	28,500	0
Liability insurance	2,800	2,800	0
Employee health insurance	22,600	21,300	1,300 U
Miscellaneous	2,130	1,400	730 U
Total expense	172,970	163,200	9,770 U
Net operating income	$ 21,230	$ 16,800	$ 4,430 F

*The revenue variance is labeled favorable (unfavorable) when the actual revenue is greater than (less than) the planning budget. The expense variances are labeled favorable (unfavorable) when the actual expense is less than (greater than) the planning budget.

operating income was actually higher than expected. For example, wages and salaries show an unfavorable variance of $4,900 because the actual wages and salaries expense was $106,900, whereas the budget called for wages and salaries of $102,000. The problem with the report, as Rick immediately realized, is that it compares revenues and costs at one level of activity (1,000 client-visits) to revenues and costs at a different level of activity (1,100 client-visits). This is like comparing apples to oranges. Because Rick had 100 more client-visits than expected, some of his costs should be higher than budgeted. From Rick's standpoint, the increase in activity was good; however, it appears to be having a negative impact on most of the costs in the report. Rick knew that something would have to be done to make the report more meaningful, but he was unsure of what to do. So he made an appointment to meet with Victoria Kho to discuss the next step.

Victoria: How is the budgeting going?

Rick: Pretty well. I didn't have any trouble putting together the budget for March. I also prepared a report comparing the actual results for March to the budget, but that report isn't giving me what I really want to know.

Victoria: Because your actual level of activity didn't match your budgeted activity?

Rick: Right. I know the level of activity shouldn't affect my fixed costs, but we had more client-visits than I had expected and that had to affect my other costs.

Victoria: So you want to know whether the higher actual costs are justified by the higher level of activity?

Rick: Precisely.

Victoria: If you leave your reports and data with me, I can work on it later today, and by tomorrow I'll have a report to show you.

How a Flexible Budget Works

A flexible budget adjusts to show what costs *should be* for the actual level of activity. To illustrate how flexible budgets work, Victoria prepared the report in Exhibit 9–5 that shows what the *revenues and costs should have been given the actual level of activity* in March. Preparing the report is straightforward. The cost formula for each cost is used to estimate what the cost should have been for 1,100 client-visits—the actual level of activity for March. For example, using the cost formula $1,500 + $0.10q, the cost of electricity in March *should have been* $1,610 (= $1,500 + $0.10 × 1,100). Also, notice that the amounts of rent ($28,500), liability insurance ($2,800), and employee health insurance ($21,300) in the flexible budget equal the corresponding amounts in the planning budget (see Exhibit 9–2). This occurs because fixed costs are not affected by the activity level.

We can see from the flexible budget that the net operating income in March *should have been* $30,510, but recall from Exhibit 9–3 that the net operating income was actually only $21,230. The results are not as good as we thought. Why? We will answer that question shortly.

To summarize to this point, Rick had budgeted for a profit of $16,800. The actual profit was quite a bit higher—$21,230. However, Victoria's analysis shows that given the

---

EXHIBIT 9–5
Flexible Budget Based on Actual Activity

Rick's Hairstyling
Flexible Budget
For the Month Ended March 31

Actual client-visits (q)	1,100
Revenue ($180.000)q	$198,000
Expenses:	
Wages and salaries ($65,000 + $37.00q)	105,700
Hairstyling supplies ($1.50q)	1,650
Client gratuities ($4.10q)	4,510
Electricity ($1,500 + $0.10q)	1,610
Rent ($28,500)	28,500
Liability insurance ($2,800)	2,800
Employee health insurance ($21,300)	21,300
Miscellaneous ($1,200 + $0.20q)	1,420
Total expense	167,490
Net operating income	$ 30,510

actual number of client-visits in March, the profit should have been even higher—$30,510. What are the causes of these discrepancies? Rick would certainly like to build on the positive factors, while working to reduce the negative factors. But what are they?

Flexible Budget Variances

To answer Rick's questions concerning the discrepancies between budgeted and actual costs, Victoria broke down the variances shown in Exhibit 9–4 into two types of variances—activity variances and revenue and spending variances. We explain how she did it in the next two sections.

Activity Variances

Part of the discrepancy between the budgeted profit and the actual profit is due to the fact that the actual level of activity in March was higher than expected. How much of this discrepancy was due to this single factor? Victoria prepared the report in Exhibit 9–6 to answer this question. In that report, the flexible budget based on the actual level of activity for the period is compared to the planning budget from the beginning of the period. The flexible budget shows what should have happened at the actual level of activity, whereas the planning budget shows what should have happened at the budgeted level of activity. Therefore, the differences between the flexible budget and the planning budget show what should have happened solely because the actual level of activity differed from what had been expected.

For example, the flexible budget based on 1,100 client-visits shows revenue of $198,000 (= $180 per client-visit × 1,100 client-visits). The planning budget based on 1,000 client-visits shows revenue of $180,000 (= $180 per client-visit × 1,000 client-visits). Because the salon had 100 more client-visits than anticipated in the

LO9–2
Calculate and interpret activity variances.

	Flexible Budget	Planning Budget	Activity Variances*
Client-visits	1,100	1,000	
Revenue ($180.00q)	$198,000	$180,000	$18,000 F
Expenses:			
Wages and salaries ($65,000 + $37.00q)	105,700	102,000	3,700 U
Hairstyling supplies ($1.50q)	1,650	1,500	150 U
Client gratuities ($4.10q)	4,510	4,100	410 U
Electricity ($1,500 + $0.10q)	1,610	1,600	10 U
Rent ($28,500)	28,500	28,500	0
Liability insurance ($2,800)	2,800	2,800	0
Employee health insurance ($21,300)	21,300	21,300	0
Miscellaneous ($1,200 + $0.20q)	1,420	1,400	20 U
Total expense	167,490	163,200	4,290 U
Net operating income	$ 30,510	$ 16,800	$13,710 F

Rick's Hairstyling
Activity Variances
For the Month Ended March 31

EXHIBIT 9–6
Activity Variances from Comparing the Flexible Budget Based on Actual Activity to the Planning Budget

*The revenue variance is labeled favorable (unfavorable) when the revenue in the flexible budget is greater than (less than) the planning budget. The expense variances are labeled favorable (unfavorable) when the expense in the flexible budget is less than (greater than) the planning budget.

planning budget, actual revenue should have been higher than planned revenue by $18,000 (= $198,000 − $180,000). This activity variance is shown on the report as $18,000 F (favorable). Similarly, the flexible budget based on 1,100 client-visits shows electricity cost of $1,610 (= $1,500 + $0.10 per client-visit × 1,100 client-visits). The planning budget based on 1,000 client-visits shows electricity cost of $1,600 (= $1,500 + $0.10 per client-visit × 1,000 client-visits). Because the salon had 100 more client-visits than anticipated in the planning budget, the actual electricity cost should have been higher than the planned cost by $10 (= $1,610 − $1,600). The activity variance for electricity is shown on the report as $10 U (unfavorable). Note that in this case, the label "unfavorable" may be a little misleading. The electricity cost *should* be $10 higher because business was up by 100 client-visits; therefore, it would be misleading to describe this variance in negative terms given that it was a necessary cost of serving more customers. For reasons such as this, we would like to caution you against assuming that unfavorable variances always indicate bad performance and favorable variances always indicate good performance.

Because all of the variances on this report are solely due to the difference between the actual level of activity and the level of activity in the planning budget from the beginning of the period, they are called **activity variances**. For example, the activity variance for revenue is $18,000 F, the activity variance for electricity is $10 U, and so on. The most important activity variance appears at the very bottom of the report; namely, the $13,710 F (favorable) variance for net operating income. This variance says that because activity was higher than expected in the planning budget, the net operating income should have been $13,710 higher. We caution against placing too much emphasis on any other single variance in this report. As we have said above, one would expect some costs to be higher as a consequence of more business. It is misleading to think of these unfavorable variances as indicative of poor performance.

On the other hand, the favorable activity variance for net operating income is important. Let's explore this variance a bit more thoroughly. First, as we have already noted, activity was up by 10%, but the flexible budget indicates that net operating income should have increased much more than 10%. A 10% increase in net operating income from the $16,800 in the planning budget would result in net operating income of $18,480 (= 1.1 × $16,800); however, the flexible budget shows much higher net operating income of $30,510. Why? The short answer is: Because of the presence of fixed costs. When we apply the 10% increase to the budgeted net operating income to estimate the profit at the higher level of activity, we implicitly assume that the revenues and *all* of the costs increase by 10%. But they do not. Note that when the activity level increases by 10%, three of the costs—rent, liability insurance, and employee health insurance—do not increase at all. These are all entirely fixed costs. So while sales do increase by 10%, these costs do not increase. This results in net operating income increasing by more than 10%. A similar effect occurs with the mixed costs, which contain fixed cost elements—wages and salaries, electricity, and miscellaneous. While sales increase by 10%, these mixed costs increase by less than 10%, resulting in an overall increase in net operating income of more than 10%. Because of the existence of fixed costs, net operating income does not change in proportion to changes in the level of activity. There is a leverage effect. The percentage changes in net operating income are ordinarily larger than the percentage increases in activity.

Revenue and Spending Variances

LO9–3

Calculate and interpret revenue and spending variances.

In the last section we answered the question "What impact did the change in activity have on our revenues, costs, and profit?" In this section we will answer the question "How well did we control our revenues, our costs, and our profit?"

Recall that the flexible budget based on the actual level of activity in Exhibit 9–5 shows what *should have happened given the actual level of activity*. Therefore, Victoria's next step was to compare actual results to the flexible budget—in essence comparing what actually happened to what should have happened. Her work is shown in Exhibit 9–7.

Rick's Hairstyling Revenue and Spending Variances For the Month Ended March 31	Actual Results	Flexible Budget	Revenue and Spending Variances[*]	
Client-visits	1,100	1,100		
Revenue($180.00q)	$194,200	$198,000	$3,800	U
Expenses:				
Wages and salaries ($65,000 + $37.00q)	106,900	105,700	1,200	U
Hairstyling supplies ($1.50q)	1,620	1,650	30	F
Client gratuities ($4.10q)	6,870	4,510	2,360	U
Electricity ($1,500 + $0.10q)	1,550	1,610	60	F
Rent ($28,500)	28,500	28,500	0	
Liability insurance ($2,800)	2,800	2,800	0	
Employee health insurance ($21,300)	22,600	21,300	1,300	U
Miscellaneous ($1,200 + $0.20q)	2,130	1,420	710	U
Total expense	172,970	167,490	5,480	U
Net operating income	$ 21,230	$ 30,510	$9,280	U

[*]The revenue variance is labeled favorable (unfavorable) when the actual revenue is greater than (less than) the flexible budget. The expense variances are labeled favorable (unfavorable) when the actual expense is less than (greater than) the flexible budget.

EXHIBIT 9–7
Revenue and Spending Variances from Comparing Actual Results to the Flexible Budget

Focusing first on revenue, the actual revenue totaled $194,200. However, the flexible budget indicates that, given the actual level of activity, revenue should have been $198,000. Consequently, revenue was $3,800 less than it should have been, given the actual number of client-visits for the month. This discrepancy is labeled as a $3,800 U (unfavorable) variance and is called a *revenue variance*. A **revenue variance** is the difference between the actual total revenue and what the total revenue should have been, given the actual level of activity for the period. If actual revenue exceeds what the revenue should have been, the variance is labeled favorable. If actual revenue is less than what the revenue should have been, the variance is labeled unfavorable. Why would actual revenue be less than or more than it should have been, given the actual level of

IN BUSINESS

THE SALES IMPLICATIONS OF THE WORLD CUP

Actual sales volumes can differ from planned sales volumes for many reasons. For example, some companies may fail to consider how sporting events such as the World Cup will affect their planned sales. **Corning** said TV sales were up 13% in Europe and 64% in Latin America during the World Cup and **Carrefour** reported a bump in sales of its beer, soft drinks, and meats during the same period. Conversely, **Whirlpool** reported lower demand for its washing machines (because the company claimed that customers were spending their disposable income on TVs) and Denny's reported a drop in full-service dining during the World Cup.

Source: Vipal Monga and Emily Chasan, "When in Doubt, Blame It on the World Cup," *The Wall Street Journal*, July 31, 2014, pp. B1 and B4.

© andresr/Getty Images RF

activity? Basically, the revenue variance is favorable if the average selling price is greater than expected; it is unfavorable if the average selling price is less than expected. This could happen for a variety of reasons including a change in selling price, a different mix of products sold, a change in the amount of discounts given, poor accounting controls, and so on.

Focusing next on costs, the actual electricity cost was $1,550; however, the flexible budget indicates that electricity costs should have been $1,610 for the 1,100 client-visits in March. Because the cost was $60 less than we would have expected for the actual level of activity during the period, it is labeled as a favorable variance, $60 F. This is an example of a *spending variance*. A **spending variance** is the difference between the actual amount of the cost and how much a cost should have been, given the actual level of activity. If the actual cost is greater than what the cost should have been, the variance is labeled as unfavorable. If the actual cost is less than what the cost should have been, the variance is labeled as favorable. Why would a cost have a favorable or unfavorable variance? There are many possible explanations including paying a higher price for inputs than should have been paid, using too many inputs for the actual level of activity, a change in technology, and so on. In the next chapter we will explore these types of explanations in greater detail.

Note from Exhibit 9–7 that the overall net operating income variance is $9,280 U (unfavorable). This means that given the actual level of activity for the period, the net operating income was $9,280 lower than it should have been. There are a number of reasons for this. The most prominent is the unfavorable revenue variance of $3,800. Next in line is the $2,360 unfavorable variance for client gratuities. Looking at this in another way, client gratuities were more than 50% larger than they should have been according to the flexible budget. This is a variance that Rick would almost certainly want to investigate further. He may find that this unfavorable variance is not necessarily a bad thing. It is possible, for example, that more lavish use of gratuities led to the 10% increase in client-visits.

Exhibit 9–7 also includes a $1,300 unfavorable variance related to employee health insurance, thereby highlighting how a fixed cost can have a spending variance. While fixed costs do not depend on the level of activity, the actual amount of a fixed cost can differ from the estimated amount included in a flexible budget. For example, perhaps Rick's employee health insurance premiums unexpectedly increased by $1,300 during March.

In conclusion, the revenue and spending variances in Exhibit 9–7 will help Rick better understand why his actual net operating income differs from what should have happened given the actual level of activity.

A Performance Report Combining Activity and Revenue and Spending Variances

LO9–4
Prepare a performance report that combines activity variances and revenue and spending variances.

Exhibit 9–8 displays Victoria's performance report that combines the activity variances (from Exhibit 9–6) with the revenue and spending variances (from Exhibit 9–7). The report brings together information from those two earlier exhibits in a way that makes it easier to interpret what happened during the period. The format of this report is a bit different from the format of the previous reports in that the variances appear between the amounts being compared rather than after them. For example, the activity variances appear between the flexible budget amounts and the planning budget amounts. In Exhibit 9–6, the activity variances appeared after the flexible budget and the planning budget.

Note two numbers in particular in the performance report—the activity variance for net operating income of $13,710 F (favorable) and the overall revenue and spending variance for net operating income of $9,280 U (unfavorable). It is worth repeating what those two numbers mean. The $13,710 favorable activity variance occurred because actual activity (1,100 client-visits) was greater than the budgeted level of activity

EXHIBIT 9–8
Performance Report Combining Activity Variances with Revenue and Spending Variances

Rick's Hairstyling
Flexible Budget Performance Report
For the Month Ended March 31

	(1) Actual Results	Revenue and Spending Variances (1) – (2)	(2) Flexible Budget	Activity Variances (2) – (3)	(3) Planning Budget
Client-visits	1,100		1,100		1,000
Revenue ($180.00q)	$194,200	$3,800 U	$198,000	$18,000 F	$180,000
Expenses:					
Wages and salaries ($65,000 + $37.00q)	106,900	1,200 U	105,700	3,700 U	102,000
Hairstyling supplies ($1.50q)	1,620	30 F	1,650	150 U	1,500
Client gratuities ($4.10q)	6,870	2,360 U	4,510	410 U	4,100
Electricity ($1,500 + $0.10q)	1,550	60 F	1,610	10 U	1,600
Rent ($28,500)	28,500	0	28,500	0	28,500
Liability insurance ($2,800)	2,800	0	2,800	0	2,800
Employee health insurance ($21,300)	22,600	1,300 U	21,300	0	21,300
Miscellaneous ($1,200 + $0.20q)	2,130	710 U	1,420	20 U	1,400
Total expense	172,970	5,480 U	167,490	4,290 U	163,200
Net operating income	$ 21,230	$9,280 U	$ 30,510	$13,710 F	$ 16,800

(1,000 client-visits). The $9,280 unfavorable overall revenue and spending variance occurred because the profit was not as large as it should have been for the actual level of activity for the period. These two different variances mean very different things and call for different types of actions. To generate a favorable activity variance for net operating income, managers must take actions to increase client-visits. To generate a favorable overall revenue and spending variance, managers must take actions to protect selling prices, increase operating efficiency, and reduce the prices of inputs.

The performance report in Exhibit 9–8 provides much more useful information to managers than a simple comparison of the planning budget with actual results as shown in Exhibit 9–4. In Exhibit 9–4, the effects of changes in activity were jumbled together with the effects of how well prices were controlled and operations were managed. The performance report in Exhibit 9–8 clearly separates these effects, allowing managers to take a much more focused approach in evaluating operations.

To get a better idea of how the performance report accomplishes this task, look at hairstyling supplies in the performance report. The actual cost of hairstyling supplies was $1,620 for the period, whereas in the planning budget, this cost was $1,500. In the comparison of the actual results to the planning budget in Exhibit 9–4, this difference is shown as an unfavorable variance of $120. Exhibit 9–4 uses a static planning budget approach that compares actual costs at one level of activity to budgeted costs at a different level of activity. As we said before, this is like comparing apples to oranges. This variance is actually a mixture of two different effects. This becomes clear in the performance report in Exhibit 9–8. The $120 difference between the actual results and the budgeted amount is composed of two different variances—a favorable spending variance of $30 and an unfavorable activity variance of $150. The favorable spending variance occurred because less was spent on hairstyling supplies than one would have expected, given the actual level of activity for the month. The activity variance occurs because activity was greater than anticipated in the planning budget, which naturally resulted in a higher total cost for this variable cost.

The flexible budget performance report in Exhibit 9–8 provides a more valid assessment of performance than simply comparing actual costs to static planning budget costs because actual costs are compared to what costs should have been at the actual level of activity. In other words, apples are compared to apples. When this is done, we see that the spending variance for hairstyling supplies is $30 F (favorable) rather than $120 U (unfavorable) as it was in the original static planning budget performance report (see Exhibit 9–4). In some cases, as with hairstyling supplies in Rick's report, an unfavorable static planning budget variance may be transformed into a favorable revenue or spending variance when an increase in activity is properly taken into account. The following discussion took place the next day at Rick's salon.

MANAGERIAL ACCOUNTING IN ACTION
THE WRAP-UP

Victoria: Let me show you what I've got. [Victoria shows Rick the flexible budget performance report in Exhibit 9–8.] I simply used the cost formulas to update the budget to reflect the increase in client-visits you experienced in March. That allowed me to come up with a better benchmark for what the costs should have been.

Rick: That's what you labeled the "flexible budget based on 1,100 client-visits"?

Victoria: That's right. Your original budget was based on 1,000 client-visits, so it understated what some of the costs should have been when you actually served 1,100 customers.

Rick: That's clear enough. These spending variances aren't quite as shocking as the variances on my first report.

Victoria: Yes, but you still have an unfavorable variance of $2,360 for client gratuities.

Rick: I know how that happened. In March there was a big political fundraising dinner that I forgot about when I prepared the March budget. To fit all of our regular clients in, we had to push them through here pretty fast. Everyone still got top-rate service, but I felt bad about not being able to spend as much time with each customer. I wanted to give my customers a little extra something to compensate them for the less personal service, so I ordered a lot of flowers, which I gave away by the bunch.

Victoria: With the prices you charge, Rick, I am sure the gesture was appreciated.

Rick: One thing bothers me about the report. When we discussed my costs before, you called rent, liability insurance, and employee health insurance fixed costs. How can I have a variance for a fixed cost? Doesn't fixed mean that it doesn't change?

Victoria: We call these costs *fixed* because they shouldn't be affected by *changes in the level of activity.* However, that doesn't mean that they can't change for other reasons. Also, the use of the term *fixed* suggests to people that the cost can't be controlled, but that isn't true. It is often easier to control fixed costs than variable costs. For example, it would be fairly easy for you to change your insurance bill by adjusting the amount of insurance you carry. It would be much more difficult for you to significantly reduce your spending on hairstyling supplies—a variable cost that is a necessary part of serving customers.

Rick: I think I understand, but it *is* confusing.

Victoria: Just remember that a cost is called variable if it is proportional to activity; it is called fixed if it does not depend on the level of activity. However, fixed costs can change for reasons unrelated to changes in the level of activity. And controllability has little to do with whether a cost is variable or fixed. Fixed costs are often more controllable than variable costs.

CHILLY SPRING WEATHER BRINGS BIG DISCOUNTS AND LOWER MARGINS

Cold temperatures can keep shoppers away from malls. When April temperatures dropped below expectations so did sales at **Victoria's Secret**, **Bath & Body Works**, and **Aeropostale**. Fewer shoppers also can lead to big discounts as Aeropostale offered 50% off shorts to those who did choose to shop in its stores.

When these types of retailers establish their budgets for the spring, it is impossible for them to foresee months in advance how the weather may influence their sales, which in turn can have an impact on their revenue activity variances.

Source: Anna Prior and Karen Talley, "Weather Holds Back Retailers," *The Wall Street Journal*, May 10, 2013, p. B2.

© Austin Bush/Getty Images

Performance Reports in Nonprofit Organizations

The performance reports in nonprofit organizations are basically the same as the performance reports we have considered so far—with one prominent difference. Nonprofit organizations usually receive a significant amount of funding from sources other than sales. For example, universities receive their funding from sales (i.e., tuition charged to students), from endowment income and donations, and—in the case of public universities—from state appropriations. This means that, like costs, the revenue in governmental and nonprofit organizations may consist of both fixed and variable elements. For example, the **Seattle Opera Company**'s revenue in a recent year consisted of grants and donations of $12,719,000 and ticket sales of $8,125,000 (or about $75.35 per ticket sold). Consequently, the revenue formula for the opera can be written as:

$$\text{Revenue} = \$12,719,000 + \$75.35q$$

where q is the number of tickets sold. In other respects, the performance report for the Seattle Opera and other nonprofit organizations would be similar to the performance report in Exhibit 9–8.

Performance Reports in Cost Centers

Performance reports are often prepared for organizations that do not have any source of outside revenue. In particular, in a large organization a performance report may be prepared for each department—including departments that do not sell anything to outsiders. For example, a performance report is very commonly prepared for production departments in manufacturing companies. Such reports should be prepared using the same principles we have discussed and should look very much like the performance report in Exhibit 9–8—with the exception that revenue, and consequently net operating income, will not appear on the report. Because the managers in these departments are responsible for costs, but not revenues, they are often called *cost centers*.

Flexible Budgets with Multiple Cost Drivers

LO9–5
Prepare a flexible budget with more than one cost driver.

At Rick's Hairstyling, we have thus far assumed that there is only one cost driver—the number of client-visits. However, in the activity-based costing chapter, we found that more than one cost driver might be needed to adequately explain all of the costs in an organization. For example, some of the costs at Rick's Hairstyling probably depend more on the number of hours that the salon is open for business than the number of client-visits. Specifically, most of Rick's employees are paid salaries, but some are paid on an hourly basis. None of the

EXHIBIT 9–9
Flexible Budget Based on More than One Cost Driver

Rick's Hairstyling Flexible Budget For the Month Ended March 31	
Actual client-visits (q_1)	1,100
Actual hours of operation (q_2)	190
Revenue ($180.00q_1$)	$198,000
Expenses:	
Wages and salaries ($65,000 + $220q_2$)	106,800
Hairstyling supplies ($1.50q_1$)	1,650
Client gratuities ($4.10q_1$)	4,510
Electricity ($390 + $0.10q_1 + $6.00q_2$)	1,640
Rent ($28,500)	28,500
Liability insurance ($2,800)	2,800
Employee health insurance ($21,300)	21,300
Miscellaneous ($1,200 + $0.20q_1$)	1,420
Total expense	168,620
Net operating income	$ 29,380

employees is paid on the basis of the number of customers actually served. Consequently, the cost formula for wages and salaries would be more accurate if it were stated in terms of the hours of operation rather than the number of client-visits. The cost of electricity is even more complex. Some of the cost is fixed—the heat must be kept at some minimum level even at night when the salon is closed. Some of the cost depends on the number of client-visits—the power consumed by hair dryers depends on the number of customers served. Some of the cost depends on the number of hours the salon is open—the costs of lighting the salon and heating it to a comfortable temperature. Consequently, the cost formula for electricity would be more accurate if it were stated in terms of both the number of client-visits and the hours of operation rather than just in terms of the number of client-visits.

Exhibit 9–9 shows a flexible budget in which these changes have been made. In that flexible budget, two cost drivers are listed—client-visits and hours of operation—where q_1 refers to client-visits and q_2 refers to hours of operation. For example, wages and salaries depend on the hours of operation and its cost formula is $65,000 + $220q_2$. Because the salon actually operated 190 hours, the flexible budget amount for wages and salaries is $106,800 (= $65,000 + $220 × 190). The electricity cost depends on

IN BUSINESS

ON-CALL SCHEDULING DRAWS THE ATTENTION OF THE NEW YORK ATTORNEY GENERAL

The New York Attorney General has warned **Target, Gap,** and 11 other companies that their on-call employee scheduling practices may violate the law. These companies are using software programs to forecast immediate-term staffing needs based on real-time sales and customer traffic information. If a store is busy it requires its on-call employees to come to work, whereas if the store is not busy the employees do not come to work and they are not paid. In other words, the employees need to plan to be available even though they may or may not be called into work or get paid.

From a flexible budgeting standpoint, the companies are trying to make their labor costs variable with respect to sales and customer traffic. From a legal standpoint, the Attorney General noted that this compensation scheme leaves employees "too little time to make arrangements for family needs, let alone to find an alternative source of income to compensate for the lost pay."

Source: Lauren Weber, "Retailers Under Fire for Work Schedules," *The Wall Street Journal*, April 13, 2015, pp. B1–B2.

both client-visits and the hours of operation and its cost formula is $\$390 + \$0.10q_1 + \$6.00q_2$. Because the actual number of client-visits was $1,100$ and the salon actually operated for 190 hours, the flexible budget amount for electricity is $\$1,640$ (= $\$390 + \$0.10 \times 1,100 + \$6.00 \times 190$). Notice that the net operating income in the flexible budget based on two cost drivers is $\$29,380$, whereas the net operating income in the flexible budget based on one cost driver (see Exhibit 9–5) is $30,510. These two amounts differ because the flexible budget based on two cost drivers is more accurate than the flexible budget based on one driver.

The revised flexible budget based on both client-visits and hours of operation can be used exactly like we used the earlier flexible budget based on just client-visits to compute activity variances as in Exhibit 9–6, revenue and spending variances as in Exhibit 9–7, and a performance report as in Exhibit 9–8. The difference is that because the cost formulas based on more than one cost driver are more accurate than the cost formulas based on just one cost driver, the variances will also be more accurate.

Some Common Errors

We started this chapter by discussing the need for managers to understand the difference between what actually happened and what was expected to happen—formalized by the planning budget. To meet this need, we developed a flexible budget that allowed us to isolate activity variances and revenue and spending variances. Unfortunately, this approach is not always followed in practice—resulting in misleading and difficult-to-interpret reports. The most common errors in preparing performance reports are to implicitly assume that all costs are fixed or to implicitly assume that all costs are variable. These erroneous assumptions lead to inaccurate benchmarks and incorrect variances.

We have already discussed one of these errors—assuming that all costs are fixed. This is the error that is made when static planning budget costs are compared to actual costs without any adjustment for the actual level of activity. Such a comparison appeared in Exhibit 9–4. For convenience, the comparison of actual to planned revenues and costs is repeated in Exhibit 9–10. Looking at that exhibit, note that the actual cost of hairstyling supplies of $\$1,620$ is directly compared to the planned cost of $\$1,500$, resulting in an unfavorable variance of $\$120$. But this comparison only makes sense if the cost of hairstyling supplies is fixed. If the cost of hairstyling supplies isn't fixed (and indeed it is not), one would *expect*

LO9–6
Understand common errors made in preparing performance reports based on budgets and actual results.

EXHIBIT 9–10
Faulty Analysis Comparing Actual Amounts to Planned Amounts (Implicitly Assumes All Income Statement Items Are Fixed)

Rick's Hairstyling For the Month Ended March 31			
	Actual Results	Planning Budget	Variances
Client-visits	1,100	1,000	
Revenue	$194,200	$180,000	$14,200 F
Expenses:			
Wages and salaries	106,900	102,000	4,900 U
Hairstyling supplies	1,620	1,500	120 U
Client gratuities	6,870	4,100	2,770 U
Electricity	1,550	1,600	50 F
Rent	28,500	28,500	0
Liability insurance	2,800	2,800	0
Employee health insurance	22,600	21,300	1,300 U
Miscellaneous	2,130	1,400	730 U
Total expense	172,970	163,200	9,770 U
Net operating income	$ 21,230	$ 16,800	$ 4,430 F

SNOW REMOVAL BUDGETS GET PLOWED UNDER

The **District of Columbia** budgeted $6.2 million for its annual snow removal needs based on an expectation of 15 inches of snow per year. So, when it received 28 inches of snow in one weekend, its snow removal budget got plowed under. During this same weekend, the **Virginia Department of Transportation** estimated that 500,000 tons of snow dropped on its northern Virginia roadways, leading to historic cost overruns in its $79 million snow removal budget.

In these types of situations, a flexible budget can help managers assess operational efficiency. For example, a manager could create a cost formula such as "the snow removal cost per inch of snow" to estimate what the total variable snow removal costs should be for the actual inches of snowfall. This "flexed" snow removal cost could be compared to the actual snow removal cost in an effort to identify sources of exceptional performance or opportunities for process improvement.

Source: Sudeep Reddy and Clare Ansberry, "States Face Big Costs to Dig Out From Blizzard," *The Wall Street Journal*, February 9, 2010, p. A6.

© Getty Images RF

the cost to go up because of the increase in activity over the planning budget. Comparing actual costs to static planning budget costs only makes sense if the cost is fixed. If the cost isn't fixed, it needs to be adjusted for any change in activity that occurs during the period.

The other common error when comparing a planning budget to actual results is to assume that all costs are variable. A report that makes this error appears in Exhibit 9–11. The variances in this report are computed by comparing actual results to the amounts in the second numerical column where *all* of the items in the planning budget have been inflated by 10%—the percentage by which activity increased. This is a perfectly valid adjustment to make if an item is strictly variable—like sales and hairstyling supplies. It is *not* a valid adjustment if the item contains any fixed element. Take, for example, rent. If the salon serves 10% more customers in a given month, would you expect the rent to increase by 10%? The answer is no. Ordinarily, the rent is fixed in advance and does not depend on the volume of business. Therefore, the amount shown in the second numerical column of $31,350 is incorrect, which leads to the erroneous favorable variance of $2,850. In fact, the actual rent paid was exactly equal to the budgeted rent, so there should be no variance at all on a valid report.

EXHIBIT 9–11
Faulty Analysis That Assumes All Items in the Planning Budget Are Variable

Rick's Hairstyling For the Month Ended March 31			
	(1) Actual Results	(2) Planning Budget × (1,100/1,000)	Variances (1) – (2)
Client-visits	1,100		
Revenue	$194,200	$198,000	$3,800 U
Expenses:			
Wages and salaries	106,900	112,200	5,300 F
Hairstyling supplies	1,620	1,650	30 F
Client gratuities	6,870	4,510	2,360 U
Electricity	1,550	1,760	210 F
Rent	28,500	31,350	2,850 F
Liability insurance	2,800	3,080	280 F
Employee health insurance	22,600	23,430	830 F
Miscellaneous	2,130	1,540	590 U
Total expense	172,970	179,520	6,550 F
Net operating income	$ 21,230	$ 18,480	$2,750 F

Directly comparing actual revenues and costs to static planning budget revenues and costs can easily lead to erroneous conclusions. Actual revenues and costs differ from budgeted revenues and costs for a variety of reasons, but one of the biggest is a change in the level of activity. One would expect actual revenues and costs to increase or decrease as the activity level increases or decreases. Flexible budgets enable managers to isolate the various causes of the differences between budgeted and actual costs.

A flexible budget is a budget that is adjusted to the actual level of activity. It is the best estimate of what revenues and costs should have been, given the actual level of activity during the period. The flexible budget can be compared to the budget from the beginning of the period or to the actual results.

When the flexible budget is compared to the planning budget, activity variances are the result. An activity variance shows how a revenue or cost should have changed in response to the difference between actual and planned activity.

When actual results are compared to the flexible budget, revenue and spending variances are the result. A favorable revenue variance indicates that revenue was larger than should have been expected, given the actual level of activity. An unfavorable revenue variance indicates that revenue was less than it should have been, given the actual level of activity. A favorable spending variance indicates that the cost was less than expected, given the actual level of activity. An unfavorable spending variance indicates that the cost was greater than it should have been, given the actual level of activity.

A flexible budget performance report combines activity variances and revenue and spending variances on one report.

Common errors in comparing actual costs to budgeted costs are to assume all costs are fixed or to assume all costs are variable. If all costs are assumed to be fixed, the variances for variable and mixed costs will be incorrect. If all costs are assumed to be variable, the variances for fixed and mixed costs will be incorrect. The variance for a cost will only be correct if the actual behavior of the cost is used to develop the flexible budget benchmark.

Review Problem: Variance Analysis Using a Flexible Budget |

Harrald's Fish House is a family-owned restaurant that specializes in Scandinavian-style seafood. Data concerning the restaurant's monthly revenues and costs appear below (q refers to the number of meals served):

	Formula
Revenue	$16.50q$
Cost of ingredients	$6.25q$
Wages and salaries	$10,400
Utilities	$800 + $0.20q$
Rent	$2,200
Miscellaneous	$600 + $0.80q$

Required:
1. Prepare the restaurant's planning budget for April assuming that 1,800 meals are served.
2. Assume that 1,700 meals were actually served in April. Prepare a flexible budget for this level of activity.
3. The actual results for April appear below. Prepare a flexible budget performance report for the restaurant for April.

Revenue	$27,920
Cost of ingredients	$11,110
Wages and salaries	$10,130
Utilities	$1,080
Rent	$2,200
Miscellaneous	$2,240

Solution to Review Problem

1. The planning budget for April appears below:

Harrald's Fish House Planning Budget For the Month Ended April 30	
Budgeted meals served (q)	1,800
Revenue ($16.50q)	$29,700
Expenses:	
Cost of ingredients ($6.25q)	11,250
Wages and salaries ($10,400)	10,400
Utilities ($800 + $0.20q)	1,160
Rent ($2,200)	2,200
Miscellaneous ($600 + $0.80q)	2,040
Total expense	27,050
Net operating income	$ 2,650

2. The flexible budget for April appears below:

Harrald's Fish House Flexible Budget For the Month Ended April 30	
Actual meals served (q)	1,700
Revenue ($16.50q)	$28,050
Expenses:	
Cost of ingredients ($6.25q)	10,625
Wages and salaries ($10,400)	10,400
Utilities ($800 + $0.20q)	1,140
Rent ($2,200)	2,200
Miscellaneous ($600 + $0.80q)	1,960
Total expense	26,325
Net operating income	$ 1,725

3. The flexible budget performance report for April appears below:

	Harrald's Fish House Flexible Budget Performance Report For the Month Ended April 30				
	(1) Actual Results	Revenue and Spending Variances (1) – (2)	(2) Flexible Budget	Activity Variances (2) – (3)	(3) Planning Budget
Meals served	1,700		1,700		1,800
Revenue ($16.50q)	$27,920	$130 U	$28,050	$1,650 U	$29,700
Expenses:					
Cost of ingredients ($6.25q)	11,110	485 U	10,625	625 F	11,250
Wages and salaries ($10,400)	10,130	270 F	10,400	0	10,400
Utilities ($800 + $0.20q)	1,080	60 F	1,140	20 F	1,160
Rent ($2,200)	2,200	0	2,200	0	2,200
Miscellaneous ($600 + $0.80q)	2,240	280 U	1,960	80 F	2,040
Total expense	26,760	435 U	26,325	725 F	27,050
Net operating income	$ 1,160	$565 U	$ 1,725	$ 925 U	$ 2,650

Activity variance The difference between a revenue or cost item in the flexible budget and the same item in the static planning budget. An activity variance is due solely to the difference between the actual level of activity used in the flexible budget and the level of activity assumed in the planning budget. (p. 420)

Flexible budget A report showing estimates of what revenues and costs should have been, given the actual level of activity for the period. (p. 415)

Management by exception A management system in which actual results are compared to a budget. Significant deviations from the budget are flagged as exceptions and investigated further. (p. 414)

Planning budget A budget created at the beginning of the budgeting period that is valid only for the planned level of activity. (p. 415)

Revenue variance The difference between the actual revenue for the period and how much the revenue should have been, given the actual level of activity. A favorable (unfavorable) revenue variance occurs because the revenue is higher (lower) than expected, given the actual level of activity for the period. (p. 421)

Spending variance The difference between the actual amount of the cost and how much the cost should have been, given the actual level of activity. A favorable (unfavorable) spending variance occurs because the cost is lower (higher) than expected, given the actual level of activity for the period. (p. 422)

9–1   What is a static planning budget?
9–2   What is a flexible budget and how does it differ from a static planning budget?
9–3   What are some of the possible reasons that actual results may differ from what had been budgeted at the beginning of a period?
9–4   Why is it difficult to interpret a difference between how much expense was budgeted and how much was actually spent?
9–5   What is an activity variance and what does it mean?
9–6   What is a revenue variance and what does it mean?
9–7   What is a spending variance and what does it mean?
9–8   What does a flexible budget performance report do that a simple comparison of budgeted to actual results does not do?
9–9   How does a flexible budget based on two cost drivers differ from a flexible budget based on one cost driver?
9–10 What assumption is implicitly made about cost behavior when actual results are directly compared to a static planning budget? Why is this assumption questionable?
9–11 What assumption is implicitly made about cost behavior when all of the items in a static planning budget are adjusted in proportion to a change in activity? Why is this assumption questionable?

The Excel worksheet form that appears below is to be used to recreate the Review Problem relating to Harrald's Fish House. Download the workbook containing this form from Connect, where you will also receive instructions about how to use this worksheet form.
     You should proceed to the requirements below only after completing your worksheet.

LO9–1, LO9–2, LO9–3, LO9–4

Required:
1.   Check your worksheet by changing the revenue in cell D4 to $16.00; the cost of ingredients in cell D5 to $6.50; and the wages and salaries in cell B6 to $10,000. The activity variance for net operating income should now be $850 U and the spending variance for total expenses should be $410 U. If you do not get these answers, find the errors in your worksheet and correct them.
   a.   What is the activity variance for revenue? Explain this variance.
   b.   What is the spending variance for the cost of ingredients? Explain this variance.

	A	B	C	D	E	F	G	H
1	Chapter 9: Applying Excel							
2								
3	**Data**							
4	Revenue				$16.50 q			
5	Cost of ingredients				$6.25 q			
6	Wages and salaries	$10,400						
7	Utilities	$800	+		$0.20 q			
8	Rent	$2,200						
9	Miscellaneous	$600	+		$0.80 q			
10								
11	Actual results:							
12	Revenue	$27,920						
13	Cost of ingredients	$11,110						
14	Wages and salaries	$10,130						
15	Utilities	$1,080						
16	Rent	$2,200						
17	Miscellaneous	$2,240						
18								
19	Planning budget activity	1,800 meals served						
20	Actual activity	1,700 meals served						
21								
22	Enter a formula into each of the cells marked with a ? below							
23	**Review Problem: Variance Analysis Using a Flexible Budget**							
24								
25	**Construct a flexible budget performance report**							
26			*Revenue*					
27			*and*					
28		*Actual*	*Spending*		*Flexible*	*Activity*		*Planning*
29		*Results*	*Variances*		*Budget*	*Variances*		*Budget*
30	Meals served	?			?			?
31	Revenue	?	?		?	?		?
32	Expenses:							
33	Cost of ingredients	?	?		?	?		?
34	Wages and salaries	?	?		?	?		?
35	Utilities	?	?		?	?		?
36	Rent	?	?		?	?		?
37	Miscellaneous	?	?		?	?		?
38	Total expenses	?	?		?	?		?
39	Net operating income	?	?		?	?		?
40								

◄ ◄ ► ► **Chapter 9 Form** / Filled in Chapter 9 Form / Chapter 9 Form ◄

2. Revise the data in your worksheet to reflect the results for the following year:

Data		
Revenue		$16.50q
Cost of ingredients		$6.25q
Wages and salaries	$10,400	
Utilities	$800 +	$0.20q
Rent	$2,200	
Miscellaneous	$600 +	$0.80q
Actual results:		
Revenue	$28,900	
Cost of ingredients	$11,300	
Wages and salaries	$10,300	
Utilities	$1,120	
Rent	$2,300	
Miscellaneous	$2,020	
Planning budget activity	1,700 meals served	
Actual activity	1,800 meals served	

Using the flexible budget performance report, briefly evaluate the company's performance for the year and indicate where attention should be focused.

■ connect **The Foundational 15**

Adger Corporation is a service company that measures its output based on the number of customers served. The company provided the following fixed and variable cost estimates that it uses for budgeting purposes and the actual results for May as shown below:

LO9–1, LO9–2, LO9–3

	Fixed Element per Month	Variable Element per Customer Served	Actual Total for May
Revenue		$5,000	$160,000
Employee salaries and wages	$50,000	$1,100	$88,000
Travel expenses		$600	$19,000
Other expenses	$36,000		$34,500

When preparing its planning budget the company estimated that it would serve 30 customers per month; however, during May the company actually served 35 customers.

Required (all computations pertain to the month of May):
1. What amount of revenue would be included in Adger's flexible budget?
2. What amount of employee salaries and wages would be included in Adger's flexible budget?
3. What amount of travel expenses would be included in Adger's flexible budget?
4. What amount of other expenses would be included in Adger's flexible budget?
5. What net operating income would appear in Adger's flexible budget?
6. What is Adger's revenue variance?
7. What is Adger's employee salaries and wages spending variance?
8. What is Adger's travel expenses spending variance?
9. What is Adger's other expenses spending variance?
10. What amount of revenue would be included in Adger's planning budget?
11. What amount of employee salaries and wages would be included in Adger's planning budget?
12. What amount of travel expenses would be included in Adger's planning budget?
13. What amount of other expenses would be included in Adger's planning budget?
14. What activity variance would Adger report with respect to its revenue?
15. What activity variances would Adger report with respect to each of its expenses?

■ connect **Exercises**

EXERCISE 9–1 Prepare a Flexible Budget LO9–1
Puget Sound Divers is a company that provides diving services such as underwater ship repairs to clients in the Puget Sound area. The company's planning budget for May appears below:

Puget Sound Divers Planning Budget For the Month Ended May 31	
Budgeted diving-hours (q)	100
Revenue ($365.00q)	$36,500
Expenses:	
Wages and salaries ($8,000 + $125.00q)	20,500
Supplies ($3.00q)	300
Equipment rental ($1,800 + $32.00q)	5,000
Insurance ($3,400)	3,400
Miscellaneous ($630 + $1.80q)	810
Total expense	30,010
Net operating income	$ 6,490

During May, the company's actual activity was 105 diving-hours.

Required:
Using Exhibit 9–5 as your guide, prepare a flexible budget for May.

EXERCISE 9–2 Activity Variances LO9–2

Flight Café prepares in-flight meals for airlines in its kitchen located next to a local airport. The company's planning budget for July appears below:

Flight Café Planning Budget For the Month Ended July 31	
Budgeted meals (q)	18,000
Revenue ($4.50q)	$81,000
Expenses:	
Raw materials ($2.40q)	43,200
Wages and salaries ($5,200 + $0.30q)	10,600
Utilities ($2,400 + $0.05q)	3,300
Facility rent ($4,300)	4,300
Insurance ($2,300)	2,300
Miscellaneous ($680 + $0.10q)	2,480
Total expense	66,180
Net operating income	$14,820

In July, 17,800 meals were actually served. The company's flexible budget for this level of activity appears below:

Flight Café Flexible Budget For the Month Ended July 31	
Budgeted meals (q)	17,800
Revenue ($4.50q)	$80,100
Expenses:	
Raw materials ($2.40q)	42,720
Wages and salaries ($5,200 + $0.30q)	10,540
Utilities ($2,400 + $0.05q)	3,290
Facility rent ($4,300)	4,300
Insurance ($2,300)	2,300
Miscellaneous ($680 + $0.10q)	2,460
Total expense	65,610
Net operating income	$14,490

Required:

1. Calculate the company's activity variances for July. (Hint: Refer to Exhibit 9–6.)
2. Which of the activity variances should be of concern to management? Explain.

EXERCISE 9–3 Revenue and Spending Variances LO9–3

Quilcene Oysteria farms and sells oysters in the Pacific Northwest. The company harvested and sold 8,000 pounds of oysters in August. The company's flexible budget for August appears below:

Quilcene Oysteria Flexible Budget For the Month Ended August 31	
Actual pounds (q)	8,000
Revenue ($4.00q)	$ 32,000
Expenses:	
Packing supplies ($0.50q)	4,000
Oyster bed maintenance ($3,200)	3,200
Wages and salaries ($2,900 + $0.30q)	5,300
Shipping ($0.80q)	6,400
Utilities ($830)	830
Other ($450 + $0.05q)	850
Total expense	20,580
Net operating income	$ 11,420

The actual results for August appear below:

Quilcene Oysteria Income Statement For the Month Ended August 31	
Actual pounds	8,000
Revenue	$35,200
Expenses:	
Packing supplies	4,200
Oyster bed maintenance	3,100
Wages and salaries	5,640
Shipping	6,950
Utilities	810
Other	980
Total expense	21,680
Net operating income	$13,520

Required:

Calculate the company's revenue and spending variances for August. (Hint: Refer to Exhibit 9–7.)

EXERCISE 9–4 Prepare a Flexible Budget Performance Report LO9–4

Vulcan Flyovers offers scenic overflights of Mount St. Helens, the volcano in Washington State that explosively erupted in 1982. Data concerning the company's operations in July appear below:

Vulcan Flyovers Operating Data For the Month Ended July 31			
	Actual Results	Flexible Budget	Planning Budget
Flights (q)	48	48	50
Revenue ($320.00q)	$13,650	$15,360	$16,000
Expenses:			
Wages and salaries ($4,000 + $82.00q)	8,430	7,936	8,100
Fuel ($23.00q)	1,260	1,104	1,150
Airport fees ($650 + $38.00q)	2,350	2,474	2,550
Aircraft depreciation ($7.00q)	336	336	350
Office expenses ($190 + $2.00q)	460	286	290
Total expense	12,836	12,136	12,440
Net operating income	$ 814	$ 3,224	$ 3,560

The company measures its activity in terms of flights. Customers can buy individual tickets for overflights or hire an entire plane for an overflight at a discount.

Required:

1. Using Exhibit 9–8 as your guide, prepare a flexible budget performance report for July that includes revenue and spending variances and activity variances.
2. Which of the variances should be of concern to management? Explain.

EXERCISE 9–5 Prepare a Flexible Budget with More Than One Cost Driver LO9–5

Alyeski Tours operates day tours of coastal glaciers in Alaska on its tour boat the Blue Glacier. Management has identified two cost drivers—the number of cruises and the number of passengers— that it uses in its budgeting and performance reports. The company publishes a schedule of day cruises that it may supplement with special sailings if there is sufficient demand. Up to 80 passengers can be accommodated on the tour boat. Data concerning the company's cost formulas appear below:

	Fixed Cost per Month	Cost per Cruise	Cost per Passenger
Vessel operating costs	$5,200	$480.00	$2.00
Advertising	$1,700		
Administrative costs	$4,300	$24.00	$1.00
Insurance	$2,900		

For example, vessel operating costs should be $5,200 per month plus $480 per cruise plus $2 per passenger. The company's sales should average $25 per passenger. In July, the company provided 24 cruises for a total of 1,400 passengers.

Required:

Using Exhibit 9–9 as your guide, prepare the company's flexible budget for July.

EXERCISE 9–6 Critique a Variance Report LO9–6

The Terminator Inc. provides on-site residential pest extermination services. The company has several mobile teams who are dispatched from a central location in company-owned trucks. The company uses the number of jobs to measure activity. At the beginning of April, the company budgeted for 100 jobs, but the actual number of jobs turned out to be 105. A report comparing the budgeted revenues and costs to the actual revenues and costs appears below:

	Actual Results	Planning Budget	Variances
The Terminator Inc.			
Variance Report			
For the Month Ended April 30			
Jobs	105	100	
Revenue	$20,520	$19,500	$ 1,020 F
Expenses:			
Mobile team operating costs	10,320	10,000	320 U
Exterminating supplies	960	1,800	840 F
Advertising	800	800	0
Dispatching costs	2,340	2,200	140 U
Office rent	1,800	1,800	0
Insurance	2,100	2,100	0
Total expense	18,320	18,700	380 F
Net operating income	$ 2,200	$ 800	$ 1,400 F

Required:

Is the above variance report useful for evaluating how well revenues and costs were controlled during April? Why, or why not?

EXERCISE 9–7 Critique a Variance Report LO9–6

Refer to the data for The Terminator Inc. in Exercise 9–6. A management intern has suggested that the budgeted revenues and costs should be adjusted for the actual level of activity in April before they are compared to the actual revenues and costs. Because the actual level of activity was 5% higher than budgeted, the intern suggested that all budgeted revenues and costs should be adjusted upward by 5%. A report comparing the budgeted revenues and costs, with this adjustment, to the actual revenues and costs appears below.

	Actual Results	Adjusted Planning Budget	Variances
The Terminator Inc.			
Variance Report			
For the Month Ended April 30			
Jobs	105	105	
Revenue	$20,520	$20,475	$ 45 F
Expenses:			
Mobile team operating costs	10,320	10,500	180 F
Exterminating supplies	960	1,890	930 F
Advertising	800	840	40 F
Dispatching costs	2,340	2,310	30 U
Office rent	1,800	1,890	90 F
Insurance	2,100	2,205	105 F
Total expense	18,320	19,635	1,315 F
Net operating income	$ 2,200	$ 840	$1,360 F

Required:

Is the above variance report useful for evaluating how well revenues and costs were controlled during April? Why, or why not?

EXERCISE 9–8 Flexible Budgets and Activity Variances LO9–1, LO9–2

Jake's Roof Repair has provided the following data concerning its costs:

	Fixed Cost per Month	Cost per Repair-Hour
Wages and salaries	$23,200	$16.30
Parts and supplies		$8.60
Equipment depreciation	$1,600	$0.40
Truck operating expenses	$6,400	$1.70
Rent	$3,480	
Administrative expenses	$4,500	$0.80

For example, wages and salaries should be $23,200 plus $16.30 per repair hour. The company expected to work 2,800 repair-hours in May, but actually worked 2,900 repair-hours. The company expects its sales to be $44.50 per repair-hour.

Required:

Compute the company's activity variances for May. (Hint: Refer to Exhibit 9–6.)

EXERCISE 9–9 Planning Budget LO9–1

Wyckam Manufacturing Inc. has provided the following information concerning its manufacturing costs:

	Fixed Cost per Month	Cost per Machine-Hour
Direct materials		$4.25
Direct labor	$36,800	
Supplies		$0.30
Utilities	$1,400	$0.05
Depreciation	$16,700	
Insurance	$12,700	

For example, utilities should be $1,400 per month plus $0.05 per machine-hour. The company expects to work 5,000 machine-hours in June. Note that the company's direct labor is a fixed cost.

Required:

Using Exhibit 9–2 as your guide, prepare the company's planning budget for June.

EXERCISE 9–10 Planning Budget LO9–1

Lavage Rapide is a Canadian company that owns and operates a large automatic car wash facility near Montreal. The following table provides data concerning the company's costs:

	Fixed Cost per Month	Cost per Car Washed
Cleaning supplies		$0.80
Electricity	$1,200	$0.15
Maintenance		$0.20
Wages and salaries	$5,000	$0.30
Depreciation	$6,000	
Rent	$8,000	
Administrative expenses	$4,000	$0.10

For example, electricity costs are $1,200 per month plus $0.15 per car washed. The company expects to wash 9,000 cars in August and to collect an average of $4.90 per car washed.

Required:

Using Exhibit 9–2 as your guide, prepare the company's planning budget for August.

EXERCISE 9–11 Flexible Budget LO9–1

Refer to the data for Lavage Rapide in Exercise 9–10. The company actually washed 8,800 cars in August.

Required:

Using Exhibit 9–5 as your guide, prepare the company's flexible budget for August.

EXERCISE 9–12 Activity Variances LO9–2

Refer to the data for Lavage Rapide in Exercise 9–10. The company actually washed 8,800 cars in August.

Required:

Calculate the company's activity variances for August. (Hint: Refer to Exhibit 9–6.)

EXERCISE 9–13 Revenue and Spending Variances LO9–3

Refer to the data for Lavage Rapide in Exercise 9–10. Also assume that the company's actual operating results for August are as follows:

Lavage Rapide Income Statement For the Month Ended August 31	
Actual cars washed	8,800
Revenue	$43,080
Expenses:	
Cleaning supplies	7,560
Electricity	2,670
Maintenance	2,260
Wages and salaries	8,500
Depreciation	6,000
Rent	8,000
Administrative expenses	4,950
Total expense	39,940
Net operating income	$ 3,140

Required:

Calculate the company's revenue and spending variances for August. (Hint: Refer to Exhibit 9–7.)

EXERCISE 9–14 Prepare a Flexible Budget Performance Report LO9–4

Refer to the data for Lavage Rapide in Exercises 9–10 and 9–13.

Required:

Using Exhibit 9–8 as your guide, prepare a flexible budget performance report that shows the company's revenue and spending variances and activity variances for August.

EXERCISE 9–15 Flexible Budget Performance Report in a Cost Center LO9–1, LO9–2, LO9–3, LO9–4

Packaging Solutions Corporation manufactures and sells a wide variety of packaging products. Performance reports are prepared monthly for each department. The planning budget and flexible budget for the Production Department are based on the following formulas, where q is the number of labor-hours worked in a month:

	Cost Formulas
Direct labor	$15.80q$
Indirect labor	$8,200 + $1.60q$
Utilities	$6,400 + $0.80q$
Supplies	$1,100 + $0.40q$
Equipment depreciation	$23,000 + $3.70q$
Factory rent	$8,400
Property taxes	$2,100
Factory administration	$11,700 + $1.90q$

The Production Department planned to work 8,000 labor-hours in March; however, it actually worked 8,400 labor-hours during the month. Its actual costs incurred in March are listed below:

	Actual Cost Incurred in March
Direct labor	$134,730
Indirect labor	$19,860
Utilities	$14,570
Supplies	$4,980
Equipment depreciation	$54,080
Factory rent	$8,700
Property taxes	$2,100
Factory administration	$26,470

Required:

1. Using Exhibit 9–2 as your guide, prepare the Production Department's planning budget for the month.
2. Using Exhibit 9–5 as your guide, prepare the Production Department's flexible budget for the month.
3. Using Exhibit 9–8 as your guide, prepare the Production Department's flexible budget performance report for March, including both the spending and activity variances.
4. What aspects of the flexible budget performance report should be brought to management's attention? Explain.

EXERCISE 9–16 Flexible Budgets and Revenue and Spending Variances LO9–1, LO9–3

Via Gelato is a popular neighborhood gelato shop. The company has provided the following cost formulas and actual results for the month of June:

	Fixed Element per Month	Variable Element per Liter	Actual Total for June
Revenue		$12.00	$71,540
Raw materials		$4.65	$29,230
Wages	$5,600	$1.40	$13,860
Utilities	$1,630	$0.20	$3,270
Rent	$2,600		$2,600
Insurance	$1,350		$1,350
Miscellaneous	$650	$0.35	$2,590

While gelato is sold by the cone or cup, the shop measures its activity in terms of the total number of liters of gelato sold. For example, wages should be $5,600 plus $1.40 per liter of gelato sold and the actual wages for June were $13,860. Via Gelato expected to sell 6,000 liters in June, but actually sold 6,200 liters.

Required:

Calculate Via Gelato revenue and spending variances for June. (Hint: Refer to Exhibit 9–7.)

EXERCISE 9–17 Flexible Budget Performance Report LO9–1, LO9–2, LO9–3, LO9–4

AirQual Test Corporation provides on-site air quality testing services. The company has provided the following cost formulas and actual results for the month of February:

	Fixed Component per Month	Variable Component per Job	Actual Total for February
Revenue		$360	$18,950
Technician wages	$6,400		$6,450
Mobile lab operating expenses	$2,900	$35	$4,530
Office expenses	$2,600	$2	$3,050
Advertising expenses	$970		$995
Insurance	$1,680		$1,680
Miscellaneous expenses	$500	$3	$465

The company uses the number of jobs as its measure of activity. For example, mobile lab operating expenses should be $2,900 plus $35 per job, and the actual mobile lab operating expenses for February were $4,530. The company expected to work 50 jobs in February, but actually worked 52 jobs.

Required:

Using Exhibit 9–8 as your guide, prepare a flexible budget performance report showing AirQual Test Corporation's revenue and spending variances and activity variances for February.

EXERCISE 9–18 Working with More Than One Cost Driver LO9–2, LO9–3, LO9–4, LO9–5

The Gourmand Cooking School runs short cooking courses at its small campus. Management has identified two cost drivers it uses in its budgeting and performance reports—the number of courses and the total number of students. For example, the school might run two courses in a month and have a total of 50 students enrolled in those two courses. Data concerning the company's cost formulas appear below:

	Fixed Cost per Month	Cost per Course	Cost per Student
Instructor wages		$3,080	
Classroom supplies			$260
Utilities	$870	$130	
Campus rent	$4,200		
Insurance	$1,890		
Administrative expenses	$3,270	$15	$4

For example, administrative expenses should be $3,270 per month plus $15 per course plus $4 per student. The company's sales should average $800 per student.

The company planned to run three courses with a total of 45 students; however, it actually ran three courses with a total of only 42 students. The actual operating results for September appear below:

	Actual
Revenue	$32,400
Instructor wages	$9,080
Classroom supplies	$8,540
Utilities	$1,530
Campus rent	$4,200
Insurance	$1,890
Administrative expenses	$3,790

Required:

Using Exhibits 9–8 and 9–9 as your guide, prepare a flexible budget performance report that shows both revenue and spending variances and activity variances for September.

Problems   

PROBLEM 9–19: Flexible Budget Performance Reports; Working Backwards LO 9–1, LO 9–2, 9–3, 9–4

Ray Company provided the following excerpts from its Production Department's flexible budget performance report:

Ray Company Production Department Flexible Budget Performance Report For the Month Ended August 31					
	Actual Results	Spending Variances	Flexible Budget	Activity Variances	Planning Budget
Labor-hours (*q*)	9,480		?		9,000
Direct labor ($?*q*)	$134,730	$?	$132,720	$?	$?
Indirect labor ($? + $1.50*q*)	?	1,780 F	21,640	?	?
Utilities ($6,500 + $?*q*)	?	1,450 U	?	336 U	12,800
Supplies ($? + $?*q*)	4,940	?	4,444	?	4,300
Equipment depreciation ($78,400)	?	0	?	?	?
Factory administration ($18,700 + $1.90*q*)	?	?	?	?	?
Total expense	$288,088	$?	$?	$?	$?

Required:
Complete the Production Department's Flexible Budget Performance Report by filling in all the question marks.

PROBLEM 9–20 Activity and Spending Variances LO9–1, LO9–2, LO9–3
You have just been hired by FAB Corporation, the manufacturer of a revolutionary new garage door opening device. The president has asked that you review the company's costing system and "do what you can to help us get better control of our manufacturing overhead costs." You find that the company has never used a flexible budget, and you suggest that preparing such a budget would be an excellent first step in overhead planning and control.

After much effort and analysis, you determined the following cost formulas and gathered the following actual cost data for March:

	Cost Formula	Actual Cost in March
Utilities	$20,600 + $0.10 per machine-hour	$24,200
Maintenance	$40,000 + $1.60 per machine-hour	$78,100
Supplies	$0.30 per machine-hour	$8,400
Indirect labor	$130,000 + $0.70 per machine-hour	$149,600
Depreciation	$70,000	$71,500

During March, the company worked 26,000 machine-hours and produced 15,000 units. The company had originally planned to work 30,000 machine-hours during March.

Required:
1. Calculate the activity variances for March. (Hint: Refer to Exhibit 9–6.) Explain what these variances mean.
2. Calculate the spending variances for March. (Hint: Refer to Exhibit 9–7.) Explain what these variances mean.

PROBLEM 9–21 More than One Cost Driver LO9–2, LO9–3, LO9–4, LO9–5
Milano Pizza is a small neighborhood pizzeria that has a small area for in-store dining as well as offering take-out and free home delivery services. The pizzeria's owner has determined that the shop has two major cost drivers—the number of pizzas sold and the number of deliveries made.
The pizzeria's cost formulas appear below:

	Fixed Cost per Month	Cost per Pizza	Cost per Delivery
Pizza ingredients		$3.80	
Kitchen staff.....................	$5,220		
Utilities	$630	$0.05	
Delivery person			$3.50
Delivery vehicle	$540		$1.50
Equipment depreciation	$275		
Rent	$1,830		
Miscellaneous	$820	$0.15	

In November, the pizzeria budgeted for 1,200 pizzas at an average selling price of $13.50 per pizza and for 180 deliveries.
Data concerning the pizzeria's actual results in November appear below:

	Actual Results
Pizzas	1,240
Deliveries	174
Revenue	$17,420
Pizza ingredients	$4,985
Kitchen staff....................	$5,281
Utilities	$984
Delivery person	$609
Delivery vehicle	$655
Equipment depreciation	$275
Rent	$1,830
Miscellaneous	$954

Required:

1. Using Exhibits 9–8 and 9–9 as your guide, prepare a flexible budget performance report that shows both revenue and spending variances and activity variances for the pizzeria for November.
2. Explain the activity variances.

PROBLEM 9–22 Critique a Report; Prepare a Performance Report LO9–1, LO9–2, LO9–3, LO9–4, LO9–6

TipTop Flight School offers flying lessons at a small municipal airport. The school's owner and manager has been attempting to evaluate performance and control costs using a variance report that compares the planning budget to actual results. A recent variance report appears below:

	Actual Results	Planning Budget	Variances
TipTop Flight School			
Variance Report			
For the Month Ended July 31			
Lessons	155	150	
Revenue	$33,900	$33,000	$900 F
Expenses:			
Instructor wages	9,870	9,750	120 U
Aircraft depreciation	5,890	5,700	190 U
Fuel	2,750	2,250	500 U
Maintenance	2,450	2,330	120 U
Ground facility expenses	1,540	1,550	10 F
Administration	3,320	3,390	70 F
Total expense	25,820	24,970	850 U
Net operating income	$ 8,080	$ 8,030	$ 50 F

After several months of using such variance reports, the owner has become frustrated. For example, she is quite confident that instructor wages were very tightly controlled in July, but the report shows an unfavorable variance.

The planning budget was developed using the following formulas, where q is the number of lessons sold:

	Cost Formulas
Revenue	$220q
Instructor wages	$65q
Aircraft depreciation	$38q
Fuel	$15q
Maintenance	$530 + $12q
Ground facility expenses	$1,250 + $2q
Administration	$3,240 + $1q

Required:

1. Should the owner feel frustrated with the variance reports? Explain.
2. Using Exhibit 9–8 as your guide, prepare a flexible budget performance report for the school for July.
3. Evaluate the school's performance for July.

PROBLEM 9–23 Performance Report for a Nonprofit Organization LO9–1, LO9–2, LO9–3, LO9–4, LO9–6

The St. Lucia Blood Bank, a private charity partly supported by government grants, is located on the Caribbean island of St. Lucia. The blood bank has just finished its operations for September, which was a very busy month due to a powerful hurricane that hit neighboring islands causing many injuries. The hurricane largely bypassed St. Lucia, but residents of St. Lucia willingly donated their blood to help people on other islands. As a consequence, the blood bank collected and processed over 20% more blood than had been originally planned for the month.

A report prepared by a government official comparing actual costs to budgeted costs for the blood bank appears below. Continued support from the government depends on the blood bank's ability to demonstrate control over its costs.

St. Lucia Blood Bank Cost Control Report For the Month Ended September 30			
	Actual Results	Planning Budget	Variances
Liters of blood collected	620	500	
Medical supplies	$ 9,250	$ 7,500	$1,750 U
Lab tests	6,180	6,000	180 U
Equipment depreciation	2,800	2,500	300 U
Rent	1,000	1,000	0
Utilities	570	500	70 U
Administration	11,740	11,250	490 U
Total expense	$31,540	$28,750	$2,790 U

The managing director of the blood bank was very unhappy with this report, claiming that his costs were higher than expected due to the emergency on the neighboring islands. He also pointed out that the additional costs had been fully covered by payments from grateful recipients on the other islands. The government official who prepared the report countered that all of the figures had been submitted by the blood bank to the government; he was just pointing out that actual costs were a lot higher than promised in the budget.

The following cost formulas were used to construct the planning budget:

	Cost Formulas
Medical supplies	$15.00q
Lab tests	$12.00q
Equipment depreciation	$2,500
Rent	$1,000
Utilities	$500
Administration	$10,000 + $2.50q

Required:

1. Using Exhibit 9–8 as your guide, prepare a flexible budget performance report for September.
2. Do you think any of the variances in the report you prepared should be investigated? Why?

PROBLEM 9–24 Critiquing a Report; Preparing a Performance Budget LO9–1, LO9–2, LO9–3, LO9–4, LO9–6

Exchange Corp. is a company that acts as a facilitator in tax-favored real estate swaps. Such swaps, know as 1031 exchanges, permit participants to avoid some or all of the capital gains taxes that would otherwise be due. The bookkeeper for the company has been asked to prepare a report for the company to help its owner/manager analyze performance. The first such report appears below:

Exchange Corp. Analysis of Revenues and Costs For the Month Ended May 31			
	Actual Unit Revenues and Costs	Planning Budget Unit Revenues and Costs	Variances
Exchanges completed	50	40	
Revenue	$385	$395	$10 U
Expenses:			
Legal and search fees	184	165	19 U
Office expenses	112	135	23 F
Equipment depreciation	8	10	2 F
Rent	36	45	9 F
Insurance	4	5	1 F
Total expense	344	360	16 F
Net operating income	$ 41	$ 35	$ 6 F

Note that the revenues and costs in the above report are *unit* revenues and costs. For example, the average office expense is $135 per exchange completed on the planning budget; whereas, the average actual office expense is $112 per exchange completed.

Legal and search fees is a variable cost; office expenses is a mixed cost; and equipment depreciation, rent, and insurance are fixed costs. In the planning budget, the fixed component of office expenses was $5,200.

All of the company's revenues come from fees collected when an exchange is completed.

Required:
1. Evaluate the report prepared by the bookkeeper.
2. Using Exhibit 9–8 as your guide, prepare a performance report that would help the owner/manager assess the performance of the company in May.
3. Using the report you created, evaluate the performance of the company in May.

PROBLEM 9–25 Critiquing a Variance Report; Preparing a Performance Report LO9–1, LO9–2, LO9–3, LO9–4, LO9–6

Several years ago, Westmont Corporation developed a comprehensive budgeting system for planning and control purposes. While departmental supervisors have been happy with the system, the factory manager has expressed considerable dissatisfaction with the information being generated by the system.

A report for the company's Assembly Department for the month of March follows:

Assembly Department Cost Report For the Month Ended March 31			
	Actual Results	Planning Budget	Variances
Machine-hours	35,000	40,000	
Variable costs:			
Supplies	$ 29,700	$ 32,000	$2,300 F
Scrap	19,500	20,000	500 F
Indirect materials	51,800	56,000	4,200 F
Fixed costs:			
Wages and salaries	79,200	80,000	800 F
Equipment depreciation	60,000	60,000	—
Total cost	$240,200	$248,000	$7,800 F

After receiving a copy of this cost report, the supervisor of the Assembly Department stated, "These reports are super. It makes me feel really good to see how well things are going in my department. I can't understand why those people upstairs complain so much about the reports."

For the last several years, the company's marketing department has chronically failed to meet the sales goals expressed in the company's monthly budgets.

Required:
1. The company's president is uneasy about the cost reports and would like you to evaluate their usefulness to the company.
2. What changes, if any, should be made in the reports to give better insight into how well departmental supervisors are controlling costs?
3. Using Exhibit 9–8 as your guide, prepare a new performance report for the quarter, incorporating any changes you suggested in question (2) above.
4. How well were costs controlled in the Assembly Department in March?

PROBLEM 9–26 Critiquing a Cost Report; Preparing a Performance Report LO9–1, LO9–2, LO9–3, LO9–4, LO9–6

Frank Weston, supervisor of the Freemont Corporation's Machining Department, was visibly upset after being reprimanded for his department's poor performance over the prior month. The department's cost control report is given below:

Freemont Corporation–Machining Department
Cost Control Report
For the Month Ended June 30

	Actual Results	Planning Budget	Variances
Machine-hours	38,000	35,000	
Direct labor wages	$ 86,100	$ 80,500	$ 5,600 U
Supplies	23,100	21,000	2,100 U
Maintenance	137,300	134,000	3,300 U
Utilities	15,700	15,200	500 U
Supervision	38,000	38,000	0
Depreciation	80,000	80,000	0
Total	$380,200	$368,700	$11,500 U

"I just can't understand all of these unfavorable variances," Weston complained to the supervisor of another department. "When the boss called me in, I thought he was going to give me a pat on the back because I know for a fact that my department worked more efficiently last month than it has ever worked before. Instead, he tore me apart. I thought for a minute that it might be over the supplies that were stolen out of our warehouse last month. But they only amounted to a couple of hundred dollars, and just look at this report. Everything is unfavorable."

Direct labor wages and supplies are variable costs; supervision and depreciation are fixed costs; and maintenance and utilities are mixed costs. The fixed component of the budgeted maintenance cost is $92,000; the fixed component of the budgeted utilities cost is $11,700.

Required:
1. Evaluate the company's cost control report and explain why the variances were all unfavorable.
2. Using Exhibit 9–8 as your guide, prepare a performance report that will help Mr. Weston's superiors assess how well costs were controlled in the Machining Department.

connect **Cases**

CASE 9–27 Ethics and the Manager LO9–3

Tom Kemper is the controller of the Wichita manufacturing facility of Prudhom Enterprises, Inc.

The annual cost control report is one of the many reports that must be filed with corporate headquarters and is due at corporate headquarters shortly after the beginning of the New Year. Kemper does not like putting work off to the last minute, so just before Christmas he prepared a preliminary draft of the cost control report. Some adjustments would later be required for transactions that occur between Christmas and New Year's Day. A copy of the preliminary draft report, which Kemper completed on December 21, follows:

Wichita Manufacturing Facility
Cost Control Report
December 21 Preliminary Draft

	Actual Results	Flexible Budget	Spending Variances
Labor-hours	18,000	18,000	
Direct labor	$ 326,000	$ 324,000	$ 2,000 U
Power	19,750	18,000	1,750 U
Supplies	105,000	99,000	6,000 U
Equipment depreciation	343,000	332,000	11,000 U
Supervisory salaries	273,000	275,000	2,000 F
Insurance	37,000	37,000	0
Industrial engineering	189,000	210,000	21,000 F
Factory building lease	60,000	60,000	0
Total expense	$1,352,750	$1,355,000	$ 2,250 F

Melissa Ilianovitch, the general manager at the Wichita facility, asked to see a copy of the preliminary draft report. Kemper carried a copy of the report to her office where the following discussion took place:

Ilianovitch: Wow! Almost all of the variances on the report are unfavorable. The only favorable variances are for supervisory salaries and industrial engineering. How did we have an unfavorable variance for depreciation?

Kemper: Do you remember that milling machine that broke down because the wrong lubricant was used by the machine operator?

Ilianovitch: Yes.

Kemper: We couldn't fix it. We had to scrap the machine and buy a new one.

Ilianovitch: This report doesn't look good. I was raked over the coals last year when we had just a few unfavorable variances.

Kemper: I'm afraid the final report is going to look even worse.

Ilianovitch: Oh?

Kemper: The line item for industrial engineering on the report is for work we hired Ferguson Engineering to do for us. The original contract was for $210,000, but we asked them to do some additional work that was not in the contract. We have to reimburse Ferguson Engineering for the costs of that additional work. The $189,000 in actual costs that appears on the preliminary draft report reflects only their billings up through December 21. The last bill they had sent us was on November 28, and they completed the project just last week. Yesterday I got a call from Laura Sunder over at Ferguson and she said they would be sending us a final bill for the project before the end of the year. The total bill, including the reimbursements for the additional work, is going to be . . .

Ilianovitch: I am not sure I want to hear this.

Kemper: $225,000

Ilianovitch: Ouch!

Kemper: The additional work added $15,000 to the cost of the project.

Ilianovitch: I can't turn in a report with an overall unfavorable variance! They'll kill me at corporate headquarters. Call up Laura at Ferguson and ask her not to send the bill until after the first of the year. We have to have that $21,000 favorable variance for industrial engineering on the report.

Required:

What should Tom Kemper do? Explain.

CASE 9–28 Critiquing a Report; Calculating Spending Variances LO9–3, LO9–5, LO9–6

Boyne University offers an extensive continuing education program in many cities throughout the state. For the convenience of its faculty and administrative staff and to save costs, the university operates a motor pool. The motor pool's monthly planning budget is based on operating 20 vehicles; however, for the month of March the university purchased one additional vehicle. The motor pool furnishes gasoline, oil, and other supplies for its automobiles. A mechanic does routine maintenance and minor repairs. Major repairs are performed at a nearby commercial garage.

The following cost control report shows actual operating costs for March of the current year compared to the planning budget for March.

Boyne University Motor Pool Cost Control Report For the Month Ended March 31			
	March Actual	Planning Budget	(Over) Under Budget
Miles	63,000	50,000	
Autos	21	20	
Gasoline	$ 9,350	$ 7,500	$(1,850)
Oil, minor repairs, parts	2,360	2,000	(360)
Outside repairs	1,420	1,500	80
Insurance	2,120	2,000	(120)
Salaries and benefits	7,540	7,540	0
Vehicle depreciation	5,250	5,000	(250)
Total	$28,040	$25,540	$(2,500)

The planning budget was based on the following assumptions:
a. $0.15 per mile for gasoline.
b. $0.04 per mile for oil, minor repairs, and parts.
c. $75 per automobile per month for outside repairs.
d. $100 per automobile per month for insurance.
e. $7,540 per month for salaries and benefits.
f. $250 per automobile per month for depreciation.

The supervisor of the motor pool is unhappy with the report, claiming it paints an unfair picture of the motor pool's performance.

Required:
1. Calculate the spending variances for March. (Hint: Refer to Exhibit 9–7.)
2. What are the deficiencies in the original cost control report? How do your calculations in part (1) above overcome these deficiencies?

(CMA, adapted)

CASE 9–29 Performance Report with More than One Cost Driver LO9–1, LO9–2, LO9–3, LO9–4, LO9–5

The Little Theatre is a nonprofit organization devoted to staging plays for children. The theater has a very small full-time professional administrative staff. Through a special arrangement with the actors' union, actors and directors rehearse without pay and are paid only for actual performances.

The Little Theatre had tentatively planned to put on six different productions with a total of 108 performances. For example, one of the productions was *Peter Rabbit,* which had a six-week run with three performances on each weekend. The costs from the current year's planning budget appear below.

The Little Theatre Costs from the Planning Budget For the Year Ended December 31	
Budgeted number of productions	6
Budgeted number of performances	108
Actors and directors wages	$216,000
Stagehands wages	32,400
Ticket booth personnel and ushers wages	16,200
Scenery, costumes, and props	108,000
Theater hall rent	54,000
Printed programs	27,000
Publicity	12,000
Administrative expenses	43,200
Total	$508,800

Some of the costs vary with the number of productions, some with the number of performances, and some are fixed and depend on neither the number of productions nor the number of performances. The costs of scenery, costumes, props, and publicity vary with the number of productions. It doesn't make any difference how many times *Peter Rabbit* is performed, the cost of the scenery is the same. Likewise, the cost of publicizing a play with posters and radio commercials is the same whether there are 10, 20, or 30 performances of the play. On the other hand, the wages of the actors, directors, stagehands, ticket booth personnel, and ushers vary with the number of performances. The greater the number of performances, the higher the wage costs will be. Similarly, the costs of renting the hall and printing the programs will vary with the number of performances. Administrative expenses are more difficult to analyze, but the best estimate is that approximately 75% of the budgeted costs are fixed, 15% depend on the number of productions staged, and the remaining 10% depend on the number of performances.

After the beginning of the year, the board of directors of the theater authorized expanding the theater's program to seven productions and a total of 168 performances. Not surprisingly, actual costs were considerably higher than the costs from the planning budget. (Grants from donors and ticket sales were also correspondingly higher, but are not shown here.) Data concerning the actual costs appear below:

The Little Theatre	
Actual Costs	
For the Year Ended December 31	
Actual number of productions	7
Actual number of performances	168
Actors and directors wages	$341,800
Stagehands wages	49,700
Ticket booth personnel and ushers wages	25,900
Scenery, costumes, and props	130,600
Theater hall rent	78,000
Printed programs	38,300
Publicity	15,100
Administrative expenses	47,500
Total	$726,900

Required:
1. Use Exhibit 9–8 as your guide, prepare a flexible budget performance report for the year that shows both spending variances and activity variances.
2. If you were on the board of directors of the theater, would you be pleased with how well costs were controlled during the year? Why, or why not?
3. The cost formulas provide figures for the average cost per production and average cost per performance. How accurate do you think these figures would be for predicting the cost of a new production or of an additional performance of a particular production?

Standard Costs and Variances

Managing Materials and Labor

© Bloomberg/Getty Images

Schneider Electric's Oxford, Ohio, plant manufactures *busways* that transport electricity from its point of entry into a building to remote locations throughout the building. The plant's managers pay close attention to direct material costs because they are more than half of the plant's total manufacturing costs. To help control scrap rates for direct materials such as copper, steel, and aluminum, the accounting department prepares direct materials quantity variances. These variances compare the amount of direct materials that were actually used to the standard quantity of direct materials that should have been used to make a product (according to computations by the plant's engineers). Keeping a close eye on these differences helps to identify and deal with the causes of excessive scrap, such as an inadequately trained machine operator, poor quality raw material inputs, or a malfunctioning machine.

Because direct labor is also a significant component of the plant's total manufacturing costs, the management team daily monitors the direct labor efficiency variance. This variance compares the actual amount of labor time used to the standard amount of labor time allowed to make a product. When idle workers cause an unfavorable labor efficiency variance, managers temporarily move workers from departments with slack to departments with a backlog of work to be done. ■

Source: Author's conversation with Doug Taylor, plant controller, Schneider Electric's Oxford, Ohio, plant.

LEARNING OBJECTIVES

After studying Chapter 10, you should be able to:

LO10–1 Compute the direct materials price and quantity variances and explain their significance.

LO10–2 Compute the direct labor rate and efficiency variances and explain their significance.

LO10–3 Compute the variable manufacturing overhead rate and efficiency variances and explain their significance.

LO10–4 *(Appendix 10A) Compute and interpret the fixed overhead budget and volume variances.*

LO10–5 *(Appendix 10B) Prepare an income statement using a standard cost system.*

In the last chapter, we investigated flexible budget variances. These variances provide feedback concerning how well an organization performed in relation to its budget. The impact on profit of a change in the level of activity is captured in the overall net operating income activity variance. The revenue and spending variances indicate how well revenues and costs were controlled—given the actual level of activity. However, with regard to spending variances, we can often get even more detail about how well costs were controlled. For example, at Rick's Hairstyling, an unfavorable spending variance for hairstyling supplies could be due to paying too much for the supplies or using too many supplies, or some combination of the two. In this chapter, we learn how to use standard costs to decompose spending variances into two parts—a part that measures how well the acquisition prices of resources were controlled and a part that measures how efficiently those resources were used.

Standard Costs—Setting the Stage

A *standard* is a benchmark for measuring performance. Standards are found everywhere. Auto service centers like **Firestone** and **Sears**, for example, often set specific labor time standards for the completion of certain tasks, such as installing a carburetor or doing a valve job, and then measure actual performance against these standards. Fast-food outlets such as **McDonald's** and **Subway** have exacting standards for the quantity of meat going into a sandwich, as well as standards for the cost of the meat. Your doctor evaluates your weight using standards for individuals of your age, height, and gender. The buildings we live in conform to standards set in building codes.

Standards also are widely used in managerial accounting where they relate to the *quantity* and acquisition *price* of inputs used in manufacturing goods or providing services. *Quantity standards* specify how much of an input should be used to make a product or provide a service. *Price standards* specify how much should be paid for each unit of the input. If either the quantity or acquisition price of an input departs significantly from the standard, managers investigate the discrepancy to find the cause of the problem and eliminate it.

Next we'll demonstrate how a company can establish quantity and price standards for direct materials, direct labor, and variable manufacturing overhead and then we'll discuss how those standards can be used to calculate variances and manage operations.

MANAGERIAL ACCOUNTING IN ACTION
THE ISSUE

Colonial Pewter Company

The Colonial Pewter Company makes only one product—an elaborate reproduction of an 18th century pewter statue. The statue is made largely by hand, using traditional metal-working tools. Consequently, the manufacturing process is labor intensive and requires a high level of skill.

Colonial Pewter has recently expanded its workforce to take advantage of unexpected demand for the statue as a gift. The company started with a small cadre of experienced pewter workers but has had to hire less experienced workers as a result of the expansion. The president of the company, J. D. Wriston, has called a meeting to discuss production problems. Attending the meeting are Tom Kuchel, the production manager; Janet Warner, the purchasing manager; and Terry Sherman, the corporate controller.

J. D.: I've got a feeling that we aren't getting the production we should out of our new people.

Tom: Give us a chance. Some of the new people have been with the company for less than a month.

Janet: Let me add that production seems to be wasting an awful lot of material—particularly pewter. That stuff is very expensive.

Tom: What about the shipment of defective pewter that you bought—the one with the iron contamination? That caused us major problems.

Janet: How was I to know it was off-grade? Besides, it was a great deal.

J. D.:   Calm down everybody. Let's get the facts before we start attacking each other.
Tom: I agree. The more facts the better.
J. D.:   Okay, Terry, it's your turn. Facts are the controller's department.
Terry: I'm afraid I can't provide the answers off the top of my head, but if you give me about a week I can set up a system that can routinely answer questions relating to worker productivity, material waste, and input prices.
J. D.:   Let's mark it on our calendars.

Setting Direct Materials Standards

Terry Sherman's first task was to prepare quantity and price standards for the company's only significant raw material, pewter ingots. The **standard quantity per unit** defines the amount of direct materials that should be used for each unit of finished product, including an allowance for normal inefficiencies, such as scrap and spoilage.[1] After consulting with the production manager, Tom Kuchel, Terry set the quantity standard for pewter at 3.0 pounds per statue.

The **standard price per unit** defines the price that should be paid for each unit of direct materials and it should reflect the final, delivered cost of those materials. After consulting with purchasing manager Janet Warner, Terry set the standard price of pewter at $4.00 per pound.

Once Terry established the quantity and price standards he computed the standard direct materials cost per statue as follows:

$$3.0 \text{ pounds per statue} \times \$4.00 \text{ per pound} = \$12.00 \text{ per statue}$$

MANAGING RAW MATERIAL COSTS IN THE APPAREL INDUSTRY

A company's raw material costs can rise for numerous and often uncontrollable reasons. For example, severe weather in China, which is the world's largest producer of cotton, can influence the cotton prices paid by **Abercrombie & Fitch**. Rising fuel costs can influence what **Maidenform Brands** pays for its petroleum-based synthetic fabrics. When farmers stop producing cotton in favor of soybeans, it increases the price **Jones Apparel Group** pays for a shrinking supply of cotton.

When faced with rising raw material costs, companies can respond three ways. First, they can maintain existing selling prices and consequently operate with lower margins. Second, they can pass the cost increases along to customers in the form of higher prices. Third, they can try to lower their raw material costs. For example, **HanesBrands** buys hedging contracts that lock in its cotton prices, thereby insulating the company from future cost increases. **J.C. Penney** is changing the blend of raw materials used in its garments, whereas Maidenform has started buying some of its raw materials from lower-cost producers in Bangladesh.

Source: Elizabeth Holmes and Rachel Dodes, "Cotton Tale: Apparel Prices Set to Rise," *The Wall Street Journal,* May 19, 2010, p. B8.

© casadaphoto/123RF

Setting Direct Labor Standards

Direct labor quantity and price standards are usually expressed in terms of labor-hours or a labor rate. The **standard hours per unit** defines the amount of direct labor-hours that should be used to produce one unit of finished goods. One approach used to determine

---

[1]   Although companies often create "practical" rather than "ideal" materials quantity standards that include allowances for normal inefficiencies such as scrap, spoilage, and rejects, this practice is often criticized because it contradicts the zero defects goal that underlies many process improvement programs. If these types of allowances are built into materials quantity standards, they should be periodically reviewed and reduced over time to reflect improved processes, better training, and better equipment.

this standard is for an industrial engineer to do a time and motion study, actually clocking the time required for each task. Throughout the chapter, we'll assume that "tight but attainable" labor standards are used rather than "ideal" standards that can only be attained by the most skilled and efficient employees working at peak effort 100% of the time. Therefore, after consulting with the production manager and considering reasonable allowances for breaks, personal needs of employees, cleanup, and machine downtime, Terry set the standard hours per unit at 0.50 direct labor-hours per statue.

The **standard rate per hour** defines the company's expected direct labor wage rate per hour, including employment taxes and fringe benefits. Using wage records and in consultation with the production manager, Terry Sherman established a standard rate per hour of $22.00. This standard rate reflects the expected "mix" of workers, even though the actual hourly wage rates may vary somewhat from individual to individual due to differing skills or seniority.

Once Terry established the time and rate standards, he computed the standard direct labor cost per statue as follows:

0.50 direct labor-hours per statue × $22.00 per direct labor-hour = $11.00 per statue

Setting Variable Manufacturing Overhead Standards

As with direct labor, the quantity and price standards for variable manufacturing overhead are usually expressed in terms of hours and a rate. The *standard hours per unit* for variable overhead measures the amount of the allocation base from a company's predetermined overhead rate that is required to produce one unit of finished goods. In the case of Colonial Pewter, we will assume that the company uses direct labor-hours as the allocation base in its predetermined overhead rate. Therefore, the standard hours per unit for variable overhead is exactly the same as the standard hours per unit for direct labor—0.50 direct labor-hours per statue.

The *standard rate per unit* that a company expects to pay for variable overhead equals *the variable portion of the predetermined overhead rate*. At Colonial Pewter, the variable portion of the predetermined overhead rate is $6.00 per direct labor-hour. Therefore, Terry computed the standard variable manufacturing overhead cost per statue as follows:

0.50 direct labor-hours per statue × $6.00 per direct-labor hour = $3.00 per statue

This $3.00 per unit cost for variable manufacturing overhead appears along with direct materials ($12 per unit) and direct labor ($11 per unit) on the *standard cost card* in Exhibit 10–1. A **standard cost card** shows the standard quantity (or hours) and standard price (or rate) of the inputs required to produce a unit of a specific product. The **standard cost per unit** for all three variable manufacturing costs is computed the same way. The standard quantity (or hours) per unit is multiplied by the standard price (or rate) per unit to obtain the standard cost per unit.

EXHIBIT 10–1
Standard Cost Card–Variable Manufacturing Costs

Inputs	(1) Standard Quantity or Hours	(2) Standard Price or Rate	Standard Cost (1) × (2)
Direct materials	3.0 pounds	$4.00 per pound	$12.00
Direct labor.	0.50 hours	$22.00 per hour	11.00
Variable manufacturing . . . . overhead	0.50 hours	$6.00 per hour	3.00
Total standard cost per unit.			$26.00

Using Standards in Flexible Budgets

Once Terry Sherman created the standard cost card shown in Exhibit 10–1, he was ready to use this information to calculate direct materials, direct labor, and variable manufacturing overhead variances. Therefore, he gathered the following data for the month of June:

Planned output in June	2,100 statues
Actual output in June	2,000 statues
Actual direct materials cost in June*	$24,700
Actual direct labor cost in June	$22,680
Actual variable manufacturing overhead cost in June	$7,140

*There were no beginning or ending inventories of raw materials in June; all materials purchased were used.

Using the above data and the standard cost data from Exhibit 10–1, Terry computed the spending and activity variances shown in Exhibit 10–2. Notice that the actual results and flexible budget columns are each based on the actual output of 2,000 statues. The planning budget column is based on the planned output of 2,100 statues. The standard costs of $12.00 per unit for materials, $11.00 per unit for direct labor, and $3.00 per unit for variable manufacturing overhead are each multiplied by the actual output of 2,000 statues to compute the amounts in the flexible budget column. For example, the standard direct labor cost per unit of $11.00 multiplied by 2,000 statues equals the direct labor flexible budget of $22,000. Similarly, the three standard variable cost figures are multiplied by 2,100 statues to compute the amounts in the planning budget column. For example, the direct labor cost for the planning budget is $23,100 (= $11.00 per unit × 2,100 units).

The spending variances shown in Exhibit 10–2 are computed by taking the amounts in the actual results column and subtracting the amounts in the flexible budget column. For all three variable manufacturing costs, this computation results in a positive number because the actual amount of the cost incurred to produce 2,000 statues exceeds the standard cost allowed for 2,000 statues. Because, in all three instances, the actual cost incurred exceeds the standard cost allowed for the actual level of output, the variance is labeled unfavorable (U). Had any of the actual costs incurred been less than the standard cost allowed for the actual level of output, the corresponding variances would have been labeled favorable (F).

The activity variances shown in the exhibit are computed by taking the amounts in the flexible budget column and subtracting the amounts in the planning budget column. For all three variable manufacturing costs, these computations result in negative numbers and what are labeled as favorable (F) variances. The label favorable is used in these instances because the standard cost allowed for the actual output is less than the standard

---

EXHIBIT 10–2
Flexible Budget Performance Report for Variable Manufacturing Costs

Colonial Pewter
Flexible Budget Performance Report—Variable Manufacturing Costs
For the Month Ended June 30

	Actual Results	Spending Variances	Flexible Budget	Activity Variances	Planning Budget
Statues produced (q)............................	2,000		2,000		2,100
Direct materials ($12.00q)........................	$24,700	$700 U	$24,000	$1,200 F	$25,200
Direct labor ($11.00q)	$22,680	$680 U	$22,000	$1,100 F	$23,100
Variable manufacturing overhead ($3.00q)	$7,140	$1,140 U	$6,000	$300 F	$6,300

cost allowed for the planned output. Had the actual level of activity been greater than the planned level of activity, all of the computations would have resulted in positive numbers and unfavorable (U) activity variances.

While the performance report in Exhibit 10–2 is useful, it would be even more useful if the spending variances could be broken down into their price-related and quantity-related components. For example, the direct materials spending variance in the report is $700 unfavorable. This means that, given the actual level of production for the period, direct materials costs were too high by $700—at least according to the standard costs. Was this due to higher than expected prices for materials? Or was it due to too much material being used? The standard cost variances we will be discussing in the rest of the chapter are designed to answer these questions.

A General Model for Standard Cost Variance Analysis

Standard cost variance analysis decomposes spending variances from the flexible budget into two elements—one due to the price paid for the input and the other due to the amount of the input that is used. A **price variance** is the difference between the actual amount paid for an input and the standard amount that should have been paid, multiplied by the actual amount of the input purchased. A **quantity variance** is the difference between how much of an input was actually used and how much should have been used for the actual level of output and is stated in dollar terms using the standard price of the input.

Why are standards separated into two categories—price and quantity? Price variances and quantity variances usually have different causes. In addition, different managers are usually responsible for buying and using inputs. For example, in the case of a raw material, the purchasing manager is responsible for its price and the production manager is responsible for the amount of the raw material actually used to make products. Therefore, it is important to clearly distinguish between deviations from price standards (the responsibility of the purchasing manager) and deviations from quantity standards (the responsibility of the production manager).

Exhibit 10–3 presents a general model that can be used to decompose the spending variance for a variable cost into a *price variance* and a *quantity variance*.[2] Column (1) in this exhibit corresponds with the Actual Results column in Exhibit 10–2. Column (3) corresponds with the Flexible Budget column in Exhibit 10–2. Column (2) has been inserted into Exhibit 10–3 to enable separating the spending variance into a price variance and a quantity variance.

Three things should be noted from Exhibit 10–3. First, it can be used to compute a price variance and a quantity variance for each of the three variable cost elements—direct materials, direct labor, and variable manufacturing overhead—even though the variances have different names. A price variance is called a *materials price variance* in the case of direct materials, a *labor rate variance* in the case of direct labor, and a *variable overhead rate variance* in the case of variable manufacturing overhead. A quantity variance is called a *materials quantity variance* in the case of direct materials, a *labor efficiency variance* in the case of direct labor, and a *variable overhead efficiency variance* in the case of variable manufacturing overhead.

Second, all three columns in the exhibit are based on the *actual amount of output* produced during the period. Even the flexible budget column (column 3) depicts the standard cost allowed for the *actual amount of output* produced during the period. The

---

[2] This general model can always be used to compute direct labor and variable manufacturing overhead variances. However, it can be used to compute direct materials variances only when the actual quantity of materials purchased equals the actual quantity of materials used in production. Later in the chapter, we will explain how to compute direct materials variances when these quantities differ.

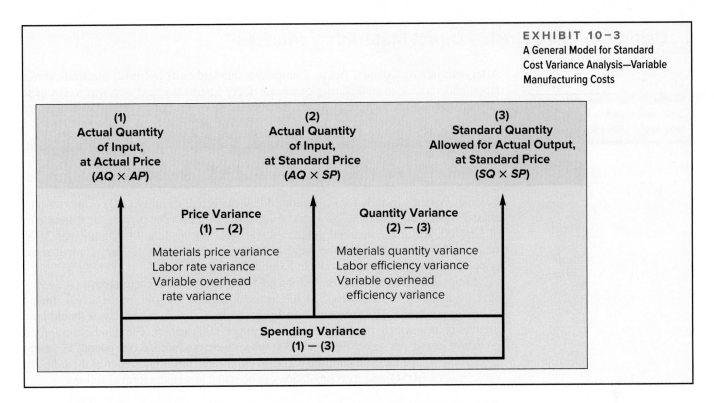

EXHIBIT 10-3
A General Model for Standard
Cost Variance Analysis—Variable
Manufacturing Costs

key to understanding the flexible budget column in Exhibit 10–3 is to grasp the meaning of the term *standard quantity allowed (SQ)*. The **standard quantity allowed** (when computing direct materials variances) or **standard hours allowed** (when computing direct labor and variable manufacturing overhead variances) refers to the amount of an input *that should have been used* to manufacture the actual output of finished goods produced during the period. It is computed by multiplying the actual output by the standard quantity (or hours) per unit. The standard quantity (or hours) allowed is then multiplied by the standard price (or rate) per unit of the input to obtain the total cost according to the flexible budget. For example, if a company actually produced 100 units of finished goods during the period and its standard quantity per unit of finished goods for direct materials is 5 pounds, then its *standard quantity allowed (SQ)* would be 500 pounds (= 100 units × 5 pounds per unit). If the company's standard cost per pound of direct materials is $2.00, then the total direct materials cost in its flexible budget would be $1,000 (= 500 pounds × $2.00 per pound).

Third, the spending, price, and quantity variances—regardless of what they are called—are computed exactly the same way regardless of whether one is dealing with direct materials, direct labor, or variable manufacturing overhead. The spending variance is computed by taking the total cost in column (1) and subtracting the total cost in column (3). The price variance is computed by taking the total cost in column (1) and subtracting the total cost in column (2). The quantity variance is computed by taking the total cost in column (2) and subtracting the total cost in column (3). In all of these variance calculations, a positive number should be labeled as an unfavorable (U) variance and a negative number should be labeled as a favorable (F) variance. An unfavorable price variance indicates that the actual price (AP) per unit of the input was greater than the standard price (SP) per unit. A favorable price variance indicates that the actual price (AP) of the input was less than the standard price per unit (SP). An unfavorable quantity variance indicates that the actual quantity (AQ) of the input used was greater than the standard quantity allowed (SQ). Conversely, a favorable quantity variance indicates that the actual quantity (AQ) of the input used was less than the standard quantity allowed (SQ).

With this general model as the foundation, we will now calculate Colonial Pewter's price and quantity variances.

Using Standard Costs—Direct Materials Variances

LO10–1

Compute the direct materials price and quantity variances and explain their significance.

After determining Colonial Pewter Company's standard costs for direct materials, direct labor, and variable manufacturing overhead, Terry Sherman's next step was to compute the company's variances for June. As discussed in the preceding section, variances are computed by comparing actual costs to standard costs. Terry referred to the standard cost card in Exhibit 10–1 that shows the standard direct materials cost per statue was computed as follows:

$$3.0 \text{ pounds per statue} \times \$4.00 \text{ per pound} = \$12.00 \text{ per statue}$$

Colonial Pewter's records for June showed that the actual quantity (AQ) of pewter purchased was 6,500 pounds at an actual price (AP) of $3.80 per pound, for a total cost of $24,700. All of the material purchased was used during June to manufacture 2,000 statues.[3] Using these data and the standard costs from Exhibit 10–1, Terry computed the price and quantity variances shown in Exhibit 10–4.

Notice that the variances in this exhibit are based on three different total costs—$24,700, $26,000, and $24,000. The first, $24,700, is the actual amount paid for the actual amount of pewter purchased. The third total cost figure, $24,000, refers to how much should have been spent on pewter to produce the actual output of 2,000 statues. The standards call for 3 pounds of pewter per statue. Because 2,000 statues were produced, 6,000 pounds of pewter should have been used. As mentioned earlier in the chapter, this is referred to as the *standard quantity allowed* (SQ) and its computation can be stated in formula form as follows:

Standard quantity allowed = Actual output × Standard quantity per unit

If 6,000 pounds of pewter had been purchased at the standard price of $4.00 per pound, the company would have spent $24,000. This is the amount that appears in the company's flexible budget for the month. The difference between the $24,700 actually spent and the $24,000 that should have been spent is the spending variance for the month of $700 U.

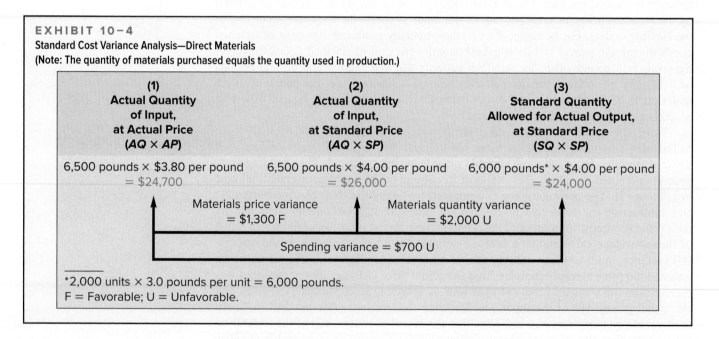

EXHIBIT 10–4

Standard Cost Variance Analysis—Direct Materials

(Note: The quantity of materials purchased equals the quantity used in production.)

(1) Actual Quantity of Input, at Actual Price (AQ × AP)	(2) Actual Quantity of Input, at Standard Price (AQ × SP)	(3) Standard Quantity Allowed for Actual Output, at Standard Price (SQ × SP)
6,500 pounds × $3.80 per pound = $24,700	6,500 pounds × $4.00 per pound = $26,000	6,000 pounds* × $4.00 per pound = $24,000

Materials price variance = $1,300 F   Materials quantity variance = $2,000 U

Spending variance = $700 U

*2,000 units × 3.0 pounds per unit = 6,000 pounds.
F = Favorable; U = Unfavorable.

---

[3] Throughout this section, we assume zero beginning and ending inventories of materials and that all materials purchased during the period are used during that period. The more general case in which there are beginning and ending inventories of materials and materials are not necessarily used during the period in which they are purchased is considered later in the chapter.

This variance is unfavorable (denoted by U) because the amount that was actually spent exceeds the amount that should have been spent. Also note that this spending variance agrees with the direct materials spending variance in Exhibit 10–2.

The second total cost figure in Exhibit 10–4, $26,000, is the key that allows us to decompose the spending variance into two distinct elements—one due to price and one due to quantity. It represents how much the company should have spent if it had purchased the actual amount of input, 6,500 pounds, at the standard price of $4.00 a pound rather than the actual price of $3.80 a pound.

The Materials Price Variance

Using the $26,000 total cost figure in column (2) of Exhibit 10–4, we can make two comparisons—one with the total cost of $24,700 in column (1) and one with the total cost of $24,000 in column (3). The difference between the $24,700 in column (1) and the $26,000 in column (2) is the *materials price variance* of $1,300, which is labeled as favorable (denoted by F). A **materials price variance** measures the difference between a direct material's actual price per unit and its standard price per unit, multiplied by the actual quantity purchased.

To understand the materials price variance, note that the actual price of $3.80 per pound of pewter is $0.20 less than the standard price of $4.00 per pound. Because 6,500 pounds were purchased, the total amount of the variance is $1,300 (= $0.20 per pound × 6,500 pounds). This variance is labeled favorable (F) because the actual purchase price per pound is less than the standard purchase price per pound. Conversely, the materials price variance would have been labeled unfavorable (U) if the actual purchase price per pound had exceeded the standard purchase price per pound.

Generally speaking, the purchasing manager has control over the price paid for materials and is therefore responsible for the materials price variance. Many factors influence materials purchase prices including the quantity and quality of materials purchased, the number of purchase orders placed with suppliers, how the purchased materials are delivered, and whether the materials are purchased in a rush order. If any of these factors deviates from what was assumed when the standards were set, a materials price variance can result. For example, purchasing second-grade materials rather than top-grade materials may result in a favorable price variance because the lower-grade materials may be less costly. However, the lower-grade materials may create production problems. It also bears emphasizing that someone other than the purchasing manager could be responsible for a materials price variance. For example, due to production problems beyond the purchasing manager's control, the purchasing manager may have to use express delivery. In these cases, the production manager should be held responsible for the resulting materials price variances.

IN BUSINESS

DIRECT MATERIAL PURCHASES: A RISK MANAGEMENT PERSPECTIVE

Shenzhen Hepalink manufactures heparin, a blood-thinning medication that is injected directly into the bloodstream of some surgical patients. The company relies on suppliers to extract its raw material, called crude heparin, from the intestines of slaughtered pigs. The harvesting of crude heparin is susceptible to contamination if the process is improperly managed and monitored. For example, **Baxter International** recently recalled tainted heparin that some people believe caused illnesses, allergic reactions, and deaths in some patients in the United States and Germany.

Shenzhen Hepalink strives to reduce contamination risks by buying crude heparin only from Chinese government-regulated slaughterhouses instead of rural unregulated slaughterhouses. The company also maintains quality assurance laboratories on each supplier's premises to ensure compliance with applicable rules. These safeguards increase Shenzhen Hepalink's raw materials cost, but they also reduce the risk of contaminated heparin eventually being injected into a patient's bloodstream.

© Jason Butcher/Getty Images RF

Source: Gordon Fairclough, "How a Heparin Maker in China Tackles Risks," *The Wall Street Journal*, March 10, 2009, pp. B1 and B5.

The Materials Quantity Variance

Referring again to Exhibit 10–4, the difference between the $26,000 in column (2) and the $24,000 in column (3) is the *materials quantity variance* of $2,000, which is labeled as unfavorable (denoted by U). The **materials quantity variance** measures the difference between the actual quantity of materials used in production and the standard quantity of materials allowed for the actual output, multiplied by the standard price per unit of materials. It is labeled as unfavorable (favorable) when the actual quantity of material used in production is greater than (less than) the quantity of material that should have been used according to the standard.

To understand the materials quantity variance, note that the actual amount of pewter used in production was 6,500 pounds. However, the standard amount of pewter allowed for the 2,000 statues that were actually produced is only 6,000 pounds. Therefore, too much pewter was used to produce the actual output—by a total of 500 pounds. To express this in dollar terms, the 500 pounds is multiplied by the standard price of $4.00 per pound to yield the quantity variance of $2,000 U. Why is the standard price of pewter, rather than the actual price, used in this calculation? The production manager is ordinarily responsible for the materials quantity variance. If the actual price were used in the calculation of the materials quantity variance, the production manager's performance evaluation would be unfairly influenced by the efficiency or inefficiency of the purchasing manager.

Excessive materials usage can result from many factors, including faulty machines, inferior materials quality, untrained workers, and poor supervision. Generally speaking, it is the responsibility of the production manager to see that material usage is kept in line with standards. There may be times, however, when the *purchasing* manager is responsible for an unfavorable materials quantity variance. For example, if the purchasing manager buys inferior materials at a lower price, the materials may be unsuitable for use and may result in excessive waste. Thus, the purchasing manager rather than the production manager would be responsible for the materials quantity variance.

Thus far, we have shown how to compute direct materials variances using the general model depicted in Exhibit 10–4; however, these variances can also be calculated using basic mathematical equations. Exhibit 10–5 shows how Colonial Pewter can compute its direct materials variances using the equations-based approach.

EXHIBIT 10–5
Direct Materials Variances: The Equations-Based Approach

Materials Price Variance:

Materials price variance = $(AQ \times AP) - (AQ \times SP)$
Materials price variance = $AQ(AP - SP)$
Materials price variance = 6,500 pounds ($3.80 per pound − $4.00 per pound)
Materials price variance = $1,300 F

Materials Quantity Variance:

Materials quantity variance = $(AQ \times SP) - (SQ \times SP)$
Materials quantity variance = $SP(AQ - SQ)$
Materials quantity variance = $4.00 per pound (6,500 pounds − 6,000 pounds)
Materials quantity variance = $2,000 U

where:
AQ = Actual quantity of inputs purchased and used in production
SQ = Standard quantity of inputs allowed for the actual output
AP = Actual price per unit of the input
SP = Standard price per unit of the input

Using Standard Costs—Direct Labor Variances

Terry Sherman's next step in determining Colonial Pewter's variances for June was to compute the direct labor variances for the month. Recall from Exhibit 10–1 that the standard direct labor cost per statue is $11, computed as follows:

$$0.50 \text{ hours per statue} \times \$22.00 \text{ per hour} = \$11.00 \text{ per statue}$$

In addition, Colonial Pewter's records for June showed that 1,050 direct labor-hours were actually worked. Given that the company paid its direct labor workers a total of $22,680 (including payroll taxes and fringe benefits), the average actual wage rate was $21.60 per hour (= $22,680 ÷ 1,050 hours). Using these data and the standard costs from Exhibit 10–1, Terry computed the direct labor rate and efficiency variances that appear in Exhibit 10–6.

Notice that the column headings in Exhibit 10–6 are the same as those used in Exhibits 10–3 and 10–4, except that in Exhibit 10–6 the terms *rate* and *hours* are used in place of the terms *price* and *quantity*.

LO10–2
Compute the direct labor rate and efficiency variances and explain their significance.

The Labor Rate Variance

Using the $23,100 total cost figure in column (2) of Exhibit 10–6, we can make two comparisons—one with the total cost of $22,680 in column (1) and one with the total cost of $22,000 in column (3). The difference between the 22,680 in column (1) and the $23,100 in column (2) is the *labor rate variance* of $420 F. The **labor rate variance** measures the difference between the actual hourly rate and the standard hourly rate, multiplied by the actual number of hours worked during the period.

To understand the labor rate variance, note that the actual hourly rate of $21.60 is $0.40 less than the standard rate of $22.00 per hour. Because 1,050 hours were actually worked, the total amount of the variance is $420 (= $0.40 per hour × 1,050 hours). The variance is labeled favorable (F) because the actual hourly rate is less than the standard hourly rate. If the actual hourly rate had been greater than the standard hourly rate, the variance would have been labeled unfavorable (U).

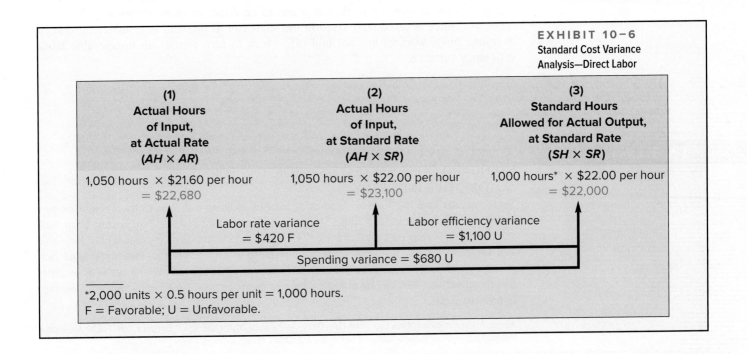

EXHIBIT 10–6
Standard Cost Variance Analysis—Direct Labor

(1) Actual Hours of Input, at Actual Rate (AH × AR)	(2) Actual Hours of Input, at Standard Rate (AH × SR)	(3) Standard Hours Allowed for Actual Output, at Standard Rate (SH × SR)
1,050 hours × $21.60 per hour = $22,680	1,050 hours × $22.00 per hour = $23,100	1,000 hours* × $22.00 per hour = $22,000

Labor rate variance = $420 F

Labor efficiency variance = $1,100 U

Spending variance = $680 U

*2,000 units × 0.5 hours per unit = 1,000 hours.
F = Favorable; U = Unfavorable.

In most companies, the wage rates paid to workers are quite predictable. Nevertheless, rate variances can arise based on how production supervisors use their direct labor workers. Skilled workers with high hourly rates of pay may be given duties that require little skill and call for lower hourly rates of pay. This will result in an unfavorable labor rate variance because the actual hourly rate of pay will exceed the standard rate specified for the particular task. In contrast, a favorable rate variance would result when workers who are paid at a rate lower than specified in the standard are assigned to the task. However, the lower-paid workers may not be as efficient. Finally, overtime work at premium rates will result in an unfavorable labor rate variance if the overtime premium is charged to the direct labor account.

The Labor Efficiency Variance

Referring back to Exhibit 10–6, the difference between the $23,100 in column (2) and the $22,000 in column (3) is the *labor efficiency variance* of $1,100 unfavorable (U). The **labor efficiency variance** measures the difference between the actual labor-hours used and the standard hours allowed for the actual output, multiplied by the standard hourly rate.

To understand Colonial Pewter's labor efficiency variance, note that the actual labor-hours used in production was 1,050 hours. However, the standard amount of hours allowed for the 2,000 statues actually produced is 1,000 hours. Therefore, the company used 50 more hours for the actual output than the standards allow. To express this in dollar terms, the 50 hours are multiplied by the standard rate of $22.00 per labor-hour to yield the efficiency variance of $1,100 U.

Possible causes of an unfavorable labor efficiency variance include poorly trained or motivated workers; poor-quality materials, requiring more labor time; faulty equipment, causing breakdowns and work interruptions; and poor supervision of workers. The managers in charge of production would usually be responsible for control of the labor efficiency variance. However, the purchasing manager could be held responsible if the purchase of poor-quality materials resulted in excessive labor processing time.

Another important cause of an unfavorable labor efficiency variance may be insufficient demand for the company's products. Managers in some companies argue that it is difficult, and perhaps unwise, to constantly adjust the workforce in response to changes in the amount of work that needs to be done. In such companies, the direct labor workforce is essentially fixed in the short run. If demand is insufficient to keep everyone busy, workers are not laid off, which in turn creates an unfavorable labor efficiency variance.

IN BUSINESS

STANDARD COST SYSTEM USAGE IN THE TURKISH AUTOMOTIVE INDUSTRY

Survey results from the Turkish automotive industry indicate that 74% of the companies surveyed use standard costing. About 55% of the companies that use standard costing base their standards on average past performance, 24% base their standards on maximum efficiency, and 21% set standards that are achievable but difficult to attain. Rather than investigating all variances, 70% of the companies only investigate variances that exceed either a dollar or percentage threshold and 27% rely on statistical control charts to determine which variances warrant further attention.

Source: A. Cemkut Badem, Emre Ergin, and Colin Drury, "Is Standard Costing Still Used? Evidence from Turkish Automotive Industry," *International Business Research*, Vol. 6, No. 7, 2013, pp. 79–90.

If customer orders are insufficient to keep the workers busy, the work center manager has two options—either accept an unfavorable labor efficiency variance or build inventory. A central lesson of Lean Production is that building inventory with no immediate prospect of sale is a bad idea. Excessive inventory—particularly work in process inventory—leads to high defect rates, obsolete goods, and inefficient operations. As a consequence, when the workforce is fixed in the short term, managers must be cautious about how labor efficiency variances are used. Some experts advocate eliminating labor efficiency variances in such situations—at least for the purposes of motivating and controlling workers on the shop floor.

Direct labor variances can also be computed using equations instead of the general model depicted in Exhibit 10–6. Exhibit 10–7 shows how Colonial Pewter can compute its direct labor variances using the equations-based approach.

EXHIBIT 10–7
Direct Labor Variances: The Equations-Based Approach

Labor Rate Variance:

Labor rate variance = $(AH \times AR) - (AH \times SR)$
Labor rate variance = $AH(AR - SR)$
Labor rate variance = 1,050 hours ($21.60 per hour − $22.00 per hour)
Labor rate variance = $420 F

Labor Efficiency Variance:

Labor efficiency variance = $(AH \times SR) - (SH \times SR)$
Labor efficiency variance = $SR(AH - SH)$
Labor efficiency variance = $22.00 per hour (1,050 hours − 1,000 hours)
Labor efficiency variance = $1,100 U

where:
AH = Actual quantity of labor-hours used in production
SH = Standard quantity of labor-hours allowed for the actual output
AR = Actual rate per direct labor-hour
SR = Standard rate per direct labor-hour

Using Standard Costs—Variable Manufacturing Overhead Variances

The final step in Terry Sherman's analysis of Colonial Pewter's variances for June was to compute the variable manufacturing overhead variances. The variable portion of manufacturing overhead can be analyzed using the same basic formulas that we used to analyze direct materials and direct labor. Recall from Exhibit 10–1 that the standard variable manufacturing overhead is $3.00 per statue, computed as follows:

0.50 hours per statue × $6.00 per hour = $3.00 per statue

Also recall that Colonial Pewter's cost records showed that the total actual variable manufacturing overhead cost for June was $7,140 and that 1,050 direct labor-hours were worked in June to produce 2,000 statues. Terry's analysis of this overhead data appears in Exhibit 10–8.

Notice the similarities between Exhibits 10–6 and 10–8. These similarities arise from the fact that direct labor-hours are being used as the base for allocating overhead cost to units of product; thus, the same hourly figures appear in Exhibit 10–8 for variable manufacturing overhead as in Exhibit 10–6 for direct labor. The main difference between the two exhibits is in the standard hourly rate being used, which in this company is much lower for variable manufacturing overhead than for direct labor.

LO10–3
Compute the variable manufacturing overhead rate and efficiency variances and explain their significance.

EXHIBIT 10–8
Standard Cost Variance Analysis—Variable
Manufacturing Overhead

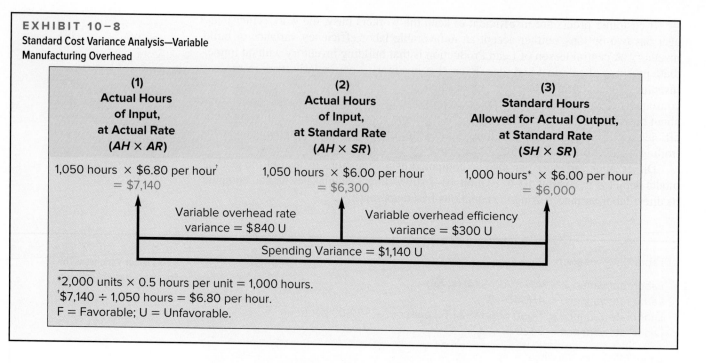

(1) Actual Hours of Input, at Actual Rate (AH × AR)	(2) Actual Hours of Input, at Standard Rate (AH × SR)	(3) Standard Hours Allowed for Actual Output, at Standard Rate (SH × SR)
1,050 hours × $6.80 per hour† = $7,140	1,050 hours × $6.00 per hour = $6,300	1,000 hours* × $6.00 per hour = $6,000

Variable overhead rate
variance = $840 U

Variable overhead efficiency
variance = $300 U

Spending Variance = $1,140 U

*2,000 units × 0.5 hours per unit = 1,000 hours.
†$7,140 ÷ 1,050 hours = $6.80 per hour.
F = Favorable; U = Unfavorable.

The Variable Manufacturing Overhead Rate and Efficiency Variances

Using the $6,300 total cost figure in column (2) of Exhibit 10–8, we can make two comparisons—one with the total cost of $7,140 in column (1) and one with the total cost of $6,000 in column (3). The difference between the $7,140 in column (1) and the $6,300 in column (2) is the *variable overhead rate variance* of $840 U. The **variable overhead rate variance** measures the difference between the actual variable overhead cost incurred during the period and the standard cost that should have been incurred based on the actual activity of the period. The difference between the $6,300 in column (2) and the $6,000 in column (3) is the *variable overhead efficiency variance* of $300 U. The **variable overhead efficiency variance** measures the difference between the actual level of activity and the standard activity allowed for the actual output, multiplied by the variable part of the predetermined overhead rate.

To understand Colonial Pewter's variable overhead efficiency variance, note that the actual amount of labor-hours used in production was 1,050 hours. However, the standard amount of labor-hours allowed for the actual output is 1,000 hours. Therefore, the company used 50 more hours for the actual output than the standards allow. To express this in dollar terms, the 50 hours are multiplied by the variable part of the predetermined overhead rate of $6.00 per labor-hour to yield the variable overhead efficiency variance of $300 U.

The interpretation of the variable overhead variances is not as clear as the direct materials and direct labor variances. In particular, the variable overhead efficiency variance is exactly the same as the direct labor efficiency variance except for one detail—the rate that is used to translate the variance into dollars. In both cases, the variance is the difference between the actual hours worked and the standard hours allowed for the actual output. In the case of the direct labor efficiency variance, this difference is multiplied by the standard direct labor rate. In the case of the variable overhead efficiency variance, this difference is multiplied by the variable portion of the predetermined overhead rate. So when direct labor is used as the overhead allocation base, whenever the direct labor efficiency variance is favorable, the variable overhead efficiency variance will also be favorable. And whenever the direct labor efficiency variance is unfavorable, the variable overhead efficiency variance will be unfavorable. Indeed, the variable overhead efficiency variance really doesn't tell us anything about how efficiently overhead resources were used. It depends solely on how efficiently direct labor was used.

EXHIBIT 10–9
Variable Manufacturing Overhead Variances: The Equations-Based Approach

Variable Overhead Rate Variance:

Variable overhead rate variance = $(AH \times AR) - (AH \times SR)$
Variable overhead rate variance = $AH(AR - SR)$
Variable overhead rate variance = 1,050 hours ($6.80 - $6.00)
Variable overhead rate variance = $840 U

Variable Overhead Efficiency Variance:

Variable overhead efficiency variance = $(AH \times SR) - (SH \times SR)$
Variable overhead efficiency variance = $SR(AH - SH)$
Variable overhead efficiency variance = $6.00 per hour (1,050 hours − 1,000 hours)
Variable overhead efficiency variance = $300 U

where:
AH = Actual quantity of labor-hours used in production
SH = Standard quantity of labor-hours allowed for the actual output
AR = Actual rate per labor-hour
SR = Standard rate per labor-hour (Variable portion of the predetermined overhead rate)

Variable manufacturing overhead variances can also be computed using equations instead of the general model depicted in Exhibit 10–8. Exhibit 10–9 shows how Colonial Pewter can compute its variable overhead variances using the equations-based approach.

In preparation for the scheduled meeting to discuss his analysis of Colonial Pewter's standard costs and variances, Terry summarized his manufacturing cost variances as follows:

Materials price variance	$ 1,300 F
Materials quantity variance	2,000 U
Labor rate variance	420 F
Labor efficiency variance	1,100 U
Variable overhead rate variance	840 U
Variable overhead efficiency variance	300 U
Total of the variances	$2,520 U

He distributed these results to the management group of Colonial Pewter, which included J. D. Wriston, the president of the company; Tom Kuchel, the production manager; and Janet Warner, the purchasing manager. J. D. Wriston opened the meeting with the following question:

MANAGERIAL ACCOUNTING IN ACTION
THE WRAP-UP

Colonial Pewter Company

J. D.: Terry, I think I understand what you have done, but just to make sure, would you mind summarizing the highlights of what you found?

Terry: As you can see, the biggest problems are the unfavorable materials quantity variance of $2,000 and the unfavorable labor efficiency variance of $1,100.

J. D.: Tom, you're the production boss. What do you think is causing the unfavorable labor efficiency variance?

Tom: It has to be the new production workers. Our experienced workers shouldn't have much problem meeting the standard of half an hour per unit. We all knew that there would be some inefficiency for a while as we brought new people on board. My plan for overcoming the problem is to pair up each of the new guys with one of our old-timers and have them work together for a while. It would slow down our older guys a bit, but I'll bet the unfavorable variance disappears and our new workers would learn a lot.

J. D.: Sounds good. Now, what about that $2,000 unfavorable materials quantity variance?

Terry: Tom, are the new workers generating a lot of scrap?

Tom: Yeah, I guess so.

J. D.:   I think that could be part of the problem. Can you do anything about it?

Tom: I can watch the scrap closely for a few days to see where it's being generated. If it is the new workers, I can have the old-timers work with them on the problem when I team them up.

J. D.:   Janet, the favorable materials price variance of $1,300 isn't helping us if it is contributing to the unfavorable materials quantity and labor efficiency variances. Let's make sure that our raw material purchases conform to our quality standards.

Janet: Will do.

J. D.:   Good. Let's reconvene in a few weeks to see what has happened. Hopefully, we can get those unfavorable variances under control.

An Important Subtlety in the Materials Variances

Most companies use the *quantity of materials purchased* to compute the materials price variance and the *quantity of materials used* in production to compute the materials quantity variance. There are two reasons for this practice. First, delaying the computation of the price variance until the materials are used would result in less timely variance reports. Second, computing the price variance when the materials are purchased allows materials to be carried in the inventory accounts at their standard cost. This greatly simplifies bookkeeping.

When we computed materials price and quantity variances for Colonial Pewter in Exhibit 10–4, we assumed that 6,500 pounds of materials were purchased and used in production. However, it is very common for a company's quantity of materials purchased to differ from its quantity used in production. When this happens, the materials price variance is computed using the *quantity of materials purchased,* whereas the materials quantity variance is computed using the *quantity of materials used* in production.

To illustrate, assume that during June Colonial Pewter purchased 7,000 pounds of materials at $3.80 per pound instead of 6,500 pounds as assumed earlier in the chapter. Also assume the company continued to use 6,500 pounds of materials in production and that the standard price remained at $4.00 per pound.

Given these assumptions, Exhibit 10–10 shows how to compute the materials price variance of $1,400 F and the materials quantity variance of $2,000 U. Note that the price variance is based on the pounds purchased whereas the quantity variance is based on the pounds used in production. Column (2) of Exhibit 10–10 contains two different total costs for this reason. When the price variance is computed, the total cost used from column (2) is $28,000—which is the cost of the pounds *purchased,* evaluated at the standard price. When the quantity variance is computed, the total cost used from column (2) is $26,000—which is the cost of the actual pounds *used,* evaluated at the standard price.

Exhibit 10–10 shows that the price variance is computed on the entire amount of material purchased (7,000 pounds), whereas the quantity variance is computed only on the amount of materials used in production during the month (6,500 pounds). What about the other 500 pounds of material that were purchased during the period, but that have not yet been used? When those materials are used in future periods, a quantity variance will be computed. However, a price variance will not be computed when the materials are finally used because the price variance was computed when the materials were purchased.

Because the price variance is based on the amount purchased and the quantity variance is based on the amount used, the two variances do not generally sum to the spending variance from the flexible budget, which is wholly based on the amount used. We would also like to emphasize that the variances depicted in Exhibit 10–10 can also be computed using the equations shown in Exhibit 10–11. The approaches shown in *Exhibits 10–10 and 10–11 can always be used to compute direct materials variances.* However, *Exhibits 10–4 and 10–5 can only be used in the special case when the quantity of materials purchased equals the quantity of materials used.*

EXHIBIT 10–10
Standard Cost Variance
Analysis—Direct Materials

(Note: The quantity of materials purchased does not equal the quantity used in production.)

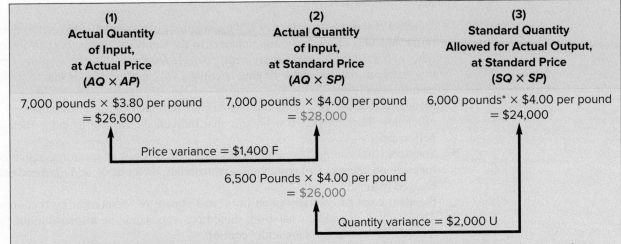

(1) Actual Quantity of Input, at Actual Price $(AQ \times AP)$	(2) Actual Quantity of Input, at Standard Price $(AQ \times SP)$	(3) Standard Quantity Allowed for Actual Output, at Standard Price $(SQ \times SP)$
7,000 pounds × $3.80 per pound = $26,600	7,000 pounds × $4.00 per pound = $28,000	6,000 pounds* × $4.00 per pound = $24,000

Price variance = $1,400 F

6,500 Pounds × $4.00 per pound = $26,000

Quantity variance = $2,000 U

In this case, the price variance and the quantity variance do not sum to the spending variance because the price variance is based on the quantity purchased whereas the quantity variance is based on the quantity used in production, and the two numbers differ.

———
*2,000 units × 3.0 pounds per unit = 6,000 pounds.
F = Favorable; U = Unfavorable.

EXHIBIT 10–11
Direct Materials Variances: The
Equations-Based Approach (when
the quantity of materials purchased
does not equal the quantity used in
production)

Materials Price Variance:

Materials price variance = $(AQ \times AP) - (AQ \times SP)$
Materials price variance = $AQ(AP - SP)$
Materials price variance = 7,000 pounds ($3.80 per pound − $4.00 per pound)
Materials price variance = $1,400 F

where:
AQ = Actual quantity of inputs *purchased*
AP = Actual price per unit of the input
SP = Standard price per unit of the input

Materials Quantity Variance:

Materials quantity variance = $(AQ \times SP) - (SQ \times SP)$
Materials quantity variance = $SP(AQ - SQ)$
Materials quantity variance = $4.00 per pound (6,500 pounds − 6,000 pounds)
Materials quantity variance = $2,000 U

where:
AQ = Actual quantity of inputs *used in production*
SQ = Standard quantity of inputs allowed for the actual output
SP = Standard price per unit of the input

Standard Costs—Managerial Implications

Advantages of Standard Costs

Standard cost systems have a number of advantages.

1. Standard costs are a key element in a management by exception approach as defined in the previous chapter. If costs conform to the standards, managers can focus on other issues. When costs are significantly outside the standards, managers are alerted that problems may exist that require attention. This approach helps managers focus on important issues.
2. Standards that are viewed as reasonable by employees can promote economy and efficiency. They provide benchmarks that individuals can use to judge their own performance.
3. Standard costs can greatly simplify bookkeeping. Instead of recording actual costs for each job, the standard costs for direct materials, direct labor, and overhead can be charged to jobs.
4. Standard costs fit naturally in an integrated system of "responsibility accounting." The standards establish what costs should be, who should be responsible for them, and whether actual costs are under control.

Potential Problems with Standard Costs

The improper use of standard costs can present a number of potential problems.

1. Standard cost variance reports are usually prepared on a monthly basis and often are released days or even weeks after the end of the month. As a consequence, the information in the reports may be so outdated that it is almost useless. Timely, frequent reports that are approximately correct are better than infrequent reports that are very precise but out of date by the time they are released. Some companies are now reporting variances and other key operating data daily or even more frequently.
2. If managers use variances only to assign blame and punish subordinates, morale may suffer. Furthermore, subordinates may be tempted to cover up unfavorable variances or take actions that are not in the best interests of the company to make sure the variances are favorable.
3. Labor-hour standards and efficiency variances make two important assumptions. First, they assume that the production process is labor-paced; if labor works faster, output will go up. However, output in many companies is not determined by how fast labor works; rather, it is determined by the processing speed of machines. Second, the computations assume that labor is a variable cost. However, direct labor can often be a fixed cost. If labor is fixed, then an undue emphasis on labor efficiency variances creates pressure to build excess inventories.
4. In some cases, a "favorable" variance can be worse than an "unfavorable" variance. For example, **McDonald's** has a standard for the amount of hamburger meat that should be in a Big Mac. A "favorable" variance would mean that less meat was used than the standard specifies. The result is substandard Big Macs and possibly numerous dissatisfied customers.
5. Too much emphasis on meeting the standards may overshadow other important objectives such as maintaining and improving quality, on-time delivery, and customer satisfaction. This tendency can be reduced by using supplemental performance measures that focus on these other objectives.
6. Just meeting standards is not sufficient because companies need to continually improve to remain competitive. For this reason, some companies focus on the trends in their standard cost variances—aiming for continual improvement rather than just meeting the standards. In other companies, engineered standards are replaced either by a rolling average of actual costs, which is expected to decline, or by very challenging target costs.

In sum, managers should exercise considerable care when using a standard cost system. It is particularly important that managers go out of their way to focus on the positive, rather than just on the negative, and to be aware of possible unintended consequences.

A LOOK AT STANDARD COST SYSTEM USAGE IN DUBAI

While many critics continue to raise credible concerns about the merits of standard costing, the data consistently show that many companies continue to use it. For example, survey results from 100 companies in Dubai indicate that 77% of industrial companies and 39% of service companies use standard cost systems. These companies believe that standard cost information aides them in budgeting, cost control and performance evaluation, computing product costs for decision making, and costing inventories. More than two-thirds of the industrial and service companies using standard costs reported that they review their standards at least semiannually to adjust them in response to changes in business conditions and performance expectations.

Source: Attiea Marie, Walid Cheffi, Rosmy Jean Louis, and Ananth Rao, "Is Standard Costing Still Relevant? Evidence from Dubai," *Management Accounting Quarterly*, Winter, 2010, pp. 1–10.

© Dinodia Photos/Alamy

Summary

A standard is a benchmark for measuring performance. Standards are set for both the quantity and the cost of inputs needed to manufacture goods or to provide services. Quantity standards indicate how much of an input, such as labor time or raw materials, should be used to make a product or provide a service. Cost standards indicate what the cost per unit of the input should be.

When standards are compared to actual performance, the difference is referred to as a *variance*. Variances are computed and reported to management on a regular basis for both the quantity and the price elements of direct materials, direct labor, and variable overhead. Price variances are computed by taking the difference between actual and standard prices and multiplying the result by the amount of input purchased. Quantity variances are computed by taking the difference between the actual amount of the input used and the amount of input that is allowed for the actual output, and then multiplying the result by the standard price per unit of the input.

Standard cost systems provide companies with a number of advantages, such as supporting the management by exception approach, simplifying bookkeeping, and providing a benchmark that employees can use to judge their own performance. However, critics of standard cost systems argue that they provide information that is outdated, they can motivate employees to make poor decisions in an effort to generate favorable variances, and they fail to adequately embrace the mindset of continuous process improvement.

Traditional standard cost variance reports are often supplemented with other performance measures to ensure that overemphasis on standard cost variances does not lead to problems in other critical areas such as product quality, inventory levels, and on-time delivery.

Review Problem: Standard Costs

Xavier Company produces a single product. Variable manufacturing overhead is applied to products on the basis of direct labor-hours. The standard cost card for one unit of product is as follows:

Inputs	(1) Standard Quantity or Hours	(2) Standard Price or Rate	Standard Cost (1) × (2)
Direct materials	6 ounces	$0.50 per ounce	$ 3.00
Direct labor.	0.6 hours	$30.00 per hour	18.00
Variable manufacturing overhead . . .	0.6 hours	$10.00 per hour	6.00
Total standard cost per unit.			$27.00

During June, 2,000 units were produced. The costs associated with June's operations were as follows:

Material purchased: 18,000 ounces at $0.60 per ounce..........	$10,800
Material used in production: 14,000 ounces	—
Direct labor: 1,100 hours at $30.50 per hour	$33,550
Variable manufacturing overhead costs incurred	$12,980

Required:

Compute the direct materials, direct labor, and variable manufacturing overhead variances.

Solution to Review Problem

Direct Materials Variances

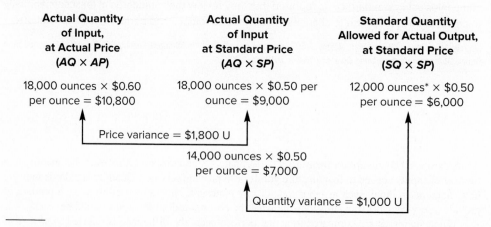

Actual Quantity of Input, at Actual Price (AQ × AP)	Actual Quantity of Input, at Standard Price (AQ × SP)	Standard Quantity Allowed for Actual Output, at Standard Price (SQ × SP)
18,000 ounces × $0.60 per ounce = $10,800	18,000 ounces × $0.50 per ounce = $9,000	12,000 ounces* × $0.50 per ounce = $6,000

Price variance = $1,800 U

14,000 ounces × $0.50 per ounce = $7,000

Quantity variance = $1,000 U

*2,000 units × 6 ounces per unit = 12,000 ounces.
F = Favorable; U = Unfavorable.

Using formulas, the same variances would be computed as follows:

$$\text{Materials price variance} = (AQ \times AP) - (AQ \times SP)$$
$$= AQ(AP - SP)$$
$$= 18,000 \text{ ounces } (\$0.60 \text{ per ounce} \times \$0.50 \text{ per ounce})$$
$$= \$1,800 \text{ U}$$
$$\text{Materials quantity variance} = (AQ \times SP) - (SQ \times SP)$$
$$= SP(AQ - SQ)$$
$$= \$0.50 \text{ per ounce } (14,000 \text{ ounces} \times 12,000 \text{ ounces})$$
$$= \$1,000 \text{ U}$$

Direct Labor Variances

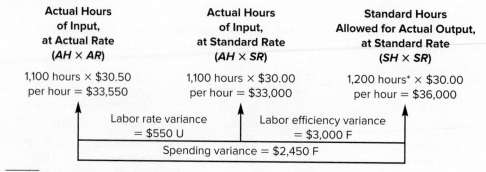

Actual Hours of Input, at Actual Rate (AH × AR)	Actual Hours of Input, at Standard Rate (AH × SR)	Standard Hours Allowed for Actual Output, at Standard Rate (SH × SR)
1,100 hours × $30.50 per hour = $33,550	1,100 hours × $30.00 per hour = $33,000	1,200 hours* × $30.00 per hour = $36,000

Labor rate variance = $550 U   Labor efficiency variance = $3,000 F

Spending variance = $2,450 F

*2,000 units × 0.6 hours per unit = 1,200 hours.
F = Favorable; U = Unfavorable.

Using formulas, the same variances can be computed as follows:

$$\text{Labor rate variance} = (AH \times AR) - (AH \times SR)$$
$$= AH(AR - SR)$$
$$= 1,100 \text{ hours } (\$30.50 \text{ per hour} - \$30.00 \text{ per hour})$$
$$= \$550 \text{ U}$$

$$\text{Labor efficiency variance} = (AH \times SR) - (SH \times SR)$$
$$= SR(AH - SH)$$
$$= \$30.00 \text{ per hour } (1,100 \text{ hours} - 1,200 \text{ hours})$$
$$= \$3,000 \text{ F}$$

Variable Manufacturing Overhead Variances

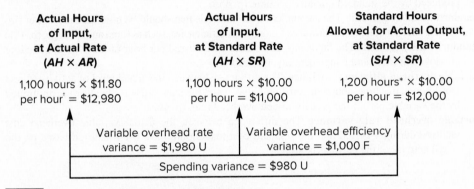

Actual Hours of Input, at Actual Rate (**AH × AR**)	Actual Hours of Input, at Standard Rate (**AH × SR**)	Standard Hours Allowed for Actual Output, at Standard Rate (**SH × SR**)
1,100 hours × $11.80 per hour† = $12,980	1,100 hours × $10.00 per hour = $11,000	1,200 hours* × $10.00 per hour = $12,000

Variable overhead rate variance = $1,980 U

Variable overhead efficiency variance = $1,000 F

Spending variance = $980 U

---

*2,000 units × 0.6 hours per unit = 1,200 hours.
†$12,980 ÷ 1,100 hours = $11.80 per hour.
F = Favorable; U = Unfavorable.

Using formulas, the same variances can be computed as follows:

$$\text{Variable overhead rate variance} = (AH \times AR) - (AH \times SR)$$
$$= AH(AR - SR)$$
$$= 1,100 \text{ hours } (\$11.80 \text{ per hour} - \$10.00 \text{ per hour})$$
$$= \$1,980 \text{ U}$$

$$\text{Variable overhead efficiency variance} = (AH \times SR) - (SH \times SR)$$
$$= SR(AH - SH)$$
$$= \$10.00 \text{ per hour } (1,100 \text{ hours} - 1,200 \text{ hours})$$
$$= \$1,000 \text{ F}$$

Glossary

Labor efficiency variance The difference between the actual labor-hours taken to complete a task and the standard hours allowed for the actual output, multiplied by the standard hourly labor rate. (p. 460)

Labor rate variance The difference between the actual hourly labor rate and the standard rate, multiplied by the number of hours worked during the period. (p. 459)

Materials price variance The difference between a direct material's actual price per unit and its standard price per unit, multiplied by the quantity purchased. (p. 457)

Materials quantity variance The difference between the actual quantity of materials used in production and the standard quantity allowed for the actual output, multiplied by the standard price per unit of materials. (p. 458)

Price variance A variance that is computed by taking the difference between the actual price and the standard price and multiplying the result by the actual quantity of the input. (p. 454)

Quantity variance A variance that is computed by taking the difference between the actual quantity of the input used and the amount of the input that should have been used for the actual level of output and multiplying the result by the standard price of the input. (p. 454)

Standard cost card A detailed listing of the standard amounts of inputs and their costs that are required to produce one unit of a specific product. (p. 452)

Standard cost per unit The standard quantity allowed of an input per unit of a specific product, multiplied by the standard price of the input. (p. 452)

Standard hours allowed The time that should have been taken to complete the period's output. It is computed by multiplying the actual number of units produced by the standard hours per unit. (p. 455)

Standard hours per unit The amount of direct labor time that should be required to complete a single unit of product, including allowances for breaks, machine downtime, cleanup, rejects, and other normal inefficiencies. (p. 451)

Standard price per unit The price that should be paid for each unit of direct materials. It should reflect the final, delivered cost of those materials. (p. 451)

Standard quantity allowed The amount of direct materials that should have been used to complete the period's actual output. It is computed by multiplying the actual number of units produced by the standard quantity per unit. (p. 455)

Standard quantity per unit The amount of direct materials that should be used for each unit of finished product, including an allowance for normal inefficiencies, such as scrap and spoilage. (p. 451)

Standard rate per hour The labor rate that should be incurred per hour of labor time, including employment taxes and fringe benefits. (p. 452)

Variable overhead efficiency variance The difference between the actual level of activity (direct labor-hours, machine-hours, or some other base) and the standard activity allowed, multiplied by the variable part of the predetermined overhead rate. (p. 462)

Variable overhead rate variance The difference between the actual variable overhead cost incurred during a period and the standard cost that should have been incurred based on the actual activity of the period. (p. 462)

Questions

10–1 What is a quantity standard? What is a price standard?

10–2 Why are separate price and quantity variances computed?

10–3 Who is generally responsible for the materials price variance? The materials quantity variance? The labor efficiency variance?

10–4 The materials price variance can be computed at what two different points in time? Which point is better? Why?

10–5 If the materials price variance is favorable but the materials quantity variance is unfavorable, what might this indicate?

10–6 Should standards be used to identify who to blame for problems?

10–7 "Our workers are all under labor contracts; therefore, our labor rate variance is bound to be zero." Discuss.

10–8 What effect, if any, would you expect poor-quality materials to have on direct labor variances?

10–9 If variable manufacturing overhead is applied to production on the basis of direct labor-hours and the direct labor efficiency variance is unfavorable, will the variable overhead efficiency variance be favorable or unfavorable, or could it be either? Explain.

10–10 Why can undue emphasis on labor efficiency variances lead to excess work in process inventories?

Applying Excel connect

LO10–1, LO10–2, LO10–3

The Excel worksheet form that appears below is to be used to recreate the main example in the text pertaining to Colonial Pewter Company. Download the workbook containing this form from Connect, where you will also receive instructions about how to use this worksheet form.

You should proceed to the requirements below only after completing your worksheet.

Required:

1. Check your worksheet by changing the direct materials standard quantity in cell B6 to 2.9 pounds, the direct labor standard quantity in cell B7 to 0.6 hours, and the variable manufacturing overhead in cell B8 to 0.6 hours. The materials spending variance should now be $1,500 U, the labor spending variance should now be $3,720 F, and the variable overhead spending variance should now be $60 F. If you do not get these answers, find the errors in your worksheet and correct them.

a. What is the materials quantity variance? Explain this variance.
b. What is the labor rate variance? Explain this variance.

	A	B	C	D	E	F	G
1	Chapter 10: Applying Excel						
2							
3	**Data**						
4	*Exhibit 10-1: Standard Cost Card*						
5	*Inputs*	*Standard Quantity*		*Standard Price*			
6	Direct materials	3.0 pounds		$4.00 per pound			
7	Direct labor	0.50 hours		$22.00 per hour			
8	Variable manufacturing overhead	0.50 hours		$6.00 per hour			
9							
10	Actual results:						
11	Actual output	2,000 units					
12	Actual variable manufacturing overhead cost	$7,140					
13		*Actual Quantity*		*Actual price*			
14	Actual direct materials cost	6,500 pounds		$3.80 per pound			
15	Actual direct labor cost	1,050 hours		$21.60 per hour			
16							
17	*Enter a formula into each of the cells marked with a ? below*						
18	**Main Example: Chapter 10**						
19							
20	*Exhibit 10-4: Standard Cost Variance Analysis–Direct Materials*						
21	Actual Quantity of Input, at Actual Price	? pounds ×		? per pound =		?	
22	Actual Quantity of Input, at Standard Price	? pounds ×		? per pound =		?	
23	Standard Quantity Allowed for the Actual Output, at Standard Price	? pounds ×		? per pound =		?	
24	Direct materials variances:						
25	Materials price variance	?					
26	Materials quantity variance	?					
27	Materials spending variance	?					
28							
29	*Exhibit 10-6: Standard Cost Variance Analysis–Direct Labor*						
30	Actual Hours of Input, at Actual Rate	? hours ×		? per hour =		?	
31	Actual Hours of Input, at Standard Rate	? hours ×		? per hour =		?	
32	Standard Hours Allowed for the Actual Output, at Standard Rate	? hours ×		? per hour =		?	
33	Direct labor variances:						
34	Labor rate variance	?					
35	Labor efficiency variance	?					
36	Labor spending variance	?					
37							
38	*Exhibit 10-8: Standard Cost Variance Analysis–Variable Manufacturing Overhead*						
39	Actual Hours of Input, at Actual Rate	? hours ×		? per hour =		?	
40	Actual Hours of Input, at Standard Rate	? hours ×		? per hour =		?	
41	Standard Hours Allowed for the Actual Output, at Standard Rate	? hours ×		? per hour =		?	
42	Variable overhead variances:						
43	Variable overhead rate variance	?					
44	Variable overhead efficiency variance	?					
45	Variable overhead spending variance	?					
46							

Chapter 10 Form | Filled in Chapter 10 Form | Chapter 10 Formulas

2. Revise the data in your worksheet to reflect the results for the subsequent period:

Data
Exhibit 10–1: Standard Cost Card

	Standard Quantity	Standard Price
Inputs.........		
Direct materials	3.0 pounds	$4.00 per pound
Direct labor......	0.50 hours	$22.00 per hour
Variable manufacturing overhead	0.50 hours	$6.00 per hour
Actual results:		
Actual output	2,100 units	
Actual variable manufacturing overhead cost	$5,100	
	Actual Quantity	Actual price
Actual direct materials cost......	6,350 pounds	$4.10 per pound
Actual direct labor cost	1,020 hours	$22.10 per hour

a.   What is the materials quantity variance? What is the materials price variance?
b.   What is the labor efficiency variance? What is the labor rate variance?
c.   What is the variable overhead efficiency variance? What is the variable overhead rate variance?

The Foundational 15   ▨ connect

LO10–1, LO10–2, LO10–3

Preble Company manufactures one product. Its variable manufacturing overhead is applied to production based on direct labor-hours and its standard cost card per unit is as follows:

Inputs	(1) Standard Quantity or Hours	(2) Standard Price or Rate	Standard Cost (1) × (2)
Direct materials	5 pounds	$8.00 per pound	$40.00
Direct labor.	2 hours	$14 per hour	28.00
Variable overhead.	2 hours	$5 per hour	10.00
Total standard cost per unit.			$78.00

The planning budget for March was based on producing and selling 25,000 units. However, during March the company actually produced and sold 30,000 units and incurred the following costs:
a.   Purchased 160,000 pounds of raw materials at a cost of $7.50 per pound. All of this material was used in production.
b.   Direct laborers worked 55,000 hours at a rate of $15.00 per hour.
c.   Total variable manufacturing overhead for the month was $280,500.

Required:
1.   What raw materials cost would be included in the company's planning budget for March?
2.   What raw materials cost would be included in the company's flexible budget for March?
3.   What is the materials price variance for March?
4.   What is the materials quantity variance for March?
5.   If Preble had purchased 170,000 pounds of materials at $7.50 per pound and used 160,000 pounds in production, what would be the materials price variance for March?
6.   If Preble had purchased 170,000 pounds of materials at $7.50 per pound and used 160,000 pounds in production, what would be the materials quantity variance for March?
7.   What direct labor cost would be included in the company's planning budget for March?
8.   What direct labor cost would be included in the company's flexible budget for March?
9.   What is the labor rate variance for March?
10. What is the labor efficiency variance for March?
11. What is the labor spending variance for March?
12. What variable manufacturing overhead cost would be included in the company's planning budget for March?
13. What variable manufacturing overhead cost would be included in the company's flexible budget for March?
14. What is the variable overhead rate variance for March?
15. What is the variable overhead efficiency variance for March?

Exercises   ▨ connect

EXERCISE 10–1 Direct Materials Variances LO10–1
Bandar Industries Berhad of Malaysia manufactures sporting equipment. One of the company's products, a football helmet for the North American market, requires a special plastic. During the quarter ending June 30, the company manufactured 35,000 helmets, using 22,500 kilograms of plastic. The plastic cost the company $171,000.
   According to the standard cost card, each helmet should require 0.6 kilograms of plastic, at a cost of $8 per kilogram.

Required:
1.   What is the standard quantity of kilograms of plastic (SQ) that is allowed to make 35,000 helmets?
2.   What is the standard materials cost allowed (SQ × SP) to make 35,000 helmets?
3.   What is the materials spending variance?
4.   What is the materials price variance and the materials quantity variance?

EXERCISE 10–2 Direct Labor Variances LO10–2

SkyChefs, Inc., prepares in-flight meals for a number of major airlines. One of the company's products is grilled salmon in dill sauce with baby new potatoes and spring vegetables. During the most recent week, the company prepared 4,000 of these meals using 960 direct labor-hours. The company paid its direct labor workers a total of $19,200 for this work, or $20.00 per hour.

According to the standard cost card for this meal, it should require 0.25 direct labor-hours at a cost of $19.75 per hour.

Required:
1. What is the standard labor-hours allowed (SH) to prepare 4,000 meals?
2. What is the standard labor cost allowed (SH × SR) to prepare 4,000 meals?
3. What is the labor spending variance?
4. What is the labor rate variance and the labor efficiency variance?

EXERCISE 10–3 Variable Overhead Variances LO10–3

Logistics Solutions provides order fulfillment services for dot.com merchants. The company maintains warehouses that stock items carried by its dot.com clients. When a client receives an order from a customer, the order is forwarded to Logistics Solutions, which pulls the item from storage, packs it, and ships it to the customer. The company uses a predetermined variable overhead rate based on direct labor-hours.

In the most recent month, 120,000 items were shipped to customers using 2,300 direct labor-hours. The company incurred a total of $7,360 in variable overhead costs.

According to the company's standards, 0.02 direct labor-hours are required to fulfill an order for one item and the variable overhead rate is $3.25 per direct labor-hour.

Required:
1. What is the standard labor-hours allowed (SH) to ship 120,000 items to customers?
2. What is the standard variable overhead cost allowed (SH × SR) to ship 120,000 items to customers?
3. What is the variable overhead spending variance?
4. What is the variable overhead rate variance and the variable overhead efficiency variance?

EXERCISE 10–4 Direct Labor and Variable Manufacturing Overhead Variances LO10–2, LO10–3

Erie Company manufactures a mobile fitness device called the Jogging Mate. The company uses standards to control its costs. The labor standards that have been set for one Jogging Mate are as follows:

Standard Hours	Standard Rate per Hour	Standard Cost
18 minutes	$17.00	$5.10

During August, 5,750 hours of direct labor time were needed to make 20,000 units of the Jogging Mate. The direct labor cost totaled $102,350 for the month.

Required:
1. What is the standard labor-hours allowed (SH) to makes 20,000 Jogging Mates?
2. What is the standard labor cost allowed (SH × SR) to make 20,000 Jogging Mates?
3. What is the labor spending variance?
4. What is the labor rate variance and the labor efficiency variance?
5. The budgeted variable manufacturing overhead rate is $4 per direct labor-hour. During August, the company incurred $21,850 in variable manufacturing overhead cost. Compute the variable overhead rate and efficiency variances for the month.

EXERCISE 10–5 Working Backwards from Labor Variances LO10–2

The auto repair shop of Quality Motor Company uses standards to control the labor time and labor cost in the shop. The standard labor cost for a motor tune-up is given below:

	Standard Hours	Standard Rate	Standard Cost
Motor tune-up	2.5	$25.00	$62.50

The record showing the time spent in the shop last week on motor tune-ups has been misplaced. However, the shop supervisor recalls that 50 tune-ups were completed during the week, and the controller recalls the following variance data relating to tune-ups:

Labor rate variance..................	$150 F
Labor spending variance..............	$200 U

Required:
1. Determine the number of actual labor-hours spent on tune-ups during the week.
2. Determine the actual hourly rate of pay for tune-ups last week. (Round your answer to the nearest cent.)

(*Hint:* A useful way to proceed would be to work from known to unknown data either by using the variance formulas in Exhibit 10–7 or by using the columnar format shown in Exhibit 10–6.)

EXERCISE 10–6 Direct Materials and Direct Labor Variances LO10–1, LO10–2
Huron Company produces a commercial cleaning compound known as Zoom. The direct materials and direct labor standards for one unit of Zoom are given below:

	Standard Quantity or Hours	Standard Price or Rate	Standard Cost
Direct materials	4.6 pounds	$2.50 per pound	$11.50
Direct labor................	0.2 hours	$18.00 per hour	$3.60

During the most recent month, the following activity was recorded:
a. Twenty thousand pounds of material were purchased at a cost of $2.35 per pound.
b. All of the material purchased was used to produce 4,000 units of Zoom.
c. 750 hours of direct labor time were recorded at a total labor cost of $14,925.

Required:
1. Compute the materials price and quantity variances for the month.
2. Compute the labor rate and efficiency variances for the month.

EXERCISE 10–7 Direct Materials Variances LO10–1
Refer to the data in Exercise 10–6. Assume that instead of producing 4,000 units during the month, the company produced only 3,000 units, using 14,750 pounds of material. (The rest of the material purchased remained in raw materials inventory.)

Required:
Compute the materials price and quantity variances for the month.

EXERCISE 10–8 Direct Materials and Direct Labor Variances LO10–1, LO10–2

Dawson Toys, Ltd., produces a toy called the Maze. The company has recently created a standard cost system to help control costs and has established the following standards for the Maze toy:

Direct materials: 6 microns per toy at $1.50 per micron
Direct labor: 1.3 hours per toy at $21 per hour

During July, the company produced 3,000 Maze toys. The toy's production data for the month are as follows:

Direct materials: 25,000 microns were purchased at a cost of $1.48 per micron. 5,000 of these microns were still in inventory at the end of the month.
Direct labor: 4,000 direct labor-hours were worked at a cost of $88,000.

Required:
1. Compute the following variances for July:
   a. The materials price and quantity variances.
   b. The labor rate and efficiency variances.
2. Prepare a brief explanation of the possible causes of each variance.

PROBLEM 10–9 Comprehensive Variance Analysis LO10–1, LO10–2, LO10–3

Marvel Parts, Inc., manufactures auto accessories. One of the company's products is a set of seat covers that can be adjusted to fit nearly any small car. The company uses a standard cost system for all of its products. According to the standards that have been set for the seat covers, the factory should work 2,850 hours each month to produce 1,900 sets of covers. The standard costs associated with this level of production are:

	Total	Per Set of Covers
Direct materials	$42,560	$22.40
Direct labor...........................	$51,300	27.00
Variable manufacturing overhead		
(based on direct labor-hours)	$6,840	3.60
		$53.00

During August, the factory worked only 2,800 direct labor-hours and produced 2,000 sets of covers. The following actual costs were recorded during the month:

	Total	Per Set of Covers
Direct materials (12,000 yards)..........	$45,600	$22.80
Direct labor...........................	$49,000	24.50
Variable manufacturing overhead	$7,000	3.50
		$50.80

At standard, each set of covers should require 5.6 yards of material. All of the materials purchased during the month were used in production.

Required:

Compute the following variances for August:

1. The materials price and quantity variances.
2. The labor rate and efficiency variances.
3. The variable overhead rate and efficiency variances.

PROBLEM 10–10 Multiple Products, Materials, and Processes LO10–1, LO10–2

Mickley Corporation produces two products, Alpha6s and Zeta7s, which pass through two operations, Sintering and Finishing. Each of the products uses two raw materials—X442 and Y661. The company uses a standard cost system, with the following standards for each product (on a per unit basis):

	Raw Material		Standard Labor Time	
Product	X442	Y661	Sintering	Finishing
Alpha6.............	1.8 kilos	2.0 liters	0.20 hours	0.80 hours
Zeta7..............	3.0 kilos	4.5 liters	0.35 hours	0.90 hours

Information relating to materials purchased and materials used in production during May follows:

Material	Purchases	Purchase Cost	Standard Price	Used in Production
X442..............	14,500 kilos	$52,200	$3.50 per kilo	8,500 kilos
Y661..............	15,500 liters	$20,925	$1.40 per liter	13,000 liters

The following additional information is available:

a. The company recognizes price variances when materials are purchased.
b. The standard labor rate is $19.80 per hour in Sintering and $19.20 per hour in Finishing.
c. During May, 1,200 direct labor-hours were worked in Sintering at a total labor cost of $27,000, and 2,850 direct labor-hours were worked in Finishing at a total labor cost of $59,850.
d. Production during May was 1,500 Alpha6s and 2,000 Zeta7s.

Required:

1. Prepare a standard cost card for each product, showing the standard cost of direct materials and direct labor.
2. Compute the materials price and quantity variances for each material.
3. Compute the labor rate and efficiency variances for each operation.

PROBLEM 10–11 Direct Materials and Direct Labor Variances; Computations from Incomplete Data LO10–1, LO10–2

Sharp Company manufactures a product for which the following standards have been set:

	Standard Quantity or Hours	Standard Price or Rate	Standard Cost
Direct materials	3 feet	$11 per foot	$33
Direct labor.	? hours	? per hour	?

During March, the company purchased direct materials at a cost of $111,300, all of which were used in the production of 3,200 units of product. In addition, 4,900 direct labor-hours were worked on the product during the month. The cost of this labor time was $95,550. The following variances have been computed for the month:

Materials quantity variance	$4,400 U
Labor spending variance	$450 F
Labor efficiency variance.	$2,000 U

Required:

1. For direct materials:
   a. Compute the actual cost per foot of materials for March.
   b. Compute the price variance and the spending variance.
2. For direct labor:
   a. Compute the standard direct labor rate per hour.
   b. Compute the standard hours allowed for the month's production.
   c. Compute the standard hours allowed per unit of product.

(*Hint:* In completing the problem, it may be helpful to move from known to unknown data either by using the columnar format shown in Exhibits 10–4 and 10–6 or by using the variance formulas in Exhibits 10–5 and 10–7.)

PROBLEM 10–12 Variance Analysis in a Hospital LO10–1, LO10–2, LO10–3

John Fleming, chief administrator for Valley View Hospital, is concerned about the costs for tests in the hospital's lab. Charges for lab tests are consistently higher at Valley View than at other hospitals and have resulted in many complaints. Also, because of strict regulations on amounts reimbursed for lab tests, payments received from insurance companies and governmental units have not been high enough to cover lab costs.

Mr. Fleming has asked you to evaluate costs in the hospital's lab for the past month. The following information is available:

a. Two types of tests are performed in the lab—blood tests and smears. During the past month, 1,800 blood tests and 2,400 smears were performed in the lab.
b. Small glass plates are used in both types of tests. During the past month, the hospital purchased 12,000 plates at a cost of $56,400. 1,500 of these plates were unused at the end of the month; no plates were on hand at the beginning of the month.

c. During the past month, 1,150 hours of labor time were recorded in the lab at a cost of $21,850.
d. The lab's variable overhead cost last month totaled $7,820.

Valley View Hospital has never used standard costs. By searching industry literature, however, you have determined the following nationwide averages for hospital labs:

Plates: Two plates are required per lab test. These plates cost $5.00 each and are disposed of after the test is completed.
Labor: Each blood test should require 0.3 hours to complete, and each smear should require 0.15 hours to complete. The average cost of this lab time is $20 per hour.
Overhead: Overhead cost is based on direct labor-hours. The average rate for variable overhead is $6 per hour.

Required:
1. Compute a materials price variance for the plates purchased last month and a materials quantity variance for the plates used last month.
2. For labor cost in the lab:
   a. Compute a labor rate variance and a labor efficiency variance.
   b. In most hospitals, one-half of the workers in the lab are senior technicians and one-half are assistants. In an effort to reduce costs, Valley View Hospital employs only one-fourth senior technicians and three-fourths assistants. Would you recommend that this policy be continued? Explain.
3. Compute the variable overhead rate and efficiency variances. Is there any relation between the variable overhead efficiency variance and the labor efficiency variance? Explain.

PROBLEM 10–13 Basic Variance Analysis; the Impact of Variances on Unit Costs LO10–1, LO10–2, LO10–3

Koontz Company manufactures a number of products. The standards relating to one of these products are shown below, along with actual cost data for May.

	Standard Cost per Unit	Actual Cost per Unit
Direct materials:		
Standard: 1.80 feet at $3.00 per foot	$ 5.40	
Actual: 1.80 feet at $3.30 per foot.		$ 5.94
Direct labor:		
Standard: 0.90 hours at $18.00 per hour.	16.20	
Actual: 0.92 hours at $17.50 per hour		16.10
Variable overhead:		
Standard: 0.90 hours at $5.00 per hour	4.50	
Actual: 0.92 hours at $4.50 per hour		4.14
Total cost per unit	$26.10	$26.18
Excess of actual cost over standard cost per unit	$0.08	

The production superintendent was pleased when he saw this report and commented: "This $0.08 excess cost is well within the 2 percent limit management has set for acceptable variances. It's obvious that there's not much to worry about with this product."

Actual production for the month was 12,000 units. Variable overhead cost is assigned to products on the basis of direct labor-hours. There were no beginning or ending inventories of materials.

Required:
1. Compute the following variances for May:
   a. Materials price and quantity variances.
   b. Labor rate and efficiency variances.
   c. Variable overhead rate and efficiency variances.
2. How much of the $0.08 excess unit cost is traceable to each of the variances computed in (1) above.
3. How much of the $0.08 excess unit cost is traceable to apparent inefficient use of labor time?
4. Do you agree that the excess unit cost is not of concern?

PROBLEM 10–14 Basic Variance Analysis LO10–1, LO10–2, LO10–3

Becton Labs, Inc., produces various chemical compounds for industrial use. One compound, called Fludex, is prepared using an elaborate distilling process. The company has developed standard costs for one unit of Fludex, as follows:

	Standard Quantity or Hours	Standard Price or Rate	Standard Cost
Direct materials	2.5 ounces	$20.00 per ounce	$50.00
Direct labor.	1.4 hours	$22.50 per hour	31.50
Variable manufacturing overhead	1.4 hours	$3.50 per hour	4.90
Total standard cost per unit.			$86.40

During November, the following activity was recorded related to the production of Fludex:

a. Materials purchased, 12,000 ounces at a cost of $225,000.
b. There was no beginning inventory of materials; however, at the end of the month, 2,500 ounces of material remained in ending inventory.
c. The company employs 35 lab technicians to work on the production of Fludex. During November, they each worked an average of 160 hours at an average pay rate of $22 per hour.
d. Variable manufacturing overhead is assigned to Fludex on the basis of direct labor-hours. Variable manufacturing overhead costs during November totaled $18,200.
e. During November, the company produced 3,750 units of Fludex.

Required:
1. For direct materials:
   a. Compute the price and quantity variances.
   b. The materials were purchased from a new supplier who is anxious to enter into a long-term purchase contract. Would you recommend that the company sign the contract? Explain.
2. For direct labor:
   a. Compute the rate and efficiency variances.
   b. In the past, the 35 technicians employed in the production of Fludex consisted of 20 senior technicians and 15 assistants. During November, the company experimented with fewer senior technicians and more assistants in order to reduce labor costs. Would you recommend that the new labor mix be continued? Explain.
3. Compute the variable overhead rate and efficiency variances. What relation can you see between this efficiency variance and the labor efficiency variance?

PROBLEM 10–15 Comprehensive Variance Analysis LO10–1, LO10–2, LO10–3

Miller Toy Company manufactures a plastic swimming pool at its Westwood Plant. The plant has been experiencing problems as shown by its June contribution format income statement below:

	Flexible Budget	Actual
Sales (15,000 pools).	$675,000	$675,000
Variable expenses:		
Variable cost of goods sold*	435,000	461,890
Variable selling expenses	20,000	20,000
Total variable expenses	455,000	481,890
Contribution margin	220,000	193,110
Fixed expenses:		
Manufacturing overhead	130,000	130,000
Selling and administrative	84,000	84,000
Total fixed expenses.	214,000	214,000
Net operating income (loss).	$ 6,000	$ (20,890)

*Contains direct materials, direct labor, and variable manufacturing overhead.

Janet Dunn, who has just been appointed general manager of the Westwood Plant, has been given instructions to "get things under control." Upon reviewing the plant's income statement, Ms. Dunn has concluded that the major problem lies in the variable cost of goods sold. She has been provided with the following standard cost per swimming pool:

	Standard Quantity or Hours	Standard Price or Rate	Standard Cost
Direct materials	3.0 pounds	$5.00 per pound	$15.00
Direct labor.	0.8 hours	$16.00 per hour	12.80
Variable manufacturing overhead	0.4 hours*	$3.00 per hour	1.20
Total standard cost per unit.			$29.00

*Based on machine-hours.

During June the plant produced 15,000 pools and incurred the following costs:
a. Purchased 60,000 pounds of materials at a cost of $4.95 per pound.
b. Used 49,200 pounds of materials in production. (Finished goods and work in process inventories are insignificant and can be ignored.)
c. Worked 11,800 direct labor-hours at a cost of $17.00 per hour.
d. Incurred variable manufacturing overhead cost totaling $18,290 for the month. A total of 5,900 machine-hours was recorded.
It is the company's policy to close all variances to cost of goods sold on a monthly basis.

Required:
1. Compute the following variances for June:
   a. Materials price and quantity variances.
   b. Labor rate and efficiency variances.
   c. Variable overhead rate and efficiency variances.
2. Summarize the variances that you computed in (1) above by showing the net overall favorable or unfavorable variance for the month. What impact did this figure have on the company's income statement? Show computations.
3. Pick out the two most significant variances that you computed in (1) above. Explain to Ms. Dunn possible causes of these variances.

PROBLEM 10–16 Comprehensive Variance Analysis LO10–1, LO10–2, LO10–3
Highland Company produces a lightweight backpack that is popular with college students. Standard variable costs relating to a single backpack are given below:

	Standard Quantity or Hours	Standard Price or Rate	Standard Cost
Direct materials	?	$6 per yard	$?
Direct labor.	?	?	?
Variable manufacturing overhead	?	$3 per direct labor-hour	?
Total standard cost per unit			$?

Overhead is applied to production on the basis of direct labor-hours. During March, 1,000 backpacks were manufactured and sold. Selected information relating to the month's production is given below:

	Materials Used	Direct Labor	Variable Manufacturing Overhead
Total standard cost allowed*	$16,800	$21,000	$4,200
Actual costs incurred	$15,000	?	$3,600
Materials price variance.	?		
Materials quantity variance	$1,200 U		
Labor rate variance.		?	
Labor efficiency variance.		?	
Variable overhead rate variance.			?
Variable overhead efficiency variance.			?

*For the month's production.

The following additional information is available for March's production:

Actual direct labor-hours	1,500
Difference between standard and actual cost per backpack produced during March	$0.15 F

Required: (Hint: It may be helpful to complete a general model diagram for direct materials, direct labor, and variable manufacturing overhead before attempting to answer any of the requirements.)
1. What is the standard cost of a single backpack?
2. What was the actual cost per backpack produced during March?
3. How many yards of material are required at standard per backpack?
4. What was the materials price variance for March if there were no beginning or ending inventories of materials?
5. What is the standard direct labor rate per hour?
6. What was the labor rate variance for March? The labor efficiency variance?
7. What was the variable overhead rate variance for March? The variable overhead efficiency variance?
8. Prepare a standard cost card for one backpack.

Cases [McGraw Hill Education] connect®

CASE 10–17 Working Backwards from Variance Data LO10–1, LO10–2, LO10–3

Vitex, Inc. manufactures a popular consumer product and it has provided the following data excerpts from its standard cost system:

Inputs	(1) Standard Quantity or Hours	(2) Standard Price or Rate	Standard Cost (1) × (2)
Direct materials	6 pounds	$3 per pound	$18.00
Direct labor.	0.8 hours	$15 per hour	12.00
Variable manufacturing overhead	0.8 hours	$3 per hour	2.40
Total standard cost per unit.			$32.40

	Total Standard Cost*	Variances Reported	
		Price or Rate	Quantity or Efficiency
Direct materials	$405,000	$6,900 F	$9,000 U
Direct labor.	$270,000	$14,550 U	$21,000 U
Variable manufacturing overhead	$54,000	$1,300 F	$? U

*Applied to Work in Process during the period.

The company's manufacturing overhead cost is applied to production on the basis of direct labor-hours. All of the materials purchased during the period were used in production. Work in process inventories are insignificant and can be ignored.

Required:
1. How many units were produced last period?
2. How many pounds of direct material were purchased and used in production?
3. What was the actual cost per pound of material?
4. How many actual direct labor-hours were worked during the period?
5. What was the actual rate paid per direct labor-hour?
6. How much actual variable manufacturing overhead cost was incurred during the period?

Appendix 10A: Predetermined Overhead Rates and Overhead Analysis in a Standard Costing System

In this appendix, we explain how the predetermined overhead rates that were discussed in the job-order costing chapters can be used in a standard costing system. Throughout this appendix, we assume that an absorption costing system is used in which *all* manufacturing costs—both variable and fixed—are included in product costs.

LO10–4
Compute and interpret the fixed overhead budget and volume variances.

MicroDrive Corporation: An Example

Exhibit 10A–1 pertains to MicroDrive Corporation, a company that produces miniature electric motors. The data within this exhibit is divided into three sections. The first section summarizes the budgeted overhead costs and budgeted machine-hours included in the company's planning budget. Note that the company's planning budget is based on producing 25,000 motors. Given that two machine-hours are allowed per motor, the planning budget allows for 50,000 machine-hours. At this level of activity, the budgeted variable manufacturing overhead is $75,000 and the budgeted fixed manufacturing overhead is $300,000.

The second section includes information that MicroDrive will use to apply overhead costs to production. Notice that the company actually produced 20,000 motors instead of the 25,000 motors included in the planning budget. Given that two machine-hours are allowed per motor, the standard machine-hours allowed for the actual production is 40,000 machine-hours. This is the quantity of machine-hours that the company will use to apply variable and fixed overhead costs to production.

The third section summarizes the company's actual variable and fixed manufacturing overhead costs for the period as well as its actual machine-hours used during the period. As we will describe in greater detail shortly, *it is very important to understand that in a standard cost system the actual hours (42,000 machine-hours) is not used to apply overhead costs to production. Variable and fixed overhead costs are applied to production using the standard hours allowed for the actual production (40,000 machine-hours).*

EXHIBIT 10A–1
MicroDrive Corporation Data

Budgeted (Planned) Overhead:	
Budgeted variable manufacturing overhead ..	$ 75,000
Budgeted fixed manufacturing overhead	300,000
Total budgeted manufacturing overhead	$375,000
Budgeted production (a)	25,000 motors
Standard machine-hours per motor (b)	2 machine-hours per motor
Budgeted machine-hours (a) × (b)	50,000 machine-hours
Applying Overhead:	
Actual production (a)......................	20,000 motors
Standard machine-hours per motor (b)	2 machine-hours per motor
Standard machine-hours allowed for the actual production (a) × (b)	40,000 machine-hours
Actual Overhead and Machine-Hours:	
Actual variable manufacturing overhead	$ 71,400
Actual fixed manufacturing overhead	308,000
Total actual manufacturing overhead........	$379,400
Actual machine-hours.....................	42,000 machine-hours

Predetermined Overhead Rates

Recall from earlier chapters that the following formula is used to establish the predetermined overhead rate at the beginning of the period:

$$\text{Predetermined overhead rate} = \frac{\text{Estimated total manufacturing overhead cost}}{\text{Estimated total amount of the allocation base}}$$

The estimated total amount of the allocation base in the formula for the predetermined overhead rate is called the **denominator activity**.

Once the predetermined overhead rate has been established, it remains unchanged throughout the period, even if the actual level of activity differs from what was estimated. Consequently, the amount of overhead applied to each unit of product is the same regardless of when it is produced during the period.

As alluded to in Exhibit 10A–1, MicroDrive Corporation uses 50,000 budgeted machine-hours as its denominator activity in the predetermined overhead rate. Consequently, the company's predetermined overhead rate would be computed as follows:

$$\text{Predetermined overhead rate} = \frac{\$375,000}{50,000 \text{ MHs}} = \$7.50 \text{ per MH}$$

This predetermined overhead rate can be broken down into its variable and fixed components as follows:

$$\text{Variable component of the predetermined overhead rate} = \frac{\$75,000}{50,000 \text{ MHs}} = \$1.50 \text{ per MH}$$

$$\text{Fixed component of the predetermined overhead rate} = \frac{\$300,000}{50,000 \text{ MHs}} = \$6.00 \text{ per MH}$$

For every standard machine-hour recorded, work in process is charged with $7.50 of manufacturing overhead, of which $1.50 represents variable manufacturing overhead and $6.00 represents fixed manufacturing overhead. In total, MicroDrive Corporation would apply $300,000 of overhead to work in process as shown below:

$$\text{Overhead applied} = \text{Predetermined overhead rate} \times \text{Standard hours allowed for the actual output}$$
$$= \$7.50 \text{ per machine-hour} \times 40,000 \text{ machine-hours}$$
$$= \$300,000$$

Overhead Application in a Standard Cost System

To understand fixed overhead variances, we first have to realize how overhead is applied to work in process in a standard cost system. Recall that in the job-order costing chapters we applied overhead to work in process on the basis of the actual level of activity (e.g., the actual direct labor-hours worked or the actual machine-hours used). This procedure was correct because at the time we were dealing with a normal cost system.[4] However, we are now dealing with a standard cost system. In such a system, overhead is applied to work in process on the basis of the *standard hours allowed for the actual output of the period* rather than on the basis of the actual number of hours worked. Exhibit 10A–2 illustrates this point. In a standard cost system, every unit of output is charged with the same amount of overhead cost, regardless of how much time the unit actually requires for processing.

---

[4] Normal cost systems are defined in the Chapters 2 and 3 glossaries.

Normal Cost System		Standard Cost System		EXHIBIT 10A–2
Manufacturing Overhead		Manufacturing Overhead		Applied Overhead Costs: Normal Cost System versus Standard Cost System
Actual overhead costs incurred.	Applied overhead costs: Actual hours × Pre-determined overhead rate.	Actual overhead costs incurred.	Applied overhead costs: Standard hours allowed for actual output × Pre-determined overhead rate.	
Underapplied or overapplied overhead		Underapplied or overapplied overhead		

Budget Variance

Two fixed manufacturing overhead variances are computed in a standard costing system—a *budget variance* and a *volume variance*. These variances are computed in Exhibit 10A–3. The **budget variance** is simply the difference between the actual fixed manufacturing overhead and the budgeted fixed manufacturing overhead for the period. The formula is:

$$\text{Budget variance} = \text{Actual fixed overhead} - \text{Budgeted fixed overhead}$$

If the actual fixed overhead cost exceeds the budgeted fixed overhead cost, the budget variance is labeled unfavorable. If the actual fixed overhead cost is less than the budgeted fixed overhead cost, the budget variance is labeled favorable.

Applying the formula to the MicroDrive Corporation data, the budget variance is computed as follows:

$$\text{Budget variance} = \$308,000 - \$300,000 = \$8,000 \text{ U}$$

According to the budget, the fixed manufacturing overhead should have been $300,000, but it was actually $308,000. Because the actual cost exceeds the budget by $8,000, the variance is labeled as unfavorable; however, this label does not automatically signal

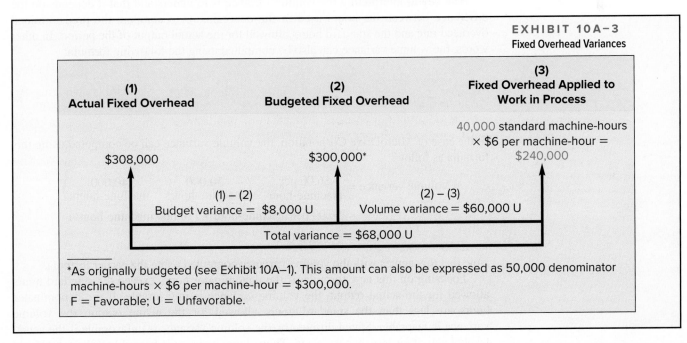

EXHIBIT 10A–3
Fixed Overhead Variances

ineffective managerial performance. For example, this variance may be the result of waste and inefficiency, or it may be due to an unforeseen yet prudent investment in fixed overhead resources that improves product quality or manufacturing cycle efficiency.

Volume Variance

The **volume variance** is defined by the following formula:

$$\text{Volume variance} = \text{Budgeted fixed overhead} - \text{Fixed overhead applied to work in process}$$

When the budgeted fixed manufacturing overhead exceeds the fixed manufacturing overhead applied to work in process, the volume variance is labeled as unfavorable. When the budgeted fixed manufacturing overhead is less than the fixed manufacturing overhead applied to work in process, the volume variance is labeled as favorable. As we shall see, caution is advised when interpreting this variance.

To understand the volume variance, we need to understand how fixed manufacturing overhead is applied to work in process in a standard costing system. As discussed earlier, fixed manufacturing overhead is applied to work in process on the basis of the standard hours allowed for the actual output of the period. In the case of MicroDrive Corporation, the company produced 20,000 motors and the standard for each motor is 2 machine-hours. Therefore, the standard hours allowed for the actual output is 40,000 machine-hours (= 20,000 motors × 2 machine-hours). As shown in Exhibit 10A–3, the predetermined fixed manufacturing overhead rate of $6.00 per machine-hour is multiplied by the 40,000 standard machine-hours allowed for the actual output to arrive at $240,000 of fixed manufacturing overhead applied to work in process. Another way to think of this is that the standard for each motor is 2 machine-hours. Because the predetermined fixed manufacturing overhead rate is $6.00 per machine-hour, each motor is assigned $12.00 (= 2 machine-hours × $6.00 per machine-hour) of fixed manufacturing overhead. Consequently, a total of $240,000 of fixed manufacturing overhead is applied to the 20,000 motors that are actually produced. Under either explanation, the volume variance according to the formula is:

$$\text{Volume variance} = \$300,000 - \$240,000 = \$60,000 \text{ U}$$

The key to interpreting the volume variance is to understand that it depends on the difference between the hours used in the denominator to compute the predetermined overhead rate and the standard hours allowed for the actual output of the period. In other words, the volume variance can also be computed using the following formula:

$$\text{Volume variance} = \text{Fixed component of the predetermined overhead rate} \times \left(\text{Denominator hours} - \text{Standard hours allowed for the actual output} \right)$$

In the case of MicroDrive Corporation, the volume variance can be computed using this formula as follows:

$$\text{Volume variance} = \$6.00 \text{ per machine-hour} \times \left(50,000 \text{ machine-hours} - 40,000 \text{ machine-hours} \right)$$

$$= \$6.00 \text{ per machine-hour} \times (10,000 \text{ machine-hours})$$

$$= \$60,000 \text{ U}$$

Note that this agrees with the volume variance computed using the earlier formula.

Focusing on this new formula, if the denominator hours exceed the standard hours allowed for the actual output, the volume variance is unfavorable. If the denominator hours are less than the standard hours allowed for the actual output, the volume variance is favorable. Stated differently, the volume variance is unfavorable if the actual level of activity is less than expected. The volume variance is favorable if the actual level of activity is greater than expected. It is important to note that the volume variance does not measure overspending or underspending. A company should incur the same dollar amount of fixed overhead cost regardless of whether the period's activity was above or below the planned (denominator) level.

The volume variance is often viewed as a measure of the utilization of facilities. If the standard hours allowed for the actual output are greater than (less than) the denominator hours, it signals efficient (inefficient) usage of facilities. However, other measures of utilization—such as the percentage of capacity utilized—are easier to compute and understand. Perhaps a better interpretation of the volume variance is that it is the error that occurs when the level of activity is incorrectly estimated and the costing system assumes fixed costs behave as if they are variable. This interpretation may be clearer in the next section that graphically analyzes the fixed manufacturing overhead variances.

Graphic Analysis of Fixed Overhead Variances

Exhibit 10A–4 shows a graphic analysis that offers insights into the fixed overhead budget and volume variances. As shown in the graph, fixed overhead cost is applied to work in process at the predetermined rate of $6.00 for each standard hour of activity. (The applied-cost line is the upward-sloping line on the graph.) Because a denominator level of 50,000 machine-hours was used in computing the $6.00 rate, the applied-cost line crosses the budget-cost line at exactly 50,000 machine-hours. If the denominator hours and the standard hours allowed for the actual output are the same, there is no volume variance. It is only when the standard hours differ from the denominator hours that a volume variance arises.

In MicroDrive's case, the standard hours allowed for the actual output (40,000 hours) are less than the denominator hours (50,000 hours). The result is an unfavorable volume variance because less cost was applied to production than was originally budgeted. If the situation had been reversed and the standard hours allowed for the actual output had exceeded the denominator hours, then the volume variance on the graph would have been favorable.

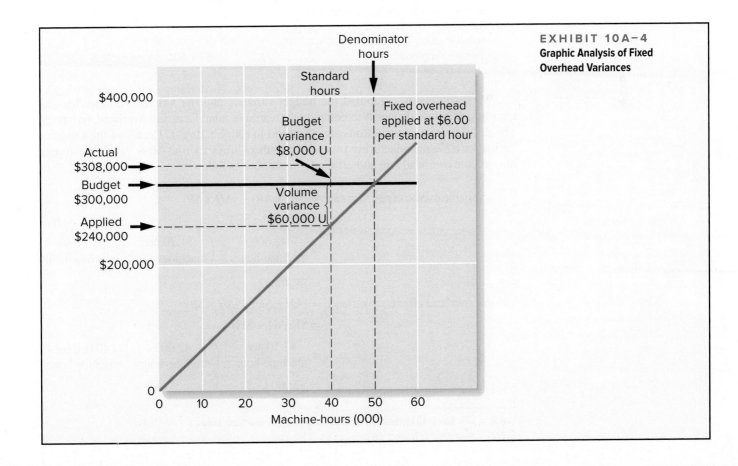

EXHIBIT 10A–4
Graphic Analysis of Fixed Overhead Variances

Cautions in Fixed Overhead Analysis

A volume variance for fixed overhead arises because when applying the costs to work in process, we act *as if* the fixed costs are variable. The graph in Exhibit 10A–4 illustrates this point. Notice from the graph that fixed overhead costs are applied to work in process at a rate of $6 per hour *as if* they are variable. Treating these costs as if they are variable is necessary for product costing purposes, but some real dangers lurk here. Managers can easily be misled into thinking that fixed costs are *in fact* variable.

Keep clearly in mind that fixed overhead costs come in large chunks. Expressing fixed costs on a unit or per hour basis, though necessary for product costing for external reports, is artificial. Increases or decreases in activity in fact have no effect on total fixed costs within the relevant range of activity. Even though fixed costs are expressed on a unit or per hour basis, they are *not* proportional to activity. In a sense, the volume variance is the error that occurs as a result of treating fixed costs as variable costs in the costing system.

Reconciling Overhead Variances and Underapplied or Overapplied Overhead

In a standard cost system, the underapplied or overapplied overhead for a period equals the sum of the overhead variances. To see this, we will return to the MicroDrive Corporation example.

As discussed earlier, in a standard cost system, overhead is applied to work in process on the basis of the standard hours allowed for the actual output of the period. The following table shows how the underapplied or overapplied overhead for MicroDrive is computed.

Predetermined overhead rate (a)	$7.50 per machine-hour
Standard machine-hours allowed for the actual production [Exhibit 10A–1] (b).	40,000 machine-hours
Manufacturing overhead applied (a) × (b).	$300,000
Total actual manufacturing overhead [Exhibit 10A–1]	$379,400
Manufacturing overhead underapplied or overapplied	$79,400 underapplied

We have already computed the budget variance and the volume variance for this company. We will also need to compute the variable manufacturing overhead variances. The data for these computations are contained in Exhibit 10A–1. Recalling the formulas for the variable manufacturing overhead variances from Exhibit 10–9, we can compute the variable overhead rate and efficiency variances as follows:

$$\text{Variable overhead rate variance} = (AH \times AR) - (AH \times SR)$$

$$= AH(AR - SR)$$

$$= \frac{42,000}{\text{machine-hours}} - \left(\frac{\$1.70 \text{ per}}{\text{machine-hour}^5} - \frac{\$1.50 \text{ per}}{\text{machine-hour}} \right)$$

$$= \$8,400 \text{ U}$$

$$\text{Variable overhead efficiency variance} = (AH \times SR) - (SH \times SR)$$

$$= SR(AH - SH)$$

$$= \frac{\$1.50 \text{ per}}{\text{machine-hour}} - \left(\frac{42,000}{\text{machine-hours}} - \frac{40,000 \text{ per}}{\text{machine-hours}} \right)$$

$$= \$3,000 \text{ U}$$

---

[5] AR = $71,400 ÷ 42,000 machine-hours = $1.70 per machine-hour.

We can now compute the sum of all of the overhead variances as follows:

Variable overhead rate variance.............	$ 8,400 U
Variable overhead efficiency variance.......	3,000 U
Fixed overhead budget variance	8,000 U
Fixed overhead volume variance	60,000 U
Total of the overhead variances	$79,400 U

Note that the total of the overhead variances is $79,400, which equals the underapplied overhead of $79,400. In general, if the overhead is underapplied, the total of the standard cost overhead variances is unfavorable. If the overhead is overapplied, the total of the standard cost overhead variances is favorable.

Glossary (Appendix 10A)

Budget variance The difference between the actual fixed overhead costs and the budgeted fixed overhead costs for the period. (p. 483)

Denominator activity The level of activity used to compute the predetermined overhead rate. (p. 482)

Volume variance The variance that arises whenever the standard hours allowed for the actual output of a period are different from the denominator activity level that was used to compute the predetermined overhead rate. It is computed by multiplying the fixed component of the predetermined overhead rate by the difference between the denominator hours and the standard hours allowed for the actual output. (p. 484)

connect   Appendix 10A: Exercises and Problems

EXERCISE 10A–1 Fixed Overhead Variances LO10–4

Primara Corporation has a standard cost system in which it applies overhead to products based on the standard direct labor-hours allowed for the actual output of the period. Data concerning the most recent year appear below:

Total budgeted fixed overhead cost for the year.................	$250,000
Actual fixed overhead cost for the year.........................	$254,000
Budgeted direct labor-hours (denominator level of activity)	25,000
Actual direct labor-hours	27,000
Standard direct labor-hours allowed for the actual output........	26,000

Required:
1. Compute the fixed portion of the predetermined overhead rate for the year.
2. Compute the fixed overhead budget variance and volume variance.

EXERCISE 10A–2 Predetermined Overhead Rate; Overhead Variances LO10–3, LO10–4

Norwall Company's budgeted variable manufacturing overhead cost is $3.00 per machine-hour and its budgeted fixed manufacturing overhead is $300,000 per month.

The following information is available for a recent month:

a. The denominator activity of 60,000 machine-hours is used to compute the predetermined overhead rate.

b. At a denominator activity of 60,000 machine-hours, the company should produce 40,000 units of product.

c. The company's actual operating results were:

Number of units produced.........................	42,000
Actual machine-hours.............................	64,000
Actual variable manufacturing overhead cost	$185,600
Actual fixed manufacturing overhead cost	$302,400

Required:

1. Compute the predetermined overhead rate and break it down into variable and fixed cost elements.
2. Compute the standard hours allowed for the actual production.
3. Compute the variable overhead rate and efficiency variances and the fixed overhead budget and volume variances.

EXERCISE 10A–3 Applying Overhead in a Standard Costing System LO10–4

Privack Corporation has a standard cost system in which it applies overhead to products based on the standard direct labor-hours allowed for the actual output of the period. Data concerning the most recent year appear below:

Budgeted variable overhead cost per direct labor-hour	$2
Total budgeted fixed overhead cost per year..................	$250,000
Budgeted direct labor-hours (denominator level of activity)	40,000
Actual direct labor-hours	39,000
Standard direct labor-hours allowed for the actual output........	38,000

Required:

1. Compute the predetermined overhead rate for the year. Be sure to include the total budgeted fixed overhead and the total budgeted variable overhead in the numerator of your rate.
2. Compute the amount of overhead that would be applied to the output of the period.

EXERCISE 10A–4 Fixed Overhead Variances LO10–4

Selected operating information on three different companies for a recent year is given below:

	Company		
	A	B	C
Full-capacity machine-hours	10,000	18,000	20,000
Budgeted machine-hours*...............	9,000	17,000	20,000
Actual machine-hours....................	9,000	17,800	19,000
Standard machine-hours allowed for actual production...................	9,500	16,000	20,000

*Denominator activity for computing the predetermined overhead rate.

Required:

For each company, state whether the company would have a favorable or unfavorable volume variance and why.

EXERCISE 10A–5 Using Fixed Overhead Variances LO10–4

The standard cost card for the single product manufactured by Cutter, Inc., is given below:

	(1) Standard Quantity or Hours	(2) Standard Price or Rate	Standard Cost (1) × (2)
Direct materials	3 yards	$6.00 per yard	$ 18
Direct labor	4 hours	$15.50 per hour	62
Variable overhead	4 hours	$1.50 per hour	6
Fixed overhead	4 hours	$5.00 per hour	20
Total standard cost per unit			$106

Manufacturing overhead is applied to production on the basis of standard direct labor-hours. During the year, the company worked 37,000 hours and manufactured 9,500 units of product. Selected data relating to the company's fixed manufacturing overhead cost for the year are shown below:

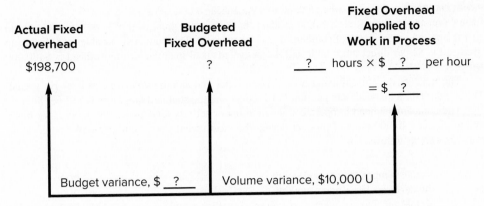

Actual Fixed Overhead	Budgeted Fixed Overhead	Fixed Overhead Applied to Work in Process
$198,700	?	<u> ? </u> hours × $<u> ? </u> per hour = $<u> ? </u>

Budget variance, $ <u> ? </u>   Volume variance, $10,000 U

Required:
1. What were the standard hours allowed for the year's production?
2. What was the amount of budgeted fixed overhead cost for the year?
3. What was the fixed overhead budget variance for the year?
4. What denominator activity level did the company use in setting the predetermined overhead rate for the year?

EXERCISE 10A–6 Predetermined Overhead Rate LO10–4

Lasser Company plans to produce 10,000 units next period at a denominator activity of 30,000 direct labor-hours. The direct labor wage rate is $12 per hour. The company's standards allow 2.5 yards of direct materials for each unit of product; the standard material cost is $8.60 per yard. The company's budget includes variable manufacturing overhead cost of $1.90 per direct labor-hour and fixed manufacturing overhead of $168,000 per period.

Required:
1. Using 30,000 direct labor-hours as the denominator activity, compute the predetermined overhead rate and break it down into variable and fixed elements.
2. Complete the standard cost card below for one unit of product:

	(1) Standard Quantity or Hours	(2) Standard Price or Rate	Standard Cost (1) × (2)
Direct materials	2.5 yards	$8.60 per yard	$21.50
Direct labor.	?	?	?
Variable manufacturing overhead	?	?	?
Fixed manufacturing overhead.	?	?	?
Total standard cost per unit.			$?

EXERCISE 10A–7 Relations Among Fixed Overhead Variances LO10–4

Selected information relating to Yost Company's operations for the most recent year is given below:

Activity:	
Denominator activity (machine-hours).	45,000
Standard hours allowed per unit.	3
Actual number of units produced.	14,000
Costs:	
Actual fixed overhead costs incurred	$267,000
Fixed overhead budget variance	$3,000 F

The company applies overhead cost to products on the basis of standard machine-hours.

Required:
1. What were the standard machine-hours allowed for the actual number of units produced?
2. What was the total budgeted fixed overhead cost for the period?
3. What was the fixed portion of the predetermined overhead rate?
4. What was the fixed overhead volume variance?

PROBLEM 10A–8 Applying Overhead; Overhead Variances LO10–3, LO10–4

Lane Company manufactures a single product that requires a great deal of hand labor. Overhead cost is applied on the basis of standard direct labor-hours. The budgeted variable manufacturing overhead is $2 per direct labor-hour and the budgeted fixed manufacturing overhead is $480,000 per year.

The standard quantity of materials is 3 pounds per unit and the standard cost is $7 per pound. The standard direct labor-hours per unit is 1.5 hours and the standard labor rate is $12 per hour.

The company planned to operate at a denominator activity level of 60,000 direct labor-hours and to produce 40,000 units of product during the most recent year. Actual activity and costs for the year were as follows:

Actual number of units produced.........................	42,000
Actual direct labor-hours worked.........................	65,000
Actual variable manufacturing overhead cost incurred.......	$123,500
Actual fixed manufacturing overhead cost incurred..........	$483,000

Required:

1. Compute the predetermined overhead rate for the year. Break the rate down into variable and fixed elements.
2. Prepare a standard cost card for the company's product; show the details for all manufacturing costs on your standard cost card.
3. Do the following:
   a. Compute the standard direct labor-hours allowed for the year's production.
   b. Complete the following Manufacturing Overhead T-account for the year:

Manufacturing Overhead

?	?
?	?

4. Determine the reason for any underapplied or overapplied overhead for the year by computing the variable overhead rate and efficiency variances and the fixed overhead budget and volume variances.
5. Suppose the company had chosen 65,000 direct labor-hours as the denominator activity rather than 60,000 hours. State which, if any, of the variances computed in (4) above would have changed, and explain how the variance(s) would have changed. No computations are necessary.

PROBLEM 10A–9 Applying Overhead; Overhead Variances LO10–3, LO10–4

Chilczuk, S.A., of Gdansk, Poland, is a major producer of classic Polish sausage. The company uses a standard cost system to help control costs. Manufacturing overhead is applied to production on the basis of standard direct labor-hours. According to the company's planning budget, the following manufacturing overhead costs should be incurred at an activity level of 35,000 labor-hours (the denominator activity level):

Variable manufacturing overhead cost.......	$ 87,500
Fixed manufacturing overhead cost..........	210,000
Total manufacturing overhead cost..........	$297,500

During the most recent year, the following operating results were recorded:

Activity:	
Actual labor-hours worked	30,000
Standard labor-hours allowed for the actual output	32,000
Cost:	
Actual variable manufacturing overhead cost incurred	$78,000
Actual fixed manufacturing overhead cost incurred	$209,400

At the end of the year, the company's Manufacturing Overhead account contained the following data:

Manufacturing Overhead

Actual	287,400	Applied	272,000
	15,400		

Management would like to determine the cause of the $15,400 underapplied overhead.

Required:

1. Compute the predetermined overhead rate. Break the rate down into variable and fixed cost elements.
2. Show how the $272,000 Applied figure in the Manufacturing Overhead account was computed.
3. Breakdown the $15,400 underapplied overhead into four components: (1) variable overhead rate variance, (2) variable overhead efficiency variance, (3) fixed overhead budget variance, and (4) fixed overhead volume variance.
4. Explain the meaning of each variance that you computed in (3) above.

PROBLEM 10A–10 Comprehensive Standard Cost Variances LO10–1, LO10–2, LO10–3, LO10–4

"Wonderful! Not only did our salespeople do a good job in meeting the sales budget this year, but our production people did a good job in controlling costs as well," said Kim Clark, president of Martell Company. "Our $18,300 overall manufacturing cost variance is only 1.2% of the $1,536,000 standard cost of products made during the year. That's well within the 3% parameter set by management for acceptable variances. It looks like everyone will be in line for a bonus this year."

The company produces and sells a single product. The standard cost card for the product follows:

Inputs	(1) Standard Quantity or Hours	(2) Standard Price or Rate	Standard Cost (1) × (2)
Direct materials	2 feet	$8.45 per foot	$16.90
Direct labor.	1.4 hours	$16 per hour	22.40
Variable overhead.	1.4 hours	$2.50 per hour	3.50
Fixed overhead	1.4 hours	$6 per hour	8.40
Total standard cost per unit.			$51.20

The following additional information is available for the year just completed:
a. The company manufactured 30,000 units of product during the year.
b. A total of 64,000 feet of material was purchased during the year at a cost of $8.55 per foot. All of this material was used to manufacture the 30,000 units produced. There were no beginning or ending inventories for the year.
c. The company worked 43,500 direct labor-hours during the year at a direct labor cost of $15.80 per hour.
d. Overhead is applied to products on the basis of standard direct labor-hours. Data relating to manufacturing overhead costs follow:

Denominator activity level (direct labor-hours).	35,000
Budgeted fixed overhead costs	$210,000
Actual variable overhead costs incurred.	$108,000
Actual fixed overhead costs incurred	$211,800

Required:

1. Compute the materials price and quantity variances for the year.
2. Compute the labor rate and efficiency variances for the year.

3. For manufacturing overhead compute:
    a. The variable overhead rate and efficiency variances for the year.
    b. The fixed overhead budget and volume variances for the year.
4. Total the variances you have computed, and compare the net amount with the $18,300 mentioned by the president. Do you agree that bonuses should be given to everyone for good cost control during the year? Explain.

PROBLEM 10A–11 Comprehensive Standard Cost Variances LO10–1, LO10–2, LO10–3, LO10–4

Flandro Company uses a standard cost system and sets its predetermined overhead rate on the basis of direct labor-hours. The following data are taken from the company's planning budget for the current year:

Denominator activity (direct labor-hours)	5,000
Variable manufacturing overhead cost	$25,000
Fixed manufacturing overhead cost..........	$59,000

The standard cost card for the company's only product is given below:

Inputs	(1) Standard Quantity or Hours	(2) Standard Price or Rate	Standard Cost (1) × (2)
Direct materials	3 yards	$4.40 per yard	$13.20
Direct labor.......................	1 hour	$12 per hour	12.00
Manufacturing overhead	1 hour	$16.80 per hour	16.80
Total standard cost per unit..........			$42.00

During the year, the company produced 6,000 units of product and incurred the following actual results:

Materials purchased, 24,000 yards at $4.80 per yard.........	$115,200
Materials used in production (in yards)	18,500
Direct labor cost incurred, 5,800 hours at $13 per hour.......	$75,400
Variable manufacturing overhead cost incurred	$29,580
Fixed manufacturing overhead cost incurred................	$60,400

Required:
1. Create a new standard cost card that separates the variable manufacturing overhead per unit and the fixed manufacturing overhead per unit.
2. Compute the materials price and quantity variances. Also, compute the labor rate and efficiency variances.
3. Compute the variable overhead rate and efficiency variances. Also, compute the fixed overhead budget and volume variances.
4. What effect, if any, does the choice of a denominator activity level have on unit standard costs? Is the volume variance a controllable variance from a spending point of view? Explain.

PROBLEM 10A–12 Selection of a Denominator; Overhead Analysis; Standard Cost Card LO10–3, LO10–4

Morton Company's budgeted variable manufacturing overhead is $4.50 per direct labor-hour and its budgeted fixed manufacturing overhead is $270,000 per year.

The company manufactures a single product whose standard direct labor-hours per unit is 2 hours. The standard direct labor wage rate is $15 per hour. The standards also allow 4 feet of raw material per unit at a standard cost of $8.75 per foot.

Although normal activity is 30,000 direct labor-hours each year, the company expects to operate at a 40,000-hour level of activity this year.

Required:

1. Assume that the company chooses 30,000 direct labor-hours as the denominator level of activity. Compute the predetermined overhead rate, breaking it down into variable and fixed cost elements.

2. Assume that the company chooses 40,000 direct labor-hours as the denominator level of activity. Compute the predetermined overhead rate, breaking it down into variable and fixed cost elements.

3. Complete two standard cost cards as outlined below.

Inputs	(1) Standard Quantity or Hours	(2) Standard Price or Rate	Standard Cost (1) × (2)
Denominator Activity: 30,000 Direct Labor-Hours			
Direct materials	4 feet	$8.75 per foot	$35.00
Direct labor.	?	?	?
Variable manufacturing overhead	?	?	?
Fixed manufacturing overhead.	?	?	?
Total standard cost per unit.			$?
Denominator Activity: 40,000 Direct Labor-Hours			
Direct materials	$4 feet	$8.75 per foot	$35.00
Direct labor.	?	?	?
Variable manufacturing overhead	?	?	?
Fixed manufacturing overhead.	?	?	?
Total standard cost per unit.			$?

4. Assume that the company actually produces 18,000 units and works 38,000 direct labor-hours during the year. Actual manufacturing overhead costs for the year are:

Variable manufacturing overhead cost	$174,800
Fixed manufacturing overhead cost.	271,600
Total manufacturing overhead cost	$446,400

Do the following:

a. Compute the standard direct labor-hours allowed for this year's production.

b. Complete the Manufacturing Overhead T-account below. Assume that the company uses 30,000 direct labor-hours (normal activity) as the denominator activity in computing predetermined overhead rates, as you have done in (1) above.

Manufacturing Overhead

Actual costs	446,400	Applied costs	?
	?		?

c. Determine the cause of the underapplied or overapplied overhead for the year by computing the variable overhead rate and efficiency variances and the fixed overhead budget and volume variances.

5. Looking at the variances you have computed, what appears to be the major disadvantage of using normal activity rather than expected actual activity as a denominator in computing the predetermined overhead rate? What advantages can you see to offset this disadvantage?

Appendix 10B: Standard Cost Systems: A Financial Reporting Perspective Using Microsoft Excel

LO10–5

Prepare an income statement using a standard cost system.

The main body of Chapter 10 and Appendix 10A focused on calculating standard cost variances for management control purposes. This appendix explains how to use a standard cost system to create a balance sheet and an income statement for financial reporting purposes. We purposely use Microsoft Excel to create these two financial statements because it enables us to teach you a valuable managerial skill—how to evaluate a transaction's impact on the balance sheet.

To set the stage for the forthcoming example, we need to review two fundamental accounting equations and specify four important assumptions.

Fundamental Accounting Equations

A company's balance sheet is based on the following accounting equation that is the bedrock of double-entry bookkeeping:

$$\text{Assets} = \text{Liabilities} + \text{Stockholders' Equity}$$

In the Excel spreadsheets that we'll be using in this appendix, one column will always be populated with an "=" sign. The accounts on the left-hand side of the "=" sign will be asset accounts and the accounts on the right-hand side will be liability and equity accounts. After we record every transaction, the amounts on the left-hand side of the "=" sign must equal the amounts on the right-hand side.

The second foundational equation relates to the Retained Earnings account on a company's balance sheet. The ending balance in retained earnings is computed using the following equation:

$$\begin{array}{c}\text{Ending balance in}\\\text{retained earnings}\end{array} = \begin{array}{c}\text{Beginning balance in}\\\text{retained earnings}\end{array} + \begin{array}{c}\text{Net}\\\text{operating}\\\text{income}\end{array} - \text{Dividends}$$

This equation highlights the connection between the balance sheet and the income statement. It explicitly recognizes the fact that net operating income from the income statement plugs into Retained Earnings on the balance sheet. In this appendix, we will not include any dividends; therefore, the only transactions that will be recorded in the Retained Earnings account will be those transactions that affect net operating income. Any transactions involving the recording of sales or the recognition of expenses will be recorded in the Retained Earnings column of the balance sheet. This approach highlights the critically important idea that a company's income statement is embedded within the Retained Earnings account in its balance sheet.

Four Key Assumptions

The first assumption that we use in this appendix is that Raw Materials, Work in Process, and Finished Goods are always carried at their *standard cost*. In other words, the standard prices paid for inputs and the standard quantities of inputs allowed for the actual level of production *will be used to flow costs through the inventory accounts*. The actual prices paid for inputs and the actual quantities of inputs that are used in production *will not affect the costs recorded in the inventory accounts*.

This approach to standard costing greatly simplifies the bookkeeping process. To enable this simplification, we will always close all standard cost variances to Cost of Goods Sold rather than closing them to the various inventory accounts *and* Cost of Goods Sold. When the closing entry increases Cost of Goods Sold we will decrease

Retained Earnings. We do this because increasing Cost of Goods Sold lowers net operating income, which in turn, lowers Retained Earnings. Conversely, when the closing entry decreases Cost of Goods Sold we will increase Retained Earnings. We do this because decreasing Cost of Goods Sold increases net operating income, which in turn, increases Retained Earnings.

The second assumption relates to the *clearing accounts* that we use to record standard cost variances. Clearing accounts always begin and end each accounting period with a zero balance. In our Excel spreadsheets, each variance will always have its own clearing account that appears on the right-hand side of the "=" sign. Putting these clearing accounts on the right-hand side of the "=" sign (rather than the left-hand side) enables us to record all favorable variances as *increases* to their respective clearing accounts and all unfavorable variances as *decreases* to their accounts. Once all variances have been recorded, the final transaction of the period will close each clearing account to Cost of Goods Sold and record the resulting change in net operating income within the Retained Earnings account.

The third assumption relates to restricting the number of general ledger accounts used in this appendix. In terms of asset accounts, we will always limit the scope of our accounts to include Cash, Raw Materials, Work in Process, Finished Goods, and Property, Plant, and Equipment, net of accumulated depreciation (which may be abbreviated as PP&E, net). With respect to liability and equity accounts, we will always use only one account—Retained Earnings.[6]

Our fourth assumption is that we'll record transactions within Microsoft Excel by using positive numbers to increase accounts and negative numbers (shown in parentheses) to decrease accounts. This is a slightly different approach than relying on the language of debits and credits. Instead of recording debits and credits, we'll identify the accounts affected by each transaction and then record increases or decreases in those accounts.

Standard Cost Systems: An Example

Dylan Corporation manufactures only one product and uses a standard cost system for internal management and financial reporting purposes. The company uses a *plantwide predetermined overhead rate* that relies on direct labor-hours as the allocation base. All of the company's manufacturing overhead costs are fixed—it does not incur any variable manufacturing overhead costs. The predetermined overhead rate is based on a cost formula that estimated $1,875,000 of fixed manufacturing overhead for an estimated allocation base of 75,000 labor-hours.

The company wants to create an ending balance sheet and an income statement for the current year. Its beginning balance sheet is shown in Exhibit 10B–1(all numbers are in thousands). Work in Process does not appear on the beginning balance sheet because Dylan Corporation does not maintain any beginning or ending work in process inventory. A standard cost card for the company's only product is shown in Exhibit 10B–2.

Summary of Transactions

During the year Dylan completed the following transactions:

a. Purchased 380,000 pounds of raw material for cash at a price of $4.75 per pound.
b. Added 365,000 pounds of raw material to work in process to produce 88,000 units.

---

[6] Ordinarily we would include a Common Stock account within the Stockholders' Equity section of the balance sheet. However, to minimize the number of columns in our spreadsheets, this appendix omits the Common Stock account and uses the term Liabilities and Equity rather than Liabilities and Stockholders' Equity.

EXHIBIT 10B–1
Dylan Corporation: Beginning Balance Sheet

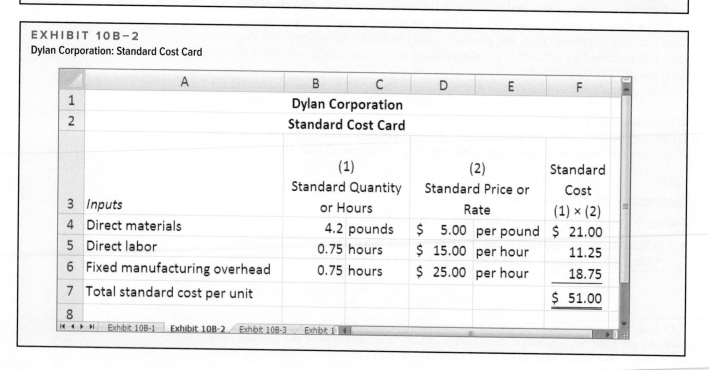

	A	B
1	Dylan Corporation	
2	Balance Sheet	
3	1/1/XX	
4	(dollars in thousands)	
5		
6	**Assets**	
7	Cash	$ 1,100
8	Raw materials inventory*	400
9	Finished goods inventory**	714
10	Property, plant and equipment, net	5,200
11	Total assets	$ 7,414
12		
13	**Liabilities and Equity**	
14	Retained earnings	7,414
15	Total liabilities and equity	$ 7,414
16		
17	* 80,000 pounds × $5.00 per pound = $400,000	
18	** 14,000 units × $51.00 per unit = $714,000	
19		

Exhibit 10B-1 / Exhibit 10B-2 / Exhib

EXHIBIT 10B–2
Dylan Corporation: Standard Cost Card

	A	B	C	D	E	F
1	Dylan Corporation					
2	Standard Cost Card					
3	*Inputs*	(1) Standard Quantity or Hours		(2) Standard Price or Rate		Standard Cost (1) × (2)
4	Direct materials	4.2	pounds	$ 5.00	per pound	$ 21.00
5	Direct labor	0.75	hours	$ 15.00	per hour	11.25
6	Fixed manufacturing overhead	0.75	hours	$ 25.00	per hour	18.75
7	Total standard cost per unit					$ 51.00
8						

Exhibit 10B-1   Exhibit 10B-2   Exhibit 10B-3   Exhibit 1

c. Assigned direct labor costs to work in process. The direct laborers (who were paid in cash) worked 72,000 hours at an average cost of $14.50 per hour to manufacture 88,000 units.

d. Applied fixed overhead to work in process using the predetermined overhead rate multiplied by the number of labor-hours allowed to manufacture 88,000 units. Actual fixed overhead costs for the year were $1,750,000. Of this total, $900,000 related to items such as insurance, utilities, and indirect labor salaries that were all paid in cash and $850,000 related to depreciation of manufacturing equipment.

e. Transferred 88,000 units from work in process to finished goods.

f. Sold (for cash) 85,000 units to customers at a price of $62.00 per unit.

g. Transferred the standard cost associated with the 85,000 units sold from finished goods to cost of goods sold.

h. Paid $450,000 of selling and administrative expenses.

i. Closed all standard cost variances to cost of goods sold.

Exhibit 10B–3 shows the spreadsheet that we'll be using to record Dylan Corporation's transactions. Notice that cell A7 depicts the beginning balance for the period (1/1) and cell A17 depicts the ending balance (12/31). In between the beginning and ending balances, rows 8 through 16 will be used to record transactions *a* through *i*. Also, note that the beginning balances shown in row 7 of the spreadsheet (in thousands) correspond to the amounts shown in the balance sheet in Exhibit 10B–1. Finally, we want to emphasize that columns H through M represent the clearing accounts that correspond to the six variances that we'll be computing shortly. Each variance account in these six columns starts with a beginning balance of zero and concludes the period with an ending balance of zero. They each record a variance for the period and then close that variance to Cost of Goods Sold at the end of the period, thereby ensuring an ending balance of zero.

EXHIBIT 10B–3

Dylan Corporation: The Transaction Template

	A	B	C	D	E	F	G	H	I	J	K	L	M	N
1								Dylan Corporation						
2								Transaction Analysis						
3								For the Year Ended 12/31/XX						
4								(dollars in thousands)						
6		Cash	Raw Materials	Work in Process	Finished Goods	PP&E (net)	=	Materials Price Variance	Materials Quantity Variance	Labor Rate Variance	Labor Efficiency Variance	Fixed Overhead Budget Variance	Fixed Overhead Volume Variance	Retained Earnings
7	1/1	$ 1,100	$ 400	$ -	$ 714	$ 5,200	=	$ -	$ -	$ -	$ -	$ -	$ -	$ 7,414
8	a.													
9	b.													
10	c.													
11	d.													
12	e.													
13	f.													
14	g.													
15	h.													
16	i.													
17	12/31													
22														

Exhibit 10B-1　Exhibit 10B-2　**Exhibit 10B-3**　Exhibit 10B-4　Exhibit 10B-5

Now we are ready to demonstrate a three-step process for preparing Dylan Corporations' income statement. First, we are going to compute all six of the company's manufacturing cost variances. Second, we will record transactions *a* through *i*. Finally, we will prepare Dylan's income statement for the year.

Calculating the Variances

For Dylan Corporation, the quantity of materials purchased (380,000 pounds) does not equal the quantity used in production (365,000 pounds); therefore, the materials price variance will be based on the *quantity of materials purchased* and the materials quantity variance will be based on the *quantity of materials used in production*. The computations of these two variances are as follows:

Materials price variance:
Materials price variance = $(AQ \times AP) - (AQ \times SP)$
Materials price variance = $AQ(AP - SP)$
Materials price variance = 380,000 pounds ($4.75 per pound − $5.00 per pound)
Materials price variance = $95,000 F

Materials quantity variance:
Materials quantity variance = $(AQ \times SP) - (SQ \times SP)$
Materials quantity variance = $SP(AQ - SQ)$
Materials quantity variance = $5.00 per pound (365,000 pounds − 369,600 pounds*)
Materials quantity variance = $23,000 F

---
*SQ = 88,000 units produced × 4.2 pounds per unit = 369,600 pounds

The materials price variance is favorable because the actual price per pound ($4.75) is less than the standard price per pound ($5.00). The materials quantity variance is favorable because the 365,000 pounds used in production are less than the 369,600 pounds (= 88,000 units × 4.2 pounds per unit) that the standards allow for the actual level of output.

The direct labor rate and efficiency variances are computed as follows:

Labor rate variance:
Labor rate variance = $(AH \times AR) - (AH \times SR)$
Labor rate variance = $AH(AR - SR)$
Labor rate variance = 72,000 hours ($14.50 per hour − $15.00 per hour)
Labor rate variance = $36,000 F

Labor efficiency variance:
Labor efficiency variance = $(AH \times SR) - (SH \times SR)$
Labor efficiency variance = $SR(AH - SH)$
Labor efficiency variance = $15.00 per hour (72,000 hours − 66,000 hours*)
Labor efficiency variance = $90,000 U

---
*SQ = 88,000 units produced × 0.75 hours per unit = 66,000 hours

The labor rate variance is favorable because the actual labor rate ($14.50) is less than the standard labor rate ($15.00). The labor efficiency variance is unfavorable because the 72,000 hours actually worked are greater than the 66,000 hours (= 88,000 units × 0.75 hours per unit) that the standards allow for the actual level of output.

The fixed overhead budget and volume variances are computed as follows:

Budget variance:

Budget variance = Actual fixed overhead − Budgeted fixed overhead

Budget variance = $1,750,000 − $1,875,000

Budget variance = $125,000 F

Volume variance:

Volume variance = Budgeted fixed overhead − Fixed overhead applied to work in process

Volume variance = $1,875,000 − $1,650,000*

Volume variance = $225,000 U

—————

*Fixed overhead applied to work in process = 66,000 hours allowed for the actual output × $25 per hour = $1,650,000

The fixed overhead budget variance of $125,000 is favorable (F) because the actual amount of fixed overhead ($1,750,000) is less than the budgeted amount of fixed overhead ($1,875,000), whereas the fixed overhead volume variance of $225,000 is unfavorable (U) because the budgeted fixed overhead ($1,875,000) is greater than the fixed overhead applied to work in process ($1,650,000). The fixed overhead applied to work in process is calculated by multiplying the predetermined overhead rate ($25.00) by the *number of direct labor-hours allowed for the actual level of production* (66,000 hours). Fixed overhead is *not* applied to production using the actual direct labor-hours worked!

Recording the Transactions

Exhibit 10B–4 shows how to properly record all of the transactions for Dylan Corporation (all amounts are in thousands). You'll notice that all favorable variances (in columns H through M) are recorded without parentheses and all unfavorable variances (in columns H through M) are recorded with parentheses. This occurs because favorable variances increase net operating income (and retained earnings) when they are closed to cost of goods sold and unfavorable variances decrease net operating income (and retained earnings) when they are closed to cost of goods sold. For example, the materials price variance of $95,000 F appears in cell H8 without parentheses. To close this variance, we record $(95,000) in cell H16, thereby bringing the ending balance in the Materials Price Variance clearing account to zero. The $(95,000) in cell H16 is offset by adding $95,000 to Retained Earnings. When all six variances are closed to Cost of Goods Sold, their combined effect is to reduce net operating income and Retained Earnings by the $(36,000) shown in cell N16.

Once all transactions are recorded, Microsoft Excel can quickly compute the ending balances for all balance sheet accounts as shown in row 17 of Exhibit 10B–4. Notice that all of the variance accounts (in columns H through M) have an ending balance of zero because they all serve as clearing accounts. Also note that the inventory accounts in the ending balance sheet are valued using *standard costs*. For example, the ending balance in Raw Materials ($475,000) consists of 95,000 pounds of materials each carried in inventory at a standard cost of $5.00 per pound. The ending balance in Finished Goods ($867,000) consists of 17,000 units each valued at a standard cost of $51.00 per unit.

EXHIBIT 10B–4

Dylan Corporation: Transaction Analysis

	A	B	C	D	E	F	G H	I	J	K	L	M	N
1							Dylan Corporation						
2							Transaction Analysis						
3							For the Year Ended 12/31/XX						
4							(dollars in thousands)						
5													
6		Cash	Raw Materials	Work in Process	Finished Goods	PP&E (net)	= Materials Price Variance	Materials Quantity Variance	Labor Rate Variance	Labor Efficiency Variance	Fixed Overhead Budget Variance	Fixed Overhead Volume Variance	Retained Earnings
7	1/1	1,100	$ 400	$ -	$ 714	$ 5,200	= $ -	$ -	$ -	$ -	$ -	$ -	$ 7,414
8	a.	(1,805)	1,900				=	95					
9	b.		(1,825)	1,848			=		23				
10	c.	(1,044)		990			=			36	(90)		
11	d.	(900)		1,650		(850)	=					125	(225)
12	e.			(4,488)	4,488		=						
13	f.	5,270					=						5,270
14	g.				(4,335)		=						(4,335)
15	h.	(450)					=						(450)
16	i.						=	(95)	(23)	(36)	90	(125)	225	(36)
17	12/31	2,171	$ 475	$ -	$ 867	$ 4,350	= $ -	$ -	$ -	$ -	$ -	$ -	$ 7,863
18													

Exhibit 10B-1 / Exhibit 10B-2 / Exhibit 10B-3 / **Exhibit 10B-4** / Exhibit 10B|

The explanations for transactions *a* through *i* (as recorded above) are as follows:

a. Cash decreases by the actual cost of the raw materials purchased, which is AQ × AP (380,000 × $4.75 = $1,805,000). Raw Materials increase by the standard cost of the raw materials purchased, which is AQ × SP (380,000 × 5 = $1,900,000). The materials price variance is $95,000 F.

b. Raw Materials decrease by the standard cost of the raw materials used in production, which is AQ × SP (365,000 × $5.00 = $1,825,000). Work in Process increases by the standard cost of the standard quantity of raw materials allowed for the actual output, which is SQ × SP (369,600 × $5.00 = $1,848,000). The materials quantity variance is $23,000 F.

c. Cash decreases by the actual amount paid to direct laborers, which is AH × AR (72,000 × $14.50 = $1,044,000). Work in Process increases by the standard cost of the standard amount of hours allowed for the actual output, which is SH × SR (66,000 × $15.00 = $990,000). The labor rate variance is $36,000 F and the labor efficiency variance is $90,000 U.

d. Cash decreases by the actual amount paid for various fixed overhead costs, which is $900,000. Work in Process increases by the standard amount of hours allowed for the actual output multiplied by the predetermined overhead rate, which is 66,000 hours × $25.00 per hour = $1,650,000. PP&E (net) decreases by the amount of depreciation for the period, which is $850,000. The fixed overhead budget variance is $125,000 F and the fixed overhead volume variance is $225,000 U.

e. Work in process decreases by the number of units transferred to Finished Goods multiplied by the standard cost per unit, which is 88,000 units × $51.00 per unit = $4,488,000. Finished Goods increases by the same amount.

f. Cash increases by the number of units sold multiplied by the selling price per unit, which is 85,000 units sold × $62.00 per unit = $5,270,000. Retained Earnings increases by the same amount.

g. Finished Goods decrease by the number of units sold multiplied by their standard cost per unit, which is 85,000 units sold × $51.00 per unit = $4,335,000. Retained Earnings decreases by the same amount.

h. Cash and Retained Earnings decrease by $450,000 to record the selling and administrative expenses.

i. All variance accounts take their balance to zero as they are closed to Cost of Goods Sold. The net effect of closing all of these variances is to increase Cost of Goods Sold by $36,000. The equation supporting this logic is as follows: $(95,000) + $(23,000) + $(36,000) + $90,000 + $(125,000) + $225,000 = $36,000. Because Cost of Goods Sold increases by $36,000, it lowers net operating income and Retained Earnings by the same amount.

EXHIBIT 10B–5
Dylan Corporation: Income Statement

	A	B	C
1	**Dylan Corporation**		
2	**Income Statement**		
3	**For Year Ended 12/31/XX**		
4	**(dollars in thousands)**		
5			
6	Sales		$ 5,270
7	Cost of goods sold at standard	$ 4,335	
8	Total variance adjustments	36	
9	Cost of goods sold		4,371
10	Gross margin		899
11	Selling and administrative expenses		450
12	Net operating income		$ 449
13			

Exhibit 10B-4 **Exhibit 10B-5**

Preparing the Income Statement

Exhibit 10B–5 shows Dylan Corporation's income statement that is derived from the Retained Earnings column of Exhibit 10B–4. The sales in the income statement of $5,270,000 come from cell N13 in Exhibit 10B–4. The cost of goods sold at standard ($4,335,000) comes from cell N14 of Exhibit 10B–4. Finally, the sum of the variance adjustments ($36,000) and the selling and administrative expenses ($450,000) come from cells N16 and N15, respectively. Although all of the numbers in Exhibit 10B–5 are shown as positive numbers, the cost of goods sold at standard ($4,335,000), the selling and administrative expenses ($450,000) and the variance adjustments ($36,000) are shown as negative numbers in column N of Exhibit 10B–4 to recognize that they each reduce retained earnings.

connect Appendix 10B: Exercises and Problems

EXERCISE 10B–1 Standard Cost Flows; Income Statement Preparation LO10–5

Forsyth Company manufactures one product, it does not maintain any beginning or ending inventories, and its uses a standard cost system. During the year, the company produced and sold 10,000 units at a price of $135 per unit. Its standard cost per unit produced is $105 and its selling and administrative expenses totaled $235,000. Forsyth does not have any variable manufacturing overhead costs and it recorded the following variances during the year:

Materials price variance...............................	$6,500 F
Materials quantity variance	$10,200 U
Labor rate variance..................................	$3,500 U
Labor efficiency variance............................	$4,400 F
Fixed overhead budget variance	$2,500 F
Fixed overhead volume variance...................	$12,000 F

Required:

1. When Forsyth closes its standard cost variances, the cost of goods sold will increase (decrease) by how much?
2. Using Exhibit 10B–5 as a guide, prepare an income statement for the year.

EXERCISE 10B–2 Standard Cost Flows; Income Statement Preparation LO10–5

Swain Company manufactures one product, it does not maintain any beginning or ending inventories, and its uses a standard cost system. The company's beginning balance in Retained Earnings is $70,000. It sells one product for $165 per unit and it generated total sales during the period of $577,500 while incurring selling and administrative expenses of $54,000. Swain Company does not have any variable manufacturing overhead costs and its standard cost card for its only product is as follows:

	(1) Standard Quantity or Hours	(2) Standard Price or Rate	Standard Cost (1) × (2)
Direct materials	7.0 pounds	$9 per pound	$ 63
Direct labor.	2.5 hours	$12 per hour	30
Fixed manufacturing overhead.	2.5 hours	$20 per hour	50
Total standard cost per unit.			$143

During the period, Swain recorded the following variances:

Materials price variance.	$3,400 U
Materials quantity variance	$9,000 F
Labor rate variance.	$3,900 U
Labor efficiency variance.	$6,600 U
Fixed overhead budget variance	$1,300 U
Fixed overhead volume variance	$5,500 F

Required:

1. When Swain closes its standard cost variances, the cost of goods sold will increase (decrease) by how much?
2. Using Exhibit 10B–5 as a guide, prepare an income statement for the year.
3. What is Swain's ending balance in Retained Earnings?

EXERCISE 10B–3 Standard Cost Flows LO10–5

Bowen Company manufactures one product, it does not maintain any beginning or ending inventories, and its uses a standard cost system. Its predetermined overhead rate includes $1,000,000 of fixed overhead in the numerator and 50,000 direct labor-hours in the denominator. The company purchased (with cash) and used 30,000 yards of raw materials at a cost of $9.80 per yard. Its direct laborers worked 20,000 hours and were paid a total of $290,000. The company started and completed 8,100 units of finished goods during the period. Bowen's standard cost card for its only product is as follows:

Inputs	(1) Standard Quantity or Hours	(2) Standard Price or Rate	Standard Cost (1) × (2)
Direct materials	3.0 yards	$10.00 per yard	$ 30.00
Direct labor.	2.4 hours	$14.00 per hour	33.60
Fixed manufacturing overhead.	2.4 hours	$20.00 per hour	48.00
Total standard cost per unit.			$111.60

Required:

1. When recording the raw material purchases:
    a. The Raw Materials inventory will increase (decrease) by how much?
    b. The Cash will increase (decrease) by how much?
2. When recording the raw materials used in production:
    a. The Raw Materials inventory will increase (decrease) by how much?
    b. The Work in Process inventory will increase (decrease) by how much?
3. When recording the direct labor costs added to production:
    a. The Work in Process inventory will increase (decrease) by how much?
    b. The Cash will increase (decrease) by how much?
4. When applying fixed manufacturing overhead to production, the Work in Process inventory will increase (decrease) by how much?
5. When transferring manufacturing costs from Work in Process to Finished Goods, the Finished Goods inventory will increase (decrease) by how much?

EXERCISE 10B–4 Standard Cost Flows LO10–5

Hartwell Company manufactures one product, it does not maintain any beginning or ending inventories, and its uses a standard cost system. Its predetermined overhead rate includes $1,760,000 of fixed manufacturing overhead in the numerator and 44,000 direct labor-hours in the denominator. The actual fixed manufacturing overhead for the period was $1,780,000.

The company purchased (with cash) and used 60,000 yards of raw materials at a cost of $11.00 per yard. Its direct laborers worked 40,000 hours and were paid a total of $600,000. The company started and completed 28,000 units of finished goods during the period. Bowen's standard cost card for its only product is as follows:

	(1) Standard Quantity or Hours	(2) Standard Price or Rate	Standard Cost (1) × (2)
Direct materials	2 yards	$12.00 per yard	$ 24.00
Direct labor.	1.5 hours	$15.00 per hour	22.50
Fixed manufacturing overhead.	1.5 hours	$40.00 per hour	60.00
Total standard cost per unit.			$106.50

Required:

1. When recording the raw material purchases (on account):
    a. The Raw Materials inventory will increase (decrease) by how much?
    b. The Cash will increase (decrease) by how much?
    c. The materials price variance will be favorable or unfavorable and by how much?
2. When recording the raw materials used in production:
    a. The Raw Materials inventory will increase (decrease) by how much?
    b. The Work in Process inventory will increase (decrease) by how much?
    c. The materials quantity variance will be favorable or unfavorable and by how much?
3. When recording the direct labor costs added to production:
    a. The Work in Process inventory will increase (decrease) by how much?
    b. The Cash will increase (decrease) by how much?
    c. The labor rate and efficiency variances will be favorable or unfavorable and by how much?
4. When applying fixed manufacturing overhead to production:
    a. The Work in Process inventory will increase (decrease) by how much?
    b. The fixed overhead budget and volume variances will be favorable or unfavorable and by how much?
5. When transferring costs from Work in Process to Finished Goods, the Finished Goods inventory will increase (decrease) by how much?

PROBLEM 10B–5 Transaction Analysis; Income Statement Preparation LO10–1, LO10–2, LO10–4, LO10–5

Wallis Company manufactures only one product and uses a standard cost system. The company uses a predetermined plantwide overhead rate that relies on direct labor-hours as the allocation base. All of the company's manufacturing overhead costs are fixed—it does not incur any variable manufacturing overhead costs. The predetermined overhead rate is based on a cost formula that estimated $2,880,000 of fixed manufacturing overhead for an estimated allocation base of 288,000 direct labor-hours. Wallis does not maintain any beginning or ending work in process inventory.

The company's beginning balance sheet is as follows:

Wallis Company	
Balance Sheet	
1/1/XX	
(dollars in thousands)	
Assets	
Cash......................................	$ 700
Raw materials inventory......................	150
Finished goods inventory	270
Property, plant, and equipment, net............	8,500
Total assets.................................	$9,620
Liabilities and Equity	
Retained earnings............................	$9,620
Total liabilities and equity....................	$9,620

The company's standard cost card for its only product is as follows:

Inputs	(1) Standard Quantity or Hours	(2) Standard Price or Rate	Standard Cost (1) × (2)
Direct materials	2 pounds	$30.00 per pound	$ 60.00
Direct labor..........................	3.00 hours	$15.00 per hour	45.00
Fixed manufacturing overhead.........	3.00 hours	$10.00 per hour	30.00
Total standard cost per unit............			$135.00

During the year Wallis completed the following transactions:

a. Purchased (with cash) 230,000 pounds of raw material at a price of $29.50 per pound.
b. Added 215,000 pounds of raw material to work in process to produce 95,000 units.
c. Assigned direct labor costs to work in process. The direct laborers (who were paid in cash) worked 245,000 hours at an average cost of $16.00 per hour to manufacture 95,000 units.
d. Applied fixed overhead to work in process inventory using the predetermined overhead rate multiplied by the number of direct labor-hours allowed to manufacture 95,000 units. Actual fixed overhead costs for the year were $2,740,000. Of this total, $1,340,000 related to items such as insurance, utilities, and salaried indirect laborers that were all paid in cash and $1,400,000 related to depreciation of equipment.
e. Transferred 95,000 units from work in process to finished goods.
f. Sold (for cash) 92,000 units to customers at a price of $170 per unit.
g. Transferred the standard cost associated with the 92,000 units sold from finished goods to cost of goods sold.
h. Paid $2,120,000 of selling and administrative expenses.
i. Closed all standard cost variances to cost of goods sold.

Required:
1. Compute all direct materials, direct labor, and fixed overhead variances for the year.
2. Using Exhibit 10B–3 as a guide, record transactions *a* through *i* for Wallis Company.
3. Compute the ending balances for Wallis Company's balance sheet.
4. Using Exhibit 10B–5 as a guide, prepare Wallis Company's income statement for the year.

PROBLEM 10B–6 Transaction Analysis; Income Statement Preparation LO10–1, LO10–2, LO10–3, LO10–4, LO10–5

Phoenix Company manufactures only one product and uses a standard cost system. The company uses a plantwide predetermined overhead rate that relies on direct labor-hours as the allocation base. The predetermined overhead rate is based on a cost formula that estimated $2,880,000 of fixed and variable manufacturing overhead for an estimated allocation base of 240,000 direct labor-hours. Phoenix does not maintain any beginning or ending work in process inventory.

The company's beginning balance sheet is as follows:

Phoenix Company	
Balance Sheet	
1/1/XX	
(dollars in thousands)	
Assets	
Cash.......................................	$ 1,200
Raw materials inventory.......................	300
Finished goods inventory	540
All other assets	12,000
Total assets..................................	$14,040
Liabilities and Equity	
Retained earnings............................	$14,040
Total liabilities and equity.....................	$14,040

The company's standard cost card for its only product is as follows:

Inputs	(1) Standard Quantity or Hours	(2) Standard Price or Rate	Standard Cost (1) × (2)
Direct materials	3 pounds	$25.00 per pound	$ 75.00
Direct labor..........................	2.00 hours	$16.00 per hour	32.00
Variable manufacturing overhead	2.00 hours	$2.00 per hour	4.00
Fixed manufacturing overhead..........	2.00 hours	$10.00 per hour	20.00
Total standard cost per unit.............			$131.00

During the year Phoenix completed the following transactions:
a. Purchased (with cash) 460,000 pounds of raw material at a price of $26.50 per pound.
b. Added 430,000 pounds of raw material to work in process to produce 125,000 units.
c. Assigned direct labor costs to work in process. The direct laborers (who were paid in cash) worked 265,000 hours at an average cost of $15.00 per hour to manufacture 125,000 units.
d. Applied variable manufacturing overhead to work in process inventory using the variable portion of the predetermined overhead rate multiplied by the number of direct labor-hours allowed to manufacture 125,000 units. Actual variable manufacturing overhead costs for the year (all paid in cash) were $480,000.
e. Applied fixed manufacturing overhead to work in process inventory using the fixed portion of the predetermined overhead rate multiplied by the number of direct labor-hours allowed to manufacture 125,000 units. Actual fixed manufacturing overhead costs for the year were $2,450,000. Of this total, $1,300,000 related to items such as insurance, utilities, and salaried indirect laborers that were all paid in cash and $1,150,000 related to depreciation of equipment.
f. Transferred 125,000 units from work in process to finished goods.
g. Sold (for cash) 123,000 units to customers at a price of $175 per unit.
h. Transferred the standard cost associated with the 123,000 units sold from finished goods to cost of goods sold.
i. Paid $3,300,000 of selling and administrative expenses.
j. Closed all standard cost variances to cost of goods sold.

Required:
1. Compute all direct materials, direct labor, variable overhead, and fixed overhead variances for the year.
2. Using Exhibit 10B–3 as a guide, record transactions *a* through *j* for Phoenix Company.
3. Compute the ending balances for Phoenix Company's balance sheet.
4. Using Exhibit 10B–5 as a guide, prepare Phoenix Company's income statement for the year.

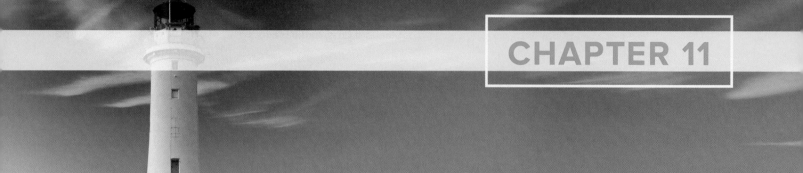

Performance Measurement in Decentralized Organizations

A Strategy of Scarcity

© Luke Sharrett/Bloomberg/Getty Images

BUSINESS FOCUS

Old Rip Van Winkle Distillery employs two people, Julian Van Winkle III and his son Preston. Its annual sales of $2 million pale in comparison to larger competitors such as **Makers' Mark** and **Wild Turkey**. Although the company could easily triple its sales volume, it chooses to limit sales to 7,000 cases of bourbon per year. Given that the company's 20-year-old aged whiskey once achieved an unprecedented "99" rating from the **Beverage Tasting Institute of Chicago**, demand for the company's products far exceeds its supply—thereby enabling regular price increases. For example, a fifth of 20-year-old Pappy Van Winkle bourbon sells for $110. As you'll learn in this chapter, the Old Rip Van Winkle Distillery purposely foregoes turnover in favor of earning large margins on its award-winning products. ∎

Source: Brian Dumaine, "Creating the Ultimate Cult Brand," *Fortune*, February 28, 2011, pp. 21–24.

LEARNING OBJECTIVES

After studying Chapter 11, you should be able to:

LO11–1 Compute return on investment (ROI) and show how changes in sales, expenses, and assets affect ROI.

LO11–2 Compute residual income and understand its strengths and weaknesses.

LO11–3 Compute throughput time, delivery cycle time, and manufacturing cycle efficiency (MCE).

LO11–4 Understand how to construct and use a balanced scorecard.

LO11–5 *(Appendix 11A) Determine the range, if any, within which a negotiated transfer price should fall.*

LO11–6 *(Appendix 11B) Charge operating departments for services provided by service departments.*

Except in very small organizations, a company's owners and its top managers must delegate decision-making authority to others. When a company's owners (e.g., stockholders) delegate decision-making authority to top managers, they employ *corporate governance systems* to direct and control the actions of those managers. When properly implemented, corporate governance systems provide incentives and feedback mechanisms to help ensure that a company's board of directors and top managers pursue goals that align with the owners' interests.[1] Similarly, when a company's top managers delegate decision-making authority to subordinates, they employ *management control systems* to direct and control the actions of those subordinates. When properly implemented, management control systems provide incentives and feedback mechanisms to help ensure that all of a company's employees pursue goals that align with its interests.

This chapter explains a variety of performance measures that a company can use to align its employees' incentives and actions with its overall interests. First, it discusses the advantages and disadvantages of decentralization. Next, it provides a brief overview of responsibility accounting systems followed by a discussion of two performance measures commonly used within those systems—return on investment (ROI) and residual income. The chapter concludes with an overview of operating performance measures and the balanced scorecard.

Decentralization in Organizations

In a **decentralized organization**, decision-making authority is spread throughout the organization rather than being confined to a few top executives. As noted above, out of necessity all large organizations are decentralized to some extent. Organizations do differ, however, in the extent to which they are decentralized. In strongly centralized organizations, decision-making authority is reluctantly delegated to lower-level managers who have little freedom to make decisions. In strongly decentralized organizations, even the lowest-level managers are empowered to make as many decisions as possible. Most organizations fall somewhere between these two extremes.

Advantages and Disadvantages of Decentralization

The major advantages of decentralization include:

1. By delegating day-to-day problem solving to lower-level managers, top-level managers can concentrate on bigger issues, such as overall strategy.
2. Empowering lower-level managers to make decisions puts the decision-making authority in the hands of those who tend to have the most detailed and up-to-date information about day-to-day operations.
3. By eliminating layers of decision making and approvals, organizations can respond more quickly to customers and to changes in the operating environment.
4. Granting decision-making authority helps train lower-level managers for higher-level positions.
5. Empowering lower-level managers to make decisions can increase their motivation and job satisfaction.

The major disadvantages of decentralization include:

1. Lower-level managers may make decisions without fully understanding the company's overall strategy.
2. If lower-level managers make their own decisions independently of each other, coordination may be lacking.

---

[1] These comments on corporate governance were adapted from the 2004 report titled OECD Principles of Corporate Governance published by the Organization for Economic Co-Operation and Development.

3. Lower-level managers may have objectives that clash with the objectives of the entire organization.[2] For example, a manager may be more interested in increasing the size of his or her department, leading to more power and prestige, than in increasing the department's effectiveness.

4. Spreading innovative ideas may be difficult in a decentralized organization. Someone in one part of the organization may have a terrific idea that would benefit other parts of the organization, but without strong central direction the idea may not be shared with, and adopted by, other parts of the organization.

Responsibility Accounting

Decentralized organizations need *responsibility accounting systems* that link lower-level managers' decision-making authority with accountability for the outcomes of those decisions. The term **responsibility center** is used for any part of an organization whose manager has control over and is accountable for cost, profit, or investments. The three primary types of responsibility centers are *cost centers, profit centers,* and *investment centers.*

Cost, Profit, and Investment Centers

Cost Center   The manager of a **cost center** has control over costs, but not over revenue or the use of investment funds. Service departments such as accounting, finance, general administration, legal, and personnel are usually classified as cost centers. In addition, manufacturing facilities are often treated as cost centers. The managers of cost centers are expected to minimize costs while providing the level of products and services needed by other parts of the organization. For example, the manager of a manufacturing facility would be evaluated at least in part by comparing actual costs to how much costs should have been for the actual level of output during the period. Standard cost variances and flexible budget variances, such as those discussed in earlier chapters, are often used to evaluate cost center performance.

Profit Center   The manager of a **profit center** has control over both costs and revenue, but not over the use of investment funds. For example, the manager in charge of a Six Flags amusement park would be responsible for both the revenues and costs, and hence the profits, of the amusement park, but may not have control over major investments in the park. Profit center managers are often evaluated by comparing actual profit to targeted or budgeted profit.

Investment Center   The manager of an **investment center** has control over cost, revenue, and investments in operating assets. For example, General Motors' vice president of manufacturing in North America would have a great deal of discretion over investments in manufacturing—such as investing in equipment to produce more fuel-efficient engines. Once General Motors' top-level managers and board of directors approve the vice president's investment proposals, he is held responsible for making them pay off. As discussed in the next section, investment center managers are often evaluated using return on investment (ROI) or residual income measures.

---

[2] Similar problems exist with top-level managers as well. The shareholders of the company delegate their decision-making authority to the top managers. Unfortunately, top managers may abuse that trust by rewarding themselves and their friends too generously, spending too much company money on palatial offices, and so on. The issue of how to ensure that top managers act in the best interests of the company's owners continues to challenge experts. To a large extent, the owners rely on performance evaluation using return on investment and residual income measures, as discussed later in the chapter, and on bonuses and stock options. The stock market is also an important disciplining mechanism. If top managers squander the company's resources, the price of the company's stock will almost surely fall–possibly resulting in a loss of prestige, bonuses, and a job. And, of course, particularly outrageous self-dealing may land a CEO in court.

Evaluating Investment Center Performance—Return on Investment

An investment center is responsible for earning an adequate return on investment. The following two sections present two methods for evaluating this aspect of an investment center's performance. The first method, covered in this section, is called *return on investment* (ROI). The second method, covered in the next section, is called *residual income.*

LO11–1
Compute return on investment (ROI) and show how changes in sales, expenses, and assets affect ROI.

The Return on Investment (ROI) Formula

Return on investment (ROI) is defined as net operating income divided by average operating assets:

$$\text{ROI} = \frac{\text{Net operating income}}{\text{Average operating assets}}$$

The higher a business segment's return on investment (ROI), the greater the profit earned per dollar invested in the segment's operating assets.

Net Operating Income and Operating Assets Defined

Note that *net operating income,* rather than net income, is used in the ROI formula. **Net operating income** is income before interest and taxes and is sometimes referred to as EBIT (earnings before interest and taxes). Net operating income is used in the formula because the base (i.e., denominator) consists of *operating assets.* To be consistent, we use net operating income in the numerator.

Operating assets include cash, accounts receivable, inventory, plant and equipment, and all other assets held for operating purposes. Examples of assets that are not included in operating assets (i.e., examples of nonoperating assets) include land held for future use, an investment in another company, or a building rented to someone else. These assets are not held for operating purposes and therefore are excluded from operating assets. The operating assets base used in the formula is typically computed as the average of the operating assets between the beginning and the end of the year.

Most companies use the net book value (i.e., acquisition cost less accumulated depreciation) of depreciable assets to calculate average operating assets. This approach has drawbacks. An asset's net book value decreases over time as the accumulated depreciation increases. This decreases the denominator in the ROI calculation, thus increasing ROI. Consequently, ROI mechanically increases over time. Moreover, replacing old depreciated equipment with new equipment increases the book value of depreciable assets and decreases ROI. Hence, using net book value in the calculation of average operating assets results in a predictable pattern of increasing ROI over time as accumulated depreciation grows and discourages replacing old equipment with new, updated equipment. An alternative to using net book value is the gross cost of the asset, which ignores accumulated depreciation. Gross cost stays constant over time because depreciation is ignored; therefore, ROI does not grow automatically over time, and replacing a fully depreciated asset with a comparably priced new asset will not adversely affect ROI.

Nevertheless, most companies use the net book value approach to computing average operating assets because it is consistent with their financial reporting practices of recording the net book value of assets on the balance sheet and including depreciation as an operating expense on the income statement. In this text, we will use the net book value approach unless a specific exercise or problem directs otherwise.

Understanding ROI

The equation for ROI, net operating income divided by average operating assets, does not provide much help to managers interested in taking actions to improve their ROI. It only offers two levers for improving performance—net operating income and average operating assets. Fortunately, ROI can also be expressed in terms of **margin** and **turnover** as follows:

$$ROI = Margin \times Turnover$$

where

$$Margin = \frac{Net\ operating\ income}{Sales}$$

and

$$Turnover = \frac{Sales}{Average\ operating\ assets}$$

Note that the sales terms in the margin and turnover formulas cancel out when they are multiplied together, yielding the original formula for ROI stated in terms of net operating income and average operating assets. So either formula for ROI will give the same answer. However, the margin and turnover formulation provides some additional insights.

Margin and turnover are important concepts in understanding how a manager can affect ROI. All other things the same, margin is ordinarily improved by increasing selling prices, reducing operating expenses, or increasing unit sales. Increasing selling prices and reducing operating expenses both increase net operating income and therefore margin. Increasing unit sales also ordinarily increases the margin because of operating leverage. As discussed in a previous chapter, because of operating leverage, a given percentage increase in unit sales usually leads to an even larger percentage increase in net operating income. Therefore, an increase in unit sales ordinarily has the effect of increasing margin. Some managers tend to focus too much on margin and ignore turnover. However, turnover incorporates a crucial area of a manager's responsibility—the investment in operating assets. Excessive funds tied up in operating assets (e.g., cash, accounts receivable, inventories, plant and equipment, and other assets) depress turnover and lower ROI. In fact, excessive operating assets can be just as much of a drag on ROI as excessive operating expenses, which depress margin.

IN BUSINESS

© Irina Mos/Shutterstock.com

HOME REMODELING ROI IS LESS THAN YOU MIGHT THINK

When it comes to home remodeling the return on investment (ROI) is calculated by taking the increase in a home's resale value due to the remodel divided by the cost of the remodeling project. While realtors often claim that remodeling projects have an ROI of at least 100% (meaning the increase in the home's resale value equals or exceeds the cost of the remodeling project), research from *Remodeling* magazine suggests otherwise. The table below summarizes the ROI of six types of remodeling projects. In each case the data indicate that homeowners would be better off selling their homes without investing in the remodeling project.

Project	(a) Increase in Resale Value	(b) Investment in Project	ROI (a) ÷ (b)
Deck addition	$20,532	$34,403	59.7%
Roofing replacement	$19,194	$33,880	56.7%
Garage addition	$44,034	$80,511	54.7%
Master-suite addition	$114,569	$220,086	52.1%
Major kitchen remodel	$64,113	$107,406	59.7%
Siding replacement (fiber-cement)	$10,379	$13,083	79.3%

Source: Sanette Tanaka, "After the Remodel, It's Payback Time," *The Wall Street Journal*, April 26, 2013, p. M12.

Many actions involve combinations of changes in sales, expenses, and operating assets. For example, a manager may make an investment in (i.e., increase) operating assets to reduce operating expenses or increase sales. Whether the net effect is favorable or not is judged in terms of its overall impact on ROI.

For example, suppose that the Montvale Burger Grill expects the following operating results next month:

Sales	$100,000
Operating expenses	$90,000
Net operating income	$10,000
Average operating assets	$50,000

The expected return on investment (ROI) for the month is computed as follows:

$$\text{ROI} = \text{Margin} \times \text{Turnover}$$

$$\text{ROI} = \frac{\text{Net operating income}}{\text{Sales}} \times \frac{\text{Sales}}{\text{Average operating assets}}$$

$$= \frac{\$10,000}{\$100,000} \times \frac{\$100,000}{\$50,000}$$

$$= 10\% \times 2 = 20\%$$

Suppose that the manager of the Montvale Burger Grill is considering investing $2,000 in a state-of-the-art soft-serve ice cream machine that can dispense a number of different flavors. This new machine would boost sales by $4,000, but would require additional operating expenses of $1,000. Thus, net operating income would increase by $3,000, to $13,000. The new ROI would be:

$$\text{ROI} = \text{Margin} \times \text{Turnover}$$

$$\text{ROI} = \frac{\text{Net operating income}}{\text{Sales}} \times \frac{\text{Sales}}{\text{Average operating assets}}$$

$$= \frac{\$13,000}{\$104,000} \times \frac{\$104,000}{\$52,000}$$

$$= 12.5\% \times 2 = 25\% \text{ (as compared to 20\% originally)}$$

In this particular example, the investment increases ROI, but that will not always happen.

E.I. du Pont de Nemours and Company (better known as DuPont) pioneered the use of ROI and recognized the importance of looking at both margin and turnover in assessing a manager's performance. ROI is now widely used as the key measure of investment center performance. ROI reflects in a single figure many aspects of the manager's responsibilities. It can be compared to the returns of other investment centers in the organization, the returns of other companies in the industry, and to the past returns of the investment center itself. DuPont also developed the diagram that appears in Exhibit 11–1. This exhibit helps managers understand how they can improve ROI.

WHIRLPOOL CHOOSES MARGIN RATHER THAN TURNOVER

Whirlpool Corporation has an industry-leading 40% market share in the U.S. when it comes to selling washers, dryers, refrigerators, dishwashers, and cooking equipment. Rather than using deep discounts to generate sales volume, the company relies on product innovations that enable price premiums and higher margins. In a recent quarter, Whirlpool's profits jumped 44% from the same quarter in the prior year due to fatter margins. In addition to margin expansion, the company also plans to boost profits by reducing capacity and cutting costs by $175 million.

Source: Bob Tita, "Whirlpool Shuns Discounts," *The Wall Street Journal*, April 25, 2013, p. B6.

EXHIBIT 11–1
Elements of Return on Investment (ROI)

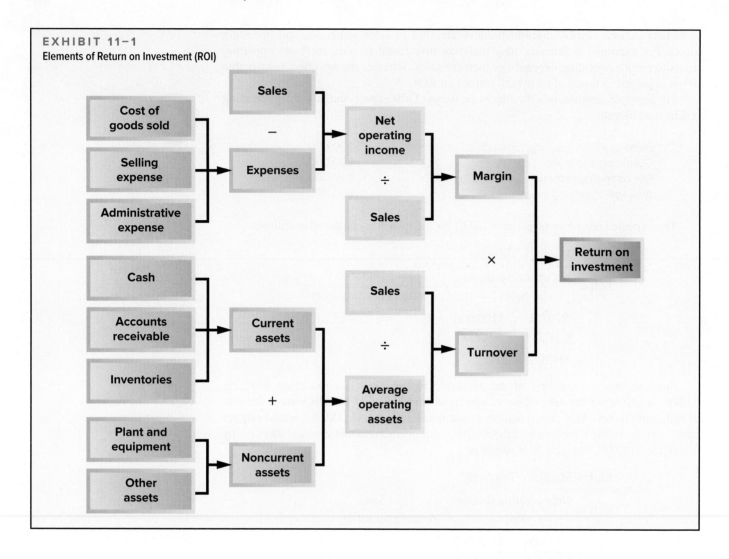

Criticisms of ROI

Although ROI is widely used in evaluating performance, it is subject to the following criticisms:

1. Just telling managers to increase ROI may not be enough. Managers may not know how to increase ROI; they may increase ROI in a way that is inconsistent with the company's strategy; or they may take actions that increase ROI in the short run but harm the company in the long run (such as cutting back on research and development). This is why ROI is best used as part of a balanced scorecard, as discussed later in this chapter. A balanced scorecard can provide concrete guidance to managers, making it more likely that their actions are consistent with the company's strategy and reducing the likelihood that they will boost short-run performance at the expense of long-term performance.

2. A manager who takes over a business segment typically inherits many committed costs over which the manager has no control. These committed costs may be relevant in assessing the performance of the business segment as an investment but they make it difficult to fairly assess the performance of the manager.

3. As discussed in the next section, a manager who is evaluated based on ROI may reject investment opportunities that are profitable for the whole company but would have a negative impact on the manager's performance evaluation.

Residual income is another approach to measuring an investment center's performance. **Residual income** is the net operating income that an investment center earns above the minimum required return on its operating assets. In equation form, residual income is calculated as follows:

$$\frac{\text{Residual}}{\text{income}} = \frac{\text{Net operating}}{\text{income}} - \left(\frac{\text{Average operating}}{\text{assets}} \times \frac{\text{Minimum required}}{\text{rate of return}}\right)$$

Economic Value Added (EVA®) is an adaptation of residual income that has been adopted by many companies.[3] Under EVA, companies often modify their accounting principles in various ways. For example, funds used for research and development are often treated as investments rather than as expenses.[4] These complications are best dealt with in a more advanced course; in this text we will not draw any distinction between residual income and EVA.

When residual income or EVA is used to measure performance, the objective is to maximize the total amount of residual income or EVA, not to maximize ROI. This is an important distinction. If the objective were to maximize ROI, then every company should divest all of its products except the single product with the highest ROI.

A wide variety of organizations have embraced some version of residual income or EVA, including **Bausch & Lomb**, **Best Buy**, **Boise Cascade**, **Coca-Cola**, **Dun and Bradstreet**, **Eli Lilly**, **Federal Mogul**, **Georgia-Pacific**, **Hershey Foods**, **Husky Injection Molding**, **J.C. Penney**, **Kansas City Power & Light**, **Olin**, **Quaker Oats**, **Silicon Valley Bank**, **Sprint**, **Toys R Us**, **Tupperware**, and the **United States Postal Service**.

For purposes of illustration, consider the following data for an investment center—the Ketchikan Division of Alaskan Marine Services Corporation.

Alaskan Marine Services Corporation Ketchikan Division Basic Data for Performance Evaluation	
Average operating assets	$100,000
Net operating income	$20,000
Minimum required rate of return	15%

Alaskan Marine Services Corporation has long had a policy of using ROI to evaluate its investment center managers, but it is considering switching to residual income. The controller of the company, who is in favor of the change to residual income, has provided the

---

[3] The basic idea underlying residual income and economic value added has been around for over 100 years. Economic value added has been popularized and trademarked by the consulting firm Stern, Stewart & Co.

[4] Over 100 different adjustments could be made for deferred taxes, LIFO reserves, provisions for future liabilities, mergers and acquisitions, gains or losses due to changes in accounting rules, operating leases, and other accounts, but most companies make only a few. For further details, see John O'Hanlon and Ken Peasnell, "Wall Street's Contribution to Management Accounting: The Stern Stewart EVA® Financial Management System," *Management Accounting Research* 9, 1998, pp. 421–444.

following table that shows how the performance of the division would be evaluated under each of the two methods:

Alaskan Marine Services Corporation Ketchikan Division		
	Alternative Performance Measures	
	ROI	Residual Income
Average operating assets (a)	$100,000	$100,000
Net operating income (b)	$ 20,000	$ 20,000
ROI, (b) ÷ (a)	20%	
Minimum required return (15% × $100,000)		15,000
Residual income		$ 5,000

The reasoning underlying the residual income calculation is straightforward. The company is able to earn a rate of return of at least 15% on its investments. Because the company has invested $100,000 in the Ketchikan Division in the form of operating assets, the company should be able to earn at least $15,000 (15% × $100,000) on this investment. Because the Ketchikan Division's net operating income is $20,000, the residual income above and beyond the minimum required return is $5,000. If residual income is adopted as the performance measure to replace ROI, the manager of the Ketchikan Division would be evaluated based on the growth in residual income from year to year.

Motivation and Residual Income

One of the primary reasons why the controller of Alaskan Marine Services Corporation would like to switch from ROI to residual income relates to how managers view new investments under the two performance measurement methods. The residual income approach encourages managers to make investments that are profitable for the entire company but that would be rejected by managers who are evaluated using the ROI formula.

To illustrate this problem with ROI, suppose that the manager of the Ketchikan Division is considering purchasing a computerized diagnostic machine to aid in servicing marine diesel engines. The machine would cost $25,000 and is expected to generate additional operating income of $4,500 a year. From the standpoint of the company, this would be a good investment because it promises a rate of return of 18% ($4,500 ÷ $25,000), which exceeds the company's minimum required rate of return of 15%.

If the manager of the Ketchikan Division is evaluated based on residual income, she would be in favor of the investment in the diagnostic machine as shown below:

Alaskan Marine Services Corporation Ketchikan Division Performance Evaluated Using Residual Income			
	Present	New Project	Overall
Average operating assets	$100,000	$25,000	$125,000
Net operating income	$20,000	$4,500	$24,500
Minimum required return	15,000	3,750*	18,750
Residual income	$ 5,000	$ 750	$ 5,750

*$25,000 × 15% = $3,750.

Because the project would increase the residual income of the Ketchikan Division by $750, the manager would choose to invest in the new diagnostic machine.

Now suppose that the manager of the Ketchikan Division is evaluated based on ROI. The effect of the diagnostic machine on the division's ROI is computed below:

Alaskan Marine Services Corporation Ketchikan Division Performance Evaluated Using ROI			
	Present	New Project	Overall
Average operating assets (a)	$100,000	$25,000	$125,000
Net operating income (b)	$20,000	$4,500	$24,500
ROI, (b) ÷ (a)	20%	18%	19.6%

The new project reduces the division's ROI from 20% to 19.6%. This happens because the 18% rate of return on the new diagnostic machine, while above the company's 15% minimum required rate of return, is below the division's current ROI of 20%. Therefore, the new diagnostic machine would decrease the division's ROI even though it would be a good investment from the standpoint of the company as a whole. If the manager of the division is evaluated based on ROI, she will be reluctant to even propose such an investment.

Generally, a manager who is evaluated based on ROI will reject any project whose rate of return is below the division's current ROI even if the rate of return on the project is above the company's minimum required rate of return. In contrast, managers who are evaluated using residual income will pursue any project whose rate of return is above the minimum required rate of return because it will increase their residual income. Because it is in the best interests of the company as a whole to accept any project whose rate of return is above the minimum required rate of return, managers who are evaluated based on residual income will tend to make better decisions concerning investment projects than managers who are evaluated based on ROI.

Divisional Comparison and Residual Income

The residual income approach has one major disadvantage. It can't be used to compare the performance of divisions of different sizes. Larger divisions often have more residual income than smaller divisions, not necessarily because they are better managed but simply because they are bigger.

As an example, consider the following residual income computations for the Wholesale Division and the Retail Division of Sisal Marketing Corporation:

	Wholesale Division	Retail Division
Average operating assets (a)	$1,000,000	$250,000
Net operating income	$120,000	$40,000
Minimum required return: 10% × (a)	100,000	25,000
Residual income	$ 20,000	$15,000

Observe that the Wholesale Division has slightly more residual income than the Retail Division, but that the Wholesale Division has $1,000,000 in operating assets as compared to only $250,000 in operating assets for the Retail Division. Thus, the Wholesale Division's greater residual income is probably due to its larger size rather than the quality of its management. In fact, it appears that the smaller division may be better managed because it has been able to generate nearly as much residual income with only one-fourth as much in operating assets. When comparing investment centers, it is probably better to focus on the percentage change in residual income from year to year rather than on the absolute amount of the residual income.

Operating Performance Measures

LO11-3
Compute throughput time, delivery cycle time, and manufacturing cycle efficiency (MCE).

In addition to financial performance measures, organizations use many nonfinancial performance measures. While financial measures reflect the *results* of what people in the organization do, they do not measure what *drives* organizational performance. For example, activity and revenue variances summarize the results of efforts aimed at increasing sales, but they do not measure the actions that actually drive sales such as improving quality, exposing more potential customers to the product, filling customer orders on time, and so on. Consequently, many organizations use a variety of nonfinancial performance measures in addition to financial measures. In this section we will discuss three examples of such measures that are critical to success in many organizations—throughput time, delivery cycle time, and manufacturing cycle efficiency (MCE). Note that while these examples focus on manufacturers, very similar measures can be used by any service organization that experiences a delay between receiving a customer request and responding to that request.

Throughput (Manufacturing Cycle) Time

The elapsed time from when production is started until finished goods are shipped to customers is called **throughput time**, or *manufacturing cycle time*. The goal is to continuously reduce this measure and the formula for computing it is as follows:

$$\text{Throughput (manufacturing cycle) time} =$$
$$\text{Process time} + \text{Inspection time} + \text{Move time} + \text{Queue time}$$

Process time is the amount of time work is actually done on the product. *Inspection time* is the amount of time spent ensuring that the product is not defective. *Move time* is the time required to move materials or partially completed products from workstation to workstation. *Queue time* is the amount of time a product spends waiting to be worked on, to be moved, to be inspected, or to be shipped. Only one of these four activities adds value to the product—process time. The other three activities—inspecting, moving, and queuing—add no value and should be eliminated as much as possible.

Delivery Cycle Time

The elapsed time from when a customer order is received until the finished goods are shipped is called **delivery cycle time**. The goal is to reduce this measure and the formula for computing it is as follows:

$$\text{Delivery cycle time} = \text{Wait time} + \text{Throughput time}$$

IN BUSINESS

THE DOCTOR WILL SEE YOU . . . LATER

When medical care reimbursement rates drop, doctors often respond by packing more patients into each day, thereby increasing patient wait times. **Press Ganey Associates** surveyed 2.4 million patients at more than 10,000 locations and determined an average wait time to see a doctor of 22 minutes. While these delays inconvenience patients, they also have financial implications for doctors. For example, Laurie Green, an obstetrician-gynecologist in San Francisco, prides herself on running an efficient medical practice because "she needs to bring in $75 every 15 minutes just to meet her office overhead."

If your doctor's office is overrun with delays, consider getting the first appointment of the day because the "early bird" not only gets the worm, but it also avoids wait time at the doctor's office!

Source: Melinda Beck, "The Doctor Will See You Eventually," *The Wall Street Journal*, October 19, 2010, pp. D1 and D4.

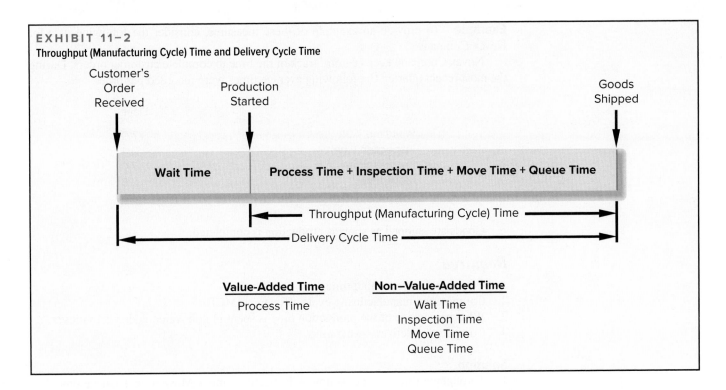

EXHIBIT 11–2
Throughput (Manufacturing Cycle) Time and Delivery Cycle Time

Wait time is the elapsed time from when a customer order is received until production of the order is started. This is a non–value-added activity that should be reduced or eliminated. When companies succeed in drastically reducing or eliminating wait time plus the non–value-added components of throughput time it often enables them to increase customer satisfaction and profits. The relation between throughput (manufacturing cycle) time and delivery cycle time is illustrated in Exhibit 11–2.

Manufacturing Cycle Efficiency (MCE)

Through concerted efforts to eliminate the *non–value-added* activities of inspecting, moving, and queuing, some companies have reduced their throughput time to only a fraction of previous levels. In turn, this has helped to reduce the delivery cycle time from months to only weeks or hours. Throughput time, which is a key measure in delivery performance, can be put into better perspective by computing the **manufacturing cycle efficiency (MCE)**. The MCE is computed by relating the value-added time to the throughput time. The goal is to increase this measure and the formula for computing it is as follows:

$$MCE = \frac{\text{Value-added time (Process time)}}{\text{Throughput (manufacturing cycle) time}}$$

Any non–value-added time results in an MCE of less than 1. An MCE of 0.5, for example, would mean that half of the total production time consists of inspection, moving, and similar non–value-added activities. In many manufacturing companies, the MCE is less than 0.1 (10%), which means that 90% of the time a unit is in process is spent on activities that do not add value to the product. Monitoring the MCE helps companies to reduce non–value-added activities and thus get products into the hands of customers more quickly and at a lower cost.

Example   To provide an example of these measures, consider the following data for Novex Company:

Novex Company keeps careful track of the time to complete customer orders. During the most recent quarter, the following average times were recorded per order:

	Days
Wait time	17.0
Inspection time	0.4
Process time	2.0
Move time	0.6
Queue time	5.0

Goods are shipped as soon as production is completed.

Required:

1. Compute the throughput time.
2. Compute the manufacturing cycle efficiency (MCE).
3. What percentage of the production time is spent in non–value-added activities?
4. Compute the delivery cycle time.

Solution

1. Throughput time = Process time + Inspection time + Move time + Queue time

$$= 2.0 \text{ days} + 0.4 \text{ days} + 0.6 \text{ days} + 5.0 \text{ days}$$

$$= 8.0 \text{ days}$$

2. Only process time represents value-added time; therefore, MCE would be computed as follows:

$$\text{MCE} = \frac{\text{Value-added time}}{\text{Throughput time}} = \frac{2.0 \text{ days}}{8.0 \text{ days}}$$

$$= 0.25$$

Thus, once put into production, a typical order is actually being worked on only 25% of the time.

3. Because the MCE is 25%, 75% (100% − 25%) of total production time is spent in non–value-added activities.

4. Delivery cycle time = Wait time + Throughput time

$$= 17.0 \text{ days} + 8.0 \text{ days}$$

$$= 25.0 \text{ days}$$

IN BUSINESS

© B Christopher/Alamy

UPS LOOKS TO SHRINK DELIVERY TIMES AND SAVE MONEY

The United Parcel Service (UPS) has invested more than 10 years and hundreds of millions of dollars developing a computer platform called Orion that is designed to identify optimal delivery routes for its drivers. The human mind cannot possibly evaluate the most efficient way for a driver to deliver 120 packages per day, so UPS has turned to 50 engineers to develop the computerized algorithms and heuristics embedded in the Orion platform.

Given that UPS drivers complete 55,000 routes per day in the U.S., if Orion can shave one mile per day off of each of these routes, it saves the company $50 million per year. Since the drivers already using Orion are actually saving seven to eight miles per day, UPS estimates that Orion will save the company $300 to $400 million per year.

Source: Steven Rosenbush and Laura Stevens, "At UPS, the Algorithm is the Driver" *The Wall Street Journal,* February 17, 2015, pp. B1 and B4.

Balanced Scorecard

Financial measures, such as ROI and residual income, and operating measures, such as those discussed in the previous section, may be included in a *balanced scorecard*. A **balanced scorecard** consists of an integrated set of performance measures that are derived from and support a company's strategy. A strategy is essentially a theory about how to achieve the organization's goals. For example, Southwest Airlines' strategy is to offer an *operational excellence* customer value proposition that has three key components—low ticket prices, convenience, and reliability. The company operates only one type of aircraft, the Boeing 737, to reduce maintenance and training costs and simplify scheduling. It further reduces costs by not offering meals, seat assignments, or baggage transfers and by booking a large portion of its passenger revenue over the Internet. Southwest also uses point-to-point flights rather than the hub-and-spoke approach of its larger competitors, thereby providing customers convenient, nonstop service to their final destination. Because Southwest serves many less-congested airports such as Chicago Midway, Burbank, Manchester, Oakland, and Providence, it offers quicker passenger check-ins and reliable departures, while maintaining high asset utilization (i.e., the company's average gate turnaround time of 25 minutes enables it to function with fewer planes and gates). Overall, the company's strategy has worked, as Southwest Airlines continues to earn substantial profits.

Under the balanced scorecard approach, top management translates its strategy into performance measures that employees can understand and influence. For example, the amount of time passengers have to wait in line to have their baggage checked might be a performance measure for the supervisor in charge of the Southwest Airlines check-in counter at the Burbank airport. This performance measure is easily understood by the supervisor, and can be improved by the supervisor's actions.

LO11–4
Understand how to construct and use a balanced scorecard.

Common Characteristics of Balanced Scorecards

Performance measures used in balanced scorecards tend to fall into the four groups illustrated in Exhibit 11–3: financial, customer, internal business processes, and learning and growth. Internal business processes are what the company does in an attempt to satisfy customers. For example, in a manufacturing company, assembling a product is an internal business process. In an airline, handling baggage is an internal business process. The idea underlying these groupings (as indicated by the vertical arrows in Exhibit 11–3) is that learning is necessary to improve internal business processes; improving business processes is necessary to improve customer satisfaction; and improving customer satisfaction is necessary to improve financial results.

Note that the emphasis in Exhibit 11–3 is on *improvement*—not on just attaining some specific objective such as profits of $10 million. In the balanced scorecard approach, continual improvement is encouraged. If an organization does not continually improve, it will eventually lose out to competitors that do.

Financial performance measures appear at the top of Exhibit 11–3. Ultimately, most companies exist to provide financial rewards to owners. There are exceptions. Some companies—for example, The Body Shop—may have loftier goals such as providing environmentally friendly products to consumers. However, even nonprofit organizations must generate enough financial resources to stay in operation.

For several reasons, financial performance measures are not sufficient in themselves—they should be integrated with nonfinancial measures in a well-designed balanced scorecard. First, financial measures are lag indicators that report on the results of past actions. In contrast, nonfinancial measures of key success drivers such as customer satisfaction are leading indicators of future financial performance. Second, top managers are ordinarily responsible for the financial performance measures—not lower-level managers. The supervisor in charge of checking in passengers can be held responsible for how long passengers have to wait in line. However, this supervisor cannot reasonably be

EXHIBIT 11–3
From Strategy to Performance
Measures: The Balanced Scorecard

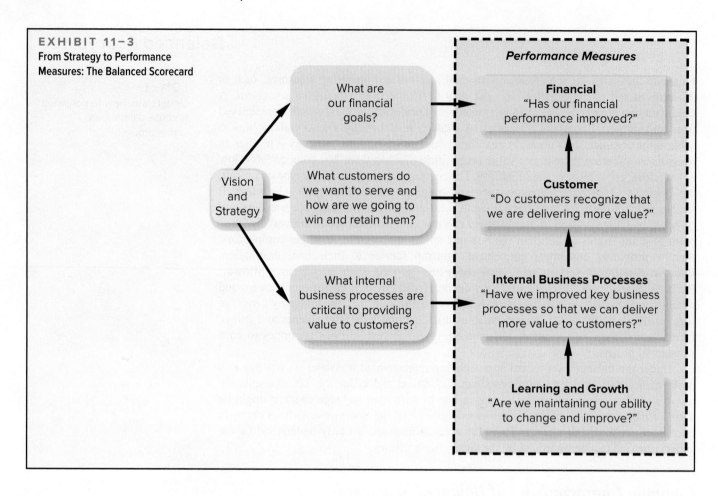

held responsible for the entire company's profit. That is the responsibility of the airline's top managers.

Exhibit 11–4 lists some examples of performance measures that can be found on the balanced scorecards of companies. However, few companies, if any, would use all of these performance measures, and almost all companies would add other performance measures. Managers should carefully select performance measures for their own company's balanced scorecard, keeping the following points in mind. First and foremost, the performance measures should be consistent with, and follow from, the company's strategy. If the performance measures are not consistent with the company's strategy, people will find themselves working at cross-purposes. Second, the performance measures should be understandable and controllable to a significant extent by those being evaluated. Third, the performance measures should be reported on a frequent and timely basis. For example, data about defects should be reported to the responsible manager at least once a day so that problems can be resolved quickly. Fourth, the scorecard should not have too many performance measures. This can lead to a lack of focus and confusion.

While the entire organization will have an overall balanced scorecard, each responsible individual will have his or her own personal scorecard as well. This scorecard should consist of items the individual can personally influence that relate directly to the performance measures on the overall balanced scorecard. The performance measures on this personal scorecard should not be overly influenced by actions taken by others in the company or by events that are outside of the individual's control. And, focusing on the performance measure should not lead an individual to take actions that are counter to the organization's objectives.

With those broad principles in mind, we will now take a look at how a company's strategy affects its balanced scorecard.

EXHIBIT 11–4
Examples of Performance Measures for Balanced Scorecards

Customer Perspective

Performance Measure	Desired Change
Customer satisfaction as measured by survey results	+
Number of customer complaints	−
Market share	+
Product returns as a percentage of sales	−
Percentage of customers retained from last period	+
Number of new customers	+

Internal Business Processes Perspective

Performance Measure	Desired Change
Percentage of sales from new products	+
Time to introduce new products to market	−
Percentage of customer calls answered within 20 seconds	+
On-time deliveries as a percentage of all deliveries	+
Work in process inventory as a percentage of sales	−
Unfavorable standard cost variances	−
Defect-free units as a percentage of completed units	+
Delivery cycle time	−
Throughput time	−
Manufacturing cycle efficiency	+
Quality costs	−
Setup time	−
Time from call by customer to repair of product	−
Percent of customer complaints settled on first contact	+
Time to settle a customer claim	−

Learning and Growth Perspective

Performance Measure	Desired Change
Suggestions per employee	+
Employee turnover	−
Hours of in-house training per employee	+

A Company's Strategy and the Balanced Scorecard

Returning to the performance measures in Exhibit 11–3, each company must decide which customers to target and what internal business processes are crucial to attracting and retaining those customers. Different companies, having different strategies, will target different customers with different kinds of products and services. Take the automobile industry as an example. **BMW** stresses engineering and handling; **Volvo**, safety; **Jaguar**, luxury detailing; and **Honda**, reliability. Because of these differences in emphasis, a one-size-fits-all approach to performance measurement won't work even within this one industry. Performance measures must be tailored to the specific strategy of each company.

Suppose, for example, that Jaguar's strategy is to offer distinctive, richly finished luxury automobiles to wealthy individuals who prize handcrafted, individualized products. To deliver this customer intimacy value proposition to its wealthy target customers,

Jaguar might create such a large number of options for details, such as leather seats, interior and exterior color combinations, and wooden dashboards, that each car becomes virtually one of a kind. For example, instead of just offering tan or blue leather seats in standard cowhide, the company may offer customers the choice of an almost infinite palette of colors in any of a number of different exotic leathers. For such a system to work effectively, Jaguar would have to be able to deliver a completely customized car within a reasonable amount of time—and without incurring more cost for this customization than the customer is willing to pay. Exhibit 11–5 suggests how Jaguar might reflect this strategy in its balanced scorecard.

If the balanced scorecard is correctly constructed, the performance measures should be linked together on a cause-and-effect basis. Each link can then be read as a hypothesis in the form "If we improve this performance measure, then this other performance measure should also improve." Starting from the bottom of Exhibit 11–5, we can read the links between performance measures as follows. If employees acquire the skills to install new options more effectively, then the company can offer more options and the options can be installed in less time. If more options are available and they are installed in less time, then customer surveys should show greater satisfaction with the range of options available. If customer satisfaction improves, then the number of cars sold should

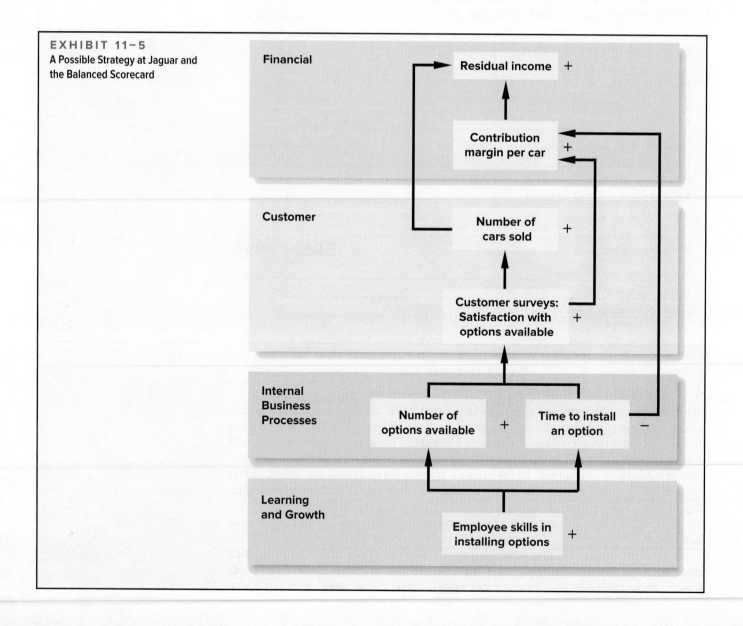

EXHIBIT 11–5
A Possible Strategy at Jaguar and the Balanced Scorecard

increase. In addition, if customer satisfaction improves, the company should be able to maintain or increase its selling prices, and if the time to install options decreases, the costs of installing the options should decrease. Together, this should result in an increase in the contribution margin per car. If the contribution margin per car increases and more cars are sold, the result should be an increase in residual income.

In essence, the balanced scorecard lays out a theory of how the company can take concrete actions to attain its desired outcomes (financial, in this case). The strategy laid out in Exhibit 11–5 seems plausible, but it should be regarded as only a theory. For example, if the company succeeds in increasing the number of options available and in decreasing the time required to install options and yet there is no increase in customer satisfaction, the number of cars sold, the contribution margin per car, or residual income, the strategy would have to be reconsidered. One of the advantages of the balanced scorecard is that it continually tests the theories underlying management's strategy. If a strategy is not working, it should become evident when some of the predicted effects (i.e., more car sales) don't occur. Without this feedback, the organization may drift on indefinitely with an ineffective strategy based on faulty assumptions.

EMPLOYEE WELLNESS DRIVES EMPLOYEE PRODUCTIVITY

When a company's employees are sick or suffering from emotional stress, it can affect their absenteeism and productivity rates. Survey results from the **Financial Fitness Group** indicate that 80% of workers in the U.S. and Puerto Rico are under moderate to high levels of financial stress. To reduce these stress levels, some companies are implementing financial wellness programs that "include finance classes, counseling sessions, and even video games designed to help staffers pay down debt, stick to a budget, and invest for their retirement."

Meredith Corporation encourages its employees to complete a financial wellness questionnaire or take a course on refinancing their mortgage in exchange for points that make them eligible for lower healthcare premiums. The company estimates that 88% of its workers who reported less money stress used no sick days in the prior year, whereas only 78% of employees who reported higher levels of stress used no sick days.

© JGI/Tom Grill/Getty Images RF

Source: Rachel Feintzeig, "Can Companies Solve Workers' Money Woes," *The Wall Street Journal,* April 8, 2015, pp. B1 and B6.

Tying Compensation to the Balanced Scorecard

Incentive compensation for employees, such as bonuses, can, and probably should, be tied to balanced scorecard performance measures. However, this should be done only after the organization has been successfully managed with the scorecard for some time—perhaps a year or more. Managers must be confident that the performance measures are reliable, sensible, understood by those who are being evaluated, and not easily manipulated. As Robert Kaplan and David Norton, the originators of the balanced scorecard concept point out, "compensation is such a powerful lever that you have to be pretty confident that you have the right measures and have good data for the measures before making the link."[5]

Summary

For purposes of evaluating performance, business units are classified as cost centers, profit centers, and investment centers. Cost and profit centers are commonly evaluated using standard cost and flexible budget variances as discussed in prior chapters. Investment centers are evaluated using the techniques discussed in this chapter.

---

[5] Lori Calabro, "On Balance: A CFO Interview," *CFO,* February 2001, pp. 73–78.

Return on investment (ROI) and residual income and its cousin EVA are widely used to evaluate the performance of investment centers. ROI suffers from the underinvestment problem—managers are reluctant to invest in projects that would decrease their ROI but whose returns exceed the company's required rate of return. The residual income and EVA approaches solve this problem by giving managers full credit for any returns in excess of the company's required rate of return.

A balanced scorecard is an integrated system of performance measures designed to support an organization's strategy. The various measures in a balanced scorecard should be linked on a plausible cause-and-effect basis from the very lowest level up through the organization's ultimate objectives. The balanced scorecard is essentially a theory about how specific actions taken by various people in the organization will further the organization's objectives. The theory should be viewed as tentative and subject to change if the actions do not in fact result in improvements in the organization's financial and other goals. If the theory changes, then the performance measures on the balanced scorecard should also change. The balanced scorecard is a dynamic measurement system that evolves as an organization learns more about what works and what doesn't work and refines its strategy accordingly.

Review Problem: Return on Investment (ROI) and Residual Income

The Magnetic Imaging Division of Medical Diagnostics, Inc., has reported the following results for last year's operations:

Sales	$25 million
Net operating income	$3 million
Average operating assets	$10 million

Required:

1. Compute the Magnetic Imaging Division's margin, turnover, and ROI.
2. Top management of Medical Diagnostics, Inc., has set a minimum required rate of return on average operating assets of 25%. What is the Magnetic Imaging Division's residual income for the year?

Solution to Review Problem

1. The required calculations follow:

$$\text{Margin} = \frac{\text{Net operating income}}{\text{Sales}}$$
$$= \frac{\$3,000,000}{\$25,000,000}$$
$$= 12\%$$

$$\text{Turnover} = \frac{\text{Sales}}{\text{Average operating assets}}$$
$$= \frac{\$25,000,000}{\$10,000,000}$$
$$= 2.5$$

$$\text{ROI} = \text{Margin} \times \text{Turnover}$$
$$= 12\% \times 2.5$$
$$= 30\%$$

2. The Magnetic Imaging Division's residual income is computed as follows:

Average operating assets	$10,000,000
Net operating income	$3,000,000
Minimum required return (25% × $10,000,000)	2,500,000
Residual income	$ 500,000

Balanced scorecard An integrated set of performance measures that are derived from and support the organization's strategy. (p. 519)

Cost center A business segment whose manager has control over cost but has no control over revenue or investments in operating assets. (p. 508)

Decentralized organization An organization in which decision-making authority is not confined to a few top executives but rather is spread throughout the organization. (p. 507)

Delivery cycle time The elapsed time from when a customer order is received until the finished goods are shipped. (p. 516)

Economic Value Added (EVA) A concept similar to residual income in which a variety of adjustments may be made to GAAP financial statements for performance evaluation purposes. (p. 513)

Investment center A business segment whose manager has control over cost, revenue, and investments in operating assets. (p. 508)

Manufacturing cycle efficiency (MCE) Process (value-added) time as a percentage of throughput time. (p. 517)

Margin Net operating income divided by sales. (p. 510)

Net operating income Income before interest and income taxes have been deducted. (p. 509)

Operating assets Cash, accounts receivable, inventory, plant and equipment, and all other assets held for operating purposes. (p. 509)

Profit center A business segment whose manager has control over cost and revenue but has no control over investments in operating assets. (p. 508)

Residual income The net operating income that an investment center earns above the minimum required return on its operating assets. (p. 513)

Responsibility center Any business segment whose manager has control over costs, revenues, or investments in operating assets. (p. 508)

Return on investment (ROI) Net operating income divided by average operating assets. It also equals margin multiplied by turnover. (p. 509)

Throughput time The elapsed time from when production is started until finished goods are shipped. (p. 516)

Turnover Sales divided by average operating assets. (p. 510)

Questions |

11–1   What is meant by the term *decentralization?*

11–2   What benefits result from decentralization?

11–3   Distinguish between a cost center, a profit center, and an investment center.

11–4   What is meant by the terms *margin* and *turnover* in ROI calculations?

11–5   What is meant by residual income?

11–6   In what way can the use of ROI as a performance measure for investment centers lead to bad decisions? How does the residual income approach overcome this problem?

11–7   What is the difference between delivery cycle time and throughput time? What four elements make up throughput time? What elements of throughput time are value-added and what elements are non–value-added?

11–8   What does a manufacturing cycle efficiency (MCE) of less than 1 mean? How would you interpret an MCE of 0.40?

11–9   Why do the measures used in a balanced scorecard differ from company to company?

11–10 Why does the balanced scorecard include financial performance measures as well as measures of how well internal business processes are doing?

Applying Excel |

LO11–1, LO11–2

The Excel worksheet form that appears below is to be used to recreate the Review Problem pertaining to the Magnetic Imaging Division of Medical Diagnostics, Inc. Download the workbook containing this form from Connect, where you will also receive instructions about how to use this worksheet form.

	A	B	C	D	E
1	Chapter 11: Applying Excel				
2					
3	Data				
4	Sales	$25,000,000			
5	Net operating income	$3,000,000			
6	Average operating assets	$10,000,000			
7	Minimum required rate of return	25%			
8					
9	Enter a formula into each of the cells marked with a ? below				
10	Review Problem: Return on Investment (ROI) and Residual Income				
11					
12	Compute the ROI				
13	Margin	?			
14	Turnover	?			
15	ROI	?			
16					
17	Compute the residual income				
18	Average operating assets	?			
19	Net operating income	?			
20	Minimum required return	?			
21	Residual income	?			
22					

|◄ ◄ ► ►| **Chapter 11 Form**   Filled in Chapter 11 Form

You should proceed to the requirements below only after completing your worksheet.

Required:

1. Check your worksheet by changing the average operating assets in cell B6 to $8,000,000. The ROI should now be 38% and the residual income should now be $1,000,000. If you do not get these answers, find the errors in your worksheet and correct them.

   Explain why the ROI and the residual income both increase when the average operating assets decrease.

2. Revise the data in your worksheet as follows:

Data	
Sales	$1,200
Net operating income	$72
Average operating assets	$500
Minimum required rate of return	15%

   a. What is the ROI?
   b. What is the residual income?
   c. Explain the relationship between the ROI and the residual income?

The Foundational 15   connect

LO11–1, LO11–2

Westerville Company reported the following results from last year's operations:

Sales	$1,000,000
Variable expenses	300,000
Contribution margin	700,000
Fixed expenses	500,000
Net operating income	$ 200,000
Average operating assets	$ 625,000

At the beginning of this year, the company has a $120,000 investment opportunity with the following cost and revenue characteristics:

Sales	$200,000
Contribution margin ratio	60% of sales
Fixed expenses	$90,000

The company's minimum required rate of return is 15%.

Required:
1. What is last year's margin?
2. What is last year's turnover?
3. What is last year's return on investment (ROI)?
4. What is the margin related to this year's investment opportunity?
5. What is the turnover related to this year's investment opportunity?
6. What is the ROI related to this year's investment opportunity?
7. If the company pursues the investment opportunity and otherwise performs the same as last year, what margin will it earn this year?
8. If the company pursues the investment opportunity and otherwise performs the same as last year, what turnover will it earn this year?
9. If the company pursues the investment opportunity and otherwise performs the same as last year, what ROI will it earn this year?
10. If Westerville's chief executive officer will earn a bonus only if her ROI from this year exceeds her ROI from last year, would she pursue the investment opportunity? Would the owners of the company want her to pursue the investment opportunity?
11. What is last year's residual income?
12. What is the residual income of this year's investment opportunity?
13. If the company pursues the investment opportunity and otherwise performs the same as last year, what residual income will it earn this year?
14. If Westerville's chief executive officer will earn a bonus only if her residual income from this year exceeds her residual income from last year, would she pursue the investment opportunity?
15. Assume that the contribution margin ratio of the investment opportunity was 50% instead of 60%. If Westerville's chief executive officer will earn a bonus only if her residual income from this year exceeds her residual income from last year, would she pursue the investment opportunity? Would the owners of the company want her to pursue the investment opportunity?

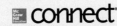 **Exercises**

EXERCISE 11–1 Compute the Return on Investment (ROI) LO11–1
Alyeska Services Company, a division of a major oil company, provides various services to the operators of the North Slope oil field in Alaska. Data concerning the most recent year appear below:

Sales	$7,500,000
Net operating income	$600,000
Average operating assets	$5,000,000

Required:
1. Compute the margin for Alyeska Services Company.
2. Compute the turnover for Alyeska Services Company.
3. Compute the return on investment (ROI) for Alyeska Services Company.

EXERCISE 11–2 Residual Income LO11–2
Juniper Design Ltd. of Manchester, England, is a company specializing in providing design services to residential developers. Last year the company had net operating income of $600,000 on sales of $3,000,000. The company's average operating assets for the year were $2,800,000 and its minimum required rate of return was 18%.

Required:
Compute the company's residual income for the year.

EXERCISE 11–3 Measures of Internal Business Process Performance LO11–3

Management of Mittel Rhein AG of Köln, Germany, would like to reduce the amount of time between when a customer places an order and when the order is shipped. For the first quarter of operations during the current year the following data were reported:

Inspection time	0.3 days
Wait time (from order to start of production)	14.0 days
Process time	2.7 days
Move time	1.0 days
Queue time......................................	5.0 days

Required:

1. Compute the throughput time.
2. Compute the manufacturing cycle efficiency (MCE) for the quarter.
3. What percentage of the throughput time was spent in non–value-added activities?
4. Compute the delivery cycle time.
5. If by using Lean Production all queue time during production is eliminated, what will be the new MCE?

EXERCISE 11–4 Building a Balanced Scorecard LO11–4

Lost Peak ski resort was for many years a small, family-owned resort serving day skiers from nearby towns. Lost Peak was recently acquired by Western Resorts, a major ski resort operator. The new owners have plans to upgrade the resort into a destination resort for vacationers. As part of this plan, the new owners would like to make major improvements in the Powder 8 Lodge, the resort's on-the-hill cafeteria. The menu at the lodge is very limited—hamburgers, hot dogs, chili, tuna fish sandwiches, pizzas, french fries, and packaged snacks. With little competition, the previous owners of the resort felt no urgency to upgrade the food service at the lodge. If skiers want lunch on the mountain, the only alternatives are the Powder 8 Lodge or a brown bag lunch brought from home.

As part of the deal when acquiring Lost Peak, Western Resorts agreed to retain all of the current employees of the resort. The manager of the lodge, while hardworking and enthusiastic, has very little experience in the restaurant business. The manager is responsible for selecting the menu, finding and training employees, and overseeing daily operations. The kitchen staff prepare food and wash dishes. The dining room staff take orders, serve as cashiers, and clean the dining room area.

Shortly after taking over Lost Peak, management of Western Resorts held a day-long meeting with all of the employees of the Powder 8 Lodge to discuss the future of the ski resort and the new management's plans for the lodge. At the end of this meeting, management and lodge employees created a balanced scorecard for the lodge that would help guide operations for the coming ski season. Almost everyone who participated in the meeting seemed to be enthusiastic about the scorecard and management's plans for the lodge.

The following performance measures were included on the balanced scorecard for the Powder 8 Lodge:

a. Weekly Powder 8 Lodge sales
b. Weekly Powder 8 Lodge profit
c. Number of menu items
d. Dining area cleanliness as rated by a representative from Western Resorts management
e. Customer satisfaction with menu choices as measured by customer surveys
f. Customer satisfaction with service as measured by customer surveys
g. Average time to take an order
h. Average time to prepare an order
i. Percentage of kitchen staff completing a basic cooking course at the local community college
j. Percentage of dining room staff completing a basic hospitality course at the local community college

Western Resorts will pay for the costs of staff attending courses at the local community college.

Required:

1. Using the above performance measures, construct a balanced scorecard for the Powder 8 Lodge. Use Exhibit 11–5 as a guide. Use arrows to show causal links and indicate with a + or − whether the performance measure should increase or decrease.

2. What hypotheses are built into the balanced scorecard for the Powder 8 Lodge? Which of these hypotheses do you believe are most questionable? Why?

3. How will management know if one of the hypotheses underlying the balanced scorecard is false?

EXERCISE 11–5 Return on Investment (ROI) LO11–1

Provide the missing data in the following table for a distributor of martial arts products:

	Division		
	Alpha	Bravo	Charlie
Sales	$?	$11,500,000	$?
Net operating income	$?	$ 920,000	$210,000
Average operating assets	$800,000	$?	$?
Margin	4%	?	7%
Turnover	5	?	?
Return on investment (ROI)	?	20%	14%

EXERCISE 11–6 Contrasting Return on Investment (ROI) and Residual Income LO11–1, LO11–2

Meiji Isetan Corp. of Japan has two regional divisions with headquarters in Osaka and Yokohama. Selected data on the two divisions follow:

	Division	
	Osaka	Yokohama
Sales	$3,000,000	$9,000,000
Net operating income	$210,000	$720,000
Average operating assets	$1,000,000	$4,000,000

Required:

1. For each division, compute the return on investment (ROI) in terms of margin and turnover. Where necessary, carry computations to two decimal places.

2. Assume that the company evaluates performance using residual income and that the minimum required rate of return for any division is 15%. Compute the residual income for each division.

3. Is Yokohama's greater amount of residual income an indication that it is better managed? Explain.

EXERCISE 11–7 Creating a Balanced Scorecard LO11–4

Ariel Tax Services prepares tax returns for individual and corporate clients. As the company has gradually expanded to 10 offices, the founder Max Jacobs has begun to feel as though he is losing control of operations. In response to this concern, he has decided to implement a performance measurement system that will help control current operations and facilitate his plans of expanding to 20 offices.

Jacobs describes the keys to the success of his business as follows:

"Our only real asset is our people. We must keep our employees highly motivated and we must hire the 'cream of the crop.' Interestingly, employee morale and recruiting success are both driven by the same two factors—compensation and career advancement. In other words, providing superior compensation relative to the industry average coupled with fast-track career advancement opportunities keeps morale high and makes us a very attractive place to work. It drives a high rate of job offer acceptances relative to job offers tendered."

"Hiring highly qualified people and keeping them energized ensures operational success, which in our business is a function of productivity, efficiency, and effectiveness. Productivity boils down to employees being billable rather than idle. Efficiency relates to the time required to complete a tax return. Finally, effectiveness is critical to our business in the sense that we cannot tolerate errors. Completing a tax return quickly is meaningless if the return contains errors."

"Our growth depends on acquiring new customers through word-of-mouth from satisfied repeat customers. We believe that our customers come back year after year because they value error-free, timely, and courteous tax return preparation. Common courtesy is an important aspect of our business! We call it service quality, and it all ties back to employee morale in the sense that happy employees treat their clients with care and concern."

"While sales growth is obviously important to our future plans, growth without a corresponding increase in profitability is useless. Therefore, we understand that increasing our profit margin is a function of cost-efficiency as well as sales growth. Given that payroll is our biggest expense, we must maintain an optimal balance between staffing levels and the revenue being generated. As I alluded to earlier, the key to maintaining this balance is employee productivity. If we can achieve cost-efficient sales growth, we should eventually have 20 profitable offices!"

Required:

1. Create a balanced scorecard for Ariel Tax Services. Link your scorecard measures using the framework from Exhibit 11–5. Indicate whether each measure is expected to increase or decrease. Feel free to create measures that may not be specifically mentioned in the chapter, but make sense given the strategic goals of the company.
2. What hypotheses are built into the balanced scorecard for Ariel Tax Services? Which of these hypotheses do you believe are most questionable and why?
3. Discuss the potential advantages and disadvantages of implementing an internal business process measure called *total dollar amount of tax refunds generated*. Would you recommend using this measure in Ariel's balanced scorecard?
4. Would it be beneficial to attempt to measure each office's individual performance with respect to the scorecard measures that you created? Why or why not?

EXERCISE 11–8 Computing and Interpreting Return on Investment (ROI) LO11–1

Selected operating data for two divisions of Outback Brewing, Ltd., of Australia are given below:

	Division	
	Queensland	New South Wales
Sales	$4,000,000	$7,000,000
Average operating assets	$2,000,000	$2,000,000
Net operating income	$360,000	$420,000
Property, plant, and equipment (net)	$950,000	$800,000

Required:

1. Compute the rate of return for each division using the return on investment (ROI) formula stated in terms of margin and turnover.
2. Which divisional manager seems to be doing the better job? Why?

EXERCISE 11–9 Return on Investment (ROI) and Residual Income Relations LO11–1, LO11–2

A family friend has asked your help in analyzing the operations of three anonymous companies operating in the same service sector industry. Supply the missing data in the table below:

	Company		
	A	B	C
Sales	$9,000,000	$7,000,000	$4,500,000
Net operating income	$?	$ 280,000	$?
Average operating assets	$3,000,000	$?	$1,800,000
Return on investment (ROI)	18%	14%	?
Minimum required rate of return:			
Percentage	16%	?	15%
Dollar amount	$?	$ 320,000	$?
Residual income	$?	$?	$ 90,000

EXERCISE 11–10 Cost-Volume-Profit Analysis and Return on Investment (ROI) LO11–1

Posters.com is a small Internet retailer of high-quality posters. The company has $1,000,000 in operating assets and fixed expenses of $150,000 per year. With this level of operating assets and fixed expenses, the company can support sales of up to $3,000,000 per year. The company's contribution margin ratio is 25%, which means that an additional dollar of sales results in additional contribution margin, and net operating income, of 25 cents.

Required:

1. Complete the following table showing the relation between sales and return on investment (ROI).

Sales	Net Operating Income	Average Operating Assets	ROI
$2,500,000	$475,000	$1,000,000	?
$2,600,000	$?	$1,000,000	?
$2,700,000	$?	$1,000,000	?
$2,800,000	$?	$1,000,000	?
$2,900,000	$?	$1,000,000	?
$3,000,000	$?	$1,000,000	?

2. What happens to the company's return on investment (ROI) as sales increase? Explain.

EXERCISE 11–11 Effects of Changes in Profits and Assets on Return on Investment (ROI) LO11–1

Fitness Fanatics is a regional chain of health clubs. The managers of the clubs, who have authority to make investments as needed, are evaluated based largely on return on investment (ROI). The company's Springfield Club reported the following results for the past year:

Sales	$1,400,000
Net operating income	$70,000
Average operating assets.	$350,000

Required:

The following questions are to be considered independently. Carry out all computations to two decimal places.

1. Compute the Springfield club's return on investment (ROI).
2. Assume that the manager of the club is able to increase sales by $70,000 and that, as a result, net operating income increases by $18,200. Further assume that this is possible without any increase in average operating assets. What would be the club's return on investment (ROI)?
3. Assume that the manager of the club is able to reduce expenses by $14,000 without any change in sales or average operating assets. What would be the club's return on investment (ROI)?
4. Assume that the manager of the club is able to reduce average operating assets by $70,000 without any change in sales or net operating income. What would be the club's return on investment (ROI)?

EXERCISE 11–12 Evaluating New Investments Using Return on Investment (ROI) and Residual Income LO11–1, LO11–2

Selected sales and operating data for three divisions of different structural engineering firms are given as follows:

	Division A	Division B	Division C
Sales	$12,000,000	$14,000,000	$25,000,000
Average operating assets	$3,000,000	$7,000,000	$5,000,000
Net operating income	$600,000	$560,000	$800,000
Minimum required rate of return	14%	10%	16%

Required:

1. Compute the return on investment (ROI) for each division using the formula stated in terms of margin and turnover.
2. Compute the residual income for each division.
3. Assume that each division is presented with an investment opportunity that would yield a 15% rate of return.
   a. If performance is being measured by ROI, which division or divisions will probably accept the opportunity? Reject? Why?
   b. If performance is being measured by residual income, which division or divisions will probably accept the opportunity? Reject? Why?

EXERCISE 11–13 Effects of Changes in Sales, Expenses, and Assets on ROI LO11–1

CommercialServices.com Corporation provides business-to-business services on the Internet. Data concerning the most recent year appear below:

Sales	$3,000,000
Net operating income	$150,000
Average operating assets	$750,000

Required:

Consider each question below independently. Carry out all computations to two decimal places.

1. Compute the company's return on investment (ROI).
2. The entrepreneur who founded the company is convinced that sales will increase next year by 50% and that net operating income will increase by 200%, with no increase in average operating assets. What would be the company's ROI?
3. The chief financial officer of the company believes a more realistic scenario would be a $1,000,000 increase in sales, requiring a $250,000 increase in average operating assets, with a resulting $200,000 increase in net operating income. What would be the company's ROI in this scenario?

Problems   connect

PROBLEM 11–14 Measures of Internal Business Process Performance LO11–3

DataSpan, Inc., automated its plant at the start of the current year and installed a flexible manufacturing system. The company is also evaluating its suppliers and moving toward Lean Production. Many adjustment problems have been encountered, including problems relating to performance measurement. After much study, the company has decided to use the performance measures below, and it has gathered data relating to these measures for the first four months of operations.

	Month			
	1	2	3	4
Throughput time (days)	?	?	?	?
Delivery cycle time (days)	?	?	?	?
Manufacturing cycle efficiency (MCE)	?	?	?	?
Percentage of on-time deliveries	91%	86%	83%	79%
Total sales (units)	3,210	3,072	2,915	2,806

Management has asked for your help in computing throughput time, delivery cycle time, and MCE. The following average times have been logged over the last four months:

	Average per Month (in days)			
	1	2	3	4
Move time per unit	0.4	0.3	0.4	0.4
Process time per unit	2.1	2.0	1.9	1.8
Wait time per order before start of production	16.0	17.5	19.0	20.5
Queue time per unit	4.3	5.0	5.8	6.7
Inspection time per unit	0.6	0.7	0.7	0.6

Required:

1. For each month, compute the following:
    a. The throughput time.
    b. The delivery cycle time.
    c. The manufacturing cycle efficiency (MCE).
2. Evaluate the company's performance over the last four months.

3. Refer to the move time, process time, and so forth, given above for month 4.

   a. Assume that in month 5 the move time, process time, and so forth, are the same as in month 4, except that through the use of Lean Production the company is able to completely eliminate the queue time during production. Compute the new throughput time and MCE.

   b. Assume in month 6 that the move time, process time, and so forth, are again the same as in month 4, except that the company is able to completely eliminate both the queue time during production and the inspection time. Compute the new throughput time and MCE.

PROBLEM 11–15 Return on Investment (ROI) and Residual Income LO11–1, LO11–2

Financial data for Joel de Paris, Inc., for last year follow:

Joel de Paris, Inc. Balance Sheet		
	Beginning Balance	Ending Balance
Assets		
Cash	$ 140,000	$ 120,000
Accounts receivable	450,000	530,000
Inventory	320,000	380,000
Plant and equipment, net	680,000	620,000
Investment in Buisson, S.A.	250,000	280,000
Land (undeveloped)	180,000	170,000
Total assets	$2,020,000	$2,100,000
Liabilities and Stockholders' Equity		
Accounts payable	$ 360,000	$ 310,000
Long-term debt	1,500,000	1,500,000
Stockholders' equity	160,000	290,000
Total liabilities and stockholders' equity	$2,020,000	$2,100,000

Joel de Paris, Inc. Income Statement		
Sales		$4,050,000
Operating expenses		3,645,000
Net operating income		405,000
Interest and taxes:		
Interest expense	$150,000	
Tax expense	110,000	260,000
Net income		$ 145,000

The company paid dividends of $15,000 last year. The "Investment in Buisson, S.A.," on the balance sheet represents an investment in the stock of another company. The company's minimum required rate of return of 15%.

Required:

1. Compute the company's average operating assets for last year.
2. Compute the company's margin, turnover, and return on investment (ROI) for last year. (Hint: Should you use net income or net operating income in your calculations?)
3. What was the company's residual income last year?

PROBLEM 11–16 Creating a Balanced Scorecard LO11–4

Mason Paper Company (MPC) manufactures commodity grade papers for use in computer printers and photocopiers. MPC has reported net operating losses for the last two years due to intense price pressure from much larger competitors. The MPC management team—including Kristen Townsend (CEO), Mike Martinez (VP of Manufacturing), Tom Andrews (VP of Marketing), and Wendy Chen (CFO)—is contemplating a change in strategy to save the company from impending bankruptcy. Excerpts from a recent management team meeting are shown below:

> **Townsend:** As we all know, the commodity paper manufacturing business is all about economies of scale. The largest competitors with the lowest cost per unit win. The limited capacity of our older machines prohibits us from competing in the high-volume commodity paper grades. Furthermore, expanding our capacity by acquiring a new paper-making machine is out of the question given the extraordinarily high price tag. Therefore, I propose that we abandon cost reduction as a strategic goal and instead pursue manufacturing flexibility as the key to our future success.
>
> **Chen:** Manufacturing flexibility? What does that mean?
>
> **Martinez:** It means we have to abandon our "crank out as many tons of paper as possible" mentality. Instead, we need to pursue the low-volume business opportunities that exist in the nonstandard, specialized paper grades. To succeed in this regard, we'll need to improve our flexibility in three ways. First, we must improve our ability to switch between paper grades. Right now, we require an average of four hours to change over to another paper grade. Timely customer deliveries are a function of changeover performance. Second, we need to expand the range of paper grades that we can manufacture. Currently, we can only manufacture three paper grades. Our customers must perceive that we are a "one-stop shop" that can meet all of their paper grade needs. Third, we will need to improve our yields (e.g., tons of acceptable output relative to total tons processed) in the nonstandard paper grades. Our percentage of waste within these grades will be unacceptably high unless we do something to improve our processes. Our variable costs will go through the roof if we cannot increase our yields!
>
> **Chen:** Wait just a minute! These changes are going to destroy our equipment utilization numbers!
>
> **Andrews:** You're right Wendy; however, equipment utilization is not the name of the game when it comes to competing in terms of flexibility. Our customers don't care about our equipment utilization. Instead, as Mike just alluded to, they want just-in-time delivery of smaller quantities of a full range of paper grades. If we can shrink the elapsed time from order placement to order delivery and expand our product offerings, it will increase sales from current customers and bring in new customers. Furthermore, we will be able to charge a premium price because of the limited competition within this niche from our cost-focused larger competitors. Our contribution margin per ton should drastically improve!
>
> **Martinez:** Of course, executing the change in strategy will not be easy. We'll need to make a substantial investment in training because ultimately it is our people who create our flexible manufacturing capabilities.
>
> **Chen:** If we adopt this new strategy, it is definitely going to impact how we measure performance. We'll need to create measures that motivate our employees to make decisions that support our flexibility goals.
>
> **Townsend:** Wendy, you hit the nail right on the head. For our next meeting, could you pull together some potential measures that support our new strategy?

Required:

1. Contrast MPC's previous manufacturing strategy with its new manufacturing strategy.
2. Generally speaking, why would a company that changes its strategic goals need to change its performance measurement system as well? What are some examples of measures that would have been appropriate for MPC prior to its change in strategy? Why would those measures fail to support MPC's new strategy?
3. Construct a balanced scorecard that would support MPC's new manufacturing strategy. Use arrows to show the causal links between the performance measures and show whether the performance measure should increase or decrease over time. Feel free to create measures that may not be specifically mentioned in the chapter, but nonetheless make sense given the strategic goals of the company.
4. What hypotheses are built into MPC's balanced scorecard? Which of these hypotheses do you believe are most questionable and why?

PROBLEM 11–17 Comparison of Performance Using Return on Investment (ROI) LO11–1

Comparative data on three companies in the same service industry are given below:

	Company		
	A	B	C
Sales	$600,000	$500,000	$?
Net operating income	$ 84,000	$ 70,000	$?
Average operating assets	$300,000	$?	$1,000,000
Margin	?	?	3.5%
Turnover	?	?	2
ROI	?	7%	?

Required:

1. What advantages are there to breaking down the ROI computation into two separate elements, margin and turnover?
2. Fill in the missing information above, and comment on the relative performance of the three companies in as much detail as the data permit. Make *specific recommendations* about how to improve the ROI.

(Adapted from National Association of Accountants,
Research Report No. 35, p. 34)

PROBLEM 11–18 Return on Investment (ROI) and Residual Income LO11–1, LO11–2

"I know headquarters wants us to add that new product line," said Dell Havasi, manager of Billings Company's Office Products Division. "But I want to see the numbers before I make any move. Our division's return on investment (ROI) has led the company for three years, and I don't want any letdown."

Billings Company is a decentralized wholesaler with five autonomous divisions. The divisions are evaluated on the basis of ROI, with year-end bonuses given to the divisional managers who have the highest ROIs. Operating results for the company's Office Products Division for this year are given below:

Sales	$10,000,000
Variable expenses	6,000,000
Contribution margin	4,000,000
Fixed expenses	3,200,000
Net operating income	$ 800,000
Divisional average operating assets	$4,000,000

The company had an overall return on investment (ROI) of 15% this year (considering all divisions). Next year the Office Products Division has an opportunity to add a new product line that would require an additional investment that would increase average operating assets by $1,000,000. The cost and revenue characteristics of the new product line per year would be:

Sales	$2,000,000
Variable expenses	60% of sales
Fixed expenses	$640,000

Required:

1. Compute the Office Products Division's ROI for this year.
2. Compute the Office Products Division's ROI for the new product line by itself.
3. Compute the Office Products Division's ROI for next year assuming that it performs the same as this year and adds the new product line.
4. If you were in Dell Havasi's position, would you accept or reject the new product line? Explain.
5. Why do you suppose headquarters is anxious for the Office Products Division to add the new product line?

6. Suppose that the company's minimum required rate of return on operating assets is 12% and that performance is evaluated using residual income.
   a. Compute the Office Products Division's residual income for this year.
   b. Compute the Office Products Division's residual income for the new product line by itself.
   c. Compute the Office Products Division's residual income for next year assuming that it performs the same as this year and adds the new product line.
   d. Using the residual income approach, if you were in Dell Havasi's position, would you accept or reject the new product line? Explain.

PROBLEM 11–19 Internal Business Process Performance Measures LO11–3

Tombro Industries is in the process of automating one of its plants and developing a flexible manufacturing system. The company is finding it necessary to make many changes in operating procedures. Progress has been slow, particularly in trying to develop new performance measures for the factory.

In an effort to evaluate performance and determine where improvements can be made, management has gathered the following data relating to activities over the last four months:

	Month			
	1	2	3	4
Quality control measures:				
Number of defects	185	163	124	91
Number of warranty claims	46	39	30	27
Number of customer complaints	102	96	79	58
Material control measures:				
Purchase order lead time	8 days	7 days	5 days	4 days
Scrap as a percent of total cost	1%	1%	2%	3%
Machine performance measures:				
Machine downtime as a percentage of availability	3%	4%	4%	6%
Use as a percentage of availability	95%	92%	89%	85%
Setup time (hours)	8	10	11	12
Delivery performance measures:				
Throughput time	?	?	?	?
Manufacturing cycle efficiency (MCE)	?	?	?	?
Delivery cycle time	?	?	?	?
Percentage of on-time deliveries	96%	95%	92%	89%

The president has read in industry journals that throughput time, MCE, and delivery cycle time are important measures of performance, but no one is sure how they are computed. You have been asked to assist the company, and you have gathered the following data relating to these measures:

	Average per Month (in days)			
	1	2	3	4
Wait time per order before start of production	9.0	11.5	12.0	14.0
Inspection time per unit	0.8	0.7	0.7	0.7
Process time per unit	2.1	2.0	1.9	1.8
Queue time per unit	2.8	4.4	6.0	7.0
Move time per unit	0.3	0.4	0.4	0.5

Required:
1. For each month, compute the following performance measures:
   a. Throughput time.
   b. MCE.
   c. Delivery cycle time.

2. Using the performance measures given in the main body of the problem and the performance measures computed in (1) above, do the following:
   a. Identify areas where the company seems to be improving.
   b. Identify areas where the company seems to be deteriorating.
3. Refer to the inspection time, process time, and so forth, given for month 4.
   a. Assume that in month 5 the inspection time, process time, and so forth, are the same as for month 4, except that the company is able to completely eliminate the queue time during production using Lean Production. Compute the new throughput time and MCE.
   b. Assume that in month 6 the inspection time, process time, and so forth, are the same as in month 4, except that the company is able to eliminate both the queue time during production and the inspection time using Lean Production. Compute the new throughput time and MCE.

PROBLEM 11–20 Return on Investment (ROI) Analysis LO11–1
The contribution format income statement for Huerra Company for last year is given below:

	Total	Unit
Sales	$4,000,000	$80.00
Variable expenses	2,800,000	56.00
Contribution margin	1,200,000	24.00
Fixed expenses	840,000	16.80
Net operating income	360,000	7.20
Income taxes @ 30%	108,000	2.16
Net income	$ 252,000	$ 5.04

The company had average operating assets of $2,000,000 during the year.

Required:
1. Compute the company's return on investment (ROI) for the period using the ROI formula stated in terms of margin and turnover.

   For each of the following questions, indicate whether the margin and turnover will increase, decrease, or remain unchanged as a result of the events described, and then compute the new ROI figure. Consider each question separately, starting in each case from the data used to compute the original ROI in (1) above.
2. Using Lean Production, the company is able to reduce the average level of inventory by $400,000. (The released funds are used to pay off short-term creditors.)
3. The company achieves a cost savings of $32,000 per year by using less costly materials.
4. The company issues bonds and uses the proceeds to purchase machinery and equipment that increases average operating assets by $500,000. Interest on the bonds is $60,000 per year. Sales remain unchanged. The new, more efficient equipment reduces production costs by $20,000 per year.
5. As a result of a more intense effort by salespeople, sales are increased by 20%; operating assets remain unchanged.
6. At the beginning of the year, obsolete inventory carried on the books at a cost of $40,000 is scrapped and written off as a loss.
7. At the beginning of the year, the company uses $200,000 of cash (received on accounts receivable) to repurchase and retire some of its common stock.

PROBLEM 11–21 Creating Balanced Scorecards that Support Different Strategies LO11–4
The Midwest Consulting Group (MCG) helps companies build balanced scorecards. As part of its marketing efforts, MCG conducts an annual balanced scorecard workshop for prospective clients. As MCG's newest employee, your boss has asked you to participate in this year's workshop by explaining to attendees how a company's strategy determines the measures that are appropriate for its balanced scorecard. Your boss has provided you with the excerpts below from the annual reports of two current MCG clients. She has asked you to use these excerpts in your portion of the workshop.

Excerpt from Applied Pharmaceuticals' annual report:

> The keys to our business are consistent and timely new product introductions and manufacturing process integrity. The new product introduction side of the equation is a function of research and development (R&D) yield (e.g., the number of marketable drug compounds created relative to the total number of potential compounds pursued). We seek to optimize our R&D yield and first-to-market capability by investing in state-of-the-art technology, hiring the highest possible percentage of the "best and the brightest" engineers that we pursue, and providing world-class training to those engineers. Manufacturing process integrity is all about establishing world-class quality specifications and then relentlessly engaging in prevention and appraisal activities to minimize defect rates. Our customers must have an awareness of and respect for our brand image of being "first to market and first in quality." If we deliver on this pledge to our customers, then our financial goal of increasing our return on stockholders' equity should take care of itself.

Excerpt from Destination Resorts International's annual report:

> Our business succeeds or fails based on the quality of the service that our front-line employees provide to customers. Therefore, it is imperative that we strive to maintain high employee morale and minimize employee turnover. In addition, it is critical that we train our employees to use technology to create one seamless worldwide experience for our repeat customers. Once an employee enters a customer preference (e.g., provide two extra pillows in the room, deliver fresh brewed coffee to the room at 8:00 A.M., etc.) into our database, our worldwide workforce strives to ensure that a customer will never need to repeat it at any of our destination resorts. If we properly train and retain a motivated workforce, we should see continuous improvement in our percentage of error-free repeat customer check-ins, the time taken to resolve customer complaints, and our independently assessed room cleanliness. This in turn should drive improvement in our customer retention, which is the key to meeting our revenue growth goals.

Required:

1. Based on the excerpts above, compare and contrast the strategies of Applied Pharmaceuticals and Destination Resorts International.
2. Select balanced scorecard measures for each company and link the scorecard measures using the framework from Exhibit 11–5. Use arrows to show the causal links between the performance measures and show whether the performance measure should increase or decrease over time. Feel free to create measures that may not be specifically mentioned in the chapter, but nonetheless make sense given the strategic goals of each company.
3. What hypotheses are built into each balanced scorecard? Why do the hypotheses differ between the two companies?

PROBLEM 11–22 Perverse Effects of Some Performance Measures LO11–4

There is often more than one way to improve a performance measure. Unfortunately, some of the actions taken by managers to make their performance look better may actually harm the organization. For example, suppose the marketing department is held responsible only for increasing the performance measure "total revenues." Increases in total revenues may be achieved by working harder and smarter, but they can also usually be achieved by simply cutting prices. The increase in volume from cutting prices almost always results in greater total revenues; however, it does not always lead to greater total profits. Those who design performance measurement systems need to keep in mind that managers who are under pressure to perform may take actions to improve performance measures that have negative consequences elsewhere.

Required:

For each of the following situations, describe actions managers might take to show improvement in the performance measure but which do not actually lead to improvement in the organization's overall performance.

1. Concerned with the slow rate at which new products are brought to market, top management of a consumer electronics company introduces a new performance measure—speed-to-market. The research and development department is given responsibility for this performance measure, which measures the average amount of time a product is in development before it is released to the market for sale.
2. The CEO of an airline company is dissatisfied with the amount of time her ground crews are taking to unload luggage from airplanes. To solve the problem, she decides to measure the

average elapsed time from when an airplane parks at the gate to when all pieces of luggage are unloaded from the airplane. For each month that an airport's ground crew can lower its "average elapsed time" relative to the prior month, the CEO pays a lump-sum bonus to be split equally among members of the crew.

3.   A manufacturing company has been plagued by the chronic failure to ship orders to customers by the promised date. To solve this problem, the production manager has been given the responsibility of increasing the percentage of orders shipped on time. When a customer calls in an order, the production manager and the customer agree to a delivery date. If the order is not completed by that date, it is counted as a late shipment.

4.   Concerned with the productivity of employees, the board of directors of a large multinational corporation has dictated that the manager of each subsidiary will be held responsible for increasing the revenue per employee of his or her subsidiary.

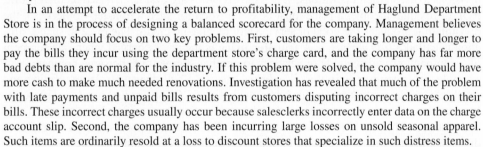

CASE 11–23 Balanced Scorecard LO11–4

Haglund Department Store is located in the downtown area of a small city. While the store had been profitable for many years, it is facing increasing competition from large national chains that have set up stores on the outskirts of the city. Recently the downtown area has been undergoing revitalization, and the owners of Haglund Department Store are somewhat optimistic that profitability can be restored.

In an attempt to accelerate the return to profitability, management of Haglund Department Store is in the process of designing a balanced scorecard for the company. Management believes the company should focus on two key problems. First, customers are taking longer and longer to pay the bills they incur using the department store's charge card, and the company has far more bad debts than are normal for the industry. If this problem were solved, the company would have more cash to make much needed renovations. Investigation has revealed that much of the problem with late payments and unpaid bills results from customers disputing incorrect charges on their bills. These incorrect charges usually occur because salesclerks incorrectly enter data on the charge account slip. Second, the company has been incurring large losses on unsold seasonal apparel. Such items are ordinarily resold at a loss to discount stores that specialize in such distress items.

The meeting in which the balanced scorecard approach was discussed was disorganized and ineffectively led—possibly because no one other than one of the vice presidents had read anything about how to build a balanced scorecard. Nevertheless, a number of potential performance measures were suggested by various managers. These potential performance measures are:

a.   Percentage of charge account bills containing errors.
b.   Percentage of salesclerks trained to correctly enter data on charge account slips.
c.   Average age of accounts receivables.
d.   Profit per employee.
e.   Customer satisfaction with accuracy of charge account bills from monthly customer survey.
f.   Total sales revenue.
g.   Sales per employee.
h.   Travel expenses for buyers for trips to fashion shows.
i.   Unsold inventory at the end of the season as a percentage of total cost of sales.
j.   Courtesy shown by junior staff members to senior staff members based on surveys of senior staff.
k.   Percentage of suppliers making just-in-time deliveries.
l.   Sales per square foot of floor space.
m.   Written-off accounts receivable (bad debts) as a percentage of sales.
n.   Quality of food in the staff cafeteria based on staff surveys.
o.   Percentage of employees who have attended the city's cultural diversity workshop.
p.   Total profit.

Required:

1.   As someone with more knowledge of the balanced scorecard than almost anyone else in the company, you have been asked to build an integrated balanced scorecard. In your scorecard, use only performance measures listed previously. You do not have to use all of the performance measures suggested by the managers, but you should build a balanced scorecard that reveals a strategy for dealing with the problems with accounts receivable and with unsold

merchandise. Construct the balanced scorecard following the format used in Exhibit 11–5. Do not be concerned with whether a specific performance measure falls within the learning and growth, internal business process, customer, or financial perspective. However, use arrows to show the causal links between performance measures within your balanced scorecard and explain whether the performance measures should show increases or decreases.

2. Assume the company adopts your balanced scorecard. After operating for a year, some performance measures show improvements, but not others. What should management do next?

3. a. Suppose customers express greater satisfaction with the accuracy of their charge account bills but the performance measures for the average age of accounts receivable and for bad debts do not improve. Explain why this might happen.

    b. Suppose the performance measures for the average age of accounts receivable, bad debts, and unsold inventory improve, but total profits do not. Explain why this might happen. Assume in your answer that the explanation lies within the company.

Appendix 11A: Transfer Pricing

Divisions in a company often supply goods and services to other divisions within the same company. For example, the truck division of Toyota supplies trucks to other Toyota divisions to use in their operations. When the divisions are evaluated based on their profit, ROI, or residual income, a price must be established for such a transfer—otherwise, the division that produces the good or service will receive no credit. The price in such a situation is called a *transfer price*. A **transfer price** is the price charged when one segment of a company provides goods or services to another segment of the same company. For example, most companies in the oil industry, such as Shell, have petroleum refining and retail sales divisions that are evaluated on the basis of ROI or residual income. The petroleum refining division processes crude oil into gasoline, kerosene, lubricants, and other end products. The retail sales division takes gasoline and other products from the refining division and sells them through the company's chain of service stations. Each product has a price for transfers within the company. Suppose the transfer price for gasoline is $0.80 a gallon. Then the refining division gets credit for $0.80 a gallon of revenue on its segment report and the retailing division must deduct $0.80 a gallon as an expense on its segment report. Clearly, the refining division would like the transfer price to be as high as possible, whereas the retailing division would like the transfer price to be as low as possible. However, the transaction has no direct effect on the entire company's reported profit. It is like taking money out of one pocket and putting it into the other.

Managers are intensely interested in how transfer prices are set because they can have a dramatic effect on the reported profitability of their divisions. Three common approaches are used to set transfer prices:

1. Allow the managers involved in the transfer to negotiate the transfer price.
2. Set transfer prices at cost using either variable cost or full (absorption) cost.
3. Set transfer prices at the market price.

We will consider each of these transfer pricing methods in turn, beginning with negotiated transfer prices. Throughout the discussion, keep in mind that *the fundamental objective in setting transfer prices is to motivate the managers to act in the best interests of the overall company*. In contrast, **suboptimization** occurs when managers do not act in the best interests of the overall company or even in the best interests of their own division.

LO11–5
Determine the range, if any, within which a negotiated transfer price should fall.

Negotiated Transfer Prices

A **negotiated transfer price** results from discussions between the selling and buying divisions. Negotiated transfer prices have several important advantages. First, this approach preserves the autonomy of the divisions and is consistent with the spirit of decentralization. Second, the managers of the divisions are likely to have much better information about the potential costs and benefits of the transfer than others in the company.

When negotiated transfer prices are used, the managers who are involved in a proposed transfer within the company meet to discuss the terms and conditions of the transfer. They may decide not to go through with the transfer, but if they do, they must agree to a transfer price. Generally speaking, we cannot predict what transfer price they will agree to. However, we can confidently predict two things: (1) the selling division will agree to the transfer only if its profits increase as a result of the transfer, and (2) the buying division will agree to the transfer only if its profits also increase as a result of the transfer. This may seem obvious, but it is an important point.

Clearly, if the transfer price is below the selling division's cost, the selling division will incur a loss on the transaction and it will refuse to agree to the transfer. Likewise, if the transfer price is set too high, it will be impossible for the buying division to make any profit on the transferred item. For any given proposed transfer, the transfer price has both a lower limit (determined by the situation of the selling division) and an upper limit (determined by the situation of the buying division). The actual transfer price agreed to by the two division managers can fall anywhere between those two limits. These limits determine the **range of acceptable transfer prices**—the range of transfer prices within which the profits of both divisions participating in a transfer would increase.

An example will help us to understand negotiated transfer prices. Harris & Louder, Ltd., owns fast-food restaurants and snack food and beverage manufacturers in the United Kingdom. One of the restaurants, Pizza Maven, serves a variety of beverages along with pizzas. One of the beverages is ginger beer, which is serves on tap. Harris & Louder has just purchased a new division, Imperial Beverages, that produces ginger beer. The managing director of Imperial Beverages has approached the managing director of Pizza Maven about purchasing Imperial Beverages' ginger beer to sell at Pizza Maven restaurants rather than its usual brand of ginger beer. Managers at Pizza Maven agree that the quality of Imperial Beverages' ginger beer is comparable to the quality of their regular brand. It is just a question of price. The basic facts are as follows:

Imperial Beverages:	
Ginger beer production capacity per month	10,000 barrels
Variable cost per barrel of ginger beer	$8 per barrel
Fixed costs per month	$70,000
Selling price of Imperial Beverages ginger beer on the outside market	$20 per barrel
Pizza Maven:	
Purchase price of regular brand of ginger beer	$18 per barrel
Monthly consumption of ginger beer	2,000 barrels

The Selling Division's Lowest Acceptable Transfer Price The selling division, Imperial Beverages, will be interested in a proposed transfer only if its profit increases. Clearly, the transfer price must not fall below the variable cost per barrel of $8. In addition, if Imperial Beverages does not have sufficient capacity to fill the Pizza Maven order while supplying its regular customers, then it would have to sacrifice some of its regular sales. Imperial Beverages would expect to be compensated for the contribution margin on any lost sales. In sum, if the transfer has no effect on fixed costs, then from the selling division's standpoint, the transfer price must cover both the variable costs of producing the transferred units and any opportunity costs from lost sales.

Seller's perspective:

$$\frac{\text{Transfer}}{\text{price}} \geq \frac{\text{Variable cost}}{\text{per unit}} + \frac{\text{Total contribution margin on lost sales}}{\text{Number of units transferred}}$$

The Buying Division's Highest Acceptable Transfer Price   The buying division, Pizza Maven, will be interested in a transfer only if its profit increases. In cases like this where a buying division has an outside supplier, the buying division's decision is simple. Buy from the inside supplier if the price is less than the price offered by the outside supplier.

$$\text{Transfer price} \leq \text{Cost of buying from outside supplier}$$

Or, if an outside supplier does not exist:

$$\text{Transfer price} \leq \text{Profit to be earned per unit sold (not including the transfer price)}$$

We will consider several different hypothetical situations and see what the range of acceptable transfer prices would be in each situation.

Selling Division with Idle Capacity   Suppose that Imperial Beverages has sufficient idle capacity to satisfy Pizza Maven's demand for ginger beer without sacrificing sales of ginger beer to its regular customers. To be specific, let's suppose that Imperial Beverages is selling only 7,000 barrels of ginger beer a month on the outside market. That leaves unused capacity of 3,000 barrels a month—more than enough to satisfy Pizza Maven's requirement of 2,000 barrels a month. What range of transfer prices, if any, would make both divisions better off with the transfer of 2,000 barrels a month?

1. The selling division, Imperial Beverages, will be interested in the transfer only if:

$$\frac{\text{Transfer}}{\text{price}} \geq \frac{\text{Variable cost}}{\text{per unit}} + \frac{\text{Total contribution margin on lost sales}}{\text{Number of units transferred}}$$

Because Imperial Beverages has enough idle capacity, there are no lost outside sales. And because the variable cost per unit is $8, the lowest acceptable transfer price for the selling division is $8.

$$\text{Transfer price} \geq \$8 + \frac{\$0}{2,000} = \$8$$

2. The buying division, Pizza Maven, can buy similar ginger beer from an outside vendor for $18. Therefore, Pizza Maven would be unwilling to pay more than $18 per barrel for Imperial Beverages' ginger beer.

$$\text{Transfer price} \leq \text{Cost of buying from outside supplier} = \$18$$

3. Combining the requirements of both the selling division and the buying division, the acceptable range of transfer prices in this situation is:

$$\$8 \leq \text{Transfer price} \leq \$18$$

Assuming that the managers understand their own businesses and that they are cooperative, they should be able to agree on a transfer price within this range.

Selling Division with No Idle Capacity   Suppose that Imperial Beverages has *no* idle capacity; it is selling 10,000 barrels of ginger beer a month on the outside market at $20 per barrel. To fill the order from Pizza Maven, Imperial Beverages would have to divert 2,000 barrels from its regular customers. What range of transfer prices, if any, would make both divisions better off transferring the 2,000 barrels within the company?

1. The selling division, Imperial Beverages, will be interested in the transfer only if:

$$\frac{\text{Transfer}}{\text{price}} \geq \frac{\text{Variable cost}}{\text{per unit}} + \frac{\text{Total contribution margin on lost sales}}{\text{Number of units transferred}}$$

Because Imperial Beverages has no idle capacity, there *are* lost outside sales. The contribution margin per barrel on these outside sales is $12 ($20 − $8).

$$\text{Transfer price} \geq \$8 + \frac{(\$20 - \$8) \times 2{,}000}{2{,}000} = \$8 + (\$20 - \$8) = \$20$$

Thus, as far as the selling division is concerned, the transfer price must at least cover the revenue on the lost sales, which is $20 per barrel. This makes sense because the cost of producing the 2,000 barrels is the same whether they are sold on the inside market or on the outside. The only difference is that the selling division loses the revenue of $20 per barrel if it transfers the barrels to Pizza Maven.

2. As before, the buying division, Pizza Maven, would be unwilling to pay more than the $18 per barrel it is already paying for similar ginger beer from its regular supplier.

$$\text{Transfer price} \leq \text{Cost of buying from outside supplier} = \$18$$

3. Therefore, the selling division would insist on a transfer price of at least $20. But the buying division would refuse any transfer price above $18. It is impossible to satisfy both division managers simultaneously; there can be no agreement on a transfer price and no transfer will take place. Is this good? The answer is yes. From the standpoint of the entire company, the transfer doesn't make sense. Why give up sales of $20 to save costs of $18?

Basically, the transfer price is a mechanism for dividing between the two divisions any profit the entire company earns as a result of the transfer. If the company as a whole loses money on the transfer, there will be no profit to divide up, and it will be impossible for the two divisions to come to an agreement. On the other hand, if the company as a whole makes money on the transfer, there will be a profit to share, and it will always be possible for the two divisions to find a mutually agreeable transfer price that increases the profits of both divisions. If the pie is bigger, it is always possible to divide it up in such a way that everyone has a bigger piece.

Selling Division Has Some Idle Capacity Suppose now that Imperial Beverages is selling 9,000 barrels of ginger beer a month on the outside market. Pizza Maven can only sell one kind of ginger beer on tap. It cannot buy 1,000 barrels from Imperial Beverages and 1,000 barrels from its regular supplier; it must buy all of its ginger beer from one source.

To fill the entire 2,000-barrel a month order from Pizza Maven, Imperial Beverages would have to divert 1,000 barrels from its regular customers who are paying $20 per barrel. The other 1,000 barrels can be made using idle capacity. What range of transfer prices, if any, would make both divisions better off transferring the 2,000 barrels within the company?

1. As before, the selling division, Imperial Beverages, will insist on a transfer price that at least covers its variable cost and opportunity cost:

$$\frac{\text{Transfer}}{\text{price}} \geq \frac{\text{Variable cost}}{\text{per unit}} + \frac{\text{Total contribution margin on lost sales}}{\text{Number of units transferred}}$$

Because Imperial Beverages does not have enough idle capacity to fill the entire order for 2,000 barrels, there *are* lost outside sales. The contribution margin per barrel on the 1,000 barrels of lost outside sales is $12 ($20 − $8).

$$\text{Transfer price} \geq \$8 + \frac{(\$20 - \$8) \times 1{,}000}{2{,}000} = \$8 + \$6 = \$14$$

Thus, as far as the selling division is concerned, the transfer price must cover the variable cost of $8 plus the average opportunity cost of lost sales of $6.

2. As before, the buying division, Pizza Maven, would be unwilling to pay more than the $18 per barrel it pays its regular supplier.

$$\text{Transfer price} \leq \text{Cost of buying from outside suppliers} = \$18$$

3. Combining the requirements for both the selling and buying divisions, the range of acceptable transfer prices is:

$$\$14 \leq \text{Transfer price} \leq \$18$$

Again, assuming that the managers understand their own businesses and that they are cooperative, they should be able to agree on a transfer price within this range.

No Outside Supplier   If Pizza Maven has no outside supplier for comparable ginger beer, the highest price the buying division would be willing to pay depends on how much the buying division expects to make on the transferred units—excluding the transfer price. If, for example, Pizza Maven expects to earn $30 per barrel of ginger beer after paying its own expenses, then it should be willing to pay up to $30 per barrel to Imperial Beverages. Remember, however, that this assumes Pizza Maven cannot buy comparable ginger beer from other sources.

Evaluation of Negotiated Transfer Prices   As discussed earlier, if a transfer within the company would result in higher overall profits for the company, there is always a range of transfer prices within which both the selling and buying division would also have higher profits if they agree to the transfer. Therefore, if the managers understand their own businesses and are cooperative, then they should always be able to agree on a transfer price if it is in the best interests of the company that they do so.

Unfortunately, not all managers understand their own businesses and not all managers are cooperative. As a result, negotiations often break down even when it would be in the managers' own best interests to come to an agreement. Sometimes that is the fault of the way managers are evaluated. If managers are pitted against each other rather than against their own past performance or reasonable benchmarks, a noncooperative atmosphere is almost guaranteed. Nevertheless, even with the best performance evaluation system, some people by nature are not cooperative.

Given the disputes that often accompany the negotiation process, many companies rely on some other means of setting transfer prices. Unfortunately, as we will see below, all of the alternatives to negotiated transfer prices have their own serious drawbacks.

Transfers at the Cost to the Selling Division

Many companies set transfer prices at either the variable cost or full (absorption) cost incurred by the selling division. Although the cost approach to setting transfer prices is relatively simple to apply, it has some major defects.

First, the use of cost—particularly full cost—as a transfer price can lead to bad decisions and thus suboptimization. Return to the example involving the ginger beer. The full cost of ginger beer can never be less than $15 per barrel, which include $8 per barrel variable cost plus $7 per barrel fixed cost at capacity (= $70,000 ÷ 10,000 barrels). What if the cost of buying the ginger beer from an outside supplier is less than $15—for example, $14 per barrel? If the transfer price were set at full cost, then Pizza Maven would never want to buy ginger beer from Imperial Beverages because it could buy its ginger beer from an outside supplier at a lower price. However, from the standpoint of the company as a whole, ginger beer should be transferred from Imperial Beverages to Pizza Maven whenever Imperial Beverages has idle capacity. Why? Because when Imperial Beverages has idle capacity, it only costs the company $8 in variable cost to produce a barrel of ginger beer, but it costs $14 per barrel to buy from outside suppliers.

Second, if cost is used as the transfer price, the selling division will never show a profit on any internal transfer. The only division that shows a profit is the division that makes the final sale to an outside party.

Third, cost-based prices do not provide incentives to control costs. If the actual costs of one division are simply passed on to the next, there is little incentive for anyone to work to reduce costs. This problem can be overcome by using standard costs rather than actual costs for transfer prices.

Despite these shortcomings, cost-based transfer prices are often used in practice. Advocates argue that they are easily understood and convenient to use.

Transfers at Market Price

Some form of competitive **market price** (i.e., the price charged for an item on the open market) is sometimes advocated as the best approach to the transfer pricing problem—particularly if transfer price negotiations routinely become bogged down.

The market price approach is designed for situations in which there is an *outside market* for the transferred product or service; the product or service is sold in its present form to outside customers. If the selling division has no idle capacity, the market price is the correct choice for the transfer price. This is because, from the company's perspective, the real cost of the transfer is the opportunity cost of the lost revenue on the outside sale. Whether the item is transferred internally or sold on the outside market, the production costs are exactly the same. If the market price is used as the transfer price, the selling division manager will not lose anything by making the transfer, and the buying division manager will get the correct signal about how much it really costs the company for the transfer to take place.

While the market price works well when the selling division has no idle capacity, difficulties occur when the selling division has idle capacity. Recalling once again the ginger beer example, the outside market price for the ginger beer produced by Imperial Beverages is $20 per barrel. However, Pizza Maven can purchase all of the ginger beer it wants from outside suppliers for $18 per barrel. Why would Pizza Maven ever buy from Imperial Beverages if Pizza Maven is forced to pay Imperial Beverages' market price? In some market price-based transfer pricing schemes, the transfer price would be lowered to $18, the outside vendor's market price, and Pizza Maven would be directed to buy from Imperial Beverages as long as Imperial Beverages is willing to sell. This scheme can work reasonably well, but a drawback is that managers at Pizza Maven will regard the cost of ginger beer as $18 rather than the $8, which is the real cost to the company when the selling division has idle capacity. Consequently, the managers of Pizza Maven will make pricing and other decisions based on an incorrect cost.

Unfortunately, none of the possible solutions to the transfer pricing problem are perfect—not even market-based transfer prices.

Divisional Autonomy and Suboptimization

The principles of decentralization suggest that companies should grant managers autonomy to set transfer prices and to decide whether to sell internally or externally. It may be very difficult for top managers to accept this principle when their subordinate managers are about to make a suboptimal decision. However, if top management intervenes, the purposes of decentralization are defeated. Furthermore, to impose the correct transfer price, top managers would have to know details about the buying and selling divisions' outside market, variable costs, and capacity utilization. The whole premise of decentralization is that local managers have access to better information for operational decisions than top managers at corporate headquarters.

Of course, if a division manager consistently makes suboptimal decisions, the performance of the division will suffer. The offending manager's compensation will be adversely affected and promotion will become less likely. Thus, a performance evaluation system based on divisional profits, ROI, or residual income provides some built-in checks and balances. Nevertheless, if top managers wish to create a culture of autonomy and independent profit responsibility, they must allow their subordinate managers to control their own destiny—even to the extent of granting their managers the right to make mistakes.

International Aspects of Transfer Pricing

The objectives of transfer pricing change when a multinational corporation is involved and the goods and services being transferred cross international borders. In this context, the objectives of international transfer pricing focus on minimizing taxes, duties, and foreign exchange risks, along with enhancing a company's competitive position and improving its relations with foreign governments. Although domestic objectives such as managerial motivation and divisional autonomy are always important, they often become secondary when international transfers are involved. Companies will focus instead on charging a transfer price that reduces its total tax bill or that strengthens a foreign subsidiary.

For example, charging a low transfer price for parts shipped to a foreign subsidiary may reduce customs duty payments as the parts cross international borders, or it may help the subsidiary to compete in foreign markets by keeping the subsidiary's costs low. On the other hand, charging a high transfer price may help a multinational corporation draw profits out of a country that has stringent controls on foreign remittances, or it may allow a multinational corporation to shift income from a country that has high income tax rates to a country that has low rates.

Appendix 11A: Review Problem: Transfer Pricing

Situation A

Collyer Products, Inc., has a Valve Division that manufactures and sells a standard valve:

Capacity in units	100,000
Selling price to outside customers	$30
Variable costs per unit	$16
Fixed costs per unit (based on capacity)	$9

The company has a Pump Division that could use this valve in one of its pumps. The Pump Division is currently purchasing 10,000 valves per year from an overseas supplier at a cost of $29 per valve.

Required:

1. Assume that the Valve Division has enough idle capacity to handle all of the Pump Division's needs. What is the acceptable range, if any, for the transfer price between the two divisions?
2. Assume that the Valve Division is selling all of the valves it can produce to outside customers. What is the acceptable range, if any, for the transfer price between the two divisions?
3. Assume again that the Valve Division is selling all of the valves it can produce to outside customers. Also assume that $3 in variable expenses can be avoided on transfers within the company, due to reduced selling costs. What is the acceptable range, if any, for the transfer price between the two divisions?

Solution to Situation A

1. Because the Valve Division has idle capacity, it does not have to give up any outside sales to take on the Pump Division's business. Applying the formula for the lowest acceptable transfer price from the viewpoint of the selling division, we get:

$$\text{Transfer price} \geq \frac{\text{Variable cost}}{\text{per unit}} + \frac{\text{Total contribution margin on lost sales}}{\text{Number of units transferred}}$$

$$\text{Transfer price} \geq \$16 + \frac{\$0}{10,000} = \$16$$

The Pump Division would be unwilling to pay more than $29, the price it is currently paying an outside supplier for its valves. Therefore, the transfer price must fall within the range:

$$\$16 \leq \text{Transfer price} \leq \$29$$

2. Because the Valve Division is selling all of the valves it can produce on the outside market, it would have to give up some of these outside sales to take on the Pump Division's business. Thus, the Valve Division has an opportunity cost, which is the total contribution margin on lost sales:

$$\text{Transfer price} \geq \frac{\text{Variable cost}}{\text{per unit}} + \frac{\text{Total contribution margin on lost sales}}{\text{Number of units transferred}}$$

$$\text{Transfer price} \geq \$16 + \frac{(\$30 - \$16) \times 10{,}000}{10{,}000} = \$16 + \$14 = \$30$$

Because the Pump Division can purchase valves from an outside supplier at only $29 per unit, no transfers will be made between the two divisions.

3. Applying the formula for the lowest acceptable transfer price from the viewpoint of the selling division, we get:

$$\text{Transfer price} \geq \frac{\text{Variable cost}}{\text{per unit}} + \frac{\text{Total contribution margin on lost sales}}{\text{Number of units transferred}}$$

$$\text{Transfer price} \geq (\$16 - \$3) + \frac{(\$30 - \$16) \times 10{,}000}{10{,}000} = \$13 + \$14 = \$27$$

In this case, the transfer price must fall within the range:

$$\$27 \leq \text{Transfer price} \leq \$29$$

Situation B

Refer to the original data in situation A above. Assume the Pump Division needs 20,000 special high-pressure valves per year. The Valve Division's variable costs to manufacture and ship the special valve would be $20 per unit. To produce these special valves, the Valve Division would have to reduce its production and sales of regular valves from 100,000 units per year to 70,000 units per year.

Required:
As far as the Valve Division is concerned, what is the lowest acceptable transfer price?

Solution to Situation B

To produce the 20,000 special valves, the Valve Division will have to give up sales of 30,000 regular valves to outside customers. Applying the formula for the lowest acceptable transfer price from the viewpoint of the selling division, we get:

$$\text{Transfer price} \geq \text{Variable cost per unit} + \frac{\text{Total contribution margin on lost sales}}{\text{Number of units transferred}}$$

$$\text{Transfer price} \geq \$20 + \frac{(\$30 - \$16) \times 30{,}000}{20{,}000} = \$20 + \$21 = \$41$$

Glossary (Appendix 11A)

Market price The price charged for an item on the open market. (p. 545)
Negotiated transfer price A transfer price agreed on between buying and selling divisions. (p. 540)
Range of acceptable transfer prices The range of transfer prices within which the profits of both the selling division and the buying division would increase as a result of a transfer. (p. 541)
Suboptimization An overall level of profits that is less than a segment or a company is capable of earning. (p. 540)
Transfer price The price charged when one division or segment provides goods or services to another division or segment of an organization. (p. 540)

Appendix 11A: Exercises, Problems, and Case

EXERCISE 11A–1 Transfer Pricing Basics LO11–5

Sako Company's Audio Division produces a speaker that is used by manufacturers of various audio products. Sales and cost data on the speaker follow:

Selling price per unit on the intermediate market	$60
Variable costs per unit	$42
Fixed costs per unit (based on capacity)	$8
Capacity in units	25,000

Sako Company has a Hi-Fi Division that could use this speaker in one of its products. The Hi-Fi Division will need 5,000 speakers per year. It has received a quote of $57 per speaker from another manufacturer. Sako Company evaluates division managers on the basis of divisional profits.

Required:

1. Assume the Audio Division is now selling only 20,000 speakers per year to outside customers.
    a. From the standpoint of the Audio Division, what is the lowest acceptable transfer price for speakers sold to the Hi-Fi Division?
    b. From the standpoint of the Hi-Fi Division, what is the highest acceptable transfer price for speakers acquired from the Audio Division?
    c. What is the range of acceptable transfer prices (if any) between the two divisions? If left free to negotiate without interference, would you expect the division managers to voluntarily agree to the transfer of 5,000 speakers from the Audio Division to the Hi-Fi Division? Why or why not?
    d. From the standpoint of the entire company, should the transfer take place? Why or why not?
2. Assume the Audio Division is selling all of the speakers it can produce to outside customers.
    a. From the standpoint of the Audio Division, what is the lowest acceptable transfer price for speakers sold to the Hi-Fi Division?
    b. From the standpoint of the Hi-Fi Division, what is the highest acceptable transfer price for speakers acquired from the Audio Division?
    c. What is the range of acceptable transfer prices (if any) between the two divisions? If left free to negotiate without interference, would you expect the division managers to voluntarily agree to the transfer of 5,000 speakers from the Audio Division to the Hi-Fi Division? Why or why not?
    d. From the standpoint of the entire company, should the transfer take place? Why or why not?

EXERCISE 11A–2 Transfer Pricing from the Viewpoint of the Entire Company LO11–5

Division A manufactures electronic circuit boards. The boards can be sold either to Division B of the same company or to outside customers. Last year, the following activity occurred in Division A:

Selling price per circuit board	$125
Variable cost per circuit board	$90
Number of circuit boards:	
Produced during the year	20,000
Sold to outside customers	16,000
Sold to Division B	4,000

Sales to Division B were at the same price as sales to outside customers. The circuit boards purchased by Division B were used in an electronic instrument manufactured by that division (one board per instrument). Division B incurred $100 in additional variable cost per instrument and then sold the instruments for $300 each.

Required:

1. Prepare income statements for Division A, Division B, and the company as a whole.
2. Assume Division A's manufacturing capacity is 20,000 circuit boards. Next year, Division B wants to purchase 5,000 circuit boards from Division A rather than 4,000. (Circuit boards of this type are not available from outside sources.) From the standpoint of the company as a whole, should Division A sell the 1,000 additional circuit boards to Division B or continue to sell them to outside customers? Explain.

EXERCISE 11A–3 Transfer Pricing Situations LO11–5

In each of the cases below, assume Division X has a product that can be sold either to outside customers or to Division Y of the same company for use in its production process. The managers of the divisions are evaluated based on their divisional profits.

	Case A	Case B
Division X:		
Capacity in units	200,000	200,000
Number of units being sold to outside customers	200,000	160,000
Selling price per unit to outside customers	$90	$75
Variable costs per unit	$70	$60
Fixed costs per unit (based on capacity)	$13	$8
Division Y:		
Number of units needed for production	40,000	40,000
Purchase price per unit now being paid to an outside supplier	$86	$74

Required:

1. Refer to the data in case A above. Assume in this case that $3 per unit in variable selling costs can be avoided on intracompany sales.
   a. What is the lowest acceptable transfer price from the perspective of the selling division?
   b. What is the highest acceptable transfer price from the perspective of the buying division?
   c. What is the range of acceptable transfer prices (if any) between the two divisions? If the managers are free to negotiate and make decisions on their own, will a transfer probably take place? Explain.
2. Refer to the data in case B above. In this case, there will be no savings in variable selling costs on intracompany sales.
   a. What is the lowest acceptable transfer price from the perspective of the selling division?
   b. What is the highest acceptable transfer price from the perspective of the buying division?
   c. What is the range of acceptable transfer prices (if any) between the two divisions? If the managers are free to negotiate and make decisions on their own, will a transfer probably take place? Explain.

PROBLEM 11A–4 Transfer Price with an Outside Market LO11–5

Hrubec Products, Inc., operates a Pulp Division that manufactures wood pulp for use in the production of various paper goods. Revenue and costs associated with a ton of pulp follow:

Selling price		$70
Expenses:		
Variable	$42	
Fixed (based on a capacity of		
50,000 tons per year)	18	60
Net operating income		$10

Hrubec Products has just acquired a small company that manufactures paper cartons. This company will be treated as a division of Hrubec with full profit responsibility. The newly formed Carton Division is currently purchasing 5,000 tons of pulp per year from a supplier at a cost of $70 per ton, less a 10% purchase discount. Hrubec's president is anxious for the Carton Division to begin purchasing its pulp from the Pulp Division if an acceptable transfer price can be worked out.

Required:

For (1) and (2) below, assume the Pulp Division can sell all of its pulp to outside customers for $70 per ton.

1.   What is the lowest acceptable transfer price from the perspective of the Pulp Division? What is the highest acceptable transfer price from the perspective of the Carton Division? What is the range of acceptable transfer prices (if any) between the two divisions? Are the managers of the Carton and Pulp Divisions likely to voluntarily agree to a transfer price for 5,000 tons of pulp next year? Why or why not?

2.   If the Pulp Division meets the price that the Carton Division is currently paying to its supplier and sells 5,000 tons of pulp to the Carton Division each year, what will be the effect on the profits of the Pulp Division, the Carton Division, and the company as a whole?

For (3)–(6) below, assume that the Pulp Division is currently selling only 30,000 tons of pulp each year to outside customers at the stated $70 price.

3.   What is the lowest acceptable transfer price from the perspective of the Pulp Division? What is the highest acceptable transfer price from the perspective of the Carton Division? What is the range of acceptable transfer prices (if any) between the two divisions? Are the managers of the Carton and Pulp Divisions likely to voluntarily agree to a transfer price for 5,000 tons of pulp next year? Why or why not?

4.   Suppose the Carton Division's outside supplier drops its price (net of the purchase discount) to only $59 per ton. Should the Pulp Division meet this price? Explain. If the Pulp Division does *not* meet the $59 price, what will be the effect on the profits of the company as a whole?

5.   Refer to (4) above. If the Pulp Division refuses to meet the $59 price, should the Carton Division be required to purchase from the Pulp Division at a higher price for the good of the company as a whole?

6.   Refer to (4) above. Assume that due to inflexible management policies, the Carton Division is required to purchase 5,000 tons of pulp each year from the Pulp Division at $70 per ton. What will be the effect on the profits of the company as a whole?

PROBLEM 11A–5 Market-Based Transfer Price LO11–5

Stavos Company's Screen Division manufactures a standard screen for high-definition televisions (HDTVs). The cost per screen is:

Variable cost per screen	$ 70
Fixed cost per screen	30*
Total cost per screen	$100

*Based on a capacity of 10,000 screens per year.

Part of the Screen Division's output is sold to outside manufacturers of HDTVs and part is sold to Stavos Company's Quark Division, which produces an HDTV under its own name. The Screen Division charges $140 per screen for all sales.

The costs, revenue, and net operating income associated with the Quark Division's HDTV are given below:

Selling price per unit		$480
Variable cost per unit:		
Cost of the screen	$140	
Variable cost of electronic parts	210	
Total variable cost		350
Contribution margin		130
Fixed costs per unit		80*
Net operating income per unit		$ 50

*Based on a capacity of 3,000 units per year.

The Quark Division has an order from an overseas source for 1,000 HDTVs. The overseas source wants to pay only $340 per unit.

Required:

1. Assume the Quark Division has enough idle capacity to fill the 1,000-unit order. Is the division likely to accept the $340 price or to reject it? Explain.
2. Assume both the Screen Division and the Quark Division have idle capacity. Under these conditions, what is the financial advantage (disadvantage) for the company as a whole (on a per unit basis) if the Quark Division *rejects* the $340 price?
3. Assume the Quark Division has idle capacity but that the Screen Division is operating at capacity and could sell all of its screens to outside manufacturers. Under these conditions, what is the financial advantage (disadvantage) for the company as a whole (on a per unit basis) if the Quark Division *accepts* the $340 unit price.
4. What conclusions do you draw concerning the use of market price as a transfer price in intra-company transactions?

PROBLEM 11A–6 Basic Transfer Pricing LO11–5

Alpha and Beta are divisions within the same company. The managers of both divisions are evaluated based on their own division's return on investment (ROI). Assume the following information relative to the two divisions:

	Case			
	1	2	3	4
Alpha Division:				
Capacity in units	80,000	400,000	150,000	300,000
Number of units now being sold to outside customers	80,000	400,000	100,000	300,000
Selling price per unit to outside customers	$30	$90	$75	$50
Variable costs per unit	$18	$65	$40	$26
Fixed costs per unit (based on capacity)	$6	$15	$20	$9
Beta Division:				
Number of units needed annually	5,000	30,000	20,000	120,000
Purchase price now being paid to an outside supplier	$27	$89	$75*	—

*Before any purchase discount.

Managers are free to decide if they will participate in any internal transfers. All transfer prices are negotiated.

Required:

1. Refer to case 1 shown above. Alpha Division can avoid $2 per unit in commissions on any sales to Beta Division.
   a. What is the lowest acceptable transfer price from the perspective of the Alpha Division?
   b. What is the highest acceptable transfer price from the perspective of the Beta Division?
   c. What is the range of acceptable transfer prices (if any) between the two divisions? Will the managers probably agree to a transfer? Explain.
2. Refer to case 2 shown above. A study indicates that Alpha Division can avoid $5 per unit in shipping costs on any sales to Beta Division.
   a. What is the lowest acceptable transfer price from the perspective of the Alpha Division?
   b. What is the highest acceptable transfer price from the perspective of the Beta Division?
   c. What is the range of acceptable transfer prices (if any) between the two divisions? Would you expect any disagreement between the two divisional managers over what the exact transfer price should be? Explain.
   d. Assume Alpha Division offers to sell 30,000 units to Beta Division for $88 per unit and that Beta Division refuses this price. What will be the loss in potential profits for the company as a whole?
3. Refer to case 3 shown above. Assume that Beta Division is now receiving an 8% price discount from the outside supplier.
   a. What is the lowest acceptable transfer price from the perspective of the Alpha Division?
   b. What is the highest acceptable transfer price from the perspective of the Beta Division?
   c. What is the range of acceptable transfer prices (if any) between the two divisions? Will the managers probably agree to a transfer? Explain

d.   Assume Beta Division offers to purchase 20,000 units from Alpha Division at $60 per unit. If Alpha Division accepts this price, would you expect its ROI to increase, decrease, or remain unchanged? Why?

4.   Refer to case 4 shown above. Assume that Beta Division wants Alpha Division to provide it with 120,000 units of a *different* product from the one Alpha Division is producing now. The new product would require $21 per unit in variable costs and would require that Alpha Division cut back production of its present product by 45,000 units annually. What is the lowest acceptable transfer price from Alpha Division's perspective?

CASE 11A–7 Transfer Pricing; Divisional Performance LO11–5

Weller Industries is a decentralized organization with six divisions. The company's Electrical Division produces a variety of electrical items, including an X52 electrical fitting. The Electrical Division (which is operating at capacity) sells this fitting to its regular customers for $7.50 each; the fitting has a variable manufacturing cost of $4.25.

The company's Brake Division has asked the Electrical Division to supply it with a large quantity of X52 fittings for only $5 each. The Brake Division, which is operating at 50% of capacity, will put the fitting into a brake unit that it will produce and sell to a large commercial airline manufacturer. The cost of the brake unit being built by the Brake Division follows:

Purchased parts (from outside vendors)	$22.50
Electrical fitting X52	5.00
Other variable costs	14.00
Fixed overhead and administration	8.00
Total cost per brake unit	$49.50

Although the $5 price for the X52 fitting represents a substantial discount from the regular $7.50 price, the manager of the Brake Division believes the price concession is necessary if his division is to get the contract for the airplane brake units. He has heard "through the grapevine" that the airplane manufacturer plans to reject his bid if it is more than $50 per brake unit. Thus, if the Brake Division is forced to pay the regular $7.50 price for the X52 fitting, it will either not get the contract or it will suffer a substantial loss at a time when it is already operating at only 50% of capacity. The manager of the Brake Division argues that the price concession is imperative to the well-being of both his division and the company as a whole.

Weller Industries uses return on investment (ROI) to measure divisional performance.

Required:

1.   What is the lowest acceptable transfer price for the Electrical Division? If you were the manager of the Electrical Division, would you supply the X52 fitting to the Brake Division for $5 each as requested? Why or why not?

2.   Assuming the airplane brakes can be sold for $50, what is the financial advantage (disadvantage) for the company as a whole (on a per unit basis) if the Electrical Division supplies fittings to the Brake Division? Explain your answer.

3.   What is the highest acceptable transfer price for the Brake Division? In principle, should it be possible for the two divisional managers to agree to a transfer price in this particular situation?

4.   Discuss the organizational behavior problems, if any, inherent in this situation. What would you advise the company's president to do in this situation?

(CMA, adapted)

Appendix 11B: Service Department Charges

LO11–6

Charge operating departments for services provided by service departments.

Most large organizations have both *operating departments* and *service departments*. The central purposes of the organization are carried out in the **operating departments**. In contrast, **service departments** do not directly engage in operating activities. Instead, they provide services or assistance to the operating departments. Examples of service departments include Cafeteria, Internal Auditing, Human Resources, Cost Accounting, and Purchasing.

Service department costs are charged to operating departments for a variety of reasons, including:

- To encourage operating departments to make wise use of service department resources. If the services were provided for free, operating managers would be inclined to waste these resources.
- To provide operating departments with more complete cost data for making decisions. Actions taken by operating departments have impacts on service department costs. For example, hiring another employee will increase costs in the human resources department. Such service department costs should be charged to the operating departments, otherwise the operating departments will not take them into account when making decisions.
- To help measure the profitability of operating departments. Charging service department costs to operating departments provides a more complete accounting of the costs incurred as a consequence of activities in the operating departments.
- To create an incentive for service departments to operate efficiently. Charging service department costs to operating departments provides a system of checks and balances in the sense that cost-conscious operating departments will take an active interest in keeping service department costs low.

In Appendix 11A, we discussed *transfer prices* that are charged within an organization when one part of an organization provides a product to another part of the organization. The service department charges considered in this appendix can be viewed as transfer prices that are charged for services provided by service departments to operating departments.

Charging Costs by Behavior

Whenever possible, variable and fixed service department costs should be charged to operating departments separately to provide more useful data for planning and control of departmental operations.

Variable Costs

Variable costs vary in total in proportion to changes in the level of service provided. For example, the cost of food in a cafeteria is a variable cost that varies in proportion to the number of persons using the cafeteria or the number of meals served.

A variable cost should be charged to operating departments according to whatever activity causes the incurrence of the cost. For example, variable costs of a maintenance department that are caused by the number of machine-hours worked in the operating departments should be charged to the operating departments on the basis of machine-hours. This will ensure that these costs are properly traced to departments, products, and customers.

Fixed Costs

The fixed costs of service departments represent the costs of making capacity available for use. These costs should be charged to operating departments in *predetermined lump-sum amounts* that are determined in advance and do not change. The lump-sum amount charged to a department can be based either on the department's peak-period or long-run average servicing needs.

The logic behind lump-sum charges of this type is as follows: When a service department is first established, its capacity will be determined by the needs of the departments it will serve. This capacity may reflect the peak-period needs of the other departments, or it may reflect their long-run average or "normal" servicing needs. Depending on how much servicing capacity is provided for, it will be necessary to make a commitment of resources, which will be reflected in the service department's fixed costs. These fixed costs should be borne by the operating departments in proportion to the amount of capacity each these departments requires. That is, if available capacity in the service department has been provided to meet the peak-period needs of operating departments, then the fixed costs of the service department should be charged in predetermined lump-sum amounts to operating departments on that basis. If available capacity has been provided only to meet "normal" or long-run average needs, then the fixed costs should be charged on that basis.

Once set, charges should not vary from period to period, because they represent the cost of having a certain level of service capacity available for each operating department. The fact that an operating department does not need the peak level or even the "normal" level of service every period is immaterial; the capacity to deliver this level of service must be available. The operating departments should bear the cost of that availability.

Should Actual or Budgeted Costs Be Charged?

The *budgeted*, rather than actual, costs of a service department should be charged to operating departments. This ensures that service departments remain solely responsible for explaining any differences between their actual and budgeted costs. If service departments could base their charges on actual costs, then operating departments would be unfairly held accountable for cost overruns in the service departments.

Guidelines for Service Department Charges

The following summarizes how service department costs should be charged to operating departments:

- Variable and fixed service department costs should be charged separately.
- Variable service department costs should be charged to operating departments by using a predetermined rate multiplied by the actual quantity of services used.
- Fixed costs represent the costs of having service capacity available. These costs should be charged in lump sums to each operating department in proportion to their peak-period needs or long-run average needs. The lump-sum amounts should be based on budgeted fixed costs, not actual fixed costs.

Example

Seaboard Airlines has two operating divisions—a Freight Division and a Passenger Division. The company has a Maintenance Department that services both divisions. Variable servicing costs are budgeted at $10 per flight-hour. The department's fixed costs are budgeted at $750,000 for the year. The fixed costs of the Maintenance Department are budgeted based on the peak-period demand, which occurs during the Thanksgiving to New Year's holiday period. The airline wants to make sure that none of its aircraft are grounded during this key period due to unavailability of maintenance facilities. Approximately 40% of the maintenance during this period is performed on the Freight Division's equipment, and 60% is performed on the Passenger Division's equipment. These figures and the budgeted flight-hours for the coming year are as follows:

	Percent of Peak Period Capacity Required	Budgeted Flight-Hours
Freight Division	40%	9,000
Passenger Division	60	15,000
Total	100%	24,000

Year-end records show that actual variable and fixed costs in the aircraft Maintenance Department for the year were $260,000 and $780,000, respectively. One division logged more flight-hours during the year than planned, and the other division logged fewer flight-hours than planned, as shown below:

	Flight-Hours	
	Budgeted	Actual
Freight Division	9,000	8,000
Passenger Division	15,000	17,000
Total flight-hours	24,000	25,000

The amount of Maintenance Department cost charged to each division for the year would be as follows:

	Actual activity	Division	
		Freight	Passenger
Variable cost charges:			
Budgeted variable rate → $10 per flight-hour × 8,000 flight-hours . . .		$ 80,000	
$10 per flight-hour × 17,000 flight-hours . . .			$170,000
Fixed cost charges:			
Peak-period capacity required → 40% × $750,000		300,000	
60% × $750,000			450,000
Total charges		$380,000	$620,000

Budgeted fixed cost

Notice that variable servicing costs are charged to the operating divisions based on the budgeted rate ($10 per hour) and the *actual activity* for the year. In contrast, the charges for fixed costs are based entirely on budgeted data. Also note that the two operating divisions are *not* charged for the actual costs of the service department, which are influenced by how well the service department is managed. Instead, the service department is held responsible for the actual costs not charged to other departments as shown below:

	Variable	Fixed
Total actual costs incurred	$260,000	$780,000
Total charges to operating departments	250,000*	750,000
Spending variance—responsibility of the Maintenance Department	$ 10,000	$ 30,000

*$10 per flight-hour × 25,000 actual flight-hours = $250,000.

Some Cautions in Allocating Service Department Costs

Pitfalls in Allocating Fixed Costs

Rather than charge fixed costs to operating departments in predetermined lump-sum amounts, some companies allocate them using a *variable* allocation base that fluctuates from period to period. This practice can distort decisions and create serious inequities between departments. The inequities arise from the fact that the fixed costs allocated to one department are heavily influenced by what happens in *other* departments.

Sales dollars is an example of a variable allocation base that is often used to allocate fixed costs from service departments to operating departments. Using sales dollars as a base is simple, straightforward, and easy to work with. Furthermore, people tend to view sales dollars as a measure of ability to pay, and, hence, as a measure of how readily costs can be absorbed from other parts of the organization.

Unfortunately, sales dollars are often a very poor base for allocating or charging costs because sales dollars vary from period to period, whereas the costs being allocated are often largely *fixed.* Therefore, a letup in sales effort in one department will shift allocated costs from that department to other, more successful departments. In effect, the departments putting forth the best sales efforts are penalized in the form of higher allocations. The result is often bitterness and resentment on the part of the managers of the better departments.

For example, let's assume that a large men's clothing store has one service department and three sales departments—Suits, Shoes, and Accessories. The service department's costs total $60,000 per period and are allocated to the three sales departments based on sales dollars. A recent period showed the following service department cost allocations:

| | Departments | | | |
	Suits	Shoes	Accessories	Total
Sales by department	$260,000	$40,000	$100,000	$400,000
Percentage of total sales	65%	10%	25%	100%
Allocation of service department costs, based on percentage of total sales	$39,000	$6,000	$15,000	$60,000

Notice that the Suits Department is responsible for 65% of total sales (= $260,000 ÷ $400,000); therefore, it is allocated 65% of the service department's costs, or $39,000 (= $60,000 × 65%).

In the following period, let's assume the manager of the Suits Department launched a successful program to expand sales in his department by $100,000. Furthermore, let's assume that sales in the other two departments remained unchanged, total service department costs remained unchanged, and the sales departments' expected usage of service department resources remained unchanged. Given these assumptions, in the following period the service department cost allocations to the sales departments would be calculated as shown below:

| | Departments | | | |
	Suits	Shoes	Accessories	Total
Sales by department	$360,000	$40,000	$100,000	$500,000
Percentage of total sales	72%	8%	20%	100%
Allocation of service department costs, based on percentage of total sales	$43,200	$4,800	$12,000	$60,000
Increase (or decrease) from prior allocation	$4,200	$(1,200)	$(3,000)	$0

Now the Suits Department is responsible for 72% of total sales (= $360,000 ÷ $500,000); therefore, it is allocated 72% of the service department's costs, or $43,200 (= $60,000 × 72%). Given these revised cost allocations, the manager of the Suits Department is likely to complain because, as a result of growing sales in his department, he is being allocated an additional 7% (= 72% – 65%) of the service department's costs.

In essence, this manager is being punished for his outstanding performance by being allocated an additional \$4,200 (= \$43,200 − \$39,000) of service department costs. On the other hand, the managers of the departments that showed no sales growth are being relieved of a portion of the costs they had been carrying. Yet, there was no change in the amount of services provided for any department across the two periods.

This example shows why a variable allocation base such as sales dollars should only be used as a base for allocating or charging costs in those cases where service department costs actually vary with the chosen allocation base. When service department costs are fixed, they should be charged to operating departments according to the guidelines mentioned earlier.

Glossary (Appendix 11B)

Operating department A department in which the central purposes of the organization are carried out. (p. 552)

Service department A department that does not directly engage in operating activities; rather, it provides services or assistance to the operating departments. (p. 552)

Appendix 11B: Exercises and Problems

EXERCISE 11B–1 Service Department Charges LO11–6

Hannibal Steel Company has a Transport Services Department that provides trucks to haul ore from the company's mine to its two steel mills—the Northern Plant and the Southern Plant. Budgeted costs for the Transport Services Department total \$350,000 per year, consisting of \$0.25 per ton variable cost and \$300,000 fixed cost. The level of fixed cost is determined by peak-period requirements. During the peak period, the Northern Plant requires 70% of the Transport Services Department's capacity and the Southern Plant requires 30%.

During the year, the Transport Services Department actually hauled the following amounts of ore for the two plants: Northern Plant, 130,000 tons; Southern Plant, 50,000 tons. The Transport Services Department incurred \$364,000 in cost during the year, of which \$54,000 was variable cost and \$310,000 was fixed cost.

Required:
1. How much of the \$54,000 in variable cost should be charged to each plant.
2. How much of the \$310,000 in fixed cost should be charged to each plant.
3. Should any of the \$364,000 in the Transport Services Department cost be treated as a spending variance and not charged to the plants? Explain.

EXERCISE 11B–2 Sales Dollars as an Allocation Base for Fixed Costs LO11–6

Konig Enterprises, Ltd., owns and operates three restaurants in Vancouver, B.C. The company allocates its fixed administrative expenses to the three restaurants on the basis of sales dollars. Last year the fixed administrative expenses totaled \$2,000,000 and were allocated as follows:

	Restaurants			
	Rick's Harborside	Imperial Garden	Ginger Wok	Total
Total sales—Last Year	\$16,000,000	\$15,000,000	\$9,000,000	\$40,000,000
Percentage of total sales ...	40%	37.5%	22.5%	100%
Allocation (based on the above percentages)	\$800,000	\$750,000	\$450,000	\$2,000,000

This year the Imperial Garden restaurant increased its sales by $10 million. The sales levels in the other two restaurants remained unchanged. The company's sales data for this year were as follows:

	Restaurants			
	Rick's Harborside	Imperial Garden	Ginger Wok	Total
Total sales—This Year	$16,000,000	$25,000,000	$9,000,000	$50,000,000
Percentage of total sales ...	32%	50%	18%	100%

Fixed administrative expenses for this year remained unchanged at $2,000,000.

Required:
1. Using sales dollars as an allocation base, show the allocation of the fixed administrative expenses among the three restaurants for this year.
2. Calculate the change in each restaurant's allocated cost from last year to this year. As the manager of the Imperial Garden, how would you feel about the amount that has been charged to you for this year?
3. Comment on the usefulness of sales dollars as an allocation base.

EXERCISE 11B–3 Service Department Charges LO11–6

Korvanis Corporation operates a Medical Services Department for its employees. Charges to the company's operating departments for the variable costs of the Medical Services Department are based on the actual number of employees in each department. Charges for the fixed costs of the Medical Services Department are based on the long-run average number of employees in each operating department.

Variable Medical Services Department costs are budgeted at $80 per employee. Fixed Medical Services Department costs are budgeted at $400,000 per year. Actual Medical Services Department costs for the most recent year were $41,000 for variable costs and $408,000 for fixed costs. Data concerning employees in the three operating departments follow:

	Cutting	Milling	Assembly
Budgeted number of employees	170	100	280
Actual number of employees for the most recent year	150	80	270
Long-run average number of employees	180	120	300

Required:
1. Determine the Medical Services Department charges for the year to each of the operating departments—Cutting, Milling, and Assembly.
2. How much, if any, of the actual Medical Services Department costs for the year should be treated as a spending variance and not charged to the operating departments?

PROBLEM 11B–4 Service Department Charges LO11–6

Sharp Motor Company has two operating divisions—an Auto Division and a Truck Division. The company has a cafeteria that serves the employees of both divisions. The costs of operating the cafeteria are budgeted at $40,000 per month plus $3 per meal served. The company pays all the cost of the meals.

The fixed costs of the cafeteria are determined by peak-period requirements. The Auto Division is responsible for 65% of the peak-period requirements, and the Truck Division is responsible for the other 35%.

For June, the Auto Division estimated it would need 35,000 meals served, and the Truck Division estimated it would need 20,000 meals served. However, due to unexpected layoffs of employees during the month, only 20,000 meals were served to the Auto Division. Another 20,000 meals were served to the Truck Division as planned.

Cost records in the cafeteria show that actual fixed costs for June totaled $42,000 and actual meal costs totaled $128,000.

Required:

1. How much cafeteria cost should be charged to each division for June?
2. Assume the company follows the practice of allocating *all* cafeteria costs incurred each month to the divisions in proportion to the number of meals served to each division during the month. On this basis, how much cost would be allocated to each division for June?
3. What criticisms can you make of the allocation method used in part (2) above?
4. If managers of operating departments know that fixed service costs are going to be allocated on the basis of peak-period requirements, what will be their probable strategy as they report their estimate of peak-period requirements to the company's budget committee? As a member of top management, what would you do to neutralize such strategies?

PROBLEM 11B–5 Service Department Charges LO11–6

Tasman Products, Ltd., of Australia has a Maintenance Department that services the equipment in the company's Forming Department and Assembly Department. The cost of this servicing is charged to the operating departments on the basis of machine-hours. Cost and other data relating to the Maintenance Department and to the other two departments for the most recent year are presented below.

Data for the Maintenance Department follow:

	Budget	Actual
Variable costs for lubricants	$96,000*	$110,000
Fixed costs for salaries and other	$150,000	$153,000

*Budgeted at $0.40 per machine-hour.

Data for the Forming and Assembly Departments follow:

	Percentage of Peak-Period Capacity Required	Machine-Hours	
		Budget	Actual
Forming Department	70%	160,000	190,000
Assembly Department	30%	80,000	70,000
Total	100%	240,000	260,000

The level of fixed costs in the Maintenance Department is determined by peak-period requirements.

Required:

Management would like data to assist in comparing actual performance to planned performance in the Maintenance Department and in the other departments.

1. How much Maintenance Department cost should be charged to the Forming Department and to the Assembly Department?
2. How much, if any, of the actual Maintenance Department costs for the year should be treated as a spending variance and not charged to the Forming and Assembly departments? Explain the rationale for your answer.

CHAPTER 12

Differential Analysis: The Key to Decision Making

Understanding the Qualitative Aspects of Decision Making

© Ian Dagnall/Alamy

SAS is a privately held $2.26 billion company located on a 200-acre campus in Cary, North Carolina. The company has an on-site medical facility (including a lab for blood tests) that is staffed by doctors, nurse practitioners, physical therapists, and a nutritionist. The company also has an infant day care, a Montessori school, a hair salon, a dry cleaning shop, a fitness center, and jogging and biking trails on campus. Employees that use the day care pay $360 per month per child for the service and SAS covers the remaining $720 per month per child that it costs to retain 120 teachers and staffers.

Although it may be difficult to quantify the benefits of these investments, SAS firmly believes that retaining happy and healthy employees is instrumental to its success. Mary Simmons, a SAS software developer says, "At lunch I will go out and bike 20 miles. Then I'll get back and all of a sudden a thought comes to my brain, and I solve something I was struggling with." ■

Source: Christopher Tkaczk, *"Offer Affordable (Awesome) Day Care," Fortune,* August 17, 2009, p. 26.

LEARNING OBJECTIVES

After studying Chapter 12, you should be able to:

LO12–1 Identify relevant and irrelevant costs and benefits in a decision.

LO12–2 Prepare an analysis showing whether a product line or other business segment should be added or dropped.

LO12–3 Prepare a make or buy analysis.

LO12–4 Prepare an analysis showing whether a special order should be accepted.

LO12–5 Determine the most profitable use of a constrained resource.

LO12–6 Determine the value of obtaining more of the constrained resource.

LO12–7 Prepare an analysis showing whether joint products should be sold at the split-off point or processed further.

LO12–8 (Appendix 12A) Compute the selling price of a product using the absorption costing approach to cost-plus pricing.

LO12–9 (Appendix 12A) Understand how customers' sensitivity to changes in price should influence pricing decisions.

LO12–10 (Appendix 12A) Analyze pricing decisions using value-based pricing.

LO12–11 (Appendix 12A) Compute the target cost for a new product or service.

This chapter discusses what may be a manager's most important responsibility—making decisions. Examples of decisions include deciding what products to sell, whether to make or buy component parts, what prices to charge, what channels of distribution to use, and whether to accept special orders at special prices. Making such decisions is often a difficult task that is complicated by numerous alternatives and massive amounts of data; however, in this chapter you will learn how to narrow your focus to the information that matters.

Decision Making: Six Key Concepts

There are six key concepts that you need to understand to make intelligent decisions. This section discusses each of those concepts and then concludes by introducing some additional terminology that was created to help you solve the exercises and problems at the end of the chapter.

LO12–1
Identify relevant and irrelevant costs and benefits in a decision.

Key Concept #1

Every decision involves choosing from among at least two alternatives. Therefore, the first step in decision making is to define the alternatives being considered. For example, if a company is deciding whether to make a component part or buy it from an outside supplier, the alternatives are *make* or *buy* the component part. Similarly, if a company is considering discontinuing a particular product, the alternatives are *keep* or *drop* the product.

Key Concept #2

Once you have defined the alternatives, you need to identify the criteria for choosing among them. The key to choosing among alternatives is distinguishing between *relevant* and *irrelevant* costs and benefits. **Relevant costs** and **relevant benefits** should be considered when making decisions. *Irrelevant costs* and *irrelevant benefits* should be ignored when making decisions. This is an important concept for two reasons. First, being able to ignore irrelevant data saves decision makers tremendous amounts of time and effort. Second, bad decisions can easily result from erroneously including irrelevant costs and benefits when analyzing alternatives.

Key Concept #3

The key to effective decision making is *differential analysis*—focusing on the future costs and benefits that differ between the alternatives. Everything else is irrelevant and should be ignored. A future cost that differs between any two alternatives is known as a **differential cost**. Differential costs are always relevant costs. Future revenue that differs between any two alternatives is known as **differential revenue**. Differential revenue is an example of a relevant benefit.

The terms *incremental cost* and *avoidable cost* are often used to describe differential costs. An **incremental cost** is an increase in cost between two alternatives. For example, if you are choosing between buying the standard model or the deluxe model of your favorite automobile, the costs of the upgrades contained in the deluxe model are incremental costs. An **avoidable cost** is a cost that can be eliminated by choosing one alternative over another. For example, assume that you have decided to watch a movie tonight; however, you are trying to choose between two alternatives—going to the movie theater or renting a movie. The cost of the ticket to get into the movie theater is an avoidable cost. You would avoid this cost by renting a movie. Similarly, the movie rental fee is an avoidable cost because you could avoid it by going to the movie theater. Avoidable costs (and incremental costs) are always relevant costs.

Differential costs and benefits can be qualitative or quantitative in nature. While qualitative differences between alternatives can have an important impact on decisions, and therefore, should not be ignored; our goal in this chapter is to hone your quantitative analysis skills. Therefore, our primary focus will be on analyzing quantitative differential costs and benefits—those that have readily measurable impacts on future cash flows.

Key Concept #4

Sunk costs are always irrelevant when choosing among alternatives. A **sunk cost** is a cost that has already been incurred and cannot be changed regardless of what a manager decides to do. Sunk costs have no impact on future cash flows and they remain the same no matter what alternatives are being considered; therefore, they are irrelevant and should be ignored when making decisions.

For example, suppose a company purchased a five-year-old truck for $12,000. The amount paid for the truck is a sunk cost because it has already been incurred and the transaction cannot be undone. The $12,000 paid for the truck is irrelevant in making decisions such as whether to keep, sell, or replace the truck. Furthermore, any accounting depreciation expense related to the truck is irrelevant in making decisions. This is true because accounting depreciation is a noncash expense that has no effect on future cash flows. It simply spreads the sunk cost of the truck over its useful life.[1]

Key Concept #5

Future costs and benefits that *do not differ between alternatives* are irrelevant to the decision-making process. So, continuing with the movie example, assume that you plan to buy a **Papa John's** pizza after watching a movie. If you are going to buy the same pizza regardless of your movie-watching venue, the cost of the pizza is irrelevant when choosing between the theater and the rental. The cost of the pizza is *not* a sunk cost because it has not yet been incurred. Nonetheless, the cost of the pizza is irrelevant to the choice of venue because it is a future cost that does not differ between the alternatives.

Key Concept #6

Opportunity costs also need to be considered when making decisions. An **opportunity cost** is the potential benefit that is given up when one alternative is selected over another. For example, if you were considering giving up a high-paying summer job to travel overseas, the forgone wages would be an opportunity cost of traveling abroad. Opportunity costs are not usually found in accounting records, but they are a type of differential cost that must be explicitly considered in every decision a manager makes.

This chapter covers various decision contexts, such as keep or drop decisions, make or buy decisions, special order decisions, and sell or process further decisions. While tackling these diverse decision contexts may seem a bit overwhelming, keep in mind that they all share a unifying theme—choosing between alternatives based on their differential costs and benefits. To emphasize this common theme, many end-of-chapter exercises and problems that span a variety of learning objectives will often use the same terminology— financial advantage (disadvantage)—when asking you to choose between alternatives. For example, numerous exercises and problems will ask questions such as:

1. What is the financial advantage (disadvantage) of closing the store?
2. What is the financial advantage (disadvantage) of buying the component part from a supplier rather than making it?
3. What is the financial advantage (disadvantage) of accepting the special order?
4. What is the financial advantage (disadvantage) of further processing the intermediate product?

---

[1] See Appendix 13C for a discussion of how depreciation expense impacts decisions when tax implications are considered.

In all of these various contexts, a financial advantage exists if pursuing an alternative, such as closing a store or accepting a special order, passes the cost/benefit test. In other words, it exists if the alternative's differential benefits (i.e., its future cash inflows) exceed its differential costs (i.e., its future cash outflows). Conversely, a financial (disadvantage) exists when an alternative fails the cost/benefit test—its differential benefits are less than its differential costs.[2]

Identifying Relevant Costs and Benefits: An Example

Cynthia is currently a student in an MBA program in Boston and would like to visit a friend in New York City over the weekend. She is trying to decide whether to drive or take the train. Because she is on a tight budget, she wants to carefully consider the costs of the two alternatives. If one alternative is far less expensive than the other, that may be decisive in her choice. By car, the distance between her apartment in Boston and her friend's apartment in New York City is 230 miles. Cynthia has compiled the following list of items to consider:

Automobile Costs		
Item	Annual Cost of Fixed Items	Cost per Mile (based on 10,000 miles per year)
(a) Annual straight-line depreciation on car [($24,000 original cost − $10,000 estimated resale value in 5 years)/5 years].................	$2,800	$0.280
(b) Cost of gasoline ($2.40 per gallon ÷ 24 miles per gallon)..		0.100
(c) Annual cost of auto insurance and license.........	$1,380	0.138
(d) Maintenance and repairs.........................		0.065
(e) Parking fees at school ($45 per month × 8 months)	$360	0.036
(f) Total average cost per mile......................		$0.619

Additional Data	
Item	
(g) Reduction in the resale value of car due solely to wear and tear........................	$0.080 per mile
(h) Cost of round-trip train ticket from Boston to New York City.....................................	$114
(i) Benefit of relaxing and being able to study during the train ride rather than having to drive...........	?
(j) Cost of putting the dog in a kennel while gone.....	$80
(k) Benefit of having a car available in New York City	?
(l) Hassle of parking the car in New York City.........	?
(m) Cost of parking the car in New York City...........	$25 per day

---

[2] Over the life of a company, cumulative net cash flows equal cumulative net income. Therefore, if a decision maximizes future net cash flows, it will also maximize future cumulative net income. However, because of accruals, in any particular period net income will usually be different from net cash flow. A decision that is based on maximizing future net cash flows might, in the short run, reduce net income, but in the long run cumulative net income will be higher than it otherwise would have been.

Which costs and benefits are relevant in this decision? Remember, only the differential costs and benefits are relevant—everything else is irrelevant and can be ignored.

Start at the top of the list with item (a): the original cost of the car is a sunk cost. This cost has already been incurred and therefore can never differ between alternatives. Consequently, it is irrelevant and should be ignored. The same is true of the accounting depreciation of $2,800 per year, which simply spreads the sunk cost across five years.

Item (b), the cost of gasoline consumed by driving to New York City, is a relevant cost. If Cynthia takes the train, she would avoid the cost of the gasoline. Hence, the cost differs between alternatives and is therefore relevant.

Item (c), the annual cost of auto insurance and license, is not relevant. Whether Cynthia takes the train or drives on this particular trip, her annual auto insurance premium and her auto license fee will remain the same.[3]

Item (d), the cost of maintenance and repairs, is relevant. While maintenance and repair costs have a large random component, over the long run they should be more or less proportional to the number of miles the car is driven. Thus, the average cost of $0.065 per mile is a reasonable estimate to use.

Item (e), the monthly fee that Cynthia pays to park at her school during the academic year is not relevant. Regardless of which alternative she selects—driving or taking the train—she will still need to pay for parking at school.

Item (f) is the total average cost of $0.619 per mile. As discussed above, some elements of this total are relevant, but some are not relevant. Because it contains some irrelevant costs, it would be incorrect to estimate the cost of driving to New York City and back by simply multiplying the $0.619 by 460 miles (230 miles each way × 2). This erroneous approach would yield a cost of driving of $284.74. Unfortunately, such mistakes are often made in both personal life and in business. Because the total cost is stated on a per-mile basis, people are easily misled. Often people think that if the cost is stated as $0.619 per mile, the cost of driving 100 miles is $61.90. But it is not. Many of the costs included in the $0.619 cost per mile are sunk and/or fixed and will not increase if the car is driven another 100 miles. The $0.619 is an average cost, not a differential cost. Beware of such unitized costs (i.e., costs stated in terms of a dollar amount per unit, per mile, per direct labor-hour, per machine-hour, and so on)—they are often misleading.

Item (g), the decline in the resale value of the car that occurs as a consequence of driving more miles, is relevant in the decision. Because she uses the car, its resale value declines, which is a real cost of using the car that should be taken into account. Cynthia estimated this cost by accessing the *Kelley Blue Book* website at **www.kbb.com**. The reduction in resale value of an asset through use or over time is often called *real* or *economic depreciation*. This is different from accounting depreciation, which attempts to match the sunk cost of an asset with the periods that benefit from that cost.

Item (h), the $114 cost of a round-trip ticket on the train, is relevant in this decision. If she drives, she would avoid the cost of the ticket.

Item (i) is relevant to the decision, even if it is difficult to put a dollar value on relaxing and being able to study while on the train. It is relevant because it is a benefit that is available under one alternative but not under the other.

Item (j), the cost of putting Cynthia's dog in the kennel while she is gone, is irrelevant in this decision. Whether she takes the train or drives to New York City, she will still need to put her dog in a kennel.

Like item (i), items (k) and (l) are relevant to the decision even if it is difficult to measure their dollar impacts.

Item (m), the cost of parking in New York City, is relevant to the decision.

---

[3] If Cynthia has an accident while driving to New York City or back, this might affect her insurance premium when the policy is renewed. The increase in the insurance premium would be a relevant cost of this particular trip, but the normal amount of the insurance premium is not relevant in any case.

Bringing together all of the relevant data, Cynthia would estimate the relevant costs of driving and taking the train as follows:

Relevant financial cost of driving to New York City:	
Gasoline (460 miles × $0.100 per mile)	$ 46.00
Maintenance and repairs (460 miles × $0.065 per mile).	29.90
Reduction in the resale value of car due solely to wear and tear (460 miles × $0.080 per mile)	36.80
Cost of parking the car in New York City (2 days × $25 per day).	50.00
Total.	$162.70
Relevant financial cost of taking the train to New York City:	
Cost of round-trip train ticket from Boston to New York City	$114.00

What should Cynthia do? From a purely financial standpoint, it would be cheaper by $48.70 ($162.70 − $114.00) to take the train than to drive. Cynthia has to decide if the convenience of having a car in New York City outweighs the additional cost and the disadvantages of being unable to relax and study on the train and the hassle of finding parking in the city.

COMPANIES WRESTLE WITH THE COSTS AND BENEFITS OF CYBERSECURITY

Quantifying the costs and benefits of alternative cybersecurity investment strategies is difficult for companies to do. On the one hand, the costs associated with insufficient spending have the potential to be enormous—**Heartland Payment Systems** paid fines and legal costs of $150 million when cyber criminals stole more than 100 million credit and debit card numbers. On the other hand, infinite spending on cybersecurity does not completely eliminate the risk of a security breach. This troubling reality is highlighted by Richard Bejtlich, Chief Security Strategist at **FireEye, Inc.**, who claims that a mere $1 million in funding would enable him to assemble a team that could hack into almost any target.

So what should companies do to manage the risk of a cyber attack? Perhaps one valuable piece of advice comes from **Gartner Inc.**'s Avivah Litan who estimates that "for every $5.62 businesses spend after a breach, they could spend $1 beforehand on encryption and network protection to prevent intrusions and minimize damage."

Source: Danny Yadron, "Companies Wrestle with the Cost of Security," *The Wall Street Journal,* February 26, 2014, p. B3.

Decision Analysis: The Total Cost and Differential Cost Approaches

The example that we just completed focused on identifying the relevant costs and benefits of taking the train versus driving—everything else was ignored. This method of decision analysis is called the *differential approach* because it focuses solely on the relevant costs and benefits. Another method of decision analysis, called the *total cost approach,* includes all of the costs and benefits—relevant or not. When done correctly, the two methods always provide the same correct answer.

To compare and contrast these two methods, let's consider Oak Harbor Woodworks, a company that is contemplating renting a new labor-saving machine for $3,000 per year.

The machine will be used on the company's butcher block production line. Data concerning the company's annual sales and costs of butcher blocks with and without the new machine are shown below:

	Current Situation	Situation with the New Machine
Units produced and sold	5,000	5,000
Selling price per unit	$40	$40
Direct materials cost per unit	$14	$14
Direct labor cost per unit	$8	$5
Variable overhead cost per unit	$2	$2
Fixed expenses, other	$62,000	$62,000
Fixed expenses, rental of new machine	—	$3,000

Given the data above, the net operating income for the product under the two alternatives can be computed, using the *total cost approach,* as shown in the first two columns of Exhibit 12–1. The net operating income in the current situation is $18,000 and the net operating income with the new machine is $30,000. The difference in the net operating incomes in these two columns indicates a $12,000 (= $30,000 – $18,000) financial advantage associated with renting the new machine. The irrelevant items (which includes sales, direct materials, variable overhead, and fixed expenses, other) appear in both columns, so they cancel each other out when isolating the $12,000 difference in favor of renting the machine.

The third column in Exhibit 12–1 uses the *differential cost approach* to derive the same financial advantage of $12,000 (= $15,000 + $(3,000)) that is associated with renting the new machine. A positive number in the Differential Costs and Benefits column indicates that the difference between the alternatives favors the new machine; a negative number indicates that the difference favors the current situation. A zero in that column simply means that the total amount for the item is exactly the same for both alternatives.

EXHIBIT 12–1
Total and Differential Costs

	Current Situation	Situation with New Machine	Differential Costs and Benefits
Sales (5,000 units × $40 per unit)	$200,000	$200,000	$ 0
Variable expenses:			
Direct materials (5,000 units × $14 per unit)	70,000	70,000	0
Direct labor (5,000 units × $8 per unit; 5,000 units × $5 per unit)	40,000	25,000	15,000
Variable overhead (5,000 units × $2 per unit)	10,000	10,000	0
Total variable expenses	120,000	105,000	
Contribution margin	80,000	95,000	
Fixed expenses:			
Other	62,000	62,000	0
Rental of new machine	0	3,000	(3,000)
Total fixed expenses	62,000	65,000	
Net operating income	$ 18,000	$ 30,000	$12,000

If we properly account for the costs and benefits that do not differ between the alternatives, they will cancel out when we compare the alternatives; hence, they can be ignored.

Rather than setting up comparative income statements, we could have arrived at the same solution much more quickly by completely ignoring the irrelevant costs and benefits.

- The selling price per unit and the number of units sold do not differ between the alternatives. Therefore, the total sales revenues are exactly the same for the two alternatives as shown in Exhibit 12–1. Because the sales revenues are exactly the same, they have no effect on the difference in net operating income between the two alternatives. That is shown in the last column in Exhibit 12–1, which shows a $0 differential benefit.
- The direct materials cost per unit, the variable overhead cost per unit, and the number of units produced and sold do not differ between the alternatives. Consequently, the total direct materials cost and the total variable overhead cost are the same for the two alternatives and can be ignored.
- The "other" fixed expenses do not differ between the alternatives, so they can be ignored as well.

Indeed, the only costs that do differ between the alternatives are direct labor costs and the fixed rental cost of the new machine. Therefore, the two alternatives can be compared based only on these relevant costs:

Financial Advantage of Renting the New Machine	
Decrease in direct labor costs (5,000 units at a cost savings of $3 per unit)	$15,000
Increase in fixed expenses	(3,000)
Financial advantage of renting the new machine	$12,000

If we focus on just the relevant costs and benefits, we get exactly the same answer ($12,000 in favor of renting the new machine) as when we listed all of the costs and benefits as shown in Exhibit 12–1—including those that do not differ between the alternatives. We get the same answer because the only costs and benefits that matter in the final comparison are those items that differ between the two alternatives and, hence, are not zero in the last column of Exhibit 12–1.

Why Isolate Relevant Costs?

In the preceding example, we used the total cost approach and the differential cost approach to derive the exact same answer. Thus, it would be natural to ask, "Why bother to isolate relevant costs when total costs will do the job just as well?" Isolating relevant costs is desirable for at least two reasons.

First, only rarely will enough information be available to prepare a detailed income statement for both alternatives. Assume, for example, that you are asked to make a decision relating to a portion of a single business process in a multidepartment, multiproduct company. Under these circumstances, it would be virtually impossible to prepare an income statement of any type. You would have to rely on your ability to recognize which costs are relevant and which are not in order to assemble the data necessary to make a decision.

Second, mingling irrelevant costs with relevant costs may cause confusion and distract attention from the information that is really critical. Furthermore, the danger always exists that an irrelevant piece of data may be used improperly, resulting in an incorrect decision. The best approach is to ignore irrelevant data and base the decision entirely on relevant data.

Adding and Dropping Product Lines and Other Segments

LO12–2

Prepare an analysis showing whether a product line or other business segment should be added or dropped.

Decisions relating to whether product lines or other segments of a company should be dropped and new ones added are among the most difficult that a manager has to make. In such decisions, many qualitative and quantitative factors must be considered. Ultimately, however, any final decision to drop a business segment or to add a new one hinges primarily on its financial impact. To assess this impact, costs must be carefully analyzed.

An Illustration of Cost Analysis

Exhibit 12–2 provides sales and cost information for the preceding month for the Discount Drug Company and its three major product lines—drugs, cosmetics, and housewares. A quick review of this exhibit suggests that dropping the housewares segment would increase the company's overall net operating income by $8,000. However, this would be a flawed conclusion because the data in Exhibit 12–2 do not distinguish between fixed expenses that can be avoided if a product line is dropped and common fixed expenses that cannot be avoided by dropping any particular product line.

In this scenario, the two alternatives under consideration are whether to *keep* the housewares product line or *drop* it. If the housewares line is dropped, then the company will lose $20,000 per month in contribution margin because all of this segment's sales and variable expenses will be eliminated. However, by dropping the housewares line it may be possible to avoid some fixed costs such as salaries or advertising costs. If dropping the housewares line enables the company to avoid more in fixed costs than it loses in contribution margin, then it would be financially advantageous to eliminate the product line. On the other hand, if the company is not able to avoid as much in fixed costs as it loses in contribution margin, then the housewares line should be kept. Thus, the company's managers need to focus their attention on identifying the costs that differ between the two alternatives (i.e., that can be avoided by dropping the housewares product line). They should be asking themselves—"What costs can we avoid if we drop this product line?"—while purposely ignoring any costs that do not differ between the alternatives.

As we have seen from our earlier discussion, not all costs are avoidable. For example, some of the costs associated with a product line may be sunk costs. Other costs may be allocated fixed costs that will not differ in total regardless of whether the product line is dropped or retained.

EXHIBIT 12–2
Discount Drug Company
Product Lines

| | Total | Product Line | | |
		Drugs	Cosmetics	House-wares
Sales	$250,000	$125,000	$75,000	$50,000
Variable expenses..............	105,000	50,000	25,000	30,000
Contribution margin	145,000	75,000	50,000	20,000
Fixed expenses:				
Salaries	50,000	29,500	12,500	8,000
Advertising..................	15,000	1,000	7,500	6,500
Utilities	2,000	500	500	1,000
Depreciation—fixtures	5,000	1,000	2,000	2,000
Rent........................	20,000	10,000	6,000	4,000
Insurance	3,000	2,000	500	500
General administrative	30,000	15,000	9,000	6,000
Total fixed expenses............	125,000	59,000	38,000	28,000
Net operating income (loss)......	$ 20,000	$ 16,000	$12,000	$ (8,000)

To show how to proceed in a product-line analysis, suppose that Discount Drug Company has analyzed the fixed costs being charged to the three product lines and determined the following:

1. The salaries expense represents salaries paid to employees working directly on the product. All of the employees working in housewares would be discharged if the product line is dropped.
2. The advertising expense represents advertisements that are specific to each product line and are avoidable if the line is dropped.
3. The utilities expense represents utilities costs for the entire company. The amount charged to each product line is an allocation based on space occupied and is not avoidable if the product line is dropped.
4. The depreciation expense represents depreciation on previously purchased fixtures that are used to display the various product lines. Although the fixtures are nearly new, they are custom-built and will have no resale value if the housewares line is dropped.
5. The rent expense represents rent on the entire building housing the company; it is allocated to the product lines on the basis of sales dollars. The monthly rent of $20,000 is fixed under a long-term lease agreement.
6. The insurance expense is for insurance carried on inventories within each of the three product lines. If housewares is dropped, the related inventories will be liquidated and the insurance premiums will decrease proportionately.
7. The general administrative expense represents the costs of accounting, purchasing, and general management, which are allocated to the product lines on the basis of sales dollars. These costs will not change if the housewares line is dropped.

With this information, management can determine that $15,000 of the fixed expenses associated with the housewares product line are avoidable and $13,000 are not:

Fixed Expenses	Total Cost Assigned to Housewares	Not Avoidable*	Avoidable
Salaries	$ 8,000		$ 8,000
Advertising	6,500		6,500
Utilities	1,000	$ 1,000	
Depreciation—fixtures	2,000	2,000	
Rent	4,000	4,000	
Insurance	500		500
General administrative	6,000	6,000	
Total	$28,000	$13,000	$15,000

*These fixed costs represent either sunk costs or future costs that will not change whether the housewares line is retained or discontinued.

As stated earlier, if the housewares product line were dropped, the company would lose the product's contribution margin of $20,000, but would save its associated avoidable fixed expenses. We now know that those avoidable fixed expenses total $15,000. Therefore, the financial disadvantage of dropping the housewares product line is $(5,000) as shown below:

Contribution margin lost if the housewares product line is discontinued (see Exhibit 12–2)	$(20,000)
Fixed expenses that can be avoided if the housewares product line is discontinued (see above)	15,000
Financial disadvantage of dropping the housewares product line	$ (5,000)

In this case, the fixed costs that can be avoided by dropping the housewares product line ($15,000) are less than the contribution margin that will be lost ($20,000). Therefore, based on the data given, the housewares line should not be discontinued unless a more profitable use can be found for the floor and counter space that it is occupying.

EXHIBIT 12–3
A Comparative Format for Product-Line Analysis

	Keep Housewares	Drop Housewares	Difference: Net Operating Income Increase (or Decrease)
Sales	$50,000	$　0	$ (50,000)
Variable expenses	30,000	0	30,000
Contribution margin	20,000	0	(20,000)
Fixed expenses:			
Salaries	8,000	0	8,000
Advertising	6,500	0	6,500
Utilities	1,000	1,000	0
Depreciation—fixtures	2,000	2,000	0
Rent	4,000	4,000	0
Insurance	500	0	500
General administrative	6,000	6,000	0
Total fixed expenses	28,000	13,000	15,000
Net operating loss	$ (8,000)	$ (13,000)	$　(5,000)

A Comparative Format

This decision can also be approached by preparing comparative income statements showing the effects of either keeping or dropping the product line. Exhibit 12–3 contains such an analysis for the Discount Drug Company. As shown in the last column of the exhibit, if the housewares line is dropped, then overall company net operating income will decrease by $5,000 each period. This is the same answer, of course, as we obtained when we focused just on the lost contribution margin and avoidable fixed costs.

Beware of Allocated Fixed Costs

Go back to Exhibit 12–2. Does this exhibit suggest that the housewares product line should be kept—as we have just concluded? No, it does not. Exhibit 12–2 suggests that the housewares product line is losing money. Why keep a product line that is showing a loss? The explanation for this apparent inconsistency lies in part with the common fixed costs that are being allocated to the product lines. One of the great dangers in allocating common fixed costs is that such allocations can make a product line (or other business segment) look less profitable than it really is. In this instance, allocating the common fixed costs among all product lines makes the housewares product line appear to be unprofitable. However, as we have just shown, there is a $5,000 financial *disadvantage* associated with dropping the product line. This point can be seen clearly if we redo Exhibit 12–2 by eliminating the allocation of the common fixed costs. Exhibit 12–4 uses the segmented approach from Chapter 6 to estimate the profitability of the product lines.

Exhibit 12–4 gives us a much different perspective of the housewares line than does Exhibit 12–2. As shown in Exhibit 12–4, the housewares line is covering all of its own traceable fixed costs and generating a $3,000 segment margin toward covering the common fixed costs of the company. Unless another product line can be found that will generate a segment margin greater than $3,000, the company would be better off keeping the housewares line rather than dropping it.

Additionally, managers may choose to retain an unprofitable product line if it helps sell other products, or if it serves as a "magnet" to attract customers. Bread, for example, may not be an especially profitable line in some food stores, but customers expect it to be available, and many of them would undoubtedly shift their buying elsewhere if a particular store decided to stop carrying it.

EXHIBIT 12–4
Discount Drug Company Product Lines—Recast in Contribution Format (from Exhibit 12–2)

	Total	Drugs	Cosmetics	House-wares
			Product Line	
Sales	$250,000	$125,000	$75,000	$50,000
Variable expenses	105,000	50,000	25,000	30,000
Contribution margin	145,000	75,000	50,000	20,000
Traceable fixed expenses:				
Salaries	50,000	29,500	12,500	8,000
Advertising	15,000	1,000	7,500	6,500
Depreciation—fixtures	5,000	1,000	2,000	2,000
Insurance	3,000	2,000	500	500
Total traceable fixed expenses	73,000	33,500	22,500	17,000
Product-line segment margin	72,000	$ 41,500	$27,500	$ 3,000*
Common fixed expenses:				
Utilities	2,000			
Rent	20,000			
General administrative	30,000			
Total common fixed expenses	52,000			
Net operating income	$ 20,000			

*If the housewares line is dropped, the company will lose the $3,000 segment margin generated by this product line. In addition, we have seen that the $2,000 depreciation on the fixtures is a sunk cost that cannot be avoided. The sum of these two figures (= $3,000 + $2,000) equals the financial disadvantage of $5,000 associated with discontinuing the housewares product line. Of course, the company may later choose to drop the product if circumstances change—such as a pending decision to replace the fixtures.

DELPHI CLOSES 42 FACTORIES

More than a decade ago, **Delphi Automotive** earned revenues of $30 billion per year and employed 47,000 people. Now the company's U. S. work force has dropped to 5,000 employees as it has closed 42 of its 47 factories. The company has dropped low margin businesses, such as its heating and cooling segment, to focus its manufacturing efforts on auto safety, navigation systems, fuel economy, and self-driving technologies. It appears that Wall Street investors agree with Delphi's efforts to trim its product lines given that the company's stock price has more than tripled since it emerged from a four-year bankruptcy.

Source: Jeff Bennett, "Delphi Sale Signals New Era for Car Suppliers," *The Wall Street Journal*, February 19, 2015, pp. B1 and B8.

Make or Buy Decisions

LO12–3
Prepare a make or buy analysis.

Providing a product or service to a customer involves many steps. For example, consider all of the steps that are necessary to develop and sell a product such as a **Fitbit** fitness watch. First, engineers need to develop the underlying electronics that provide customers with capabilities such as real-time GPS tracking, heart rate monitoring, and activity monitoring. In addition, they need to design a wrist watch that not only houses the electronic circuitry, but that also meets the customers' needs in terms of aesthetics, durability, and functionality. Second, the watches need to be assembled, tested, individually packaged, and then boxed in larger quantities to enable shipping. Third, the finished goods need to be transported to retail sales locations and eventually sold to customers. Finally, the company needs to provide after-sale service such as Internet and phone-based help lines, warranty claims, and product returns. All of these activities, from development, to production, to after-sales service are called a *value chain*.

Separate companies may carry out each of the activities in the value chain or a single company may carry out several. When a company is involved in more than one activity in the entire value chain, it is **vertically integrated**. Some companies control all of the activities in the value chain from producing basic raw materials right up to the final distribution of finished goods and provision of after-sales service. Other companies are content to integrate on a smaller scale by purchasing many of the parts and materials that go into their finished products. A decision to carry out one of the activities in the value chain internally, rather than to buy externally from a supplier, is called a **make or buy decision**. Quite often these decisions involve whether to buy a particular part or to make it internally. Make or buy decisions also involve decisions concerning whether to outsource development tasks, after-sales service, or other activities.

Strategic Aspects of the Make or Buy Decision

Vertical integration provides certain advantages. An integrated company is less dependent on its suppliers and may be able to ensure a smoother flow of parts and materials for production than a nonintegrated company. For example, a strike against a major parts supplier can interrupt the operations of a nonintegrated company for many months, whereas an integrated company that is producing its own parts would be able to continue operations. Also, some companies feel that they can control quality better by producing their own parts and materials, rather than by relying on the quality control standards of outside suppliers. In addition, an integrated company realizes profits from the parts and materials that it is "making" rather than "buying," as well as profits from its regular operations.

The advantages of vertical integration are counterbalanced by the advantages of using external suppliers. By pooling demand from a number of companies, a supplier may be able to enjoy economies of scale. These economies of scale can result in higher quality and lower costs than would be possible if the company were to attempt to make the parts or provide the service on its own. A company must be careful, however, to retain control over activities that are essential to maintaining its competitive position. For example, **Hewlett-Packard** controls the software for laser printers that it makes in cooperation with **Canon Inc.** of Japan. The present trend appears to be toward less vertical integration, with companies like **Oracle** and Hewlett-Packard concentrating on hardware and software design and relying on outside suppliers for almost everything else in the value chain.

An Example of a Make or Buy Decision

To provide an illustration of a make or buy decision, consider Mountain Goat Cycles. The company is currently making the heavy-duty gear shifters that it installs on its most popular line of mountain bikes. The company's Accounting Department reports the following costs of making 8,000 shifters each year:

	Per Unit	8,000 Units
Direct materials	$ 6	$ 48,000
Direct labor	4	32,000
Variable overhead	1	8,000
Supervisor's salary	3	24,000
Depreciation of special equipment	2	16,000
Allocated general overhead	5	40,000
Total cost	$21	$168,000

An outside supplier has offered to sell 8,000 shifters a year to Mountain Goat Cycles for a price of only $19 each, or a total of $152,000 (= 8,000 shifters × $19 each). Should the company stop making the shifters internally and buy them from the outside supplier? As always, the decision should depend on the relevant costs—those that differ between the alternatives. And the costs that differ between the alternatives consist of the costs that could be avoided by buying the shifters from the outside supplier. If the costs that can be avoided by buying the shifters from the outside supplier total less than $152,000, then the company should continue to make its own shifters and reject the outside supplier's offer. On the other hand, if the costs that can be avoided by buying the shifters from the outside supplier total more than $152,000 the outside supplier's offer should be accepted.

ASHLEY FURNITURE MANAGES ITS OWN FLEET OF DELIVERY TRUCKS

Many manufacturers choose to outsource truck deliveries in the name of cost savings. However, **Ashley Furniture Industries** in Arcadia, Wisconsin, takes a different approach. It owns 800 delivery trucks and employs 3,000 people in warehousing and transportation based on the belief that delivering furniture from its warehouses to the retailers that sell its products improves customer relations and service. Ashley pays its drivers an average of $70,000 per year and it strives to provide them with predictable delivery schedules that enable them to be home more often. Ashley's vice-president of transportation, Larry Corey, says that he needs to review 100 applications to find one good truck driver. Keith Koenig, who owns furniture stores in southern Florida says that Ashley's delivery times and reliability are unbeatable.

© Imaginechina/ AP Images

Source: James R. Hagerty, "A Radical Idea: Own Your Supply Chain," *The Wall Street Journal,* April 30, 2015, pp. B1–B2.

Exhibit 12–5 contains the relevant cost analysis of the make or buy decision related to the gear shifters. The direct materials ($48,000), direct labor ($32,000), and variable overhead ($8,000) are all relevant costs because each cost could be avoided by purchasing the shifters from the outside supplier. In other words, Mountain Goat Cycles would no longer incur these variable manufacturing costs if it stopped making the shifters. In addition, we will assume that the supervisor of the gear shifter manufacturing process would not be retained if the company stops making the shifters; thus, the supervisory

	Total Relevant Costs—8,000 units	
	Make	Buy
Direct materials (8,000 units × $6 per unit)	$ 48,000	
Direct labor (8,000 units × $4 per unit).	32,000	
Variable overhead (8,000 units × $1 per unit).	8,000	
Supervisor's salary	24,000	
Depreciation of special equipment (not relevant)		
Allocated general overhead (not relevant)		
Outside purchase price		$152,000
Total cost.	$112,000	$152,000
Financial advantage of making the gear shifters.	$40,000	

EXHIBIT 12–5
Mountain Goat Cycles Make or Buy Analysis

salary of $24,000 would be avoided if the company decides to buy the gear shifters from an outside supplier. [4]

The depreciation of special equipment of $16,000 (as shown in the original data) is an irrelevant cost because the equipment has already been purchased; thus, the cost incurred to buy the equipment is a sunk cost. The depreciation charge of $16,000 simply spreads this sunk cost over the equipment's useful life. If the equipment could be sold, its salvage value would be relevant. Or if the equipment could be used to make other products, this could be relevant as well. However, we will assume that the equipment has no salvage value and that it has no other use except making the heavy-duty gear shifters.

The allocated general overhead of $40,000 (as shown in the original data) is also an irrelevant cost in this decision context. We draw this conclusion because we are assuming that these allocated costs are common to all items produced in the factory and would continue unchanged even if the shifters were bought from an outside supplier. Throughout this chapter, you should assume that these types of allocated common costs are irrelevant to the decision unless you are explicitly told otherwise. If you are explicitly told that a portion of allocated common costs can be avoided by choosing one alternative over another, then by all means, treat the explicitly identified avoidable costs as relevant costs. Otherwise, err on the side of ignoring allocated common costs when choosing between alternatives.

Because the avoidable costs related to making the shifters is $40,000 less than the total amount that would be paid to buy them from the outside supplier, Mountain Goat Cycles should reject the outside supplier's offer. However, the company may wish to consider one additional factor before coming to a final decision—the opportunity cost of the space that it currently uses to produce the shifters.

Opportunity Cost

If the space now being used to produce the shifters *would otherwise be idle,* then Mountain Goat Cycles should continue to make its own shifters and the supplier's offer should be rejected, as stated above. Idle space that has no alternative use has an opportunity cost of zero.

But what if the space now being used to make shifters could be used for some other purpose? In that case, the space would have an opportunity cost equal to the segment margin that could be derived from the best alternative use of the space.

To illustrate, assume that the space now being used to make shifters could be used to produce a new cross-country bike that would generate a segment margin of $60,000 per year. Under these conditions, Mountain Goat Cycles would be $20,000 better off by choosing to buy the shifters from the outside supplier (rather than making them) and using the newly available space to produce the cross-country bike:

	Make	Buy
Total annual cost (see Exhibit 12–5)	$112,000	$152,000
Opportunity cost—segment margin forgone on a potential new product line	60,000	
Total cost.	$172,000	$152,000
Financial advantage of buying the gear shifters from the outside supplier		$20,000

---

[4] Many companies adhere to a "no layoffs" policy because they believe it improves employee morale, organizational learning, customer satisfaction, and financial results. Furthermore, in some countries, such as France, Germany, and Japan, labor regulations and cultural norms may limit management's ability to reduce the size of the labor force. In these contexts, it would be incorrect to assume that direct labor and supervision are automatically avoidable costs in make or buy decisions. Nonetheless, for the sake of consistency, within this chapter you should assume that direct labor and supervisory salaries are avoidable costs when analyzing make or buy decisions unless you are explicitly told otherwise.

Opportunity costs are not recorded in the organization's general ledger because they do not represent actual dollar outlays. Rather, they represent economic benefits that are *forgone* as a result of pursuing some course of action. The opportunity cost for Mountain Goat Cycles is sufficiently large in this case to change the decision.

IS THERE SUCH A THING AS A $1 BUS TICKET?

When **Megabus** and **Greyhound's Bolt Bus** sell tickets for $1 it begs the question—how can that be profitable? The answer lies in understanding the concept of opportunity costs. The bus companies use computer algorithms to determine how many empty seats ordinarily exist on a given bus route. Since the incremental cost of allowing a customer to occupy a seat that would otherwise be empty is zero, the $1 price provides bus companies with additional contribution margin. Of course, only a few $1 tickets are available for each trip on a given bus route. Furthermore, these deeply discounted tickets must be purchased well in advance of the travel date. All other customers pay a higher fare that enables the bus company to earn a profit on its routes.

© Kelly Sillaste/Getty Images RF

Source: Anne VanderMey, "What's Up With $1 Bus Tickets?" *Fortune,* November 7, 2011, p. 27.

Special Order Decisions

Managers must often evaluate whether a *special order* should be accepted, and if the order is accepted, the price that should be charged. A **special order** is a one-time order that is not considered part of the company's normal ongoing business. To illustrate, Mountain Goat Cycles has just received a request from the Seattle Police Department to produce 100 specially modified mountain bikes at a price of $558 each. The bikes would be used to patrol some of the more densely populated residential sections of the city. Mountain Goat Cycles can easily modify its City Cruiser model to fit the specifications of the Seattle Police. The normal selling price of the City Cruiser bike is $698, and its unit product cost is $564 as shown below:

LO12–4
Prepare an analysis showing whether a special order should be accepted.

Direct materials	$372
Direct labor.	90
Manufacturing overhead	102
Unit product cost.	$564

The variable portion of the above manufacturing overhead is $12 per unit. The order would have no effect on the company's total fixed manufacturing overhead costs.

The modifications requested by the Seattle Police Department consist of welded brackets to hold radios, nightsticks, and other gear. These modifications would require $34 in incremental variable costs. In addition, the company would have to pay a graphics design studio $2,400 to design and cut stencils that would be used for spray painting the Seattle Police Department's logo and other identifying marks on the bikes. The company's managers believe that this order will have no effect on the company's other sales and it can be produced without disrupting any of the company's regular scheduled production.

To quantify the financial advantage (disadvantage) of accepting the Seattle Police Department's order, Mountain Goat Cycles should focus its attention on the incremental costs and benefits associated with the order. Because the existing fixed manufacturing overhead costs would not be affected by the order, they are not relevant. The financial advantage (disadvantage) of the special order would be computed as follows:

	Per Unit	Total 100 Bikes
Incremental revenue (a)	$558	$55,800
Less incremental costs:		
Variable costs:		
Direct materials...........................	372	37,200
Direct labor...............................	90	9,000
Variable manufacturing overhead	12	1,200
Special modifications	34	3,400
Total variable cost.........................	$508	50,800
Fixed cost:		
Purchase of stencils		2,400
Total incremental cost (b)		53,200
Financial advantage of accepting the order (a) − (b)...		$ 2,600

Therefore, even though the $558 price on the special order is below the normal $564 unit product cost and the order would require additional costs, the company is still better off accepting the order. In general, a special order should be accepted if the incremental revenue from the special order exceeds the incremental costs of the order. However, it is important to make sure that there is indeed idle capacity and that the special order does not cut into normal unit sales or undercut prices on normal sales. For example, if the company was operating at capacity, opportunity costs would have to be taken into account, as well as the incremental costs that have already been detailed above.

Volume Trade-Off Decisions

Companies are forced to make *volume trade-off decisions* when they do not have enough capacity to produce all of the products and sales volumes demanded by their customers. In these situations, companies must trade off, or sacrifice production of some products in favor of others in an effort to maximize profits. The key questions become: how should companies manage those trade-offs? Which products should they produce and sell and which sales opportunities should they intentionally bypass?

To answer these questions, our discussion of volume trade-off decisions will proceed in three steps. First, we'll define the meaning of a constraint. Second, we'll explain how to determine the most profitable use of a constrained resource. Third, we'll discuss how to determine the value of obtaining more of a constrained resource and how to manage constraints to increase profits.

What Is a Constraint?

A **constraint** is anything that prevents you from getting more of what you want. Every individual and every organization faces at least one constraint, so it is not difficult to find examples of constraints.[5] You may not have enough time to study thoroughly for every subject *and* to go out with your friends on the weekend, so time is your constraint. **United Airlines** has only a limited number of loading gates available at its busy Chicago O'Hare hub, so its constraint is loading gates. **Vail Resorts** has only a limited amount of land to develop as homesites and commercial lots at its ski areas, so its constraint is land.

---

[5] In this chapter, we always assume that the company has only one constraint. When companies have more than one constraint, the optimal production mix can be found using a quantitative method known as linear programming, which is covered in more advanced courses.

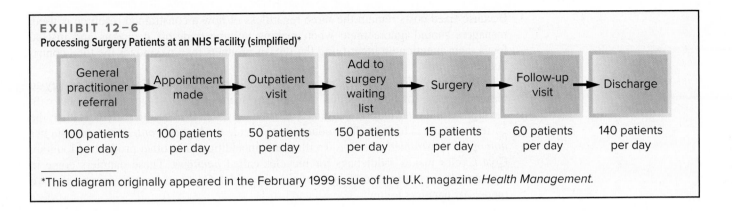

EXHIBIT 12–6
Processing Surgery Patients at an NHS Facility (simplified)*

General practitioner referral	Appointment made	Outpatient visit	Add to surgery waiting list	Surgery	Follow-up visit	Discharge
100 patients per day	100 patients per day	50 patients per day	150 patients per day	15 patients per day	60 patients per day	140 patients per day

*This diagram originally appeared in the February 1999 issue of the U.K. magazine *Health Management.*

As an example, long waiting periods for surgery are a chronic problem in the **National Health Service (NHS)**, the government-funded provider of health care in the United Kingdom. The diagram in Exhibit 12–6 illustrates a simplified version of the steps followed by a surgery patient. The number of patients who can be processed through each step in a day is indicated in the exhibit. For example, appointments for outpatient visits can be made for as many as 100 referrals from general practitioners in a day.

The constraint, or **bottleneck**, in the system is determined by the step that limits total output because it has the smallest capacity—in this case surgery. The total number of patients processed through the entire system cannot exceed 15 per day—the maximum number of patients who can be treated in surgery. No matter how hard managers, doctors, and nurses try to improve the processing rate elsewhere in the system, they will never succeed in driving down wait lists until the capacity of surgery is increased. In fact, improvements elsewhere in the system—particularly before the constraint—are likely to result in even longer waiting times and more frustrated patients and health care providers. Thus, to be effective, improvement efforts must be focused on the constraint. A business process, such as the process for serving surgery patients, is like a chain. If you want to increase the strength of a chain, what is the most effective way to do this? Should you concentrate your efforts on strengthening the strongest link, all the links, or the weakest link? Clearly, focusing your effort on the weakest link will bring the biggest benefit.

The procedure to follow to strengthen the chain is clear. First, identify the weakest link, which is the constraint. In the case of the NHS, the constraint is surgery. Second, do not place a greater strain on the system than the weakest link can handle—if you do, the chain will break. In the case of the NHS, more referrals than surgery can accommodate lead to unacceptably long waiting lists. Third, concentrate improvement efforts on strengthening the weakest link. In the case of the NHS, this means finding ways to increase the number of surgeries that can be performed in a day. Fourth, if the improvement efforts are successful, eventually the weakest link will improve to the point where it is no longer the weakest link. At that point, the new weakest link (i.e., the new constraint) must be identified, and improvement efforts must be shifted over to that link. This simple sequential process provides a powerful strategy for optimizing business processes.

Utilizing a Constrained Resource to Maximize Profits

Managers routinely face the challenge of managing constrained resources in a manner that maximizes profits. A department store, for example, has a limited amount of floor space and therefore cannot stock every product that may be available. A manufacturer has a limited number of machine-hours and a limited number of direct labor-hours at its disposal. When companies face these types of constraints their managers must decide which products or services make the most profitable use of those limited resources.

LO12–5
Determine the most profitable use of a constrained resource.

Because fixed costs remain the same regardless of how a constrained resource is used, managers should ignore them when making volume trade-off decisions and instead focus their attention on identifying the mix of products that maximizes the total contribution margin.

Given that some products must be cut back when a constraint exists, the key to maximizing the total contribution margin may seem obvious—favor the products with the highest unit contribution margins. Unfortunately, that is not quite correct. Rather, the correct solution is to favor the products that provide the highest *contribution margin per unit of the constrained resource*. To illustrate, in addition to its other products, Mountain Goat Cycles makes saddlebags for bicycles called *panniers*. These panniers come in two models—a touring model and a mountain model. Cost and revenue data for the two models of panniers follow:

	Mountain Pannier	Touring Pannier
Selling price per unit.....................	$25	$30
Variable cost per unit	10	18
Contribution margin per unit.............	$15	$12
Contribution margin (CM) ratio	60%	40%

The mountain pannier appears to be much more profitable than the touring pannier. It has a $15 per unit contribution margin as compared to only $12 per unit for the touring model, and it has a 60% CM ratio as compared to only 40% for the touring model.

But now let us add one more piece of information—the plant that makes the panniers is operating at capacity. This does not mean that every machine and every person in the plant is working at the maximum possible rate. Because machines have different capacities, some machines will be operating at less than 100% of capacity. However, if the plant as a whole cannot produce any more units, some machine or process must be operating at capacity. The machine or process that is limiting overall output is called the bottleneck—it is the constraint.

At Mountain Goat Cycles, the bottleneck (i.e., constraint) is a stitching machine. The mountain pannier requires two minutes of stitching time per unit, and the touring pannier requires one minute of stitching time per unit. The stitching machine is available for 12,000 minutes per month, and the company can sell up to 4,000 mountain panniers and 7,000 touring panniers per month. Producing up to this demand for both products would require 15,000 minutes, as shown below:

	Mountain Pannier	Touring Pannier	Total
Monthly demand (a)	4,000 units	7,000 units	
Stitching machine time required to produce one unit (b)........	2 minutes	1 minute	
Total stitching time required (a) × (b)	8,000 minutes	7,000 minutes	15,000 minutes

Producing up to demand would require 15,000 minutes, but only 12,000 minutes are available. This simply confirms that the stitching machine is the bottleneck. By definition, because the stitching machine is a bottleneck, the stitching machine does not have enough capacity to satisfy the existing demand for mountain panniers and touring panniers Therefore, some orders for the products will have to be turned down. Naturally, managers will want to know which product is less profitable. To answer this question, they should focus on the contribution margin per unit of the constrained resource.

This figure is computed by dividing a product's contribution margin per unit by the amount of the constrained resource required to make a unit of that product. These calculations are carried out below for the mountain and touring panniers:

	Mountain Pannier	Touring Pannier
Contribution margin per unit (a)	$15.00	$12.00
Stitching machine time required to produce one unit (b)	2 minutes	1 minute
Contribution margin per unit of the constrained resource, (a) ÷ (b)	$7.50 per minute	$12.00 per minute

It is now easy to decide which product is less profitable and should be deemphasized. Each minute on the stitching machine that is devoted to the touring pannier results in an increase of $12.00 in contribution margin and profits. The comparable figure for the mountain pannier is only $7.50 per minute. Therefore, the touring model should be emphasized. Even though the mountain model has the larger contribution margin per unit and the larger CM ratio, the touring model provides the larger contribution margin in relation to the constrained resource.

To verify that the touring model is indeed the more profitable product, suppose an hour of additional stitching time is available and that unfilled orders exist for both products. The additional hour on the stitching machine could be used to make either 30 mountain panniers (60 minutes ÷ 2 minutes per mountain pannier) or 60 touring panniers (60 minutes ÷ 1 minute per touring pannier), with the following profit implications:

	Mountain Pannier	Touring Pannier
Contribution margin per unit (a)	$ 15	$ 12
Additional units that can be processed in one hour (b)	30	60
Additional contribution margin (a) × (b)	$450	$720

Because the additional contribution margin would be $720 for the touring panniers and only $450 for the mountain panniers, the touring panniers make the most profitable use of the company's constrained resource—the stitching machine.

The stitching machine is available for 12,000 minutes per month, and producing the touring panniers is the most profitable use of the stitching machine. Therefore, to maximize profits, the company should produce all of the touring panniers the market will demand (7,000 units) and use any remaining capacity to produce mountain panniers. The computations to determine how many mountain panniers can be produced are as follows:

Monthly demand for touring panniers (a)	7,000 units
Stitching machine time required to produce one touring pannier (b).	1 minute
Total stitching time required to produce touring panniers (a) × (b)	7,000 minutes
Remaining stitching time available (12,000 minutes − 7,000 minutes) (c).	5,000 minutes
Stitching machine time required to produce one mountain pannier (d).	2 minutes
Production of mountain panniers (c) ÷ (d)	2,500 units

Therefore, profit would be maximized by producing 7,000 touring panniers and then using the remaining capacity to produce 2,500 mountain panniers. With this product mix the company can earn a total contribution margin of $121,500 computed as follows:

	Mountain Pannier	Touring Pannier	Total
Contribution margin per unit (a)	$15	$12	
Number of units produced (b)	2,500	7,000	
Contribution margin (a) × (b)	$37,500	$84,000	$121,500

This example clearly shows that looking at each product's unit contribution margin alone is not enough; the contribution margin must be viewed in relation to the amount of the constrained resource each product requires.

IN BUSINESS

SUBARU RESPONDS TO A PRODUCTION CONSTRAINT

When demand for **Subaru**'s vehicles jumped unexpectedly the automaker missed many sales opportunities because of insufficient production capacity. The company responded by expanding its Japanese production capacity by 15% and investing $400 million to increase the output of its U.S. plant in Lafayette, Indiana, by 76%. Subaru is contemplating building a new plant that could produce 200,000 more vehicles; however, because this volume represents more than 25% of Subaru's global output, it presents some risks. If sales take a downturn, Subaru could be left with a large amount of unused capacity costs.

Source: Yoshio Takahashi and Yoree Koh, "Subaru's Got a Big Problem: It's Selling Too Many Cars," *The Wall Street Journal*, August 21, 2013, pp. B1 and B2.

© Kristoffer Tripplaar/Alamy

Managing Constraints

LO12–6

Determine the value of obtaining more of the constrained resource.

Effectively managing an organization's constraints is a key to increasing profits. As discussed above, when a constraint exists in the production process, managers can increase profits by producing the products with the highest contribution margin per unit of the constrained resource. However, they can also increase profits by increasing the capacity of the bottleneck operation.

When a manager increases the capacity of the bottleneck, it is called **relaxing (or elevating) the constraint**. In the case of Mountain Goat Cycles, the company is currently working one eight-hour shift. To relax the constraint, the stitching machine operator could be asked to work overtime. No one else would have to work overtime. Because all of the other operations involved in producing panniers have excess capacity, up to a point, the additional panniers processed through the stitching machine during overtime could be finished during normal working hours in the other operations.

The benefits from relaxing the constraint are often enormous and can be easily quantified—the key is the contribution margin per unit of the constrained resource that we have already computed. This number, which was originally stated in terms of minutes in the Mountain Goat Cycles example, is restated below in terms of hours for easier interpretation:

	Mountain Pannier	Touring Pannier
Contribution margin per minute of the constrained resource (a)	$7.50 per minute	$12.00 per minute
Minutes per hour (b)	60 minutes	60 minutes
Contribution margin per hour of the constrained resource (a) × (b)	$450 per hour	$720 per hour

So what is the value of relaxing the constraint—the time on the stitching machine? The manager should first ask, "What would I do with additional capacity at the bottleneck if it were available?" If the time were to be used to make additional mountain panniers, it would be worth $450 per hour. If the time were to be used to make additional touring panniers, it would be worth $720 per hour. In this latter case, the company should be willing to pay an overtime *premium* to the stitching machine operator of up to $720 per hour! Suppose, for example, that the stitching machine operator is paid $20 per hour during normal working hours and time-and-a-half, or $30 per hour, for overtime. In this case, the premium for overtime is only $10 per hour, whereas in principle, the company should be willing to pay a premium of up to $720 per hour. The difference between what the company should be willing to pay as a premium, $720 per hour, and what it would actually have to pay, $10 per hour, is pure profit of $710 per hour.

To reinforce this concept, suppose that there are only unfilled orders for the mountain pannier. How much would it be worth to the company to run the stitching machine overtime in this situation? Because the additional capacity would be used to make the mountain pannier, the value of that additional capacity would drop to $7.50 per minute or $450 per hour. Nevertheless, the value of relaxing the constraint would still be quite high and the company should be willing to pay an overtime premium of up to $450 per hour.

These calculations indicate that managers should pay great attention to the bottleneck operation. If a bottleneck machine breaks down or is ineffectively utilized, the losses to the company can be quite large. In our example, for every minute the stitching machine is down due to breakdowns or setups, the company loses between $7.50 and $12.00.[6] The losses on an hourly basis are between $450 and $720! In contrast, there is no such loss of contribution margin if time is lost on a machine that is not a bottleneck—such machines have excess capacity anyway.

The implications are clear. Managers should focus much of their attention on managing the bottleneck. As we have discussed, managers should emphasize products that make the most profitable use of the constrained resource. They should also make sure that products are processed smoothly through the bottleneck, with minimal lost time due to breakdowns and setups. And they should try to find ways to increase the capacity at the bottleneck.

The capacity of a bottleneck can be effectively increased in a number of ways, including:

- Working overtime on the bottleneck.
- Subcontracting some of the processing that would ordinarily be done at the bottleneck.
- Investing in additional machines at the bottleneck.
- Shifting workers from processes that are not bottlenecks to the process that is the bottleneck.
- Focusing business process improvement efforts on the bottleneck.
- Reducing defective units. Each defective unit that is processed through the bottleneck and subsequently scrapped takes the place of a good unit that could have been sold.

The last three methods of increasing the capacity of the bottleneck are particularly attractive because they are essentially free and may even yield additional cost savings.

Joint Product Costs and Sell or Process Further Decisions

In some industries, two or more products, known as **joint products**, are produced from a single raw material input. For example, in the petroleum refining industry a large number of joint products are extracted from crude oil, including gasoline, jet fuel, home heating

LO12–7
Prepare an analysis showing whether joint products should be sold at the split-off point or processed further.

---

[6] Setups are required when production switches from one product to another. For example, consider a company that makes automobile side panels. The panels are painted before shipping them to an automobile manufacturer for final assembly. The customer might require 100 blue panels, 50 black panels, and 20 yellow panels. Each time the color is changed, the painting equipment must be purged of the old paint color, cleaned with solvents, and refilled with the new paint color. This takes time. In fact, some equipment may require such lengthy and frequent setups that it is unavailable for actual production more often than not.

oil, lubricants, asphalt, and various organic chemicals. The point in a manufacturing process where joint products (such as gasoline and jet fuel) can be recognized as separate products is referred to as the **split-off point**.

Quite often joint products can be sold at the split-off point or they can be processed further and sold for a higher price. A decision as to whether a joint product should be sold at the split-off point or processed further is known as a **sell or process further decision**. To make these decisions, managers need to follow a three step process. First, they should always ignore all **joint costs**, which include all costs incurred up to the split-off point. These costs should be ignored because they remain the same under both alternatives—whether the manager chooses to sell a joint product at the split-off point or process it further.

The second step is to determine the incremental revenue that is earned by further processing the joint product. This computation is performed by taking the revenue earned after further processing the joint product and subtracting the revenue that could be earned by selling the joint product at the split-off point.

The third step is to take the incremental revenue from step two and subtract the incremental costs associated with processing the joint product beyond the split-off point. If the resulting answer is positive, then the joint product should be processed further and sold for a higher price. If the answer is negative, then the joint product should be sold at the split-off point without any further processing.

Santa Maria Wool Cooperative: An Example

Santa Maria Wool Cooperative buys raw wool from local sheepherders, separates the wool into three grades—coarse, fine, and superfine—and then dyes the wool using traditional methods that rely on pigments from local materials. Exhibit 12–7 contains a diagram of the company's production process.

The company's joint costs include $200,000 for the raw wool and $40,000 for separating the raw wool into three intermediate products. The three types of undyed wool are called intermediate products because they are not finished at this point. Nevertheless, a market does exist for undyed wool—although at a significantly lower price than finished, dyed wool. More specifically and as shown in Exhibit 12–7, the undyed course wool, undyed fine wool, and undyed superfine wool each can be sold at the split-off point for $120,000, $150,000, and $60,000 respectively.

Exhibit 12–7 also shows that the cost of further processing the undyed coarse wool, undyed fine wool, and undyed superfine wool is $50,000, $60,000, and $10,000 respectively. Furthermore, the sales values of dyed coarse wool, dyed fine wool, and dyed superfine wool are $160,000, $240,000, and $90,000, respectively.

If Santa Maria Wool Cooperative chooses to further process all three of its intermediate products, it will earn a profit of $130,000 as shown below:

Analysis of the profitability of the overall operation:		
Combined final sales value ($160,000 + $240,000 + $90,000)		$490,000
Less costs of producing the end products:		
Cost of wool	$200,000	
Cost of separating wool	40,000	
Combined costs of dyeing ($50,000 + $60,000 + $10,000)	120,000	360,000
Profit		$130,000

Note that the joint costs of buying the wool ($200,000) and separating the wool ($40,000) are relevant when considering the profitability of the entire operation. This is because these joint costs could be avoided if the entire operation were shut down.

While Santa Maria can make a profit of $130,000 if it further processes all three products, the questions we want to explore further are: should the company further process all three products? Could the company be financially better off by selling one or more of the three products at the split-off point?

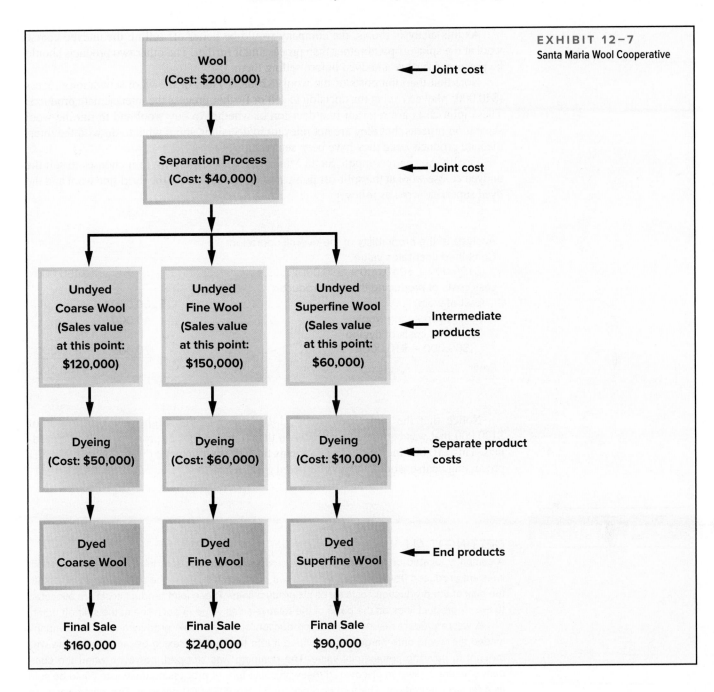

EXHIBIT 12–7
Santa Maria Wool Cooperative

The appropriate way to answer these sell-or-process-further questions is to compare the incremental revenues and incremental costs for each of the joint products as follows:

Analysis of sell or process further:	Coarse Wool	Fine Wool	Superfine Wool
Final sales value after further processing........	$160,000	$240,000	$90,000
Less sales value at the split-off point............	120,000	150,000	60,000
Incremental revenue from further processing	40,000	90,000	30,000
Less cost of further processing (dyeing).........	50,000	60,000	10,000
Financial advantage (disadvantage) of further processing	$ (10,000)	$ 30,000	$20,000

As this analysis shows, the company would be better off selling the undyed coarse wool at the split-off point rather than processing it further. The other two products should be processed further and dyed before selling them.

Note that the joint costs of the wool ($200,000) and of the wool separation process ($40,000) play no role in the decision to sell or further process the intermediate products. These joint costs are relevant in a decision of whether to buy wool and to run the wool separation process, but they are not relevant in decisions about what to do with the intermediate products once they have been separated.

Finally, we can recompute Santa Maria's overall profitability if it chooses to sell the undyed coarse wool at the split-off point and to further process the dyed fine wool and the dyed superfine wool as follows:

Analysis of the profitability of the overall operation:		
Combined final sales value		
($120,000 + $240,000 + $90,000)		$450,000
Less costs of producing the end products:		
Cost of wool	$200,000	
Cost of separating wool	40,000	
Combined costs of dyeing		
($60,000 + $10,000)	70,000	310,000
Profit		$140,000

Notice that the revised profit of $140,000 is $10,000 higher than the profit of $130,000 that was computed earlier when the company further processes all three products. This $10,000 increase in profit equals the $10,000 financial disadvantage of further processing coarse wool that was computed earlier.

IN BUSINESS

GETTING IT ALL WRONG

A company located on the Gulf of Mexico produces soap products. Its six main soap product lines are produced from common inputs. Joint product costs up to the split-off point constitute the bulk of the production costs for all six product lines. These joint product costs are allocated to the six product lines on the basis of the relative sales value of each line at the split-off point.

A waste product results from the production of the six main product lines. The company loaded the waste onto barges and dumped it into the Gulf of Mexico because the waste was thought to have no commercial value. The dumping was stopped, however, when the company's research division discovered that with some further processing the waste could be sold as a fertilizer ingredient. The further processing costs $175,000 per year. The waste was then sold to fertilizer manufacturers for $300,000.

The accountants responsible for allocating manufacturing costs included the sales value of the waste product along with the sales value of the six main product lines in their allocation of the joint product costs at the split-off point. This allocation resulted in the waste product being allocated $150,000 in joint product cost. This $150,000 allocation, when added to the further processing costs of $175,000 for the waste, made it appear that the waste product was unprofitable—as shown in the table below. When presented with this analysis, the company's management decided that further processing of the waste should be stopped. The company went back to dumping the waste in the Gulf.

Sales value of the waste product after further processing	$300,000
Less costs assigned to the waste product	325,000
Net loss	$ (25,000)

Activity-Based Costing and Relevant Costs

As discussed in an earlier chapter, activity-based costing can be used to help identify potentially relevant costs for decision-making purposes. Activity-based costing improves the traceability of costs by focusing on the activities caused by a product or other segment. However, managers should exercise caution against reading more into this "traceability" than really exists. People have a tendency to assume that if a cost is traceable to a segment, then the cost is automatically an avoidable cost. That is not true because the costs provided by a well-designed activity-based costing system are only *potentially* relevant. Before making a decision, managers must still decide which of the potentially relevant costs are actually avoidable. Only those costs that are avoidable are relevant and the others should be ignored.

To illustrate, refer again to the data relating to the housewares line in Exhibit 12–4. The $2,000 fixtures depreciation is a traceable cost of the housewares lines because it directly relates to activities in that department. We found, however, that the $2,000 is not avoidable if the housewares line is dropped. The key lesson here is that the method used to assign a cost to a product or other segment does not change the basic nature of the cost. A sunk cost such as depreciation of old equipment is still a sunk cost regardless of whether it is traced directly to a particular segment on an activity basis, allocated to all segments on the basis of labor-hours, or treated in some other way in the costing process. Regardless of the method used to assign costs to products or other segments, the principles discussed in this chapter must be applied to determine the costs that are avoidable in each situation.

Summary

Everything in this chapter consists of applications of one simple but powerful idea—only those costs and benefits that differ between alternatives are relevant in a decision. All other costs and benefits are irrelevant and should be ignored. In particular, sunk costs are irrelevant as are future costs that do not differ between alternatives.

This simple idea was applied in a variety of situations including decisions that involve adding or dropping a product line, making or buying a component, accepting or rejecting a special order, using a constrained resource, and further processing joint products. This list includes only a small sample of the possible applications of the differential cost concept. Indeed, any decision involving costs hinges on the proper identification and analysis of the differential costs. We will continue to focus on the concept of differential costs in the following chapter where long-term investment decisions are considered.

Review Problem: Differential Analysis

Charter Sports Equipment manufactures round, rectangular, and octagonal trampolines. Sales and expense data for the past month follow:

	Total	Trampoline		
		Round	Rectangular	Octagonal
Sales	$1,000,000	$140,000	$500,000	$360,000
Variable expenses....................	410,000	60,000	200,000	150,000
Contribution margin	590,000	80,000	300,000	210,000
Fixed expenses:				
Advertising—traceable..............	216,000	41,000	110,000	65,000
Depreciation of special equipment ...	95,000	20,000	40,000	35,000
Line supervisors' salaries............	19,000	6,000	7,000	6,000
General factory overhead*...........	200,000	28,000	100,000	72,000
Total fixed expenses.................	530,000	95,000	257,000	178,000
Net operating income (loss)...........	$ 60,000	$ (15,000)	$ 43,000	$ 32,000

*A common fixed cost that is allocated on the basis of sales dollars.

Management is concerned about the continued losses shown by the round trampolines and wants a recommendation as to whether or not the line should be discontinued. The special equipment used to produce the trampolines has no resale value. If the round trampoline model is dropped, the two line supervisors assigned to the model would be discharged.

Required:

1. What is the financial advantage (disadvantage) of discontinuing the round trampolines? The company has no other use for the capacity now being used to produce the round trampolines. Show computations to support your answer.
2. Recast the above data in a format that would be more useful to management in assessing the profitability of the various product lines.

Solution to Review Problem

1. No, production and sale of the round trampolines should not be discontinued. Computations to support this answer follow:

Contribution margin lost if the round trampolines are discontinued		$(80,000)
Less fixed expenses that can be avoided:		
Advertising—traceable..........	$41,000	
Line supervisors' salaries..........	6,000	47,000
Financial (disadvantage) of discontinuing the round trampolines.........		$(33,000)

The depreciation of the special equipment is a sunk cost, and therefore, it is not relevant to the decision. The general factory overhead is allocated and will presumably continue regardless of whether or not the round trampolines are discontinued; thus, it is not relevant.

2. If management wants a clearer picture of the profitability of the segments, the general factory overhead should not be allocated. It is a common cost and, therefore, should be deducted from the total product-line segment margin. A more useful income statement format would be as follows:

		Trampoline		
	Total	Round	Rectangular	Octagonal
Sales	$1,000,000	$140,000	$500,000	$360,000
Variable expenses..........	410,000	60,000	200,000	150,000
Contribution margin	590,000	80,000	300,000	210,000
Traceable fixed expenses:				
Advertising—traceable..........	216,000	41,000	110,000	65,000
Depreciation of special equipment ...	95,000	20,000	40,000	35,000
Line supervisors salaries	19,000	6,000	7,000	6,000
Total traceable fixed expenses..........	330,000	67,000	157,000	106,000
Product-line segment margin	260,000	$ 13,000	$143,000	$104,000
Common fixed expenses..........	200,000			
Net operating income..........	$ 60,000			

Glossary

Avoidable cost A cost that can be eliminated by choosing one alternative over another in a decision. This term is synonymous with *differential cost* and *relevant cost.* (p. 561)

Bottleneck A machine or some other part of a process that limits the total output of the entire system. (p. 577)

Constraint A limitation under which a company must operate, such as limited available machine time or raw materials, that restricts the company's ability to satisfy demand. (p. 576)

Differential cost A future cost that differs between any two alternatives. (p. 561)

Differential revenue Future revenue that differs between any two alternatives. (p. 561)

Incremental cost An increase in cost between two alternatives. (p. 561)

Joint costs Costs that are incurred up to the split-off point in a process that produces joint products. (p. 582)

Joint products Two or more products that are produced from a common input. (p. 581)

Make or buy decision A decision concerning whether an item should be produced internally or purchased from an outside supplier. (p. 572)

Opportunity cost The potential benefit that is given up when one alternative is selected over another. (p. 562)

Relaxing (or elevating) the constraint An action that increases the amount of a constrained resource. Equivalently, an action that increases the capacity of the bottleneck. (p. 580)

Relevant benefit A benefit that should be considered when making decisions. (p. 561)

Relevant cost A cost that should be considered when making decisions. (p. 561)

Sell or process further decision A decision as to whether a joint product should be sold at the split-off point or sold after further processing. (p. 582)

Special order A one-time order that is not considered part of the company's normal ongoing business. (p. 575)

Split-off point That point in the manufacturing process where some or all of the joint products can be recognized as individual products. (p. 582)

Sunk cost A cost that has already been incurred and that cannot be changed by any decision made now or in the future. (p. 562)

Vertical integration The involvement by a company in more than one of the activities in the entire value chain from development through production, distribution, sales, and after-sales service. (p. 572)

Questions

12–1 What is a *relevant cost?*

12–2 Define the following terms: *incremental cost, opportunity cost,* and *sunk cost.*

12–3 Are variable costs always relevant costs? Explain.

12–4 "Sunk costs are easy to spot—they're the fixed costs associated with a decision." Do you agree? Explain.

12–5 "Variable costs and differential costs mean the same thing." Do you agree? Explain.

12–6 "All future costs are relevant in decision making." Do you agree? Why?

12–7 Prentice Company is considering dropping one of its product lines. What costs of the product line would be relevant to this decision? What costs would be irrelevant?

12–8 "If a product is generating a loss, then it should be discontinued." Do you agree? Explain.

12–9 What is the danger in allocating common fixed costs among products or other segments of an organization?

12–10 How does opportunity cost enter into a make or buy decision?

12–11 Give at least four examples of possible constraints.

12–12 How will relating product contribution margins to the amount of the constrained resource they consume help a company maximize its profits?

12–13 Define the following terms: *joint products, joint costs,* and *split-off point.*

12–14 From a decision-making point of view, should joint costs be allocated among joint products?

12–15 What guideline should be used in determining whether a joint product should be sold at the split-off point or processed further?

12–16 Airlines sometimes offer reduced rates during certain times of the week to members of a businessperson's family if they accompany him or her on trips. How does the concept of relevant costs enter into the decision by the airline to offer reduced rates of this type?

 Applying Excel

The Excel worksheet form that appears below is to be used to recreate the example in the text related to Santa Maria Wool Cooperative. Download the workbook containing this form from Connect, where you will also receive instructions about how to use this worksheet form.

LO12–7

	A	B	C	D	E
1	Chapter 12: Applying Excel				
2					
3	Data				
4	Exhibit 12-7 Santa Maria Wool Cooperative				
5	Cost of wool	$200,000			
6	Cost of separation process	$40,000			
7	Sales value of intermediate products at split-off point:				
8	Undyed coarse wool	$120,000			
9	Undyed fine wool	$150,000			
10	Undyed superfine wool	$60,000			
11	Costs of further processing (dyeing) intermediate products:				
12	Undyed coarse wool	$50,000			
13	Undyed fine wool	$60,000			
14	Undyed superfine wool	$10,000			
15	Sales value of end products:				
16	Dyed coarse wool	$160,000			
17	Dyed fine wool	$240,000			
18	Dyed superfine wool	$90,000			
19					
20	Enter a formula into each of the cells marked with a ? below				
21	Example: Joint Product Costs and the Contribution Approach				
22					
23	Analysis of the profitability of the overall operation:				
24	Combined final sales value			?	
25	Less costs of producing the end products:				
26	Cost of wool	?			
27	Cost of separation process	?			
28	Combined costs of dyeing	?		?	
29	Profit			?	
30					
31	Analysis of sell or process further:				
32		Coarse	Fine	Superfine	
33		Wool	Wool	Wool	
34	Final sales value after further processing	?	?	?	
35	Less sales value at the split-off point	?	?	?	
36	Incremental revenue from further processing	?	?	?	
37	Less cost of further processung (dyeing)	?	?	?	
38	Financial advantage (disadvantage) of further processing	?	?	?	
39					

Chapter 12 Form   Chapter 12 Form

You should proceed to the requirements below only after completing your worksheet.

Required:

1. Check your worksheet by changing the cost of further processing undyed coarse wool in cell B12 to $30,000. The overall profit from processing all intermediate products into final products should now be $150,000 and the financial advantage of further processing coarse wool should now be $10,000. If you do not get these answers, find the errors in your worksheet and correct them.

   How should operations change in response to this change in cost?

2. In industries that process joint products, the costs of the raw materials inputs and the sales values of intermediate and final products are often volatile. Change the data area of your worksheet to match the following:

Data	
Exhibit 12–7 Santa Maria Wool Cooperative	
Cost of wool..	$290,000
Cost of separation process	$40,000
Sales value of intermediate products at split-off point:	
Undyed coarse wool..............................	$100,000
Undyed fine wool	$110,000
Undyed superfine wool	$90,000
Costs of further processing (dyeing) intermediate products:	
Undyed coarse wool..............................	$50,000
Undyed fine wool	$60,000
Undyed superfine wool	$10,000
Sales value of end products:	
Dyed coarse wool...............................	$180,000
Dyed fine wool.................................	$210,000
Dyed superfine wool............................	$90,000

a. What is the overall profit if all intermediate products are processed into final products?

b. What is the financial advantage (disadvantage) from further processing each of the intermediate products?

c. With these new costs and selling prices, what recommendations would you make concerning the company's operations? If your recommendation is followed, what should be the overall profit of the company?

---

connect   **The Foundational 15**

Cane Company manufactures two products called Alpha and Beta that sell for $120 and $80, respectively. Each product uses only one type of raw material that costs $6 per pound. The company has the capacity to annually produce 100,000 units of each product. Its average cost per unit for each product at this level of activity are given below:

LO12–2, LO12–3, LO12–4, LO12–5, LO12–6

	Alpha	Beta
Direct materials	$ 30	$ 12
Direct labor...................................	20	15
Variable manufacturing overhead	7	5
Traceable fixed manufacturing overhead	16	18
Variable selling expenses	12	8
Common fixed expenses........................	15	10
Total cost per unit	$ 100	$ 68

The company considers its traceable fixed manufacturing overhead to be avoidable, whereas its common fixed expenses are unavoidable and have been allocated to products based on sales dollars.

Required:

(Answer each question independently unless instructed otherwise.)

1. What is the total amount of traceable fixed manufacturing overhead for each of the two products?
2. What is the company's total amount of common fixed expenses?
3. Assume that Cane expects to produce and sell 80,000 Alphas during the current year. One of Cane's sales representatives has found a new customer who is willing to buy 10,000 additional Alphas for a price of $80 per unit. What is the financial advantage (disadvantage) of accepting the new customer's order?
4. Assume that Cane expects to produce and sell 90,000 Betas during the current year. One of Cane's sales representatives has found a new customer who is willing to buy 5,000 additional Betas for a price of $39 per unit. What is the financial advantage (disadvantage) of accepting the new customer's order?
5. Assume that Cane expects to produce and sell 95,000 Alphas during the current year. One of Cane's sales representatives has found a new customer who is willing to buy 10,000 additional Alphas for a price of $80 per unit; however pursuing this opportunity will decrease Alpha sales to regular customers by 5,000 units. What is the financial advantage (disadvantage) of accepting the new customer's order?

6. Assume that Cane normally produces and sells 90,000 Betas per year. What is the financial advantage (disadvantage) of discontinuing the Beta product line?
7. Assume that Cane normally produces and sells 40,000 Betas per year. What is the financial advantage (disadvantage) of discontinuing the Beta product line?
8. Assume that Cane normally produces and sells 60,000 Betas and 80,000 Alphas per year. If Cane discontinues the Beta product line, its sales representatives could increase sales of Alpha by 15,000 units. What is the financial advantage (disadvantage) of discontinuing the Beta product line?
9. Assume that Cane expects to produce and sell 80,000 Alphas during the current year. A supplier has offered to manufacture and deliver 80,000 Alphas to Cane for a price of $80 per unit. What is the financial advantage (disadvantage) of buying 80,000 units from the supplier instead of making those units?
10. Assume that Cane expects to produce and sell 50,000 Alphas during the current year. A supplier has offered to manufacture and deliver 50,000 Alphas to Cane for a price of $80 per unit. What is the financial advantage (disadvantage) of buying 50,000 units from the supplier instead of making those units?
11. How many pounds of raw material are needed to make one unit of each of the two products?
12. What contribution margin per pound of raw material is earned by each of the two products?
13. Assume that Cane's customers would buy a maximum of 80,000 units of Alpha and 60,000 units of Beta. Also assume that the raw material available for production is limited to 160,000 pounds. How many units of each product should Cane produce to maximize its profits?
14. If Cane follows your recommendation in requirement 13, what total contribution margin will it earn?
15. If Cane uses its 160,000 pounds of raw materials as you recommended in requirement 13, up to how much should it be willing to pay per pound for additional raw materials?

Exercises

EXERCISE 12-1 Identifying Relevant Costs LO12-1

Svahn, AB, is a Swedish manufacturer of sailing yachts. The company has assembled the information shown below that pertains to two independent decision-making contexts called Case A and Case B:

Case A:

The company chronically has no idle capacity and the old Model B100 machine is the company's constraint. Management is considering purchasing a Model B300 machine to use in addition to the company's present Model B100 machine. The old Model B100 machine will continue to be used to capacity as before, with the new Model B300 machine being used to expand production. This will increase the company's production and sales. The increase in volume will be large enough to require increases in fixed selling expenses and in general administrative overhead, but not in the fixed manufacturing overhead.

Case B:

The old Model B100 machine is not the company's constraint, but management is considering replacing it with a new Model B300 machine because of the potential savings in direct materials with the new machine. The Model B100 machine would be sold. This change will have no effect on production or sales, other than some savings in direct materials costs due to less waste.

Required:

Copy the information below onto your answer sheet and place an X in the appropriate column to indicate whether each item is relevant or irrelevant to the decision context described in Case A and Case B.

Item	Case A Relevant	Case A Irrelevant	Case B Relevant	Case B Irrelevant
a. Sales revenue				
b. Direct materials				
c. Direct labor				
d. Variable manufacturing overhead				
e. Depreciation—Model B100 machine				
f. Book value—Model B100 machine				
g. Disposal value—Model B100 machine				
h. Market value—Model B300 machine (cost)				
i. Fixed manufacturing overhead (general)				
j. Variable selling expense				
k. Fixed selling expense				
l. General administrative overhead				

EXERCISE 12–2 Dropping or Retaining a Segment LO12–2

The Regal Cycle Company manufactures three types of bicycles—a dirt bike, a mountain bike, and a racing bike. Data on sales and expenses for the past quarter follow:

	Total	Dirt Bikes	Mountain Bikes	Racing Bikes
Sales	$300,000	$90,000	$150,000	$60,000
Variable manufacturing and selling expenses	120,000	27,000	60,000	33,000
Contribution margin	180,000	63,000	90,000	27,000
Fixed expenses:				
Advertising, traceable...................	30,000	10,000	14,000	6,000
Depreciation of special equipment	23,000	6,000	9,000	8,000
Salaries of product-line managers	35,000	12,000	13,000	10,000
Allocated common fixed expenses*.......	60,000	18,000	30,000	12,000
Total fixed expenses.....................	148,000	46,000	66,000	36,000
Net operating income (loss)...............	$ 32,000	$17,000	$ 24,000	$ (9,000)

*Allocated on the basis of sales dollars.

Management is concerned about the continued losses shown by the racing bikes and wants a recommendation as to whether or not the line should be discontinued. The special equipment used to produce racing bikes has no resale value and does not wear out.

Required:

1. What is the financial advantage (disadvantage) per quarter of discontinuing the Racing Bikes?
2. Should the production and sale of racing bikes be discontinued?
3. Prepare a properly formatted segmented income statement that would be more useful to management in assessing the long-run profitability of the various product lines.

EXERCISE 12–3 Make or Buy Decision LO12–3

Troy Engines, Ltd., manufactures a variety of engines for use in heavy equipment. The company has always produced all of the necessary parts for its engines, including all of the carburetors. An outside supplier has offered to sell one type of carburetor to Troy Engines, Ltd., for a cost of $35 per unit. To evaluate this offer, Troy Engines, Ltd., has gathered the following information relating to its own cost of producing the carburetor internally:

	Per Unit	15,000 Units per Year
Direct materials	$14	$210,000
Direct labor	10	150,000
Variable manufacturing overhead	3	45,000
Fixed manufacturing overhead, traceable	6*	90,000
Fixed manufacturing overhead, allocated	9	135,000
Total cost	$42	$630,000

*One-third supervisory salaries; two-thirds depreciation of special equipment (no resale value).

Required:

1. Assuming the company has no alternative use for the facilities that are now being used to produce the carburetors, what would be the financial advantage (disadvantage) of buying 15,000 carburetors from the outside supplier?
2. Should the outside supplier's offer be accepted?
3. Suppose that if the carburetors were purchased, Troy Engines, Ltd., could use the freed capacity to launch a new product. The segment margin of the new product would be $150,000 per year. Given this new assumption, what would be financial advantage (disadvantage) of buying 15,000 carburetors from the outside supplier?
4. Given the new assumption in requirement 3, should the outside supplier's offer be accepted?

EXERCISE 12–4 Special Order Decision LO12–4

Imperial Jewelers manufactures and sells a gold bracelet for $189.95. The company's accounting system says that the unit product cost for this bracelet is $149.00 as shown below:

Direct materials	$ 84.00
Direct labor.	45.00
Manufacturing overhead	20.00
Unit product cost.	$149.00

The members of a wedding party have approached Imperial Jewelers about buying 20 of these gold bracelets for the discounted price of $169.95 each. The members of the wedding party would like special filigree applied to the bracelets that would require Imperial Jewelers to buy a special tool for $250 and that would increase the direct materials cost per bracelet by $2.00. The special tool would have no other use once the special order is completed.

To analyze this special order opportunity, Imperial Jewelers has determined that most of its manufacturing overhead is fixed and unaffected by variations in how much jewelry is produced in any given period. However, $4.00 of the overhead is variable with respect to the number of bracelets produced. The company also believes that accepting this order would have no effect on its ability to produce and sell jewelry to other customers. Furthermore, the company could fulfill the wedding party's order using its existing manufacturing capacity.

Required:

1. What is the financial advantage (disadvantage) of accepting the special order from the wedding party?
2. Should the company accept the special order?

EXERCISE 12–5 Volume Trade-Off Decisions LO12–5

Outdoor Luggage, Inc., makes high-end hard-sided luggage for sports equipment. Data concerning three of the company's most popular models appear below.

	Ski Guard	Golf Guard	Fishing Guard
Selling price per unit.	$200	$300	$255
Variable cost per unit	$60	$140	$55
Plastic injection molding machine processing time required to produce one unit.	2 minutes	5 minutes	4 minutes
Pounds of plastic pellets per unit.	7 pounds	4 pounds	8 pounds

Required:

1. If we assume that the total time available on the plastic injection molding machine is the constraint in the production process, how much contribution margin per minute of the constrained resource is earned by each product?
2. Which product offers the most profitable use of the plastic injection molding machine?
3. If we assume that a severe shortage of plastic pellets has required the company to cut back its production so much that its new constraint has become the total available pounds of plastic pellets, how much contribution margin per pound of the constrained resource is earned by each product?
4. Which product offers the most profitable use of the plastic pellets?
5. Which product has the largest contribution margin per unit? Why wouldn't this product be the most profitable use of the constrained resource in either case?

EXERCISE 12–6 Managing a Constrained Resource LO12–6

Portsmouth Company makes fine colonial reproduction furniture. Upholstered furniture is one of its major product lines and the bottleneck on this production line is time in the upholstery shop. Upholstering is a craft that takes years of experience to master and the demand for upholstered furniture far exceeds the company's capacity in the upholstering shop. Information concerning three of the company's upholstered chairs appears below:

	Recliner	Sofa	Love Seat
Selling price per unit.	$1,400	$1,800	$1,500
Variable cost per unit	$800	$1,200	$1,000
Upholstery shop time required to produce one unit.	8 hours	10 hours	5 hours

Required:

1. More time could be made available in the upholstery shop by asking the employees who work in this shop to work overtime. Assuming that this extra time would be used to produce sofas, up to how much of a premium should the company be willing to pay in terms of an overtime premium per hour to keep the upholstery shop open after normal working hours?
2. A small nearby upholstering company has offered to upholster furniture for Portsmouth at a fixed charge of $45 per hour. The management of Portsmouth is confident that this upholstering company's work is high quality and their craftsmen can work as quickly as Portsmouth's own craftsmen on the simpler upholstering jobs such as the Love Seat. How much additional contribution margin per hour can Portsmouth earn if it hires the nearby upholstering company to make Love Seats?
3. Should Portsmouth hire the nearby upholstering company? Explain.

EXERCISE 12–7 Sell or Process Further Decisions LO12–7

Dorsey Company manufactures three products from a common input in a joint processing operation. Joint processing costs up to the split-off point total $350,000 per quarter. For financial reporting purposes, the company allocates these costs to the joint products on the basis of their relative sales value at the split-off point. Unit selling prices and total output at the split-off point are as follows:

Product	Selling Price	Quarterly Output
A....................	$16 per pound	15,000 pounds
B....................	$8 per pound	20,000 pounds
C....................	$25 per gallon	4,000 gallons

Each product can be processed further after the split-off point. Additional processing requires no special facilities. The additional processing costs (per quarter) and unit selling prices after further processing are given below:

Product	Additional Processing Costs	Selling Price
A.................	$63,000	$20 per pound
B.................	$80,000	$13 per pound
C.................	$36,000	$32 per gallon

Required:

1. What is the financial advantage (disadvantage) of further processing each of the three products beyond the split-off point?
2. Based on your analysis in requirement 1, which product or products should be sold at the split-off point and which product or products should be processed further?

EXERCISE 12–8 Volume Trade-Off Decisions LO12–5, LO12–6

Barlow Company manufactures three products—A, B, and C. The selling price, variable costs, and contribution margin for one unit of each product follow:

	Product		
	A	B	C
Selling price	$180	$270	$240
Variable expenses:			
Direct materials	24	80	32
Other variable expenses	102	90	148
Total variable expenses	126	170	180
Contribution margin	$ 54	$100	$ 60
Contribution margin ratio...............	30%	37%	25%

The same raw material is used in all three products. Barlow Company has only 6,000 pounds of raw material on hand and will not be able to obtain any more of it for several weeks due to a strike in its supplier's plant. Management is trying to decide which product(s) to concentrate on next week in filling its backlog of orders. The material costs $8 per pound.

Required:

1. Calculate the contribution margin per pound of the constraining resource for each product.
2. Assuming that Barlow has unlimited demand for each of its three products, what is the maximum contribution margin the company can earn when using the 6,000 pounds of raw material on hand?
3. Assuming that Barlow's estimated customer demand is 500 units per product line, what is the maximum contribution margin the company can earn when using the 6,000 pounds of raw material on hand?
4. A foreign supplier could furnish Barlow with additional stocks of the raw material at a substantial premium over the usual price. Assuming Barlow's estimated customer demand is 500 units per product line and that the company has used its 6,000 pounds of raw material in an optimal fashion, what is the highest price Barlow Company should be willing to pay for an additional pound of materials? Explain.

EXERCISE 12–9 Special Order Decision LO12–4

Delta Company produces a single product. The cost of producing and selling a single unit of this product at the company's normal activity level of 60,000 units per year is:

Direct materials	$5.10
Direct labor.	$3.80
Variable manufacturing overhead	$1.00
Fixed manufacturing overhead.	$4.20
Variable selling and administrative expense	$1.50
Fixed selling and administrative expense.	$2.40

The normal selling price is $21 per unit. The company's capacity is 75,000 units per year. An order has been received from a mail-order house for 15,000 units at a special price of $14.00 per unit. This order would not affect regular sales or the company's total fixed costs.

Required:

1. What is the financial advantage (disadvantage) of accepting the special order?
2. As a separate matter from the special order, assume the company's inventory includes 1,000 units of this product that were produced last year and that are inferior to the current model. The units must be sold through regular channels at reduced prices. What unit cost is relevant for establishing a minimum selling price for these units? Explain.

EXERCISE 12–10 Make or Buy Decision LO12–3

Futura Company purchases the 40,000 starters that it installs in its standard line of farm tractors from a supplier for the price of $8.40 per unit. Due to a reduction in output, the company now has idle capacity that could be used to produce the starters rather than buying them from an outside supplier. However, the company's chief engineer is opposed to making the starters because the production cost per unit is $9.20 as shown below:

	Per Unit	Total
Direct materials	$3.10	
Direct labor	2.70	
Supervision	1.50	$60,000
Depreciation	1.00	$40,000
Variable manufacturing overhead	0.60	
Rent	0.30	$12,000
Total production cost	$9.20	

If Futura decides to make the starters, a supervisor would have to be hired (at a salary of $60,000) to oversee production. However, the company has sufficient idle tools and machinery such that no new equipment would have to be purchased. The rent charge above is based on space utilized in the plant. The total rent on the plant is $80,000 per period. Depreciation is due to obsolescence rather than wear and tear.

Required:

What is the financial advantage (disadvantage) of making the 40,000 starters instead of buying them from an outside supplier?

EXERCISE 12–11 Make or Buy Decision LO12–3

Han Products manufactures 30,000 units of part S–6 each year for use on its production line. At this level of activity, the cost per unit for part S–6 is:

Direct materials	$ 3.60
Direct labor	10.00
Variable manufacturing overhead	2.40
Fixed manufacturing overhead	9.00
Total cost per part	$25.00

An outside supplier has offered to sell 30,000 units of part S–6 each year to Han Products for $21 per part. If Han Products accepts this offer, the facilities now being used to manufacture part S–6 could be rented to another company at an annual rental of $80,000. However, Han Products has determined that two-thirds of the fixed manufacturing overhead being applied to part S–6 would continue even if part S–6 were purchased from the outside supplier.

Required:

What is the financial advantage (disadvantage) of accepting the outside supplier's offer?

EXERCISE 12–12 Volume Trade-Off Decisions LO12–5

Benoit Company produces three products—A, B, and C. Data concerning the three products follow (per unit):

	Product		
	A	B	C
Selling price	$80	$56	$70
Variable expenses:			
Direct materials	24	15	9
Other variable expenses	24	27	40
Total variable expenses	48	42	49
Contribution margin	$32	$14	$21
Contribution margin ratio	40%	25%	30%

The company estimates that it can sell 800 units of each product per month. The same raw material is used in each product. The material costs $3 per pound with a maximum of 5,000 pounds available each month.

Required:

1. Calculate the contribution margin per pound of the constraining resource for each product.
2. Which orders would you advise the company to accept first, those for A, B, or C? Which orders second? Third?
3. What is the maximum contribution margin that the company can earn per month if it makes optimal use of its 5,000 pounds of materials?

EXERCISE 12–13 Sell or Process Further Decision LO12–7

Wexpro, Inc., produces several products from processing 1 ton of clypton, a rare mineral. Material and processing costs total $60,000 per ton, one-fourth of which is allocated to product X15. Seven thousand units of product X15 are produced from each ton of clypton. The units can either be sold at the split-off point for $9 each, or processed further at a total cost of $9,500 and then sold for $12 each.

Required:

1. What is the financial advantage (disadvantage) of further processing product X15?
2. Should product X15 be processed further or sold at the split-off point?

EXERCISE 12–14 Identification of Relevant Costs LO12–1

Kristen Lu purchased a used automobile for $8,000 at the beginning of last year and incurred the following operating costs:

Depreciation ($8,000 ÷ 5 years)	$1,600
Insurance	$1,200
Garage rent	$360
Automobile tax and license	$40
Variable operating cost	$0.14 per mile

The variable operating cost consists of gasoline, oil, tires, maintenance, and repairs. Kristen estimates that, at her current rate of usage, the car will have zero resale value in five years, so the annual straight-line depreciation is $1,600. The car is kept in a garage for a monthly fee.

Required:

1. Kristen drove the car 10,000 miles last year. Compute the average cost per mile of owning and operating the car.
2. Kristen is unsure about whether she should use her own car or rent a car to go on an extended cross-country trip for two weeks during spring break. What costs above are relevant in this decision? Explain.
3. Kristen is thinking about buying an expensive sports car to replace the car she bought last year. She would drive the same number of miles regardless of which car she owns and would rent the same parking space. The sports car's variable operating costs would be roughly the same as the variable operating costs of her old car. However, her insurance and automobile tax and license costs would go up. What costs are relevant in estimating the incremental cost of owning the more expensive car? Explain.

EXERCISE 12–15 Dropping or Retaining a Segment LO12–2

Thalassines Kataskeves, S.A., of Greece makes marine equipment. The company has been experiencing losses on its bilge pump product line for several years. The most recent quarterly contribution format income statement for the bilge pump product line follows:

Thalassines Kataskeves, S.A. Income Statement—Bilge Pump For the Quarter Ended March 31		
Sales		$850,000
Variable expenses:		
Variable manufacturing expenses	$330,000	
Sales commissions	42,000	
Shipping	18,000	
Total variable expenses		390,000
Contribution margin		460,000
Fixed expenses:		
Advertising (for the bilge pump product line)	270,000	
Depreciation of equipment (no resale value)	80,000	
General factory overhead	105,000*	
Salary of product-line manager	32,000	
Insurance on inventories	8,000	
Purchasing department	45,000†	
Total fixed expenses		540,000
Net operating loss		$ (80,000)

*Common costs allocated on the basis of machine-hours.
†Common costs allocated on the basis of sales dollars.

Discontinuing the bilge pump product line would not affect sales of other product lines and would have no effect on the company's total general factory overhead or total Purchasing Department expenses.

Required:

What is the financial advantage (disadvantage) of discontinuing the bilge pump product line?

EXERCISE 12–16 Identification of Relevant Costs LO12–1

Bill has just returned from a duck hunting trip. He brought home eight ducks. Bill's friend, John, disapproves of duck hunting, and to discourage Bill from further hunting, John presented him with the following cost estimate per duck:

Camper and equipment:	
Cost, $12,000; usable for eight seasons; 10 hunting trips per season	$150
Travel expense (pickup truck):	
100 miles at $0.31 per mile (gas, oil, and tires—$0.21 per mile; depreciation and insurance—$0.10 per mile)	31
Shotgun shells (two boxes per hunting trip)	20
Boat:	
Cost, $2,320, usable for eight seasons; 10 hunting trips per season	29
Hunting license:	
Cost, $30 for the season; 10 hunting trips per season	3
Money lost playing poker:	
Loss, $24 (Bill plays poker every weekend whether he goes hunting or stays at home)	24
Bottle of whiskey:	
Cost, $15 per hunting trip (used to ward off the cold)	15
Total cost	$272
Cost per duck ($272 ÷ 8 ducks)	$ 34

Required:

1. Assuming the duck hunting trip Bill has just completed is typical, what costs are relevant to a decision as to whether Bill should go duck hunting again this season?
2. Suppose Bill gets lucky on his next hunting trip and shoots 10 ducks using the same amount of shotgun shells he used on his previous hunting trip to bag 8 ducks. How much would it have cost him to shoot the last two ducks? Explain.
3. Which costs are relevant in a decision of whether Bill should give up hunting? Explain.

EXERCISE 12–17 Dropping or Retaining a Segment LO12–2

Bed & Bath, a retailing company, has two departments—Hardware and Linens. The company's most recent monthly contribution format income statement follows:

		Department	
	Total	Hardware	Linens
Sales	$4,000,000	$3,000,000	$1,000,000
Variable expenses	1,300,000	900,000	400,000
Contribution margin	2,700,000	2,100,000	600,000
Fixed expenses	2,200,000	1,400,000	800,000
Net operating income (loss)	$ 500,000	$ 700,000	$ (200,000)

A study indicates that $340,000 of the fixed expenses being charged to Linens are sunk costs or allocated costs that will continue even if the Linens Department is dropped. In addition, the elimination of the Linens Department will result in a 10% decrease in the sales of the Hardware Department.

Required:

What is the financial advantage (disadvantage) of discontinuing the Linens Department?

Problems

PROBLEM 12–18 Relevant Cost Analysis in a Variety of Situations LO12–2, LO12–3, LO12–4

Andretti Company has a single product called a Dak. The company normally produces and sells 60,000 Daks each year at a selling price of $32 per unit. The company's unit costs at this level of activity are given below:

Direct materials	$10.00	
Direct labor	4.50	
Variable manufacturing overhead	2.30	
Fixed manufacturing overhead	5.00	($300,000 total)
Variable selling expenses	1.20	
Fixed selling expenses	3.50	($210,000 total)
Total cost per unit	$26.50	

A number of questions relating to the production and sale of Daks follow. Each question is independent.

Required:

1. Assume that Andretti Company has sufficient capacity to produce 90,000 Daks each year without any increase in fixed manufacturing overhead costs. The company could increase its unit sales by 25% above the present 60,000 units each year if it were willing to increase the fixed selling expenses by $80,000. What is the financial advantage (disadvantage) of investing an additional $80,000 in fixed selling expenses? Would the additional investment be justified?

2. Assume again that Andretti Company has sufficient capacity to produce 90,000 Daks each year. A customer in a foreign market wants to purchase 20,000 Daks. If Andretti accepts this order it would have to pay import duties on the Daks of $1.70 per unit and an additional $9,000 for permits and licenses. The only selling costs that would be associated with the order would be $3.20 per unit shipping cost. What is the break-even price per unit on this order?

3. The company has 1,000 Daks on hand that have some irregularities and are therefore considered to be "seconds." Due to the irregularities, it will be impossible to sell these units at the normal price through regular distribution channels. What is the unit cost figure that is relevant for setting a minimum selling price? Explain.

4. Due to a strike in its supplier's plant, Andretti Company is unable to purchase more material for the production of Daks. The strike is expected to last for two months. Andretti Company has enough material on hand to operate at 30% of normal levels for the two-month period. As an alternative, Andretti could close its plant down entirely for the two months. If the plant were closed, fixed manufacturing overhead costs would continue at 60% of their normal level during the two-month period and the fixed selling expenses would be reduced by 20% during the two-month period.

   a. How much total contribution margin will Andretti forgo if it closes the plant for two months?

   b. How much total fixed cost will the company avoid if it closes the plant for two months?

   c. What is the financial advantage (disadvantage) of closing the plant for the two-month period?

   d. Should Andretti close the plant for two months?

5. An outside manufacturer has offered to produce 60,000 Daks and ship them directly to Andretti's customers. If Andretti Company accepts this offer, the facilities that it uses to produce Daks would be idle; however, fixed manufacturing overhead costs would be reduced by 75%. Because the outside manufacturer would pay for all shipping costs, the variable selling expenses would be only two-thirds of their present amount. What is Andretti's avoidable cost per unit that it should compare to the price quoted by the outside manufacturer?

PROBLEM 12–19 Dropping or Retaining a Segment LO12–2

Jackson County Senior Services is a nonprofit organization devoted to providing essential services to seniors who live in their own homes within the Jackson County area. Three services are provided for seniors—home nursing, Meals On Wheels, and housekeeping. Data on revenue and expenses for the past year follow:

	Total	Home Nursing	Meals On Wheels	House-keeping
Revenues	$900,000	$260,000	$400,000	$240,000
Variable expenses	490,000	120,000	210,000	160,000
Contribution margin	410,000	140,000	190,000	80,000
Fixed expenses:				
Depreciation	68,000	8,000	40,000	20,000
Liability insurance	42,000	20,000	7,000	15,000
Program administrators' salaries	115,000	40,000	38,000	37,000
General administrative overhead* ...	180,000	52,000	80,000	48,000
Total fixed expenses	405,000	120,000	165,000	120,000
Net operating income (loss)	$ 5,000	$ 20,000	$ 25,000	$ (40,000)

*Allocated on the basis of program revenues.

The head administrator of Jackson County Senior Services, Judith Miyama, considers last year's net operating income of $5,000 to be unsatisfactory; therefore, she is considering the possibility of discontinuing the housekeeping program.

The depreciation in housekeeping is for a small van that is used to carry the housekeepers and their equipment from job to job. If the program were discontinued, the van would be donated to a charitable organization. None of the general administrative overhead would be avoided if the housekeeping program were dropped, but the liability insurance and the salary of the program administrator would be avoided.

Required:

1. What is the financial advantage (disadvantage) of discontinuing the Housekeeping program? Should the Housekeeping program be discontinued? Explain.
2. Prepare a properly formatted segmented income statement that would be more useful to management in assessing the long-run financial viability of its various services.

PROBLEM 12–20 Sell or Process Further Decision LO12–7

(Prepared from a situation suggested by Professor John W. Hardy.) Lone Star Meat Packers is a major processor of beef and other meat products. The company has a large amount of T-bone steak on hand, and it is trying to decide whether to sell the T-bone steaks as they are initially cut or to process them further into filet mignon and the New York cut.

If the T-bone steaks are sold as initially cut, the company figures that a 1-pound T-bone steak would yield the following profit:

Selling price ($7.95 per pound)	$7.95
Less joint costs incurred up to the split-off point where	
T-bone steak can be identified as a separate product...	3.80
Profit per pound	$4.15

If the company were to further process the T-bone steaks, then cutting one side of a T-bone steak provides the filet mignon and cutting the other side provides the New York cut. One 16-ounce T-bone steak cut in this way will yield one 6-ounce filet mignon and one 8-ounce New York cut; the remaining ounces are waste. It costs $0.55 to further process one T-bone steak into the filet mignon and New York cuts. The filet mignon can be sold for $12.00 per pound, and the New York cut can be sold for $8.80 per pound.

Required:

1. What is the financial advantage (disadvantage) of further processing one T-bone steak into filet mignon and New York cut steaks?
2. Would you recommend that the T-bone steaks be sold as initially cut or processed further? Why?

PROBLEM 12–21 Dropping or Retaining a Flight LO12–2

Profits have been decreasing for several years at Pegasus Airlines. In an effort to improve the company's performance, the company is thinking about dropping several flights that appear to be unprofitable.

A typical income statement for one round-trip of one such flight (flight 482) is as follows:

Ticket revenue (175 seats × 40% occupancy × $200 ticket price)	$14,000	100.0%
Variable expenses ($15 per person)	1,050	7.5
Contribution margin	12,950	92.5%
Flight expenses:		
Salaries, flight crew	1,800	
Flight promotion	750	
Depreciation of aircraft	1,550	
Fuel for aircraft	5,800	
Liability insurance	4,200	
Salaries, flight assistants	1,500	
Baggage loading and flight preparation	1,700	
Overnight costs for flight crew and assistants at destination	300	
Total flight expenses	17,600	
Net operating loss	$ (4,650)	

The following additional information is available about flight 482:
a. Members of the flight crew are paid fixed annual salaries, whereas the flight assistants are paid based on the number of round trips they complete.
b. One-third of the liability insurance is a special charge assessed against flight 482 because in the opinion of the insurance company, the destination of the flight is in a "high-risk" area. The remaining two-thirds would be unaffected by a decision to drop flight 482.
c. The baggage loading and flight preparation expense is an allocation of ground crews' salaries and depreciation of ground equipment. Dropping flight 482 would have no effect on the company's total baggage loading and flight preparation expenses.
d. If flight 482 is dropped, Pegasus Airlines has no authorization at present to replace it with another flight.
e. Aircraft depreciation is due entirely to obsolescence. Depreciation due to wear and tear is negligible.
f. Dropping flight 482 would not allow Pegasus Airlines to reduce the number of aircraft in its fleet or the number of flight crew on its payroll.

Required:
1. What is the financial advantage (disadvantage) of discontinuing flight 482?
2. The airline's scheduling officer has been criticized because only about 50% of the seats on Pegasus' flights are being filled compared to an industry average of 60%. The scheduling officer has explained that Pegasus' average seat occupancy could be improved considerably by eliminating about 10% of its flights, but that doing so would reduce profits. Explain how this could happen.

PROBLEM 12–22 Special Order Decisions LO12–4
Polaski Company manufactures and sells a single product called a Ret. Operating at capacity, the company can produce and sell 30,000 Rets per year. Costs associated with this level of production and sales are given below:

	Unit	Total
Direct materials	$15	$ 450,000
Direct labor	8	240,000
Variable manufacturing overhead	3	90,000
Fixed manufacturing overhead	9	270,000
Variable selling expense	4	120,000
Fixed selling expense	6	180,000
Total cost	$45	$1,350,000

The Rets normally sell for $50 each. Fixed manufacturing overhead is $270,000 per year within the range of 25,000 through 30,000 Rets per year.

Required:

1. Assume that due to a recession, Polaski Company expects to sell only 25,000 Rets through regular channels next year. A large retail chain has offered to purchase 5,000 Rets if Polaski is willing to accept a 16% discount off the regular price. There would be no sales commissions on this order; thus, variable selling expenses would be slashed by 75%. However, Polaski Company would have to purchase a special machine to engrave the retail chain's name on the 5,000 units. This machine would cost $10,000. Polaski Company has no assurance that the retail chain will purchase additional units in the future. What is the financial advantage (disadvantage) of accepting the special order?

2. Refer to the original data. Assume again that Polaski Company expects to sell only 25,000 Rets through regular channels next year. The U.S. Army would like to make a one-time-only purchase of 5,000 Rets. The Army would pay a fixed fee of $1.80 per Ret, and it would reimburse Polaski Company for all costs of production (variable and fixed) associated with the units. Because the army would pick up the Rets with its own trucks, there would be no variable selling expenses associated with this order. What is the financial advantage (disadvantage) of accepting the U.S. Army's special order?

3. Assume the same situation as described in (2) above, except that the company expects to sell 30,000 Rets through regular channels next year. Thus, accepting the U.S. Army's order would require giving up regular sales of 5,000 Rets. Given this new information, what is the financial advantage (disadvantage) of accepting the U.S. Army's special order?

PROBLEM 12–23 Make or Buy Decision LO12–3

Silven Industries, which manufactures and sells a highly successful line of summer lotions and insect repellents, has decided to diversify in order to stabilize sales throughout the year. A natural area for the company to consider is the production of winter lotions and creams to prevent dry and chapped skin.

After considerable research, a winter products line has been developed. However, Silven's president has decided to introduce only one of the new products for this coming winter. If the product is a success, further expansion in future years will be initiated.

The product selected (called Chap-Off) is a lip balm that will be sold in a lipstick-type tube. The product will be sold to wholesalers in boxes of 24 tubes for $8 per box. Because of excess capacity, no additional fixed manufacturing overhead costs will be incurred to produce the product. However, a $90,000 charge for fixed manufacturing overhead will be absorbed by the product under the company's absorption costing system.

Using the estimated sales and production of 100,000 boxes of Chap-Off, the Accounting Department has developed the following manufacturing cost per box:

Direct material	$3.60
Direct labor	2.00
Manufacturing overhead	1.40
Total cost	$7.00

The costs above relate to making both the lip balm and the tube that contains it. As an alternative to making the tubes for Chap-Off, Silven has approached a supplier to discuss the possibility of buying the tubes. The purchase price of the supplier's empty tubes would be $1.35 per box of 24 tubes. If Silven Industries stops making the tubes and buys them from the outside supplier, its direct labor and variable manufacturing overhead costs per box of Chap-Off would be reduced by 10% and its direct materials costs would be reduced by 25%.

Required:

1. If Silven buys its tubes from the outside supplier, how much of its own Chap-Off manufacturing costs per box will it be able to avoid? (Hint: You need to separate the manufacturing overhead of $1.40 per box that is shown above into its variable and fixed components to derive the correct answer.)

2. What is the financial advantage (disadvantage) per box of Chap-Off if Silven buys its tubes from the outside supplier?

3. What is the financial advantage (disadvantage) in total (not per box) if Silven buys 100,000 boxes of tubes from the outside supplier?

4. Should Silven Industries make or buy the tubes?
5. What is the maximum price that Silven should be willing to pay the outside supplier for a box of 24 tubes? Explain.
6. Instead of sales of 100,000 boxes, revised estimates show a sales volume of 120,000 boxes. At this higher sales volume, Silven would need to rent extra equipment at a cost of $40,000 per year to make the additional 20,000 boxes of tubes. Assuming that the outside supplier will not accept an order for less than 120,000 boxes, what is the financial advantage (disadvantage) in total (not per box) if Silven buys 120,000 boxes of tubes from the outside supplier? Given this new information, should Silven Industries make or buy the tubes?
7. Refer to the data in (6) above. Assume that the outside supplier will accept an order of any size for the tubes at a price of $1.35 per box. How many boxes of tubes should Silven make? How many boxes of tubes should it buy from the outside supplier?
8. What qualitative factors should Silven Industries consider in determining whether they should make or buy the tubes?

(CMA, adapted)

PROBLEM 12–24 Shutting Down or Continuing to Operate a Plant LO12–2

Birch Company normally produces and sells 30,000 units of RG–6 each month. The selling price is $22 per unit, variable costs are $14 per unit, fixed manufacturing overhead costs total $150,000 per month, and fixed selling costs total $30,000 per month.

Employment-contract strikes in the companies that purchase the bulk of the RG–6 units have caused Birch Company's sales to temporarily drop to only 8,000 units per month. Birch Company estimates that the strikes will last for two months, after which time sales of RG–6 should return to normal. Due to the current low level of sales, Birch Company is thinking about closing down its own plant during the strike, which would reduce its fixed manufacturing overhead costs by $45,000 per month and its fixed selling costs by 10%. Start-up costs at the end of the shutdown period would total $8,000. Because Birch Company uses Lean Production methods, no inventories are on hand.

Required:
1. What is the financial advantage (disadvantage) if Birch closes its own plant for two months?
2. Should Birch close the plant for two months? Explain.
3. At what level of unit sales for the two-month period would Birch Company be indifferent between closing the plant or keeping it open? (Hint: This is a type of break-even analysis, except that the fixed cost portion of your break-even computation should include only those fixed costs that are relevant [i.e., avoidable] over the two-month period.)

PROBLEM 12–25 Volume Trade-Off Decisions LO12–5, LO12–6

The Walton Toy Company manufactures a line of dolls and a sewing kit. Demand for the company's products is increasing, and management requests assistance from you in determining an economical sales and production mix for the coming year. The company has provided the following data:

Product	Demand Next Year (units)	Selling Price per Unit	Direct Materials	Direct Labor
Debbie	50,000	$16.70	$4.30	$6.40
Trish	42,000	$7.50	$1.10	$4.00
Sarah	35,000	$26.60	$6.44	$11.20
Mike	40,000	$14.00	$2.00	$8.00
Sewing kit	325,000	$9.60	$3.20	$3.20

The following additional information is available:
a. The company's plant has a capacity of 130,000 direct labor-hours per year on a single-shift basis. The company's present employees and equipment can produce all five products.
b. The direct labor rate of $16 per hour is expected to remain unchanged during the coming year.
c. Fixed costs total $520,000 per year. Variable overhead costs are $2 per direct labor-hour.
d. All of the company's nonmanufacturing costs are fixed.
e. The company's finished goods inventory is negligible and can be ignored.

Required:

1. How many direct labor hours are used to manufacture one unit of each of the company's five products?
2. How much variable overhead cost is incurred to manufacture one unit of each of the company's five products?
3. What is the contribution margin per direct labor-hour for each of the company's five products?
4. Assuming that direct labor-hours is the company's constraining resource, what is the highest total contribution margin that the company can earn if it makes optimal use of its constrained resource?
5. Assuming that the company has made optimal use of its 130,000 direct labor-hours, what is the highest direct labor rate per hour that Walton Toy Company would be willing to pay for additional capacity (that is, for added direct labor time)?
6. Identify changes that the company could make to enable it to satisfy the customers' demand for *all* of its products.

(CMA, adapted)

PROBLEM 12–26 Close or Retain a Store LO12–2

Superior Markets, Inc., operates three stores in a large metropolitan area. A segmented absorption costing income statement for the company for the last quarter is given below:

	Total	North Store	South Store	East Store
Superior Markets, Inc.				
Income Statement				
For the Quarter Ended September 30				
Sales	$3,000,000	$720,000	$1,200,000	$1,080,000
Cost of goods sold	1,657,200	403,200	660,000	594,000
Gross margin	1,342,800	316,800	540,000	486,000
Selling and administrative expenses:				
Selling expenses	817,000	231,400	315,000	270,600
Administrative expenses	383,000	106,000	150,900	126,100
Total expenses	1,200,000	337,400	465,900	396,700
Net operating income (loss)	$ 142,800	$(20,600)	$ 74,100	$ 89,300

The North Store has consistently shown losses over the past two years. For this reason, management is giving consideration to closing the store. The company has asked you to make a recommendation as to whether the store should be closed or kept open. The following additional information is available for your use:

a. The breakdown of the selling and administrative expenses that are shown above is as follows:

	Total	North Store	South Store	East Store
Selling expenses:				
Sales salaries	$239,000	$ 70,000	$ 89,000	$ 80,000
Direct advertising	187,000	51,000	72,000	64,000
General advertising*	45,000	10,800	18,000	16,200
Store rent	300,000	85,000	120,000	95,000
Depreciation of store fixtures ...	16,000	4,600	6,000	5,400
Delivery salaries	21,000	7,000	7,000	7,000
Depreciation of delivery				
equipment	9,000	3,000	3,000	3,000
Total selling expenses	$817,000	$231,400	$315,000	$270,600

*Allocated on the basis of sales dollars.

	Total	North Store	South Store	East Store
Administrative expenses:				
Store managers' salaries	$ 70,000	$ 21,000	$ 30,000	$ 19,000
General office salaries*	50,000	12,000	20,000	18,000
Insurance on fixtures and inventory	25,000	7,500	9,000	8,500
Utilities	106,000	31,000	40,000	35,000
Employment taxes	57,000	16,500	21,900	18,600
General office—other*	75,000	18,000	30,000	27,000
Total administrative expenses	$383,000	$106,000	$150,900	$126,100

*Allocated on the basis of sales dollars.

b. The lease on the building housing the North Store can be broken with no penalty.

c. The fixtures being used in the North Store would be transferred to the other two stores if the North Store were closed.

d. The general manager of the North Store would be retained and transferred to another position in the company if the North Store were closed. She would be filling a position that would otherwise be filled by hiring a new employee at a salary of $11,000 per quarter. The general manager of the North Store would continue to earn her normal salary of $12,000 per quarter. All other managers and employees in the North store would be discharged.

e. The company has one delivery crew that serves all three stores. One delivery person could be discharged if the North Store were closed. This person's salary is $4,000 per quarter. The delivery equipment would be distributed to the other stores. The equipment does not wear out through use, but does eventually become obsolete.

f. The company pays employment taxes equal to 15% of their employees' salaries.

g. One-third of the insurance in the North Store is on the store's fixtures.

h. The "General office salaries" and "General office—other" relate to the overall management of Superior Markets, Inc. If the North Store were closed, one person in the general office could be discharged because of the decrease in overall workload. This person's compensation is $6,000 per quarter.

Required:

1. How much employee salaries will the company avoid if it closes the North Store?
2. How much employment taxes will the company avoid if it closes the North Store?
3. What is the financial advantage (disadvantage) of closing the North Store?
4. Assuming that the North Store's floor space can't be subleased, would you recommend closing the North Store?
5. Assume that the North Store's floor space can't be subleased. However, let's introduce three more assumptions. First, assume that if the North Store were closed, one-fourth of its sales would transfer to the East Store, due to strong customer loyalty to Superior Markets. Second, assume that the East Store has enough capacity to handle the increased sales that would arise from closing the North Store. Third, assume that the increased sales in the East Store would yield the same gross margin as a percentage of sales as present sales in the East store. Given these new assumptions, what is the financial advantage (disadvantage) of closing the North Store?

PROBLEM 12–27 Sell or Process Further Decisions LO12–7

Come-Clean Corporation produces a variety of cleaning compounds and solutions for both industrial and household use. While most of its products are processed independently, a few are related, such as the company's Grit 337 and its Sparkle silver polish.

Grit 337 is a coarse cleaning powder with many industrial uses. It costs $1.60 a pound to make, and it has a selling price of $2.00 a pound. A small portion of the annual production of Grit 337 is retained in the factory for further processing. It is combined with several other ingredients to form a paste that is marketed as Sparkle silver polish. The silver polish sells for $4.00 per jar.

This further processing requires one-fourth pound of Grit 337 per jar of silver polish. The additional direct variable costs involved in the processing of a jar of silver polish are:

Other ingredients	$0.65
Direct labor	1.48
Total direct cost	$2.13

Overhead costs associated with processing the silver polish are:

Variable manufacturing overhead cost	25% of direct labor cost
Fixed manufacturing overhead cost (per month):	
Production supervisor	$3,000
Depreciation of mixing equipment	$1,400

The production supervisor has no duties other than to oversee production of the silver polish. The mixing equipment is special-purpose equipment acquired specifically to produce the silver polish. It can produce up to 15,000 jars of polish per month. Its resale value is negligible and it does not wear out through use.

Advertising costs for the silver polish total $4,000 per month. Variable selling costs associated with the silver polish are 7.5% of sales.

Due to a recent decline in the demand for silver polish, the company is wondering whether its continued production is advisable. The sales manager feels that it would be more profitable to sell all of the Grit 337 as a cleaning powder.

Required:

1. How much incremental revenue does the company earn per jar of polish by further processing Grit 337 rather than selling it as a cleaning powder?
2. How much incremental contribution margin does the company earn per jar of polish by further processing Grit 337 rather than selling it as a cleaning powder?
3. How many jars of silver polish must be sold each month to exactly offset the avoidable fixed costs incurred to produce and sell the polish? Explain.
4. If the company sells 9,000 jars of polish, what is the financial advantage (disadvantage) of choosing to further process Grit 337 rather than selling is as a cleaning powder?
5. If the company sells 11,500 jars of polish, what is the financial advantage (disadvantage) of choosing to further process Grit 337 rather than selling is as a cleaning powder?

(CMA, adapted)

PROBLEM 12–28 Make or Buy Decisions LO12–3

"In my opinion, we ought to stop making our own drums and accept that outside supplier's offer," said Wim Niewindt, managing director of Antilles Refining, N.V., of Aruba. "At a price of $18 per drum, we would be paying $5 less than it costs us to manufacture the drums in our own plant. Since we use 60,000 drums a year, that would be an annual cost savings of $300,000." Antilles Refining's current cost to manufacture one drum is given below (based on 60,000 drums per year):

Direct materials	$10.35
Direct labor	6.00
Variable overhead	1.50
Fixed overhead ($2.80 general	
company overhead, $1.60 depreciation	
and, $0.75 supervision)	5.15
Total cost per drum	$23.00

A decision about whether to make or buy the drums is especially important at this time because the equipment being used to make the drums is completely worn out and must be replaced. The choices facing the company are:

Alternative 1: Rent new equipment and continue to make the drums. The equipment would be rented for $135,000 per year.

Alternative 2: Purchase the drums from an outside supplier at $18 per drum.

The new equipment would be more efficient than the equipment that Antilles Refining has been using and, according to the manufacturer, would reduce direct labor and variable overhead costs by 30%. The old equipment has no resale value. Supervision cost ($45,000 per year) and direct materials cost per drum would not be affected by the new equipment. The new equipment's capacity would be 90,000 drums per year.

The company's total general company overhead would be unaffected by this decision.

Required:

1. Assuming that 60,000 drums are needed each year, what is the financial advantage (disadvantage) of buying the drums from an outside supplier?
2. Assuming that 75,000 drums are needed each year, what is the financial advantage (disadvantage) of buying the drums from an outside supplier?
3. Assuming that 90,000 drums are needed each year, what is the financial advantage (disadvantage) of buying the drums from an outside supplier?
4. What other factors would you recommend that the company consider before making a decision?

Cases   connect

CASE 12–29 Sell or Process Further Decision LO12–7

The Scottie Sweater Company produces sweaters under the "Scottie" label. The company buys raw wool and processes it into wool yarn from which the sweaters are woven. One spindle of wool yarn is required to produce one sweater. The costs and revenues associated with the sweaters are given below:

		Per Sweater
Selling price		$30.00
Cost to manufacture:		
Raw materials:		
Buttons, thread, lining	$2.00	
Wool yarn	16.00	
Total raw materials	18.00	
Direct labor	5.80	
Manufacturing overhead	8.70	32.50
Manufacturing profit (loss)		$ (2.50)

Originally, all of the wool yarn was used to produce sweaters, but in recent years a market has developed for the wool yarn itself. The yarn is purchased by other companies for use in production of wool blankets and other wool products. Since the development of the market for the wool yarn, a continuing dispute has existed in the Scottie Sweater Company as to whether the yarn should be sold simply as yarn or processed into sweaters. Current cost and revenue data on the yarn are given below:

		Per Spindle of Yarn
Selling price		$20.00
Cost to manufacture:		
Raw materials (raw wool)	$7.00	
Direct labor	3.60	
Manufacturing overhead	5.40	16.00
Manufacturing profit		$ 4.00

The market for sweaters is temporarily depressed, due to unusually warm weather in the western states where the sweaters are sold. This has made it necessary for the company to discount the selling price of the sweaters to $30 from the normal $40 price. Since the market for wool yarn has remained strong, the dispute has again surfaced over whether the yarn should be sold outright rather than processed into sweaters. The sales manager thinks that the production of sweaters should be discontinued; she is upset about having to sell sweaters at a $2.50 loss when the yarn could be sold for a $4.00 profit. However, the production superintendent does not want to close down a large portion of the factory. He argues that the company is in the sweater business, not the yarn business, and the company should focus on its core strength.

All of the manufacturing overhead costs are fixed and would not be affected even if sweaters were discontinued. Manufacturing overhead is assigned to products on the basis of 150% of direct labor cost. Materials and direct labor costs are variable.

Required:

1. What is the financial advantage (disadvantage) of further processing one spindle of wool yarn into a sweater?
2. Would you recommend that the wool yarn be sold outright or processed into sweaters? Explain.
3. What is the lowest price that the company should accept for a sweater? Support your answer with appropriate computations and explain your reasoning.

CASE 12–30 Ethics and the Manager; Shut Down or Continue Operations LO12–2

Haley Romeros had just been appointed vice president of the Rocky Mountain Region of the Bank Services Corporation (BSC). The company provides check processing services for small banks. The banks send checks presented for deposit or payment to BSC, which records the data on each check in a computerized database. BSC then sends the data electronically to the nearest Federal Reserve Bank check-clearing center where the appropriate transfers of funds are made between banks. The Rocky Mountain Region has three check processing centers, which are located in Billings, Montana; Great Falls, Montana; and Clayton, Idaho. Prior to her promotion to vice president, Ms. Romeros had been the manager of a check processing center in New Jersey.

Immediately after assuming her new position, Ms. Romeros requested a complete financial report for the just-ended fiscal year from the region's controller, John Littlebear. Ms. Romeros specified that the financial report should follow the standardized format required by corporate headquarters for all regional performance reports. That report follows:

		Check Processing Centers		
Bank Services Corporation (BSC) **Rocky Mountain Region** **Financial Performance**	Total	Billings	Great Falls	Clayton
Sales	$50,000,000	$20,000,000	$18,000,000	$12,000,000
Operating expenses:				
Direct labor	32,000,000	12,500,000	11,000,000	8,500,000
Variable overhead	850,000	350,000	310,000	190,000
Equipment depreciation	3,900,000	1,300,000	1,400,000	1,200,000
Facility expense*	2,800,000	900,000	800,000	1,100,000
Local administrative expense[†]	450,000	140,000	160,000	150,000
Regional administrative expense[‡]	1,500,000	600,000	540,000	360,000
Corporate administrative expense[§]	4,750,000	1,900,000	1,710,000	1,140,000
Total operating expense	46,250,000	17,690,000	15,920,000	12,640,000
Net operating income (loss)	$ 3,750,000	$ 2,310,000	$ 2,080,000	$ (640,000)

*Includes building rental expense for the Billings and Great Falls locations and building depreciation for the Clayton location

[†]Local administrative expenses are the administrative expenses incurred at the check processing centers.

[‡]Regional administrative expenses are allocated to the check processing centers based on sales.

[§]Corporate administrative expenses are charged to segments of the company such as the Rocky Mountain Region and the check processing centers at the rate of 9.5% of their sales.

Upon seeing this report, Ms. Romeros summoned John Littlebear for an explanation.

Romeros: What's the story on Clayton? It didn't have a loss the previous year did it?

Littlebear: No, the Clayton facility has had a nice profit every year since it opened six years ago, but Clayton lost a big contract this year.

Romeros: Why?

Littlebear: One of our national competitors entered the local market and bid very aggressively on the contract. We couldn't afford to meet the bid. Clayton's costs—particularly their facility expenses— are just too high. When Clayton lost the contract, we had to lay off a lot of employees, but we could not reduce the fixed costs of the Clayton facility.

Romeros: Why is Clayton's facility expense so high? It's a smaller facility than either Billings or Great Falls and yet its facility expense is higher.

Littlebear: The problem is that we are able to rent suitable facilities very cheaply at Billings and Great Falls. No such facilities were available at Clayton; we had them built. Unfortunately, there were big cost overruns. The contractor we hired was inexperienced at this kind of work and in fact went bankrupt before the project was completed. After hiring another contractor to finish the work, we were way over budget. The large depreciation charges on the facility didn't matter at first because we didn't have much competition at the time and could charge premium prices.

Romeros: Well we can't do that anymore. The Clayton facility will obviously have to be shut down. Its business can be shifted to the other two check processing centers in the region.

Littlebear: I would advise against that. The $1,100,000 in facility depreciation at the Clayton location is misleading. That facility should last indefinitely with proper maintenance. And it has no resale value; there is no other commercial activity around Clayton.

Romeros: What about the other costs at Clayton?

Littlebear: If we shifted Clayton's sales over to the other two processing centers in the region, we wouldn't save anything on direct labor or variable overhead costs. We might save $90,000 or so in local administrative expense, but we would not save any regional administrative expense and corporate headquarters would still charge us 9.5% of our sales as corporate administrative expense.

In addition, we would have to rent more space in Billings and Great Falls in order to handle the work transferred from Clayton; that would probably cost us at least $600,000 a year. And don't forget that it will cost us something to move the equipment from Clayton to Billings and Great Falls. And the move will disrupt service to customers.

Romeros: I understand all of that, but a money-losing processing center on my performance report is completely unacceptable.

Littlebear: And if you shut down Clayton, you are going to throw some loyal employees out of work.

Romeros: That's unfortunate, but we have to face hard business realities.

Littlebear: And you would have to write off the investment in the facilities at Clayton.

Romeros: I can explain a write-off to corporate headquarters; hiring an inexperienced contractor to build the Clayton facility was my predecessor's mistake. But they'll have my head at headquarters if I show operating losses every year at one of my processing centers. Clayton has to go. At the next corporate board meeting, I am going to recommend the Clayton facility be closed.

Required:

1. From the standpoint of the company as a whole, what is the financial advantage (disadvantage) of closing the Clayton processing center and redistributing its work to other processing centers in the region? Explain.

2. Why might it be in Haley Romeros's self-interest to shut down the Clayton facility? Do you think Haley Romeros is conducting herself in an ethical fashion? Explain.

3. What influence should the depreciation on the facilities at Clayton have on prices charged by Clayton for its services?

CASE 12–31 Integrative Case: Relevant Costs; Pricing LO12–1, LO12–4

Wesco Incorporated's only product is a combination fertilizer/weedkiller called GrowNWeed. GrowNWeed is sold nationwide to retail nurseries and garden stores.

Zwinger Nursery plans to sell a similar fertilizer/weedkiller compound through its regional nursery chain under its own private label. Zwinger does not have manufacturing facilities of its own, so it has asked Wesco (and several other companies) to submit a bid for manufacturing and delivering a 20,000-pound order of the private brand compound to Zwinger. While the chemical composition of the Zwinger compound differs from that of GrowNWeed, the manufacturing processes are very similar.

The Zwinger compound would be produced in 1,000-pound lots. Each lot would require 25 direct labor-hours and the following chemicals:

Chemicals	Quantity in Pounds
AG–5	300
KL–2	200
CW–7	150
DF–6	175

The first three chemicals (AG–5, KL–2, and CW–7) are all used in the production of GrowN-Weed. DF–6 was used in another compound that Wesco discontinued several months ago. The supply of DF–6 that Wesco had on hand when the other compound was discontinued was not discarded. Wesco could sell its supply of DF–6 at the prevailing market price less $0.10 per pound selling and handling expenses.

Wesco also has on hand a chemical called BH–3, which was manufactured for use in another product that is no longer produced. BH–3, which cannot be used in GrowNWeed, can be substituted for AG–5 on a one-for-one basis without affecting the quality of the Zwinger compound. The BH–3 in inventory has a salvage value of $600.

Inventory and cost data for the chemicals that can be used to produce the Zwinger compound are shown below:

Raw Material	Pounds in Inventory	Actual Price per Pound When Purchased	Current Market Price per Pound
AG–5	18,000	$1.15	$1.20
KL–2	6,000	$1.10	$1.05
CW–7	7,000	$1.35	$1.35
DF–6	3,000	$0.80	$0.70
BH–3	3,500	$0.90	(Salvage)

The current direct labor wage rate is $14 per hour. The predetermined overhead rate is based on direct labor-hours (DLH). The predetermined overhead rate for the current year, based on a two-shift capacity with no overtime, is as follows:

Variable manufacturing overhead	$ 3.00	per DLH
Fixed manufacturing overhead	10.50	per DLH
Combined predetermined overhead rate	$13.50	per DLH

Wesco's production manager reports that the present equipment and facilities are adequate to manufacture the Zwinger compound. Therefore, the order would have no effect on total fixed manufacturing overhead costs. However, Wesco is within 400 hours of its two-shift capacity this month. Any additional hours beyond the 400 hours must be done in overtime. If need be, the Zwinger compound could be produced on regular time by shifting a portion of GrowNWeed production to overtime. Wesco's direct labor wage rate for overtime is $21 per hour. There is no allowance for any overtime premium in the predetermined overhead rate.

Required:

1. Wesco has decided to submit a bid for the 20,000 pound order of Zwinger's new compound. The order must be delivered by the end of the current month. Zwinger has indicated that this is a one-time order that will not be repeated. Calculate the lowest price that Wesco could bid for the order and still exactly cover its incremental manufacturing costs.

2. Refer to the original data. Assume that Zwinger Nursery plans to place regular orders for 20,000-pound lots of the new compound. Wesco expects the demand for GrowNWeed to remain strong. Therefore, the recurring orders from Zwinger would put Wesco over its two-shift capacity. However, production could be scheduled so that 90% of each Zwinger order could be completed during regular hours. As another option, some GrowNWeed production could be shifted temporarily to overtime so that the Zwinger orders could be produced on regular time. Current market prices are the best available estimates of future market prices.

   Wesco's standard markup policy for new products is 40% of the full manufacturing cost, including fixed manufacturing overhead. Calculate the price that Wesco, Inc., would quote Zwinger Nursery for each 20,000 pound lot of the new compound, assuming that it is to be treated as a new product and this pricing policy is followed.

(CMA, adapted)

CASE 12–32 Make or Buy Decisions; Volume Trade-Off Decisions LO12–1, LO12–3, LO12–5

TufStuff, Inc., sells a wide range of drums, bins, boxes, and other containers that are used in the chemical industry. One of the company's products is a heavy-duty corrosion-resistant metal drum, called the WVD drum, used to store toxic wastes. Production is constrained by the capacity of an automated welding machine that is used to make precision welds. A total of 2,000 hours of welding time is available annually on the machine. Because each drum requires 0.4 hours of welding machine time, annual production is limited to 5,000 drums. At present, the welding machine is used exclusively to make the WVD drums. The accounting department has provided the following financial data concerning the WVD drums:

WVD Drums		
Selling price per drum		$149.00
Cost per drum:		
Direct materials	$52.10	
Direct labor ($18 per hour)	3.60	
Manufacturing overhead	4.50	
Selling and administrative expense	29.80	90.00
Margin per drum		$ 59.00

Management believes 6,000 WVD drums could be sold each year if the company had sufficient manufacturing capacity. As an alternative to adding another welding machine, management has considered buying additional drums from an outside supplier. Harcor Industries, Inc., a supplier of quality products, would be able to provide up to 4,000 WVD-type drums per year at a price of $138 per drum, which TufStuff would resell to its customers at its normal selling price after appropriate relabeling.

Megan Flores, TufStuff's production manager, has suggested the company could make better use of the welding machine by manufacturing bike frames, which would require only 0.5 hours of welding machine time per frame and yet sell for far more than the drums. Megan believes that TufStuff could sell up to 1,600 bike frames per year to bike manufacturers at a price of $239 each. The accounting department has provided the following data concerning the proposed new product:

Bike Frames		
Selling price per frame		$239.00
Cost per frame:		
Direct materials	$99.40	
Direct labor ($18 per hour)	28.80	
Manufacturing overhead	36.00	
Selling and administrative expense	47.80	212.00
Margin per frame		$ 27.00

The bike frames could be produced with existing equipment and personnel. Manufacturing overhead is allocated to products on the basis of direct labor-hours. Most of the manufacturing overhead consists of fixed common costs such as rent on the factory building, but some of it is variable. The variable manufacturing overhead has been estimated at $1.35 per WVD drum and $1.90 per bike frame. The variable manufacturing overhead cost would not be incurred on drums acquired from the outside supplier.

Selling and administrative expenses are allocated to products on the basis of revenues. Almost all of the selling and administrative expenses are fixed common costs, but it has been estimated that variable selling and administrative expenses amount to $0.75 per WVD drum whether made or purchased and would be $1.30 per bike frame.

All of the company's employees—direct and indirect—are paid for full 40-hour work weeks and the company has a policy of laying off workers only in major recessions.

Required:
1. Would you be comfortable relying on the financial data provided by the accounting department for making decisions related to the WVD drums and bike frames? Why?
2. Assuming direct labor is a fixed cost, compute the contribution margin per unit for:
   a. Purchased WVD drums.
   b. Manufactured WVD drums.
   c. Manufactured bike frames.
3. Assuming direct labor is a fixed cost, compute the contribution margin per welding hour for:
   a. Manufactured WVD drums.
   b. Manufactured bike frames.

4. Assuming direct labor is a fixed cost, determine the number of WVD drums (if any) that should be purchased and the number of WVD drums and/or bike frames (if any) that should be manufactured. What is the increase (decrease) in net operating income that would result from this plan over current operations?

As soon as your analysis was shown to the top management team at TufStuff, several managers got into an argument concerning how direct labor costs should be treated when making this decision. One manager argued that direct labor is always treated as a variable cost in textbooks and in practice and has always been considered a variable cost at TufStuff. After all, "direct" means you can directly trace the cost to products. "If direct labor is not a variable cost, what is?" Another manager argued just as strenuously that direct labor should be considered a fixed cost at TufStuff. No one had been laid off in over a decade, and for all practical purposes, everyone at the plant is on a monthly salary. Everyone classified as direct labor works a regular 40-hour workweek and overtime has not been necessary since the company adopted Lean Production techniques. Whether the welding machine is used to make drums or frames, the total payroll would be exactly the same. There is enough slack, in the form of idle time, to accommodate any increase in total direct labor time that the bike frames would require.

5. Assuming direct labor is a variable cost, compute the contribution margin per unit for:
   a. Purchased WVD drums.
   b. Manufactured WVD drums.
   c. Manufactured bike frames.
6. Assuming direct labor is a variable cost, compute the contribution margin per welding hour for:
   a. Manufactured WVD drums.
   b. Manufactured bike frames.
7. Assuming direct labor is a variable cost, determine the number of WVD drums (if any) that should be purchased and the number of WVD drums and/or bike frames (if any) that should be manufactured. What is the increase (decrease) in net operating income that would result from this plan over current operations?
8. What do you think is the correct way to treat direct labor cost in this situation—as variable or as fixed? Explain.

CASE 12–33 Plant Closing Decision LO12–1, LO12–2

QualSupport Corporation manufactures seats for automobiles, vans, trucks, and various recreational vehicles. The company has a number of plants around the world, including the Denver Cover Plant, which makes seat covers.

Ted Vosilo is the plant manager of the Denver Cover Plant but also serves as the regional production manager for the company. His budget as the regional manager is charged to the Denver Cover Plant.

Vosilo has just heard that QualSupport has received a bid from an outside vendor to supply the equivalent of the entire annual output of the Denver Cover Plant for $35 million. Vosilo was astonished at the low outside bid because the budget for the Denver Cover Plant's operating costs for the upcoming year was set at $52 million. If this bid is accepted, the Denver Cover Plant will be closed down.

The budget for Denver Cover's operating costs for the coming year is presented below.

Denver Cover Plant Annual Budget for Operating Costs		
Materials		$14,000,000
Labor:		
Direct	$13,100,000	
Supervision	900,000	
Indirect plant	4,000,000	18,000,000
Overhead:		
Depreciation—equipment	3,200,000	
Depreciation—building	7,000,000	
Pension expense	5,000,000	
Plant manager and staff	800,000	
Corporate expenses*	4,000,000	20,000,000
Total budgeted costs		$52,000,000

*Fixed corporate expenses allocated to plants and other operating units based on total budgeted wage and salary costs.

Additional facts regarding the plant's operations are as follows:

a.   Due to Denver Cover's commitment to use high-quality fabrics in all of its products, the Purchasing Department was instructed to place blanket purchase orders with major suppliers to ensure the receipt of sufficient materials for the coming year. If these orders are canceled as a consequence of the plant closing, termination charges would amount to 20% of the cost of direct materials.

b.   Approximately 400 plant employees will lose their jobs if the plant is closed. This includes all of the direct laborers and supervisors as well as the plumbers, electricians, and other skilled workers classified as indirect plant workers. Some would be able to find new jobs while many others would have difficulty. All employees would have difficulty matching Denver Cover's base pay of $18.80 per hour, which is the highest in the area. A clause in Denver Cover's contract with the union may help some employees; the company must provide employment assistance to its former employees for 12 months after a plant closing. The estimated cost to administer this service would be $1.5 million for the year.

c.   Some employees would probably choose early retirement because QualSupport has an excellent pension plan. In fact, $3 million of the annual pension expense would continue whether Denver Cover is open or not.

d.   Vosilo and his staff would not be affected by the closing of Denver Cover. They would still be responsible for administering three other area plants.

e.   If the Denver Cover Plant were closed, the company would realize about $3.2 million salvage value for the equipment and building. If the plant remains open, there are no plans to make any significant investments in new equipment or buildings. The old equipment is adequate and should last indefinitely.

Required:

1.   Without regard to costs, identify the advantages to QualSupport Corporation of continuing to obtain covers from its own Denver Cover Plant.

2.   QualSupport Corporation plans to prepare a financial analysis that will be used in deciding whether or not to close the Denver Cover Plant. Management has asked you to identify:

a.   The annual budgeted costs that are relevant to the decision regarding closing the plant (show the dollar amounts).

b.   The annual budgeted costs that are *irrelevant* to the decision regarding closing the plant and explain why they are irrelevant (again show the dollar amounts).

c.   Any nonrecurring costs that would arise due to the closing of the plant, and explain how they would affect the decision (again show any dollar amounts).

3.   Looking at the data you have prepared in (2) above, what is the financial advantage (disadvantage) of closing the plant? Show computations and explain your answer.

4.   Identify any revenues or costs not specifically mentioned in the problem that QualSupport should consider before making a decision.

(CMA, adapted)

Appendix 12A: Pricing Decisions

Some products have an established market price. Consumers will not pay more than this price and there is no reason for a supplier to charge less—the supplier can sell all that it produces at this price. Under these circumstances, the supplier simply charges the prevailing market price for the product. Markets for basic raw materials such as farm products and minerals follow this pattern.

In this appendix, we are concerned with the more common situation in which a business needs to set its own prices. For example, **Delta Airlines** has to establish ticket prices for all of its flights. **Accenture** needs to establish bid prices when it responds to inquiries from prospective consulting clients. **Procter & Gamble** has to set prices for Bounty, Tide, Pampers, Crest, and its many other product lines. If these companies choose prices that are too high or too low it can dramatically decrease profits.

Factors That Influence Pricing Decisions

Many factors can influence how companies establish their selling prices. In this section, we'd like to discuss three of those factors—customers, competitors, and costs.

Customers   Customers usually possess two things—latitude and private information—that complicate the pricing process. In terms of latitude, the customer can choose to buy your product, or a competitor's product, or nothing at all. Customers also have private information regarding their level of interest in your product or service and how much they might be willing to pay for it.

For example, consider a scenario where a prospective customer invites numerous suppliers to place competitive bids in hopes of winning a contract. The customer has access to private information because it can compare and choose among the bids submitted by each supplier. If a particular supplier sets a bid price that is too high, the customer will award the contract to a competitor. Conversely, if that same supplier is awarded the contract based on a bid price that is much lower than its competitors, it may forgo revenue that the customer would have been willing to pay.

Many companies do not continuously set bid prices for individual contracts; instead, they sell products and services to large volumes of diverse customers who do not have an identical willingness to pay a particular price for a given product. In these situations, companies are keenly interested in quantifying the customers' *price elasticity of demand*. The **price elasticity of demand** measures the degree to which a change in price affects unit sales. Demand for a product or service is said to be *inelastic* if a change in price has little effect on the number of units sold. On the other hand, demand for a product or service is *elastic* if a change in price has a substantial effect on the volume of units sold. Generally speaking, managers should set higher prices when demand is inelastic and lower prices when demand is elastic.

Competitors   Competitors have an important effect on a company's pricing decisions because they provide *reference prices* that influence the price elasticity of demand. For example, gasoline buyers usually have readily available reference prices when buying fuel. If a gas station raises its prices higher than the reference price of its competitor across the street, then demand is likely to drop significantly. In this instance, demand is elastic because gasoline is a commodity; therefore, customers are unwilling to pay more than the competitor's reference price. If the same gas station lowered its prices expecting elastic demand to create market share gains, the competitor across the street would probably match the price reduction, thereby holding each gas station's market share constant while lowering both competitors' profits.

If a company wants to charge higher prices than its competitors, then the company must differentiate its products or services from competing choices in a manner that motivates its customers to accept higher prices. For example, brands such as **Prada**, **Rolex**, and **Rolls Royce** have created product quality and an elite social status that differentiates their products from competitors and creates inelastic demand among wealthy customers willing to pay extremely high prices.

Costs   Customers and competitors play important roles in determining the *price ceiling* for a company's products and services. The price ceiling represents the highest price that customers are willing to pay. A company's *price floor* is determined by its incremental costs. The price floor represents the lowest price that a company can charge and still make incremental profit on the sales transaction.

It is important to recognize that if a company prices all of its products above the price floor, it does not guarantee the company will earn a profit. This is because the total sales revenue earned minus incremental costs may not cover the company's fixed costs. A company increases its likelihood of covering all of its costs and maximizing profits if it is capable of choosing optimal prices based on customer demand data rather than computing prices that are arbitrarily chosen without the benefit of customer feedback.

Cost-Plus Pricing

Companies frequently use a pricing approach where they *markup* cost.[7] A product's **markup** is the difference between its selling price and its cost and is usually expressed as a percentage of cost.

$$\text{Selling price} = (1 + \text{Markup percentage}) \times \text{Cost}$$

For example, a company that uses a markup of 50% adds 50% to the costs of its products to determine selling prices. If a product costs $10, then the company would apply a markup of $5 to derive a selling price of $15 for the product. This approach is called **cost-plus pricing** because a predetermined markup percentage is applied to a cost base to determine the selling price.

Companies can define the cost base that they use for cost-plus pricing in a variety of ways. For example, some companies may use absorption costing to define a cost base that includes direct materials, direct labor, variable manufacturing overhead, and fixed manufacturing overhead whereas other companies may rely on a product's variable cost as the cost base. Furthermore, companies can use various types of cost systems, such as normal costing or standard costing, when quantifying the cost base. If a company uses normal costing for its absorption approach, it would calculate unit product costs based on actual direct materials and direct labor costs plus applied overhead. A company that uses standard costing for its absorption approach would derive unit product costs based on standard direct materials and direct labor costs per unit plus the amount of applied overhead that is allowed per unit produced.

In the next section, we will discuss the absorption costing approach to cost-plus pricing. As the name implies, the absorption approach uses an absorption-based unit product cost for the cost base when calculating the markup percentage.

The Absorption Costing Approach to Cost-Plus Pricing

LO12–8
Compute the selling price of a product using the absorption costing approach to cost-plus pricing.

Surveys consistently reveal that many managers use the absorption costing approach to cost-plus pricing. This method can be explained in a three-step process.

First, a company needs to calculate its *unit product costs* (including direct materials, direct labor, variable manufacturing overhead, and fixed manufacturing overhead). Second, it needs to determine its markup percentage on absorption cost. Third, it needs to multiply a product's unit product cost by the sum of one plus the markup percentage to determine the product's selling price.

Ritter Company: An Example

Let's assume that Ritter Company wants to set the selling price on a product that has just undergone some design modifications. The company has invested $100,000 in operating assets to sell an estimated sales volume of 10,000 units. Its required return on investment (ROI) in its operating assets is 20%. The accounting department has provided the following cost estimates for the redesigned product:

	Per Unit	Total
Direct materials	$6	
Direct labor	$4	
Variable manufacturing overhead	$3	
Fixed manufacturing overhead		$70,000
Variable selling and administrative expenses	$2	
Fixed selling and administrative expenses		$60,000

[7] There are some legal restrictions on prices. Antitrust laws prohibit "predatory" prices, which are generally interpreted by the courts to mean a price below average variable cost. "Price discrimination"—charging different prices to customers in the same market for the same product or service—is also prohibited by the law.

In step one of its absorption cost-plus pricing process, Ritter Company would compute the redesigned product's unit product cost as follows (absorption basis):

Direct materials	$ 6
Direct labor	4
Variable manufacturing overhead	3
Fixed manufacturing overhead ($70,000 ÷ 10,000 units)	7
Unit product cost	$20

Ritter's second step would be to determine the markup percentage that will be multiplied by the unit product cost ($20) to derive the selling price. The formula that is used to determine the markup percentage is as follows:

$$\text{Markup percentage on absorption cost} = \frac{(\text{Required ROI} \times \text{Investment}) + \text{Selling and administrative expenses}}{\text{Unit product cost} \times \text{Unit sales}}$$

Referring to Ritter's background information, the markup percentage on absorption cost would be calculated as follows:

$$\text{Markup percentage on absorption cost} = \frac{(20\% \times \$100{,}000) + (\$2 \text{ per unit} \times 10{,}000 \text{ units} + \$60{,}000)}{\$20 \text{ per unit} \times 10{,}000 \text{ units}}$$

$$= \frac{(\$20{,}000) + (\$80{,}000)}{\$200{,}000}$$

$$= 50\%$$

Notice that the 50% markup on absorption cost is designed to provide the company's required return on investment (20% × $100,000 = $20,000) and to cover the product's selling and administrative expenses ($2 per unit × 10,000 units + $60,000 = $80,000).

The third step is to establish the selling price per unit using the cost-plus pricing equation that was introduced earlier:

$$\text{Selling price} = (1 + \text{Markup percentage}) \times \text{Cost}$$

$$= (1 + 50\%) \times \$20$$

$$= \$30$$

The selling price of $30 covers the unit product cost of $20 plus it provides $10 more dollars to cover selling and administrative expenses and to provide the required ROI.

As shown in Exhibit 12A–1, *if Ritter actually realizes its forecasted sales of 10,000 units,* the product will indeed earn a net operating income of $20,000 and an ROI of 20%. However, if it turns out that more than 10,000 units are sold at this price, the ROI will be greater than 20%. If less than 10,000 units are sold, the ROI will be less than 20%. *The required ROI will be attained only if the forecasted unit sales volume is attained.*

Problems with the Absorption Costing Approach

The absorption costing approach makes pricing look deceptively simple. All a company needs to do is compute its unit product cost, decide how much profit it wants, and then set its price. It appears that a company can ignore customer demand and arrive at a price that will safely yield whatever profit it wants. Given that the absorption approach forecasts unit sales *before* establishing a selling price, it appears to operate on the faulty assumption that customers have no latitude—that they are required to buy the product at whatever price the seller deems appropriate. That is not true! Customers have a choice. If the price is too high they can buy from a competitor or they may choose not to buy at all.

EXHIBIT 12A–1

Income Statement and ROI Analysis—Ritter Company Actual Unit Sales = 10,000 Units; Selling Price = $30

Direct materials	$ 6
Direct labor	4
Variable manufacturing overhead	3
Fixed manufacturing overhead ($70,000 ÷ 10,000 units)	7
Unit product cost	$20

Absorption Costing Income Statement

Sales ($30 per unit × 10,000 units)	$300,000
Cost of goods sold ($20 per unit × 10,000 units)	200,000
Gross margin	100,000
Selling and administrative expenses ($2 per unit × 10,000 units + $60,000)	80,000
Net operating income	$ 20,000

ROI

$$ROI = \frac{\text{Net operating income}}{\text{Average operating assets}}$$

$$= \frac{\$20,000}{\$100,000}$$

$$= 20\%$$

Suppose, for example, that when Ritter Company sets its price at $30, it sells only 7,000 units rather than the forecasted volume of 10,000 units. As shown in Exhibit 12A–2, this lower sales volume would cause the unit product cost to increase from $20 to $23. Furthermore, and as also shown in Exhibit 12A–2, the company would have a loss of $25,000 on the product instead of a profit of $20,000.

EXHIBIT 12A–2

Income Statement and ROI Analysis—Ritter Company Actual Unit Sales = 7,000 Units; Selling Price = $30

Direct materials	$ 6
Direct labor	4
Variable manufacturing overhead	3
Fixed manufacturing overhead ($70,000 ÷ 7,000 units)	10
Unit product cost	$23

Absorption Costing Income Statement

Sales ($30 per unit × 7,000 units)	$210,000
Cost of goods sold ($23 per unit × 7,000 units)	161,000
Gross margin	49,000
Selling and administrative expenses ($2 per unit × 7,000 units + $60,000)	74,000
Net operating loss	$ (25,000)

ROI

$$ROI = \frac{\text{Net operating income}}{\text{Average operating assets}}$$

$$= \frac{-\$25,000}{\$100,000}$$

$$= -25\%$$

If Ritter responds to this situation by raising its price in an effort to restore profitability at a sales volume of 7,000 units, it would recalculate the markup percentage on absorption cost as follows:

$$\frac{\text{Markup percentage}}{\text{on absorption cost}} = \frac{(20\% \times \$100,000) + (\$2 \text{ per unit} \times 7,000 \text{ units} + \$60,000)}{\$23 \text{ per unit} \times 7,000 \text{ units}}$$

$$= \frac{(\$20,000) + (\$74,000)}{\$161,000}$$

$$= 58.4\%$$

This higher markup percentage would in turn raise the price on the redesigned product from $30.00 to $36.43, which is calculated as follows:

$$\text{Selling price} = (1 + \text{Markup percentage}) \times \text{Cost}$$

$$= (1 + 58.4\%) \times \$23$$

$$= \$36.43$$

While Ritter may hope that a price increase of $6.43 (= $36.43 − $30.00) will restore profitability, in all likelihood, the price hike will cause additional customer defections and lower profits. This is because Ritter's customers are not required to pay whatever price is necessary for Ritter to meet its financial goals. The customers have the latitude to reject Ritter's price and spend their money elsewhere.

Pricing and Customer Latitude

As discussed in the previous section, customers have latitude in their purchasing decisions. They can purchase a competitor's product or allocate their spending budget to some other product altogether. This latitude should be taken into account when setting prices. To illustrate, consider Nature's Garden, a company that sells many products including Apple-Almond Shampoo. The company has provided the following data regarding this product:

LO12–9
Understand how the customers' sensitivity to changes in price should influence pricing decisions.

	Apple-Almond Shampoo
Unit sales (a)	200,000
Selling price per unit	$5.00
Variable cost per unit	2.00
Contribution margin per unit (b)	$3.00
Total contribution margin (a) × (b)	$600,000
Traceable fixed expenses	570,000
Net operating income	$ 30,000

Management is considering increasing the price of Apple-Almond Shampoo from $5.00 to $5.50, but is fully aware that this 10% increase in price [= ($5.50 − $5.00) ÷ $5.00] will result in a decline in unit sales because of the latitude that customers have in their purchasing decisions. If unit sales drop too much, profit (i.e., net operating income) may actually decline despite the increase in the selling price. The company's marketing managers have estimated that this price hike could decrease unit sales by as much as 15%, from 200,000 units to 170,000 units.

The question the company would like to answer is which price ($5.00 or $5.50) will generate higher profits? To answer this question, the company can use the following equation to calculate Apple-Almond Shampoo's profit at each price:

$$\text{Profit} = (P - V) \times Q - \text{Fixed expenses}$$

where P is the selling price per unit, V is the variable cost per unit, and Q is the unit sales.

At a price of \$5.00 and a sales volume of 200,000 units Apple-Almond Shampoo earns a profit of \$30,000 as shown below:

$$\text{Profit} = (P - V) \times Q - \text{Fixed expenses}$$
$$= (\$5.00 - \$2.00) \times 200,000 - \$570,000$$
$$= \$3.00 \times 200,000 - \$570,000$$
$$= \$600,000 - \$570,000$$
$$= \$30,000$$

At a price of \$5.50 and a sales volume of 170,000 units, assuming that fixed expenses are not affected by the decrease in unit sales, Apple-Almond Shampoo earns a profit of \$25,000 as shown below:

$$\text{Profit} = (P - V) \times Q - \text{Fixed expenses}$$
$$= (\$5.50 - \$2.00) \times 170,000 - \$570,000$$
$$= \$3.50 \times 170,000 - \$570,000$$
$$= \$595,000 - \$570,000$$
$$= \$25,000$$

Given these results, Nature's Garden should not raise the price of this product to \$5.50 because its profits would be \$5,000 higher (= \$30,000 – \$25,000) at the lower price of \$5.00.

Customer Latitude: A Closer Look

Thus far, our example assumed that management has only two options: either keep the price of Apple-Almond Shampoo at \$5.00 or increase it to \$5.50 with a resulting drop in unit sales of 15%. However, keep in mind that the 15% figure is an estimate not a certainty. Based on our previous calculations, we know that increasing the price from \$5.00 to \$5.50 would reduce profits if unit sales decrease by 15%. If unit sales decrease by more than 15%, profits will decline even more. But what would be the financial implications if unit sales actually decreased by something *less than* 15%?

Management could explore this possibility by calculating the unit sales (Q) needed at the higher price (\$5.50) to achieve the same profit (\$30,000) that is earned at the lower price (\$5.00). Assuming that fixed expenses remain unchanged, that critical value of unit sales (Q) can be solved for as follows:

$$\text{Profit} = (P - V) \times Q - \text{Fixed expenses}$$
$$\$30,000 = (\$5.50 - \$2.00) \times Q - \$570,000$$
$$\$600,000 = \$3.50Q$$
$$Q = 171,429 \text{ units (rounded)}$$

This calculation tells us that if the company sells 171,249 units at the selling price of \$5.50, the company will earn the same profit that it earned at the lower price of \$5.00. But if the company sells *more* than 171,249 units, then increasing the selling price by 10% will *increase* profit. However, if the company sells *fewer* than 171,429 units, then increasing the selling price by 10% will *decrease* profit. The critical value of 171,249 units is sort of a break-even in this situation.

The sales volume of 171,429 units reflects a percentage change in sales of −14.3% [= (171,429 – 200,000) ÷ 200,000]. Thus, if management believes unit sales will drop by *less* than 14.3% it should choose a price of \$5.50. If management believes unit sales will drop by *more* than 14.3% it should choose a price of \$5.00. Let's suppose that management believes unit sales will drop by less than 14.3% and therefore the selling price is increased to \$5.50. Further suppose that management is correct and after increasing the price, unit sales drop by only 13%—from 200,000 units to 174,000 units. Then Apple-Almond Shampoo would earn a profit of \$39,000 as shown below:

$$\text{Profit} = (P - V) \times Q - \text{Fixed expenses}$$

$$= (\$5.50 - \$2.00) \times 174{,}000 - \$570{,}000$$

$$= \$3.50 \times 174{,}000 - \$570{,}000$$

$$= \$39{,}000$$

In this case, because unit sales drop by only 13%, the higher price of $5.50 causes profits to increase by $9,000 (= $39,000 – $30,000).

Choosing Optimal Prices: The Influence of Customer Latitude

If we assume a 10% increase in the price of Apple-Almond Shampoo causes a 13% decrease in unit sales, then a price of $5.50 will generate $9,000 (= $39,000 – $30,000) of additional profit compared to a price of $5.00. However, it would be incorrect to conclude that $5.50 is the *optimal price* for Apple-Almond Shampoo; in other words, the price that would maximize profit.

A price of $5.50 is not necessarily the optimal price because Nature's Garden is not limited to choosing a price of either $5.00 or $5.50. Perhaps the company would be better off considering an 8% or 12% price increase rather than just a 10% increase. For that matter, the company can establish any price it wants for Apple-Almond Shampoo. It could establish a very low price, such as $2.00 per unit, or a very high price, such as $50 per unit, or anything in between. The low price of $2.00 would be a bad idea because it equals the product's variable cost per unit and would lead to a loss of $570,000, whereas, the high price of $50 per unit may be a bad idea because very few customers, if any, would pay $50 for a bottle of shampoo. Thus, the management challenge becomes leveraging knowledge of how customers will respond to changes in price to determine the selling price that will maximize profits—keeping in mind that this optimal price could be higher or lower than the current price of $5.00.

Exhibit 12A–3 uses Microsoft Excel to illustrate a pricing model that calculates an optimal price for any product or service once the percentage change in price and percentage change in unit sales have been specified.[8] The specific calculations shown in Exhibit 12A–3 relate to Nature Garden's Apple-Almond Shampoo assuming that a 10% increase in price causes a 13% decrease in unit sales.

	A	B	C	D	E	F
1		Optimal Pricing Model				
2	Apple-Almond Shampoo:					
3	Current unit sales	200,000				
4	Current selling price per unit	$5.00				
5	Variable cost per unit	$2.00				
6	Traceable fixed costs	$570,000				
7						
8	Percentage change in selling price	10%				
9	Percentage change in unit sales	-13%				
10						
11		Per Unit		Unit Sales		Total
12	Sales	$ 6.34	×	141,467	=	$ 896,481
13	Variable expenses	2.00	×	141,467	=	282,934
14	Contribution margin	$ 4.34	×	141,467	=	613,547
15	Traceable fixed expenses					570,000
16	Net operating income					$ 43,547
17						

H ◀ ▶ H   Chapter 12 Form ╱ Chapter 12 Form ◀

EXHIBIT 12A–3
Nature's Garden Apple-Almond Shampoo: An Optimal Pricing Model

Note: The price shown in cell B12 is rounded to the nearest penny, whereas Excel used the unrounded price (which is approximately $6.337) to compute the total sales in cell F12.

---

[8] This pricing model assumes a constant elasticity demand curve and fixed expenses that are unaffected by the changes in unit sales. Other demand curves, such as a linear demand curve, could be assumed. While there is some empirical support for using the constant elasticity demand curve, it should be acknowledged that the "optimal" selling price will depend on the demand curve that is assumed. Because of this, as well as the uncertainty that usually surrounds estimates of customer responses to price changes, the "optimal" price produced by this model should be viewed as an estimate and not taken too literally.

The first thing to notice with respect to the output from our optimal price calculations shown in Exhibit 12A–3 is that the optimal price is not $5.00 or $5.50. It is $6.34 as shown in cell B12. At this price the company earns a profit of $43,547 (cell F16), which is $4,547 (= $43,547 – $39,000) higher than the previously computed profit obtained at a price of $5.50. While the mathematics underlying this pricing model are beyond the scope of this course, if you choose to download the model and familiarize yourself with it, we want you to understand how to input data into the model and how to interpret the results.[9]

To input data into the model, you should follow a four-step process. First, input the product's current unit sales (cell B3), current selling price (cell B4), variable cost per unit (cell B5), and traceable fixed costs (cell B6). Second, input the percentage change in selling price (cell B8) and the percentage change in unit sales (cell B9). Third, input the current selling price in cell B12. Fourth, click on the Data tab in Microsoft Excel and select Solver in the upper right-hand portion of your screen.[10] When the Solver window opens, click "Solve" and the optimal price will be calculated and automatically inserted into cell B12. In addition, the optimal profit will be automatically calculated in cell F16.

A Visual Perspective of the Optimal Pricing Model

Exhibit 12A–4 plots Apple Almond Shampoo's net operating income as a function of the selling price when we assume that a 10% increase in price decreases unit sales by 13%.[11]

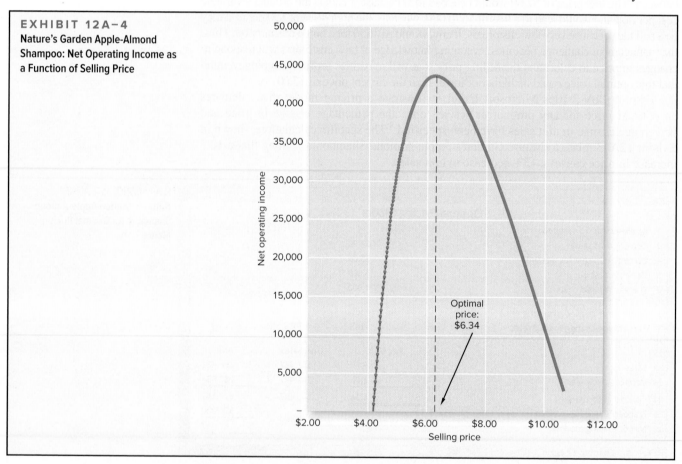

EXHIBIT 12A–4
Nature's Garden Apple-Almond Shampoo: Net Operating Income as a Function of Selling Price

---

[9] To obtain a copy of this Excel-based pricing model go to www.mhhe.com/garrison_opm.

[10] Solver is an Add-in offered within Microsoft Excel. To activate Solver if you do not see it in your Data tab, click the File tab and select Options. Within the Excel Options menu that appears on your screen, click Add-ins and then select Solver Add-in and click OK.

[11] As with the Solver solution to the optimal pricing problem, this graph assumes a constant elasticity demand curve and that the fixed expenses are constant throughout the entire range of unit sales that result from the various prices.

This plot provides a visual aid in understanding what the optimal pricing model is doing. Essentially, Excel Solver efficiently searches along this graph for the price that maximizes the profit, which in this case is a selling price of $6.34 that results in a total profit of $43,547.

For a variety of reasons, this optimal selling price should not be taken too literally. A prudent manager would make a small change in price in the direction of the optimal price and then observe what happens to unit sales and to the net operating income. Nevertheless, the Excel workbook can provide us with important insights into pricing. If we wanted to adjust the percentage change in unit sales or the percentage change in selling price, we could re-run the Solver function to automatically compute the revised optimal selling price.[12] For example, the table below summarizes the results for three scenarios illustrating different customer sensitivities to a 10% increase in price for Apple-Almond Shampoo:

Percentage change in selling price	+10%	+10%	+10%
Percentage change in unit sales	−12%	−13%	−15%
Optimal selling price	$7.86	$6.34	$4.84
Unit sales	109,009	141,467	211,685
Net operating income	$68,908	$43,547	$30,390

In general, the more sensitive customers are to price, the lower the optimal selling price will be and the less sensitive customers are to price, the higher the optimal selling price will be. For example, when customers respond to a 10% increase in price with a 12% decrease in unit sales the optimal price is $7.86, which is $2.86 above the current price of $5.00. Conversely, when customers respond to a 10% increase in price with a 15% decrease in unit sales the optimal price is $4.84, which is $0.16 below the current price of $5.00. This large swing in prices illustrates how a small change in the customers' sensitivity to price can have a big impact on the optimal selling price.

Value-Based Pricing

An alternative to cost-plus pricing is *value-based pricing*. Companies that use **value-based pricing** establish selling prices based on the economic value of the benefits that their products and services provide to customers.

LO12–10
Analyze pricing decisions using value-based pricing.

One approach to value-based pricing relies on a concept known as the *economic value to the customer (EVC)*. A product's **economic value to the customer** is the price of the customer's best available alternative plus the value of what differentiates the product from that alternative. The price of the best available alternative is known as the *reference value*, whereas the value of what differentiates a product from the best available alternative is known as the *differentiation value*[13].

A product's differentiation value can arise in either of two ways. First, a product may differentiate itself by enabling customers to generate more sales and contribution margin than the best available alternative. Second, a product may differentiate itself by enabling customers to realize greater cost savings than the best available alternative.

---

[12] If Solver is unable to find a solution, the most likely cause is that the combination of the percentage change in price and the percentage change in unit sales that you have inputted has resulted in an infinite optimal price. For example, if a 10% increase in price always leads to only a 5% decrease in units sold and fixed costs are constant, then profits always go up when the price is increased. This obviously cannot happen in practice. At some point customers will stop buying the product altogether.

[13] The terms reference value and differentiation value, as well as the forthcoming example grounded in the magazine publishing industry, were adapted from *The Strategy and Tactics of Pricing: A Guide to Profitable Decision Making* by Thomas T. Nagle and Reed K. Holden, 2002, Pearson Education, Upper Saddle River, New Jersey.

In equation form, the EVC is computed as follows:

$$\text{Economic value to the customer} = \text{Reference value} + \text{Differentiation value}$$

Once the seller computes the EVC, it seeks to negotiate a value-based selling price with the customer that falls within the following range:

$$\text{Reference value} \leq \text{Value-based price} \leq \text{EVC}$$

Economic Value to the Customer: An Example

The managers of Hike America magazine want to establish a selling price for a one-month full-page advertisement in their magazine. While their primary competitor, Hiking Trails magazine, charges $5,000 per month for a full-page ad, the managers of Hike America believe that they can justify a higher selling price by quantifying the EVC of a full-page ad in their magazine. To enable their analysis, the managers gathered the following data pertaining to the two magazines:

	Hike America	Hiking Trails
Number of readers	200,000	300,000
Percent of readers who buy advertised products each month	.002	.001
Monthly spending per reader who buys advertised products	$100	$80
Contribution margin ratio of advertisers	25%	25%

Although Hike America has fewer readers than Hiking Trails magazine (200,000 vs. 300,000), a higher percentage of Hike America's "hard core" subscribers buy advertised products each month (.002 vs. .001) and they spend more per person on advertised products ($100 vs. $80). Given the assumption that advertisers in both magazines earn a contribution margin ratio of 25% on all merchandise sales, Hike America's managers computed the differentiation value of an ad placed in their magazine as follows:

	Hike America	Hiking Trails
Number of readers (a)	200,000	300,000
Percent of readers who buy advertised products each month (b)	.002	.001
Number of readers per month buying advertised products (a) × (b)	400	300
Monthly sales per reader who buys advertised products (a)	$100	$80
Contribution margin ratio (b)	25%	25%
Monthly contribution margin per reader who buys advertised products (a) × (b)	$25	$20
Number of readers per month buying advertised products (a)	400	300
Monthly contribution margin per reader who buys advertised products (b)	$25	$20
Contribution margin per month provided by a full-page ad (a) × (b)	$10,000	$6,000
Differentiation value	$4,000	

Given that Hike America 's reference value is $5,000—the price charged by Hiking Trails for a full-page ad—the EVC would be computed as follows:

Economic value to the customer = Reference value + Differentiation value
$$= \$5,000 + \$4,000$$
$$= \$9,000$$

Hike America would seek to negotiate a value-based selling price for a full-page advertisement within the following range:

Reference value $\leq$ Value-based price $\leq$ EVC
$$\$5,000 \leq \text{Value-based price} \leq \$9,000$$

It bears emphasizing that the EVC of $9,000 does not necessarily represent the price that Hike America should charge customers for a full-page advertisement. Instead, it provides the magazine's managers a starting point for understanding the economic benefit (in terms of additional contribution margin) that a full-page ad in their magazine can offer to prospective customers. In fact, the data shown below suggest that Hike America probably needs to establish a price less than $9,000.

	Hike America		
	Price = $9,000	Price = $8,000	Hiking Trails
Contribution margin provided by the ad	$10,000	$10,000	$6,000
Investment in the ad (a)	9,000	8,000	5,000
Incremental profit from the ad (b)	$ 1,000	$ 2,000	$1,000
Return on investment (b) / (a)	11%	25%	20%

Notice that the right-hand column of numbers shows that Hiking Trails magazine provides its customers with a 20% ROI for a full-page advertisement. Conversely, the left-hand column of numbers shows that Hike America's customers would only earn an 11% ROI if they paid $9,000 for a full-page ad. Thus, if Hike America established a price of $9,000 it would provide advertisers with a lower ROI than they could earn by placing a full-page ad in Hiking Trails magazine. However, Hike America might consider touting a lower price, such as $8,000, to its prospective customers. As shown in the middle column of data, this lower price would provide prospective advertisers with an ROI of 25%, which compares favorably with Hiking Trails' ROI of 20%.

Target Costing

Our discussion thus far has presumed that a product has already been developed, has been costed, and is ready to be marketed as soon as a price is set. In many cases, the sequence of events is just the reverse. That is, the company already *knows* what price should be charged, and the problem is to *develop* a product that can be marketed profitably at the desired price. Even in this situation, where the normal sequence of events is reversed, cost is still a crucial factor. The company can use an approach called *target costing*. **Target costing** is the process of determining the maximum allowable cost for a new product and then developing a prototype that can be profitably made for that maximum target cost figure. A number of companies have used target costing, including **Compaq, Culp, Cummins Engine, Daihatsu Motors, Chrysler, Ford, Isuzu Motors, ITT Automotive, Komatsu, Matsushita Electric, Mitsubishi Kasei, NEC, Nippodenso, Nissan, Olympus, Sharp, Texas Instruments,** and **Toyota**.

LO12–11
Compute the target cost for a new product or service.

The target cost for a product is computed by starting with the product's anticipated selling price and then deducting the desired profit, as follows:

$$\text{Target cost} = \text{Anticipated selling price} - \text{Desired profit}$$

The product development team is then given the responsibility of designing the product so that it can be made for no more than the target cost.

Reasons for Using Target Costing

The target costing approach was developed in recognition of two important characteristics of markets and costs. The first is that many companies have less control over price than they would like to think. The market (i.e., supply and demand) really determines price, and a company that attempts to ignore this does so at its peril. Therefore, the anticipated market price is taken as a given in target costing.

The second observation is that most of a product's cost is determined in the design stage. Once a product has been designed and has gone into production, not much can be done to significantly reduce its cost. Most of the opportunities to reduce cost come from designing the product so that it is simple to make, uses fewer parts, and is robust and reliable. If the company has little control over market price and little control over cost once the product has gone into production, then it follows that the major opportunities for affecting profit come during a product's design stage. So that is where the effort is concentrated—in designing and developing cost effective products that possess features valued by customers.

The difference between target costing and other approaches to product development is profound. Instead of designing the product and then finding out how much it costs, the target cost is set first and then the product is designed so that the target cost is attained.

An Example of Target Costing

To provide a simple example of target costing, assume the following situation: Handy Company wishes to invest $2,000,000 to design, develop, and produce a new hand mixer. The company's Marketing Department surveyed the features and prices of competing products and determined that a price of $30 would enable Handy to sell an estimated 40,000 hand mixers per year. Because the company desires a 15% ROI, the target cost to manufacture, sell, distribute, and service one mixer is $22.50 as computed below:

Projected sales (40,000 mixers × $30 per mixer)	$1,200,000
Less desired profit (15% × $2,000,000)	300,000
Target cost for 40,000 mixers	$ 900,000
Target cost per mixer ($900,000 ÷ 40,000 mixers)	$22.50

This $22.50 target cost would be broken down into target costs for the various functions: manufacturing, marketing, distribution, after-sales service, and so on. Each functional area would be responsible for keeping its actual costs within target.

Summary (Appendix 12A)

Pricing involves a delicate balancing act. Higher prices result in more revenue per unit but drive down unit sales. Exactly where to set prices to maximize profit is a difficult problem.

Managers often rely on cost-plus pricing to establish selling prices. The absorption approach to cost-plus pricing applies a markup to the absorption costing unit product cost that is intended to cover nonmanufacturing costs and to provide an adequate return on investment. With the absorption approach, costs will be covered and the return on investment will be adequate *only* if the unit sales forecast used in the cost-plus formula is accurate. If applying the cost-plus formula results in a price that is too high, the unit sales forecast will not be attained.

Customers have latitude in their purchasing decisions. They can choose to buy your product, a competitor's product, or nothing at all. This latitude should be taken into account when setting prices. The customers' sensitivity to price is said to be *inelastic* if a change in price has little effect on the number of units sold. On the other hand, the customers' sensitivity to price is *elastic* if a change in price has a substantial effect on the volume of units sold. In general, the more sensitive customers are to price, the lower the optimal selling price will be and the less sensitive customers are to price, the higher the optimal selling price will be.

Value-based pricing is an alternative to cost-plus pricing. Companies that use value-based pricing establish selling prices based on the economic value of the benefits that their products and services provide to customers. One approach to value-based pricing relies on quantifying the *economic value to the customer (EVC)*. A product's EVC is the price of the customer's best alternative (the reference value) plus the value of what differentiates the seller's product from that alternative (the differentiation value). Once the seller computes the EVC, it establishes a value-based selling price that falls between the reference value and the EVC.

Companies that use target costing estimate what a new product's market price is likely to be based on its anticipated features and the prices of products already on the market. They subtract desired profit from the estimated market price to arrive at the product's target cost. The design and development team is then given the responsibility of ensuring that the actual cost of the new product does not exceed the target cost.

Glossary (Appendix 12A)

Cost-plus pricing A pricing method in which a predetermined markup is applied to a cost base to determine the target selling price. (p. 614)

Economic value to the customer (EVC) The price of a customer's best alternative (called the reference value) plus the value of what differentiates a product from that alternative (called the differentiation value). (p. 621)

Markup The difference between the selling price of a product or service and its cost. The markup is usually expressed as a percentage of cost. (p. 614)

Price elasticity of demand A measure of the degree to which a change in price affects the unit sales of a product or service. (p. 613)

Target costing The process of determining the maximum allowable cost for a new product and then developing a prototype that can be profitably made for that maximum target cost figure. (p. 623)

Value-based pricing A pricing method in which a company establishes selling prices based on the economic value of the benefits that their products and services provide to customers. (p. 621)

connect   Appendix 12A: Exercises and Problems

EXERCISE 12A–1 Absorption Costing Approach to Cost-Plus Pricing LO12–8
Martin Company uses the absorption costing approach to cost-plus pricing. It is considering the introduction of a new product. To determine a selling price, the company has gathered the following information:

Number of units to be produced and sold each year	14,000
Unit product cost	$25
Estimated annual selling and administrative expenses	$50,000
Estimated investment required by the company	$750,000
Desired return on investment (ROI)	12%

Required:
1. Compute the markup percentage on absorption cost required to achieve the desired ROI.
2. Compute the selling price per unit.

EXERCISE 12A–2 Customer Latitude and Pricing LO12–9

Maria Lorenzi owns an ice cream stand that she operates during the summer months in West Yellowstone, Montana. She is unsure how to price her ice cream cones and has experimented with two prices in successive weeks during the busy August season. The number of people who entered the store was roughly the same each week. During the first week, she priced the cones at $3.50 and 1,800 cones were sold. During the second week, she priced the cones at $4.00 and 1,400 cones were sold. The variable cost of a cone is $0.80 and consists solely of the costs of the ice cream and the cone itself. The fixed expenses of the ice cream stand are $2,675 per week.

Required:
1. What profit did Maria earn during the first week when her price was $3.50?
2. At the start of the second week, Maria increased her selling price by what percentage? What percentage did unit sales decrease? (Round your answers to one-tenth of a percent.)
3. What profit did Maria earn during the second week when her price was $4.00?
4. What was Maria's increase (decrease) in profits from the first week to the second week?

EXERCISE 12A–3 Value-Based Pricing LO12–10

McDermott Company has developed a new industrial component called IC–75. The company is excited about IC–75 because it offers superior performance relative to the comparable component sold by McDermott's primary competitor. The competing part sells for $1,200 and needs to be replaced after 2,000 hours of use. It also requires $200 of preventive maintenance during its useful life.

The IC–75's performance capabilities are similar to its competing product with two important exceptions—it needs to be replaced after 4,000 hours of use and it requires $300 of preventive maintenance during its useful life.

Required:
From a value-based pricing standpoint:
1. What is the reference value that McDermott should consider when pricing IC–75?
2. What is the differentiation value offered by IC–75 relative the competitor's offering for each 4,000 hours of usage?
3. What is IC–75's economic value to the customer over its 4,000-hour life?
4. What range of possible prices should McDermott consider when setting a price for IC–75?

EXERCISE 12A–4 Target Costing LO12–11

Shimada Products Corporation of Japan is anxious to enter the electronic calculator market. Management believes that in order to be competitive in world markets, the price of the electronic calculator that the company is developing cannot exceed $15. Shimada's required rate of return is 12% on all investments. An investment of $5,000,000 would be required to purchase the equipment needed to produce the 300,000 calculators that management believes can be sold each year at the $15 price.

Required:
Compute the target cost of one calculator.

EXERCISE 12A–5 Customer Latitude and Optimal Pricing LO12–9

Northport Company manufactures numerous products, one of which is called Sea Breeze Skin Cleanser. The company has provided the following data regarding this product:

Unit sales (a)	120,000
Selling price per unit	$20.00
Variable cost per unit	13.00
Contribution margin per unit (b)	$ 7.00
Total contribution margin (a) × (b)	$840,000
Traceable fixed expenses	800,000
Net operating income	$ 40,000

Management is considering increasing the price of Sea Breeze by 20%, from $20.00 to $24.00. The company's marketing managers estimate that this price hike could decrease unit sales by as much as 30%, from 120,000 units to 84,000 units.

Required:
In all of the below requirements, assume that the traceable fixed expenses are not affected by the pricing decision.
1. Assuming the marketing managers' estimate is accurate, what profit will Sea Breeze Skin Cleanser earn at a price of $24.00?
2. How many units would Northport need to sell at a price of $24.00 to earn the exact same profit that it currently earns at a price of $20.00? (Round your answer up to the nearest whole number.)

3.   If Northport raises the price of Sea Breeze Skin Cleanser to $24.00, what percentage decrease in unit sales could be absorbed while still providing the same profit currently being earned at a price of $20.00? (Round your answer to the nearest one-tenth of a percent.)

4.   Download the optimal pricing model from www.mhhe.com/garrison_opm. Input all of the pertinent data related to Sea Breeze Skin Cleanser into the model (including the assumptions that a 20% increase in selling price will cause a 30% decrease in unit sales). Be sure to input the current price in cell B12. Click on the Data tab in Microsoft Excel and select Solver in the upper right-hand portion of your screen. When the Solver window opens, click "Solve."

  a.   What is the optimal selling price?

  b.   What profit is earned at the optimal selling price?

  c.   How much additional profit is earned at the optimal price compared to a price of $24.00?

5.   Assume that a 20% increase in selling price would actually cause a 35% decline in unit sales instead of a 30% drop. Using the optimal pricing model, determine your answers to the following questions:

  a.   What is the optimal selling price and optimal profit if unit sales decline by 35% instead of 30%?

  b.   Is the optimal price from requirement 5a higher or lower than your answer in requirement 4a? Why?

  c.   If a 20% increase in price causes unit sales to decrease by 35% instead of 30%, would you recommend retaining a price of $20 or implementing your optimal price from requirement 5a? Why?

EXERCISE 12A–6 Value-Based Pricing; Absorption Costing Approach to Cost-Plus Pricing LO12–8, LO12–10

Valmont Company has developed a new industrial piece of equipment called the XP–200. The company is considering two methods of establishing a selling price for the XP–200—absorption cost-plus pricing and value-based pricing.

Valmont's cost accounting system reports an absorption unit product cost for XP–200 of $8,400. Its markup percentage on absorption cost is 85%. The company's marketing managers have expressed concerns about the use of absorption cost-plus pricing because it seems to overlook the fact that the XP–200 offers superior performance relative to the comparable piece of equipment sold by Valmont's primary competitor. More specifically, the XP–200 can be used for 20,000 hours before replacement. It only requires $1,000 of preventive maintenance during its useful life and it consumes $120 of electricity per 1,000 hours used.

These figures compare favorably to the competing piece of equipment that sells for $15,000, needs to be replaced after 10,000 hours of use, requires $2,000 of preventive maintenance during its useful life and consumes $140 of electricity per 1,000 hours used.

Required:

1.   If Valmont uses absorption cost-plus pricing, what price will it establish for the XP–200?

2.   What is XP–200's economic value to the customer (EVC) over its 20,000-hour life?

3.   If Valmont uses value-based pricing, what range of possible prices should it consider when setting a price for the XP–200?

4.   What advice would you give Valmont's managers when choosing between absorption cost-plus pricing and value-based pricing?

EXERCISE 12A–7 Customer Latitude and Pricing LO12–9

The postal service of St. Vincent, an island in the West Indies, obtains a significant portion of its revenues from sales of special souvenir sheets to stamp collectors. The postal service purchases the souvenir sheets from a supplier for $0.80 each. St. Vincent has been selling the souvenir sheets for $8.00 each and ordinarily sells about 80,000 units. To test the market, the postal service recently priced a new souvenir sheet at $7.00 and sales increased to 93,600 units.

Required:

1.   What total contribution margin did the postal service earn when it sold 80,000 sheets at a price of $8.00 each?

2.   By what percentage did the St. Vincent post office decrease its selling price? By what percentage did unit sales increase? (Round your answers to one-tenth of a percent.)

3.   What total contribution margin did the postal service earn when it sold 93,600 sheets at a price of $7.00 each?

4.   What was the postal service's increase (decrease) in total contribution margin going from the higher price of $8.00 to the lower price of $7.00?

5.   How many sheets would the postal service have to sell at the lower price of $7.00 to equal the total contribution margin earned at the higher price of $8.00? (Round your answer up to the nearest whole number.)

6. What percentage increase in the number of sheets sold at $7.00 must be achieved to equal the total contribution margin earned at the higher price of $8.00? (Round your answer up to the nearest one-tenth of a percent.)

7. A financial manager at the postal service has suggested that a more accurate comparison of the two pricing alternatives ($8.00 vs. $7.00) should include an allocation of the postal service's common fixed costs. A portion of the common fixed costs would be allocated to each alternative using total sales dollars as the cost allocation base. He contends that this approach would help ensure that the postal service's common fixed costs are covered by the prices that it charges customers. Do you agree?

PROBLEM 12A–8 Standard Costs; Absorption Costing Approach to Cost-Plus Pricing LO12–8

Wilderness Products, Inc., has designed a self-inflating sleeping pad for use by backpackers and campers. The following information is available about the new product:

a. An investment of $1,350,000 will be necessary to carry inventories and accounts receivable and to purchase some new equipment needed in the manufacturing process. The company's required rate of return is 24% on all investments.

b. A standard cost card has been prepared for the sleeping pad, as shown below:

	Standard Quantity or Hours	Standard Price or Rate	Standard Cost
Direct materials.....................	4.0 yards	$2.70 per yard	$10.80
Direct labor	2.4 hours	$8.00 per hour	19.20
Manufacturing overhead (20% variable)..	2.4 hours	$12.50 per hour	30.00
Total standard cost per pad			$60.00

c. The only variable selling and administrative expense will be a sales commission of $9 per pad. The fixed selling and administrative expenses will be $732,000 per year.

d. Because the company manufactures many products, no more than 38,400 direct labor-hours per year can be devoted to production of the new sleeping pads.

e. Manufacturing overhead costs are allocated to products on the basis of direct labor-hours.

Required:

1. Assume that the company uses the absorption approach to cost-plus pricing.
   a. Compute the markup percentage that the company needs on the pads to achieve a 24% return on investment (ROI) if it sells all of the pads it can produce.
   b. What selling price per sleeping pad will the company establish if it uses a markup percentage on absorption cost?
   c. Assume that the company is able to sell all of the pads that it can produce. Prepare an income statement for the first year of activity. Compute the company's ROI based on the first year of activity.

2. After marketing the sleeping pads for several years, the company is experiencing a falloff in demand due to an economic recession. A large retail outlet will make a bulk purchase of pads if its label is sewn in and if an acceptable price can be worked out. What is the minimum acceptable price for this special order?

PROBLEM 12A–9 Absorption Costing Approach to Cost-Plus Pricing LO12–8

Aldean Company wants to use absorption cost-plus pricing to set the selling price on a new product. The company plans to invest $200,000 in operating assets to produce and sell 16,000 units. Its required return on investment (ROI) in its operating assets is 18%. The accounting department has provided cost estimates for the new product as shown below:

	Per Unit	Total
Direct materials	$7	
Direct labor	$5	
Variable manufacturing overhead	$2	
Fixed manufacturing overhead		$116,000
Variable selling and administrative expenses ...	$1	
Fixed selling and administrative expenses		$50,000

Required:

1. What is the unit product cost for the new product?
2. What is the markup percentage on absorption cost for the new product?
3. What selling price would the company establish for its new product using a markup percentage on absorption cost? (Round your answer to the nearest penny.)

PROBLEM 12A–10 Absorption Costing Approach to Cost-Plus Pricing LO12–8

Currington Company wants to use absorption cost-plus pricing to set the selling price on a newly remodeled product. The company plans to invest $150,000 in operating assets to produce and sell 12,000 units. Its required return on investment (ROI) in its operating assets is 16%. The accounting department has provided cost estimates for the new product as follows:

	Per Unit	Total
Direct materials	$4	
Direct labor	$3	
Variable manufacturing overhead	$1	
Fixed manufacturing overhead		$66,000
Variable selling and administrative expenses . . .	$1	
Fixed selling and administrative expenses		$45,000

Required:

1. What is the unit product cost for the remodeled product?
2. What is the markup percentage on absorption cost for the remodeled product?
3. What selling price would the company establish for its remolded product using a markup percentage on absorption cost?
4. Suppose the company actually sold only 10,000 units (instead of its planned sales volume of 12,000 units) at the selling price that you derived in requirement 3. What ROI did the company actually earn at this lower sales volume?
5. Assume that the company wants to raise the price of its newly remodeled product with the intention of achieving the product's desired ROI at the lower sales volume of 10,000 units. Using absorption cost-plus pricing, what would be the revised selling price at this lower sales volume? How might customers react to this new price?

PROBLEM 12A–11 Target Costing LO12–11

National Restaurant Supply, Inc., sells restaurant equipment and supplies throughout most of the United States. Management is considering adding a machine that makes sorbet to its line of ice cream making machines. Management will negotiate the purchase price of the sorbet machine with its Swedish manufacturer.

Management of National Restaurant Supply believes the sorbet machine can be sold to its customers in the United States for $4,950. At that price, annual sales of the sorbet machine should be 100 units. If the sorbet machine is added to National Restaurant Supply's product lines, the company will have to invest $600,000 in inventories and special warehouse fixtures. The variable cost of selling the sorbet machines would be $650 per machine.

Required:

1. If National Restaurant Supply requires a 15% return on investment (ROI), what is the maximum amount the company would be willing to pay the Swedish manufacturer for the sorbet machines?
2. The manager who is flying to Sweden to negotiate the purchase price of the machines would like to know how the purchase price of the machines would affect National Restaurant Supply's ROI. Construct a chart that shows National Restaurant Supply's ROI as a function of the purchase price of the sorbet machine. Put the purchase price on the X-axis and the resulting ROI on the Y-axis. Plot the ROI for purchase prices between $3,000 and $4,000 per machine.
3. After many hours of negotiations, management has concluded that the Swedish manufacturer is unwilling to sell the sorbet machine at a low enough price so that National Restaurant Supply is able to earn its 15% required ROI. Apart from simply giving up on the idea of adding the sorbet machine to National Restaurant Supply's product lines, what could management do?

PROBLEM 12A–12 Absorption Costing Approach to Cost-Plus Pricing; Customer Latitude and Pricing LO12–8, LO12–9

Messina Company wants to use absorption cost-plus pricing to establish the selling price for a new product. The company plans to invest $650,000 in operating assets that provide the capacity to make 30,000 units. Its required return on investment (ROI) in its operating assets is 20%. Messina's Accounting Department set a goal of producing and selling 20,000 units during the new product's first year of availability. It also provided the following cost estimates for the new product:

	Per Unit	Total
Direct materials	$12	
Direct labor	$8	
Variable manufacturing overhead	$3	
Fixed manufacturing overhead		$100,000
Variable selling and administrative expenses	$1	
Fixed selling and administrative expenses		$60,000

Required:

1. If the company plans to produce and sell 20,000 units, what is the absorption unit product cost for its new product?
2. At a planned sales volume of 20,000 units, what is the markup percentage on absorption cost for the new product?
3. Using absorption cost-plus pricing and assuming a planned sales volume of 20,000 units, what selling price would the company establish for its new product?
4. Using an absorption format, calculate Messina's net operating income if it actually produces and sells only 19,000 units (instead of 20,000 units) at the absorption cost-plus price from requirement 3. Calculate the return on investment (ROI) at this lower sales volume.
5. Assume that Messina's controller recommends raising the new product's selling price in an effort to achieve the desired ROI at the lower sales volume of 19,000 units.
   a) What would become the new markup percentage? (Round your answer to the nearest one-tenth of a percent.)
   b) What would become the new selling price? (Round your calculations and answer to the nearest penny.)
6. Download the optimal pricing model from www.mhhe.com/garrison_opm. Suppose Messina's Marketing Department surveyed its customers and estimated that an 8% increase in the price of this new product would cause its unit sales to decrease by 22%. The company's marketing managers also believe that Messina's total fixed costs will be unaffected by the pricing decision. Assuming that the new product's actual sales volume was 19,000 units and the marketing managers' estimates and assumptions are correct, input all of the pertinent data into the pricing model. Be sure to input the current price (as calculated in requirement 3) in cell B12. Click on the Data tab in Microsoft Excel and select Solver in the upper right-hand portion of your screen. When the Solver window opens, click "Solve."
   a) What is the optimal selling price?
   b) What profit is earned at the optimal selling price?
   c) Comment on the wisdom of the controller's recommendation to increase the new product's selling price.

PROBLEM 12A–13 Value-Based Pricing LO12–10

The managers of *Midwest Whitetails* magazine (a magazine dedicated to deer hunters) want to establish a price for customers wishing to place a full-page advertisement in their magazine for one month. To help with the price setting decision, the managers intend to compute the economic value to the customer (EVC) of a full-page ad in their magazine. They have gathered the following data pertaining to *Midwest Whitetails* magazine as well as their primary competitor, *Trophy Whitetails* magazine:

	Midwest Whitetails	Trophy Whitetails
Number of readers	130,000	200,000
Percent of readers who buy advertised products each month	.007	.005
Monthly spending per reader who buys advertised products	$120	$100
Contribution margin ratio of advertisers	40%	40%

Trophy Whitetails magazine charges $4,000 per month for a full-page ad. *Midwest Whitetails'* managers believe they can charge more than $4,000 by quantifying the economic value to its customers of placing an ad in their magazine.

Although *Midwest Whitetails* has fewer readers than *Trophy Whitetails* (130,000 vs. 200,000), *Midwest Whitetails* attracts a segment of hunters that is more likely to buy advertisers' products than the casual hunters that tend to subscribe to *Trophy Whitetails*. Therefore, a higher percentage of *Midwest Whitetails* subscribers buy advertised products (.007 vs. .005) and they spend more per person on advertised products ($120 vs. $100). The managers of *Midwest Whitetails* assume that advertisers in both magazines earn an average contribution margin ratio of 40% on all of their merchandise sales.

Required:

From a value-based pricing standpoint:

1. What is the reference value that *Midwest Whitetails* should consider when setting the price of a full-page ad in its magazine?
2. What is the differentiation value offered by a full-page ad placed in *Midwest Whitetails* magazine?
3. What is the economic value to the customer (EVC) of a full-page ad in *Midwest Whitetails* magazine?
4. What range of possible prices should *Midwest Whitetails* consider when setting a price for a full-page ad?

CHAPTER 13

Capital Budgeting Decisions

Commercial Delivery Fleets Adopt Electric Trucks

© David Goldman/AP Images

Staples, Frito-Lay, and **AT&T** have begun purchasing electric delivery trucks even though they cost $30,000 more than diesel delivery trucks. Staples is willing to make the more expensive up-front investment because it expects each electric truck to incur lower operating costs. For example, it estimates that electric trucks will save $2,450 per year in maintenance costs and $6,500 per year in fuel costs. It also expects to replace each electric truck's brakes every four or five years instead of every one or two years with diesel trucks. In total, Staples expects each electric delivery truck to save $60,000 over its 10-year useful life. ■

Source: Mike Ramsey, "As Electric Vehicles Arrive, Firms See Payback in Trucks," *The Wall Street Journal,* December 8, 2010, pp. B1–B2.

LEARNING OBJECTIVES

After studying Chapter 13, you should be able to:

LO13–1 Determine the payback period for an investment.

LO13–2 Evaluate the acceptability of an investment project using the net present value method.

LO13–3 Evaluate the acceptability of an investment project using the internal rate of return method.

LO13–4 Evaluate an investment project that has uncertain cash flows.

LO13–5 Rank investment projects in order of preference.

LO13–6 Compute the simple rate of return for an investment.

LO13–7 *(Appendix 13A) Understand present value concepts and the use of present value tables.*

LO13–8 *(Appendix 13C) Include income taxes in a net present value analysis.*

Managers often consider decisions that involve an investment today in the hope of realizing future profits. For example, **Yum! Brands, Inc.**, makes an investment when it opens a new Pizza Hut restaurant. **L. L. Bean** makes an investment when it installs a new computer to handle customer billing. **Ford** makes an investment when it redesigns a vehicle such as the F–150 pickup truck. **Merck & Co.** invests in medical research. **Amazon.com** makes an investment when it redesigns its website. All of these investments require spending money now to realize future net cash inflows.

The term **capital budgeting** is used to describe how managers plan significant investments in projects that have long-term implications such as the purchase of new equipment or the introduction of new products. Most companies have many more potential projects than they can actually fund. Hence, managers must carefully select those projects that promise the greatest future return. How well managers make these capital budgeting decisions is a critical factor in the long-run financial health of the organization. This chapter discusses four methods for making capital budgeting decisions—the *payback method,* the *net present value method,* the *internal rate of return method,* and the *simple rate of return method.*

Capital Budgeting—An Overview

Typical Capital Budgeting Decisions

Any decision that involves a cash outlay now to obtain a future return is a capital budgeting decision. Typical capital budgeting decisions include:

1. Cost reduction decisions. Should new equipment be purchased to reduce costs?
2. Expansion decisions. Should a new plant, warehouse, or other facility be acquired to increase capacity and sales?
3. Equipment selection decisions. Which of several available machines should be purchased?
4. Lease or buy decisions. Should new equipment be leased or purchased?
5. Equipment replacement decisions. Should old equipment be replaced now or later?

Capital budgeting decisions fall into two broad categories—*screening decisions* and *preference decisions.* **Screening decisions** relate to whether a proposed project is acceptable—whether it passes a preset hurdle. For example, a company may have a policy of accepting projects only if they provide a return of at least 20% on the investment. The required rate of return is the minimum rate of return a project must yield to be acceptable. **Preference decisions**, by contrast, relate to selecting from among several acceptable alternatives. To illustrate, a company may be considering several different machines to replace an existing machine on the assembly line. The choice of which machine to purchase is a preference decision.

Cash Flows versus Net Operating Income

The first three capital budgeting methods discussed in the chapter—the payback method, the net present value method, and internal rate of return method—all focus on analyzing the *cash flows* associated with capital investment projects, whereas the simple rate of return method focuses on *incremental net operating income.* To better prepare you to apply the payback, net present value, and internal rate of return methods, we'd like to define the most common types of cash outflows and cash inflows that accompany capital investment projects.

Typical Cash Outflows   Most projects have at least three types of cash outflows. First, they often require an immediate cash outflow in the form of an initial investment in equipment, other assets, and installation costs. Any salvage value realized from the sale of old equipment can be recognized as a reduction in the initial investment or as a cash inflow. Second, some projects require a company to expand its working capital. **Working capital** is current assets (e.g., cash, accounts receivable, and inventory) less current liabilities.

When a company takes on a new project, the balances in the current asset accounts often increase. For example, opening a new **Nordstrom**'s department store requires additional cash in sales registers and more inventory. These additional working capital needs are treated as part of the initial investment in a project. Third, many projects require periodic outlays for repairs and maintenance and additional operating costs.

Typical Cash Inflows   Most projects also have at least three types of cash inflows. First, a project will normally increase revenues or reduce costs. Either way, the amount involved should be treated as a cash inflow for capital budgeting purposes. Notice that from a cash flow standpoint, a reduction in costs is equivalent to an increase in revenues. Second, cash inflows are also frequently realized from selling equipment for its salvage value when a project ends, although the company actually may have to pay to dispose of some low-value or hazardous items. Third, any working capital that was tied up in the project can be released for use elsewhere at the end of the project and should be treated as a cash inflow at that time. Working capital is released, for example, when a company sells off its inventory or collects its accounts receivable.

The Time Value of Money

Beyond defining a capital project's cash outflows and inflows, it is also important to consider when those cash flows occur. For example, if someone offered to give you $1,000 dollars today that you could save toward your eventual retirement or $1,000 dollars a year from now that you could save toward your future retirement, which alternative would you choose? In all likelihood, you would choose to receive $1,000 today because you could invest it and have more than $1,000 dollars a year from now. This simple example illustrates an important capital budgeting concept known as *the time value of money*. The **time value of money** recognizes that a dollar today is worth more than a dollar a year from now if for no other reason than you could put the dollar in a bank today and have more than a dollar a year from now. Because of the time value of money, capital investments that promise earlier cash flows are preferable to those that promise later cash flows.

Although the payback method focuses on cash flows, it does not recognize the time value of money. In other words, it treats a dollar received today as being of equal value to a dollar received at any point in the future. Conversely, the net present value and internal rate of return methods not only focus on cash flows, but they also recognize the time value of those cash flows. These two methods use a technique called *discounting cash flows* to translate the value of future cash flows to their present value. If you are not familiar with the concept of discounting cash flows and the use of present value tables, you should read Appendix 13A: The Concept of Present Value, at the end of the chapter, before studying the net present value and internal rate of return methods.

© Royalty-Free/Corbis

IN BUSINESS

INVESTING IN A VINEYARD: A CASH FLOWS PERSPECTIVE

When Michael Evans was contemplating moving to Buenos Aires, Argentina, to start a company called the **Vines of Mendoza**, he had to estimate the project's initial cash outlays and compare them to its future net cash inflows. The initial cash outlays included $2.9 million to buy 1,046 acres of land and to construct a tasting room, $300,000 for a well and irrigation system, $30,000 for underground power lines, and $285,000 for 250,000 grape plants. The annual operating costs included $1,500 per acre for pruning, mowing, and irrigation and $114 per acre for harvesting.

In terms of future cash inflows, Evans hopes to sell his acreage to buyers who want to grow their own grapes and make their own wine while avoiding the work involved with doing so. He intends to charge buyers a one-time fee of $55,000 per planted acre. The buyers also would reimburse Evans for his annual operating costs per acre plus a 25% markup. In a good year, buyers should be able to get 250 cases of wine from their acre of grapevines.

Source: Helen Coster, "Planting Roots," *Forbes*, March 1, 2010, pp. 42–44.

The Payback Method

The payback method of evaluating capital budgeting projects focuses on the *payback period*. The **payback period** is the length of time that it takes for a project to recover its initial cost from the net cash inflows that it generates. This period is sometimes referred to as "the time that it takes for an investment to pay for itself." The basic premise of the payback method is that the more quickly the cost of an investment can be recovered, the more desirable is the investment.

LO13-1

Determine the payback period for an investment.

The payback period is expressed in years. *When the annual net cash inflow is the same every year,* the following formula can be used to compute the payback period:

$$\text{Payback period} = \frac{\text{Investment required}}{\text{Annual net cash inflow}} \qquad (1)$$

To illustrate the payback method, consider the following data:

Example A: York Company needs a new milling machine. The company is considering two machines: machine A and machine B. Machine A costs $15,000, has a useful life of ten years, and will reduce operating costs by $5,000 per year. Machine B costs only $12,000, will also reduce operating costs by $5,000 per year, but has a useful life of only five years.

Required:
Which machine should be purchased according to the payback method?

$$\text{Machine A payback period} = \frac{\$15,000}{\$5,000} = 3.0 \text{ years}$$

$$\text{Machine B payback period} = \frac{\$12,000}{\$5,000} = 2.4 \text{ years}$$

According to the payback calculations, York Company should purchase machine B because it has a shorter payback period than machine A.

Evaluation of the Payback Method

The payback method is not a true measure of the profitability of an investment. Rather, it simply tells a manager how many years are required to recover the original investment. Unfortunately, a shorter payback period does not always mean that one investment is more desirable than another.

To illustrate, refer back to Example A. Machine B has a shorter payback period than machine A, but it has a useful life of only 5 years rather than 10 years for machine A. Machine B would have to be purchased twice—once immediately and then again after the fifth year—to provide the same service as just one machine A. Under these circumstances, machine A would probably be a better investment than machine B, even though machine B has a shorter payback period. Unfortunately, the payback method ignores all cash flows that occur after the payback period.

A further criticism of the payback method is that it does not consider the time value of money. A cash inflow to be received several years in the future is weighed the same as a cash inflow received right now. To illustrate, assume that for an investment of $8,000 you can purchase either of the two following streams of cash inflows:

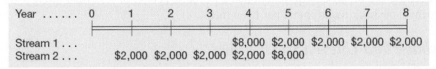

Year	0	1	2	3	4	5	6	7	8
Stream 1 . . .					$8,000	$2,000	$2,000	$2,000	$2,000
Stream 2 . . .		$2,000	$2,000	$2,000	$2,000	$8,000			

Which stream of cash inflows would you prefer to receive in return for your $8,000 investment? Each stream has a payback period of 4.0 years. Therefore, if payback alone is used to make the decision, the streams would be considered equally desirable. However, from a time value of money perspective, stream 2 is much more desirable than stream 1.

On the other hand, under certain conditions the payback method can be very useful. For one thing, it can help identify which investment proposals are in the "ballpark." That is, it can be used as a screening tool to help answer the question, "Should I consider this proposal further?" If a proposal doesn't provide a payback within some specified period, then there may be no need to consider it further. In addition, the payback period is often important to new companies that are "cash poor." When a company is cash poor, a project with a short payback period but a low rate of return might be preferred over another project with a high rate of return but a long payback period. The reason is that the company may simply need a faster return of its cash investment. And finally, the payback method is sometimes used in industries where products become obsolete very rapidly—such as consumer electronics. Because products may last only a year or two, the payback period on investments must be very short.

An Extended Example of Payback

As shown by formula (1) from earlier in the chapter, the payback period is computed by dividing the investment in a project by the project's annual net cash inflows. If new equipment is replacing old equipment, then any salvage value to be received when disposing of the old equipment should be deducted from the cost of the new equipment, and only the *incremental* investment should be used in the payback computation. In addition, any depreciation deducted in arriving at the project's net operating income must be added back to obtain the project's expected annual net cash inflow. To illustrate, consider the following data:

Example B: Goodtime Fun Centers, Inc., operates amusement parks. Some of the vending machines in one of its parks provide very little revenue, so the company is considering removing the machines and installing equipment to dispense soft ice cream. The equipment would cost $80,000 and have an eight-year useful life with no salvage value. Incremental annual revenues and costs associated with the sale of ice cream would be as follows:

Sales	$150,000
Variable expenses	90,000
Contribution margin	60,000
Fixed expenses:	
Salaries	27,000
Maintenance	3,000
Depreciation	10,000
Total fixed expenses	40,000
Net operating income	$ 20,000

The vending machines can be sold for a $5,000 scrap value. The company will not purchase the equipment unless it has a payback period of three years or less. Does the ice cream dispenser pass this hurdle?

Exhibit 13–1 computes the payback period for the ice cream dispenser. Several things should be noted. First, depreciation is added back to net operating income to obtain the annual net cash inflow from the new equipment. Depreciation is not a cash outlay; thus, it must be added back to adjust net operating income to a cash basis. Second, the payback computation deducts the salvage value of the old machines from the cost of the new equipment so that only the incremental investment is used in computing the payback period.

Because the proposed equipment has a payback period of less than three years, the company's payback requirement has been met.

Payback and Uneven Cash Flows

When the cash flows associated with an investment project change from year to year, the simple payback formula that we outlined earlier cannot be used. Instead, the payback period can be computed as follows (assuming that cash inflows occur evenly throughout

Step 1:	*Compute the annual net cash inflow.* Because the annual net cash inflow is not given, it must be computed before the payback period can be determined:	

Net operating income	$20,000
Add: Noncash deduction for depreciation	10,000
Annual net cash inflow	$30,000

Step 2:	*Compute the payback period.* Using the annual net cash inflow from above, the payback period can be determined as follows:

Cost of the new equipment	$80,000
Less salvage value of old equipment	5,000
Investment required	$75,000

$$\text{Payback period} = \frac{\text{Investment required}}{\text{Annual net cash inflow}}$$

$$= \frac{\$75,000}{\$30,000} = 2.5 \text{ years}$$

EXHIBIT 13–1
Computation of the Payback Period

the year): Payback period = Number of years up to the year in which the investment is paid off + (Unrecovered investment at the beginning of the year in which the investment is paid off ÷ Cash inflow in the period in which the investment is paid off). To illustrate how to apply this formula, consider the following data:

Year	Investment	Cash Inflow
1	$4,000	$1,000
2		$0
3		$2,000
4	$2,000	$1,000
5		$500
6		$3,000
7		$2,000

What is the payback period on this investment? The answer is 5.5 years, computed as follows: 5 + ($1,500 ÷ $3,000) = 5.5 years. In essence, we are tracking the unrecovered investment year by year as shown in Exhibit 13–2. By the middle of the sixth year, sufficient cash inflows will have been realized to recover the entire investment of $6,000 ($4,000 + $2,000).

EXHIBIT 13–2
Payback and Uneven Cash Flows

Year	Investment	Cash Inflow	Unrecovered Investment*
1	$4,000	$1,000	$3,000
2		$0	$3,000
3		$2,000	$1,000
4	$2,000	$1,000	$2,000
5		$500	$1,500
6		$3,000	$0
7		$2,000	$0

*Year X unrecovered investment = Year X–1 unrecovered investment + Year X investment – Year X cash inflow

The Net Present Value Method

LO13–2

Evaluate the acceptability of an investment project using the net present value method.

As previously mentioned, the *net present value method* and the *internal rate of return method* use discounted cash flows to analyze capital budgeting decisions. The net present value method is discussed in this section followed by a discussion of the internal rate of return method.

The Net Present Value Method Illustrated

The net present value method compares the present value of a project's cash inflows to the present value of its cash outflows. The difference between the present value of these cash flows, called the **net present value**, determines whether or not a project is an acceptable investment.

When performing net present value analysis, managers usually make two important assumptions. First, they assume that all cash flows other than the initial investment occur at the end of periods. This assumption is somewhat unrealistic because cash flows typically occur *throughout* a period rather than just at its end; however, it simplifies the computations considerably. Second, managers assume that all cash flows generated by an investment project are immediately reinvested at a rate of return equal to the rate used to discount the future cash flows, also known as the *discount rate*. If this condition is not met, the net present value computations will not be accurate.

To illustrate net present analysis, consider the following data:

Example C: Harper Company is contemplating buying a new machine that will cost $50,000 and last for five years. The new machine will enable the company to reduce its labor costs by $18,000 per year. At the end of the five-year period, the company will sell the machine for its salvage value of $5,000. Harper Company requires a minimum pretax return of 18% on all investment projects.[1]

Should the machine be purchased? Harper Company must determine whether a cash investment now of $50,000 can be justified if it will result in an $18,000 cost reduction in each of the next five years. The answer may seem obvious given that the total cost savings is $90,000 ($18,000 per year × 5 years); however, the company can earn an 18% return by investing its money elsewhere. It is not enough that the annual cost reductions cover just the original cost of the machine; they must also yield a return of at least 18% or the company would be better off investing the money elsewhere.

To determine whether the investment is desirable, the stream of annual $18,000 cost savings and the machine's salvage value of $5,000 should be discounted to their present values and then compared to the cost of the new machine. Exhibits 13–3, 13–4, and 13–5 demonstrate three distinct but equivalent ways of performing these calculations. The approaches in Exhibits 13–3 and 13–4 rely on the discount factors shown in Appendix 13B that have been rounded to three decimal places. The method shown in Exhibit 13–5 derives its answer using unrounded discount factors.

Cell B8 of Exhibit 13–3 calculates the present value of Harper Company's initial cash outlay of $(50,000) by multiplying $(50,000) by 1.000, the present value factor for any cash flow that occurs immediately. Cell C8 calculates the present value of the annual cost savings of $56,286 by multiplying $18,000 by 3.127, the present value factor of a five-year annuity at the discount rate of 18% (see Exhibit 13B–2). Cell D8 calculates the present value of the machine's salvage value of $2,185 by multiplying $5,000 by 0.437, the present value factor of a single sum to be received in five years at the discount rate of 18% (see Exhibit 13B–1). Finally, cells B8 through D8 are added together to derive the net present value in cell B9 of $8,471.

---

[1] For simplicity, we ignore inflation and taxes. The impact of income taxes on capital budgeting decisions is discussed in Appendix 13C.

	A	B	C	D	
1			Year(s)		
2		Now	1-5	5	
3	Initial investment	$ (50,000)			
4	Annual cost savings		$ 18,000		
5	Salvage value of the new machine			$ 5,000	
6	Total cash flows (a)	$ (50,000)	$ 18,000	$ 5,000	
7	Discount factor (18%) (b)	1.000	3.127	0.437	
8	Present value of the cash flows (a) × (b)	$ (50,000)	$ 56,286	$ 2,185	
9	Net present value (SUM B8:D8)	$ 8,471			
10					
11	Note: The discount factors come from Exhibits 13B-1 and 13B-2 in Appendix 13B.				
12					

EXHIBIT 13–3
Net Present Value Analysis Using Discount Factors from Exhibits 13B–1 and 13B–2 in Appendix 13B

Exhibit 13–4 shows another way to calculate the net present value of $8,471. Under this approach Cell B8 calculates the present value of the initial cash outlay of $(50,000) by multiplying $(50,000) by 1.000—just as was done in Exhibit 13–3. However, rather than calculating the present value of the annual cost savings using a discount factor of 3.127 from Exhibit 13B–2, the approach used in Exhibit 13–4 discounts the annual cost savings in Years 1–5 *and* the machine's salvage value in Year 5 to their present values using the discount factors from Exhibit 13B–1. For example, the $18,000 cost savings in Year 3 (cell E6) is multiplied by the discount factor of 0.609 (cell E7) to derive this future cash flow's present value of $10,962 (cell E8). As another example, the $23,000 of total cash flows in Year 5 (cell G6) is multiplied by the discount factor of 0.437 (cell G7) to determine these future cash flows' present value of $10,051 (cell G8). The present values in cells B8 through G8 are then added together to compute the project's net present value of $8,471(cell B9).

The methods described in Exhibits 13–3 and 13–4 are mathematically equivalent—they both produced a net present value of $8,471. The only difference between these two exhibits relates to the discounting of the annual labor cost savings. In Exhibit 13–3, the labor cost savings are discounted to their present value using the annuity factor of 3.127, whereas in Exhibit 13–4, these cost savings are discounted using five separate factors that sum to 3.127 (0.847 + 0.718 + 0.609 + 0.516 + 0.437 = 3.127).

EXHIBIT 13–4
Net Present Value Analysis Using Discount Factors from Exhibit 13B–1 in Appendix 13B

	A	B	C	D	E	F	G	
1					Year			
2		Now	1	2	3	4	5	
3	Initial investment	$ (50,000)						
4	Annual labor cost savings		$ 18,000	$ 18,000	$ 18,000	$ 18,000	$ 18,000	
5	Salvage value of new machine						$ 5,000	
6	Total cash flows (a)	$ (50,000)	$ 18,000	$ 18,000	$ 18,000	$ 18,000	$ 23,000	
7	Discount factor (18%) (b)	1.000	0.847	0.718	0.609	0.516	0.437	
8	Present value of cash flows (a) × (b)	$ (50,000)	$ 15,246	$ 12,924	$ 10,962	$ 9,288	$ 10,051	
9	Net present value (SUM B8:G8)	$ 8,471						
10								
11	Note: The discount factors come from Exhibits 13B-1 in Appendix 13B.							
12								

It bears reemphasizing that the net present values in Exhibits 13–3 and 13–4 are calculated using the *rounded* discount factors from Appendix 13B. However, net present value calculations can also be performed using *unrounded* discount factors. One approach to using unrounded discount factors would be to replace the rounded discount factors shown in row 7 of Exhibits 13–3 and 13–4 with formulas that compute unrounded discount factors. Another approach, as shown in Exhibit 13–5, is to use Microsoft Excel's NPV function to perform the calculations. The NPV function automatically calculates the net present value after specifying three parameters—the discount rate (0.18), the annual cash flows (C6:G6), and the initial cash outlay (+B6). Notice that the net present value in Exhibit 13–5 of $8,475 is $4 higher than the net present value shown in Exhibits 13–3 and 13–4. The trivial $4 difference arises because Microsoft Excel's NPV function uses unrounded discount factors.

EXHIBIT 13–5

Net Present Value Analysis Using Microsoft Excel's NPV Function

	A	B	C	D	E	F	G
1					Year		
2		Now	1	2	3	4	5
3	Initial investment	$ (50,000)					
4	Annual labor cost savings		$ 18,000	$ 18,000	$ 18,000	$ 18,000	$ 18,000
5	Salvage value of new machine						$ 5,000
6	Total cash flows (a)	$ (50,000)	$ 18,000	$ 18,000	$ 18,000	$ 18,000	$ 23,000
7	Net present value (SUM B8:G8)	$ 8,475					
8							
9	Note: The net present value is computed using the formula: =NPV(0.18,C6:G6)+B6						
10							

Exhibit 13-3   Exhibit 13-4   **Exhibit 13-5**   Exhibit 13-6   Exh

---

During your career you should feel free to use any of the methods discussed thus far to perform net present value calculations. However, throughout this chapter and its forthcoming exercises and problems, we'll be using the approaches illustrated in Exhibits 13–3 and 13–4 accompanied by the rounded discount factors in Appendix 13B.

Once you have computed a project's net present value, you'll need to interpret your findings. For example, because Harper Company's proposed project has a positive net present value of $8,471, it implies that the company should purchase the new machine. A positive net present value indicates that the project's return exceeds the discount rate. A negative net present value indicates that the project's return is less than the discount rate. Therefore, if the company's minimum required rate of return is used as the discount rate, a project with a positive net present value has a return that exceeds the minimum required rate of return and is acceptable. Conversely, a project with a negative net present value has a return that is less than the minimum required rate of return and is unacceptable. In sum:

If the Net Present Value Is . . .	Then the Project Is . . .
Positive	Acceptable because its return is greater than the required rate of return.
Zero	Acceptable because its return is equal to the required rate of return.
Negative	Not acceptable because its return is less than the required rate of return.

A company's *cost of capital* is usually regarded as its minimum required rate of return. The **cost of capital** is the average rate of return that the company must pay to its long-term creditors and its shareholders for the use of their funds. If a project's rate of return is less than the cost of capital, the company does not earn enough to compensate its creditors and shareholders. Therefore, any project with a rate of return less than the cost of capital should be rejected.

The cost of capital serves as a *screening device*. When the cost of capital is used as the discount rate in net present value analysis, any project with a negative net present value does not cover the company's cost of capital and should be discarded as unacceptable.

Recovery of the Original Investment

The net present value method automatically provides for return of the original invest-ment. Whenever the net present value of a project is positive, the project will recover the original cost of the investment plus sufficient excess cash inflows to compensate the organization for tying up funds in the project. To demonstrate this point, consider the fol-lowing situation:

Example D: Carver Hospital is considering the purchase of an attachment for its X-ray machine that will cost $3,170. The attachment will be usable for four years, after which time it will have no salvage value. It will increase net cash inflows by $1,000 per year in the X-ray department. The hospital's board of directors requires a rate of return of at least 10% on such investments.

A net present value analysis of the desirability of purchasing the X-ray attachment (using a discount factor of 3.170 from Exhibit 13B–2) is presented in Exhibit 13–6. Notice that the attachment has exactly a 10% return on the original investment because the net present value is zero at a 10% discount rate.

Each annual $1,000 cash inflow arising from use of the attachment is made up of two parts. One part represents a recovery of a portion *of* the original $3,170 paid for the attachment, and the other part represents a return *on* this investment. The breakdown of each year's $1,000 cash inflow between recovery *of* investment and return *on* investment is shown in Exhibit 13–7.

The first year's $1,000 cash inflow consists of a return *on* investment of $317 (a 10% return *on* the $3,170 original investment), plus a $683 return *of* that investment. Because the amount of the unrecovered investment decreases each year, the dollar amount of the return on investment also decreases each year. By the end of the fourth year, all $3,170 of the original investment has been recovered.

EXHIBIT 13–6
Carver Hospital—Net Present Value Analysis of X-Ray Attachment

	A	B	C
1			Years
2		Now	1-4
3	Initial investment	$ (3,170)	
4	Annual cost savings		$ 1,000
5	Total cash flows (a)	$ (3,170)	$ 1,000
6	Discount factor (10%) (b)	1.000	3.170
7	Present value of the cash flows (a) × (b)	$ (3,170)	$ 3,170
8	Net present value (SUM B7:C7)	$ 0	
9			
10	Note: The discount factor comes from Exhibits 13B-2 in Appendix 13B.		
11			

Exhibit 13-6 / Exhibit 13-7

EXHIBIT 13–7
Carver Hospital—Breakdown of Annual Cash Inflows

	A	B	C	D	E	F
1		(1)	(2)	(3)	(4)	(5)
2	Year	Investment Outstanding during the Year	Cash Inflow	Return on Investment (1) × 10%	Recovery of Investment during the Year (2) – (3)	Unrecovered Investment at the End of the Year (1) – (4)
3	1	$3,170	$1,000	$317	$683	$2,487
4	2	$2,487	$1,000	$249	$751	$1,736
5	3	$1,736	$1,000	$173	$827	$909
6	4	$909	$1,000	$91	$909	$0
7	Total investment recovered				$3,170	

Exhibit 13-6   **Exhibit 13-7**   Exhibit 13-8   Exhibit 13-9   Exh

COOLING SERVERS NATURALLY

Google consumes more than 2 terawatt hours of electricity per year, which is greater than the annual electricity consumption of 200,000 American homes. A large part of Google's electricity consumption relates to running and cooling its huge number of servers. In an effort to lower its electricity bill, Google invested €200 million to build a server storage facility in the Baltic Sea coastal community of Hamina, Finland. Hamina's low electricity rates coupled with its persistently low ambient air temperatures will lower Google's annual electricity bills considerably. Shortly after Google's facility opened in Hamina, **Facebook** opened a five-acre data center in Luleå, Sweden, where the average temperature is 35 degrees Fahrenheit.

Source: Sven Grunberg and Niclas Rolander, "For Data Center, Google Goes for the Cold," *The Wall Street Journal,* September 12, 2011, p. B10.

An Extended Example of the Net Present Value Method

Example E provides an extended example of how the net present value method is used to analyze a proposed project. This example helps tie together and reinforce many of the ideas discussed thus far.

Example E: Under a special licensing arrangement, Swinyard Corporation has an opportunity to market a new product for a five-year period. The product would be purchased from the manufacturer, with Swinyard responsible for promotion and distribution costs. The licensing arrangement could be renewed at the end of the five-year period. After careful study, Swinyard estimated the following costs and revenues for the new product:

Cost of equipment needed	$60,000
Working capital needed	$100,000
Overhaul of the equipment in four years	$5,000
Salvage value of the equipment in five years	$10,000
Annual revenues and costs:	
Sales revenues	$200,000
Cost of goods sold	$125,000
Out-of-pocket operating costs (for salaries,	
advertising, and other direct costs)	$35,000

EXHIBIT 13–8
The Net Present Value Method—An Extended Example

	A	B	C	D	E	F	G
1					Year		
2		Now	1	2	3	4	5
3	Purchase of equipment	$ (60,000)					
4	Investment in working capital	$ (100,000)					
5	Sales		$ 200,000	$ 200,000	$ 200,000	$ 200,000	$ 200,000
6	Cost of goods sold		$ (125,000)	$ (125,000)	$ (125,000)	$ (125,000)	$ (125,000)
7	Out-of-pocket costs for salaries, advertising, etc.		$ (35,000)	$ (35,000)	$ (35,000)	$ (35,000)	$ (35,000)
8	Overhaul of equipment					$ (5,000)	
9	Salvage value of the equipment						$ 10,000
10	Working capital released						$ 100,000
11	Total cash flows (a)	$ (160,000)	$ 40,000	$ 40,000	$ 40,000	$ 35,000	$ 150,000
12	Discount factor (14%) (b)	1.000	0.877	0.769	0.675	0.592	$ 0.519
13	Present value of cash flows (a) × (b)	$ (160,000)	$ 35,080	$ 30,760	$ 27,000	$ 20,720	$ 77,850
14	Net present value (SUM B13:G13)	$ 31,410					
15							
16	Note: The discount factors come from Exhibit 13B-1 in Appendix 13B.						
17							

Exhibit 13-3 / Exhibit 13-4 / Exhibit 13-5 / Exhibit 13-6 / Exhibit 13-7 / **Exhibit 13-8** / Exhibit

At the end of the five-year period, if Swinyard decides not to renew the licensing arrangement the working capital would be released for investment elsewhere. Swinyard uses a 14% discount rate. Would you recommend that the new product be introduced?

This example involves a variety of cash inflows and cash outflows. The solution (using discount factors from Exhibit 13B–1) is given in Exhibit 13–8.

Notice how the working capital is handled in this exhibit. It is counted as a cash outflow at the beginning of the project (cell B4) and as a cash inflow when it is released at the end of the project (cell G10). Also notice how the sales revenues, cost of goods sold, and out-of-pocket costs are handled. **Out-of-pocket costs** are actual cash outlays for salaries, advertising, and other operating expenses.

Because the net present value of the proposal is positive, the new product is acceptable.

IN BUSINESS

SHOULD EGG FARMERS INVEST IN CAGE-FREE FACILITIES OR BIGGER CAGES?

Egg farmers are facing an interesting capital budgeting question: should they invest in building cage-free facilities for their hens or should they buy bigger cages? Investing in bigger cages costs less than cage-free farming and it complies with new animal welfare laws; however, it does not satisfy the demands of many customers and animal-rights advocates. For example, Nestlé, Starbucks, Burger King, and Aramark have pledged to eliminate the use of eggs from caged hens.

Rose Acre Farms has committed to raising all of its hens in cage-free facilities. Farmers estimate that building a cage-free farm for 100,000 birds costs $1 million more than it would cost to build a large-cage facility for these same birds. Since only 6% of the U.S. flock is currently cage-free, egg farmers can command a price premium for eggs produced in a free-roaming farm.

Source: David Kesmodel, "Flap Over Eggs: Whether to Go Cage-Free," *The Wall Street Journal*, March 16, 2015, pp. B1–B2.

The Internal Rate of Return Method

LO13–3
Evaluate the acceptability of an investment project using the internal rate of return method.

The **internal rate of return** is the rate of return of an investment project over its useful life. The internal rate of return is computed by finding the discount rate that equates the present value of a project's cash outflows with the present value of its cash inflows. In other words, the internal rate of return is the discount rate that results in a net present value of zero.

The Internal Rate of Return Method Illustrated

To illustrate the internal rate of return method, consider the following data:

Example F: Glendale School District is considering the purchase of a large tractor-pulled lawn mower. At present, the lawn is mowed using a small hand-pushed gas mower. The large, tractor-pulled mower will cost $16,950 and will have a useful life of 10 years. It will have a negligible scrap value, which can be ignored. The tractor-pulled mower would do the job faster than the old mower, resulting in labor savings of $3,000 per year.

To compute the internal rate of return of the new mower, we must find the discount rate that will result in a zero net present value. How do we do this? The simplest and most direct approach *when the net cash inflow is the same every year* is to divide the investment in the project by the expected annual net cash inflow. This computation yields a factor from which the internal rate of return can be determined. The formula is as follows:

$$\text{Factor of the internal rate of return} = \frac{\text{Investment required}}{\text{Annual net cash inflow}} \qquad (2)$$

The factor derived from formula (2) is then located in Exhibit 13B–2 in Appendix 13B to see what rate of return it represents. Using formula (2) and the data for the Glendale School District's proposed project, we get:

$$\frac{\text{Investment required}}{\text{Annual net cash inflow}} = \frac{\$16,950}{\$3,000} = 5.650$$

Thus, the discount factor that will equate a series of $3,000 cash inflows with a present investment of $16,950 is 5.650. Now we need to find this factor in Exhibit 13B–2 in Appendix 13B to see what rate of return it represents. We should use the 10-period line in Exhibit 13B–2 because the cash flows for the project continue for 10 years. If we scan along the 10-period line, we find that a factor of 5.650 represents a 12% rate of return. Therefore, the internal rate of return of the mower project is 12%. We can verify this by computing the project's net present value using a 12% discount rate as shown in Exhibit 13–9.

Notice from Exhibit 13–9 that using a 12% discount rate equates the present value of the annual cost savings with the present value of the initial investment required for the project, leaving a zero net present value. The 12% rate therefore represents the internal rate of return of the project.

Once the Glendale School District computes the project's internal rate of return of 12%, it would accept or reject the project by comparing this percentage to the school district's minimum required rate of return. If the internal rate of return is equal to or greater than the required rate of return, then the project is acceptable. If the internal rate of return is less than the required rate of return, then the project is rejected. For example, if we assume that Glendale's minimum required rate of return is 15%, then the school district would reject this project because the 12% internal rate of return does not clear the 15% *hurdle rate*.

EXHIBIT 13–9
Evaluation of the Mower Using a 12% Discount Rate

	A	B	C
1			Years
2		Now	1-10
3	Initial investment	$ (16,950)	
4	Annual cost savings		$ 3,000
5	Total cash flows (a)	$ (16,950)	$ 3,000
6	Discount factor (12%) (b)	1.000	5.650
7	Present value of the cash flows (a) × (b)	$ (16,950)	$ 16,950
8	Net present value (SUM B7:C7)	$ 0	
9			
10	Note: The discount factor comes from Exhibits 13B-2 in Appendix 13B.		
11			

Exhibit 13-8   Exhibit 13 9   Exhibit

Comparison of the Net Present Value and Internal Rate of Return Methods

This section compares the net present value and internal rate of return methods in three ways. First, both methods use the cost of capital to screen out undesirable investment projects. When the internal rate of return method is used, the cost of capital is used as the hurdle rate that a project must clear for acceptance. If the internal rate of return of a project is not high enough to clear the cost of capital hurdle, then the project is ordinarily rejected. When the net present value method is used, the cost of capital is the discount rate used to compute the net present value of a proposed project. Any project yielding a negative net present value is rejected unless other factors are significant enough to warrant its acceptance.

Second, the net present value method is often simpler to use than the internal rate of return method, particularly when a project does not have identical cash flows every year. For example, if a project has some salvage value at the end of its life in addition to its annual cash inflows, the internal rate of return method requires a trial-and-error process to find the rate of return that will result in a net present value of zero. While computer software can be used to perform this trial-and-error process in seconds, it is still a little more complex than using spreadsheet software to perform net present value analysis.

Third, the internal rate of return method makes a questionable assumption. Both methods assume that cash flows generated by a project during its useful life are immediately reinvested elsewhere. However, the two methods make different assumptions concerning the rate of return that is earned on those cash flows. The net present value method assumes the rate of return is the discount rate, whereas the internal rate of return method assumes the rate of return earned on cash flows is the internal rate of return on the project. Specifically, if the internal rate of return of the project is high, this assumption may not be realistic. It is generally more realistic to assume that cash inflows can be reinvested at a rate of return equal to the discount rate—particularly if the discount rate is the company's cost of capital or an opportunity rate of return. For example, if the discount rate is the company's cost of capital, this rate of return can be actually realized by paying off the company's creditors and buying back the company's stock with cash flows from the project. In short, when the net present value method and the internal rate of return method do not agree concerning the attractiveness of a project, it is best to go with the net present value method. Of the two methods, it makes the more realistic assumption about the rate of return that can be earned on cash flows from the project.

Expanding the Net Present Value Method

So far, all of our examples have involved an evaluation of a single investment project. In the following section we use the *total-cost approach* to explain how the net present value method can be used to evaluate two alternative projects.

The total-cost approach is the most flexible method for comparing competing projects. To illustrate the mechanics of the approach, consider the following data:

Example G: Harper Ferry Company operates a high-speed passenger ferry service across the Mississippi River. One of its ferryboats is in poor condition. This ferry can be renovated at an immediate cost of $200,000. Further repairs and an overhaul of the motor will be needed three years from now at a cost of $80,000. In all, the ferry will be usable for 5 years if this work is done. At the end of 5 years, the ferry will have to be scrapped at a salvage value of $60,000. The scrap value of the ferry right now is $70,000. It will cost $300,000 each year to operate the ferry, and revenues will total $400,000 annually.

As an alternative, Harper Ferry Company can purchase a new ferryboat at a cost of $360,000. The new ferry will have a life of 5 years, but it will require some repairs costing $30,000 at the end of 3 years. At the end of 5 years, the ferry will have a scrap value of $60,000. It will cost $210,000 each year to operate the ferry, and revenues will total $400,000 annually.

Harper Ferry Company requires a return of at least 14% on all investment projects.

Should the company purchase the new ferry or renovate the old ferry? Exhibit 13–10 shows the solution using the total-cost approach and discount factors from Exhibit 13B–1.

Two points should be noted from the exhibit. First, *all* cash inflows and *all* cash outflows are included in the solution under each alternative. No effort has been made to isolate those cash flows that are relevant to the decision and those that are irrelevant. The inclusion of all cash flows associated with each alternative gives the approach its name—the *total-cost* approach.

Second, notice that a net present value is computed for each alternative. This is a strength of the total-cost approach because an unlimited number of alternatives can be compared side by side to determine the best option. For example, another alternative for Harper Ferry Company would be to get out of the ferry business entirely. If management desired, the net present value of this alternative could be computed to compare with the alternatives shown in Exhibit 13–10. Still other alternatives might be available to the company. In the case at hand, given only two alternatives, the data indicate that the net present value in favor of buying the new ferry is $252,630.[2]

Least-Cost Decisions

Some decisions do not involve any revenues. For example, a company may be trying to decide whether to buy or lease an executive jet. The choice would be made on the basis of which alternative—buying or leasing—would be least costly. In situations such as these, where no revenues are involved, the most desirable alternative is the one with the

---

[2] The alternative with the highest net present value is not always the best choice, although it is the best choice in this case. For further discussion, see the section Preference Decisions—The Ranking of Investment Projects.

EXHIBIT 13–10
The Total-Cost Approach to Project Selection

	A	B	C	D	E	F	G
					Year		
1	Keep the old ferry:						
2		Now	1	2	3	4	5
3	Renovation	$(200,000)					
4	Annual revenues		$ 400,000	$ 400,000	$ 400,000	$ 400,000	$ 400,000
5	Annual cash operating costs		$(300,000)	$(300,000)	$(300,000)	$(300,000)	$(300,000)
6	Repairs in three years				$ (80,000)		
7	Salvage value of old ferry						$ 60,000
8	Total cash flows (a)	$(200,000)	$ 100,000	$ 100,000	$ 20,000	$ 100,000	$ 160,000
9	Discount factor (14%) (b)	1.000	0.877	0.769	0.675	0.592	0.519
10	Present value of cash flows (a) × (b)	$(200,000)	$ 87,700	$ 76,900	$ 13,500	$ 59,200	$ 83,040
11	Net present value (SUM B10:G10)	$ 120,340					
12							
13	Buy the new ferry:				Year		
14		Now	1	2	3	4	5
15	Initial investment	$(360,000)					
16	Salvage value of the old ferry	$ 70,000					
17	Annual revenues		$ 400,000	$ 400,000	$ 400,000	$ 400,000	$ 400,000
18	Annual cash operating costs		$(210,000)	$(210,000)	$(210,000)	$(210,000)	$(210,000)
19	Repairs in three years				$ (30,000)		
20	Salvage value of new ferry						$ 60,000
21	Total cash flows (a)	$(290,000)	$ 190,000	$ 190,000	$ 160,000	$ 190,000	$ 250,000
22	Discount factor (14%) (b)	1.000	0.877	0.769	0.675	0.592	0.519
23	Present value of cash flows (a) × (b)	$(290,000)	$ 166,630	$ 146,110	$ 108,000	$ 112,480	$ 129,750
24	Net present value (SUM B23:G23)	$ 372,970					
25							
26	Net present value in favor of buying the new ferry (B24-B11)	$ 252,630					
27							
28	Note: The discount factors come from Exhibit 13B-1 in Appendix 13B.						
29							

Exhibit 13-10 / Exhibit 13-11 / Exhibit 13C-1

least total cost from a present value perspective. Hence, these are known as least-cost decisions. To illustrate a least-cost decision, consider the following data:

Example H: Val-Tek Company is considering replacing an old threading machine with a new threading machine that would substantially reduce annual operating costs. Selected data relating to the old and new machines are presented below:

	Old Machine	New Machine
Purchase cost when new	$200,000	$250,000
Salvage value now	$30,000	—
Annual cash operating costs	$150,000	$90,000
Overhaul needed immediately	$40,000	—
Salvage value in six years	$0	$50,000
Remaining life	6 years	6 years

Val-Tek Company uses a 10% discount rate.

Exhibit 13–11 analyzes the alternatives using the total-cost approach and discount factors from Exhibits 13B–1 and 13B–2. Because this is a least-cost decision, the present values are negative for both alternatives. However, the present value of the alternative of buying the new machine is $109,500 lower than the other alternative. Therefore, buying the new machine is the less costly alternative.

EXHIBIT 13-11
Least-Cost Decision: A Net Present Value Analysis

	A	B	C	D
1	Keep the old machine:		Year(s)	
2		Now	1-6	6
3	Overhaul needed now	$ (40,000)		
4	Annual cash operating costs		$ (150,000)	
5	Total cash flows (a)	$ (40,000)	$ (150,000)	
6	Discount factor (10%) (b)	1.000	4.355	
7	Present value of the cash flows (a) × (b)	$ (40,000)	$ (653,250)	
8	Net present value (SUM B7:C7)	$ (693,250)		
9				
10	Buy the new machine:		Year(s)	
11		Now	1-6	6
12	Initial investment	$ (250,000)		
13	Salvage value of old machine	$ 30,000		
14	Annual cash operating costs		$ (90,000)	
15	Salvage value of new machine			$ 50,000
16	Total cash flows (a)	$ (220,000)	$ (90,000)	$ 50,000
17	Discount factor (10%) (b)	1.000	4.355	0.564
18	Present value of the cash flows (a) × (b)	$ (220,000)	$ (391,950)	$ 28,200
19	Net present value (SUM B18:D18)	$ (583,750)		
20				
21	Net present value in favor of buying the new machine	$ 109,500		
22				
23	Note: The discount factors come from Exhibits 13B-1 and 13B-2 in Appendix 13B.			
24				

Exhibit 13-10   **Exhibit 13-11**   Exhibit 13C-1

IN BUSINESS

© Ken James/Bloomberg/Getty Images

UNITED PARCEL SERVICE FOCUSES ITS ATTENTION ON DECEMBER 22nd

When **United Parcel Service** (UPS) failed to deliver millions of packages by Christmas Day, it needed to devise a solution so that the same problems would not be repeated next year. The company's answer was a $500 million capital investment in an automated system that it calls the "Next Generation Sort Aisle." The new system rapidly identifies zip codes, thereby enabling employees to process 15% more packages per day. The system can also quickly reroute packages in the event of bad weather. UPS hopes that its new automated system also will enable it to save $500 million per year on employee training. But, perhaps more importantly, the company also hopes that the new system will enable it to deliver the 34 million packages that it receives on December 22 to its anxious recipients by Christmas Day.

Source: Laura Stevens, "One Day, 34 Million Packages at UPS," *The Wall Street Journal*, December 22, 2014, pp. B1–B2.

Thus far, we have assumed that all future cash flows are known with certainty. However, future cash flows are often uncertain or difficult to estimate. A number of techniques are available for handling this complication. Some of these techniques are quite technical—involving computer simulations or advanced mathematical skills—and are beyond the scope of this book. However, we can provide some very useful information to help managers deal with uncertain cash flows without getting too technical.

LO13–4
Evaluate an investment project that has uncertain cash flows.

An Example

As an example of difficult-to-estimate future cash flows, consider the case of investments in automated equipment. The up-front costs of automated equipment and the tangible benefits, such as reductions in operating costs and waste, tend to be relatively easy to estimate. However, the intangible benefits, such as greater reliability, greater speed, and higher quality, are more difficult to quantify in terms of future cash flows. These intangible benefits certainly impact future cash flows—particularly in terms of increased sales and perhaps higher selling prices—but the cash flow effects are difficult to estimate. What can be done?

A fairly simple procedure can be followed when the intangible benefits are likely to be significant. Suppose, for example, that a company with a 12% discount rate is considering purchasing automated equipment that would have a 10-year useful life. Also suppose that a discounted cash flow analysis of just the tangible costs and benefits shows a negative net present value of $226,000. Clearly, if the intangible benefits are large enough, they could turn this negative net present value into a positive net present value. In this case, the amount of additional cash flow per year from the intangible benefits that would be needed to make the project financially attractive can be computed as follows:

Net present value excluding the intangible benefits (negative)	$(226,000)
Present value factor for an annuity at 12% for 10 periods (from Exhibit 13B–2 in Appendix 13B)	5.650

$$\frac{\text{Negative net present value to be offset, } \$226{,}000}{\text{Present value factor, } 5.650} = \$40{,}000$$

Thus, if the intangible benefits of the automated equipment are worth at least $40,000 a year to the company, then the automated equipment should be purchased. If, in the judgment of management, these intangible benefits are not worth $40,000 a year, then the automated equipment should not be purchased.

This technique can be used in other situations in which future cash flows are difficult to estimate. For example, this technique can be used when the salvage value is difficult to estimate. To illustrate, suppose that all of the cash flows from an investment in a supertanker have been estimated—other than its salvage value in 20 years. Using a discount rate of 12%, management has determined that the net present value of all of these cash flows is a negative $1.04 million. This negative net present value would be offset by the salvage value of the supertanker. How large would the salvage value have to be to make this investment attractive?

Net present value excluding salvage value (negative)	$(1,040,000)
Present value factor at 12% for 20 periods (from Exhibit 13B–1 in Appendix 13B)	0.104

$$\frac{\text{Negative net present value to be offset, } \$1{,}040{,}000}{\text{Present value factor, } 0.104} = \$10{,}000{,}000$$

Thus, if the salvage value of the tanker in 20 years is at least $10 million, its net present value would be positive and the investment should be made. However, if management believes the salvage value is unlikely to be as large as $10 million, the investment should not be made.

Preference Decisions—The Ranking of Investment Projects

LO13–5

Rank investment projects in order of preference.

Recall that when considering investment opportunities, managers must make two types of decisions—screening decisions and preference decisions. Screening decisions, which come first, pertain to whether or not a proposed investment is acceptable. Preference decisions come *after* screening decisions and attempt to answer the following question: "How do the remaining investment proposals, all of which have been screened and provide an acceptable rate of return, rank in terms of preference? That is, which one(s) would be *best* for the company to accept?"

Sometimes preference decisions are called rationing decisions, or ranking decisions. Limited investment funds must be rationed among many competing alternatives. Hence, the alternatives must be ranked. Either the internal rate of return method or the net present value method can be used in making preference decisions. However, as discussed earlier, if the two methods are in conflict, it is best to use the net present value method, which is more reliable.

Internal Rate of Return Method

When using the internal rate of return method to rank competing investment projects, the preference rule is: *The higher the internal rate of return, the more desirable the project.* An investment project with an internal rate of return of 18% usually is considered preferable to another project that has a return of only 15%. Internal rate of return is widely used to rank projects.

Net Present Value Method

The net present value of one project cannot be directly compared to the net present value of another project unless the initial investments are equal. For example, assume that a company is considering two competing investments, as shown below:

	Investment	
	A	B
Investment required	$(10,000)	$(5,000)
Present value of cash inflows	11,000	6,000
Net present value	$ 1,000	$ 1,000

Although each project has a net present value of $1,000, the projects are not equally desirable if the funds available for investment are limited. The project requiring an investment of only $5,000 is much more desirable than the project requiring an investment of $10,000. This fact can be highlighted by dividing the net present value of the project by the investment required. The result, shown below in equation form, is called the **project profitability index**.

$$\text{Project profitability index} = \frac{\text{Net present value of the project}}{\text{Investment required}} \quad (3)$$

The project profitability indexes for the two investments above would be computed as follows:

	Investment	
	A	B
Net present value (a)	$1,000	$1,000
Investment required (b)	$10,000	$5,000
Project profitability index, (a) ÷ (b)	0.10	0.20

When using the project profitability index to rank competing investments projects, the preference rule is: *The higher the project profitability index, the more desirable the project.*[3] Applying this rule to the two investments above, investment B should be chosen over investment A.

The project profitability index is an application of the techniques for utilizing constrained resources discussed in an earlier chapter. In this case, the constrained resource is the limited funds available for investment, and the project profitability index is similar to the contribution margin per unit of the constrained resource.

A few details should be clarified with respect to the computation of the project profitability index. The "Investment required" refers to any cash outflows that occur at the beginning of the project, reduced by any salvage value recovered from the sale of old equipment. The "Investment required" also includes any investment in working capital that the project may need.

The Simple Rate of Return Method

LO13–6
Compute the simple rate of return for an investment.

The **simple rate of return** method is the final capital budgeting technique discussed in the chapter. This method also is often referred to as the accounting rate of return or the unadjusted rate of return. We will begin by explaining how to compute the simple rate of return followed by a discussion of this method's limitations and its impact on the behavior of investment center managers.

To obtain the simple rate of return, the annual incremental net operating income generated by a project is divided by the initial investment in the project, as shown below.

$$\text{Simple rate of return} = \frac{\text{Annual incremental net operating income}}{\text{Initial investment}} \quad (4)$$

The annual incremental net operating income included in the numerator should be reduced by the depreciation charges that result from making the investment. Furthermore, the initial investment shown in the denominator should be reduced by any salvage value realized from the sale of old equipment.

Example I: Brigham Tea, Inc., is a processor of low-acid tea. The company is contemplating purchasing equipment for an additional processing line that would increase revenues by $90,000 per year. Incremental cash operating expenses would be $40,000 per year. The equipment would cost $180,000 and have a nine-year life with no salvage value.

To apply the formula for the simple rate of return, we must first determine the annual incremental net operating income from the project:

Annual incremental revenues		$90,000
Annual incremental cash operating expenses ...	$40,000	
Annual depreciation ($180,000 − $0) ÷ 9	20,000	
Annual incremental expenses		60,000
Annual incremental net operating income		$30,000

---

[3] Because of the "lumpiness" of projects, the project profitability index ranking may not be perfect. Nevertheless, it is a good starting point.

Given that the annual incremental net operating income from the project is $30,000 and the initial investment is $180,000, the simple rate of return is 16.7% as shown below:

$$\text{Simple rate of return} = \frac{\text{Annual incremental net operating income}}{\text{Initial investment}}$$

$$= \frac{\$30,000}{\$180,000}$$

$$= 16.7\%$$

Example J: Midwest Farms, Inc., hires people on a part-time basis to sort eggs. The cost of hand sorting is $30,000 per year. The company is investigating an egg-sorting machine that would cost $90,000 and have a 15-year useful life. The machine would have negligible salvage value, and it would cost $10,000 per year to operate and maintain. The egg-sorting equipment currently being used could be sold now for a scrap value of $2,500.

This project is slightly different from the preceding project because it involves cost reductions with no additional revenues. Nevertheless, the annual incremental net operating income can be computed by treating the annual cost savings as if it were incremental revenues as follows:

Annual incremental cost savings		$ 30,000
Annual incremental cash operating expenses	$10,000	
Annual depreciation ($90,000 – $0) ÷ 15	6,000	
Annual incremental expenses		16,000
Annual incremental net operating income		$ 14,000

Thus, even though the new equipment would not generate any additional revenues, it would reduce costs by $14,000 a year. This would have the effect of increasing net operating income by $14,000 a year.

Finally, the salvage value of the old equipment offsets the initial cost of the new equipment as follows:

Cost of the new equipment	$90,000
Less salvage value of the old equipment	2,500
Initial investment	$87,500

Given the annual incremental net operating income of $14,000 and the initial investment of $87,500, the simple rate of return is 16.0% computed as follows:

$$\text{Simple rate of return} = \frac{\text{Annual incremental net operating income}}{\text{Initial investment}}$$

$$= \frac{\$14,000}{\$87,500}$$

$$= 16.0\%$$

The simple rate of return suffers from two important limitations. First, it focuses on accounting net operating income rather than cash flows. Thus, if a project does not have constant incremental revenues and expenses over its useful life, the simple rate of return will fluctuate from year to year, thereby possibly causing the same project to appear desirable in some years and undesirable in others. Second, the simple rate of return method does not involve discounting cash flows. It considers a dollar received 10 years from now to be as valuable as a dollar received today.

Given these limitations, it is reasonable to wonder why we bothered discussing this method. First of all, in spite of its limitations, some companies use the simple rate of return to evaluate capital investment proposals. Therefore, you should be familiar with this approach so you can properly critique it in the event that you encounter it in practice. More importantly, you need to understand how the simple rate of return method influences the behavior of investment center managers who are evaluated and rewarded based on their return on investment (ROI).

For example, assume the following three facts. First, assume you are an investment center manager whose pay raises are based solely on ROI. Second, assume that last year your division had an ROI of 20%. Third, assume your division has the chance to pursue a capital budgeting project that will have a positive net present value and a simple rate of return of 17%. Given these three assumptions, would you choose to accept this project or reject it? Although the company would want you to accept it because of its positive net present value, you would probably choose to reject it because the simple rate of return of 17% is less than your prior year's ROI of 20%. This basic example illustrates how a project's simple rate of return can influence the decisions made by investment center managers. It also highlights an important challenge faced by organizations, namely designing performance measurement systems that align employee actions with organizational goals.

Postaudit of Investment Projects

After an investment project has been approved and implemented, a *postaudit* should be conducted. A **postaudit** involves checking whether or not expected results are actually realized. This is a key part of the capital budgeting process because it helps keep managers honest in their investment proposals. Any tendency to inflate the benefits or downplay the costs in a proposal should become evident after a few postaudits have been conducted. The postaudit also provides an opportunity to reinforce and possibly expand successful projects and to cut losses on floundering projects.

The same capital budgeting method should be used in the postaudit as was used in the original approval process. That is, if a project was approved on the basis of a net present value analysis, then the same procedure should be used in performing the postaudit. However, the data used in the postaudit analysis should be *actual observed data* rather than estimated data. This gives management an opportunity to make a side-by-side comparison to see how well the project has succeeded. It also helps assure that estimated data received on future proposals will be carefully prepared because the persons submitting the data knows that their estimates will be compared to actual results in the postaudit process. Actual results that are far out of line with original estimates should be carefully reviewed.

Summary

The payback method of evaluating capital investment projects focuses on the payback period. The payback period is the length of time that it takes for a project to recover its initial cost from the net cash inflows that it generates. The basic premise of the payback method is that the more quickly the cost of an investment can be recovered, the more desirable is the investment.

Investment decisions should take into account the time value of money because a dollar received today is more valuable than a dollar received in the future. The net present value and internal rate of return methods both reflect this fact. In the net present value method, future cash flows are discounted to their present value. The difference between the present value of the cash inflows and the present value of the cash outflows is called a project's net present value. If the net present value of a project is negative, the project is rejected. The discount rate in the net present value method is usually based on a minimum required rate of return such as a company's cost of capital.

The internal rate of return is the rate of return that equates the present value of the cash inflows and the present value of the cash outflows, resulting in a zero net present value. If the internal rate of return is less than a company's minimum required rate of return, the project is rejected.

After rejecting projects whose net present values are negative or whose internal rates of return are less than the minimum required rate of return, more projects may remain than can be supported with available funds. The remaining projects can be ranked using either the project profitability index or internal rate of return. The project profitability index is computed by dividing the net present value of the project by the required initial investment.

The simple rate of return is determined by dividing a project's annual incremental net operating income by the initial investment in the project. While this method has important limitations, it can influence the decision-making process of investment center managers who are evaluated and rewarded based on their return on investment (ROI).

Review Problem: Comparison of Capital Budgeting Methods

Lamar Company is considering a project that would have a five-year life and require a $2,400,000 investment in equipment. At the end of five years, the project would terminate and the equipment would have no salvage value. The project would provide net operating income each year as follows:

Sales		$3,200,000
Variable expenses		1,800,000
Contribution margin		1,400,000
Fixed expenses:		
Advertising, salaries, and other fixed out-of-pocket costs	$700,000	
Depreciation	300,000	
Total fixed expenses		1,000,000
Net operating income		$ 400,000

The company's discount rate is 12%.

Required:

1. Compute the annual net cash inflow from the project.
2. Compute the project's net present value. Is the project acceptable?
3. Find the project's internal rate of return to the nearest whole percent.
4. Compute the project's payback period.
5. Compute the project's simple rate of return.

Solution to Review Problem

1. The annual net cash inflow can be computed by deducting the cash expenses from sales:

Sales	$3,200,000
Variable expenses	1,800,000
Contribution margin	1,400,000
Advertising, salaries, and other fixed out-of-pocket costs	700,000
Annual net cash inflow	$ 700,000

Or the annual net cash inflow can be computed by adding depreciation back to net operating income:

Net operating income	$400,000
Add: Noncash deduction for depreciation	300,000
Annual net cash inflow	$700,000

2. The net present value is computed as follows:

	A	B	C	D	E	F	G
					Year		
1							
2		Now	1	2	3	4	5
3	Initial investment	$ (2,400,000)					
4	Sales		$ 3,200,000	$ 3,200,000	$ 3,200,000	$ 3,200,000	$ 3,200,000
5	Variable expenses		$ (1,800,000)	$ (1,800,000)	$ (1,800,000)	$ (1,800,000)	$ (1,800,000)
6	Fixed out-of-pocket costs		$ (700,000)	$ (700,000)	$ (700,000)	$ (700,000)	$ (700,000)
7	Total cash flows (a)	$ (2,400,000)	$ 700,000	$ 700,000	$ 700,000	$ 700,000	$ 700,000
8	Discount factor (12%) (b)	1.000	0.893	0.797	0.712	0.636	0.567
9	Present value of cash flows (a) × (b)	$ (2,400,000)	$ 625,100	$ 557,900	$ 498,400	$ 445,200	$ 396,900
10	Net present value (SUM B9:G9)	$ 123,500					
11							
12	Note: The discount factors come from Exhibit 13B-1 in Appendix 13B.						

Sheet1 / Sheet2 / Sheet3

Or, it can also be computed as follows:

	A	B	C
			Years
1			
2		Now	1-5
3	Initial investment	$ (2,400,000)	
4	Sales		$ 3,200,000
5	Variable expenses		$ (1,800,000)
6	Fixed out-of-pocket costs		$ (700,000)
7	Total cash flows (a)	$ (2,400,000)	$ 700,000
8	Discount factor (12%) (b)	1.000	3.605
9	Present value of the cash flows (a) × (b)	$ (2,400,000)	$2,523,500
10	Net present value (SUM B9:C9)	$123,500	
11			
12	Note: The discount factor comes from Exhibit 13B-2 in Appendix 13B.		

Sheet1 / Sheet2 / Sheet3

Yes, the project is acceptable because it has a positive net present value.

3. The formula for computing the factor of the internal rate of return is:

$$\text{Factor of the internal rate of return} = \frac{\text{Investment required}}{\text{Annual net cash flow}}$$

$$= \frac{\$2,400,000}{\$700,000} = 3.429$$

Looking in Exhibit 13B–2 in Appendix 13B at the end of the chapter and scanning along the 5-period line, we find that a factor of 3.429 is closest to a factor of 3.433, which corresponds to a rate of return of 14%.

4. The formula for the payback period is:

$$\text{Payback period} = \frac{\text{Investment required}}{\text{Annual net cash flow}}$$

$$= \frac{\$2,400,000}{\$700,000}$$

$$= 3.4 \text{ years (rounded)}$$

5. The formula for the simple rate of return is:

$$\text{Simple rate of return} = \frac{\text{Annual incremental net operating income}}{\text{Initial investment}}$$

$$= \frac{\$400,000}{\$2,400,000}$$

$$= 16.7\%$$

Glossary

Capital budgeting The process of planning significant investments in projects that have long-term implications such as the purchase of new equipment or the introduction of a new product. (p. 633)

Cost of capital The average rate of return a company must pay to its long-term creditors and shareholders for the use of their funds. (p. 640)

Internal rate of return The discount rate at which the net present value of an investment project is zero; the rate of return of a project over its useful life. (p. 644)

Net present value The difference between the present value of an investment project's cash inflows and the present value of its cash outflows. (p 638)

Out-of-pocket costs Actual cash outlays for salaries, advertising, repairs, and similar costs. (p. 643)

Payback period The length of time that it takes for a project to fully recover its initial cost out of the net cash inflows that it generates. (p. 635)

Postaudit The follow-up after a project has been approved and implemented to determine whether expected results were actually realized. (p. 653)

Preference decision A decision in which the acceptable alternatives must be ranked. (p. 633)

Project profitability index The ratio of the net present value of a project's cash flows to the investment required. (p. 650)

Screening decision A decision as to whether a proposed investment project is acceptable. (p. 633)

Simple rate of return The rate of return computed by dividing a project's annual incremental net operating income by the initial investment required. (p. 651)

Time value of money The concept that a dollar today is worth more than a dollar a year from now. (p. 634)

Working capital Current assets less current liabilities. (p. 633)

Questions

13–1 What is the difference between capital budgeting screening decisions and capital budgeting preference decisions?

13–2 What is meant by the term *time value of money?*

13–3 What is meant by the term *discounting?*

13–4 Why isn't accounting net income used in the net present value and internal rate of return methods of making capital budgeting decisions?

13–5 Why are discounted cash flow methods of making capital budgeting decisions superior to other methods?

13–6 What is net present value? Can it ever be negative? Explain.

13–7 Identify two simplifying assumptions associated with discounted cash flow methods of making capital budgeting decisions.

13–8 If a company has to pay interest of 14% on long-term debt, then its cost of capital is 14%. Do you agree? Explain.

13–9 What is meant by an investment project's internal rate of return? How is the internal rate of return computed?

13–10 Explain how the cost of capital serves as a screening tool when using (*a*) the net present value method and (*b*) the internal rate of return method.

13–11 As the discount rate increases, the present value of a given future cash flow also increases. Do you agree? Explain.

13–12 Refer to Exhibit 13–8. Is the return on this investment proposal exactly 14%, more than 14%, or less than 14%? Explain.

13–13 How is the project profitability index computed, and what does it measure?

13–14 What is meant by the term *payback period?* How is the payback period determined? How can the payback method be useful?

13–15 What is the major criticism of the payback and simple rate of return methods of making capital budgeting decisions?

 **Applying Excel**

The Excel worksheet form that appears below is to be used to recreate Example E and Exhibit 13–8. Download the workbook containing this form from Connect, where you will also receive instructions about how to use this worksheet form.

LO13–2, LO13–3

	A	B	C	D	E	F	G
1	Chapter 13: Applying Excel						
2							
3	Data						
4	Example E						
5	Cost of equipment needed	$60,000					
6	Working capital needed	$100,000					
7	Overhaul of equipment in four years	$5,000					
8	Salvage value of the equipment in five years	$10,000					
9	Annual revenues and costs:						
10	Sales revenues	$200,000					
11	Cost of goods sold	$125,000					
12	Out-of-pocket operating costs	$35,000					
13	Discount rate	14%					
14							
15	*Enter a formula into each of the cells marked with a ? below*						
16	Exhibit 13-8						
17					Years		
18		Now	1	2	3	4	5
19	Purchase of equipment	?					
20	Investment in working capital	?					
21	Sales		?	?	?	?	?
22	Cost of goods sold		?	?	?	?	?
23	Out-of-pocket operating costs		?	?	?	?	?
24	Overhaul of equipment					?	
25	Salvage value of the equipment						?
26	Working capital released						?
27	Total cash flows (a)	?	?	?	?	?	?
28	Discount factor (14%) (b)	?	?	?	?	?	?
29	Present value of cash flows (a) x (b)	?	?	?	?	?	?
30	Net present value	?					
31							
32	*Use the formulas from Appendix 13B:						
33	Present value of $1 = 1/(1+r)^n						
34	Present value of an annuity of $1 = (1/r)*(1-(1/(1+r)^n))						
35	where n is the number of years and r is the discount rate						
36							

Chapter 13 Form / Filled in Chapter 13 Form / Chapter 13 Formu

You should proceed to the requirements below only after completing your worksheet. Note that you may get a slightly different net present value from that shown in the text due to the precision of the calculations.

Required:

1. Check your worksheet by changing the discount rate to 10%. The net present value should now be between $56,495 and $56,518—depending on the precision of the calculations. If you do not get an answer in this range, find the errors in your worksheet and correct them.

    Explain why the net present value has increased as a result of reducing the discount rate from 14% to 10%.

2. The company is considering another project involving the purchase of new equipment. Change the data area of your worksheet to match the following:

Data	
Example E	
Cost of equipment needed	$120,000
Working capital needed	$80,000
Overhaul of equipment in four years	$40,000
Salvage value of the equipment in five years	$20,000
Annual revenues and costs:	
Sales revenues	$255,000
Cost of goods sold	$160,000
Out-of-pocket operating costs	$50,000
Discount rate	14%

a. What is the net present value of the project?
b. Experiment with changing the discount rate in one percent increments (e.g., 13%, 12%, 15%, etc.). At what interest rate does the net present value turn from negative to positive?
c. The internal rate of return is between what two whole discount rates (e.g., between 10% and 11%, between 11% and 12%, between 12% and 13%, between 13% and 14%, etc.)?
d. Reset the discount rate to 14%. Suppose the salvage value is uncertain. How large would the salvage value have to be to result in a positive net present value?

The Foundational 15   connect

LO13–1, LO13–2, LO13–3, LO13–5, LO13–6

Cardinal Company is considering a five-year project that would require a $2,975,000 investment in equipment with a useful life of five years and no salvage value. The company's discount rate is 14%. The project would provide net operating income in each of five years as follows:

Sales	$2,735,000
Variable expenses	1,000,000
Contribution margin	1,735,000
Fixed expenses:	
Advertising, salaries, and other fixed	
out-of-pocket costs	$735,000
Depreciation	595,000
Total fixed expenses	1,330,000
Net operating income	$ 405,000

Required:

(Answer each question by referring to the original data unless instructed otherwise.)

1. Which item(s) in the income statement shown above will not affect cash flows?
2. What are the project's annual net cash inflows?
3. What is the present value of the project's annual net cash inflows?

4. What is the project's net present value?
5. What is the project profitability index for this project? (Round your answer to the nearest whole percent.)
6. What is the project's internal rate of return to the nearest whole percent?
7. What is the project's payback period?
8. What is the project's simple rate of return for each of the five years?
9. If the company's discount rate was 16% instead of 14%, would you expect the project's net present value to be higher than, lower than, or the same as your answer to requirement 4? No computations are necessary.
10. If the equipment had a salvage value of $300,000 at the end of five years, would you expect the project's payback period to be higher than, lower than, or the same as your answer to requirement 7? No computations are necessary.
11. If the equipment had a salvage value of $300,000 at the end of five years, would you expect the project's net present value to be higher than, lower than, or the same as your answer to requirement 3? No computations are necessary.
12. If the equipment had a salvage value of $300,000 at the end of five years, would you expect the project's simple rate of return to be higher than, lower than, or the same as your answer to requirement 8? No computations are necessary.
13. Assume a postaudit showed that all estimates (including total sales) were exactly correct except for the variable expense ratio, which actually turned out to be 45%. What was the project's actual net present value?
14. Assume a postaudit showed that all estimates (including total sales) were exactly correct except for the variable expense ratio, which actually turned out to be 45%. What was the project's actual payback period?
15. Assume a postaudit showed that all estimates (including total sales) were exactly correct except for the variable expense ratio, which actually turned out to be 45%. What was the project's actual simple rate of return?

 **Exercises**

EXERCISE 13–1 Payback Method LO13–1

The management of Unter Corporation, an architectural design firm, is considering an investment with the following cash flows:

Year	Investment	Cash Inflow
1	$15,000	$1,000
2	$8,000	$2,000
3		$2,500
4		$4,000
5		$5,000
6		$6,000
7		$5,000
8		$4,000
9		$3,000
10		$2,000

Required:
1. Determine the payback period of the investment.
2. Would the payback period be affected if the cash inflow in the last year were several times as large?

EXERCISE 13–2 Net Present Value Analysis LO13–2

The management of Kunkel Company is considering the purchase of a $27,000 machine that would reduce operating costs by $7,000 per year. At the end of the machine's five-year useful life, it will have zero salvage value. The company's required rate of return is 12%.

Required:
1. Determine the net present value of the investment in the machine.
2. What is the difference between the total, undiscounted cash inflows and cash outflows over the entire life of the machine?

EXERCISE 13–3 Internal Rate of Return LO13–3

Wendell's Donut Shoppe is investigating the purchase of a new $18,600 donut-making machine. The new machine would permit the company to reduce the amount of part-time help needed, at a cost savings of $3,800 per year. In addition, the new machine would allow the company to produce one new style of donut, resulting in the sale of 1,000 dozen more donuts each year. The company realizes a contribution margin of $1.20 per dozen donuts sold. The new machine would have a six-year useful life.

Required:

1. What would be the total annual cash inflows associated with the new machine for capital budgeting purposes?
2. What discount factor should be used to compute the new machine's internal rate of return?
3. Using Exhibit 13B–2 in Appendix 13B as a reference, what is the new machine's internal rate of return to the nearest whole percent?
4. In addition to the data given previously, assume that the machine will have a $9,125 salvage value at the end of six years. Under these conditions, what is the internal rate of return to the nearest whole percent? (Hint: You may find it helpful to use the net present value approach; find the discount rate that will cause the net present value to be closest to zero.)

EXERCISE 13–4 Uncertain Future Cash Flows LO13–4

Lukow Products is investigating the purchase of a piece of automated equipment that will save $400,000 each year in direct labor and inventory carrying costs. This equipment costs $2,500,000 and is expected to have a 15-year useful life with no salvage value. The company's required rate of return is 20% on all equipment purchases. Management anticipates that this equipment will provide intangible benefits such as greater flexibility and higher-quality output that will result in additional future cash inflows.

Required:

1. What is the net present value of the piece of equipment *before* considering its intangible benefits?
2. What minimum dollar value per year must be provided by the equipment's intangible benefits to justify the $2,500,000 investment?

EXERCISE 13–5 Preference Ranking LO13–5

Information on four investment proposals is given below:

	Investment Proposal			
	A	B	C	D
Investment required	$(90,000)	$(100,000)	$(70,000)	$(120,000)
Present value of cash inflows	126,000	138,000	105,000	160,000
Net present value	$ 36,000	$ 38,000	$ 35,000	$ 40,000
Life of the project	5 years	7 years	6 years	6 years

Required:

1. Compute the project profitability index for each investment proposal.
2. Rank the proposals in terms of preference.

EXERCISE 13–6 Simple Rate of Return Method LO13–6

The management of Ballard MicroBrew is considering the purchase of an automated bottling machine for $120,000. The machine would replace an old piece of equipment that costs $30,000 per year to operate. The new machine would cost $12,000 per year to operate. The old machine currently in use could be sold now for a salvage value of $40,000. The new machine would have a useful life of 10 years with no salvage value.

Required:

1. What is the annual depreciation expense associated with the new bottling machine?
2. What is the annual incremental net operating income provided by the new bottling machine?
3. What is the amount of the initial investment associated with this project that should be used for calculating the simple rate of return?
4. What is the simple rate of return on the new bottling machine?

EXERCISE 13–7 Net Present Value Analysis of Two Alternatives LO13–2

Perit Industries has $100,000 to invest. The company is trying to decide between two alternative uses of the funds. The alternatives are:

	Project A	Project B
Cost of equipment required	$100,000	$0
Working capital investment required	$0	$100,000
Annual cash inflows	$21,000	$16,000
Salvage value of equipment in six years	$8,000	$0
Life of the project	6 years	6 years

The working capital needed for project B will be released at the end of six years for investment elsewhere. Perit Industries' discount rate is 14%.

Required:
1. Compute the net present value of Project A.
2. Compute the net present value of Project B.
3. Which investment alternative (if either) would you recommend that the company accept?

EXERCISE 13–8 Payback Period and Simple Rate of Return LO13–1, LO13–6

Nick's Novelties, Inc., is considering the purchase of new electronic games to place in its amusement houses. The games would cost a total of $300,000, have an eight-year useful life, and have a total salvage value of $20,000. The company estimates that annual revenues and expenses associated with the games would be as follows:

Revenues		$200,000
Less operating expenses:		
Commissions to amusement houses	$100,000	
Insurance	7,000	
Depreciation	35,000	
Maintenance	18,000	160,000
Net operating income		$ 40,000

Required:
1. What is the payback period for the new electronic games? Assume that Nick's Novelties, Inc., will not purchase new games unless they provide a payback period of five years or less. Would the company purchase the new games?
2. What is the simple rate of return promised by the games? If the company requires a simple rate of return of at least 12%, will the games be purchased?

EXERCISE 13–9 Net Present Value Analysis and Simple Rate of Return LO13–2, LO13–6

Derrick Iverson is a divisional manager for Holston Company. His annual pay raises are largely determined by his division's return on investment (ROI), which has been above 20% each of the last three years. Derrick is considering a capital budgeting project that would require a $3,000,000 investment in equipment with a useful life of five years and no salvage value. Holston Company's discount rate is 15%. The project would provide net operating income each year for five years as follows:

Sales		$2,500,000
Variable expenses		1,000,000
Contribution margin		1,500,000
Fixed expenses:		
Advertising, salaries, and other fixed		
out-of-pocket costs	$600,000	
Depreciation	600,000	
Total fixed expenses		1,200,000
Net operating income		$ 300,000

Required:
1. Compute the project's net present value.
2. Compute the project's simple rate of return.
3. Would the company want Derrick to pursue this investment opportunity? Would Derrick be inclined to pursue this investment opportunity? Explain.

EXERCISE 13–10 Net Present Value Analysis LO13–2

Kathy Myers frequently purchases stocks and bonds, but she is uncertain how to determine the rate of return that she is earning. For example, three years ago she paid $13,000 for 200 shares of Malti Company's common stock. She received a $420 cash dividend on the stock at the end of each year for three years. At the end of three years, she sold the stock for $16,000. Kathy would like to earn a return of at least 14% on all of her investments. She is not sure whether the Malti Company stock provided a 14% return and would like some help with the necessary computations.

Required:
1. Compute the net present value that Kathy earned on her investment in Malti Company stock. Round your answer to the nearest whole dollar.
2. Did the Malti Company stock provide a 14% return?

EXERCISE 13–11 Preference Ranking of Investment Projects LO13–5

Oxford Company has limited funds available for investment and must ration the funds among four competing projects. Selected information on the four projects follows:

Project	Investment Required	Net Present Value	Life of the Project (years)	Internal Rate of Return
A	$160,000	$44,323	7	18%
B	$135,000	$42,000	12	16%
C	$100,000	$35,035	7	20%
D	$175,000	$38,136	3	22%

The net present values above have been computed using a 10% discount rate. The company wants your assistance in determining which project to accept first, second, and so forth.

Required:
1. Compute the project profitability index for each project.
2. In order of preference, rank the four projects in terms of:
    a. Net present value.
    b. Project profitability index.
    c. Internal rate of return.
3. Which ranking do you prefer? Why?

EXERCISE 13–12 Uncertain Cash Flows LO13–4

The Cambro Foundation, a nonprofit organization, is planning to invest $104,950 in a project that will last for three years. The project will produce net cash inflows as follows:

Year 1	$30,000
Year 2	$40,000
Year 3	?

Required:
Assuming that the project will yield exactly a 12% rate of return, what is the expected net cash inflow for Year 3?

EXERCISE 13–13 Payback Period and Simple Rate of Return Computations LO13–1, LO13–6

A piece of labor-saving equipment has just come onto the market that Mitsui Electronics, Ltd., could use to reduce costs in one of its plants in Japan. Relevant data relating to the equipment follow:

Purchase cost of the equipment	$432,000
Annual cost savings that will be provided by the equipment	$90,000
Life of the equipment	12 years

Required:

1. What is the payback period for the equipment? If the company requires a payback period of four years or less, would the equipment be purchased?
2. What is the simple rate of return on the equipment? Use straight-line depreciation based on the equipment's useful life. Would the equipment be purchased if the company's required rate of return is 14%?

EXERCISE 13–14 Comparison of Projects Using Net Present Value LO13–2

Labeau Products, Ltd., of Perth, Australia, has $35,000 to invest. The company is trying to decide between two alternative uses for the funds as follows:

	Invest in Project X	Invest in Project Y
Investment required	$35,000	$35,000
Annual cash inflows	$12,000	
Single cash inflow at the end of 6 years		$90,000
Life of the project	6 years	6 years

The company's discount rate is 18%.

Required:

1. Compute the net present value of Project X.
2. Compute the net present value of Project Y.
3. Which project would you recommend the company accept?

EXERCISE 13–15 Internal Rate of Return and Net Present Value LO13–2, LO13–3

Henrie's Drapery Service is investigating the purchase of a new machine for cleaning and blocking drapes. The machine would cost $137,320, including freight and installation. Henrie's estimated the new machine would increase the company's cash inflows, net of expenses, by $40,000 per year. The machine would have a five-year useful life and no salvage value.

Required:

1. What is the machine's internal rate of return to the nearest whole percent?
2. Using a discount rate of 14%, what is the machine's net present value? Interpret your results.
3. Suppose the new machine would increase the company's annual cash inflows, net of expenses, by only $37,150 per year. Under these conditions, what is the internal rate of return to the nearest whole percent?

 **Problems**

PROBLEM 13–16 Net Present Value Analysis LO13–2

Windhoek Mines, Ltd., of Namibia, is contemplating the purchase of equipment to exploit a mineral deposit on land to which the company has mineral rights. An engineering and cost analysis has been made, and it is expected that the following cash flows would be associated with opening and operating a mine in the area:

Cost of new equipment and timbers	$275,000
Working capital required	$100,000
Annual net cash receipts	$120,000*
Cost to construct new roads in three years	$40,000
Salvage value of equipment in four years	$65,000

*Receipts from sales of ore, less out-of-pocket costs for salaries, utilities, insurance, and so forth.

The mineral deposit would be exhausted after four years of mining. At that point, the working capital would be released for reinvestment elsewhere. The company's required rate of return is 20%.

Required:

What is the net present value of the proposed mining project? Should the project be accepted? Explain.

PROBLEM 13–17 Net Present Value Analysis; Internal Rate of Return; Simple Rate of Return LO13–2, LO13–3, LO13–6

Casey Nelson is a divisional manager for Pigeon Company. His annual pay raises are largely determined by his division's return on investment (ROI), which has been above 20% each of the last three years. Casey is considering a capital budgeting project that would require a $3,500,000 investment in equipment with a useful life of five years and no salvage value. Pigeon Company's discount rate is 16%. The project would provide net operating income each year for five years as follows:

Sales		$3,400,000
Variable expenses		1,600,000
Contribution margin		1,800,000
Fixed expenses:		
Advertising, salaries, and other fixed		
out-of-pocket costs	$700,000	
Depreciation	700,000	
Total fixed expenses		1,400,000
Net operating income		$ 400,000

Required:

1. What is the project's net present value?
2. What is the project's internal rate of return to the nearest whole percent?
3. What is the project's simple rate of return?
4. Would the company want Casey to pursue this investment opportunity? Would Casey be inclined to pursue this investment opportunity? Explain.

PROBLEM 13–18 Net Present Value Analysis LO13–2

Oakmont Company has an opportunity to manufacture and sell a new product for a four-year period. The company's discount rate is 15%. After careful study, Oakmont estimated the following costs and revenues for the new product:

Cost of equipment needed	$130,000
Working capital needed	$60,000
Overhaul of the equipment in two years	$8,000
Salvage value of the equipment in four years	$12,000
Annual revenues and costs:	
Sales revenues	$250,000
Variable expenses	$120,000
Fixed out-of-pocket operating costs	$70,000

When the project concludes in four years the working capital will be released for investment elsewhere within the company.

Required:

Calculate the net present value of this investment opportunity.

PROBLEM 13–19 Simple Rate of Return; Payback Period LO13–1, LO13–6

Paul Swanson has an opportunity to acquire a franchise from The Yogurt Place, Inc., to dispense frozen yogurt products under The Yogurt Place name. Mr. Swanson has assembled the following information relating to the franchise:

a. A suitable location in a large shopping mall can be rented for $3,500 per month.
b. Remodeling and necessary equipment would cost $270,000. The equipment would have a 15-year life and an $18,000 salvage value. Straight-line depreciation would be used, and the salvage value would be considered in computing depreciation.
c. Based on similar outlets elsewhere, Mr. Swanson estimates that sales would total $300,000 per year. Ingredients would cost 20% of sales.

d. Operating costs would include $70,000 per year for salaries, $3,500 per year for insurance, and $27,000 per year for utilities. In addition, Mr. Swanson would have to pay a commission to The Yogurt Place, Inc., of 12.5% of sales.

Required:

1. Prepare a contribution format income statement that shows the expected net operating income each year from the franchise outlet.
2. Compute the simple rate of return promised by the outlet. If Mr. Swanson requires a simple rate of return of at least 12%, should he acquire the franchise?
3. Compute the payback period on the outlet. If Mr. Swanson wants a payback of four years or less, will he acquire the franchise?

PROBLEM 13–20 Net Present Value Analysis; Uncertain Cash Flows LO13–2, LO13–4

"I'm not sure we should lay out $250,000 for that automated welding machine," said Jim Alder, president of the Superior Equipment Company. "That's a lot of money, and it would cost us $80,000 for software and installation, and another $36,000 per year just to maintain the thing. In addition, the manufacturer admits it would cost $45,000 more at the end of three years to replace worn-out parts."

"I admit it's a lot of money," said Franci Rogers, the controller. "But you know the turnover problem we've had with the welding crew. This machine would replace six welders at a cost savings of $108,000 per year. And we would save another $6,500 per year in reduced material waste. When you figure that the automated welder would last for six years, I'm sure the return would be greater than our 16% required rate of return."

"I'm still not convinced," countered Mr. Alder. "We can only get $12,000 scrap value out of our old welding equipment if we sell it now, and in six years the new machine will only be worth $20,000 for parts. But have your people work up the figures and we'll talk about them at the executive committee meeting tomorrow."

Required:

1. Compute the annual net cost savings promised by the automated welding machine.
2. Using the data from (1) above and other data from the problem, compute the automated welding machine's net present value. Would you recommend purchasing the automated welding machine? Explain.
3. Assume that management can identify several intangible benefits associated with the automated welding machine, including greater flexibility in shifting from one type of product to another, improved quality of output, and faster delivery as a result of reduced throughput time. What minimum dollar value per year would management have to attach to these intangible benefits in order to make the new welding machine an acceptable investment?

PROBLEM 13–21 Preference Ranking of Investment Projects LO13–5

The management of Revco Products is exploring four different investment opportunities. Information on the four projects under study follows:

	Project Number			
	1	2	3	4
Investment required	$(270,000)	$(450,000)	$(360,000)	$(480,000)
Present value of cash inflows at a 10% discount rate	336,140	522,970	433,400	567,270
Net present value	$ 66,140	$ 72,970	$ 73,400	$ 87,270
Life of the project	6 years	3 years	12 years	6 years
Internal rate of return	18%	19%	14%	16%

Because the company's required rate of return is 10%, a 10% discount rate has been used in the present value computations above. Limited funds are available for investment, so the company can't accept all of the available projects.

Required:

1. Compute the project profitability index for each investment project.
2. Rank the four projects according to preference, in terms of:
   a. Net present value
   b. Project profitability index
   c. Internal rate of return
3. Which ranking do you prefer? Why?

PROBLEM 13–22 Net Present Value Analysis LO13–2

The Sweetwater Candy Company would like to buy a new machine that would automatically "dip" chocolates. The dipping operation currently is done largely by hand. The machine the company is considering costs $120,000. The manufacturer estimates that the machine would be usable for five years but would require the replacement of several key parts at the end of the third year. These parts would cost $9,000, including installation. After five years, the machine could be sold for $7,500.

   The company estimates that the cost to operate the machine will be $7,000 per year. The present method of dipping chocolates costs $30,000 per year. In addition to reducing costs, the new machine will increase production by 6,000 boxes of chocolates per year. The company realizes a contribution margin of $1.50 per box. A 20% rate of return is required on all investments.

Required:
1.   What are the annual net cash inflows that will be provided by the new dipping machine?
2.   Compute the new machine's net present value. Round all dollar amounts to the nearest whole dollar.

PROBLEM 13–23 Comprehensive Problem LO13–1, LO13–2, LO13–3, LO13–5, LO13–6

Lou Barlow, a divisional manager for Sage Company, has an opportunity to manufacture and sell one of two new products for a five-year period. His annual pay raises are determined by his division's return on investment (ROI), which has exceeded 18% each of the last three years. He has computed the cost and revenue estimates for each product as follows:

	Product A	Product B
Initial investment:		
Cost of equipment (zero salvage value)	$170,000	$380,000
Annual revenues and costs:		
Sales revenues	$250,000	$350,000
Variable expenses	$120,000	$170,000
Depreciation expense	$34,000	$76,000
Fixed out-of-pocket operating costs	$70,000	$50,000

The company's discount rate is 16%.

Required:
1.   Calculate the payback period for each product.
2.   Calculate the net present value for each product.
3.   Calculate the internal rate of return for each product.
4.   Calculate the project profitability index for each product.
5.   Calculate the simple rate of return for each product.
6.   Which of the two products should Lou's division pursue? Why?

PROBLEM 13–24 Simple Rate of Return; Payback Period; Internal Rate of Return LO13–1, LO13–3, LO13–6

The Elberta Fruit Farm of Ontario always has hired transient workers to pick its annual cherry crop. Janessa Wright, the farm manager, just received information on a cherry picking machine that is being purchased by many fruit farms. The machine is a motorized device that shakes the cherry tree, causing the cherries to fall onto plastic tarps that funnel the cherries into bins. Ms. Wright has gathered the following information to decide whether a cherry picker would be a profitable investment for the Elberta Fruit Farm:

a.   Currently, the farm is paying an average of $40,000 per year to transient workers to pick the cherries.
b.   The cherry picker would cost $94,500, and it would have an estimated 12-year useful life. The farm uses straight-line depreciation on all assets and considers salvage value in computing depreciation expense. The estimated salvage value of the cherry picker is $4,500.
c.   Annual out-of-pocket costs associated with the cherry picker would be: cost of an operator and an assistant, $14,000; insurance, $200; fuel, $1,800; and a maintenance contract, $3,000.

Required:
1.   Determine the annual savings in cash operating costs that would be realized if the cherry picker were purchased.
2.   Compute the simple rate of return expected from the cherry picker. Would the cherry picker be purchased if Elberta Fruit Farm's required rate of return is 16%?

3. Compute the payback period on the cherry picker. The Elberta Fruit Farm will not purchase equipment unless it has a payback period of five years or less. Would the cherry picker be purchased?
4. Compute (to the nearest whole percent) the internal rate of return promised by the cherry picker. Based on this computation, does it appear that the simple rate of return is an accurate guide in investment decisions?

PROBLEM 13–25 Net Present Value Analysis of a Lease or Buy Decision LO13–2

The Riteway Ad Agency provides cars for its sales staff. In the past, the company has always purchased its cars from a dealer and then sold the cars after three years of use. The company's present fleet of cars is three years old and will be sold very shortly. To provide a replacement fleet, the company is considering two alternatives:

Purchase alternative: The company can purchase the cars, as in the past, and sell the cars after three years of use. Ten cars will be needed, which can be purchased at a discounted price of $17,000 each. If this alternative is accepted, the following costs will be incurred on the fleet as a whole:

Annual cost of servicing, taxes, and licensing	$3,000
Repairs, first year	$1,500
Repairs, second year	$4,000
Repairs, third year	$6,000

At the end of three years, the fleet could be sold for one-half of the original purchase price.

Lease alternative: The company can lease the cars under a three-year lease contract. The lease cost would be $55,000 per year (the first payment due at the end of Year 1). As part of this lease cost, the owner would provide all servicing and repairs, license the cars, and pay all the taxes. Riteway would be required to make a $10,000 security deposit at the beginning of the lease period, which would be refunded when the cars were returned to the owner at the end of the lease contract.

Riteway Ad Agency's required rate of return is 18%.

Required:
1. What is the net present value of the cash flows associated with the purchase alternative? Round all dollar amounts to the nearest whole dollar.
2. What is the net present value of the cash flows associated with the lease alternative? Round all dollar amounts to the nearest whole dollar.
3. Which alternative should the company accept?

PROBLEM 13–26 Simple Rate of Return; Payback LO13–1, LO13–6

Sharkey's Fun Center contains a number of electronic games as well as a miniature golf course and various rides located outside the building. Paul Sharkey, the owner, would like to construct a water slide on one portion of his property. Mr. Sharkey gathered the following information about the slide:

a. Water slide equipment could be purchased and installed at a cost of $330,000. According to the manufacturer, the slide would be usable for 12 years after which it would have no salvage value.
b. Mr. Sharkey would use straight-line depreciation on the slide equipment.
c. To make room for the water slide, several rides would be dismantled and sold. These rides are fully depreciated, but they could be sold for $60,000 to an amusement park in a nearby city.
d. Mr. Sharkey concluded that about 50,000 more people would use the water slide each year than have been using the rides. The admission price would be $3.60 per person (the same price the Fun Center has been charging for the old rides).
e. Based on experience at other water slides, Mr. Sharkey estimates that annual incremental operating expenses for the slide would be: salaries, $85,000; insurance, $4,200; utilities, $13,000; and maintenance, $9,800.

Required:
1. Prepare an income statement showing the expected net operating income each year from the water slide.
2. Compute the simple rate of return expected from the water slide. Based on this computation, would the water slide be constructed if Mr. Sharkey requires a simple rate of return of at least 14% on all investments?
3. Compute the payback period for the water slide. If Mr. Sharkey accepts any project with a payback period of five years or less, would the water slide be constructed?

PROBLEM 13–27 Net Present Value Analysis LO13–2

In five years, Kent Duncan will retire. He is exploring the possibility of opening a self-service car wash. The car wash could be managed in the free time he has available from his regular occupation, and it could be closed easily when he retires. After careful study, Mr. Duncan determined the following:

a.   A building in which a car wash could be installed is available under a five-year lease at a cost of $1,700 per month.

b.   Purchase and installation costs of equipment would total $200,000. In five years the equipment could be sold for about 10% of its original cost.

c.   An investment of an additional $2,000 would be required to cover working capital needs for cleaning supplies, change funds, and so forth. After five years, this working capital would be released for investment elsewhere.

d.   Both a wash and a vacuum service would be offered. Each customer would pay $2.00 for a wash and $1.00 for access to a vacuum cleaner.

e.   The only variable costs associated with the operation would be 20 cents per wash for water and 10 cents per use of the vacuum for electricity.

f.   In addition to rent, monthly costs of operation would be: cleaning, $450; insurance, $75; and maintenance, $500.

g.   Gross receipts from the wash would be about $1,350 per week. According to the experience of other car washes, 60% of the customers using the wash would also use the vacuum.

Mr. Duncan will not open the car wash unless it provides at least a 10% return.

Required:

1.   Assuming the car wash will be open 52 weeks a year, compute the expected annual net cash receipts (gross cash receipts less cash disbursements) from its operation. (Do not include the cost of the equipment, the working capital, or the salvage value in these computations.)

2.   What is the net present value of the investment in the car wash? Would you advise Mr. Duncan to open the car wash? Round all dollar figures to the nearest whole dollar.

PROBLEM 13–28 Net Present Value Analysis LO13–2

Bilboa Freightlines, S.A., of Panama, has a small truck that it uses for intracity deliveries. The truck is worn out and must be either overhauled or replaced with a new truck. The company has assembled the following information:

	Present Truck	New Truck
Purchase cost (new)	$21,000	$30,000
Remaining book value	$11,500	
Overhaul needed now	$7,000	
Annual cash operating costs	$10,000	$6,500
Salvage value-now	$9,000	
Salvage value-five years from now	$1,000	$4,000

If the company keeps and overhauls its present delivery truck, then the truck will be usable for five more years. If a new truck is purchased, it will be used for five years, after which it will be traded in on another truck. The new truck would be diesel-operated, resulting in a substantial reduction in annual operating costs, as shown above.

The company computes depreciation on a straight-line basis. All investment projects are evaluated using a 16% discount rate.

Required:

1.   What is the net present value of the "keep the old truck" alternative? Round to the nearest whole dollar.

2.   What is the net present value of the "purchase the new truck" alternative? Round to the nearest whole dollar.

3.   Should Bilboa Freightlines keep the old truck or purchase the new one?

PROBLEM 13–29 Net Present Value Analysis LO13–2

Linda Clark received $175,000 from her mother's estate. She placed the funds into the hands of a broker, who purchased the following securities on Linda's behalf:

a.   Common stock was purchased at a cost of $95,000. The stock paid no dividends, but it was sold for $160,000 at the end of three years.

b.   Preferred stock was purchased at its par value of $30,000. The stock paid a 6% dividend (based on par value) each year for three years. At the end of three years, the stock was sold for $27,000.

c.   Bonds were purchased at a cost of $50,000. The bonds paid annual interest of $6,000. After three years, the bonds were sold for $52,700.

The securities were all sold at the end of three years so that Linda would have funds available to open a new business venture. The broker stated that the investments had earned more than a 16% return, and he gave Linda the following computations to support his statement:

Common stock:	
Gain on sale ($160,000 – $95,000)	$65,000
Preferred stock:	
Dividends paid (6% × $30,000 × 3 years)	5,400
Loss on sale ($27,000 – $30,000)	(3,000)
Bonds:	
Interest paid ($6,000 × 3 years)	18,000
Gain on sale ($52,700 – $50,000)	2,700
Net gain on all investments	$88,100

$$\frac{\$88,100 \div 3 \text{ years}}{\$175,000} = 16.8\%$$

Required:

1.   Using a 16% discount rate, compute the net present value of each of the three investments. On which investment(s) did Linda earn a 16% rate of return? (Round computations to the nearest whole dollar.)

2.   Considering all three investments together, did Linda earn a 16% rate of return? Explain.

3.   Linda wants to use the $239,700 proceeds ($160,000 + $27,000 + $52,700 = $239,700) from sale of the securities to open a retail store under a 12-year franchise contract. What minimum annual net cash inflow must the store generate for Linda to earn a 14% return over the 12-year period? Round computations to the nearest whole dollar.

PROBLEM 13–30 Net Present Value Analysis; Uncertain Future Cash Flows; Postaudit LO13–2, LO13–4
Saxon Products, Inc., is investigating the purchase of a robot for use on the company's assembly line. Selected data relating to the robot are provided below:

Cost of the robot	$1,600,000
Installation and software	$450,000
Annual savings in inventory carrying costs	$210,000
Annual increase in power and maintenance costs	$30,000
Salvage value in 5 years	$70,000
Useful life	5 years

In addition to the data above, engineering studies suggest that use of the robot will result in a savings of 25,000 direct labor-hours each year. The labor rate is $16 per hour. Also, the smoother work flow made possible by the use of automation will allow the company to reduce the amount of inventory on hand by $400,000. This inventory reduction will take place at the end of the first year of operation; the released funds will be available for use elsewhere in the company. Saxon Products has a 20% required rate of return.

Required:

1.   Determine the *annual net* cost savings if the robot is purchased. (Do not include the $400,000 inventory reduction or the salvage value in this computation.)

2.   Compute the net present value of the proposed investment in the robot. Based on these data, would you recommend that the robot be purchased? Explain.

3.   Assume that the robot is purchased. However, due to unforeseen problems, software and installation costs were $75,000 more than estimated and direct labor could only be reduced by 22,500 hours per year, rather than the original estimate of 25,000 hours. Assuming that all other cost data is accurate, what would a postaudit suggest is the actual net present value of this investment? Does it appear that the company made a wise investment?

4.   Upon seeing your analysis in (3) above, Saxon's president stated, "That robot is the worst investment we've ever made. And now we'll be stuck with it for years."

   a.   Explain to the president what benefits other than cost savings might accrue from using the new automated equipment.

   b.   Compute for the president the minimum dollar amount of annual cash inflow that would be needed from the benefits in (a) above for the automated equipment to yield a 20% rate of return.

Cases

CASE 13–31 Ethics and the Manager

The Fore Corporation is an integrated food processing company that has operations in over two dozen countries. Fore's corporate headquarters are in Chicago, and the company's executives frequently travel to visit Fore's foreign and domestic facilities.

Fore has a fleet of aircraft that consists of two business jets with international range and six smaller turboprop aircraft that are used on shorter flights. Company policy is to assign aircraft to trips on the basis of minimizing cost; however, the practice has been to assign the aircraft based on the organizational rank of the traveler. Fore offers its aircraft for short-term lease or for charter by other organizations whenever Fore itself does not plan to use the aircraft. Fore surveys the market often in order to keep its lease and charter rates competitive.

William Earle, Fore's vice president of finance, has claimed that a third business jet can be justified financially. However, some people in the controller's office have surmised that the real reason for a third business jet was to upgrade the aircraft used by Earle. Presently, the people outranking Earle keep the two business jets busy with the result that Earle usually flies in smaller turboprop aircraft.

The third business jet would cost $11 million. A capital expenditure of this magnitude requires a formal proposal with projected cash flows and net present value computations using Fore's minimum required rate of return. If Fore's president and the finance committee of the board of directors approve the proposal, it will be submitted to the full board of directors. The board has final approval on capital expenditures exceeding $5 million and has established a firm policy of rejecting any discretionary proposal that has a negative net present value.

Earle asked Rachel Arnett, assistant corporate controller, to prepare a proposal on a third business jet. Arnett gathered the following data:

- Acquisition cost of the aircraft, including instrumentation and interior furnishing.
- Operating cost of the aircraft for company use.
- Projected avoidable commercial airfare and other avoidable costs from company use of the plane.
- Projected value of executive time saved by using the third business jet.
- Projected contribution margin from incremental lease and charter activity.
- Estimated resale value of the aircraft.

When Earle reviewed Arnett's completed proposal and saw the large negative net present value figure, he returned the proposal to Arnett. With a glare, Earle commented, "You must have made an error. The proposal should look better than that."

Feeling some pressure, Arnett went back and checked her computations; she found no errors. However, Earle's message was clear. Arnett discarded her projections that she believed were reasonable and replaced them with figures that had a remote chance of actually occurring but were more favorable to the proposal. For example, she used first-class airfares to refigure the avoidable commercial airfare costs, even though company policy was to fly coach. She found revising the proposal to be distressing.

The revised proposal still had a negative net present value. Earle's anger was evident as he told Arnett to revise the proposal again, and to start with a $100,000 positive net present value and work backwards to compute supporting projections.

Required:

1. Explain whether Rachel Arnett's revision of the proposal was in violation of the IMA's Statement of Ethical Professional Practice.
2. Was William Earle in violation of the IMA's Statement of Ethical Professional Practice by telling Arnett specifically how to revise the proposal? Explain your answer.
3. Identify specific internal controls that Fore Corporation could implement to prevent unethical behavior on the part of the vice president of finance.

(CMA, adapted)

CASE 13–32 Net Present Value Analysis of a New Product LO13–2

Matheson Electronics has just developed a new electronic device it believes will have broad market appeal. The company has performed marketing and cost studies that revealed the following information:

a. New equipment would have to be acquired to produce the device. The equipment would cost $315,000 and have a six-year useful life. After six years, it would have a salvage value of about $15,000.
b. Sales in units over the next six years are projected to be as follows:

Year	Sales in Units
1	9,000
2	15,000
3	18,000
4–6	22,000

c. Production and sales of the device would require working capital of $60,000 to finance accounts receivable, inventories, and day-to-day cash needs. This working capital would be released at the end of the project's life.

d. The devices would sell for $35 each; variable costs for production, administration, and sales would be $15 per unit.

e. Fixed costs for salaries, maintenance, property taxes, insurance, and straight-line depreciation on the equipment would total $135,000 per year. (Depreciation is based on cost less salvage value.)

f. To gain rapid entry into the market, the company would have to advertise heavily. The advertising costs would be:

Year	Amount of Yearly Advertising
1–2	$180,000
3	$150,000
4–6	$120,000

g. The company's required rate of return is 14%.

Required:

1. Compute the net cash inflow (incremental contribution margin minus incremental fixed expenses) anticipated from sale of the device for each year over the next six years.

2. Using the data computed in (1) above and other data provided in the problem, determine the net present value of the proposed investment. Would you recommend that Matheson accept the device as a new product?

Appendix 13A: The Concept of Present Value

A dollar received today is more valuable than a dollar received a year from now for the simple reason that if you have a dollar today, you can put it in the bank and have more than a dollar a year from now. Because dollars today are worth more than dollars in the future, cash flows that are received at different times must be valued differently.

LO13–7
Understand present value concepts and the use of present value tables.

The Mathematics of Interest

If a bank pays 5% interest, then a deposit of $100 today will be worth $105 one year from now. This can be expressed as follows:

$$F_1 = P(1 + r) \qquad (1)$$

where F_1 = the balance at the end of one period, P = the amount invested now, and r = the rate of interest per period.

In the case where $100 is deposited in a savings account that earns 5% interest, $P = \$100$ and $r = 0.05$. Under these conditions, $F_1 = \$105$.

The $100 present outlay is called the **present value** of the $105 amount to be received in one year. It is also known as the *discounted value* of the future $105 receipt. The $100 represents the value in present terms of $105 to be received a year from now when the interest rate is 5%.

Compound Interest   What if the $105 is left in the bank for a second year? In that case, by the end of the second year the original $100 deposit will have grown to $110.25:

Original deposit	$100.00
Interest for the first year: $100 × 0.05	5.00
Balance at the end of the first year	105.00
Interest for the second year: $105 × 0.05	5.25
Balance at the end of the second year	$110.25

Notice that the interest for the second year is $5.25, as compared to only $5.00 for the first year. This difference arises because interest is being paid on interest during the second year. That is, the $5.00 interest earned during the first year has been left in the account and has been added to the original $100 deposit when computing interest for the second year. This is known as **compound interest**. In this case, the compounding is annual. Interest can be compounded on a semiannual, quarterly, monthly, or even more frequent basis. The more frequently compounding is done, the more rapidly the balance will grow.

We can determine the balance in an account after n periods of compounding using the following equation:

$$F_n = P(1 + r)^n \qquad (2)$$

where n = the number of periods of compounding.

If $n = 2$ years and the interest rate is 5% per year, then the balance in two years will be computed as follows:

$$F_2 = \$100(1 + 0.05)^2$$
$$F_2 = \$110.25$$

Present Value and Future Value   Exhibit 13A–1 shows the relationship between present value and future value. As shown in the exhibit, if $100 is deposited in a bank at 5% interest compounded annually, it will grow to $127.63 by the end of five years.

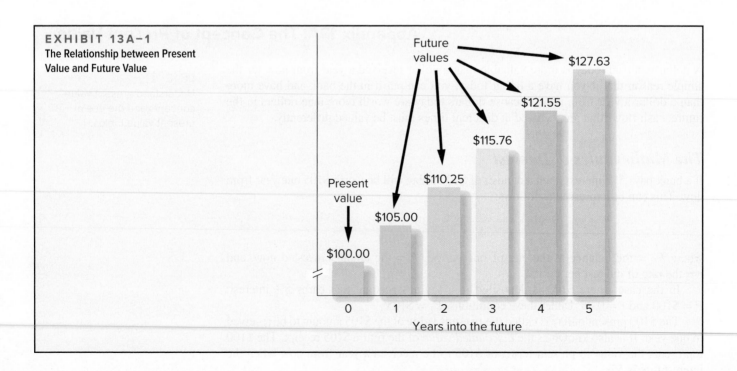

EXHIBIT 13A–1
The Relationship between Present Value and Future Value

Computation of Present Value

An investment can be viewed in two ways—either in terms of its future value or in terms of its present value. We have seen from our computations above that if we know the present value of a sum (such as our $100 deposit), the future value in n years can be computed by using equation (2). But what if the situation is reversed and we know the *future* value of some amount but we do not know its present value?

For example, assume that you are to receive $200 two years from now. You know that the future value of this sum is $200 because this is the amount that you will be receiving in two years. But what is the sum's present value—what is it worth *right now?* The present value of any sum to be received in the future can be computed by turning equation (2) around and solving for P:

$$P = \frac{F_n}{(1 + r)^n} \qquad (3)$$

In our example, $F_n = \$200$ (the amount to be received in the future), $r = 0.05$ (the annual rate of interest), and $n = 2$ (the number of years in the future that the amount will be received).

$$P = \frac{\$200}{(1 + 0.05)^2}$$

$$P = \frac{\$200}{1.1025}$$

$$P = \$181.40$$

As shown by the computation above, the present value of a $200 amount to be received two years from now is $181.40 if the interest rate is 5%. In effect, $181.40 received *right now* is equivalent to $200 received two years from now.

The process of finding the present value of a future cash flow, which we have just completed, is called **discounting**. We have *discounted* the $200 to its present value of $181.40. The 5% interest we used to find this present value is called the **discount rate**. Discounting future sums to their present value is a common practice in business, particularly in capital budgeting decisions.

If you have a power key (y^x) on your calculator, the above calculations are fairly easy. However, some of the present value formulas we will be using are more complex. Fortunately, tables are available in which many of the calculations have already been done. For example, Exhibit 13B–1 in Appendix 13B shows the discounted present value of $1 to be received at various periods in the future at various interest rates. The table indicates that the present value of $1 to be received two periods from now at 5% is 0.907. Because in our example we want to know the present value of $200 rather than just $1, we need to multiply the factor in the table by $200:

$$\$200 \times 0.907 = \$181.40$$

This answer is the same as we obtained earlier using the formula in equation (3).

Present Value of a Series of Cash Flows

Although some investments involve a single sum to be received (or paid) at a single point in the future, other investments involve a *series* of cash flows. A series of identical cash flows is known as an **annuity**. To provide an example, assume that a company has just purchased some government bonds. The bonds will yield interest of $15,000 each year and will be held for five years. What is the present value of the stream of interest receipts from the bonds? As shown in Exhibit 13A–2, if the discount rate is 12%, the present value of this stream is $54,075. The discount factors used in this exhibit were taken from Exhibit 13B–1 in Appendix 13B.

Exhibit 13A–2 illustrates two important points. First, the present value of the $15,000 interest declines the further it is into the future. The present value of $15,000 received a year from now is $13,395, as compared to only $8,505 if received five years from now. This point underscores the time value of money.

EXHIBIT 13A–2
Present Value of a Series of Cash Receipts

Year	Factor at 12% (Exhibit 13B–1)	Interest Received	Present Value
1	0.893	$15,000	$13,395
2	0.797	$15,000	11,955
3	0.712	$15,000	10,680
4	0.636	$15,000	9,540
5	0.567	$15,000	8,505
			$54,075

The second point is that the computations used in Exhibit 13A–2 involved unnecessary work. The same present value of $54,075 could have been obtained more easily by referring to Exhibit 13B–2 in Appendix 13B. Exhibit 13B–2 contains the present value of $1 to be received each year over a *series* of years at various interest rates. Exhibit 13B–2 has been derived by simply adding together the factors from Exhibit 13B–1, as follows:

Year	Factors at 12% (from Exhibit 13B–1)
1	0.893
2	0.797
3	0.712
4	0.636
5	0.567
	3.605

The sum of these five factors is 3.605. Notice from Exhibit 13B–2 that the factor for $1 to be received each year for five years at 12% is also 3.605. If we use this factor and multiply it by the $15,000 annual cash inflow, then we get the same $54,075 present value that we obtained earlier in Exhibit 13A–2.

$$\$15,000 \times 3.605 = \$54,075$$

Therefore, when computing the present value of a series of equal cash flows that begins at the end of period 1, Exhibit 13B–2 should be used.

To summarize, the present value tables in Appendix 13B should be used as follows:

Exhibit 13B–1: This table should be used to find the present value of a single cash flow (such as a single payment or receipt) occurring in the future.

Exhibit 13B–2: This table should be used to find the present value of a series of identical cash flows beginning at the end of the current period and continuing into the future.

The use of both of these tables is illustrated in various exhibits in the main body of the chapter. *When a present value factor appears in an exhibit, you should take the time to trace it back into either Exhibit 13B–1 or Exhibit 13B–2 to get acquainted with the tables and how they work.*

Appendix 13A: Review Problem: Basic Present Value Computations

Each of the following situations is independent. Work out your own solution to each situation, and then check it against the solution provided.

1. John plans to retire in 12 years. Upon retiring, he would like to take an extended vacation, which he expects will cost at least $40,000. What lump-sum amount must he invest now to have $40,000 at the end of 12 years if the rate of return is:
   a. Eight percent?
   b. Twelve percent?

2. The Morgans would like to send their daughter to a music camp at the end of each of the next five years. The camp costs $1,000 a year. What lump-sum amount would have to be invested now to have $1,000 at the end of each year if the rate of return is:
   a. Eight percent?
   b. Twelve percent?
3. You have just received an inheritance from a relative. You can either receive a $200,000 lump-sum amount at the end of 10 years or receive $14,000 at the end of each year for the next 10 years. If your discount rate is 12%, which alternative would you prefer?

Solution to Review Problem

1. a. The amount that must be invested now would be the present value of the $40,000, using a discount rate of 8%. From Exhibit 13B–1 in Appendix 13B, the factor for a discount rate of 8% for 12 periods is 0.397. Multiplying this discount factor by the $40,000 needed in 12 years will give the amount of the present investment required: $40,000 × 0.397 = $15,880.
   b. We will proceed as we did in (a) above, but this time we will use a discount rate of 12%. From Exhibit 13B–1 in Appendix 13B, the factor for a discount rate of 12% for 12 periods is 0.257. Multiplying this discount factor by the $40,000 needed in 12 years will give the amount of the present investment required: $40,000 × 0.257 = $10,280.

   Notice that as the discount rate (desired rate of return) increases, the present value decreases.

2. This part differs from (1) above in that we are now dealing with an annuity rather than with a single future sum. The amount that must be invested now is the present value of the $1,000 needed at the end of each year for five years. Because we are dealing with an annuity, or a series of annual cash flows, we must refer to Exhibit 13B–2 in Appendix 13B for the appropriate discount factor.
   a. From Exhibit 13B–2 in Appendix 13B, the discount factor for 8% for five periods is 3.993. Therefore, the amount that must be invested now to have $1,000 available at the end of each year for five years is $1,000 × 3.993 = $3,993.
   b. From Exhibit 13B–2 in Appendix 13B, the discount factor for 12% for five periods is 3.605. Therefore, the amount that must be invested now to have $1,000 available at the end of each year for five years is $1,000 × 3.605 = $3,605.

   Again, notice that as the discount rate increases, the present value decreases. When the rate of return increases, less must be invested today to yield a given amount in the future.

3. For this part we will need to refer to both Exhibits 13B–1 and 13B–2 in Appendix 13B. From Exhibit 13B–1, we will need to find the discount factor for 12% for 10 periods, then apply it to the $200,000 lump sum to be received in 10 years. From Exhibit 13B–2, we will need to find the discount factor for 12% for 10 periods, then apply it to the series of $14,000 payments to be received over the 10-year period. Whichever alternative has the higher present value is the one that should be selected.

$$\$200,000 \times 0.322 = \$64,400$$
$$\$14,000 \times 5.650 = \$79,100$$

Thus, you should prefer to receive the $14,000 per year for 10 years rather than the $200,000 lump sum. This means that you could invest the $14,000 received at the end of each year at 12% and have *more* than $200,000 at the end of 10 years.

Glossary (Appendix 13A)

Annuity A series of identical cash flows. (p. 673)
Compound interest The process of paying interest on interest in an investment. (p. 672)
Discount rate The rate of return that is used to find the present value of a future cash flow. (p. 673)
Discounting The process of finding the present value of a future cash flow. (p. 673)
Present value The value now of an amount that will be received in some future period. (p. 671)

Appendix 13A: Exercises   connect

EXERCISE 13A–1 Basic Present Value Concepts [LO13–7]

Annual cash inflows that will arise from two competing investment projects are given below:

Year	Investment A	Investment B
1	$ 3,000	$12,000
2	6,000	9,000
3	9,000	6,000
4	12,000	3,000
	$30,000	$30,000

The discount rate is 18%.

Required:

Compute the present value of the cash inflows for each investment.

EXERCISE 13A–2 Basic Present Value Concepts LO13–7

Julie has just retired. Her company's retirement program has two options as to how retirement benefits can be received. Under the first option, Julie would receive a lump sum of $150,000 immediately as her full retirement benefit. Under the second option, she would receive $14,000 each year for 20 years plus a lump-sum payment of $60,000 at the end of the 20-year period.

Required:

If she can invest money at 12%, which option would you recommend that she accept? Use present value analysis.

EXERCISE 13A–3 Basic Present Value Concepts LO13–7

In three years, when he is discharged from the Air Force, Steve wants to buy an $8,000 power boat.

Required:

What lump-sum amount must Steve invest now to have the $8,000 at the end of three years if he can invest money at:
1.   Ten percent?
2.   Fourteen percent?

EXERCISE 13A–4 Basic Present Value Concepts LO13–7

Fraser Company will need a new warehouse in five years. The warehouse will cost $500,000 to build.

Required:

What lump-sum amount should the company invest now to have the $500,000 available at the end of the five-year period? Assume that the company can invest money at:
1.   Ten percent.
2.   Fourteen percent.

EXERCISE 13A–5 Basic Present Value Concepts LO13–7

The Atlantic Medical Clinic can purchase a new computer system that will save $7,000 annually in billing costs. The computer system will last for eight years and have no salvage value.

Required:

What is the maximum price (i.e., the price that exactly equals the present value of the annual savings in billing costs) that the Atlantic Medical Clinic should be willing to pay for the new computer system if the clinic's required rate of return is:
1.   Sixteen percent?
2.   Twenty percent?

EXERCISE 13A–6 Basic Present Value Concepts LO13–7

The Caldwell Herald newspaper reported the following story: Frank Ormsby of Caldwell is the state's newest millionaire. By choosing the six winning numbers on last week's state lottery, Mr. Ormsby won the week's grand prize totaling $1.6 million. The State Lottery Commission indicated that Mr. Ormsby will receive his prize in 20 annual installments of $80,000 each.

Required:

1.   If Mr. Ormsby can invest money at a 12% rate of return, what is the present value of his winnings?
2.   Is it correct to say that Mr. Ormsby is the "state's newest millionaire"? Explain your answer.

Appendix 13B: Present Value Tables

EXHIBIT 13B–1

Present Value of \$1; $\dfrac{1}{(1 + r)^n}$

Periods	4%	5%	6%	7%	8%	9%	10%	11%	12%	13%	14%	15%	16%	17%	18%	19%	20%	21%	22%	23%	24%	25%
1	0.962	0.952	0.943	0.935	0.926	0.917	0.909	0.901	0.893	0.885	0.877	0.870	0.862	0.855	0.847	0.840	0.833	0.826	0.820	0.813	0.806	0.800
2	0.925	0.907	0.890	0.873	0.857	0.842	0.826	0.812	0.797	0.783	0.769	0.756	0.743	0.731	0.718	0.706	0.694	0.683	0.672	0.661	0.650	0.640
3	0.889	0.864	0.840	0.816	0.794	0.772	0.751	0.731	0.712	0.693	0.675	0.658	0.641	0.624	0.609	0.593	0.579	0.564	0.551	0.537	0.524	0.512
4	0.855	0.823	0.792	0.763	0.735	0.708	0.683	0.659	0.636	0.613	0.592	0.572	0.552	0.534	0.516	0.499	0.482	0.467	0.451	0.437	0.423	0.410
5	0.822	0.784	0.747	0.713	0.681	0.650	0.621	0.593	0.567	0.543	0.519	0.497	0.476	0.456	0.437	0.419	0.402	0.386	0.370	0.355	0.341	0.328
6	0.790	0.746	0.705	0.666	0.630	0.596	0.564	0.535	0.507	0.480	0.456	0.432	0.410	0.390	0.370	0.352	0.335	0.319	0.303	0.289	0.275	0.262
7	0.760	0.711	0.665	0.623	0.583	0.547	0.513	0.482	0.452	0.425	0.400	0.376	0.354	0.333	0.314	0.296	0.279	0.263	0.249	0.235	0.222	0.210
8	0.731	0.677	0.627	0.582	0.540	0.502	0.467	0.434	0.404	0.376	0.351	0.327	0.305	0.285	0.266	0.249	0.233	0.218	0.204	0.191	0.179	0.168
9	0.703	0.645	0.592	0.544	0.500	0.460	0.424	0.391	0.361	0.333	0.308	0.284	0.263	0.243	0.225	0.209	0.194	0.180	0.167	0.155	0.144	0.134
10	0.676	0.614	0.558	0.508	0.463	0.422	0.386	0.352	0.322	0.295	0.270	0.247	0.227	0.208	0.191	0.176	0.162	0.149	0.137	0.126	0.116	0.107
11	0.650	0.585	0.527	0.475	0.429	0.388	0.350	0.317	0.287	0.261	0.237	0.215	0.195	0.178	0.162	0.148	0.135	0.123	0.112	0.103	0.094	0.086
12	0.625	0.557	0.497	0.444	0.397	0.356	0.319	0.286	0.257	0.231	0.208	0.187	0.168	0.152	0.137	0.124	0.112	0.102	0.092	0.083	0.076	0.069
13	0.601	0.530	0.469	0.415	0.368	0.326	0.290	0.258	0.229	0.204	0.182	0.163	0.145	0.130	0.116	0.104	0.093	0.084	0.075	0.068	0.061	0.055
14	0.577	0.505	0.442	0.388	0.340	0.299	0.263	0.232	0.205	0.181	0.160	0.141	0.125	0.111	0.099	0.088	0.078	0.069	0.062	0.055	0.049	0.044
15	0.555	0.481	0.417	0.362	0.315	0.275	0.239	0.209	0.183	0.160	0.140	0.123	0.108	0.095	0.084	0.074	0.065	0.057	0.051	0.045	0.040	0.035
16	0.534	0.458	0.394	0.339	0.292	0.252	0.218	0.188	0.163	0.141	0.123	0.107	0.093	0.081	0.071	0.062	0.054	0.047	0.042	0.036	0.032	0.028
17	0.513	0.436	0.371	0.317	0.270	0.231	0.198	0.170	0.146	0.125	0.108	0.093	0.080	0.069	0.060	0.052	0.045	0.039	0.034	0.030	0.026	0.023
18	0.494	0.416	0.350	0.296	0.250	0.212	0.180	0.153	0.130	0.111	0.095	0.081	0.069	0.059	0.051	0.044	0.038	0.032	0.028	0.024	0.021	0.018
19	0.475	0.396	0.331	0.277	0.232	0.194	0.164	0.138	0.116	0.098	0.083	0.070	0.060	0.051	0.043	0.037	0.031	0.027	0.023	0.020	0.017	0.014
20	0.456	0.377	0.312	0.258	0.215	0.178	0.149	0.124	0.104	0.087	0.073	0.061	0.051	0.043	0.037	0.031	0.026	0.022	0.019	0.016	0.014	0.012
21	0.439	0.359	0.294	0.242	0.199	0.164	0.135	0.112	0.093	0.077	0.064	0.053	0.044	0.037	0.031	0.026	0.022	0.018	0.015	0.013	0.011	0.009
22	0.422	0.342	0.278	0.226	0.184	0.150	0.123	0.101	0.083	0.068	0.056	0.046	0.038	0.032	0.026	0.022	0.018	0.015	0.013	0.011	0.009	0.007
23	0.406	0.326	0.262	0.211	0.170	0.138	0.112	0.091	0.074	0.060	0.049	0.040	0.033	0.027	0.022	0.018	0.015	0.012	0.010	0.009	0.007	0.006
24	0.390	0.310	0.247	0.197	0.158	0.126	0.102	0.082	0.066	0.053	0.043	0.035	0.028	0.023	0.019	0.015	0.013	0.010	0.008	0.007	0.006	0.005
25	0.375	0.295	0.233	0.184	0.146	0.116	0.092	0.074	0.059	0.047	0.038	0.030	0.024	0.020	0.016	0.013	0.010	0.009	0.007	0.006	0.005	0.004
26	0.361	0.281	0.220	0.172	0.135	0.106	0.084	0.066	0.053	0.042	0.033	0.026	0.021	0.017	0.014	0.011	0.009	0.007	0.006	0.005	0.004	0.003
27	0.347	0.268	0.207	0.161	0.125	0.098	0.076	0.060	0.047	0.037	0.029	0.023	0.018	0.014	0.011	0.009	0.007	0.006	0.005	0.004	0.003	0.002
28	0.333	0.255	0.196	0.150	0.116	0.090	0.069	0.054	0.042	0.033	0.026	0.020	0.016	0.012	0.010	0.008	0.006	0.005	0.004	0.003	0.002	0.002
29	0.321	0.243	0.185	0.141	0.107	0.082	0.063	0.048	0.037	0.029	0.022	0.017	0.014	0.011	0.008	0.006	0.005	0.004	0.003	0.002	0.002	0.002
30	0.308	0.231	0.174	0.131	0.099	0.075	0.057	0.044	0.033	0.026	0.020	0.015	0.012	0.009	0.007	0.005	0.004	0.003	0.003	0.002	0.002	0.001
40	0.208	0.142	0.097	0.067	0.046	0.032	0.022	0.015	0.011	0.008	0.005	0.004	0.003	0.002	0.001	0.001	0.001	0.000	0.000	0.000	0.000	0.000

EXHIBIT 13B-2

Present Value of an Annuity of $1 in Arrears; $\dfrac{1}{r}\left[1 - \dfrac{1}{(1+r)^n}\right]$

Periods	4%	5%	6%	7%	8%	9%	10%	11%	12%	13%	14%	15%	16%	17%	18%	19%	20%	21%	22%	23%	24%	25%
1	0.962	0.952	0.943	0.935	0.926	0.917	0.909	0.901	0.893	0.885	0.877	0.870	0.862	0.855	0.847	0.840	0.833	0.826	0.820	0.813	0.806	0.800
2	1.886	1.859	1.833	1.808	1.783	1.759	1.736	1.713	1.690	1.668	1.647	1.626	1.605	1.585	1.566	1.547	1.528	1.509	1.492	1.474	1.457	1.440
3	2.775	2.723	2.673	2.624	2.577	2.531	2.487	2.444	2.402	2.361	2.322	2.283	2.246	2.210	2.174	2.140	2.106	2.074	2.042	2.011	1.981	1.952
4	3.630	3.546	3.465	3.387	3.312	3.240	3.170	3.102	3.037	2.974	2.914	2.855	2.798	2.743	2.690	2.639	2.589	2.540	2.494	2.448	2.404	2.362
5	4.452	4.329	4.212	4.100	3.993	3.890	3.791	3.696	3.605	3.517	3.433	3.352	3.274	3.199	3.127	3.058	2.991	2.926	2.864	2.803	2.745	2.689
6	5.242	5.076	4.917	4.767	4.623	4.486	4.355	4.231	4.111	3.998	3.889	3.784	3.685	3.589	3.498	3.410	3.326	3.245	3.167	3.092	3.020	2.951
7	6.002	5.786	5.582	5.389	5.206	5.033	4.868	4.712	4.564	4.423	4.288	4.160	4.039	3.922	3.812	3.706	3.605	3.508	3.416	3.327	3.242	3.161
8	6.733	6.463	6.210	5.971	5.747	5.535	5.335	5.146	4.968	4.799	4.639	4.487	4.344	4.207	4.078	3.954	3.837	3.726	3.619	3.518	3.421	3.329
9	7.435	7.108	6.802	6.515	6.247	5.995	5.759	5.537	5.328	5.132	4.946	4.772	4.607	4.451	4.303	4.163	4.031	3.905	3.786	3.673	3.566	3.463
10	8.111	7.722	7.360	7.024	6.710	6.418	6.145	5.889	5.650	5.426	5.216	5.019	4.833	4.659	4.494	4.339	4.192	4.054	3.923	3.799	3.682	3.571
11	8.760	8.306	7.887	7.499	7.139	6.805	6.495	6.207	5.938	5.687	5.453	5.234	5.029	4.836	4.656	4.486	4.327	4.177	4.035	3.902	3.776	3.656
12	9.385	8.863	8.384	7.943	7.536	7.161	6.814	6.492	6.194	5.918	5.660	5.421	5.197	4.988	4.793	4.611	4.439	4.278	4.127	3.985	3.851	3.725
13	9.986	9.394	8.853	8.358	7.904	7.487	7.103	6.750	6.424	6.122	5.842	5.583	5.342	5.118	4.910	4.715	4.533	4.362	4.203	4.053	3.912	3.780
14	10.563	9.899	9.295	8.745	8.244	7.786	7.367	6.982	6.628	6.302	6.002	5.724	5.468	5.229	5.008	4.802	4.611	4.432	4.265	4.108	3.962	3.824
15	11.118	10.380	9.712	9.108	8.559	8.061	7.606	7.191	6.811	6.462	6.142	5.847	5.575	5.324	5.092	4.876	4.675	4.489	4.315	4.153	4.001	3.859
16	11.652	10.838	10.106	9.447	8.851	8.313	7.824	7.379	6.974	6.604	6.265	5.954	5.668	5.405	5.162	4.938	4.730	4.536	4.357	4.189	4.033	3.887
17	12.166	11.274	10.477	9.763	9.122	8.544	8.022	7.549	7.120	6.729	6.373	6.047	5.749	5.475	5.222	4.990	4.775	4.576	4.391	4.219	4.059	3.910
18	12.659	11.690	10.828	10.059	9.372	8.756	8.201	7.702	7.250	6.840	6.467	6.128	5.818	5.534	5.273	5.033	4.812	4.608	4.419	4.243	4.080	3.928
19	13.134	12.085	11.158	10.336	9.604	8.950	8.365	7.839	7.366	6.938	6.550	6.198	5.877	5.584	5.316	5.070	4.843	4.635	4.442	4.263	4.097	3.942
20	13.590	12.462	11.470	10.594	9.818	9.129	8.514	7.963	7.469	7.025	6.623	6.259	5.929	5.628	5.353	5.101	4.870	4.657	4.460	4.279	4.110	3.954
21	14.029	12.821	11.764	10.836	10.017	9.292	8.649	8.075	7.562	7.102	6.687	6.312	5.973	5.665	5.384	5.127	4.891	4.675	4.476	4.292	4.121	3.963
22	14.451	13.163	12.042	11.061	10.201	9.442	8.772	8.176	7.645	7.170	6.743	6.359	6.011	5.696	5.410	5.149	4.909	4.690	4.488	4.302	4.130	3.970
23	14.857	13.489	12.303	11.272	10.371	9.580	8.883	8.266	7.718	7.230	6.792	6.399	6.044	5.723	5.432	5.167	4.925	4.703	4.499	4.311	4.137	3.976
24	15.247	13.799	12.550	11.469	10.529	9.707	8.985	8.348	7.784	7.283	6.835	6.434	6.073	5.746	5.451	5.182	4.937	4.713	4.507	4.318	4.143	3.981
25	15.622	14.094	12.783	11.654	10.675	9.823	9.077	8.422	7.843	7.330	6.873	6.464	6.097	5.766	5.467	5.195	4.948	4.721	4.514	4.323	4.147	3.985
26	15.983	14.375	13.003	11.826	10.810	9.929	9.161	8.488	7.896	7.372	6.906	6.491	6.118	5.783	5.480	5.206	4.956	4.728	4.520	4.328	4.151	3.988
27	16.330	14.643	13.211	11.987	10.935	10.027	9.237	8.548	7.943	7.409	6.935	6.514	6.136	5.798	5.492	5.215	4.964	4.734	4.524	4.332	4.154	3.990
28	16.663	14.898	13.406	12.137	11.051	10.116	9.307	8.602	7.984	7.441	6.961	6.534	6.152	5.810	5.502	5.223	4.970	4.739	4.528	4.335	4.157	3.992
29	16.984	15.141	13.591	12.278	11.158	10.198	9.370	8.650	8.022	7.470	6.983	6.551	6.166	5.820	5.510	5.229	4.975	4.743	4.531	4.337	4.159	3.994
30	17.292	15.372	13.765	12.409	11.258	10.274	9.427	8.694	8.055	7.496	7.003	6.566	6.177	5.829	5.517	5.235	4.979	4.746	4.534	4.339	4.160	3.995
40	19.793	17.159	15.046	13.332	11.925	10.757	9.779	8.951	8.244	7.634	7.105	6.642	6.233	5.871	5.548	5.258	4.997	4.760	4.544	4.347	4.166	3.999

Appendix 13C: Income Taxes and the Net Present Value Method

This appendix discusses the impact of income taxes on the net present value method of making capital budgeting decisions. We ignored income taxes throughout the chapter for two reasons. First, many organizations do not pay income taxes. Non-profit organizations, such as hospitals and charitable foundations, and government agencies are exempt from income taxes. Second, capital budgeting is complex and best absorbed in small doses. Now that we have a solid foundation in the concept of discounting cash flows, we can explore the impact of income taxes on the net present value method.

> **LO13–8**
> Include income taxes in a net present value analysis.

To keep this discussion within reasonable bounds, we make a number of simplifying assumptions. We assume that a company's taxable income equals its net income for financial reporting purposes and that straight-line depreciation with zero salvage value is used. We also assume that the tax rate is a flat percentage of taxable income and that there are no gains or losses on the sale of noncurrent assets.

Key Concepts

This appendix takes everything that you have already learned about the net present value method and simply adds one more type of cash flow to the computations—it adds income tax expense as a *cash outflow*. To calculate the amount of income tax expense associated with a capital budgeting project, we'll be using a two-step process. The first step is to calculate the incremental net income earned during each year of the project. The second step is to multiply each year's incremental net income by the tax rate to determine the income tax expense. Each year's income tax expense is then discounted to its present value along with all other cash flows realized over the life of the project.

A capital budgeting project's incremental net income computation *includes* annual revenues minus annual cash operating expenses (including variable expenses and fixed out-of-pocket costs), annual depreciation expense, and any one-time expenses. Notice that *depreciation expense is included in the computation of incremental net income.* Although depreciation expense is a noncash expense, it does impact the computation of taxable income, which in turn affects the cash outflows pertaining to income tax expense. A capital budgeting project's incremental net income computation *does not include* immediate cash outflows in the form of initial investments in equipment, other assets, and installation costs. It also *does not include* investments in working capital, the release of working capital at the end of a project, and the proceeds from selling a noncurrent asset when no gain or loss is realized on the sale.

To summarize, the items that should be included and excluded from a capital budgeting project's incremental net income computations are as follows:

Include in the computation of incremental net income:
Annual revenues
Annual cash operating expenses
Annual depreciation expense
One-time expenses

Exclude from the computation of incremental net income:
Initial investments in equipment, other assets, and installation costs
Investment in working capital
Release of working capital at the end of a project
Proceeds from selling noncurrent assets when no gain or loss is realized

Income Taxes and Net Present Value Analysis: An Example

Holland Company owns the mineral rights to land that has a deposit of ore. The company is uncertain if it should purchase equipment and open a mine on the property. After careful study, the company gathered the following data:

Initial investment in equipment	$275,000
Initial investment in working capital	$50,000
Estimated annual sales of ore	$250,000
Estimated annual cash operating expenses	$150,000
Cost of road repairs needed in 3 years	$30,000

The ore in the mine would be exhausted after five years, at which time the mine would be closed and the working capital would be released and redeployed by the company. The equipment has a useful life of five years and a salvage value of zero. The company uses straight-line depreciation for financial reporting and tax purposes. Its after-tax cost of capital is 12% and its tax rate is 30%. To be consistent, when we take the net present value of after-tax cash flows, we use the *after-tax* cost of capital as the discount rate.

Should Holland Company purchase the equipment and open a mine on the property? Exhibit 13C–1 shows a net present value analysis that incorporates the impact of income taxes on this decision. The top portion of the exhibit computes the project's incremental net income for Years 1–5 and the income tax expense for each of those years. The incremental net income computations include the annual sales ($250,000), the annual cash operating expenses ($150,000), the road repairs in Year 3 ($30,000), and the annual depreciation expense of $55,000 ($275,000 ÷ 5 years = $55,000 per year). Each year's incremental net income is multiplied by the tax rate of 30% to determine the income tax expense.

The bottom portion of Exhibit 13C–1 calculates the net present value of the mining project. The cash flows summarized in this portion of the exhibit include the initial

EXHIBIT 13C–1
Holland Company: Income Taxes and Net Present Value Analysis

	A	B	C	D	E	F	G
1					Year		
2		Now	1	2	3	4	5
3	*Calculate the annual tax expense:*						
4	Sales		$ 250,000	$ 250,000	$ 250,000	$ 250,000	$ 250,000
5	Cash operating expenses		$ (150,000)	$ (150,000)	$ (150,000)	$(150,000)	$ (150,000)
6	Road repairs				$ (30,000)		
7	Depreciation expense		$ (55,000)	$ (55,000)	$ (55,000)	$ (55,000)	$ (55,000)
8	Incremental net income		$ 45,000	$ 45,000	$ 15,000	$ 45,000	$ 45,000
9	Tax rate		30%	30%	30%	30%	30%
10	Income tax expense		$ (13,500)	$ (13,500)	$ (4,500)	$ (13,500)	$ (13,500)
11							
12	*Calculate the net present value:*						
13	Purchase of equipment	$ (275,000)					
14	Investment in working capital	$ (50,000)					
15	Sales		$ 250,000	$ 250,000	$ 250,000	$ 250,000	$ 250,000
16	Cash operating expenses		$ (150,000)	$ (150,000)	$ (150,000)	$(150,000)	$ (150,000)
17	Road repairs				$ (30,000)		
18	Release of working capital						$ 50,000
19	Income tax expense		$ (13,500)	$ (13,500)	$ (4,500)	$ (13,500)	$ (13,500)
20	Total cash flows (a)	$ (325,000)	$ 86,500	$ 86,500	$ 65,500	$ 86,500	$ 136,500
21	Discount factor (12%) (b)	1.000	0.893	0.797	0.712	0.636	0.567
22	Present value of cash flows (a) × (b)	$ (325,000)	$ 77,245	$ 68,941	$ 46,636	$ 55,014	$ 77,396
23	Net present value (SUM B22:G22)	$ 232					
24							
25	Note: The discount factors come from Exhibit 13B-1 in Appendix 13B.						
26							

outlays for the purchase of equipment ($275,000) and the investment in working capital ($50,000), the annual sales ($250,000), the annual cash operating expenses ($150,000), the road repairs in Year 3 ($30,000), the release of working capital in Year 5 ($50,000), and the annual income tax expense. Notice that the amounts of income tax expense shown in cells C19 through G19 come directly from the calculations previously performed in cells C10 through G10. Each year's total cash flows in cells B20 through G20 are multiplied by the appropriate discount factor for 12% to compute their present value. The present values in cells B22 through G22 are combined to determine the project's net present value of $232. Because the net present value is positive, it indicates that Holland Company should proceed with the mining project.

Summary (Appendix 13C)

Unless the organization is tax-exempt, such as a nonprofit school or a governmental body, income taxes should be considered when using net present value analysis to make capital budgeting decisions. Calculating the amount of income tax expense associated with a capital budgeting project is a two-step process. The first step is to calculate the incremental net income earned during each year of the project. The second step is to multiply each year's incremental net income by the tax rate to determine the income tax expense. Each year's income tax expense is then discounted to its present value along with all other cash flows realized over the life of the project.

A capital budgeting project's incremental net income computation includes annual revenues minus annual cash operating expenses, annual depreciation expense, and any one-time expenses. It does not include immediate cash outflows in the form of initial investments in equipment, other assets, and installation costs, as well as investments in working capital, the release of working capital at the end of a project, and the proceeds from selling a noncurrent asset where no gain or loss is realized on the sale.

■ connect   Appendix 13C: Exercises and Problems

EXERCISE 13C–1 Income Taxes and Net Present Value Analysis LO13–8
Gaston Company is considering a capital budgeting project that would require a $2,000,000 investment in equipment with a useful life of five years and no salvage value. The company's tax rate is 30% and its after-tax cost of capital is 13%. It uses the straight-line depreciation method for financial reporting and tax purposes. The project would provide net operating income each year for five years as follows:

Sales		$2,800,000
Variable expenses		1,600,000
Contribution margin		1,200,000
Fixed expenses:		
Advertising, salaries, and other fixed		
out-of-pocket costs	$500,000	
Depreciation	400,000	
Total fixed expenses		900,000
Net operating income		$ 300,000

Required:
Compute the project's net present value.

EXERCISE 13C–2 Income Taxes and Net Present Value Analysis LO13–8
Winthrop Company has an opportunity to manufacture and sell a new product for a five-year period. To pursue this opportunity, the company would need to purchase a piece of equipment for $130,000. The equipment would have a useful life of five years and zero salvage value. It would be

depreciated for financial reporting and tax purposes using the straight-line method. After careful study, Winthrop estimated the following annual costs and revenues for the new product:

Annual revenues and costs:	
Sales revenues	$250,000
Variable expenses	$120,000
Fixed out-of-pocket operating costs	$70,000

The company's tax rate is 30% and its after-tax cost of capital is 15%.

Required:
1. Calculate the annual income tax expense that will arise as a result of this investment.
2. Calculate the net present value of this investment opportunity.

PROBLEM 13C–3 Income Taxes and Net Present Value Analysis LO13–8
Lander Company has an opportunity to pursue a capital budgeting project with a five-year time horizon. After careful study, Lander estimated the following costs and revenues for the project:

Cost of equipment needed	$250,000
Working capital needed	$60,000
Repair the equipment in two years	$18,000
Annual revenues and costs:	
Sales revenues	$350,000
Variable expenses	$180,000
Fixed out-of-pocket operating costs	$80,000

The piece of equipment mentioned above has a useful life of five years and zero salvage value. Lander uses straight-line depreciation for financial reporting and tax purposes. The company's tax rate is 30% and its after-tax cost of capital is 12%. When the project concludes in five years the working capital will be released for investment elsewhere within the company.

Required:
1. Calculate the annual income tax expense for each of years 1 through 5 that will arise as a result of this investment opportunity.
2. Calculate the net present value of this investment opportunity.

PROBLEM 13C–4 Income Taxes and Net Present Value Analysis LO13–8
Rosman Company has an opportunity to pursue a capital budgeting project with a five-year time horizon. After careful study, Rosman estimated the following costs and revenues for the project:

Cost of new equipment needed	$420,000
Sale of old equipment no longer needed	$80,000
Working capital needed	$65,000
Equipment maintenance in each of Years 3 and 4	$20,000
Annual revenues and costs:	
Sales revenues	$410,000
Variable expenses	$175,000
Fixed out-of-pocket operating costs	$100,000

The new piece of equipment mentioned above has a useful life of five years and zero salvage value. The old piece of equipment mentioned above would be sold at the beginning of the project and there would be no gain or loss realized on its sale. Rosman uses the straight-line depreciation method for financial reporting and tax purposes. The company's tax rate is 30% and its after-tax cost of capital is 12%. When the project concludes in five years the working capital will be released for investment elsewhere within the company.

Required:
1. Calculate the annual income tax expense for each of years 1 through 5 that will arise as a result of this investment opportunity.
2. Calculate the net present value of this investment opportunity.

PROBLEM 13C–5 Income Taxes and Net Present Value Analysis LO13–5, LO13–8

Shimano Company has an opportunity to manufacture and sell one of two new products for a five-year period. The company's tax rate is 30% and its after-tax cost of capital is 14%. The cost and revenue estimates for each product are as follows:

	Product A	Product B
Initial investment in equipment	$400,000	$550,000
Initial investment in working capital	$85,000	$60,000
Annual sales	$370,000	$390,000
Annual cash operating expenses	$200,000	$170,000
Cost of repairs needed in three years	$45,000	$70,000

The equipment pertaining to both products has a useful life of five years and no salvage value. The company uses the straight-line depreciation method for financial reporting and tax purposes. At the end of five years, each product's working capital will be released for investment elsewhere within the company.

Required:
1. Calculate the annual income tax expense for each of years 1 through 5 that will arise if Product A is introduced.
2. Calculate the net present value of the investment opportunity pertaining to Product A.
3. Calculate the annual income tax expense for each of years 1 through 5 that will arise if Product B is introduced.
4. Calculate the net present value of the investment opportunity pertaining to Product B.
5. Calculate the project profitability index for Product A and Product B. Which of the two products should the company pursue? Why?

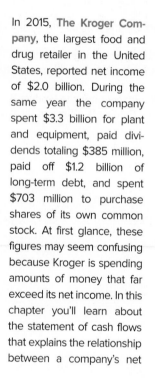

Statement of Cash Flows

Understanding Cash Flows

© Bloomberg/Getty Images

In 2015, **The Kroger Company**, the largest food and drug retailer in the United States, reported net income of $2.0 billion. During the same year the company spent $3.3 billion for plant and equipment, paid dividends totaling $385 million, paid off $1.2 billion of long-term debt, and spent $703 million to purchase shares of its own common stock. At first glance, these figures may seem confusing because Kroger is spending amounts of money that far exceed its net income. In this chapter you'll learn about the statement of cash flows that explains the relationship between a company's net income and its cash inflows and outflows. ∎

Source: The Kroger Company, 2015 Form 10–K Annual Report, www.sec.gov/edgar/searchedgar/companysearch.html.

LEARNING OBJECTIVES

After studying Chapter 14, you should be able to:

LO14–1 Classify cash inflows and outflows as relating to operating, investing, or financing activities.

LO14–2 Prepare a statement of cash flows using the indirect method to determine the net cash provided by operating activities.

LO14–3 Compute free cash flow.

LO14–4 *(Appendix 14A) Use the direct method to determine the net cash provided by operating activities.*

Three major financial statements are required for external reports—an income statement, a balance sheet, and a statement of cash flows. The **statement of cash flows** highlights the major activities that impact cash flows and, hence, affect the overall cash balance. Managers focus on cash for a very good reason—without sufficient cash at the right times, a company may miss golden investment opportunities or may even go bankrupt.

The statement of cash flows answers questions that cannot be easily answered by looking at the income statement and balance sheet. For example, where did **Delta Airlines** get the cash to pay a dividend of nearly $140 million in a year in which, according to its income statement, it lost more than $1 billion? How was **The Walt Disney Company** able to invest nearly $800 million to expand and renovate its theme parks despite a loss of more than $500 million on its investment in EuroDisney? Where did **The Kroger Company** get $3.3 billion to invest in plant and equipment in a year when its net income was only $2.0 billion? The answers to such questions can be found on the statement of cash flows.

The statement of cash flows is a valuable analytical tool for managers as well as for investors and creditors, although managers tend to be more concerned with forecasted statements of cash flows that are prepared as part of the budgeting process. The statement of cash flows can be used to answer crucial questions such as:

1. Is the company generating sufficient positive cash flows from its ongoing operations to remain viable?
2. Will the company be able to repay its debts?
3. Will the company be able to pay its usual dividend?
4. Why do net income and net cash flow differ?
5. To what extent will the company have to borrow money in order to make needed investments?

Managers prepare the statement of cash flows by applying a fundamental principle of double-entry bookkeeping—the change in the cash balance must equal the changes in all other balance sheet accounts besides cash.[1] This principle ensures that properly analyzing the changes in all noncash balance sheet accounts always quantifies the cash inflows and outflows that explain the change in the cash balance. Our goal in this chapter is to translate this fairly complex principle into a small number of concepts and steps that simplify the process of preparing and interpreting a statement of cash flows.

Before delving into the specifics of how to prepare the statement of cash flows, we need to review two basic equations that apply to all asset, contra-asset, liability, and stockholders' equity accounts:

Basic Equation for Asset Accounts
Beginning balance + Debits − Credits = Ending balance

Basic Equation for Contra-Asset, Liability, and Stockholders' Equity Accounts
Beginning balance − Debits + Credits = Ending balance

These equations will help you compute various cash inflows and outflows that are reported in the statement of cash flows and they'll be referred to throughout the chapter.

---

[1] The statement of cash flows is based on the following fundamental balance sheet and income statement equations:

(1) Change in cash + Changes in noncash assets = Changes in liabilities + Changes in stockholders' equity
(2) Net cash flow = Change in cash
(3) Changes in stockholders' equity = Net income − Dividends + Changes in capital stock
These three equations can be used to derive the following equation:
(4) Net cash flow = Net income − Changes in noncash assets + Changes in liabilities − Dividends + Changes in capital stock
Essentially, the statement of cash flows, which explains net cash flow, is constructed by starting with net income and then adjusting it for changes in noncash balance sheet accounts.

The Statement of Cash Flows: Key Concepts

The statement of cash flows summarizes all of a company's cash inflows and outflows during a period, thereby explaining the change in its cash balance. In a statement of cash flows, cash is broadly defined to include both cash and cash equivalents. **Cash equivalents** consist of short-term, highly liquid investments such as Treasury bills, commercial paper, and money market funds that are made solely for the purpose of generating a return on temporarily idle funds. Most companies invest their excess cash reserves in these types of interest-bearing assets that can be easily converted into cash. Because such assets are equivalent to cash, they are included with cash in a statement of cash flows.

The remainder of this section discusses four key concepts that you'll need to understand to prepare a statement of cash flows. These four concepts include organizing the statement of cash flows, distinguishing between the direct and indirect methods of preparing a portion of the statement of cash flows, completing the three-step process underlying the indirect method, and recording gross cash flows where appropriate within a statement of cash flows.[2]

IN BUSINESS

© David Paul Morris/Bloomberg/Getty Images

SAMSUNG'S ENVIABLE CASH FLOWS

Samsung's cash and cash equivalents have reached $40 billion. The company is likely to use its cash for various purposes including research and development, marketing, making acquisitions in software and medical equipment, funding an increase in dividend payments, and buying back shares of its own stock. Samsung's cash hoard mirrors the types of enormous cash balance maintained by Apple. Apple's investors eventually pressured the company to increase its dividend per share and its stock repurchases.

Source: Daisuke Wakabayashi and Min-Jeong Lee, "Samsung's Sweet Problem? Nearly $40 Billion in Cash," *The Wall Street Journal*, May 8, 2013, pp. B1 and B4.

LO14–1

Classify cash inflows and outflows as relating to operating, investing, or financing activities.

Organizing the Statement of Cash Flows

To make it easier to compare data from different companies, U.S. generally accepted accounting principles (GAAP) and International Financial Reporting Standards (IFRS) require companies to follow prescribed rules when preparing the statement of cash flows. One of these rules requires organizing the statement into three sections that report cash flows resulting from *operating activities, investing activities,* and *financing activities.* **Operating activities** generate cash inflows and outflows related to revenue and

---

[2] Another concept that relates to the statement of cash flows is direct exchange transactions, which refer to transactions where noncurrent balance sheet items are swapped. For example, a company might issue common stock in a direct exchange for property. Direct exchange transactions are not reported on the statement of cash flows; however, they are disclosed in a separate schedule that accompanies the statement. More advanced accounting courses cover this topic in greater detail. We will not include direct exchange transactions in this chapter.

	Cash Inflow	Cash Outflow
Operating activities		
Collecting cash from customers.........................	√	
Paying suppliers for inventory purchases.................		√
Paying bills to insurers, utility providers, etc		√
Paying wages and salaries to employees		√
Paying taxes to governmental bodies		√
Paying interest to lenders		√
Investing activities		
Buying property, plant, and equipment		√
Selling property, plant, and equipment	√	
Buying stocks and bonds as a long-term investment		√
Selling stocks and bonds held for long-term investment.......	√	
Lending money to another entity		√
Collecting the principal on a loan to another entity...........	√	
Financing activities		
Borrowing money from a creditor	√	
Repaying the principal amount of a debt		√
Collecting cash from the sale of common stock	√	
Paying cash to repurchase your own common stock..........		√
Paying a dividend to stockholders		√

EXHIBIT 14–1
Cash Inflows and Outflows Resulting from Operating, Investing, and Financing Activities

expense transactions that affect net income. **Investing activities** generate cash inflows and outflows related to acquiring or disposing of noncurrent assets such as property, plant, and equipment, long-term investments, and loans to another entity. **Financing activities** generate cash inflows and outflows related to borrowing from and repaying principal to creditors and completing transactions with the company's owners, such as selling or repurchasing shares of common stock and paying dividends. The most common types of cash inflows and outflows resulting from these three activities are summarized in Exhibit 14–1.[3]

Operating Activities: Direct or Indirect Method?

U.S. GAAP and IFRS allow companies to compute the net amount of cash inflows and outflows resulting from operating activities, which is known formally as the **net cash provided by operating activities**, using either the *direct* or *indirect* method. Both of these methods have the same purpose, which is to translate accrual-based net income to a cash basis. However, they approach this task in two different ways.

Under the **direct method**, the income statement is reconstructed on a cash basis from top to bottom. For example, cash collected from customers is listed instead of sales, and payments to suppliers is listed instead of cost of goods sold. In essence, cash receipts are counted as sales and cash disbursements pertaining to operating activities are counted as expenses. The difference between the cash receipts and cash disbursements is the net cash provided by operating activities.

Under the **indirect method**, net income is adjusted to a cash basis. That is, rather than directly computing cash sales, cash expenses, and so forth, these amounts are derived

---

[3] Operating cash inflows can also include interest income and dividend income; however, in this chapter we will limit our scope to cash receipts from sales to customers.

indirectly by removing from net income any items that do not affect cash flows. The indirect method has an advantage over the direct method because it shows the reasons for any differences between net income and net cash provided by operating activities.

Although both methods result in the same amount of net cash provided by operating activities, the overwhelming majority of companies uses the indirect method for external reporting purposes. If a company uses the direct method to prepare its statement of cash flows, then it must also provide a supplementary report that uses the indirect method. However, if a company chooses to use the indirect method, there is no requirement that it also report results using the direct method. Because the direct method requires more work, very few companies choose this approach. Therefore, we will explain the direct method in Appendix 14A, and we will cover the indirect method in the main body of the chapter.

The Indirect Method: A Three-Step Process

The indirect method adjusts net income to net cash provided by operating activities using a three-step process.

Step 1   The first step is to *add depreciation charges* to net income. Depreciation charges are the credits to the Accumulated Depreciation account during the period—the sum total of the entries that have increased Accumulated Depreciation. Why do we do this? Because Accumulated Depreciation is a noncash balance sheet account and we must adjust net income for all of the changes in the noncash balance sheet accounts that have occurred during the period.

To compute the credits to the Accumulated Depreciation account we use the equation for contra-assets that was mentioned earlier:

Basic Equation for Contra-Asset Accounts
Beginning balance − Debits + Credits = Ending balance

For example, assume the Accumulated Depreciation account had beginning and ending balances of $300 and $500, respectively. Also, assume that the company sold equipment with accumulated depreciation of $70 during the period. Given that we use debits to the Accumulated Depreciation account to record accumulated depreciation on assets that have been sold or retired, the depreciation that needs to be added to net income is computed as follows:

$$\text{Beginning balance} - \text{Debits} + \text{Credits} = \text{Ending balance}$$
$$\$300 - \$70 + \text{Credits} = \$500$$
$$\text{Credits} = \$500 - \$300 + \$70$$
$$\text{Credits} = \$270$$

The same logic can be depicted using an Accumulated Depreciation T-account. Given that we know the account's beginning and ending balances and the amount of the debit that would have been recorded for the sale of equipment, the credit side of the T-account must equal $270.

Accumulated Depreciation

	Beg. Bal.	$300
Sale of equipment 70		270
	End. Bal.	$500

For service and merchandising companies, the credits to the Accumulated Depreciation T-account equal the debits to the Depreciation Expense account. For these companies, the adjustment in step one consists of adding depreciation expense to net income.

However, for manufacturing companies, some of the credits to the Accumulated Depreciation T-account relate to depreciation on production assets that are debited to work in process inventories rather than depreciation expense. For these companies, the depreciation charges do not simply equal depreciation expense.

Because depreciation is added back to net income on the statement of cash flows, some people erroneously conclude that a company can increase its cash flow by simply increasing its depreciation expense. This is false; a company cannot increase its net cash provided by operating activities by increasing its depreciation expense. If it increases its depreciation expense by X dollars, then net income will decline by X dollars and the amount of the adjustment in step one of this process will increase by X dollars. The decline in net income and the increase in the amount of the adjustment in step one exactly offset each other, resulting in zero impact on the net cash provided by operating activities.

Step 2   The second step is to *analyze net changes in noncash balance sheet accounts* that impact net income. Exhibit 14–2 provides general guidelines for how to analyze current asset and current liability accounts.[4] For each account shown in the exhibit, you'll begin by referring to the balance sheet to compute the change in the account balance from the beginning to the end of the period. Then, you will either add each of these amounts to net income or subtract them from net income as shown in Exhibit 14–2. Notice that changes in all current asset accounts (Accounts Receivable, Inventory, and Prepaid Expenses) result in the same type of adjustment to net income. If an asset account balance increases during the period, then the amount of the increase is subtracted from net income. If an asset account balance decreases during the period, then the amount of the decrease is added to net income. The current liability accounts (Accounts Payable, Accrued Liabilities, and Income Taxes Payable) are handled in the opposite fashion. If a liability account balance increases, then the amount of the increase is added to net income. If a liability account balance decreases, then the amount of the decrease is subtracted from net income.

Keep in mind that the purpose of these adjustments is to translate net income to a cash basis. For example, the change in the Accounts Receivable balance measures the difference between credit sales and cash collections from customers who purchased on account. When the Accounts Receivable balance increases it means that the amount of credit sales exceeds the amount of cash collected from customers. In this case, the change in the Accounts Receivable balance is subtracted from net income because it reflects the amount by which credit sales exceeds cash collections from customers. When the Accounts Receivable balance decreases it means that cash collected from customers

	Increase in Account Balance	Decrease in Account Balance
Current Assets		
Accounts receivable..................	Subtract	Add
Inventory............................	Subtract	Add
Prepaid expenses....................	Subtract	Add
Current Liabilities		
Accounts payable....................	Add	Subtract
Accrued liabilities	Add	Subtract
Income taxes payable................	Add	Subtract

EXHIBIT 14–2
General Guidelines for Analyzing How Changes in Noncash Balance Sheet Accounts Affect Net Income on the Statement of Cash Flows

---

[4] Other accounts such as Interest Payable can impact these computations. However, for simplicity, in this chapter we will focus on the accounts shown in Exhibit 14–2.

exceeds credit sales. In this case, the change in the Accounts Receivable balance is added to net income because it reflects the amount by which cash collections from customers exceeds credit sales.

The other accounts shown in Exhibit 14–2 have a similar underlying logic. The Inventory and Accounts Payable adjustments translate cost of goods sold to cash paid for inventory purchases. The Prepaid Expenses and Accrued Liabilities adjustments translate selling and administrative expenses to a cash basis. The Income Taxes Payable adjustment translates income tax expense to a cash basis.

Step 3   The third step in computing the net cash provided by operating activities is to *adjust for gains/losses* included in the income statement. Under U.S. GAAP and IFRS rules, the cash proceeds from the sale of noncurrent assets must be included in the investing activities section of the statement of cash flows. To comply with these rules, the gains and losses pertaining to the sale of noncurrent assets must be removed from net income as reported in the operating activities section of the statement of cash flows. To make this adjustment, subtract gains from net income and add losses to net income in the operating activities section.

SEARS' SUPPLIERS WANT THEIR MONEY SOONER

Some of **Sears'** suppliers want to be paid in 15 days instead of their usual norms of 30–60 days. The suppliers are seeking quicker payments to compensate them for the risk of selling merchandise to the troubled retailer who is experiencing annual losses in excess of $1 billion. From a cash flow perspective, faster payments to suppliers will decrease Sears' accounts payable balance, which in turn lowers its net cash provided by operating activities.

Source: Suzanne Kapner, "Jittery Suppliers Press Sears to Pay Up Faster," *The Wall Street Journal,* March 19, 2015, pp. B1–B2.

Investing and Financing Activities: Gross Cash Flows

U.S. GAAP and IFRS require that the investing and financing sections of the statement of cash flows disclose gross cash flows. To illustrate, suppose **Macy's Department Stores** purchases $50 million in property during the year and sells other property for $30 million. Instead of showing the net change of $20 million, the company must show the gross amounts of both the purchases and sales. The $50 million purchase would be disclosed as a cash outflow and the $30 million sale would be reported as a cash inflow in the investing section of the statement of cash flows. Similarly, if **Alcoa** receives $80 million from selling long-term bonds and then pays out $30 million to retire other bonds, the two transactions must be reported separately in the financing section of the statement of cash flows rather than being netted against each other.

The gross method of reporting cash flows is not used in the operating activities section of the statement of cash flows, where debits and credits are netted against each other. For example, if **Sears** adds $600 million to its accounts receivable as a result of sales during the year and $520 million of accounts receivable are collected, only the net increase of $80 million is reported on the statement of cash flows.

To compute gross cash flows for the investing and financing activities sections of the statement of cash flows, you'll begin by calculating the changes in the balance of each applicable balance sheet account. As with the current assets, when a noncurrent asset account balance (including Property, Plant, and Equipment; Long-Term Investments; and Loans to Other Entities) increases, it signals the need to subtract cash outflows in the investing activities section of the statement of cash flows. If the balance in a noncurrent asset account decreases during the period, then it signals the need to add cash inflows.

	Increase in Account Balance	Decrease in Account Balance	
Noncurrent Assets (Investing activities)			EXHIBIT 14–3
Property, plant, and equipment	Subtract	Add	General Guidelines for Analyzing
Long-term investments	Subtract	Add	How Changes in Noncash Balance
Loans to other entities	Subtract	Add	Sheet Accounts Affect the Investing
Liabilities and Stockholders' Equity (Financing activities)			and Financing Sections of the Statement of Cash Flows
Bonds payable	Add	Subtract	
Common stock	Add	Subtract	
Retained earnings	*	*	

*Requires further analysis to quantify cash dividends paid.

The liability and equity accounts (Bonds Payable and Common Stock) are handled in the opposite fashion. If a liability or equity account balance increases, then it signals a need to add cash inflows to the financing activities section of the statement of cash flows. If a liability or equity account balance decreases, then it signals a need to subtract cash outflows. Exhibit 14–3 summarizes these general guidelines.

While these guidelines provide a helpful starting point, to properly calculate each account's *gross* cash inflows and outflows you'll need to analyze the transactions that occurred within that account during the period. We will illustrate how to do this using Property, Plant, and Equipment and Retained Earnings.

Property, Plant, and Equipment When a company purchases property, plant, or equipment it debits the Property, Plant, and Equipment account for the amount of the purchase. When it sells or disposes of these kinds of assets, it credits the Property, Plant, and Equipment account for the original cost of the asset. To compute the cash outflows related to Property, Plant, and Equipment we use the basic equation for assets mentioned earlier:

Basic Equation for Asset Accounts
Beginning balance + Debits − Credits = Ending balance

For example, assume a company's beginning and ending balances in its Property, Plant, and Equipment account are $1,000 and $1,800, respectively. In addition, during the period the company sold a piece of equipment for $40 cash that originally cost $100 and had accumulated depreciation of $70. The company recorded a gain on the sale of $10, which had been included in net income.

We start by calculating the $800 increase in the Property, Plant, and Equipment account. This increase signals the need to subtract cash outflows in the investing activities section of the statement of cash flows. In fact, it may be tempting to conclude that the proper way to analyze Property, Plant, and Equipment in this instance is to record an $800 cash outflow corresponding with the $800 increase in the account balance. However, that would only be correct if the company did not sell any property, plant, and equipment during the year. Because the company did sell equipment, we must use the basic equation for asset accounts to compute the cash outflows as follows:

$$\text{Beginning balance} + \text{Debits} - \text{Credits} = \text{Ending balance}$$
$$\$1{,}000 + \text{Debits} - \$100 = \$1{,}800$$
$$\text{Debits} = \$1{,}800 - \$1{,}000 + \$100$$
$$\text{Debits} = \$900$$

The same logic can be depicted using a Property, Plant, and Equipment T-account. Given that we know the account's beginning and ending balances and the amount of the credit that would have been recorded to write off the *original cost* of the equipment that was sold, the additions to the account, as summarized on the debit side of the T-account, must equal $900.

Property, Plant, and Equipment

Beg. Bal.	$1,000		
Additions	900	Sale of equipment	100
End. Bal.	$1,800		

So, instead of reporting an $800 cash outflow pertaining to Property, Plant, and Equipment in the investing activities section of the statement of cash flows, the proper accounting requires subtracting the $10 gain on the sale of equipment from net income in the operating activities section of the statement. It also requires disclosing a $40 cash inflow from the sale of equipment and a $900 cash outflow for additions to Property, Plant, and Equipment in the investing activities section of the statement.

Retained Earnings   When a company earns net income it credits the Retained Earnings account and when it pays a dividend it debits the Retained Earnings account. To compute the amount of a cash dividend payment we use the basic equation for stockholders' equity accounts mentioned earlier:

Basic Equation for Stockholders' Equity Accounts
Beginning balance − Debits + Credits = Ending balance

For example, assume a company's beginning and ending balances in its Retained Earnings account are $2,000 and 3,000, respectively. In addition, the company reported net income of $1,200 and paid a cash dividend. To determine the amount of the dividend, we start by calculating the $1,000 increase in the Retained Earnings account. However, given that this amount reflects the net income earned during the period as well as the amount of the dividend payment, we must use the equation above to calculate the amount of the dividend payment as follows:

Beginning balance − Debits + Credits = Ending balance

$2,000 − Debits + $1,200 = $3,000

$3,200 = $3,000 + Debits

Debits = $200

The same logic can be depicted using a Retained Earnings T-account. Given that we know the account's beginning and ending balances and the net income that would have been recorded on the credit side of the T-account, the dividend, as reported on the debit side of the T-account, must equal $200.

Retained Earnings

		Beg. Bal.	$2,000
Dividend	200	Net income	1,200
		End. Bal.	$3,000

So, instead of erroneously reporting a $1,000 cash flow pertaining to the overall change in Retained Earnings, the proper accounting requires disclosing net income of $1,200 within the operating activities section of the statement of cash flows and a $200 cash dividend in the financing activities section of the statement.

Summary of Key Concepts

Exhibit 14–4 summarizes the four key concepts just discussed. The first key concept is that the statement of cash flows is divided into three sections: operating activities, investing activities, and financing activities. The net cash used or provided by these three types of activities is combined to derive the net increase/decrease in cash and cash equivalents, which explains the change in the cash balance. The second key concept is that the operating activities section of the statement of cash flows can be prepared

EXHIBIT 14–4
Summary of Key Concepts Needed to Prepare a Statement of Cash Flows

Key Concept #1

The statement of cash flows is divided into three sections:

Operating activities
Net cash provided by (used in) operating activities — $xx

Investing activities
Net cash provided by (used in) investing activities — xx

Financing activities
Net cash provided by (used in) financing activities — xx

Net increase/decrease in cash and cash equivalents — xx
Beginning cash and cash equivalents — xx
Ending cash and cash equivalents — $xx

Key Concept #2

U.S. GAAP and IFRS allow two methods for preparing the operating activities section of the statement of cash flows:

Direct Method (Appendix 14A)
Cash receipts from customers — $ xx
Cash paid for inventory purchases — (xx)
Cash paid for selling and administrative expenses — (xx)
Cash paid for income taxes — (xx)
Net cash provided by (used in) operating activities — $ xx

Indirect Method
Net income — $ xx
Various adjustments (+/−) — xx
Net cash provided by (used in) operating activities — $ xx

Key Concept #3

Computing the net cash provided by operating activities using the indirect method is a three step process:

Operating activities
Net income — $xx
Adjustments to convert net income to a cash basis:

Step 1 — Add: Depreciation — xx

Step 2 — Analyze net changes in noncash balance sheet accounts:
Increase in current asset accounts — (xx)
Decrease in current asset accounts — xx
Increase in current liability accounts — xx
Decrease in current liability accounts — (xx)

Step 3 — Adjust for gains/losses:
Gain on sale — (xx)
Loss on sale — xx
Net cash provided by (used in) operating activities — $xx

Key Concept #4

The investing and financing sections of the statement of cash flows must report gross cash flows:

Net cash provided by (used in) operating activities — $xx

Investing activities
Purchase of property, plant, and equipment — (xx)
Sale of property, plant, and equipment — xx
Purchase of long-term investments — (xx)
Sale of long-term investments — xx
Net cash provided by (used in) investing activities — (xx)

Financing activities
Issuance of bonds payable — xx
Repaying principal on bonds payable — (xx)
Issuance of common stock — xx
Purchase own shares of common stock — (xx)
Paying a dividend — (xx)
Net cash provided by (used in) financing activities — xx
Net increase/decrease in cash and cash equivalents — xx
Beginning cash and cash equivalents — xx
Ending cash and cash equivalents — $xx

using the direct or indirect method. The direct method translates sales, cost of goods sold, selling and administrative expenses, and income tax expense to a cash basis. The indirect method begins with accrual-based net income and adjusts it to a cash basis. The third key concept is that the indirect method requires three steps to compute net cash provided by operating activities. The first step is to add back depreciation to net income. The second step is to analyze net changes in noncash balance sheet accounts that impact net income. The third step is to adjust for gains or losses included in the income statement. The fourth key concept is to record gross (rather than net) cash inflows and outflows in the investing and financing activities sections of the statement of cash flows.[5]

An Example of a Statement of Cash Flows

LO14–2

Prepare a statement of cash flows using the indirect method to determine the net cash provided by operating activities.

To illustrate the ideas introduced in the preceding section, we will now construct a statement of cash flows for a merchandising company called Apparel, Inc. The company's income statement and balance sheet are shown in Exhibits 14–5 and 14–6.

Let's also assume the following facts with respect to Apparel, Inc.:

1. The company sold a store that had an original cost of $15 million and accumulated depreciation of $10 million. The cash proceeds from the sale were $8 million. The gain on the sale was $3 million.
2. The company did not issue any new bonds during the year.
3. The company did not repurchase any of its own common stock during the year.
4. The company paid a cash dividend during the year.

Notice that the balance sheet in Exhibit 14–6 includes the amount of the change in each balance sheet account. For example, the beginning and ending balances in Cash and Cash Equivalents are $29 million and $91 million, respectively. This is a $62 million increase in the account balance. A similar computation is performed for all other balance

EXHIBIT 14–5
Apparel, Inc., Income Statement

Apparel, Inc. Income Statement (dollars in millions)	
Sales	$3,638
Cost of goods sold	2,469
Gross margin	1,169
Selling and administrative expenses	941
Net operating income	228
Nonoperating items: Gain on sale of store	3
Income before taxes	231
Income taxes	91
Net income	$ 140

---

[5] This chapter adopts two simplifications related to common stock transactions. First, it always assumes that companies issue no-par value common stock, thus the chapter excludes Additional Paid-In Capital. Second, the chapter assumes that stock repurchases are recorded with a debit to the Common Stock account rather than a debit to the contra-equity account called Treasury Stock.

EXHIBIT 14–6
Apparel, Inc., Balance Sheet

Apparel, Inc.
Comparative Balance Sheet
(dollars in millions)

	Ending Balance	Beginning Balance	Change
Assets			
Current assets:			
Cash and cash equivalents	$ 91	$ 29	+62
Accounts receivable.	637	654	−17
Inventory	586	537	+49
Total current assets.	1,314	1,220	
Property, plant, and equipment	1,517	1,394	+123
Less accumulated depreciation	654	561	+93
Net property, plant, and equipment	863	833	
Total assets	$2,177	$2,053	
Liabilities and Stockholders' Equity			
Current liabilities:			
Accounts payable	$ 264	$ 220	+44
Accrued liabilities	193	190	+3
Income taxes payable	75	71	+4
Total current liabilities	532	481	
Bonds payable	479	520	−41
Total liabilities	1,011	1,001	
Stockholders' equity:			
Common stock	157	155	+2
Retained earnings.	1,009	897	+112
Total stockholders' equity	1,166	1,052	
Total liabilities and stockholders' equity	$2,177	$2,053	

sheet accounts. Study the changes in these account balances because we will be referring to them later. For example, keep in mind that the purpose of Apparel's statement of cash flows is to disclose the operating, investing, and financing cash flows underlying the $62 million increase in Cash and Cash Equivalents shown in Exhibit 14–6. *Also, please be advised that although the changes in account balances are computed for you in Exhibit 14–6, you'll ordinarily need to compute these amounts yourself before attempting to construct the statement of cash flows.*

Operating Activities

This section uses the three-step process explained earlier to construct Apparel's operating activities section of the statement of cash flows.

Step 1   The first step in computing Apparel's net cash provided by operating activities is to *add depreciation* to net income. The balance sheet in Exhibit 14–6 shows Apparel's Accumulated Depreciation account had beginning and ending balances of $561 million and $654 million, respectively. We also know from the assumptions mentioned earlier that Apparel sold a store during the year that had $10 million of accumulated depreciation. Given these facts, we can use the basic equation for contra-assets to determine that Apparel needs to add $103 million of depreciation to its net income:

$$\text{Beginning balance} - \text{Debits} + \text{Credits} = \text{Ending balance}$$

$$\$561 \text{ million} - \$10 \text{ million} + \text{Credits} = \$654 \text{ million}$$

$$\text{Credits} = \$654 \text{ million} - \$561 \text{ million} + \$10 \text{ million}$$

$$\text{Credits} = \$103 \text{ million}$$

Step 2   The second step in computing net cash provided by operating activities is to *analyze net changes in noncash balance sheet accounts* that impact net income. Exhibit 14–7 explains the five adjustments Apparel needs to make to complete this step. For your ease of reference, the top half of Exhibit 14–7 reproduces an excerpt of the general guidelines for completing this step that were previously summarized in Exhibit 14–2. The bottom half of Exhibit 14–7 applies the general guidelines from the top half of the exhibit to Apparel's balance sheet. For example, Exhibit 14–6 shows that Apparel's Accounts Receivable balance decreased by $17 million. The top half of Exhibit 14–7 says that decreases in accounts receivable are added to net income. This explains why the bottom half of Exhibit 14–7 includes a plus sign in front of Apparel's $17 million decrease in Accounts Receivable. Similarly, Exhibit 14–6 shows that Apparel's Inventory balance increased by $49 million. When inventory increases, the amount of the increase is subtracted from net income. This explains why the bottom half of Exhibit 14–7 includes a minus sign in front of Apparel's $49 million increase in Inventory. Similar logic can be used to explain why the increases from Exhibit 14–6 in Accounts Payable (+44), Accrued Liabilities (+3), and Income Taxes Payable (+4) all result in the additions to Apparel's net income that are shown in the bottom half of Exhibit 14–7.

EXHIBIT 14–7
Apparel, Inc.: Analyzing How Net Changes in Noncash Balance Sheet Accounts Affect Net Income on the Statement of Cash Flows

	Increase in Account Balance	Decrease in Account Balance
General Guidelines from Exhibit 14–2		
Current Assets:		
Accounts receivable	Subtract	Add
Inventory	Subtract	Add
Current Liabilities:		
Accounts payable	Add	Subtract
Accrued liabilities	Add	Subtract
Income taxes payable	Add	Subtract
	Increase in Account Balance	Decrease in Account Balance
Apparel's Account Analysis		
Current Assets:		
Accounts receivable		+17
Inventory	–49	
Current Liabilities:		
Accounts payable	+44	
Accrued liabilities	+3	
Income taxes payable	+4	

Step 3   The third step in computing the net cash provided by operating activities is to *adjust for gains/losses* included in the income statement. Apparel reported a $3 million gain on its income statement in Exhibit 14–5; therefore, this amount needs to be subtracted from net income. Subtracting the gain on sale removes the gain from the operating activities section of the statement of cash flows. The entire amount of the cash proceeds related to this sale will be recorded in the investing activities section of the statement.

Exhibit 14–8 shows the operating activities section of Apparel's statement of cash flows. Take a moment to trace each of the numbers that we just computed to this exhibit. The total amount of the adjustments to net income is $119 million, which results in net cash provided by operating activities of $259 million.

	Apparel, Inc. (dollars in millions)		
	Operating Activities		
	Net income		$140
	Adjustments to convert net income to a cash basis:		
Step 1 ⟶	Depreciation	103	
	Decrease in accounts receivable	17	
	Increase in inventory	(49)	
Step 2 ⟶	Increase in accounts payable	44	
	Increase in accrued liabilities	3	
	Increase in income taxes payable	4	
Step 3 ⟶	Gain on sale of store	(3)	119
	Net cash provided by (used in) operating activities .		$259

EXHIBIT 14–8
Apparel, Inc.: Operating Activities Section of the Statement of Cash Flows

Investing Activities

Apparel's investing cash flows pertain to its Property, Plant, and Equipment account, which according to Exhibit 14–6 had beginning and ending balances of $1,394 million and $1,517 million, respectively, for an increase of $123 million. This increase suggests that Apparel purchased equipment; however, it does not capture the gross cash flows that need to be reported in the statement of cash flows.

The previously defined assumptions say that Apparel sold a store that had an original cost of $15 million for $8 million in cash. The cash inflow from this sale needs to be recorded in the investing activities section of the statement of cash flows. To compute the cash outflows related to purchases of property, plant, and equipment we use the basic equation for assets that was mentioned in the beginning of the chapter:

$$\text{Beginning balance} + \text{Debits} - \text{Credits} = \text{Ending balance}$$

$$\$1{,}394 \text{ million} + \text{Debits} - \$15 \text{ million} = \$1{,}517 \text{ million}$$

$$\text{Debits} = \$1{,}517 \text{ million} - \$1{,}394 \text{ million} + \$15 \text{ million}$$

$$\text{Debits} = \$138 \text{ million}$$

Notice the credits in the equation above include the original cost of the store that was sold. When the cash outflows of $138 million for purchases of property, plant, and equipment are combined with the $8 million of cash proceeds from the sale of the store, Apparel's net cash used in investing activities is $130 million.

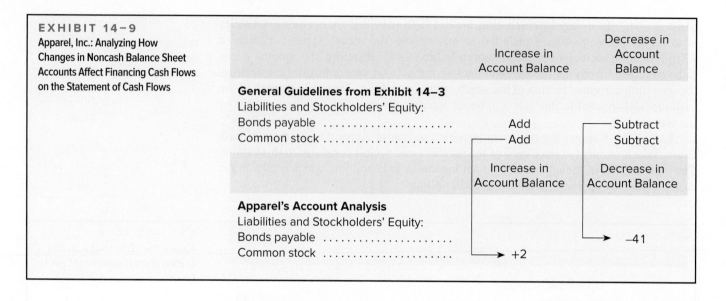

EXHIBIT 14–9
Apparel, Inc.: Analyzing How Changes in Noncash Balance Sheet Accounts Affect Financing Cash Flows on the Statement of Cash Flows

Financing Activities

Exhibit 14–9 explains how to compute Apparel's financing cash flows related to its Bonds Payable and Common Stock balance sheet accounts. The top half of the exhibit reproduces an excerpt of the general guidelines for analyzing financing cash flows that was previously summarized in Exhibit 14–3. The bottom half of Exhibit 14–9 applies the general guidelines from the top half of the exhibit to these two accounts from Apparel's balance sheet. We will analyze each account in turn.

Exhibit 14–6 shows that Apparel's Bonds Payable balance decreased by $41 million. Because, as stated earlier, Apparel did not issue any bonds during the year, we can conclude that the $41 million decrease in the account is due solely to retiring bonds payable. The top half of Exhibit 14–9 says that a decrease in Bonds Payable signals the need to subtract cash outflows in the investing activities section of the statement of cash flows. This explains why the bottom half of the exhibit includes a minus sign in front of Apparel's $41 million decrease in Bonds Payable. Similarly, Exhibit 14–6 shows that Apparel's Common Stock balance increased by $2 million. Because, as stated earlier, Apparel did not repurchase any of its own stock during the year, we can conclude that the $2 million increase in the account is due solely to issuing common stock. The top half of Exhibit 14–9 says that increases in common stock signal the need to add cash inflows in the investing activities section of the statement of cash flows. This explains why the bottom half of the exhibit includes a plus sign in front of Apparel's $2 million increase in Common Stock.

The final financing cash outflow for Apparel is its dividend payment to common stockholders. The dividend payment can be computed using the basic equation for stockholders' equity accounts mentioned at the beginning of the chapter:

$$\text{Beginning balance} - \text{Debits} + \text{Credits} = \text{Ending balance}$$
$$\$897 \text{ million} - \text{Debits} + \$140 \text{ million} = \$1{,}009 \text{ million}$$
$$\$1{,}037 \text{ million} = \$1{,}009 \text{ million} + \text{Debits}$$
$$\text{Debits} = \$28 \text{ million}$$

When the cash outflows of $69 million (= $41 million + $28 million) are combined with the cash inflows of $2 million, Apparel's net cash used in financing activities is $67 million.

Exhibit 14–10 shows Apparel's statement of cash flows. The operating activities section of this statement is carried over from Exhibit 14–8. Take a moment to trace the investing

EXHIBIT 14–10
Apparel, Inc. Statement of Cash Flows

Apparel, Inc.
Statement of Cash Flows—Indirect Method
(dollars in millions)

Operating Activities

Net income.		$140
Adjustments to convert net income to a cash basis:		
Depreciation.	103	
Decrease in accounts receivable.	17	
Increase in inventory	(49)	
Increase in accounts payable.	44	
Increase in accrued liabilities.	3	
Increase in income taxes payable	4	
Gain on sale of store.	(3)	119
Net cash provided by (used in) operating activities		259

Investing Activities

Additions to property, plant, and equipment	(138)	
Proceeds from sale of store	8	
Net cash provided by (used in) investing activities		(130)

Financing Activities

Retirement of bonds payable	(41)	
Issuance of common stock	2	
Cash dividends paid.	(28)	
Net cash provided by (used in) financing activities		(67)
Net increase in cash and cash equivalents.		62
Beginning cash and cash equivalents.		29
Ending cash and cash equivalents.		$ 91

and financing cash flows just discussed to Exhibit 14–10. Notice that the net change in cash and cash equivalents ($62 million) is calculated using the following equation:

$$\begin{array}{l} \text{Net change in} \\ \text{cash and cash} \\ \text{equivalents} \end{array} = \begin{array}{l} \text{Net cash provided} \\ \text{by (used in)} \\ \text{operating activities} \end{array} + \begin{array}{l} \text{Net cash provided} \\ \text{by (used in)} \\ \text{investing activities} \end{array} + \begin{array}{l} \text{Net cash provided} \\ \text{by (used in)} \\ \text{financing activities} \end{array}$$

$$\begin{array}{l} \text{Net change in} \\ \text{cash and cash} \\ \text{equivalents} \end{array} = \$259 \text{ million} + \$(130) \text{ million} + \$(67) \text{ million}$$

$$\begin{array}{l} \text{Net change in} \\ \text{cash and cash} \\ \text{equivalents} \end{array} = \$62 \text{ million}$$

This amount agrees with the $62 million change in the Cash and Cash Equivalents account shown on the balance sheet in Exhibit 14–6.

Seeing the Big Picture

In the beginning of the chapter, we mentioned that a statement of cash flows is prepared by analyzing the changes in noncash balance sheet accounts. We then presented a method of preparing a statement of cash flows. This method simplified the process of creating the statement of cash flows, and now we will show that it is equivalent to analyzing the changes in noncash balance sheet accounts.

Exhibit 14–11 uses T-accounts to summarize how the changes in Apparel, Inc.'s noncash balance sheet accounts quantify the cash inflows and outflows that explain the change in its cash balance. The top portion of the exhibit is Apparel's Cash T-account and the bottom portion provides T-accounts for the company's remaining balance sheet accounts. Notice that the net cash provided by operating activities of $259 million and the net increase in cash and cash equivalents of $62 million shown in the Cash T-account agree with the corresponding figures in the statement of cash flows shown in Exhibit 14–10.

We will explain Exhibit 14–11 in five steps. Entry (1) records Apparel's net income of $140 million in the credit side of the Retained Earnings account and the debit side of the Cash account. The net income of $140 million shown in the Cash T-account will be adjusted until it reflects the $62 million net increase in cash and cash equivalents. Entry (2) adds the depreciation of $103 million to net income. Entries (3) through (7) adjust net income for the changes in the current asset and current liability accounts. Entries (8) through (11) summarize the cash outflows and inflows related to the additions to

---

EXHIBIT 14–11

T-Accounts after Posting of Account
Changes—Apparel, Inc. (in millions)

Cash

Net income	(1)	140	49	(4)	Increase in inventory	
Depreciation	(2)	103	3	(12)	Gain on sale of store	
Decrease in accounts receivable	(3)	17				
Increase in accounts payable	(5)	44				
Increase in accrued liabilities	(6)	3				
Increase in income taxes payable	(7)	4				
Net cash provided by operating activities		259				
Proceeds from sale of store	(12)	8	138	(8)	Additions to property, plant, and equipment	
Increase in common stock	(11)	2	41	(9)	Decrease in bonds payable	
			28	(10)	Cash dividends paid	
Net increase in cash and cash equivalents		62				

Accounts Receivable

Bal.	654			
		17	(3)	
Bal.	637			

Inventory

Bal.	537			
(4)	49			
Bal.	586			

Property, Plant, and Equipment

Bal.	1,394			
(8)	138	15	(12)	
Bal.	1,517			

Accumulated Depreciation

		561	Bal.	
(12)	10	103	(2)	
		654	Bal.	

Accounts Payable

	220	Bal.	
	44	(5)	
	264	Bal.	

Accrued Liabilities

	190	Bal.	
	3	(6)	
	193	Bal.	

Income Taxes Payable

	71	Bal.	
	4	(7)	
	75	Bal.	

Bonds Payable

		520	Bal.
(9)	41		
		479	Bal.

Common Stock

		155	Bal.
		2	(11)
		157	Bal.

Retained Earnings

		897	Bal.
(10)	28	140	(1)
		1,009	Bal.

property, plant, and equipment, the retirement of bonds payable, the payment of the cash dividend, and the issuance of common stock. Entry (12) records the sale of the store. Notice that the gain on the sale of $3 million is recorded in the credit side of the Cash T-account. This is equivalent to subtracting the gain from net income so that the entire amount of the cash proceeds from the sale of $8 million can be recorded in the investing activities section of the statement of cash flows.

IN BUSINESS

FOUR SEASONS HOTELS STRUGGLE TO MANAGE THEIR DEBT

When the **Four Seasons Maui**'s occupancy rate fell from 79% to 60%, its net cash flow plummeted to $10.9 million in the first three quarters of the year. The hotel's owner was unable to make its annual debt payment of $23.6 million, so it worked with lenders to restructure the terms of their loan agreement. Other Four Seasons hotels faced similar problems. For example, the **Four Seasons San Francisco** teetered on the brink of foreclosure until its owner brought in a new co-owner called **Westbrook Partners LLC** to pay $35 million of its $90 million mortgage. Similarly, the owner of the **Four Seasons Dallas** faced a cash shortage that forced it to restructure the terms of its $183 million mortgage.

Source: Kris Hudson, "Four Seasons Maui on Ropes," *The Wall Street Journal*, March 22, 2010, p. B2.

Interpreting the Statement of Cash Flows

Managers can derive many useful insights by studying the statement of cash flows. In this section, we will discuss two guidelines managers should use when interpreting the statement of cash flows.

Consider a Company's Specific Circumstances

A statement of cash flows should be evaluated in the context of a company's specific circumstances. To illustrate this point, let's consider two examples related to start-up companies and companies with growing versus declining sales. Start-up companies usually are unable to generate positive cash flows from operations; therefore, they rely on issuing stock and taking out loans to fund investing activities. This means that start-up companies often have negative net cash provided by operating activities and large spikes in net cash used for investing activities and net cash provided by financing activities. However, as a start-up company matures, it should begin generating enough cash to sustain day-to-day operations and maintain its plant and equipment without issuing additional stock or borrowing money. This means the net cash provided by operating activities should swing from a negative to a positive number. The net cash used for investing activities should decline somewhat and stabilize and the net cash provided by financing activities should decrease.

A company with growing sales would understandably have an increase in its accounts receivable, inventory, and accounts payable balances. On the other hand, if a company with declining sales has increases in these account balances, it could signal trouble. Perhaps accounts receivable is increasing because the company is attempting to boost sales by selling to customers who can't pay their bills. Perhaps the increase in inventory suggests the company is stuck with large amounts of obsolete inventory. Accounts payable may be increasing because the company is deferring payments to suppliers in an effort to inflate its net cash provided by operating activities. Notice that the plausible interpretations of these changes in account balances depend on the company's circumstances.

Consider the Relationships among Numbers

While each number in a statement of cash flows provides useful information, managers derive the most meaningful insights by examining the relationships among numbers.

For example, some managers study their company's trends in cash flow margins by comparing the net cash provided by operating activities to sales. The goal is to continuously increase the operating cash flows earned per sales dollar. If we refer back to Apparel's income statement in Exhibit 14–5 and its statement of cash flows in Exhibit 14–10, we can determine that its cash flow margin is about $0.07 per dollar of sales (= $259 ÷ $3,638). Managers also compare the net cash provided by operating activities to the ending balance of current liabilities. If the net cash provided by operating activities is greater than (less than) the current liabilities, it indicates the company did (did not) generate enough operating cash flow to pay its bills at the end of the period. Apparel's net cash provided by operating activities of $259 million (see Exhibit 14–10) was not enough to pay its year-end current liabilities of $532 million (see Exhibit 14–6).

As a third example, managers compare the additions to property, plant, and equipment in the investing activities section of the statement of cash flows to the depreciation included in the operating activities section of the statement. If the additions to property, plant, and equipment are consistently less than depreciation, it suggests the company is not investing enough money to maintain its noncurrent assets. If we refer back to Apparel's statement of cash flows in Exhibit 14–10, its additions to property, plant, and equipment ($138 million) are greater than its depreciation ($103 million). This suggests that Apparel is investing more than enough money to maintain its noncurrent assets.

LO14–3
Compute free cash flow.

Free Cash Flow   *Free cash flow* is a measure used by managers to look at the relationship among three numbers from the statement of cash flows—net cash provided by operating activities, additions to property, plant, and equipment (also called capital expenditures), and dividends. **Free cash flow** measures a company's ability to fund its capital expenditures for property, plant, and equipment and its cash dividends from its net cash provided by operating activities.[6] The equation for computing free cash flow is as follows:

$$\text{Free cash flow} = \begin{array}{c} \text{Net cash provided} \\ \text{by operating} \\ \text{activities} \end{array} - \text{Capital expenditures} - \text{Dividends}$$

Using this equation and the statement of cash flows shown in Exhibit 14–10, we can compute Apparel's free cash flow (in millions) as follows:

$$\text{Free cash flow} = \$259 - \$138 - \$28$$
$$= \$93$$

The interpretation of free cash flow is straightforward. A positive number indicates that the company generated enough cash flow from its operating activities to fund its capital expenditures and dividend payments. A negative number suggests that the company needed to obtain cash from other sources, such as borrowing money from lenders or issuing shares of common stock, to fund its investments in property, plant,

---

[6] For a summary of alternative definitions of free cash flow, see John Mills, Lynn Bible, and Richard Mason, "Defining Free Cash Flow," *CPA Journal,* January 2002, pp. 36–42.

and equipment and its dividend payments. Negative free cash flow does not automatically signal poor performance. As previously discussed, a new company with enormous growth prospects would be expected to have negative free cash flow during its start-up phase. However, even new companies will eventually need to generate positive free cash flow to survive.

Earnings Quality Managers and investors often look at the relationship between net income and net cash provided by operating activities to help assess the extent to which a company's earnings truly reflects operational performance. Managers generally perceive that earnings are of higher quality, or more indicative of operational performance, when the earnings (1) are not unduly influenced by inflation, (2) are computed using conservative accounting principles and estimates, and (3) are correlated with net cash provided by operating activities. When a company's net income and net cash provided by operating activities move in tandem with one another (in other words, are correlated with one another), it suggests that earnings result from changes in sales and operating expenses. Conversely, if a company's net income is steadily increasing and its net cash provided by operating activities is declining, it suggests that net income is being influenced by factors unrelated to operational performance, such as nonrecurring transactions or aggressive accounting principles and estimates.

PANERA INCREASES ITS STOCK BUYBACK

Panera Bread Company announced plans to spend $750 million to repurchase shares of its own stock. The company intends to take on $500 million in new debt and it plans to sell 73 of its 925 company-owned stores to fund the stock repurchase. When Panera's plans were made public its stock price jumped 12% to $182.89. The company also plans to bolster its financial performance by taking steps to grow sales outside the lunch hour and by implementing operational efficiencies that reduce food preparation time and the length of the lines at its checkout counters.

© Helen Sessions/Alamy

Source: Ilan Brat, "Panera to Expand Buyback and Sell Some Stores," *The Wall Street Journal*, April 17, 2015, p. B3.

Summary

The statement of cash flows is one of three major financial statements prepared by organizations. It explains how cash was generated and how it was used during a period. The statement of cash flows is widely used as a tool for assessing the financial health of organizations.

For external reporting purposes, the statement of cash flows must be organized in terms of operating, investing, and financing activities. The net cash provided by operating activities is an important measure because it indicates how successful a company is in generating cash on a continuing basis. The indirect method of computing the net cash provided by operating activities is a three-step process. The first step is to add depreciation to net income. The second step is to analyze net changes in noncash balance sheet accounts that impact net income. The third step is to adjust for gains or losses included in the income statement.

The investing and financing sections of the statement of cash flows must report gross cash flows. The statement of cash flows summarizes the net increase/decrease in cash and cash equivalents during the period, which explains the change in the cash balance.

Review Problem

Rockford Company's comparative balance sheets for this year and last year and the company's income statement for this year follow:

Rockford Company
Comparative Balance Sheet
(dollars in millions)

	This Year	Last Year
Assets		
Current assets:		
Cash and cash equivalents	$ 26	$ 10
Accounts receivable	180	270
Inventory	205	160
Prepaid expenses	17	20
Total current assets	428	460
Property, plant, and equipment	430	309
Less accumulated depreciation	218	194
Net property, plant, and equipment	212	115
Long-term investments	60	75
Total assets	$700	$650
Liabilities and Stockholders' Equity		
Current liabilities:		
Accounts payable	$230	$310
Accrued liabilities	70	60
Income taxes payable	15	8
Total current liabilities	315	378
Bonds payable	135	40
Total liabilities	450	418
Stockholders' equity:		
Common stock	140	140
Retained earnings	110	92
Total stockholders' equity	250	232
Total liabilities and stockholders' equity	$700	$650

Rockford Company
Income Statement
For This Year Ended December 31
(dollars in millions)

Sales	$1,000
Cost of goods sold	530
Gross margin	470
Selling and administrative expenses	352
Net operating income	118
Nonoperating items:	
Loss on sale of equipment	4
Income before taxes	114
Income taxes	48
Net income	$ 66

Additional data:
1. This year Rockford paid a cash dividend.
2. The $4 million loss on sale of equipment reflects a transaction in which equipment with an original cost of $12 million and accumulated depreciation of $5 million was sold for $3 million in cash.
3. Rockford did not purchase any long-term investments during the year. There was no gain or loss on the sale of long-term investments.
4. This year Rockford did not retire any bonds payable, or issue or repurchase any common stock.

Required:
1. Using the indirect method, determine the net cash provided by operating activities for this year.
2. Construct a statement of cash flows for this year.

Solution to Review Problem
The first task you should complete before turning your attention to the problem's specific requirements is to compute the changes in each balance sheet account as shown below (all amounts are in millions):

Rockford Company
Comparative Balance Sheet
(dollars in millions)

	This Year	Last Year	Change
Assets			
Current assets:			
Cash and cash equivalents	$ 26	$ 10	+16
Accounts receivable	180	270	−90
Inventory	205	160	+45
Prepaid expenses	17	20	−3
Total current assets	428	460	
Property, plant, and equipment	430	309	+121
Less accumulated depreciation	218	194	+24
Net property, plant, and equipment	212	115	
Long-term investments	60	75	−15
Total assets	$700	$650	
Liabilities and Stockholders' Equity			
Current liabilities:			
Accounts payable	$230	$310	−80
Accrued liabilities	70	60	+10
Income taxes payable	15	8	+7
Total current liabilities	315	378	
Bonds payable	135	40	+95
Total liabilities	450	418	
Stockholders' equity:			
Common stock	140	140	+0
Retained earnings	110	92	+18
Total stockholders' equity	250	232	
Total liabilities and stockholders' equity	$700	$650	

Requirement 1:
You should perform three steps to compute the net cash provided by operating activities.

Step 1: Add depreciation to net income.
To complete this step, apply the following equation:

$$\text{Beginning balance} - \text{Debits} + \text{Credits} = \text{Ending balance}$$

$194 \text{ million} - \$5 \text{ million} + \text{Credits} = \$218 \text{ million}$

$\text{Credits} = \$218 \text{ million} - \$194 \text{ million} + \$5 \text{ million}$

$\text{Credits} = \$29 \text{ million}$

Step 2: Analyze net changes in noncash balance sheet accounts that affect net income.
        To complete this step, apply the logic from Exhibit 14–2 as follows:

	Increase in Account Balance	Decrease in Account Balance
Current Assets:		
Accounts receivable		+90
Inventory	−45	
Prepaid expenses		+3
Current Liabilities:		
Accounts payable		−80
Accrued liabilities	+10	
Income taxes payable	+7	

Step 3: Adjust for gains/losses included in the income statement.
        Rockford's $4 million loss on the sale of equipment must be added to net income.

Having completed these three steps, the operating activities section of the statement of cash flows would appear as follows:

Rockford Company
Statement of Cash Flows—Indirect Method
For This Year Ended December 31
(dollars in millions)

Operating Activities		
Net income		$66
Adjustments to convert net income to a cash basis:		
Depreciation	$29	
Decrease in accounts receivable	90	
Increase in inventory	(45)	
Decrease in prepaid expenses	3	
Decrease in accounts payable	(80)	
Increase in accrued liabilities	10	
Increase in income taxes payable	7	
Loss on sale of equipment	4	18
Net cash provided by (used in) operating activities		$84

Requirement 2:
To finalize the statement of cash flows, we must complete the investing and financing sections of the statement. This requires analyzing the Property, Plant, and Equipment, Long-Term Investments, Bonds Payable, Common Stock, and Retained Earnings accounts. The table below is based on Exhibit 14–3 and it captures the changes in four account balances for Rockford.

	Increase in Account Balance	Decrease in Account Balance
Noncurrent Assets (Investing activities)		
Property, plant, and equipment	−121	
Long-term investments		+15
Liabilities and Stockholders' Equity		
(Financing activities)		
Bonds payable	+95	
Common stock	No change	No change
Retained earnings	*	*

*Requires further analysis to quantify cash dividends paid.

        The data at the beginning of the problem state that Rockford did not purchase any long-term investments during the year and that there was no gain or loss on the sale of long-term investments. This means that the $15 million decrease in Long-Term Investments corresponds with a $15 million cash inflow from the sale of long-term investments that is recorded in the investing section of the statement of cash flows. The data also state that Rockford did not retire any bonds payable during the year; therefore, the $95 million increase in Bonds Payable must be due to issuing bonds payable. This cash inflow is recorded in the financing section of the statement of cash flows.

The Common Stock account had no activity during the period, so it does not impact the statement of cash flows. This leaves two accounts that require further analysis—Property, Plant, and Equipment and Retained Earnings.

The company sold equipment that had an original cost of $12 million for $3 million in cash. The cash proceeds from the sale need to be recorded in the investing activities section of the statement of cash flows. The cash outflows related to Rockford's investing activities can be computed using the following equation:

$$\text{Beginning balance} + \text{Debits} - \text{Credits} = \text{Ending balance}$$
$$\$309 \text{ million} + \text{Debits} - \$12 \text{ million} = \$430 \text{ million}$$
$$\text{Debits} = \$430 \text{ million} - \$309 \text{ million} + \$12 \text{ million}$$
$$\text{Debits} = \$133 \text{ million}$$

Rockford's Retained Earnings account and the basic equation for stockholders' equity can be used to compute the company's dividend payment as follows:

$$\text{Beginning balance} - \text{Debits} + \text{Credits} = \text{Ending balance}$$
$$\$92 \text{ million} - \text{Debits} + \$66 \text{ million} = \$110 \text{ million}$$
$$\$158 \text{ million} = \$110 \text{ million} + \text{Debits}$$
$$\text{Debits} = \$48 \text{ million}$$

The company's complete statement of cash flows is shown below. Notice that the net increase in cash and cash equivalents of $16 million equals the change in the Cash and Cash Equivalents account balance.

Rockford Company		
Statement of Cash Flows—Indirect Method		
For This Year Ended December 31		
(dollars in millions)		
Operating Activities		
Net income		$ 66
Adjustments to convert net income to a cash basis:		
Depreciation	$ 29	
Decrease in accounts receivable	90	
Increase in inventory	(45)	
Decrease in prepaid expenses	3	
Decrease in accounts payable	(80)	
Increase in accrued liabilities	10	
Increase in income taxes payable	7	
Loss on sale of equipment	4	18
Net cash provided by (used in) operating activities		84
Investing Activities		
Additions to property, plant, and equipment	(133)	
Proceeds from sale of long-term investments	15	
Proceeds from sale of equipment	3	
Net cash provided by (used in) investing activities		(115)
Financing Activities		
Issuance of bonds	95	
Cash dividends paid	(48)	
Net cash provided by (used in) financing activities		47
Net increase in cash and cash equivalents		16
Beginning cash and cash equivalents		10
Ending cash and cash equivalents		$ 26

Glossary

Cash equivalents Short-term, highly liquid investments such as Treasury bills, commercial paper, and money market funds, that are made solely for the purpose of generating a return on temporarily idle funds. (p. 686)

Direct method A method of computing the net cash provided by operating activities in which the income statement is reconstructed on a cash basis from top to bottom. (p. 687)

Financing activities These activities generate cash inflows and outflows related to borrowing from and repaying principal to creditors and completing transactions with the company's owners, such as selling or repurchasing shares of common stock and paying dividends. (p. 687)

Free cash flow A measure that assesses a company's ability to fund its capital expenditures and dividends from its net cash provided by operating activities. (p. 702)

Indirect method A method of computing the net cash provided by operating activities that starts with net income and adjusts it to a cash basis. (p. 687)

Investing activities These activities generate cash inflows and outflows related to acquiring or disposing of noncurrent assets such as property, plant, and equipment, long-term investments, and loans to another entity. (p. 687)

Net cash provided by operating activities The net result of the cash inflows and outflows arising from day-to-day operations. (p. 687)

Operating activities These activities generate cash inflows and outflows related to revenue and expense transactions that affect net income. (p. 686)

Statement of cash flows A financial statement that highlights the major activities that impact cash flows and, hence, affect the overall cash balance. (p. 685)

Questions

14–1   What is the purpose of a statement of cash flows?

14–2   What are *cash equivalents,* and why are they included with cash on a statement of cash flows?

14–3   What are the three major sections on a statement of cash flows, and what type of cash inflows and outflows should be included in each section?

14–4   What general guidelines can you provide for interpreting the statement of cash flows?

14–5   If an asset is sold at a gain, why is the gain subtracted from net income when computing the net cash provided by operating activities under the indirect method?

14–6   Why aren't transactions involving accounts payable considered to be financing activities?

14–7   Assume that a company repays a $300,000 loan from its bank and then later in the same year borrows $500,000. What amount(s) would appear on the statement of cash flows?

14–8   How do the direct and the indirect methods differ in their approach to computing the net cash provided by operating activities?

14–9   A business executive once stated, "Depreciation is one of our biggest operating cash inflows." Do you agree? Explain.

14–10 If the Accounts Receivable balance increases during a period, how will this increase be recognized using the indirect method of computing the net cash provided by operating activities?

14–11 Would a sale of equipment for cash be considered a financing activity or an investing activity? Why?

14–12 What is the difference between net cash provided by operating activities and free cash flow?

The Foundational 15   connect

LO14–1, LO14–2

Ravenna Company is a merchandiser that uses the indirect method to prepare the operating activities section of its statement of cash flows. Its balance sheet for this year is as follows:

	Ending Balance	Beginning Balance
Cash and cash equivalents	$ 48,000	$ 57,000
Accounts receivale	41,000	44,000
Inventory	55,000	50,000
Total current assets	144,000	151,000
Property, plant, and equipment	150,000	140,000
Less accumulated depreciation	50,000	35,000
Net property, plant, and equipment	100,000	105,000
Total assets	$244,000	$256,000
Accounts payable	$ 32,000	$ 57,000
Income taxes payable	25,000	28,000
Bonds payable	60,000	50,000
Common stock	70,000	60,000
Retained earnings	57,000	61,000
Total liabilities and stockholders' equity	$244,000	$256,000

During the year, Ravenna paid a $6,000 cash dividend and it sold a piece of equipment for $3,000 that had originally cost $6,000 and had accumulated depreciation of $4,000. The company did not retire any bonds or repurchase any of its own common stock during the year.

Required:
1. What is the amount of the net increase or decrease in cash and cash equivalents that would be shown on the company's statement of cash flows?
2. What net income would the company include on its statement of cash flows?
3. How much depreciation would the company add to net income on its statement of cash flows?
4. (To help answer this question, create an Accounts Receivable T-account and insert the beginning and ending balances.) If the company debited Accounts Receivable and credited Sales for $600,000 during the year, what is the total amount of credits recorded in Accounts Receivable during the year? What does the amount of these credits represent?
5. What is the amount and direction (+ or −) of the accounts receivable adjustment to net income in the operating activities section of the statement of cash flows? What does this adjustment represent?
6. (To help answer this question, create T-accounts for Inventory and Accounts Payable and insert their beginning and ending balances.) If the company debited Cost of Goods Sold and credited Inventory for $400,000 during the year, what is the total amount of inventory purchases recorded on the debit side of the Inventory T-account and the credit side of the Accounts Payable T-account? What is the total amount of the debits recorded in the Accounts Payable T-account during the year? What does the amount of these debits represent?
7. What is the combined amount and direction (+ or −) of the inventory and accounts payable adjustments to net income in the operating activities section of the statement of cash flows? What does this amount represent?
8. (To help answer this question, create an Income Taxes Payable T-account and insert the beginning and ending balances.) If the company debited Income Tax Expense and credited Income Taxes Payable $700 during the year, what is the total amount of the debits recorded in the Income Taxes Payable account? What does the amount of these debits represent?
9. What is the amount and direction (+ or −) of the income taxes payable adjustment to net income in the operating activities section of the statement of cash flows? What does this adjustment represent?
10. Would the operating activities section of the company's statement of cash flows contain an adjustment for a gain or a loss? What would be the amount and direction (+ or −) of the adjustment?
11. What is the amount of net cash provided by operating activities in the company's statement of cash flows?
12. What is the amount of gross cash outflows reported in the investing section of the company's statement of cash flows?
13. What is the company's net cash provided by (used in) investing activities?

14. What is the amount of gross cash inflows reported in the financing section of the company's statement of cash flows?
15. What is the company's net cash provided by (used in) financing activities?

Exercises   connect

EXERCISE 14–1 Classifying Transactions LO14–1

Below are certain events that took place at Hazzard, Inc., last year:

a. Collected cash from customers.
b. Paid cash to repurchase its own stock.
c. Borrowed money from a creditor.
d. Paid suppliers for inventory purchases.
e. Repaid the principal amount of a debt.
f. Paid interest to lenders.
g. Paid a cash dividend to stockholders.
h. Sold common stock.
i. Loaned money to another entity.
j. Paid taxes to the government.
k. Paid wages and salaries to employees.
l. Purchased equipment with cash.
m. Paid bills to insurers and utility providers.

Required:

Prepare an answer sheet with the following headings:

	Activity		
Transaction	Operating	Investing	Financing
a.			
b.			
Etc.			

Enter the cash inflows and outflows above on your answer sheet and indicate how each of them would be classified on a statement of cash flows. Place an X in the Operating, Investing, or Financing column as appropriate.

EXERCISE 14–2 Net Cash Provided by Operating Activities LO14–2

For the just completed year, Hanna Company had net income of $35,000. Balances in the company's current asset and current liability accounts at the beginning and end of the year were as follows:

| | December 31 ||
	End of Year	Beginning of Year
Current assets:		
Cash and cash equivalents	$30,000	$40,000
Accounts receivable	$125,000	$106,000
Inventory	$213,000	$180,000
Prepaid expenses	$6,000	$7,000
Current liabilities:		
Accounts payable	$210,000	$195,000
Accrued liabilities	$4,000	$6,000
Income taxes payable	$34,000	$30,000

The Accumulated Depreciation account had total credits of $20,000 during the year. Hanna Company did not record any gains or losses during the year.

Required:

Using the indirect method, determine the net cash provided by operating activities for the year.

EXERCISE 14–3 Calculating Free Cash Flow LO14–3

Apex Company prepared the statement of cash flows for the current year that is shown below:

Apex Company Statement of Cash Flows—Indirect Method		
Operating activities		
Net income		$ 40,000
Adjustments to convert net income to cash basis:		
Depreciation	$ 22,000	
Increase in accounts receivable	(60,000)	
Increase in inventory	(25,000)	
Decrease in prepaid expenses	9,000	
Increase in accounts payable	55,000	
Decrease in accrued liabilities	(12,000)	
Increase in income taxes payable	5,000	(6,000)
Net cash provided by (used in) operating activities		34,000
Investing activities		
Proceeds from the sale of equipment	14,000	
Loan to Thomas Company	(40,000)	
Additions to plant and equipment	(110,000)	
Net cash provided by (used in) investing activities		(136,000)
Financing activities		
Increase in bonds payable	90,000	
Increase in common stock	40,000	
Cash dividends	(30,000)	
Net cash provided by (used in) financing activities		100,000
Net decrease in cash and cash equivalents		(2,000)
Beginning cash and cash equivalents		27,000
Ending cash and cash equivalents		$ 25,000

Required:

Compute Apex Company's free cash flow for the current year.

EXERCISE 14–4 Prepare a Statement of Cash Flows LO14–1, LO14–2

The following changes took place last year in Pavolik Company's balance sheet accounts:

Asset and Contra-Asset Accounts			Liabilities and Stockholders' Equity Accounts		
Cash and cash equivalents	$5	D	Accounts payable	$35	I
Accounts receivable	$110	I	Accrued liabilities	$4	D
Inventory	$70	D	Income taxes payable	$8	I
Prepaid expenses	$9	I	Bonds payable	$150	I
Long-term investments	$6	D	Common stock	$80	D
Property, plant, and equipment ...	$185	I	Retained earnings	$54	I
Accumulated depreciation	$60	I			

D = Decrease; I = Increase

Long-term investments that cost the company $6 were sold during the year for $16 and land that cost $15 was sold for $9. In addition, the company declared and paid $30 in cash dividends during the year. Besides the sale of land, no other sales or retirements of plant and equipment took place during the year. Pavolik did not retire any bonds during the year or issue any new common stock.

The company's income statement for the year follows:

Sales	$700
Cost of goods sold	400
Gross margin	300
Selling and administrative expenses	184
Net operating income	116
Nonoperating items:	
Loss on sale of land .... $(6)	
Gain on sale of investments 10	4
Income before taxes	120
Income taxes	36
Net income	$ 84

The company's beginning cash balance was $90 and its ending balance was $85.

Required:
1. Use the indirect method to determine the net cash provided by operating activities for the year.
2. Prepare a statement of cash flows for the year.

EXERCISE 14–5 Net Cash Provided by Operating Activities LO14–2

Changes in various accounts and gains and losses on the sale of assets during the year for Argon Company are given below:

Item	Amount
Accounts receivable.................	$90,000 decrease
Inventory...........................	$120,000 increase
Prepaid expenses....................	$3,000 decrease
Accounts payable	$65,000 decrease
Accrued liabilities	$8,000 increase
Income taxes payable................	$12,000 increase
Sale of equipment...................	$7,000 gain
Sale of long-term investments	$10,000 loss

Required:
Prepare an answer sheet using the following column headings:

Item	Amount	Add	Subtract

For each item, place an X in the Add or Subtract column to indicate whether the dollar amount should be added to or subtracted from net income under the indirect method when computing the net cash provided by operating activities for the year.

EXERCISE 14–6 Prepare a Statement of Cash Flows; Free Cash Flow LO14–1, LO14–2, LO14–3

Comparative financial statement data for Carmono Company follow:

	This Year	Last Year
Assets		
Cash and cash equivalents	$ 3	$ 6
Accounts receivable	22	24
Inventory	50	40
Total current assets	75	70
Property, plant, and equipment	240	200
Less accumulated depreciation	65	50
Net property, plant, and equipment	175	150
Total assets	$250	$220
Liabilities and Stockholders' Equity		
Accounts payable	$ 40	$ 36
Common stock	150	145
Retained earnings	60	39
Total liabilities and stockholders' equity	$250	$220

For this year, the company reported net income as follows:

Sales	$275
Cost of goods sold	150
Gross margin	125
Selling and administrative expenses	90
Net income	$ 35

This year Carmono declared and paid a cash dividend. There were no sales of property, plant, and equipment during this year. The company did not repurchase any of its own stock this year.

Required:
1. Using the indirect method, prepare a statement of cash flows for this year.
2. Compute Carmono's free cash flow for this year.

Problems

PROBLEM 14–7 Prepare a Statement of Cash Flows LO14–1, LO14–2
Comparative financial statements for Weaver Company follow:

Weaver Company Comparative Balance Sheet at December 31	This Year	Last Year
Assets		
Cash and cash equivalents	$ 9	$ 15
Accounts receivable	340	240
Inventory	125	175
Prepaid expenses	10	6
Total current assets	484	436
Property, plant, and equipment	610	470
Less accumulated depreciation	93	85
Net property, plant, and equipment	517	385
Long-term investments	16	19
Total assets	$1,017	$840
Liabilities and Stockholders' Equity		
Accounts payable	$ 310	$230
Accrued liabilities	60	72
Income taxes payable	40	34
Total current liabilities	410	336
Bonds payable	290	180
Total liabilities	700	516
Common stock	210	250
Retained earnings	107	74
Total stockholders' equity	317	324
Total liabilities and stockholders' equity	$1,017	$840

Weaver Company
Income Statement
For This Year Ended December 31

Sales		$800
Cost of goods sold		500
Gross margin		300
Selling and administrative expenses		213
Net operating income		87
Nonoperating items:		
Gain on sale of investments	$7	
Loss on sale of equipment	(4)	3
Income before taxes		90
Income taxes		27
Net income		$ 63

During this year, Weaver sold some equipment for $20 that had cost $40 and on which there was accumulated depreciation of $16. In addition, the company sold long-term investments for $10 that had cost $3 when purchased several years ago. Weaver paid a cash dividend this year and the company repurchased $40 of its own stock. This year Weaver did not retire any bonds.

Required:
1. Using the indirect method, determine the net cash provided by operating activities for this year.
2. Using the information in (1) above, along with an analysis of the remaining balance sheet accounts, prepare a statement of cash flows for this year.

PROBLEM 14–8 Classification of Transactions LO14–1
Below are several transactions that took place in Seneca Company last year:
a. Paid suppliers for inventory purchases.
b. Bought equipment for cash.
c. Paid cash to repurchase its own stock.
d. Collected cash from customers.
e. Paid wages to employees.
f. Equipment was sold for cash.
g. Common stock was sold for cash to investors.
h. Cash dividends were declared and paid.
i. A long-term loan was made to a supplier.
j. Income taxes were paid to the government.
k. Interest was paid to a lender.
l. Bonds were retired by paying the principal amount due.

Required:
Prepare an answer sheet with the following headings:

	Activity			Cash	Cash
Transaction	Operating	Investing	Financing	Inflow	Outflow
a.					
b.					
Etc.					

Enter the transactions above on your answer sheet and indicate how each of them would be classified on a statement of cash flows. As appropriate, place an X in the Operating, Investing, or Financing column. Also, place an X in the Cash Inflow or Cash Outflow column.

PROBLEM 14–9 Understanding a Statement of Cash Flows LO14–1, LO14–2
Brock Company is a merchandiser that prepared the statement of cash flows and income statement provided below:

Brock Company Statement of Cash Flows—Indirect Method		
Operating Activities		
Net income		$275
Adjustments to convert net income to a cash basis:		
Depreciation	140	
Increase in accounts receivable	(24)	
Decrease in inventory	39	
Decrease in accounts payable	(45)	
Decrease in accrued liabilities	(5)	
Increase in income taxes payable	6	
Gain on sale of equipment	(4)	107
Net cash provided by (used in) operating activities		382
Investing Activities		
Additions to property, plant, and equipment	(150)	
Proceeds from sale of equipment	19	
Net cash provided by (used in) investing activities		(131)
Financing Activities		
Issuance of bonds payable	40	
Issuance of common stock	4	
Cash dividends paid	(35)	
Net cash provided by (used in) financing activities		9
Net increase in cash and cash equivalents		260
Beginning cash and cash equivalents		170
Ending cash and cash equivalents		$430

Brock Company Income Statement	
Sales	$5,200
Cost of goods sold	2,980
Gross margin	2,220
Selling and administrative expenses	1,801
Net operating income	419
Nonoperating items: Gain on sale of equipment	4
Income before taxes	423
Income taxes	148
Net income	$ 275

Required:

Assume you have been asked to teach a workshop to the employees within Brock Company's Marketing Department. The purpose of your workshop is to explain how the statement of cash flows differs from the income statement. Your audience is expecting you to explain the logic underlying each number included in the statement of cash flows. Prepare a memo that explains the format of the statement of cash flows and the rationale for each number included in Brock's statement of cash flows.

PROBLEM 14–10 Prepare a Statement of Cash Flows; Free Cash Flow LO14–1, LO14–2, LO14–3

Joyner Company's income statement for Year 2 follows:

Sales	$900,000
Cost of goods sold	500,000
Gross margin	400,000
Selling and administrative expenses	328,000
Net operating income	72,000
Nonoperating items:	
Gain on sale of equipment	8,000
Income before taxes	80,000
Income taxes	24,000
Net income	$ 56,000

Its balance sheet amounts at the end of Years 1 and 2 are as follows:

	Year 2	Year 1
Assets		
Cash and cash equivalents	$ 4,000	$ 21,000
Accounts receivable	250,000	170,000
Inventory	310,000	260,000
Prepaid expenses	7,000	14,000
Total current assets	571,000	465,000
Property, plant, and equipment	510,000	400,000
Less accumulated depreciation	132,000	120,000
Net property, plant, and equipment	378,000	280,000
Loan to Hymans Company	40,000	0
Total assets	$989,000	$745,000
Liabilities and Stockholders' Equity		
Accounts payable	$310,000	$250,000
Accrued liabilities	20,000	30,000
Income taxes payable	45,000	42,000
Total current liabilities	375,000	322,000
Bonds payable	190,000	70,000
Total liabilities	565,000	392,000
Common stock	300,000	270,000
Retained earnings	124,000	83,000
Total stockholders' equity	424,000	353,000
Total liabilities and stockholders' equity	$989,000	$745,000

Equipment that had cost $40,000 and on which there was accumulated depreciation of $30,000 was sold during Year 2 for $18,000. The company declared and paid a cash dividend during Year 2. It did not retire any bonds or repurchase any of its own stock.

Required:
1. Using the indirect method, compute the net cash provided by operating activities for Year 2.
2. Prepare a statement of cash flows for Year 2.
3. Compute the free cash flow for Year 2.
4. Briefly explain why cash declined so sharply during the year.

PROBLEM 14–11 Missing Data; Statement of Cash Flows LO14–1, LO14–2

Yoric Company listed the net changes in its balance sheet accounts for the past year as follows:

	Debits > Credits by:	Credits > Debits by:
Cash and cash equivalents	$ 17,000	
Accounts receivable	110,000	
Inventory		$ 65,000
Prepaid expenses		8,000
Long-term loans to subsidiaries		30,000
Long-term investments	80,000	
Plant and equipment	220,000	
Accumulated depreciation		5,000
Accounts payable		32,000
Accrued liabilities	9,000	
Income taxes payable		16,000
Bonds payable		400,000
Common stock	170,000	
Retained earnings		50,000
	$606,000	$606,000

The following additional information is available about last year's activities:
a. Net income for the year was $ _____?_____ .
b. The company sold equipment during the year for $15,000. The equipment originally cost $50,000 and it had $37,000 in accumulated depreciation at the time of sale.
c. Cash dividends of $20,000 were declared and paid during the year.
d. The beginning and ending balances in the Plant and Equipment and Accumulated Depreciation accounts are given below:

	Beginning	Ending
Plant and equipment	$1,580,000	$1,800,000
Accumulated depreciation	$675,000	$680,000

e. The balance in the Cash account at the beginning of the year was $23,000; the balance at the end of the year was $ _____?_____ .
f. If data are not given explaining the change in an account, make the most reasonable assumption as to the cause of the change.

Required:
Using the indirect method, prepare a statement of cash flows for the year.

PROBLEM 14–12 Prepare a Statement of Cash Flows LO14–1, LO14–2

A comparative balance sheet and an income statement for Burgess Company are given below:

Burgess Company Comparative Balance Sheet (dollars in millions)	Ending Balance	Beginning Balance
Assets		
Current assets:		
Cash and cash equivalents	$ 49	$ 79
Accounts receivable	645	580
Inventory	660	615
Total current assets	1,354	1,274
Property, plant, and equipment	1,515	1,466
Less accumulated depreciation	765	641
Net property, plant, and equipment	750	825
Total assets	$2,104	$2,099
Liabilities and Stockholders' Equity		
Current liabilities:		
Accounts payable	$ 250	$ 155
Accrued liabilities	190	165
Income taxes payable	76	70
Total current liabilities	516	390
Bonds payable	450	620
Total liabilities	966	1,010
Stockholders' equity:		
Common stock	161	161
Retained earnings	977	928
Total stockholders' equity	1,138	1,089
Total liabilities and stockholders' equity	$2,104	$2,099

Burgess Company Income Statement (dollars in millions)	
Sales	$3,600
Cost of goods sold	2,550
Gross margin	1,050
Selling and administrative expenses	875
Net operating income	175
Nonoperating items: Gain on sale of equipment	3
Income before taxes	178
Income taxes	63
Net income	$ 115

Burgess also provided the following information:

1. The company sold equipment that had an original cost of $13 million and accumulated depreciation of $8 million. The cash proceeds from the sale were $8 million. The gain on the sale was $3 million.
2. The company did not issue any new bonds during the year.
3. The company paid a cash dividend during the year.
4. The company did not complete any common stock transactions during the year.

Required:

1. Using the indirect method, prepare a statement of cash flows for the year.

2. Assume that Burgess had sales of $3,800, net income of $135, and net cash provided by operating activities of $150 in the prior year (all numbers are stated in millions). Prepare a memo that summarizes your interpretations of Burgess's financial performance.

PROBLEM 14–13 Prepare and Interpret a Statement of Cash Flows; Free Cash Flow LO14–1, LO14–2, LO14–3

Mary Walker, president of Rusco Company, considers $14,000 to be the minimum cash balance for operating purposes. As can be seen from the following statements, only $8,000 in cash was available at the end of this year. Since the company reported a large net income for the year, and also issued both bonds and common stock, the sharp decline in cash is puzzling to Ms. Walker.

Rusco Company Comparative Balance Sheet at July 31		
	This Year	Last Year
Assets		
Current assets:		
Cash and cash equivalents	$ 8,000	$ 21,000
Accounts receivable	120,000	80,000
Inventory	140,000	90,000
Prepaid expenses	5,000	9,000
Total current assets	273,000	200,000
Long-term investments	50,000	70,000
Plant and equipment	430,000	300,000
Less accumulated depreciation	60,000	50,000
Net plant and equipment	370,000	250,000
Total assets	$693,000	$520,000
Liabilities and Stockholders' Equity		
Current liabilities:		
Accounts payable	$123,000	$ 60,000
Accrued liabilities	8,000	17,000
Income taxes payable	20,000	12,000
Total current liabilities	151,000	89,000
Bonds payable	70,000	0
Total liabilities	221,000	89,000
Stockholders' equity:		
Common stock	366,000	346,000
Retained earnings	106,000	85,000
Total stockholders' equity	472,000	431,000
Total liabilities and stockholders' equity	$693,000	$520,000

Rusco Company Income Statement For This Year Ended July 31		
Sales		$500,000
Cost of goods sold		300,000
Gross margin		200,000
Selling and administrative expenses		158,000
Net operating income		42,000
Nonoperating items:		
Gain on sale of investments	$10,000	
Loss on sale of equipment	(2,000)	8,000
Income before taxes		50,000
Income taxes		20,000
Net income		$ 30,000

The following additional information is available for this year.
a.   The company declared and paid a cash dividend.
b.   Equipment was sold during the year for $8,000. The equipment originally cost $20,000 and had accumulated depreciation of $10,000.
c.   Long-term investments that cost $20,000 were sold during the year for $30,000.
d.   The company did not retire any bonds payable or repurchase any of its common stock.

Required:
1.   Using the indirect method, compute the net cash provided by operating activities for this year.
2.   Using the data from (1) above, and other data from the problem as needed, prepare a statement of cash flows for this year.
3.   Compute free cash flow for this year.
4.   Explain the major reasons for the decline in the company's cash balance.

PROBLEM 14–14 Prepare and Interpret a Statement of Cash Flows LO14–1, LO14–2
A comparative balance sheet for Lomax Company containing data for the last two years is as follows:

Lomax Company Comparative Balance Sheet		
	This Year	Last Year
Assets		
Current assets:		
Cash and cash equivalents	$ 61,000	$ 40,000
Accounts receivable	710,000	530,000
Inventory	848,000	860,000
Prepaid expenses	10,000	5,000
Total current assets	1,629,000	1,435,000
Property, plant, and equipment	3,170,000	2,600,000
Less accumulated depreciation	810,000	755,000
Net property, plant, and equipment	2,360,000	1,845,000
Long-term investments	60,000	110,000
Loans to subsidiaries	214,000	170,000
Total assets	$4,263,000	$3,560,000
Liabilities and Stockholders' Equity		
Current liabilities:		
Accounts payable	$ 970,000	$ 670,000
Accrued liabilities	65,000	82,000
Income taxes payable	95,000	80,000
Total current liabilities	1,130,000	832,000
Bonds payable	820,000	600,000
Total liabilities	1,950,000	1,432,000
Stockholders' equity:		
Common stock	1,740,000	1,650,000
Retained earnings	573,000	478,000
Total stockholders' equity	2,313,000	2,128,000
Total liabilities and stockholders' equity	$4,263,000	$3,560,000

The following additional information is available about the company's activities during this year:
a.   The company declared and paid a cash dividend this year.
b.   Bonds with a principal balance of $350,000 were repaid during this year.
c.   Equipment was sold during this year for $70,000. The equipment cost $130,000 and had $40,000 in accumulated depreciation on the date of sale.

d. Long-term investments were sold during the year for $110,000. These investments cost $50,000 when purchased several years ago.
e. The subsidiaries did not repay any outstanding loans during the year.
f. Lomax did not repurchase any of its own stock during the year.

The company reported net income this year as follows:

Sales		$2,000,000
Cost of goods sold		1,300,000
Gross margin		700,000
Selling and administrative expenses . . .		490,000
Net operating income		210,000
Nonoperating items:		
Gain on sale of investments	$60,000	
Loss on sale of equipment	(20,000)	40,000
Income before taxes		250,000
Income taxes		80,000
Net income		$ 170,000

Required:
1. Using the indirect method, prepare a statement of cash flows for this year.
2. What problems relating to the company's activities are revealed by the statement of cash flows that you have prepared?

Appendix 14A: The Direct Method of Determining the Net Cash Provided by Operating Activities

To compute the net cash provided by operating activities under the direct method, we must reconstruct the income statement on a cash basis from top to bottom. Exhibit 14A–1 shows the adjustments that must be made to adjust sales, expenses, and so forth, to a cash basis. To illustrate, we have included in the exhibit the Apparel, Inc., data from the chapter.

> **LO14–4**
> Use the direct method to determine the net cash provided by operating activities.

Note that the net cash provided by operating activities of $259 million agrees with the amount computed in the chapter by the indirect method. The two amounts agree because the direct and indirect methods are just different roads to the same destination. The investing and financing activities sections of the statement will be exactly the same as shown for the indirect method in Exhibit 14–10. The only difference between the indirect and direct methods is in the operating activities section.

Similarities and Differences in the Handling of Data

Although we arrive at the same destination under either the direct or indirect method, not all data are handled the same way in the two adjustment processes. Stop for a moment, flip back to the bottom half of Exhibit 14–7 and compare the adjustments described in that exhibit to the adjustments made for the direct method in Exhibit 14A–1. The adjustments for accounts that affect sales (which includes only accounts receivable in our example) are handled the same way in the two methods. In either case, increases in the accounts are subtracted and decreases are added. However, the adjustments for accounts that affect expenses (which include all remaining accounts in Exhibit 14–7) are handled in opposite

EXHIBIT 14A–1
General Model: Direct Method of Determining the Net Cash Provided by Operating Activities

Revenue or Expense Item	Add (+) or Deduct (–) to Adjust to a Cash Basis	Illustration— Apparel, Inc. (in millions)	
Sales (as reported)		$3,638	
Adjustments to a cash basis:			
Increase in accounts receivable	–		
Decrease in accounts receivable	+	+17	$3,655
Cost of goods sold (as reported)		2,469	
Adjustments to a cash basis:			
Increase in inventory	+	+49	
Decrease in inventory	–		
Increase in accounts payable	–	–44	
Decrease in accounts payable	+	_____	2,474
Selling and administrative expenses (as reported)		941	
Adjustments to a cash basis:			
Increase in prepaid expenses	+		
Decrease in prepaid expenses	–		
Increase in accrued liabilities	–	–3	
Decrease in accrued liabilities	+		
Depreciation	–	–103	835
Income tax expense (as reported)		91	
Adjustments to a cash basis:			
Increase in income taxes payable	–	–4	
Decrease in income taxes payable	+	_____	87
Net cash provided by (used in) operating activities ...			$ 259

ways in the indirect and direct methods. This is because under the indirect method the adjustments are made to *net income,* whereas under the direct method the adjustments are made to the *expense accounts* themselves.

To illustrate this difference, note the handling of inventory and depreciation in the indirect and direct methods. Under the indirect method (Exhibit 14–7), an increase in the inventory account ($49) is *subtracted* from net income in computing the amount of net cash provided by operating activities. Under the direct method (Exhibit 14A–1), an increase in inventory is *added* to cost of goods sold. The reason for the difference can be explained as follows: An increase in inventory means that the period's inventory purchases exceeded the cost of goods sold included in the income statement. Therefore, to adjust net income to a cash basis, we must either subtract this increase from net income (indirect method) or we must add this increase to cost of goods sold (direct method). Either way, we will end up with the same figure for net cash provided by operating activities. Similarly, depreciation is added to net income under the indirect method to cancel out its effect (Exhibit 14–8), whereas it is subtracted from selling and administrative expenses under the direct method to cancel out its effect (Exhibit 14A–1). These differences in the handling of data are true for all other expense items in the two methods.

In the matter of gains and losses on sale of assets, no adjustments are needed under the direct method. These gains and losses are simply ignored because they are not part of sales, cost of goods sold, selling and administrative expenses, or income taxes. Observe that in Exhibit 14A–1, Apparel's $3 million gain on the sale of the store is not listed as an adjustment in the operating activities section.

Special Rules—Direct and Indirect Methods

As stated earlier, when the direct method is used, U.S. GAAP and IFRS require a reconciliation between net income and the net cash provided by operating activities, as determined by the indirect method. Thus, *when a company elects to use the direct method, it must also present the indirect method* in a separate schedule accompanying the statement of cash flows.

On the other hand, if a company elects to use the indirect method to compute the net cash provided by operating activities, then it also must provide a special breakdown of data. The company must provide a separate disclosure of the amount of interest and the amount of income taxes paid during the year. This separate disclosure is required so that users can take the data provided by the indirect method and make estimates of what the amounts for sales, income taxes, and so forth, would have been if the direct method had been used instead.

---

connect   **Appendix 14A: Exercises and Problems**

EXERCISE 14A–1 Adjust Net Income to a Cash Basis LO14–4
Refer to the data for Pavolik Company in Exercise 14–4.

Required:
Use the direct method to convert the company's income statement to a cash basis.

EXERCISE 14A–2 Net Cash Provided by Operating Activities LO14–4
Wiley Company's income statement for Year 2 follows:

Sales	$150,000
Cost of goods sold	90,000
Gross margin	60,000
Selling and administrative expenses	40,000
Income before taxes	20,000
Income taxes	8,000
Net income	$ 12,000

The company's selling and administrative expense for Year 2 includes $7,500 of depreciation expense. Selected balance sheet accounts for Wiley at the end of Years 1 and 2 are as follows:

	Year 2	Year 1
Current Assets		
Accounts receivable	$40,000	$30,000
Inventory	$54,000	$45,000
Prepaid expenses	$8,000	$6,000
Current Liabilities		
Accounts payable	$35,000	$28,000
Accrued liabilities	$5,000	$8,000
Income taxes payable	$2,000	$2,500

Required:
1. Using the direct method, convert the company's income statement to a cash basis.
2. Assume that during Year 2 Wiley had a $9,000 gain on sale of investments and a $3,000 loss on the sale of equipment. Explain how these two transactions would affect your computations in (1) above.

EXERCISE 14A–3 Net Cash Provided by Operating Activities LO14–4

Refer to the data for Carmono Company in Exercise 14–6.

Required:

Using the direct method, convert the company's income statement to a cash basis.

EXERCISE 14A–4 Net Cash Provided by Operating Activities LO14–4

Refer to the data for Hanna Company in Exercise 14–2. The company's income statement for the year appears below:

Sales	$350,000
Cost of goods sold	140,000
Gross margin	210,000
Selling and administrative expenses	160,000
Income before taxes	50,000
Income taxes	15,000
Net income	$ 35,000

Required:

Using the direct method (and the data from Exercise 14–2), convert the company's income statement to a cash basis.

PROBLEM 14A–5 Prepare and Interpret a Statement of Cash Flows LO14–1, LO14–4

Refer to the financial statements for Rusco Company in Problem 14–13. Because the Cash account decreased so dramatically during this year, the company's executive committee is anxious to see how the income statement would appear on a cash basis.

Required:

1. Using the direct method, adjust the company's income statement for this year to a cash basis.
2. Using the data from (1) above, and other data from the problem as needed, prepare a statement of cash flows for this year.
3. Briefly explain the major reasons for the sharp decline in cash during this year.

PROBLEM 14A–6 Prepare a Statement of Cash Flows LO14–1, LO14–4

Refer to the financial statement data for Weaver Company in Problem 14–7.

Required:

1. Using the direct method, adjust the company's income statement for this year to a cash basis.
2. Using the information obtained in (1) above, along with an analysis of the remaining balance sheet accounts, prepare a statement of cash flows for this year.

PROBLEM 14A–7 Prepare and Interpret a Statement of Cash Flows LO14–1, LO14–4

Refer to the financial statement data for Joyner Company in Problem 14–10. Sam Conway, president of the company, considers $15,000 to be the minimum cash balance for operating purposes. As can be seen from the balance sheet data, only $4,000 in cash was available at the end of the current year. The sharp decline is puzzling to Mr. Conway, particularly because sales and profits are at a record high.

Required:

1. Using the direct method, adjust the company's income statement to a cash basis for Year 2.
2. Using the data from (1) above and other data from the problem as needed, prepare a statement of cash flows for Year 2.
3. Explain why cash declined so sharply during the year.

CHAPTER 15

Financial Statement Analysis

Coca-Cola Looks to Trim the Fat

© Lionel Bonaventure/AFP/Getty Images

Coca-Cola's operating expenses as a percentage of sales is 39%, which compares unfavorably with the likes of **Colgate** (35%), **Nestlé** (32%), **Proctor & Gamble** (31%), and **Anheuser-Busch InBev** (27%). The company plans to cut $3 billion in costs over five years by pursuing a variety of actions such as eliminating 1,000–2,000 jobs, dropping its lavish Christmas party, and tightening its travel and entertainment budget. Coke also plans to implement zero-based budgeting, which requires managers to justify all proposed annual expenditures rather than having to merely justify increases in spending relative to the prior year. Investors are skeptical whether Coke, which has historically focused on sales growth, can shift gears and reduce its spending. When Coke announced its cost-cutting plan its share price dropped 2.2%. ■

Source: Mike Esterl, "Austerity Is the New Flavor at Coca-Cola," *The Wall Street Journal*, December 24, 2014, pp. B1–B2.

LEARNING OBJECTIVES

After studying Chapter 15, you should be able to:

LO15–1 Prepare and interpret financial statements in comparative and common-size form.

LO15–2 Compute and interpret financial ratios that managers use to assess liquidity.

LO15–3 Compute and interpret financial ratios that managers use for asset management purposes.

LO15–4 Compute and interpret financial ratios that managers use for debt management purposes.

LO15–5 Compute and interpret financial ratios that managers use to assess profitability.

LO15–6 Compute and interpret financial ratios that managers use to assess market performance.

Stockholders, creditors, and managers are examples of stakeholders that use *financial statement analysis* to evaluate a company's financial health and future prospects. Stockholders and creditors analyze a company's financial statements to estimate its potential for earnings growth, stock price appreciation, making dividend payments, and paying principal and interest on loans. Managers use financial statement analysis for two reasons. First, it enables them to better understand how their company's financial results will be interpreted by stockholders and creditors for the purposes of making investing and lending decisions. Second, financial statement analysis provides managers with valuable feedback regarding their company's performance. For example, managers may study trends in their company's financial statements to assess whether performance has been improving or declining. Or, they may use financial statement analysis to benchmark their company's performance against world-class competitors.

In this chapter, we'll explain how managers prepare financial statements in comparative and common-size form and how they use financial ratios to assess their company's liquidity, asset management, debt management, profitability, and market performance.

Limitations of Financial Statement Analysis

This section discusses two limitations of financial statement analysis that managers should always keep in mind—comparing financial data across companies and looking beyond ratios when formulating conclusions.

Comparing Financial Data across Companies

Comparisons of one company with another can provide valuable clues about the financial health of an organization. Unfortunately, differences in accounting methods between companies sometimes make it difficult to compare their financial data. For example, if one company values its inventories by the LIFO method and another company by the average cost method, then direct comparisons of their financial data such as inventory valuations and cost of goods sold may be misleading. Sometimes enough data are presented in footnotes to the financial statements to restate data to a comparable basis. Otherwise, managers should keep in mind any lack of comparability. Even with this limitation in mind, comparing key ratios with other companies and with industry averages often helps managers identify opportunities for improvement.

Looking beyond Ratios

Ratios should not be viewed as an end, but rather as a *starting point*. They raise many questions and point to opportunities for further analysis, but they rarely answer any questions by themselves. In addition to financial ratios, managers should consider various internal factors, such as employee learning and growth, business process performance, and customer satisfaction as well as external factors like industry trends, technological changes, changes in consumer tastes, and changes in broad economic indicators.

Statements in Comparative and Common-Size Form

LO15–1
Prepare and interpret financial statements in comparative and common-size form.

An item on a balance sheet or income statement has little meaning by itself. Suppose a company's sales for a year were $250 million. In isolation, that is not particularly useful information. How does that stack up against last year's sales? How do the sales relate to the cost of goods sold? In making these kinds of comparisons, three analytical techniques are widely used:

1. Dollar and percentage changes on statements (*horizontal analysis*).
2. Common-size statements (*vertical analysis*).
3. Ratios.

The first and second techniques are discussed in this section; the third technique is discussed in the remainder of the chapter. Throughout the chapter, we will illustrate these analytical techniques using the financial statements of Brickey Electronics, a producer of specialized electronic components.

Dollar and Percentage Changes on Statements

Horizontal analysis (also known as **trend analysis**) involves analyzing financial data over time, such as computing year-to-year dollar and percentage changes within a set of financial statements. Exhibits 15–1 and 15–2 show Brickey Electronics' financial

EXHIBIT 15–1

			Increase (Decrease)	
Brickey Electronics Comparative Balance Sheet (dollars in thousands)	This Year	Last Year	Amount	Percent
Assets				
Current assets:				
Cash	$ 1,200	$ 2,350	$(1,150)	(48.9)%*
Accounts receivable, net	6,000	4,000	2,000	50.0%
Inventory	8,000	10,000	(2,000)	(20.0)%
Prepaid expenses	300	120	180	150.0%
Total current assets	15,500	16,470	(970)	(5.9)%
Property and equipment:				
Land	4,000	4,000	0	0.0%
Buildings and equipment, net	12,000	8,500	3,500	41.2%
Total property and equipment	16,000	12,500	3,500	28.0%
Total assets	$31,500	$28,970	$ 2,530	8.7%
Liabilities and Stockholders' Equity				
Current liabilities:				
Accounts payable	$ 5,800	$ 4,000	$ 1,800	45.0%
Accrued liabilities	900	400	500	125.0%
Notes payable, short term	300	600	(300)	(50.0)%
Total current liabilities	7,000	5,000	2,000	40.0%
Long-term liabilities:				
Bonds payable, 8%	7,500	8,000	(500)	(6.3)%
Total liabilities	14,500	13,000	1,500	11.5%
Stockholders' equity:				
Common stock, $12 par	6,000	6,000	0	0.0%
Additional paid-in capital	3,000	3,000	0	0.0%
Total paid-in capital	9,000	9,000	0	0.0%
Retained earnings	8,000	6,970	1,030	14.8%
Total stockholders' equity	17,000	15,970	1,030	6.4%
Total liabilities and stockholders' equity	$31,500	$28,970	$ 2,530	8.7%

*The changes between this year and last year are expressed as a percentage of the dollar amount for last year. For example, Cash decreased by $1,150 between this year and last year. This decrease expressed in percentage form is computed as follows: $1,150 ÷ $2,350 = 48.9%. Other percentage figures in this exhibit and Exhibit 15–2 are computed in the same way.

EXHIBIT 15–2

Brickey Electronics
Comparative Income Statement and Reconciliation of Retained Earnings
(dollars in thousands)

	This Year	Last Year	Increase (Decrease) Amount	Increase (Decrease) Percent
Sales	$52,000	$48,000	$4,000	8.3%
Cost of goods sold	36,000	31,500	4,500	14.3%
Gross margin	16,000	16,500	(500)	(3.0)%
Selling and administrative expenses:				
Selling expenses	7,000	6,500	500	7.7%
Administrative expenses	5,860	6,100	(240)	(3.9)%
Total selling and administrative expenses	12,860	12,600	260	2.1%
Net operating income	3,140	3,900	(760)	(19.5)%
Interest expense	640	700	(60)	(8.6)%
Net income before taxes	2,500	3,200	(700)	(21.9)%
Income taxes (30%)	750	960	(210)	(21.9)%
Net income	1,750	2,240	$ (490)	(21.9)%
Dividends to common stockholders, $1.44 per share	720	720		
Net income added to retained earnings	1,030	1,520		
Beginning retained earnings	6,970	5,450		
Ending retained earnings	$ 8,000	$ 6,970		

statements in this *comparative form.* The dollar changes highlight the changes that are the most important economically; the percentage changes highlight the changes that are the most unusual.

Horizontal analysis can be even more useful when data from a number of years are used to compute *trend percentages.* To compute **trend percentages**, a base year is selected and the data for all years are stated as a percentage of that base year. To illustrate, consider the sales and net income of **McDonald's Corporation**, the world's largest food service retailer, with more than 31,000 restaurants worldwide:

	2006	2007	2008	2009	2010	2011	2012	2013	2014	2015
Sales (millions)	$20,895	$22,787	$23,522	$22,745	$24,075	$27,006	$27,567	$28,106	$27,441	$25,413
Net income (millions) ...	$3,544	$2,395	$4,313	$4,551	$4,946	$5,503	$5,465	$5,586	$4,758	$4,529

By simply looking at these data, you can see that sales increased every year except 2009, 2014, and 2015 and net income increased every year except 2007, 2012, 2014, and 2015. However, recasting these data into trend percentages aids interpretation:

	2006	2007	2008	2009	2010	2011	2012	2013	2014	2015
Sales	100%	109%	113%	109%	115%	129%	132%	135%	131%	122%
Net income	100%	68%	122%	128%	140%	155%	154%	158%	134%	128%

In the above table, both sales and net income have been restated as a percentage of the 2006 sales and net income. For example, the 2008 sales of $23,522 are 113% of the 2006 sales of $20,895. This trend analysis is easier to analyze when the data are plotted as in Exhibit 15–3. McDonald's experienced modest but reasonably constant sales growth through 2013 and then sales dropped in 2014 and 2015. Net income plummeted in 2007, fully recovered in 2008, reached a record-high in 2013, and then dipped again in 2014 and 2015.

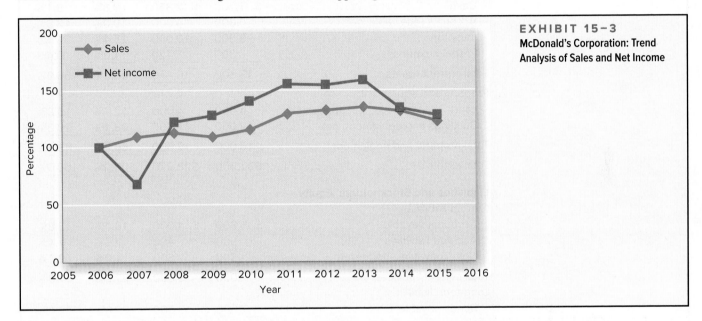

EXHIBIT 15–3
McDonald's Corporation: Trend Analysis of Sales and Net Income

Common-Size Statements

Horizontal analysis, which was discussed in the previous section, examines changes in financial statement accounts over time. **Vertical analysis** focuses on the relations among financial statement accounts at a given point in time. A **common-size financial statement** is a vertical analysis in which each financial statement account is expressed as a percentage. In income statements, all items are usually expressed as a percentage of sales. In balance sheets, all items are usually expressed as a percentage of total assets. Exhibit 15–4 contains Brickey Electronics' common-size balance sheet and Exhibit 15–5 contains its common-size income statement.

Notice from Exhibit 15–4 that placing all assets in common-size form clearly shows the relative importance of the current assets as compared to the noncurrent assets. It also shows that significant changes have taken place in the composition of the current assets over the last year. For example, accounts receivable have increased in relative importance and both cash and inventory have declined in relative importance. Judging from the sharp increase in accounts receivable, the deterioration in the cash balance may be a result of an inability to collect from customers.

The common-size income statement in Exhibit 15–5 states each line item as a percentage of sales. For example, the administrative expenses were 12.7% of sales last year and 11.3% of sales this year. If the quality and efficiency of Brickey's administrative services is holding constant or improving over time, then these two percentages suggest that this year Brickey managed its administrative resources more cost-effectively than last year. Beyond administrative expenses, managers also have a keen interest in other percentages disclosed in a common-size income statement and those will be discussed in a later section related to profitability ratios.

EXHIBIT 15-4

	Brickey Electronics Common-Size Comparative Balance Sheet (dollars in thousands)		Common-Size Percentages	
	This Year	Last Year	This Year	Last Year
Assets				
Current assets:				
Cash	$ 1,200	$ 2,350	3.8%*	8.1%
Accounts receivable, net	6,000	4,000	19.0%	13.8%
Inventory	8,000	10,000	25.4%	34.5%
Prepaid expenses	300	120	1.0%	0.4%
Total current assets	15,500	16,470	49.2%	56.9%
Property and equipment:				
Land	4,000	4,000	12.7%	13.8%
Buildings and equipment, net	12,000	8,500	38.1%	29.3%
Total property and equipment	16,000	12,500	50.8%	43.1%
Total assets	$31,500	$28,970	100.0%	100.0%
Liabilities and Stockholders' Equity				
Current liabilities:				
Accounts payable	$ 5,800	$ 4,000	18.4%	13.8%
Accrued liabilities	900	400	2.9%	1.4%
Notes payable, short term	300	600	1.0%	2.1%
Total current liabilities	7,000	5,000	22.2%	17.3%
Long-term liabilities:				
Bonds payable, 8%	7,500	8,000	23.8%	27.6%
Total liabilities	14,500	13,000	46.0%	44.9%
Stockholders' equity:				
Common stock, $12 par	6,000	6,000	19.0%	20.7%
Additional paid-in capital	3,000	3,000	9.5%	10.4%
Total paid-in capital	9,000	9,000	28.6%	31.1%
Retained earnings	8,000	6,970	25.4%	24.0%
Total stockholders' equity	17,000	15,970	54.0%	55.1%
Total liabilities and stockholders' equity	$31,500	$28,970	100.0%	100.0%

*Each asset account on a common-size statement is expressed as a percentage of total assets, and each liability and equity account is expressed as a percentage of total liabilities and stockholders' equity. For example, the percentage figure above for this year's Cash balance is computed as follows: $1,200 ÷ $31,500 = 3.8%. All common-size percentages have been rounded to one decimal place; therefore, the figures as shown may not fully reconcile down each column.

EXHIBIT 15–5

Brickey Electronics
Common-Size Comparative Income Statement
(dollars in thousands)

	This Year	Last Year	Common-Size Percentages* This Year	Common-Size Percentages* Last Year
Sales	$52,000	$48,000	100.0%	100.0%
Cost of goods sold	36,000	31,500	69.2%	65.6%
Gross margin	16,000	16,500	30.8%	34.4%
Selling and administrative expenses:				
Selling expenses	7,000	6,500	13.5%	13.5%
Administrative expenses	5,860	6,100	11.3%	12.7%
Total selling and administrative expenses	12,860	12,600	24.7%	26.3%
Net operating income	3,140	3,900	6.0%	8.1%
Interest expense	640	700	1.2%	1.5%
Net income before taxes	2,500	3,200	4.8%	6.7%
Income taxes (30%)	750	960	1.4%	2.0%
Net income	$ 1,750	$ 2,240	3.4%	4.7%

*Note that the percentage figures for each year are expressed as a percentage of total sales for the year. For example, the percentage figure for this year's cost of goods sold is computed as follows: $36,000 ÷ $52,000 = 69.2%. All common-size percentages have been rounded to one decimal place; therefore, the figures as shown may not fully reconcile down each column.

Ratio Analysis—Liquidity

LO15–2
Compute and interpret financial ratios that managers use to assess liquidity.

Liquidity refers to how quickly an asset can be converted to cash. Liquid assets can be converted to cash quickly, whereas ill-liquid assets cannot. Companies need to continuously monitor the amount of their liquid assets relative to the amount that they owe short-term creditors, such as suppliers. If a company's liquid assets are not enough to support timely payments to short-term creditors, this presents an important management problem that, if not remedied, can lead to bankruptcy.

This section uses Brickey Electronics' financial statements to explain one measure and two ratios that managers use to analyze their company's liquidity and its ability to pay short-term creditors. *As you proceed through this section, keep in mind that all calculations are performed for this year rather than last year.*

Working Capital

The excess of current assets over current liabilities is known as **working capital**.

$$\text{Working capital} = \text{Current assets} - \text{Current liabilities}$$

The working capital for Brickey Electronics is computed as follows:

$$\text{Working capital} = \$15,500,000 - \$7,000,000 = \$8,500,000$$

Managers need to interpret working capital from two perspectives. On one hand, if a company has ample working capital, it provides some assurance that the company can pay its creditors in full and on time. On the other hand, maintaining large amounts of working capital isn't free. Working capital must be financed with long-term debt and equity—both of which are expensive. Furthermore, a large and growing working capital balance may indicate troubles, such as excessive growth in inventories. Therefore, managers often want to minimize working capital while retaining the ability to pay short-term creditors.

Current Ratio

A company's working capital is frequently expressed in ratio form. A company's current assets divided by its current liabilities is known as the **current ratio**:

$$\text{Current ratio} = \frac{\text{Current assets}}{\text{Current liabilities}}$$

For Brickey Electronics, the current ratio is computed as follows:

$$\text{Current ratio} = \frac{\$15,500,000}{\$7,000,000} = 2.21$$

Although widely regarded as a measure of short-term debt-paying ability, the current ratio must be interpreted with great care. A *declining* ratio might be a sign of a deteriorating financial condition, or it might be the result of eliminating obsolete inventories or other stagnant current assets. An *improving* ratio might be the result of stockpiling inventory, or it might indicate an improving financial situation. In short, the current ratio is useful, but tricky to interpret.

The general rule of thumb calls for a current ratio of at least 2. However, many companies successfully operate with a current ratio below 2. The adequacy of a current ratio depends heavily on the *composition* of the assets. For example, as we see in the table below, both Worthington Corporation and Greystone, Inc., have current ratios of 2. However, they are not in comparable financial condition. Greystone is more likely to have difficulty meeting its current financial obligations because almost all of its current assets consist of inventory rather than more liquid assets such as cash and accounts receivable.

	Worthington Corporation	Greystone, Inc.
Current assets:		
Cash	$ 25,000	$ 2,000
Accounts receivable, net	60,000	8,000
Inventory	85,000	160,000
Prepaid expenses	5,000	5,000
Total current assets (a)	$175,000	$175,000
Current liabilities (b)	$ 87,500	$ 87,500
Current ratio, (a) ÷ (b)	2	2

Acid-Test (Quick) Ratio

The **acid-test (quick) ratio** is a more rigorous test of a company's ability to meet its short-term debts than the current ratio. Inventories and prepaid expenses are excluded from total current assets, leaving only the more liquid (or "quick") assets to be divided by current liabilities.

$$\text{Acid-test ratio} = \frac{\text{Cash} + \text{Marketable securities} + \text{Accounts receivable} + \text{Short-term notes receivable}}{\text{Current liabilities}}$$

The acid-test ratio measures how well a company can meet its obligations without having to liquidate or depend too heavily on its inventory. Ideally, each dollar of liabilities should be backed by at least $1 of quick assets. However, acid-test ratios as low as 0.3 are common.

The acid-test ratio for Brickey Electronics is computed below:

$$\text{Acid-test ratio} = \frac{\$1,200,000 + \$0 + \$6,000,000 + \$0}{\$7,000,000} = 1.03$$

Although Brickey Electronics' acid-test ratio is within the acceptable range, a manager might be concerned about several trends revealed in the company's balance sheet. Notice in Exhibit 15–1 that short-term debts are rising, while the cash balance is declining. Perhaps the lower cash balance is a result of the substantial increase in accounts receivable. In short, as with the current ratio, the acid-test ratio should be interpreted with one eye on its basic components.

Ratio Analysis—Asset Management

LO15–3
Compute and interpret financial ratios that managers use for asset management purposes.

A company's assets are funded by lenders and stockholders, both of whom expect those assets to be deployed efficiently and effectively. In this section, we'll describe various measures and ratios that managers use to assess their company's asset management performance. *All forthcoming calculations will be performed for this year.*

Accounts Receivable Turnover

The *accounts receivable turnover* and *average collection period* ratios measure how quickly credit sales are converted into cash. The **accounts receivable turnover** is computed by dividing sales on account (i.e., credit sales) by the average accounts receivable balance for the year:

$$\text{Accounts receivable turnover} = \frac{\text{Sales on account}}{\text{Average accounts receivable balance}}$$

Assuming that all of Brickey Electronics' sales were on account, its accounts receivable turnover is computed as follows:

$$\text{Accounts receivable turnover} = \frac{\$52,000,000}{(\$6,000,000 + \$4,000,000)/2} = 10.4$$

The accounts receivable turnover can then be divided into 365 days to determine the average number of days required to collect an account (known as the **average collection period**).

$$\text{Average collection period} = \frac{365 \text{ days}}{\text{Accounts receivable turnover}}$$

The average collection period for Brickey Electronics is computed as follows:

$$\text{Average collection period} = \frac{365 \text{ days}}{10.4} = 35.1 \text{ days}$$

This means that on average it takes 35 days to collect a credit sale. Whether this is good or bad depends on the credit terms Brickey Electronics is offering its customers. Many customers will tend to withhold payment for as long as the credit terms allow. If the credit terms are 30 days, then a 35-day average collection period would usually be viewed as very good. On the other hand, if the company's credit terms are 10 days, then a 35-day average collection period is worrisome. A long collection period may result from having too many old uncollectible accounts, failing to bill promptly or follow up on late accounts, lax credit checks, and so on. In practice, average collection periods ranging all the way from 10 days to 180 days are common, depending on the industry.

Inventory Turnover

The **inventory turnover ratio** measures how many times a company's inventory has been sold and replaced during the year. It is computed by dividing the cost of goods sold by the average level of inventory [(Beginning inventory balance + Ending inventory balance) ÷ 2]:

$$\text{Inventory turnover} = \frac{\text{Cost of goods sold}}{\text{Average inventory balance}}$$

Brickey's inventory turnover is computed as follows:

$$\text{Inventory turnover} = \frac{\$36,000,000}{(\$8,000,000 + \$10,000,000)/2} = 4.0$$

The number of days needed on average to sell the entire inventory (called the **average sale period**) can be computed by dividing 365 by the inventory turnover:

$$\text{Average sale period} = \frac{365 \text{ days}}{\text{Inventory turnover}}$$

$$= \frac{365 \text{ days}}{4 \text{ times}} = 91.3 \text{ days}$$

The average sale period varies from industry to industry. Grocery stores, with significant perishable stocks, tend to turn over their inventory quickly. On the other hand, jewelry stores tend to turn over their inventory slowly. In practice, average sale periods of 10 days to 90 days are common, depending on the industry.

A company whose inventory turnover ratio is much slower than the average for its industry may have too much inventory or the wrong sorts of inventory. Some managers argue that they must buy in large quantities to take advantage of quantity discounts. But these discounts must be compared to the added costs of insurance, taxes, financing, and risks of obsolescence and deterioration that result from carrying added inventories.

Operating Cycle

The **operating cycle** measures the elapsed time from when inventory is received from suppliers to when cash is received from customers. It is computed as follows:

$$\text{Operating cycle} = \text{Average sale period} + \text{Average collection period}$$

Brickey Electronics' operating cycle is computed as follows:

$$\text{Operating cycle} = 91.3 \text{ days} + 35.1 \text{ days} = 126.4 \text{ days}$$

A manager's goal is to reduce the operating cycle because it puts cash receipts in the company's possession sooner. In fact, if a company can shrink its operating cycle to fewer days than its average payment period for suppliers, it means the company is receiving cash from customers before it has to pay suppliers for inventory purchases. For example, if a company's operating cycle is 10 days and its average payment period to suppliers is 30 days, the company is receiving cash from customers 20 days before it pays its suppliers. In this example, the company could earn interest income on cash collections for

20 days before paying a portion of those receipts to suppliers. Conversely, if a company's operating cycle is much longer than its average payment period for suppliers, it creates the need to borrow money to fund its inventories and accounts receivable. In the case of Brickey Electronics, its operating cycle is very high, thereby suggesting that it needs to borrow money to fund its working capital.

INVENTORY MANAGEMENT IN THE APPAREL INDUSTRY

Many apparel retailers such as **Aéropostale** are practicing a three-step inventory management tactic known as chasing. First, the retailer orders very small quantities of its new clothing styles from its suppliers. Second, the retailer determines which of its new clothing styles are popular with customers. Third, the retailer chases consumer demand by asking suppliers to very quickly ramp-up production of its most popular clothing styles. This tactic, if properly executed, enables retailers to not only reduce their average sale period and operating cycle, but it also helps them minimize price markdowns related to excess inventories and forgone sales related to out-of-stock items. Of course, tension inevitably arises with suppliers who greatly prefer large order quantities and 6–9 month lead times.

Source: Elizabeth Holmes, "Tug-of-War in Apparel World," *The Wall Street Journal*, July 16, 2010, pp. B1–B2.

Total Asset Turnover

The **total asset turnover** is a ratio that compares total sales to average total assets. It measures how efficiently a company's assets are being used to generate sales. This ratio expands beyond current assets to include noncurrent assets, such as property, plant, and equipment. It is computed as follows:

$$\text{Total asset turnover} = \frac{\text{Sales}}{\text{Average total assets}}$$

Brickey Electronics' total asset turnover is computed as follows:

$$\text{Total asset turnover} = \frac{\$52,000,000}{(\$31,500,000 + \$28,970,000)/2} = 1.72$$

A company's goal is to increase its total asset turnover. To do so, it must either increase sales or reduce its investment in assets. If a company's accounts receivable turnover and inventory turnover are increasing, but its total asset turnover is decreasing, it suggests the problem may relate to noncurrent asset utilization and efficiency. It also bears emphasizing that if all else holds constant, a company's total asset turnover will increase over time simply because the accumulated depreciation on plant and equipment grows over time.

Ratio Analysis—Debt Management

Managers need to evaluate their company's debt management choices from the vantage point of two stakeholders—long-term creditors and common stockholders. Long-term creditors are concerned with a company's ability to repay its loans over the long-run. For example, if a company paid out all of its available cash in the form of dividends, then nothing would be left to pay back creditors. Consequently, creditors often seek protection by requiring that borrowers agree to various restrictive covenants, or rules. These restrictive covenants typically include restrictions on dividend payments as well as rules stating that the company must maintain certain financial ratios at specified levels. Although

LO15–4
Compute and interpret financial ratios that managers use for debt management purposes.

restrictive covenants are widely used, they do not ensure that creditors will be paid when loans come due. The company still must generate sufficient earnings to cover payments.

Stockholders look at debt from a *financial leverage* perspective. **Financial leverage** refers to borrowing money to acquire assets in an effort to increase sales and profits. A company can have either positive or negative financial leverage depending on the difference between its rate of return on total assets and the rate of return that it must pay its creditors. If the company's rate of return on total assets exceeds the rate of return the company pays its creditors, *financial leverage is positive*. If the rate of return on total assets is less than the rate of return the company pays its creditors, *financial leverage is negative*. We will explore whether Brickey Electronics has positive or negative financial leverage later in the chapter. For now, you need to understand that if a company has positive financial leverage, having debt can substantially benefit common stockholders. Conversely, if a company has negative financial leverage, common stockholders suffer. Given the potential benefits of maintaining positive financial leverage, managers do not try to avoid debt, rather they often seek to maintain a level of debt that is considered to be normal within their industry.

In this section, we explain three ratios that managers use for debt management purposes, times interest earned ratio, debt-to-equity ratio, and the equity multiplier. *All calculations are performed for this year.*

Times Interest Earned Ratio

The most common measure of a company's ability to provide protection to its long-term creditors is the **times interest earned ratio**. It is computed by dividing earnings before interest expense and income taxes (i.e., net operating income) by interest expense:

$$\text{Times interest earned ratio} = \frac{\text{Earnings before interest expense and income taxes}}{\text{Interest expense}}$$

For Brickey Electronics, the times interest earned ratio for this year is computed as follows:

$$\text{Times interest earned} = \frac{\$3,140,000}{\$640,000} = 4.91$$

The times interest earned ratio is based on earnings before interest expense and income taxes because that is the amount of earnings that is available for making interest payments. Interest expenses are deducted *before* income taxes are determined; creditors have first claim on the earnings before taxes are paid.

A times interest earned ratio of less than 1 is inadequate because interest expense exceeds the earnings that are available for paying that interest. In contrast, a times interest earned ratio of 2 or more may be considered sufficient to protect long-term creditors.

Debt-to-Equity Ratio

The **debt-to-equity ratio** is one type of leverage ratio that indicates the relative proportions of debt and equity at one point in time on a company's balance sheet. As the debt-to-equity ratio increases, it indicates that a company is increasing its financial leverage. In other words, it is relying on a greater proportion of debt rather than equity to fund its assets. The debt-to-equity ratio is measured as follows:

$$\text{Debt-equity ratio} = \frac{\text{Total liabilities}}{\text{Stockholders' equity}}$$

Brickey's debt-to-equity ratio for this year is computed as follows:

$$\text{Debt-to-equity ratio} = \frac{\$14,500,000}{\$17,000,000} = 0.85$$

At the end of this year, Brickey Electronics' creditors were providing 85 cents for each $1 being provided by stockholders.

Creditors and stockholders have different views about the optimal debt-to-equity ratio. Ordinarily, stockholders would like a lot of debt to take advantage of positive financial leverage. On the other hand, because equity represents the excess of total assets over total liabilities, and hence a buffer of protection for creditors, creditors would like to see less debt and more equity. In practice, debt-to-equity ratios from 0.0 (no debt) to 3.0 are common. Generally speaking, in industries with little financial risk, managers maintain high debt-to-equity ratios. In industries with more financial risk, managers maintain lower debt-to-equity ratios.

Equity Multiplier

The **equity multiplier** is another type of leverage ratio that indicates the portion of a company's assets funded by equity. Similar to the debt-to-equity ratio, as the equity multiplier increases, it indicates that a company is increasing its financial leverage. In other words, it is relying on a greater proportion of debt rather than equity to fund its assets. Instead of measuring amounts in the numerator and denominator at one point in time (as is done with the debt-to-equity ratio), the equity multiplier focuses on average amounts maintained throughout the year and it is measured as follows:

$$\text{Equity multiplier} = \frac{\text{Average total assets}}{\text{Average stockholders' equity}}$$

Brickey's equity multiplier for this year is computed as follows:

$$\text{Equity multiplier} = \frac{(\$31,500,000 + \$28,970,000)/2}{(\$17,000,000 + \$15,970,000)/2} = 1.83$$

The debt-to-equity ratio and the equity multiplier provide signals about how a company is managing its mix of debt and equity. We have introduced the equity multiplier because it will be used in the next section of the chapter to provide further insight into how companies measure and interpret what will be defined as return on equity (ROE).

Ratio Analysis—Profitability

Managers pay close attention to the amount of profits that their companies earn. However, when analyzing ratios, they tend to focus on the amount of profit earned relative to some other amount such as sales, total assets, or total stockholder's equity. When profits are stated as a percentage of another number, such as sales, it helps managers draw informed conclusions about how the organization is performing over time. For example, if a company had profits in Years 1 and 2 of $10 and $20, respectively, it would be naïve to immediately assume that the company's performance has improved. In other words, if we further assume that sales in Year 1 are $100 and sales in Year 2 are $1,000, it would be troubling to see that the company converted $900 of additional sales into only $10 dollars of additional profit. In this section, we develop this idea further by discussing four profitability ratios commonly used by managers—gross margin percentage, net profit margin percentage, return on total assets, and return on equity. *All forthcoming calculations are performed for this year.*

LO15–5
Compute and interpret financial ratios that managers use to assess profitability.

Gross Margin Percentage

Exhibit 15–5 shows that Brickey's cost of goods sold as a percentage of sales increased from 65.6% last year to 69.2% this year. Or looking at this from a different viewpoint, the *gross margin percentage* declined from 34.4% last year to 30.8% this year. Managers and investors pay close attention to this measure of profitability. The **gross margin percentage** is computed as follows:

$$\text{Gross margin percentage} = \frac{\text{Gross margin}}{\text{Sales}}$$

The gross margin percentage should be more stable for retailing companies than for other companies because the cost of goods sold in retailing excludes fixed costs. When fixed costs are included in the cost of goods sold, the gross margin percentage should increase and decrease with sales volume. With increases in sales volume, fixed costs are spread across more units and the gross margin percentage should improve.

IN BUSINESS

HAS ABERCROMBIE & FITCH LOST ITS CACHET?

Over the past five years, **Abercrombie & Fitch** (A&F) has earned gross margin percentages in the low-to-mid 60% range, whereas **American Eagle Outfitters** and **Aéropostale** have earned gross margin percentages below 40%. Part of the reason for A&F's huge margins has been its strong brand recognition among teenagers, who were willing to pay high prices for apparel donning the company's logo. However, now that the fickle teen market has declared logos a fashion faux pas, it presents A&F with an interesting challenge—maintaining its margins by selling logo-less apparel. The financial stakes are high given that each 1% drop in the company's gross margin percentage translates to a 14% drop in net operating income.

Source: Miriam Gottfried, "Abercrombie's Margins Aren't Cool," *The Wall Street Journal,* December 9, 2014, p. C10.

Net Profit Margin Percentage

Exhibit 15–5 shows that Brickey's *net profit margin percentage* decreased from 4.7% last year to 3.4% this year. The **net profit margin percentage** is widely used by managers and it is computed as follows:

$$\text{Net profit margin percentage} = \frac{\text{Net income}}{\text{Sales}}$$

The gross profit margin percentage and the net profit margin percentage state the gross margin and net income as a percentage of sales. The gross margin percentage focuses on only one type of expense (cost of goods sold) and its impact on performance, whereas the net profit margin percentage also looks at how selling and administrative expenses, interest expense, and income tax expense have influenced performance. The remaining ratios in this section look at profitability relative to amounts reported on the balance sheet rather than sales.

IN BUSINESS

© Mark Summerfield/Alamy

ALLEGIANT TRAVEL COMPANY THRIVES SERVING SMALL CITIES

Allegiant Travel Company earns the highest profit margins in the U.S. airline industry by flying customers from 75 small city markets, such as Minot, North Dakota, Allentown, Pennsylvania, and Casper, Wyoming, to 14 warm-weather destinations, such as Tampa, Florida, Honolulu, Hawaii, and Las Vegas, Nevada. Over a five-year span, Allegiant's stock price has risen by over 360% and in a recent quarter, the company earned a pre-tax profit margin of 18.5% on sales of $900 million.

Its enviable financial results are accompanied by the industry's worst on-time arrival rating—with more than 30% of its flights arriving late to their destinations. These contradictory statistics raise an interesting question: how can a company with the worst on-time arrival rate in the airline industry achieve market-leading profit margins? Perhaps part of the answer to this question is that Allegiant's small-city strategy removes competitors from 186 of its 203 routes.

Source: Jack Nicas, "From Toledo to Profitability," *The Wall Street Journal,* June 5, 2013, pp. B1 and B7.

Return on Total Assets

The **return on total assets** is a measure of operating performance that is defined as follows:

$$\text{Return on total assets} = \frac{\text{Net income} + [\text{Interest expense} \times (1 - \text{Tax rate})]}{\text{Average total assets}}$$

Interest expense is added back to net income to show what earnings would have been if the company had no debt. With this adjustment, a manager can evaluate his company's return on total assets over time without the analysis being influenced by changes in the company's mix of debt and equity over time. Furthermore, this adjustment enables managers to draw more meaningful comparisons with other companies that have differing amounts of debt. Notice that the interest expense is placed on an after-tax basis by multiplying it by the factor $(1 - \text{Tax rate})$.

The return on total assets for Brickey Electronics is computed as follows (from Exhibits 15–1 and 15–2):

$$\text{Return on total assets} = \frac{\$1,750,000 + [\$640,000 \times (1 - 0.30)]}{(\$31,500,000 + \$28,970,000)/2} = 7.3\%$$

Brickey Electronics has earned a return of 7.3% on average total assets employed during this year.

Return on Equity

The return on total assets looks at profits relative to total assets, whereas the *return on equity* looks at profits relative to the book value of stockholders' equity. The **return on equity** is computed as follows:

$$\text{Return on equity} = \frac{\text{Net income}}{\text{Average stockholders' equity}}$$

Brickey Electronics' return on equity for this year would be computed as follows:

$$\text{Return on equity} = \frac{\$1,750,000}{(\$17,000,000 + \$15,970,000)/2} = 10.6\%$$

Now that we have computed return on total assets and return on equity, we can take a moment to see financial leverage in operation for Brickey Electronics. Notice from Exhibit 15–1 that the company pays 8% interest on its bonds payable. The after-tax interest cost of these bonds is only 5.6% [8% interest rate $\times (1 - 0.30) = 5.6\%$]. As shown earlier, the company's after-tax return on total assets is 7.3%. Because the return on total assets of 7.3% is greater than the 5.6% after-tax interest cost of the bonds, leverage is positive and the difference goes to the stockholders. This explains in part why the return on equity of 10.6% is greater than the return on total assets of 7.3%.

It also bears emphasizing that many managers and investors take a more in-depth look at return on equity using principles pioneered by **E.I. du Pont de Nemours and Company** (better known as DuPont). This approach recognizes that return on equity is influenced by three elements—operating efficiency (as measured by net profit margin percentage), asset usage efficiency (as measured by total asset turnover), and financial leverage (as measured by the equity multiplier). The following equation computes Brickey Electronics' return on equity using these three elements:

$$\text{Return on equity} = \frac{\text{Net profit margin}}{\text{percentage}} \times \frac{\text{Total asset}}{\text{turnover}} \times \frac{\text{Equity}}{\text{multiplier}}$$

$$\text{Return on equity} = \frac{\text{Net income}}{\text{Sales}} \times \frac{\text{Sales}}{\text{Average total assets}} \times \frac{\text{Average total assets}}{\text{Average stockholders' equity}}$$

$$\text{Return on equity} = 3.37\% \times 1.72 \times 1.83 = 10.6\%$$

Notice that the sales and average total asset figures cancel, so we are left with net income divided by average stockholders' equity. While this equation is a little bit more complex, its return on equity of 10.6% agrees with the initial return on equity computation performed earlier. Also notice that this equation uses a net profit margin percentage of 3.37% rather than the rounded net profit margin percentage of 3.4% shown in Exhibit 15–5. The total asset turnover of 1.72 and the equity multiplier of 1.83 were previously computed earlier in the chapter.

Ratio Analysis—Market Performance

LO15–6
Compute and interpret financial ratios that managers use to assess market performance.

This section summarizes five ratios that common stockholders use to assess a company's performance. Given that common stockholders are the ones who own the company, it logically follows that managers should have a thorough understanding of the measures that their owners will use to judge their performance. *All calculations are performed for this year.*

Earnings per Share

An investor buys a stock in the hope of realizing a return in the form of either dividends or future increases in the value of the stock. Because earnings form the basis for dividend payments and future increases in the value of shares, investors are interested in a company's *earnings per share.*

Earnings per share is computed by dividing net income by the average number of common shares outstanding during the year.

$$\text{Earnings per share} = \frac{\text{Net income}}{\text{Average number of common shares outstanding}}$$

Using the data in Exhibits 15–1 and 15–2, Brickey Electronics' earnings per share would be computed as follows:

$$\text{Earnings per share} = \frac{\$1,750,000}{(500,000 \text{ shares*} + 500,000 \text{ shares})/2} = \$3.50 \text{ per share}$$

*$6,000,000 total par value ÷ $12 par value per share = 500,000 shares.

© RosalreneBetancourt 10/Alamy

IN BUSINESS

MCDONALD'S FACES FINANCIAL CHALLENGES

McDonald's posted a 4.6% drop in monthly same-store sales—its biggest such decline in more than 14 years. The fast-food chain is losing customers to fast-casual chains such as **Chick-fil-A** and **Five Guys Holdings** that offer fewer menu items and faster service. A survey of investment analysts showed that they expect McDonald's sales to drop by 3% and its earnings per share to drop by 9%.

McDonald's U.S.A, President Mike Andres said, "What has worked for McDonald's U.S. for the past decade is not sufficient to propel the business forward in the future." In that spirit, McDonald's has taken steps to better serve local tastes by creating a new organizational structure that divides the U.S. into four geographic regions. The new structure acknowledges that menu-item preferences can differ by geographic region and that McDonald's should be responsive to these differences.

Source: Julie Jargon, "Sales Drop at McDonald's Worsens," *The Wall Street Journal,* December 9, 2014, p. B2.

Price-Earnings Ratio

The **price-earnings ratio** expresses the relationship between a stock's market price per share and its earnings per share. If we assume that Brickey Electronics' stock has a market price of $40 per share at the end of this year, then its price-earnings ratio would be computed as follows:

$$\text{Price-earnings ratio} = \frac{\text{Market price per share}}{\text{Earnings per share}}$$

$$= \frac{\$40 \text{ per share}}{\$3.50 \text{ per share}} = 11.43$$

The price-earnings ratio is 11.43; that is, the stock is selling for about 11.43 times its current earnings per share.

A high price-earnings ratio means that investors are willing to pay a premium for the company's stock—presumably because the company is expected to have higher than average future earnings growth. Conversely, if investors believe a company's future earnings growth prospects are limited, the company's price-earnings ratio would be relatively low. In the late 1990s, the stock prices of some dot.com companies—particularly those with little or no earnings—were selling at levels that resulted in huge and nearly unprecedented price-earnings ratios. Many commentators cautioned that these price-earnings ratios were unsustainable in the long run—and they were right. The stock prices of almost all dot.com companies subsequently crashed.

Dividend Payout and Yield Ratios

Investors in a company's stock make money in two ways—increases in the market value of the stock and dividends. In general, earnings should be retained in a company and not paid out in dividends as long as the rate of return on funds invested inside the company exceeds the rate of return that stockholders could earn on alternative investments outside the company. Therefore, companies with excellent prospects of profitable growth often pay little or no dividend. Companies with little opportunity for profitable growth, but with steady, dependable earnings, tend to pay out a higher percentage of their cash flow from operations as dividends.

The Dividend Payout Ratio   The **dividend payout ratio** quantifies the percentage of current earnings being paid out in dividends. This ratio is computed by dividing the dividends per share by the earnings per share for common stock:

$$\text{Dividend payout ratio} = \frac{\text{Dividends per share}}{\text{Earnings per share}}$$

For Brickey Electronics, the dividend payout ratio is computed as follows:

$$\text{Dividend payout ratio} = \frac{\$1.44 \text{ per share (see Exhibit 15–2)}}{\$3.50 \text{ per share}} = 41.1\%$$

There is no such thing as a "right" dividend payout ratio, although the ratio tends to be similar for companies within the same industry. As noted above, companies with ample growth opportunities at high rates of return tend to have low payout ratios, whereas companies with limited reinvestment opportunities tend to have higher payout ratios.

The Dividend Yield Ratio   The **dividend yield ratio** is computed by dividing the current dividends per share by the current market price per share:

$$\text{Dividend yield ratio} = \frac{\text{Dividends per share}}{\text{Market price per share}}$$

Because the market price for Brickey Electronics' stock is $40 per share, the dividend yield is computed as follows:

$$\text{Dividend yield ratio} = \frac{\$1.44 \text{ per share}}{\$40 \text{ per share}} = 3.6\%$$

The dividend yield ratio measures the rate of return (in the form of cash dividends only) that would be earned by an investor who buys common stock at the current market price. A low dividend yield ratio is neither bad nor good by itself.

Book Value per Share

Book value per share measures the amount that would be distributed to holders of each share of common stock if all assets were sold at their balance sheet carrying amounts (i.e., book values) and if all creditors were paid off. Book value per share is based entirely on historical costs. The formula for computing it is:

$$\text{Book value per share} = \frac{\text{Total stockholders' equity}}{\text{Number of common shares outstanding}}$$

The book value per share of Brickey Electronics' common stock is computed as follows:

$$\text{Book value per share} = \frac{\$17,000,000}{500,000 \text{ shares}} = \$34 \text{ per share}$$

If this book value is compared with the $40 market value of Brickey Electronics' stock, then the stock may appear to be overpriced. However, as we discussed earlier, market prices reflect expectations about future earnings and dividends, whereas book value largely reflects the results of events that have occurred in the past. Ordinarily, the market value of a stock exceeds its book value. For example, in one year, **Microsoft**'s common stock often traded at over 4 times its book value, and **Coca-Cola**'s market value was over 17 times its book value.

Summary of Ratios and Sources of Comparative Ratio Data

Exhibit 15–6 contains a summary of the ratios discussed in this chapter. The formula for each ratio and a summary comment on each ratio's significance are included in the exhibit.

Exhibit 15–7 contains a listing of public sources that provide comparative ratio data organized by industry. These sources are used extensively by managers, investors, and analysts. The **EDGAR** database listed in Exhibit 15–7 is a particularly rich source of data. It contains copies of all reports filed by companies with the SEC since about 1995—including annual reports filed as Form 10–K.

EXHIBIT 15–6
Summary of Ratios

Ratio	Formula	Significance
Liquidity:		
Working capital	Current assets − Current liabilities	Measures the company's ability to repay current liabilities using only current assets
Current ratio	Current assets ÷ Current liabilities	Test of short-term debt-paying ability
Acid-test ratio	(Cash + Marketable securities + Accounts receivable + Short-term notes receivable) ÷ Current liabilities	Test of short-term debt-paying ability without having to rely on inventory
Asset Management:		
Accounts receivable turnover	Sales on account ÷ Average accounts receivable balance	Measures how many times a company's accounts receivable have been turned into cash during the year
Average collection period	365 days ÷ Accounts receivable turnover	Measures the average number of days taken to collect an account receivable
Inventory turnover	Cost of goods sold ÷ Average inventory balance	Measures how many times a company's inventory has been sold during the year
Average sale period	365 days ÷ Inventory turnover	Measures the average number of days taken to sell the inventory one time
Operating cycle	Average sale period + Average collection period	Measures the elapsed time from when inventory is received from suppliers to when cash is received from customers
Total asset turnover	Sales ÷ Average total assets	Measures how efficiently assets are being used to generate sales
Debt Management:		
Times interest earned ratio	Earnings before interest expense and income taxes ÷ Interest expense	Measures the company's ability to make interest payments
Debt-to-equity ratio	Total liabilities ÷ Stockholders' equity	Measures the amount of assets being provided by creditors for each dollar of assets being provided by the stockholders
Equity multiplier	Average total assets ÷ Average stockholders' equity	Measures the portion of a company's assets funded by equity
Profitability:		
Gross margin percentage	Gross margin ÷ Sales	Measures profitability before selling and administrative expenses
Net profit margin percentage	Net income ÷ Sales	A broad measure of profitability
Return on total assets	{Net income + [Interest expense × (1 − Tax rate)]} ÷ Average total assets	Measures how well assets have been employed by management
Return on equity	Net income ÷ Average stockholders' equity	When compared to the return on total assets, measures the extent to which financial leverage is working for or against common stockholders
Market Performance:		
Earnings per share	Net income ÷ Average number of common shares outstanding	Affects the market price per share, as reflected in the price-earnings ratio
Price-earnings ratio	Market price per share ÷ Earnings per share	An index of whether a stock is relatively cheap or relatively expensive in relation to current earnings
Dividend payout ratio	Dividends per share ÷ Earnings per share	An index showing whether a company pays out most of its earnings in dividends or reinvests the earnings internally
Dividend yield ratio	Dividends per share ÷ Market price per share	Shows the return in terms of cash dividends being provided by a stock
Book value per share	Total stockholders' equity ÷ Number of common shares outstanding	Measures the amount that would be distributed to common stockholders if all assets were sold at their balance sheet carrying amounts and if all creditors were paid off

EXHIBIT 15–7
Sources of Financial Ratios

Source	Content
Almanac of Business and Industrial Financial Ratios, Aspen Publishers; published annually	An exhaustive source that contains common-size income statements and financial ratios by industry and by the size of companies within each industry.
AMA Annual Statement Studies, Risk Management Association; published annually	A widely used publication that contains common-size statements and financial ratios on individual companies; the companies are arranged by industry.
EDGAR, Securities and Exchange Commission; website that is continually updated; **www.sec.gov**	An exhaustive Internet database that contains reports filed by companies with the SEC; these reports can be downloaded.
FreeEdgar, EDGAR Online, Inc.; web site that is continually updated; **www.freeedgar.com**	A site that allows you to search SEC filings; financial information can be downloaded directly into Excel worksheets.
Hoover's Online, Hoovers, Inc.; website that is continually updated; **www.hoovers.com**	A site that provides capsule profiles for 10,000 U.S. companies with links to company websites, annual reports, stock charts, news articles, and industry information.
Industry Norms & Key Business Ratios, Dun & Bradstreet; published annually	Fourteen commonly used financial ratios are computed for over 800 major industry groupings.
Mergent Industrial Manual and Mergent Bank and Finance Manual; published annually	An exhaustive source that contains financial ratios on all companies listed on the New York Stock Exchange, the American Stock Exchange, and regional American exchanges.
Sandard & Poor's Industry Survey, Standard & Poor's; published annually	Various statistics, including some financial ratios, are given by industry and for leading companies within each industry grouping.

Summary

The data contained in financial statements represent a quantitative summary of a company's operations and activities. A manager who is skillful at analyzing these statements can learn much about his company's strengths, weaknesses, emerging problems, operating efficiency, profitability, and so forth.

Many techniques are available to analyze financial statements and to assess the direction and importance of trends and changes. In this chapter, we have discussed three such analytical techniques—dollar and percentage changes in statements (horizontal analysis), common-size statements (vertical analysis), and ratio analysis. Refer to Exhibit 15–6 for a detailed listing of the ratios.

Review Problem: Selected Ratios and Financial Leverage

Mulligan Corporation's financial statements are as follows:

Mulligan Corporation Comparative Balance Sheet (dollars in millions)	This Year	Last Year
Assets		
Current assets:		
Cash	$ 281	$ 313
Marketable securities	157	141
Accounts receivable	288	224
Inventories	692	636
Other current assets	278	216
Total current assets	1,696	1,530
Property and equipment, net	2,890	2,288
Other assets	758	611
Total assets	$5,344	$4,429
Liabilities and Stockholders' Equity		
Current liabilities:		
Accounts payable	$ 391	$ 341
Short-term bank loans	710	700
Accrued liabilities	757	662
Other current liabilities	298	233
Total current liabilities	2,156	1,936
Long-term liabilities	904	265
Total liabilities	3,060	2,201
Stockholders' equity:		
Common stock and additional paid-in capital	40	40
Retained earnings	2,244	2,188
Total stockholders' equity	2,284	2,228
Total liabilities and stockholders' equity	$5,344	$4,429

Mulligan Corporation Income Statement (dollars in millions)	This Year
Sales	$9,411
Cost of goods sold	3,999
Gross margin	5,412
Selling and administrative expenses:	
Store operating expenses	3,216
Other operating expenses	294
Depreciation and amortization	467
General and administrative expenses	489
Total selling and administrative expenses	4,466
Net operating income	946
Plus interest and other income	110
Interest expense	0
Net income before taxes	1,056
Income taxes (about 36%)	384
Net income	$ 672

Required:

1. Compute the return on total assets.
2. Compute the return on equity.
3. Is Mulligan's financial leverage positive or negative? Explain.
4. Compute the current ratio.
5. Compute the acid-test ratio.
6. Compute the inventory turnover.
7. Compute the average sale period.
8. Compute the debt-to-equity ratio.
9. Compute the total asset turnover.
10. Compute the net profit margin percentage.

Solution to Review Problem

1. Return on total assets:

$$\text{Return on total assets} = \frac{\text{Net income} + [\text{Interest expense} \times (1 - \text{Tax rate})]}{\text{Average total assets}}$$

$$= \frac{\$672 + [\$0 \times (1 - 0.36)]}{(\$5,344 + \$4,429)/2} = 13.8\% \text{ (rounded)}$$

2. Return on equity:

$$\text{Return on equity} = \frac{\text{Net income}}{\text{Average stockholders' equity}}$$

$$= \frac{\$672}{(\$2,284 + \$2,228)/2} = 29.8\% \text{ (rounded)}$$

3. The company has positive financial leverage because the return on equity of 29.8% is greater than the return on total assets of 13.8%. The positive financial leverage was obtained from current and long-term liabilities.

4. Current ratio:

$$\text{Current ratio} = \frac{\text{Current assets}}{\text{Current liabilities}}$$

$$= \frac{\$1,696}{\$2,156} = 0.79 \text{ (rounded)}$$

5. Acid-test ratio:

$$\text{Acid-test ratio} = \frac{\text{Cash} + \text{Marketable securities} + \text{Accounts receivable} + \text{Short-term notes receivable}}{\text{Current liabilities}}$$

$$= \frac{\$281 + \$157 + \$288 + \$0}{\$2,156} = 0.34 \text{ (rounded)}$$

6. Inventory turnover:

$$\text{Inventory turnover} = \frac{\text{Cost of goods sold}}{\text{Average inventory balance}}$$

$$= \frac{\$3,999}{(\$692 + \$636)/2} = 6.0 \text{ (rounded)}$$

7. Average sale period:

$$\text{Average sale period} = \frac{365 \text{ days}}{\text{Inventory turnover}}$$

$$= \frac{365 \text{ days}}{6.0} = 60.8 \text{ days (rounded)}$$

8. Debt-to-equity ratio:

$$\text{Debt-to-equity ratio} = \frac{\text{Total liabilities}}{\text{Stockholders' equity}}$$

$$= \frac{\$3,060}{\$2,284} = 1.34 \text{ (rounded)}$$

9. Total asset turnover:

$$\text{Total asset turnover} = \frac{\text{Sales}}{\text{Average total assets}}$$

$$\text{Total asset turnover} = \frac{\$9,411}{(\$5,344 + \$4,429)/2} = 1.93 \text{ (rounded)}$$

10. Net profit margin percentage:

$$\text{Net profit margin percentage} = \frac{\text{Net income}}{\text{Sales}}$$

$$\text{Net profit margin percentage} = \frac{\$672}{\$9,411} = 7.1\% \text{ (rounded)}$$

Glossary

(Note: Definitions and formulas for all financial ratios are shown in Exhibit 15–6. These definitions and formulas are not repeated here.)

Common-size financial statements A statement that shows the items appearing on it in percentage form as well as in dollar form. On the income statement, the percentages are based on total sales revenue; on the balance sheet, the percentages are based on total assets. (p. 729)

Financial leverage A difference between the rate of return on assets and the rate paid to creditors. (p. 736)

Horizontal analysis A side-by-side comparison of two or more years' financial statements. (p. 727)

Trend analysis See *Horizontal analysis.* (p. 727)

Trend percentages Several years of financial data expressed as a percentage of performance in a base year. (p. 728)

Vertical analysis The presentation of a company's financial statements in common-size form. (p. 729)

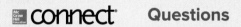 **Questions**

15–1 Distinguish between horizontal and vertical analysis of financial statement data.

15–2 What is the basic purpose for examining trends in a company's financial ratios and other data? What other kinds of comparisons might an analyst make?

15–3 Assume that two companies in the same industry have equal earnings. Why might these companies have different price-earnings ratios? If a company has a price-earnings ratio of 20 and reports earnings per share for the current year of $4, at what price would you expect to find the stock selling on the market?

15–4 Would you expect a company in a rapidly growing technological industry to have a high or low dividend payout ratio?

15–5 What is meant by the dividend yield on a common stock investment?

15–6 What is meant by the term financial leverage?

15–7 The president of a plastics company was quoted in a business journal as stating, "We haven't had a dollar of interest-paying debt in over 10 years. Not many companies can say that." As a stockholder in this company, how would you feel about its policy of not taking on debt?

15–8 If a stock's market value exceeds its book value, then the stock is overpriced. Do you agree? Explain.

15–9 A company seeking a line of credit at a bank was turned down. Among other things, the bank stated that the company's 2 to 1 current ratio was not adequate. Give reasons why a 2 to 1 current ratio might not be adequate.

The Foundational 15

Markus Company's common stock sold for $2.75 per share at the end of this year. The company paid a common stock dividend of $0.55 per share this year. It also provided the following *data excerpts* from this year's financial statements:

LO15–2, LO15–3, LO15–4, LO15–5, LO15–6

	Ending Balance	Beginning Balance
Cash	$35,000	$30,000
Accounts receivable	$60,000	$50,000
Inventory	$55,000	$60,000
Current assets	$150,000	$140,000
Total assets	$450,000	$460,000
Current liabilities	$60,000	$40,000
Total liabilities	$130,000	$120,000
Common stock, $1 par value	$120,000	$120,000
Total stockholders' equity	$320,000	$340,000
Total liabilities and stockholders' equity	$450,000	$460,000

	This Year
Sales (all on account)	$700,000
Cost of goods sold	$400,000
Gross margin	$300,000
Net operating income..................	$140,000
Interest expense	$8,000
Net income...........................	$92,400

Required:
1. What is the earnings per share?
2. What is the price-earnings ratio?
3. What is the dividend payout ratio and the dividend yield ratio?
4. What is the return on total assets (assuming a 30% tax rate)?
5. What is the return on equity?
6. What is the book value per share at the end of this year?
7. What is the amount of working capital and the current ratio at the end of this year?
8. What is the acid-test ratio at the end of this year?
9. What is the accounts receivable turnover and the average collection period?
10. What is the inventory turnover and the average sale period?
11. What is the company's operating cycle?
12. What is the total asset turnover?
13. What is the times interest earned ratio?
14. What is the debt-to-equity ratio at the end of this year?
15. What is the equity multiplier?

Exercises

EXERCISE 15–1 Common-Size Income Statement LO15–1

A comparative income statement is given below for McKenzie Sales, Ltd., of Toronto:

McKenzie Sales, Ltd. Comparative Income Statement		
	This Year	Last Year
Sales	$8,000,000	$6,000,000
Cost of goods sold	4,984,000	3,516,000
Gross margin	3,016,000	2,484,000
Selling and administrative expenses:		
Selling expenses	1,480,000	1,092,000
Administrative expenses	712,000	618,000
Total expenses	2,192,000	1,710,000
Net operating income	824,000	774,000
Interest expense	96,000	84,000
Net income before taxes	$ 728,000	$ 690,000

Members of the company's board of directors are surprised to see that net income increased by only $38,000 when sales increased by $2,000,000.

Required:

1. Express each year's income statement in common-size percentages. Carry computations to one decimal place.
2. Comment briefly on the changes between the two years.

EXERCISE 15–2 Financial Ratios for Assessing Liquidity LO15–2

Comparative financial statements for Weller Corporation, a merchandising company, for the year ending December 31 appear below. The company did not issue any new common stock during the year. A total of 800,000 shares of common stock were outstanding. The interest rate on the bond payable was 12%, the income tax rate was 40%, and the dividend per share of common stock was $0.75 last year and $0.40 this year. The market value of the company's common stock at the end of this year was $18. All of the company's sales are on account.

Weller Corporation Comparative Balance Sheet (dollars in thousands)	This Year	Last Year
Assets		
Current assets:		
Cash	$ 1,280	$ 1,560
Accounts receivable, net	12,300	9,100
Inventory	9,700	8,200
Prepaid expenses	1,800	2,100
Total current assets	25,080	20,960
Property and equipment:		
Land	6,000	6,000
Buildings and equipment, net	19,200	19,000
Total property and equipment	25,200	25,000
Total assets	$50,280	$45,960
Liabilities and Stockholders' Equity		
Current liabilities:		
Accounts payable	$ 9,500	$ 8,300
Accrued liabilities	600	700
Notes payable, short term	300	300
Total current liabilities	10,400	9,300
Long-term liabilities:		
Bonds payable	5,000	5,000
Total liabilities	15,400	14,300
Stockholders' equity:		
Common stock	800	800
Additional paid-in capital	4,200	4,200
Total paid-in capital	5,000	5,000
Retained earnings	29,880	26,660
Total stockholders' equity	34,880	31,660
Total liabilities and stockholders' equity	$50,280	$45,960

Weller Corporation Comparative Income Statement and Reconciliation (dollars in thousands)		
	This Year	Last Year
Sales	$79,000	$74,000
Cost of goods sold	52,000	48,000
Gross margin	27,000	26,000
Selling and administrative expenses:		
Selling expenses	8,500	8,000
Administrative expenses	12,000	11,000
Total selling and administrative expenses	20,500	19,000
Net operating income	6,500	7,000
Interest expense	600	600
Net income before taxes	5,900	6,400
Income taxes	2,360	2,560
Net income	3,540	3,840
Dividends to common stockholders	320	600
Net income added to retained earnings	3,220	3,240
Beginning retained earnings	26,660	23,420
Ending retained earnings	$29,880	$26,660

Required:
Compute the following financial data and ratios for this year:
1. Working capital.
2. Current ratio.
3. Acid-test ratio.

EXERCISE 15–3 Financial Ratios for Asset Management LO15–3
Refer to the data in Exercise 15–2 for Weller Corporation.

Required:
Compute the following financial data for this year:
1. Accounts receivable turnover. (Assume that all sales are on account.)
2. Average collection period.
3. Inventory turnover.
4. Average sale period.
5. Operating cycle.
6. Total asset turnover.

EXERCISE 15–4 Financial Ratios for Debt Management LO15–4
Refer to the data in Exercise 15–2 for Weller Corporation.

Required:
Compute the following financial ratios for this year:
1. Times interest earned ratio.
2. Debt-to-equity ratio.
3. Equity multiplier.

EXERCISE 15–5 Financial Ratios for Assessing Profitability LO15–5
Refer to the data in Exercise 15–2 for Weller Corporation.

Required:
Compute the following financial data for this year:
1. Gross margin percentage.
2. Net profit margin percentage.
3. Return on total assets.
4. Return on equity.

EXERCISE 15–6 Financial Ratios for Assessing Market Performance LO15–6

Refer to the data in Exercise 15–2 for Weller Corporation.

Required:
Compute the following financial data for this year:
1. Earnings per share.
2. Price-earnings ratio.
3. Dividend payout ratio.
4. Dividend yield ratio.
5. Book value per share.

EXERCISE 15–7 Trend Percentages LO15–1

Rotorua Products, Ltd., of New Zealand markets agricultural products for the burgeoning Asian consumer market. The company's current assets, current liabilities, and sales over the last five years (Year 5 is the most recent year) are as follows:

	Year 1	Year 2	Year 3	Year 4	Year 5
Sales	$1,800,000	$1,980,000	$2,070,000	$2,160,000	$2,250,000
Cash	$ 50,000	$ 65,000	$ 48,000	$ 40,000	$ 30,000
Accounts receivable, net	300,000	345,000	405,000	510,000	570,000
Inventory	600,000	660,000	690,000	720,000	750,000
Total current assets	$ 950,000	$1,070,000	$1,143,000	$1,270,000	$1,350,000
Current liabilities	$ 400,000	$ 440,000	$ 520,000	$ 580,000	$ 640,000

Required:
1. Express all of the asset, liability, and sales data in trend percentages. (Show percentages for each item.) Use Year 1 as the base year and carry computations to one decimal place.
2. Comment on the results of your analysis.

EXERCISE 15–8 Selected Financial Ratios LO15–2, LO15–3, LO15–4

The financial statements for Castile Products, Inc., are given below:

Castile Products, Inc. Balance Sheet December 31	
Assets	
Current assets:	
Cash	$ 6,500
Accounts receivable, net	35,000
Merchandise inventory	70,000
Prepaid expenses	3,500
Total current assets	115,000
Property and equipment, net	185,000
Total assets	$300,000
Liabilities and Stockholders' Equity	
Liabilities:	
Current liabilities	$ 50,000
Bonds payable, 10%	80,000
Total liabilities	130,000
Stockholders' equity:	
Common stock, $5 per value	30,000
Retained earnings	140,000
Total stockholders' equity	170,000
Total liabilities and stockholders' equity	$300,000

Castile Products, Inc. Income Statement For the Year Ended December 31	
Sales	$420,000
Cost of goods sold	292,500
Gross margin	127,500
Selling and administrative expenses	89,500
Net operating income	38,000
Interest expense	8,000
Net income before taxes	30,000
Income taxes (30%)	9,000
Net income	$ 21,000

Account balances at the beginning of the year were: accounts receivable, $25,000; and inventory, $60,000. All sales were on account.

Required:
Compute the following financial data and ratios:
1. Working capital.
2. Current ratio.
3. Acid-test ratio.
4. Debt-to-equity ratio.
5. Times interest earned ratio.
6. Average collection period.
7. Average sale period.
8. Operating cycle.

EXERCISE 15–9 Financial Ratios for Assessing Profitability and Managing Debt LO15–4, LO15–5
Refer to the financial statements for Castile Products, Inc., in Exercise 15–8. Assets at the beginning of the year totaled $280,000, and the stockholders' equity totaled $161,600.

Required:
Compute the following:
1. Gross margin percentage.
2. Net profit margin percentage.
3. Return on total assets.
4. Return on equity.
5. Was financial leverage positive or negative for the year? Explain.

EXERCISE 15–10 Financial Ratios for Assessing Market Performance LO15–6
Refer to the financial statements for Castile Products, Inc., in Exercise 15–8. In addition to the data in these statements, assume that Castile Products, Inc., paid dividends of $2.10 per share during the year. Also assume that the company's common stock had a market price of $42 at the end of the year and there was no change in the number of outstanding shares of common stock during the year.

Required:
Compute financial ratios as follows:
1. Earnings per share.
2. Dividend payout ratio.
3. Dividend yield ratio.
4. Price-earnings ratio.
5. Book value per share.

EXERCISE 15–11 Financial Ratios for Assessing Profitability and Managing Debt LO15–4, LO15–5
Selected financial data from the June 30 year-end statements of Safford Company are given below:

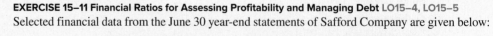

Total assets	$3,600,000
Long-term debt (12% interest rate)	$500,000
Total stockholders' equity	$2,400,000
Interest paid on long-term debt	$60,000
Net income	$280,000

Total assets at the beginning of the year were $3,000,000; total stockholders' equity was $2,200,000. The company's tax rate is 30%.

Required:
1. Compute the return on total assets.
2. Compute the return on equity.
3. Is financial leverage positive or negative? Explain.

EXERCISE 15–12 Selected Financial Measures for Assessing Liquidity LO15–2

Norsk Optronics, ALS, of Bergen, Norway, had a current ratio of 2.5 on June 30 of the current year. On that date, the company's assets were:

Cash	$ 90,000
Accounts receivable, net	260,000
Inventory	490,000
Prepaid expenses	10,000
Plant and equipment, net	800,000
Total assets	$1,650,000

Required:
1. What was the company's working capital on June 30?
2. What was the company's acid-test ratio on June 30?
3. The company paid an account payable of $40,000 immediately after June 30.
   a. What effect did this transaction have on working capital? Show computations.
   b. What effect did this transaction have on the current ratio? Show computations.

connect   Problems

PROBLEM 15–13 Effects of Transactions on Various Financial Ratios LO15–2, LO15–3, LO15–4, LO15–5, LO15–6

In the right-hand column below, certain financial ratios are listed. To the left of each ratio is a business transaction or event relating to the operating activities of Delta Company (each transaction should be considered independently).

Business Transaction or Event	Ratio
1. Declared a cash dividend.	Current ratio
2. Sold inventory on account at cost.	Acid-test ratio
3. Issued bonds with an interest rate of 8%. The company's return on assets is 10%.	Return on equity
4. Net income decreased by 10% between last year and this year. Long-term debt remained unchanged.	Times interest earned
5. Paid a previously declared cash dividend.	Current ratio
6. The market price of the company's common stock dropped from $24.50 to $20.00. The dividend paid per share remained unchanged.	Dividend payout ratio
7. Obsolete inventory totaling $100,000 was written off as a loss.	Inventory turnover ratio
8. Sold inventory for cash at a profit.	Debt-to-equity ratio
9. Changed customer credit terms from 2/10, n/30 to 2/15, n/30 to comply with a change in industry practice.	Accounts receivable turnover ratio
10. Issued a stock dividend to common stockholders.	Book value per share
11. The market price of the company's common stock increased from $24.50 to $30.00.	Book value per share
12. Paid $40,000 on accounts payable.	Working capital
13. Issued a stock dividend to common stockholders.	Earnings per share
14. Paid accounts payable.	Debt-to-equity ratio
15. Purchased inventory on account.	Acid-test ratio
16. Wrote off an uncollectible account against the Allowance for Bad Debts.	Current ratio
17. The market price of the company's common stock increased from $24.50 to $30.00. Earnings per share remained unchanged.	Price-earnings ratio
18. The market price of the company's common stock increased from $24.50 to $30.00. The dividend paid per share remained unchanged.	Dividend yield ratio

Required:

Indicate the effect that each business transaction or event would have on the ratio listed opposite to it. State the effect in terms of increase, decrease, or no effect on the ratio involved, and give the reason for your answer. In all cases, assume that the current assets exceed the current liabilities both before and after the event or transaction. Use the following format for your answers:

Effect on Ratio	Reason for Increase, Decrease, or No Effect
1.	
Etc.	

PROBLEM 15–14 Effects of Transactions on Various Ratios LO15–2

Denna Company's working capital accounts at the beginning of the year follow:

Cash	$50,000
Marketable securities	$30,000
Accounts receivable, net	$200,000
Inventory	$210,000
Prepaid expenses	$10,000
Accounts payable.....................	$150,000
Notes due within one year	$30,000
Accrued liabilities	$20,000

During the year, Denna Company completed the following transactions:

Ex. Paid a cash dividend previously declared, $12,000.
a. Issued additional shares of common stock for cash, $100,000.
b. Sold inventory costing $50,000 for $80,000, on account.
c. Wrote off uncollectible accounts in the amount of $10,000, reducing the accounts receivable balance accordingly.
d. Declared a cash dividend, $15,000.
e. Paid accounts payable, $50,000.
f. Borrowed cash on a short-term note with the bank, $35,000.
g. Sold inventory costing $15,000 for $10,000 cash.
h. Purchased inventory on account, $60,000.
i. Paid off all short-term notes due, $30,000.
j. Purchased equipment for cash, $15,000.
k. Sold marketable securities costing $18,000 for cash, $15,000.
l. Collected cash on accounts receivable, $80,000.

Required:

1. Compute the following amounts and ratios as of the beginning of the year:
   a. Working capital.
   b. Current ratio.
   c. Acid-test ratio.
2. Indicate the effect of each of the transactions given above on working capital, the current ratio, and the acid-test ratio. Give the effect in terms of increase, decrease, or none. Item *Ex* is given below as an example of the format to use:

	The Effect on		
Transaction	Working Capital	Current Ratio	Acid-Test Ratio
Ex. Paid a cash dividend previously declared	None	Increase	Increase

PROBLEM 15–15 Comprehensive Ratio Analysis LO15–2, LO15–3, LO15–4, LO15–5, LO15–6

You have just been hired as a financial analyst for Lydex Company, a manufacturer of safety helmets. Your boss has asked you to perform a comprehensive analysis of the company's financial statements, including comparing Lydex's performance to its major competitors. The company's financial statements for the last two years are as follows:

Lydex Company
Comparative Balance Sheet

	This Year	Last Year
Assets		
Current assets:		
Cash	$ 960,000	$ 1,260,000
Marketable securities	0	300,000
Accounts receivable, net	2,700,000	1,800,000
Inventory	3,900,000	2,400,000
Prepaid expenses	240,000	180,000
Total current assets	7,800,000	5,940,000
Plant and equipment, net	9,300,000	8,940,000
Total assets	$17,100,000	$14,880,000
Liabilities and Stockholders' Equity		
Liabilities:		
Current liabilities...................	$ 3,900,000	$ 2,760,000
Note payable, 10%.................	3,600,000	3,000,000
Total liabilities	7,500,000	5,760,000
Stockholders' equity:		
Common stock, $78 par value	7,800,000	7,800,000
Retained earnings	1,800,000	1,320,000
Total stockholders' equity	9,600,000	9,120,000
Total liabilities and stockholders' equity .	$17,100,000	$14,880,000

Lydex Company
Comparative Income Statement and Reconciliation

	This Year	Last Year
Sales (all on account)	$15,750,000	$12,480,000
Cost of goods sold	12,600,000	9,900,000
Gross margin	3,150,000	2,580,000
Selling and administrative expenses ...	1,590,000	1,560,000
Net operating income	1,560,000	1,020,000
Interest expense	360,000	300,000
Net income before taxes	1,200,000	720,000
Income taxes (30%)	360,000	216,000
Net income	840,000	504,000
Common dividends	360,000	252,000
Net income retained	480,000	252,000
Beginning retained earnings	1,320,000	1,068,000
Ending retained earnings	$ 1,800,000	$ 1,320,000

To begin your assignment you gather the following financial data and ratios that are typical of companies in Lydex Company's industry:

Current ratio	2.3
Acid-test ratio	1.2
Average collection period	30 days
Average sale period	60 days
Return on assets	9.5%
Debt-to-equity ratio	0.65
Times interest earned ratio	5.7
Price-earnings ratio	10

Required:

1. You decide first to assess the company's performance in terms of debt management and profitability. Compute the following for both this year and last year:
   a. The times interest earned ratio.
   b. The debt-to-equity ratio.
   c. The gross margin percentage.
   d. The return on total assets. (Total assets at the beginning of last year were $12,960,000.)
   e. The return on equity. (Stockholders' equity at the beginning of last year totaled $9,048,000. There has been no change in common stock over the last two years.)
   f. Is the company's financial leverage positive or negative? Explain.

2. You decide next to assess the company's stock market performance. Assume that Lydex's stock price at the end of this year is $72 per share and that at the end of last year it was $40. For both this year and last year, compute:
   a. The earnings per share.
   b. The dividend yield ratio.
   c. The dividend payout ratio.
   d. The price-earnings ratio. How do investors regard Lydex Company as compared to other companies in the industry? Explain.
   e. The book value per share of common stock. Does the difference between market value per share and book value per share suggest that the stock at its current price is a bargain? Explain.

3. You decide, finally, to assess the company's liquidity and asset management. For both this year and last year, compute:
   a. Working capital.
   b. The current ratio.
   c. The acid-test ratio.
   d. The average collection period. (The accounts receivable at the beginning of last year totaled $1,560,000.)
   e. The average sale period. (The inventory at the beginning of last year totaled $1,920,000.)
   f. The operating cycle.
   g. The total asset turnover. (The total assets at the beginning of last year totaled $12,960,000.)

4. Prepare a brief memo that summarizes how Lydex is performing relative to its competitors.

PROBLEM 15–16 Common-Size Financial Statements LO15–1

Refer to the financial statement data for Lydex Company given in Problem 15–15.

Required:

For both this year and last year:
1. Present the balance sheet in common-size format.
2. Present the income statement in common-size format down through net income.
3. Comment on the results of your analysis.

PROBLEM 15–17 Interpretation of Financial Ratios LO15–2, LO15–3, LO15–6

Pecunious Products, Inc.'s financial results for the past three years are summarized below:

	Year 3	Year 2	Year 1
Sales trend	128.0	115.0	100.0
Current ratio	2.5	2.3	2.2
Acid-test ratio	0.8	0.9	1.1
Accounts receivable turnover	9.4	10.6	12.5
Inventory turnover	6.5	7.2	8.0
Dividend yield	7.1%	6.5%	5.8%
Dividend payout ratio	40%	50%	60%
Dividends paid per share*	$1.50	$1.50	$1.50

*There have been no changes in common stock outstanding over the three-year period.

Your boss has asked you to review these results and then answer the following questions:
a. Is it becoming easier for the company to pay its bills as they come due?
b. Are customers paying their accounts at least as fast now as they were in Year 1?
c. Is the total of the accounts receivable increasing, decreasing, or remaining constant?
d. Is the level of inventory increasing, decreasing, or remaining constant?

e.   Is the market price of the company's stock going up or down?

f.   Is the earnings per share increasing or decreasing?

g.   Is the price-earning ratio going up or down?

Required:

Provide answers to each of the questions raised by your boss.

PROBLEM 15–18 Common-Size Statements and Financial Ratios for a Loan Application LO15–1, LO15–2, LO15–3, LO15–4

Paul Sabin organized Sabin Electronics 10 years ago to produce and sell several electronic devices on which he had secured patents. Although the company has been fairly profitable, it is now experiencing a severe cash shortage. For this reason, it is requesting a $500,000 long-term loan from Gulfport State Bank, $100,000 of which will be used to bolster the Cash account and $400,000 of which will be used to modernize equipment. The company's financial statements for the two most recent years follow:

Sabin Electronics Comparative Balance Sheet	This Year	Last Year
Assets		
Current assets:		
Cash	$ 70,000	$ 150,000
Marketable securities	0	18,000
Accounts receivable, net	480,000	300,000
Inventory	950,000	600,000
Prepaid expenses	20,000	22,000
Total current assets	1,520,000	1,090,000
Plant and equipment, net	1,480,000	1,370,000
Total assets	$3,000,000	$2,460,000
Liabilities and Stockholders' Equity		
Liabilities:		
Current liabilities	$ 800,000	$ 430,000
Bonds payable, 12%	600,000	600,000
Total liabilities	1,400,000	1,030,000
Stockholders' equity:		
Common stock, $15 par	750,000	750,000
Retained earnings	850,000	680,000
Total stockholders' equity	1,600,000	1,430,000
Total liabilities and stockholders' equity ...	$3,000,000	$2,460,000

Sabin Electronics Comparative Income Statement and Reconciliation	This Year	Last Year
Sales	$5,000,000	$4,350,000
Cost of goods sold	3,875,000	3,450,000
Gross margin	1,125,000	900,000
Selling and administrative expenses ..	653,000	548,000
Net operating income	472,000	352,000
Interest expense	72,000	72,000
Net income before taxes	400,000	280,000
Income taxes (30%)	120,000	84,000
Net income	280,000	196,000
Common dividends	110,000	95,000
Net income retained	170,000	101,000
Beginning retained earnings	680,000	579,000
Ending retained earnings	$ 850,000	$ 680,000

During the past year, the company introduced several new product lines and raised the selling prices on a number of old product lines in order to improve its profit margin. The company also hired a new sales manager, who has expanded sales into several new territories. Sales terms are 2/10, n/30. All sales are on account.

Required:

1. To assist in approaching the bank about the loan, Paul has asked you to compute the following ratios for both this year and last year:
   a. The amount of working capital.
   b. The current ratio.
   c. The acid-test ratio.
   d. The average collection period. (The accounts receivable at the beginning of last year totaled $250,000.)
   e. The average sale period. (The inventory at the beginning of last year totaled $500,000.)
   f. The operating cycle.
   g. The total asset turnover. (The total assets at the beginning of last year were $2,420,000.)
   h. The debt-to-equity ratio.
   i. The times interest earned ratio.
   j. The equity multiplier. (The total stockholders' equity at the beginning of last year totaled $1,420,000.)

2. For both this year and last year:
   a. Present the balance sheet in common-size format.
   b. Present the income statement in common-size format down through net income.

3. Paul Sabin has also gathered the following financial data and ratios that are typical of companies in the electronics industry:

Current ratio	2.5
Acid-test ratio	1.3
Average collection period	18 days
Average sale period	60 days
Debt-to-equity ratio	0.90
Times interest earned ratio	6.0

Comment on the results of your analysis in (1) and (2) above and compare Sabin Electronics' performance to the benchmarks from the electronics industry. Do you think that the company is likely to get its loan application approved?

PROBLEM 15–19 Financial Ratios for Assessing Profitability and Market Performance LO15–5, LO15–6
Refer to the financial statements and other data in Problem 15–18. Assume Paul Sabin has asked you to assess his company's profitability and stock market performance.

Required:

1. You decide first to assess the company's stock market performance. For both this year and last year, compute:
   a. The earnings per share. There has been no change in common stock over the last two years.
   b. The dividend yield ratio. The company's stock is currently selling for $40 per share; last year it sold for $36 per share.
   c. The dividend payout ratio.
   d. The price-earnings ratio. How do investors regard Sabin Electronics as compared to other companies in the industry if the industry norm for the price-earnings ratio is 12? Explain.
   e. The book value per share of common stock. Does the difference between market value and book value suggest that the stock is overpriced? Explain.

2. You decide next to assess the company's profitability. Compute the following for both this year and last year:
   a. The gross margin percentage.
   b. The net profit margin percentage.

c. The return on total assets. (Total assets at the beginning of last year were $2,420,000.)
d. The return on equity. (Stockholders' equity at the beginning of last year was $1,420,000.)
e. Is the company's financial leverage positive or negative? Explain.
3. Comment on the company's profit performance and stock market performance over the two-year period.

PROBLEM 15–20 Ethics and the Manager LO15–2, LO15–4

Venice InLine, Inc., was founded by Russ Perez to produce a specialized in-line skate he had designed for doing aerial tricks. Up to this point, Russ has financed the company with his own savings and with cash generated by his business. However, Russ now faces a cash crisis. In the year just ended, an acute shortage of high-impact roller bearings developed just as the company was beginning production for the Christmas season. Russ had been assured by his suppliers that the roller bearings would be delivered in time to make Christmas shipments, but the suppliers were unable to fully deliver on this promise. As a consequence, Venice InLine had large stocks of unfinished skates at the end of the year and was unable to fill all of the orders that had come in from retailers for the Christmas season. Consequently, sales were below expectations for the year, and Russ does not have enough cash to pay his creditors.

Well before the accounts payable were due, Russ visited a local bank and inquired about obtaining a loan. The loan officer at the bank assured Russ that there should not be any problem getting a loan to pay off his accounts payable—providing that on his most recent financial statements the current ratio was above 2.0, the acid-test ratio was above 1.0, and net operating income was at least four times the interest on the proposed loan. Russ promised to return later with a copy of his financial statements.

Russ would like to apply for a $80,000 six-month loan bearing an interest rate of 10% per year. The unaudited financial reports of the company appear below:

Venice InLine, Inc. Comparative Balance Sheet As of December 31 (dollars in thousands)		
	This Year	Last Year
Assets		
Current assets:		
Cash	$ 70	$150
Accounts receivable, net	50	40
Inventory	160	100
Prepaid expenses	10	12
Total current assets	290	302
Property and equipment	270	180
Total assets	$560	$482
Liabilities and Stockholders' Equity		
Current liabilities:		
Accounts payable.......................	$154	$ 90
Accrued liabilities	10	10
Total current liabilities	164	100
Long-term liabilities	—	—
Total liabilities	164	100
Stockholders' equity:		
Common stock and additional paid-in capital	100	100
Retained earnings	296	282
Total stockholders' equity	396	382
Total liabilities and stockholders' equity	$560	$482

Venice InLine, Inc.
Income Statement
For the Year Ended December 31
(dollars in thousands)

	This Year
Sales (all on account)	$420
Cost of goods sold	290
Gross margin	130
Selling and administrative expenses:	
Selling expenses	42
Administrative expenses	68
Total selling and administrative expenses	110
Net operating income	20
Interest expense	—
Net income before taxes	20
Income taxes (30%)	6
Net income	$ 14

Required:
1. Based on the unaudited financial statements and the statement made by the loan officer, would the company qualify for the loan?
2. Last year Russ purchased and installed new, more efficient equipment to replace an older plastic injection molding machine. Russ had originally planned to sell the old machine but found that it is still needed whenever the plastic injection molding process is a bottleneck. When Russ discussed his cash flow problems with his brother-in-law, he suggested to Russ that the old machine be sold or at least reclassified as inventory on the balance sheet because it could be readily sold. At present, the machine is carried in the Property and Equipment account and could be sold for its net book value of $45,000. The bank does not require audited financial statements. What advice would you give to Russ concerning the machine?

PROBLEM 15–21 Incomplete Statements; Ratios Analysis LO15–2, LO15–3, LO15–4, LO15–5, LO15–6
Incomplete financial statements for Pepper Industries follow:

Pepper Industries
Balance Sheet
March 31

Current assets:	
Cash	$?
Accounts receivable, net	?
Inventory	?
Total current assets	?
Plant and equipment, net	?
Total assets	$?
Liabilities:	
Current liabilities	$320,000
Bonds payable, 10%	?
Total liabilities	?
Stockholders' equity:	
Common stock, $5 par value	?
Retained earnings	?
Total stockholders' equity	?
Total liabilities and stockholders' equity	$?

Pepper Industries Income Statement For the Year Ended March 31	
Sales	$4,200,000
Cost of goods sold	?
Gross margin	?
Selling and administrative expenses	?
Net operating income	?
Interest expense	80,000
Net income before taxes	?
Income taxes (30%)	?
Net income	$?

The following additional information is available about the company:

a. All sales during the year were on account.

b. There was no change in the number of shares of common stock outstanding during the year.

c. The interest expense on the income statement relates to the bonds payable; the amount of bonds outstanding did not change during the year.

d. Selected balances at the *beginning* of the current year were:

Accounts receivable	$270,000
Inventory	$360,000
Total assets	$1,800,000

e. Selected financial ratios computed from the statements above for the current year are:

Earnings per share	$2.30
Debt-to-equity ratio	0.875
Accounts receivable turnover	14.0
Current ratio	2.75
Return on total assets	18.0%
Times interest earned ratio	6.75
Acid-test ratio	1.25
Inventory turnover	6.5

Required:

Compute the missing amounts on the company's financial statements. (*Hint:* What's the difference between the acid-test ratio and the current ratio?)

Integration Exercises: An Overview

Successful managers rely on an integrated set of managerial accounting competencies to solve complex real-world problems. Therefore, we have created 13 integration exercises to help you develop these critically important managerial skills. This collective group of exercises will enable you to see how the learning objectives throughout the book interrelate with one another. As you begin to understand "how it all fits together," you will start the exciting evolution from "number cruncher" to a manager-in-training.

Integration Exercises

INTEGRATION EXERCISE 1 Activity Variance, Spending Variance, Materials Price Variance, Materials Quantity Variance LO9–1, 9–2, LO9–3, LO10–1

Southside Pizzeria wants to improve its ability to manage the ingredient costs associated with making and selling its pizzas. For the month of June, the company plans to make 1,000 pizzas. It has created a planning budget that includes a cost formula for mozzarella cheese of $2.40 per pizza. At the end of June, Southside actually sold 1,100 pizzas and the actual cost of the cheese that it used during the month was $2,632.

Required:
1. What is the mozzarella cheese activity variance for June?
2. What is the mozzarella cheese spending variance for June?
3. Assume that the company establishes a price standard of $0.30 per ounce for mozzarella cheese and a quantity standard of eight ounces of cheese per pizza. Also, assume that Southside actually used 9,400 ounces of cheese during the month to make 1,100 pizzas.
   a. What is the materials price variance for mozzarella cheese for June?
   b. What is the materials quantity variance for mozzarella cheese for June?
   c. What is the materials spending variance for mozzarella cheese for June?

INTEGRATION EXERCISE 2 Different Costs for Different Purposes, Cost-Volume-Profit-Relationships
LO1–1, LO1–2, LO1–3, LO1–4, LO1–5, LO1–6, LO5–1, LO5–3, LO5–5, LO5–7, LO5–8

Hixson Company manufactures and sells one product for $34 per unit. The company maintains no beginning or ending inventories and its relevant range of production is 20,000 units to 30,000 units. When Hixson produces and sells 25,000 units, its unit costs are as follows:

	Amount per Unit
Direct materials	$8.00
Direct labor	$5.00
Variable manufacturing overhead	$1.00
Fixed manufacturing overhead	$6.00
Fixed selling expense	$3.50
Fixed administrative expense	$2.50
Sales commissions	$4.00
Variable administrative expense	$1.00

Required:
1. For financial accounting purposes, what is the total amount of product costs incurred to make 25,000 units? What is the total amount of period costs incurred to sell 25,000 units?
2. If 24,000 units are produced, what is the variable manufacturing cost per unit produced? What is the average fixed manufacturing cost per unit produced?

3. If 26,000 units are produced, what is the variable manufacturing cost per unit produced? What is the average fixed manufacturing cost per unit produced?

4. If 27,000 units are produced, what are the total amounts of direct and indirect manufacturing costs incurred to support this level of production?

5. What total incremental manufacturing cost will Hixson incur if it increases production from 25,000 to 25,001 units?

6. What is Hixson's contribution margin per unit? What is its contribution margin ratio?

7. What is Hixson's break-even point in unit sales? What is its break-even point in dollar sales?

8. How much will Hixson's net operating income increase if it can grow production and sales from 25,000 units to 26,500 units?

9. What is Hixson's margin of safety at a sales volume of 25,000 units?

10. What is Hixson degree of operating leverage at a sales volume of 25,000 units?

INTEGRATION EXERCISE 3 Absorption Costing, Variable Costing, Cost-Volume-Profit-Relationships

LO5–4, LO5–5, LO5–7, LO6–1, LO6–2

Newton Company manufactures and sells one product. The company assembled the following projections for its first year of operations:

Variable costs per unit:	
Manufacturing:	
Direct materials	$20
Direct labor.....................................	$16
Variable manufacturing overhead	$4
Variable selling and administrative................	$2
Fixed costs per year:	
Fixed manufacturing overhead...................	$450,000
Fixed selling and administrative expenses.........	$70,000

During its first year of operations Newton expects to produce 25,000 units and sell 20,000 units. The budgeted selling price of the company's only product is $66 per unit.

Required (answer each question independently by referring to the original data):

1. Assuming that Newton's projections are accurate, what will be its absorption costing net operating income in its first year of operations?

2. Newton is considering investing in a higher quality raw material that will increase its direct materials cost by $1 per unit. It estimates that the higher quality raw material will increase sales by 1,000 units. What will be the company's revised absorption costing net operating income if it invests in the higher quality raw material and continues to *produce* 25,000 units?

3. Newton is considering raising its selling price by $1.00 per unit with an expectation that it will lower unit sales by 1,500 units. What will be the company's revised absorption costing net operating income if it raises its price by $1.00 and continues to *produce* 25,000 units?

4. Assuming that Newton's projections are accurate, what will be its variable costing net operating income in its first year of operations?

5. Newton is considering investing in a higher quality raw material that will increase its direct materials cost by $1 per unit. It estimates that the higher quality raw material will increase sales by 1,000 units. What will be the company's revised variable costing net operating income if it invests in the higher quality raw material and continues to *produce* 25,000 units?

6. Newton is considering raising its selling price by $1.00 per unit with an expectation that it will lower unit sales by 1,500 units. What will be the company's revised variable costing net operating income if it raises its price by $1.00 and continues to *produce* 25,000 units?

7. What is Newton's break-even point in unit sales? What is its break-even point in dollar sales?
8. What is the company's projected margin of safety in its first year of operations?

INTEGRATION EXERCISE 4 Cash Budget, Income Statement, Balance Sheet, Statement of Cash Flows, Ratio Analysis LO8–2, LO8–3, LO8–4, LO8–8, LO8–9, LO8–10, LO14–2, LO15–3

Millen Corporation is a merchandiser that is preparing a master budget for the month of July. The company's balance sheet as of June 30 is shown below:

Millen Corporation Balance Sheet June 30	
Assets	
Cash	$120,000
Accounts receivable...........................	166,000
Inventory.....................................	37,200
Plant and equipment, net of depreciation	554,800
Total assets	$878,000
Liabilities and Stockholders' Equity	
Accounts payable	$93,000
Common stock.................................	586,000
Retained earnings.............................	199,000
Total liabilities and stockholders' equity	$878,000

Millen's managers have made the following additional assumptions and estimates:
1. Estimated sales for July and August are $310,000 and $330,000, respectively.
2. Each month's sales are 20% cash sales and 80% credit sales. Each month's credit sales are collected 30% in the month of sale and 70% in the month following the sale. All of the accounts receivable at June 30 will be collected in July.
3. Each month's ending inventory must equal 20% of the cost of next month's sales. The cost of goods sold is 60% of sales. The company pays for 40% of its merchandise purchases in the month of the purchase and the remaining 60% in the month following the purchase. All of the accounts payable at June 30 will be paid in July.
4. Monthly selling and administrative expenses are always $70,000. Each month $10,000 of this total amount is depreciation expense and the remaining $60,000 relates to expenses that are paid in the month they are incurred.
5. The company does not plan to buy or sell any plant and equipment during July. It will not borrow any money, pay a dividend, issue any common stock, or repurchase any of its own common stock during July.

Required:
1. Calculate the expected cash collections for July.
2. Calculate the expected cash disbursements for merchandise purchases for July.
3. Prepare a cash budget for July.
4. Prepare a budgeted income statement for the month ended July 31. Use an absorption format.
5. Prepare a budgeted balance sheet as of July 31.
6. Calculate the estimated accounts receivable turnover and inventory turnover for the month of July.
7. Calculate the estimated operating cycle for the month of July. (Hint: Use 30 days in the numerator to calculate the average collection period and the average sales period.)
8. Using the indirect method, calculate the estimated net cash provided by operating activities for July.

INTEGRATION EXERCISE 5 Statement of Cash Flows; Ratio Analysis LO14–1, LO14–2, LO14–3, LO15–2, LO15–3, LO15–4, LO15–5, LO15–6

A comparative balance sheet and an income statement for Rowan Company are given below:

Rowan Company
Comparative Balance Sheet
(dollars in millions)

	Ending Balance	Beginning Balance
Assets		
Current assets:		
Cash and cash equivalents	$ 70	$ 91
Accounts receivable.	536	572
Inventory.	620	580
Total current assets.	1,226	1,243
Property, plant, and equipment.	1,719	1,656
Less accumulated depreciation	640	480
Net property, plant, and equipment.	1,079	1,176
Total assets.	$ 2,305	$ 2,419
Liabilities and Stockholders' Equity		
Current liabilities:		
Accounts payable	$ 205	$ 180
Accrued liabilities	94	105
Income taxes payable.	72	88
Total current liabilities.	371	373
Bonds payable.	180	310
Total liabilities.	551	683
Stockholders' equity:		
Common stock.	800	800
Retained earnings.	954	936
Total stockholders' equity	1,754	1,736
Total liabilities and stockholders' equity	$ 2,305	$ 2,419

Rowan Company
Income Statement
For the Year Ended December 31
(dollars in millions)

Sales	$4,350
Cost of goods sold	3,470
Gross margin	880
Selling and administrative expenses	820
Net operating income.	60
Nonoperating items: Gain on sale of equipment	4
Income before taxes.	64
Income taxes	22
Net income.	$ 42

Rowan also provided the following information:
1. The company sold equipment that had an original cost of $16 million and accumulated depreciation of $9 million. The cash proceeds from the sale were $11 million. The gain on the sale was $4 million.
2. The company did not issue any new bonds during the year.

3. The company paid a cash dividend during the year.
4. The company did not complete any common stock transactions during the year.

Required:
1. Using the indirect method, prepare a statement of cash flows for the year.
2. Calculate the free cash flow for the year.
3. To help Rowan assess its liquidity at the end of the year, calculate the following:
   a. Current ratio
   b. Acid-test (quick) ratio
4. To help Rowan assess its asset management, calculate the following:
   a. Average collection period (assuming all sales are on account)
   b. Average sale period
5. To help Rowan assess its debt management, calculate the following:
   a. Debt-to-equity ratio at the end of the year
   b. Equity multiplier
6. To help Rowan assess its profitability, calculate the following:
   a. Net profit margin percentage
   b. Return on equity
7. To help Rowan assess its market performance, calculate the following (assume the par value of the company's common stock is $10 per share):
   a. Earnings per share
   b. Dividend payout ratio

INTEGRATION EXERCISE 6 Plantwide and Departmental Overhead Allocation; Activity-Based Costing; Segmented Income Statements LO2–1, LO2–2, LO2–3, LO2–4, LO6–4, LO6–5, LO7–1, LO7–3, LO7–4

Koontz Company manufactures two models of industrial components—a Basic model and an Advanced Model. The company considers all of its manufacturing overhead costs to be fixed and it uses plantwide manufacturing overhead cost allocation based on direct labor-hours. Koontz's controller prepared the segmented income statement that is shown below for the most recent year (he allocated selling and administrative expenses to products based on sales dollars):

	Basic	Advanced	Total
Number of units produced and sold	20,000	10,000	30,000
Sales	$3,000,000	$2,000,000	$5,000,000
Cost of goods sold	2,300,000	1,350,000	3,650,000
Gross margin	700,000	650,000	1,350,000
Selling and administrative expenses.............	720,000	480,000	1,200,000
Net operating income (loss)	$ (20,000)	$ 170,000	$ 150,000

Direct laborers are paid $20 per hour. Direct materials cost $40 per unit for the Basic model and $60 per unit for the Advanced model. Koontz is considering a change from plantwide overhead allocation to a departmental approach. The overhead costs in the company's Molding Department would be allocated based on machine-hours and the overhead costs in its Assemble and Pack Department would be allocated based on direct labor-hours. To enable further analysis, the controller gathered the following information:

	Molding	Assemble and Pack	Total
Manufacturing overhead costs	$787,500	$562,500	$1,350,000
Direct labor-hours:			
Basic	10,000	20,000	30,000
Advanced........................	5,000	10,000	15,000
Machine-hours:			
Basic	12,000	-	12,000
Advanced........................	10,000	-	10,000

Required:

1. Using the plantwide approach:
   a. Calculate the plantwide overhead rate.
   b. Calculate the amount of overhead that would be assigned to each product.
2. Using a departmental approach:
   a. Calculate the departmental overhead rates.
   b. Calculate the total amount of overhead that would be assigned to each product.
   c. Using your departmental overhead cost allocations, redo the controller's segmented income statement (continue to allocate selling and administrative expenses based on sales dollars).
3. Koontz's production manager has suggested using activity-based costing instead of either the plantwide or departmental approaches. To facilitate the necessary calculations, she assigned the company's total manufacturing overhead cost to five activity cost pools as follows:

Activity Cost Pool	Activity Measure	Manufacturing Overhead
Machining	Machine-hours in Molding	$ 417,500
Assemble and pack	Direct labor-hours in Assemble and Pack	282,500
Order processing	Number of customer orders	230,000
Setups	Setup hours	340,000
Other (unused capacity)		80,000
		$1,350,000

She also determined that the average order size for the Basic and Advanced models is 400 units and 50 units, respectively. The molding machines require a setup for each order. One setup hour is required for each customer order of the Basic model and three hours are required to setup for an order of the Advanced model.

The company pays a sales commissions of 5% for the Basic model and 10% for the Advanced model. Its traceable fixed advertising costs include $150,000 for the Basic model and $200,000 for the Advanced model. The remainder of the company's selling and administrative costs are organization-sustaining in nature.

Using the additional information provided by the production manager, calculate:
   a. An activity rate for each activity cost pool.
   b. The total manufacturing overhead cost allocated to the Basic model and the Advanced model using the activity-based approach.
   c. The total selling and administrative cost traced to the Basic model and the Advanced model using the activity-based approach.
4. Using your activity-based cost assignments from requirement 3, prepare a contribution format segmented income statement that is adapted from Exhibit 6–8. (Hint: Organize all of the company's costs into three categories: variable expenses, traceable fixed expenses, and common fixed expenses.)
5. Using your contribution format segmented income statement from requirement 4, calculate the break-even point in dollar sales for the Advanced model.
6. Explain how Koontz's activity-based costing approach differs from its plantwide and departmental approaches.

INTEGRATION EXERCISE 7 Normal Costing versus Actual Costing LO2–1, LO2–2, LO2–3, LO3–3, LO3–4, LO6–1, LO6–2

Darwin Company manufactures only one product that it sells for $200 per unit. The company uses plantwide overhead cost allocation based on the number of units produced. It provided the following estimates at the beginning of the year:

Number of units produced	50,000
Total fixed manufacturing overhead costs	$1,000,000
Variable manufacturing overhead per unit produced	$12

During the year, the company had no beginning inventories of any kind and no ending raw materials or work in process inventories. All raw materials were used in production as direct materials. An unexpected business downturn caused annual sales to drop to 38,000 units. In response to the decline in sales, Darwin decreased its annual production to 40,000 units. The company's actual costs for the year were as follows:

Variable costs per unit:	
Manufacturing:	
Direct materials	$78
Direct labor.	$60
Variable manufacturing overhead	$12
Variable selling and administrative	$15
Fixed costs per year:	
Fixed manufacturing overhead.	$1,000,000
Fixed selling and administrative expenses.	$350,000

Required:

1. Assuming the company uses normal costing (as described in Chapters 2 and 3):
   a. Compute the plantwide predetermined overhead rate.
   b. Compute the unit product cost for each unit produced during the year.
   c. Prepare a schedule of cost of goods manufactured and a schedule of cost of goods sold. Assume that any underapplied or overapplied overhead is closed entirely to cost of goods sold.
   d. Compute absorption costing net operating income for the year.
2. Assuming the company uses actual costing (as described in Chapter 6):
   a. Compute the unit product cost for each unit produced during the year.
   b. Compute absorption costing net operating income for the year.
3. Are your normal costing and actual costing net operating incomes the same? Why? Support your answer with computations.

INTEGRATION EXERCISE 8 Capital Budgeting, Return on Investment, Residual Income LO11–1, LO11–2, LO13–2

Simmons Company is a merchandiser with multiple store locations. One of its store managers is considering a shift in her store's product mix in anticipation of a strengthening economy. Her store would invest $800,000 in more expensive merchandise (an increase in its working capital) with the expectation that it would increase annual sales and variable expenses by $400,000 and $250,000, respectively for three years. At the end of the three-year period, the store manager believes that the economic surge will subside; therefore, she will release the additional investment in working capital. The store manager's pay raises are largely determined by her store's return on investment (ROI), which has exceeded 22% each of the last three years.

Required:

1. Assuming the company's discount rate is 16%, calculate the net present value of the store manager's investment opportunity.
2. Calculate the annual margin, turnover, and return on investment (ROI) provided by the store manager's investment opportunity.
3. Assuming that the company's minimum required rate of return is 16%, calculate the residual income earned by the store manager's investment opportunity for each of years 1 through 3.
4. Do you think the store manager would choose to pursue this investment opportunity? Do you think the company would want the store manager to pursue it? Why?
5. Using a discount rate of 16%, calculate the present value of your residual incomes for years 1 through 3. Is your answer greater than, less than, or equal to the net present value that you computed in (1) above? Why? Support your explanation with computations.

INTEGRATION EXERCISE 9 Master Budgeting LO8–2, LO8–3, LO8–4, LO8–5, LO8–6, LO8–7, LO8–8, LO8–9, LO8–10

Endless Mountain Company manufactures a single product that is popular with outdoor recreation enthusiasts. The company sells its product to retailers throughout the northeastern quadrant of the United States. It is in the process of creating a master budget for 2017 and reports a balance sheet at December 31, 2016, as follows:

	A	B	C	
1	**Endless Mountain Company**			
2	**Balance Sheet**			
3	**December 31, 2016**			
4				
5	**Assets**			
6	Current assets:			
7	Cash	$ 46,200		
8	Accounts receivable	260,000		
9	Raw materials inventory (4,500 yards)	11,250		
10	Finished goods inventory (1,500 units)	32,250		
11	Total current assets		$349,700	
12	Plant and equipment:			
13	Buildings and equipment	900,000		
14	Accumulated depreciation	(292,000)		
15	Plant and equipment, net		608,000	
16	Total assets		$957,700	
17				
18	**Liabilities and Stockholders' Equity**			
19	Current liabilities:			
20	Accounts payable		$158,000	
21	Stockholders' equity:			
22	Common stock	$ 419,800		
23	Retained earnings	379,900		
24	Total stockholders' equity		799,700	
25	Total liabilities and stockholders' equity		$957,700	
26				

Beginning Balance Sheet / Budgeting Assum

The company's chief financial officer (CFO), in consultation with various managers across the organization has developed the following set of assumptions to help create the 2017 budget:

1. The budgeted unit sales are 12,000 units, 37,000 units, 15,000 units, and 25,000 units for quarters 1–4, respectively. Notice that the company experiences peak sales in the second and fourth quarters. The budgeted selling price for the year is $32 per unit. The budgeted unit sales for the first quarter of 2018 is 13,000 units.

2. All sales are on credit. Uncollectible accounts are negligible and can be ignored. Seventy-five percent of all credit sales are collected in the quarter of the sale and 25% are collected in the subsequent quarter.

3. Each quarter's ending finished goods inventory should equal 15% of the next quarter's unit sales.

4. Each unit of finished goods requires 3.5 yards of raw material that costs $3.00 per yard. Each quarter's ending raw materials inventory should equal 10% of the next quarter's production needs. The estimated ending raw materials inventory on December 31, 2017, is 5,000 yards.

5. Seventy percent of each quarter's purchases are paid for in the quarter of purchase. The remaining 30% of each quarter's purchases are paid in the following quarter.

6. Direct laborers are paid $18 an hour and each unit of finished goods requires 0.25 direct labor-hours to complete. All direct labor costs are paid in the quarter incurred.

7. The budgeted variable manufacturing overhead per direct labor-hour is $3.00. The quarterly fixed manufacturing overhead is $150,000 including $20,000 of depreciation on equipment. The number of direct labor-hours is used as the allocation base for the budgeted plantwide overhead rate. All overhead costs (excluding depreciation) are paid in the quarter incurred.

8. The budgeted variable selling and administrative expense is $1.25 per unit sold. The fixed selling and administrative expenses per quarter include advertising ($25,000), executive salaries ($64,000), insurance ($12,000), property tax ($8,000), and depreciation expense ($8,000). All selling and administrative expenses (excluding depreciation) are paid in the quarter incurred.

9. The company plans to maintain a minimum cash balance at the end of each quarter of $30,000. Assume that any borrowings take place on the first day of the quarter. To the extent possible, the company will repay principal and interest on any borrowings on the last day of the fourth quarter. The company's lender imposes a simple interest rate of 3% per quarter on any borrowings.

10. Dividends of $15,000 will be declared and paid in each quarter.

11. The company uses a last-in, first-out (LIFO) inventory flow assumption. This means that the most recently purchased raw materials are the "first-out" to production and the most recently completed finished goods are the "first-out" to customers.

Required:

The company's CFO has asked you to use Microsoft Excel to prepare the 2017 master budget. Your Excel file should include a tab that contains the December 31, 2016, balance sheet, a tab that summarizes the budgeting assumptions, and tabs corresponding to the following budget schedules and financial statements:

1. Quarterly sales budget including a schedule of expected cash collections.
2. Quarterly production budget.
3. Quarterly direct materials budget including a schedule of expected cash disbursements for purchases of materials.
4. Quarterly direct labor budget.
5. Quarterly manufacturing overhead budget.
6. Ending finished goods inventory budget at December 31, 2017.
7. Quarterly selling and administrative expense budget.
8. Quarterly cash budget.
9. Income statement for the year ended December 31, 2017.
10. Balance sheet at December 31, 2017.

INTEGRATION EXERCISE 10 Statement of Cash Flows LO14–1, 14–2

Refer to the information pertaining to Endless Mountain Company that is provided in Integration Exercise 9. In addition to the budget schedules that you prepared in Integration Exercise 9, insert a new tab in your Microsoft Excel worksheet titled "Statement of Cash Flows."

Required:

1. Using the indirect method, calculate Endless Mountain Company's estimated net cash provided by operating activities for 2017.
2. Prepare the company's budgeted statement of cash flows for the year ended December 31, 2017.

INTEGRATION EXERCISE 11 Financial Statement Ratio Analysis LO15–2, LO15–3, LO15–4, LO15–5

Refer to the information pertaining to Endless Mountain Company that is provided in Integration Exercise 9. In addition to the budget schedules that you prepared in Integration Exercise 9, insert a new tab in your Microsoft Excel worksheet titled "Ratio Analysis."

Required (For all questions, be sure to use formulas that link to the other tabs in your Microsoft Excel worksheet when performing your calculations):

1. To help assess the company's liquidity, calculate the following at December 31, 2017:
   a. Working capital
   b. Current ratio
2. To help assess the company's asset management, calculate the following for 2017:
   a. Accounts receivable turnover
   b. Average collection period
   c. Inventory turnover
   d. Average sale period
   e. Operating cycle

3. To help assess the company's debt management, calculate the following for 2017:
   a. Times interest earned ratio
   b. Equity multiplier
4. To help assess the company's profitability, calculate the following for 2017:
   a. Net profit margin percentage
   b. Return on equity
5. For each of the measures and ratios that you computed in requirements 1 through 4, indicate whether, generally speaking, management would prefer to see it increase or decrease over time. Support each answer with an explanation.

INTEGRATION EXERCISE 12 Cost-Volume-Profit Relationships, Variable Costing LO1–4, LO5–1, LO5–5, LO5–7, LO5–8, LO6–1, LO6–2, LO6–3

Refer to the information pertaining to Endless Mountain Company that is provided in Integration Exercise 9. In addition to the budget schedules that you prepared in Integration Exercise 9, insert two new tabs in your Microsoft Excel worksheet titled "CVP Analysis" and "Variable Costing."

Required (For all questions, be sure to use formulas that link to the other tabs in your Microsoft Excel worksheet when performing your calculations):

1. Calculate the following budgeted figures for 2017:
   a. The total fixed cost.
   b. The variable cost per unit sold.
   c. The contribution margin per unit sold.
   d. The break-even point in unit sales and dollar sales.
   e. The margin of safety.
   f. The degree of operating leverage
2. Calculate the following budgeted figures for 2017:
   a. A variable costing income statement. Stop your computations at net operating income.
   b. A reconciliation that explains the difference in the absorption costing and variable costing net operating incomes.

INTEGRATION EXERCISE 13 Master Budgeting, Statement of Cash Flows, Ratio Analysis, Cost-Volume-Profit Relationships, Variable Costing LO5–5, LO6–2, LO8–5, LO8–6, LO8–8, LO8–9, LO8–10, LO14–2, LO15–3

Refer to the information pertaining to Endless Mountain Company that is provided in Integration Exercise 9 as well as the schedules that you prepared in answering Integration Exercises 9 through 12.

Required:

1. Assume that the company expects to collect all of its credit sales in the quarter of sale rather than the original assumption that it will collect 75% of credit sales in the quarter of sale and the remaining 25% in the subsequent quarter. *Without changing any of the underlying assumptions in your budgeting assumptions tab*, calculate the following revised figures related to the 2017 budget:
   a. Net income (absorption basis)
   b. Accounts receivable turnover
   c. Net cash provided by operating activities
2. Go to the Budgeting Assumptions tab in your Microsoft Excel worksheet. Change the percentage of sales that are collected in the quarter of sale to 100% and the percentage of sales that are collected in the quarter after sale to 0%. Do your answers to 1a through 1c match the numbers that appear in your Excel worksheet? If not, why?
3. Refer to the original budgeting assumptions from Integration Exercise 9. Assume that the company expects to pay its direct laborers $19 per hour instead of the original estimate of $18 per hour. *Without changing any of the underlying assumptions in your budgeting assumptions tab*, calculate the following revised figures related to the 2017 budget:
   a. Ending finished goods inventory at December 31, 2017.
   b. The break-even point in unit sales.
   c. Variable costing net operating income
4. Go to the Budgeting Assumptions tab in your Microsoft Excel worksheet. Change the direct labor cost per hour from $18 to $19. Do your answers to 3a through 3c match the numbers that appear in your Excel worksheet? If not, why?

Index